lonely planet

LONELY PLANET PUBLICATIONS
Melbourne • Oakland • London • Paris

RUSSIA, UKRAINE & BELARUS

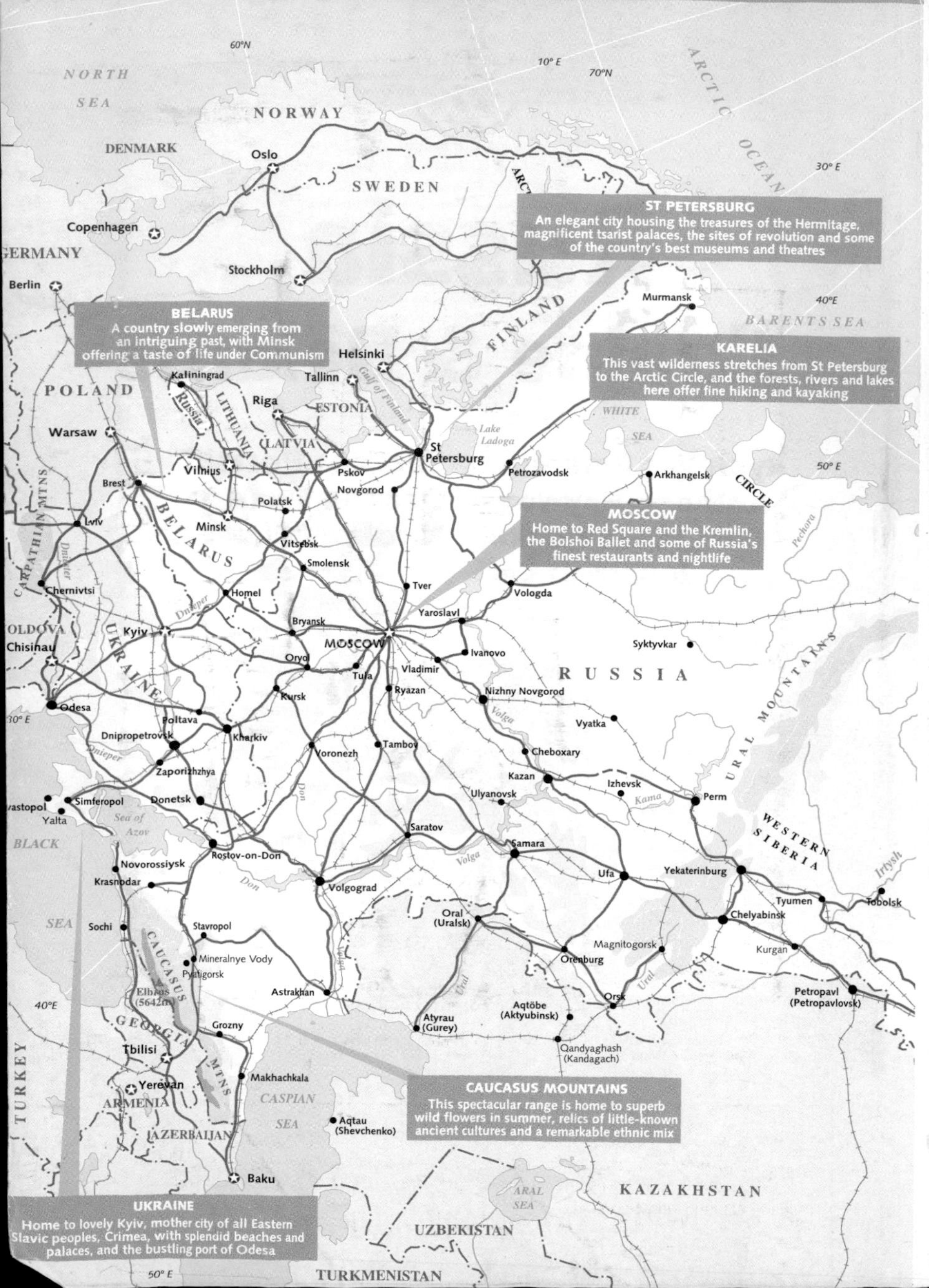
ST PETERSBURG
An elegant city housing the treasures of the Hermitage, magnificent tsarist palaces, the sites of revolution and some of the country's best museums and theatres
BELARUS
A country slowly emerging from an intriguing past, with Minsk offering a taste of life under Communism
KARELIA
This vast wilderness stretches from St Petersburg to the Arctic Circle, and the forests, rivers and lakes here offer fine hiking and kayaking
MOSCOW
Home to Red Square and the Kremlin, the Bolshoi Ballet and some of Russia's finest restaurants and nightlife
CAUCASUS MOUNTAINS
This spectacular range is home to superb wild flowers in summer, relics of little-known ancient cultures and a remarkable ethnic mix
UKRAINE
Home to lovely Kyiv, mother city of all Eastern Slavic peoples, Crimea, with splendid beaches and palaces, and the bustling port of Odesa
NORTH SEA
NORWAY
DENMARK
SWEDEN
FINLAND
GERMANY
POLAND
ESTONIA
LATVIA
LITHUANIA
Russia
BELARUS
UKRAINE
MOLDOVA
RUSSIA
GEORGIA
ARMENIA
AZERBAIJAN
TURKEY
KAZAKHSTAN
UZBEKISTAN
TURKMENISTAN
ARCTIC OCEAN
BARENTS SEA
WHITE SEA
BLACK SEA
Sea of Azov
CASPIAN SEA
ARAL SEA
ARCTIC CIRCLE
CARPATHIAN MTNS
CAUCASUS MTNS
URAL MOUNTAINS
WESTERN SIBERIA
Gulf of Finland
Lake Ladoga
Elbrus (5642m)
Dniester
Dnieper
Don
Volga
Kama
Ural
Pechora
Irtysh
60°N
70°N
10° E
30° E
40°E
50° E
Oslo
Copenhagen
Stockholm
Berlin
Helsinki
Tallinn
Riga
Kaliningrad
Warsaw
Vilnius
Brest
Minsk
Polatsk
Vitsebsk
Homel
Lviv
Chernivtsi
Chisinau
Kyiv
Odesa
Poltava
Kharkiv
Dnipropetrovsk
Zaporizhzhya
Donetsk
Simferopol
Sevastopol
Yalta
Novorossiysk
Krasnodar
Sochi
Stavropol
Mineralnye Vody
Pyatigorsk
Grozny
Tbilisi
Yerevan
Makhachkala
Baku
Aqtau (Shevchenko)
Astrakhan
Atyrau (Gurey)
Aqtöbe (Aktyubinsk)
Qandyaghash (Kandagach)
Orsk
Orenburg
Oral (Uralsk)
Magnitogorsk
Chelyabinsk
Kurgan
Petropavl (Petropavlovsk)
Tyumen
Tobolsk
Yekaterinburg
Ufa
Samara
Saratov
Volgograd
Rostov-on-Don
Voronezh
Tambov
Kursk
Oryol
Tula
Bryansk
Smolensk
MOSCOW
Tver
Ryazan
Vladimir
Ivanovo
Yaroslavl
Vologda
Nizhny Novgorod
Cheboxary
Kazan
Ulyanovsk
Izhevsk
Perm
Vyatka
Syktyvkar
Arkhangelsk
Petrozavodsk
Murmansk
St Petersburg
Pskov
Novgorod

Contents – Text

GETTING AROUND 584

WESTERN SIBERIA 589

EASTERN SIBERIA 635

THE RUSSIAN FAR EAST 672

UKRAINE

FACTS ABOUT UKRAINE 715

FACTS FOR THE VISITOR 737

BELARUS

Contents – Maps

EUROPEAN RUSSIA

FACTS ABOUT EUROPEAN RUSSIA

MOSCOW

AROUND MOSCOW

ST PETERSBURG

AROUND ST PETERSBURG

WESTERN EUROPEAN RUSSIA

NORTHERN EUROPEAN RUSSIA

VOLGA REGION

CAUCASUS

TRANS-SIBERIAN RAILWAY

TRANS-SIBERIAN RAILWAY

SIBERIA & THE RUSSIAN FAR EAST

WESTERN SIBERIA

EASTERN SIBERIA

THE RUSSIAN FAR EAST

UKRAINE

FACTS ABOUT UKRAINE

KYIV

WESTERN UKRAINE

SOUTHERN UKRAINE

CRIMEA

EASTERN UKRAINE

BELARUS

FACTS ABOUT BELARUS

MINSK

ELSEWHERE IN BELARUS

RUSSIA, UKRAINE & BELARUS MAP INDEX

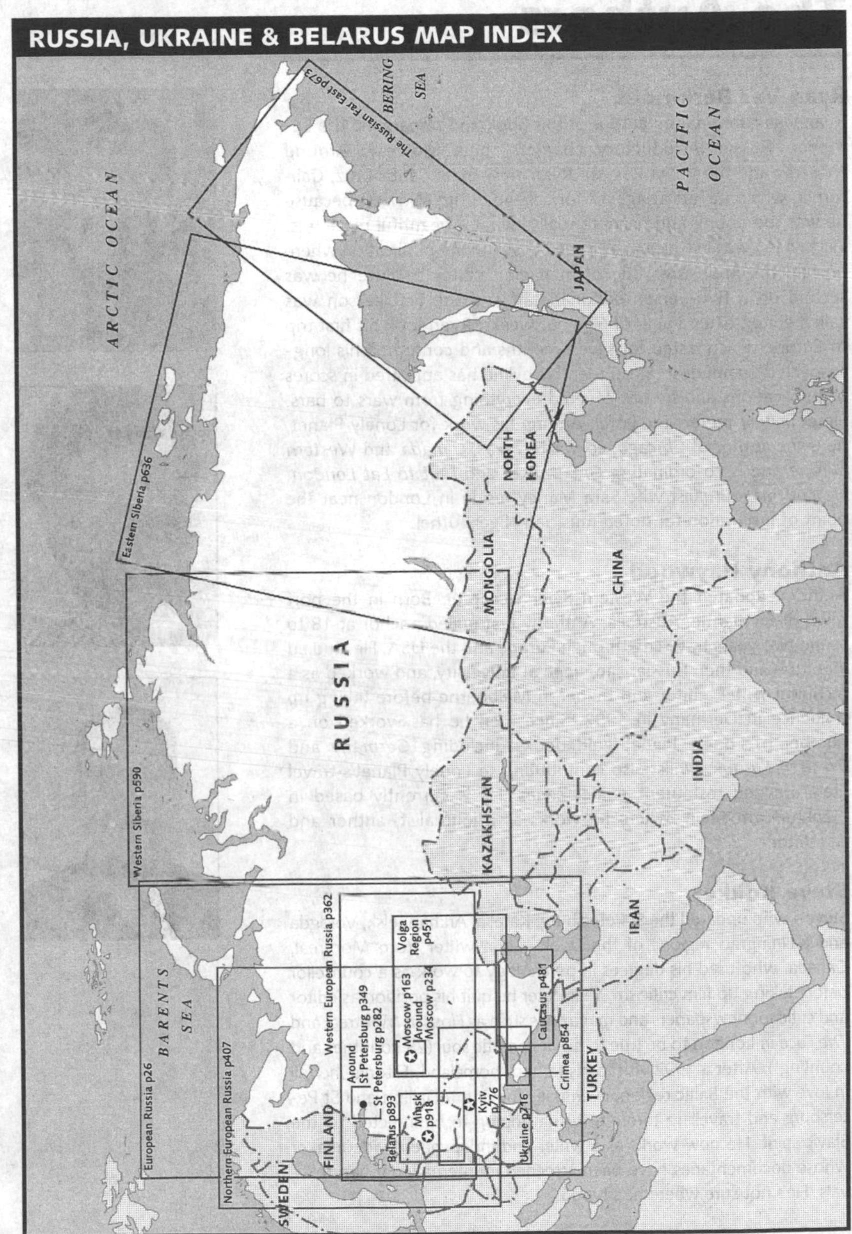

The Authors

Ryan Ver Berkmoes

Ryan was coordinating author of this book and researched the European Russia introductory chapters, plus Moscow, Around Moscow and the Volga Region. Ryan grew up in Santa Cruz, California, which he left at age 17 for college in the Midwest because he was too young and naive to realise what a beautiful place it is. His first job was in Chicago at a small muckraking publication where he had the impressive title of managing editor because he was second on a two-person editorial staff and the first person was called editor. After a year of 60-hour weeks, Ryan took his first trip to Europe which lasted for seven months and confirmed his long-suspected wanderlust. Since then his byline has appeared in scores of publications and he has covered everything from wars to bars. He definitely prefers the latter. Among his work for Lonely Planet, he is the author of *Chicago*, co-wrote *Texas*, *Canada* and *Western Europe* and is co-ordinating *Great Lakes* and *Out to Eat London*. He and his journalist wife Sara Marley reside in London near the point of inspiration for noted musician Nigel Tufnel.

Anthony Haywood

Anthony updated the Western Siberia chapter. Born in the port town of Fremantle, Australia, Anthony first pulled anchor at 18 to spend two years travelling through Europe and the USA. He studied literature and then Russian language at university, and worked as a technical writer, editor and trainer in Melbourne before taking up residence in Germany in 1992. Since then he has worked on a number of Lonely Planet guidebooks, including *Germany* and *Western Europe*, whilst also contributing to Lonely Planet's travel literature and restaurant guides series. He is currently based in Frankfurt am Main, where he works as a journalist, author and translator.

Steve Kokker

Steve – who updated the St Petersburg, Karelia, Arkhangelsk, Vologda and Kaliningrad regions of this book – is a writer from Montreal, Canada, who used his degrees in psychology to work as a counsellor before taking up film criticism. Years later he quit his position as editor and critic for newspapers and magazines such as *Hour* in Montreal and *The Face* in London to be true to his peripatetic soul (23 countries and counting!). After a 1992 visit to his father's homeland, Estonia, he fell in love with the Baltic region, eventually moving to Tallinn and St Petersburg and travelling through Russia hoping to be infected by the Slavic spirit. He now works as a writer and independent videomaker whose documentaries have been screened in international film festivals. He's not sure where he's based.

Jonathan Leff

Jonathan updated the Belarus section of this book. As an Okie transplant to California, he helped expand the Berkeley Guides to cover the Baltic States of Estonia, Latvia and Lithuania before deciding he liked Vilnius well enough to move there. He made several forays into Luka-land from the Lithuanian capital on long weekends away from his full-time job at Reuters, each time hoping for a small coup to cover, but each time disappointed.

Suzanne Possehl

Suzanne updated the Western European Russia, Caucasus, Trans-Siberian Railway, Easterm Siberia and Russian Far East chapters. Born and raised in the wilds of New York and schooled in Boston, Suzanne ditched her first and only nine to five job, as an editor for a Washington DC, CIA funded think tank, and moved to Russia in 1991 to study literature at Leningrad State University. Bread lines, protests and the overall chaos soon lured her out of the library and onto the street. She began reporting for several newspapers and magazines including *The New York Times* and *USNews & World Report*. Fluent in Russian and with a Russian-stitched rucksack, she travelled through much of the Soviet bloc, including three crossings of Siberia – the latest as co-author for *Russia, Ukraine & Belarus*. Once the dust from the collapse of communism settled, Suzanne moved back to New York with her Russian-born husband Georgi Shablovsky, a photographer, computer hack and biologist. They now live in Montreal, Canada, where Suzanne teaches at McGill University.

Deanna Swaney

Deanna updated the Kola Peninsula section. After her university studies (which included a brief attempt to learn Russian), Deanna made a shoestring tour of Europe and has been addicted to travel ever since. Despite an erstwhile career in computer programming, she avoided encroaching yuppiedom in the Arctic wastes of midtown Anchorage by making a break for South America, where she wrote Lonely Planet's *Bolivia* guide. Subsequent travels led through a circuit of island paradises – Arctic and tropical – and resulted in three more guides: *Tonga*, *Samoa* and *Iceland, Greenland & the Faroe Islands*. Back on dry land, she wrote *Zimbabwe, Botswana & Namibia* and *Norway* and, in between, assisted with a guide to the Trans-Siberian Railway and contributed to Lonely Planet's guides to *Brazil*, *Mauritius, Réunion & Seychelles*, *Madagascar & Comoros* and *Southern Africa*, as well as shoestring guides to Africa, South America and Scandinavia. Her time is now divided between travelling, writing and finding time to work on various construction projects around her home base in Alaska's Susitna Valley.

Nicola Williams

Nicola updated the Ukraine section. A journalist by training, Nicola first hit the road in 1990 when she bussed and boated it from Jakarta to East Timor and back again. Following a two year stint at the *North Wales Weekly News*, Nicola moved to Latvia to bus it round the Baltics as features editor of the English-language newspaper *Baltic Times*. Following a happy 12 months exploring the Baltics and its big red neighbours as editor-in-chief of the *In Your Pocket* city-guide series, she traded in Lithuanian *cepelinai* for Lyonnaise *andouillette*.

Nicola graduated from Kent and did an MA in Islamic Societies & Cultures at London's School of Oriental & African Studies. She updated Lonely Planet's *Estonia, Latvia & Lithuania*, authored *Romania & Moldova* and *Provence & the Côte d'Azur* and, very sensibly, returned east in freezing weather to research the Ukraine chapters of this book.

FROM THE AUTHORS

Ryan Ver Berkmoes Thanks firstly to my translator Alevtina Chernorukova whose many talents revealed themselves like a matryoshka doll: just when I thought I'd seen them all, more were revealed. Thanks as well to Artyom Popov, who illustrates well my fascination with all things Russian.

Numerous people were very generous with their time and resources. They include Monika Warburton, Deana Mash, Irina Kulagina, Jeroen Gerrese, Jan Passoff, Andrey Abadjidi and Marion Gardiner. Antonia Bryson provided both a comfy couch and entry to Moscow's café society.

I'm indebted to the tremendous skill and enthusiasm of Nicola Williams, Steve Kokker, Anthony Haywood, Deanna Swaney and the rest of the *Russia, Ukraine & Belarus* author team. I'm also indebted to John Noble, John King, Andrew Humphreys, Richard Nebesky and the others whose excellent work on earlier editions of this book proved both tough to equal but easy to follow. And Nick Selby deserves special mention not just for his previous Russia work but for encouraging me to pursue the project in the first place.

At LP I'd like to thank Jane Fitzpatrick, Liz Filleul, Marcel Gaston, Adrian Persoglia and of course Carolyn Bain, who understands that the best meetings take place out of the office.

Finally thanks to Sara Marley for always giving me reason to curtail my wanderlust and return home.

Anthony Haywood Anthony would like to thank first and foremost the kind, mostly anonymous, Russians who ensured that research went smoothly. Many of these were travelling companions on trains who were not only knowledgeable about their region but also fine company when it counted. Thanks also to John Noble, who provided the excellent basis for this research and to Carolyn Bain and everyone else at LP who worked on the book. Special

thanks go to Masha, Vasya and Anya in Moscow, Jan Passoff, staff at the Travellers Guest House in Moscow, Olga and Konstantin Brylyakov in Yekaterinburg, Surgey Kurgin, and Anna Byrova. Vanessa Locke and Irina Nevskaya were a great help with everything Turkic, and I'm indebted to Sergey and Olga Kass for providing the safety nets. Last but not least, heartfelt thanks again to friends and family, who helped out with a finger in the dike on more than one occasion.

Steve Kokker Special thanks to Henri (meie mees) Kaasik-Aaslav. To Pasha for his grammar and skill at breaking noses, and to Katri Kaasik-Aaslav for keeping me grounded whenever I get spirited away. In St Pete, hugs to Oxana, Vova and Princess Irina; to Andrei Udalov and his many temptations; Lena at the Oktyabrskaya; Ivan Zaporozhets, a very fine cadet; Valery Fomin for showing me Saturn; Sasha Bogdanov; Alexander Kukharsky, the first person I ever met in that strange country; and to 'Vanessa Mae' (Ven), whose sweet melodies I will hum forever. In Lapland, thanks to Lena, my Princess of the North. In magical Arkhangelsk, huge thanks to Valentin Chiptsov, Alexey Golenishchev, and Vassily Matonin; also to Vladimir and Tanya Zykov in Severodvinsk. In Vologda, thanks to the Circus for their fine acrobats. In Kaliningrad, big thanks to the Tumanov family (may Slava take to the skies!), and to Andrei and Katya for a dream come true. Back at LP, many thanks to my favourite and observant editor Carolyn Bain. Bear hugs to Mother Russia for all her eccentric children, my parents for their patience, and to the city on the Neva for showing me how life was meant to be lived.

Jonathan Leff Thanks above all to Catherine Belonogoff, editor of Minsk in Your Pocket and life companion. Also Petruccio Kalachin, for pointing out the glaring omission of St Efrossinia Monastery in Polatsk; the staff at the Svislach Hotel in Minsk for always finding room for one more; Andrei for the speedy trip to Mir; Nickolay Takounov at Belintourist; Anna and Valdimir at Reuters in Minsk for putting me onto what's hot and what's not; Stefan and Elisabeth for their good dining suggestions; Greek ambassador Panayotis Goumas for his valuable views on his 'neighbour'; and Peter Kasaty for his helpful Web site, A Belarus Miscellany (solar.rtd.utk.edu/~kasaty/miscellany.html). And to mom and dad, for not believing every single thing they read in the papers about Belarus.

Suzanne Possehl First and foremost my thanks to the KGB officers in Mirny for making this, my third trip across Siberia, the most memorable. Who knows where else I may have gone if they had not so kindly exiled me back to Moscow? My gratitude also to all the psycho drunkards, evil hotel administrators, crazy Aeroflot sales clerks and the like who tried their best to ruin my journey from Kamchatka to the Caucasus but ended up helping anyway. As for the souls back home – and you know who you are – a million *spasibos* for your thoughts on the guide and support during its preparation. Thanks also to all the unnamed travellers met on the road who shared their insights and stories. Finally, to the finest team of hacks, hackers and designers to put their pens to New Russia – Jane Fitzpatrick, Liz Filleul and Carolyn Bain, Marcel Gaston, Mark Griffiths, Russia co-authors Ryan, Steve, Anthony and our lively and lovely predecessors from RUB1. I want to pour you all a big hearty toast! I'll bring the vodka, you pick the time, the place.

Deanna Swaney The work on my portion of this book would have been considerably more difficult without the assistance of Steve Kokker, who graciously kept me up to date with all the latest Kola happenings. In addition, Valentin Petrov in Apatity, Tatiana Bolod in Murmansk, Rune Rafaelsen in Kirkenes, and Audhild and Børge at Sovjetrejser all provided invaluable and hard-to-find information. I must also thank Robert Strauss, who first introduced me to Russia, and as always, my love and best wishes to Earl, Dean, Kim, Jennifer and Lauren Swaney, in Fresno; to Keith & Holly Hawkings in Anchorage; and to Dave Dault, who most admirably continues to keep things humming back home.

Nicola Williams My chunk of this book is dedicated to (1) fellow Ukraine-bound travellers who, like me, will slash this guide in half to shed several kilos (2) husband Matthias Lüfkens who proffered his taxi haggling and translating skills for 4909km of my trip. Beyond that, in Kyiv very sincere thanks to Jane Bleddyn, Ken Kinzer and their fabulous gang for making Kyiv nightlife memorable; Andrea Godfrey and Julia Ivanova of European Travel Services for providing me a roof over my head and much more; Trudy Burrow, Kevin Hills, Heidi Stivland, Anna Grenot and Melissa McDonald; driver Igor Romanchuk; and Irina Stanichuk of TACIS.

In Donetsk, thank you Michelle Ann Hanson and husband Emmanuel Justus for dinner and oodles of inside info (don't miss *The Dejurnaya*), and their cool gang – Julia Holdsworth; Mike Chambert (Donetsk) and Winsor Lewis (Rostov) of the British Know How Fund; and Svetlana Zanrevska. Heading into the Carpathians, thank you Juniper Neil of the Carpathian Agency for Regional Development in Rakhiv; Sam Axelrod of the Carpathian National Natural Park HQ in Yaremche; and Ioura Ruznak of Uzhhorod's Pid Zamkom (Ukraine's coolest cafe).

Further afield, thanks to Neil McGowan from the Russia Experience, Neil Taylor of Regent Holidays, DTI Belarus & Ukraine desk office Simon Bryan, and Paul Gowen of RAC Motoring Services. Within the realm of LP, particular thanks to Jen Loy (US) and Leonie (Oz) who chased up a lot of the GT&A facts. At home in France, a warm thank you to Ukraine's most fervent fans, Bruno Cadene of Radio France Isère, wife Galina who hails from Donetsk and baby Mathieu.

This Book

This second edition of Russia, Ukraine & Belarus was updated, using material from the title's first edition, by Ryan Ver Berkmoes, Anthony Haywood, Steve Kokker, Jonathan Leff, Suzanne Possehl, Deanna Swaney and Nicola Williams. Caroline Liou and Paul Greenway contributed material on Beijing and Ulaan Baatar for the Trans-Siberian Railway chapter. The first edition of this title was researched by John Noble, Andrew Humphreys, Richard Nebesky, Nick Selby, George Wesely and John King.

FROM THE PUBLISHER

This 2nd edition of Russia, Ukraine & Belarus was produced at Lonely Planet's Melbourne office and coordinated by Adrian Persoglia (mapping and design) and Carolyn Bain (editorial).

On the editing front, assistance was provided by Ada Cheung, Anne Mulvaney, Darren O'Connell, Helen Yeates, Jocelyn Harewood, Kalya Ryan, Liz Filleul, Lyn McGaurr and Susie Ashworth. Shelley Muir assisted with proofing, wrote the aside on Dostoevsky and helped to steer the book through layout.

Cartographic assistance and support was provided by Ann Jeffree, Birgit Jordan, Celia Wood, Csanád Csutoros, Lisa Borg, Marcel Gaston, Mark Griffiths, Paul Dawson, Sarah Sloane and Yvonne Bischofberger.

Many thanks to Quentin Frayne for the language section, and to Valentina Kremenchutskaya and Inna Zaitseva for their language expertise. Thanks to Dan Levin for help with the temperamental Cyrillic font.

Thanks also to Leonie Mugavin for her help with travel information, Matt King for assistance with illustrations, Valerie Tellini for help with images, Jenny Joy Jones for producing the metro maps, Maria Vallianos for creating the cover, Tim Uden for his Quarkful expertise and help in getting everything together, and Rachel Imeson for the final round of checking.

THANKS
Many thanks to the travellers who used the last edition and wrote to us with helpful hints, advice and interesting anecdotes. Your names appear in the back of this book.

Foreword

ABOUT LONELY PLANET GUIDEBOOKS

The story begins with a classic travel adventure: Tony and Maureen Wheeler's 1972 journey across Europe and Asia to Australia. Useful information about the overland trail did not exist at that time, so Tony and Maureen published the first Lonely Planet guidebook to meet a growing need.

From a kitchen table, then from a tiny office in Melbourne (Australia), Lonely Planet has become the largest independent travel publisher in the world, an international company with offices in Melbourne, Oakland (USA), London (UK) and Paris (France).

Today Lonely Planet guidebooks cover the globe. There is an ever-growing list of books and there's information in a variety of forms and media. Some things haven't changed. The main aim is still to help make it possible for adventurous travellers to get out there – to explore and better understand the world.

At Lonely Planet we believe travellers can make a positive contribution to the countries they visit – if they respect their host communities and spend their money wisely. Since 1986 a percentage of the income from each book has been donated to aid projects and human rights campaigns.

Updates Lonely Planet thoroughly updates each guidebook as often as possible. This usually means there are around two years between editions, although for more unusual or more stable destinations the gap can be longer. Check the imprint page (following the colour map at the beginning of the book) for publication dates.

Between editions up-to-date information is available in two free newsletters – the paper *Planet Talk* and email *Comet* (to subscribe, contact any Lonely Planet office) – and on our Web site at www.lonelyplanet.com. The *Upgrades* section of the Web site covers a number of important and volatile destinations and is regularly updated by Lonely Planet authors. *Scoop* covers news and current affairs relevant to travellers. And, lastly, the *Thorn Tree* bulletin board and *Postcards* section of the site carry unverified, but fascinating, reports from travellers.

Correspondence The process of creating new editions begins with the letters, postcards and emails received from travellers. This correspondence often includes suggestions, criticisms and comments about the current editions. Interesting excerpts are immediately passed on via newsletters and the Web site, and everything goes to our authors to be verified when they're researching on the road. We're keen to get more feedback from organisations or individuals who represent communities visited by travellers.

Lonely Planet gathers information for everyone who's curious about the planet – and especially for those who explore it first-hand. Through guidebooks, phrasebooks, activity guides, maps, literature, newsletters, image library, TV series and Web site we act as an information exchange for a worldwide community of travellers.

Research Authors aim to gather sufficient practical information to enable travellers to make informed choices and to make the mechanics of a journey run smoothly. They also research historical and cultural background to help enrich the travel experience and allow travellers to understand and respond appropriately to cultural and environmental issues.

Authors don't stay in every hotel because that would mean spending a couple of months in each medium-sized city and, no, they don't eat at every restaurant because that would mean stretching belts beyond capacity. They do visit hotels and restaurants to check standards and prices, but feedback based on readers' direct experiences can be very helpful.

Many of our authors work undercover, others aren't so secretive. None of them accept freebies in exchange for positive write-ups. And none of our guidebooks contain any advertising.

Production Authors submit their raw manuscripts and maps to offices in Australia, USA, UK or France. Editors and cartographers – all experienced travellers themselves – then begin the process of assembling the pieces. When the book finally hits the shops, some things are already out of date, we start getting feedback from readers and the process begins again ...

WARNING & REQUEST

Things change – prices go up, schedules change, good places go bad and bad places go bankrupt – nothing stays the same. So, if you find things better or worse, recently opened or long since closed, please tell us and help make the next edition even more accurate and useful. We genuinely value all the feedback we receive. Julie Young coordinates a well travelled team that reads and acknowledges every letter, postcard and email and ensures that every morsel of information finds its way to the appropriate authors, editors and cartographers for verification.

Everyone who writes to us will find their name in the next edition of the appropriate guidebook. They will also receive the latest issue of *Planet Talk*, our quarterly printed newsletter, or *Comet*, our monthly email newsletter. Subscriptions to both newsletters are free. The very best contributions will be rewarded with a free guidebook.

Excerpts from your correspondence may appear in new editions of Lonely Planet guidebooks, the Lonely Planet Web site, *Planet Talk* or *Comet*, so please let us know if you *don't* want your letter published or your name acknowledged.

Send all correspondence to the Lonely Planet office closest to you:

Australia: PO Box 617, Hawthorn, Victoria 3122
USA: 150 Linden St, Oakland, CA 94607
UK: 10A Spring Place, London NW5 3BH
France: 1 rue du Dahomey, 75011 Paris

Or email us at: talk2us@lonelyplanet.com.au

For news, views and updates see our Web site: www.lonelyplanet.com

HOW TO USE A LONELY PLANET GUIDEBOOK

The best way to use a Lonely Planet guidebook is any way you choose. At Lonely Planet we believe the most memorable travel experiences are often those that are unexpected, and the finest discoveries are those you make yourself. Guidebooks are not intended to be used as if they provide a detailed set of infallible instructions!

Contents All Lonely Planet guidebooks follow roughly the same format. The Facts about the Destination chapters or sections give background information ranging from history to weather. Facts for the Visitor gives practical information on issues like visas and health. Getting There & Away gives a brief starting point for researching travel to and from the destination. Getting Around gives an overview of the transport options when you arrive.

The peculiar demands of each destination determine how subsequent chapters are broken up, but some things remain constant. We always start with background, then proceed to sights, places to stay, places to eat, entertainment, getting there and away, and getting around information – in that order.

Heading Hierarchy Lonely Planet headings are used in a strict hierarchical structure that can be visualised as a set of Russian dolls. Each heading (and its following text) is encompassed by any preceding heading that is higher on the hierarchical ladder.

Entry Points We do not assume guidebooks will be read from beginning to end, but that people will dip into them. The traditional entry points are the list of contents and the index. In addition, however, some books have a complete list of maps and an index map illustrating map coverage.

There may also be a colour map that shows highlights. These highlights are dealt with in greater detail in the Facts for the Visitor chapter, along with planning questions and suggested itineraries. Each chapter covering a geographical region usually begins with a locator map and another list of highlights. Once you find something of interest in a list of highlights, turn to the index.

Maps Maps play a crucial role in Lonely Planet guidebooks and include a huge amount of information. A legend is printed on the back page. We seek to have complete consistency between maps and text, and to have every important place in the text captured on a map. Map key numbers usually start in the top left corner.

Although inclusion in a guidebook usually implies a recommendation we cannot list every good place. Exclusion does not necessarily imply criticism. In fact there are a number of reasons why we might exclude a place – sometimes it is simply inappropriate to encourage an influx of travellers.

Introduction

Russia, Ukraine and Belarus, the three core republics of the old Soviet Union, have found that old ties still bind. Although they were the countries which finally killed off the USSR when they proclaimed independence in 1991, they have remained close, and talk of a grand reunion – albeit mostly from politicians with their own agendas – continues to swirl about.

The three countries have many differences but also much in common. Their peoples form the three branches of the Eastern Slav group, with a shared heritage which goes back to the Kyivan (Kievan) Rus state founded in the 9th century. Their languages are distinct but closely related. Most of Ukraine and Belarus were part of the Russian Empire for over a century before they became founding members of the USSR in 1922. Today, all three countries are facing the same challenges as they struggle to adapt to the massive changes of the 1990s which have been nowhere near as easy or as beneficial as optimists had once hoped.

Hardship, uncertainty, tension and conflict – between regions, religions and ethnic groups – have arisen. Russia in particular has seen strife as some of its panoply of ethnic and religious groups have decided that independence is preferable to cohabitation.

The much-vaunted free-market economy has stalled somewhere between the stifling old state-controlled system with its shortages and queues and a genuinely free market where incomes rise to match prices and anyone can participate in seeking riches. Instead, the only shortage is money for the masses of citizens struggling to survive in a world of Soviet-era wages and Western-style prices. They can buy anything in the kiosks and stores which have appeared everywhere but they probably can't afford it.

Politics too is stalled somewhere between the totalitarian state and genuine democracy. Sure there are elections, but they are often rigged and even sworn democrats have shown a rapacious hunger for power once they've assumed office.

The territory the three countries cover stretches almost halfway round the globe, across 11 time zones. At the same moment as potato farmers in Belarus climb down from their tractors after a day's work, reindeer herders in Kamchatka, in Russia's Far East, may be rousing their herds for the next day's grazing. As well as endless tracts of forest, steppe and plain, these countries contain great variety of landscape and fauna.

This whole canvas is spread open for travellers. Despite stories in Western media about economic collapse, ethnic conflict, escalating crime and deathtrap aircraft, travel in Russia, Ukraine and Belarus is no more daunting than in most of the rest of the world. The biggest challenge will be budgeting – not your money, but your time. With patience, diligence and a big sense of adventure you can get almost anywhere, it just may take forever.

Costs can be tailored to almost any budget. Away from the major cities of Moscow and St Petersburg, you will find prices are quite cheap as goods and services have to be priced for locals rather than the occasional tourist.

This book divides its territory into four – European Russia (west of the Ural Mountains); Siberia and the Russian Far East; Ukraine; and Belarus. There's also a special chapter for Trans-Siberian rail travellers.

European Russia is the heartland of the world's biggest country, and contains its two major cities and four-fifths of its population. Also within European Russia are the Volga River, a historic highway whose basin is home to many non-Russian peoples such as the Muslim Tatars; and the northern side of the spectacular Caucasus mountains striding across from the Black Sea to the Caspian.

This is a land of snow and deadly winters, but also of rivers that meander across meadows and 24-hour midsummer daylight in northern latitudes. A composite of the extravagant glories of old Russia and the drab legacies of the Soviet era, it's home to the mysteries of the Orthodox Church, to rusting industrial cities and millions of people who still work the land, and to the 'New Russians', the flashy capitalists making the most of the anything-goes post-Soviet era. Its people, in the words of one of their own proverbs, 'love to suffer', yet they also love to party and can be disarmingly warm-hearted and hospitable.

From Russia's European heartland the old tsarist empire spread out to absorb hundreds of neighbouring peoples – across Siberia to the Pacific, westward into Ukraine and Belarus, and south to other areas now again independent of Russia, the Transcaucasus and Central Asia.

Siberia, for generations a place of snow-bound exile for those out of favour with the rulers in Moscow or St Petersburg, today has its share of industrial development and cities, but remains mostly untamed and empty of people. Famed among travellers as the reason for the world's longest train ride, it's also dotted with some of the globe's major natural wonders – the exquisite Altay Mountains; serene Lake Baikal, the world's deepest and, some say, most beautiful lake; the volcanoes and geysers of Kamchatka – and unexpected pockets of non-Russian culture such as those of the Buddhist Buryats and Tuvans or the shamanist Yakuts.

Ukraine is a land of great economic potential. Its rolling, fertile steppe supports both big industrial cities and innumerable villages of picket fences and duck ponds that seem to come from a bygone age. Kyiv (Kiev), the mother city of all the Eastern Slav civilisations, is full of history and a bit of swagger as the national capital. The west of the country, focused on Lviv, is the most distinctively Ukrainian region, almost Central European in character and with Russian influence at its weakest. On Ukraine's long, warm Black Sea coast, the Crimean peninsula presents a big contrast with its mountains and relaxed seaside resorts, while the port of Odesa remains a crossroads city with an indefinable atmosphere of excitement and mystery.

Belarus is a flat, in-between land, its people the victims of centuries of wars between Russians, Germans, Lithuanians,

Poles and others. Born for the first time as an independent state in 1991, it's hardly a mainstream tourist attraction, but it can surprise those who take time to explore it. Its modern capital, Minsk, is an increasingly cosmopolitan city, while other cities such as Hrodna and Polatsk preserve the imprint of the past, and the countryside has a haunting, old-fashioned beauty.

The opening up of this Eastern Slavic realm emphasises perhaps more than anything its differences from the outside world. The unique landscapes, ways of life and histories here constantly surprise and challenge the outsider. To explore these countries, all you need is a sense of curiosity and, when appropriate, small measures of caution, determination and tolerance of discomfort.

Last-Minute Addition

At the time of going to press, there was political upheaval yet again in Russia. On New Year's Eve 1999, in a move that surprised everyone, Russian President Boris Yeltsin announced his immediate resignation. In his speech, Yeltsin said he was not leaving for health reasons but because of the need for Russia to 'enter the new millennium with new politicians, new faces, new intelligent, strong and energetic people'.

Yeltsin signed a decree entrusting the caretaker duties of the president to Vladimir Putin, the Russian prime minister. He made a clear endorsement of Putin, a candidate in the presidential election originally scheduled for June 2000 but now to take place on 26 March. It is anticipated that Putin will win this – as prime minister, his strong handling of the war in Chechnya and no-nonsense manner has appealed to many Russians. Only if things go badly for the Russian forces in Chechnya is he likely to lose his popularity with voters.

There are also a number of references in this book to the December 1999 Russian parliamentary elections. The two surprise successes of these elections – for the newly formed Unity party (winning 72 of the 450 seats) and the Union of Right Wing Forces (29 seats) – appear to have come about as a result of Putin's overwhelming popularity. Though the Communists, with 113 seats, are likely to remain the largest single parliamentary faction, for the first time they will be outnumbered by representatives of centrist and pro-reform parties.

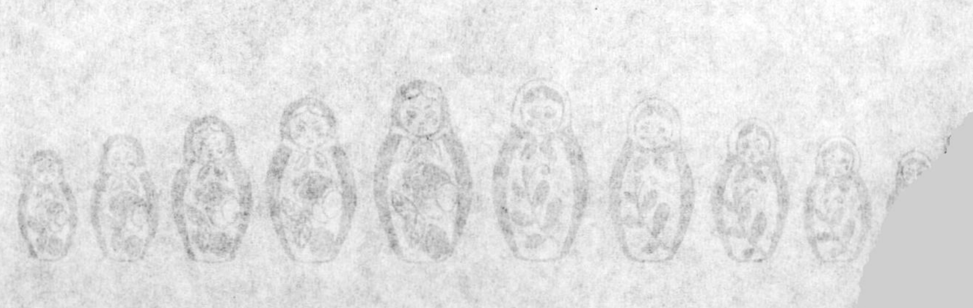

EUROPEAN RUSSIA

Facts about European Russia

European Russia – Russia west of the Ural Mountains – comprises only a quarter of Russia but is still bigger than any other European country. With four-fifths of Russia's population, it's very much the country's hub. It is a land of much variety, stretching from the frozen tundra that borders the Arctic Ocean to the peaks of the Caucasus, Europe's highest mountains, 3000km south. Between these extremes lie Russia's two greatest cities and much more.

During the Soviet years, only pockets of this huge country were truly open to foreigners. Even today, when virtually all of it can be freely explored by anyone, much remains little known to the outside world.

Russia's most vital cities are Moscow, in the historic heartland at the centre of European Russia, and St Petersburg, established less than 300 years ago on the Gulf of Finland as Russia's gateway to Europe. In these two places tsars reigned and the world's greatest communist state was born, Russia's unique architecture flowered, and the mysteries of the Russian Orthodox Church flourished, as they do today. Here too, the impact of all the modern changes is most evident – as any traveller can experience in hotels, shops and restaurants or while sampling the nightlife. Within a few hundred kilometres of these cities are dozens of smaller places where you can witness the country's historic grandeur together with the beauty of its gentle countryside and the perennial, bitter hardness of Russian life.

To the north lie tracts of forest, lakes, marshes and tundra – a vast new world for hikers, skiers and campers. As well, the north is dotted with intriguing human enclaves such as the Arctic ports of Murmansk and Arkhangelsk, Kizhi Island with its extraordinary assemblage of old wooden architecture, remnants of Gulag labour camps, and the venerable churches and monasteries of Vologda and elsewhere.

East from Moscow, then south, flows the Volga River. The Volga is one of Russia's historic highways and links many cities of both ancient and modern importance – among them Yaroslavl, Nizhny Novgorod, Kazan, Ulyanovsk, Saratov, Volgograd (once Stalingrad) and Astrakhan – along its course to the Caspian Sea. Numerous ethnic minorities, whose religious beliefs range from Islam to Buddhism to animism, live in or near to the Volga basin, reminders of European Russia's proximity to Asia and the many former Soviet republics.

European Russia's other great waterway, the Don River, flows south from near Moscow to the Sea of Azov, an offshoot of the Black Sea, near Rostov-on-Don. Between the two rivers begins European Russia's steppe, part of the great rolling grasslands – now largely given over to agriculture – which stretch across the northern hemisphere from Mongolia to Hungary.

The steppe gives way on European Russia's southern fringe to the Caucasus Mountains. Stretching between the Black and Caspian seas, the Caucasus is a range of spectacular beauty and home to an incredible jigsaw of ethnic groups. Many of these groups were not conquered by Russia until the 19th century; today some are tragically mired in bloody conflicts with each other or with Russia.

There is even a coastal riviera, where the Caucasus Mountains meet the Black Sea, to which Russians flock for summer holidays.

Though the practicalities of travel outside the main cities may demand some patience

EUROPEAN RUSSIA
0°
10°
20°
30°
40°
50°
60°
70°
80°
75°
70°
65°
0
500
1000km
Novaya Zemlya
BARENTS SEA
KARA SEA
Arctic Circle
NORWAY
SWEDEN
FINLAND
Murmansk
Vorkuta
Salekhard
Pechora
Arkhangelsk
Syktyvkar
Petrozavodsk
STOCKHOLM
HELSINKI
Vyborg
Tallinn
St Petersburg
BALTIC SEA
ESTONIA
Novgorod
Vologda
Vyatka
Perm
Yekaterinburg
RIGA
Pskov
LATVIA
Yaroslavl
Kostroma
Ivanovo
Volga
Yoshkar-Ola
Izhevsk
LITHUANIA
Tver
MOSCOW
Kaliningrad
VILNIUS
Vitsebsk
Vladimir
Nizhny Novgorod
Kazan
Cheboxary
Ufa
Smolensk
Ryazan
Ulyanovsk
MINSK
Kaluga
Tula
Tolyatti
WARSAW
BELARUS
Bryansk
Saransk
Samara
Penza
Oryol
Tambov
Orenburg
Orsk
POLAND
Homel
Oral (Uralsk)
Aqtobe (Aktyubinsk)
Kursk
Saratov
Voronezh
KYIV
Belgorod
UKRAINE
Kharkiv
Don
Volga
KAZAKHSTAN
Volgograd
MOLDOVA
Atyrau (Gurev)
CHISINAU
Donetsk
Don
ROMANIA
Rostov-on-Don
Astrakhan
Aral Sea
Odesa
Elista
BUCHAREST
Krasnodar
Stavropol
CASPIAN SEA
Simferopol
UZBEKISTAN
Novorossiysk
Caucasus Mtns
Mineralnye Vody
Sochi
Grozny
BULGARIA
BLACK SEA
Makhachkala
Mt Elbrus (5642m)
Vladikavkaz
TURKMENISTAN
GEORGIA
TBILISI
TURKEY
ARMENIA
AZERBAIJAN
BAKU
URAL MOUNTAINS

and persistence, Russia never fails to surprise, not least with its people's bizarre combination of gloom and high spirits, rudeness and warm hospitality, secrecy and openness. In the end you'll have shed your own shaft of light on the place that Winston Churchill characterised as 'a riddle wrapped in a mystery inside an enigma'.

HISTORY

Early History

European Russia's earliest known people inhabited the basin of the Don River about 20,000 BC. By 2000 BC a basic agriculture, relying on hardy cereals, had penetrated from the Danube region as far east as the Moscow area and the southern Ural Mountains. At about the same time, peoples in Ukraine and southern areas of European Russia domesticated the horse and developed a nomadic, pastoral lifestyle.

While central and northern European Russia remained a complete backwater for almost 3000 years, the south was subject to a succession of invasions by nomads from the east. The first written records, by the 5th century BC Greek historian Herodotus, concern a people called the Scythians, who probably originated in the Altay region of Siberia and Mongolia and were feared for their riding and battle skills. They spread as far west as southern Russia and Ukraine by the 7th century BC. The Scythian empire, which stretched south as far as Egypt, ended with the arrival of another people from the east, the Sarmatians, in the 3rd century BC.

The Sarmatians were followed in the 4th century AD by the Huns, also from the Altay region, then by the Huns' relations the Avars, then by the Khazars, a grouping of Turkic and Iranian tribes from the Caucasus, who occupied the lower Volga and Don basins and the steppes to the east and west between the 7th and 10th centuries. The crafty and talented Khazars brought stability and religious tolerance to areas under their control. Their capital was Itil, near the mouth of the Volga. In the 9th century they converted to Judaism. By the 10th century they had mostly settled down to farming and trade.

Slavs

The migrants who were to give Russia its predominant character, however, were the Slavs. There is some disagreement about where the Slavs originated, but in the first few centuries AD they expanded rapidly to the east, west and south from the vicinity of present-day northern Ukraine and southern Belarus. The Eastern Slavs were the ancestors of the Russians; they were still spreading eastward across the central Russian woodland belt in the 9th century. From the Western Slavs came the Poles, Czechs, Slovaks and others. The Southern Slavs became the Serbs, Croats, Slovenes and Bulgarians.

The Slavs' conversion to Christianity in the 9th and 10th centuries was accompanied by the introduction of an alphabet devised by Cyril, a Greek missionary (now St Cyril), and simplified a few decades later by a fellow missionary, Methodius. The forerunner of Cyrillic, it was based on the Greek alphabet, with a dozen or so additional characters. The Bible was translated into the Southern Slav dialect. This became known as Church Slavonic and is the language of the Russian Orthodox Church's liturgy to this day.

Vikings & Kyivan Rus

The crucial factor in the creation of the first Russian state was the potential for trade on river routes across Eastern Slavic areas – between the Baltic and Black seas and, to a lesser extent, between the Baltic and the Volga. Vikings from Scandinavia, called Varyagi (Varangians) by the Slavs, had been nosing east from the Baltic since the 6th century AD, trading and raiding for furs, slaves and amber, and coming into conflict with the Khazars and with Constantinople (Istanbul), the eastern centre of Christianity, as they went. To secure their hold on the trade routes, the Vikings made themselves masters of settlements in key areas – places such as Novgorod, Smolensk and Kyiv (Kiev in Russian). Though by no means united themselves, they created a loose confederation of city states in the Eastern Slavic areas. The founding of Novgorod in 862 by Rurik of Jutland is traditionally taken as the birth of the Russian state. Rurik's successor,

Oleg, became Kyiv's ruler two decades later, and the Rurikid dynasty, though soon Slavicised, maintained its hold to produce the dominant rulers in Eastern Slavic areas until the end of the 16th century.

The name Rus may have been that of the dominant Kyivan Viking clan. In later years the term Russian or Great Russian came to be used for Eastern Slavs in the north, while those to the south or west were identified as Ukrainians or Belarusians.

Prince Svyatoslav made Kyiv the dominant regional power by campaigning against quarrelling Varangian princes and dealing the Khazars a series of fatal blows. After his death, his son Vladimir made further conquests, and persuaded the Patriarch of Constantinople to establish an episcopal see – a Church 'branch' – in Kyiv in 988, marking the birth of the Russian Orthodox Church. He also introduced the beginnings of a feudal structure to replace clan allegiances, though some principalities – including Novgorod, Pskov and Vyatka (north of Kazan) – were ruled democratically by popular assemblies *(veches)*.

Kyiv's supremacy was broken by new invaders from the east – first the Pechenegs, then the Polovtsy, who sacked Kyiv in 1093 – and by the effects of the European crusades from the late 11th century onwards, which broke the Arab hold on southern Europe and the Mediterranean, reviving west-east trade routes and making Rus a commercial backwater.

Novgorod & Rostov-Suzdal

The northern Rus principalities began breaking from Kyiv after about 1050. The merchants of Novgorod joined the emerging Hanseatic League, a federation of city-states that controlled Baltic and North Sea trade. Novgorod became the League's gateway to the lands east and south-east.

As Kyiv declined, the Russian population shifted northwards and the fertile Rostov-Suzdal region north-east of Moscow began to be developed. Vladimir Monomakh of Kyiv founded the town of Vladimir there in 1108 and gave the Rostov-Suzdal principality to his son Yury Dolgoruky, who is credited with founding the little settlement of Moscow in 1147. Rostov-Suzdal grew so rich and strong that Yury's son Andrey Bogolyubov sacked Kyiv in 1169 and moved the court to Vladimir. The Church's headquarters remained in Kyiv until 1300. Rostov-Suzdal began to gear up for a challenge to the hold on the Volga-Ural Mountains region of the Bulgars. The Bulgars were a people who had originated farther east several centuries before and had since converted to Islam. Their capital, Bolgar, was near modern Kazan, on the Volga.

Tatars & the Golden Horde

It's hard to overstate the fear instilled by the Tatars, the name used by Slavs for the mostly Mongolian invaders who suddenly thundered out of Asia in the 13th century. Within 30 years these horsemen built the largest land empire the world has ever seen, slaughtering as many as a quarter of their new subjects in the process.

This was the work of a Mongolian warlord called Temuchin (1167-1227), from south of Lake Baikal, in present-day eastern Siberia, who by 1206 had forged a powerful tribal alliance centred at Karakorum in present-day Mongolia, and named himself Jenghis Khan (Great Ruler).

After his armies overran north China and Korea they went west through Central Asia, Afghanistan, Iran and the Caucasus and into the plains between the Volga and Don rivers. There they met the armies of the Russian princes and thrashed them at the Battle of Kalka River in 1223. This push was cut short by the death of Jenghis Khan, but his grandson Batu Khan returned in 1236 to finish the job, laying waste to Bolgar and Rostov-Suzdal and annihilating most of the other Russian principalities, including Kyiv, within four years. Novgorod was saved only by spring floods that prevented the invaders from crossing the marshes around the city.

Batu and his successors ruled the Golden Horde – one of the khanates into which the empire of Jenghis had broken – from Saray on the Volga (near modern Volgograd). The Horde's control over its subjects was indirect: though it raided them in traditional fashion if they grew uppity, it mainly used local princes to keep order, provide soldiers and collect taxes.

Alexander Nevsky & the Rise of Moscow

One such 'collaborator' was Alexander Nevsky, Prince of Novgorod, a Russian hero (and later a saint of the Russian Church) for his resistance to invaders from the west – German crusaders and Swedes. His victory in 1240 over the Swedes on the Neva River, near present-day St Petersburg, earned him his nickname, Nevsky. Batu Khan put him on the throne as Grand Prince of Vladimir.

Nevsky and his successors acted as intermediaries between the Tatars and other Russian princes. By shrewd diplomacy the princes of Moscow obtained and hung on to the title of Grand Prince from the early 14th century while other princes resumed their feuding. The Church provided backing to Moscow by moving there from Vladimir in the 1320s, and was in turn favoured with exemption from Tatar taxation.

But Moscow proved to be the Tatars' nemesis. With a new-found Russian confidence, Grand Prince Dmitry put Moscow at the head of a coalition of princes and took on the Tatars, defeating them in a great battle at Kulikovo on the Don River in 1380. For this he became Dmitry Donskoy ('of the Don') and was canonised after his death.

The Tatars crushed this uprising in a three-year campaign but their days were numbered. Weakened by internal dissension, they fell at the end of the 14th century to the Turkic Empire of Timur (Tamerlane), which was based in Samarkand. Yet the Russians, themselves divided as usual, remained Tatar vassals until 1480.

Moscow vs Lithuania

Moscow – or Muscovy, as its expanding lands came to be known – was champion of the Russian cause after Kulikovo, though it had rivals, especially Novgorod and Tver. More ominous was the rise of the Grand Duchy of Lithuania, which had started to expand into old Kyivan Rus lands in the 14th century. At first just a headache for Moscow, it became a threat in 1386 when the Lithuanian ruler Jogaila married the Polish queen Jadwiga and became king of Poland, thus joining two of Europe's most powerful states.

With Jogaila's coronation as Wladyslaw II of Poland, the previously pagan Lithuanian ruling class embraced Catholicism. The Russian Church portrayed the struggle against Lithuania as one against the Pope in Rome. After Constantinople, centre of the Greek Orthodox Church, was taken by the Turks in 1453, the metropolitan or head of the Russian Church declared Moscow the 'third Rome', the true heir of Christianity.

Meanwhile, with the death of Dmitry Donskoy's son in 1425, Muscovy suffered a dynastic war. The old Rurikids got the upper hand – ironically with Lithuanian and Tatar help – but it was only with Ivan III's forceful reign from 1462 to 1505 that the other principalities ceased to oppose Muscovy.

Ivan III (the Great)

Ivan III brought most of the Great Russian principalities to heel. Novgorod was first, in 1478, as it was no longer able to rely on the Tatars as a diversion. Two years later a Russian army faced the Tatars at the Ugra River south-west of Moscow. Though they parted without a fight, after that Ivan simply stopped paying tribute to the Golden Horde.

Tver fell to Moscow in 1485, far-flung Vyatka in 1489. Pskov and Ryazan, the only states still independent at the end of Ivan's reign, were mopped up by his successor, Vasily III. Lithuania and Poland, however, remained thorns in Russia's side.

Servants & Serfs

When Ivan III took Novgorod he installed a governor, exiled the city's influential families and ejected the Hanseatic merchants, closing Russia's 'window on the West' for two centuries. The exiles were replaced with Ivan's administrators, who got temporary title to confiscated lands for good performance. This new approach to land tenure, called *pomestie* (estate), characterised Ivan's rule. Previously, the greater nobles *(boyars)* had held land under a system of patrimony

Rulers of Russia – Rurik to Yeltsin

Following is a list of the major rulers of Russia or the Soviet Union. In line with common usage, rulers' names before 1700 are directly transliterated, but are Anglicised from Peter the Great until 1917, and transliterated after that – thus Vasily not Basil, Mikhail not Michael, Alexey not Alexis; but Peter not Pyotr, Catherine not Yekaterina etc.

Ivan the Terrible was the first ruler to have himself formally called tsar. Peter the Great began using emperor, though tsar remained in use. In this book we use empress for a female ruler; a tsar's wife who does not become ruler is a tsarina. A tsar's son is a tsarevich and his daughter a tsarevna.

Rurik of Novgorod	862-82
Oleg of Kyiv	882-912
Svyatoslav	962-72
Vladimir I	980-1015
Yaroslav the Wise	1019-54
Vladimir II Monomakh	1113-25
Yury Dolgoruky	1149-57
Andrey Bogolyubov	1157-74
Alexander Nevsky	1252-63
Daniil of Moscow	1276-1303
Ivan I (Kalita)	1325-40
Dmitry Donskoy	1359-89
Ivan III (the Great)	1462-1505
Vasily III	1505-33
Yelena (Regent)	1533-47
Ivan IV (the Terrible)	1547-84
Fyodor I	1584-98
Boris Godunov	1598-1605
False Dmitry	1605-06
Vasily Shuysky	1606-10
Mikhail Romanov	1613-45
Alexey	1645-76
Fyodor III	1676-82
Peter I & Ivan V (Regent: Sofia)	1682-89
Peter I & Ivan V	1689-96
Peter I (the Great)	1696-1725
Catherine I	1725-27
Peter II	1727-30
Anna	1730-40
Elizabeth	1741-61
Peter III	1761-62
Catherine II (the Great)	1762-96
Paul	1796-1801
Alexander I	1801-25
Nicholas I	1825-55
Alexander II	1855-81
Alexander III	1881-94
Nicholas II	1894-1917
Alexandr Kerensky	1917
Vladimir Lenin	1917-24
Josef Stalin	1929-53
Nikita Khrushchev	1957-64
Leonid Brezhnev	1964-82
Yury Andropov	1982-84
Konstantin Chernenko	1984-85
Mikhail Gorbachev	1985-91
Boris Yeltsin	1991-99
(Vladimir Putin, Acting President pending March 2000 elections)	

(votchina) giving them unlimited control and inheritance rights over their lands and the people on them. The freedom to shift allegiance to other princes had given them political clout too. Now, with few alternative princes left, the boyars' influence declined in favour of the new landholding civil servants.

This increased central control spread to the lower levels of society with the growth of serfdom. Before the 1500s, peasants could work for themselves after meeting their masters' needs, and could even change jobs during the two weeks around St George's Day in November. These rights were less frequently bestowed by the new masters, who lacked the old sense of obligation, and peasants became a permanent fixture on the land.

Cossacks

The word 'Cossack', from the Turkic *kazak*, meaning free man, adventurer or horseman, was first applied to residual Tatar groups and later to serfs, paupers and drop-outs who started fleeing south from Russia, Poland

and Lithuania in the 15th century. They organised themselves into self-governing communities in the Don basin, on the Dnipro (Dnepr in Russian) River in Ukraine, and in western Kazakhstan. Those in a given region, eg the Don Cossacks, were not just a tribe; its men constituted an army *(voysko)*, within which each village-regiment *(stanitsa)* elected a leader *(ataman)*.

Mindful of their skill as fighters, the Russian government treated the Cossacks carefully, offering autonomy in return for military service. Cossacks were the wedge that opened Siberia in the 17th century. By the 19th century there were a dozen Cossack armies from Ukraine to the Far East.

But they still raised hell when things didn't suit them. Three peasant uprisings in the Volga-Don region – 1670, 1707 and 1773 – were Cossack-led. After 1917 the Bolsheviks abolished Cossack institutions (though some cavalry units were revived in WWII).

Ivan IV (the Terrible)

Vasily III's son, Ivan IV, took the throne in 1533 at age three, with his mother as regent. After 13 years of court intrigues he had himself crowned 'Tsar of all the Russias'. The word 'tsar', from the Latin *caesar*, had previously been used only for a Great Khan or for the Emperor of Constantinople.

Ivan IV's marriage to Anastasia, who was from the Romanov boyar family, was a happy one – unlike the five that followed her death in 1560, which was a turning point in his life. Believing her to have been poisoned, he instituted a reign of terror that earned him the sobriquet *grozny* (literally 'awesome' but in this case translated as 'Terrible') and nearly destroyed all his earlier good works. In a fit of rage he even killed his eldest son and heir, Ivan.

His subsequent career was indeed terrible, though he was admired for upholding Russian interests and tradition. During his active reign (1547-84) Russia defeated the surviving Tatar khanates of Kazan and Astrakhan, thus acquiring the whole Volga region and a chunk of Caspian Sea coast and opening the way to Siberia. His campaign against the Crimean Tatars, however, nearly ended with the loss of Moscow. Ivan's interest in the West and obsession with reaching the Baltic Sea foreshadowed Peter the Great, but he failed to break through, and only antagonised the Lithuanians, Poles and Swedes, setting the stage for the Time of Troubles. His growing paranoia led to a savage attack on Novgorod that finally snuffed out that city's golden age.

Boris Godunov & the Time of Troubles

When Ivan died of poisoning in 1584, rule passed to his second son, the hopeless Fyodor I, who had the sense to leave government to his brother-in-law, Boris Godunov, a skilled 'prime minister' who repaired much of Ivan's damage. Fyodor died childless in 1598, ending the 700-year Rurikid dynasty, and Boris ruled as tsar for seven more years.

Then a Polish-backed Catholic pretender arrived on the scene claiming to be Dmitry (another son of Ivan the Terrible), who had died in obscure circumstances – murdered on Boris Godunov's orders, some said. This 'False Dmitry' gathered a huge ragtag army as he advanced on Moscow. Boris Godunov conveniently died, his son was lynched and the boyars acclaimed the pretender tsar.

Thus began the Time of Troubles, or Smuta (1606-13), a spell of anarchy, dynastic chaos and foreign invasions. At its heart was a struggle between feudal landholders (the boyars) and central government (the tsar). The False Dmitry was murdered in a popular revolt and succeeded by Vasily Shuysky (1606-10), another boyar puppet. A second False Dmitry (claiming to be both the previous Dmitrys) challenged Shuysky; Swedish and Polish invaders fought each other over claims to the Russian throne; Shuysky was dethroned by the boyars and in 1610-12 the Poles occupied Moscow.

Eventually a popular army, rallied by the Church and supported by Cossack mercenaries, removed the Poles. In 1613 a Zemsky Sobor, or Assembly of the Land, with representatives of the political classes of the day, elected 16-year-old Mikhail Romanov tsar, the first of a new dynasty that was to rule until 1917.

17th Century Russia

Though the first three Romanov rulers – Mikhail (1613-45), Alexey (1645-76) and Fyodor III (1676-82) – provided continuity and stability, there were also big changes that foretold the downfall of 'old' Russia.

Acquisitions The 17th century saw a huge growth in Russian lands. The 'opening' of Siberia, begun by the Stroganov merchant family and Cossack mercenaries under Ataman Yermak Timofeevich, remains one of history's biggest and most explosive territorial expansions.

Additionally, when Cossacks in Ukraine appealed for help against the Poles, Tsar Alexey couldn't resist their pleas, and in 1667 Smolensk, Kyiv and lands east of the Dnepr came under Russian control.

Serfdom Authority in the countryside had collapsed during the Time of Troubles. Thousands of peasants fled to Cossack areas or to Siberia, where serfdom was unknown. Landlords, in despair, found support from the government. The peasants' right to move freely was abolished in 1646. In 1675 they lost all rights to the land and, in a uniquely Russian version of serfdom, could be sold separately from the estates they worked. They were, in effect, slaves.

In 1670-71 Cossacks, runaway serfs and adventurers joined in a huge uprising in the Volga-Don region, led by the Cossack Stepan (Stenka) Razin. Razin's army of 200,000 seized the entire lower Volga basin before he was captured and killed. He remains a folk hero today.

The Church Internal conflicts transformed the Church into a friend of authority, distrusted as much as the government was. In the mid-17th century, Patriarch Nikon tried to bring rituals and texts into line with the 'pure' Greek Orthodox Church, horrifying those attached to traditional Russian forms.

The result was a bitter schism between Nikon's New Believers and Old Believers who, under government persecution, formed a widespread, occasionally fanatical religious underground. In the end Nikon himself was sacked by Tsar Alexey over the issue of Church authority in the newly acquired Ukrainian territories, while Old Believers survive to this day.

Peter the Great

Peter I, known as 'the Great' for his commanding 2.24m frame and his equally commanding victory over the Swedes, dragged Russia kicking and screaming into Europe, made it a major world power and insulted all his administrators and soldiers by shaving off their beards.

Born to Tsar Alexey's second wife in 1672, Peter spent much of his youth in royal residences in the countryside, organising his playmates into military regiments. Energetic, inquisitive and comfortable in any circle, he often visited Moscow's European district to learn about the West. Dutch and British ship captains in Arkhangelsk gave him navigation lessons on the White Sea.

When Fyodor III died in 1682, Peter became tsar, along with his feeble-minded half-brother Ivan V, under the regency of Ivan's ambitious sister, Sofia. She had the support of a leading statesman of the day, Prince Vasily Golitsyn. The boyars, annoyed by Golitsyn's institution of a stringent ranking system, schemed successfully to have Sofia sent to a monastery in 1689 and replaced as regent by Peter's unambitious mother.

Few doubted that Peter was the true monarch, and when he became sole ruler, after his mother's death in 1694 and Ivan's in 1696, he embarked on a modernisation campaign, symbolised by his fact-finding mission to Europe in 1697-98 – he was the first Muscovite ruler ever to go there. Historical literature abounds with tales of his spirited visits to hospitals, workshops and trading houses, his stint as a ship's carpenter in Amsterdam and his hiring of some 1000 experts for service in Russia.

He was also busy negotiating alliances. In 1695 he had sent Russia's first navy down the Don River and captured the Black Sea port of Azov from the Crimean Tatars, vassals of the Ottoman Turks. His European allies weren't interested in the Turks but

shared his concern about the Swedes, who held most of the Baltic coast and had penetrated deep into Europe.

Peter's alliance with Poland and Denmark led to the Great Northern War against Sweden (1700-21), the focal point of his career. The rout of Charles XII's forces at the Battle of Poltava (1709) heralded Russia's power and the collapse of the Swedish Empire. The Treaty of Nystadt (1721) gave Peter control of the Gulf of Finland and the eastern shores of the Baltic Sea. In the midst of this (1707), he put down another peasant rebellion, led by the Don Cossack Kondraty Bulavin.

On land taken from the Swedes, Peter founded a new city, which he named St Petersburg after his patron saint. In 1712 he made it the capital, symbol of a new, Europe-facing Russia.

Peter's Legacy Peter succeeded in mobilising Russian resources to compete on equal terms with the West – a startling achievement. His territorial gains were small, but the strategic Baltic territories also added ethnic variety, including a new upper class of German traders and administrators who formed the backbone of Russia's commercial and military expansion.

Peter was also to have the last word on the authority of the Church. When it resisted his reforms he simply blocked the appointment of a new patriarch, put bishops under a government department and in effect became head of the Church himself.

Vast sums were needed to build St Petersburg, pay a growing civil service, modernise the army and launch naval and commercial fleets. But money was scarce in an economy based on serf labour, so Peter slapped taxes on everything from coffins to beards, including an infamous 'Soul Tax' on all lower-class adult males. The lot of serfs worsened, as they bore the main tax burden.

But even the upper classes had to chip in: aristocrats could either serve in the army or the civil service, or lose their titles and land. Birth counted for little, as state servants were subject to Peter's Table of Ranks, a performance-based ladder of promotion with the upper grades conferring hereditary nobility. Some aristocrats lost all they had, while capable state employees of humble origin, and even foreigners, became Russian nobles.

Peter died in 1725 without naming a successor, and the matter was again decided by intrigue and force. If it hadn't been for a government structure built on the Table of Ranks and a professional bureaucracy with a vested interest in its preservation, Peter's reforms might well have died with him.

After Peter

For 37 years after Peter's death, Russia suffered ineffectual rulers. Day-to-day administration was handled by a governing body called the Supreme Privy Council, staffed by many of Peter's leading administrators. Dominated by the Dolgoruky and Golitsyn boyar families, the council elected Peter's niece Anna of Courland (a small principality in present-day Latvia) to the throne, with a contract stating that the council had the final say in policy decisions. Anna ended this experiment in constitutional monarchy by disbanding the council.

Anna ruled from 1730 to 1740, appointing a Baltic German baron, Ernst Johann von Bühren, to handle affairs of state. His name was Russified to Biron, but his heavy-handed, corrupt style came to symbolise the German influence on the royal family that had begun with Peter the Great.

During the reign of Peter's daughter, Elizabeth (1741-61), German influence waned and restrictions on the nobility were loosened. Some aristocrats began to dabble in manufacture and trade.

Catherine II (the Great)

Daughter of a German prince, Catherine came to Russia at the age of 15 to marry Empress Elizabeth's heir-apparent, her nephew Peter III. Intelligent and ambitious, Catherine learned Russian, embraced the Orthodox Church and devoured the writings of European political philosophers. This was the time of the Enlightenment, when talk of human rights, social contracts and the separation of powers abounded.

Catherine II (the Great)

Catherine later said of Peter III, 'I believe the Crown of Russia attracted me more than his person'. Six months after he ascended the throne she had him overthrown in a palace coup led by her current lover (it has been said that she had more lovers than the average serf had hot dinners), and he was murdered shortly afterwards.

Enlightened Despotism Catherine embarked on a program of reforms, though she made it clear that she had no intention of limiting her own authority. She drafted a new legal code, limited the use of torture and supported religious tolerance. But any ideas she might have had of improving the lot of serfs went overboard with the rebellion of 1773-74, led by the Don Cossack Yemelyan Pugachev.

Pugachev claimed he was Peter III. His rebellion, which spread from the Ural Mountains to the Caspian Sea and along the Volga, was Russia's most violent peasant uprising. Hundreds of thousands responded to his promises to end serfdom and taxation, but were beaten by famine and government armies. Pugachev was executed and Catherine put an end to Cossack autonomy.

In the cultural sphere, Catherine increased the number of schools and colleges and expanded publishing. Her vast collection of paintings forms the core of the present-day Hermitage collection. A critical elite gradually developed, alienated from most uneducated Russians but also increasingly at odds with central authority – a 'split personality' common among future Russian radicals.

Territorial Gains Catherine's reign saw major expansion at the expense of the weakened Ottoman Turks and Poles, engineered by her 'prime minister' and foremost lover, Grigory Potyomkin. War with the Turks began in 1768, peaked with the naval victory at Çesme (Chesma) and ended with a 1774 treaty giving Russia control of the north coast of the Black Sea, freedom of shipping through the Dardanelles to the Mediterranean and 'protectorship' of Christian interests in the Ottoman Empire – a pretext for later incursions into the Balkans. Crimea was annexed in 1783.

Poland had spent the previous century collapsing into semi-independent units with a figurehead king in Warsaw. Catherine manipulated events with divide-and-rule tactics and even had a former lover, Stanislas Poniatowski, installed as king. Austria and Prussia proposed sharing Poland among the three powers, and in 1772, 1793 and 1795 the country was carved up, ceasing to exist as an independent state until 1918. Eastern Poland and the Grand Duchy of Lithuania – roughly, present-day Lithuania, Belarus and western Ukraine – came under Russian rule.

Alexander I

When Catherine died in 1796 the throne passed to her son, Paul I. An old-school autocrat, he antagonised the gentry with attempts to reimpose compulsory state service, and was killed in a coup in 1801. His son and successor, Alexander I, Catherine's favourite grandson, who had been trained by the best European tutors, kicked off his reign with several reforms, including an expansion of the school system that brought education within reach of the lower middle classes. But he was soon preoccupied with the wars against Napoleon which were to dominate his career.

After Napoleon defeated him at Austerlitz, north of Vienna, in 1805 and then at Friedland, near modern Kaliningrad, Alexander began to consider negotiating. The Treaty of Tilsit (1807) left Napoleon in charge as Emperor of the West and Alexander as Emperor of the East, united (in theory) against England.

1812 & Aftermath The alliance lasted only until 1810, when Russia resumed trade with England. A furious Napoleon decided to crush the tsar with his Grand Army of 700,000, the largest force the world had ever seen for a single military operation.

The vastly outnumbered Russian forces retreated across their own countryside through the summer of 1812, scorching the earth in an attempt to deny the French sustenance and fighting some successful rearguard actions. Napoleon set his sights on Moscow, the symbolic heart of Russia. In September, with the lack of provisions beginning to bite on the French, the Russian general Mikhail Kutuzov finally decided to turn and fight at Borodino, 130km from Moscow. The battle was extremely bloody, but inconclusive, with the Russians withdrawing in good order.

Before the month was out, Napoleon entered a deserted Moscow; the same day, the city began to burn down around him (whether by Russian or French hand, or by accident, has never been established). Alexander ignored his overtures to negotiate. With winter coming and his supply lines overstretched, Napoleon ordered a retreat – he was unable to do anything else. His troops starved and were picked off by Russian partisans. Only one in 20 made it back to the relative safety of Poland, and the Russians pursued them all the way to Paris.

At the Congress of Vienna, where the victors met in 1814-15 to establish a new order after Napoleon's final defeat, Alexander championed the cause of the old monarchies. His legacies were a hazy Christian fellowship of European kings, called the Holy Alliance, and a system of pacts to guard against future Napoleons – or any revolutionary change.

More Territorial Gains Meanwhile the Russian Empire was inching outwards. Russian merchants had arrived in Alaska in 1784 and established a solid trading community. Russian ships dropped anchor in San Francisco Bay in 1806, capping their explorations of the Pacific coast.

The kingdom of Georgia united with Russia in 1801. After a war with Sweden in 1807-09, Alexander became Grand Duke of Finland. Russia argued with Turkey over the Danube principalities of Bessarabia (essentially, modern Moldova) and Wallachia (now in Romania), taking Bessarabia in 1812. Persia ceded northern Azerbaijan a year later and Yerevan (in Armenia) in 1828.

Decembrists

Alexander died in 1825 without leaving a clear heir, sparking the usual crisis. His reform-minded brother Constantine, married to a Pole and living happily in Warsaw, had no interest in the throne.

Officers who had brought back liberal ideas from Paris in 1815 preferred Constantine to Alexander's youngest brother, the militaristic Nicholas, who was due to be crowned on 26 December 1825. Their rally in St Petersburg was squashed by troops loyal to Nicholas; several of these so-called Decembrists (Dekabristy) were executed and over 100 – mostly aristocrats and officers – were sent into Siberian exile.

This was the tsarist elite's first cry for change. Officers, intellectuals and children of the clergy formed secret societies. Many looked to the American and French revolutions for inspiration. Others drifted towards the typically Russian solution of anarchism – which would in the future be represented by gurus such as Mikhail Bakunin and Pyotr Kropotkin, who loathed all authority and upheld the virtues of the village commune.

Political debate revealed two trends: 'Westernisers' wanted to rebuild Russia on European lines; 'Slavophiles', generally Orthodox, believed the tsarist tradition could be revitalised with the old idea of the Zemsky Sobor consultative assembly.

Nicholas I

The reign of Nicholas I (1825-55) was a time of stagnation and repression under a tsar who put his faith in his army. The social revolutions that shook Europe in 1830 and 1848 passed Russia by.

There were positive developments, however. The economy grew, and grain exports increased. Nicholas detested serfdom, if only because he detested the serf-owning class. Peasants on state lands, nearly half the total, were given title to their land and, in effect, freed.

In foreign policy, Nicholas' meddling in the Balkans was eventually to destroy Russian credibility in Europe. Bad diplomacy led to the Crimean War of 1854-56 against Ottoman Turkey, Britain and France, who declared war after Russian troops marched into the Ottoman provinces of Moldavia and Wallachia – ostensibly to protect Christian communities there. At Sevastopol an Anglo-French-Turkish force besieged the Russian naval headquarters. Inept command on both sides led to a bloody, stalemated war.

Alexander II & Alexander III

The 'Great Reforms' Nicholas died in 1855. His son, Alexander II, saw the Crimean War stirring up discontent within Russia and accepted peace on unfavourable terms. The war had revealed the backwardness behind the post-1812 imperial glory, and the time for reform had come.

The serfs were freed in 1861. Of the land they had worked, roughly a third was kept by established landholders. The rest went to village communes, which assigned it to the individual ex-serfs in return for 'redemption payments' to compensate former landholders – a system that pleased nobody.

The abolition of serfdom opened the way for a market economy, capitalism and an industrial revolution. Railways and factories were built, and cities expanded as peasants left the land. Foreign investment in Russia grew during the 1880s and 1890s. But nothing was done to modernise farming, and very little to help the peasants. By 1914, 85% of the Russian population was still rural, but their lot had barely improved in 50 years.

Revolutionary Movements The reforms raised hopes that were not satisfied. The tsar refused to set up a representative assembly for all of Russia. Peasants were angry at having to pay for land they considered theirs by right. Radical students, known as *narodniki* or Populists, took to the countryside in the 1870s to rouse the peasants, but the students and the peasants proved to be worlds apart and the campaign failed.

Other Populists saw more value in cultivating revolution among the growing urban working class, or proletariat, while yet others turned to terrorism: one secret society, the People's Will, blew up Alexander II in 1881.

Not all opponents to tsarism were radical revolutionaries. Some moderates, well off and with much to lose from a revolution, called themselves liberals and advocated constitutional reform along Western European lines, with universal suffrage and a national parliament *(duma)*.

The terrorist groups were genuinely surprised that there was no uprising after Alexander II's assassination. Most were rounded up and executed or exiled, and the reign of his son Alexander III was marked by repression of revolutionaries and liberals alike.

Discontent was sometimes directed at Jews and took the form of violent mass attacks, or pogroms. At their height in the 1880s, these were often fanned by the authorities to unload social tension onto a convenient scapegoat. Tending towards intellectual and commercial professions, Jews were hated as shopkeepers and industrialists by the lower classes and as political radicals by the authorities.

Territorial Expansion During the reigns of Alexander II (1855-81) and Alexander III (1881-94), Central Asia (modern Kazakhstan, Uzbekistan, Turkmenistan, Kyrgyzstan and Tajikistan) came fully under Russian control.

In the east, Russia acquired a long strip of Pacific coast from China and built the port of Vladivostok, but sold the 'worthless' Alaskan territories to the USA in 1867 for just US$7.2 million.

Marxism

Many revolutionaries fled abroad. Two who went to Switzerland, Georgy Plekhanov and Pavel Axelrod, were converted to Marxism and founded the Russian Social Democratic Party in 1883. As Marxists they believed that Russia was passing through a capitalist phase on its way to socialism, and that the urban proletariat was the only class with revolutionary potential.

One of their converts was young, upper-middle-class Vladimir Ulyanov, better known by his later pseudonym, Lenin. In 1895 he took charge of Russia's first Marxist cell in St Petersburg, which earned him three years of Siberian exile. On his release in 1899 he went to Europe, where he remained (except for a few secret visits) until 1917, rising to joint leadership of the Party with Plekhanov.

Social democrats in Europe were being elected to parliaments and developing Marxism into 'parliamentary socialism', improving the lot of workers through legislation. The question of what to do in Russia, where there was no parliament, only an active secret police, came to a head at a meeting of the Socialist International movement in London in 1903.

Among Russian socialists, Lenin stood for violent overthrow of the government by a small, committed, well organised Party, while Plekhanov stood for mass membership and cooperation with other political forces. Lenin won the vote through clever manoeuvring, and his faction came to be known as the Bolsheviks, or majority people; Plekhanov's faction became the Mensheviks, or minority people. The Mensheviks actually outnumbered the Bolsheviks in the Party, but Lenin clung to the name, for obvious reasons. The two factions coexisted until 1912, when the Bolsheviks set up their own party.

Back at home, in 1900 the Populist movement became the Social Revolutionary Party, which was the main revolutionary

Lenin, leader of the 1917 Bolshevik Revolution and founder of Russia's Communist Party

force in rural Russia. Liberal politicians formed the Union of Liberation in 1903, and this soon became the Constitutional Democrats (Kadets).

Russo-Japanese War

Nicholas II, who succeeded his father, Alexander III, in 1894, was a weak man who commanded less respect than his father, but was equally opposed to representative government.

The first serious blow to his position was a humiliating defeat by Japan. Though in 1875 Russia and Japan had managed to agree on who should have Sakhalin Island (Russia) and who should get the Kuril Islands (Japan), by the turn of the century they were at odds over their respective 'spheres of influence' – Russia's in Manchuria, Japan's in Korea. As in the Crimea 50 years before, poor diplomacy led to war. In 1904 Japan attacked the Russian naval base at Port Arthur (Dalian) in China.

Defeat followed defeat for Russia on land and sea. The ultimate disaster came in May 1905, when the entire Baltic fleet, which had sailed halfway around the world to relieve Port Arthur, was sunk in the Tsushima Straits off Japan.

1905 Revolution

In Russia, unrest became widespread after the fall of Port Arthur. On 9 January 1905, a priest named Georgy Gapon led a crowd of 200,000 workers – men, women and children – to the Winter Palace in St Petersburg to petition the tsar for better working conditions. Singing 'God save the Tsar', they were met by imperial guards, who opened fire and killed several hundred. This was 'Bloody Sunday'.

After the Tsushima Straits debacle the country broke into anarchy, with wild strikes, pogroms, mutinies and killings of landowners and industrialists. Social democrat activists formed *soviets* in St Petersburg and Moscow. These workers' councils, with representatives chosen by acclaim, proved remarkably successful: the St Petersburg Soviet, led by Mensheviks under Leon Trotsky, declared a general strike, which brought the whole country to a standstill in October.

The tsar gave in and promised a duma (parliament). General elections in April 1906 gave it a leftist majority and it demanded further reforms. The tsar disbanded it. New elections in 1907 pushed the duma farther to the left. It was again disbanded and a new electoral law, limiting the vote to the upper classes and ethnic Russians, ensured that the third and fourth dumas were more cooperative with the tsar, who continued to choose the prime minister and Cabinet.

The capable prime minister, Pyotr Stolypin, abolished the hated redemption payments in the countryside. Enterprising peasants were now able to acquire decent parcels of land, which could be worked efficiently; this led to the creation of a new class of 'big farmers' *(kulaks)*, and to a series of good harvests. It also made it easier for peasants to leave their villages, providing a mobile labour force for industry. Radical activists lost their following.

But Stolypin was assassinated in 1911, and the tsarist regime again lost touch with the people. Nicholas became a puppet of his strong-willed, eccentric wife, Alexandra, who herself fell under the spell of a sinister Siberian peasant named Rasputin. Rasputin was eventually killed by court nobles in December 1916.

WWI

Russia's involvement with the Balkans made it a main player in the world war that began there in 1914. The war was badly managed from the start. Heavy defeats in Prussia were followed in 1915 by German advances deep into Russia itself. By the time the Germans halted, to concentrate on trench warfare in France, an estimated two million Russian troops had been killed and Germany controlled Poland and much of the Baltic coast, Belarus and Ukraine.

The tsar responded to protests by disbanding the duma and assuming personal command in the field, where he couldn't make much headway. At home, the disorganised government failed to introduce rationing, and in February 1917 in Petrograd (the new, less 'German' name for St Petersburg), discontent in the food queues turned to riots. Soldiers and police mutinied, refusing to fire on demonstrators. A new Petrograd Soviet of Workers' & Soldiers' Deputies was formed on the 1905 model, and more sprang up elsewhere. The reconvened duma ignored an order to disband itself and set up a committee to assume government.

Now there were two alternative power bases in the capital. The soviet was a rallying and debating point for factory workers and soldiers; the duma committee attracted the educated and commercial elite. In February the two reached agreement on a provisional government that would demand the tsar's abdication. The tsar tried to return to Petrograd but was blocked by his own troops. On 1 March he abdicated.

1917 Bolshevik Revolution

The provisional government announced general elections for November, and continued the war despite a collapse of discipline in the army and popular demands for peace. On 3 April Lenin and other exiled Bolsheviks returned to Petrograd via Scandinavia in a sealed railway carriage provided by the German army. Though well and truly in the minority in the soviets, the Bolsheviks were organised and committed. They won many over with a demand for immediate 'peace, land and bread', and believed the soviets should seize power at once. But a series of violent mass demonstrations in July (the 'July Days'), inspired by the Bolsheviks, was in the end not fully backed by them and was quelled. Lenin fled to Finland, and Alexander Kerensky, a moderate Social Revolutionary, became prime minister.

In September the Russian military chief of staff, General Kornilov, sent cavalry to Petrograd to crush the soviets. Kerensky turned to the left for support against this insubordination, even courting the Bolsheviks, and the counter-revolution was defeated. After this, public opinion massively favoured the Bolsheviks, who quickly took control of the Petrograd Soviet (chaired by Trotsky, who had joined them) and, by extension, all the soviets in the land. Lenin decided it was time to seize power, and returned from Finland in October.

During the night of 24-25 October 1917, Bolshevik workers and soldiers in Petrograd seized government buildings and communication centres, and arrested the provisional government, which was meeting in the Winter Palace. (Kerensky managed to escape, eventually dying in the USA in 1970.) Within hours, an All-Russian Congress of Soviets, meeting in Petrograd, made the soviets the ruling councils in Russia, headed by a 'parliament' called the Soviet Central Executive Committee. A Council of People's Commissars became the government, headed by Lenin, with Trotsky as commissar for foreign affairs and the Georgian Josef Stalin as commissar for nationalities.

Local soviets elsewhere in Russia seized power relatively easily, but the coup in Moscow took six days of fighting. The general elections scheduled for November could not be stopped, however. More than half Russia's male population voted. Roughly 55% chose Kerensky's rural Socialist party and only 25% voted for the Bolsheviks – so, when the new assembly met in January, the Bolsheviks disbanded it after its first day in session.

Civil War

The Soviet government wasted no time introducing sweeping measures. It redistributed land to those who worked it, signed an armistice with the Germans in December 1917 and set up the Cheka, a secret police force; Trotsky, now military commissar, founded the Red Army in January 1918. In March the Bolshevik Party renamed itself the Communist Party and moved the capital to Moscow.

In March 1918, the Treaty of Brest-Litovsk surrendered Poland, the Baltic provinces, Ukraine, Finland and Transcaucasia to Germany and its allies, enabling the Soviet regime to concentrate on internal enemies. These were becoming numerous in the countryside because of food requisitions by armed trade-union detachments.

In July the former tsar and his family, who had been interned for months, were killed by their Communist guards in Yekaterinburg. Two months later, the Cheka began a systematic program of arrests, torture and executions.

Those hostile to the Bolsheviks, collectively termed 'Whites', had developed strongholds in the south and east of the country. But they lacked unity, as they ranged from tsarist stalwarts to landlord-killing Social Revolutionaries (who were opposed to the Brest-Litovsk treaty), from Finnish partisans to Japanese troops. The Bolsheviks had the advantage of controlling the heart of Russia, including its war industry and communications. Full-scale civil war broke out in early 1918 and lasted almost three years. The main centres of opposition to the Bolsheviks were:

- In the south, tsarist and liberal sympathisers under generals Kornilov and Denikin, plus Cossacks clamouring for autonomy.
- Ukraine, which was under German control until November 1918, and then was occupied

variously by nationalists, the army of newly independent Poland, and Denikin's troops.

- Admiral Kolchak's government of 'all Russia' in Omsk, Siberia, which was supported by 40,000 Czech prisoners of war, the most formidable fighting force the Red Army had to deal with.
- The Baltic provinces and Finland, which waged successful wars of independence.
- British, French, US and Japanese troops who made mischief round the periphery. The Japanese were the biggest threat as they established themselves in large tracts of the Far East, but they eventually pulled out in 1922.
- Uprisings by peasants, as a result of famine in 1920-21; and by sailors at the Kronstadt naval base near Petrograd in 1921, against the Soviet monopoly of power. These sailors had been among the first supporters of the revolution, but the Cheka executed them in their thousands.

By 1921, the Communist Party had firmly established one-party rule, thanks to the Red Army and the Cheka, which continued to eliminate opponents. Some of them escaped, joining an estimated 1.5 million citizens in exile.

'War Communism'

During the civil war, a system called 'War Communism' subjected every aspect of society to the aim of victory. This meant sweeping nationalisations in all economic sectors and strict administrative control by the Soviet government, which in turn was controlled by the Communist Party.

The Party itself was restructured to reflect Lenin's creed of 'Democratic Centralism', which held that Party decisions should be obeyed all the way down the line. A new political bureau, the Politburo, was created for Party decision-making, and a new secretariat supervised Party appointments, ensuring that only loyal members were given responsibility (Stalin became Party general secretary in 1922).

War Communism was also a form of social engineering to create a classless society. To an extent it worked, in that many 'class enemies' were eliminated by execution or exile, but the economic consequences were disastrous: forced food requisitions and hostility towards the larger, more efficient farmers, combined with drought and a breakdown of infrastructure, led to the enormous famine of 1920-21, when between four and five million people died.

The New Economic Policy

Lenin suggested a strategic compromise with capitalism. The New Economic Policy, or NEP, was adopted by the 10th Party Congress in 1921 and remained in force until 1927. The state continued to own the 'commanding heights' of the economy – large-scale industry, banks, transport – but allowed private enterprise to re-emerge. Farm output improved as the kulaks consolidated their holdings and employed landless peasants as wage-earners. Farm surplus was sold to the cities in return for industrial products, giving rise to a new class of traders and small-scale industrialists called 'Nepmen'.

In the state sectors, wages were allowed to reflect effort as professional managers replaced Party administrators. By the late 1920s, agricultural and industrial production had reached prewar levels.

But the political tide was set the other way. At the 1921 Party congress, Lenin outlawed debate within the Party as 'factionalism' and launched the first systematic purge among Party members. The Cheka was reorganised as the GPU (State Political Administration) in 1922, with much greater powers to operate outside the law; for the time being it limited its activities to targeting political opponents. The Union of Soviet Socialist Republics (USSR), a federation of theoretically independent Soviet Socialist Republics (SSRs), was established in 1922. The initial members were the Russian, Ukrainian, Belarusian and Transcaucasian SSRs. By 1940 the number had reached 11 with the splitting of the Transcaucasian SSR into Georgian, Armenian and Azerbaijani SSRs and the addition of five Central Asian republics.

Stalin vs Trotsky

In May 1922, Lenin suffered the first of a series of paralysing strokes that removed him from effective control of the Party and government. He died aged 54 in January 1924. His embalmed remains were put on display in Moscow, Petrograd became Leningrad in his honour, and a personality cult was built around him – all orchestrated by Stalin.

Lenin had failed to name a successor, although he expressed a low opinion of 'too rude' Stalin. The charismatic Trotsky, hero of the civil war and second only to Lenin as an architect of the revolution, wanted collectivisation of agriculture – an extension of War Communism – and worldwide revolution. He attacked Party 'bureaucrats' who wished to concentrate on socialism in the Soviet Union. But even before Lenin's death, the powers that mattered in the Party and soviets had backed a three-man leadership of Zinoviev, Kamenev and Stalin, in which Stalin already pulled the strings. As Party general secretary, he controlled all appointments and had installed his supporters wherever it mattered. His influence grew with a recruiting drive that doubled Party membership to over a million.

Trotsky and his diminishing group of supporters were expelled from the Party in 1927. In 1929 he went into exile, ending up in Mexico, where an agent of Stalin wielding an ice pick finished him off in 1940.

Five-Year Plans & Farm Collectivisation

With Trotsky out of the way, Stalin took up Trotsky's farm collectivisation idea as part of a grand plan to turn the USSR into an industrial power. The first Five-Year Plan, launched in 1929, called for a quadrupling of output by heavy industry, such as power stations, mines, steelworks and railways. Agriculture was to be collectivised to get the peasants to fulfil production quotas, which would feed the growing cities and provide food exports to pay for imported heavy machinery.

The forced collectivisation of agriculture destroyed the country's peasantry (who were still 80% of the population) as a class and as a way of life. Farmers were required to pool their land and resources into collective farms *(kolkhozy)*, usually consisting of about 75 households and dozens of square kilometres in area, which became their collective property, in return for compulsory quotas of produce. These kolkhozy covered two-thirds of all farmland, supported by a network of Machine Tractor Stations that dispensed machinery and advice (political or otherwise). Another farm organisation was the *sovkhoz*, a state-owned business for large-scale farming of single crops by paid staff.

Farmers who resisted – and most kulaks did, especially in Ukraine and the Volga and Don regions, which had the biggest grain surpluses – were killed or deported to labour camps in their millions. Farmers slaughtered their animals rather than hand them over, leading to the loss of half the national livestock. A drought and continued grain requisitions led to famine in the same three regions in 1932-33, in which a further six million or more people died. Some say Stalin deliberately orchestrated this to wipe out opposition. An estimated 20 million country people had left for the cities by 1939, by which time virtually all those left were 'collectivised'.

In heavy industry, if not in consumer goods, the first two Five-Year Plans produced faster growth than any Western country ever showed. By 1939 only the USA and Germany had higher industrial output.

The Gulag & Purges

Many of these new mines and factories were in Central Asia or the resource-rich, but thinly populated, region of Siberia. A key labour force was provided by the network of concentration camps – now referred to as the Gulag, from **G**lavnoe **U**pravlenie **Lag**erey (Main Administration for Camps) – which stretched from the north of European Russia through Siberia and Central Asia to the Far East.

Many of the early camp inmates were farmers caught up in the collectivisation, but in the 1930s the terror shifted to Party members and other influential people not enthusiastic enough about Stalin. In 1934 Sergey Kirov, the popular Leningrad Party secretary and Stalin's second-in-command, who favoured alleviating the lot of the peasants and producing more consumer goods for urban workers, was murdered by an agent of the secret police (now called the NKVD, the People's Commissariat of Internal Affairs).

This launched the biggest series of purges yet. That year 100,000 Party members, intellectuals and 'enemies of the people' disappeared or were executed in Leningrad alone. In 1936 the former Party leaders Zinoviev and Kamenev made absurd public confessions, admitting to murdering Kirov and plotting to kill Stalin, and were executed.

This was the first of the Moscow show trials, whose charges ranged from murder plots and capitalist sympathies to Trotskyist conspiracies. The biggest was staged in 1938 against 17 leading Bolsheviks, including the Party theoretician Bukharin. Throughout 1937 and 1938 the NKVD's 'black raven' vans continued quietly to take victims from their homes at night; most were never heard of again. In the non-Russian republics of the USSR, virtually the whole Party apparatus was eliminated for 'bourgeois nationalism'. The ghastly business clawed its way into all sectors and levels of society – even 400 of the Red Army's 700 generals were shot. Its victims are thought to have totalled 8.5 million.

The Gulag population grew from 30,000 in 1928 to eight million in 1938. Prisoners were underfed, mistreated and literally worked to death; the average life expectancy was about two years, and 90% of inmates didn't come out alive. The Gulag continued well after WWII, and Boris Yeltsin announced the release of Russia's 'last 10' political prisoners from a camp near Perm in 1992.

The German-Soviet Pact

In 1939 the UK and France tried to persuade Stalin to join them in declaring war on Germany if it should invade Poland. They were coolly received. If the Germans were to walk into Poland they would be on the Soviet border, not far from Minsk, and ready, if the USSR was hostile, to roll on to Moscow. Stalin needed time to prepare his country for war, and saw a deal with the Germans as a route to making territorial gains in Poland.

On 23 August 1939, the Soviet and German foreign ministers, Molotov and Ribbentrop, stunned the world by signing a nonaggression pact. A secret protocol stated that any future rearrangement would divide Poland between them; Germany would have a free hand in Lithuania, and the Soviet Union in Estonia, Latvia, Finland and Bessarabia, which had been lost to Romania in 1918.

Germany invaded Poland on 1 September; the UK and France declared war on Germany on 3 September. Stalin traded the Polish provinces of Warsaw and Lublin with Hitler for most of Lithuania, and the Red Army marched into the newly acquired territories less than three weeks later. The Soviet gains in Poland, many of which were areas inhabited by non-Polish speakers and had been under Russian control before WWI, were quickly incorporated into the Belarusian and Ukrainian republics of the USSR.

The Baltic States were made republics of the USSR in 1940 (along with Moldavia, they brought the total of SSRs up to its final number of 15). But the Finns offered fierce resistance, fighting the Red Army to a standstill.

The Great Patriotic War

When Hitler put his secret plans for an invasion of the Soviet Union into effect as 'Operation Barbarossa' on 22 June 1941, the Soviet Union was not completely unprepared for war. The second and third Five-Year Plans had given priority to arms industries, the army budget had increased 40-fold between 1933 and 1940, and universal military service had been introduced in 1939. But Stalin in one of the great blunders of all time refused to believe that the Germans were preparing to attack, even as reports came to Moscow of massive German preparations along the border. The disorganised Red Army was no match for the

German war machine, which advanced on three fronts. Within four months the Germans had overrun Minsk and Smolensk and were just outside Moscow; they had marched through the Baltic States and laid siege to Leningrad; and had captured Kyiv and most of Ukraine. Only an early, severe winter halted the advance.

The Soviet commander, General Zhukov, used the winter to push the Germans back from Moscow. Leningrad held out – and continued to do so for 2¼ years, during which over half a million of its civilians died, mainly from hunger. In 1942 Hitler ordered a new southern offensive towards the Caucasus oilfields, which became bogged down in the battle for Stalingrad (now Volgograd). Well aware of the symbolism of a city named after the Great Leader, both Hitler and Stalin ordered that there be no retreat. (See the boxed text 'A Battle to the Death' in the Volga Region chapter.)

The Germans, with insecure supply lines along a front that stretched more than 1600km from north to south, also faced scorched earth and guerrilla warfare. Their atrocities against the population stiffened resistance. Stalin appealed to old-fashioned patriotism and eased restrictions on the Church, ensuring that the whole country rallied to the cause with incredible endurance. Military goods supplied by the Allies through the northern ports of Murmansk and Arkhangelsk were invaluable in the early days of the war. All Soviet military industry was packed up, moved east of the Ural Mountains, and worked by women and Gulag labour.

The Soviet forces slowly gained the upper hand at Stalingrad, and on 2 February 1943 Field Marshal von Paulus surrendered what was left of the encircled German Sixth Army. It was the turning point of the war. The Red Army had driven the Germans out of most of the Soviet Union by the end of the year; it reached Berlin in April 1945.

The USSR had borne the brunt of the war. Its total losses, civilian and military, may never be known, but they probably reached at least 26 million. Recent estimates by some Western historians have put the figure as high as 40 million, or one-quarter of the Soviet Union's population – an astonishing statistic. The battle for Stalingrad alone cost an estimated one million Soviet troops, more than the combined US casualties in all theatres of the war, and the Smolensk-Moscow campaign of 1941 took the lives of 1.5 million.

The Red Army's successes meant that the US and British leaders, Roosevelt and Churchill, had to observe Stalin's wishes in the postwar settlement. At Tehran (November 1943) and Yalta (February 1945), the three agreed each to govern the areas they liberated until free elections could be held.

Soviet troops liberating Eastern Europe propped up local communist movements, which formed 'action committees' that either manipulated the elections or simply seized power when election results were unfavourable.

Postwar Stalinism

Control over Eastern Europe, and a postwar modernisation of industry with the aid of German factories and engineers seized as war booty, made the Soviet Union one of the two major world powers. The development of a Soviet atomic bomb as early as September 1949 demonstrated industry's new power. But the first postwar Five-Year Plan was military and strategic (more heavy industry); consumer goods and agriculture remained low priorities.

A Cold War was shaping up between the communist and capitalist worlds, and in the USSR the new demon became 'cosmopolitanism' – warm feelings towards the West. The first victims were the estimated two million Soviet citizens repatriated by the Allies in 1945 and 1946. Some were former prisoners of war or forced labourers taken by the Germans; others were refugees or people who had taken the chance of war to escape the USSR. They were sent straight to the Gulag in case their stay abroad had contaminated them.

Party and government purges continued as Stalin's reign came to resemble that of Ivan the Terrible, with unpredictable, often shattering decisions.

In 1947 US President Harry Truman initiated a policy of 'containment' of Soviet influence within its 1947 limits. The US, British and French forces occupying western zones of Germany unified their areas. The Soviet troops in eastern Germany retaliated by blockading western Berlin, controlled by the Western powers, in 1948; it had to be supplied from the air for a year. This led to the long-term division of Germany.

In 1949 the North Atlantic Treaty Organization (NATO) was set up to protect Western Europe against invasion. The Soviet Union replied with a series of military alliances that led to the Warsaw Pact in 1955.

The Khrushchev Era

Stalin died, allegedly of a stroke, in 1953. An estimated 20 million people had died in his purges, forced famines and labour camps, yet he had become something of a god in his own lifetime. Churchill commented that when Stalin took Russia on, it only had the wooden plough, but he left it with nuclear weapons.

Power passed to a combined leadership of five Politburo members. One, Lavrenty Beria, the head of the NKVD, was secretly tried and shot (and the NKVD was reorganised as the KGB, the Committee for State Security, which was to remain firmly under Party control). In 1954 another, Nikita Khrushchev, a pragmatic Ukrainian who had helped carry out 1930s purges, launched the Virgin Lands campaign, bringing vast tracts of Kazakhstan and Central Asia under cultivation. A series of good harvests did his reputation no harm.

During the 20th Party congress in 1956, Khrushchev made a famous 'secret speech' about crimes committed under Stalin. It was the beginning of de-Stalinisation, marked by the release of some Gulag prisoners and a thaw in the political and intellectual climate. The congress also approved peaceful coexistence between communist and non-communist regimes. The Soviet Union, Khrushchev argued, would soon triumph over the 'imperialists' by economic means. Despite the setback of the 1956 Hungarian rebellion, which was put down by Soviet troops, in 1957 he emerged the unchallenged leader of the USSR.

In October 1957, the world listened to radio 'blips' from the first space satellite, Sputnik 1, and in 1961 Yury Gagarin became the first person in space. The Soviet Union seemed to be going places. But foreign crises undermined Khrushchev. In 1961 Berlin was divided by the Wall to stop an exodus from eastern Germany. In 1962, on the pretext of supplying the USSR's Caribbean ally Cuba with defensive weapons, Khrushchev stationed medium-range missiles with nuclear capability on the US doorstep. After some tense calling of bluff that brought the world to the brink of nuclear war, he withdrew the missiles.

A rift opened between the Soviet Union and China, itself now on the road to superpower status. The two competed for the allegiance of newly independent Third World nations and came into conflict over areas in Central Asia and the Far East that had been conquered by the tsars.

At home, the agricultural sector performed poorly and Khrushchev upset Party colleagues by decentralising economic decision-making. After a disastrous harvest in 1963 forced the Soviet Union to buy wheat from Canada, the Central Committee relieved Khrushchev of his posts in 1964, because of 'advanced age and poor health'.

The Brezhnev Reaction

The new 'collective' leadership of Leonid Brezhnev (first secretary) and Alexey Kosygin (premier) soon devolved into a one-man show under conservative Brezhnev. Stalin was once again portrayed as a national hero and Khrushchev's administrative reforms were rolled back. Economic stagnation was the predictable result, despite the exploitation of huge Siberian oil and gas reserves. But despite increased repression, the 'dissident' movement grew, along with underground publishing *(samizdat)*. Prison terms and forced labour did not seem to have the desired effect, and in 1972 the KGB chief, Yury Andropov, introduced new measures that included forced emigration and the use of psychiatric institutions.

The growing government and Party elite, known as the list of nominees *(nomenklatura)*, enjoyed lavish lifestyles, with access to goods that were unavailable to the average citizen. So did military leaders and some approved engineers and artists. But the ponderous, overcentralised economy, with its suffocating bureaucracy, was providing fewer and fewer improvements in general living standards. Incentive and initiative were dead; corruption began to spread in the Party and a cynical malaise began to spread through society.

Repression extended to countries under the Soviet wing. The 1968 Prague Spring, when new Czechoslovak Party leader Alexander Dubcek promised 'Socialism with a human face', was crushed by Soviet troops. The invasion was later defended by the 'Brezhnev Doctrine' that the Soviet Union had the right to defend its interests among countries that fell within its sphere of influence. In 1979 Afghanistan would be one such country. Relations with China fell to an all-time low with border clashes in 1969. The military build-up between the two countries was only toned down in the late 1980s.

Ironically, the Brezhnev era also included the easing of superpower tensions, known as détente. US president Richard Nixon visited Moscow and the two superpowers signed the first Strategic Arms Limitation Talks (SALT) treaty, restricting the number of nuclear ballistic weapons.

Andropov & Chernenko

Brezhnev was rarely seen in public after his health declined in 1979. Before he died in 1982, he came to symbolise the lifeless state of affairs in the country. The average age of Politburo members was 69.

Brezhnev's successor, the former KGB chief Yury Andropov, replaced some officials with young technocrats and began campaigns against alcoholism (which was costing the economy dearly) and corruption. He also clamped down on dissidents and increased defence spending, while the economy continued to decline.

Andropov died in February 1984, only 14 months after coming to power. The geriatric generation tried to cling to power by choosing the frail, 72-year-old Konstantin Chernenko as his successor. But Chernenko had only a year to live.

Gorbachev

Glasnost Mikhail Gorbachev, a 54-year-old Andropov protégé from Stavropol on Russia's southern steppes, was waiting to step up as general secretary. Articulate and energetic, he understood that the Soviet economy badly needed sparking back into life, and soon departed radically from the policies of his predecessors with greater openness at home and abroad. He launched an immediate turnover in the Politburo, bureaucracy and military, replacing many of the Brezhnevite 'old guard' with his own, younger supporters, and he clamped down vigorously on alcohol abuse. 'Acceleration' in the economy, and openness *(glasnost)*, first manifested in press criticism of poor economic management and past Party failings, were his initial slogans. The aim was to spur the dangerously stagnant economy by encouraging some management initiative, rewarding efficiency and letting bad practices be criticised.

Foreign Affairs In foreign policy, Gorbachev discontinued the isolationist, confrontational and economically costly policies of his predecessors. Most of the world was delighted to find an active intelligence at the helm of the Soviet Union. The constructive Georgian Eduard Shevardnadze replaced the dour Andrey Gromyko as foreign minister. At his first meeting with US president Ronald Reagan in Geneva in 1985, Gorbachev suggested a 50% cut in long-range nuclear weapons. By 1987 the two superpowers had agreed to remove all medium-range missiles from Europe; other significant cuts in arms and troop numbers followed. The 'new thinking' also put an end, in 1988-89, to the Soviet Union's 'Vietnam', the now-unpopular Afghan war. Relations with China improved too.

Perestroika At home, Gorbachev soon found that he could not expect a program of limited reform to proceed smoothly and that he had some hard choices to make. The Chornobyl (Chernobyl in Russian) nuclear disaster in April 1986 led to one step along this road. Gorbachev announced there would be greater openness in reporting embarrassing things such as disasters; it had taken the authorities 18 days to admit the extent of the disaster at the power station in Ukraine, and even when they did, it was in a heavily expurgated form.

The anti-alcohol campaign was very unpopular and won little support. The end result was a huge growth in illegal distilling. Before long it was abandoned.

But above all it was becoming clear that no leader who relied on the Party could survive as a reformer. Many Party officials, with their privileged positions and (in some cases) opportunities for corruption, were a hindrance to, not a force for, change. In the economy *perestroika* (restructuring) became the new slogan. This meant limited private enterprise and private property, not unlike Lenin's NEP, plus further efforts to push decision-making and responsibility out towards the grass roots. New laws were enacted in both these fields in 1988, but their application met resistance from the centralised bureaucracy.

Glasnost was supposed to tie in with perestroika as a way to encourage new ideas and counter the Brezhnev legacy of cynicism. The release at the end of 1986 of a famous dissident, Nobel Peace Prizewinner Andrey Sakharov, from internal exile in Nizhny Novgorod was the start of a general freeing of political prisoners. Religions were allowed to operate more and more freely.

Political Reform In 1988 Gorbachev appealed over the Party's head to the people by announcing a new 'parliament', the Congress of People's Deputies, with two-thirds of its members to be elected directly by the people, thus reducing the power of the bureaucracy and Party. The elections were held and the congress convened, to outspoken debate and national fascination, in 1989. Though dominated by Party apparatchiks, the parliament also contained outspoken critics of the government such as Sakharov.

End of the Empire Gorbachev sprang repeated surprises, including sudden purges of difficult opponents, but the forces unleashed by his opening up of society grew impossible to control. From 1988 onwards, the reduced threat of repression and the experience of electing even semirepresentative assemblies spurred a growing clamour for independence in the Soviet satellite states in Eastern Europe, then in the USSR's Baltic republics, then in Moldova, then in the Transcaucasian republics. The Eastern European countries threw off their Soviet puppet regimes one by one in the autumn of 1989. The Berlin Wall fell on 9 November. The Brezhnev Doctrine, Gorbachev's spokesperson said, had given way to the 'Sinatra Doctrine' – letting them do it *their* way. The formal reunification of Germany on 3 October 1990 marked the effective end of the Cold War.

In 1990 the three Baltic republics of the USSR also declared (or, as they would have it, reaffirmed) their independence – an independence that for the time being remained more theoretical than real. Before long, most other Soviet republics either followed suit or declared 'sovereignty' – the precedence of their own laws over the Soviet Union's. Gorbachev's proposal for an ill-defined new federal system, to hold the Soviet Union together, won few friends.

The Rise of Yeltsin Also in 1990, the populist reformer Boris Yeltsin won the chairmanship of the parliament of the giant Russian Republic, which had three-quarters of the USSR's area and more than half its population. Soon after coming to power, Gorbachev had promoted Yeltsin to head the Communist Party in Moscow, but had then dumped him in 1987-88 in the face of opposition to his reforms there from the Party's old guard. Yeltsin had already by that time declared perestroika a failure, and these events produced a lasting personal enmity between the two men. Gorbachev struggled increasingly from then on to hold together the radical reformers and the conservative old guard in the Party.

Once chosen as chairman of the Russian parliament, Yeltsin proceeded to taunt and jockey for power with Gorbachev. He seemed already to have concluded that real change was impossible not only under the Communist Party but also within a centrally controlled Soviet Union, the members of which were in any case showing severe centrifugal tendencies. Yeltsin resigned from the Communist Party and his parliament proclaimed the sovereignty of the Russian Republic.

At street level, organised crime and black-marketeering boomed, profiting from a slackening of the law-and-order system, and preying on many of the fledgling private businesses by running protection rackets.

In early 1990 Gorbachev persuaded the Communist Party to vote away its own constitutional monopoly on power, and parliament chose him for the newly created post of executive president, which further distanced the organs of government from the Party. But these events made little difference to the crisis into which the USSR was sliding.

Economic Collapse & Old-Guard Reaction Gorbachev's economic reforms, while wounding the old centralised command system badly enough to prevent it reaching even Brezhnevite levels of efficiency, were not profound enough to yield a healthy private sector or a sound, decentralised state sector. The old system was crippled but had not been replaced.

Prices went up, supplies of goods went down, people got angry. Some wanted all-out capitalism immediately; others wanted to go back to the suddenly rosy old days. Gorbachev tried to steer a middle course to prevent a showdown between the radical reformers and the conservatives in the Party and the armed forces – a tack which achieved nothing and pleased no-one.

Much of the record 1990 harvest was left to rot in fields and warehouses because the Party could no longer mobilise the machinery and hands to bring it in, while private enterprise was not yet advanced enough to do so. When Gorbachev, still trying to keep a balance, backed down in September 1990 from implementing the radical '500 Day Plan' – to shift to a fully fledged market economy within 500 days – many saw it as submission to the growing displeasure of the old guard, and the loss of his last chance to save reform.

His Nobel Peace Prize, awarded in the bleak winter of 1990-91, when fuel and food were disappearing from many shops, left the average Soviet citizen literally cold. The army, the security forces and the Party hardliners called with growing confidence for the restoration of law and order to save the country. Foreign minister Shevardnadze, long one of Gorbachev's staunchest partners but now under constant old-guard sniping for 'losing Eastern Europe', resigned, warning of impending hardline dictatorship.

Fall of the Soviet Union

By spring 1991 Gorbachev appeared increasingly weak, directionless and under the old guard's thumb, with his popularity at an all-time low. Boris Yeltsin, committed to ending Communist power and resigned to letting the republics – many of which now demanded full independence – go their own way, was already arguably more powerful than Gorbachev. In June Yeltsin was voted president of the Russian Republic in the country's first-ever direct presidential elections. Yeltsin demanded devolution of power from the Soviet Union to the republics, and banned Communist Party cells from government offices and workplaces in Russia. Gorbachev won some respite by fashioning a new union treaty, transferring greater power to the republics, which was to be signed on 20 August.

The Coup Matters were taken out of Gorbachev's hands, however, on 18 August, when a delegation from the 'Committee for the State of Emergency in the USSR' arrived at the Crimean dacha where he was taking a holiday and demanded that he declare a state of emergency and transfer power to the vice-president, Gennady

Yanaev. Gorbachev refused and was put under house arrest. The old-guard coup had begun.

The eight-person State of Emergency Committee, which included Gorbachev's defence minister, his prime minister and his KGB chief, planned to restore the Communist Party and the Soviet Union to their former status. On 19 August tanks appeared on Moscow's streets and it was announced that Yanaev had assumed the president's powers.

But things didn't go according to the plot. Boris Yeltsin escaped arrest and went to the Moscow 'White House', seat of the Russian parliament, to rally opposition. Crowds gathered at the White House, persuaded some of the tank crews to switch sides, and started to build barricades. Yeltsin climbed on a tank to declare the coup illegal and call for a general strike. Troops ordered to storm the White House refused to do so.

The following day huge crowds opposed to the coup gathered in Moscow and Leningrad. The leaders of Ukraine and Kazakhstan rejected the coup. Estonia declared full independence from the Soviet Union. Coup leaders started to quit or fall ill. On 21 August the tanks withdrew; the coup leaders fled and were arrested.

Demolition Gorbachev flew back to Moscow on 22 August, but his time was up. The old-style Soviet Union and the Communist Party were already suffering the consequences of their humiliation in the failed coup. Yeltsin had announced that all state property in the Russian Republic was under the control of Russia, not the Soviet Union. On 23 August he banned the Communist Party in Russia. Gorbachev resigned as the USSR Party's leader the following day, ordering that its property be transferred to the Soviet parliament.

Latvia had followed Estonia by declaring independence on 21 August (Lithuania had already done so). Most of the other republics of the USSR followed suit. International, and finally Soviet, recognition of the Baltic States' independence followed by early September.

Gorbachev embarked on a last-ditch bid to save the Soviet Union with proposals for a looser union of independent states. In September the Soviet parliament abolished the centralised Soviet state, vesting power in three temporary governing bodies until a new union treaty could be signed. But Yeltsin was steadily transferring control over everything that mattered in Russia from Soviet hands into Russian ones.

On 8 December Yeltsin and the leaders of Ukraine and Belarus, meeting near Brest in Belarus, announced that the USSR no longer existed. They proclaimed a new Commonwealth of Independent States (CIS), a vague alliance of fully independent states with no central authority. Russia kicked the Soviet government out of the Kremlin on 19 December. Two days later, at a meeting in Almaty, Kazakhstan, eight more republics joined the CIS, and the USSR was pronounced finally dead. (The only absentees among the 15 republics of the USSR were the three Baltic States and Georgia. Georgia joined the CIS later.)

Gorbachev, a president without a country, formally resigned on 25 December, the day the white, blue and red Russian flag replaced the Soviet red flag over the Kremlin.

Russia Under Yeltsin

Economic Reform & Regional Tensions

Yeltsin was quick to announce plans to move to a free-market economy in Russia. Changes included the phasing out of state subsidies, freeing of prices, reduction in government spending, and privatisation of state businesses, housing, land and agriculture. In November 1991 Yeltsin had appointed a reforming government to carry this out. He gave himself the jobs of prime minister and defence minister, as well as president, as an emergency measure.

With the economy already in chaos, and the 1991 harvest the lowest in years because the distribution system had broken down, some local regions of Russia started hoarding scarce foodstuffs or declaring autonomy and control over their own economic resources. All the 20 nominally autonomous ethnic regions scattered across Russia, some of them rich in resources vital to the Russian economy, declared themselves autonomous republics, leading to fears that Russia might disintegrate as the USSR had just done. These worries were eventually defused, however, by a 1992 federative treaty between the central government and the republics; by a new constitution in 1993, which handed the other regions increased rights; and by changes in the tax system (see the later Government & Politics section for more information).

Conflict with the Old Guard The parliament, although it had supported Yeltsin against the coup in 1991, could not tolerate the fast pace of his economic reforms, the weakening of Russian power that stemmed from his demolition of the Soviet Union, his arms-reduction agreements with the USA and his need for Western economic aid. Elected in 1990 under Gorbachev-era voting rules, the parliament was dominated by communists and Russian nationalists, both opposed to the course things were taking.

As early as April 1991, Yeltsin's ministers were complaining that their reforms were being stymied by contradictory legislation from the parliament. As the austerity caused by economic reform continued to bite – though there was more in the shops, ordinary people could buy less – Yeltsin's popularity began to fall and his opponents in parliament launched a series of increasingly serious challenges to his position. Another complaint was a steady rise in organised crime, which was to some extent the result of the opening up of the economy – though corruption in the bureaucracy, which was now deeply mixed up in embezzling and smuggling state property, even oil, went back at least as far as the Brezhnev era.

Yeltsin was forced to sacrifice key ministers such as Yegor Gaidar, architect of the economic reforms, and to compromise on the pace of reform. In December 1992 parliament chose Viktor Chernomyrdin, an oil and gas-industry apparatchik, as prime minister to replace Gaidar. It continued to issue resolutions contradicting Yeltsin's presidential decrees, leaving overall policy heading nowhere. Though the president had strong executive powers, Russia's confused, much-amended, Soviet-era constitution failed to make clear the division of powers between president and parliament.

In April 1993 a national referendum gave Yeltsin a big vote of confidence, both in his presidency and in his economic reform policies. But the National Salvation Front, an aggressive communist-nationalist group with strong links to parliament, continued to stir trouble, including May Day riots in Moscow that left 600 people injured. Yeltsin started moves towards framing a new constitution that would kill off the existing parliament and define more clearly the roles of president and legislature.

White House Showdown Finally, with neither party having demonstrable constitutional right on its side, matters came down to a trial of strength. In September 1993 parliament convened with plans to remove many of the president's powers. Yeltsin 'dissolved' the parliament, which in turn 'stripped' Yeltsin of all his powers. Yeltsin sent troops to blockade the White House, ordering the members to leave it by 4 October. Many did, but on 2 and 3 October the National Salvation Front attempted an insurrection, overwhelming the troops around the White House and attacking Moscow's Ostankino TV centre, where 62 people died. Though Yeltsin enjoyed only patchy support from the armed forces, next morning loyal tanks and troops stormed the White House, leaving at least 70 dead. Yeltsin's use of force won him few friends.

1993 Elections Elections to a new form of parliament were held in December 1993. The name of the more influential lower house, the State Duma, consciously echoed that of tsarist Russia's parliaments. The so-called Liberal Democratic Party, led by the neofascist Vladimir Zhirinovsky, won a sizable chunk of seats, though not enough to dominate the Duma, which was split between Communists (whose party had been legalised again in 1992), nationalists and reformers. Zhirinovsky blamed Jews and foreigners for Russia's troubles, courted Saddam Hussein and had advocated, among other things, executing gangsters and resurrecting the Russian empire by annexing most of the old Soviet Union and even portions of Poland, Finland and Alaska. The size of his vote was interpreted more as a protest against falling living standards and rising crime than as a positive endorsement of his views.

At the same time as the elections, a national referendum gave the go-ahead to a new Yeltsin-drafted constitution, which gave the president a clear upper hand over parliament. The constitution also enshrines the rights to free trade and competition, private ownership of land and property, freedom of conscience, and free movement in and out of Russia, and bans censorship, torture and the establishment of any official ideology.

The new Cabinet, picked by Chernomyrdin (still prime minister) after the elections, left out any leading economic reformers, but the pragmatic and increasingly influential Chernomyrdin turned out to be more of a reformer and less of an old-guard hack than many had expected. The year 1994 saw some benefits of economic reform take hold in a few big cities, notably Moscow and St Petersburg (the name to which Leningrad had reverted in 1991), where a market economy was taking root and an enterprise culture was developing among the younger generations.

The Mafia The big problem preoccupying everybody was crime and corruption. The 'Mafia' – a broad term encompassing the many thousands of corrupt officials (including many Yeltsin-era appointees), businesspeople, financiers and police, as well as small and big-time gangsters – had spread into every corner and level of society. Yeltsin had described them as a 'threat to Russia's strategic interests and national security' in 1993. By 1994 about one in every 5000 citizens in Russia was being murdered each year, about twice as many as in the USA and about 10 times more than in Britain. Politicians, industrialists, financiers, even TV stars were among the victims of contract killings. One of Yeltsin's advisers reported in 1994: 'Every, repeat every, owner of a shop or kiosk pays a racketeer'. The FBI opened an office in Moscow to help fight international organised crime and drug trafficking, in which Russia was a rising 'star'.

Gangsters had not only profited from economic liberalisation through being some of the few people with capital to invest, but also hindered it by scaring off potential entrepreneurs. No-one was able to do a thing about it, least of all Yeltsin, despite some blustery pronouncements. With the problem reaching such high levels of society, the only possible solution seemed to many to be an all-out war on crime – a prospect that raised the spectres of suspended civil rights and a deepening of Yeltsin's dictatorial tendencies.

War in Chechnya Foreign policy reflected the growing mood of conservative nationalism at home. Russia was concentrating on making most of the former Soviet Union into its 'sphere of influence'. While the need for a buffer zone between Russia and the outside world was one reason for this, the millions of ethnic Russians living in the former Soviet republics, many of them already moving to Russia as political tides turned against them, were also a concern. Russian troops had intervened in fighting in Georgia, Moldova and Tajikistan with the aim of strengthening Russia's hand in those regions, and by early 1995 Russian forces were stationed in varying numbers in all the other former republics except Estonia and Lithuania.

But the Russian military's most significant adventure since the Afghan War was a disaster. This was the war in Chechnya, intended to bring to heel this Muslim republic of around one million people in the Caucasus, which had declared independence from Russia in 1991. Chechnya, prone to internal conflicts and noted as the homeland of many of the most powerful and violent gangsters in Russia, also sat across the routes of the pipelines that bring oil from the Caspian Sea to Russia. Its leader, Jokar Dudaev, seemed to enjoy taunting Moscow and flouting its laws.

Attempts to negotiate a settlement or have Dudaev deposed had got nowhere by the end of 1994. Yeltsin, perhaps hoping to cash in on the nationalist mood in Russia, ordered his army and air force into Chechnya for what was meant to be a quick operation to restore Russian control. But the Chechens, whose fighting tradition goes back to 19th-century wars against imperial Russian forces, fought bitterly. Their resistance was also fuelled by an anti-Russian resentment stemming from 1943-45, when the Chechens were among six peoples from the Caucasus region deported en masse to Central Asia for alleged collaboration with the invading Germans (the surviving Chechens were allowed back in the 1950s).

By mid-1995 at least 25,000 people, mostly civilians, were dead, and the Russians had only just gained full control of the Chechen capital, Grozny, which had been reduced to rubble by bombing, shelling and house-to-house fighting. Some 300,000 or more people had fled their homes, Dudaev was still holding out in southern Chechnya, and the guerrilla warfare was continuing unabated. Criticism of Yeltsin surged and in national elections in December 1995, Communists and nationalists won control of 45% of the Duma.

1996 Elections

By early 1996, Yeltsin seemed a shadow of the man who had leapt into world prominence by leaping atop that tank in August 1991. Frequent bouts of various ill-defined sicknesses kept him from public view. Worse for his hold on power, when he was seen in public he often seemed confused and unstable. Rumours – not all spread by his political opponents – said he was a dying alcoholic.

But even as the Communists under Gennady Zyuganov seemed set to rise from the dead on a wave of discontent, the powers that had grown rich under Russia's five-year flirtation with capitalism came to Yeltsin's aid. The media moguls and financiers made certain that the only message the Russian voters received was Yeltsin's. The Communists were kept off television. Meanwhile one of Yeltsin's young protégés – Anatoly Chubais – ran a brilliant campaign that among other things had a temporarily revived Yeltsin appear on stage dancing at a rock concert to show his supposed strength.

In the June 1996 elections, Zyuganov and a tough-talking ex-general, Alexander Lebed, split the opposition vote and Yeltsin easily defeated Zyuganov in a run-off in early July (although the strain of dancing at concerts and other stunts had taken their toll because Yeltsin again disappeared from view for several weeks). The Communists and other opposition parties returned to their grousing in the Duma, while Lebed unwisely accepted an offer from Yeltsin to try to negotiate an end to the fighting in Chechnya. Given little leeway, Lebed proved to be the fall guy for the entire botched affair and his political star was greatly dimmed by the time a peace settlement was reached and Russian troops began withdrawing in late 1996.

Meanwhile Yeltsin's health woes had grown to the point where even the Kremlin had to admit he might be suffering from something worse than 'a cold'. In November an American-led team of surgeons

Boris shaking off yet another 'cold' (with the medicinal help of vodka)

carried out quintuple heart bypass surgery on him. While Yeltsin slowly recuperated, much of 1997 saw a series of financial shenanigans and deals that became known variously as the 'War of the Oligarchs' or the 'War of the Bankers'. These were nothing more than power grabs by the various Russian billionaires, the most prominent of whom was Boris Berezovsky, a mysterious man who seemed to have his hands in every deal.

Underneath the rarely seen Yeltsin, there was constant jockeying for power by the so-called young reformers like Chubais and Boris Nemtsov and those held sway by the billionaires who saw little profit in economic reform. On occasion Yeltsin would make a grand show of exerting his authority, as he did in 1998 when he sacked his government for its bad economic management.

Economic Collapse

If Nero fiddled while Rome burned, then it can be said that Yeltsin sniffled while Russia collapsed. A series of 'colds' including one 'bad cold' kept him away from the Kremlin. As the various political forces inside and outside the Yeltsin government jockeyed for power, events elsewhere were sounding grave warnings for the economy. The Asian economic crisis had already humbled countries such as Thailand and Malaysia, whose economies had been far healthier than Russia's.

While Yeltsin and the Duma fought over his nomination of Sergei Kiriyenko as prime minister of a new government in the spring of 1998, signs that the Russian economy was in deep trouble were everywhere. Coal miners went on strike over months of unpaid wages that were part of more than $300 billion that was owed to workers across the country. This, added to well over $100 billion in foreign debt, meant that Russia was effectively bankrupt. Proposals by the Yeltsin government to stave off default were largely ridiculed by the Communists in the Duma.

During the summer of 1998, the foreign investors who had propped up the Russian economy fled. On 17 August, the Yeltsin government took the inevitable but fateful step of devaluing the rouble. Instantly, all the money in Russia was worth far less. In a repeat of scenes that had shaken the West during the Depression of 1929, large numbers of Russian banks closed, leaving their depositors with nothing. Worst hit were members of the burgeoning middle class, the very people the West had been counting on to bring political stability to the country. From dreams of owning cars and houses, they were reduced to living in poverty, like most other Russians.

Yeltsin's gesture of firing Kiriyenko on August 23 was seen as the hollow move it was. Days of political wrangling followed while the economy virtually collapsed. Foreign firms that had pumped money into places like Moscow began withdrawing and firing their employees. In September, Yevgeney Primakov was approved as the new prime minister – a promotion akin to being made commander of the *Titanic* after the last lifeboat had sailed away.

Late 1998 proved to be a grim time throughout Russia. In remote areas – which had barely benefited from the years of a market economy – the sporadic government aid that had kept communities afloat dried up. In the north and in Siberia whole towns had to be evacuated because there was no food or fuel for heat. A nationwide poll found that 97% of the population felt their standard of living had declined in 1998 while 51% saw 1999 as 'ominous'.

As the economic situation worsened, old allies in the Yeltsin government took to sniping at each other. Berezovsky was accused of corruption, a development that reminded many people of the scene in *Casablanca* in which Claude Raines declares his 'shock' that there is gambling at Rick's even as he is being handed his winnings.

In May 1999 Yeltsin fired Primakov (the third prime minister fired in 14 months) and replaced him with a little-known lackey, Sergei Stephashin, who was in turn sacked after only 82 days in office. Veteran KGB officer Vladimir Putin was named the fifth prime minister in only 17 months.

By now such changes in government were fooling no-one and contributing to a growing cynicism about democracy on the part of the long-suffering populace.

Rise of the Nationalists

With the economy in shambles and the vast majority of Russians leading worse lives than they had led before democracy and the so-called 'market economy', it is no surprise that various nationalist groups like the Communists would enjoy growing support. Their cause received a major boost on 24 March 1999 when NATO forces led by the USA began bombing Yugoslavia over the Kosovo crisis. This attack on the Serbs, who are regarded by Russians as ethnic kin, inflamed long-dormant passions among Russians, who turned out in Moscow to stone the US embassy.

Prior to the NATO attacks, a poll had shown that 57% of Russians had favourable feelings about the Western democracies. After 24 March, that figure fell to 14%. This has given parties like the Communists renewed hope for Duma elections late in 1999

From Superpower to Stuporpower

In 1999 the entire Russian military budget was $4 billion. In the USA the military budget was $260 billion. This disparity shows the levels to which the armed forces in Russia have sunk since the end of the Cold War. While decreased money for the military might be good news to those who oppose such spending, it holds several dangers in itself.

During the Cold War, Russia's army, navy and air force were so strong that the only way the USA and NATO thought that they could counter the threat was by stockpiling huge numbers of nuclear weapons. Now, in an ironic twist, the roles have been reversed. The Russian military has been humbled by numerous embarrassments including its failure against Chechen rebels in its own backyard and its humbling in Kosovo in 1999. There, after an initial bluster by a mere 200 troops who challenged NATO's command, the army was forced to ask NATO for supplies such as water because the Russians had none of their own.

With its armed forces in tatters, Russia's only hope of remaining an international power is by heavy reliance on nuclear weapons. Without its still substantial arsenal, it wields no force at all. As proof, the Defence Ministry has abandoned its oft-repeated line from the Soviet era that it would never be the first to use nuclear weapons. The danger is that with little in the way of conventional military might, Russia will feel compelled to use nuclear weapons over a relatively minor conflict.

Meanwhile the other great danger of the Russian military collapse lies rotting throughout the former Soviet Union. Hundreds of ships, planes, bombs and other weapons have been abandoned to the elements. There is the obvious fear that some of the material will fall into unscrupulous hands, but more insidious is the environmental threat. One especially bad example is the more than 100 atomic submarines rusting away in fjords around the Kola Peninsula. All are full of deadly nuclear fuel and there is almost no money to properly decommission them and process the radioactive material. After years of dumping nuclear waste in the ocean, the navy seems unsure of how to handle this huge menace safely. The government has ignored the growing piles of waste and instead has focused its energies on jailing two officials who went public with news of the danger.

Several decayed submarines in Murmansk are said to be in danger of exploding and releasing at least half the radiation released at Chornobyl (Chernobyl). A sign near the centre displays the current level of airborne radiation. Other threats to the environment include the vast stockpiles of ageing nuclear warheads and unstable chemical weapons scattered throughout Russia.

and the presidential elections of 2000. Few expect Yeltsin to have the stamina to run again (in June 1999 a close ally admitted the president was lucid perhaps 10% of the time), but no-one expects the Yeltsin political bloc cheerfully to give up power, especially to the Communists. The nationalists have even led a campaign to recreate a part of the old Soviet Union by reuniting with Ukraine and/or Belarus, although the likelihood of this is greatly in doubt.

In September 1999 a series of explosions in Moscow left more than 200 people dead. This unprecedented terrorism in the nation's capital fuelled unease and xenophobia. The Moscow government introduced oppressive measures against ethnic minorities, especially those from the southern republics such as Chechnya. There was a widespread belief, although unproven, that Chechen terrorists were responsible for the bombings.

Seizing upon public opinion, the Russian government launched a brutal new military campaign centred on Grozny, the Chechen capital. Tens of thousands of civilians fled to the countryside to escape the bombardment and there was a huge number of casualties.

See the boxed text on p.21 for an update on Yeltsin's surprise resignation.

GEOGRAPHY

European Russia dwarfs all other European countries in size but still makes up only a quarter of the 17 million sq km area of Russia – the world's biggest country. The border between Europe and Asia runs down the western side of the Ural Mountains, 1300km east of Moscow. Cities and towns are concentrated chiefly across the middle half of European Russia, thinning out in the frozen north and the southern steppe.

Boundaries

In the north, European Russia faces the Arctic Kara and Barents seas and the White Sea (an inlet of the Barents Sea), and has a short border with Norway and a longer one with Finland. The Novaya Zemlya and Zemlya Frantsa-Iosifa island groups, the latter stretching to the edge of the permanent Arctic icecap, are also part of European Russia.

South of Finland, Russia opens on the Gulf of Finland, an inlet of the Baltic Sea. St Petersburg stands at the eastern end of this gulf. In the west and south-west, Russia borders Estonia, Latvia, Belarus and Ukraine. The small Kaliningrad region of Russia lies disconnected from the rest of the country, between Lithuania, Poland and the Baltic Sea. East of Ukraine, stretches of Russian coast on the Sea of Azov, an inlet of the Black Sea, and on the Black Sea itself, intervene before Russia's borders with Georgia and Azerbaijan in the Caucasus Mountains. East of the Caucasus, Russia faces the Caspian Sea, and north of the Caspian its border with Kazakhstan runs up to the Ural Mountains.

Topography

Most of the country is flat. The Ural Mountains rise no higher than 1900m. The plains to their west are never more than 500m high, averaging just 170m. Only in the Caucasus, stretching between the Black and Caspian seas on European Russia's southern fringe, are major elevations reached. Here, just on the Russian side of the border with Georgia, stands 5642m Elbrus, Europe's highest peak.

Rivers & Lakes

Hundreds of rivers snake across the plains. The biggest is the 3690km Volga, Europe's longest river and until the 20th century one of Russia's major highways. The Volga rises north-west of Moscow, then flows eastward for about half its length before turning south at Kazan and emptying into the Caspian Sea near Astrakhan. Long stretches of the river are now reservoirs for hydroelectric purposes. The Volga also has the biggest drainage basin (1.38 million sq km) of any European river. The next-longest rivers are the 1870km Don, which rises south of Moscow and flows south into the Sea of Azov, and the 1810km Pechora, which flows from the Ural Mountains to the Barents Sea.

With all these 'highests' and 'longests', you might bet on Europe's biggest lake being in Russia, too. In fact Russia contains the two biggest, both north-east of St Petersburg: Lake Ladoga (18,390 sq km) and Lake Onega (9600 sq km).

CLIMATE

The central fact of the Russian climate, which has a deep effect on the national psyche, is its long, dark, very cold winters, whose severity is explained by the fact that so much of the country is so far north and so far from the open sea.

Moscow & St Petersburg

The two main cities are warm from about mid-May to early September. Summer days in these northern latitudes are long – so long that at midsummer in St Petersburg there's no real darkness. Autumn is brief, and by the end of November Moscow is frozen most of the time. Serious snow arrives in December and stays till late March/early April. St Petersburg, beside an arm of the Baltic Sea, is a few degrees milder than Moscow in winter but in midwinter is reduced to about five hours of murky light a day. Spring arrives fast, with a great thaw a month or so long, in March and April, and people go a touch crazy. Thousands of extra cars emerge from winter storage onto city streets.

The South

South of Moscow the inland climate is similar to that in Moscow, though perhaps a few degrees warmer in summer. The Black Sea coast is mild – it rarely freezes, and typical mid-May to early September temperatures reach between 20°C and 27°C. Coastal waters of the Black Sea itself are usually in the low 20°Cs from June to September.

The North

Up north, as you'd expect, it gets even colder than in Moscow. Arkhangelsk, despite being on the coast, averages around 5°C below Moscow's temperatures, and inland it's even more bitter. Murmansk, which benefits from the dying eddies of the Gulf Stream, is a bit warmer, and its port is ice-free all year round – but here, 200km inside the Arctic Circle, there's permanent darkness in December and January.

Rainfall

July and August, the warmest months, are also the wettest months in most places, with

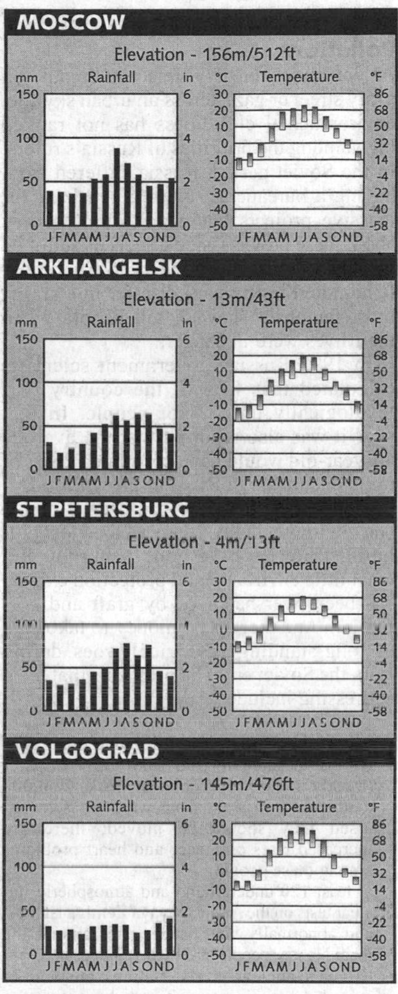

as many as one rainy day in three. But only the Caucasus region receives really serious precipitation.

The area between Moscow and St Petersburg is marginally wetter than most of the rest of European Russia, but it still gets only half as much rain in a year as New York, and even receives less than Rome. The lower Volga region, from around Saratov, is a bit drier.

ECOLOGY & ENVIRONMENT

Pollution

As you'll notice every time you breathe on a city street or gaze across an urban skyline, environmental cleanliness has not ranked high among the priorities of Russia's rulers. In the Soviet period, Russia suffered from having a bureaucracy with a penchant for massive projects but which didn't worry about these projects' side effects or admit its mistakes – or even, as the 1986 Chornobyl (Chernobyl in Russian) disaster in Ukraine most famously showed, tell people when their lives were in danger.

In 1992 Russian government scientists calculated that 15% of the country was 'ecologically unsafe' for people. In that year it was also reported that the average 40-year-old would have consumed 28kg of toxic chemicals in Russian-grown food.

The market economy has been a mixed bag environmentally. Many of the most polluting factories have gone bankrupt, but what little environmental protection existed has been overshadowed by graft and corruption. And there is no money to take care of long-standing ecological woes dating from the Soviet era. The problems that need addressing include:

- up to 2.7 million people still living in areas of Russia affected by the Chornobyl disaster (mostly in the west around Bryansk); 400,000 of them are in areas from which it is recognised they should be moved; there are increased rates of cancer and heart problems among these people;
- at least 120 underground and atmospheric nuclear tests on the Arctic Novaya Zemlya islands, and abnormally high cancer rates among the local Nentsy people and their reindeer herds;
- Russia's nuclear power stations are widely regarded as accidents waiting to happen, especially as money to run and maintain them becomes scarce;
- desertification of the Kalmyk Steppe areas around the northern Caspian Sea because of overgrazing by sheep;
- erosion of fertile black-earth steppe lands because of excessive cultivation;
- severe pollution of the Volga by industrial waste, sewage, pesticides and fertilisers; and a chain of hydroelectric dams along the river, blocking fish spawning routes and slowing the current, which encourages fish parasites (it now takes water 18 months to flow from Rybinsk to Volgograd, instead of the one month it used to take);
- all main rivers, including the Volga, Don, Kama, Kuban and Oka, have 10 to 100 times the permitted viral and bacterial levels;
- chronic overfishing of the Arctic Barents Sea, pollution of both the Baltic and Black seas, and the near extermination of life in the Sea of Azov as a result of overfishing, salination and industrial pollution;
- many cities with excessive toxins in their air.

Conservation

Russian wildlife has always been hunted – for furs as much as for meat – and some species are now also threatened by pollution. Poaching is one of the greatest threats and a plethora of species of game and fish are suffering from rampant poaching. Often the worst offenders are the former conservation officers themselves.

FLORA & FAUNA

European Russia's natural vegetation falls into several east-west bands. Northernmost is the tundra, which covers the northern 150km or so of mainland and southern Novaya Zemlya. (Northern Novaya Zemlya and Zemlya Frantsa-Iosifa are mostly ice-covered.) Delicate lichens, mosses, grasses, flowers and a few low shrubs and trees grow in the tundra on the permafrost, a frozen bog hundreds of metres deep. Seals, walruses and polar bears live on or near the coasts; lemmings, polar foxes, wolves and (sometimes domesticated) reindeer live inland.

Next is the taiga, the northern pine, fir, spruce and larch forest, that stretches from the Arctic Circle to the latitudes of St Petersburg and Yaroslavl. The vast stretches of forest and tundra across the country serve as a major carbon sink, which helps to minimise the release of carbon compounds that contribute to global warming. It is estimated that the taiga removes 500 million tonnes of carbon from the atmosphere each year. These huge forests shelter elk, some reindeer, wolves, brown bears (also native to the mixed forest farther south), beaver, lynx, foxes and many smaller furry animals.

Farther south, stretching in the west from around St Petersburg almost to Ukraine, is a band of mixed forest roughly 500km wide, in which broad-leaved species (predominantly birch) steadily replace conifers as you move south. Deer, wolves, lynx and foxes are among its fauna. Moscow lies in this belt.

From the latitudes of Voronezh and Saratov down into the Kuban area north of the Caucasus stretches the steppe (from *stepi*, meaning plain), the flat or gently rolling band of low grassland, mostly treeless except along river banks, which runs intermittently all the way from Mongolia to Hungary. Since much of the steppe is on humus-rich black earth *(chyornozyom)*, superb for grain growing, most of it is cultivated and no longer in its natural state. Fauna of the steppe are mostly small, but herds of the small saiga (a type of antelope), an ancient animal which once grazed all the way from Britain to Alaska, still roam the more arid steppe regions around the northern Caspian Sea. These areas are being desertified because of the huge herds of sheep grazed on them.

The delta through which the Volga River enters the Caspian is, in contrast to the surrounding area, very rich in flora and fauna. Huge carpets of the pink or white Caspian lotus flower spread across the waters in summer, many millions of birds of over 200 species frequent the delta, and wild boar and 30 other mammal species roam the land.

The steppe gives way to alpine regions in the Caucasus, a botanist's wonderland with 6000 highly varied plant species and glorious wild flowers in summer. Among the animals of the Caucasus are the tur (a mountain goat), the bezoar (wild goat), the endangered mouflon (mountain sheep), the chamois (an antelope), the brown bear and the reintroduced European bison. The lammergeier (bearded vulture), the endangered griffon vulture, the imperial eagle, the peregrine falcon, the goshawk and the snowcock are among the Caucasus' most spectacular birds. Both types of vulture will occasionally attack a live tur.

State Nature Reserves

Many of the former USSR's 160 state nature reserves, ranging in size up to several thousand square kilometres, are in European Russia. These are areas set aside to protect fauna and flora, often habitats of endangered or unique species, where controls are very strict. There's also a class of *zakazniki*, areas where protection is limited to specific species or seasons.

These reserves were once the pride of the Soviet government, and were – by Russian standards – lavished with resources. Scientists had ample funding to study the biological diversity of the reserves and conservation laws were strictly enforced.

But, as with reserves in developing countries, the entire network is in danger of collapse due to a shortage of funds. The remaining conservation officers and scientists often grow their own food so they can eat. Some reserves are open to visitors; and unlike in the old days, when your ramblings were strictly controlled, today you can often hire the staff to show you around. Information on some reserves and how to visit them is included in regional sections of this book. A visit to one of the reserves is usually a fascinating experience and a boon to the reserves and the people who work on them – your money goes a very long way here.

GOVERNMENT & POLITICS

Russia is governed by an executive president and a two-house legislature or parliament. This system was ushered in by the new constitution of 1993. One of the constitutional flaws that has been regularly revealed is that the president and the parliament can (and do) both make laws and can effectively block each other's actions, producing political stalemate.

The president is the head of state and has broad powers. All government ministers are appointed by the president, including the premier, who is effectively number two and who would assume the presidency should the president die or become incapacitated. (Given that Yeltsin's worst 'cold', which could only be cured with open-heart surgery, didn't result in powers being handed over, it

The Political Circus

Given the tumultuous nature of Russian politics, you can never be sure who is doing which job. But at any given time you can be fairly certain that the following cast of characters will be involved in the fray: (See also the boxed text on p.21 for an update on Yeltsin's surprise resignation.)

Boris Yeltsin

It's been all downhill for Yeltsin since he stood on that tank in 1991. Political squabbles, a resurgent Communist Party, murky back-room dealings by associates and the virtual bankruptcy of his nation have all taken their toll on Russia's first president. He has not been helped by numerous bouts of serious illness that have, in the best Kremlin traditions, been officially described as 'colds'. Still, Yeltsin should not be counted out as he seems to thrive on political brinkmanship even after it has been said that he has no more tricks up his sleeve. He is attended to by a vast and murky crowd of advisers and hangers-on known as 'the family', which includes his daughters Tatyana and Lena. Many of these people have been at the centre of corruption charges that have plagued the later years of the presidency.

Vladimir Putin

An unknown bureaucrat when he was named prime minister by Yeltsin in August 1999, Putin quickly showed that he didn't have a grey persona to match his grey hair. The former KGB spy and head of internal security has benefited from having no prior reputation with the cynical Russian populace. He took command of the late 1999 war in Chechnya and made other strong statements about the need for order that won plaudits from Russians tired of the turbulent 1990s. Observers have been impressed by Putin's quick consolidation of power and his savvy political skills, as well as his popularity among the populace. From a spy in the shadows, he seems to be flourishing in the spotlight and is a very strong contender for the presidential elections in 2000.

Boris Berezovsky

A multibillionaire with interests in a wide range of Russian businesses, Berezovsky has been called the 'Rasputin' of the Kremlin owing to his deep and mysterious influence on Yeltsin and his cronies. His large media empire has been used to Yeltsin's advantage, especially during the 1996 presidential elections. Perhaps this makes it fitting that Berezovsky is pals with that other media tycoon Rupert Murdoch. His arch-enemy and rival for Yeltsin's ear is Yevgeny Primakov, who scored points while prime minister in early 1999 by getting Yeltsin to oust Berezovsky as executive secretary of the Commonwealth of Independent States (CIS) and had corruption charges brought against him.

Yevgeny Primakov

An old reformer from the Gorbachev era, Primakov was the nominal link between Yeltsin and the Communist Party. A leading contender for the presidency owing to his ties with supporters of both, Primakov is a harsh critic of the unfettered capitalism as practised by Berezovsky. This kind of stance is popular with the long-suffering Russian populace, which gave him high ratings as prime minister even as the country's finances collapsed in the months after August 1998.

can be inferred that the only incapacitation that might be acknowledged is death.) The rub in this scheme is that the Duma has to approve the president's appointees, which can and has led to showdowns. Presidential elections are held every four years.

The parliament has two houses. The upper house, the Federation Council (Sovet Federatsii), has 178 seats, occupied by two representatives from each of Russia's 89 administrative districts, including small regions, autonomous areas and the cities of

The Political Circus

Anatoly Chubais

With the Russian economy in tatters, the man who was the architect of privatisation and the move to a market economy has a lot to answer for. Relegated to roles in the background of the Yeltsin regime, Chubais is widely regarded as a wizard of politics who masterminded Yeltsin's return from political if not physical near-death in the 1996 elections. Although his lack of popularity precludes a public appointment, he is greatly feared by opponents for his manoeuvrings behind the scenes.

Sergei Kiriyenko

A relative unknown when he was made prime minister in March 1998, Kiriyenko rapidly learned the ways of the Kremlin. Although known for his management skills in industry, running Russia proved too much a challenge for the youthful Kiriyenko, who was fired by Yeltsin after the rouble collapsed. Still, he is being kept around as the designated hatchet man against Moscow's mayor, Yuri Luzhkov, who is another contender for the presidency. Kiriyenko is in charge of a hotline people can phone with word of Luzhkov's misdeeds and he has said he himself would like to be Moscow's mayor.

Yuri Luzhkov

A big city boss of the big city of Moscow, Luzhkov is fairly drooling with anticipation at the thought of gaining the presidency. As head of his Fatherland Party he has stoked nationalism among his supporters with occasional anti-Western rhetoric. However as mayor of Moscow, Luzhkov has given a warm welcome to any Western firm willing to invest in the city and give his regime a piece of the action. His commitment to democracy appears limited to its uses as a means to gain power. His trademark grin and strong leadership may be an unbeatable combination for voters tired of a nation adrift.

Alexander Lebed

From a contender for the presidency in 1996, the blunt-faced ex-general has ended up in near political exile in Siberia. In one of his shrewder moves Yeltsin co-opted Lebed's opposition by giving him a job in government. That this job was to settle matters in Chechnya first time around (in the mid-1990s) and that it was probably hopeless didn't stop Lebed from accepting the post, which brought him no glory. In 1998 he won the governorship of the Siberian province of Krasnoyarsk vowing to knock things into shape and send corrupt financiers and officials scuttling for cover. Instead of propelling him into the Kremlin as he had hoped, his term as governor became his own Gulag. Things haven't improved in the province and his star is fading fast.

Gennady Zyuganov

The leader of the Communist Party, Zyuganov commands the largest block of votes in the Duma. Although he ran a strong campaign against Yeltsin in 1996, he lost the run-off election by a wide margin. He regularly calls for a return to the Soviet days and in 1998 was widely criticised for openly anti-Semitic remarks. Although his bluster is loud, Zyuganov has accomplished little in real terms. He did block financial reforms in 1998, which only helped worsen the rouble's collapse, but his calls for street protests over various issues have drawn mostly party hacks.

Moscow and St Petersburg. Representatives are the top officials from these areas and as such are not elected to this body. The Federation Council has most of the responsibility for legislation on the relationship between central government and the regions.

The State Duma (Gosudarstvennaya Duma) oversees economic legislation. Its 450 members are equally divided between representatives elected from single-member districts and those elected from party lists. Obviously this gives extra clout to the major parties, and efforts to replace its system of representation with a purely proportional system have been shunned. Elections are held every four years in the December preceding the presidential elections.

Political Parties

There are numerous political parties in Russia, but just a few hold a concentration of power. The coalition of pro-market democrats is led by the Yabloko Bloc party. This group of liberals has seen its fortunes wane with those of the market economy. The centre is dominated by the evocatively named Our Home is Russia Party led by Viktor Chernomyrdin. This is the faction most closely allied with Yeltsin.

The conservative and nationalist groups are dominated by Gennady Zyuganov's Communist Party of the Russian Federation and the far right (and misleadingly named) Liberal Democratic Party of Russia whose leader, the not exactly stable Vladimir Zhirinovsky, regularly advocates invading Poland, expelling foreigners and the like. The last two parties garnered 22% and 11% of the seats in the Duma respectively in the 1995 elections.

See the boxed text on p.21 for an update on the 1999 parliamentary election results and Yeltsin's surprise resignation.

Republics & Regions

Russia is officially known as the Russian Federation, a name that acknowledges the existence of 21 semi-autonomous republics within it. The rest of Russia is divided into 68 regions *(oblasti)* and territories *(krai)*. About two-thirds of the republics, regions and territories are in European Russia; the rest fall east of the Ural Mountains.

The republics exist as a result of the old Soviet system of nominally autonomous republics for many minority ethnic groups. In Soviet times those autonomous republics that lay surrounded by, or next to, Russia were grouped with it in a 'federation' that made up the USSR's Russian Republic. After the collapse of the Soviet Union, all these republics declared varying degrees of autonomy from Russia, the most extreme being Chechnya, in the Caucasus, which unilaterally declared full independence.

Yeltsin struck deals with the republics, which largely pacified them, and the 1993 constitution awarded regions and territories much the same status as republics and declared that federal laws always took precedence over local ones.

ECONOMY

Russia is a country blessed with astonishing resources. Russian economics is the attempt to avoid an equally astonishing failure to capitalise on those resources.

Legacy of the Past

The centralised, state-run 'command economy' of the Soviet era, based on large single-product units with priority given to military and heavy industrial development, turned a nation of peasants into a superpower and the world's number two industrial giant. But by the 1980s this system, with its dated industrial plant and few incentives for workers other than corruption, was becoming less and less efficient. Gorbachev's attempts at reform disrupted the planned economy but were not drastic enough to develop a workable substitute.

Market Reform & Industry

The new government of independent Russia in 1991 was strongly pro-market and aimed for a quick transition to capitalism. But the economy it had to start with was a shambles. The food distribution system and trade with other ex-Soviet republics had more or less collapsed, and there was a huge budget deficit.

The reformers' first task was to make enough food available to stave off starvation. This they did by removing state controls on most prices – goods reappeared in the shops at much higher prices as trading, rather than hoarding, became worthwhile again. The reformers were heavily criticised for the increased prices of basic foodstuffs, with average citizens realising that it is better to wait in long queues for food one can afford than have easy access to food that's unaffordable.

One of the main battles was over military and heavy industry. There was an 80% cut in military procurement spending in 1992, and further cuts after that. This helped to spark conservative resistance to cuts in other government spending on industry. Inefficient, 'rust-bucket' factories – some producing goods they could not sell, others not even producing anything – were kept open with government subsidies as the old bureaucracy fought to prop up the sources of its privileges. The economic slump at the end of the decade meant that the economy was contracting at a rate of 5% a year, while annual inflation had gone from a stable 11% to 80%.

Much of Russian commerce is conducted by an immense barter system that is a way around the lack of cash. Factories pay workers in the products they produce, the workers trade those products for food. Local governments trade tax credits with the electric company for power, and on and on it goes. The result is a false economy without capital or taxes to pay for investment or services. The economic situation stagnates as everybody does whatever they can just to get by.

Privatisation

Privatisation proceeded steadily and by 1994 around 100,000 of the 180,000 state businesses had been sold off – with, inevitably, a measure of corruption among those in charge of the process. However, the economic crisis has wiped out the value of the shares that were sold or, often, given to employees in lieu of wages. In addition, local governments are once again becoming involved in local businesses as investors or de facto owners. In Moscow, for instance, the city government ensures that it has an interest in almost every project it approves.

Western Aid

Russia has continued to need large-scale Western loans to help meet its budget deficits. The International Monetary Fund (IMF) regularly loans (read 'gives', since Russia's foreign debt is so enormous it's unlikely ever to be able to pay it off) billions of dollars to keep the country afloat. In addition the USA, Germany, the European Union (EU) and other bodies chime in with a variety of economic aid. The net result of this is to make Russia beholden to the West. Russia was strongly against foreign involvement in the Kosovo crisis of mid-1999, unsurprising given the close cultural and religious ties between Russia and Serbia. When push came to shove, however, the Yeltsin government knew it desperately needed Western cash and in the end moderated its stance. In 1999, Russia owed $17.3 billion in various foreign debt payments yet had only $10 billion in reserves.

Living Standards

Living standards for the average Russian are bleak in monetary terms. Pensioners are lucky to receive $20 a month. The average wage for workers is $50 a month and a quarter of the population is owed back wages. About 44 million people live below the official poverty line of $32 a month and at least nine million are unemployed, although many others considered 'employed' have jobs with little work and less pay. Life for the average Russian has become much harder since 1991, with the prices of most goods far higher and incomes much lower. One consequence of these declining living standards is that the best and brightest young Russians are emigrating with their talents.

One important way that people survive is by growing all manner of produce on small plots of land. On sunny summer weekends you'll see hordes of people carefully tending the food they'll be eating all winter. Over 100 million people feed themselves this way.

Agriculture

Russia's harvest in 1998 was the worst in 45 years and the Kremlin had to request five million tonnes of food aid from the USA and EU. Efforts to privatise the old collective farms have met with little success. Rural dwellers, deprived of any system that rewarded initiative, were reluctant to begin producing independently. In the meantime, farm supplies such as tractors, seeds and fertiliser stopped arriving from the government. Without vital resources needed to grow food there was no food to sell and thus no money to buy the vital resources – an unbreakable cycle. The August 1998 crisis destroyed the few banks that were willing to make farm loans.

POPULATION & PEOPLE

Some 112 million of Russia's 147 million people live in European Russia. Three-quarters of European Russia's people live in towns and cities, the most densely populated areas being around Moscow (population nine million) and St Petersburg (five million), and the areas stretching east of Moscow as far as Kazan and Samara, and south to Voronezh and Saratov. The biggest cities after Moscow and St Petersburg, all with populations of one to 1.5 million, are Nizhny Novgorod, Samara, Kazan, Perm, Ufa, Rostov-on-Don and Volgograd.

Life expectancy of Russians continues to fall: at current rates the population will decline to 123 million by 2030. Much of this is due to the population's staggering health problems. Alcoholism is rampant – as you may notice when you see what seems like everybody over the age of 10 wandering around with a beer on a warm day or clutching a bottle of vodka on a cold day. According to the Russian Ministry of Health, Russians consume on average 12L of pure alcohol a year, which is three times the average for the rest of the developed world. Besides the many health problems inherent to a diet high in alcohol and fat, accidental deaths due to drunkenness are frequent. On a warm summer weekend people drown in the rivers and lakes at a rate four times greater than anywhere else in the West, primarily because of drunkenness. The average life expectancy for a Russian man is 58 years, for a woman 71.

About 81% of European Russia's people are Russians. The rest belong to dozens of smaller ethnic groups, all with their own languages and cultural traditions (in varying degrees of usage), and varied religions. Their complex distribution has been shaped by war, forced movements and migration over many thousands of years. Most of the major ethnic groups have their own republics within Russia, some of which – notably Tatarstan – have developed societies with a character different from the rest of European Russia.

More information on minority peoples can be found in the regional chapters.

Middle Volga Minorities

The region east of Moscow, around the middle section of the Volga River and its tributaries, contains the biggest ethnic minorities, though they're still outnumbered about three to one in the region by Russians. The system of republics in this region stems from Soviet attempts to limit the influence of the Tatars, historical rivals of the Russians.

The region's, and European Russia's, biggest minority is the Tatars themselves, who are descended from the Mongol-Tatar armies of Jenghis Khan and his successors and from earlier Hunnic, Turkic and Finno-Ugric settlers on the middle Volga. The Tatars are mostly Muslim, and some 1.8 million of them form nearly half the population of the Tatarstan republic, whose capital is Kazan, on the Volga. A million or so Tatars live in other parts of European Russia, while a further million or so live elsewhere in the CIS.

Two other important groups in the middle Volga region are the Chuvash (1.8 million) and the Bashkirs (1.5 million). The Chuvash, descendants of the pre-Mongol-Tatar settlers in the region, are Orthodox Christian and form a majority in Chuvashia (capital: Cheboxary). The Bashkirs are a partly Turkic people, nominally Muslim, about half of whom live in the Bashkortostan republic (capital: Ufa). Here, however, they are outnumbered both by Russians and by Tatars.

The other four major groups of the region are Finno-Ugric peoples, descendants of its earliest known inhabitants, and distant relatives of the Estonians, Hungarians and Finns: the 1.2 million Orthodox or Muslim Mordvins, a quarter of whom live in Mordovia (capital: Saransk); the 800,000 Udmurts or Votyaks, predominantly Orthodox, two-thirds of whom live in Udmurtia (capital: Izhevsk); the 700,000 Mari or Cheremys, with an animist/shamanist religion, nearly half of whom live in Mary-El (capital: Yoshkar-Ola); and the 350,000 Komi, Orthodox, most of whom live in the Komi republic (capital: Syktyvkar).

Northern Minorities

About 140,000 members of another Finno-Ugric people, the Karelians, live in European Russia. Some 80,000 of them form 10% of the population of the Karelia republic north of St Petersburg. More Karelians live across the border in Finland.

Southern Minorities

The northern Caucasus, which is in Russia, is a real ethnic jigsaw of at least 19 local nationalities. Several of them have been involved in ethnic conflicts in recent years, some of which stem from Stalinist gerrymandering of their territories. Resentments were also fuelled by Stalin's deportation of four entire Caucasus peoples – the Chechens, Ingush, Balkars and Karachay – to Central Asia in 1943-45, allegedly for collaboration with the German invaders. Those who had not died were allowed to return in the 1950s.

The Chechens, a Muslim people almost one million strong, are renowned for their fierce nationalism. This prompted Chechnya to declare independence from Russia in 1991 and, four years later, led to a savage war, in which Russia attempted to regain control of Chechnya.

Cossacks

The Cossacks, particularly in places north of the Caucasus such as Krasnodar, Stavropol and Novocherkassk, have been reasserting their identity. After the Bolshevik Revolution the Cossacks, who had mostly sided with the Whites in the civil war, suffered massacres, deportations and victimisation and were not recognised as a separate ethnic group. They were registered under other nationalities, usually Russian or Ukrainian. Cossacks are trying to revive their military traditions and have strong Russian nationalist tendencies, merging into xenophobia and anti-Semitism. In 1920 there were about four million Cossacks, but it's difficult to estimate the number of Cossacks today.

Jews

Of the approximately one million Jews in Russia in 1989, only some 500,000 remained in 1998. Most are in urban European Russia, but there's also a small, conservative community of 17,000 'Mountain Jews' in the Caucasus. A relaxation of exit rules since the mid-1980s has sparked an exodus of Russian Jews to Germany and the USA, and also to Israel, where they have become a sizable force in Israeli politics.

After Kyiv's destruction of the Judaic Khazar Empire, Russia had few Jews until the 1772-95 partitions of Poland brought in half a million, who were confined by law to the occupied lands – roughly, present-day Ukraine, Belarus, Lithuania and eastern Poland, the so-called Pale of Settlement. The notion of a 'Jewish problem' grew in the 19th century, exploding in the 1880s into pogroms and massive emigration to Western Europe and the USA.

On top of Soviet antireligious policies, Stalin devoted himself after WWII to the destruction of Jewish cultural life, shutting schools, theatres and publishing houses. The denial of Jewish applications for emigration in the early 1980s gave rise to the issue of 'refuseniks'. With its new religious freedoms, glasnost also brought an upsurge in grass-roots anti-Semitism, and emigration grew to a flood.

EDUCATION

One of the Soviet Union's greatest achievements was education. From an agrarian society in which literacy was limited to the few in the upper classes, the USSR achieved a literacy rate of 98%, among the best in the world. Russia continues to benefit from this legacy, although mandatory schooling has fallen to eight years from the Soviet Union's 11. However this has been in part attributed to the fact that fully 25% of coursework under the Soviet system involved ideological subjects such as Marxism and the like.

Russian schools today emphasise basics such as reading and mathematics, and the high literacy rate has been maintained. Students wishing to attend a further two years of secondary education must pass rigorous tests. The hurdles are even tougher for those wishing to attend a university. Technical subjects such as science and mathematics are valued and bright students are encouraged to specialise in a particular area from a young age. This has been criticised because it limits a student's educational choice. While Russian teachers and professors are held in high regard by their international peers, at home they are among the worst victims of the economic hardships. Their government-paid salaries are among the lowest in the land.

ARTS

Ballet

Russian ballet grew out of dance schools set up in 18th century St Petersburg and Moscow. Though the dancers were initially of low status (in Moscow they came from an orphanage), their performances were patronised by the tsars. In the 19th century, French and Italian teachers and dancers brought new techniques, and ballet developed far more prestige in Russia than in Western Europe, where it was often second to opera on the bill. Under the Frenchman Marius Petipa, the St Petersburg Imperial Ballet rose to world prominence. He choreographed over 60 works, including *Swan Lake*, *The Nutcracker* and *The Sleeping Beauty*, and developed ballet as a large-scale spectacle. Anna Pavlova, Mikhail Fokine and Vaslav Nijinsky, all graduates of the Imperial Ballet school, came to the fore in the early 20th century.

Fokine, who has *Les Sylphides*, *The Firebird* and *Petrushka* to his credit, succeeded Petipa as the leading choreographer. Influenced by the World of Art group (see the Painting section in this chapter), he saw ballet as a synthesis of the arts. The Ballets Russes, with designs by Leon Bakst, took Paris by storm in 1909 and brought about a revival of ballet in Europe as a whole.

After the revolution, though many leading lights went West, Soviet ballet maintained its technical standards. Socialist Realism demanded a good story line: new works included *The Red Poppy* (1927) and Prokofiev's *Romeo and Juliet* (1946). The first outstanding dancers of the Soviet period were Galina Ulanova and Maya Plisetskaya.

In the 1950s, Moscow's Bolshoi Ballet, which emphasised drama where Leningrad's Kirov Ballet focused on elegance, made its first triumphant tours of the West. Yury Grigorovich emerged as its bright, new choreographer, with *Spartacus*, *Ivan the Terrible* and other successes.

But by the late 1980s, Grigorovich was at loggerheads with leading dancers such as Plisetskaya, Yekaterina Maximova, Vladimir Vasiliev and Gediminas Taranda; he was accused of stifling choreographers and dancers he did not favour – including Vasiliev and Plisetskaya – and his style was earning such epithets as 'brutal' and 'Stalinist'. Leading Soviet dancers including Rudolf Nureyev, Natalia Makarova and Mikhail Baryshnikov – all from the Kirov – had been moving to the West since the 1960s for greater challenges and more money, and the Bolshoi feuds, combined with glasnost, sped up this process. Plisetskaya and Irek Mukhamedov, both of whom left in 1990, were only two of its leading lights to go West.

The row went on, with both President Yeltsin and the State Duma, Russia's parliament, getting involved, before Grigorovich finally resigned in 1995, prompting dancers loyal to him to stage the Bolshoi's first-ever strike. He was replaced by Vasiliev who has since then struggled to keep his company together in the face of the allure of decamping to the West and its huge fees. The star ballerina Nina Ananiashvili earns $200 a month with the Bolshoi; performing in New York she could easily collect $15,000 per performance.

Things are booming at the Kirov, where director Valery Gergiev has earned international kudos. Both St Petersburg and Moscow have several other ballet companies in addition to the Kirov and Bolshoi.

Music

Classical The roots of Russian music lie in folk song and dance and Orthodox Church chants. Mikhail Glinka (1804-57), in operas that include *Ivan Susanin* (or *A Life for the Tsar*) and *Ruslan and Lyudmila*, was the first to merge these with Western forms. He influenced the composers known as the Mighty Handful, who lacked formal musical training until adulthood and were concerned to explore and develop Slav roots. Their orchestral works include *Pictures at an Exhibition* by Modest Mussorgsky (1839-81) and *Scheherazade* by Nikolai Rimsky-Korsakov (1844-1908). *Boris Godunov* by Mussorgsky and *Prince Igor* by Alexander Borodin (1833-87) are two of the best loved Russian operas.

Pyotr Tchaikovsky (1840-93) also used folk motifs but was closer to the Western tradition. His *1812 Overture*, his concertos and symphonies, the ballets *Swan Lake*, *The Sleeping Beauty* and *The Nutcracker*, and his opera *Yevgeny Onegin* are still among the world's most popular works.

The next generation included the great bass singer and pianist Fyodor Chaliapin (1873-1938), the pianist-composer Alexander Scriabin (1872-1915), the Romantic composer Sergey Rachmaninov (1873-1943) and the innovator Igor Stravinsky (1882-1971). The last two fled the revolution. Stravinsky's *The Rite of Spring* – which created a furore at its first performance in Paris – and *The Firebird* were influenced by Russian folk music. Sergey Prokofiev (1891-1953), who also left but returned in 1934, wrote the scores for Eisenstein's films *Alexander Nevsky* and *Ivan the Terrible*, the ballet *Romeo and Juliet*, and *Peter and the Wolf*, beloved of teachers of music to young children. His work was condemned for 'formalism' towards the end of his life.

Dmitry Shostakovich (1906-75) won international acclaim, chiefly for his symphonies, while working, not without conflict, in the Soviet Union. Other innovative composers were silenced. Major performers to emerge in the Soviet era – though some left for the West – included violinist David Oystrakh (1908-74), pianist Svyatoslav Richter (born 1914), cellist/conductor Mstislav Rostropovich (born 1927) and pianist/conductor Vladimir Ashkenazy.

Progressive new music surfaced only slowly in the post-Stalin era, with outside contacts limited. Alfred Schnittke's *First Symphony*, probably the most important work of this major experimental modern Russian composer, had to be premiered by its champion, conductor Gennady Rozhdestvensky, in the provincial city of Gorky (now Nizhny Novgorod) in 1974 and was not played in Moscow till 1986.

Among the best recent composers have been Andrey Volkonsky, Sofia Gubaydulina, Edison Denisov, Valentin Silvestrov and, in the newest generation, Alexander Knayfel, Dmitry Smirnov and Yelena Firsova.

Rock Russian rock was born in the 1960s, when the 'bourgeois' Beatles filtered through despite official disapproval. Rock developed underground, starved of decent equipment and the chance to record or perform to big audiences, but gathered a huge following among the disaffected, distrustful youth of the 1970s (the Soviet hippy era) and 1980s.

Bands in the 1970s started by imitating Western counterparts, but eventually a home-grown music emerged, whose lyrics often reflected real social issues. Some artists, like Boris Grebenshikov – a kind of Russian Bob Dylan cum John Lennon – and his band Akvarium (Aquarium), became household names but still needed other jobs to get by. Music was circulated by illegal tapes known as *magizdat*, the musical equivalent of samizdat; concerts were held, if at all, in remote halls in city suburbs, and even to attend them could be risky.

Punk and heavy metal came into fashion in the early 1980s. Under glasnost, the authorities eventually allowed the true voices of youth to sound out: rock festivals were held in outlying Soviet republics such as Georgia and Estonia, big concerts took place in major cities, and the state record company, Melodia, started to produce albums by previously unacceptable groups.

Come glasnost, rock initially flowered, with New Wave music, fashionable from about the mid-1980s, appealing to a Russian taste for theatricality. The tone of many of the more 'serious' groups of the 1980s was one of protest about, or a gloomy resignation to, the frustration and alienation of Soviet life. The tortured dronings of Viktor Tsoy and the chunky riffs of his band Kino were archetypal.

Other leading 1980s bands were Akvarium; Va Bank from Moscow and DDT from St Petersburg, both punk-influenced; Orkestr Populyarnaya Mekhanika (Popular Mechanics Orchestra), a St Petersburg 'performance rock' outfit; and Nautilus Pompilius, an electronic New Wave band from Yekaterinburg. Many of these groups can still be found touring Russia and Europe.

The latest popular rock groups include Kino, Nautilus Pompilus, Mummy Troll, Splin and Alicia. On the contemporary hits band of your radio dial you're likely to find Linda, Natasha Korolyeva and Hi Fi. Possibly unlistenable unless you're just getting spots for the first time are shameless pop stars Tatyana Bulanova, Leontiev, Na-Na, and lots of other screechers you're likely to hear in any cab you hail.

Literature

19th Century The poet Alexander Pushkin (1799-1837) is revered as the father of Russian literature. Almost every step he took – and he travelled *very* widely around tsarist Russia – is marked by a monument or museum. *Yevgeny Onegin*, a verse novel, was his major work. For the 200th anniversary of his birth, Moscow engaged in an orgy of Pushkin-mania that included decrees mandating the display of pictures of the writer in all store windows.

The first, and probably shortest, important Russian novel, *A Hero of Our Time* by Mikhail Lermontov (1814-41), makes a great travelling companion in the Caucasus, where it's set. Its cynical antihero, Pechorin, is an indirect comment on the climate of the times. Pushkin and Lermontov launched a long tradition of conflict between writers and the state, and both died in duels widely perceived as set up by the authorities. The satirical *The Government Inspector* by Nikolai Gogol (1809-52), who also wrote the novel *Dead Souls*, was the first major Russian play.

Ivan Turgenev (1818-83) was the first of the three great novelists of the second half of the 19th century. Bazarov, hero of his *Fathers and Sons*, became a symbol for the antitsarist nihilist movement. *The Possessed* by Fyodor Dostoevsky (1821-81) is both a satire of provincial society and an analysis of political violence. Like his other great works – *Crime and Punishment*, set in the St Petersburg slums, *The Idiot* and *The Brothers Karamazov* – it combines profound treatment of questions of morality and faith with deep psychological probing. *War and Peace* by Leo Tolstoy (1828-1910) is a panorama of Russia during the Napoleonic Wars. It's a pinnacle of world literature but it won't leave you much time for seeing today's Russia if you read it while you're there. On a slightly smaller scale, *Anna Karenina* is the tragedy of a woman who violates the rigid sexual code of her time.

Chekhov & Gorky The plays of Anton Chekhov (1860-1904) – *The Seagull*, *Three Sisters*, *The Cherry Orchard*, *Uncle Vanya* – look tragicomically at the angst of the provincial middle class in the stagnating late 19th century. They owed much of their early success to 'realist' productions at the Moscow Art Theatre by Konstantin Stanislavsky, which aimed to show life as it really was. Maxim Gorky (1868-1936) painted a graphic picture of urban poverty and brutality from the same era in his autobiographical *My Childhood* and in the play *The Lower Depths*.

Revolutionary Period The Futurist poets who emerged as the revolution approached used shock tactics – slang, eroticism, abrupt switches of tack – to stir people out of complacency. Though many supported the revolution, their lives often ended in tragedy. Vladimir Mayakovsky (1893-1930), almost the revolution's official bard for a long time, committed suicide; Anna Akhmatova (1888-1966) was persecuted into silence for most of her later life; Osip Mandelstam (1892-1938) died in a Stalinist transit camp near Vladivostok. Akhmatova's and Mandelstam's lives are painfully recorded by Nadezhda Mandelstam in her autobiographical *Hope Against Hope*.

Boris Pasternak (1890-1960) was another persecuted Futurist poet, best known in the West for his novel *Dr Zhivago*. Less of an outcast was Alexandra Kollontay (1872-1952), a senior Party figure and feminist, renowned for commenting that sex was like scratching yourself – it relieved an itch. Her novels include *A Great Love*, based on Lenin's affair with Inessa Armand, and *Love of Worker Bees*.

Soviet Era In 1932 the Party officially demanded Socialist Realism from art and literature. This meant 'concrete representation of reality in its revolutionary development ... in accordance with ... ideological training of the workers in the spirit of Socialism'. Writers had to convey the Party's messages – and please Stalin.

Mikhail Sholokhov (born 1905), with his sagas of revolution and war among the Don Cossacks, *And Quiet Flows the Don* and *The Don Flows Home to the Sea*, was one of the few decent writers to win approval. *The Master and Margarita* by the great satirist Mikhail Bulgakov (1891-1940) was banned for ages. It's a wacky comic novel with a serious twist, in which the Devil turns up in Moscow to cause all manner of anarchy and make idiots of the system and its lackeys.

The Khrushchev thaw saw the emergence of poets like Yevgeny Yevtushenko and Andrey Voznesensky (both born in 1933), who managed to remain on the right side of the authorities, and the novelist Alexander Solzhenitsyn (born 1918), who didn't. *One Day in the Life of Ivan Denisovich*, a short tale of Gulag life, was published in the USSR in 1962, but Solzhenitsyn fell foul of the Brezhnev clampdown and was exiled in 1974. He went to the USA and finally returned to Russia in 1994. His *Cancer Ward* and *The First Circle*, both written before his departure, are powerful accounts of the 1930s, but *The Gulag Archipelago* is his major work. One Russian said of it to us: 'You read this book, *then* you come to this country'. Through interviews and the testimony of hundreds of Gulag prisoners, Solzhenitsyn brings to light some of the most heinous prison conditions the world has ever known, in a style so familiar that you're enveloped in the stories before you're quite aware of it.

Glasnost brought forth a flood of writing previously suppressed. Two of the chief new talents to emerge since then are Viktor Yerofeev, whose erotic novel *Russian Beauty* has been translated into 27 languages, and Tatyana Tolstaya, whose *On the Golden Porch*, a collection of stories about big souls in little Moscow flats, made her an international name when published in the West in 1989.

Recent years have seen a flowering of Russian publishing and the traditional Russian love of books seems as strong as ever. Just note the number of people reading novels to while away the minutes on the Moscow metro. Viktor Dotsenko sells almost one million of his popular crime fiction novels a year. Other authors such as Irina Ratushinskaya have found sales world-wide. Her *Fictions and Lies* (1999) shows a cast of characters held hostage by the sly methods of the KGB. Viktor Pelevin's novels such as *The Yellow Arrow* (1997) have been widely translated and he has been compared to the great Mikhail Bulgakov.

Theatre productions are also hanging on with an estimated 1000 professional troupes performing throughout the land, double that of 1991.

Architecture

Until Soviet times most building was in wood. The *izbà*, or single-storey wooden cottage, still fairly common in the countryside, was the typical Russian dwelling. Stone and brick were usually the preserves of the Church, royalty and nobility.

Early Russia Kyivan Rus adopted the 'cross in square' church plan developed in Byzantium in the 9th century. At its simplest this consisted of three aisles, each with an eastern apse (semicircular end), a dome or 'cupola' over the central aisle next to its apse, and high vaulted roofs forming a crucifix shape centred on the dome.

As Russian culture moved north, Novgorod, Pskov and Vladimir-Suzdal developed the pattern with varying emphases in the 11th and 12th centuries. Roofs grew steeper to prevent heavy northern snows collecting and crushing them, and windows grew narrower to keep the cold out. Pskov invented the little *kokoshnik* gable, which was semicircular or spade-shaped and was usually found in rows supporting a dome or drum.

Stone often replaced brick, and in Vladimir-Suzdal was carved into a glorious kaleidoscope of decorative images. Another Vladimir-Suzdal hallmark was the 'blind arcade' – a wall decoration resembling a row of arches.

Moscow Moscow in the 15th century looked to these earlier centres for inspiration in its grand building program. Though the architects of two of the Kremlin's three great cathedrals built between 1475 and 1510 were Italian, they took Vladimir's churches as their models; the third cathedral was by builders from Pskov.

Later in the 16th century the translation into brick of north Russian wooden church features, such as the tent roof *(shatyor)* and the onion dome on a tall drum, added up to a new, uniquely Russian architecture, more vertical in effect than the Byzantine shape. St Basil's Cathedral, the Ivan the Great Belltower in the Moscow Kremlin and the Ascension Church at Kolomenskoe are three high points of this era.

In the 17th century builders in Moscow added tiers of kokoshniki, colourful tiles and brick patterning to create jolly, merchant-financed churches such as St Nicholas of the Weavers, and the Trinity in Nikitniki. In mid-century Patriarch Nikon outlawed such frippery, but elaboration returned later in the century with Western-influenced Moscow baroque, which featured ornate white detailing on red-brick walls. The Church of the Intercession at Fili is a high point of this.

Baroque Mainstream baroque reached Russia with Peter the Great's opening up to Western influences. The focus was on his new capital, St Petersburg, as he banned new stone buildings elsewhere. The great baroque architect was an Italian, Bartolomeo Rastrelli, who created an inspired series of buildings, the style of which merged into rococo, for Empress Elizabeth. Three of the most brilliant were the Winter Palace and Smolny Cathedral, both in St Petersburg, and Catherine Place at nearby Pushkin.

Classicism In the later 18th century, Catherine the Great turned away from rococo 'excess' toward Europe's new wave of

St Basil's Cathedral, Red Square, Moscow

classicism – an attempt to re-create the ambience of an idealised ancient Rome and Greece with their mathematical proportions, rows of columns, pediments and domes. Catherine and her successors built waves of grand classical edifices in a bid to make St Petersburg the continent's most imposing capital.

From the simpler classicism of her own reign, exemplified by the Pavlovsk Palace near St Petersburg, the more grandiose Russian Empire style developed under Alexander, with such buildings as the Admiralty and Kazan Cathedral in St Petersburg. The heavy St Isaac's Cathedral, built for Nicholas I, was the last big project of this wave of classicism in St Petersburg. Moscow abounds with Empire-style buildings since much of it had to be rebuilt after the fire of 1812.

Revivals A series of architectural revivals, notably of early Russian styles, began in the later 19th century. The first, pseudo-Russian phase produced the GUM (Gosudarstvenny Univermag), or state department store, the History Museum and the Leningrad Station in Moscow, and the Moscow Station and the Resurrection Church in St Petersburg. The early 20th century neo-Russian movement brought forth the extraordinary Kazan Station in Moscow, which imitates no fewer than seven earlier styles, while Style Moderne (Russian Art Nouveau) yielded the bizarre Yaroslavl Station on the other side of the same square.

Soviet Era The revolution gave rein to young Constructivist architects, who rejected superficial decoration in favour of buildings whose appearance was a direct function of their uses and materials – a new architecture for a new society. They used lots of glass and concrete in uncompromising geometric forms.

Konstantin Melnikov was probably the most famous Constructivist and his own house off ulitsa Arbat in Moscow is one of the most interesting examples of the style. Moscow's *Pravda* and *Izvestia* offices are others. In the 1930s the Constructivists were denounced, and a 400m-high design by perpetrators of yet another revival – monumental classicism – was chosen for Stalin's pet project, a Palace of Soviets in Moscow, which mercifully never got off the ground.

Like the US and German governments of the 1930s, Stalin favoured neoclassical architecture, which echoed ancient Athens – 'the only culture of the past to approach the ideal', according to Anatoly Lunacharsky, the first Soviet Commissar of Education. Stalin liked it to be on a gigantic scale to underline the might of the Soviet state. Convict labour was used, with a high death toll, to create enormous structures around the country. They reached their apogee in the 'Seven Sisters', seven skyscrapers, Gothic in effect, which popped up around Moscow soon after WWII.

Then in 1955 came a decree ordering architects to avoid 'excesses', after which a bland International Modern style – Constructivism without the spark, you might say – was used for prestigious buildings, while drab blocks of cramped flats sprouted countrywide to house the people. The past few years have seen big architectural energies going into restoration of decayed churches and monasteries.

'New Russian' The same folks who drive way too fast, talk on mobile phones in theatres and have their thugs knock you out of the way in restaurants are responsible for some horrid and gaudy buildings in Moscow and St Petersburg. Featuring bright metals and mirrored glass, they tend to be plopped down in the middle of otherwise unassuming vintage buildings. 'Lego buildings' is a phrase popular with some locals for these quickly assembled and brightly coloured monstrosities. Many would say the reconstructed Cathedral of Christ the Saviour, the brainchild of Moscow Mayor Yuri Luzhkov, is a prime example.

Painting

Icons Icons – images intended to aid the veneration of the holy subjects they depict, and sometimes believed able to grant luck, wishes or even miracles – were the key art form up to the time of Peter the Great, though only in the 20th century did they really come to be seen as 'works of art'. They're most commonly found on the iconostasis of a church, a large screen in front of the east-end sanctuary.

Icons were originally painted by monks as a spiritual exercise, and Byzantine rules decreed that only Christ, the Virgin, the angels, saints and scriptural events could be painted – all of which were supposed to be copies of a limited number of approved prototype images. Christ images include the Pantokrator (All-Ruler) and the Mandilion, the latter called 'not made by hand' because it was supposedly developed from the imprint of Christ's face on St Veronica's handkerchief. Icons were traditionally painted in tempera – inorganic pigment mixed with a binder such as egg yolk – on wood. When they faded they were often touched up, obscuring the original work.

The first 'Russian' icons were painted by Byzantine monks in Kyiv. The beginning of a distinct Russian icon tradition came when artists in Novgorod started to draw on local folk art in their representation of people, producing sharply outlined figures with softer faces and introducing lighter colours including pale yellows and greens.

The earliest outstanding painter was Theophanes the Greek (Feofan Grek, about 1340-1405), who worked in Byzantium, then Novgorod, then Moscow, and brought a new delicacy and grace to the form. His finest works are in the Annunciation Cathedral of the Moscow Kremlin.

Andrey Rublyov, a monk at the Trinity Monastery of St Sergius, Sergiev Posad, and the Andronikov Monastery, Moscow, and 20 years Theophanes' junior, was the greatest Russian icon painter. His most famous work is the dreamy *Old Testament Trinity*, in Moscow's Tretyakov Gallery.

The layman Dionysius, the leading late-15th century painter, elongated his figures and refined the use of colour. Sixteenth century icons grew smaller and more crowded, their figures more realistic and Russian-looking. In 17th century Moscow, Simon Ushakov moved towards Western religious painting with the use of perspective and architectural backgrounds.

Peredvizhniki In the 18th century, when Peter the Great encouraged Western trends in Russian art, Dmitry Levitsky's portraits were the outstanding achievement. The major artistic force of the 19th century was the Peredvizhniki (Wanderers) movement, which saw art as a force for national awareness and social change. The movement gained its name from the touring exhibitions with which it widened its audience. Patronised by the industrialists Savva Mamontov – whose Abramtsevo estate near Moscow became an artists' colony – and Pavel Tretyakov, they included Vasily Surikov, who painted vivid Russian historical scenes, Nikolai Ge (biblical and historical scenes), and Ilya Repin, perhaps the best loved of all Russian artists, who ranged from social criticism *(Volga Bargemen)* through history *(Zaporozhie Cossacks Writing a Letter to the Turkish Sultan)* to portraits of the famous.

Isaak Levitan, who revealed the beauty of the Russian landscape, was one of many others associated with the Peredvizhniki. The end-of-century genius Mikhail Vrubel, inspired by sparkling Byzantine and Venetian mosaics, showed early traces of Western influence.

Futurism Around the turn of the century the World of Art (Mir Iskusstva) movement in St Petersburg, led by Alexander Benois and Sergey Diaghilev under the motto 'Art pure and unfettered', opened Russia up to Western innovations such as Impressionism, Art Nouveau and Symbolism. From about 1905 Russian art became a maelstrom of groups, styles and 'isms' as it absorbed decades of European change in a few years before giving birth to its own avant-garde Futurist movements, which in turn helped Western art go head over heels.

Mikhail Larionov and Natalia Goncharova were the centre of the Cézanne-influenced Knave of Diamonds group (with which Vasily Kandinsky was associated) before developing Neo-Primitivism, based on popular arts and primitive icons.

In 1915 Kazimir Malevich announced the arrival of Suprematism, declaring that his utterly abstract geometrical shapes – with the black square representing the ultimate 'zero form' – finally freed art from having to depict the material world and made it a doorway to higher realities. Another famed Futurist, who managed to escape subordinate isms, was Vladimir Mayakovsky, who was also a major poet.

Soviet Era Futurists turned to the needs of the revolution – education, posters, banners – with enthusiasm. They had a chance to act on their theories of how art shapes society. But at the end of the 1920s, Formalist (abstract) art fell out of favour. The Communist Party wanted Socialist Realism (see the Literature section). Images of striving workers, heroic soldiers and inspiring leaders took over; two million sculptures of Lenin and Stalin dotted the country; Malevich ended up painting portraits (penetrating ones) and doing designs for Red Square parades; Mayakovsky committed suicide.

After Stalin, an avant-garde 'Conceptualist' underground was allowed to form. Ilya Kabakov painted or sometimes just arranged the debris of everyday life to show the gap between the promises and realities of Soviet existence. Erik Bulatov's 'Sotsart' pointed to the devaluation of language by ironically reproducing Soviet slogans or depicting words disappearing over the horizon. In 1962 the authorities set up a show of such 'unofficial' art at the Moscow Manezh; Khrushchev called it 'dogshit' and sent it back underground. In the mid-1970s it resurfaced in the Moscow suburbs – only to be literally bulldozed back down.

Eventually a thaw set in and the avant-garde became international big business. In 1988, *A Fundamental Lexicon* by Grisha Bruskin, a multipanelled iconostasis-like work satirising both Soviet propaganda and the Church, sold for UK£242,000 at a Sotheby's sale in Moscow.

Most contemporary painters of any note have left Russia for the riches – and possibly coffeehouses – of the West. A few specialist art galleries are listed in the shopping sections of the Moscow and St Petersburg chapters. At these you can find the latest works by Russians within and without the motherland.

The most popular painter in Russia is the religious artist Ilya Glazunov, a staunch defender of the Russian Orthodox cultural tradition. Hundreds of thousands of people visit exhibitions of his work.

Moscow's newly expanded Tretyakov Gallery and St Petersburg's Russian Museum have the country's chief collections of Russian art, while the Hermitage (St Petersburg) and the Pushkin Fine Arts Museum (Moscow) have world-famous Western European collections. Both cities also stage dozens of temporary exhibitions.

Cinema

Russian – or rather Soviet – cinema first flourished shortly after the revolution. Sergey Eisenstein's *Battleship Potemkin* (1925) remains one of the landmarks of world cinema, its famous Odesa Steps sequence possibly the most cribbed three minutes on celluloid (see the boxed text '192 Steps' in the Odesa section of the Southern Ukraine chapter); Charlie Chaplin described it as 'the best film in the world'. Eisenstein's *Alexander Nevsky* (1938) contains one of cinema's great battle scenes; his *Ivan the Terrible* (1945) shows the coming to power of the great tsar amid intrigues and his eventual triumph over his enemies – a discreet commentary on Stalinism.

Mikhail Kalatozov's *The Cranes are Flying* (1957) – a love story set during WWII – was judged Best Film at Cannes in 1958. Of later Soviet directors, probably the dominant figure was Andrey Tarkovsky, whose films include *Andrey Rublyov* (1966), *Solaris* (1972) – the Russian answer to *2001* – and *Stalker* (1980), which summed up the Brezhnev era pretty well with its characters wandering puzzled through a landscape of clanking trains, rusting metal and overgrown concrete. Tarkovsky died in exile in 1987. In Russia, Alexey German's *My Friend Ivan Lapshin* (1982) is widely reckoned to be one of the best Soviet films: set in 1935, it shows with a light touch the amorous and professional ups and downs of a provincial police investigator, yet catches the real horror of life under Stalin with its underlying sense of impending terror.

Glasnost brought new excitement as film-makers were allowed to reassess Soviet life with unprecedented freedom, and audiences flocked to see the latest exposure of youth culture or Stalinism. (There was also a steady stream of releases of previously banned films.) Vasily Pichul's *Little Vera* caused a sensation in 1989 with its frank portrayal of a family in chaos (exhausted wife, drunken husband, rebellious daughter) and its sexual frankness – mild by Western standards but startling to the Soviet audience. Since then pornography has become commonplace.

Russian film production suffered during the 1990s. At the beginning of the decade the average Russian went to the movies 14 times a year. By 1996 competition for leisure time from TV and rising ticket prices had reduced this figure to 0.4, which means that many Russians didn't go at all. Lenfilm's former output of over 40 films a year from its St Petersburg studios has been slashed. Still, some movies are being made: *Brat* (Brother, 1997) by Alexei Balabanov was very popular. Other film-makers to watch for include Nikita Mikhalkov, whose *Burnt by the Sun* won an Oscar in 1994, Pavel Chukhrai (*Vor*; The Thief, 1997) and Alexander Sokurov (*Molokh*, 1999).

Folk Culture

Loosely defined, 'folk culture' is what ordinary people have traditionally done to enrich their lives in a way that distinguishes them from other groups or regions. Russian folk culture is still very visible, especially in music, dance, and applied and decorative art.

Big music and dance ensembles such as the Igor Moiseev Folk Dance Ensemble, the Osipov Russian Folk Orchestra and the Pyatnitsky Russian Folk Chorus have repertoires with roots as old as Kyivan Rus, including heroic ballads and the familiar Slavic *trepak* or stamping dances. Smaller bands in restaurants may do similar things – or put on Roma (gypsy) song-and-dance shows, once the traditional accompaniment of tsarist officers on drinking and womanising binges.

Isolated by vast distances and long winters, Russians evolved an amazing spectrum of richly decorated folk art. Perhaps most familiar are the intricately painted, enamelled wood boxes called Palekh, after the village east of Moscow that's famous for them; and *finift*, luminous enamelled metal miniatures from Rostov-Veliky. From Gzhel, also east of Moscow, came glazed earthenware in the 18th century and its trademark blue-and-white porcelain in the 19th. Gus-Khrustalny, south of Vladimir, maintains a glass-making tradition as old as Rus. Every region also has its own style of embroidery and some specialise in knitted and other fine fabrics.

Most common is woodcarving, represented by toys, distaffs and gingerbread moulds in the museums, and in its most cliched form by the nested *matryoshka* dolls – surely the most familiar symbol of Russia – and the red, black and gold lacquered-pine bowls called *khokhloma* that overflow from souvenir shops. Most uniquely Slavic are the 'gingerbread' houses of western and northern Russia and Siberia with their carved window frames, lintels and trim. The art of carpentry flourished in 17th and 18th century houses and churches.

Late in the Soviet period, these things could increasingly be found only in homes or in museum collections. But the coming of the free market and a revived interest in national traditions has brought much more good craftwork into the open. The process is also being catalysed by the restoration of churches and mosques and their artwork.

Circus

Russian popular culture is not confined to TV soap operas, discos and video halls. At the circus, despite economic difficulties since the demise of support from the Soviet state, you'll still see adults as well as children at ease and in unreserved good humour. The Russian circus tradition has roots in the medieval travelling minstrels called *skomorokhi*. The country's first permanent circus was established in St Petersburg in 1877.

While Western circuses grow smaller and more scarce, the Russian versions are like those from childhood stories – prancing horses with acrobats on their backs, snarling lions and tigers, heart-stopping high-wire artists and clowns that are hilarious in spite of the language barrier. Many cities have their own troupes and most at least have an arena for visiting companies. Best known is the Moscow Circus, which is really several troupes, with 7000 artists in all. In summer, circuses go on tour to each other's cities.

However, there are many concerns about the treatment of animals used not only in the circuses but also in zoos. The major troupes have cleaned up their records on the strength of tourist money but especially in rural areas you will see animals forced to perform many cruel acts.

SOCIETY & CONDUCT

Traditional Culture

With its myriad of ethnic groups, Russia has a rich stew of cultures, many of which are discussed in the relevant regional chapters of this book. Many old customs are being revived through the Russian Orthodox Church: Russian women are liable to be pointed at or given a tongue lashing by a babushka if they don't cover their heads in a church. (Tourists, however, will not be expected to follow this custom.)

Hospitality is a delightful tradition. If you are offered some you can expect to be regaled with stories, to be drowned in vodka, to offer and receive many toasts and to eat loads of food off small plates. This may seem foreign if the only Russians you've met previously have been gruff bureaucrats, but if a Russian decides to invite you into his or her home, you can expect a bear hug of an embrace, both physically and mentally. This can be especially true far from the big cities, where you'll meet locals determined to share everything they have with you, however meagre.

The Dacha At least 30% of Russians have one of these small country homes. Usually they don't have electricity or running water but do have a fertile spot that's at least figuratively far away from the city. Often little more than a hut, these retreats offer Russians refuge from life and as such figure prominently in the national psyche. On half-warm weekends, places like Moscow begin to empty out early on Friday as people head to the country.

One of the most important aspects of dacha life is gardening. Families grow all manner of vegetables and fruits to eat over the winter. A cherry tree will be fussed over for years; hearty crops of potatoes and cabbage will be nurtured through the summer. Flowers also play an important part in creating the proper dacha ambience and even among people who have no need to grow food the contact with the soil provides an important balm for the Russian soul.

Dos & Don'ts

Should you be lucky enough to be invited to a Russian's home, bring a gift. Wine, confectionary or a cake are all appropriate. Flowers are also popular but make certain there's an odd number because even numbers are for funerals. Also be prepared to remove your shoes once inside the door. Once the festivities begin you can't refuse any food or drink offered unless you wish to cause grave offence. When you are in any setting with other people, even strangers such as those in a train compartment, you should offer to share anything you have to eat, drink or smoke.

Men will find that traditional gentlemanly behaviour is not just appreciated but expected, as you will notice when you see women standing in front of closed doors waiting for something to happen. Giving up your seat on the metro or a bus will also garner many favourable nods except from the dolts not giving up theirs.

RELIGION

The Russian constitution enshrines religious freedom. A law passed in 1997 recognises the Russian Orthodox Church as the leading faith and promises to respect Islam, Judaism and Buddhism. A clause gives courts the power to ban groups inciting hatred or intolerant behaviour.

Russian Orthodox Church

After decades of closures and confiscations of property, victimisation, deportations and executions of believers under the Soviet regime, the Russian Orthodox Church (Russkaya Pravoslavnaya Tserkov) is enjoying a big revival. By 1991 it already had an estimated 50 million members. The rise in churchgoers has been linked to the growth of Russian nationalism, for the Church is an intimate part of many Russians' notions of Russia and 'Russianness'.

Closed and neglected churches are being restored all over the country, and churches and monasteries that had been turned into museums, archive stores, even prisons, have been returned to Church hands. There are probably now close to 25,000 active churches in the whole country, as against fewer than 7000 in 1988.

In 1917 Russia had over 50,000 churches. Lenin adapted Marx's view of religion as 'the opium of the people' to a Russian context, and likened it to home brew. Stalin seemed to be trying to wipe it out altogether until 1941, when he decided the war effort needed the patriotism religion could stir up. Khrushchev returned to the attack in the 1950s, closing about 15,000 churches, some of which became museums of atheism!

History & Hierarchy Constantinople (modern Istanbul, ancient Byzantium, the capital of the Eastern Roman Empire after 395 AD) was the eastern centre of Christianity in the Middle Ages, and Rome was its western centre. For doctrinal, cultural and political reasons, the two gradually drew apart. The final date of the split between the 'Eastern Orthodox' and 'Roman Catholic' churches is usually put at 1054.

Prince Vladimir of Kyiv effectively founded the Russian Orthodox Church in 988 by adopting Christianity from Constantinople. The Church's headquarters stayed at Kyiv until 1300, when it moved north to Vladimir. In the 1320s it moved again, from Vladimir to Moscow.

Patriarch Alexy of Moscow & All Russia is head of the Church. The Patriarch's residence is the Danilov Monastery, Moscow, though some Church business is still conducted at the Trinity Monastery of St Sergius at Sergiev Posad, his residence until the late 1980s. The Yelokhovsky Cathedral is currently the senior church in Moscow. The Church's senior bishops bear the title Metropolitan. The Russian Orthodox Church is one of the main fellowships of 15 autocephalous ('self-headed') Orthodox churches, in which Istanbul is a kind of first among equals.

Beliefs & Practice Russian Orthodoxy is highly traditional, and the atmosphere inside a church is formal and solemn. Priests dress imposingly, the smell of candles and incense permeates the air, old women bustle about sweeping and polishing. Churches have no seats, no music (only melodic chanting) and no statues – but many icons (see Painting under Arts earlier in this chapter), before which people will often be seen praying, and even kissing the ground. Men bare their heads and women usually cover theirs.

As a rule, working churches are open to one and all, but as a visitor take care not to disturb any devotions or offend sensibilities. Hands in pockets attract frowns. Women visitors can often get away without covering their heads but miniskirts are unwelcome and even trousers sometimes attract disapproval. Photography at services is generally not welcome, though you might get a yes if you ask. At other times you should still feel out the situation first and ask if in doubt.

GEOGI SHABLOVSKY

Orthodox religious icon

The Virgin Mary (*Bogomater*, Mother of God) is greatly honoured. The language of the liturgy is 'Church Slavonic', the old Bulgarian dialect into which the Bible was first translated for Slavs. Easter (Paskha) is the focus of the Church year, with festive midnight services to launch Easter Day. Christmas (Rozhdestvo) falls on 7 January because the Church still uses the Julian calendar that the Soviet state abandoned in 1918.

In most churches, Divine Liturgy (Bozhestvennaya Liturgia), lasting about two hours, is at 8, 9 or 10 am Monday to Saturday, and usually at 7 and 10 am on Sunday and festival days. Most churches also hold services at 5 or 6 pm daily. Some include an akathistos *(akafist)*, a series of chants to the Virgin or saints.

Church Design Churches are decorated with frescoes, mosaics and icons with the aim of conveying Christian teachings and assisting veneration. Different subjects are assigned traditional places in the church (the Last Judgement, for instance, appears on the western wall). An often elaborately decorated iconostasis (icon stand) divides the main body of the church from the sanctuary, or altar area, at the eastern end, which is off limits to all but the priest. During a service the priest comes and goes through the Holy or Royal Door, an opening in the middle of the iconostasis.

The iconostasis is composed of up to six tiers of icons. The biggest is the deesis row *(deisusnyy ryad)*, whose central group of icons, known as the deesis, consists of Christ enthroned as the judge of the world, with the Virgin and John the Baptist interceding for humanity on either side. Archangels, apostles and Eastern Church fathers may also appear on this row. Below the deesis row are one or two rows of smaller icons: the bottom one is the local row *(mestnyy ryad)* showing saints with local links. Above the deesis row are the festival row *(prazdnichnyy ryad)* showing the annual festivals of the Church, then the prophet row *(prorocheskiy ryad)* showing Old Testament prophets, and sometimes a further patriarch row *(praotecheskyy ryad)* showing the Old Testament patriarchs.

Church Names In Russian, *sobor* means cathedral; *tserkov* and *khram* mean church. Common church names include:

Blagoveshchenskaya	(Annunciation)
Borisoglebskaya	(SS Boris & Gleb)
Nikolskaya	(St Nicholas)
Petropavlovskaya	(SS Peter & Paul)
Pokrovskaya	(Intercession of the Virgin)
Preobrazhenskaya	(Transfiguration)
Rizopolozhenskaya	(Deposition of the Holy Robe)
Rozhdestvenskaya	(Nativity)
Troitskaya	(Trinity)
Uspenskaya	(Assumption or Dormition)
Vladimirskaya	(St Vladimir)
Voskresenskaya	(Resurrection)
Voznesenskaya	(Ascension)
Znamenskaya	(Holy Sign)

Old Believers The Russian Church was split in 1653 by the reforms of Patriarch Nikon, who thought it had departed from its roots. He insisted, among other things, that the translation of the Bible be altered to conform with the Greek original, and that the sign of the cross be made with three fingers, not two. Those who couldn't accept these changes became known as Old Believers *(Starovery)* and came in for persecution. Some fled to the Siberian forests or remote parts of Central Asia, where one group who had never heard of Lenin, electricity or the revolution was found in the 1980s. Only in 1771-1827, 1905-18 and again recently have Old Believers had real freedom of worship. They probably now number over one million, but in 1917 there were as many as 20 million.

Other Christian Churches

Russia has small numbers of Roman Catholics, and Lutheran and Baptist Protestants, mostly among the German and other non-Russian ethnic groups. Other groups such as the Mormons, Seventh-Day Adventists and Salvation Army are sending hordes of missionaries. Not all groups are being welcomed. Courts have tried to use the 1997 religion law to ban the Pentecostalist Church, the Jehovah's Witnesses and other Christian faiths seen as threats by the Russian Orthodox Church.

Islam

European Russia has about 12 million active and nominal Muslims, mainly among the Tatar and Bashkir peoples east of Moscow and several of the Caucasus ethnic groups (see Population & People). Nearly all are Sunni Muslims, except for some Shiah in Dagestan. Soviet 'militant atheism' led to the closure of nearly all the mosques and *madrassas* (Muslim religious schools) in Russia. Under Stalin there were mass deportations and liquidation of the Muslim elite. Policies eased marginally after WWII.

Islam has, like Christianity, enjoyed growth since the mid-1980s. Though it has been some Muslim peoples – notably the Chechens and Tatars – who have been the most resistant of Russia's minorities to being brought within the Russian national fold since the fall of the Soviet Union in 1991, nationalism has played at least as big a part as religion in this, and militant Islam has as yet barely raised its head in Russia.

Islam in Russia is fairly secularised – eg women are not veiled, the Friday Sabbath is not a commercial holiday.

Working mosques are closed to women and often to non-Muslim men, though men may occasionally be invited in. There seems to be no way around this. If you are asked in, you'll have to take your shoes off (and hope your socks are clean! – dirty socks, like dirty feet, may be an insult to the mosque).

Judaism

Many of Russia's 500,000 or so Jews have been assimilated into Russian culture and do not seriously practise Judaism. However, there are approximately 30 synagogues. Unlike the country's other religious groups, Jews have no central coordinating body, though a yeshiva, or rabbinical academy, opened in Moscow in 1956.

There has been a disturbing rise in anti-Semitism not only in far-right political groups with neo-Nazi overtones but also in the Communist Party. In 1998, party leader Gennady Zyuganov, who finished second in the 1996 presidential election, accused Jews of causing 'mass impoverishment' and 'extinction' in Russia. However, to date these sentiments have not swept the populace. A poll taken after Zyuganov's statements showed that 83% of people found them 'unacceptable'.

Buddhism

The 145,000 Kalmyks – the largest ethnic group in the Kalmyk republic, north-west of the Caspian Sea – are traditionally members of the Gelugpa or 'Yellow-Hat' sect of Tibetan Buddhism, whose spiritual leader is the Dalai Lama. The Kalmyks fled to their present region in the 17th century from wars in western Mongolia, where Buddhism had reached them not long before. Buddhism was tolerated by the Soviet state until Stalin nearly wiped it out in the 1930s. Today temples are being rebuilt throughout the Kalmyk Republic.

Shamanism

The religion of most of the 700,000 Mari and some of the 800,000 Udmurts, both Finno-Ugric peoples in the middle Volga region, remains largely animist and shamanist. Animism is a belief in the presence of spirits or spiritual qualities in objects of the natural world. People contact these spirits for guidance through a medium or shaman ('witch doctor').

LANGUAGE

Just about everyone in Russia speaks Russian, although there are also dozens of other languages spoken by ethnic minorities. Russian and most of the other languages are written in variants of the Cyrillic alphabet. Russian grammar may be daunting, but your travels will be far more interesting if you at least take the time to learn the Cyrillic alphabet, so that you can read maps and street signs.

It's easy to find English-speakers in the big cities but no so easy in small towns (sometimes not even in tourist hotels).

For more information, as well as a list of useful Russian words and phrases, see the Language chapter located near the back of this book.

Facts for the Visitor

The Soviet legacy of an inefficient tourism infrastructure, Byzantine visa procedures and a lack of standard information outlets means that making plans for a trip to Russia is a challenging business. Of course, these difficulties mean that except at the Kremlin in Moscow or the Hermitage in St Petersburg you won't see hordes of tourists. And away from these cities you may see none at all.

HIGHLIGHTS

Moscow and St Petersburg are by far Russia's two most fascinating cities – and a big contrast, so try to fit both into your plans. As well as the best palaces, museums and theatres, they have the best restaurants, the best nightlife and the best accommodation across a range of budgets.

There are many excellent short trips to be made from both cities, too – especially to the 'Golden Ring' area of historic towns to the east of Moscow and the magnificent tsarist palaces and parks a short distance outside St Petersburg.

North of St Petersburg, the forests, rivers and lakes of Karelia offer some fine hiking and kayaking, as well as an extraordinary collection of old Russian wooden buildings on Kizhi Island in Lake Onega. Still farther north, there's the curiosity of a port city inside the Arctic Circle (Murmansk) and some good climbing and skiing on the Kola Peninsula.

From Arkhangelsk you can visit the Solovetsky Islands in the White Sea, with their monastery that was once one of Stalin's most infamous Gulag camps, and get a glimpse of decaying nuclear submarines at Severodvinsk (watch for the glow ...).

The mighty Volga is not so mighty now that it has been harnessed for hydroelectricity but you can see it in a relatively unfettered state at Golden Ring towns such as Yaroslavl or, farther east, Nizhny Novgorod. Astrakhan, near the delta where the Volga enters the Caspian Sea, is an old Russian city but has reminders that Central Asia is close.

In the deep south are the spectacularly beautiful Caucasus Mountains, with superb wild flowers in summer, relics of little-known ancient cultures and a fascinating ethnic mix among their modern inhabitants – though the conflicts that some of these have been embroiled in mean you shouldn't travel to parts of the Caucasus.

SUGGESTED ITINERARIES

When planning a trip, remember that transport between sights that seem close is often very slow or infrequent.

One week
: Visit Moscow and St Petersburg, ideally beginning in one and ending in the other. There will, perhaps, be time to stop off in one of the cities within close range of Moscow, such as Tver, which is on the train line linking the two major cities.

Two weeks
: The trip would be the same as that suggested for one week, with an extra day in Moscow and St Petersburg as well as a few days exploring the historic towns of the Golden Ring around Moscow.

One month
: This would allow a more leisurely exploration of the Golden Ring as well as journeys into parts of western or northern European Russia. Alternatively, you could combine the two week itinerary above with a journey east on one of the Trans-Siberian routes.

Two months
: This would be an optimal trip for someone who really wanted to explore Russia. One month could be spent in European Russia; in the summer a trip to northern European Russia would be good sojourn. The second month could be used for a detailed exploration of the Ural Mountains and Siberia. Alternatively you could use a few weeks for camping and trekking in the Ural Mountains.

Six months
: This trip would be both a major adventure and an endurance test. You could count on seeing a fair number of the destinations described in this book.

PLANNING

When to Go

July and August are the warmest months and the main holiday season for both foreigners and Russians. They're also the dampest months in most parts of European Russia, with as many as one rainy day in three. For these reasons, early summer (May and June) and late summer/early autumn (September and the first half of October) are many people's favourite seasons. Early autumn brings stunning colours as the leaves turn; locals disappear into the forests to gather buckets of mushrooms and berries.

Winter, if you're prepared for it, can be a great season. The theatres open, the furs and vodka come out, the snow makes everything picturesque, and the insides of buildings are kept warm. Least liked everywhere are the first snows and the spring thaw, which turn everything to slush and mud.

What Kind of Trip

One important thing to keep in mind as you plan is that you should make an effort to see at least a bit of Russia outside Moscow or St Petersburg. Even the historic towns of the Golden Ring are relatively free from tourists and you will be rewarded with a slice of rural Russian life that is far from the frenetic pace of the cities.

Group Travel Despite the many virtues of independent travel, group travel in Russia has some advantages worth noting. Budget group travel is a very cheap way to see European Russia. Getting around is obviously much easier for groups with their prearranged transport. Most special-interest travel is done in groups.

Tours can start at home or in Russia, last for a long weekend or for months, offer conditions that range from spartan to shamefully luxurious, with full board or do-it-yourself meals.

Individual Travel To head out on your own equipped with a few Russian phrases and a map is not impossible and is certainly the most exciting, if not absolutely the cheapest, way to see any part of Russia. The important factor to note about individual travel is that your enjoyment will be directly in proportion to your ability to speak Russian. Away from the major cities your odds of meeting anyone who speaks English are slim. Without an ability to speak Russian you will find everything you attempt both more costly and more difficult.

Excursions Excursions and trips can be booked wherever you are. These can make for a good hybrid journey with your major travels being independent but your specialised trips involving a guide or tour. Throughout Russia you will find locals ready to escort you on nature expeditions, treks, tours and the like. Many interesting places are far off the beaten path and the best way to reach them is often through a local guide or travel agent. Many of these instances are noted in the destination listing.

Maps

Maps of Moscow and St Petersburg are available from a myriad sources in those two cities and outside Russia. Country maps of Russia are also readily available. For other city maps or detailed regional maps useful for hiking or other activities, your choices are more limited.

Russian Sources Good, topographically accurate Russian maps of many cities and regions are cheap, but availability is very patchy. Most cities of any size have good maps but they can be hard to find. Try hotels, bookshops, kiosks and the like.

In Moscow, good sources for Russian language maps are the kiosks in the underpass from the Okhotny Ryad metro station to the Kremlin and the Torgovy Dom Biblio-Globus bookshop, Myasnitskaya ulitsa 6, near the Lubyanka metro station.

Overseas Sources The CIS map from the German publisher Hallwag is one of the clearest all-Russia maps, covering the whole country and the rest of the CIS (main roads and railways included) on one sheet at a scale of 1:7,000,000 (1cm to 70km). A minor disadvantage to English-language users is that it uses an unfamiliar transliteration system. *Hildebrand's Travel Map CIS* is also good.

Bartholomew publishes a European Russia map at 1:2,000,000. Freytag & Berndt's CIS map has European Russia at 1:2,000,000 on one side, and the whole country at 1:8,000,000 on the other. National Geographic produces far and away the best-looking wall map of Russia.

The most accurate commercially available maps of smaller regions of Russia are produced by the United States Defense Mapping Agency. These maps show parts of rural Russia in detail that is unavailable elsewhere. They're available for $13.95 each (the country's broken into many sections) from A Galaxy of Maps (toll-free ☎ 800-388 6588, fax 954-267 9007, sales@galaxymaps.com) in Ft Lauderdale, FL, USA. It will happily mail or fax you the complete listing of what's available.

What to Bring

Luggage Unless you're here to trek it doesn't much matter what you carry it all in, just make certain you can carry it over long distances. As always, the less you have the better, as train and bus storage can be tight and you'll find no-one to help you. A light day-pack is very useful for excursions. But strap-on bumbags (fanny packs), flags, English-language patches and other 'Hi, I'm a foreigner' accoutrements should not be used. To really fit in, use a plastic bag as a day-pack.

Clothing Brightly coloured clothes mark you out as a foreigner and may attract unwanted attention. Russians mostly wear really dull colours – grey, dark blue, brown and black.

For winter you'll need a thick, windproof coat, preferably long; a hat with ear-flaps to guard against frostbite; gloves and scarf; and thermal underwear. Because buildings are well heated inside, many light, removable layers work better than a few heavy ones. Footwear should be warm, thick-soled and waterproof (even insulated, for the north or Siberia).

In spring, summer and autumn, come equipped for sudden chills and rain. In autumn you'll need a hat and a raincoat or light overcoat. Late autumn and early winter tend to be wet and slushy. Shoes should be stout and water-resistant. When it's hot Russians wear as little as possible, although shorts are less common in rural areas.

Except for some posh restaurants in Moscow and St Petersburg you can dress casually for an evening out. You'll need something modest for visiting churches and mosques, possibly including a head-scarf for women.

Other Items Western toiletries are readily available, even in small towns, so you should only pack extra if there's a brand you absolutely have to have. The same goes for tampons and condoms. Don't trust Russian-made birth-control pills.

Unless you are going to spend all your nights in four-star Western hotels bring a small towel for trains or hotels that lack such a luxury. By all means carry toilet paper with you as you will rarely find any when you need it. But don't bring a lot from home as adequate brands (meaning soft) are widely sold.

An electric water-heating element enables you to purify water and make inexpensive hot drinks at will. A Thermos flask, mug and spoon are a boon for long train or road journeys. Other items to consider are a bottle opener and corkscrew, a small torch (flashlight), matches, Swiss army knife, universal bathroom plug, laundry soap, washing line and a few clothes pegs, sunglasses, compass (for hiking), sunscreen and lip salve, and a travel alarm clock.

In summer you'll need strong insect repellent at almost any latitude. St Petersburg is renowned for its huge mosquitoes as is most of the countryside such as northern Karelia and on the Kola Peninsula. Make certain that whatever brand you bring has a high concentration of DEET (diethyl-m-toluamid).

For suggestions of health-related items to pack, see the boxed text 'Medical Kit Check List' under Health later in this chapter.

TOURIST OFFICES

Local Tourist Offices

Tourist offices of the kind that travellers in the West are used to do not exist in Russia. Instead you're dependent for information mainly on the moods of hotel receptionists/administrators, service bureaus and travel firms. Service bureaus and travel firms exist primarily to sell services such as accommodation, excursions and transport. If you don't look as though you're thinking of booking something, they may or may not be willing to answer questions.

There is no official source of tourist information outside Russia.

Tourist Offices Abroad

Russia has no tourist offices abroad and most of its consulates and embassies do not have much practical country information. Foreign travel agencies specialising in Russian travel can be useful (see the later European Russia Getting There & Away chapter).

VISAS & DOCUMENTS

All foreigners visiting Russia need visas. To get one you must technically have confirmed accommodation for every night you'll be in the country, though in practice there are countless ways around this.

At the time of writing, a Russian visa was a passport-sized paper document; but nothing goes into your passport. The visa lists entry/exit dates, your passport number, any children travelling with you, and visa type (see Types of Visa later). It's an exit permit too, so if you lose it (or overstay), leaving the country can be harder than getting in.

The following sections give general information about visa procedures – before you go to Russia and once you're there. Despite changes in details here and there, these guidelines have remained essentially static since the fall of the Soviet Union and the last edition of this book.

Processing Fees

Each Russian consulate charges as much as it can, so rates fluctuate depending on where and when you apply. Note, too, that US citizens pay more than anyone else for their visas – a retaliatory measure imposed by Russians who have been shamefully treated when applying for US visas. The US State Department continually announces it will streamline procedures and give clerks sensitivity training, but until that actually happens, Russians are trying, with some success, to treat US citizens as poorly as the USA treats Russians. When you get upset about it, consider this: however poor the treatment is that you receive, the Russians are no doubt being far nicer to you than the US consulate would be to them. The Moscow embassy is an especially egregious offender.

Registration

When you check in at a hotel, camping ground or hostel, you surrender your passport and visa so the hotel can register you with OVIR *(Otdel Viz i Registratsii)*, the Department of Visas & Registration. You'll get your documents back the next morning – you'll usually need to ask, as nobody seems to remember to return them to you. A safer alternative is to tell staff at the front desk you need your passport back in five minutes so you can change some money. They'll usually register it right then.

All Russian visas must be registered with OVIR within three business days of your arrival in Russia. No ifs or buts about it. Some travel agencies claim that their 'visas needn't be registered'. This is not true, so be highly suspicious of any company that tells you it is. Sometimes you have to pay a registration fee of $5 to $10. In Moscow, you can avoid a trip to OVIR and get your visa registered for free at Andrews Consulting (☎ 095-258 51 98) at Novaya ploshchad 10, 5th floor, near the Lubyanka metro station.

Extending a visa that's not registered can be impossible, and getting out of the country with an unregistered visa could be a very expensive proposition. On the other hand, you may get out with just a lecture or even unhindered. But travellers have reported that fines of up to $500 have been levied at the Finnish and Norwegian borders.

Registration Problems The company or organisation that invites you to Russia is responsible for your registration, and no other company can support your visa. You can't take a visa that was issued on the invitation of, say, the HI Hostel in St Petersburg and have it registered in Moscow by the Travellers Guest House.

If you're not sure which organisation invited you (if the sponsorship line – on tourist visas this begins with the words *V uchrezhdenie* – has a name you've never heard of), the simplest option is to spend a night at one of the major hotels, which will register your visa for you right at the front desk. There may be a fee involved, but usually the cost of the room will suffice.

HIV/AIDS Testing

At the time of writing, HIV/AIDS testing was required for foreigners staying in the Russian Federation longer than three months. By definition, this does not affect tourist visas, which are only issued for shorter stays. The medical certificate must be in English and in Russian. Consult the company sponsoring your business visa for the latest regulations.

Types of Visa

Six types of visa are available to foreign visitors and are listed below. For all visas you'll need:

- a passport valid for at least a month beyond your return date. You may be able to get away with giving the embassy or consulate only photocopies of the data pages of your passport;
- three passport-size (4cm by 4.5cm), full-face photos, not more than a year old. Vending-machine photos with white background are fine if they're essentially identical;
- a completed application form, including entry/exit dates;
- a handling fee (an amount that varies from country to country and depending on your citizenship).

Tourist Visa A tourist visa is issued to, well, tourists: those who have booked hotel or hostel beds and are in Russia for purposes other than business. These are the most straightforward and inflexible visas available. In theory you're supposed to have booked accommodation for every night you'll be in the country, but in practice you can often get away with only booking a few, even just one – ask the travel agent, hotel or hostel you're booking through.

Extending a tourist visa is hugely difficult and the extension, if granted, will usually be only for a short time. Tourist visas are best for trips when you know exactly what you're doing and when, where and for how long you'll be doing it. To obtain a tourist visa, you will need, in addition to the above items:

- confirmation of hotel reservations, which can be a faxed copy on hotel letterhead signed and stamped by the hotel; or confirmation of bookings from a travel agent; or
- a visa-support letter from a youth hostel/guesthouse. (See the business visa section for tourist visa support fees charged by some hostels and guesthouses.)

Business Visa Far more flexible and desirable for the independent traveller is a business (or commercial) visa supported by a Russian company. The invitation eliminates the need for pre-arranged hotel confirmations because the company inviting you ostensibly puts you up for the duration of your stay. While a visa to Russia supposedly allows you to travel anywhere, holders of tourist visas may have a harder time getting accommodation in smaller regional cities that are not listed on their visas than will holders of business visas doing the same thing.

To obtain a business visa you must have a letter of invitation from a registered Russian company guaranteeing to provide accommodation during the entire length of your stay, and a covering letter from your company (or you) stating the purpose of your trip.

There are many organisations that will send you a business invitation for a fee – usually not an outrageous amount. You will need to send them a fax or email containing your name as it appears in your passport, date and place of birth, nationality, passport number and expiry date, dates of entry to and exit from Russia (these can be approximate) and the name of the consulate at which you intend to apply for your visa. Sample fees for visa-support services include:

HI St Petersburg Hostel (☎ 812-329 80 18, fax 329 80 19, ryh@ryh.ru), 3-ya Sovetskaya ulitsa 28, St Petersburg. Organised through the hostel, a tourist visa (with reservation for accommodation booked, plus two weeks of added time in country) costs $25 including registration, plus $10 for the fax. The hostel will require credit card or other payment in advance.

IRO Travel (☎ 095-234 65 53), Bolshoy Pereyaslavskaya ulitsa 50, Moscow, at the Travellers Guest House. This organisation charges $48.50 for a tourist invitation for up to 25 days maximum, $88 for a one-month business visa invitation, and $201 for three-month multiple entry business visa support (21-day processing time required).

RTT Matkapalvelut Travel Agency (☎ 09-659 052), Laivasillankatu 14, Helsinki, near the Russian embassy. This agency charges US citizens $86 for an invitation and all visa processing at the Helsinki consulate for five-day service, and $190 for same-day service. Other nationalities pay less. Note that its prices include the Russian consulate's visa fees in addition to RTT's invitation fees.

There are scores of companies in Russia willing to issue commercial visa invitations, some cheaper, some more expensive. Those we've listed are known to be reliable and will follow through with registration.

Student Visa Student visas can be wonderful things; they're flexible and extendable and they even entitle you to pay Russian prices for air fares, train fares and other items affected under the country's dual-pricing system (see Costs later in this chapter). You'll need proof of enrolment at an accredited Russian school or university, which usually requires prepayment.

'Private' Visa This is the visa you get for a visit by personal invitation, and it's also referred to as an 'ordinary' visa by some authorities. The visa itself is as easy to get as a tourist visa but getting the invitation is a complex matter.

The person who is inviting you must go to their local office of OVIR and fill out an invitation form for approval of the invitation. Approval, which takes several weeks, comes in the form of a notice of permission *(izveshchenie)*, good for one year, which the person inviting you must then send to you. You will need this invitation approval notice together with the standard application form to apply for the visa, which is valid for as many as 60 days in your host's town.

'On-the-Spot' Visa These are fast-track business visas, freed from the requirement for advance invitations. Individuals arriving at Moscow's Sheremetevo-2 or St Petersburg's Pulkovo-2 airports can get short-term visas at a special consular office before going through passport control. To get one of these visas, you'll have to have a copy of a Ministry of Foreign Affairs (MID) invitation and have a representative of your inviting company meet you at the airport. Note, however, that airlines may not necessarily let you board your flight to Russia, because if you're turned down for the fast-track visa the airline is responsible for bringing you out again – so check with the airlines in advance.

This kind of visa is good for up to a month and attracts fees from about $150 to $250. Though expensive and problematic, it may be one way around the paper chase.

Transit Visa This is for 'passing through', which is loosely interpreted. For transit by air it's usually good for 48 hours. For a non-stop Trans-Siberian Railway journey it's valid for 10 days, giving westbound passengers a few days in Moscow without the obligatory hotel prebooking (those heading east can't linger in Moscow). Under certain circumstances, travellers transiting Russia and holding valid entry/exit visas to Armenia, Belarus, Kazakhstan, Kyrgyzstan, Tajikistan or Uzbekistan need not apply for a Russian transit visa. The requirements on this are sketchy, and while a Russian consulate may say it's unnecessary, the odds of being allowed into or out of Russia on the premise that you're holding a Tajik visa are slim. Many border guards are not familiar with the latest regulations handed down in Moscow, so it's always best to play it safe, especially when travelling to border crossings in remote areas.

When to Apply

Apply as soon as you have all the documents you need (but not more than two months ahead). Business, tourist, private and student visas all take the same amount of time to process once you have the paperwork – be it invitation, confirmation or izveshchenie. This ought to be 10 working days, but can vary. You can pay a higher fee for quicker service at most embassies.

Transit visas normally take seven working days but may take as little as a few hours at the Russian embassy in Beijing.

How to Apply

Individuals can arrange their own visas, though long queues at embassies and consulates are common in the high season and Russian consular officials are sometimes somewhat less than bright and perky – and they rarely answer the telephone. If you're booking your flight or accommodation through a travel agency, they'll get your visa too for an extra fee, usually between $5 and $30 (agencies in Hong Kong, which must go through the embassy in Bangkok for visas, charge you more). For group tours, the agency does the work.

Visa Agencies Certain agencies specialise in getting visas: in the USA, Visa Services, Inc (☎ 202-387 0300), 1519 Connecticut Ave NW, Washington DC 20036, and Travel Document Systems (☎ 202-638 3800, toll-free within the USA ☎ 800-874 5100, info@traveldocs.com), 734 15th St NW, Suite 400, Washington DC 20005; in the UK, Worldwide Visas (☎ 020-8995 2492), 9 Adelaide St, Charing Cross, London WC2 N4HZ. Unless you're really pressed for time or especially badly affected by impersonal bureaucracies, it seems a bit extravagant really. An agency will put your paperwork together and forward it to the embassy for you – for a fee of up to $65.

In Person To apply for a visa yourself, go to the nearest Russian embassy or consulate (see the following By Mail section if you're not near one). Bring your passport or photocopies of the pages covering your personal information and passport validity, your photographs and your hotel confirmation, hostel or business invitation, proof of enrolment, izveshchenie or transit tickets. Ask for, and complete, the visa application, and then wait.

How long you wait depends on how much you're willing to pay. Rush fees vary not just by country but by individual consulate; next-day service can cost several times the cost of 10-day service.

While Russian consular officials in some locations are friendly and even smile once in a while, those at others are often not. Unfortunately there's not much you can do except be very polite and get out of there as quickly as you can. You *do* have the right to shop around.

By Mail It's possible to do it all by mail, with stamped, self-addressed envelopes or, if you have them, FedEx, Airborne, DHL or TNT airbills, complete with your account number for all requested forms and completed documents. When you receive the visa, check it carefully – especially the expiry, entry and exit dates and any restrictions on entry or exit points.

Fax-Back Service For callers in the UK, the Russian embassy's consular section in London offers an interactive recorded message about visas (☎ 0891-171 271). This is a premium-rate number that costs UK£0.49 per minute peak, UK£0.38 per minute cheap rate, but it tells you most of what you'll need to know in five to 10 minutes. You then have to visit or write to the consulate to get the relevant forms. Even if (by some administrative oversight) you were so lucky as to get through on the main consulate number, you'd be referred to this recording anyway.

Visa Extensions & Changes

Extensions have become time-consuming, if not downright difficult. A tourist visa can now only be extended through official hotels (not hostels) and with a great deal of advance notice (and perhaps of money).

Where Can You Go?

Some cities in Russia are still off-limits to foreigners but these are few and far between. Technically, any visa is valid for all of Russia except these closed cities. Practically speaking, no-one cares where you go.

You may have trouble with a tourist visa in a hotel in a strange city (ie a city not listed on the visa), though this can usually be talked around. If you will be venturing off the beaten path, it's best to play it safe and get a business visa, the authoritative appearance of which effectively grants you the run of the country.

Lost or Stolen Documents

In order to facilitate replacement of your documents it is imperative that you make and carry photocopies of them, especially your Russian visa (see Photocopies later in this section for further hints). Without this photocopy, replacing a lost or stolen visa can be a nightmare – sometimes you'll even have to contact the issuing embassy and ask it to track down your visa number. Good luck.

Your embassy or consulate in Russia can replace a lost or stolen passport, but if you lose your visa you must go to the local visa office, OVIR. A Russian travel agent, your hotel service bureau or the youth hostels can help with this, including reporting the loss to the police. Again, both procedures are much easier if you've stashed away a few passport-sized photos, your visa number and photocopies of your visa and your passport's personal information and validity pages.

Travel Insurance

Make sure that you have adequate health insurance. A travel insurance policy to cover theft, loss and medical problems is a wise idea. There is a wide variety of policies and your travel agent will have recommendations. Make certain that your policy will cover medical evacuation back to your home country from any part of Russia where you are likely to travel.

Youth, Student & Senior Cards

Full-time students and people aged under 26 or over 59 tend to get a substantial discount on admissions, transport and perhaps even hotels. Always try flashing your ID before paying.

For about $6, full-time students can get an ISIC from student agencies worldwide. If you're not a student but you are under 26, ask a student agency at home for an ISIC Youth Card.

Railways in Britain and the American Association for Retired People issue identification cards for seniors, and similar organisations exist in other Western countries.

Photocopies

All important documents (passport data page and visa page, credit cards, travel insurance policy, air/bus/train tickets, driving licence etc) should be photocopied before you leave home. Leave one copy with someone at home and keep another with you, separate from the originals. Also take some spare passport photos. After you have entered Russia, try to get a photocopy of your customs declaration *(deklaratsia)*. All these will be very useful if your documents go astray.

It's also a good idea to store details of your vital travel documents in Lonely Planet's free online Travel Vault, in case you lose the photocopies or can't be bothered with them. Your password-protected Travel Vault is accessible online anywhere in the world – create it at www.ekno.lonelyplanet.com.

EMBASSIES & CONSULATES

It's important to realise what your own embassy – the embassy of the country of which you are a citizen – can and can't do to help you if you get into trouble.

Generally speaking, it won't be much help in emergencies if the trouble you're in is remotely your own fault. Remember that you are bound by the laws of the country you are in. Your embassy will not be sympathetic if you end up in jail after committing a crime locally, even if such actions are legal in your own country.

In genuine emergencies you might get some assistance, but only if other channels have been exhausted. For example, if you need to get home urgently, a free ticket is exceedingly unlikely – the embassy would expect you to have insurance. If you have all your money and documents stolen, the embassy might assist with getting a new passport, but a loan for onward travel is out of the question.

Russian Embassies Abroad

Australia
Embassy:
(☎ 02-6295 9033/9474, fax 6295 1847)
78 Canberra Ave, Griffith, ACT 2603
Consulate:
(☎ 02-9326 1866)
7 Fullerton St, Woollahra, NSW 2025

Azerbaijan
Embassy:
(☎ 8922-98 60 16, fax 9822-98 60 83)
Hotel Azerbaijan, 370133 Baku

Belarus
Embassy:
(☎ 0172-345 497, fax 503 664)
vulitsa Staravilenskaya 48, 220002 Minsk

Canada
Embassy:
(☎ 613-235 4341, fax 236 6342)
285 Charlotte St, Ottawa, Canada
Visa Department:
(☎ 613-236 7220/6215, fax 238 6158)
Consulate:
(☎ 514-843 5901 or ☎ 842 5343, fax 842 2012)
3655 Ave Du Musée, Montreal, Quebec, H3G 2EI

China
Embassy:
(☎ 10-532 2051, visa section ☎ 532 1267)
4 Baizhongjie, Beijing 100600
Consulate:
(☎ 21-324 2682)
20 Huangpu Lu, Shanghai 200080

Estonia
Embassy:
(☎ 22-44 30 14, fax 44 37 73)
Pikk 19, EE-0200 Tallinn
Consulate:
(☎/fax 235-3 13 67)
Vilde 8, EE-2020 Narva

Finland
Embassy:
(☎ 09-66 14 49, ☎ 66 18 76/77 or ☎ 60 70 50, fax 66 10 06)
Tehtaankatu 1B, FIN-00140 Helsinki

France
Embassy:
(☎ 1-45 04 05 50 or ☎ 45 04 71 71, fax 45 04 17 65)
40-50 Boulevard Lannes, F-75116 Paris
Consulate:
(☎ 91-77 15 25, fax 77 34 54)
8 Rue Ambrois Pare, F-13008 Marseille

Germany
Embassy:
(☎ 0228-312 08 5/6/7 or ☎ 312 52 9, fax 311 56 3)
Waldstrasse 42, 53177 Bonn
Consular affairs:
(☎ 0228-312 08 3, fax 384 56 1)
Consulates:
(☎ 030 229 14 20, fax 2299 397)
Unter den Linden 63-65, 10117 Berlin
(☎ 040-229 52 01, fax 229 77 27)
Am Feenteich 20, 22085 Hamburg
(☎ 0341-518 76, fax 585 24 04)
Kickerlingsberg 18, 04105 Leipzig
(☎ 089-592 50 3, fax 550 38 28)
Seidelstrasse 8, 80335 Munich
(☎ 0381-226 42, fax 227 43)
Tuhnenstrasse 3, 18057 Rostock

Ireland
Embassy:
(☎ 01-494 3525 or ☎ 492 2048, fax 492 3525)
186 Orwell Rd, Rathgar, Dublin 6

Kazakhstan
Embassy:
(☎ 3272-44 83 32 or ☎ 44 66 44)
ulitsa Dzhandosova 4, Almaty

Kyrgyzstan
Embassy:
(☎ 3312-22 16 91, fax 22 18 23, 22 17 10)
ulitsa Pervomayskaya 17, Bishkek

Latvia
Embassy:
(☎ 2-33 21 51 or ☎ 22 06 93, fax 21 25 79)
Paeglesiela 2, LV-1397 Riga

Lithuania
Embassy:
(☎ 22-35 17 63, fax 35 38 77)
Juozapaviciaus gatve 11, LT-2000 Vilnius

Moldova
Embassy:
(☎/fax 2-23 26 00)
bulvar Stefan del Mare 151, 277019 Chisinau

Mongolia
Embassy:
(☎ 1-7 28 51, ☎ 2 68 36 or ☎ 2 75 06)
Friendship St A 6, Ulaan Baatar

Netherlands
Embassy:
(☎ 070-345 13 00/01, ☎ 346 88 88 or ☎ 34 10 75 06, fax 361 79 60)
Andries Bickerweg 2, NL-2517 JP The Hague

New Zealand
Embassy:
(☎ 04-476 6113)
57 Messines Rd, Karori, Wellington

Poland
Embassy:
(☎ 022-621 55 75)
ulica Belwederska 49, PL-00-761 Warsaw
Consulates:
(☎ 058-41 42 00 or ☎ 41 96 39)
ulica Batorego 15, PL-80-251 Gdansk-Wrzeszcz
(☎ 012-22 26 47, ☎ 22 92 33 or ☎ 22 83 88)
ulica Westerplatte 11, PL-31-033 Krakow
(☎ 061-41 75 23 or ☎ 41 77 40)
ulica Dukowska 53A, PL-60-567 Poznan
(☎ 091-22 22 45, ☎ 22 48 77, ☎ 22 21 19 or ☎ 22 03 33)
ulica P Skargi 14, PL-71-422 Szczecin

Turkmenistan
Embassy:
(☎ 3632-25 39 57 or ☎ 29 84 66, fax 29 84 66)
11 Turkmenbashy Shaely, 744004 Ashkhabad

UK
Embassy:
(☎ 020-7229 3628/29, fax 7727 8624/25 or 7299 5804)
13 Kensington Palace Gardens, London W8 4QX
Consular Section:
(☎ 020-7229 8027, visa information message ☎ 0891-171 271, fax 020-7229 3215)
5 Kensington Palace Gardens, London W8 4QS
Consulate:
(☎ 0131-225 7098, fax 225 9587)
9 Coates Crescent, Edinburgh E13 7RL

Ukraine
Embassy:
(☎ 044-294 79 36, fax 292 66 31)
vulitsya Kutuzova 8, UKR-252000 Kyiv

USA
Embassy:
(☎ 202-298 5700/5772, fax 298 5749)
2650 Wisconsin Ave, NW, Washington DC 20007
Visa Department:
(☎ 202-939 8907, fax 939 8909)
1825 Phelps Place NW, Washington DC 20008
Consulates:
(☎ 212-348 0926, fax 831 9162)
9 East 91 St, New York, NY 10128
(☎ 415-928 6878, fax 929 0306)
2790 Green St, San Francisco, CA 94123
(☎ 206-728 1910, fax 728 1871)
2323 Westin Building, 2001 Sixth Ave, Seattle, WA 98121-2617

Uzbekistan
Embassy:
(☎ 3712-54 36 41, ☎ 55 92 18 or ☎ 55 91 57, fax 55 87 74)
ulitsa Nukusskaya (formerly ulitsa Proletarskaya) 83, 750015 Tashkent

Embassies in Moscow

The area code for the telephone numbers in the following list is ☎ 095.

Armenia
(☎ 924 12 69)
Armyansky pereulok 2

Australia
(☎ 956 60 70)
Kropotkinsky pereulok 13

Azerbaijan
(☎ 229 16 49)
Leontevsky pereulok 16

Belarus
(☎ 924 70 31 or, for visa inquiries, ☎ 924 70 95)
Maroseyka ulitsa 17/6

Canada
(☎ 956 66 66)
Starokonyushenny pereulok 23

China
(☎ 143 15 40 or, for visa inquiries, ☎ 143 15 43)
ulitsa Druzhby 6

Czech Republic
(☎ 251 05 40)
ulitsa Yuliusa Fuchika 12/14

Estonia
(☎ 290 46 55 or ☎ 290 50 13)
Kalashny pereulok 8

Finland
(☎ 246 40 27)
Kropotkinsky pereulok 15/17

France
(☎ 236 00 03)
Bolshaya Yakimanka ulitsa 45

Georgia
(☎ 291 66 02 or ☎ 291 69 02)
Nozhovy pereulok 6
Consular section:
(☎ 241 97 67)
ulitsa Arbat 42

Germany
(☎ 956 10 80)
ulitsa Mosfilmovskaya 56
Consular section:
(☎ 936 24 01)
Leninsky prospekt 95A

Ireland
(☎ 288 41 01 or ☎ 230 27 63)
Grokholsky pereulok 5
Israel
(☎ 238 27 32 or ☎ 230 67 00)
ulitsa Bolshaya Ordynka 56
Japan
(☎ 291 85 00)
Kalashny pereulok 12
Kazakhstan
(☎ 208 98 52 or ☎ 927 18 36)
Chistoprudny bulvar 3A
Kyrgyzstan
(☎ 237 44 81 or ☎ 237 48 82)
ulitsa Bolshaya Ordynka 64
Latvia
(☎ 925 27 07)
ulitsa Chaplygina 3
Lithuania
(☎ 291 26 43)
Borisoglebsky pereulok 10
Moldova
(☎ 928 54 05)
ulitsa Kuznetsky Most 18
Mongolia
(☎ 290 67 92)
Borisoglebsky pereulok 11
Consular section (for visas):
(☎ 244 78 67)
Spasopeskovsky pereulok 7
Netherlands
(☎ 291 29 99)
Kalashny pereulok 6
New Zealand
(☎ 956 35 79)
Povarskaya ulitsa 44
North Korea
(☎ 143 62 49)
ulitsa Mosfilmovskaya 72
Norway
(☎ 290 38 72)
Povarskaya ulitsa 7
Poland
(☎ 255 00 17 or, for the visa section, ☎ 254 36 21)
ulitsa Klimashkina 4
Romania
(☎ 143 04 24/27)
ulitsa Mosfilmovskaya 64
Slovakia
(☎ 251 05 40 or ☎ 251 10 70)
ulitsa Yuliusa Fuchika 12/14
South Africa
(☎ 230 68 69)
Bolshoy Strochenovsky pereulok 22/25
Sweden
(☎ 956 12 00)
ulitsa Mosfilmovskaya 60
Tajikistan
(☎ 290 61 02)
Skatertny pereulok 19
Turkey
(☎ 245 67 35)
7-y Rostovsky pereulok 12
Turkmenistan
(☎ 291 66 36)
Filippovsky pereulok 22
UK
(☎ 956 74 00)
Sofiyskaya naberezhnaya (formerly naberezhnaya Morisa Toreza) 14
Ukraine
(☎ 229 10 79)
Leontevsky pereulok 18
USA
(☎ 252 24 51 or, for after-hours emergencies, ☎ 956 42 61)
Novinsky bulvar 19/23
Uzbekistan
(☎ 230 00 76, ☎ 238 98 11 or, for visa inquiries, 230 00 54)
Pogorelsky pereulok 12

Consulates in St Petersburg

The area code for St Petersburg is ☎ 812.

Canada
(☎ 325 84 48 or ☎ 316 72 22) Malodetskoselsky prospekt 32
China
(☎ 114 62 30)
naberezhnaya Kanala Griboedova 134
Estonia
(☎ 238 18 04)
Bolshaya Monetnaya ulitsa 14
Finland
(☎ 273 73 21)
ulitsa Chaykovskogo 71
France
(☎ 312 11 30 or ☎ 311 85 11)
naberezhnaya reki Moyki 15
Germany
(☎ 327 31 11)
ulitsa Furshtadtskaya 39
Latvia
(☎ 327 60 53)
10-ya Linia 11 (Vasilevsky Side)
Poland
(☎ 274 41 70)
5-ya Sovetskaya ulitsa 12/14
UK
(☎ 325 60 36 or ☎ 325 61 66)
ploshchad Proletarskoy Diktatury 5
USA
(☎ 275 17 01)
ulitsa Furshtadtskaya 15

CUSTOMS

Russian customs laws and regulations are in a state of flux and are not consistently enforced. Travellers to Russia should declare all items of value on a deklaratsia upon arrival and keep this form until their departure from Russia.

If you are arriving by air, the airline will probably give you two customs forms in English. Keep one to fill out when you leave. Border posts and airports rarely have forms in English. The first six lines ask: your full name, citizenship, the country you are arriving from, the country that's your destination, the purpose of your visit (the answers can be short: business, tourism, private etc) and how many pieces of luggage (including hand luggage) you're carrying. The next five lines have Roman numerals. The first three ask if you are carrying (I) weapons and ammunition; (II) narcotics and appliances to use them – note that if you have prescribed syringes you mention them here; and (III) antiques and objects of art. The next (IV) asks you to list any Russian roubles, state loan bonds or Russian lottery tickets you are carrying. Item five (V) is a table in which you list all currency you are bringing in. You write the type of currency then the amount in digits and words. The next item asks you to name any roubles, other currency or valuables you are bringing in that belong to another person. Finally, just above where you give the date and sign your name you list how many pieces of luggage – if any – you've sent separately.

If the total value of what you've listed is $500 or more (or is even close to this amount) you must go through a red lane and have the form stamped by a customs official, who may also check your luggage. In practice this is a formality, but it is important that you respect it. If the total value of your declared items is comfortably below $500, you can use a green line, if one exists.

When you leave Russia you will have to fill out an identical form declaring what you are removing from the country. If you have a stamped customs form, your exit customs form cannot show you are leaving with more than you brought in. If you did not get your form stamped on the way in, your exit form cannot show you are taking out items with a total value of more than $500.

Lost Customs Form

Treat a stamped customs declaration as carefully as you treat your passport. If you should lose it then you will need a police report confirming the loss, which you present to customs when you leave Russia.

What You Can Bring In

You may bring in modest amounts of anything for personal use except, obviously, illegal drugs and weapons. Cameras, notebook computers, video cameras, radios and Walkmans, and video and audio tapes are OK. If you're bringing in hypodermic needles, make sure you bring in a prescription for them and declare them under the line 'Narcotics and appliances for use thereof'.

Up to 250 cigarettes are fine but large amounts of anything saleable are suspect. Food is allowed (except for some fresh fruit and vegetables), as is a litre of hard liquor or wine.

What You Can Take Out

Anything bought from a legitimate shop or department store can go out, but save your receipts. Technically, you can't take Russian currency with you, though officials won't usually check your pockets or wallet, and in 1999 we routinely listed modest amounts on our customs forms without any problems.

Anything vaguely 'arty', such as manuscripts, instruments, coins, jewellery, antiques or antiquarian books (meaning those published before 1975) must be assessed by the Ministry of Culture at Neglinnaya 8/10, office 29 in Moscow and at Malaya Morskaya 17 in St Petersburg. There the bureaucrats will issue a receipt for tax paid (usually 100% of the purchase price – bring your sales receipt), which you show to customs on your way out of the country. If you buy something large, a photograph will usually be fine for assessment purposes.

A painting bought at a tourist art market, in a department store or from a commercial gallery should be declared and receipts should be kept. Generally speaking, customs in airports is much more strict and thorough than at any border crossing.

MONEY

All prices in this book are listed in US dollars (abbreviated to $). For rules on taking money in/out of the country, see the Customs section earlier.

Currency

Russian currency is the rouble *(ROO-bl)*, written as рубль or abbreviated as ру or р. There are 100 kopecks in the rouble, and these come in small coins worth one, 10 and 50 kopecks.

The rouble was revalued in 1998 by a factor of 1000 to one. Notes dating from prior to the revaluation are no longer valid, so if you see rouble notes with lots of zeros in them, be very dubious or treat them as souvenirs. Roubles are issued in coins in amounts of one, two and five roubles. Banknotes come in values of 10, 50, 100 and 500 roubles. In practice the 500 notes are the easiest to carry, but they will be hard to use for small purchases, as the seller may not have change.

It is illegal to make purchases in any currency other than roubles. When you run into prices in dollars – or the favoured pseudonym, 'units' – in expensive restaurants and hotels you will still be presented with a final bill in roubles.

Exchange Rates

Many prices in Russia track the exchange rate of the US dollar, so when the rouble loses value, prices rise to compensate. Before the devaluation in August 1998 six roubles were worth $1.

country	unit		rouble (R)
Australia	A$1	=	R17.28
Canada	C$1	=	R18.17
China	Y10	=	R32.37
euro	€1	=	R27.06
Finland	10 mk	=	R45.51
France	10FF	=	R41.26
Germany	DM1	=	R13.84
Ireland	IR£1	=	R34.36
Japan	¥100	=	R26.38
Netherlands	f1	=	R12.28
New Zealand	NZ$1	=	R13.83
Norway	10 Nkr	=	R33.58
UK	UK£1	=	R43.16
Ukraine	10 hv	=	R51.24
USA	US$1	=	R26.80

Exchanging Money

Cash US dollars, German Deutschmarks and Russian roubles can be easily exchanged anywhere; other currencies such as the British pound or French franc can be hard/impossible to change outside Moscow and St Petersburg. Note that most EU currencies (the British pound is a notable exception) will be replaced by the euro in January 2002. At the time of print it was difficult to foresee how the euro would be accepted in Russia and how easily it will be exchanged for roubles. It is likely that the Russians will be deeply suspicious of the euro and hence your safest bet after early 2002 will be to travel with US dollars.

Whatever currency you bring should be in pristine condition. Banks and exchanges do not accept old, tatty bills with rips or tears. Dollars are the most commonly used exchange currency and the easiest to find in other parts of the world before your trip. Make certain that besides looking and smelling newly minted, they are of the new design, which has the large off-set portrait. Most people carry $100 bills, changing just a few at a time.

Every town of any size will have at least one bank or exchange office. Be prepared to fill out a lengthy form and show your passport. Your receipt is for your own records as customs officials no longer require documentation of your currency transactions. As anywhere, rates can vary from one establishment to the next so it's always worth shopping around.

Travellers Cheques Travellers cheques can be difficult to exchange outside the largest cities. Also, the process is a lengthy (and confusing) one, involving trips to numerous different cashiers in the bank, each responsible for a different part of the transaction. Expect to pay at least a 2% commission. Unless you will be spending all your time in Moscow and St Petersburg it's not a good idea to carry your fortune in travellers cheques because you might not be able to use them.

Not all travellers cheques are treated as equal by Russian establishments willing to handle them. In descending order of acceptance are American Express (Amex), Thomas Cook and Visa. You'll have little or no luck with other brands.

ATMs Automatic teller machines (ATMs) are an ideal solution for travellers who don't want to carry wads of cash. Using a credit card or the same card you use in ATMs at home, you can obtain cash as you need it. Unfortunately many of the banks with ATMs died after August 1998. Most sizable towns usually have at least one operating ATM that will accept cards from outside Russia. Sometimes this can border on the bizarre, such as in Volgograd where during the summer of 1999 the only working ATM was in a perfume store. Look for signs that say *bankomat* (БАНКОМАТ).

If you are going to rely on ATMs for obtaining cash on your trip, make certain you always have a few days' supply of cash at hand in case you can't find a working machine. Also, obtain and memorise PINs for virtually all of the credit and cash cards you intend to carry. This will increase your odds of finding a machine that will give you cash on one of your cards.

The ATMs we note in the city listings are linked up to one or more of the following international networks: Amex, Cirrus, Eurocard, MasterCard and Visa. The machines dispense roubles only and sometimes won't part with more than the equivalent of $100 per transaction.

Credit Cards The crash of the Russian economy wreaked havoc with credit card acceptance. In the summer of 1999 few establishments besides luxury hotels would accept plastic of any kind. This included travel agents, expensive restaurants, boutiques and other normally credit card friendly establishments. With the rouble falling, merchants are afraid that they will lose money between the time of the charge and when the credit card company reimburses them. However, if the monetary situation stabilises, credit cards should become more acceptable.

Most sizable cities have banks that will give you a cash advance on your credit card, but be prepared for a tangle of paperwork.

International Transfers Larger cities will have at least one bank that can handle Western Union money wires. Ask at any bank for this information – we found they were happy to steer you to whichever bank in town handled wire transfers.

Black Market Because the rouble floats – some cynics will say sinks – freely on international exchange markets, there is no reason for the black market to exist. Should some shadowy character offer to exchange money for you, remember that they can't give you a better rate than banks and profit. Thus they are either crooks or insane.

Security

Don't leave money – in any form – lying around your room. Preferably, keep it in several different places about your person and baggage. When you go out, carry what you'll need in your pockets (but avoid eye-catching wallet bulges), with any extra tucked away under your clothing – best in a money belt, shoulder wallet or ankle pouch. Wrapping cash carefully in plastic and tucking it under the insole of your shoe is another good idea.

Costs

Depending on where you go, Russia can be a budget traveller's dream or a corporate accountant's nightmare.

Moscow can seem like the most expensive city in the world. Since few of the local workers can *ever* afford to eat out due to their low salaries, the restaurants, bars and cafes target their prices at well-paid expats and free-spending visitors. Food and drink prices here easily outpace even those in London and New York. Expect to pay at least $20 a head for a meal in a simple restaurant. Lodgings prices are very high as well. The simple but cheap hotels found in Western Europe don't exist here. Besides the hostels, there's little to choose from between the mammoth Communist-era hotels charging $100 or more a night and the large Western chains who charge $250 or more a night. The only bargains are activities you'll share with the locals such as riding the metro ($0.15).

St Petersburg is a bit better. Prices here are more typical of those charged in major cities in the West. You can find a fine meal for $10 and not bad rooms outside hostels for $50.

Away from these two cities, prices plummet. With few tourists lurking about to exploit, local businesses have to charge rates affordable by all. Meals can be had for $1 and rooms in shabby but passable old hotels go for under $15. Transport costs throughout the country are not high, even in instances where foreigners are charged more. See the European Russia Getting Around chapter for details.

Dual-Pricing System Hotels (except the most expensive Western ones), museums, the railway, domestic airlines and museums all frequently have a two-tier pricing system with foreigners paying more. In hotels the difference can be as much as 50%, although if the room costs only $8 to begin with that's not too bad. Foreigner charges on the myriad domestic airlines vary but can be as low as $1 in difference.

The highest mark-up, percentage wise, is made by museums. But since that $5 you pay represents about the same portion of your income as the $0.20 a Russian pays, there's a certain fairness. And that extra money you shell out is desperately needed to protect the very works of art you've come to see.

Tipping & Bargaining

A lasting bequest of communism is that tipping is not as widespread in Russia as it could be. It's standard in the better restaurants (count on leaving 10%), whereas elsewhere 5% to 10% of the total is fine. Tipping your guide, if you have one, is an accepted practice. Generally about $5 to $10 for a day would be a good tip. Small gifts, like a bottle of skin cream, a box of imported chocolates or a cassette or CD, are appropriate if the service has been great, but remember that the gifts of yore (packets of Marlboro, badges and pins etc) are no longer of value here.

Prices in stores are usually firm. In markets, food vendors will sometimes offer a deal that is their best offer. Take it or you will be quibbling over something like $0.05. For other goods in markets and souvenir stalls, you can make a counter bid that is somewhat lower than the price the merchant is asking, but Russia is not a place where you can expect protracted haggling.

Taxes

The Value Added Tax (VAT, in Russian NDS) is 20% and is usually included in the price listed for purchases, but ask just to make sure.

POST & COMMUNICATIONS

Post

Pochtamt (почтамт) refers to any post office. A main post office is a *glavpochtamt*, while an international one is a *mezhdunarodnyy glavpochtamt*. The main offices are open from 8 am to 8 or 9 pm, with shorter hours on Saturday and Sunday; in big cities one office will possibly stay open 24 hours a day.

Sending Mail Outward post is slow but fairly reliable. Airmail letters take two to three weeks from Moscow and St Petersburg to the UK, longer from other cities, and three to four weeks to the USA or Australasia. A standard-sized airmail letter to any place abroad costs $0.25.

You can address outgoing international mail as you would from any country, in your own language, though it might help to *precede* it with the country name in Cyrillic. Some Cyrillic country names are:

America (USA)	–	Америка (США)
Australia	–	Австралия
Canada	–	Канада
France	–	Франция
Germany	–	Германия
Great Britain	–	Великобритания
Ireland	–	Ирландия
New Zealand	–	Новая Зеландия

In major cities you can usually find the services of at least one of the following express carriers: Fedex, UPS, DHL International and TNT Express Worldwide.

Receiving Mail Incoming mail is so unreliable that many companies, hotels and even private individuals use private services that have addresses in either Germany or Finland. The mail completes its journey to its Russian destination with a private carrier. Other than availing yourself of one of these services if you plan a longer hotel stay, your *reliable* options for receiving mail in Russia are nil. Anything addressed to poste restante should be considered lost before it is sent.

Embassies and consulates won't hold mail for transient visitors.

Should you decide to send mail to Russia or try to receive it, note that addresses should be written in reverse order: Russia (Россия), postal code (if known), city, street address, name.

Telephone

Russian city codes are listed in this book under the relevant section heading. The telephone country code for Russia is ☎ 7.

The world of international and even domestic telecommunications has changed immensely since 1991; it's now possible to do all sorts of magical things like dial a number in another country and have it connect. But with the improvement in services there's been an explosion of providers, which can be confusing and, if you're not careful, expensive.

Private Telephones From a private phone in Russia, dialling outside the country is very simple, but the prices keep rising and are now even higher than prices for equivalent calls from the West to Russia. To call internationally dial ☎ 8, wait for the second tone, then dial ☎ 10 plus the country and city codes, then the number. Omit any noughts (zeroes) from the city code (eg to call Sydney the code would be ☎ 8 (tone) 10 61 2 and then the phone number).

At the time of writing, daytime telephone prices per minute were $0.75 to Europe, $1 to the USA and Canada and $1.50 to Australasia. Some useful country codes are:

Australia	☎ 61
Belarus	☎ 375
Canada	☎ 1
China	☎ 86
Estonia	☎ 372
Finland	☎ 358
France	☎ 33
Germany	☎ 49
Ireland	☎ 353
Japan	☎ 81
Latvia	☎ 371
Lithuania	☎ 370
Netherlands	☎ 31
New Zealand	☎ 64
Norway	☎ 47
UK	☎ 44
Ukraine	☎ 380
USA	☎ 1

Pay Phones Pay phones (таксофон, *taksofon*) are located throughout most cities and are sometimes in working order. Most take prepaid phonecards, which are available from metro token booths or from kiosks. There are several types of card phones, and not all cards are interchangeable. Card phones can be used for local and domestic or international long distance calls.

Some older phone booths accept metal tokens *(zhetony)* as payment. Place the token in the slot on top of the phone and dial the number; when the party answers, the token should drop. A series of beeps means you must place another token in the slot or risk disconnection.

Domestic (which means within Russia or to any former Soviet republic) long-distance calls may be made from pay phones marked Междугородный *(mezhdugorodnyy)*, using different, wrinkled-metal tokens available only in telephone offices. They work on a similar principle, but you need to push the Ответ *(otvet)* button on the phone's face when your party answers. Dial ☎ 8, wait for the second tone, then dial the city code (including noughts) and the number.

State/Central Telephone Offices State-run long-distance telephone offices are found in almost all towns and cities, usually in the same building as or near a post office. In most you leave a deposit with an attendant and are assigned a private booth where you dial your number directly as outlined above. In a few you still give your number to an attendant who dials the number and then sends you to a booth to take the call. Whichever way you do this, you either pay an outstanding balance or collect change from your deposit when you leave. Rates are similar to home services.

Satellite Phone Centres In many cities you can now find privately run phone centres that boast satellite links to the outside world. These have an advantage over the state offices because they offer much more reliable connections, more comfortable surroundings and competitive rates.

Country Direct This service allows you to dial a toll-free number in Moscow or St Petersburg for connection with a service provider such as AT&T, MCI or Sprint, which can put through collect or calling-card calls to numbers outside Russia. Note that you pay for this reliability and convenience with high rates. The access numbers for these services change frequently so check the number with the provider before you leave for Russia.

Hotel Phones At most traditional Russian hotels local calls are free. Placing long-distance calls can be more difficult and you'll have to work the details out with the front desk. Calls from expensive Western hotels are, well, expensive. A direct-dialled call abroad from your room can cost over $100 for 20 minutes of chatting. If you or your company don't want to pay this kind of rate, you'll either have to use a country direct service (which, while expensive, will be cheaper than hotel phones) or go outside.

Most hotel-room telephones have a direct-dial number for incoming calls, which saves you having to be connected through the switchboard. However, this can lead to unwanted disturbances. See Dangers & Annoyances later in this chapter.

Cellular Service Here, as in the rest of Eastern Europe, cell (or mobile) phones are popular with affluent citizens who want to bypass the antiquated state system. You may be able to use your regular cell phone while you are in Russia: check with your service provider for details. But remember, the cost of 'roaming' is high.

Fax

Faxes can be sent from most post offices and better hotels. Rates at post offices are usually $3 a page to Europe and $5 a page anywhere else.

Email & Internet Access

A substantial number of Russians are adept email and Internet users. In many cities you will find cybercafes, which are sprouting up throughout the country. Expect to pay about $2 an hour for online access. If there is not yet a cybercafe in the town you are visiting, track down the local Internet provider, who will most likely allow you to send/receive email messages. Ask at any store you see selling computer goods or at a local university.

To access your home email account from computers in Russia, you'll need to carry three pieces of information with you: your incoming (POP or IMAP) mail server name, your account name and your password. Your ISP or network supervisor will be able to give you these. Armed with this information, you should be able to access your Internet mail account from any net-connected machine in the world, provided it runs some kind of email software (remember that

Netscape and Internet Explorer both have mail modules). It pays to become familiar with the process for doing this before you leave home.

An even easier option to send mail is to open a free eKno Web-based email account online at www.ekno.lonelyplanet.com. You can then access your mail from anywhere in the world from any net-connected machine running a standard Web browser. Other services offering Web-based free email accounts are hotmail.com, nettaxi.com and yahoo.com.

INTERNET RESOURCES

A good starting place for links about Russia is Lonely Planet Online (www.lonelyplanet.com), our award-winning travel Web site, which has destination profiles, feature stories, reports from travellers on the road, and much more.

The sites below are good starting points for further research:

Bucknell Russian Studies Department
  www.departments.bucknell.edu/russian/
  (Bucknell University in the USA runs this huge award-winning site with links to just about any topic on Russia you can imagine)

Russian Culture
  russianculture.tqn.com/mbody.htm
  (a moderated page on the about.com site that collects unusual and off-beat links to various aspects of Russian life)

Russia Today
  www.russiatoday.com
  (daily news and current events written by Russians)

Kremlinkam
  www.kremlinkam.com
  (this enjoyable site has live pictures from the capital and even manages to have fun with Lenin's tomb; it's good for a real-time weather check of Moscow)

Russia Tourism Pages
  russia-tourism.com
  (an encyclopaedia of tourism-related sites with links on a myriad subjects including travel agents, hotels and much more)

Washington Post Russia Special Report
  www.washingtonpost.com/wpsrv/inatl/longterm/russiagov/russiagov.htm
  (a comprehensive collection of Washington Post stories from the best team of foreign correspondents covering Russia)

Russian Consular Information Sheet
  travel.state.gov/russia.html
  (the official US State Department information page on Russia, with the most up-to-date information on visas, safety issues, trouble spots and other practical matters)

BOOKS

Lonely Planet

Lonely Planet's *St Petersburg* is a comprehensive, practical city guide. In 2000, it will be joined by a city guide to *Moscow*. The *Russian phrasebook* has detailed language information geared to the traveller. Lonely Planet also has guides to many neighbouring countries including Finland, Norway, Scandinavian & Baltic Europe, Estonia, Latvia & Lithuania, Eastern Europe, Poland, the Czech & Slovak Republics, Hungary, Romania & Moldova, Georgia, Armenia & Azerbaijan, Central Asia, Mongolia and China.

Guidebooks

The *Trans-Siberian Handbook* by Bryn Thomas, published by Trailblazer, is a detailed guide to the various routes across the continent. *Russia by Rail with Belarus and Ukraine* by Athol Yates follows several major train routes radiating from Moscow. It lists sights that can be seen from trains kilometre by kilometre. *A Travel Guide to Jewish Russia & Ukraine* by Ben G Frank was published in 1999 and is an impressive work documenting the Jewish culture and its effects on these lands. *Live & Work in Russia and Eastern Europe* by Jonathan Packer is a good reference for people hoping to find a job or start a business in Russia.

Travellers' Tales

Several years before glasnost, Colin Thubron taught himself Russian and drove just about every open motor route alone, visiting many of today's most frequented destinations. The result, *Among the Russians* (published in some countries as *Where Nights Are Longest*), is a rather humourless but precise and eloquent account of the personal experience of travel in Soviet times – and a lot hasn't changed since.

Letters From Russia by the Marquis de Custine is a French aristocrat's rather jollier account of visiting St Petersburg and Moscow and hobnobbing with the tsar and high society in 1839. His description of St Basil's Cathedral hasn't been bettered yet: 'a sort of irregular fruit bristling with excrescences, a cantaloup melon with embroidered edges ... a crystallisation of a thousand colours ... this confectionery box'.

Caucasian Journey, by wandering fisherman Negley Farson, describes journeys among the northern Caucasian tribal peoples in the 1920s, before the full force of Bolshevism hit them. In the 1990s Negley's son Daniel Farson took off down the Volga to the same destination and the result is *A Dry Ship to the Mountains* (1994).

A slew of travellers' tales hit bookshops in the late 1990s, as writers took advantage of the relaxed travel restrictions to explore Russia. The results are mixed. Best of the current lot of travel narratives is *Hooked* by Fen Montaigne. A skilled travel writer, Montaigne uses the excuse that he wants to fly fish the untamed wild rivers of rural Russia to explore the psyche and lives of people light years away from Moscow and St Petersburg.

The Spirit-Wrestlers by Philip Marsden delves into the spiritual world of southern Russia where mystics and miracle-workers are part of life and the secular state is a mere distraction. *Open Lands* by Mark Taplin travels deep into parts of Russia that were closed to foreigners for decades under the Soviets. Here he finds both life unchanged for 100 years and disturbing trends for the future. *Around the Sacred Sea* by Bartle Bull is an interesting account of a journey around the huge Caspian Sea by horseback. Nicely illustrated, it can't quite shake the fact that it's really about a bunch of rich Harvard graduates on an adventure.

History & Politics

General & Pre-Soviet Era Sir Fitzroy Maclean, a Scot whose lifetime affair with Russia and other ex-Soviet republics goes back to days as a diplomat in Moscow in the 1930s, has written several entertaining, intelligent books on the country. His *Holy Russia* (1978) is a good short Russian history by a great storyteller, plus a walk through Moscow, St Petersburg and other history-rich cities. His *All the Russias: The End of an Empire* (1992) covers the whole ex-USSR. The USSR section of his *Eastern Approaches* (which also covers WWII adventures elsewhere) focuses mainly on travels in outlying republics but does include a chilling account of the 1938 show trial of the veteran revolutionary Bukharin.

A History of Russia by Nicholas Riasanovsky is one of the best single-volume versions of the whole Russian story through the end of the Soviet Union.

A Traveller's History of Russia & the USSR by Peter Neville is good on pre-Gorbachev Russia, but, despite its supposed post-Soviet timing, it repeatedly refers to the USSR in the present tense.

One of the best books on any single strand of pre-Soviet history is *Peter the Great – His Life & World* by Robert K Massie – a good read about one of Russia's most famous and influential rulers. *Catherine the Great: Life and Legend* by John T Alexander is a highly readable account of the empress, that best of all makes a case for some of the more salacious tales of her life.

Soviet Era *The Rise & Fall of the Soviet Empire* by Stephen Dalziel describes what its title says it does in lively style, covering the years 1917-92, with some good photos. *A History of the Soviet Union* by Geoffrey Hosking is a dense, analytical look at the Soviet era up to 1985. If you need to know why Kamenev fell out with Kalinin or why Left SRs loathed Kadets, Hosking's your man.

Ten Days That Shook the World is a melodramatic, enthusiastic, contemporary account of the Bolsheviks' 1917 power grab by US journalist John Reed, who himself ended up entombed on Red Square.

The 900 Days: The Siege of Leningrad by Harrison Salisbury tells of that city's sufferings in WWII. *Stalingrad* by Anthony Beevor is a superb work that uses new access to long-secret archives to concentrate on the human cost of this savage battle.

Recent History *Lenin's Tomb* by David Remnick, the *Washington Post*'s Moscow correspondent from 1988 to 1992, won a Pulitzer Prize for its flowing account of the Gorbachev era and its end, combining analytic history with hundreds of interviews. *Eternal Russia* by Jonathan Steele, the *Guardian*'s Moscow correspondent from 1988, covers the Gorbachev years and continues up to the 1993 White House shoot-out and subsequent elections, analysing whether Russia can ever really become the true capitalist democracy that Western politicians long for. *An Empire's New Clothes* by former *Times of London* correspondent Bruce Clark is an astute assessment of how the Yeltsin crowd's ambitions may help re-create a Russian empire (if only that rouble would stop falling).

Martin Walker's Russia, a collection of articles by Steele's *Guardian* predecessor in Moscow, is worth reading for the excitement it conveys of early glasnost. Walker was encouraged to write about daily life as much as politics. *The Waking Giant* is Walker's more considered account of the Gorbachev revolution. Though written before Gorbachev's limitations became clear, it's still fascinating.

New books about recent events continue to hit the shelves as so many foreign correspondent assigned to cover Russia mark the end of their assignment with a book.

General Much of *USSR: From an Original Idea by Karl Marx* by Marc Polonsky & Russell Taylor is still all too relevant. It's a 1980s street-wise look at the headaches of travel by authors experienced in organising 'real life' Soviet tours – funny enough to keep you up when the trip gets you down.

Imperium by Ryszard Kapuscinski is a 1994 collection of essays, journalism and recollections of the Soviet empire by the Polish correspondent and travel writer. Kapuscinski's boyhood town, Pinsk, was in the part of Poland taken over by the USSR in 1939 (it's in Belarus today). His teacher and some classmates were then deported, and the experience left him with a loathing of the Soviet system that comes across strongly.

Women's Glasnost vs Naglost by Tatyana Mamonova (1994) combines essays by this Russian women's movement leader with interviews of a cross-section of women in a country where wife-beating and abortion reach incredible levels.

A History of Russian Architecture by William Craft Brumfield is the definitive work on the topic, from wooden huts to the bombastic last gasps of the Soviet Union. *Russian Art of the Avant-Garde* is a collection of essays that shows that Soviet artists weren't painting in a vacuum and led the West in many trends.

Towards Another Shore by Aileen M Kelly is a brilliant examination of the development of Russian ideological thinking. *The Sexual Revolution in Russia* by Igor S Kon is considered the authoritative history of sexual mores and habits among the Russians throughout history. *Pushkin's Button* by Serena Vitale is a fascinating recounting of the writer/poet's duel in which he was killed.

NEWSPAPERS & MAGAZINES

Russian-Language

Russia is the kind of place that William Randolph Hearst would love: free-wheeling newspapers doing the bidding of proprietors with political agendas. Moscow has at least 15 dailies that among them present a spectrum of opinion that makes the range of papers in London seem narrow by comparison: opinions expressed extend from far-left socialist to fascist. Amid this cacophony the government makes certain that its views are heard as well: various Russian governmental bodies own almost 20% of the nation's newspapers. And the potential power of the press has not been lost on those in power after the Russian media almost single-handedly brought Boris Yeltsin back from the political dead.

Given shifting loyalty and ownership, the character of the newspapers changes regularly. This was shown in 1999 when *Kommersant*, which had been regarded as the most serious and independent of the dailies, was bought by a mysterious investment group with obscure ties to the Russian power structure.

continued on page 113

FOOD & DRINK

GEORGI SHABLOVSKY

FOOD

Things keep improving for dining in Russia. Restaurants serving decent and reasonably priced food have popped up in many towns. Travellers to Moscow, St Petersburg and other large cities will find a choice of good places for a meal.

But in many towns there aren't that many places to eat. Remember, in all of Russia *less* than 1% of the population eat *more* than one meal at a restaurant each year. Not only can't people afford to eat out, but there aren't many places in which they could eat out even if they could afford to. Things are different in Moscow and St Petersburg, where there are scores of good – if pricey – places to eat.

Meals in some of the better new restaurants can be fine renditions of Russian classics made with fresh and tasty ingredients. In contrast, food in run-of-the-mill, old-style Russian restaurants tends to be bland, rich, heavy on meat, potatoes and overboiled or pickled vegetables, and light on fresh vegetables, dairy products and fresh fruit. Try to get into the Russian way of starting with a few hors d'oeuvres *(zakuski)*, which are often the most interesting items on the menu. 'Main' courses are smaller than Westerners are used to and can be uninspired. A good way to decide if a place is a worthy choice is by the time-honoured 'smell test'. If you stick your nose in and it smells like old cabbage, old socks or something worse, give it a miss.

There's been a big growth in non-Russian restaurants and in Moscow or St Petersburg you can eat excellent Italian, Indian, French and many other cuisines. Most of these have foreign management and foreign standards of service – though at a price. Moscow is one of the world's most expensive cities for a restaurant meal. Outside the major cities, entrepreneurs have started restaurants, many of which are excellent. Much more common are street cafes with plastic furniture provided by warring soft drink companies and simple menus of drinks and snacks.

Don't miss the cuisine of the former Soviet republic of Georgia, with unique, spicy dishes that do justice to both meat and vegetables. There are quite a few Georgian restaurants in European Russia.

Dress in all but the top-end restaurants is informal. The biggest gripe beyond a possibly huge bill will be the flashy new Russians yacking away on their mobile phones.

Food Shops

Moscow, St Petersburg and other large cities have lots of supermarkets and food stores where you can get a big range of goods. Most are pretty well stocked, often with imported as well as Russian food. The old food stores with the infuriating system whereby you have to queue three times for each purchase – once to find out its price, once to pay, and once to collect it – are fast converting at least to one-stop service if not to full supermarket-style shopping.

Title page: Tins of Russian caviar (Photo by Jonathan Smith).
Facing page: One of the best cafes in Sochi, on top of Mt Bolshoy Akhun, Caucasus.

One inexpensive staple Russian food you might want to buy for long journeys is *kolbasa*, a salami-like sausage, which is eaten cold, in slices, and can go down pretty well with bread, tomato and raw onion. It comes in various types and guises – thin or fat, herby or garlicky, but it's always long.

Markets

Every sizable town has a market (рынок, *RIH-nuk*), where locals sell spare potatoes and carrots from their dacha plots and bigger traders offload truckfuls of melons, oranges, bananas – you name it – often from the Transcaucasus or Central Asia. You'll often find dried fruit, cheese, nuts, honey, meat and other foods in markets too. Take your own shopping bag. Markets are colourful places to visit even if you don't need to buy; go early in the morning for the liveliest scene and best selection.

You can usually bargain a bit over prices. Watch carefully that the vendor doesn't select the most rotten or shrivelled items to pop into your bag.

GEORGI SHABLOVSKY

Left: Market in St Petersburg.

Hotel Restaurants

All Soviet-era hotels, except a few bottom-end places, always had somewhere you could eat. But these places, which were once known for tired food and tired smells, are facing competition from independent places elsewhere in town. Many have closed, others have improved their standards while others are limping along with the same foods and smells known to generations.

The Western-run luxury hotels have a choice of fine and expensive restaurants. Sometimes they offer lunch buffets that are good value.

Stolovaya & Bufet

A *stolovaya* is like a cafeteria, the common person's eatery. It's dreary but cheap (you can often fill up for under $1) with a small, less-than-mouthwatering choice of cutlet or fish or meatballs, soup, boiled vegetables, bread, tea and coffee. Slide your tray along the counter and the staff will ladle out what you point at. You'll often find them in market or station areas. They have poetic names such as Stolovaya No 32. Some are decent, some very grotty.

A *bufet* (plural *bufety*) is similar to a stolovaya. It's a snack bar, usually in a hotel, selling cheap cold meats, boiled eggs, salads, bread, pastries etc.

GEORGI SHABLOVSKY

Right: An old-fashioned Soviet-style cafeteria in Sochi, on the Black Sea.

Fast Food

Western fast-food chains have hit Moscow, St Petersburg and other cities, where they're incredibly popular. McDonald's is expanding rapidly. Russian imitators are getting in on the act with outlets that may be a street kiosk or even a van, or may be a cafe with tables. Pizza and kebabs (often the Russian *shashlyk* form) are common fare.

Kiosks

Around parks and markets, on streets and near train and bus stations are cheap, often stand-up places selling one or two items plus a drink. They're usually a poor introduction to their respective products but they're handy and cheap. 'Takeaway' is на вынос *(na VIH-nus)*. Types of snack shop include:

Блинная *(BLEE-nuh-yuh)* serves *bliny* – pancakes with savoury or sweet fillings;

Бутербродная *(bu-tir-BROD-nuh-yuh)* serves little open sandwiches;

Закусочная *(zuh-KU-such-nuh-yuh)* serves miscellaneous snacks;
Пельменная *(pil-MYEN-uh-yuh)* serves *pelmeni* – meat ravioli;
Пирожковая *(pi-ra-SHKO-vuh-yuh)* serves *pirozhki* – deep-fried meat or vegetable turnovers;
Чебуречная *(chi-bu-RECH-nuh-yuh)* serves Georgian or Armenian *chebureki* – spicy, deep-fried mutton pies;
Шашлычная *(shush-LICH-nuh-yuh)* serves *shashlyk* – charcoal-grilled meat kebab.

Ice-Cream Parlours

Russians love ice cream, bought anywhere you see the label мороженое (morozhenoe, *ma-ROH-zhi-nah-yuh*). It's not unusual to see people gobbling dishfuls of it at outdoor tables in freezing weather. An ice-cream parlour is a *kafe-morozhenoe*. There's a lot of imported ice cream now, but the Russian variety is good too. Some of the best are the simple pre-filled cones sold by street vendors. Although the cone is something akin to edible cardboard, the ice cream is a traditional Russian variety that isn't too sweet but is very creamy. They cost $0.10. Sadly, in Moscow you can no longer get the traditional variety – only Nestlé-made copies that cost more but aren't as creamy. Progress ...

CLINT CURÉ

Ordering & Paying

Restaurants with foreign customers often have English-language menus. If a menu is in Russian only, you *may* in some places get some translation help from the waiter. Otherwise you are left to your own devices, especially at some of the new places away from the major cities where they never see a non-Russian customer.

If the menu defeats you – as it often does – you can just say 'What do you recommend?' (Что вы посоветуете? *shto vih pa-sa-VYEH-tu-yeh-tyeh?*). Or you could point at what other diners are having.

If a waiter – or your food – is taking an eternity to appear, ponder on a word Russian has given to the universal vocabulary of eating. After the victory over Napoleon, impatient Russian soldiers in Paris cafes would bang their tables and shout *bystro, bystro!* (quickly, quickly!), from which came the word bistro.

waiter, waitress	официант, официантка *ah-fit-si-AHNT, ah-fit-si-AHNT-kuh*
menu	меню *min-YU*
hot	горячий *gar-YA-chi*
cold	холодный *kha-LOHD-ni*
more	ещё *yee-SHCHO*
May we order?	Можно заказать? *MOZH-na zuh-kuh-ZAHT?*
Please bring…	Принесите, пожалуйста... *pri-nyeh-SEE-tyeh, pa-ZHAHL-stuh...*
That's all.	Всё. *Vsyo*
Bon appétit!	Приятного аппетита *pri-AHT-na-va ah-pih-TEET-a!*

When you're done you'll have to chase up the bill (счёт, *schyot*). If there's a service charge – noted on the menu by the words за обслуживание (for service) – there's no need to tip further unless the service has been exceptional (see also Tipping earlier in the chapter).

Breakfast

Breakfast (завтрак, *zavtrak, ZAHF-truk*) in hotels can range from a large help-yourself buffet spread to bread, butter, jam, tea and a boiled egg or nothing at all. Items you might find include:

Блины *(blee-NIH)* – bliny (as блинчики *(blinchiki)* they are rolled around meat or cheese and browned)
Каша – *kasha* or Russian-style buckwheat porridge
Сырники *(SEER-ni-ki)* – fritters of cottage cheese, flour and egg
Творог *(tva-ROK)* – cottage cheese
Кефир *(kyi-FEER)* – yogurt-like sour milk, served as a drink

Яйцо *(yai-TSOH)* – egg
    всмятку *(FSMYAT-ku)* – soft-boiled
    крутое *(kru-TOY-eh)* – hard-boiled
    омлет *(ahm-LYET)* – omelette
    яичница *(yuh-EECH-nit-suh)* – fried

Bliny, kasha and syrniki can be delicious if topped with some combination of jam, sugar and the universal Russian condiment, sour cream (сметана, *smi-TAH-nuh*).

Lunch & Dinner

Russians often like a fairly heavy early-afternoon meal (обед, *obed, ah-BYET*) and a lighter evening meal (ужин, *uzhin, OO-zhin*), but a night-out supper can go on and on.

Meals (and menus) are divided into courses:

Закуски – *zakuski* or appetisers, often grouped into cold zakuski (холодные закуски) and hot zakuski (горячие закуски)
Первые блюда – first courses, usually soups
Вторые блюда – second courses or 'main' dishes, also called hot courses (горячие блюда)
Сладкие блюда – sweet courses or desserts

Main dishes may be further divided into:

Фирменные – house specials
Национальные – national or ethnic dishes
Порционные – special orders
Мясные – meat
Рыбные – fish
Птица – poultry
Овощные – vegetable

Appetisers

The fancier zakuski rival main courses for price. Of course try the caviar (икра, *ee-KRA*). The best is black (sturgeon) caviar *(ikra chyornaya*, also called *zernistaya)*. Much cheaper and saltier is red (salmon) caviar *(ikra krasnaya*, also called *ketovaya)*. Russians spread it on buttered toast or bliny and wash it down with a slug of vodka. There's also ersatz caviar made entirely from eggplant or other vegetables.

A few other zakuski worth trying are:

Блины со сметаной *(blee-NIH sa-smi-TA-noy)* – bliny with sour cream
Рыба солёная *(RIH-buh sahl-YO-nuh-yuh)* – salted fish
Сёмга копчёная *(SYOM-guh kahp-CHO-nuh-yuh)* – smoked salmon

Грибы в сметане *(gree-BIH fsmi-TA-nyeh)* or жульен из грибов *(zhool-YEN eez gree-BOF)* – mushrooms baked in sour cream, obscenely good

Salad (салат, *suh-LAHT*) is an appetiser too. Most likely you'll be offered one with tomatoes (из помидоров *eez pa-mi-DOR-uf*) or cucumbers (из огурцов, *eez a-goort-SOF*), or the ubiquitous салат столичный *(suh-LAHT sta-LEECH-ni)*, comprised of vegetable and beef bits, potato and egg in sour cream and mayonnaise.

Soup

Rich soups may be the pinnacle of Slavic cooking. There are dozens of varieties, often served with a dollop of sour cream. Most are made from meat stock. The Russian word for soup sounds the same, суп.

Among the most common soups are:

Борщ *(borshch)* – beetroot with vegetables and meat
Лапша *(LAHP-shuh)* – chicken noodle
Окрошка *(a-KROHSH-kuh)* – cold or hot soup made from cucumbers, sour cream, potatoes, egg, meat and *kvas* (a beer-like drink)
Рассольник *(rah-SOL-nik)* – pickled cucumber and kidney
Солянка *(sahl-YAHNK-uh)* – thick meat or fish soup with salted cucumbers and other vegetables
Уха *(OO-khuh)* – fish soup with potatoes and vegetables
Харчо *(khar-CHOH)* – garlicky mutton, Caucasian-style
Щи *(shchi)* – cabbage or sauerkraut (many varieties)

Poultry & Meat

Poultry (птица, *PTEET-suh*) is usually chicken (курица, *KOO-rit-suh*, or цыплёнок, *tsi-PLYOH-nuk*). Meat (мясо, *MYA-suh*) is usually:

Баранина *(buh-RA-ni-nuh)* – mutton
Говядина *(gav-YA-di-nuh)* – beef
Свинина *(sfi-NEE-nuh)* – pork

Cooking Styles

Words you might spot on the menu are:

Варёный *(var-YOH-ni)* – boiled
Жареный *(ZHAR-ih-ni)* – roasted or fried
Отварной *(aht-var-NOY)* – poached or boiled
Печёный *(pi-CHOH-ni)* – baked
Фри *(free)* – fried

Dishes

The list of possible dishes (and possible names) is huge, but following are some common meat and poultry dishes:

Антрекот *(ahn-tri-KOHT)* – entrecote, boned sirloin steak
Бефстроганов *(byef-STRO-guh-nof)* – beef Stroganoff, beef slices in a rich sauce
Бифштекс *(bif-SHTEKS)* – 'steak', usually a glorified hamburger filling
Голубцы *(ga-loop-TSIH)* – *golubtsy*, cabbage rolls stuffed with meat
Жаркое *(zhar-KOY-eh)* – meat or poultry stewed in a clay pot; most common seems to be жаркое по-домашнему *(...pa-da-MAHSH-ni-mu)*, 'home-style', with mushrooms, potatoes and vegetables
Котлета *(kaht-LYET-uh)* – this is usually a croquette of ground meat; котлета пожарская *(...pa-ZHAR-ska-ya)* is minced chicken
Котлета по-киевски *(kaht-LYET-uh pa-KEE-iv-ski)* – chicken Kyiv (or Kiev), fried boneless chicken breast stuffed with butter (watch out, it squirts!)
Пельмени *(pil-MYEN-i)* – *pelmeni* or Siberian-style meat dumplings
Плов – *plov* or pilaf, rice with mutton bits, from Central Asia
Цыплёнок табака *(tsi-PLYOH-nuk tuh-buh-KAH)* – chicken Tabaka, grilled chicken Caucasian-style
Шашлык – *shashlyk*, skewered and grilled mutton or other meat, adapted from Central Asia and Transcaucasia

Fish

Fish is рыба *(RIH-buh)*. Some common varieties are:

Омуль *(OH-mool)* – omul, like salmon, from Lake Baikal
Осётр *(a-SYOTR)*, осетрина *(a-si-TREE-nuh)* or севрюга *(siv-RYU-guh)* – sturgeon
Сёмга *(SYOM-guh)* – salmon
Судак *(su-DAHK)* – pike perch
Форель *(far-YEL)* – trout

Two good sturgeon dishes are:

Осетрина отварная *(a-si-TREE-nuh aht-VAR-nuh-yuh)* – poached sturgeon
Осетрина с грибами *(a-si-TREE-nuh zgree-BUH-mi)* – with mushrooms

Vegetables

Vegetables are овощи *(OH-va-shchi)*; greens are зелень *(ZYEH-lin)*. A garnish is гарниры *(gar-NEE-ri)*. Common vegetables include:

Горох *(ga-ROKH)* – peas
Капуста *(kuh-POOS-tuh)* – cabbage
Картошка *(kar-TOSH-kuh)*, картофель *(kar-TOF-il)* – potato
Морковь *(mar-KOF)* – carrots
Огурец *(a-gur-YETS)* – cucumber
Помидор *(pa-mi-DOR)* – tomato

Fruit

Fruit is фрукты *(FROOK-ti)*:

Абрикос *(uh-bri-KOS)* – apricot
Арбуз *(ar-BOOS)* – watermelon
Виноград *(vi-na-GRAHT)* – grapes
Груша *(GROO-shuh)* – pear
Дыня *(DIN-yuh)* – melon
Яблоко *(YA-bla-ka)* – apple

Other Foods

On every table are stacks of bread (хлеб, *khlep*). Best is Russian 'black' bread, a vitamin-rich sour rye.

Russians are mad about wild mushrooms (грибы, *gree-BIH*); in late summer and early autumn they troop into the woods with their buckets. Other items are:

Рис *(rees)* – rice
Сыр *(seer)* – cheese
Масло *(MAHS-la)* – butter
Перец *(PYER-its)* – pepper
Сахар *(SA-khar)* – sugar
Соль *(sol)* – salt

Desserts

Perhaps most Russians are exhausted or drunk by dessert time, since this is the least imaginative course. Most likely you'll get ice cream, мороженое *(ma-ROH-zhi-nah yuh)*. Other possibilities are:

Блинчики *(BLEEN-chi-ki)* – bliny with jam or other sweet filling
Кисель *(ki-SEL)* – fruit jelly (jell-o to Yanks)
Компот *(kahm-POHT)* – fruit in syrup (probably from a tin)
Оладьи *(a-LAH-dyi)* – fritters topped with syrup or sour cream
Пирожное *(pi-ROZH-na-yuh)* – pastries

Vegetarian Food

Russia is rough on a vegetarian – though some private restaurants have caught on, particularly in Moscow, St Petersburg and other large cities. Main dishes are heavy on meat and poultry, vegetables are boiled to death and even the good vegetable and fish soups are usually made from meat stock.

If you're vegetarian, say so, early and often. You'll see a lot of cucumber and tomato salads, and will develop an eagle eye for the rare good fish and dairy dishes. Zakuski include quite a lot of meatless things like eggs, salted fish and mushrooms. If you spot fresh (raw) vegetables (овощи свежие) on the menu, you're in luck!

Menus often have a category like vegetable, milk, egg and flour dishes (овощные, молочные, яичные, мучные блюда) – but don't get your hopes up. You may have to just run down the names of things you can eat, rather than relying on the waiter to think of something.

By the way, potatoes *(kartoshka, kartofel)* aren't filed under 'vegetable' in the Russian mind, so you must name them separately: 'potatoes and vegetables'.

I'm a vegetarian (f).	Я вегетарианка. *ya vi-gi-ta-ri-AHN-ka*
I'm a vegetarian (m).	Я вегетарианец. *ya vi-gi-ta-ri-AHN-yets*
I cannot eat meat.	Я не ем мясного. *ya ni yem myis-NOH-va*
without meat	без мяса *bis MYA-suh*
only vegetables	только овощи *TOL-ka OH-va-shchi*

DRINKS

Drinking is the joy of the Rus. We cannot live without it. With these words Vladimir of Kyiv, the father of the Russian state, is said to have rejected abstinent Islam on his people's behalf in the 10th century. And who wouldn't want to bend their minds now and then during those long, cold, dark winters? Russians sometimes drink vodka in moderation, but more often it's tipped down in swift shots, with a beer, with the aim of getting legless.

The *average* Russian drinks more than 12L of pure alcohol a year – equivalent to over a bottle of vodka a week – and men drink much more than women.

The nearest thing to a pub is a *traktir* (tavern), but these are not common. Nor, except in hotels, are bars that serve nothing but drink. A lot of public drinking (other than on park benches) goes on in restaurants and cafes – and, since many of these are in hotels, the average tourist is likely to encounter quite a lot of it. If you find yourself sharing a table with locals, it's odds-on they'll press you to drink with them. Even people from distant tables, spotting foreigners, may be seized with hospitable urges. If it's vodka that's being drunk, they'll want a man to down the shot – neat of course – in one; women are usually excused. This can be fun to start with as you toast international friendship etc, but vodka has a knack of creeping up on you from behind and the consequences can be appalling. A slice of heavily buttered bread before each shot, or a beer the morning after, are reckoned to be vodka antidotes.

Refusing a drink can be very difficult. Russians may continue to insist until they win you over, especially on some train rides. If you can't manage to stand quite firm, take it in small gulps with copious thanks, while saying how you'd love to indulge but have to be up early in the morning etc. And if you're really not in the mood, the only tested and true method of warding off all offers (as well as making them feel quite awful) is to say *'Ya alkogolik'* (*alkogolichka* for women) – 'I'm an alcoholic'.

Alcohol

You can buy it everywhere. Kiosks, shops, bars, restaurants – you name it. Foreign brands as well as Russian are common. But be very suspicious of kiosk spirits. There's a lot of bad cheap stuff around that can

GEORGI SHABLOVSKY

Right: Fancy a shot? Various brands of Vodka.

make you ill. Only buy screw-top bottles and always check to see that the seal is not broken. Taste carefully any liquor you've bought at a kiosk to make sure it's really what it's supposed to be, and that it hasn't been diluted or tampered with. Err on the side of caution.

Vodka

Vodka is distilled from wheat, rye or occasionally potatoes. The word comes from *voda* (water), and means something like 'a wee drop'. Its flavour (if any) comes from what's added after distillation. Two common 'plain' vodkas are Stolichnaya, which is in fact slightly sweetened with sugar, and Moskovskaya, which has a touch of sodium bicarbonate. Tastier, more colourful and rarer are Shuiskaya Classic,

Zolotoe Koltso (Golden Ring), Pertsovka (pepper vodka), Starka (with apple and pear leaves), Limonnaya (lemon vodka), and Okhotnichya (Hunter's), which has about a dozen ingredients, including peppers, juniper berries, ginger and cloves.

Sure enough, the fashion for Western products has extended even unto vodka. The more popular imports are Smirnoff (made in the USA), Absolut (and all its varieties), Gorbachow, Rasputin and New Yorkskaya.

Supermarket and liquor store prices range from around $1 for half a litre of Stolichnaya or Moskovskaya to $20 for the most exotic brands.

Beer

For the imbiber, beer is one of the best bits of news to come out of Russia. Scores of the old traditional breweries with their foul-smelling product that went 'off' after three days (if it had ever been on) are vanishing. In their place are old traditional breweries that have learned new ways – such as how to brew tasty beer – and a number of joint ventures with Western brewers.

The market leader is Baltika, a Scandinavian joint-venture with Russian management based in St Petersburg. It makes no less than nine excellent brews, fittingly labelled '1' through '9'. Just about every brewing style is represented and its worth drinking your way through the range to find a favourite. No 3 is the most commonly sold and is a light and clean lager; No 5 is a full-bodied ale. Baltika is sold in bottles and available on tap and can be found throughout the country for a mere $0.30.

Western brands being brewed in Russia include Belgium's Stella Artois, Germany's Holsten and Turkey's Efes.

Champagne, Wine & Brandy

Champagne (it's still frequently called 'Soviet Champagne') comes very dry *(bryut)*, dry *(sukhoe)*, semidry *(polusukhoe)*, semisweet *(polusladkoe)* and sweet *(sladkoe)*. Anything above dry is sweet enough to turn your mouth inside out. A 750g bottle is about $7 in a restaurant and $4 in a supermarket, kiosk or liquor store. Most other wine comes from outside the CIS (Eastern European brands are the cheapest), though you can find Georgian, Moldovan and Crimean wine.

Brandy is popular and it's all called *konyak*, though local varieties certainly aren't Cognac. The best non-Western konyak in Russia is Armenian, and anything classified five star is usually fine.

Kvas

Kvas is fermented rye bread water, dispensed on the street for a few kopecks a dose from big, wheeled tanks with Квас printed on the side. It's mildly alcoholic, tastes not unlike ginger beer, and is cool and refreshing in summer.

Alcohol Glossary

alcohol	алкоголь *al-ka-GOHL*
glass	стакан *stuh-KAHN*
bottle	бутылка *bu-TIL-kuh*
50g	пятьдесят грамм *pit-dis-YAHT grahm*
200g	двести грамм *DVYES-t i grahm*
750g	семьсот пятьдесят грамм *sim-SOT pit-dis-YAHT grahm*
1L	литр *LEE-tr*
vodka	водка *VOHT-kuh*
Soviet champagne	Советское шампанское *sav-YET-ska-yuh sham-PAN-ska-yuh*
very dry	брют *bryut*
dry	сухое *soo-KHOY-eh*
semidry	полусухое *pah-loo-soo-KHOY-eh*
semisweet	полусладкое *pah-loo-SLAT-kah-yeh*
sweet	сладкое *SLAT-kah-yeh*
wine	вино *vi-NOH*
white wine	белое вино *BYEL-ah-yuh vi-NOH*
red wine	красное вино *KRAHS-na-yuh vi-NOH*
dry (wine)	сухой *soo-KHOY*
sweet (wine)	сладкий *SLAT-ky*
brandy	коньяк *ka-NYAK*
beer	пиво *PEE-vah*
beer bar	пивной бар *piv-NOY bar*
kvas	квас *kvahs*

takeaway	с собой *sa-BOY*
To your health!	За ваше здоровье! *za VA-sheh zda-ROH-vyeh!*

Nonalcoholic Drinks

Water & Mineral Water

Tap water is suspect in some cities and should definitely be avoided in St Petersburg. Many people stick to mineral water, which is ubiquitous and cheap. See the Health section in European Russia Facts for the Visitor.

Tea & Coffee

These normally come black, though warm, milky coffee turns up in some places in winter.

The traditional Russian tea-making method is to brew an extremely strong pot, pour small shots of it into glasses and fill the glasses with hot water from the *samovar*, an urn with an inner tube filled with hot charcoal. The pot is kept warm on top of the samovar. Modern samovars have electric elements, like a kettle, instead of the charcoal tube. Putting jam, instead of sugar, in tea is quite common.

Coffee comes in small cups and is supposed to be thick, but quality – and sometimes supplies – are erratic. Almost any cafe, restaurant or bufet, and some bakery shops, will offer tea or coffee or both.

If you're a serious coffee or tea drinker, carry a Thermos, mug, your own tea bags and/or coffee, and powdered milk and sugar if you use them. It's easy to get the Thermos filled with boiling water by your *dezhurnaya* (floor lady) or at a hotel bufet.

Sok, Napitok & Limonad

Sok is juice – of a kind – usually sweetened, flavoured and heavily diluted. It never resembles the original fruit, but a jugful with a meal often goes down a treat. *Napitok* means beverage but in practice it's often a fancy sok, maybe with some real fruit thrown in. *Limonad* (literally 'lemonade') is a fizzy drink apparently made from industrial waste and tasting like mouthwash.

Other Drinks

Jugs of yogurt-like sour milk *(kefir)* are served as a breakfast drink. Milk is common and is sold cheaply in dairy shops *(molochnaya)* but is often not pasteurised. Pepsi, Coke and their relatives are widely available.

Alcohol-Free Glossary

water	вода *va-DAH*
boiled water	кипячёная вода *ki-pya-CHO-nuh-yuh va-DAH*

mineral water	минеральная вода *mi-ni-RAL-nuh-yuh va-DAH*
soda water	газированная вода *ga-zi-ROH-va-nuh-yuh va-DAH*
coffee	кофе *KOF-yeh*
tea	чай *chai*
with sugar	с сахаром *s SAKH-ar-am*
with jam	с вареньем *s far-YEN-yim*
juice	сок *sohk*
apple juice	яблочный сок *YAHB-luch-ny sohk*
orange juice	апельсиновый сок *ah-pil-SIN-ah-vy sohk*
grape juice	виноградный сок *vi-na-GRAD-ny sohk*
beverage	напиток *na-PEET-ak*
'lemonade'	лимонад *li-ma-NAHD*
soft drink	безалкогольный напиток *biz-al-ka-GOHL-ni nuh-PEE-tuk*
milk	молоко *ma-la-KOH*

continued from page 96

Following are some of the main papers you're likely to find on sale in Moscow and throughout the country.

Ivestiya An old name in Russian newspapers dating from the Soviet era, this now bland daily supports large business interests.

Kommersant As mentioned above, this paper was one of the best regarded, but murky ownership has sullied its reputation for independence.

Komsomolskaya Pravda The third best-selling daily, it has a street-smart sense that appeals to young people and a pro-Yuri Luzhkov stance owing to its partial ownership by the Moscow city government.

Moscow Komsomolets A hugely popular Moscow-based daily in the mould of London's *The Sun*, *The New York Post* and breast-fixated tabloids everywhere.

Noviye Ivestiyu As the name hints, this readable daily was started by disgruntled *Ivestiya* journalists. Since these were some of Russia's better writers, it's very readable, although its editorial decisions are coloured by its financial support from Boris Berezovsky.

Pravda The former official mouthpiece of the Soviet era remains faithfully loyal to the Communist Party.

Segodnya A respected daily that competes with *Kommersant* for the quality market.

Another newspaper that won't escape your notice is *Argumenty i Fakty*, a weekly phenomenon that sells over 30 million copies and prints 16 regional editions. Its content is considered relatively free from outside influence.

You'll also notice many familiar Western magazine titles such as *Elle* and *Playboy* produced in Russia under licence.

English-Language

Western hotels usually have day-old copies of the *International Herald-Tribune*, *The European Wall Street Journal*, *Financial Times* and occasionally some of the British broadsheets. The same newsstands will have the top news weeklies, such as *The Economist*, *Time* and *Newsweek*. But other than in these expensive hotels – primarily in Moscow and St Petersburg – imported English-language newspapers and magazines are a rarity due to the paucity of English speakers and the high cover prices.

In Moscow, the undisputed king of the hill in locally published English-language news is the *Moscow Times*, a first-rate daily staffed by top-notch journalists and editors covering Russian and international issues. It's available free at hotels, business centres and restaurants, and also by subscription. This paper is must reading but unfortunately is hard to find outside Moscow without a subscription. Another Moscow daily, the *Moscow Tribune*, always seems to be on the verge of closing.

In St Petersburg, *St Petersburg Times* is a biweekly with the same high standards as its Moscow sibling.

A few English-language business journals come and go from the Moscow scene but they mostly dish up the same tepid stories designed to appeal to advertisers while not challenging the readers.

RADIO & TV

Russian-Language Radio

Private Russian-language radio has come a long way and it's worth listening to, though it's rare to hear any Russian bands other than oldies-but-goodies like Akvarium, Kino and Time Machine. Radio in Russia is broken into three bands, AM, UKV (the lower band of FM from 66 to 77 MHz) and FM (100-107 MHz). A Western-made FM radio usually won't go lower than 85 MHz.

English-Language Radio

The clearest BBC World Service shortwave (SW) frequencies in the morning, late evening and at night are near 9410, 12,095 (the best) and 15,070 MHz – though the exact setting varies with location in Russia. The BBC broadcasts at the following times and frequencies:

from 2 to 5 am at 9410
from 3 to 5 am at 6195
from 5 am to 9 pm at 12,095
from 6 am to 3 pm at 15,565
from 7 am to 3 pm at 17,640
from 3 to 9 pm at 9410
from 3 to 5 pm at 15,575
from 6 to 8 pm at 6195

Russian-Language TV
Russia's TV networks are part of the nation's power structure. Don't look for independent analysis here, although you will get no shortage of stations slagging off their owner's opponents. Various governmental bodies own at least 20% of the stations.

ORT and RTR are national channels and support whoever is at the top. News programs are dedicated to the status quo. NTV has the best news, although *Itogy* (Summary) on Sunday nights drags on for about two hours, which is surely too long for a program of this name. Political programs always occupy prime time on most channels as politics has always been a major entertainment in the country.

TV 6 shows lots of US-style talk shows and series from *Dynasty* to *Babylon-5*. The dubbing at times is atrocious. Kultura (Culture) is heavy on classical music, theatre, culture news and old Soviet and Western movies. It claims to be the only noncommercial channel, as it doesn't show any commercials.

Most of the stations fill out their schedules with home-grown and imported soaps and game shows.

English-Language TV
Long-term residents can subscribe to various satellite systems that bring in the usual suspects of English-language expat life everywhere: CNN International, BBC World, CNBC and other information-heavy and entertainment-deprived channels. The same can be found in expensive hotels.

VIDEO SYSTEMS
The predominant video format in Russia and the countries of the former Soviet Union is SECAM, a system incompatible with that used in most of Europe (France and Greece are among the exceptions) and Australia, and that used in the USA.

PHOTOGRAPHY & VIDEO
Film & Equipment
Major brands of print film are widely available throughout Russia at prices typical for Western Europe. As anywhere else, slide film is not widely sold. Whatever film you purchase, check the expiration date carefully. Any town or city of any size will have at least one place to get your film processed.

The same uncommon specialist shops that sell slide film also will have a smattering of camera gear by leading brands like Nikon and Canon.

Technical Tips
Avoid running films through airport x-ray machines. No matter what the attendant says, these machines are not film-safe; effects are cumulative and too much will fog your pictures. Lead 'film-safe' pouches help, but the best solution is to have your film and camera inspected by hand. You can minimise officials' annoyance by having all film in a few clear plastic bags.

Cold Weather Camera batteries get sluggish in the cold. Carry your camera inside your coat and keep some spare batteries warm in your pocket. In the prolonged Siberian winter you may be better off with a manual camera than an automatic battery-operated one; film gets brittle at very low temperatures and a motor drive's fast advance or rewind can break it. It may also leave static marks on the film. Frame-filling expanses of snow come out a bit grey unless you deliberately *overexpose* about one-half to one stop. Deep cold can play tricks with exposure, so 'bracket' your best pictures with additional shots about one stop underexposed and overexposed.

Hot Weather To avoid magenta-tinted pictures of hot territories, protect film from fierce summer heat. If you don't like leaving it at the hotel, line a stuff-sack with a piece cut from an aluminised Mylar 'survival blanket'; film will stay cool inside all day.

Restrictions
Use common sense when deciding what to photograph. Military and other sensitive sites may provoke a negative reaction from officials. When in doubt ask permission and the guard who was thinking about arresting you may suddenly pose for your camera.

Some museums and galleries forbid flash pictures, some ban all photos. Caretakers in a few churches and other historical buildings charge mercilessly for the privilege of using a still or video camera.

Photographing People

When taking photographs of people, it's always better to ask first; if people don't want to be photographed, respect their privacy.

A lifetime with the KGB may make older people uneasy about having their picture taken. A (genuine) offer to send a copy can loosen a subject up. Many people are touchy about your photographing embarrassing things like drunks, run-down housing or other signs of social decay.

The Russian for 'may I take a photograph?' is *fotografirovat mozhno? (fa-ta-gruh-FEE-ra-vut MOZH-na?)*. You can also use the more informal *mozhno vas snimat (MOZH-na vas sni-MAHT)*, but this can also be construed as flirting with someone, so make sure you hold your camera high when you say it.

TIME

From the early hours of the last Sunday in September to the early hours of the last Sunday in March, Moscow and St Petersburg time is GMT/UTC plus three hours. From the last Sunday in March to the last Sunday in September, 'summer time' is in force and it's GMT/UTC plus four hours.

Most of European Russia is in the same time zone as Moscow and St Petersburg. The exceptions are the Kaliningrad region in the west, which operates on Moscow time minus one hour, and also some regions in the east, where Samara and Izhevsk are on Moscow time plus one hour, and Ufa, Perm and Orenburg are on Moscow time plus two hours.

East of the Ural Mountains, Yekaterinburg is on Moscow time plus two hours, Irkutsk on Moscow time plus five hours, Vladivostok on Moscow time plus seven hours, and Petropavlovsk-Kamchatsky on Moscow time plus nine hours.

Russian train timetables (except for suburban train timetables) are mostly in Moscow time everywhere – and so are station clocks in most places. See the boxed text 'Amok Time' in the Volga Region chapter for an amusing take on this.

The following international relationships will be wrong by an hour for short periods when other cities change to 'summer time' on different dates.

When it's noon in Moscow and St Petersburg, it's ...

1 am in San Francisco;
4 am in New York and Toronto;
9 am in London;
10 am in Paris, Berlin, Vilnius, Warsaw, Prague and Budapest;
11 am in Helsinki, Tallinn, Riga, Minsk, Kyiv, Chisinau, Bucharest and Ankara;
1 pm in Tbilisi, Yerevan and Baku;
2 pm in Bishkek and Tashkent;
5 pm in Beijing and Ulaan Baatar;
7 pm in Sydney;
9 pm in Auckland.

ELECTRICITY

Standard voltage is 220V, 50Hz AC, though a few places still have an old 127V system. Sockets require a continental or European plug with two round pins. Travel adaptors will enable many appliances from countries with different electrical setups to work in Russia. Look for voltage (V) and frequency (Hz) labels on your appliances. Some trains and hotel bathrooms have 110V and 220V shaver plugs.

WEIGHTS & MEASURES

Russia operates on the metric system (see the back of the book for conversions from other units). Restaurant menus often list the weight of food and drink servings in grams, and in particular you order drinks by weight; a teacup is about 200g, a shot-glass about 50g. The unit of items sold by the piece, such as eggs, is *shtuka* or *sht*, which literally means 'thing' or 'piece'.

A verst *(versta)*, an old Russian unit of measurement you come across in 19th century novels etc, is 1.067km. It's divided into 500 *sazheni*; a *sazhen* is divided into three *arshiny*; and an *arshin* is divided into 16 *vershoky*.

LAUNDRY

Self-service laundries are almost unheard of, but you can get laundry done in most hotels. Ask the floor attendant. It usually takes two days. If you're doing it yourself, bring along a universal sink plug.

TOILETS

Hotel room toilets are generally fine but those in common areas of older hotels can be dreadful. Elsewhere public toilets are rare and, where they do exist, often disgusting, even in otherwise good restaurants. McDonald's is an honourable exception here and this is one of the main reasons we try to list as many as possible in the text. It's always a good idea to carry your own toilet paper, which you'll find can be easily bought anywhere.

Pay toilets are identified by the words платный туалет (*platny tualet*). In any toilet Ж stands for women's *(zhenskiy)*, while M stands for men's *(muzhskoy)*.

HEALTH

Travel health depends on your predeparture preparations, your daily health care while travelling and how you handle any medical problem that does develop. While the potential dangers can seem quite frightening, in reality few travellers experience anything more than an upset stomach.

Predeparture Planning

Immunisations There are no vaccination requirements for travel to Russia, Ukraine or Belarus but some vaccinations are recommended for a healthy trip. It is recommended you seek medical advice at least six weeks before travel. Discuss your requirements with your doctor: vaccinations you should consider include the following (for more details about the diseases themselves, see the individual disease entries later in this section).

Diphtheria & Tetanus Vaccinations for these two diseases are usually combined and are recommended for everyone. After an initial course of three injections (usually given in childhood), booster injections are necessary every 10 years.

Polio Everyone should keep up to date with this vaccination, which is normally given in childhood. A booster every 10 years maintains immunity.

Hepatitis A Hepatitis A vaccine (eg Avaxim, Havrix 1440 or VAQTA) provides long-term immunity (possibly for more than 10 years) after an initial injection and a booster at six to 12 months. Alternatively, an injection of gamma globulin can provide short-term protection against hepatitis A – two to six months, depending on the dose given. It is not a vaccine but a ready-made antibody collected from blood donations. It is reasonably effective, and unlike the vaccine, it is protective immediately, but because it is a blood product, there are current concerns about its long-term safety. Hepatitis A vaccine is also available in a combined form, Twinrix, with hepatitis B vaccine. Three injections over a six month period are required, the first two providing substantial protection against hepatitis A.

Typhoid Vaccination against typhoid may be required if you are travelling for more than a couple of weeks in most parts of Asia, Africa, Central and South America and Central and Eastern Europe. It is now available either as an injection or as capsules to be taken orally.

Hepatitis B Travellers who should consider vaccination against hepatitis B include those on a long trip, as well as those visiting countries where there are high levels of hepatitis B infection, where blood transfusions may not be adequately screened or where sexual contact or needle sharing is a possibility. Vaccination involves three injections, with a booster at 12 months. More rapid courses are available if necessary.

Tuberculosis The risk of TB to travellers is usually very low unless they are living with or closely associated with local people. Vaccination against TB (BCG) is recommended for children and young adults living in these areas for three months or more.

Health Insurance Make sure that you have adequate health insurance to cover you in case of emergencies. See Travel Insurance under Visas & Documents earlier in this chapter.

Other Preparations Make sure you're healthy before you start travelling. If you are going on a long trip make sure your teeth are OK. If you wear glasses take a spare pair and your prescription.

If you require a particular medication take an adequate supply, as it may not be available locally. Take part of the packaging showing the generic name rather than the brand, which will make getting replacements easier. It's a good idea to have a legible prescription or letter from your doctor to show that you legally use the medication to avoid any problems.

Basic Rules

Food & Drink Being cautious about what you eat and drink is the best protection against diseases of insanitation such as diarrhoea, giardiasis, cholera and hepatitis A. There have been many reported cases of unfit food being sold, but there's no need to get too paranoid about these.

In some Russian cities tap water is safe to drink; in others – notably St Petersburg – it definitely isn't. To play safe, don't drink it; that includes avoiding ice in your drinks and brushing your teeth with it. However, five-star hotels should have their own water purifying systems. Other decent hotels and restaurants should have safe bottled mineral water. Mineral water from shops and kiosks may not be pure. Imported bottled water is available in some shops in larger towns. An electric water heating element is a useful thing to carry for boiling your own water.

Cheap vodka bought from shops or kiosks can make you ill. Look for name brands in unopened bottles.

In tourist hotels and good restaurants, food can be considered safe. But choose food from street vendors and cafeterias *(stolovaya)* with care. Go for hot, fresh-looking dishes. Don't eat anything you don't like the look, taste or smell of. Avoid salads. Be suspicious of fish and shellfish and avoid undercooked meat. Peel fruit yourself or wash it in water you trust. Ice cream is OK, except possibly the soft extruded kind. In remote areas milk may be unpasteurised (with a risk of tuberculosis), although yogurt and sour milk *(kefir)* are usually hygienic.

If the place is clean and the vendor looks clean and healthy then the food is probably safe. Busy places are usually OK.

Medical Kit Check List

Following is a list of items you should consider including in your medical kit – consult your pharmacist for brands available in your country.

- ☐ **Aspirin** or **paracetamol** (acetaminophen in the USA) – for pain or fever
- ☐ **Antihistamine** – for allergies, eg hay fever; to ease the itch from insect bites or stings; and to prevent motion sickness
- ☐ **Antibiotics** – consider including these if you're travelling well off the beaten track; see your doctor, as they must be prescribed, and carry the prescription with you
- ☐ **Loperamide** or **diphenoxylate** – 'blockers' for diarrhoea; **prochlorperazine** or **metaclopramide** for nausea and vomiting
- ☐ **Rehydration mixture** – to prevent dehydration, eg due to severe diarrhoea; particularly important when travelling with children
- ☐ **Insect repellent**, **sunscreen**, **lip balm** and **eye drops**
- ☐ **Calamine lotion**, **sting relief spray** or **aloe vera** – to ease irritation from sunburn and insect bites or stings
- ☐ **Antifungal cream** or **powder** – for fungal skin infections and thrush
- ☐ **Antiseptic** (such as povidone-iodine) – for cuts and grazes
- ☐ **Bandages**, **Band-Aids (plasters)** and other wound dressings
- ☐ **Water purification tablets** or **iodine**
- ☐ **Scissors**, **tweezers** and a **thermometer** (note that mercury thermometers are prohibited by airlines)
- ☐ **Syringes** and **needles** – in case you need injections in a country with medical hygiene problems. Ask your doctor for a note explaining why you have them.
- ☐ **Cold** and **flu tablets**, **throat lozenges** and **nasal decongestant**
- ☐ **Multivitamins** – consider for long trips, when dietary vitamin intake may be inadequate

Water Purification The simplest way of purifying water is to boil it thoroughly. Vigorous boiling should be satisfactory; however, at high altitude water boils at a lower temperature, so germs are less likely to be killed. Boil it for longer in these environments.

Consider purchasing a water filter for a long trip. There are two main kinds of filter. Total filters take out all parasites, bacteria and viruses and make water safe to drink. They are often expensive, but they can be more cost effective than buying bottled water. Simple filters (which can even be nylon mesh bags) take dirt and larger foreign bodies out of the water so that chemical solutions can work much more effectively; if water is dirty, chemical solutions may not work at all. It's very important when buying a filter to read the specifications, so that you know exactly what it removes from the water and what it doesn't. Simple filtering will not remove all dangerous organisms, so if you cannot boil water it should be treated chemically. Chlorine tablets will kill many pathogens, but not some parasites like giardia and amoebic cysts. Iodine is more effective in purifying water and is available in tablet form. Follow the directions carefully and remember that too much iodine can be harmful.

Medical Problems & Treatment

Self-diagnosis and treatment can be risky, so you should always seek medical help. An embassy, consulate or five star hotel can usually recommend a local doctor or clinic. Although we do give drug dosages in this section, they are for emergency use only. Correct diagnosis is vital. In this section we have used the generic names for medications – check with a pharmacist for brands available locally.

Note that antibiotics should ideally be administered only under medical supervision. Take only the recommended dose at the prescribed intervals and use the whole course, even if the illness seems to be cured earlier. Stop immediately if there are any serious reactions and don't use the antibiotic at all if you are unsure that you have the correct one. Some people are allergic to commonly prescribed antibiotics such as penicillin; carry this information (eg on a bracelet) when travelling.

Environmental Hazards

Altitude Sickness Lack of oxygen at high altitudes (over 2500m) affects most people to some extent. The effect may be mild or severe and occurs because less oxygen reaches the muscles and the brain at high altitude, requiring the heart and lungs to compensate by working harder. Symptoms of Acute Mountain Sickness (AMS) usually develop during the first 24 hours at altitude but may be delayed up to three weeks. Mild symptoms include headache, lethargy, dizziness, difficulty sleeping and loss of appetite. AMS may become more severe without warning and can be fatal. Severe symptoms include breathlessness, a dry, irritating cough (which may progress to the production of pink, frothy sputum), severe headache, lack of coordination and balance, confusion, irrational behaviour, vomiting, drowsiness and unconsciousness. There is no hard-and-fast rule as to what height is too high: People have died from AMS at 3000m, although 3500m to 4500m is the usual range at which it can be fatal.

Treat mild symptoms by resting at the same altitude until recovery, usually a day or two. Paracetamol or aspirin can be taken for headaches. If symptoms persist or become worse, however, *immediate descent is necessary*; even 500m can help. Drug treatments should never be used to avoid descent or to enable further ascent.

Hypothermia If you are trekking at high altitudes or simply taking a long bus trip over mountains, particularly at night, be prepared for the conditions.

Hypothermia occurs when the body loses heat faster than it can produce it and the core temperature of the body falls. It is surprisingly easy to progress from very cold to dangerously cold due to a combination of wind, wet clothing, fatigue and hunger, even if the air temperature is above freezing. It is best to dress in layers; silk, wool and some of the new artificial fibres are all good insulating materials. A hat is important, as a lot of heat is lost through the head. A strong, waterproof outer layer (and a 'space' blanket for emergencies) is essential. Carry basic supplies, including food containing simple sugars to generate heat quickly and fluid to drink.

Symptoms of hypothermia are exhaustion, numb skin (particularly toes and fingers), shivering, slurred speech, irrational or violent behaviour, lethargy, stumbling, dizzy spells, muscle cramps and violent bursts of energy. Irrationality may take the form of sufferers claiming they are warm and trying to take off their clothes.

To treat mild hypothermia, first get the person out of the wind and/or rain, remove their clothing if it's wet and replace it with dry, warm clothing. Give them hot liquids – not alcohol – and some high-kilojoule, easily digestible food. Do not rub victims: instead, allow them to warm themselves slowly. This should be enough to treat the early stages of hypothermia. The early recognition and treatment of mild hypothermia is the only way to prevent severe hypothermia, which is a critical condition.

Motion Sickness Eating lightly before and during a trip will reduce the chances of motion sickness. If you are prone to motion sickness try to find a place that minimises movement – near the wing on aircraft, close to midships on boats, near the centre on buses. Fresh air usually helps; reading and cigarette smoke don't. Commercial motion-sickness preparations, which can cause drowsiness, have to be taken before the trip commences. Ginger (available in capsule form) and peppermint (including mint-flavoured sweets) are natural preventatives.

Sunburn You can get sunburnt surprisingly quickly, even through cloud. Use a sunscreen, a hat, and a barrier cream for your nose and lips. Calamine lotion or a commercial after-sun preparation are good for mild sunburn. Protect your eyes with good quality sunglasses, particularly if you will be near water, sand or snow.

Infectious Diseases

Diarrhoea Simple things like a change of water, food or climate can all cause a mild bout of diarrhoea, but a few rushed toilet trips with no other symptoms is not indicative of a major problem.

Dehydration is the main danger with any diarrhoea, particularly in children or the elderly as dehydration can occur quite quickly. Under all circumstances *fluid replacement* (at least equal to the volume being lost) is the most important thing to remember. Weak black tea with a little sugar, soda water, or soft drinks allowed to go flat and diluted 50% with clean water are all good in this situation.

With severe diarrhoea a rehydrating solution is preferable to replace minerals and salts lost. Commercially available oral rehydration salts (ORS) are very useful; add them to boiled or bottled water. In an emergency you can make up a solution of six teaspoons of sugar and a half teaspoon of salt to a litre of boiled or bottled water. You need to drink at least the same volume of fluid that you are losing in bowel movements and vomiting.

Urine is the best guide to the adequacy of replacement – if you have small amounts of concentrated urine, you need to drink more. Keep drinking small amounts often. Stick to a bland diet as you recover.

Gut-paralysing drugs such as loperamide or diphenoxylate can be used to bring relief from the symptoms, although they do not actually cure the problem. Only use these drugs if you do not have access to toilets, eg if you *must* travel. Note also that these drugs are not recommended for children under 12 years.

In certain situations antibiotics may be required: diarrhoea with blood or mucus (dysentery), any diarrhoea with fever, profuse watery diarrhoea, persistent diarrhoea not improving after 48 hours and severe diarrhoea. These suggest a more serious cause of diarrhoea and in these situations gut-paralysing drugs should be avoided.

Two other causes of persistent diarrhoea experienced by travellers are giardiasis and amoebic dysentery.

Giardiasis is caused by a common parasite, *Giardia lamblia*. Symptoms include stomach cramps, nausea, a bloated stomach, watery, foul-smelling diarrhoea and frequent gas. Giardiasis can appear several weeks after you have been exposed to the parasite. The symptoms may disappear for a few days and then return; this can go on for several weeks.

Amoebic dysentery, caused by the protozoan *Entamoeba histolytica*, is characterised by a gradual onset of low-grade diarrhoea, often with blood and mucus. Cramping abdominal pain and vomiting are less likely than in other types of diarrhoea, and fever may not be present. It will persist until treated and can recur and cause other health problems.

You should seek medical advice if you think you have giardiasis or amoebic dysentery, but where this is not possible, tinidazole or metronidazole are the recommended drugs. Treatment is a 2g single dose of tinidazole or 250mg of metronidazole three times daily for five to 10 days.

Hepatitis Hepatitis is a general term for inflammation of the liver. There are several different viruses that cause hepatitis, and they differ in the way that they are transmitted. The symptoms are similar in all forms of the illness, and include fever, chills, headache, fatigue, feelings of weakness and aches and pains, followed by loss of appetite, nausea, vomiting, abdominal pain, dark urine, light-coloured faeces, jaundiced (yellow) skin and yellowing of the whites of the eyes. People who have had hepatitis should avoid alcohol for some time after the illness, as the liver needs time to recover.

Hepatitis A is transmitted by contaminated food and drinking water. You should seek medical advice, but there is not much you can do except rest, drink lots of fluids, eat lightly and avoid fatty foods. Hepatitis E is transmitted in the same way as hepatitis A; it can be particularly serious in pregnant women.

There are almost 300 million chronic carriers of **hepatitis B** in the world. It is spread through contact with infected blood, blood products or body fluids, for example through sexual contact, unsterilised needles and blood transfusions, or contact with blood via small breaks in the skin. You can become infected by being shaved, tattooed or body-pierced with contaminated equipment. The symptoms of hepatitis B may be more severe than type A and the disease can lead to long term problems such as chronic liver damage, liver cancer or a long term carrier state. Hepatitis C and D are spread in the same way as hepatitis B and can also lead to long term complications.

There are vaccines against hepatitis A and B, but there are currently no vaccines against the other types of hepatitis. Following the basic rules about food and water (hepatitis A and E) and avoiding risk situations (hepatitis B, C and D) are important preventative measures.

HIV & AIDS Infection with the human immunodeficiency virus (HIV) may lead to acquired immune deficiency syndrome (AIDS), which is a fatal disease. Any exposure to blood, blood products or body fluids may put the individual at risk. The disease is often transmitted through sexual contact or dirty needles – vaccinations, acupuncture, tattooing and body piercing can be potentially as dangerous as intravenous drug use. HIV/AIDS can also be spread through infected blood transfusions; Russia's record of blood-screening is not perfect.

If you do need an injection, ask to see the syringe unwrapped in front of you, or take a needle and syringe pack with you.

Fear of HIV infection should certainly never preclude treatment for serious medical conditions.

Sexually Transmitted Diseases HIV/AIDS and hepatitis B can be transmitted through sexual contact – see the relevant sections earlier for more details. Other STDs include gonorrhoea, herpes and syphilis; sores, blisters or rashes around the genitals and discharges or pain when urinating are common symptoms. In some STDs, such as wart virus or chlamydia, symptoms may be less marked or not observed at all, especially in women. Chlamydia infection can cause infertility in men and women before any symptoms have been noticed. Syphilis symptoms eventually disappear completely but the disease continues and can cause severe problems in later years. While abstinence from sexual contact is the only 100% effective prevention, using condoms is also effective. The treatment of gonorrhoea and syphilis is with antibiotics. The different sexually transmitted diseases each require specific antibiotics.

Cholera The current injectable vaccine against cholera is poorly protective and has many side effects, so it is not recommended for travellers. Cholera is the worst of the watery diarrhoeas and medical help should be sought. Outbreaks of cholera are generally widely reported, so you can avoid such problem areas. *Fluid replacement is the most vital treatment* – the risk of dehydration is severe as you may lose up to 20L a day. If there is a delay in getting to hospital, then begin taking tetracycline. The adult dose is 250mg four times a day. It is not recommended for children under nine years nor for pregnant women. Tetracycline may help shorten the illness, but adequate fluids are required to save lives.

Diphtheria There have been extensive epidemics of diphtheria in the region over the past few years. The disease can be potentially fatal and is generally transmitted by the inhalation of infected cough or sneeze droplets. There is a higher risk of catching the disease in urban areas. Symptoms include coughing, shortness of breath and swelling around the throat. Medical help must be sought. Vaccination against the disease is available.

Typhoid Typhoid fever is a dangerous gut infection caused by contaminated water and food. Medical help must be sought.

In its early stages sufferers may feel they have a bad cold or flu on the way, as early symptoms are a headache, body aches and a fever that rises a little each day until it is around 40°C (104°F) or more. The victim's pulse is often slow relative to the degree of fever present – unlike a normal fever where the pulse increases. There may also be symptoms of vomiting, abdominal pain, diarrhoea or constipation.

In the second week the high fever and slow pulse continue and a few pink spots may appear on the body; trembling, delirium, weakness, weight loss and dehydration may occur. Complications such as pneumonia, a perforated bowel or meningitis may also occur.

Tuberculosis (TB) TB is a bacterial infection usually transmitted from person to person by coughing but which may also be transmitted through consumption of unpasteurised milk. Milk that has been boiled is normally safe to drink, and the souring of milk to make yogurt or cheese also kills the bacilli.

Travellers are usually not at great risk as close household contact with the infected person is usually required before the disease is passed on. You may need to have a TB test before you travel as this can help diagnose the disease later if you become ill.

Insect-Borne Diseases

Ticks You should always check all over your body if you have been walking through a potentially tick-infested area as ticks can cause skin infections and other more serious diseases. If a tick is found attached to your body, press down around the tick's head with tweezers, grab the head and gently pull upwards. Avoid pulling the rear of the body as this may squeeze the tick's gut contents through the attached mouth parts into the skin, increasing the risk of infection and disease. Smearing chemicals on the tick will not make it let go and is not recommended.

You might want to consider a vaccination against tick-borne encephalitis if you plan to do extensive hiking between May and September. In Europe, you can get a tick-borne encephalatis vaccination as a series of two or three injections; it takes about 10 days to receive all three shots. The vaccination is not available in the USA or Australia.

Lyme Disease This is a tick-transmitted infection that may be acquired throughout the region. The illness usually begins with a spreading rash at the site of the tick bite and is accompanied by fever, headache, extreme fatigue, aching joints and muscles and mild neck stiffness. If untreated, these symptoms usually resolve over several weeks but over subsequent weeks or months disorders of the nervous system, heart and joints may develop. There is no vaccination against Lyme disease. Treatment works best early in the illness and medical help should be sought

Cuts, Bites & Stings

Cuts & Scratches Wash well and treat any cut with an antiseptic such as povidone-iodine. Where possible avoid bandages and Band-Aids, which can keep wounds wet.

Bedbugs & Lice Bedbugs live in various places, but particularly in dirty mattresses and bedding, evidenced by spots of blood on bedclothes or on the wall. Bedbugs leave itchy bites in neat rows. Calamine lotion or a sting relief spray may help.

All lice cause itching and discomfort. They make themselves at home in your hair (head lice), your clothing (body lice) or in your pubic hair (crabs). You catch lice through direct contact with infected people or by sharing combs, clothing and the like. Powder or shampoo treatment will kill the lice and infected clothing should then be washed in very hot, soapy water and left in the sun to dry.

Bites & Stings Bee and wasp stings are usually painful rather than dangerous. However, in people who are allergic to them severe breathing difficulties may occur and require urgent medical care. Applying Calamine lotion or a sting relief spray will give relief and ice packs will reduce the pain and swelling.

Rabies This fatal viral infection is found in rural areas. Many animals can be infected (such as dogs, cats and bats) and it is their saliva that is infectious. Any bite, scratch or even lick from an animal should be cleaned immediately and thoroughly. Scrub with soap and running water, and then apply alcohol or iodine solution. Medical help should be sought promptly to receive a course of injections to prevent the onset of symptoms and further complications.

Women's Health

Gynaecological Problems Antibiotic use, synthetic underwear, sweating and contraceptive pills can lead to fungal vaginal infections, especially when travelling in hot climates. Fungal infections are characterised by a rash, itch and discharge and can be treated with a vinegar or lemon-juice douche, or with yogurt. Nystatin, miconazole or clotrimazole pessaries or vaginal cream are the usual treatment. Maintaining good personal hygiene and wearing loose-fitting clothes and cotton underwear may help prevent these infections.

Sexually transmitted diseases are a major cause of vaginal problems. Symptoms include a smelly discharge, painful intercourse and sometimes a burning sensation when urinating. Medical attention should be sought and male sexual partners must also be treated.

For more details see the section on Sexually Transmitted Diseases earlier. Besides abstinence, the best thing is to practise safer sex using condoms.

Pregnancy Most miscarriages occur during the first three months of pregnancy. Miscarriage is not uncommon and can occasionally lead to severe bleeding. The last three months should also be spent within reasonable distance of good medical care. A baby born as early as 24 weeks stands a chance of survival, but only in a good modern hospital.

Pregnant women should avoid all unnecessary medication, although vaccinations and malarial prophylactics should still be taken where needed. Additional care should be taken to prevent illness and particular attention should be paid to diet and nutrition. Alcohol and nicotine, for example, should be avoided.

WOMEN TRAVELLERS

Bring sanitary towels or tampons only if there is a brand you absolutely must use. Otherwise you can find locally produced Western brands like Tampax everywhere. Western and Russian-made soap and other toiletries are widely available but you might want to bring your own soap as hotels supply meagre quantities.

Attitudes Towards Women

You're unlikely to experience sexual harassment on the streets in most parts of the country, though sexual stereotyping remains strong. However, in places such as Makhachkala in southern European Russia we have seen Russian women being harassed by non-Russian men. In remoter areas, the idea that women are somehow less capable than men may persist, and in some Muslim areas women are treated as second-class people. In rural areas of the country, revealing clothing will probably attract unwanted attention (whereas on hot days in Moscow women wear as little as possible).

Safety Precautions

With lawlessness and crime on the rise, you need to be wary; a woman alone should certainly avoid private taxis at night. Never get in any taxi with more than one person – the driver – already in it. Any young or youngish woman alone in or near flashy bars frequented by foreigners risks being mistaken for a prostitute.

GAY & LESBIAN TRAVELLERS

While girls walking hand in hand and drunken men being affectionate are common sights throughout Russia, open displays of same-sex love are not condoned. In general, the idea of homosexual acts is well tolerated by the younger generation, though overt gay behaviour is frowned upon.

There is an active gay and lesbian scene in Moscow and St Petersburg as memories of the Soviet ban on homosexuals fade. Newspapers such as the *Moscow Times* and the *St Petersburg Times* have shown an interest in publicising gay and lesbian issues and events. They also contain listings of gay clubs and bars. Away from the two major cities, however, the gay scene is much less open.

The *Spartacus* guide lists several organisations, clubs, cruising areas and health services, though their listings tend to be dated: some gay travellers have reported problems when relying on an out-of-date listing, so be sure to confirm details.

The Web sites www.gayrussia.msk.ru and www.vmt.com/gayrussia have good links and other information. Kremlin Tours Travel Agency (☎ 095-276 7274, kremln@dol.ru) is a full-service travel agency in Moscow that specialises in gay clients. It organises tours, homestays, visas etc. St Petersburg's Krilija (Wings; ☎ 812-312 31 80, krilija@ilga.org, www.geocities.com/TheTropics/Cove/6377) is Russia's oldest officially registered gay and lesbian community organisation that also runs the Neva Banks Gay Travel Agency and is happy to assist travellers with information (in English), accommodation and tours. On the women's side, things are less organised, but the Club of Independent Women (☎ 812-355 88 40) should be able to provide assistance.

Cracks in the Iron Closet: Travels in Gay & Lesbian Russia by David Tuller and Frank Browning is a fascinating account of the gay and lesbian scene in modern Russia. A combination of travel memoir and social commentary, it reveals an emerging homosexual culture that is surprisingly different from its US counterpart.

DISABLED TRAVELLERS

Inaccessible transport, lack of ramps and lifts and no centralised policy for people with physical limitations make Russia a challenging destination for wheelchair-bound visitors. More mobile travellers will have a relatively easier time, but keep in mind that there are obstacles along the way. Toilets are frequently accessed from stairs in restaurants and museums; distances are great; public transport extremely crowded; and many footpaths are in a poor condition and hazardous even for the mobile.

Readers who use wheelchairs report that Russians are anxious to help but don't know how, thus either speaking Russian or having a translator is essential. In museums, staff may say that most floors are inaccessible because they don't want to suggest the freight elevator for fear of offending.

Organisations

There are a number of organisations and tour providers around the world that specialise in the needs of disabled travellers.

Australia

Independent Travellers (☎ 08-232 2555, toll-free ☎ 008-811 355, fax 232 6877), 167 Gilles St, Adelaide SA 5000, is a travel agent that provides specialised advice for disabled travellers to a number of destinations.

Russia

The All-Union Association for the Rehabilitation of the Disabled (☎ 095-298 87 37, fax 230 24 07) is at 1 Kuibyahera ploshchad, Moscow.

UK

RADAR (☎ 020-7250 3222), 250 City Rd, London, is a good resource centre.

USA

Twin Peaks Press (☎ 202-694 2462, or toll-free in the USA and Canada ☎ 800-637 2256) publishes several useful handbooks for disabled travellers, including *Travel for the Disabled* and the *Directory of Travel Agencies* for the Disabled. It can be contacted at PO Box 129, Vancouver, WA 98666.

Access, the Foundation for Accessibility by the Disabled (☎ 516-887 5798), can be contacted at PO Box 356, Malverne, NY 11565.

The Information Center for Individuals with Disabilities (☎ 617-727 5540, TTY 345 9743 or toll-free ☎ 800-248 3737) is at Fort Point Place, 1st Floor, 27-43 Wormwood Street, Boston, MA 02210. Call or write for their free listings and travel advice.

Mobility International USA (☎ TDD 503-343 1284, fax 343-6812; miusa@igc.apc.org), PO Box 3551, Eugene, OR 97403, advises disabled travellers on mobility issues. It also runs an exchange program, and has run several programs in Russia.

SATH, Society for the Advancement of Travel for the Handicapped (☎ 212-447 7284), is at 347 Fifth Ave No 610, New York, NY 10016.

Handicapped Travel Newsletter (☎/fax 903-677 1260) is a nonprofit, bimonthly publication with good information on travelling around the world. Subscriptions are $10 annually. Its address is PO Drawer 269, Athens, TX 75751.

Internet Resources

The Internet is brimming with information on the subject of physical disabilities. EKA (Evan Kemp Associates), a company selling products for the disabled, runs a good site with lots of links. It's at www.eka.com. Disabled Peoples' International has a home page at www.dpi.org. It's a nonprofit and well done Web site with tons of listings and great links; those behind it are based in Canada and seem to think truly globally.

SENIOR TRAVELLERS

Travellers over the age of 60 can expect senior citizen discounts and good treatment from Russian ticket agents. Respect for the elderly is far more ingrained in Russia than in some countries, such as the USA. Organisations in your home country, like the American Association of Retired Persons (www.aarp.org), which you can join even if you're not retired or a senior, can assist with age-specific information before you leave.

TRAVEL WITH CHILDREN

Moscow and St Petersburg have a fair number of attractions that will entertain children. Elsewhere, diversions are more problematic. Add to this the lack of English-language publications or outlets for familiar toys and you have a challenge for parents. But travelling in Russia with children can be fun as long as you come well prepared with the right attitudes, equipment and patience. Lonely Planet's *Travel with Children* by Maureen Wheeler contains useful advice on how to cope with kids on the road and what to bring to make things go more smoothly.

DANGERS & ANNOYANCES

Danger Regions

It's obviously foolish to go where there's fighting going on or bandits on the loose. The Caucasus is the most volatile area. No-one needs reminding about Chechnya. Dagestan has also been a scene of civil unrest and general lawlessness.

If you're going anywhere you think might be dangerous, check with your government's foreign affairs ministry at home or your embassy in Russia.

Transport Safety

See the European Russia Getting Around chapter for information on the hazards of flying and precautions to consider taking on some trains.

Crime

The 'Mafia' The Western media have had a field day talking about the dangers of the Russian Mafia, painting a portrait of a country inundated with Al Capone types who race through the streets indiscriminately firing Kalashnikovs. In fact, the organised crime problem in Russia is far more complex, and far less of a threat to visitors, than one might guess from reading an issue of *Newsweek*.

Street Crime Moscow and St Petersburg's streets are about as safe, or as dangerous, as those of New York, London or Amsterdam. There's petty theft, pocket-picking, purse-snatching and all the other crimes that are endemic in big cities anywhere in the world. Travellers have reported muggings in broad daylight along Moscow's Novy Arbat and St Petersburg's Nevsky prospekt. Many have reported problems with groups of children who surround foreigners, ostensibly to beg, and end up closing in, with dozens of hands probing Westerners' pockets or worse.

The key here is to be neither paranoid nor insouciant. Common sense must be applied, and you should be aware that it's pretty obvious you're a Westerner. Anything you can do to try to fit in such as shunning bumbags (fanny packs), bright Western clothes and the like is a good idea. Even better is to scrap the day-pack and carry your goods in a plastic bag.

Burglary Break-ins to flats and cars are epidemic so don't leave anything of worth – this includes sunglasses, cassette tapes, windscreen wipers and cigarettes – in a car. Valuables lying around hotel rooms are also tempting providence. At camp sites watch for things being stolen from clotheslines or even cabins. If you'll be living in a flat, invest in a steel door.

Annoyances

The single most annoying thing the majority of travellers encounter in Russia is that combination of bureaucracy and apathy that turns some people in 'service' industries into surly, ill-mannered, obstructive goblins. Things have improved somewhat with the introduction of private enterprise, but at times you still have to contend with hotel desk staff struck deaf, or at best monosyllabic, by your arrival, shop 'assistants' with strange paralyses that make them unable to turn to face customers, and so on. In general, however, customer service is much improved.

One thing you can't do anything about is the tangle of opening hours whereby every shop, museum and cafe seems to be having its lunch or afternoon break, or day off, or is *remont* (closed for repairs), or is simply closed full stop, just when you want to visit.

Other things you might find annoying are alcoholic late-night comings, goings and door banging in hotel corridors; engine-revving, car-alarm testing, tyre-screeching and more door-banging outside hotels after the restaurant closes; the brain-numbing volume of restaurant bands and the clouds of cigarette smoke that billow from most gatherings of Russian citizens.

Given that prostitution is legal, don't be surprised to see a lot of prostitutes about: busy streets, hotel lobbies, bars, clubs and virtually any place else there might be somebody willing to pay for sex are all haunts. And prostitutes still sometimes walk into or telephone your hotel room offering sex. If this happens raise a ruckus with everyone working in the hotel.

Discrimination

Overt hostility is almost unheard of, though a high level of entrenched racist attitudes exists in Russia. What is most surprising is that racist attitudes or statements can come from otherwise highly educated Russians. Jews, targets of state-sponsored anti-Semitism during the Communist reign, are more distrusted than hated, though the hatred certainly exists, especially that stirred up by right-wing political parties. Gypsies, also known as Roma or Travellers, however, are openly reviled.

LEGAL MATTERS

Do your best to avoid contact with the myriad types of police. Some are known to bolster their puny incomes by robbing foreigners either outright or through sham 'fines'. There would seem to be no age limit at all for alcohol consumption. There is zero tolerance of any alcohol consumption by drivers. The age of consent for both sexes is 16.

Arrest

If you are arrested, the Russian authorities are obliged to inform your embassy or consulate immediately and allow you to communicate with it without delay. You can insist on seeing an embassy or consular official straight away. Be polite and respectful towards officials and things will go far more smoothly for you. *'Pa-ZHAHL-stuh, ya kha-TYEL bi pahz-vah-NEET v pah-SOLST-vih ma-YEY STRAHN-ih'* means 'I'd like to call my embassy'.

BUSINESS HOURS

Government offices, should you need them, open from 9 or 10 am to 5 or 6 pm weekdays. Banks usually open from 9 am to noon Monday to Friday; those in major cities often also open from 1 to 6 pm. Currency-exchange booths open long hours, and on Saturday and sometimes Sunday too.

Most shops are open Monday to Saturday. Food shops tend to open from 8 am to 8 pm except for a break *(pereryv)* from 1 to 2 pm or 2 to 3 pm; some close later, some open Sunday until 5 pm. Other shops mostly operate from 10 or 11 am to 7 or 8 pm with a 2 to 3 pm break. Department stores may run from 8 am to 8 or 9 pm without a break. A few shops stay open through the weekend and close on Monday.

In major cities there are more and more 24-hour kiosks selling food and drink. Restaurants typically open from noon to midnight except for a break between afternoon and evening meals.

Museum hours change often, as do their weekly days off. Most shut entrance doors 30 minutes or an hour before closing time and may have shorter hours on the day before their day off.

PUBLIC HOLIDAYS & SPECIAL EVENTS

Public Holidays

The main public holidays are:

New Year's Day
1 January
Russian Orthodox Christmas Day
7 January
International Women's Day
8 March
International Labour Day/Spring Festival
1 & 2 May
Victory (1945) Day
9 May
Russian Independence Day
12 June
Day of Reconciliation and Accord (the rebranded Revolution Day)
7 November

Other days that are widely celebrated are 23 February – Defenders of the Motherland Day, Easter Monday and 12 December – Constitution Day. Much of Russia shuts down for the first half of May and its wealth of holidays.

Special Events

The Russians do a delightful job of finding reasons to hold a festival. Some of the more important are:

January

Russian Orthodox Christmas *(Rozhdestvo)*
7 January – begins with midnight church services.

February to April

Goodbye Russian Winter *(Maslennitsa)*
Late February and/or early March – folk shows and games to celebrate the beginning of the end of winter.

Festival of the North
Last week of March – Murmansk and other northern towns hold reindeer races, ski marathons etc.

Easter *(Paskha)*
The main festival of Orthodox Church year, held in March/April. Easter Day begins with celebratory midnight services, after which people eat special dome-shaped cakes called *kulichy* and curd-cakes called *paskha*, and may exchange painted wooden Easter eggs. The devout deny themselves meat, milk, alcohol and sex in the 40 day pre-Easter fasting period of Lent.

May

Graduates Day

Held on or near the 24th – a day when those finishing school parade about their hometowns in traditional student garb.

June

St Petersburg White Nights

Last 10 days of June – general merrymaking and staying out late, plus dance festival. Many other northern towns have their own version.

November

Great October Socialist Revolution Anniversary

7 November – now that the holiday has been taken over by the noncommunists (see Public Holidays earlier), this is a big day for marches by the Communist Party.

December

Sylvestr and New Year

31 December & 1 January – the main winter and gift-giving festival. Gifts are put under the traditional fir tree *(yolka)*. See out the old year with vodka and welcome the new one with champagne while listening to the Kremlin chimes on TV.

ACTIVITIES

Camping, hiking, skiing, canoeing and other outdoor activities are all popular with Russians. However, unlike in Western countries, the infrastructure here for most activities is rudimentary. Sporting goods stores, adventure travel firms, organised tours and the like are all hard to find. See the Organised Tours section of the European Russia Getting There & Away chapter for details on adventure travel companies operating trips to Russia.

The best strategy for obtaining information about outdoor activities is to inquire locally. Quite often there will be a group of enthusiasts who are more than happy to share their knowledge and even equipment with a visitor. Local inquiries are also a good way to locate guides for trekking or other activities where detailed local knowledge is essential.

Cycling

Deteriorated roads and manic drivers are two of the main hazards to cyclists. Otherwise you will find rural Russians quite fascinated and friendly towards long-distance riders. Just make certain you have a bike designed for the harshest of conditions and that you carry plenty of spare parts.

Skiing

A few simple downhill ski slopes can be found scattered through the country. A more common activity is cross-country skiing, which attracts legions of skiers during the long winters. Given the wealth of open space even near cities like Moscow, you won't have a problem finding a place to hit the trail. The few sporting goods stores that exist carry decent, inexpensive Russian-made equipment.

Hiking

Those same open lands good for cross-country skiing are also good for hiking. Among the best areas for hiking are the Lapland Nature Reserve in Northern European Russia and the Elbrus area of the Caucasus. See the relevant regional chapters for more details. The western Ural Mountains are another popular place for longer hikes.

The difficulty in finding reliable maps means that it's especially important to seek out local advice, information and even guides.

Mountaineering

The dramatic peaks of the Elbrus area are a natural magnet for climbers. See the Caucasus chapter for details and note that these types of trip are best organised before arrival in Russia.

Boating

Although many rivers have water quality that discourages even getting near the water, the coasts offer many canoeing and kayaking possibilities. The Solovetsky Islands in Northern European Russia are an example of the remote and fascinating places that can be explored by boat during the summer. The Volga River delta with its fascinating flora and fauna below Astrakhan is another good place for exploring.

In towns and parks with clean lakes there are usually rowing boats available for rent during the warmer months.

Ice Skating

Russians skate with abandon during the long winter. Outdoor rinks are common and easy to find and equipment rentals are cheap. There are also many indoor rinks open throughout the year.

LANGUAGE COURSES

Although it's useful to speak Russian before you arrive, there are plenty of opportunities for language study once there. The English-language publications in Moscow and St Petersburg (see Newspapers & Magazines earlier in the chapter) regularly carry listings of and advertisements for Russian-language schools and tutors. The cost of formal course work varies widely, but one-on-one tutoring can be a bargain given the low local wage levels. Numerous professors and other highly skilled people are anxious to augment their incomes teaching you Russian.

Another option for learning Russian is through one of the many international universities operating in Moscow and St Petersburg. These are usually affiliated with a school in either Britain or the USA. To find out about what programs are available, inquire at any college or university, which will have reams of information on international study programs worldwide.

WORK

The August 1998 crash also meant a crash of jobs for foreigners. Far from hiring, companies in Russia that employed foreigners have sent them home in droves. In addition, scores of Russians with the same skills have been sent to the ranks of the unemployed. Thus the chances for foreigners to find work in Russia are slim. The odds of starting a profitable business are also small; certainly much lower than they were in the early 1990s when Westerners – especially US citizens – flocked to set up businesses in Moscow and St Petersburg.

Should you actually find work in Russia or be sent there by your company, you should be given the resources of a professional relocation firm who can navigate the thicket of rules and regulations surrounding foreign employment in Russia.

ACCOMMODATION

You're usually free to stay in any type of accommodation you can find in Russia. Gone are the days when tourists were restricted to specified hotels and a few grotty camp sites, all of which had to be booked before you could even get a visa. You may find it useful to book a few nights in advance for Moscow and St Petersburg, although tourism has been way down since the uncertainties of August 1998. Other than in these two cities, accommodation usually does not need to be booked in advance, albeit reservations themselves are often problematic.

Camping

Camping in the wild is legal in many places, except those signposted Не разбивать палатку (No putting up of tents) and/or Не разжигать костов (No camp fires); if you're off the beaten track it is usually legal and fine just to put up a tent and hit the hay. Check with locals if you're in doubt.

Organised camp sites *(kempingi)* are increasingly rare and are usually open only from some time in June to some time in September. They're not quite like camp sites in the West: small wooden cabins often take up much of the space, leaving little room for tents. Some kempingi are on the fringes of cities but may be in quite attractive woodland settings; however, communal toilets and washrooms are often filthy and other facilities few.

Tourbases

A tourbase *(turbaza)* is a holiday camp for Russians, usually owned by a factory or large company for the use of its employees. They range from absolutely spartan to somewhat luxurious, and many are now open to foreign tourists. Lodging options usually consist of a large common room with six or more beds, smaller doubles and private cottages. All are cheap: usually $10 to $15 or less. There are reasons – many have no indoor plumbing, and usually the only place to eat is a canteen *(stolovoya)*. But if you bring a good supply of food and a sense of adventure, these are a great way to get a feel for the average Russian's holi-

GEORGI SHABLOVSKY

Peter & Paul Fortress

JONATHAN SMITH

Church of the Resurrection of Christ

JONATHAN SMITH

Detail of Bankovsky Most (Bank Bridge) over Griboedova Canal

JONATHAN SMITH

Bankovsky Most over Griboedova Canal, St Petersburg

JONATHAN SMITH

Pushkin & the Russian Museum

JONATHAN SMITH

Ah, the old Kasparov gambit, good move

JONATHAN SMITH

Heads, I drive the boat, tails, you drive the boat

GEORGI SHABLOVSKY

St Petersburg folk dancers

day. At some, you can arrange boating, skiing, hiking or mountaineering.

Hostels

Moscow and St Petersburg each have one or more youth or backpackers' hostels, all more or less in the international mould and able to offer visa support. See the individual city listings for details. The rest of Russia is ripe for hostel development both for foreigners and locals but so far no hostel movement has emerged.

University Accommodation

In Moscow, St Petersburg and other cities with large universities it's possible to stay in Russian student accommodation. Prices range from about $2 to $15 a night. The accommodation is not unlike the kind you find in hostels and guesthouses. Getting in can sometimes be a bit iffy – it depends on availability or even the administrator's mood. A student card, and looking like a student, certainly help. See the city listings for further information or, alternatively, ask around at a university campus in Russia.

Hotels

Russian hotels run the gamut from flyblown lice-traps where for a couple of dollars you can, if you wish, share a room (and a single unflushable toilet down the corridor) with a gang of male market traders from the 'southern republics', to international five-star palaces full of Western businesspeople whose slumbers cost their companies $400 a night.

Most hotels have one price for Russians and another, higher price for foreigners. There's little you can do about this (even if you go with Russian friends you'll often still have to pay the foreigner price). The only exceptions are a few hotels, mostly in out-of-the-way places, that get very few foreigners and haven't heard there are such things as foreigner prices. In this book we list the prices hotels charge for foreigners when there is a dual-pricing system.

At most hotels, you can just walk in and get a room on the spot. If you can't, it will probably be for one of four reasons:

- the hotel is genuinely full (extremely rare);
- the receptionist/administrator thinks that because you haven't got their town named on your visa you can't stay there (almost as rare) – they're wrong, but there may not be much you can do about it;
- they say their hotel doesn't take foreigners – either because they think it's so bad you couldn't possibly want to stay there (they can usually be persuaded otherwise, though when you've seen round some places you might agree with them); or because they didn't take foreigners in Soviet times and they don't know times have changed (this happens more often in out-of-the-way places);
- or the hotel belongs to some institute or organisation and only takes people booked in through special channels.

Procedures At virtually all hotels you have to show your passport and visa when you check in – and staff may keep it till next day to register your presence with the local OVIR. Don't worry about this – it's normal – but do remember to get your passport and visa back before you leave. Better yet, tell them you need your passport to change money: they should then complete the paperwork in five minutes.

In most hotels except the cheapest and the expensive new foreign ones, each floor has a floor lady *(dezhurnaya)* to keep an eye on it. They're well worth making friends with. Often the dezhurnaya and the room cleaners are the nicest people in the place, almost always able to supply you with snacks, bottled drinks or boiled water.

Hotels with significant numbers of foreigners attract prostitutes – which is what any well-dressed young Russian woman hanging around a lobby or bar and making continuous eye-contact with you is likely to be.

Checkout time is usually noon, but it's unlikely that anyone will mind if you stay an extra hour or two. If you want to store your luggage somewhere safe for a late departure, arrange it with the dezhurnaya or front desk.

Rooms Many hotels have a range of rooms at widely differing prices but may automatically offer foreigners the most expensive, often claiming that cheaper ones are 'not suitable'. Given that away from the major cities room prices may average about $10 you may be happy with their idea of 'best'. But feel free to look around and ask about cheaper options.

Not all hotels have genuine single rooms and 'single' prices often refer to single occupancy of a double room. Some hotels, mainly in the bottom end and lower middle range, have rooms for three or four people where the price per person comes to much less than in a single or double. Beds are always single.

An average hotel room measures about 4m by 5m and has its own bathroom containing a toilet, washbasin, shower and/or bath, toilet paper, soap and a couple of small towels. Hot water supplies are fairly reliable: but since hot water is supplied on a district basis, whole neighbourhoods can be without it for a month or more in summer when the system is shut down for maintenance (the best hotels manage to avoid this).

A *lyux* room is a kind of suite, with a sitting room in addition to the bedroom and bathroom.

Budget Rooms may have their own toilet, washbasin or shower, or you may have to use facilities shared by the whole corridor. Some places are clean, if musty, and even run to TV or a fridge in the rooms; others are decaying, dirty and smelly and lack decent toilets and washing facilities. In some cheap hotels you do have to take care with security. Prices range from $40 in Moscow to just a couple of dollars elsewhere.

Mid-Range These are mainly Soviet-era tourist hotels, typically concrete and glass rectangles, though some of the older ones have a bit of style. They have clean, reasonably comfortable rooms with bathrooms and often small balconies. They'll have a restaurant plus a couple of bars or the snack bars called *bufety*. A casino haunted by mafiosi is a common feature. These are the most common type of hotel you'll find in much of the country. Except in Moscow and St Petersburg (where they can cost $70 to $100) you'll pay $5 to $20 for a mid-range single.

To date, Russia has disappointingly few of the small, cosy, moderately priced hotels found elsewhere in Europe.

Top End The top end consists of Western-run luxury hotels, nearly all in Moscow and St Petersburg. These are up to the best international standards, with very comfortable rooms boasting satellite TV, minibars, fawning service, fine restaurants, health clubs, and prices to match, from around $200/250 to $350/400 a single/double.

Outside the two big cities the 'top end', where it exists, is composed mainly of the very best Soviet-era tourist hotels, along with the occasional former Communist Party hotel or small, new private venture. You may pay from $60/100 to $130/150.

You may get better prices for top-end hotels if you prebook through a travel agent in Russia or abroad. In the months following August 1998 deals offering 50% off or more were commonplace.

Private Homes

It's not hard in many places to find a room in a private flat, shared with the owners. One good point about this type of accommodation – often referred to as 'bed & breakfast' (B&B) or 'homestay' – is that it enables you to glimpse how Russians really live. Typically you get a two-bed room, use of a bathroom, and possibly cooking facilities. Most flats that take in guests are clean and respectable – though they're rarely large! If you stay in a few you'll be surprised, despite outward similarities, how different their owners can make them.

Moscow and St Petersburg have organisations specifically geared to accommodate foreign visitors in private flats at around $20 or $30 per person, normally with English-speaking hosts, breakfast included and other services such as excursions and extra meals available. Many travel agencies and tourism firms in these and other cities can also find you a place for something like $15 per person, but the price may depend on things like how far the flat is from the city centre, whether the hosts speak English, and whether any meals are provided.

It's also possible to pay the price Russians pay for staying in a private flat – about $7 a night – by going with one of the people who approach travellers arriving off major trains in Moscow and St Petersburg, or finding a *kvartirnoe byuro*, which is an agency that places short-term guests in private flats. You'll want to be sure that you trust anyone who approaches you at a station (many of them really are genuine folks just in need of some extra cash) and establish how far from the city centre their place is before accompanying them. It's better to avoid committing yourself before you actually see the place. Kvartirnye byura are usually located in airports or Aeroflot offices and sometimes train or bus stations. In some places home-owners also wait around the entrances or lobbies of certain hotels offering rooms in their flats. Always establish the location first. If you're alone, it's possible you'll find yourself sharing the room with another guest.

Booking Homestays from Overseas

You can contact many Russian homestay agents from overseas (if you do, check that they can provide visa support too), but you can also book through many travel agencies in your own country.

One Russian organisation we have had good reports about is the St Petersburg-based Host Families Association (HOFA; ☎/fax 812-275 19 92, alexei@hofak.hop.stu.neva.ru, www.spb.ru/homestays), which can provide places in St Petersburg, Moscow, Pskov, Saratov, Volgograd, some Siberian cities and nine cities in other CIS countries. It offers visa support.

In Australia, the Russia Travel Centre (☎ 02-9262 1144) in Sydney and Passport Travel Services (☎ 03-9867 3888) in Melbourne can book rooms in Russia. In the UK, try Interchange (☎ 020-8681 3612, interchange@interchange.uk.com) which offers homestays in Moscow and St Petersburg.

In the USA, Moscow Bed & Breakfast (☎ 603-585 3347, fax 585 3347, jkates@top.monad.net) represents rooms in Moscow and beyond and also offers visa support. Russian Home Travel (toll-free ☎ 800-861 9335, russiahome@aol.com) has visa support and represents hosts in Moscow and St Petersburg. American-International Homestays (☎ 303-642 3088 or toll-free ☎ 800-876 2048, fax 303-642 3365, www.spectravel.com/homes) arranges individual or group trips with accommodation in the homes of host families which are supervised by the organisation.

Normal prices are between $25 and $50 per person a night, usually with breakfast and English-speaking hosts included. Some of these companies also offer more expensive packages including excursions, all meals, and so on. There are also discounts for longer stays. It's worth knowing that your host family usually only gets a small fraction of the price you pay the agent.

ENTERTAINMENT

There's no shortage of entertainment in the two major cities. The relevant chapters list many options as well as sources of local information about what's on. Elsewhere options are more limited.

Information & Tickets

The entertainment listings in the English-language publications in Moscow and St Petersburg greatly simplify the process of finding out what's on in those cities. Elsewhere, the ability to decipher Cyrillic is a huge advantage. A lot of information, including that about rock and sports events, is published on posters. You can also learn a lot from the what's-on charts that you'll find in hotel service bureaus, at concierge desks and in the ticket kiosks that dot sizable cities (these kiosks are identified by the words Театральная касса *(teatralnaya kassa)* or just Театр *(teatr)*). But again, note that reading Cyrillic is all but mandatory at these places.

You can buy face-value tickets from the *kassa* (ticket office) at the venue itself (typically open for advance or same-day sales from early afternoon till the start of the evening show), or a teatralnaya kassa, or any other outlets listed on posters – look for words like sale (**продажа**) and tickets (**билеты**). It can be surprisingly easy to get tickets this way with a few words of Russian.

If these avenues fail, you can resort to a hotel service bureau or a ticket agency. Here you'll often pay a huge premium over the face value of the ticket (which is usually tiny). For things like the Bolshoi Ballet, $50 to $65 for a $15 ticket is not unusual. Still, service bureaus and concierges generally get better tickets than you otherwise could, and for some events they might be the only places able to sell you a ticket.

Then there are the touts. It's standard practice when tickets are scarce for people with spares, as well as the professional touts, to sell a few outside the main entrance before starting time. Prices are a free-for-all and of course you run the risk of obstructed view, wrong date and other hazards, but sellers will normally let you have a look at the ticket before you pay for it. Make sure that the ticket's for the date, performance and section you want (see the boxed text).

Music

Classical, jazz and rock music, ballet, opera and drama all thrive in Russia, the cultural flagships being St Petersburg's Kirov Ballet & Opera, Moscow's Bolshoi Ballet & Opera, and orchestras including the State Symphony Orchestra, the Russian National Symphony Orchestra and the St Petersburg Philharmonic. Many major cities have their own ballet and opera companies and orchestras.

Useful Theatre Words & Phrases

theatre	*teatr*	театр
opera & ballet theatre	*teatr opery i baleta*	театр оперы и балета
drama theatre	*dramaticheskiy teatr*	драматический театр
concert hall	*kontsertnyy zal*	концертный зал
circus	*tsirk*	цирк
cinema	*kinoteatr, kino*	кинотеатр, кино
Have you got tickets for...?	*u vas bilety (bil-YET-i) na...?*	У вас билеты на...?
Extra tickets?	*Lishnie bilety?*	Лишние билеты?
cheap tickets	*deshyovye bilety*	дешёвые билеты
best tickets	*luchshchie bilety*	лучшие билеты
stalls, lowest tier of seating	*amfiteatr, parter, kresla*	амфитеатр, партер, кресла
dress circle (one tier up from stalls)	*bel-etazh*	бель-этаж
box	*lozha*	ложа
balcony	*balkon*	балкон
first tier (eg of balcony)	*pervyy yarus*	первый (1-й) ярус
second tier	*vtoroy (fta-ROY) yarus*	второй (2-ой) ярус
third tier	*tretiy yarus*	третий (3-й) ярус
row	*ryad (ryat)*	ряд
inconvenient place (eg obstructed view)	*neudobnoe mesto (nye-oo-DOHB-nah-yeh MYEST-ah)*	неудобное место
matinee	*utrenniy kontsert*	утренний концерт
cloakroom	*garderob (gar-di-ROP)*	гардероб
guest stars	*gastroli*	гастроли
Swan Lake	*Lebedinoe ozero*	Лебединое озеро
Sleeping Beauty	*Spyachkaya krasavitsa*	Спячкая красавица
The Nutcracker	*Shchelkunchik*	Щелкунчик

Ээ

Rock and pop music are popular and you'll see posters for local performances at stadiums, clubs and bars in every town. Live jazz is limited to the largest cities while finding authentic folk music can be more of a challenge. The best way to track down more esoteric music beyond Russian rock outside Moscow and St Petersburg is to ask around.

Much culture and entertainment lies dormant between about June and September as companies go away on tour or holiday.

See the Arts section of the preceding Facts about European Russia chapter for more details on music.

Theatre

Live theatre is popular throughout Russia and you can find companies hard at work in all but the smallest towns. Obviously with the exception of a few places in the major cities the performances will be in Russian, but that's really the only way to see Chekhov. The works being performed range from Russian classics, Soviet standards and new works as well as plays by foreigners.

Bars & Clubs

Friendly bars and clubs abound in Moscow and St Petersburg, as do unfriendly ones. Many of the latter are overrun with that peculiar species of 'new Russian' known as the 'flat-head'. Basically these are goonish guys whose IQs match their neck size (and that's in inches, not centimetres). If you're in a place with these louts, ignore them. Another phenomenon is that many otherwise low-key places will stage strip shows aimed at both sexes. Many bars and clubs have live music many nights. The quality ranges from dreadful to inspired and runs the gamut from pop to techno and beyond.

Finding a quiet place to sip a beer while dashing off some prose may be hard but if you're looking for places where the mood builds to wild abandon, then you'll have no problems. There are no real serving hours – and if there were they'd just be bribed away – so many places are open 24 hours a day. Clubs with audience participation strip shows, open prostitution and numerous other vices are common.

Away from Moscow and St Petersburg, it can be hard to find bars given that there was no tradition of pubs in Russia. Clubs are another matter, with most cities of any size having several places of varying character and respectability where people can party until dawn and beyond.

In larger Russian cities, the Irish equivalent of McDonald's, the 'authentic Irish pub', is popping up as fast as the factories in the Old Sod can pop them out. During the summer months, the ubiquitous simple street cafes can be fine places to while away the warm nights.

SPECTATOR SPORTS

Once-proud sports facilities dot Russia. Built during Soviet times for the scores of semiprofessional and amateur sports clubs, youth leagues and all the rest of the state apparatus that reached its pinnacle during the USSR's dominance of the Olympics, this huge infrastructure is going to seed in a hurry. Many of the sports halls and stadiums have found new uses as shopping complexes, nightclubs and other decidedly unhealthy pursuits.

This limits opportunities to see teams in action primarily to football and ice hockey. The premier football league, Vysshaya Liga, consists of 16 teams, the best of which include Moscow's Spartak, Lokomotiv, TsSKA, Torpedo and Dinamo as well as Alaniya (Vladikavkaz), Rostselmash (Rostov-on-Don), Zenit (St Petersburg), and another Lokomotiv (Nizhni Novgorod).

The top ice hockey league (Super Liga) has 20 teams. The perennial top 10 are: Ak Bars (Kazan), Amur (Khabarovsk), Metallurg (Magnitogorsk), Dinamo (Moscow), Metallurg (Novokuznetsk), Avangard (Omsk), Molot-Prikamye (Perm), Lada (Tolyatti), Salavat Yulayev (Ufa) and Torpedo (Yaroslavl).

When asked about women's spectator sports, one Russian woman thought for a moment and said, 'There's ice skating, but you have to starve yourself.' Watch listings for word of ice skating competitions for both genders. The best talent performs in Russia as part of the never-ending world tours.

SHOPPING

You can buy just about anything in Russian cities that you can buy in comparable-sized cities in the West. If you have the cash – and we mean cash – than you can probably find what you're looking for at the ever-growing array of kiosks, shops, markets, department stores and malls.

There are plenty of attractive things to buy if you know where to look. Most regions still have some local craft specialities, even if the Soviet years have killed off others.

What to Look For

The trademark Russian souvenir is the matryoshka, the set of wooden dolls within dolls. Glasnost enabled them to become something of a true folk art, with all manner of intricate painted designs. But recent-vintage matryoshkas can be seedy little things, poorly painted dolls depicting Soviet and Russian leaders, the Keystone Cops – you name it. Although some of the better ones can display typically biting Russian wit such as the Clinton doll that revealed another one of his alleged and admitted sexual partners with each nested doll.

These days you can buy small, mass-produced sets for a couple of dollars but the best examples may set you back $100. For this price you can also take along a family photo to Izmaylovsky Park in Moscow and come back the following week to collect your very own personalised matryoshka set.

Quality is similarly varied with the enamelled wooden boxes known as *palekh* (after the town east of Moscow where they originated), each with an intricate scene painted in its lid – but they're usually even more expensive. Several hundred dollars are asked for the best. Cheaper but cheerful are the gold, red and black wooden bowls, mugs and spoons from Khokhloma, a bit farther east, which are widely available.

Another attractive Russian craft is the blue-and-white ornamental china called Gzhel (after its home town, east of Moscow).

The trademark Russian textile is the 'Babushka scarf' – officially the Pavlovsky Posad kerchief *(platok Pavlovo Posad)*, again named after its home town east of Moscow. These fine woollen scarves with floral designs go for anything from $2 to $10 or more in shops. Other Russian textiles include wool shawls so fine they look almost like lace.

LEE FOSTER

The ubiquitous matryoshka doll

Amber *(yantar)* from the Baltic coast is a jewellery speciality, though beware of fake stuff in St Petersburg and Moscow markets and shops. A good necklace or ring might be $50 to $200. Russian records and cassettes – rock, jazz, classical – are a bargain at about $1 to $2. For the same price you can get all manner of pirated CDs, video cassettes and software. But you deserve what you get if you buy one of these numbers only to discover that the CD actually has military music instead of Deep Purple, the video of *Star Wars Episode I – The Phantom Menace* was shot in a movie theatre using a handheld camcorder or that your new copy of Windows 98 is mostly a breeding ground for viruses.

More ideas: paintings from street artists and art markets (some talent amid the kitsch); art and children's books from bookshops; posters, both old Socialist exhortation and modern social commentary, from bookshops or specialist poster *(plakat)* shops; and little Lenin busts for $5 to $10 at street stands and in tourist markets.

Getting There & Away

European Russia has land borders with 11 other countries. You do not have to use the same agent to book your transport into the country as the one you're using to arrange any ground services in Russia – you can get there by the cheapest or most desirable means you can find.

One happy situation is that, with the exception of transit visas, the success of your visa application does not hinge on transport into *or out of* the country. Unless you have a transit visa, you can always enter Russia on a one-way ticket (even if your visa is only good for one day, no-one will ever ask to see your outgoing ticket), so you have a great deal of flexibility once inside Russia to determine the cheapest way of getting out again.

Information on travel between European Russia and Ukraine and Belarus is also given in the Ukraine and Belarus Getting There & Away chapters; information on travel between European Russia and Siberia, the Russian Far East, Mongolia and China is given in the Trans-Siberian Railway chapter and/or the Siberia & the Russian Far East Getting There & Away chapter.

AIR

There's daily service to Moscow from all major European capitals and New York, as well as frequent service from Hong Kong and other Asian travel centres. There's also daily service from several European cities to St Petersburg. There isn't any direct service to European Russia from Australasia; you'll need to get to an Asian, European or US gateway and proceed from there.

If you are flying to another city in European Russia or elsewhere in the nation your best connection will be through Moscow, which has the bulk of domestic flights. However, this will inevitably require a change of airports, which can mean a potentially costly, inconvenient and time-consuming adventure.

Warning

The information in this chapter is particularly vulnerable to change: Prices for international travel are volatile, routes are introduced and cancelled, schedules change, special deals come and go, and rules and visa requirements are amended. Airlines and governments seem to take a perverse pleasure in making price structures and regulations as complicated as possible. You should check directly with the airline or a travel agent to make sure you understand how a fare (and ticket you may buy) works. In addition, the travel industry is highly competitive and there are many lurks and perks.

The upshot of this is that you should get opinions, quotes and advice from as many airlines and travel agents as possible before you part with your hard-earned cash. The details given in this chapter should be regarded as pointers and are not a substitute for your own careful, up-to-date research.

Airports

Moscow's Sheremetevo-2 airport handles all international flights. It has improved a bit in recent years and is now about on a par with other average international airports in the world, although the arrivals level 'taxi mafia' remain. Unfortunately for those travelling on to another Russian destination, domestic flights depart from four domestic airports that are 30 minutes to two hours away from Sheremetevo-2. See the Getting Around section in the Moscow chapter for further details.

In St Petersburg, the international airport, Pulkovo-2, is also separate from the domestic airport, Pulkovo-1. But at least here the two are not far apart. See the Getting There & Away section in the St Petersburg chapter for details.

Air Travel Glossary

Baggage Allowance This will be written on your ticket and usually includes one 20kg item to go in the hold, plus one item of hand luggage.

Bucket Shops These are unbonded travel agencies specialising in discounted airline tickets.

Bumped Just because you have a confirmed seat doesn't mean you're going to get on the plane (see Overbooking).

Cancellation Penalties If you have to cancel or change a discounted ticket, there are often heavy penalties involved; insurance can sometimes be taken out against these penalties. Some airlines impose penalties on regular tickets as well, particularly against 'no-show' passengers.

Check-In Airlines ask you to check in a certain time ahead of the flight departure (usually one to two hours on international flights). If you fail to check in on time and the flight is overbooked, the airline can cancel your booking and give your seat to somebody else.

Confirmation Having a ticket written out with the flight and date you want doesn't mean you have a seat until the agent has checked with the airline that your status is 'OK' or confirmed. Meanwhile you could just be 'on request'.

Courier Fares Businesses often need to send urgent documents or freight securely and quickly. Courier companies hire people to accompany the package through customs and, in return, offer a discount ticket which is sometimes a phenomenal bargain. In effect, what the companies do is ship their freight as your luggage on regular commercial flights. This is a legitimate operation, but there are two shortcomings – the short turnaround time of the ticket (usually not longer than a month) and the limitation on your luggage allowance. You may have to surrender all your allowance and take only carry-on luggage.

Full Fares Airlines traditionally offer 1st class (coded F), business class (coded J) and economy class (coded Y) tickets. These days there are so many promotional and discounted fares available that few passengers pay full economy fare.

ITX An ITX, or 'independent inclusive tour excursion', is often available on tickets to popular holiday destinations. Officially it's a package deal combined with hotel accommodation, but many agents will sell you one of these for the flight only and give you phoney hotel vouchers in the unlikely event that you're challenged at the airport.

Lost Tickets If you lose your airline ticket an airline will usually treat it like a travellers cheque and, after inquiries, issue you with another one. Legally, however, an airline is entitled to treat it like cash and if you lose it then it's gone forever. Take good care of your tickets.

MCO An MCO, or 'miscellaneous charge order', is a voucher that looks like an airline ticket but carries no destination or date. It can be exchanged through any International Association of Travel Agents (IATA) airline for a ticket on a specific flight. It's a useful alternative to an onward ticket in those countries that demand one, and is more flexible than an ordinary ticket if you're unsure of your route.

No-Shows No-shows are passengers who fail to show up for their flight. Full-fare passengers who fail to turn up are sometimes entitled to travel on a later flight. The rest are penalised (see Cancellation Penalties).

Air Travel Glossary

On Request This is an unconfirmed booking for a flight.

Onward Tickets An entry requirement for many countries is that you have a ticket out of the country. If you're unsure of your next move, the easiest solution is to buy the cheapest onward ticket to a neighbouring country or a ticket from a reliable airline which can later be refunded if you do not use it.

Open Jaw Tickets These are return tickets where you fly out to one place but return from another. If available, this can save you backtracking to your arrival point.

Overbooking Airlines hate to fly empty seats and since every flight has some passengers who fail to show up, airlines often book more passengers than they have seats. Usually excess passengers make up for the no-shows, but occasionally somebody gets 'bumped' onto the next available flight. Guess who it is most likely to be? The passengers who check in late.

Point-to-Point Tickets These are discount tickets that can be bought on some routes in return for passengers waiving their rights to a stopover.

Promotional Fares These are officially discounted fares, available from travel agencies or direct from the airline.

Reconfirmation If you don't reconfirm your flight at least 72 hours prior to departure, the airline may delete your name from the passenger list. Ring to find out if your airline requires reconfirmation.

Restrictions Discounted tickets often have various restrictions on them – such as needing to be paid for in advance and incurring a penalty to be altered. Others are restrictions on the minimum and maximum period you must be away, such as a minimum of 14 days or a maximum of one year.

Round-the-World Tickets RTW tickets give you a limited period (usually a year) in which to circumnavigate the globe. You can go anywhere the carrying airlines go, as long as you don't backtrack. The number of stopovers or total number of separate flights is decided before you set off and they usually cost a bit more than a basic return flight.

Stand-by This is a discounted ticket where you only fly if there is a seat free at the last moment. Stand-by fares are usually available only on domestic routes.

Transferred Tickets Airline tickets cannot be transferred from one person to another. Travellers sometimes try to sell the return half of their ticket, but officials can ask you to prove that you are the person named on the ticket. This is less likely to happen on domestic flights, but on an international flight tickets are compared with passports.

Travel Agencies Travel agencies vary widely and you should choose one that suits your needs. Some simply handle tours, while full-service agencies handle everything from tours and tickets to car rental and hotel bookings. If all you want is a ticket at the lowest possible price, then go to an agency specialising in discounted fares.

Travel Periods Ticket prices vary with the time of year. There is a low (off-peak) season and a high (peak) season, and often a low-shoulder season and a high-shoulder season as well. Usually the fare depends on your outward flight – if you depart in the high season and return in the low season, you pay the high-season fare.

Airlines

Aeroflot Russian International Airlines (www.aeroflot.com) is the main Russian carrier to the rest of the world. It has improved a fair amount from its notorious Soviet days. It flies a large fleet with many Boeings and Airbuses and has a passable business class and acceptable economy class. It should not be confused with the scores of domestic airlines cast off from the old Aeroflot.

Transaero is a private Russian airline offering Western-style service on mostly Western-made aircraft. It has a limited schedule of flights to Europe.

To/From Ukraine Air Ukraine and Aeroflot fly between Moscow and Kyiv (Kiev in Russian) as well as to/from Dnepropetrovsk and Donetsk. Aerosweet is a new Ukrainian airline with Western-style service and aeroplanes. It flies between Kyiv and Moscow's Vnukovo airport.

To/From Europe Aeroflot has daily flights between most of the major cities in Europe and Moscow and limited service to/from St Petersburg.

Air France has daily flights between Paris and Moscow and St Petersburg.

Austrian Airlines has daily flights between Vienna and Moscow and frequent flights to St Petersburg. It also has numerous flights to the nations surrounding Russia such as Georgia and the Baltic States.

British Airways has daily flights between London Heathrow and Moscow and frequent service between London Gatwick and Moscow and St Petersburg.

Czech Airlines has daily flights between Prague and Moscow.

Finnair has daily flights between Helsinki and Moscow and St Petersburg.

KLM has daily service between Amsterdam and Moscow.

LOT Polish Airlines has daily flights between Warsaw and Moscow and two flights a week to/from St Petersburg.

Lufthansa has an extensive schedule of flights linking Russia. There are daily flights between Frankfurt, Munich, Berlin and Dusseldorf and Moscow and daily service from Frankfurt to St Petersburg. In addition there are several flights a week linking Frankfurt with Nizhny Novgorod, Perm, Kazan, Samara and Yekaterinburg.

MALEV Hungarian Airlines has daily flights between Budapest and Moscow.

Sabena has daily flights between Brussels and Moscow.

Scandinavian Airlines has daily flights between Copenhagen and Stockholm and Moscow and frequent service between those cities and St Petersburg.

Swissair has daily flights between Geneva and Zurich and Moscow and frequent service between Zurich and St Petersburg.

Transaero has daily flights between Frankfurt and Moscow and less frequent service to/from London Gatwick.

Turkish Airlines has daily flights between Istanbul and Moscow.

To/From North America Delta has a daily flight between New York and Moscow. Aeroflot flies between Moscow and New York, Chicago, Miami, Los Angeles, San Francisco, Toronto and Montreal with varying degrees of regularity.

To/From Asia Japan Airlines has a weekly flight between Tokyo and Moscow. Air China flies twice a week between Beijing and Moscow. And showing that old ideological ties can linger on, Vietnam Airlines has a weekly flight between Hanoi and Moscow. Otherwise the only nonstop flights to/from Asia are the sporadic services offered by Aeroflot to major cities such as Delhi, Bangkok, Hong Kong, Singapore, Hanoi and Tokyo.

To/From Australasia There is no great option for flying between Australia and New Zealand and Russia. You either have to fly to an Asian city and transfer to an Aeroflot flight or go via one of the European hub airports.

To/From the Rest of the World Aeroflot has infrequent flights to a few cities in South America and Africa. If you intend to use other airlines you'll have to travel via a European hub airport. Aeroflot has frequent flights to/from the capitals of the countries of the former Soviet Union.

Buying Tickets

An air ticket alone can gouge a great slice out of anyone's budget, but you can reduce the cost by finding discounted fares. Stiff competition has resulted in widespread discounting – good news for travellers! The only people likely to be paying full fare these days are travellers flying in first or business class. Passengers flying in economy can usually manage some sort of discount. But unless you buy carefully and flexibly, it is still possible to end up paying exorbitant amounts for a journey.

For long-term travel there are plenty of discount tickets valid for 12 months, allowing multiple stopovers with open dates. For short-term travel cheaper fares are available if you are prepared to travel midweek, stay away at least one Saturday night or take advantage of short-lived promotional offers.

When you're looking for bargain air fares, go to a travel agent rather than directly to the airline. From time to time, airlines do have promotional fares and special offers but generally they only sell fares at the official listed price. This is especially true with travel to Russia, where airlines rarely have promotional fares but make many seats available at bargain rates through travel agents.

Another good source of bargain fares is the Internet. Many airlines, full-service and no-frills, offer some excellent fares to Web surfers. They may sell seats by auction or simply cut prices to reflect the reduced cost of electronic selling. Many travel agents around the world have Web sites, which can make the Internet a quick and easy way to compare prices, a good starting point for when you're ready to negotiate with your favourite travel agent. Online ticket sales work well if you are doing a simple one-way or return trip on specified dates. However, online superfast fare generators are no substitute for a travel agent who knows all about special deals, has strategies for avoiding layovers and can offer advice on everything from which airline has the best vegetarian food to the best travel insurance to bundle with your ticket.

The days when some travel agents would routinely fleece travellers by running off with their money are, happily, almost over. Paying by credit card generally offers protection, as most card issuers provide refunds if you can prove you didn't get what you paid for. Similar protection can be obtained by buying a ticket from a bonded agent, such as one covered by the Air Transport Operators License (ATOL) scheme in the UK. Agents who only accept cash should hand over the tickets straight away and not tell you to 'come back tomorrow'. After you've made a booking or paid your deposit, call the airline and confirm that the booking was made. It's generally not advisable to send money (even cheques) through the post unless the agent is very well established – some travellers have reported being ripped off by fly-by-night mail-order ticket agents.

You may decide to pay more than the rock-bottom fare by opting for the safety of a better known travel agent. Firms such as STA Travel, which has offices worldwide, Council Travel in the USA and USIT Campus (formerly Campus Travel) in the UK are not going to disappear overnight and they do offer good prices to most destinations.

If you purchase a ticket and later want to make changes to your route or get a refund, you need to contact the original travel agent. Airlines only issue refunds to the purchaser of a ticket – usually the travel agent who bought the ticket on your behalf. Many travellers change their routes halfway through their trips, so think carefully before you buy a ticket that is not easily refunded.

Student & Youth Fares Full-time students and people under 26 have access to better deals than other travellers. The better deals may not always be cheaper fares but can include more flexibility to change flights and/or routes. You have to show a document proving your date of birth or a valid International Student Identity Card (ISIC) when you're buying your ticket and boarding the plane. There are plenty of places around the world where nonstudents can get fake student cards, but if you get caught using a fake card you could have your ticket confiscated.

Courier Flights Courier flights are a great bargain if you're lucky enough to find one. Air freight companies expedite delivery of urgent items by sending them with you as your baggage allowance. You are permitted to bring along a carry-on bag, but that's all. In return, you get a steeply discounted ticket. Given the unreliability of the Russian post, many companies use air freight companies, so you may find a courier flight.

There are other restrictions: courier tickets are sold for a fixed date and schedule changes can be difficult to make. If you buy a return ticket, your schedule will be even more rigid. You need to clarify before you fly what restrictions apply to your ticket, and don't expect a refund once you've paid.

Booking a courier ticket takes some effort. They are not readily available and arrangements have to be made a month or more in advance. You won't find courier flights on all routes either – just on the major air routes.

Courier flights are occasionally advertised in the newspapers, or you could contact air freight companies listed in the phone book. You may even have to actually go to the air freight company to get an answer – the companies aren't always keen to give out information over the phone. *Travel Unlimited* (PO Box 1058, Allston, MA 02134, USA) is a monthly travel newsletter from the USA that publishes many courier flight deals from destinations worldwide. A 12-month subscription to the newsletter costs US$25, or US$35 for residents outside the USA. Another possibility (at least for US residents) is to join the International Association of Air Travel Couriers (IAATC). The membership fee of US$45 gets members a bimonthly update of air courier offerings, access to a fax-on-demand service with daily updates of last-minute specials and the bimonthly newsletter *Shoestring Traveler*. For more information, contact IAATC (☎ 561-582 8320, www.courier.org). But be aware that joining this organisation does not guarantee that you'll get a courier flight.

Ticketless Travel Ticketless travel, whereby your reservation details are contained within an airline computer, is becoming more common. On simple return trips the absence of a ticket can be a benefit – it's one less thing to worry about; however, if you are planning a complicated itinerary that you may wish to amend en route, there is no substitute for the good old paper version.

Travellers with Special Needs

Most international airlines can cater for people with special needs – travellers with disabilities, people with young children and even children travelling alone.

Special dietary preferences (vegetarian, kosher etc) can be catered for with advance notice. If you are travelling in a wheelchair, most international airports can provide an escort from check-in desk to plane where needed, and ramps, lifts, toilets and phones are generally available.

Airlines usually carry babies up to two years of age at 10% of the adult fare, although a few may carry them free of charge. Reputable international airlines usually provide nappies (diapers), tissues, talcum and all the other paraphernalia needed to keep babies clean, dry and half-happy. For children between the ages of two and 12, the fare on international flights is usually 50% of the regular fare or 67% of a discounted fare.

Departure Tax

Russian departure taxes are usually included in the price of the ticket.

The USA

Discount travel agents in the USA are known as consolidators (although you won't see a sign on the door saying Consolidator). San Francisco is the ticket consolidator capital of the USA, although some good deals can be found in Los Angeles,

New York and other big cities. Consolidators can be found through the *Yellow Pages* or the major daily newspapers. The *New York Times*, the *Los Angeles Times*, the *Chicago Tribune* and the *San Francisco Examiner* all produce weekly travel sections in which you will find a number of travel agency ads.

Council Travel, the USA's largest student travel organisation, has around 60 offices throughout that country; its head office (toll-free ☎ 800-226 8624, www.ciee.org) is at 205 E 42nd St, New York, NY 10017. STA Travel (toll-free ☎ 800-777 0112, www.statravel.com) has offices in Boston, Chicago, Miami, New York, Philadelphia, San Francisco and other major cities.

Economy class air fares to Moscow from the East Coast range from US$700 to US$1200 depending on the season. Expect to pay about US$200 more for West Coast departures. However, travel agents may be able to do much better.

Canada

Canadian discount air ticket sellers are also known as consolidators and their air fares tend to be about 10% higher than those sold in the USA. The *Globe & Mail*, the *Toronto Star*, the *Montreal Gazette* and the *Vancouver Sun* carry travel agents' ads and are a good place to look for cheap fares.

Travel CUTS (toll-free ☎ 800-667 2887, www.travelcuts.com) is Canada's national student travel agency and has offices in all major cities.

Prices for flights from Canada to Moscow are about the same as those listed earlier from the USA.

Australia

Cheap flights from Australia to Europe generally go via South-East Asian capitals, involving stopovers at Kuala Lumpur, Bangkok or Singapore. If a long stopover between connections is necessary, transit accommodation is sometimes included in the price of the ticket. If the fare requires you to pay for transit accommodation yourself, it may be worth considering a more expensive ticket.

Quite a few travel offices specialise in discount air tickets. Some travel agents, particularly smaller ones, advertise cheap air fares in the travel sections of weekend newspapers, such as *The Age* in Melbourne and *The Sydney Morning Herald*.

Two well known agents for cheap fares are STA Travel and Flight Centre. STA Travel (☎ 03-9349 2411, www.statravel.com.au) has its main office at 224 Faraday St, Carlton, VIC 3053, and offices in all major cities and on many university campuses. Call ☎ 131 776 Australia-wide for the location of your nearest branch. Flight Centre (☎ 131 600 Australia-wide, www.flightcentre.com.au) has a central office at 82 Elizabeth St, Sydney, and there are dozens of offices throughout Australia.

Published air fares to Moscow can be an uninspiring A$2000 or more, but you may find return low-season fares for around A$1500. It definitely pays to shop around.

New Zealand

The *New Zealand Herald* has a travel section in which travel agents advertise fares. Flight Centre (☎ 09-309 6171) has a large central office in Auckland at National Bank Towers (corner Queen and Darby Sts) and many branches throughout the country. STA Travel (☎ 09-309 0458) has its main office at 10 High St, Auckland, and has other offices in Auckland as well as in Hamilton, Palmerston North, Wellington, Christchurch and Dunedin. The Web address is www.statravel.com.au.

Air fares from New Zealand to Russia are as expensive as those from Australia.

The UK

Airline ticket discounters are known as bucket shops in the UK. Despite the somewhat disreputable name, there is nothing under-the-counter about them. Discount air travel is big business in London. Advertisements for many travel agents appear in the travel pages of the weekend broadsheets, such as the *Independent* on Saturday and the *Sunday Times*. Look out for the free magazines, such as *TNT*, which are widely available in London – start by looking outside the main railway and underground stations. *Time Out* is another excellent source of bargain air fares.

For students or travellers under 26, popular travel agencies in the UK include STA Travel (☎ 020-7361 6161, www.statravel.co.uk), which has an office at 86 Old Brompton Rd, London SW7 3LQ, and other offices in London and Manchester. USIT Campus Travel (☎ 020-7730 3402, www.usitcampus.com), 52 Grosvenor Gardens, London SW1WOAG, has branches throughout the UK. Both of these agencies sell tickets to all travellers but cater especially to young people and students.

Other recommended bucket shops in London include: Trailfinders (☎ 020-7938 3939), 194 Kensington High St, London W8 7RG; Bridge the World (☎ 020-7734 7447), 4 Regent Place, London W1R 5FB; as well as Flightbookers (☎ 020-7757 2000), 177-178 Tottenham Court Rd, London W1P 9LF.

Fregata Travel (☎ 020-7940 1700, fax 7940 1701, fregata@natex.co.uk), 4 Tanner St, London SE1 3LD, is good for all manner of independent travel arrangements.

Shop around and you should find return tickets between London and Moscow and St Petersburg for under £200.

Continental Europe

Though London is the travel discount capital of Europe, there are several other cities in which you will find a range of good deals. Generally, there is not much variation in air fare prices from the main European cities. All the major airlines are usually offering some sort of deal and travel agents generally have a number of deals on offer, so shop around.

Across Europe many travel agencies have ties with STA Travel, where cheap tickets can be purchased and STA-issued tickets can be altered (usually for a US$25 fee). Outlets in major cities include: Voyages Wasteels (☎ 08 03 88 70 04 (this number can only be dialled from within France), fax 01 43 25 46 25), 11 rue Dupuytren, 756006 Paris; STA Travel (☎ 030-311 0950, fax 313 0948), Goethestrasse 73, 10625 Berlin; Passaggi (☎ 06-474 0923, fax 482 7436), Stazione Termini FS, Galleria Di Tesla, Rome; and ISYTS (☎ 01-322 1267, fax 323 3767), 11 Nikis St, Upper Floor, Syntagma Square, Athens.

France has a network of student travel agencies that can supply discount tickets to travellers of all ages. OTU Voyages (☎ 01 44 41 38 50, www.otu.fr) has a central Paris office at 39 Ave Georges Bernanos (5e) and another 42 offices around the country. Acceuil des Jeunes en France (☎ 01 42 77 87 80), 119 rue Saint Martin (4e), is another popular discount travel agency.

General travel agencies in Paris that offer some of the best services and deals include Nouvelles Frontières (☎ 08 03 33 33 33, www.nouvelles-frontieres.com), 5 Ave de l'Opéra (1er); and Voyageurs du Monde (☎ 01 42 86 16 00) located at 55 rue Sainte Anne (2e).

Belgium, Switzerland, the Netherlands and Greece are also good places for buying discount air tickets. In Belgium Acotra Student Travel Agency (☎ 02-512 86 07) at rue de la Madeline, Brussels, and WATS Reizen (☎ 03-226 16 26) at de Keyserlei 44, Antwerp, are both well known agencies. In Switzerland SSR Voyages (☎ 01-297 11 11, www.ssr.ch) specialises in student, youth and budget fares. In Zurich there is a branch at Leonhardstrasse 10 and there are branches in most major cities.

In the Netherlands NBBS Reizen is the official student travel agency. You can find it in Amsterdam (☎ 020-624 09 89) at Rokin 66 and there are several other agencies around the city. Another recommended travel agent in Amsterdam is Malibu Travel (☎ 020-626 32 30) at Prinsengracht 230.

In Athens check the many travel agencies in the backstreets between Syntagma and Omonia Squares. For student and non-concessionary fares try Magic Bus (☎ 01-323 7471, fax 322 0219).

For travel agencies in European Russia see the relevant listings in the city sections.

Europe's major national airlines may publish air fares to/from Moscow and St Petersburg of US$400 to US$600 but you should be able to find deals for much less.

Asia

Although most Asian countries are now offering fairly competitive air fare deals, Bangkok, Singapore and Hong Kong are still the best places to shop around for discount tickets. Hong Kong's travel market can be unpredictable, but some excellent bargains are available if you are lucky.

Khao San Rd in Bangkok is the budget travellers' headquarters. Bangkok has a number of excellent travel agents but there are also some suspect ones; ask the advice of other travellers before handing over your cash. STA Travel (☎ 02-236 0262), 33 Surawong Rd, is a good and reliable place to start.

In Singapore STA Travel (☎ 737 7188) in the Orchard Parade Hotel, 1 Tanglin Rd, offers competitive discount fares for Asian destinations and beyond. Singapore, like Bangkok, has hundreds of travel agents, so you can compare prices on flights. Chinatown Point shopping centre on New Bridge Rd has a good selection of travel agents.

Hong Kong has a number of excellent, reliable travel agencies and some not so reliable ones. A good way to check on a travel agent is to look it up in the phone book: fly-by-night operators don't usually stay around long enough to get listed. Many travellers use the Hong Kong Student Travel Bureau (☎ 2730 3269), 8th floor, Star House, Tsimshatsui. You could also try Phoenix Services (☎ 2722 7378), 7th floor, Milton Mansion, 96 Nathan Rd, Tsimshatsui. Global Union Express (☎ 2868 3231, fax 2845 5078, guehk@netvigator.com), Room 22-23 New Henry House, 10 Ice House St, Central, books budget accommodation including the Traveller's Guest House in Moscow.

Published air fares from places like Tokyo to Moscow can top US$2000, but again, you should be able to find something for about half that.

LAND

Border Crossings

Russian visas are not issued at the border. Upon entry and exit you will have to fill out a customs declaration form. (see Customs in the European Russia Facts for the Visitor chapter for details).

Train & Bus Border crossings are a straightforward but drawn-out affair, with a steady stream of customs and ticket personnel scrutinising your passport and visa.

Car & Motorcycle You'll first pass the neighbouring country's border point, where you'll need to show your vehicle registration and insurance papers, your driving licence, passport and visa. These formalities are usually minimal for Western citizens.

On the Russian side, chances are your vehicle will be subjected to a cursory inspection by border guards (your life will be made much easier if you open all doors and the boot yourself, and shine a torch for the guards at night). You pass through customs separately from your car, walking through a metal detector and possibly having hand luggage x-rayed.

Visas

Norway US citizens, Canadians, UK citizens, Irish citizens, Australians and New Zealanders do not need a visa to enter Norway.

Finland US citizens, Canadians, UK citizens, Irish citizens, Australians and New Zealanders do not need a visa to enter Finland.

Estonia US citizens, UK citizens, Irish citizens, Australians and New Zealanders do not need a visa to enter Estonia. Canadians do.

Latvia US citizens, UK citizens and the Irish do not need a visa to enter Latvia. Canadians, Australians and New Zealanders need a visa if they do not already have one for Estonia or Lithuania.

Lithuania US citizens, Canadians, UK citizens, Irish citizens and Australians do not need a visa to enter Lithuania. New Zealand citizens do.

Poland US citizens, UK citizens and Irish citizens and do not need a visa to enter Poland. Canadians, Australians and New Zealanders do.

Belarus See the Visas section of the Belarus Facts for the Visitor chapter for details on document requirements.

Ukraine See the Visas section of the Ukraine Facts for the Visitor chapter for details on document requirements.

Georgia All travellers needs a visa to enter Georgia.

Azerbaijan All travellers needs a visa to enter Azerbaijan.

Kazakhstan All travellers needs a visa to enter Kazakhstan.

Train

Train fares for trips to/from Russia listed under individual countries in this section are for a berth in a four-berth compartment. Where applicable, they are the fares foreigners are charged (in US dollars).

Finland There are daily night trains between Helsinki and Moscow's Oktyabrskaya station. The trip costs $96 and takes 14 hours.

On the heavily travelled Helsinki-Vyborg-St Petersburg corridor the rail crossing is at Vainikkala (Luzhayka on the Russian side). There are two daily daytime trains between St Petersburg and Helsinki that take five hours. See Getting There & Away in the St Petersburg chapter.

Estonia Daily trains between Tallinn and St Petersburg cost $45 and take 11 hours.

Latvia Two trains run daily between Riga and Moscow ($50, 17 hours), crossing into Russia east of Ludza. Between Riga and St Petersburg, the daily train takes 12 hours.

Lithuania A train leaves Vilnius for Kaliningrad (seven hours) five times a day, for Moscow ($36, 18 hours) three times a day and for St Petersburg (15-17 hours) four times a day. The St Petersburg trains cross Latvia, the Moscow ones cross Belarus (see the Transit Visa section of the Belarus Facts for the Visitor chapter for transit visa details).

Poland There is one train daily linking Kaliningrad to Gdansk (six hours). There's a service twice a day between Warsaw and Moscow (20 or 24 hours), and a daily service between Warsaw and St Petersburg (29 hours). The Moscow trains enter Belarus near Brest. The St Petersburg trains leave Poland at Kuznica, which is near Hrodna (Grodno in Russian) in Belarus. Changing the wheels to/from Russia's wider gauge adds three hours to the journey.

Belarus See the Getting There & Away section of the Minsk chapter for details on train services between Russia and Belarus.

Ukraine See the Ukraine Getting There & Away chapter for details of trains crossings between Russia and Ukraine.

Georgia Hostilities in Georgia in 1999 caused all train service to/from Russia to be suspended. When the trains are running, there is overnight service between Rostov-on-Don and Tbilisi.

Azerbaijan There are trains every two days running between Moscow and Baku via Rostov-on-Don. This marathon journey takes 54 hours.

Kazakhstan & Uzbekistan There are trains every two days between Moscow and Tashkent ($97, 36 hours) and Almaty ($110, 50 hours). These trains are actually some of the better long-distance trains in Russia. Other train lines link Astrakhan with Oktyabrsk, and Novosibirsk with Tashkent and Almaty.

Bus

Norway A bus leaves Kirkenes on Wednesday, Friday and Sunday at 3 pm from the Rica Arctic Hotel and from the Hotel Polyarnye Zory in Murmansk at 9 am on the same days (the trip from Norway takes seven hours, but thanks to more efficient border crossings on the return journey, the trip *to* Norway takes only four hours). Due to military exercises along the route, it's only open to foreigners – even those with their own vehicles – on Monday, Wednesday, Friday and Sunday, from 7 am to 9 pm Norwegian time (9 am to 11 pm Kola time).

Finland Buses between Helsinki and St Petersburg take seven hours. See Getting There & Away in the St Petersburg chapter for details.

Estonia There is a bus to St Petersburg leaving from Tallinn's Autobussijaam every night. Expect to arrive in St Petersburg rumpled and cranky, with limbs aching, nine hours later.

Latvia There are daily buses between Riga and Kaliningrad that take 10 hours.

Poland See the Getting There & Away section in the Kaliningrad section of the Western European Russia chapter for details on buses to/from towns in Poland.

Azerbaijan There are buses between Derbent and Makhachkala, the capital of Dagestan, and Baku.

Car & Motorcycle

Foreigners can legally drive on almost all of Russia's highways and can even ride motorcycles. On the down side, driving in Russia is truly an unfiltered Russian experience. Poor roads, maddeningly inadequate signposting, low-quality petrol and keen highway patrolmen can lead to frustration and dismay. See the European Russia Getting Around chapter for specific driving tips and information on road rules and fuel.

The Basics To be allowed to drive your own or a rented car/motorcycle in Russia you'll need to be 18 years old and have a full driving licence. In addition, you'll need an International Driving Permit with a Russian translation of your licence, or a certified Russian translation of your full licence (you can certify translations at a Russian embassy or consulate).

You will also need your vehicle's registration papers and proof of insurance. Be sure your insurance covers you in Russia. Your insurance agent at home or one in Finland may also be able to get you a policy covering driving in Russia. In the UK, Black Sea and Baltic Insurance (☎ 020-7709 9202) can provide you with all you need.

Finally, a customs declaration promising that you will take your vehicle with you when you leave is also required.

Departure Tax A departure road tax of about US$10 is collected at the border.

Finland Highways cross at the Finnish border posts of Nuijamaa and Vaalimaa (Brusnichnoe and Torfyanovka respectively on the Russian side). From these towns to St Petersburg the road is said to be infested with modern-day highwaymen (though we've driven it dozens of times and never had any difficulties). Don't stop for anybody, fill up with petrol on the Finnish side (preferably before you get to the border filling station, which is more expensive than others and closes early). There's a radar speed-trap just outside the St Petersburg city line where the limit is 60km/h (hint: radar detectors are legal in Russia). Be sure and watch for all road signs; a few involve tricky curves and signposting is not all it should be. It's best to make this drive for the first time during daylight hours.

Estonia The nearest border crossing from Tallinn is at Narva and the road from there to St Petersburg is uneventful, if not particularly fast.

Latvia The M9 Riga-Moscow road crosses the border east of Rezekne (Latvia). The A212 road from Riga leads to Pskov, crossing a corner of Estonia en route.

Lithuania The A229 to Kaliningrad crosses the border at Kybartai. Most roads to the rest of Russia cross Belarus.

Poland The main border crossing between Poland and Kaliningrad is near Bagrationovsk on the A195 highway. Lines can be very long.

Belarus See the Belarus Getting There & Away chapter for details on road links between Russia and Belarus.

Ukraine See the Ukraine Getting There & Away chapter for details on road links between Russia and Ukraine.

Georgia There are two main routes between Russia and Georgia. One route heads south along the Black Sea from Sochi from where it is 629km to Tbilisi. The other is the spectacular Georgian Military Hwy through the Caucasus – it's 220km from Vladikavkaz to Tbilisi.

Azerbaijan The same road used by the Dagestan-Baku buses can be used by cars although the various wars in the area should give drivers pause for thought.

Kazakhstan Roads into Kazakhstan head east from Astrakhan, and south from Samara, Chelyabinsk and Omsk.

SEA

Opportunities to reach European Russia by sea have dried up. There is no scheduled passenger service on the Baltic Sea and nothing at all on the Black or Caspian seas.

There is a four day return cruise from Helsinki to St Petersburg run by Kristina Cruises (☎ 09-5211 144, fax 5211 4500, www.kristinatours.com). The costs range from US$410 to US$975 per person. Its US agent is EuroCruises (☎ 212-691 2099, toll-free ☎ 800-688 3876, fax 212-366 4747), 303 W 13th St, New York, NY 10014.

ORGANISED TOURS

Nowadays, virtually any travel agent in the world can assist you with bookings, confirmations and domestic travel tickets for many areas of Russia. You needn't go through a Russia specialist or Intourist to book your trip, though the more experience your agent has, the better off you'll probably be.

The following agencies provide a range of tours and travel services to Russia. Numerous more Russian-based agencies can provide tours once you are there.

Australia

Eastern Europe Travel Bureau (☎ 02-9262 1144, fax 9262 4479), 75 King St, Sydney, NSW 2000 – does budget tours to European Russia.

Gateway Travel (☎ 02-9745 3333, fax 9745 3237, gatrav@magna.com.au), 48 The Boulevarde, Strathfield, NSW 2135 – one of the best agencies, with a wide variety of specialised tours, excursions and services, including budget group tours.

Passport Travel (☎ 03-9867 3888, fax 9867 1055, passport@travelcentre.com.au), Suite 11, 410 St Kilda Rd, Melbourne, VIC 3004 – arranges visa invitations, independent travel, language courses, trans-Siberia travel and more.

Canada

RJ's Tours (☎ 780-415 5633 or ☎ 877-353 5633, fax 780-415 5639, ttravel@connect.ab.ca), 11708 – 135A St, Edmonton, AB Canada T5M-1L5 – tours galore.

The UK

Exodus Adventure (☎ 020-8675 5550, fax 8673 0779, www.exodustravels.co.uk), 9 Weir Rd, London SW12 0LT – organises adventure travel throughout Russia.

GW Travel Ltd (☎ 0161-928 9410, fax 941 6101, www.gwtravel.co.uk), 6 Old Market Place, Altrincham, Cheshire WA14 4NP – offers rail tours of Russia on private trains.

Inntel Moscow (☎ 020-7937 7207, fax 7938 2912, inntelmoscow@inntel-moscow.co.uk, www.inntel-moscow.co.uk), 167-169 High St Kensington, London W8 6SH – arranges all manner of trips.

Page & Moy Holidays (☎ 0116-250 7979), 136-140 London Rd, Leicester LE2 1ED – specialises in river cruises.

Russia Experience (☎ 020-8566 8846, fax 8566 8843, www.trans-siberian.co.uk) – has years of experience in Russia and can help you with transport, tours and bookings, or put together an all-inclusive adventure.

Scotts Tours (☎ 020-7383 5353, fax 7383 3709, sales@scottstours.co.uk), 141 Whitfield St, London W1P 5RY – makes independent touring arrangements and specialises in arranging internal travel details.

Travel For The Arts (☎ 020-7483 4466, fax 7586 0639, www.travelforthearts.co.uk), 117 Regent's Park Rd, London NW1 8UR – organises luxury culture-based tours to Russia (particularly St Petersburg) and other European destinations for people with a specific interest in opera and ballet.

Voyages Jules Verne (☎ 020-7616 1000), 21 Dorset Square, London NW1 6QG – organises numerous Russian boat tours.
Wallace Arnold Tours (☎ 0113-231 0739, fax 231 0563), Gelderd Rd, Leeds LS12 6DH – operates bus tours between the UK and Russia aimed at older travellers.

The USA

Cruise Marketing International (toll-free ☎ 800-578 7742, www.cruiserussia.com), 200-A Industrial Rd, San Carlos, CA 94070 – books tours on cruises along Russian waterways such as the Volga River.
Departures International (☎ 415-563 5959, fax 563 5935), 1793 Union St, San Francisco, CA 94123 – leads gay and lesbian groups to Moscow and St Petersburg.
General Tours (☎ 603-357 5033, toll-free ☎ 800-221 2216), 53 Summer St, Keene, NH 03431 – is a well established company offering 'to your right is the Kremlin'-style packages to Moscow, St Petersburg and the Golden Ring for a wide range of prices.
Russiatours (☎ 813-987 2477, fax 988 6420, www.russiatours.com), 13312 N 56th St, Suite 102, Tampa, FL 33617 – offers luxurious group tours.
Russia Travel Bureau (☎ 212-986 1500, fax 490 1650, russtvl@interserv.com), 225 East 44th St, New York, NY 10017 – provides a full range of cruises, all-inclusive tours and other arrangements.

Intourist

Intourist is no longer the monolithic monopoly it once was (although a few bureaus may still act like it). The following companies are all related to the surviving Intourist structure to some extent. They usually have an extensive selection of tours and other services available.

Asia
Intourist Japan (☎ 03-3238 9118, fax 3238 9110), 5F Daihachi-Tanaka Bldg 5-1 Goban-cho, Chiyoda-Ku, Tokyo, Japan
Intourist Bangkok (☎ 662 236 9800, fax 662 236 9789), 2 KCC Building, 5th Floor, Silom Soi 9, Silom Rd, Bangkok 10500, Thailand
Canada
Intours Corporation (☎ 416-566 4720, fax 766 8507, intours@pathcom.com), 2051 Bloor St, Suite 308, West Toronto, TM6S 1M8
The UK
Intourist Travel Ltd (☎ 020-7538 8600, fax 7538 5967, info@intourist.co.uk, www.intourist.co.uk) 219 Marsh Wall, London E14 9FJ
The USA
Intourist USA (☎ 561-586 5305, fax 586 1353, info@intourist-usa.com), 12 South Dixie Hwy, Lake Worth, Fl 33460

Adventure Travel

The following Russian travel companies specialise in adventure travel to some of the remoter and wilder parts of Russia.

Pilgrim Tours (☎ 095-208 1040, fax 207 3243, pilgrim@glasnet.ru), ulitsa Neglinnaya, strovenie 2, Moscow 103031 – has a range of itineraries.
Sputnik Russia (☎ 095-939 8031, fax 938 1946), ulitsa Kosygina 15, Moscow – has many plans including horse riding tours of the Altay Mountains.
Team Gorky Adventure Travel Company (☎ 8312-65 19 99, fax 63 24 44, teamgork@ray.unn.runnet.ru), ulitsa 40 Let Oktiabria 1a, Nizhny Novgorod 603062 – organises outdoor travel in Russia, including Siberia.
Via Logo (☎/fax 095-132 7409), Leningradsky prospekt 87A, office 305, Moscow 117313 – has hiking, white-water rafting and other adventures.

Getting Around

Many of the memories of your Russian travels that last you a lifetime will stem from the efforts you make to get around the world's largest country.

AIR

The former Soviet state airline, Aeroflot, has been decentralised into hundreds of smaller airlines ('baby-flots'). These come and go with such a rapidity that not even the Russian Department of Air Transport (RDAT) can say how many exist. Sometimes a new baby-flot is created when a few pilots take over a disused plane and announce they are going to fly somewhere and start selling tickets. The same airline may vanish from the scene about the time the first fuel bill is due.

The upshot of this orgy of aerobatic entrepreneurship is virtually unregulated skies and a bad safety record. Tales of Russian airline safety lapses are common, though often apocryphal. Getting reliable statistics is difficult but people familiar with the Russian aviation scene say that the safety of domestic airlines differs widely.

Generally, Aeroflot Russian International Airlines is thought to have the highest standards. This airline took over the old international routes of the Soviet-era Aeroflot and today offers Western-style services on mostly Western-made aircraft such as the Boeing 777. The airline also offers domestic services on many routes, so it may be worth determining if the Aeroflot you're thinking of flying is the international one or one of the hundreds of 'baby-flots' – many of whom apparently can't afford the paint to eradicate the old Aeroflot logos from their planes. Check out the Web site at www.aeroflot.com for further information.

The question is how to decide if an airline is safe enough to fly? If Aeroflot Russian International Airlines and Transaero Airlines are considered to have the best record (despite an Aeroflot accident over Thailand in 1994 when the pilot allowed his young son to take the controls of the Airbus with predictably fatal results), then how can you determine which airlines are worst? The simple answer is you can't. Whether or not to fly domestically in Russia is a choice only you can make: you will most likely arrive in one piece, but is it worth the risk? When making up your mind, consider that alternatives such as travelling by road might be even more unsafe. And certainly there may be times when, faced with a 55 hour train ride, you will opt for a three hour flight.

Domestic Air Services

Forget everything you know about flying elsewhere in the world: flying in Russia is like the country itself – unique.

Timetables These are often fantasy-based. Many flights (except those between major cities) are delayed, often for hours and with no explanation offered.

If you're lucky enough to see a domestic flights timetable, and able to decipher it, you'll find that all the airlines are listed together (if you look very closely you'll see that each has a different flight code). You may never actually know which airline you're flying on because they generally share the same ticket outlets and check-in facilities – and many of them still haven't got round to writing their own names on their planes in place of Aeroflot.

Some routes are served by two or even three different airlines, others by just one. Some have names that make determining their routes easy, such as Astrakhan Air.

Buying Tickets Air tickets for virtually all domestic Russian airlines, and airlines of former Soviet republics, can be purchased from offices in cities all over Russia (see city chapters for locations) and through travel agents in Russia or abroad. Note that the city ticket offices often still have a huge Aeroflot sign over the door even if none of the airlines serving that town actually uses that name.

Generally speaking, you'll do better booking internal flights once you arrive in Russia, where more flights and flight information are available, and where prices may be lower.

Whenever you book airline tickets in Russia you'll need your passport and visa. Most Aeroflot offices in the country have a special window for foreigners and international flights, so you won't have to wait in huge queues, though you will pay foreigner rates unless you have a student or diplomatic visa. At crowded ticket offices it's a good idea to get to any window you can and show your passport, making it clear that you're a foreigner. Since foreigners have to pay more for their tickets, staff are often keen to sell to foreigners and may even find seats on supposedly full planes. Flight tickets can also be purchased at the airport right up to the departure of the plane and sometimes even if the city/town centre office says that the plane is full.

Costs Although foreigners continue to be charged higher fares on most routes, at the time of research this differential was often as low as $1. Fares can be very reasonable – sometimes little more than a berth on a train.

Return fares are usually just double the one-way fares. The following approximate one-way foreigner fares (in US dollars) and flying times from Moscow to other Russian cities are representative of those throughout the country:

destination	cost	duration (hours)
Arkhangelsk	$45	3
Astrakhan	$64	2¼
Irkutsk	$90	7½
Murmansk	$54	3
Novgorod	$33	1½
Novosibirsk	$70	4
Sochi	$130	2½
St Petersburg	$41	1½ (Transaero)
Vladivostok	$112	9
Yekaterinburg	$53	2½

Check-In & Luggage Check-in is 90 to 40 minutes before departure and airlines are entitled to bump you if you come later than that. To minimise the danger of loss or theft, try not to check in any baggage: many planes have special stowage areas for large carry-on pieces. Also note that you put your carry-on luggage under your own seat, not the one in front of you.

Have your passport and ticket handy throughout the various security and ticket checks that can last right up until you find a seat. Some flights have assigned seats, others do not. On the latter, seating is a free-for-all.

Service We've had good reports of the service on Aeroflot Russian International Airlines and Transaero. On all others, service can vary as widely as everything else. Some airlines are known for parsimoniously handing out a few cups of water and maybe a boiled egg. Others supply meals of varying quality. On one we were presented with an impressive selection of snacks and drinks. Only as the plane began its descent were we handed a bill.

TRAIN

European Russia is crisscrossed with an extensive rail network that makes rail a viable means of getting to practically anywhere. Train journeys are cheap and relatively comfortable but they usually take a long, long time. If you like trains, and if you or your travelling partner speaks good Russian, they're an excellent way to get around, see the countryside and meet Russians from all walks of life. A good 1st or 2nd class berth on a Russian sleeper train could prove more civilised than one in Western Europe, as they're often larger and more comfortable.

Trains have a remarkable on-time record. A 55 hour journey will depart and leave every station to the minute, something British and American train travellers can hardly fathom. However, there are underlying reasons for this punctuality. Managers have a large part of their pay determined by the timeliness of their trains. This not only inspires promptness, but it results in the creation of schedules that are at best forgiving. You'll notice this when you find your train stationary for hours in the middle of nowhere only suddenly to start up and roll into the next station right on time.

Another inconvenience of Russian train travel is that, like roads and Rome, all train lines seem to lead to Moscow. Thus journeys to cities that are geographically close but lie on two different lines can be very long, as the train goes part way to Moscow before joining the line to its destination. Think of the spokes of a large wheel without the rim.

Foreigners are also expected to purchase special foreigner tickets at two to three times the normal price.

Types of Train

There is nothing quite like the smell of a Russian train: it's a mixture of coal smoke and coffee, cigarettes and sweat, sausage and vodka, garlic and beef pie and dozens of other elements that combine to form an aroma that's neither bad nor good but so distinctive it will be permanently etched in your mind's nose.

Long Distance The regular long-distance service is a fast train *(skoryy poezd)*. It stops more often than the typical intercity train in the West and rarely gets up enough speed really to merit the 'fast' label. Foreigners booking rail tickets through agencies are usually put on a skoryy train. The best skoryy trains often have names. These name trains *(firmennye poezdy)* generally have cleaner cars, polite(er) attendants and more convenient arrival/departure hours; they sometimes also have fewer stops, more 1st class accommodation or functioning restaurants.

A passenger train *(passazhirskiy poezd)* is an intercity stopping train, found mostly on routes of 1000km or less. These can take an awfully long time, as they clank and lurch from one small town to the next.

Short Distance A suburban train *(prigorodnyy poezd*, also called an *elektrichka)* is a local service linking a city and its suburbs or nearby towns, or groups of adjacent towns – often useful for day trips, though they can be fearfully crowded. There's no need to book ahead for these – just buy your ticket and go. In bigger stations there may be separate timetables, ticket halls (usually called the *prigorodnyy zal*) and platforms for these trains.

Classes

With a reservation, your ticket will normally give the numbers of your carriage *(vagon)* and seat *(mesto)*.

1st Class Compartments in a 1st class carriage, also called soft class *(myagkiy)* or sleeping car *(spalnyy vagon, SV* or *lyux)*, have upholstered seats and convert to comfortable sleeping compartments for two people. You will be given two sheets, a washcloth, a pillowcase and a blanket. Your mattress will be rolled up on the seats at the beginning of the journey. On some name trains they even now give you a little amenity kit.

2nd Class Compartments in a 2nd class carriage, also called compartmentalised *(kupeynyy* or *kupe)* or hard class *(zhyostkiy)*, are four-person (occasionally three-person) couchettes. The four and three-person varieties are sometimes given as 2/4 and 2/3 on fare lists (1/2 is 1st class, two person). Seats are leather or plastic and also form the lower pair of bunks. You have to pay a fee (usually about $1) to the conductor *(provodnik)* for your bedding.

Other Classes Reserved-place *(platskartnyy)*, sometimes also called hard class or 3rd class, has open bunk accommodation. Groups of hard bunks are partitioned, but not closed off, from each other, and many more are squeezed in than in 1st or 2nd class. This class is low on comfort, privacy and security.

General *(obshchiy)*, also called 4th class, is unreserved bench-type seating. At times there might be room to lie down, while at other times there might not be enough room to sit. Prigorodnyy trains normally have only this type of accommodation. On a few daytime-only intercity trains there are higher grade obshchiy carriages with more comfortable, reserved chairs. Obshchiy is rare on skoryy trains.

Timetables

The whole Russian rail network mostly runs on Moscow time. You'll usually find timetables and station clocks on Moscow time, but if in doubt confirm these details carefully. The only general exception is suburban rail services, which stick to local time.

Most stations have an information window that charges for information. Expect the attendant to speak only Russian, to give only a bare minimum of information and to demand additional money (usually $0.10) if your first question doesn't elicit a satisfactory answer and you are forced to ask another question.

See the boxed text 'Reading a Train Timetable' for ways to crack these railroad Rosetta stones.

Buying Tickets

Except in St Petersburg and Moscow (see those city chapters), getting tickets for the Russian price is generally not much more difficult than getting Russian train tickets of any description – an art in and of itself, because most train station ticket windows are maddeningly inefficient, and long waits are the rule.

As far as paying the Russian price, it's quite a simple matter of being able to speak Russian and act like a local. Note, however, that many car attendants and conductors will check to see that you have a foreigner ticket if they suspect you are a foreigner; on many trains they check everybody's passport. Foreigners caught with a Russian ticket will have to pay a fine – either real or invented – on the spot. Given the cheap cost of tickets (see Costs later in this section) it may not be worth the hassle of trying to use a Russian ticket.

There are several ticket windows in larger stations: usually one or more general ticket windows (for the purchase of all ticket types) and one or more 'special' windows exclusively for veterans, the elderly or infirm, heroes of the Great Patriotic War, passengers travelling with children and foreigners. Queuing at one of the special windows means risking a long wait only to be told you're in the wrong queue.

Once you get to the front of the queue, you can usually get the ticket you want fairly easily provided you have all the information you need – your destination, the train number, the date and time of departure, the type of accommodation and the number of tickets – and even more easily if you have all this written down in Cyrillic. Use ordinary (Arabic) numerals for the day of the month and Roman numerals for the month. See the boxed text 'Reading a Train Timetable' for more information.

You can usually get a seat on a 'sold-out' train by speaking with a carriage attendant (*provodnik* (male) or *provodnitsa* (female)). If you don't have a ticket, try to find a friendly provodnik, state your destination, and offer a price. To estimate prices for Russian citizens, subtract a third to a half from the prices in the table. Offer the face ticket price first and move slowly upwards from there – you can usually come to some sort of agreement.

Suburban Trains Tickets for these – which are very cheap – are often sold at separate windows. There are also machines *(avtomaticheskie kassy)* that sometimes work. A table beside the machine tells you which price zone *(zona)* your destination is in.

Costs

Foreigners are supposed to pay higher fares than those Russians pay. The difference between foreigner and Russian fares goes up and down – and also varies from route to route: at the time of writing foreigner fares were mostly 50% to 100% higher than Russian fares.

First class fares are generally 60% to 100% higher than 2nd class; 3rd class is about 40% less than 2nd class; 4th class is about 60% less than 2nd class. If you have children, one child under five travels free; other children under 10 pay half fare.

Reading a Train Timetable

Russian train timetables vary from place to place but generally list: a destination; train number; category of train; frequency of service; and time of departure and arrival, in *Moscow time* unless otherwise noted (see the following information on arrival and departure times).

Trains in smaller city stations generally begin somewhere else, so you'll see a starting point and a destination on the timetable. For example, when catching a train from Petrozavodsk to Murmansk, the timetable may list Moscow as an origination point and Murmansk as the destination. The following are a few key points to look out for.

Number Номер *(Nomer)*. The higher the number of a train, the slower it is; anything over 900 is likely to be a mail train.

Category Скорый, Пассажирский, Почтовый-багажный, Пригородный *(Skory, Passazhirsky, Pochtovy-bagazhny, Prigorodny)*, and various abbreviations thereof, are train categories and refer, respectively, to fast, passenger, post-cargo and suburban trains. There may also be the name of the train, usually in Russian quotation marks, eg "Нижегородец„ *('Nizhegorodets')*.

Frequency Ежедневно (*yezhednevno*, daily); чётные (*chyotnye*, even dates); нечётные (*nechyotnye*, odd dates); отменён (*otmenyon*, cancelled). All of these, as well, can appear in various abbreviations. Days of the week are listed usually as numbers (where 1 is Monday and 7 Sunday) or as abbreviations of the name of the day (Пон, Вт, Ср, Чт, Пт, Сб and Вск are, respectively, Monday to Sunday).

On some trains, frequency depends on the time of year, in which case details are usually given in hard-to-decipher, abbreviated, small print: eg '27/VI – 31/VIII Ч; 1/IX – 25/VI 2,5' means that from 27 June to 31 August the train runs on even dates, while from 1 September to 25 June it runs on Tuesday and Friday.

Arrival & Departure Times Most train times are given in a 24-hour time format, and almost always in Moscow time (Московское время, *Moskovskoe vremya*). But suburban trains are usually marked in local time (местное время, *mestnoe vremya*). From here in it gets tricky (as though the rest wasn't), so don't confuse the following:

время отправления *(vremya otpravlenia)*, which means time of departure;
время отправления с началного пункта *(vremya otpravlenia s nachalnogo punkta)*, the time of departure from the train's starting point;
время прибытия *(vremya pribytia)*, the time of arrival at the station you're in;
время прибытия на конечный пункт *(vremya pribytia na konechny punkt)*, the time of arrival at the destination;
время в пути *(vremya v puti)*, the duration of the journey.

Corresponding trains running in opposite directions on the same route may appear on the same line of the timetable. In this case you may find route entries like время отправления с конечного пункта *(vremya otpravlenia s konechnogo punkta)*, or the time the return train leaves its station of origin.

Distance You may sometimes see the растнояние *(rastoyanie)* – distance in kilometres – on the timetable as well, but they're probably lying.

Fares are frequently hiked upward by large amounts to compensate for inflation. In this book we don't generally give train fares in regional chapters, as they tend to be so variable.

The following table is a rough guide only. At the time of writing, these were typical prices (in US dollars) for foreigner 2nd class fares on skoryy trains between Moscow and a number of Russian cities, purchased from train stations or other official sources:

destination	cost
Arkhangelsk	$26
Astrakhan	$36
Irkutsk	$104
Kaliningrad	$54
Kazan	$28
Khabarovsk	$74
Kursk	$16
Murmansk	$38
Nizhny Novgorod	$22
Novgorod	$21
Novosibirsk	$41
Oryol	$12
Perm	$40
Pskov	$20
Pyatigorsk	$52
Rostov-on-Don	$42
Smolensk	$14
Sochi	$52
St Petersburg	$26
Ulan-Ude	$116
Vladikavkaz	$46
Vladivostok	$140
Vologda	$18
Vyborg	$22
Yekaterinburg	$38

On the Journey

The compartments are comfortable but can get a little close after several hours. You can stow your luggage in the steel bins beneath the lower bunks or above the door – the bins are safer. Smoking is forbidden in the compartments, but permitted in the spaces at the ends of the cars, past the toilets or the attendant's room.

The provodnik or provodnitsa may not smile too often, but they are generally among the best hearted service workers in the country, providing cups of tea from their samovars – though you shouldn't rely on these for all your liquid intake – and often a wake-up call (or bellow) on arrival. On long trips it's well worth your while to be friendly to the attendant.

Sleeping compartments are mixed sex; when women show that they want to change or get out of bed, men go out and loiter in the corridor. Be aware that toilets can be locked long before and after station stops.

Food & Drink Take as much food and drink with you as you think you'll need for the whole trip. The food in restaurant cars, if there is any, is not good, and you're unlikely to find much edible at halts along the way. On long trips Russian travellers bring great bundles of food that they spread out and – as dictated by railway etiquette – offer to each other; you should do the same. Always remember to bring along bottled water for the trip as there'll be none available on the train. Almost every train in Russia has a samovar at the end of the carriage filled with boiling water that's safe to drink.

At many stations, hawkers will come aboard selling beer, soft drinks, sandwiches and other food and, near borders, cigarettes and vodka. Be suspicious of all food sold like this.

Left Luggage

Many train stations have either a left-luggage room (камера хранения, *kamera khranenia)* or left-luggage lockers (автоматические камеры хранения, *avtomaticheskie kamery khranenia*). These are generally secure, but make sure you note down their opening and closing hours and, if in doubt, establish how long you can leave your stuff for.

Here is how to work the left-luggage lockers (they're generally the same everywhere). Be suspicious of people who offer to help you work them, above all when it comes to selecting your combination.

1. Buy two tokens *(zhetony)* from the attendant.
2. Find an empty locker and put your stuff in.
3. Decide on a combination of one Russian letter and three numbers and write it down.
4. Set the combination on the inside of the locker door.
5. Put one token in the slot.
6. Close the locker.

To open the locker, set your combination on the outside of your locker door. Note that even though it seems as if the knobs on the outside of the door should correspond directly with those on the inside, the letter is always the left-most knob, followed by three numbers, on both the inside and the outside. After you've set your combination, put a token in the slot, wait a second or two for the electrical humming sound and then pull open the locker.

Dangers & Annoyances

Some intercity trains have been plagued by midnight rip-offs. Make certain on all sleepers that your baggage is stowed, preferably in the steel bins beneath the lower bunks. When you lock your door, remember that it can be unlocked with a rather simple key; on the left side of the door about three-quarters of the way up there's a small steel switch that flips up, blocking the door from opening more than a few centimetres. Flip this switch up and make sure to stuff a piece of cork in the cavity so it can't be flipped back down by a bent coat-hanger.

Generally, Russians love speaking with foreigners; on long train rides, they love drinking with them as well. Turning this down is not always as easy as it would seem. Choose your drinking partners very carefully on trains, and only drink from new bottles and only when you can watch the seal being broken. If you have a bad feeling about someone, saying '*Ya alkogolik/alkogolichka*' ('I'm an alcoholic', in masculine and feminine forms) will usually stop them from pressing you further.

BUS

Russian buses are a great but slow way to travel between small towns. In some regions, like border areas, central Karelia, south-western Russia and the Kola Peninsula, bus travel may be the only option you have. There are no foreigner prices on buses – you pay the same as Russians. But Russia's long-distance bus stations – like those everywhere – are scoundrel magnets, and are rarely pleasant places to visit after dark.

Buying Tickets

Most cities have a main intercity bus station (автовокзал, *avtovokzal*, *af-tah-vahk-ZAHL*), usually called the central bus station *(tsentralnyy avtovokzal)* even if it's on the edge of town. Prices are comparable to Russian-price 2nd class train fares; journey times depend on road conditions but probably average somewhere between those of a *skoryy* and a *passazhirskiy* train.

Tickets are sold at the station, where smouldering queues wait quasi-patiently for the window to begin selling seats. This usually happens an hour or two before a bus is scheduled to depart. Ticket prices are normally listed on the timetable and posted on a wall. As often as not you'll get a ticket with a seat assignment.

If tickets seem to be sold out, you can, of course, negotiate with the driver. Note that it's illegal for buses to carry more passengers than they have seats; drivers may ask those standing to duck when the bus passes road checkpoints.

Costs

At the time of research, the average bus fare seemed to equate to roughly US$1 for every hour of scheduled journey time.

HIRED CARS

These are private cars operating as cabs over long distances. Since they take the most direct route between cities the savings in time can be considerable over slow trains and meandering buses.

Typically you will find drivers offering this service outside of bus terminals. Someone in your party must speak Russian to negotiate a price with the driver that typically works out to about $0.12 a kilometre. This can be a great deal with a 500km journey costing $60 for up to three people.

Select your driver carefully, look over his car and try to assess his sobriety before setting off.

CAR & MOTORCYCLE

Driving in Russia isn't everybody's cup of tea but if you've got a sense of humour and don't mind some fairly rugged road conditions, a few hassles finding petrol, and getting lost now and then, it's an adventurous way to see European Russia. You experience at least one aspect of Russian reality as the locals do, see more of the countryside, and have total independence from the Russian transportation system until you run out of petrol.

Motorbikes will undergo vigorous scrutiny by border officials and highway police, especially if you're riding anything vaguely Ninja-ish. But one traveller said that while riding his hand-built motorcycle across Russia, the only attention he attracted from the police consisted of admiring questions and comments.

It's definitely not wise to ride a motorcycle in major cities, where crime is high and traffic police are widespread. Finally, while foreign automobile companies now have an established presence in Moscow, St Petersburg and other cities, motorcycles in the former Soviet Union are almost exclusively Russian or East German-made – it is to be doubted that a Ural-brand carb will fit your Hog.

See the Car & Motorcycle section of the European Russia Getting There & Away chapter for information on planning and preparing a trip to Russia with your own vehicle and details on border crossings.

Road Rules

Russians drive on the right and traffic coming from the right has the right of way. Speed limits are generally 60km/h in towns and between 80 and 110km/h on highways. There may be a 90km/h zone, enforced by speed traps, as you leave a city. Children under 12 may not travel in the front seat, and safety belt use is mandatory. Motorcycle riders (and passengers) must wear crash helmets.

Technically the maximum legal blood-alcohol content is 0.04%, but in practice it is illegal to drive after consuming *any* alcohol at all. This is a rule that is strictly enforced. The normal way of establishing alcohol in the blood is by a blood test but apparently you can be deemed under its influence even without any test.

Traffic lights that flicker green are about to change to yellow, then red.

The GAI The State Automobile Inspectorate, GAI (*gah-yee*, short for Gosudarstvennaya Avtomobilnaya Inspektsia), skulks about on the roadsides, waiting for speeding, headlightless or other miscreant vehicles. Officers of the GAI are authorised to stop you (they do this by pointing their striped, sometimes lighted, stick at you and waving you towards the side), issue on-the-spot fines (in roubles only – you should get a receipt) and, worst of all, shoot at your car if you refuse to pull over.

The GAI also hosts the occasional speed trap – the Moscow-Brest, Moscow-Oryol and Vyborg-St Petersburg roads have reputations for this. In cities, the GAI is everywhere, stopping cars for no discernible reason and collecting 'fines' on the spot. There are permanent GAI checkpoints at the boundary of many Russian cities and towns. For serious infractions, the GAI can confiscate your licence, which you'll have to retrieve from the main station. GAI guys have been known to shake down foreigners. Don't give them any hard currency. Get receipts for any fine you pay and if you think you've been ripped off, head for the nearest GAI office and complain. Get the shield number of the 'arresting' officer.

On the Road

Russian main roads are a mixed bag – sometimes smooth, straight dual carriageways, sometimes rough, narrow, winding and choked with the diesel fumes of the slow, heavy vehicles that make up a high proportion of Russian traffic. Driving much more than 300km in a day is pretty tiring.

Russian drivers use indicators far less than they should, and like to overtake everything on the road – on the inside. Priority rules at roundabouts seem to vary from area to area: all you can do is follow local practice. Russian drivers rarely switch on anything more than sidelights – and often not even those – until it's pitch black at night. Some say this is to avoid dazzling others, as for some reason dipping headlights is not a common practice.

Fuel

Joint-venture and other Western-style gas stations are becoming common. Petrol comes in four main grades – 76, 93, 95 and 98 octane. Prices are cheap by European standards: $0.12 a litre for 76 octane and $0.27 a litre for 98 octane. Unleaded gas is becoming available in major cities – BP or Castrol gas stations usually always have it. Diesel *(dizel)* is available. Petrol stations aren't often more than 100km apart, but don't rely on it.

Car Rental

You can rent self-drive cars in Moscow and St Petersburg – see the relevant city chapters for details. Elsewhere, renting a car that comes with a driver is the norm. This can be a blessing given the nature of Russian roads. Away from the largest cities you can rent a car and driver for about $5 an hour through hotels and travel agencies.

HITCHING

Hitching is never entirely safe in any country in the world, and Lonely Planet doesn't recommend it. Travellers who hitch should understand that they are taking a small but potentially serious risk. People who do choose to hitch will be safer if they travel in pairs and let someone know where they are planning to go.

That said, hitching in Russia is a very common method of getting around. In cities, hitching rides is called hailing a cab, no matter what type of vehicle stops (see Taxis in the Local Transport section later in this chapter). In the countryside, especially in remote areas not well served by public transport, hitching is a major mode of transport. Rides are hailed by standing at the side of the road and flagging passing vehicles with a low, up-and-down wave (not an extended thumb). You're expected to pitch in for petrol; paying what would be the normal bus fare for a long-haul ride is considered appropriate.

While hitching is widely accepted here – and therefore safer than in some other countries – there are always yahoos and lunatics puttering down the nation's highways and byways. Use common sense and keep safe. Avoid hitching at night. Women should exercise extreme caution and everyone should avoid hitching alone.

BOAT

The great rivers that wind across the flat expanses of Russia are the country's oldest highways. A millennium ago the early Russians based their power on control of the waterborne trade between the Baltic and Black seas. River transport remains important and in summer it's possible to travel long distances across Russia on passenger boats. You can do this either by taking a cruise, bookable through agencies in the West (often expensive) or in Russia, or by using scheduled river passenger services. The season runs from late May to mid-October but is shorter on some routes.

The biggest problem with travelling by boat is that the economic crisis has severely reduced services. In many cases the only way to find out what's running will be to go down to the river station *(rechnoy vokzal)* and see for yourself.

On timetables and fare tables, Raketa, Kometa and Meteor are all types of hydrofoil; fast *(skoraya)* usually refers to steamships, high-speed *(gidrofoyl, skorostnaya)* or underwater-winged *(na podvodnykh krylyakh)* to hydrofoils. *Vverkh* means upstream and *vnizu* downstream, while *tuda* means one way and *krugovoy* return.

Major Routes

European Russia's main waterway network extends from St Petersburg to Astrakhan, near the Volga's delta on the Caspian Sea, via the Neva, Svir and Volga rivers and a series of linking canals. Moscow is part of this system.

Moscow to St Petersburg There are numerous boats plying the routes between Moscow and St Petersburg. Many of these boats stop at some of the Golden Ring cities on the way.

Most of the trips are aimed at foreign tourists. See the Organised Tours section of the European Russia Getting There & Away chapter for the names of many travel companies that can book such trips.

You can also sail on a boat aimed at Russian holiday-makers. The price is much less than for the foreigner cruises but the food and accommodation are also less lavish. A Moscow travel agency, Cruise-Service (☎ 095-153 1074, fax 272 9998), Ulansky pereulok, 22, markets river sailings aboard the *Zoshima Shashkov*. A return Moscow-St Petersburg cruise takes 18 days – including four days spent in St Petersburg – and costs $45 a day per person in a double room with private bathroom. This includes all meals and guided tours.

South of Moscow Trips south of Moscow along the Volga and Don rivers to Astrakhan and Rostov-on-Don are popular. See the Volga Region chapter for details.

Other Routes Other river or sea passenger services in Russia, some served by hydrofoil, include: along the Neva River and the Gulf of Finland from St Petersburg to Petrodvorets, Kronstadt and Lomonosov; from St Petersburg to Valaam in Lake Ladoga; on Lake Onega, from Petrozavodsk to Kizhi; from Kem (Karelia) and Arkhangelsk to the Solovetsky Islands; from Pskov to Tartu (Estonia); between Novgorod and Staraya Russa; along the Kuban River from Krasnodar; and along the Black Sea coast between Sochi, Novorossiysk and other places.

LOCAL TRANSPORT

Most cities have good public transport systems combining bus, trolleybus and tram; the biggest cities also have metro systems. Public transport is very cheap, and is easy to use, especially if you are able to decipher some Cyrillic.

Taxis are fairly plentiful, and are usually cheap by Western standards.

Metro

Moscow and St Petersburg have metro systems. If the rest of the Soviet Union had worked as efficiently as these metros, it would have kicked Western butt: these metros leave their Western counterparts in the dust. The only confusing element is that a metro station can have several names – one for each different line that crosses at that station. See the Getting Around sections of the relevant city chapters for details on riding these systems.

Bus, Trolleybus & Tram

These three forms of transport are often the only means of getting around towns, and even in cities with metros you often need above-ground transport, too. Services are frequent in city centres, but more erratic as you move out towards the edges. They can get jam-packed in the late afternoon or on poorly served routes.

A stop is usually marked by a roadside A *(avtobus, uf-TOH-boos)* sign for buses, T for trolleybuses *(tra-LEY-boos)*, and ТРАМВАЙ *(trum-VAI)* or a T hanging over the road for trams. The normal fare is somewhere under $0.10.

Payment methods vary from city to city, but the most common method is to punch a ticket in little machines fixed inside the vehicle. You buy the tickets (талоны, *talony, tuh-LOHN-i*) in strips of five or 10 from drivers – a sign in the window between the driver's compartment and the passenger area saying Талоны нет *(talony nyet)* means that the driver's out of tickets – or from street kiosks displaying them in the window, or sometimes from sellers outside metro or train stations. Other payment methods include depositing a coin in a box and rolling out a ticket, or paying your fare to an absurdly dressed conductor (usually a woman with several rolls of tickets hanging from a rope round her neck).

On crowded transport people usually give up seats to women with children or a lot of baggage, and to old people.

Taxi

There are two main types of taxis in Russia: the official ones (four-door sedans with a chequerboard strip down the side and a green light in the front window); and 'private' taxis (any other vehicle you may see; see also Hitching earlier in this chapter).

Official taxis have a meter that they sometimes use, though you can always negotiate an off-the-meter price. There's a flag fall, and the number on the meter must be multiplied by the multiplier listed on a sign that *should* be on the dashboard or somewhere visible. Extra charges are incurred for radio calls and some night-time calls. The official taxis outside of luxury hotels often demand usurious rates.

Unofficial or private taxis are anything you can stop. Stand at the side of the road, extend your arm and wait until something stops – it could be an ambulance, off-duty city bus, army jeep or just a passenger car. When someone stops for you, it's common to negotiate destination and fare. State your destination, and if the driver's game, one of a couple of things will happen. If the driver asks you to sit down *(saditse)*, just get in and when you reach the destination you pay what you feel the ride was worth. If the driver states a price, you can negotiate; your offer has been rejected if the driver takes off in a huff.

Lastly, the driver may just ask you how much it's worth to you. For this you'll need to have spoken with locals to determine the average taxi fare in that city at the time of your visit; taxi prices around the country vary widely. Practise saying your destination and the amount you want to pay so it comes out properly. The more smoothly you speak, the lower the fare. If possible, let a Russian friend negotiate for you: they'll do better than you will.

Risks & Precautions Now and then tales crop up of rip-offs or robberies in taxis. Avoid taxis lurking outside foreign-run establishments, luxury hotels etc. They charge far too much and get uppity when you try to talk them down. Know your route: be familiar with how to get there and how long it should take. Never get into a taxi with more than one person in it, especially after dark.

Keep your fare money in a separate pocket to avoid flashing large wads of cash. Have the taxi stop at the corner nearest your destination, not the exact address, if you're staying at a private residence. Trust your instincts. If a driver looks creepy, take the next car. Check the back seat of the car for hidden friends before you get in.

Boat

In St Petersburg, Moscow and several other cities on rivers, coasts, lakes or reservoirs, public ferries and water excursions give a different perspective on the place. For details, see Getting Around in the relevant chapters or sections.

ORGANISED TOURS

Once you're in Russia, you'll find many travel agencies that specialise in city tours and excursions throughout the country. Sometimes these are the best way to visit out-of-the-way sights. See the travel agencies and organised tours listed in the relevant city sections. The European Russia Getting There & Away chapter lists Russian-based companies specialising in adventure travel within the country.

Moscow
Москва

☎ 095 • pop 9 million

Some people love Moscow. Some hate it. Most do both. It's glittering, it's grey. It's friendly, it's surly. It's beautiful, it's bleak. It's hedonistic, it's religious.

It's the epicentre of the new Russia, with shops, restaurants and nightlife that most provincial Russians can still only dream about. As never before in the lifetimes of its people, Moscow is a city of excitement and opportunity where anything can happen. It also epitomises what's wrong with Russia, growing street crime and rising prices, riddled with corruption, and spattered with large numbers of drunks and beggars.

Much more than most major cities, Moscow rewards those who take the time and trouble to get to know it. For the capital of the world's biggest country, to many newcomers it seems oddly quiet and village-like. You may be dazzled by the wild nightlife in the clubs and bars but it will take more effort to find the pulse of the city.

The slur that St Petersburgers cast on Moscow – that it's 'just a big village, not a real city' – is partly true. Moscow indeed began life as a provincial outpost and grew slowly, with different neighbourhoods taking distinct identities. Now, it's more like several thousand villages. Each street, courtyard and staircase has its own character. Moscow has its great buildings, historic sites, seats of the high and mighty, broad avenues, famous theatres, busy restaurants, parks and squares, but the real flavour of this city is in its small nooks and crannies, each of them unique.

Pass beneath the Kremlin walls and stroll around the historic precinct within. Walk through Red Square and feast your eyes on St Basil's Cathedral. Then start to explore wherever your fancy takes you. Markets, parks, quiet streets off the main avenues. The beautiful old convent of Novodevichy and the cemetery next door, where famous multitudes are buried. The Tretyakov or Pushkin fine art museums that house world famous collections of Russian and impressionist art. The old royal palace of Kolomenskoe on its bluff above the sinuous Moscow River. Take a boat ride along the river itself. Go to a concert or go wild at a

HIGHLIGHTS

- Pondering the sweep of history from Red Square
- Wandering the backstreets on the south banks of the Moscow River
- Commiserating with the redundant Soviet statues in the Sculptures Park
- Seeing the Kremlin from a Moscow River boat cruise
- Smelling the spring flowers at Kolomenskoe
- Surviving the sybaritic Moscow nightlife

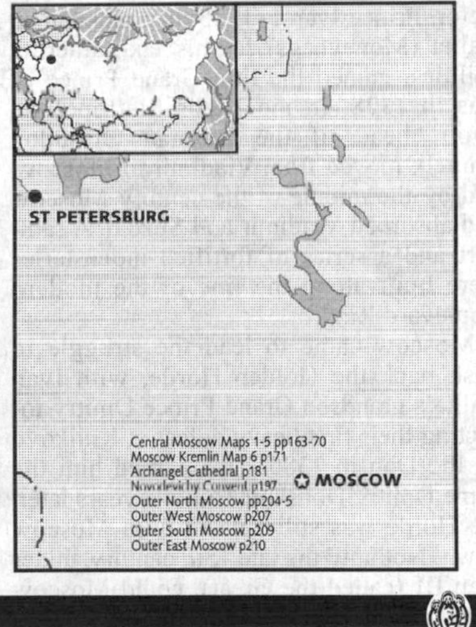

club. Or go underground where parts of the famed metro really deserve the adjective 'elegant'. Soon you may just be entranced.

HISTORY

First Settlers

The Kremlin and its surrounds were probably settled by the 11th century, but the founding of Moscow is traditionally ascribed to Yury Dolgoruky, Prince of Suzdal, who is recorded as giving a feast here, on what was the western fringe of his realm, in 1147. In 1237-38 Moscow was sacked along with the rest of the Vladimir-Suzdal realm by Tatars led by Batu, Jenghis Khan's grandson. These Tatars set up a capital at Saray on the southern Volga and became known as the Golden Horde. Moscow, near river trade routes, survived to become a princedom in its own right from the time of Daniil (1276-1303), and emerged as the Golden Horde's chief northern tribute collector. Prince Ivan I (1325-40), nicknamed Kalita (Moneybags) for his tax-gathering abilities, gained the title Grand Prince of Rus in 1328. In the 1320s Metropolitan Pyotr, head of the Russian Orthodox Church, moved from Vladimir to Moscow, and by the middle of the century Moscow had absorbed Vladimir and Suzdal. A rampart and a series of fortified monasteries were built along the line of the modern Boulevard Ring.

Moscow came to lead the struggle to push back the Golden Horde, with Ivan Kalita's grandson Grand Prince Dmitry inflicting their first heavy defeat at Kulikovo on the Don in 1380. This earned him the name Dmitry Donskoy. But two years later, the Horde was still able to burn Moscow down. Not until the late 15th century, under Ivan III (called the Great), could Moscow cease paying tribute to the Horde.

By the end of Ivan's reign, Moscow's control stretched from Novgorod in the west to Tula in the south, towards the Urals in the east and to the Barents Sea in the north. Ivan brought Italian architects to build cathedrals in the Kremlin and styled himself 'ruler of all Russia' as he set about reuniting the lands of old Kyivan (Kievan) Rus.

Ivan the Terrible

Ivan IV (1533-84), named Grozny (literally 'Awesome', but for this man translated as 'Terrible'), became grand prince at the age of three and spent his childhood amid vicious palace power struggles in which his mother was murdered. He had himself crowned tsar (caesar) at 16 and went on to marry six times (though Elizabeth I of England turned him down), terrorise the nobles and kill his eldest son in a fit of rage. He expanded Muscovite territory by launching the conquest of Siberia and winning control of the Volga from the Golden Horde khanates of Kazan and Astrakhan – St Basil's Cathedral was built in celebration – but he failed to win the Baltic region.

By 1571, when the Crimean Tatars burnt all Moscow except the Kremlin, the city probably had over 100,000 people and was one of the biggest in the world. The Kitay-Gorod, east of the Kremlin, was the main part of the town. By 1600 a 9km white stone wall with 27 towers stood round the line of the Boulevard Ring, and a 16km rampart around the Garden Ring. The area inside the white wall came to be known as the Bely Gorod (White City).

Tsar Boris Godunov (1598-1605) – formerly an adviser to Ivan the Terrible's son and successor, Fyodor – faced both famine and the Polish-backed invasion of the first False Dmitry. The seven years after Boris' death were the Time of Troubles – characterised by the first False Dmitry proclaiming himself tsar then being murdered, a second False Dmitry popping up, civil wars, invasions and Moscow being occupied by Poland. Finally, the Poles were driven out, and 16-year-old Mikhail Romanov was elected tsar by a council of nobles, launching the 300-year Romanov dynasty and a period of consolidation during which Muscovy's territory spread southwards.

Peter the Great

Peter I (the Great), impressed in his youth by visits to Moscow's foreigners' quarter on the Yauza River, toured Europe in 1697-98. He built a new capital, St Petersburg, on the Baltic to open Russia up to Western trade and ideas, and consolidated military victories over Sweden. He disliked Moscow, where as a boy he had seen his uncle and his mother's advisers killed in a palace coup.

But Moscow remained important enough to be Napoleon's main goal when his troops marched on Russia in 1812. After the bloody Battle of Borodino 130km west of the city, the Russians abandoned Moscow and allowed Napoleon to march in and install himself in the Kremlin. The night he arrived a great fire broke out that burnt most of the city, including the stores. With winter coming, the French had to pull out little more than a month after they had arrived.

Moscow was feverishly rebuilt in just a few years, and it was around this time that its two outer defensive rings were replaced by the tree-lined Boulevard Ring and Garden Ring roads. As new industrial suburbs grew up beyond the 'class barrier' of the Garden Ring, the city's population increased from 350,000 in the 1840s to 1.4 million in 1914.

Revolution

October 1917 saw more savage street fighting in Moscow than in St Petersburg. In 1918 the government moved back to Moscow after two centuries' absence, fearing that Petrograd (as St Petersburg was then called) might come under German attack. Moscow became the epicentre of the total reorganisation – in some cases devastation – of a huge country, and scene of its main 1930s show trials.

Under Stalin, one of the world's first comprehensive urban plans was devised for Moscow. The first line of the metro was completed in 1935. The broad thoroughfares he deemed necessary for his capital were created in the 1930s. In the late 1940s and early 1950s the 'Seven Sisters' or 'Stalin Wedding Cakes', seven great, grey neo-Gothic skyscrapers (see Landmarks under Orientation), were erected. Meanwhile, by some estimates, Stalin had had half of Moscow's artistic and historical landmarks demolished – most notoriously the enormous Cathedral of Christ the Saviour, a major city landmark which is now rebuilt.

German troops came within about 30km of the Kremlin in December 1941. A huge monument marks the spot where they were halted near the entrance road to Sheremetevo-2 airport. After WWII, huge housing estates grew up round the outskirts: the less high-rise ones hurriedly erected under Khrushchev in the mid-1950s are nicknamed *khrushchoby*, after *trushchoby* (slums); later blocks were built higher as planners tried to keep the city within its outer ring road.

Reform & Glasnost

Moscow has been in the forefront of political change, and a thorn in the flesh of the national leaders, since the first whispers of glasnost in the mid-1980s. Boris Yeltsin was made the city's new Communist Party chief in 1985 and became hugely popular as he sacked hundreds of corrupt commercial managers and permitted demonstrations to be held in the city. This last move was too much for the Communist old guard and led to Yeltsin's resignation in 1987.

When Moscow elected a new, reforming city council in 1990, with the economist Gavriil Popov as mayor, Popov embarked on the 'decommunisation' of the city, selling off housing and state businesses and restoring pre-revolutionary street names.

It was the rallying of Muscovites behind Yeltsin at Moscow's 'White House', seat of the parliament of the Russian Republic, that foiled the old guard coup in 1991 and precipitated the ultimate collapse of the Soviet Union. Two years later, when disenchantment with Yeltsin and politics had set in, Muscovites attended another confrontation at the White House – between the tanks sent by Yeltsin, now Russian president, and his obstructive foes in parliament. This time the people were spectators, not participants.

'New' Moscow

By the mid-1990s Moscow was the vanguard of the 'new Russia', filling up with all the things Russians had expected capitalism to bring but which had barely begun to percolate down to the provinces: banks, stock exchanges, casinos, BMWs, advertising, bright new shops, hotels, restaurants and nightlife.

While the 'new Russians' luxuriated in excess, most of the population could not afford these diversions and could only look on with wonder and envy. Moscow is one of the most expensive cities in the world while the people are among the poorest paid. This is why there are so few restaurants and bars aimed at the masses – less than 1% eat out more than once a year.

The election of Yuri Luzhkov as mayor in 1992 set the stage for the creation of a big city boss in the grandest of traditions. Through a web of financial interests, ownerships and the city's firm grip on land ownership, Luzhkov is not so much a man of the people as the CEO of a vast monopoly whose interests range from the media to manufacturing to just about all of the five-star hotels. He has engaged in many populist acts such as cleaning the streets and planting trees, as well as openly capitalistic acts such as building a huge shopping mall next to the Kremlin.

The economic crash that culminated in August 1998 has slowed things down a bit: fortunes have been lost, BMWs repossessed, expensive clubs closed and profit-seeking expats sent packing. But Moscow remains the most free-wheeling city in Russia: to a jaded population there are no surprises and to the ambitious there are no limits.

ORIENTATION

Picture Moscow as four road rings that spread out from this centre. Radial roads spear out across the rings, and the Moscow River meanders across everything from north-west to south-east with the Kremlin sitting at the northern tip of its biggest loop.

The Kremlin, a north-pointing triangle with 750m sides, is at Moscow's heart in every way. Red Square lies along its eastern side, the Moscow River flows to the south.

Four Rings

The first of the four rings, a semicircle to the north of the Kremlin, between 250 and 750m out, is formed by the streets Mokhovaya ulitsa, Okhotny ryad and Teatralny proezd, and the Novaya ploshchad and Staraya ploshchad squares. Three other important squares, Manezhnaya ploshchad, Teatralnaya ploshchad and Lubyanskaya ploshchad, punctuate this ring.

Next is the Boulevard Ring (Bulvarnoe Koltso), three-quarters of a circle 750 to 1500m from the Kremlin. It's mostly dual carriageway, with a park strip down the middle. Each section has a different name, always ending in 'bulvar'. The Boulevard Ring ends as it approaches the Moscow River in the south-west and south-east.

Third is the Garden Ring (Sadovoe Koltso), a full circle between 2 and 2.5km out, which crosses the river twice. Most of its northern sections are called Sadovaya-something (Garden-something) ulitsa; several of its southern sections are called ulitsa-something-val, recalling its origins as a rampart (*val*). And the difference between the Garden and Boulevard rings? The Garden Ring is the one *without* any gardens.

The fourth ring, much farther out, is Moscow's outer ring road, the Moskovskaya Koltsevaya Avtomobilnaya Doroga, some 15km from the Kremlin in the east and west, and 19km north and south. A few protuberances apart, it forms the city limits.

Landmarks

The only elevation worth the name in the whole flat expanse is the Sparrow Hills, 6km south-west of the Kremlin, topped by the Moscow University skyscraper. The Sparrow Hills afford the most panoramic view the city has to offer except for the Ostankino TV tower in the north.

Moscow's most prominent buildings are Stalin's 'Seven Sisters' skyscrapers – the Ukraina and Leningradsky hotels, the university tower on the Sparrow Hills, the Foreign Affairs and Agriculture ministries, the Kudrinskaya ploshchad and the Kotelnicheskaya apartment buildings – but you could easily mistake one for another.

Maps

It is a challenge to find up-to-date, non-Cyrillic maps of Moscow reflecting all the street name changes of the early 1990s. The

continued on page 173

To Tver &
St Petersburg
To Sergiev
Posad &
Yaroslavl
Khinki
Reservoir
Sheremetevo
Airports 1 & 2
A104
M10
M8
Moscow Canal
Moskovskaya Koltsevaya Avtomobilnaya Doroga
Outer North Moscow
Losiny
Ostrov
Park
Leningradskoe shosse
Dmitrovskoe shosse
Botanical
Gardens
Timiryazeva
Academy
Park
A103
Volokolamskoe schosse
Sokolniki
Park
shosse
Outer East
Moscow
To
Riga
M9
Leningradsky prospekt
prospekt Mira
Shchyolkovskoe
To
Vladimir
MAP 2
MAP 3
Izmaylovsky
Park
M7
Moscow River
A105
Outer West
Moscow
schosse Entuziastov
Park
Pobedy
MAP 4
MAP 5
Ryazansky prospekt
Kuskovo
Park
Kutuzovsky prospekt
Outer South Moscow
Volgogradsky prospekt
To
Bykovo
Airport
prospekt Vernadskogo
A100
M1
M5
Leninsky prospekt
Profsoyuznaya ulitsa
shosse
Kashirskoe shosse
Moscow River
To
Ryazan
To Smolensk
& Minsk
Varshavskoe
Moskovskaya Koltsevaya Avtomobilnaya Doroga
Vnukovo
Airport
M3
To Bryansk
& Kyiv
M4
To
Domodedevo
Airport (7km)
M4
A101
M2
0
5
10 km
To Tula &
Oryol
To
Voronezh

Hippodrome
0
200
400 km
Belorusskaya
Belorussky Vokzal
Tverskaya Zatava Plashchad
Begovaya
Ulitsa 1905 Goda
Krasnopresnenskaya
Barrikadnaya
Kudrinskaya ploshchad
Park Krasnaya Presnya
Moscow River
Leningradsky prospekt
Khodynskaya ul
Zvenigorodskoe shosse
ul Krasnaya Presnya
Barrikadnaya ul
Bolshaya Gruzinskaya ul
Novy Arbat ul
Kutuzovsky prospekt
Kalininsky most
Krasnopresnenskaya nab
Konyushkovskaya ulitsa
Novinsky bulvar
Sadovaya-Kudrinskaya ul
Povarskaya ul
Rochdelskaya ul
ul Mantulinskaya
Smolenskaya nab
Ukrainsky bulvar
nab Tarasa Shevchenko
pr Shlomina
MAP 4

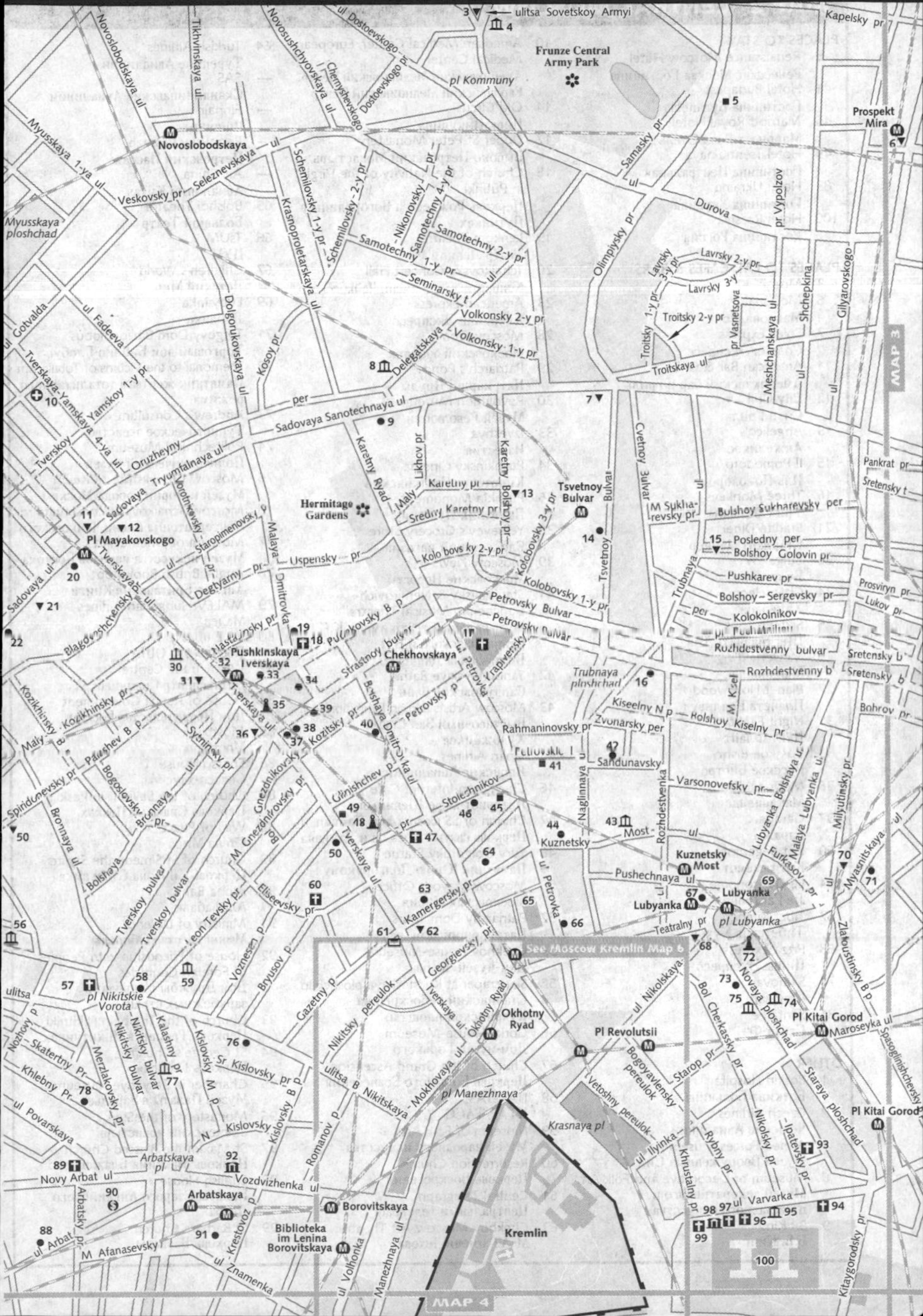

ulitsa Sovetskoy Armyi
Kapelsky pr
Frunze Central Army Park
pl Kommuny
ul Dostoevskogo
Dostoevskogo pr
Novosushchyovskaya ul
Chernyshevskogo
Novoslobodskaya ul
Tikhvinskaya ul
Novoslobodskaya
Seleznevskaya ul
Myusskaya 1-ya ul
Veskovsky pr
Myusskaya ploshchad
Schemilovsky 2-y pr
Schemilovsky 1-y pr
Krasnoproletarskaya ul
Nikonovsky pr
Samotechny 4-y pr
Samotechny 2-y pr
Samotechny 1-y pr
Seminarsky t
Samarsky pr
Durova ul
Olimpiysky pr
pr Vypolzov
Prospekt Mira
Lavrsky 2-y pr
Lavrsky 3-y pr
Troitsky 2-y pr
Troitsky 1-y pr
pr Vasnetsova
Meshchanskaya ul
Shchepkina ul
Gilyarovskogo ul
Troitskaya ul
ul Gotvalda
ul Fadeeva
Tverskoy-Yamskoy 1-y pr
Tverskaya-Yamskaya 4-ya ul
Dolgorukovskaya ul
Kosoy pr
Delegatskaya ul
Volkonsky 2-y pr
Volkonsky 1-y per
Sadovaya Sanotechnaya ul
Oruzheyny per
Tryumfalnaya ul
Sadovaya
Vorotnikovsky per
Staropimenovsky per
Pl Mayakovskogo
Sadovaya ul
Karetny Ryad
Maly Likhov pr
Karetny pr
Sredny Karetny pr
Karetny Bolshoy pr
Kolobovsky 3-y pr
Kolobovsky 2-y pr
Kolobovsky 1-y pr
Hermitage Gardens
Uspensky pr
Degtyarny pr
Malaya Dmitrovka
Tsvetnoy Bulvar
Tsvetnoy Bulvar
Cvetnoy Bulvar
M Sukharevsky pr
Bolshoy Sukharevsky per
Posledny per
Bolshoy Golovin pr
Pushkarev pr
Bolshoy Sergevsky pr
Kolokolnikov per
Pankrat pr
Sretensky t
Prosviryn pr
Lukov pr
Trubnaya ul
Petrovsky Bulvar
Blagoveshchensky per
Nastasyinsky per
Pushkinskaya
Tverskaya
Chekhovskaya
Strastnoy bulvar
Putinkovsky B p
Petrovka
Krapivensky per
Rozhdestvenny bulvar
Rozhdestvenny b
Sretensky b
Bobrov pr
Trubnaya ploshchad
Kiseelny N p
Bolshoy Kiseelny pr
Zvonarsky per
Rahmaninovsky pr
Petrovskie l
Sandunavsky
Naglinnaya ul
Varsonovefsky pr
Rozhdestvenka ul
Bolshaya Lubyanka ul
Malaya Lubyanka ul
Milyutinsky pr
Kozikhinsky pr
Maly Kozikhinsky pr
Palashev B p
Sytninsky pr
Spiridonevsky pr
Bogoslovsky pr
Bronnaya ul
Bolshaya Dmitrovka ul
Kozitsky pr
Petrovsky p
Gnezdnikovsky
Glinishchev pr
Stoleshnikov pr
Kuznetsky Most ul
Kuznetsky Most
Pushechnaya ul
Furkasov pr
Myasnitskaya ul
Lubyanka
pl Lubyanka
Teatralny pr
Zlatoustinsky B p
Bolshaya Bronnaya
M Gnezdnikovsky pr
Tverskoy bulvar
Leon Tevsky pr
Eliseevsky pr
Kamergersky pr
Georgievsky pr
See Moscow Kremlin Map 6
Voznesensky pr
Bryusov p
ulitsa
pl Nikitskie Vorota
Nozhovy p
Skatertny Pr
Khlebny Pr
ul Povarskaya
Merzlyakovsky pr
Nikitsky bulvar
Kalashny pr
Kislovsky M p
Sr Kislovsky pr
Kislovsky B p
Gazetny p
Nikitsky pereulok
Tverskaya ul
Okhotny Ryad ul
Okhotny Ryad
ulitsa B Nikitskaya
Mokhovaya ul
pl Manezhnaya
ul Nikolskaya
Pl Revolutsii
Bogoyavlensky pereulok
Vetoshny pereulok
Krasnaya pl
Bol Cherkassky pr
Starop pr
Novaya ploshchad
Staraya ploshchad
Pl Kitai Gorod
Maroseyka ul
Spasoglinishchevsky
Ilyinka ul
Khrustalny pr
Rybny pr
Nikolsky pr
Ipatevsky pr
Varvarka ul
Kitaygorodsky pr
Kremlin
Arbatskaya
Novy Arbat ul
Arbatsky
Vozdvizhenka ul
Arbatskaya
Borovitskaya
Biblioteka im Lenina
Borovitskaya
Romanov p
Manezhnaya ul
ul Volkhonka
ul Arbat
M Afanasevsky
Krestovoz p
ul Znamenka
MAP 3
MAP 4

MAP 2 CENTRAL MOSCOW

PLACES TO STAY

5 Renaissance Moscow Hotel
Ренессанс Москва Гостиница
41 Hotel Budapest
Гостиница Будапешт
45 Marriott Royal Hotel
Марриотт Роял Отель
49 Hotel Tsentralnaya
Гостиница Центральная
83 Hotel Ukraina
Гостиница Украина
100 Hotel Rossiya
Гостиница Россия

PLACES TO EAT, CAFES & BARS

3 Moosh
6 McDonald's
Макдоналдс
7 Soleil Express
Солейл Экспресс
11 American Bar & Grill
Американский бар и гриль
12 City Grill
Сити Гриль
13 Angelico's
Анжеликос
15 Il Pomodoro
Иль Помодоро
16 Three Monkeys
Три Обезьяны
21 Starlite Diner
Старлайт Дайнер
22 Bulgakov
Булгаков
24 Chameleon
Хамелеон
25 Sixteen Tons
Шестнадцать Тон
26 McDonald's
Макдоналдс
27 Planet Hollywood
Планета Голливуд
31 Night Flight
Найт Флайт
33 Russkoe Bistro
Русское Бистро
36 McDonald's
Макдоналдс
37 Garage
Гараж
50 Kot Begemot
Кот Бегемот
54 Le Gastronome
Ле Гастроном
62 Tibet Kitchen
Тибетская Кухня
68 Pizza Express
Пицца Экспресс
70 Samovar
Самовар
81 Santa Fe
Санта-Фэ

OTHER

1 Botkin Hospital
Боткина Больница
2 Czech Airlines
Чешские Авиалинии
4 Armed Forces Museum
Музей Вооруженных Сил
8 Museum of Decorative and Folk Art
Музей декоративного и прикладного искусства
9 BB King
Б.Б. Кинг
10 American Medical Center, European Medical Center
Американский Медицинский Центр, Европейский Медицинский Центр
14 Old Circus
Цирк Никулина
17 Upper St Peter Monastery
Высоко-Петровский Монастырь
18 Church of the Nativity of the Virgin in Putinki
Церковь Рождества Богородицы в Путинках
19 Lenkom Theatre
Театр Ленком
20 Tchaikovsky Concert Hall
Концертный зал имени Чайковского
23 American Express
Американ Экспресс
28 Moscow Zoo
Московский зоопарк
29 Patriarch's Pond
Патриарши Пруды
30 Revolution Museum
Музей Революции
33 Izvestiya
Известия
34 Pushkinsky Cinema
Кинотеатр Пушкинский
35 Pushkin Monument
Памятник Пушкину
38 Yeliseyev's Grocery Store
Елисеевский магазин
39 Moscow News
Московские Новости
41 Stanislavsky & Nemirovich-Danchenko Musical Theatre
Музыкальный театр имени К.С. Станиславского и В.И. Немировича-Данченко
42 Sandunovskiye Baths
Сандуновские бани
43 Moscow Artists' Union Exhibition Hall
Выставочный Зал Союза Художников
44 Japan Airlines
Японские Авиалинии
46 Chevignon Internet Café
Интернет-кафе Шевиньон
47 Church of SS Cosma and Damian
Церковь святых Косьмы и Дамиана
48 Yury Dolgoruky Statue
Памятник Юрию Долгорукому
50 Moscow Mayor's Office
Московская Мэрия
52 Patriarshy Dom Tours
Патриарший Дом
53 Chekhov House-Museum
Дом-музей Чехова
55 Skyscraper at Kudrinskaya ploshchad
Сталинский небоскреб на Кудринской площади
56 Gorky House-Museum
Дом-музей Горького
57 Church of the Grand Ascension
Церковь Большого Вознесения
58 ITAR-TASS
ИТАР-ТАСС
59 Museum of Folk Art
Музей народного искусства
60 Resurrection Church
Церковь Воскресения
61 Central Telegraph
Центральный телеграф
63 Chekhov Moscow Art Theatre
МсАТ имени Чехова
64 Turkish Airlines
Турецкие Авиалинии
— SAS
Скандининавские Авиалинии
— Finnair
Финнэр
— Petrovsky Passazh
Петровский Пассаж
— Air China
Авиалинии Китая
65 Bolshoi Theatre
Большой Театр
66 TsUM
ЦУМ
67 Children's World
Детский Мир
69 Lubyanka
Лубянка
71 Torgovy Dom Biblio-Globus
Торговый дом Библио-Глобус
72 Memorial to the Victims of Totaliarism
Памятник жертвам тоталитарного режима
73 Andrew's Consulting
Туристическое агенство
74 Politechnical Museum
Политехнический музей
75 Moscow City History Museum
Музей истории города Москвы
76 Moscow Tchaikovsky Conservatoire
Консерватопия имени Чайковского
77 Museum of Oriental Art
Музей искусства народов Востока
78 Anglia British Bookshop
Англия Британские Книги
79 MALEV Hungarian Airlines
Малев
80 US Embassy
Посольство США
82 World Trade Centre
Бизнесцентр Совинцентра
84 House of Russia Government
Дом Правительства России
85 Mostbank
Мостбанк
86 Spasso House
Спассо-хаус
87 Church of the Saviour in Peski
Церковь Спаса на Песках
88 Wall of Peace
Стена Мира
89 Church of St Simeon the Stylite
Церковь Симеона Стольника
90 Alpha Bank
Альфабанк
91 Ministry of Defence
Министерство Обороны
92 House of Friendship with Peoples of Foreign Countries
Дом Дружбы с народами зарубежных стран
93 Church of the Trinity in Nikitniki
Церковь Троицы в Никитниках
94 St George's Church
Церковь Георгия
95 Chamber in Zaryadye Museum
Музей Палаты в Зарядье
96 Monastery of the Sign
Знаменский монастырь
97 St Maxim the Blessed Church
Церковь Максима Блаженного
98 English House
Палаты Старого Английского Двора
99 St Barbara Church
Церковь Варвары

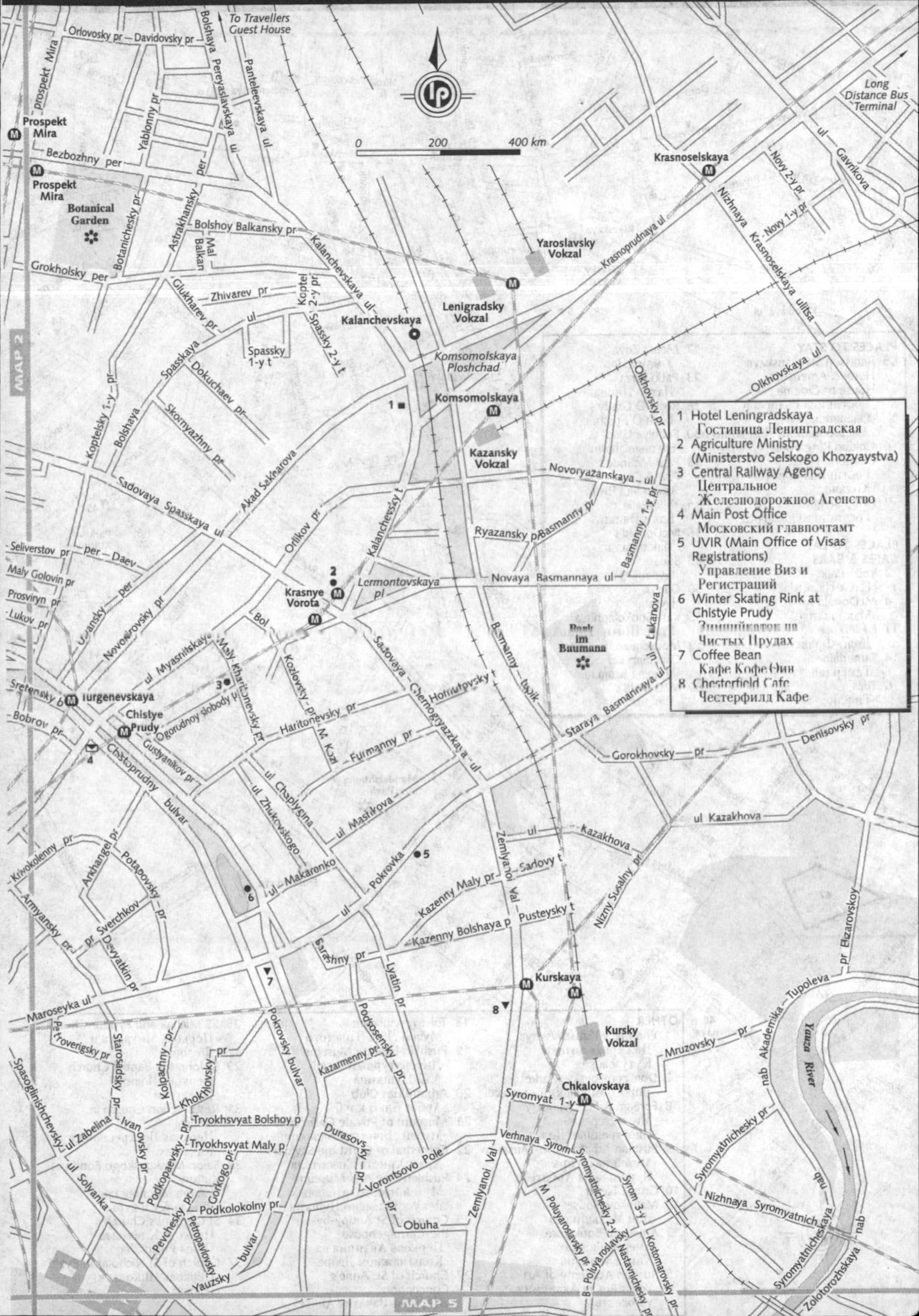

1 Hotel Leningradskaya
Гостиница Ленинградская
2 Agriculture Ministry
(Ministerstvo Selskogo Khozyaystva)
3 Central Railway Agency
Центральное
Железнодорожное Агенство
4 Main Post Office
Московский главпочтамт
5 UVIR (Main Office of Visas Registrations)
Управление Виз и Регистраций
6 Winter Skating Rink at Chistyie Prudy
Зиннийкатов на Чистых Прудах
7 Coffee Bean
Кафе Кофе Бин
8 Chesterfield Cafe
Честерфилд Кафе

0 200 400 km

To Travellers Guest House
Long Distance Bus Terminal
Prospekt Mira
Botanical Garden
Krasnoselskaya
Yaroslavsky Vokzal
Lenigradsky Vokzal
Kalanchevskaya
Komsomolskaya Ploshchad
Komsomolskaya
Kazansky Vokzal
Krasnye Vorota
Lermontovskaya pl
Turgenevskaya
Chistye Prudy
Park im Baumana
Kurskaya
Kursky Vokzal
Chkalovskaya
Yauza River

Orlovosky pr – Davidovsky pr
prospekt Mira
Bolshaya Pereyaslavskaya ul
Panteleevskaya ul
Yablonny pr
Bezbozhny per
Botanichesky pr
Astrakhansky per
Bolshoy Balkansky pr
Mal Balkan
Grokholsky per
Kalanchevskaya ul
Glukharev pr
Zhivarev pr
Koptel 2-y pr
Spassky 2-y t
Spassky 1-y t
Spasskaya
Dokuchaev pr
Skornyazhny pr
Koptelsky 1-y pr
Bolshaya
Akad Sakharova
Sadovaya Spasskaya ul
Seliverstov pr
per – Daev
Maly Golovin pr
Prosviryn pr
Lukov pr
Ulansky per
Novoryazanskaya ul
Krasnoprudnaya ul
Olkhovsky pr
Olkhovskaya ul
Nizhnaya Krasnoselskaya ulitsa
Novy 2-y pr
Novy 1-y pr
Gavrikova ul
Basmanny pr
Basmanny 1-y pr
Ryazansky pr
Novaya Basmannaya ul
Orlikov pr
Kalanchevsky t
Novorozovsky pr
Bol
ul Myasnitskaya
Maly Kharitonevsky pr
Kozlovsky pr
Sadovaya Chernogryazzkaya ul
Basmanny tupik
Lukanova
Staraya Basmannaya ul
Sretensky b
Bobrov pr
Ogorodnoy slobody p
Haritonevsky pr
Hohlutovsky t
M Kazi
Furmanny pr
Gorokhovsky pr
Denisovsky pr
Chistoprudny bulvar
Gusyatnikov pr
ul Chaplygina
ul Zhukovskogo
ul Mashkova
ul Kazakhova
Krivokolenny pr
Arkhangel pr
Potapovsky pr
ul Makarenko
ul Pokrovka
Zemlyanoi Val
Sadovy t
Nizhny Susalny pr
Kazenny Maly pr
Kazenny Bolshaya p
Pusteysky t
Armyansky pr
Sverchkov pr
Devyatkin pr
Barashny pr
Lyatin pr
Elizarovsky pr
Akademika Tupoleva nab
Maroseyka ul
Petroverigsky pr
Starosadsky pr
Kolpachny pr
Khokhlovsky pr
Pokrovsky bulvar
Podsosensky pr
Kazarmenny pr
Mruzovsky pr
Syromyat 1-y
Spasoglinishchevsky pr
ul Zabelina
Ivanovsky pr
Tryokhsvyat Bolshoy p
Tryokhsvyat Maly p
Durasovsky pr
Vorontsovo Pole
Verhnaya Syrom
Syromyatnichesky pr
Syromyatnichesky 2-y
Syrom 3-y
Nizhnaya Syromyatnicheskaya
Syromyatnicheskaya nab
ul Solyanka
Podkopaevsky pr
Gorkogo pr
Pevchesky pr
Petropavlovsky pr
Podkolokolny pr
Obuha
Yauzsky bulvar
M Poluyaroslavsky pr
B Poluyaroslavsky pr
Nastavnichesky pr
Kostomarovsky pr
Zolotorozhskaya nab

MAP 2
MAP 5

MAP 4 CENTRAL MOSCOW

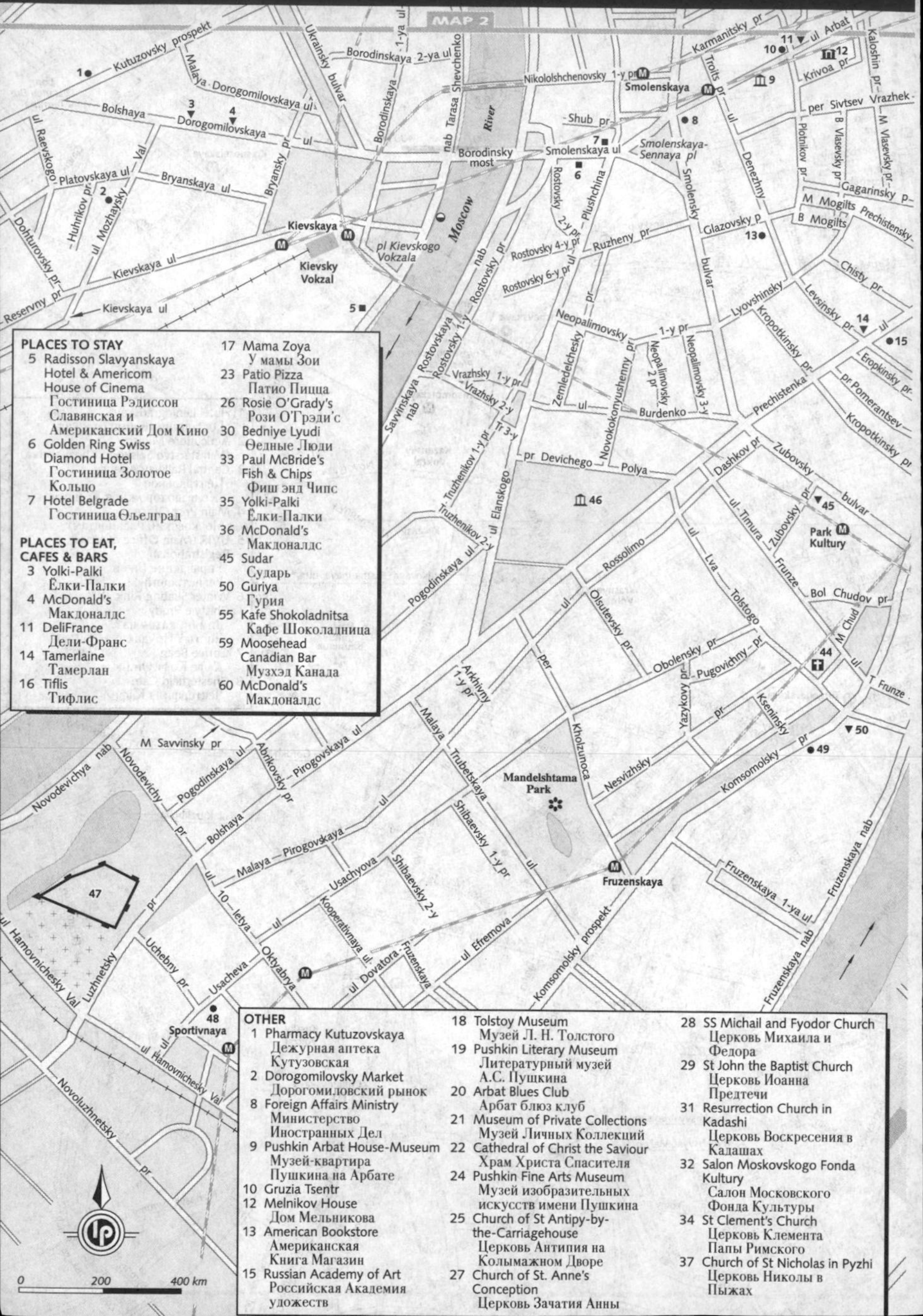

PLACES TO STAY

5 Radisson Slavyanskaya Hotel & Americom House of Cinema
Гостиница Рэдиссон Славянская и Американский Дом Кино

6 Golden Ring Swiss Diamond Hotel
Гостиница Золотое Кольцо

7 Hotel Belgrade
Гостиница Өљелград

PLACES TO EAT, CAFES & BARS

3 Yolki-Palki
Ёлки-Палки

4 McDonald's
Макдоналдс

11 DeliFrance
Дели-Франс

14 Tamerlaine
Тамерлан

16 Tiflis
Тифлис

17 Mama Zoya
У мамы Зои

23 Patio Pizza
Патио Пицца

26 Rosie O'Grady's
Рози О'Грэди'с

30 Bedniye Lyudi
Өедные Люди

33 Paul McBride's Fish & Chips
Фиш энд Чипс

35 Yolki-Palki
Ёлки-Палки

36 McDonald's
Макдоналдс

45 Sudar
Сударь

50 Guriya
Гурия

55 Kafe Shokoladnitsa
Кафе Шоколадница

59 Moosehead Canadian Bar
Музхэд Канада

60 McDonald's
Макдоналдс

OTHER

1 Pharmacy Kutuzovskaya
Дежурная аптека Кутузовская

2 Dorogomilovsky Market
Дорогомиловский рынок

8 Foreign Affairs Ministry
Министерство Иностранных Дел

9 Pushkin Arbat House-Museum
Музей-квартира Пушкина на Арбате

10 Gruzia Tsentr

12 Melnikov House
Дом Мельникова

13 American Bookstore
Американская Книга Магазин

15 Russian Academy of Art
Российская Академия удожеств

18 Tolstoy Museum
Музей Л. Н. Толстого

19 Pushkin Literary Museum
Литературный музей А.С. Пушкина

20 Arbat Blues Club
Арбат блюз клуб

21 Museum of Private Collections
Музей Личных Коллекций

22 Cathedral of Christ the Saviour
Храм Христа Спасителя

24 Pushkin Fine Arts Museum
Музей изобразительных искусств имени Пушкина

25 Church of St Antipy-by-the-Carriagehouse
Церковь Антипия на Колымажном Дворе

27 Church of St. Anne's Conception
Церковь Зачатия Анны

28 SS Michail and Fyodor Church
Церковь Михаила и Федора

29 St John the Baptist Church
Церковь Иоанна Предтечи

31 Resurrection Church in Kadashi
Церковь Воскресения в Кадашах

32 Salon Moskovskogo Fonda Kultury
Салон Московского Фонда Культуры

34 St Clement's Church
Церковь Клемента Папы Римского

37 Church of St Nicholas in Pyzhi
Церковь Николы в Пыжах

0 200 400 km

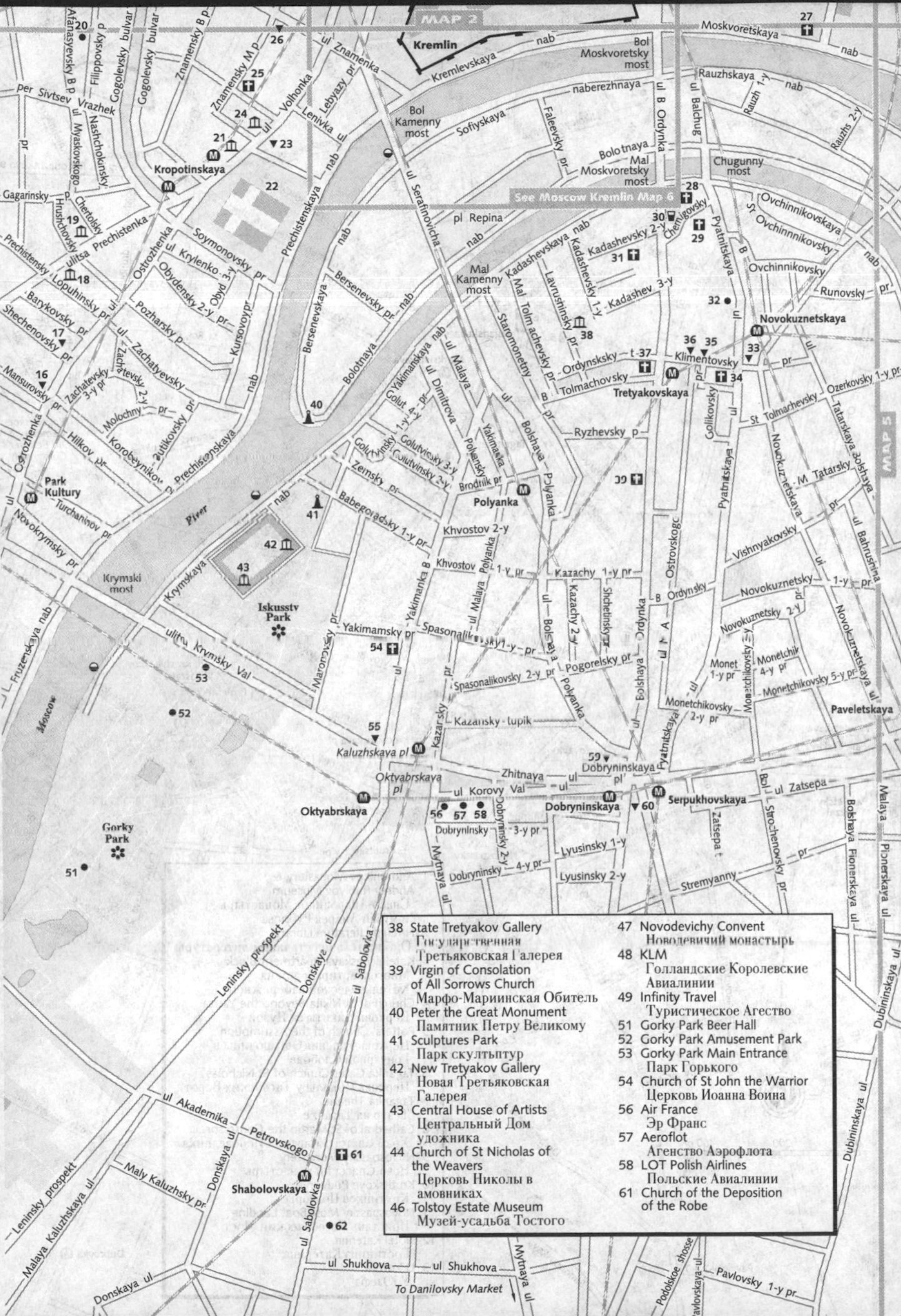
MAP 2
Kremlin
See Moscow Kremlin Map 6
MAP 5
Kropotinskaya
Park Kultury
Polyanka
Tretyakovskaya
Novokuznetskaya
Paveletskaya
Oktyabrskaya
Dobryninskaya
Serpukhovskaya
Shabolovskaya
Kaluzhskaya pl
Iskusstv Park
Gorky Park
Krymski most
Bol Kamenny most
Mal Kamenny most
Bol Moskvoretsky most
Mal Moskvoretsky most
Chugunny most
Moscow River
Kremlevskaya nab
Moskvoretskaya nab
Prechistenskaya nab
Bersenevskaya nab
Yakimanskaya nab
Krymskaya nab
Frunzenskaya nab
Ovchinnikovskaya nab
ulitsa Prechistenka
Ostrozhenka
Volhonka
ul Znamenka
Gogolevsky bulvar
ul Serafimovicha
ul B Ordynka
ul Bolshaya Polyanka
ul B Yakimanka
ul Malaya Polyanka
ul Pyatnitskaya
ul Bolshaya Ordynka
Novokuznetskaya ul
ul Krymsky Val
Leninsky prospekt
ul Akademika Petrovskogo
Donskaya ul
ul Sabolovka
Mytnaya ul
ul Korovy Val
Zhitnaya ul
ul Zatsepa
ul Shukhova
Malaya Kaluzhskaya ul
Maly Kaluzhsky pr
Pavlovsky 1-y pr
To Danilovsky Market
38 State Tretyakov Gallery
Государственная Третьяковская Галерея
39 Virgin of Consolation of All Sorrows Church
Марфо-Мариинская Обитель
40 Peter the Great Monument
Памятник Петру Великому
41 Sculptures Park
Парк скультптур
42 New Tretyakov Gallery
Новая Третьяковская Галерея
43 Central House of Artists
Центральный Дом удожника
44 Church of St Nicholas of the Weavers
Церковь Николы в амовниках
46 Tolstoy Estate Museum
Музей-усадьба Тостого
47 Novodevichy Convent
Новодевичий монастырь
48 KLM
Голландские Королевские Авиалинии
49 Infinity Travel
Туристическое Агество
51 Gorky Park Beer Hall
52 Gorky Park Amusement Park
53 Gorky Park Main Entrance
Парк Горького
54 Church of St John the Warrior
Церковь Иоанна Воина
56 Air France
Эр Франс
57 Aeroflot
Агенство Аэрофлота
58 LOT Polish Airlines
Польские Авиалинии
61 Church of the Deposition of the Robe

1 Andronikov Monastery & Andrey Rublyov Museum
Спасо-Андроников Монастырь и музей Андрея Рублева
2 Foreign Literature Library
Фиблиотека иностранной литературы
3 Kotelnicheskaya Apartment Block
Многоквартирый дом на Котельнической набережной
4 Church of St Nikita Beyond the Yauza
Церковь Никиты за Яузой
5 Potters' Church of the Assumption
Церковь Успения Фогородицы в Гончарной Слободе
6 Taganka Gates Church of St Nicholas
Церковь Николы у Таганских Ворот
7 Taganka Theatre
Театр на Таганке
8 Cathedral of St Martin the Confessor
Храм Святого Мартина Исповедника
9 Novospassky Monastery
Ново-Спасский монастырь
10 Krutitskoye Podvorye
Крутицкое Подворье
11 Novospassky Most Boat Landing
Пристань Новоспасский Мост
12 Hotel Katerina
Гостиница Катерина
13 U Yuzefa
У Юзефа

Teatralny pr
Gazetny pr
Georgievsky p
Nikitsky pereulok
Tverskaya ulitsa
Okhotny Ryad
ulitsa Nikolskaya
Bogoyavlensky pereulok
Starop p
Mokhovaya ulitsa
ulitsa B Nikitskaya
pl Manezhnaya
Vetoshny pereulok
KITAY - GOROD
Romanov pr
Krasnaya ploshchad
ulitsa Ilyinka
Khrustalny p
Alexandrovsky Gardens
Vozdvizhenka ulitsa
Kremlin
Manezhnaya ulitsa
ulitsa Volhonka
Moskvoretskaya
Kremlevskaya nab
ulitsa Znamenka
Bol Moskvoretsky most
Lebyazy p
Sofiyskaya naberezhnaya
ulitsa B Ordynka
ulitsa Balchug
Bol Kamenny most
Lenivka ulitsa
nab
Prechistenskaya
ulitsa Serafinovicha
Faleevsky p
nab Bolotnaya
Mal Moskvoretsky most

MAP 6 MOSCOW KREMLIN

PLACES TO STAY & EAT, CAFES & BARS

7 Territoria
Территория
12 Hotel Moskva
Гостиница Москва
15 Hotel Intourist
Гостиница Интурист
16 Hotel National
Гостиница Националь
67 Hotel Baltschug Kempinski
Гостиница Балчуг Кемпински

MOSCOW KREMLIN

29 Moscow State University
Московский Государственный Университет
33 Saviour Gate Tower
Спасская башня
34 Supreme Soviet
Верховный Совет
34 Senate
Сенат
35 Manezh Central Exhibition Hall
Центральный Выставочный Зал Манеж
36 Kutafya Tower
Кутафья Башня
37 Trinity Gate Tower
Троицкая Башня
38 Arsenal
Арсенал
39 Supreme Soviet building
Здание Верховного Совета
43 Tsar Tower
Царская башня
44 Tsar Cannon
Царь-пушка
45 Assumption Cathedral
Успенский Собор
46 Patriarch's Palace
Патриарший Дворец
47 Kremlin Palace of Congresses
Кремлевский Дворец Съездов
48 Poteshny Palace
Потешный Дворец
49 Kremlin Ticket Offices
Кассы музеев Кремля
51 Russian State Library
Российская Государственная Библиотека
54 Pashkov House
Дом Пашкова
55 Terem Palace
Теремной Дворец
56 Hall of Facets
Грановитая Палата
57 Church of the Deposition of the Robe
Церковь Ризоположения
58 Ivan the Great Bell Tower
Колокольня Ивана Великого
59 Tsar Bell
Царь-колокол
60 Konstantin and Yelena Tower
Константино-Еленинская башня
61 Archangel Cathedral
Архангельский Собор
62 Annuciation Cathedral
Благовещенский Собор
63 Great Kremlin Palace
Большой Кремлевский Дворец
64 Armoury & Diamond Fund Exhibition
Оружейная Палата и Выставка Алмазного Фонда
65 Annuciation Tower
Благовещенская башня
66 Secrets Tower
Тайницкая башня

METRO STATIONS

2 Teatralnaya
Театральная
14 Okhotny Ryad
Охотный Ряд
13 Okhotny Ryad
Охотный Ряд
18 Okhotny Ryad
Охотный Ряд
20 Teatralnaya & Ploshchad Revolyutsii
Театральная и Площадь Революции
21 Ploshchad Revolyutsii
Площадь Революции
52 Borovitskaya
Боровицкая
50 Alexandrovsy Sad, Borovitskaya & Biblioteka imeni Lenina
Александровский Сад, Боровицкая и Библиотека имени Ленина
53 Borovitskaya & Biblioteka imeni Lenina
Боровицкая и Библиотека имени Ленина

OTHER

1 Global USA
Глобал США
3 Maly Theatre
Малый Драматический Театр
4 Pharmacy Ferrein
Дежурная аптека Феррейн
5 Karl Marx Statue
Памятник Карлу Марксу
6 House of Unions
Дом Союзов
8 Focus Photoshop
Фотомагазин Фокус
9 State Duma
Государственная Дума
10 Printing House
Печатный Двор
11 Zaikonospassky Monastery
Заиконоспасский монастырь
17 Transaero
Трансаэро
19 Central Lenin Museum
Центральный музей В. И. Ленина
22 Monastery of Epiphany
Богоявленский монастырь
23 Kazan Cathedral
Казанский Собор
24 Resurrection Gate & Chapel of the Iverian Virgin
Воскресениские ворота и часовня Иверской Богоматери
25 State History Museum
Государственный Исторический Музей
26 Tomb of the Unknown Soldier
Могила Неизвестнного Солдата
27 Okhotny Ryad Shopping Mall
Охотный Ряд
28 Intourist
Интурист
29 Lenin's Tomb
Мавзолей В.И. Ленина
30 Place of Skulls
Лобное место
31 GUM
ГУМ (Государственный Универсальный Магазин)
32 Old Stock Exchange
Бывшая Биржа
41 Kuzma Minin and Dmitry Pozharsky Statue
Памятник Минину и Пожарскому
42 St Basil's Cathedral
Собор Василия Бладенного

continued from page 162

normally accurate Falk products are woefully out of date. Better are the maps from Cartographia and Kummerly & Fry that are both sensibly called the *Moscow City Map*. The best map of the city is the 2nd edition of *The New Moscow City Map and Guide* published by Russia Information Services of Montpelier, Vermont, USA.

Accurate maps in Cyrillic are widely sold in Moscow and cost $1 to $3. Good sources are the kiosks in the underpass from the Okhotny Ryad metro station to the Kremlin and Torgovy Dom Biblio-Globus (Map 2; ☎ 928 3567), Myasnitskaya ulitsa 6. See the Bookshops section later in the chapter for sources of non-Cyrillic maps in Moscow.

INFORMATION

Tourist Offices

Moscow has no tourist offices in the normal sense of places where you can obtain a map, inquire about places to stay, opening times of sights, and so on. Many travel agencies including Intourist offer information but it's weighted to their self-interest. If you're in a pinch, staff at the large hotels will usually help with simple requests.

Visas & Documents

See European Russia Facts for the Visitor for general information on Russian visas.

Registration Normally your visa's sponsor will register your visa for you. You can ask whether this is being done. If you have a tourist visa without a sponsor and are staying in a private home, then your host will usually know where the local OVIR office is to register your visa, a normally simple procedure. If you have a visa but noone to register it, you can avail yourself of the free registration service offered by Andrew's Consulting (Map 2; ☎ 258 5198, fax 258 5199), Novaya ploshchad 10, 5th floor.

For all other visa matters such as extending a tourist or transit visa or replacing a lost visa, check with UVIR (Upravlenia Viz i Registratsii; Map 3; ☎ 200 8497), the city's main visa and registration office, at ulitsa Pokrovka 42. The staff are used to dealing with foreigners and speak English. UVIR is open from 10 am to 1 pm and 3 to 6 pm Monday, Tuesday and Thursday; from 10 am to 1 pm and 3 to 5 pm Friday; and from 10 am to 1 pm on Saturday for emergencies only. It's closed Wednesday and Sunday. Go early to avoid the crowds.

Money

You will find hundreds of banks and exchange counters around Moscow starting at Sheremetevo-2 airport. If you are exchanging more than a small sum, it can be worthwhile shopping around. You may be approached by Russians who want to exchange money on the street. Often these are people who simply need your dollars and want to complete an exchange *sans* the middle man so you both get a better rate. But exercise all the usual cautions so you don't fall prey to a scamster.

Except at a few exchange counters in hotels and near the Kremlin, currencies other than US dollars and Deutschmarks will either be impossible to exchange or yield very bad rates. Travellers cheques are another problem – most exchange counters and stores won't accept them.

Banks Two of Moscow's most established banks are Alfa Bank (Map 2; ☎ 230 3696), ulitsa Arbat 4/1, open from 8.30 am to 7.30 pm daily (closing at 3 pm Sunday), and Most Bank (Map 2; ☎ 290 8206), Novy Arbat 36, open from 9.30 am to 7 pm weekdays and 9.30 am to 2.30 pm Saturday. Both offer services including credit card advances, travellers cheque cashing and ATMs.

Credit Cards Don't count on being able to use these anywhere outside of Western hotels.

American Express American Express (Map 2; ☎ 755 9000) is on the western Garden Ring at Sadovaya-Kudrinskaya ulitsa 21A; it's open from 9 am to 5 pm Monday to Friday, 9 am to 1 pm Saturday. It cashes American Express travellers cheques and offers client mail-holding and travel services. There is an ATM for Amex cards.

ATMs You can find ATMs in the walls of most banks throughout central Moscow. They only dispense roubles.

Wire Transfers Call Western Union (☎ 119 8266) to find out which banks will accept wire transfers of money.

Post

The usual warnings about delays and disappearances of incoming and outgoing mail apply to Moscow. See the Post section of European Russia Facts for the Visitor for all the dire details.

A convenient, central post office is in the Central Telegraph (Tsentralny Telegraf; Map 2) at Tverskaya ulitsa 7, just up the hill from Hotel Intourist. Postal counters are open from 8 am to 10 pm daily. Moscow's main post office (Moskovsky Glavpochtamt; Map 3) is at Myasnitskaya ulitsa 26, on the corner of Chistoprudny bulvar. It's open from 8 am to 8 pm weekdays, 9 am to 7 pm weekends, and has a philatelic counter.

Express Services The major air courier services operating in Moscow include: DHL Worldwide Express (☎ 956 1000), Fedex (☎ 234 3400), TNT (☎ 931 9640) and UPS (☎ 961 2211). They can advise on drop-off locations and arrange pick-ups.

Telephone

Many of the older hotels don't charge for local calls. The same cannot be said for the large Western hotels which charge extortionate prices for a call down the street. International calls are easily arranged – if not dialled directly – at most hotels and aren't cheap at any. If making an international call to Moscow, dial the entire ☎ 095 area code, including the 0.

Major Western telephone service companies have access code telephone numbers for Moscow that allow you to call home using your own long-distance service. These can change frequently, so check with your server before you leave home.

Pay Phones Most of the pay phones you will find in Moscow are modern blue-and-white units fielded by the Moscow State Telephone Network (МГТС). They are operated by cards widely available in shops and kiosks in a range of units; international calls will require at least 100 units.

Follow these steps to make a call:

Step One: Lift the receiver and check for a dial tone.

Step Two: Press the button above the green one that bears a stylised flag until the display screen shows English.

Step Three: Follow the directions on the display screen for inserting your card and dialling.

Step Four: Press the button on the right that bears the speaker symbol when your party answers the phone.

See the Telephone section of European Russia Facts for the Visitor for dialling details for international calls. Dial ☎ 09 for Moscow directory enquiries.

Telephone Office The convenient Central Telegraph (Tsentralny Telegraf; Map 2) at Tverskaya ulitsa 7, just up the hill from Hotel Intourist, is open for calls 24 hours. You can't make collect calls but you can use the fax service.

Email & Internet Access

You can sip a Coke and surf the net at Chevignon Internet Café (Map 2; ☎ 733 9205), Baza 14, Stoleshnikov pereulok 14. Above a clothing store, it's open 24 hours. It has fast computers and there's usually no queue. Access costs $5 an hour. For considerably more money ($20 an hour) you can have your own little room with very fast access at Sovincenter Business Center (Map 2; ☎ 253 2884) which is in the World Trade Centre at Krasnopresnenskaya nab 12. It's open from 9 am to 9 pm daily.

Internet Resources

Moscow is well represented on the Internet. See the Internet Resources section of the European Russia Facts for the Visitor chapter for a list of mostly Moscow-based sites. One, www.kremlinkam.com, bears repeating as its live views of the Kremlin are just about the best way to get an up-to-the-minute look at Moscow's weather. It also lists the current exchange rate.

The official Web site run by the Moscow government is www.moscow-guide.ru. It's huge and frequently updated with information on a range of topics from transport to culture Another good source of links and information is the Traveller's Yellow Pages On-Line for Moscow at www.infoservices.com/moscow.

Travel Agencies

Andrew's Consulting (Map 2; ☎ 258 5198, fax 258 5199), Novaya ploshchad 10, 5th floor, offers a full range of services aimed at business travellers. Infinity Travel (Map 4; ☎ 234 6555, fax 234 6556, info@infinity.ru, www.infinity.ru), formerly IRO Travel, Komsomolsky prospekt 13, is affiliated with the Travellers Guest House. It offers domestic and international rail and air tickets (including cheap international airfares), visa support service, trans-Siberian and Central Asia packages.

Kremlin Tours Travel Agency (☎ 276 7274, kremln@dol.ru) specialises in gay and lesbian travel in Russia and organises tours, homestays and the like.

See the Adventure Travel section of the European Russia Getting There & Away chapter for several Moscow-based travel companies offering tours and arrangements for active travellers.

Bookshops

You won't have a problem finding a good selection of English-language books at Anglia British Bookshop (Map 2; ☎ 203 5802), Khlebny pereulok 2/3. There's an excellent and wide variety of books including a lot of travel titles from fine publishers such as Lonely Planet. It's open from 10 am to 7 pm daily (until 5 pm Sunday). The American Bookstore (Map 4; ☎ 241 4224), Denezhny pereulok 8/10, also has a wide selection of books, mostly from US publishers. It's open from 10 am to 7 pm from Monday to Saturday.

Torgovy Dom Biblio-Globus (Map 2; ☎ 928 3567), Myasnitskaya ulitsa 6, is a Russian bookshop with lots of art and photography books, some in English, and dictionaries. There's also a good selection of maps and travel guides.

Newspapers & Magazines

The *Moscow Times* (www.moscowtimes.ru) is an excellent, free, English-language newspaper that would be a good daily any place in the world. It does a good job of covering local news such as the turbulent and entertaining political scene. The paper has a number of good writers including columnist Helen Womack, whose essays turn everyday life in Moscow into poetry. The weekly entertainment section published on Friday has comprehensive listings of what's on as well as restaurant, bar and club listings. The paper is distributed in many hotels, restaurants and stores.

The *Moscow Tribune* is a distant second in the English-language stakes. Its content and advertising support are quite thin.

The *Exile* is a weekly newspaper published by a group of Americans who manage with each issue to be preppy and misogynist as well as just plain stupid and amateur. Think of the paper you would have published with your pals when you were 13. It does have extensive entertainment listings that have won it a large following with the expat community, although these are slanted towards readers whose sexual encounters involve payment.

Numerous other English-language weeklies and monthlies seem to appear at random, last a few issues and then vanish. One very useful established monthly is the *Moscow Business Telephone Guide*, a free, invaluable, bilingual phone book. It can be found in the same places as the aforementioned publications. The *Russia Business Review* is a free glossy monthly with good and imaginative articles about local economic conditions and decent restaurant listings as well.

Libraries & Cultural Centres

The Foreign Literature Library (Map 5; ☎ 915 3636), Nikoloyamskaya ulitsa 1, is home to several international libraries and cultural centres including the American

Cultural Center Library (☎ 915 3669), open from 10 am to 8 pm Monday to Friday; the French Cultural Centre (☎ 915 3669), open from 1 to 6 pm Monday to Friday; and the British Council Resource Centre (☎ 915 3511), open from 10 to 8 pm Monday to Friday. Take your passport.

The Russian State Library (Rossiyskaya Gosudarstvennaya Biblioteka; Map 6) at ulitsa Vozdvizhenka 3 on the corner of Mokhovaya ulitsa, is one of the world's largest, with over 20 million volumes. If you seriously want to peruse some of these, take along your passport and one passport photo. You have to fill in a form or two at the library's information office in order to get a free reader's card *(chitatelsky bilet)*. The library's opening hours are from 9 am to 9 pm daily (closed the last Monday of each month).

Laundry

Coin and self-service laundries are unheard of in Moscow. However, you'll find that virtually every place of accommodation offers laundry services.

Toilets

Public toilets – when you can find them – are better left unfound. Your best bets are large hotels, restaurants and McDonald's, of which Moscow has many.

Left Luggage

All the major train stations have luggage lockers and/or left-luggage services. You can also check your bags in at most of the major hotels.

Medical Services

Although Moscow's tap water is considered safe to drink, locals regard it with deep suspicion and usually boil it first. The other common health concern is the air, which is filled with pollution and wind-blown dirt, although several other huge cities would rival Moscow in the dirty air department.

Several foreign-run health services are available in Moscow, offering Western standards of treatment. They are very expensive and can be fiscally ruinous without valid insurance coverage, although if trouble strikes you may not have a choice.

American Medical Center (Map 2; ☎ 956 3366, fax 956 2306), 2-y Tverskoy-Yamskoy pereulok 10, offers wide-ranging facilities, including 24 hour emergency and various specialists such as paediatricians and psychiatrists. It also has a pharmacy and dental services.

European Medical Center (Map 2; ☎ 956-7999), 2-y Tverskoy-Yamskoy pereulok 10, is a separate organisation in the same building as the American Medical Center that also has a wide range of medical services and specialities including 24 hour house calls. Medical evacuation can be arranged from anywhere in Russia.

The best Russian facility is:

Botkin Hospital (Map 2; ☎ 945 0045), 2-y Botkinsky proezd 5, the main Moscow hospital for foreigners, is well equipped by Russian standards, with emergency and after-hours services.

You'll find that embassies usually maintain lists of local doctors who speak the language of their citizens.

Pharmacies The American Medical Center has a pharmacy stocked with Western medicines. The following two pharmacies are both centrally located, open 24 hours and stock both Russian and Western medicines, most available without prescription:

Pharmacy Ferrein (Map 6; ☎ 921 4942), Nikolskaya ulitsa 19-21

Pharmacy Kutuzovskaya (Map 4; ☎ 243 1601), Kutuzovsky prospekt 19-21

Emergency

Emergency telephone numbers are: ☎ 01 for fire, ☎ 02 for police, and ☎ 03 for ambulance. These numbers have Russian-speaking operators only. To report crime, call Petrovka 38, the state police, on ☎ 200 8924 for an English-speaking officer. The English-Language Crisis Line is a 24 hour hotline staffed by professionals. Call ☎ 244 3449, say 'crisis line', leave your number and a counsellor will call back.

CRAIG PERSHOUSE

Today Moscow, tomorrow the world

CHRIS MELLOR

... and if I push this button I get an E minor

CHRIS MELLOR

The seething masses of Moscow's shopping precinct

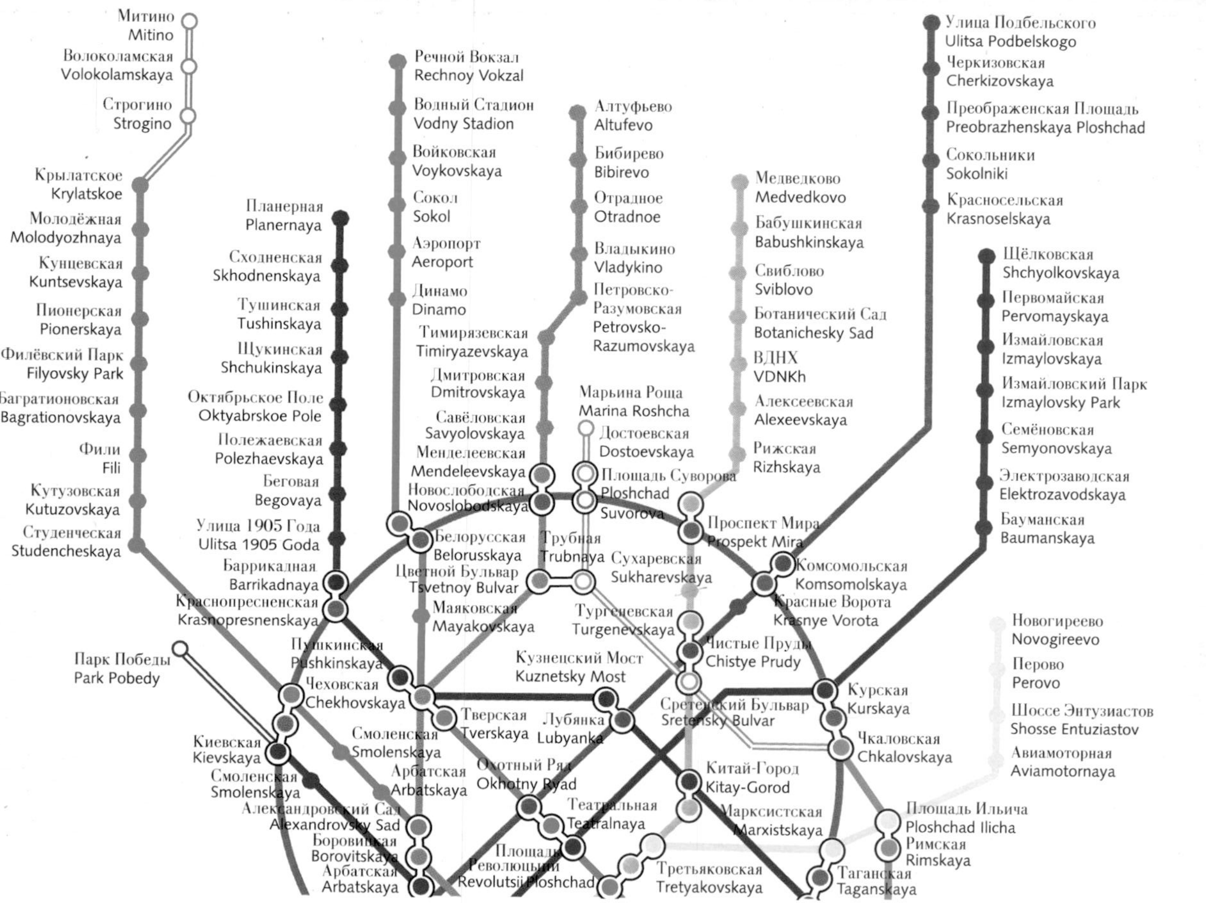
Митино
Mitino
Волоколамская
Volokolamskaya
Строгино
Strogino
Крылатское
Krylatskoe
Молодёжная
Molodyozhnaya
Кунцевская
Kuntsevskaya
Пионерская
Pionerskaya
Филёвский Парк
Filyovsky Park
Багратионовская
Bagrationovskaya
Фили
Fili
Кутузовская
Kutuzovskaya
Студенческая
Studencheskaya
Планерная
Planernaya
Сходненская
Skhodnenskaya
Тушинская
Tushinskaya
Щукинская
Shchukinskaya
Октябрьское Поле
Oktyabrskoe Pole
Полежаевская
Polezhaevskaya
Беговая
Begovaya
Улица 1905 Года
Ulitsa 1905 Goda
Баррикадная
Barrikadnaya
Краснопресненская
Krasnopresnenskaya
Речной Вокзал
Rechnoy Vokzal
Водный Стадион
Vodny Stadion
Войковская
Voykovskaya
Сокол
Sokol
Аэропорт
Aeroport
Динамо
Dinamo
Тимирязевская
Timiryazevskaya
Дмитровская
Dmitrovskaya
Савёловская
Savyolovskaya
Менделеевская
Mendeleevskaya
Новослободская
Novoslobodskaya
Белорусская
Belorusskaya
Алтуфьево
Altufevo
Бибирево
Bibirevo
Отрадное
Otradnoe
Владыкино
Vladykino
Петровско-Разумовская
Petrovsko-Razumovskaya
Марьина Роща
Marina Roshcha
Достоевская
Dostoevskaya
Площадь Суворова
Ploshchad Suvorova
Медведково
Medvedkovo
Бабушкинская
Babushkinskaya
Свиблово
Sviblovo
Ботанический Сад
Botanichesky Sad
ВДНХ
VDNKh
Алексеевская
Alexeevskaya
Рижская
Rizhskaya
Проспект Мира
Prospekt Mira
Улица Подбельского
Ulitsa Podbelskogo
Черкизовская
Cherkizovskaya
Преображенская Площадь
Preobrazhenskaya Ploshchad
Сокольники
Sokolniki
Красносельская
Krasnoselskaya
Щёлковская
Shchyolkovskaya
Первомайская
Pervomayskaya
Измайловская
Izmaylovskaya
Измайловский Парк
Izmaylovsky Park
Семёновская
Semyonovskaya
Электрозаводская
Elektrozavodskaya
Бауманская
Baumanskaya
Трубная
Trubnaya
Цветной Бульвар
Tsvetnoy Bulvar
Сухаревская
Sukharevskaya
Комсомольская
Komsomolskaya
Красные Ворота
Krasnye Vorota
Маяковская
Mayakovskaya
Тургеневская
Turgenevskaya
Чистые Пруды
Chistye Prudy
Новогиреево
Novogireevo
Перово
Perovo
Шоссе Энтузиастов
Shosse Entuziastov
Авиамоторная
Aviamotornaya
Парк Победы
Park Pobedy
Пушкинская
Pushkinskaya
Чеховская
Chekhovskaya
Кузнецкий Мост
Kuznetsky Most
Сретенский Бульвар
Sretensky Bulvar
Курская
Kurskaya
Киевская
Kievskaya
Смоленская
Smolenskaya
Тверская
Tverskaya
Лубянка
Lubyanka
Чкаловская
Chkalovskaya
Смоленская
Smolenskaya
Арбатская
Arbatskaya
Охотный Ряд
Okhotny Ryad
Китай-Город
Kitay-Gorod
Александровский Сад
Alexandrovsky Sad
Театральная
Teatralnaya
Марксистская
Marxistskaya
Площадь Ильича
Ploshchad Ilicha
Римская
Rimskaya
Боровицкая
Borovitskaya
Арбатская
Arbatskaya
Площадь Революции
Revolutsii Ploshchad
Третьяковская
Tretyakovskaya
Таганская
Taganskaya

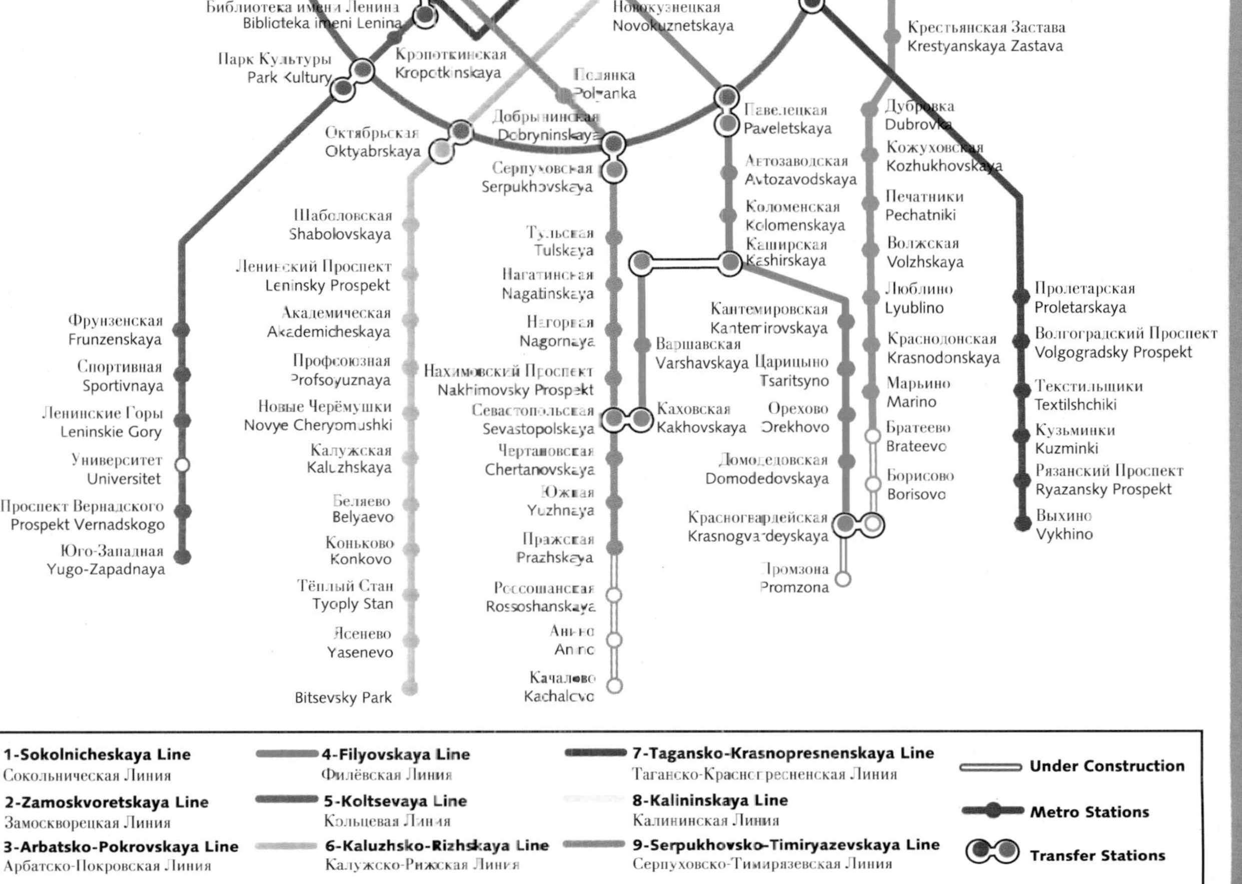
Библиотека имени Ленина
Biblioteka imeni Lenina
Парк Культуры
Park Kultury
Кропоткинская
Kropotkinskaya
Новокузнецкая
Novokuznetskaya
Полянка
Polyanka
Октябрьская
Oktyabrskaya
Добрынинская
Dobryninskaya
Серпуховская
Serpukhovskaya
Павелецкая
Paveletskaya
Крестьянская Застава
Krestyanskaya Zastava
Дубровка
Dubrovka
Кожуховская
Kozhukhovskaya
Печатники
Pechatniki
Волжская
Volzhskaya
Люблино
Lyublino
Краснодонская
Krasnodonskaya
Марьино
Marino
Братеево
Brateevo
Борисово
Borisovo
Автозаводская
Avtozavodskaya
Коломенская
Kolomenskaya
Каширская
Kashirskaya
Кантемировская
Kantemirovskaya
Царицыно
Tsaritsyno
Орехово
Orekhovo
Домодедовская
Domodedovskaya
Красногвардейская
Krasnogvardeyskaya
Промзона
Promzona
Варшавская
Varshavskaya
Каховская
Kakhovskaya
Пролетарская
Proletarskaya
Волгоградский Проспект
Volgogradsky Prospekt
Текстильщики
Textilshchiki
Кузьминки
Kuzminki
Рязанский Проспект
Ryazansky Prospekt
Выхино
Vykhino
Фрунзенская
Frunzenskaya
Спортивная
Sportivnaya
Ленинские Горы
Leninskie Gory
Университет
Universitet
Проспект Вернадского
Prospekt Vernadskogo
Юго-Западная
Yugo-Zapadnaya
Шаболовская
Shabolovskaya
Ленинский Проспект
Leninsky Prospekt
Академическая
Akademicheskaya
Профсоюзная
Profsoyuznaya
Новые Черёмушки
Novye Cheryomushki
Калужская
Kaluzhskaya
Беляево
Belyaevo
Коньково
Konkovo
Тёплый Стан
Tyoply Stan
Ясенево
Yasenevo
Bitsevsky Park
Тульская
Tulskaya
Нагатинская
Nagatinskaya
Нагорная
Nagornaya
Нахимовский Проспект
Nakhimovsky Prospekt
Севастопольская
Sevastopolskaya
Чертановская
Chertanovskaya
Южная
Yuzhnaya
Пражская
Prazhskaya
Россошанская
Rossoshanskaya
Анино
Anino
Качалово
Kachalovo
1-Sokolnicheskaya Line
Сокольническая Линия
2-Zamoskvoretskaya Line
Замоскворецкая Линия
3-Arbatsko-Pokrovskaya Line
Арбатско-Покровская Линия
4-Filyovskaya Line
Филёвская Линия
5-Koltsevaya Line
Кольцевая Линия
6-Kaluzhsko-Rizhskaya Line
Калужско-Рижская Линия
7-Tagansko-Krasnopresnenskaya Line
Таганско-Краснопресненская Линия
8-Kalininskaya Line
Калининская Линия
9-Serpukhovsko-Timiryazevskaya Line
Серпуховско-Тимирязевская Линия
Under Construction
Metro Stations
Transfer Stations

LIZ THOMPSON

All dressed up with no space to go – monument to Soviet space flight

JOHN NOBLE

Domes of St Basil's Cathedral

GEORGI SHABLOVSKY

Inside GUM, Moscow

CRAIG PERSHOUSE

One of Moscow's Seven Sisters

LIZ THOMPSON

Going underground – a station of the Moscow metro

Dangers & Annoyances

Crime Despite Muscovites' paranoia about rising crime in the city, visitors generally have little to fear from big-time organised crime, which tends to concentrate on other targets. However, you certainly need to always be on your guard against pickpockets and muggers.

The most common hazard is violent and xenophobic drunks. Be on your guard and avoid them as much as possible. Certain members of the police force will also bug anybody who doesn't look like a fair-haired Muskovite. Practical advice from a Moscow synagogue is 'cover your kippa'. Also watch out for gangs of children, generally referred to as 'gypsy kids', who are after your bag, camera, or anything loose on your person. These come in groups of eight, 10 or more and may be as young as seven or eight years old.

Unsavoury Characters The new money in Moscow has bred a new breed of thug known commonly as 'flatheads'. These large, ill-tempered men are typically employed by someone with lots of money who pays them to look after their interests with as little grace as possible. You're likely to run into them as guards at shops, clubs and restaurants, when they knock you aside so their patron can jump the queue, and when you are nearly run over by one of their cars. These are not difficult to spot because they bear flashing blue lights which show they have bought a permit from the Moscow government that allows them to flout all traffic laws.

Even in the poshest Western five-star hotel you will see lobbies full of prostitutes. They can also be found in clubs, on the street and just about anywhere else. One glance and you will have their unwavering attention. They may try to follow you to your room, show up unexpectedly or otherwise force their charms upon you. Given that there is usually some flathead-like character nearby who may try to shake you down, you should immediately complain to the management. On the street, just keep walking briskly.

KREMLIN (MAP 6)

The Moscow Kremlin (Kreml) is the kernel of its city and country, the place to which all Russian roads lead and from which most political power emanates. From here Ivan the Terrible and Stalin orchestrated their terrors, Napoleon watched Moscow burn, Lenin fashioned the dictatorship of the proletariat, Khrushchev led communism in the Cold War, Gorbachev unleashed perestroika, and Yeltsin ruled with colour, if not always vigour.

In what was for decades a den of militant atheism, it may come as a surprise that the Kremlin's chief glories, the bases from which most of its famous gold domes rise, are cathedrals. The Kremlin was once the centre of Russia's Church as well as State.

The Kremlin occupies a roughly triangular plot of land covering little Borovitsky Hill on the north bank of the Moscow River, probably first settled in the 11th century. Today it's enclosed by high walls 2.25km long, with Red Square outside the east wall. The best views of the Kremlin are from Sofiyskaya naberezhnaya, across the river, and the upper floors of the Rossiya and Intourist hotels.

A kremlin is a town's fortified stronghold, and the first low, wooden wall around Moscow's was built in the 1150s. The Kremlin grew with the importance of Moscow's princes and in the 1320s became the headquarters of the Russian Church, which shifted from Vladimir. The 'White Stone Kremlin' – which had limestone walls – was built in the 1360s with almost the same boundaries as today. This lasted till the 1475-1516 rebuilding launched by Ivan the Great, when master builders from Pskov and Italy came to supervise new walls and towers (most of which still stand), the three great cathedrals and more. Other buildings have been added piecemeal since then.

Even after Peter the Great shifted his capital and Church headquarters to St Petersburg, tsars were crowned here. But nothing of today's Kremlin would be standing if Catherine the Great hadn't run out of money and interest after drawing up plans for a new, classical Kremlin in the 1770s, or

MOSCOW

if Napoleon's troops hadn't been prevented by rain and the timely arrival of Russian soldiers from blowing the whole place up as they retreated in 1812.

Admission

The Kremlin is open to visitors from 10 am to 5 pm daily except Thursday. Don't wear shorts or they won't let you in.

The main visitors' entrance is the Kutafya Tower on Manezhnaya ulitsa (metro: Alexandrovsky Sad, Borovitskaya or Biblioteka imeni Lenina). Kremlin ticket offices (kassy muzeyev Kremlya; ☎ 921 4720), which close at 4.30 pm, are on either side of the Kutafya tower and in the Alexandrovsky Garden a short distance to the south. Beneath the Kutafya Tower is a left-luggage office (kamera khranenia), open from 9 am to 6.30 pm, where you must leave large bags or backpacks for $0.30 apiece.

A ticket for the grounds is $8, and it costs extra for tickets to the cathedrals and museums inside; you can get these either at the ticket offices or at the door of each venue that you decide to visit. The foreigner charges were $6 each for the six buildings clustered around the Kremlin's central Cathedral Square (Sobornaya ploshchad) – the Assumption, Archangel and Annunciation cathedrals, the Church of the Deposition of the Robe, the Patriarch's Palace, and the Ivan the Great Bell Tower – and $10 for the Armoury. An ISIC gets you half-price tickets. Prices for Russians are about 10% of the foreigner prices, but the cashiers are very adept at distinguishing non-Russian accents. Also note that foreigner prices are continually adjusted to allow for currency revaluations or domestic economic collapse, so don't expect any bargains.

Inside the grounds, police blow whistles to stop you straying into out-of-bounds areas, including the government buildings.

Tours Kremlin tours are among the main offerings of the companies selling guided tours of Moscow. See Organised Tours later in this chapter for details. Expect to pay $20 (including entry fee) on average for a tour of the Kremlin that will cover the grounds and the Armoury. Numerous freelance guides tout their services near Kutafya Tower. Prices and quality vary widely.

Northern & Western Buildings

The **Kutafya Tower** (Kutafya bashnya), which forms the main visitors' entrance today, stands away from the Kremlin's west wall, at the end of a ramp over the Alexandrovsky Garden. The ramp was once a bridge over the Neglinnaya River, which used to be part of the Kremlin's defences but has flowed underground, beneath the Alexandrovsky Garden, since the early 19th century. The Kutafya Tower is the last survivor of a number of outer bridge towers that once stood on this side of the Kremlin.

From the Kutafya Tower, walk up the ramp and pass through the Kremlin walls beneath the **Trinity Gate Tower** (Troitskaya bashnya). On your way to Sobornaya ploshchad you pass the following buildings that are closed to visitors.

The lane to the right (south), immediately inside the Trinity Gate Tower, runs between the 17th century **Poteshny Palace** (Poteshny dvorets) where Stalin lived, and the bombastic marble, glass and concrete **Kremlin Palace of Congresses** (Kremlyovksy Dvorets Syezdov), built in 1960-61 for Communist Party congresses and as a concert and ballet auditorium which holds 6000 people. North of the Kremlin Palace of Congresses, the 18th century **Arsenal** is ringed with 800 captured Napoleonic cannon. The ultimate seat of power in the modern Kremlin, the offices of the president of Russia, are in the yellow, triangular former **Senate** (Senat) building, a fine 18th century classical edifice, east of the Arsenal. Next to the Senate is a 1930s **Supreme Soviet** (Verkhovny Soviet) building.

Assumption Cathedral

The first building open to visitors that you reach, just past the State Kremlin Palace, is the **Patriarch's Palace** (Patriarshy dvorets), but you'll probably prefer to pass over it for the time being and continue into Sobornaya ploshchad, the heart of the Kremlin, surrounded by magnificent buildings.

On the northern side of Sobornaya ploshchad, with five golden helmet domes and four semicircular gables facing the square, is the Assumption Cathedral (Uspensky sobor), the focal church of prerevolutionary Russia and burial place of most of the heads of the Russian Orthodox Church from the 1320s to 1700.

The cathedral was built between 1475 and 1479 after the Bolognese architect Aristotle Fioravanti had toured Novgorod, Suzdal and Vladimir to acquaint himself with Russian architecture. His design is based on the Assumption Cathedral at Vladimir, with some Western features. It replaced a smaller 1326 cathedral on the same site.

In 1812 French troops used the cathedral as a stable and looted 295kg of gold and over five tonnes of silver, but much of it was recovered. Occasional special services are now held in the Assumption Cathedral after a gap from 1918 to 1989.

A striking 1660s fresco of the Virgin Mary faces Sobornaya ploshchad above the door once used for royal processions. The visitors' entrance is at the western end. The interior is unusually bright and spacious, full of warm golds, reds and blues. The tombs of many of the leaders of the Russian Church (metropolitans up to 1590, patriarchs from 1590 to 1700) are against the north, west and south walls.

Near the south wall is a tent-roofed wooden throne made in 1551 for Ivan the Terrible. It's commonly known as the **Throne of Monomakh** because of its carved scenes from the career of 12th century Grand Prince Vladimir Monomakh of Kyiv.

The **iconostasis** dates from 1652 but its lowest level contains some older icons. Among them are, second from the right, the 1340s *Saviour with the Angry Eye (Spas yaroe oko)* and, on the left of the central door, the *Virgin of Vladimir (Vladimirskaya Bogomater)*, an early 15th century Rublyov school copy of Russia's most revered image, the *Vladimir Icon of the Mother of God (Vladimirskaya Ikona Bogomateri)*. The 12th century original, now in the Tretyakov Gallery, stood in the Assumption Cathedral from the 1480s to 1930. One of the oldest Russian icons, the 12th century red-clothed *St George (Svyatoy Georgy)* from Novgorod, formerly positioned to the right of the iconostasis' south door, was removed for restoration when we last visited.

Most of the existing murals on the cathedral walls were painted on a gilt base in the 1640s, but three grouped together on the south wall – *The Apocalypse (Apokalipsis), The Life of Metropolitan Pyotr (Zhitie Mitropolita Petra)* and *All Creatures Rejoice in Thee (O tebe raduetsya)* – are attributed to Dionysius and his followers, the cathedral's original 15th century mural painters.

Church of the Deposition of the Robe

This delicate little single domed church (Tserkov Rizpolozhenia), beside the west door of the Assumption Cathedral, was built between 1484 and 1486 in exclusively Russian style as the private chapel of the heads of the Church, who tended to be highly suspicious of such people as Italian architects. Later, the tsars used it. The interior walls, ceilings and pillars are covered with 17th century frescoes. It houses an exhibition of 15th to 17th century woodcarvings.

Ivan the Great Bell Tower

With its two golden domes rising above the eastern side of Sobornaya ploshchad, the Ivan the Great Bell Tower (Kolokolnya Ivana Velikogo) is the Kremlin's tallest structure – a Moscow landmark visible 30km away. Before the 20th century it was forbidden to build any higher in Moscow.

The southern tower had just two octagonal tiers beneath a drum and dome when designed by the Italian Marco Bono in 1505-08. Boris Godunov raised it to 81m (which the inscription just below the dome explains at some length). The building's central section, with gilded single dome and a 65 tonne bell, dates from between 1532 and 1542. The tent-roofed annexe next to the belfry was commissioned by Patriarch Filaret in 1642 and bears his name. Exhibitions from the Kremlin collections are shown on the ground level.

The Tsar Bell, broken before it was ever rung

Tsar Bell

Beside the bell tower stands the world's biggest bell, the Tsar-kolokol, a 202 tonne monster that never rang. It was cast in the 1730s for Empress Anna Ivanovna using the remains of Tsar Alexey's 130 tonne 1655 version, which had shattered in a fall from its own special belfry in a 1701 fire. The bell was cooling off in the foundry casting pit in 1737 when water that was being poured on one of the fires nearby came into contact with the bell, causing an 11 tonne chunk to chip off.

Tsar Cannon

North of the bell tower is the Tsar Cannon (Tsar-pushka). It was cast in 1586 for Fyodor I, whose portrait is on the barrel. Shot has never sullied its 89cm bore – certainly not the cannonballs beside it, which are too big even for this elephantine firearm.

Archangel Cathedral

Back on Sobornaya ploshchad, the Archangel Cathedral (Arkhangelsky sobor) at the square's south-eastern corner was for centuries the coronation, wedding and burial church of tsars. The tombs of all Muscovy's rulers from the 1320s to the 1690s are here bar one (the absentee is Boris Godunov, who is buried at Sergiev Posad).

The cathedral was built between 1505 and 1508 by the Italian Alevisio Novi and dedicated to the Archangel Michael, guardian of Moscow's princes. Like the Assumption Cathedral, it is five domed and essentially Byzantine-Russian in style. But the exterior has many Venetian Renaissance features – notably the distinctive scallop shell gables.

The rows of sarcophagi which take up much of the floor space were carved in the 17th century. Tsarevich Dmitry, a son of Ivan the Terrible who died mysteriously in 1591 and was impersonated by the False Dmitrys during the Time of Troubles, lies beneath a painted stone canopy. Frustratingly, Ivan's own tomb is out of sight behind the iconostasis, along with those of his other sons: Ivan (whom he killed), and Fyodor (who succeeded him). From Peter the Great onwards, emperors and empresses were buried in St Petersburg; the exception was Peter II, who died in Moscow in 1730 and is here.

The murals – revealed from under later layers during 1950s restorations – are from the 17th century. The south wall depicts many of those buried here; on the pillars are some of their predecessors, including Andrey Bogolyubsky, Prince Daniil and his father, Alexander Nevsky.

Annunciation Cathedral

The Annunciation Cathedral (Blagoveshchensky sobor) at the south-western corner of Sobornaya ploshchad, contains probably the greatest icons of possibly the greatest icon painter, Theophanes the Greek. They have a timeless beauty which appeals even to those usually left cold by icons.

This cathedral, built between 1484 and 1489 by Pskov masters, was the royal family's private chapel. Originally it had just three domes and an open gallery round three sides. Ivan the Terrible, whose taste was more elaborate, added six more domes and chapels at each corner, enclosed the gallery and gilded the roof. His fourth marriage disqualified him under Orthodox law from

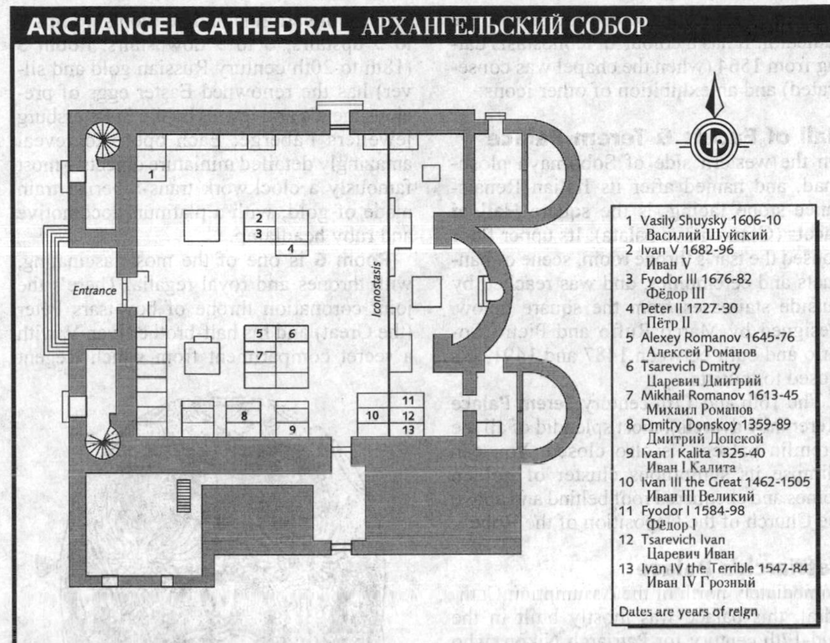

entering the church proper, so he had the southern arm of the gallery converted into the Archangel Gabriel Chapel, from which he could watch services through a grille.

Many of the murals in the gallery date from the 1560s. Among them are the *Capture of Jericho* in the porch, *Jonah and the Whale* on the south side of the northern arm of the gallery, *Virgin* on the west arm's west wall, the *Trinity* on its east wall, and the *Tree of Jesse* (showing Christ's ancestors) on its ceiling.

The small central part of the cathedral has a lovely jasper floor and several 16th century frescoes – including Russian princes on the north pillar and Byzantine emperors on the south, both with Apocalypse scenes above them. But its real treasure is the iconostasis, where 1920s restorers uncovered early 15th century icons probably painted for a previous church on the site by three of the greatest medieval Russian artists.

Theophanes is usually thought to have painted the six icons at the right-hand end of the deesis row, the biggest of the iconostasis' six tiers. From left to right, these are the *Virgin Mary*, *Christ Enthroned*, *St John the Baptist*, the *Archangel Gabriel*, the *Apostle Paul* and *St John Chrysostom*. What sets them apart from most other icons is the genuine emotion visible in their faces and movements. These are real people, not cardboard cutouts.

The third icon from the left, *Archangel Michael*, is ascribed to Andrey Rublyov, who may also have painted the adjacent *St Peter.* Rublyov is also reckoned to be the artist of the first, second, sixth, seventh and probably the third and fifth icons from the left of the festival row, above the deesis row. Prokhor of Gorodets is thought to have painted the seven at the right-hand end.

The **Archangel Gabriel Chapel** (Pridel Arkhangela Gavriila) can be entered either from the southern end of the western arm of the gallery or from the central part of the cathedral. It has a colourful iconostasis dating from 1564 (when the chapel was consecrated) and an exhibition of other icons.

Hall of Facets & Terem Palace

On the western side of Sobornaya ploshchad, and named after its Italian Renaissance stone facing, is the square **Hall of Facets** (Granovitaya palata). Its upper floor housed the tsar's throne room, scene of banquets and ceremonies, and was reached by outside staircases from the square below. Designed by Marco Ruffo and Pietro Solario and built between 1487 and 1491, it's closed to tourists.

The 16th and 17th century **Terem Palace** (Teremnoy dvorets), most splendid of all the Kremlin palaces, is also closed. You can glimpse its sumptuous cluster of golden domes and chequered roof behind and above the Church of the Deposition of the Robe.

Patriarch's Palace

Immediately north of the Assumption Cathedral, this palace was mostly built in the mid-17th century for Patriarch Nikon, who ordered a return to the early Moscow style. It contains a **Museum of 17th Century Russian Applied Art & Life**. This houses mostly church vestments, icons, illuminated books and so on, but also incorporates the five domed **Church of the Twelve Apostles** (Tserkov Dvenadtsati Apostolov), which Nikon had built as a new patriarch's chapel, and the large **Hall of the Cross** (Krestovaya Palata), once the patriarch's official reception hall.

Armoury

A numbingly opulent collection of treasures accumulated over centuries by the Russian State and Church is housed in the Armoury (Oruzheynaya palata) in the south-west corner of the Kremlin. Normally you can enter (with a ticket) any time the Kremlin is open, but during some busy periods entry may be restricted to specific times, posted at the Armoury door or the Kutafya Tower ticket offices. In such cases your ticket will be for one particular entry time *(seans)*.

The collection is in nine rooms: **rooms 1** to **5** upstairs, **6** to **9** downstairs. **Room 3** (18th to 20th century Russian gold and silver) has the renowned Easter eggs of precious metals and jewels by the St Petersburg jewellers Fabergé. Each opens to reveal amazingly detailed miniature objects – most famously a clockwork trans-Siberian train made of gold, with a platinum locomotive and ruby headlamp.

Room 6 is one of the most fascinating, with thrones and royal regalia. There's the joint coronation throne of boy tsars Peter (the Great) and his half-brother Ivan V, with a secret compartment from which Regent

Fabergé egg

Sofia would prompt them; the 800-diamond throne of Peter's father, Tsar Alexey; the jewel-studded, sable-trimmed, gold Cap of Monomakh, worn for coronations for two centuries until 1682; and the coronation dresses of 18th century empresses. (Empress Elizabeth, we're told, had 15,000 other dresses, and lots of unpaid bills.)

Among the coaches in **room 9** is the sleigh in which Elizabeth rode from St Petersburg to Moscow for her coronation, pulled by 23 horses at a time – about 800 in all for the trip.

Between the Armoury and the Annunciation Cathedral stretches the 700 room **Great Kremlin Palace** (Bolshoy Kremlyovsky dvorets), built in the period from 1838 to 1849 as an imperial residence. Now it is an official residence of the Russian president and is used for official state visits and receptions. It's not open to the public.

Diamond Fund Exhibition

If the Armoury hasn't sated your diamond lust, there are more in the separate Diamond Fund Exhibition (Vystavka almaznogo fonda) in the same building, but you have to pre-book a group tour to see them (see the Getting In section). The collection, mainly of precious stones and jewellery garnered by tsars and empresses, includes such weighty beasts as the 190 carat diamond given to Catherine the Great by her lover Grigory Orlov.

Towers

The Kremlin walls have 19 distinctive towers, mostly built between 1485 and 1500, with tent roofs added in the 17th century. Some towers had to be rebuilt after Napoleonic vandalism.

The **Saviour Gate Tower** (Spasskaya bashnya) over the Kremlin's 'official' exit on to Red Square is Moscow's Big Ben – its chimes are relayed over state radio. This gate was used for processions in tsarist days. Ivan the Terrible watched executions nearby, where the **Tsar Tower** (Tsarskaya bashnya) was later built.

The **Konstantin and Yelena Tower** (Konstantino-Yeleninskaya bashnya) is also known as the Torture Tower. The **Secrets Tower** (Taynitskaya bashnya) facing the river was both a gate and the start of a secret passage to the river. Ivan the Terrible used the **Annunciation Tower** (Blagoveshchenskaya bashnya), the next along, as a prison.

Alexandrovsky Garden

This park (Alexandrovsky Sad) along the Kremlin's western wall, open free to everybody, is a pleasant spot in which to cool down on a hot day.

The **Tomb of the Unknown Soldier** (Mogila neizvestnogo soldata) at its north end is a kind of national pilgrimage spot, where newlyweds bring flowers and have their pictures taken. The tomb contains the remains of one soldier who died in December 1941 at Km 41 of Leningradskoe shosse – the nearest the Nazis came to Moscow. The inscription reads 'Your name is unknown, your deeds immortal'. There's an eternal flame, and other inscriptions listing the Soviet hero cities of WWII and honouring 'those who fell for the motherland' between 1941 and 1945. The changing of the guard happens every hour from 10 am to 7 pm in summer; to 3 pm during winter.

CITY CENTRE

The heart of the city lies in the arc round the Kremlin bound by Mokhovaya ulitsa, Okhotny ryad, Teatralny proezd and Lubyansky proezd.

Red Square (Map 6)

Red Square (Krasnaya ploshchad) lies immediately outside the Kremlin's north-eastern wall. As you step on to the square, feast your eyes on the building that, more than any other, says 'Russia' – St Basil's Cathedral, which rises from the slope at the southern end of the square.

Red Square is closed to traffic except for the limousines that whiz in and out of the Kremlin's Saviour Gate from time to time. Most people here are sightseers but that doesn't reduce the frisson of walking on these 400m by 150m of cobbles so central to Russian history. It's particularly atmospheric when floodlit at night.

Red Square used to be a market square and has always been a place where the Kremlin's occupants chose to make points to their people. Ivan the Terrible publicly confessed his misdeeds here in 1547, built St Basil's to commemorate his victories in the 1550s, and later had numerous perceived enemies executed here. The Cossack rebel Stepan Razin was dismembered here in 1671, and 2000 members of Peter the Great's mutinous palace guard, the Streltsy, were executed en masse here in 1698.

Soviet rulers chose Red Square for their main twice-yearly military parades: perhaps most poignantly on 7 November 1941, when tanks rolled straight off to the front line outside Moscow; and during the Cold War, when lines of ICBMs rumbled across the square to remind the West of Soviet military might.

The name Krasnaya ploshchad has nothing to do with either communism or the blood that's flowed here. *Krasnyy* originally meant beautiful: only in the 20th century did it come to mean 'red' too.

The best way to enter the Red Square is through the **Resurrection Gate** (Voskresenskiye Vorota). Rebuilt in 1995 with its twin red towers topped by green tent spires, it's an exact copy of the original completed on this site in 1680. The first gateway was destroyed in 1931 because Stalin considered it an impediment to the parades and demonstrations held in the Red Square.

Within the gateway is a bright **Chapel of the Iverian Virgin** (Chasovnya Iverskoy Boromateri), originally built in the late 18th century to house the icon.

Lenin's Tomb The granite tomb of Lenin (Mavzoley V I Lenina) stands at the foot of the Kremlin wall, which somewhat dwarfs it. Despite calls by Mayor Luzhkov and others, including the Church, for Lenin to be removed to both a more secluded and more politically palatable resting place, the

Russia's Most Famous Corpse

The sallow figure lying in repose in Lenin's Tomb certainly could be that of the famous Communist ... then again, there has been speculation that what's on show in the brightly lit chamber may not be Lenin at all – or even human.

Certainly what you see on your quick walk-through far more resembles a display at Madame Tussaud's in London than it does your typical human body several decades after death. What is known is that budget cuts in 1991 decimated the cadre of workers who used to care for the body.

In the heyday of the Soviet era, nary a bit of fungus could grow or the odd digit decompose before skilled technicians were there, wielding special potions and other tools. Nowadays, with visits down and maintenance curtailed, it's hard not to compare the yellowish figure behind the glass with a skilfully created bowl of wax fruit.

Still the ruse continues; in 1999 the figure was given a new coat and tie even though a poll taken at the time showed that 55% of Russians thought Lenin should be given a grave beside his mother in St Petersburg, as he himself had requested. They've been talking of burying him for 10 years and the talk is likely to continue for a long time. Most leaders, ie Yeltsin and Luzhkov, want him in the ground, but they have better things to do than battle the hardliners, who are happy with him where he is.

CLINT CURÉ

Kremlin Wall

Some of the worthies given the honour of burial beneath the Kremlin Wall include:

Felix Dzerzhinsky	The founder of the Cheka (forerunner of the KGB)
Yakov Sverdlov	A key organiser of the revolution and the first official head of the Soviet State
Andrey Zhdanov	Stalin's cultural chief and the second most powerful man in the USSR immediately after WWII
Mikhail Frunze	The Red Army leader who secured Central Asia for the Soviet Union in the 1920s
Inessa Armand	Lenin's lover
John Reed (Dzhon Rid)	The American author of *Ten Days that Shook the World*, a first-hand account of the revolution

Plaques in the wall mark the spots where the ashes of many more heroes lie, including:

Yury Gagarin	The first astronaut
Marshal Georgy Zhukov	The commander who defeated Hitler
Alexey Kosygin	Brezhnev's initial partner in power in the 1960s
Igor Kurchatov	The leader of the team that developed the Soviet hydrogen bomb

embalmed leader remained on display in 1999 as he had since 1924 (apart from a retreat to Siberia during WWII). From 1953 to 1961 Lenin shared the tomb with Stalin, who had initiated the tradition of Soviet leaders standing on the tomb to inspect the annual May Day and 7 November parades.

The tomb is open to the public, free of charge, from 10 am to 1 pm daily except Monday and Friday, although the hours have become erratic as interest in the former leader has waned and crowds have thinned. Join the queue at the north-western corner of Red Square and within a few minutes you'll be descending the stairs into the tomb.

Humourless guards ensure that visitors remain respectful. Without stopping, you walk round three sides of the glass case in which Lenin lies; a surprisingly small figure who looks as real as the fake carnations decorating the tombs outside. Note that the tomb is air-conditioned, which makes it a nice refuge on a hot day. For a discussion of just what you see in the tomb, see the boxed text, 'Russia's Most Famous Corpse'.

From the tomb you emerge into a plot beneath the Kremlin wall where lie the remains of many more Soviet luminaries. Special notables are represented by busts above their graves in a special plot between Lenin's tomb and the Kremlin wall. These include Stalin and Soviet Communist Party general secretaries Leonid Brezhnev, Yury Andropov and Konstantin Chernenko. See the 'Kremlin Wall' boxed text for others buried or commemorated here.

St Basil's Cathedral No picture can prepare you for St Basil's (Sobor Vasilia Blazhennogo), which rises like a fairy tale at the southern end of Red Square. This building's unique cluster of colours and shapes, in some lights ominous and forbidding, in others joyous and playful, is the ultimate symbol of Russia; and, despite its Oriental turban domes, the cathedral is in fact the culmination in brick of a wholly Russian style that had been developed in building wooden churches.

St Basil's was created between 1555 and 1561, replacing an existing church on the site, to celebrate Ivan the Terrible's taking of the Tatar stronghold of Kazan on 1 October 1552, the feast of the Intercession – hence its official name, the Pokrovsky (Intercession) Cathedral. The architect is thought to have been called Posnik Yakovlev. Legend has it that Ivan had this genius blinded so that he could never build anything comparable.

The cathedral owes its usual name to the barefoot holy fool Vasily (Basil) the Blessed, who predicted Ivan's damnation and added (correctly), as the army left for Kazan, that Ivan would murder a son. Vasily died while Kazan was under siege and was buried beside the church which St Basil's soon replaced. He was later canonised.

St Basil's apparent anarchy of shapes in fact hides a comprehensible plan of nine main chapels: the tall, tent-roofed one in the centre; four big, octagonal-towered ones, topped with the four biggest domes, on the north, south, east and west; and four smaller ones in between. A couple of extra tent roofs on the stairways, an extra north-eastern chapel over Vasily the Blessed's grave, and a tent-roofed south-eastern bell tower were added later. Only in the 1670s were the domes patterned and St Basil's given its present, highly colourful appearance.

The interior is open to visitors from 10 am to 6 pm daily except Tuesday (foreigner admission $4). The ground level holds a small exhibition on St Basil's itself, and there are some lovely frescoes of flower patterns and saints.

In front of St Basil's stands a **statue** of the butcher Kuzma Minin and Prince Dmitry Pozharsky (pamyatnik Mininu i Pozharskomu), who together raised and led the army that ejected the occupying Poles from the Kremlin in 1612. Just up the slope is the round, walled **Place of Skulls** (Lobnoe Mesto), the spot where Ivan the Terrible made his public confession and also where the Streltsy were executed by Peter the Great.

GUM The Gosudarstvenny Universalny Magazin (State Department Store), which lines the north-eastern side of Red Square, was built in the 19th century to house over 1000 shops. GUM once symbolised all that was bad about Soviet shopping – long queues and shelves empty of all but a few drab goods.

A remarkable transformation has taken place since perestroika, and today, GUM is a bright, bustling place full of attractive shops stocked with imported and Russian goods of all kinds. Benetton, Yves Rocher, Galerie Lafayette and many other big foreign names are here. There are a few snack places, and pay toilets at the southern end of the ground level. See Shopping later in this chapter for further information.

Kazan Cathedral The tiny Kazan Cathedral (Kazansky sobor) on the corner of Red Square and Nikolskaya ulitsa opposite the northern end of GUM, looks, and is, simultaneously old and brand new. Founded in 1636 in thanks for the 1612 expulsion of Polish invaders, it housed for two centuries the *Virgin of Kazan* icon which had supposedly helped to rout the Poles, and became a highly venerated symbol of Moscow's and Russia's survival.

Then in 1936 it was completely demolished, allegedly because it impeded the flow of celebrating workers in May Day and Revolution Day parades. In 1993, with the revival of the Church, it was rebuilt as before. It's open to visitors from 8 am to 7 pm daily, and evening service is held at 8 pm on Monday.

State History Museum The State History Museum (Gosudarstvenny Istorichesky Muzey; ☎ 292 4019) is located at the northern end of Red Square and has an enormous collection covering the whole Russian empire from the Stone Age on. The building, which dates from the late 19th century, is itself an attraction. Each room is in the style of a different period or region, some with highly decorated walls which echo old Russian churches. Reopened in 1997, each year sees the addition of a few more galleries. The museum is open from 11 am to 7 pm daily except Tuesday. Admission is $3.

The former Central Lenin Museum across the street at ploshchad Revolyutsii 2, once the big daddy of all the Lenin museums, was closed in 1993 after the White House shoot-out.

Kitay-Gorod

The narrow old streets east of Red Square are known as the Kitay-Gorod, which means 'Chinatown', but it has nothing to do with China. The name derives from '*kita*' which means wattle, after the palisades that reinforced the earthen ramp erected around this early Kremlin suburb. This is one of the oldest parts of Moscow, settled since the 13th century and long a trade and financial centre.

Nikolskaya ulitsa, which leaves Red Square between GUM and the Kazan Cathedral and leads to Lubyanskaya ploshchad, is the Kitay-Gorod's busiest street, lined with numerous shops and thronged with pedestrians. It used to be the centre of a busy trade in icons, and had three monasteries.

The dilapidated, but occasionally active, church of the **Zaikonospassky Monastery** (Zaikonospassky monastyr; Map 6), built between 1661 and 1720, stands in the courtyard of No 9. The ornate green and white building a block east, with a lion and unicorn above its entrance, is the old **Printing House** (pechatny dvor; Map 6) where in 1563-64 Ivan Fyodorov reputedly produced Russia's first printed book, the *Acts of the Apostles*, and in 1703 the first Russian newspaper, *Vedomosti*, was printed.

The **Monastery of Epiphany** (Bogoyavlenky Monastyr; Map 6) is just up the road and around the corner, past the Stariy Gorod kiosk row. Its Epiphany Cathedral was constructed in the 1690s; the monastery itself dates back to the 13th century and is the second oldest in Moscow.

Moscow's financial heart used to be along ulitsa Ilyinka a block south of Nikolskaya ulitsa: the **old stock exchange** (byvshaya birzha; Map 6) is at No 2.

Ulitsa Varvarka has the Kitay-Gorod's greatest concentration of interesting buildings, though they're grotesquely dwarfed by Hotel Rossiya. The pink and white **St Barbara's Church** (Tserkov Varvary; Map 2), now government offices, dates from the years 1795 to 1804. The reconstructed 16th century **English House** (Palaty starogo angliyskogo dvora; Map 2), white with peaked wooden roofs, was the residence of England's first emissaries to Russia (sent by Elizabeth I to Ivan the Terrible) and the base for English merchants who were allowed to trade duty free in exchange for military supplies to Ivan. It's open from 11 am to 6 pm daily except Monday; admission is $0.40.

Built in 1698, the yellow **St Maxim the Blessed's Church** (Tserkov Maxima Blazhennogo; Map 2) at ulitsa Varvarka 4 is now a folk-art exhibition hall. Next along is the pointed bell tower of the 17th century **Monastery of the Sign** (Znamensky monastyr; Map 2); between the street and the western half of Hotel Rossiya's access ramp are the monastery's monks' building (now a crafts shop) and a golden domed cathedral.

Between the street and the eastern half of the ramp is the small but interesting **Chambers in Zaryadie Museum** (Muzey Palaty v Zaryadie; Map 2), devoted to the lives of the Romanov family before they became tsars and were mere *boyars* (nobles). The house was built by Nikita Romanov, who was Ivan the Terrible's first brother-in-law, and whose grandson Mikhail later became the first of the 300-year Romanov dynasty. It's open from 11 am to 6 pm Wednesday, and 10 am to 5 pm Thursday to Monday; it's closed on Tuesday and the first Monday of the month; admission is $3. The entrance is on the Hotel Rossiya side.

The colourful **St George's Church** (Tserkov Georgiya; Map 2) at ulitsa Varvarka 12, another crafts gallery, dates from 1658. Off the south-eastern corner of Hotel Rossiya is the pretty little 15th and 16th century Pskov style **Church of St Anne's Conception** (Tserkov Zachatiya Anny; Map 4).

Opposite St George's Church, Ipatyevsky pereulok leads to the 1630s **Church of the Trinity in Nikitniki** (Tserkov Troitsy v Nikitnikakh; Map 2), one of Moscow's finest, with onion domes and lovely tiers of red and white spade gables rising from a square tower. The interior is covered with 1650s gospel frescoes by Simon Ushakov and others which reveal much about 17th century Russia. A carved doorway leads into St Nikita the Martyr's chapel, above the vault of the Nikitnikov merchant family, one of whom built the church. The church is open again for services but hours are erratic.

Around Manezhnaya Ploshchad (Map 6)

Wide Manezhnaya ploshchad north of the State History Museum, at the northern end of Red Square where several key Moscow streets converge, has been transformed into the vast underground **Okhotny Ryad Shopping Mall** (☎ 737 8409), which makes its presence known in the square with a series of half-domes and balustrades, and a network of fountains and sculptures. One of Mayor Luzkhov's grand projects, the mall has an excess of gilt and marble and hosts a variety of overpriced boutiques and several eateries on the lower level.

The long, low building on the south-western side of the square is the **Manezh Central Exhibition Hall** (Tsentralny vystavochny zal Manezh; ☎ 202 8976), home to some of Moscow's most popular art exhibitions, open from 11 am to 8 pm daily. Prices vary depending on what is on show. It was built in 1825 as a military riding school. On the north-western side of the square are the fine old edifices of **Moscow State University** (Moskovsky gosudarstvenny universitet), built in 1793; the grandiose 1934 **Intourist headquarters**, formerly the US embassy; and Hotel National, built in 1903 and now sumptuously remodelled.

The 1930s **Hotel Moskva**, fronting the north-eastern side of the square, is half constructivist, half Stalinist. The story goes that Stalin was shown two possible designs for the hotel. Not realising they were alternatives, he approved both of them. Not daring to point out his error, the builders built half in each style, with predictably incongruous results.

On Mokhovaya ulitsa, at the intersection with ulitsa Vozdvizhenka, is the **Russian State Library** (Rossiyskaya gosudarstvennaya biblioteka), one of the world's biggest with over 20 million volumes. It incorporates one of Moscow's finest classical buildings, the 1784-87 **Pashkov House** (Dom Pashkova), named after its original owner, at the southern end of Mokhovaya ulitsa. For details on visiting this grand but financially troubled institution, see the Libraries section earlier in this chapter.

North-east of Manezhnaya ploshchad, Okhotny ryad passes between Hotel Moskva and the glowering **State Duma** (Gosudarstvennaya duma), where Russia's parliament now sits. This building was erected in the 1930s for Gosplan (the Soviet State Planning Department), and was the source of the USSR's Five-Year Plans. Next door is the green-columned **House of Unions** (Dom Soyuzov), which dates from the 1780s and used to be the Nobles' Club. Its Hall of Columns (originally a ballroom, now a concert hall) was in 1938 the scene of one of Stalin's most grotesque show trials, that of Nikolai Bukharin, a leading Communist Party theorist who had been a close associate of Lenin.

Teatralnaya Ploshchad

Teatralnaya ploshchad opens out on both sides of Okhotny ryad, 200m from Manezhnaya ploshchad. The northern half of the square is dominated by the **Bolshoi Theatre** (Map 2). There has been a theatre here since the late 18th century and Tchaikovsky's *Swan Lake* was premiered (unsuccessfully) here in 1877. Initially overshadowed by St Petersburg's Mariinsky Theatre, the Bolshoi didn't really hit the high notes until the 1950s, when foreign tours won great acclaim for its ballet and opera companies.

The busy streets behind the Bolshoi constitute Moscow's main shopping centre (see the Inner North section). Across ulitsa Petrovka from the 'Big' Bolshoi, is the 'Small' **Maly Theatre** (Map 6), a drama theatre. On the southern half of Teatralnaya ploshchad is the tiled, sculptured facade of the luxury **Hotel Metropol**. A **Karl Marx Statue** (Pamyatnik Karlu Marxu; Map 6) remains in the square in front.

Around Lubyanskaya Ploshchad (Map 2)

For several decades the broad square at the top of Teatralny proezd meant just three chilling letters to most Russians: KGB, the initials of the Komitet Gosudarstvennoy Bezopasnosti (Committee for State Security). Today the red and grey building looming on its north-eastern side, known to one and all as the **Lubyanka**, is the headquarters of the KGB's successor, the FSB (Federalnaya Sluzhba Bezopasnosti – Federal Security Service). The FSB doesn't operate foreign spies as the KGB did (that's now done by a separate External Intelligence Service, the SVR). The main entrance is round the back, on Furkasovsky pereulok, but except for the KGB Museum, the building is not open to the public.

Behind the Lubyanka at Bolshaya Lubyanka ulitsa 12/1 is a four room **KGB Museum** devoted to the history, propaganda and paraphernalia of the Soviet intelligence services. The museum is not open to casual callers but Patriarshy Dom (see Organised Tours later in the chapter) occasionally takes groups there.

From 1926 to 1990 Lubyanskaya ploshchad was called ploshchad Dzerzhinskogo, after Felix Dzerzhinsky, who founded the Cheka, the KGB's ancestor, soon after the revolution. A tall statue of Dzerzhinsky which dominated the square was memorably removed by angry crowds, with the assistance of a couple of cranes, when the 1991 coup collapsed. Now you can see the statue in every detail in the park behind the Central House of Artists, where it stands among the others fallen from grace.

The much humbler **Memorial to the Victims of Totalitarianism** (Pamyatnik zhertvam totalitarnogo rezhima) stands in the little garden on the south-eastern side of the square. This single stone slab comes from the territory of an infamous 1930s labour camp on the Solovetsky Islands in the White Sea. The inscription records that it was placed here in 1990 'in memory of the millions of victims of the totalitarian regime' by Memorial, an organisation devoted to digging out the truth about Stalinism.

The little **Moscow City History Museum** (Muzey istorii goroda Moskvy; ☎ 924 8490) at Novaya ploshchad 12 faces the huge **Polytechnical Museum** (Politekhnichesky muzey; ☎ 923 0756), which occupies a whole block at No 3/4. The former, open from 11 am to 6 pm daily except Monday ($3), shows how the city has spread from its starting point at the Kremlin. The Polytechnical Museum, open from 10 am to 5.30 pm daily except Monday and the last Thursday of the month ($2), covers the history of Russian science, technology and industry.

INNER NORTH (MAP 2)

The area that stretches about 2km north of the Bolshoi Theatre is full of narrow, winding streets and intriguing nooks and crannies. In this part of the city are a range of eateries, several theatres, the Old Circus and, just behind the Bolshoi, Moscow's glossiest central shopping area (see also the Shopping section later in this chapter).

Ulitsa Petrovka

Now restored to its pre-revolutionary fashionable status, ulitsa Petrovka begins beside the Bolshoi Theatre. The big department store **TsUM** at No 2 is, like GUM, a bright, busy place now given over to multitudes of separate shops.

The **Upper St Peter Monastery** (Vysoko-Petrovsky monastyr) at the corner of ulitsa Petrovka and Petrovsky bulvar (part of the Boulevard Ring) was founded in the 1380s as part of an early defensive ring round Moscow. Its buildings date mostly from the late 17th century. Enter from Petrovsky bulvar or Krapivensky pereulok. The grounds are open from 9 am to 7 pm daily. Churches only open for services; admission is free.

The main **Virgin of Bogolyubovo Church** (Tserkov vo imya Bogolubskoi Ikony Bozhiey Materi) has five onion domes on towers above spade gables. The loveliest structure is the brick **Cathedral of Metropolitan Pyotr** (Sobor Petra Mitropolita) in the middle of the grounds, restored with a shingle roof. It was built in 1690 by Peter the Great's mother in thanks for his ousting of the Regent Sofia.

Ulitsa Kuznetsky Most

Fashionable ulitsa Kuznetsky Most has some interesting shops. The grand 19th century **Sandunovskiye Baths** (Sandunovskie bany, Sanduny for short), north of ulitsa Kuznetsky Most on Zvonarsky pereulok, is Moscow's most famous public bathhouse. See Activities later in this chapter for details.

Bolshaya Dmitrovka Ulitsa

Bolshaya Dmitrovka ulitsa, which runs north from Okhotny ryad, is a good street for eateries and has a few theatres too. Moscow's most famous drama theatre, plus a few better eateries and interesting shops, are in adjoining streets such as Kamergersky pereulok and Stoleshnikov pereulok.

The **Chekhov Moscow Art Theatre** (MKhAT imeni Chekhova) at Kamergersky pereulok 3 gave the world Chekhov, revolutionised Russian drama, and heavily influenced Western theatre. The theatre is known by its Russian initials MKhAT, short for Moskovsky Khudozhestvenny Akademichesky Teatr (Moscow Academic Art Theatre).

Founded by actor-director Konstantin Stanislavsky and playwright-director Vladimir Nemirovich-Danchenko over an 18 hour restaurant lunch in 1898, the Art Theatre adopted a 'realist' approach which stressed truthful portrayal of characters and society, teamwork by the cast (not relying on stars), and respect for the writer. 'We declared war on all the conventionalities of the theatre ... in the acting, the properties, the scenery, or the interpretation of the play', Stanislavsky wrote.

This treatment of *The Seagull* rescued Chekhov from despair after the play had flopped in St Petersburg. *Uncle Vanya*, *Three Sisters* and *The Cherry Orchard* were all premiered here. Gorky's *The Lower Depths* was another success. Chekhov is still staged here regularly. See Entertainment later in this chapter for performance information.

North of the Boulevard Ring

Moscow's **Old Circus** (Tsirk Tsvetnom) is at Tsvetnoy bulvar 13, down the street from Tsvetnoy Bulvar metro. An oasis of light and chattering children on dark winter nights, it has been here since 1880, though the existing building is modern, having been rebuilt in 1989.

Farther north, just beyond the Garden Ring, the **Museums of Decorative & Folk Art** (Muzei dekorativnogo i narodnogo iskusstva; ☎ 923 7725) are at Delegatskaya ulitsa 3 and 5. There is a good, two room Palekh collection as well as lots of regional folk art. It's open from 10 am to 6 pm daily (closed Friday); admission is $0.30.

The **Armed Forces Museum** (Muzey vooruzhennykh sil; ☎ 281 4877), ulitsa Sovietskoy Armii 2, contains the history of Soviet and Russian forces since 1917. Among the highlights are parts of the American U-2 spy plane brought down over Siberia in 1960, plus many tanks, planes, guns, etc. Open from 10 am to 4.30 pm Wednesday to Sunday (admission approximately $0.30), the museum is a 1.25km hike west from the Novoslobodskaya metro.

INNER NORTH-WEST (MAP 2)

The area that stretches north-west from the city centre lies between two of Moscow's busiest arteries: Tverskaya ulitsa, which runs north-west from Manezhnaya ploshchad; and ulitsa Novy Arbat, which heads west to Kalininsky Most over the Moscow River. Between the two is a network of quiet, old streets dotted with artistic venues and museums. On the bank of the Moscow River, towards the area's western extremity, stands the Moscow White House.

Inner Tverskaya Ulitsa

In spite of soulless reconstruction in the 1930s, it's hard to imagine Moscow without Tverskaya ulitsa, the beginning of the road to St Petersburg. The bottom end of the street, by the National and Intourist hotels, is regarded as the city's hub by many tourists. Numerous places to eat and some of Moscow's classier shops are dotted up the slope to the intersection with the Boulevard Ring at Pushkinskaya ploshchad. Trolleybus Nos 12 and 20 run up and down Tverskaya ulitsa as far as the Belorussia Station.

Through the arch across the start of Bryusov pereulok is the unexpected little gold domed **Church of the Resurrection** (Tserkov Voskresenia). The main building, built in 1629, is full of fine icons saved from churches torn down during the Soviet era. The refectory and bell tower date from 1820.

A bit farther up Tverskaya ulitsa is Tverskaya ploshchad with its **statue of Yury Dolgoruky**, traditionally considered Moscow's founder. The buffed up five-storey building that faces it is the **Moscow Mayor's Office** (Moskovskaya meriya). Behind the statue to the right is the 17th century **Church of SS Cosma and Damian** (Tserkov Svyatykh Kosmy i Damiana).

On the eastern side of Tverskaya ulitsa at No 14, shortly before Pushkinskaya ploshchad, is the ornate **Yeliseev's Grocery Store** – Yeliseevsky Magazin – named after its founding owner, Pyotr Yeliseev, whose bust can be seen in the central hall. Originally a mansion, it was remodelled in 1901 as a kind of Russian Harrods, with chandeliers, stained glass and marble columns and has been restored to its former splendour.

Around Pushkinskaya Ploshchad

The parks that open out on either side of Tverskaya ulitsa at the intersection with the Boulevard Ring constitute Pushkinskaya ploshchad, with a **Pushkin statue** (pamyatnik Pushkinu) facing Tverskaya ulitsa. Behind the statue there is the recently renamed **Pushkinsky Cinema** (kinoteatr Pushkinsky) – the former Rossiya – which is the main venue of Russian film makers and celebrities. To top it all, there is also Pushkinskaya metro station underneath. It seems Pushkin has been chosen to take the place of Lenin in the new Russian ideology.

The square is also famous as the site of Russia's original **McDonald's**, still popular for its predictable food and predictably clean toilets. Pushkinskaya ploshchad is also the nearest thing to a Russian Fleet Street. On the northern side, east of Tverskaya ulitsa, squat the offices of *Izvestia* (News), formerly the newspaper of the USSR Supreme Soviet, now a bland daily. Opposite Izvestia on the southern side of Pushkinskaya ploshchad is **Moskovskie Novosti** (Moscow News), a weekly published in several languages and a standard-bearer of reform.

Just off Pushkinskaya ploshchad at Malaya Dmitrovka ulitsa 4 stand the multiple tent roofs of the **Church of the Nativity of the Virgin in Putinki** (Tserkov rozhdestva Bogoroditsy v Putinkakh). Curiously, these contributed to a ban on tent roofs on churches by Patriarch Nikon in 1652, the year this church was completed. Nikon thought them too Russian and secular, too far from the Church's Byzantine roots. Next to the Church of the Nativity up the road, the **Lenkom Theatre** (Teatr Lenkom) occupies the former Merchants' Club, built in 1909.

Boulevard Ring

Pushkinskaya ploshchad forms part of Moscow's oddest-shaped park, 8km long and 20m wide, between the two carriageways of the Boulevard Ring (Bulvarnoe Koltso). Though hemmed in by traffic, the shady path down the middle of the road makes a great stroll, with intriguing 'bench people', families and viola-toting musicians.

The Boulevard Ring was created in the late 18th and early 19th centuries, replacing Moscow's old defensive walls with boulevards and terraces of handsome buildings, and some of that era's elegance lingers in the neighbourhoods south-west of Pushkinskaya ploshchad, off Tverskoy bulvar – the oldest section – and Nikitsky bulvar (formerly Suvorovsky bulvar).

Trolleybus Nos 15 and 31 run both ways along the ring between Trubnaya ploshchad, 1.25km east of Pushkinskaya ploshchad, and Kropotkinskaya metro 2.75km south.

Patriarch's Pond

Beside outer Malaya Bronnaya ulitsa, a pleasant 1km walk west from Pushkinskaya ploshchad, is the Patriarch's Pond (Patriarshy prudy), a peaceful fishpond (and winter skating rink). It was immortalised by the writer Mikhail Bulgakov, who had the devil appear here in *The Master and Margarita*, one of the most loved 20th century Russian novels. There are some pleasant small cafes and restaurants nearby.

Outer Tverskaya Ulitsa

North of Pushkinskaya ploshchad at Tverskaya ulitsa 21 is the **Revolution Museum** (Muzey revolyutsii), which has a wrecked trolleybus in its forecourt, a reminder of the 1991 coup and a fitting metaphor for the whole ideology. Inside, a mish-mash of material tries to provide an honest account of Soviet history from the 1905 and 1917 revolutions up to the 1980s. Look for the picture of the giant Palace of Soviets (Dvorets Sovietov) that Stalin was going to build on the site of the blown-up – and now rebuilt – Cathedral of Christ the Saviour (Khram Khrista Spasitelya). The museum is open from 10 am to 6 pm daily, but is closed on Monday and the last Friday of each month. Foreigner admission is $1. There's a good souvenir shop with lots of nifty Bolshie posters.

Tverskaya ulitsa crosses the Garden Ring at Triumfalnaya ploshchad, with several restaurants, the **Tchaikovsky Concert Hall** (Kontsertny zal imeni Chaykovskogo) and a few theatres clustered nearby. Though revolutionary bard Vladimir Mayakovsky no longer lends his name to the square, his statue still surveys it and the metro station beneath is still called Mayakovskaya.

Bolshaya Nikitskaya Ulitsa

Bolshaya Nikitskaya ulitsa dissects the Inner North-West area, running from the Moscow State University buildings on Mokhovaya ulitsa out to the Garden Ring. In the backstreets along here many old mansions have survived, some renovated, some dilapidated. Most of those inside the Boulevard Ring were built by the 18th century aristocracy, and most of those outside by rising 19th century industrialists. With little traffic, this is an excellent area for a quiet ramble.

The **Moscow Tchaikovsky Conservatoire** (Konservatoria imeni Chaykovskogo; Map 2) at No 13 is one of Russia's leading music schools for musicians, with two concert halls of its own.

At Leontevsky pereulok 7, north of Bolshaya Nikitskaya ulitsa, is the **Museum of Folk Art** (Muzey narodnogo iskusstva; ☎ 291 8718), a one room sampler of traditional and contemporary Russian handicrafts. It's open from 10 am to 5 pm Tuesday to Saturday; admission is $0.40. Across the street at Leontevsky pereulok 6 is the **Stanislavsky House-Museum** (Dom-muzey Stanislavskogo), open from noon to 5 pm, and closed Monday and Tuesday. Admission is $0.80.

Ploshchad Nikitskie Vorota, where Bolshaya Nikitskaya ulitsa crosses the Boulevard Ring, is named after the Nikitsky Gates in the city walls which the ring has replaced. On its eastern side is the headquarters of the Russian news agency **ITAR-TASS**, with its windows full of news photos.

South down the Boulevard Ring, the **Museum of Oriental Art** (Muzey iskusstva narodov vostoka) at Nikitsky bulvar 12A mounts professional exhibitions from a large collection of art and religious artefacts from Asia and Africa. It's open from 11 am to 8 pm daily except Monday and the last Friday of the month; admission is $2.

In 1831 the poet Alexander Pushkin married Natalia Goncharova in the **Church of the Grand Ascension** (Tserkov Bolshogo Voznesenia) on the western side of ploshchad Nikitskie Vorota. Six years later he died in St Petersburg, defending her honour in a duel.

Immediately north, at Malaya Nikitskaya ulitsa 6/2, is the fascinating 1906 Art Nouveau **Gorky House-Museum** (Dom-muzey Gorkogo). It's fascinating more for its design than for Gorky. Designed by Fyodor Shekhtel for a banker named Ryabushinsky and given to Gorky in 1931, the house is a visual fantasy from the sculpted doorways, ceiling murals, stained glass and carved stone staircase to the exterior tilework. There's a tale that Stalin hastened Gorky's death (in 1936) by having the walls of the small, ground-level bedroom covered with toxic paint. Opening hours are from 10 am to 5 pm Thursday, Saturday and Sunday and from noon to 7 pm Wednesday and Friday. The museum is free; enter at the back.

Garden Ring

The **skyscraper** at Kudrinskaya ploshchad, where Bolshaya Nikitskaya ulitsa meets the Garden Ring, is an apartment block, one of the Stalinist neo-Gothic monstrosities often called the 'Seven Sisters'. This wide, noisy stretch of the Garden Ring makes it easy to believe the story that the ring's widening and tree felling in the 1930s was done to enable warplanes to land. These alterations robbed the ring, created in the early 19th century as a tree-lined boulevard in place of Moscow's old outer rampart, of its charm.

If you fancy a trip round the entire 16km of the Garden Ring, hop onto trolleybus No б in either direction. It'll eventually bring you back to where you started (though you may have to change to another No б at Kursk Station).

Barrikadnaya, the neighbourhood around Kudrinskaya ploshchad, saw heavy street fighting during the 1905 and 1917 uprisings. Just north, on the inner side of the Garden Ring at Sadovaya-Kudrinskaya ulitsa 6, is the **Chekhov House-Museum** (Dom-muzey Chekhova; ☎ 291 6154), where Chekhov forsook medicine for writing. It's open from 11 am to 6 pm on Tuesday, Thursday and Saturday, 2 pm to 7 pm on Wednesday and Friday. Admission is $0.20.

Behind Kudrinskaya ploshchad at the corner of Barrikadnaya ulitsa and Bolshaya Gruzinskaya ulitsa (opposite metro Krasnopresnenskaya) is the main entrance to the big **Moscow Zoo** (Moskovsky zoopark; ☎ 255 5375), which is vaguely depressing but set among trees. It's open from 9 am to 8 pm daily in summer, till 6 pm in spring and autumn and 5 pm in winter; admission is $0.80.

A block south of Kudrinskaya ploshchad, on the Garden Ring at Novinsky bulvar 19/23, is the **US Embassy** – easy to spot by the crowds of anxious visa applicants.

White House

Moscow's White House (Bely dom), scene of two crucial episodes in recent Russian history, stands at Krasnopresnenskaya naberezhnaya 2, just north of Kalininsky Most, a short walk west of the US embassy (Krasnopresnenskaya and Barrikadnaya are the nearest metro stations).

It was here that Boris Yeltsin rallied the opposition that confounded the 1991 hardline coup, then two years later sent in tanks and troops to blast out conservative rivals – some of them the same people who backed him in 1991. The images of Yeltsin climbing on a tank in front of the White House in 1991, and of the same building ablaze after the 1993 assault, are among the most unforgettable from those tumultuous years.

The White House – now back to its original colour and officially called the House of Government of the Russian Federation (Dom pravitelstva Rossiyskoy federatsii) – fronts one of the Moscow River's stateliest bends, with the Stalinist Hotel Ukraina rising on the far bank. This corner of Moscow is particularly appealing when these buildings and Kalininsky Most are lit up at night.

INNER SOUTH-WEST

The south-western segment of inner Moscow, bound by ulitsa Novy Arbat to the north and stretching down a long tongue of land within a great loop of the Moscow River, is packed with interest, from the shops, buskers and restaurants of pedestrianised ulitsa Arbat to Moscow's top foreign art collection in the Pushkin Fine Arts Museum, and the historic, beautiful Novodevichy Convent and Cemetery. Within the Garden Ring is a web of old streets with some fine churches and other good museums, which is a delight to wander through (but not alone!) after dark when many of its buildings are subtly lit.

Ulitsa Vozdvizhenka & Ulitsa Novy Arbat (Map 2)

Ulitsa Vozdvizhenka, running west from the Kremlin, and ulitsa Novy Arbat, its continuation to the Moscow River, form the start of the road west to Smolensk.

The 'Moorish Castle' studded with seashells at ulitsa Vozdvizkenka 16 was built in 1899 for an eccentric merchant named Arseny Morozov, who was inspired by a real one in Spain. The inside is sumptuous and equally over the top. It's now the **House of Friendship with Peoples of Foreign Countries** (Dom druzhby s narodom zarubezhnykh stran). Ask really, really nicely during office hours and staff might let you in to see for yourself why, according to one story, Morozov's mother said when she saw it, 'Until now, only I knew you were mad; now everyone will'.

Ulitsa Novy Arbat, which begins beyond the Boulevard Ring, was created in the 1960s, with four matching ministry highrises. During Soviet times Novy Arbat was

Moscow's 'modern' shopping centre, and still is due to recent renovations. At the corner of Novy Arbat and Povarskaya ulitsa there is a 24-storey high-rise and the small **Church of St Simeon the Stylite** (tserkov Simeona Stolpnika), built in the middle of the 17th century.

Ulitsa Arbat

Ulitsa Arbat is a 1.25km pedestrian mall which stretches from Arbatskaya ploshchad (metro: Arbatskaya) on the Boulevard Ring to Smolenskaya ploshchad (metro: Smolenskaya) on the Garden Ring. There's a street art market, complete with instant portrait painters, soapbox poets and jugglers as well as buskers (and some pickpockets). The Arbat is an interesting walk, dotted with old, pastel coloured merchant houses and tourist-oriented shops and cafes.

Until the 1960s ulitsa Arbat was Moscow's main westward artery. Then a swathe was bulldozed through streets to its north to create the present ulitsa Novy Arbat, taking out the old Arbatskaya ploshchad, a monastery and half a dozen churches. Ulitsa Arbat itself lay like a severed limb until restored as a pedestrian precinct in the 1980s.

The evocative names of nearby lanes – Khlebny (Bread), Skatertny (Tablecloth), Serebryany (Silver), Plotnikov (Carpenters') – and that of the peaceful quarter south of the Arbat, called Staraya Konyushennaya (Old Stables), identify the area as an old settlement of court attendants. These were eventually displaced by artists and aristocrats.

At Spasopeskosky pereulok, one of the side lanes, there is the 17th century **Church of the Saviour in Peski** (Tserkov Spasa na Peskakh; Map 2). At the far end of the lane is the elegant **Spaso House** (Map 2), the residence of the US ambassador.

Near ulitsa Arbat's eastern end is the **Wall of Peace** (Stena Mira; Map 2), composed of hundreds of individually painted tiles on a theme of international friendship. In a side street at Krivoarbatsky pereulok 10 stands the refreshingly bizarre **Melnikov House** (Dom Melnikova; Map 4). This concoction of brick, plaster and lozenge-shaped windows was built in 1927 by Konstantin Melnikov, the great constructivist architect who was denounced in the 1930s and banned from ever working again. Melnikov continued to live in the house, one of the few privately owned houses in the USSR, until his death in 1974.

Towards the western end of the Arbat is the **Gruzia Tsentr** (Map 4), a Georgian cultural centre with a small wax museum housing figures of Stalin and Gorbachev (but for Lenin you have to go you know where ...). At the western end of the street is the **Pushkin Arbat House-Museum** (Muzey-kvartira Pushkina na Arbate; Map 4; ☎ 241 4212), a house where the Pushkins lived after they married. It's open from 11 am to 6 pm daily (closed Monday). Across the street there is a tacky, gilded sculpture of the couple by none other than Zarub Tsereteli (see the boxed text 'An Unholy Alliance').

The street ends with one of Stalin's 'Seven Sisters', the **Foreign Affairs Ministry** (Ministerstvo innostrannykh del; Map 4), whose upper reaches look like a fairy-tale castle when floodlit after dark.

Pushkin Fine Arts Museum (Map 4)

Moscow's premier foreign art museum is just a skip from the south-western corner of the Kremlin at ulitsa Volkhonka 12 (metro: Kropotkinskaya). The Pushkin Museum (Muzey izobrazitelnykh iskusstv imeni A S Pushkina; ☎ 203 9578) is famous for its impressionist and post-impressionist paintings, but also has a broad selection of European works from the Renaissance onward – mostly appropriated from private collections after the revolution – and a good display of ancient Egyptian art. There is also an amazing (read: mind-numbing) array of statues through the ages which will trigger the memories of survivors of the Vatican museums' statuary purgatory.

Keep an eye open for any special exhibitions at the Pushkin, too; in recent years the museum, like the Hermitage in St Petersburg, has revealed some fabulous art hoards kept secret since they were seized by the

Red Army from Germany at the end of WWII. The museum is also making an effort to mount some ambitious temporary exhibitions from its vast legitimate holdings.

The highlight of the museum's permanent display is certainly the four rooms of impressionist and post-impressionist paintings and sculpture. **Room 22** has 11 Monets and several Renoirs; **18** has many Gauguins and Cézannes; **17** has Picasso, Matisse and Rousseau; **21** has several Van Goghs and Degas. But don't neglect the Italian Renaissance paintings (**4** & **5**) the 17th century Dutch and Flemish paintings, including six Rembrandt portraits (**8, 9 & 10**), and the ancient Egyptian collection in **room 1** (enter via rooms 3, 4 & 2). Some rooms have labels in English.

The museum is open from 10 am to 6 pm daily except Monday. Foreign admission is $7/4 for adults/students. An audio guide in English is available for $4. There's a snack bar downstairs next to the cloakroom. Pick up the free map as you go in.

Around the Pushkin Fine Arts Museum

Next door to the Pushkin Fine Arts Museum at ulitsa Volkhonka 14 is the **Museum of Private Collections** (Muzey lichnykh kollektsiy; Map 4; ☎ 203 7798). This shows art collections donated by private individuals, many of whom amassed the works during the Soviet era. The collectors/donors are featured as well as the art. The museum is open from 10 am to 4 pm Wednesday to Sunday; admission is $5.

The lopsided church beside the Pushkin at Kolymazhnaya ulitsa 8 is **St Antipy-by-the-Carriagehouse** (Tserkov Antipia na kolymazhnom dvore; Map 4). It was supposedly commissioned by Malyuta Skuratov, the psychopath who ran Ivan the Terrible's secret police.

The gigantic block a couple of streets farther back on ulitsa Znamenka at the Boulevard Ring is the **Ministry of Defence** (Ministerstvo oborony; Map 2) – Russia's Pentagon.

Looming like something out of a Las Vegas impresario's fantasy, the **Cathedral of Christ the Saviour** (Khram Khrista Spasitelya; Map 4; ☎ 203 3823) is actually the dream of Moscow mayor Yuri Luzhkov come true. It sits on the site of an earlier and similar church of the same name, built in 1839-83 to commemorate Russia's victory over Napoleon, which was blown up during Stalin's orgy of explosive secularism. He planned to replace it with a 315m-high 'Palace of Soviets' – including a 100m statue of Lenin – but the project literally never got off the ground.

IAMSIN WILSON

The original Cathedral of Christ the Saviour

This time largely completed in a mere two years in time for Moscow's 850th birthday in 1997, the new church has aroused many reactions from Muscovites. They range from pious devotion from the legions of babushkas who donated money to the cause, to abject horror from those appalled by the presence of this gaudy symbol of the new Moscow – and the mayor's hegemony.

Besides raising the spirits of the devout, the church is good at lifting the hordes of tourists who ride elevators to the roof for a panoramic view of Moscow that features another example of the Luzhkov-Tsereteli artistic marriage, the statue of Peter the Great. (See the boxed text 'An Unholy Alliance'.) The church occupies the block between ulitsa Volkhonka 4 and the Moscow

An Unholy Alliance

Just as Francois Mitterand left his mark on Paris through a series of mega-projects such as the Louvre pyramids and La Défense, so too Mayor Yuri Luzhkov wants to leave his mark on Moscow. However, to date his 'mark' has been more akin to what canines do to signal their territory – at least from an aesthetic view.

Luzhkov has thrown millions, possibly billions, of roubles at a string of huge projects, many of which have had the dubious creative input of his court artist Zarub Tsereteli, a former Soviet hack who's found the ultimate client in the mayor. The Okhotny Ryad shopping mall next to the Kremlin, the gaudy Cathedral of Christ the Saviour and many smaller projects have given Luzhkov a chance to spend the public's millions (with some cash input from a web of shadowy 'investors', but that's another story) and Tsereteli a chance to exercise his creativity.

The culmination of their 1990s works is the **Statue of Peter the Great** on the Moscow River across from the Cathedral of Christ the Saviour. Impossibly ugly, ungainly, and lots of other unfavourable adjectives, the 60m statue allegedly depicts the Russian ruler on the prow of a stylised boat. In reality, the monstrous pile shows a strange blob of a man on an even blobbier boat with sails which look like so many sheets hung out to dry. Unveiled in 1998, the statue soon attracted the attention of critics who unsuccessfully tried to blow it up. Today a 24-hour guard stands watch.

Undaunted by the critics, Luzhkov and Tsereteli have announced their next grand project for a spot near the Kremlin: a 'Crystal Chapel', which the unflappable mayor and presidential contender has already dubbed 'The Eighth Wonder of the World'.

River and is open from 10 am to 6 pm daily. The elevator ride is part of a $6 tour for one to 10 people. English-language tours are sometimes available – call ☎ 201 4565 or inquire at the kiosk by the entrance to the lower church.

Prechistenka Ulitsa & Beyond (Map 4)

Prechistenka ulitsa, which heads south-west from Kropotkinskaya metro, is virtually a museum of classical mansions, most of which date from the empire-style rebuilding after the great fire of 1812.

Have a look at No 12, which houses the **Pushkin Literary Museum** (Literaturny muzey Pushkina; ☎ 201 3256), devoted to the poet's life and work. It is open from 11 am to 6 pm daily (2 pm to 7 pm on Thursday, closed Monday); admission is $0.40. No 11 is now a **Tolstoy Museum** (Muzey Tolstogo; ☎ 201 5811) containing the writer's manuscripts, letters and sketches. It's open from 11 am to 6 pm daily except Monday and the last Friday of the month; admission is $0.40. At No 19-21, the **Russian Academy of Art** (Rossiyskaya akademia khudozhestv) has an exhibition hall.

There's more Tolstoyana across the busy Garden Ring from the end of Prechistenka ulitsa. Down the second street on the left – opposite the shady **Skver Devichego Polya** (Maiden's Field) park, with its brooding Tolstoy statue – is the interesting **Tolstoy Estate-Museum** (Muzey-usadba Tolstogo; metro: Park Kultury) at ulitsa Lva Tolstogo 21. The house was the writer's winter home in the 1880s and 90s. It's neither particularly big nor especially opulent, but fitting for junior nobility, which Tolstoy was. Rachmaninov and Rimsky-Korsakov played the piano in the upstairs reception room; Tolstoy's training weights and bicycle repose outside his study. You can wander around without a guide and there are explanatory notices in English. The house is open from 10 am to 6 pm, closed Monday and last Friday of the month. Entrance is $2.

At the southern end of ulitsa Lva Tolstogo, the beautiful **Church of St Nicholas**

of the Weavers (Tserkov Nikoli v Khamovnikakh) vies with St Basil's Cathedral as the most colourful in Moscow. Commissioned by the Moscow weavers' guild in 1676, it indeed looks like a great, jolly, green and orange tapestry. Inside are equally rich frescoes and icons.

Novodevichy Convent (Map 4)

A cluster of sparkling domes behind handsome turreted walls near a bank of the Moscow River, Novodevichy Convent (Novodevichy monastyr; ☎ 246 8526) is one of the city's most beautiful examples of architecture, and is rich with history and treasures. The adjacent Novodevichy Cemetery is Moscow's most prestigious resting place after the Kremlin wall, with many famous tombs. The name 'Novodevichy' (New Maidens) probably originates from a market, once held in the locality, where Tatars bought Russian girls to sell to Muslim harems.

Trolleybus Nos 5 and 15 come here down Prechistenka ulitsa and Bolshaya Pirogovskaya ulitsa from Kropotkinskaya metro station. Sportivnaya metro is 500m to the south.

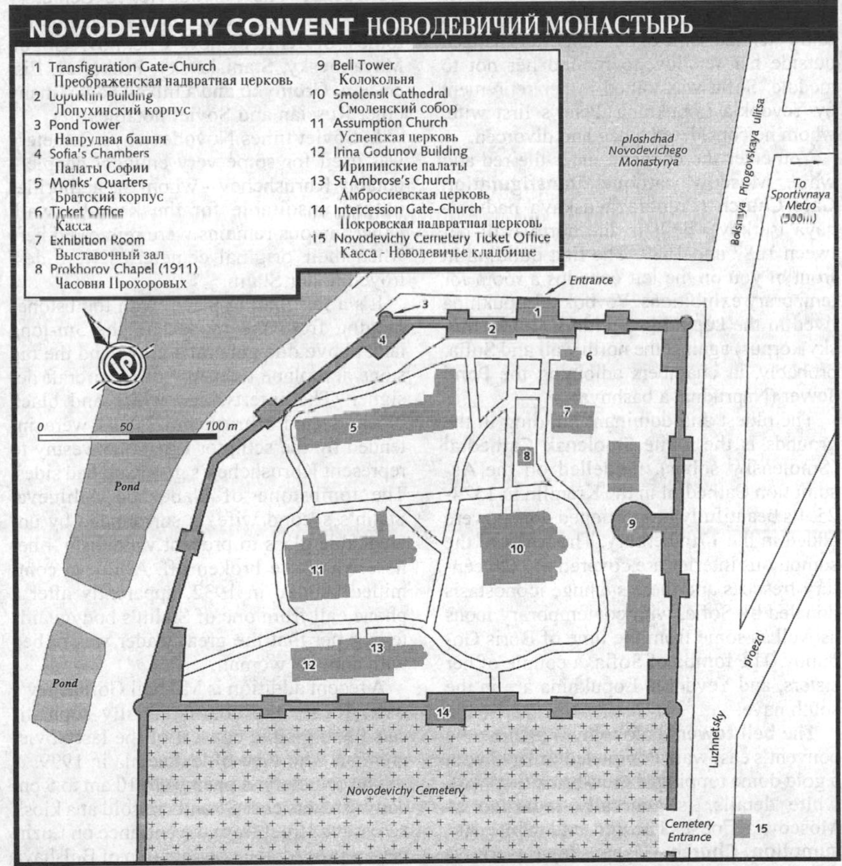

Convent The convent entrance is on ploshchad Novodevichego Monastyrya beside Bolshaya Pirogovskaya ulitsa. The best views are from across the pond to the north.

The convent was founded in 1524 to celebrate the taking of Smolensk from Lithuania, an important step in Moscow's conquest of the old Kyivan Rus lands. Novodevichy was rebuilt by Peter the Great's half-sister Sofia, who used it as a second residence when she ruled Russia as regent in the 1680s.

When Peter, aged 17, deposed Sofia in 1689, he confined her to Novodevichy, and in 1698 she was imprisoned here for life after being implicated in the Streltsy rebellion. It's said Peter had some of her supporters hanged outside her window to remind her not to meddle. Sofia was joined in her retirement by Yevdokia Lopukhina, Peter's first wife, whom he considered a nag and divorced.

You enter the convent under the red and white Moscow baroque **Transfiguration Gate-Church** (Preobrazhenskaya nadvratnaya tserkov), built in the north wall between 1687 and 1689. The first building in front of you on the left contains a room for temporary exhibitions. Yevdokia Lopukhina lived in the **Lopukhin Building** (Lopukhinsky korpus) against the north wall and Sofia, probably, in chambers adjoining the **Pond Tower** (Naprudnaya bashnya).

The oldest and dominant building in the grounds is the white **Smolensk Cathedral** (Smolensky sobor), modelled on the Assumption Cathedral in the Kremlin in 1524-25. Its beautifully proportioned domes were added in the 17th century. The walls of the sumptuous interior are covered in 16th century frescoes and there's a huge iconostasis donated by Sofia, with contemporary icons as well as some from the time of Boris Godunov. The **tombs** of Sofia, a couple of her sisters, and Yevdokia Lopukhina are in the south nave.

The **bell tower** (kolokolnya) against the convent's east wall, completed in 1690 with a gold dome topping six red-brick tiers with white details, is generally regarded as Moscow's finest. The red and white **Assumption Church** (Uspenskaya tserkov) and its refectory date from 1685 to 1687. The 16th century **St Ambrose's Church** (Ambrosievskaya tserkov) is adjoined by another refectory and the **Irina Godunov Building** (Irininskie palaty), where Boris Godunov's sister lived.

The complex has been returned to the Church and is open to visitors from 8 am to 6 pm daily for $1. One or two rooms house temporary exhibits of various kinds, for which tickets are sold at the ticket office inside the grounds. These are often closed on weekends.

Cemetery The Novodevichye Cemetery (Novodevichiye kladbishche) contains the tombs of Khrushchev, Chekhov, Gogol, Mayakovsky, Stanislavsky, Prokofiev, Eisenstein, Gromyko and a mixed bag of many other Russian and Soviet notables.

In Soviet times Novodevichye Cemetery was used for some very eminent people – notably Khrushchev – whom the authorities judged unsuitable for the Kremlin wall. Other famous remains were reinterred here when their original cemeteries were destroyed under Stalin.

It's a fascinating place, with tombstones ranging from the modest to the 3m-long tank above one general's grave and the big stone aeroplane over that of an aircraft designer. The intertwined white and black blocks round Khrushchev's bust were intended by the sculptor Ernst Neizvestny to represent Khrushchev's good and bad sides. The tombstone of Nadezhda Allilueva, Stalin's second wife, is surrounded by unbreakable glass to prevent vandalism – her nose was once broken off. Allilueva committed suicide in 1932, apparently after a phone call from one of Stalin's bodyguards telling her that the great leader was in bed with another woman.

A recent addition is Mikhail Gorbachev's wife, Raisa, the controversially sophisticated and visible consort of the last Soviet premier, who died of leukaemia in 1999.

The cemetery is open from 10 am to 5 pm daily. Tickets cost $1 and are sold at a kiosk across the street from the entrance on Luzhnetsky proezd, the continuation of Bolshaya

Pirogovskaya ulitsa. If you want to investigate this place in depth, buy the Russian map on sale at the kiosk, which pinpoints nearly 200 graves.

Luzhniki (Map: Outer South Moscow)

The area within the river bend south-west of Novodevichy contains a group of sporting stadiums collectively known as Luzhniki ('Marshes', what the area used to be). The main 80,000 capacity Luzhniki Stadium was the chief venue for the 1980 Olympics, and had a huge renovation in the late 1990s. Coincidentally, the contract for the new seats went to a company controlled by the mayor's wife.

INNER SOUTH

The Zamoskvorechie ('Beyond-Moscow-River Area') stretches south from opposite the Kremlin, inside a big river loop. In this part of the city you'll find Moscow's most famous park, its premier gallery of Russian art, and the current headquarters of the Russian Orthodox Church.

The Vodootvodny (Drainage) Canal slices across the top of the Zamoskvorechie, preventing spring floods in the city centre and creating a sliver of island opposite the Kremlin. South was the direction from which Tatars used to attack, so Moscow's defensive forces were stationed in the Zamoskvorechie, along with merchants and quarters devoted to servicing the royal court.

After the Tatar threat abated and the court moved to St Petersburg, the merchants were joined by nobles, then by 19th century factories and their workers. Little damaged by Stalin, it's still a varied, intriguing area. From almost any place here you can see the giant Peter the Great sculpture. For more on this modern monolith, see the boxed text 'An Unholy Alliance'.

Gorky Park (Map 4)

Stretching almost 3km along the river upstream of Krymsky Most, Gorky Park is full of that sometimes rare species, the happy Russian. Officially the Central Park of Culture & Rest named after Maxim Gorky (Tsentralny Park Kultury i Otdykha imeni A M Gorkogo), it's the original Soviet culture park. Part of it is straight ornamental park, with black swans cruising between the pedal boats, making even Australians feel a little bit at home.

But that's not all. Gorky Park has a small Western amusement park with two Western roller coasters and almost a dozen other terror-inducing attractions (aside from the Peter the Great statue). Space buffs can shed a tear for the *Buran*, the Soviet space shuttle which never carried anyone into space because the USSR itself crashed before it could blast off. Now it's a kiddie attraction. Most of the rides cost about $0.50. One sad row of hawkers features chained animals – many endangered – who morosely pose for snapshots with giggling adolescents.

The park has a number of snack bars and, behind the amusement park, a 2000 seat German beer hall, complete with litre glasses and excellent grilled chicken. In winter the ponds freeze and the paths are flooded to make a giant skating rink – you can rent skates if you take along some ID such as a passport. The park's main entrance is on ulitsa Krymsky Val, 500m from either Park Kultury or Oktyabrskaya metro. Admission to the park is $0.40.

Around Gorky Park (Map 4)

The big block at ulitsa Krymsky Val 10, opposite Gorky Park's main entrance, houses the **Central House of Artists** (Tsentralny dom khudozhnika) and the **New Tretyakov Gallery** (Novaya Tretyakovskaya galereya). The Central House of Artists, facing the road, puts on good contemporary art shows. Behind it, the New Tretyakov Gallery has an excellent collection of 20th century Russian art, which is much more than heroic images of muscle-bound men wielding scythes and busty women milking cows. Both are open from 10 am to 9 pm (closed Monday). Foreigner admission for each gallery is $7/3.50 for adults/students. There's a busy art market in the nearby arcade.

Behind the complex is the wonderful and moody **Sculptures Park** (Park Skulptur), a collection of Soviet statues – Stalin,

MOSCOW

Dzerzhinsky, a selection of Lenins and Brezhnevs – put out to pasture here when they were ripped from their pedestals in the wave of anti-Soviet feeling after 1991. These discredited icons have now been joined by contemporary work, including an eerie bust of Stalin surrounded by heads representing millions of purge victims.

Nearby on Bolshaya Yakimanka ulitsa stands the finest of all Zamoskvorechie churches, **St John the Warrior** (Tserkov Ivana voina), with its colourful, tiled domes. Said to have been partly designed by Peter the Great in thanks for his 1709 victory over Sweden at Poltava, it mixes Moscow and European baroque styles. It's a working church but often locked; the big, 17th century iconostasis is reputedly a masterpiece. You can see the Kremlin in the distance.

Tretyakov Gallery (Map 4)

The State Tretyakov Gallery (Gosudarstvennaya Tretyakovskaya galereya; ☎ 951 1362) is nothing short of spectacular, with the world's best collection of Russian icons and an outstanding collection of other prerevolutionary Russian art, particularly the 19th century Peredvizhniki (see the Painting section in the Facts about European Russia chapter). There may be more masterpieces per square metre here than anywhere else.

The collection is based on that of the 19th century industrialist brothers Pavel and Sergey Tretyakov; Pavel was a patron of the Peredvizhniki. The original part of the building was created in the likeness of an old boyar castle by Viktor Vasnetsov between 1900 and 1905.

Much of the Tretyakov's collection of religious art was confiscated from churches during the Soviet era. Now that the Church wants its icons back, the Tretyakov has had to battle to keep its most precious treasures. For the moment at least, it has fended off the pressure by also restoring the **Church of St Nicholas** within its grounds. About 200 icons are displayed there, and the building functions as both church and museum.

Orientation The 62 rooms are numbered, and progress in chronological order from rooms 1 to 54. The next eight rooms hold icons and jewellery. The exhibits begin on the ground level. Most Peredvizhniki are in **rooms 20, 23** and **24**, except in those cases where a Peredvizhniki artist has a hall dedicated to exhibiting his work (they were all men). Icons reside on the ground floor in **rooms 55** to **62**. Two masterpieces, Rublev's *Trinity* (1420s) and Vrubel's *Demon Seated* (1890), are in **rooms 60** and **33** respectively.

The entrance to the gallery is through a lovely courtyard; show up early to beat the queues. Thanks to a lavish renovation during the early 1990s, the entire gallery is accessible to wheelchairs.

The Tretyakov is open from 10 am to 7.30 pm daily (closed Monday); the ticket counter closes at 6.30 pm. It is 1km south of the Kremlin at Lavrushinsky pereulok 10 (metro: Tretyakovskaya). Foreigner admission is $8/4 for adults/students.

Ulitsa Bolshaya Ordynka & Pyatnitskaya Ulitsa (Map 4)

The atmosphere of 19th century Moscow lives on in the low buildings, old courtyards and clusters of onion domes along narrow ulitsa Bolshaya Ordynka, which runs 2km down the middle of the Zamoskvorechie to Serpukhovskaya ploshchad, and on Pyatnitskaya ulitsa, which is roughly parallel 200m to the east. The many churches make up a scrapbook of Moscovite architectural styles. The name 'Ordynka' comes from *orda* (horde): until the 16th century this was the start of the road to the Golden Horde's capital on the Volga, where Tatar ambassadors lived.

If you head south from Maly Moskvoretsky Most, the first lane on the right, 2-y Kadashevsky pereulok, contains the tall **Resurrection Church in Kadashi** (Tserkov Voskresenia v Kadashakh), which is a restoration centre for other churches. Its rich, late 17th century decoration is a fine example of so-called Moscow baroque.

In Chernigovsky pereulok, the small, white **SS Mikhail & Fyodor Church** (Tserkov Mikhaila i Fyodora) has two rows of spade gables and five domes on a thin tower, while the larger **St John the Baptist Church**

(Tserkov Ioanna Predtechi) houses an exhibition of unusual Russian glassware. Both date from the late 17th century, though St John's bell tower, a Zamoskvorechie landmark which fronts Pyatnitskaya ulitsa, was added in 1753.

The empire-style **Virgin of Consolation of All Sorrows Church** (Tserkov ikony Bogomateri Vsekh Skorbyashchikh Radost) at ulitsa Bolshaya Ordynka 20, dates mostly from between 1828 and 1833. Klimentovsky pereulok leads to **St Clement's Church** (Tserkov Klementa Papy Rimskogo), built between 1742 and 1774, at Pyatnitskaya ulitsa 26 (lately closed for rebuilding), a rare Moscow example of the true baroque style favoured by Empress Elizabeth.

The blue and white **Church of St Nicholas in Pyzhi** (Tserkov Nikoly v Pyzhakh), a working church at ulitsa Bolshaya Ordynka 27A, is a typical five domed, mid-17th century church, with spade gables and thin onion domes. **SS Martha & Mary Convent** (Marfo-Mariiskaya obitel) at No 34A, with its pretty, single domed Intercession Church (now housing church restoration offices), was founded in the early 20th century.

Donskoy Monastery (Map: Outer South Moscow)

The youngest of Moscow's fortified monasteries, founded in 1591, is a five minute walk from Shabolovskaya metro. The Don Monastery (Donskoy monastyr) was built to house the *Virgin of the Don* icon (now in the Tretyakov Gallery), revered for its help at the 1380 battle of Kulikovo and again in 1591 when, it's said, the Tatar Khan Giri retreated without a fight after the icon showered him with burning arrows in a dream.

Most of the monastery, surrounded by a brick wall with 12 towers, was built between 1684 and 1733 under Regent Sofia and Peter the Great. From 1918 to 1927 it was the Russian Orthodox Church headquarters, then it was closed as a monastery, falling into neglect despite being used as an architecture museum. Restored in 1990 and 1991, it's now back in Church hands.

The **Virgin of Tikhvin Church** (Tserkov Tikhvinskoy Bogomateri) over the north gate, built in 1713 and 1714, is one of the last examples of Moscow baroque. In the centre of the grounds is the large, brick **New Cathedral** (Novy Sobor), built between 1684 and 1693; just to its south is the smaller **Old Cathedral** (Stary Sobor), dating from 1591 to 1593.

When burials in central Moscow were banned after a plague in 1771, the Donskoy Monastery became a graveyard for the nobility, and it is littered with elaborate tombs and chapels. At ulitsa Donskaya leading north from the monastery there is the **Church of the Deposition of the Robe** (Tserkov Rizopolozheniya), built in 1701.

Danilovsky Monastery (Map 4)

The headquarters of the Russian Orthodox Church stands behind white fortress walls on ulitsa Danilovsky Val, five minutes' walk east of Tulskaya metro. The Danilov Monastery (Svyato-Danilovsky monastyr) was built in the late 13th century by Daniil, the first Prince of Moscow, as an outer city defence. Ivan the Terrible rebuilt it, and it was later repeatedly altered. After the revolution it spent time as a factory.

It was restored in time to replace Sergiev Posad as the Church's spiritual and administrative centre and the official residence of its head, the Patriarch of Moscow & All Russia, during the Russian Orthodoxy's millennium celebrations in 1988. Today it radiates an air of purpose befitting the Church's role in modern Russia. The grounds are open 7am to 7 pm daily and admission is free.

On holy days in particular the place seethes with worshippers crossing themselves, lighting candles and ladling holy water into jugs at the tiny chapel inside the gates. You enter beneath the pink **St Simeon Stylites Gate-Church** (Nadvratnaya tserkov Simeona Stolpnika) on the north wall on ulitsa Danilovsky Val. Its bells are the first in Moscow to ring on holy days. The bell tower was rebuilt in 1984.

The monastery's oldest and busiest church is the **Church of the Holy Fathers of the Seven Ecumenical Councils** (Tserkov sv ottsov semi vselenskikh soborov), where worship is held continuously from 10 am to

5 pm daily. Founded in the 17th century and rebuilt repeatedly, the church contains several chapels on two floors: the main one upstairs is flanked by side chapels to St Daniil (the prince, on the northern side) and SS Boris & Gleb (south). On the ground level, the small main chapel is dedicated to the Protecting Veil, and the northern one to the prophet Daniil. Many of the church's icons are new; others have been brought from other churches.

The yellow, neoclassical **Trinity Cathedral** (Troitsky sobor), built in the 1830s, is an austere counterpart to the other buildings.

INNER SOUTH-EAST

Around Taganskaya Ploshchad (Map 5)

Taganskaya ploshchad (metro: Taganskaya) on the Garden Ring is a monster intersection – loud, dusty and crowded. But it's the hub of the Zayauzie, the area south of the little Yauza River, and the territory of the 17th century blacksmiths guild and other guilds. Later it became an Old Believers' quarter. The square's character disappeared with a reconstruction in the 1970s and 1980s, but traces remain in the streets that radiate from it.

The great block on Taganskaya ploshchad at Verkhnyaya Radishchevskaya ulitsa is the **Taganka Theatre** (Teatr na Taganke), famous in the Soviet era for director Yury Lyubimov's vaguely subversive repertoire, from updated Chekhov to modern Russian and Western works, which annoyed the Soviet authorities and delighted everyone else.

Behind metro Taganskaya is the sombre 1712 **Taganka Gates Church of St Nicholas** (Tserkov Nikoly u Taganskikh Vorot). More fetching is the **Potters' Church of the Assumption** (Tserkov Uspenia Bogoroditsy v goncharovoy Slobode), built in 1654, with its star-spangled domes, a block away at Goncharnaya ulitsa 29. Note the tilework under the 'extra' refectory dome.

Goncharnaya ulitsa leads north to two impressive classical mansions at No 12 and No 16, and the **Church of St Nikita Beyond the Yauza** (Tserkov Nikoly za Yauzoy), which has 15th century foundations, 16th century walls, 17th century chapels and an 18th century bell tower. The church is dwarfed by the **Kotelnicheskaya apartment block** (Mnogokvartirny dom na Kotelnicheskoy naberezhnoy), one of the Stalinist Gothic 'Seven Sisters' skyscrapers built around 1950.

North-east of Taganskaya, at Bolshaya Kommunisticheskaya ulitsa 15, you can't miss the grand **Cathedral of St Martin the Confessor** (Khram sv Martina Ispovednika), built in 1792 in shameless imitation of St Paul's Cathedral in London. Though it was badly neglected during the Soviet period, it's now open and being renovated. This whole neighbourhood has a look of abandoned grace.

Andronikov Monastery & Andrey Rublyov Museum (Map 5)

The fortified Andronikov Monastery (Spaso-Andronikov monastyr) on the banks of the Yauza at Andronyevskaya ploshchad (metro: Ploshchad Ilyicha), just over a kilometre north-east of Taganskaya ploshchad, dates from 1360. It's famous because Andrey Rublyov, the master of icon painting, was a monk here in the 15th century. Rublyov is buried in the grounds; no-one quite knows where.

In the centre of the grounds, topped by a posy of *kokoshnik* gables, is the compact **Saviour's Cathedral** (Spassky Sobor), built in 1427, the oldest stone building in Moscow. To the left is the combined rectory and 17th century Moscow baroque **Church of the Archangel Michael** (Tserkov Arkhangela Mikhaila). To the right, in the old monks' quarters, is the **Andrey Rublyov Museum of Early Russian Culture & Art** (Muzey Drevnerusskoy Kultury i Iskusstva imeni Andreya Rublyova), a museum of icons but with nothing by Rublyov himself. What there is, however, is lovely, including a few strong, luminous 14th to 16th century works interestingly juxtaposed.

The museum (☎ 278 1467) and monastery grounds are open from 11 am to 6 pm daily except Wednesday and the last Friday of the month. The grounds are free; tickets for the exhibitions are $2.50.

Novospassky Monastery (Map 5)

One kilometre south of Taganskaya ploshchad, on Verkhny Novospassky proezd (metro: Proletarskaya), is another of Moscow's fort-monasteries. The New Monastery of the Saviour (Novospassky monastyr) dates from the 15th century, when it was relocated from inside the Kremlin. Under restoration for at least 30 years, it became a working monastery again in the early 1990s. During the day you are welcome to walk in beneath the 18th century wedding-cake bell tower.

The centrepiece is the **Transfiguration Cathedral** (Spaso-Preobrazhensky Sobor), built by the imperial Romanov family in the 1640s in imitation of the Kremlin's Assumption Cathedral. Frescoes depict the history of Christianity in Russia, with the Romanov family tree, which goes as far back as the Viking Prince Rurik, climbing one wall.

To the left is the 1675 **Intercession Church** (Pokrovskaya Tserkov), which is joined to the refectory (*trapezny*) and bakery buildings. Outside near the river is a pond. Under the river bank, beneath one of the monastery towers, is the site of a mass grave for thousands of victims of Stalin.

The monastery (☎ 276 9570) is open to visitors from 7 am to 5 pm daily. Admission is free.

Krutitskoe Podvorye (Map 5)

Across the road south of Novospassky is a sumptuous *podvoryie* (ecclesiastical residence) used by the Moscow metropolitans from the 16th century, when they lost their place in the Kremlin after the founding of the Russian patriarchate.

At the northern end of the grounds is the **Assumption Cathedral** (Uspensky Sobor), a symphony of brickwork. But the best part is nearby – an extraordinary Moscow baroque **gate tower** (teremok), with friezes in unexpected yellows and blues, and frescoes of the Saviour, Virgin and (possibly) John the Baptist.

You can visit from 10 am to 6 pm (closed Tuesday and the first Monday of the month); it's free of charge.

Rogozhskoe Cemetery & Old Believers' Community

One of Russia's most atmospheric religious centres is the **Old Believers' community** (Staroobryadcheskaya Obshchina), located at Rogozhskoe, 3km east of Taganskaya ploshchad. The Old Believers split from the main Russian Orthodox Church in 1653 when they refused to accept certain reforms – they have maintained old forms of worship and customs, such as the wearing of beards, ever since.

In the late 18th century, during a brief period free of persecution, rich Old Believer merchants set up what is perhaps the most important Old Believers' community around their **Rogozhskoe Cemetery** (Rogozhskoe kladbishche), and the place remains an island of old Russia to this day, with dark, mysterious churches.

To get there take trolleybus No 16 or 26, or bus No 51, east from Taganskaya ploshchad along Taganskaya ulitsa and Nizhegorodskaya ulitsa, and get off after crossing a railway. Rogozhskoe's tall, green-domed 20th century **bell tower** is clearly visible to the north (left). The yellow classical-style **Intercession Church** (Tserkov Pokrova) contains one of Moscow's finest collections of icons, all dating from before 1653. The oldest is the 14th century *Saviour with the Angry Eye (Spas yaroe oko)*, protected behind glass near the south door.

The complex is open from 9 am to 6 pm daily (closed Monday); admission is free.

INNER NORTH-EAST (MAP 3)

Around Komsomolskaya Ploshchad

This area, with three main rail terminuses, 750m outside the Garden Ring, is proof that Moscow really is the place where Europe and Asia meet. Komsomolskaya ploshchad is also an amazing architectural variety show of bizarre styles. Leave your valuables at home (unless you have to take them on a train) as the crowds constantly passing through include some dubious characters.

Leningrad Station (Leningradsky vokzal) on the northern side of the square, with its tall clock tower, is Moscow's oldest, built in

MOSCOW

OUTER NORTH MOSCOW МОСКВА, ВНЕШНЯЯ СЕВЕРНАЯ ЧАСТЬ

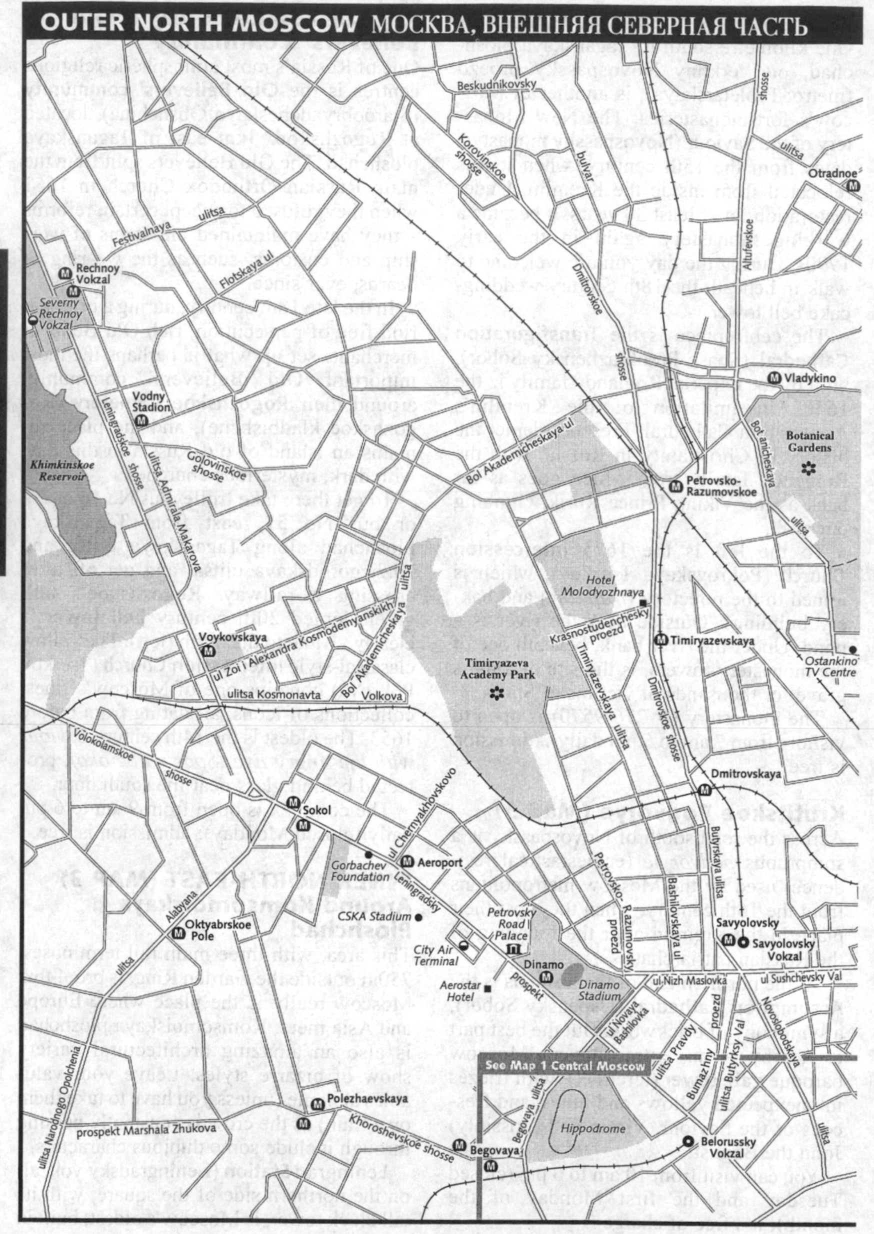

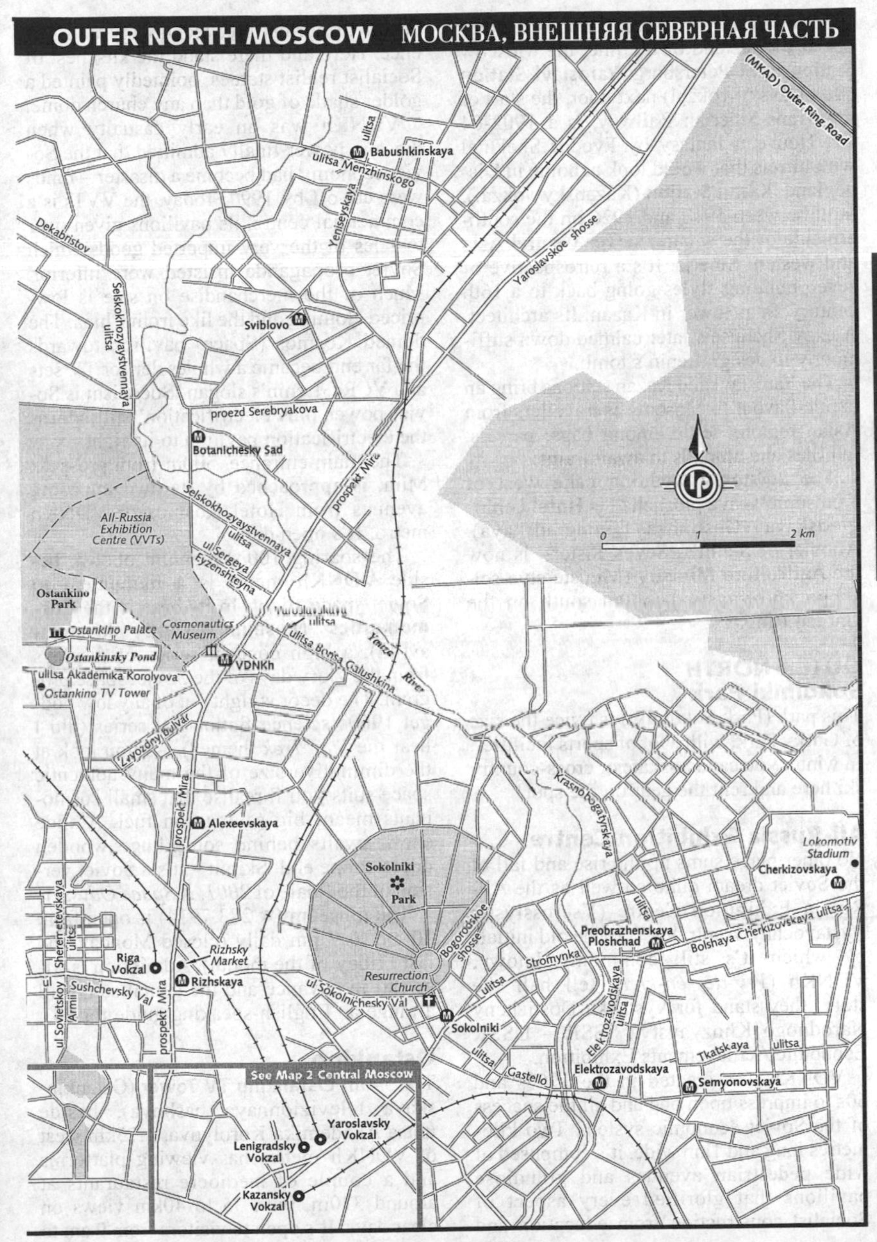

OUTER NORTH MOSCOW
МОСКВА, ВНЕШНЯЯ СЕВЕРНАЯ ЧАСТЬ
(MKAD) Outer Ring Road
Babushkinskaya
ulitsa Menzhinskogo
Yeniseyskaya ulitsa
Dekabristov
Yaroslavskoe shosse
Selskokhozyaystvennaya ulitsa
Sviblovo
proezd Serebryakova
Botanichesky Sad
prospekt Mira
Selskokhozyaystvennaya ulitsa
All-Russia Exhibition Centre (VVTs)
ul Sergeya Eyzenshteyna
0
1
2 km
Ostankino Park
Ostankino Palace
Cosmonautics Museum
Ostankinsky Pond
VDNKh
ulitsa Borisa Galushkina
Yauza River
ulitsa Akademika Korolyova
Ostankino TV Tower
Lvovozdny bulvar
Krasnobogatyrskaya
prospekt Mira
Alexeevskaya
Lokomotiv Stadium
Cherkizovskaya
Sokolniki Park
Preobrazhenskaya Ploshchad
Bolshaya Cherkizovskaya ulitsa
Bogorodskoe shosse
ulitsa Stromynka
Riga Vokzal
Rizhsky Market
Rizhskaya
ul Sheremetevskaya ulitsa
Sushchevsky Val
ul Sovietskoy Armii
prospekt Mira
Resurrection Church
ul Sokolnichesky Val
Sokolniki
Elektrozavodskaya ulitsa
ulitsa Gastello
Tkatskaya ulitsa
Elektrozavodskaya
Semyonovskaya
See Map 2 Central Moscow
Yaroslavsky Vokzal
Lenigradsky Vokzal
Kazansky Vokzal
MOSCOW

1851, and very similar to its opposite number at the far end of the line, the Moscow Station in St Petersburg. **Yaroslavl Station** (Yaroslavsky vokzal) next door, the start of the Trans-Siberian Railway, is a 1902-04 Art Nouveau fantasy by Fyodor Shekhtel with turrets that would look at home in Disneyland. **Kazan Station** (Kazansky vokzal), built between 1912 and 1926 on the southern side of the square, serves Central Asia and western Siberia. It's a retrospective of seven building styles going back to a 16th century Tatar tower in Kazan. Its architect, Alexey Shchusev, later calmed down sufficiently to design Lenin's tomb.

The Yaroslavl and Kazan stations bring an exotic flavour to Moscow as travellers from Asian regions settle among bags, parcels, families and animals to await trains.

The 26-storey wedding cake west of Komsomolskaya ploshchad is **Hotel Leningradskaya** (Gostinitsa Leningradskaya). Another of Stalin's 'Seven Sisters' is now the **Agriculture Ministry** (Ministerstvo selskogo khozyaystva), 600m south on the Garden Ring.

OUTER NORTH

Sokolniki Park

This park (Park Sokolniki) is twice the size of Gorky Park, with a lot of sports facilities. In winter you can ice-skate or cross-country ski here and rent the gear on the spot.

All-Russia Exhibition Centre

No other place sums up the rise and fall of the Soviet dream quite so well as the All-Russia Exhibition Centre (Vserossiysky Vystavochny Tsentr, VVTs). The old initials by which it's still commonly known, VDNKh (*Vey-dey-en-kha*), tell half the story: they stand for Vystavka Dostizheny Narodnogo Khozyaystva SSSR – USSR Economic Achievements Exhibition.

VDNKh was created in the 1950s and 60s to impress upon one and all the success of the Soviet economic system. Two kilometres long and 1km wide, it's composed of wide pedestrian avenues and grandiose pavilions that glorified every aspect of Socialist construction from education and health to agriculture, technology and science. Here and there stand the kitschest of Socialist realist statues, pointedly painted a golder shade of gold than any church dome.

VDNKh was an early casualty when those in power finally admitted that the Soviet economy had become a disaster – funds were cut off by 1990. Today, the VVTs is a commercial centre, its pavilions given over to sales of the very imported goods which Soviet propaganda insisted were inferior. Much of the merchandise on sale is low-priced clothing and the like from China. The domed Kosmos (Space) pavilion towards the far end became a wholesaler for TV sets and VCRs. Lenin's slogan 'Socialism is Soviet power plus electrification' still adorns the electrification pavilion to its right.

The main entrance, 500m from prospekt Mira, is approached by its own imposing avenues from Hotel Kosmos or VDNKh metro. It's open daily.

The soaring 100m titanium obelisk beside VDNKh metro is a monument to Soviet space flight. In its base is the **Cosmonautics Museum** (Muzey kosmonavtiki), a high concept series of displays from the glory days of the Soviet space program. The decor is right out of any low budget 1960s science fiction TV series (did I hear the *Star Trek* theme?). As you look at the diminutive size of the many authentic space suits you'll realise that small cosmonauts meant big savings on fuel. A slide show awaits behind some huge wooden doors at one end. Skip it – it's a Soviet version of the finale of *2001: A Space Odyssey*.

The museum (☎ 283 7914) is open from 10 am to 7 pm daily (closed Monday and last Friday of the month). Admission is $1, or call in advance and the genial staff will arrange an English-speaking guide for $6.

Ostankino

The 540m **Ostankino TV Tower** (Ostankinskaya televizionnaya bashnya), beside ulitsa Akademika Korolyova, 1.75km west of VDNKh metro, has viewing platforms and a couple of mediocre restaurants at around 330m, with 35 to 40km views on clear days. It's open to visitors from 9 am to

8.30 pm daily except Monday. To get a ticket ($2), take your passport and visa to the grey building beside the tower. Then walk over to the tower, pass through security control, and the lift will whisk you up to the viewing level at 25km/h.

North of the **Ostankinsky Pond** (Ostankinsky prud) is the pink and white **Ostankino Palace** (Ostankinsky dvorets), a wooden mansion with a stucco exterior made to resemble stone. It was built in the 1790s as the chief summer pad of Count Nikolai Sheremetev, probably Russia's richest aristocrat of the time.

Today the palace is the **Ostankino House-Museum** (Ostankinsky dvorets-muzey). Its lavish interior, with hand-painted wallpaper and intricate parquet floors, houses the count's art treasures. The centrepiece is the oval theatre-ballroom built for the Sheremetevs' troupe of 250 serf actors (see also Kuskovo in the Outer East section). In 1801 Count Nikolai married one of the troupe, Praskovia Zhemchugova, and the two retired to Ostankino to avoid court gossip. Praskovia died in childbirth two years later and the count abandoned the place.

Only the **Italian Pavilion** is open for visits. The limited hours (☎ 286 6288) are from 10 am to 5 pm from May 18 to October 1 (closed Monday and Tuesday, and on days when it rains or the humidity is over 80%); admission is $1.

To reach this cluster of sights, walk west from VDNKh metro across the car parks to pick up tram No 7 or 11, or trolleybus No 13, 36, 69 or 73 west along ulitsa Akademika Korolyova.

Petrovsky Palace

Leningradsky prospekt, which slices northwest through the suburbs towards the Sheremetevo airports and St Petersburg, is a fairly uninspiring avenue. The oddest sight along it, opposite the Aerostar Hotel approach road about 500m north of Dinamo metro and the Dinamo stadium, is the **Petrovsky Road-Palace** (Petrovsky dvorets), one of the many staging posts Catherine the Great built for her trips between St Petersburg and Moscow. This one was also Napoleon's headquarters after Moscow burned down. It's a fantastic cocktail of pseudo-Gothic, Moorish and traditional Russian styles, and is still in good shape. For about 50 years it housed the Air Force Engineering Academy and it is now being restored.

OUTER WEST

Following a vicious but inconclusive battle at Borodino (see the Borodino section in the Around Moscow chapter) in August 1812, Moscow's defenders retreated along what are now Kutuzovsky prospekt and ulitsa Arbat, pursued by Napoleon's Grand Army.

About 3km west of Kalininsky Most and Hotel Ukraina, near where the Russian commander Mikhail Kutuzov stopped for a war council, you'll now find the **Borodino Panorama** (Muzey-panorama Borodinskaya bitva), a pavilion with a giant 360° painting of the Borodino battle. Standing inside this tableau of bloodshed – an unprecedented 70,000 were killed in 15 hours – is an impressive, if idealised, way to visualise the event. See if you can spot Napoleon on his white horse. The panorama at Kutuzovsky prospekt 38 (☎ 148 1967, metro:

Kutuzovskaya) is open from 10 am to 6 pm daily (closed Friday and the last Thursday of the month); admission is $2.

The **Triumphal Arch** (Triumfalnaya arka), farther out on Kutuzovsky prospekt, celebrates Napoleon's eventual defeat. It was demolished at its original site in front of Belorussia Station in the 30s and reconstructed here in a fit of post-WWII public spirit.

From here you can get to **Victory Park** (Park Pobedy), a huge complex including the Museum of the Great Patriotic War, endless fountains, a church and several typically kitsch Tsereteli-designed monuments.

About 1.5km north of the Borodino Panorama in the neighbourhood called Fili is the 1690s **Church of the Intercession** (Tserkov Pokrova v Filyakh), a beautiful red-brick, Moscow baroque confection (gold dome atop octagonal tower above square tier, on a rosette base with four more gold domes) in otherwise dreary surroundings. It's open from 11 am to 5.30 pm (closed Wednesday and last Friday each month); admission is $2. From Fili metro, walk 500m north on Novozavodskaya ulitsa – it's impossible to miss.

OUTER SOUTH

The best view over Moscow with your feet on the ground is from Universitetskaya ploshchad on the **Sparrow Hills** (Vorobyovy Gory), just across the river bend from Luzhniki. From here most of the city spreads out before you and there's a ski jump in the parkland which runs down to the river. Trolleybus No 7 runs here from Kievskaya or Leninsky Prospekt metro.

Immediately behind Universitetskaya ploshchad rises the 36-storey Stalinist main spire of **Moscow University** (Moskovsky gosudarstvenny universitet), another 'Seven Sister' visible from most places in the city thanks to its elevated site; it was built by convict labour between 1949 and 1953. Bus Nos 1, 113 and 119 travel between the back of the main building and Universitet metro.

Kolomenskoe Museum-Reserve

Kolomenskoe, an ancient royal country seat amid 4 sq km of parkland on a bluff above a bend of the Moscow River, is the best excursion to the outer suburbs. It's 10 minutes walk from Kolomenskaya metro: go about 400m east on ulitsa Novinki and then south on Bolshaya ulitsa, which becomes ulitsa Shtatnaya Sloboda.

From ulitsa Shtatnaya Sloboda, you enter what's officially Kolomenskoe Museum-Reserve (Muzey-zapovednik Kolomenskoe) by the 17th century **Saviour Gate** (Spasskaya vorota) built in the time of Tsar Alexey, at the rear of the grounds. Inside the gate, to the left of the main path, the **Kazan Church** (Kazanskaya tserkov), also built by Alexey, faces the site of his great wooden palace demolished in 1768 by Catherine the Great. Ahead, the white, tent-roofed 17th century **Front Gate & Clock Tower** mark the edge of the old inner palace precinct. A golden double-headed eagle, symbol of the Romanov dynasty, tops the gate. The adjacent buildings house an interesting **museum** with a bit of everything: a model of Alexey's wooden palace, material on rebellions associated with Kolomenskoe, and Russian crafts from clocks and tiles to woodcarving and metalwork.

Outside the front gate, overlooking the river, rises Kolomenskoe's loveliest structure, the tall, almost rocket-like **Ascension Church** (Voznesenskaya tserkov), which is nearly as quintessentially Russian as St Basil's Cathedral. The Ascension Church was built between 1530 and 1532 for Grand Prince Vasily III, probably to celebrate the birth of his heir – Ivan the Terrible. It was an important development in Russian architecture, and paved the way for St Basil's 25 years later by reproducing the shapes of wooden churches in brick for the first time. Immediately south of it are the round 16th century **St George's Bell Tower** (Kolokolnya Georgia) and a 17th century falcon or water **tower** – no-one seems sure which.

Some 300m farther south across a gully, the white **St John the Baptist Church** (Tserkov Ioanna Predtechi), built for Ivan the Terrible in the 1540s or 1550s, has four corner chapels which make it a stylistic 'quarter-way house' between the Ascension Church and St Basil's.

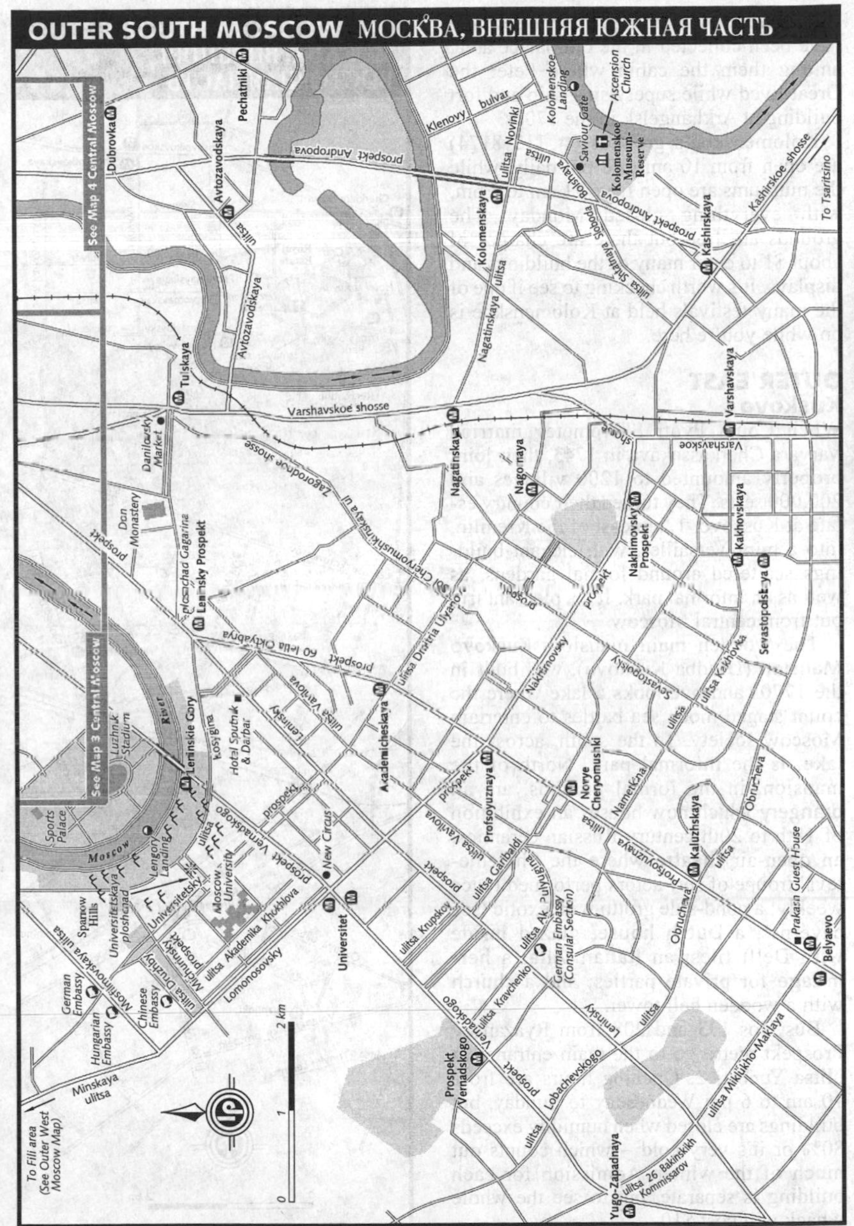
OUTER SOUTH MOSCOW МОСКВА, ВНЕШНЯЯ ЮЖНАЯ ЧАСТЬ
See Map 4 Central Moscow
Dubrovka
Pechatniki
Avtozavodskaya
prospekt Andropova
Klenovy bulvar
Kolomenskoe Landing
Ascension Church
Saviour Gate
Kolomenskoe Museum-Reserve
ulitsa Novinki
Bolshaya ulitsa
Kolomenskaya
Kashirskaya
Kashirskoe shosse
To Tsaritsino
Nagatinskaya ulitsa
Tulskaya
Varshavskoe shosse
Danilovsky Market
Nagatinskaya
Varshavskaya
Nagornaya
Don Monastery
ploshchad Gagarina
Leninsky Prospekt
Zagorodnoe shosse
Kakhovskaya
Nakhimovsky Prospekt
Sevastopolskaya
See Map 3 Central Moscow
Luzhniki Stadium
Moscow River
Leninskie Gory
Hotel Sputnik & Darbar
60 letia Oktyabrya
ulitsa Dmitria Ulyanova
ulitsa Vavilova
Akademicheskaya
Profsoyuznaya
Novye Cheryomushki
Nametkina
Obrucheva
Kaluzhskaya
Sports Palace
Lengory Landing
Sparrow Hills
Universitetskaya ploshchad
Moscow University
prospekt Vernadskogo
New Circus
Universitet
ulitsa Krupskoy
ulitsa Garibaldi
ulitsa Akademika Khokhlova
Lomonosovsky
ulitsa Druzhby
Michurinsky prospekt
Mosfilmovskaya ulitsa
German Embassy
Hungarian Embassy
Chinese Embassy
German Embassy (Consular Section)
Minskaya ulitsa
To Fili area (See Outer West Moscow Map)
0 1 2 km
ulitsa Kravchenko
Prospekt Vernadskogo
ulitsa Lobachevskogo
Yugo-Zapadnaya
ulitsa 26 Bakinskikh Kommissarov
ulitsa Miklukho-Maklaya
Belyaevo
Prakash Guest House

Old **wooden buildings** from elsewhere have been collected in the old palace area, among them the cabin where Peter the Great lived while supervising ship and fort building at Arkhangelsk in the 1700s.

Kolomenskoe's grounds (☎ 112 8174) are open from 10 am to 8 pm daily, while the museums are open from 11 am to 5 pm, with everything closed Monday. The grounds are free but there are charges of about $1 to enter many of the buildings and displays. It's worth checking to see if one of the many festivals held at Kolomenskoe is on while you're here.

OUTER EAST

Kuskovo

When Count Pyotr Sheremetev married Varvara Cherkassakava in 1743, their joint property amounted to 1200 villages and 200,000 serfs. They turned their country estate at Kuskovo, 12km east of the Kremlin, into a mini Versailles, with elegant buildings scattered around formal gardens, as well as an informal park. It's a pleasant trip out from central Moscow.

The wooden main mansion, **Kuskovo Mansion** (Usadba Kuskovo), was built in the 1770s and overlooks a lake where the count staged mock sea battles to entertain Moscow society. To the south, across the lake, is the informal park. North of the mansion, in the formal grounds, are an **orangery** which now houses an exhibition of 18th to 20th century Russian ceramics; an open-air **theatre** where the Sheremetevs' troupe of serf actors performed twice weekly; a pond-side grotto with exotic 'sea caverns'; a **Dutch house**, glazed inside with Delft tiles; an **Italian villa**; a **hermitage** for private parties; and a **church** with a wooden bell tower.

Bus Nos 133 and 208 from Ryazansky Prospekt metro go to the main entrance at ulitsa Yunosti 2. Opening hours are from 10 am to 6 pm Wednesday to Sunday, but buildings are closed when humidity exceeds 80% or it's very cold – which counts out much of the winter. Admission for each building is separate, but to see the whole whack will cost $10.

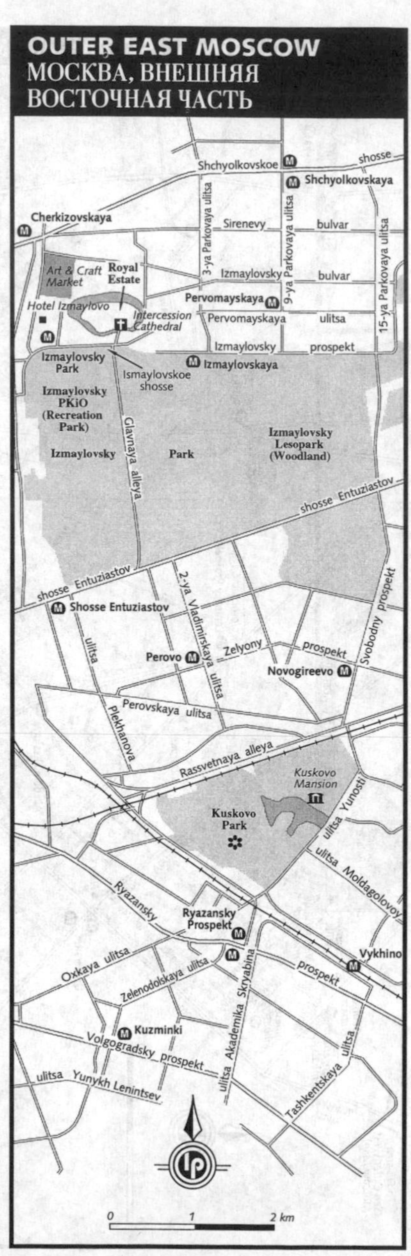

Izmaylovo

Izmaylovsky Park, a former royal hunting preserve 10km east of the Kremlin, is the nearest large tract of undeveloped land to central Moscow. Its 15 sq km contain a recreation park at the western end, and a much larger expanse of woodland (Izmaylovsky Lesopark) east of Glavnaya alleya, the road which cuts north-south across the park. Most people visit this area for the huge weekend Izmaylovo crafts market (see Shopping later in this chapter), but the parks and the nearby old royal estate are worth visiting too.

From Izmaylovsky Park metro, head south (away from the giant Hotel Izmaylovo) for the recreation park, and north (the same direction as the craft market) for the **royal estate**. Opposite Hotel Izmaylovo's Korpus Delta (Delta Building), walk down a small path to the right, and across a bridge on to a moated island. Tsar Alexey had an experimental farm here in the 17th century, where Western farming methods and cottage industries were tried. It was on the farm ponds that his son Peter learnt to sail in a little boat, which (like several others he used later!) came to be called the Grandfather of the Russian Navy.

You pass an extensive 18th century barracks, now partly occupied by the police, to reach the beautiful, five-domed 1679 **Intercession Cathedral** (Pokrovsky Sobor), now closed. The nearby triple arched, tent-roofed **Ceremonial Gates** (1682) and the squat brick **bridge tower** (1671) are the only other original buildings remaining. The original palace and accompanying buildings are gone.

ACTIVITIES

River Trips

A boat ride on the Moscow River is a fine way to see things from another angle. The main route runs between the Kiev Station landing (Map 4) and the Novospassky Most landings which is near the Novospassky Monastery, 1km west of Proletarskaya metro (Map 5). There are six intermediate stops: at the foot of Sparrow Hills (Map: Outer South Moscow), Frunzenskaya towards the southern end of Frunzenskaya naberezhnaya, Gorky Park (Map 4), Krimean Most, Bolshoy Kamenny Most opposite the Kremlin (Map 6) and Ustinsky Most near Hotel Rossiya and Red Square (Map 5).

The boats seat about 200 and cheap drinks are sold aboard. The views are great and this is one of the better things to do with a free afternoon in Moscow. The boats are operated by the Capital Shipping Company (☎ 277 3902) and run from late April to early October.

Check at the landings for the limited weekday schedules; on weekends they run as often as every 20 minutes in either direction. The fare is $1 whether you ride the entire length (90 minutes) or just go one stop. You buy a new ticket from a landing kiosk each time you board.

Banya

What better way to cope with Moscow than to have it steamed, washed and beaten out of you? There are traditional *banyas* (Russian baths) all over town. The oldest and a work of art themselves are **Sandunovskiye Baths** (Map 2; ☎ 925 4631) at ulitsa Neglinnaya 14. The Gothic Room has rich wood carving and the main shower room has an almost aristocratic Roman feel to it. For a detailed look at the traditions and workings of a Russian banya, see the boxed text 'A Russian Banya' in the Northern European Russia chapter.

The facility is open from 8 am to 10 pm daily (closed Tuesday). Admission varies from $10 for general access to $20 for a session on the top floor in the pool with Roman columns.

Winter Sports

There's no shortage of winter in Moscow, so take advantage of it. You can rent ice skates and see where all those great Russian figure skaters come from at **Gorky Park** (Map 4), the winter skating rink at **Chistyie Prudy** (Map 3), the lovely, secluded **Patriarch's Pond** (Map 2) and in the north at **Sokolniki Park** (Map: Outer North Moscow), where you can also rent cross-country skis.

Swimming

Public pools are difficult places to take the plunge if you are a foreigner because they all insist on a Russian doctor's certificate of your good health before they'll let you in. Alternatively, the large hotels with pools listed under Places to Stay often will allow people to use their facilities for a fee of $10 to $20.

On hot summer days you can join much of the city and head to the many beaches at Serebryaniy Bor, a series of lakes and channels on the Moscow River 20km north of the city (a key detail since nothing from Moscow has yet *flushed* into the water). There are areas that are unofficially dedicated to families, gays, nudists and even disco dancers.

To reach the beaches, take the metro to Sokol and then ride trolleybus No 65 to the end of the line.

LANGUAGE COURSES

The *Moscow Times* carries lots of small ads from tutors and colleges offering short-term Russian-language lessons. Many will teach you their Russian in return for your sharing your English. Le Cref (☎ 784 6369) is an organisation that can arrange all sorts of formal classroom courses or individual tutors in Russian.

ORGANISED TOURS

Patriarshy Dom (Map 2; ☎ 795 0927) runs a varied and interesting program of English-language tours in and around Moscow. Two or three different tours are offered each day and it has several tours to places such as the KGB Museum where you can't otherwise get access.

Tours within Moscow normally last around two or three hours and cost from $8 to $20 per person; excursions outside the city are longer, more expensive and may include lunch.

Intourist (Map 6; ☎ 292 1278, fax 292 2475) runs several mainstream tours geared for large groups that visit places like the Kremlin and Pushkin Museum. The large central office is located near the National Hotel at ulitsa Mokhovaya 13.

SPECIAL EVENTS

See the Special Events section of European Russia Facts for the Visitor for a list of Russian special events that are invariably celebrated in spectacular ways in Moscow.

Mayor Luzhkov has been a keen proponent of bread and circuses for the masses. However, the festivals have been an ever-changing lot year to year; consult the newspapers while you are in Moscow to see what might be on.

For details on the International Tchaikovsky Competition, see the Entertainment section later in this chapter. Otherwise, three festivals that are long established are:

Contemporary Music Festival
Held at venues all over the city for a few weeks in late May and early June. Top Russian and international acts perform.

December Nights Festival
Held at the main performance halls, theatres and museums from mid-December to early January. Classical music at its best is performed in classy surroundings by the best Russian and foreign talent.

Winter Festival
An outdoor funfest for those with antifreeze in their veins (and you can bet plenty of people are using the vodka kind) during early January. Teams compete to build elaborate ice sculptures in front of the Pushkin Museum and on Red Square. But the real nutters (or those who have far too much antifreeze in their veins) can be found punching holes in the ice on the Moscow River and plunging in for a dip. Do this and you're a member of the 'Walrus Club'. And you can take consolation that it's probably too cold for the usual legions of germs.

PLACES TO STAY

Moscow is not a cheap place to stay. The sort of small and simple hotels found elsewhere in Europe just don't exist yet. During the 1990s investment was limited to luxury properties. Hotels in the mid-priced and budget range are exclusively older Soviet-era properties that have weathered the transition to a market economy with varying measures of grace. Many are huge labyrinths (like the Rossiya) that lack any charm; however, with a bit of spirit, a stay in these places can be part of the Russian adventure.

Moscow has no central homestay agency. However, you can arrange to stay in private homes before you arrive by booking from abroad – see the Homestays section of the European Russia Facts for the Visitor chapter for a list of agencies.

Unless noted, the places listed below all have air-conditioning for those scorching Moscow summers.

PLACES TO STAY – BUDGET

Camping

There are no camping grounds in or near Moscow worthy of consideration.

Guesthouses

The ***Travellers Guest House*** *(Map 3; ☎ 280 8562, fax 280 7686, tgh@glasnet.ru, Bolshaya Pereyaslavskaya ulitsa 50, floor 10)* is to date the only guesthouse in Moscow that's really geared to international budget travellers. It's a 10 minute walk north of Prospekt Mira metro. The only sign on the building says ЦМИПКС. The guesthouse can take up to 140 people, at $15 for a place in a five-bed dorm, or $30/45 for singles/doubles. Rooms are basic but clean; each shares a toilet and bathroom with one other room. There's a common room, a kitchen, useful notice boards and a place to leave luggage. It offers good visa support service, international airline tickets, rail tickets at foreigner prices, and trans-Siberian and Central Asia packages through their Infinity Travel Agency affiliate. You should book ahead in the summer.

Prakash Guest House *(Outer South Moscow Map; ☎/fax 334 2598, Profsoyuznaya ulitsa 83/1)* offers similar accommodation, though without the communal facilities. It's run by an Indian team just a minute's walk north of Belyaevo metro. A place in a four-bed dormitory costs $15; singles/doubles with breakfast, TV and phone are $30/45. Some pairs of rooms share a bathroom and toilet. Meals are available. There's room for about 70 guests, but it's worth calling first to check availability. Prakash offers visa support, domestic travel bookings and airport transfers. Use entrance two on the south side of the building; there are no signs.

Hotels

Hotels in the cheapest price range are mostly grey places that were poor relations even in Soviet times. Note that the following prices are subject to fluctuation.

Centre ***Hotel Tsentralnaya*** *(Map 2; ☎ 229 8957, fax 292 1221, Tverskaya ulitsa 10)* has large, drab rooms and shared facilities. Singles/doubles cost $38/58, a price which won't get you a single smile from the staff (maybe it's the lack of air-con). Pushkinskaya and Tverskaya metros are five minutes' walk north.

North ***Hotel Leningradskaya*** *(Map 3; ☎ 975 1815, fax 975 1802, Kalanchevskaya ulitsa 21/40)* is in the shortest of Stalin's 'Seven Sisters'. Its once grand lobby is as faded as Joe's dream of a socialist empire; dull rooms cost $45/58. The location is convenient to three train stations: Kalanchevskaya, Leningrad and Kazan. This is good for transport but bad if you want to avoid the seedy folk whom train stations attract. Komsomolskaya metro is also close by.

Outer South ***Hotel Sputnik*** *(Outer South Moscow Map; ☎ 938 7106, fax 938 7096, Leninsky prospekt 38)* is a 1970s tower that has basic rooms with shower for $35/55. Leninsky Prospekt metro is a 15 minute walk, or take bus No 111 or trolleybus No 4, 33, 62 or 84.

PLACES TO STAY – MID-RANGE

These hotels are Soviet era constructions and 20 years ago were about the best Moscow could offer. Their prices have been kept in check, and service standards pepped up a bit by competition from the wave of superior top end hotels.

This is the category where prices vary the widest. Sometimes they change by the minute or at whim, as happened at one place where we were given a price list that was different from the prices posted which in turn was different from that quoted by the desk clerk. Consider the prices below as averages.

Centre

Hotel Moskva *(Map 6; ☎ 960 2020, fax 960 5938, Okhotny ryad 2)* occupies the block between Manezhnaya ploshchad and Teatralnaya ploshchad. Here you can feel like a member of the Politburo as this was the hostelry of choice for visiting Communist Party apparatchiks. The atmosphere is appropriately sombre – apart from a smattering of prostitutes and pimps in the lobby – but the rooms are comfortable. Singles/doubles cost $60/70. West-facing rooms have views of the Kremlin.

Hotel Rossiya *(Map 2; ☎ 232 5000, 232 6262, ulitsa Varvarka 6)* has over 5000 beds. This grotesquely enormous 1960s block, with sides 250m long, dwarfs the neighbouring old churches and mansions of the Kitay-Gorod. Rooms vary widely in quality – if you can find them in this maze. Expect to pay about $80 for a single/double. The location is great, but avoid the hotel's bars and restaurants.

Hotel Intourist *(Map 6; ☎ 956 8400, fax 956 8450, Tverskaya ulitsa 3/5)* is a landmark 22-storey eyesore that is the haunt of tour groups and others who enjoy the location near Red Square. The antiseptic rooms have the standard conveniences of TV, private bath etc and cost $90/150.

Hotel Budapest *(Map 2; ☎ 921 1060, fax 921 1266, Petrovskie linii 2/18)* is 1km north of the Kremlin. It is the pick of the mid-range hotels with just 125 comfortable rooms for $120/150, all with cable TV, private bathroom and more.

West

Hotel Belgrad *(Map 4; ☎ 248 2841, fax 248 2814, Smolenskaya ulitsa 8)* has poky singles/doubles for $70/90 but is functional and conveniently situated near the western end of ulitsa Arbat.

Hotel Ukraina *(Map 2; ☎ 243 3030, fax 956 2078, Kutuzovsky prospekt 2/1)* is a 1000 room Stalinist 'Seven Sister' by Kalininsky Most, facing the White House across the Moscow River. It's among the best value of the mid-range hotels and is also the most atmospheric, with echoes of Stalinist pomp in its spacious hallways and comfortable, modernised, almost stately rooms. Mostly with terrific views, these go for $85/105, including cable TV.

PLACES TO STAY – TOP END

Moscow's top end hotels offer international standard comfort and service. Nearly all are new, or are older hotels that have undergone dramatic upgradings. Most are managed by Western hotel chains and you can book these easily from abroad. Businesspeople make up the majority of the clientele.

Expect satellite TV, international direct dial phones, air-con, minibars and room service in very comfortable modern or modernised rooms, and a range of expensive restaurants, shops, bars and services. Many hotels have health clubs or exercise rooms with pool, sauna, massage and the like.

With the downturn in business travel to Moscow you should consider the prices below as 'soft'. A travel agent can probably find numerous deals for you to choose from.

Centre

The ***Renaissance Moscow Hotel*** *(Map 2; ☎ 931 9000, fax 931 9076, Olimpiysky prospekt 18)*, 4km north of the Kremlin, was built for the 1980 Olympics, as was the enormous indoor Olympic Sports Complex across the road. It was upgraded with Lufthansa's help in around 1990 and is now German-run. The 500 rooms and suites cost from $250/290. Thanks to its athletic origins, it boasts probably the best hotel fitness club in Moscow, with a 22m pool. You can't miss the eponymous Dome Cinema, which shows English-language movies.

Hotel National *(Map 6; ☎ 258 7000, fax 258 7100, Okhotny ryad 14/1)* occupies the choicest location, facing the Kremlin across Manezhnaya ploshchad, at the foot of Tverskaya ulitsa. Built in 1903, its chandeliers and frescoed ceilings survived the revolution and after a careful renovation it is one of the best hotels. It's owned by the city of Moscow and is affiliated with Forte Hotels.

Many of the rooms in the old wing are museums in themselves and the hotel publishes a guide to its antiques. Rooms in the old wing ($300 to $450) are actually slightly smaller than the standard rooms ($350 to $390) in the new wing, but warrant the higher tariff because their views of Red Square are spectacular. The National has a small pool, whirlpool and health club.

The ***Marriott Royal Hotel*** *(Map 2; ☎ 937 1000, fax 937 1001, ulitsa Petrovka 11/20)* is the most ambitious of the American company's three hotels in Moscow. Located near the Bolshoi, it has large, comfortable rooms and staff who are remarkably anxious to please. When we were there, the Norwegian prime minister was strolling through the lobby so you'll probably manage to avoid rubbing shoulders with riffraff. The basement pool is quite large. Rooms cost from $320 a single/double.

Hotel Baltschug Kempinski *(Map 6; ☎ 230 6500, fax 230 6502, ulitsa Balchug 1)* is on the Moscow River, opposite the Kremlin from where it commands spectacular views. First built in 1898, it has 234 high-ceilinged rooms filled with state-of-the-art gizmos from around $320/350; and there is a pool as well as a casino in the basement. The breakfast buffet has food to match the views.

West (Map 4)

The bright ***Radisson Slavyanskaya Hotel*** *(☎ 941 8020, fax 240 6915, Berezhkovskaya naberezhnaya 2)* is 3.5km west of the Kremlin by Kiev Station. It's almost a village in itself with a large business centre, its own shopping mall, a host of cafes and restaurants, a big pool and the Americom House of Cinema. There are 430 rooms and suites priced from $180/210 for a single/double room.

The ***Golden Ring Swiss Diamond Hotel*** *(☎ 725 0100, fax 725 0101, ulitsa Smolenskaya 5)* was reopened in 1998 after a long refitting. It is close to the White House and the river and has numerous amenities. The rooms are very modern and cost $190/225. There is an emphasis on security throughout the place.

East (Map 5)

Hotel Katerina *(☎ 795 2444, fax 795 2443, Shluzovaya Naberezhnaya 6)* is a welcome addition. It has Scandinavian management and comes the closest to being an intimate European-style hotel of any place in town. The small lobby has a comfy fireplace where staff will serve you a glass of wine, and the neighbourhood itself is quiet and leafy. Singles/doubles cost from $165/205, including a buffet breakfast.

Outer North

The ***Moscow Aerostar Hotel*** *(Outer North Moscow Map; ☎ 213 9000, fax 213 9001, Leningradsky prospekt 37)* is fairly convenient, just 6km from the Kremlin on the road from Sheremetevo-2 airport. Originally built for the 1980 Olympics, the 415 rooms cost $270/300. There's also a fully serviced business centre.

At Sheremetevo-2 airport itself, the ***Novotel*** *(☎ 926 5900, fax 926 5903)* is a good place to stay if you're stuck between flights; otherwise it's a long trek to the centre even with the free shuttle bus. There's a good atrium pool and a few restaurants and bars. Rooms are about $160/200.

PLACES TO EAT

You can get any kind of meal you want in Moscow, so long as you're willing to pay for it. Sticker shock is common at Moscow restaurants where prices are geared to free-spending new Russians and flush expats rather than the average person.

Unfortunately, the places to eat that are geared to the masses typically embody the old motto: 'you get what you pay for'. These can be nameless canteens or shabby cafes which your nose will find faster than your eyes. Even at better places, don't expect standards of food to be quite up there with their Western counterparts. Many ingredients have to be imported and the journey is not always the kindest to quality.

You will also soon realise that the divisions between what constitutes a restaurant, bar or club are often quite blurred. For example, Night Flight is renowned for its steaks, salad bar and lunch specials. But at night it's renowned as the priciest brothel-cum-nightclub in Moscow. In the same vein, the city's Planet Hollywood – a chain known for its family friendly atmosphere elsewhere – stages regular strip shows by both professionals and patrons. Like everything else, nothing in Moscow is as you'd expect. For this reason, we've grouped places to eat with cafes and bars in the map keys. Just because a place is known for its tasty snacks doesn't mean you'll always get a meal.

Only at the top places and those in luxury hotels can you expect to be able to use a credit card. The hard working cooks of Moscow never take a day off so unless otherwise stated, all of the following are open from noon to midnight daily.

Restaurants

Places in this category are listed by cuisine and in roughly ascending order of price.

Russian ***Yolki-Palki*** *(Map 4; ☎ 953 9130, 14 Klimentovsky pereulok)* is one of several outlets for this fun Russian chain which specialises in simple and traditional food like *shashlyk* (grilled kebabs) and *golubtsy* (minced meat in cabbage) served in a homy atmosphere meant to evoke a country cottage. Nothing's over $5, the staff are young and enthusiastic and the beer cheap. At the heart of their schtick is a huge wagon in the dining room that is laden with fresh salads which can be a meal alone for only $4. Another Yolki Palki *(Map 4; ☎ 243 2019, B. Dorogomilovskaya 12A)* is near Kiev Station.

Chicken is the specialty at ***Kot Begemot*** *(Map 2; ☎ 209 6463, Spiridonyevsky pereulok 10A)*, but all meat dishes are nicely seasoned and filling. Order anything with mushrooms and sit back and enjoy the quiet ambience. Lunch specials are a mere $4; you can have dinner for under $15 easily.

Actors abound at ***Tram*** *(☎ 299 0770, ulitsa Malaya Dmitrovka 6)*. This cosy basement bistro is under the Lenkom Theatre (Map 2) and the dishes are named after plays (although the roast pig's trotters stand on their own, so to speak). You can dine for $15 and it's open 24 hours a day.

Samovar *(Map 2; ☎ 921 4688, ulitsa Myasnitskaya 13)* is one of the best all-round Russian restaurants in town. The menu is heavy with classic renditions of standards such as *pelmeni* and *bliny*. On a higher note, you can opt for the excellent fish in champagne sauce. Bills average about $30 a head, but the draught beer is only $2. It's open from 1 pm to 1 am.

Moscow expats take visiting relatives to ***Sudar*** *(Map 4; ☎ 247 1157, Zubovsky Proyezd 2)*. And for good reason, because this is another place that brings out the best in Russian cooking such as the many mushroom dishes and the warming borsch. Parents from anywhere will love the old standards played live in the lounge. Expect to pay about $32 each.

Few actual scribes can afford the exquisite fare at the ***Central House of Writers*** *(Map 2; ☎ 291 1515, ulitsa Povarskaya 50)*, which has a lovely carved wood dining room which figured in *The Master and Margarita*. This is the place for caviar, champagne, and every other hedonistic tradition of a regal Russian meal. Oh – and make somebody else pay the $100 plus per person (including quality wines, of course).

Caucasian The food from Russia's southern neighbours is very popular in Moscow, probably because it's usually spicy and tasty and the wines are good and cheap.

The bargain-priced beer ($1) is just one of the inducements at ***Guriya*** *(Map 4; ☎ 246 0378, Komsomolsky prospekt 7/3)* which has very good, albeit simple, renditions of the eggplant and grilled meat dishes of Georgian cooking. You can escape for under $10 a person, which is why there's often a queue. It's open from 11 am to 11 pm.

Armenia inspires the menu at ***Moosh*** *(Map 2; ☎ 284 3670, ulitsa Oktyabrskaya 2/4)*. The sturgeon shashlyks are memorable and the spicy meatballs and flat bread are tops. You can feast for under $10 and the draught Baltika's $1. It's a 15 minute walk west of the Prospekt Mira metro station.

Copies of this book abound at ***Mama Zoya*** *(Map 4; ☎ 201 7743, Sechenovsky pereulok 8)*, a budget Georgian restaurant that moved to new quarters, but took its delightfully kitsch decor along. This is a favourite of backpackers and expats who smile when the help yells at them.

One of the most pleasant places in Moscow, ***Tiflis*** *(Map 4; ☎ 290 2897, ulitsa Ostozhenka 32)* is housed in a traditional grand Georgian house. The balconies are the perfect place for dining on warm days. The *khachapuri* (a cheesy bread) is the best in town and the mixed shashlyks are perfectly seasoned. With plenty of wine, you'll pay at least $35 a head (credit cards are accepted).

European ***U Yuzefa*** *(Map 5; ☎ 238 4646, ulitsa Dubininskaya 11/17)* was one of the first Jewish restaurants in Moscow. It retains much of its old charm and, better yet, retains many of its old prices. About half of the menu is kosher and the rest of the food is simple and fresh. The salads are good and all are under $3. Wash it down with drinkable wine for $6 a bottle.

Everything is cheap and cheery at ***Soleil Express*** *(Map 2; ☎ 725 6474, ulitsa Sadovaya-Samotechnaya 24/27)*, including the phone, which is free for local calls. The sandwiches and salads are fresh, and coffee is $1. It's open from 8.30 am to 11 pm.

Paul McBride's Fish & Chips *(Map 4; ☎ 959 5454, ulitsa Pyatnitskaya 29/8)* is at least as good as you'll find in old Blighty. The prices are good (from $9), the fish fresh and the chips piled high. It features clean design and, well, cleanliness. It's open from noon to 11 pm (on Friday and Saturday night it stays open until 6 am) and serves classic fry-ups for $5.

Rosie O'Grady's *(Map 4; ☎ 203 9087, ulitsa Znamenka 9/12)* is a delightful rendition of the Irish theme bar (see Entertainment). The menu is quite good and has excellent burgers, chicken sandwiches ($9) and other food to fill your hands and stomach. It's open until 1 am.

Come for lunch to ***Night Flight*** *(Map 2; ☎ 229 4165, ulitsa Tverskaya 17)* and you'll enjoy excellent multi-course $15 specials that include an excellent salad bar and prime steak. But come later and the menu changes dramatically as Night Flight becomes one of the most notorious nightclubs in town (see Entertainment). It's open for lunch from noon to 4 pm.

You can decamp for the Mediterranean at ***Angelico's*** *(Map 2; ☎ 299 3696, Karetny Bolshoy pereulok)*. In fact, during the long winter this is as close as you can get to the sunny climes. The grilled shrimp with tomatoes and pesto is typical of the dishes that capture the taste of Provence. The stylish interior is highlighted by works from local artists. Expect to pay more than $30 per person. It's open until 2 am.

Stalin never dreamed of a place like ***Le Gastronome*** *(Map 2; ☎ 255 4433, Kudrinskaya ploshchad 1)* when he ordered his 'Seven Sisters' skyscrapers. But this is an excellent European restaurant in the restored splendour of what was a grand food hall. The wide-ranging menu has everything from gourmet burgers ($12) to live lobsters (don't ask). Brunch specials are not bad at $8 and everything is 25% off before 5 pm. The bar is a treat (see Entertainment).

Asian Only the dimmest are in doubt about the menu at ***It's Sushi*** *(Map 2; ☎ 299 4236, Triumfalnaya ploshchad 4/31)* which has surprisingly fresh examples for as little as $1 a pop. You'll have to really gorge yourself to top $15 here, in the foyer of the Tchaikovsky Concert Hall. It's open until 11 pm, and more branches are planned.

You can tell ***Darbar*** *(Outer South Moscow Map; ☎ 930 2925, 38 Leninsky prospekt)* is on the mark because it's filled with Indian families enjoying the Indian cuisine. The samosas, curries, dhal and anything with chicken all get raves. Expect to pay $15 a head before you hit the draught beer. Darbar is off the lobby of Hotel Sputnik.

Ponder the large mural of its namesake country while you await great food at ***Tibet Kitchen*** *(Map 2; ☎ 923 2422, Kamergersky pereulok 5/6)*. The vegetarian spring rolls have many fans, as do the lovely, friendly staff. The menu abounds with many classic Chinese dishes (average $9) as well.

Tamerlaine *(Map 4; ☎ 202 5649, ulitsa Prechistenka 30)* is one of those Mongolian barbecues where you choose from a long list of ingredients and the chefs then stir-fry it up for you. The bread may look like a deflated football, but it tastes great. When in doubt, stick with the recommended combinations. Expect to pay at least $35 a person with drinks. It's open until 11 pm.

Italian You can't miss ***Patio Pizza*** *(Map 4; ☎ 298-2530, ulitsa Volkhonka 13a)* – they're all over town – but this branch across from the Pushkin Museum is considered the best. The staff are cheerful and the pizzas (from $8) come hot from wood ovens. The salad bar is huge. It gets crowded on weekends.

Pizza Express *(Map 2; ☎ 937 2397, ulitsa Nikolskaya 25)* is legendary for cheap gourmet pizzas served in stunning surroundings in London and they're hoping for the same reputation in Moscow. Everything is fresh and flawless; the individual pizzas cost from $8.

Il Pomodoro *(Map 2; ☎ 924 2931, 5 Bolshoy Golovin pereulok)* is a classic family-run Italian trattoria with a long menu of reasonable and good pastas and sauces. The salads are huge and a meal in themselves. Expect to pay about $30 a person with wine. It's open until 11 pm.

American The original location of ***The Starlite Diner*** *(Map 2; ☎ 290 9638, ulitsa bolshaya Sadovaya 16)* is the best as it has a wonderful, leafy outdoor seating area. Year-round (and around the clock), however, you can't beat this ersatz American diner's thick and creamy milkshakes ($5), cheese fries ($3) burgers ($7) and more. One of our friends swears by the shakes as a hangover cure.

There's surprisingly good value at ***City Grill*** *(Map 2; ☎ 299 5519, ulitsa Sadovaya-Triumfalnaya 2/30)*. Order the torpedo sandwich with a choice of ingredients for a filling $8 treat. People love the pork chops and mashed potatoes which go for $10. It also has good, non-meaty salads.

The ***Moosehead Canadian Bar*** *(Map 4; ☎ 230 7333, ulitsa Bolshaya Polyanka)* has good bar food such as chicken wings. The Wednesday burrito special ($5) is a treat. (Also see Entertainment.)

The ***American Bar and Grill*** *(Map 2; ☎ 251 0150, ulitsa 1st Tverskaya-Yamskaya 2/1)* is open 24 hours and is known for good breakfasts ($8), large lunches and excellent steaks ($15); the vegetarian lasagne is renowned ($11). The bar area hops at night (see Entertainment).

Margaritas are tops at ***Santa Fe*** *(Map 2; ☎ 256 1487, ulitsa Mantulinskaya 5/1)* where raucous tequila-fuelled crowds wolf down huge plates of reasonably authentic Mexican standards like burritos and fajitas. You can eat for $15, but the margaritas ($6) will quickly add to that. It's until 2 am.

The ***Chesterfield Cafe*** *(Map 3; ☎ 917 0150, Zemlyanoi Val)* is a good and fun place when crowded but feels a bit cavernous when not. There's live sports from around the world on satellite TVs and the ribs are excellent ($18). It's all like an American sports bar, except you can get beer and food 24 hours daily. There's a good garden out the back, too.

Cafes

There are scores of cafes along the pedestrian zones of ulitsa Arbat and Stoleshnikov pereulok. There are several scattered about inside GUM when you need a break from Red Square. Elsewhere, when the weather's nice and warm, small impromptu sidewalk cafes appear on just about any large patch of pavement.

The ***Coffee Bean*** *(Map 3; ☎ 923 9793, ulitsa Pokrovka 18)* is a classic coffee bar: high ceilings, newspapers laying around and nice mugs of Joe ($1.50) or his various Italian cousins like Cappuccino. There are also a few cakes and simple sandwiches. There's no smoking and the patio is a great place to while away the hours.

Relive the past at ***Kafe Shokoladnitsa*** *(Map 4; ☎ 238 2734, Krymsky Val 2/4)* on Kaluzhskaya ploshchad. Veteran Soviet-era waitresses will curtly inform you that half of the menu is unavailable, but don't despair – the house speciality, bliny with chocolate sauce, is usually available. It's open until 10.30 pm.

The ***DeliFrance*** *(Map 4; ☎ 202 6721, ulitsa Arbat 16/3)* has authentic croissants thanks to frequent deliveries of special dough from France, and everyone raves about the lemon tarts ($4). There's another branch inside the lobby of the Tchaikovsky Concert Hall.

Brunch Sunday brunch at the luxury hotels is an institution for many expats and wealthy Russians. You can while away the hours while you gorge yourself on a feast of international foods.

Moscow Aerostar Hotel *(Outer North Moscow Map;* ☎ *213 9000, Leningradsky prospekt 37)* has an excellent brunch in the Cafe Taiga that has more Asian selections than many others for $31. ***Hotel Baltschug Kempinski*** *(Map 6;* ☎ *230 6500, ulitsa Balchug 1)* has the best view and, like the others, includes champagne in the $33 price. The ***Radisson Slavyanskaya Hotel*** *(Map 4;* ☎ *941 8020, Berezhkovskaya naberezhnaya 2)* sets up its groaning tables in the ballroom around huge ice sculptures. It costs $34.

Fast Food

First came McDonald's, then came Yuri. Deciding that Moscow needed a home-grown version of the Golden Arches, Mayor Luzhkov decreed the creation of the ***Russkoe Bistro***, a sort of 'pirozhki in a hurry concept'. With the city driving its growth, you can find the merry red and gold Grenadier logo all over town at dozens of locations.

To give you an idea of just how many Russkoe Bistros there are, the branch at ulitsa Tverskaya 23 (Map 2) is one of four within a 200m radius.

The pirozhki are quite good and come with a huge variety of fillings for under $1 each. Staff also serve the tasty fermented drink called *kvas*, as well as cheap beer. Many of the locations have nice patios. However, unlike their grinning brethren at the American competition, the youthful Russkoe Bistro employees have quickly realised that they are in fact civil servants – no smiles here.

Although not as ubiquitous as Yuri's favourite, ***McDonald's*** has many locations – you'll pass four between Sheremetevo-2 and central Moscow. The original branch *(Map 2; ulitsa Bolshaya Bronnaya 29)* is the most famous, but is now simply another busy outlet. Prices are similar to the West (a Big Mac is $2) so the real allure lies in two areas: familiar fare and clean toilets. Other convenient outlets can be found at:

prospekt Mira 39 (Map 2)
ulitsa B Dorogomilovskaya 8 (Map 4)
Klimentovsky pereulok 16/21 (Map 4)
ulitsa B Serpukhovskaya 4/3 (Map 4)
ulitsa Krasnaya Presnya 31 (Map 2)

Self-Catering

If you want to eat like a Muscovite, you should buy your food, take it home, cook it and eat it. While this may not be feasible if you're staying in a hotel, visits to Russian food markets can be entertaining and if nothing else you can buy the ingredients for a good picnic.

If you're just looking for a bottle of water, a cold beer or some packaged food, you'll find small food stores and kiosks everywhere. Many are open 24 hours.

If you have a hankering for food from home, ***Global USA*** *(Map 6;* ☎ *229 8786, ulitsa Tverskaya 6)* carries groceries imported from around the world. Its opening hours are from 10 am to 10 pm and credit cards are accepted.

Markets Moscow's food markets *(rynky)* are full of interest as well as fruit, vegetables, cheese, honey and meat. Many of the traders and their goods are from southern CIS republics. Take your own bag. Prices are good if you bargain a bit – and keep an eye on the quality of the items that are being popped into your bag. The most central markets are:

Danilovsky Market
  Mytnaya ulitsa 74 (Outer South Moscow Map; metro: Tulskaya)
Rizhsky Market
  prospekt Mira 94-96 (Outer North Moscow Map; metro: Rizhskaya)
Dorogomilovsky Market
  ulitsa Mozhaysky Val 10, with an overflow along Kievskaya ulitsa to the Kiev Station (Map 4)

ENTERTAINMENT

Moscow can keep anyone entertained for months. A ballet at the Bolshoi, a concert in the Kremlin or a night at the Moscow circus is a unique experience – and there's a lively club scene, too.

Unfortunately for summer visitors, much of the entertainment industry goes on holiday or tour from late June to early September, so choice is limited and quality drops.

Information

The key to finding out what's on is the comprehensive weekly entertainment section in the Friday *Moscow Times*. For a laugh, you can also try *Exile*, but if it doesn't involve debauchery of some kind, they won't recommend it.

Theatre and concert programs are also displayed in Russian at the venues themselves, on street posters, and on charts at ticket kiosks around the city. For further information, see Entertainment in the European Russia Facts for the Visitor chapter.

Classical Music

The largest concert venue is ***Tchaikovsky Concert Hall*** *(Map 2; ☎ 299 0378, Triumfalnaya ploshchad 4/31)*, which seats over 1600 and is the home of the famous State Symphony Orchestra (Gosudarstvenny Akademichesky Simfonichesky Orkestr). The ***Moscow Tchaikovsky Conservatoire*** *(Map 2; ☎ 229 8183, Bolshaya Nikitskaya ulitsa 13)* is the country's largest music school and has two venues: the Great Hall (Bolshoy Zal) and the Small Hall (Maly Zal).

Every four years hundreds of musicians gather at the Conservatoire to compete for the titles of top pianist, singer, cellist and violinist at the International Tchaikovsky Competition (the next is in 2002).

Tickets? Anyone for Tickets?

Tickets for most Moscow concerts and stage and sports events are easy enough to get, though, as happens anywhere in the world, a few very popular events sell out early. Service bureaus and concierges in hotels sell tickets for a few main events – and sometimes have tickets when other outlets have run out – but often charge very hefty commissions on what are usually very cheap face values. It's cheaper just to go along to the ticket office at the venue (most are open for advance or same-day sales for several hours most days, right up to the start of the performance if there are tickets left), or a street ticket kiosk.

The street kiosks are marked *teatralnaya kassa* or just *teatr* (театральная касса or театр) and sell tickets for concerts, circuses, theatres, shows and sports events at close to their face value. Often the tickets they have available are displayed in the window. Locations of some useful kiosks are: Manezhnaya ploshchad in front of Intourist headquarters; ploshchad Revolyutsii near the metro exit; the west side of Teatralnaya ploshchad; ulitsa Petrovka opposite the Bolshoi Theatre; Tverskaya ulitsa opposite the Hotel National; Pushkinskaya ploshchad near the corner of Malaya Dmitrovka ulitsa; and outside Prospekt Mira circle line metro station.

Typical face-value prices for theatres and classical concerts are $2 or less, and for the circuses $1 to $2. If your Russian is inadequate, copy the name of the event and the date on a piece of paper and show it to the cashier. Often there will be a range of ticket prices available.

Tickets for the Bolshoi, the circuses and a few other things are a bit harder – but still quite possible – to come by. You'll be extremely lucky to pay the face value for a Bolshoi ticket. A common practice when tickets are hard to get is to go to the venue half an hour before the show starts and look for someone with spare tickets to sell. At the Bolshoi, you can find touts around the theatre throughout the day. Exercise caution when buying the tickets so that you don't buy ones for a show that was, say, last year.

Almost all evening theatre, concert and circus performances start at 7 pm.

Opera & Ballet

Bolshoi An evening at the ***Bolshoi*** *(Map 2; ☎ 292 9986, Teatralnaya ploshchad 1, www.bolshoi.ru)* remains one of Moscow's best nights out. The atmosphere in the glittering, six-tier auditorium is electric. However, the 18th century theatre, whose foundations are sinking, was due to close for restoration in 1999 (but this keeps being pushed back), with performances shifting to a new auditorium adjoining Teatralnaya ploshchad.

Both the ballet and opera companies, with several hundred artists between them, perform a range of Russian and foreign works. Sometimes other Russian companies perform here, too – it's always wise to check that it's the actual Bolshoi Ballet or Opera that you're paying to see.

Under artistic director Vladimir Vasiliev, the Bolshoi has staged a remarkable turnaround from the chaos that marked the final years of the authoritarian rule of its previous director, Yuri Grigorovich. Big names to watch for in the Bolshoi company include Nina Anaiashvili, Dmitri Belogolovtsev, Sergei Filin and Svetlana Lunkina.

Normally, you can't get Bolshoi tickets from the theatre's box office or from a *teatralnaya kassa* (theatre ticket office). You might conceivably be lucky a week or more in advance – or at 3.30 pm on the day of the performance, when any unsold tickets may go on sale at the box office. Generally, you either have to buy a ticket from one of a few specific outlets (as far ahead as you can, though you might still be lucky on the day), or hang around outside the theatre before the performance and get one from a tout (see the boxed text 'Tickets? Anyone for Tickets?').

Other Companies The Bolshoi does not have a monopoly on ballet and opera in Moscow. Leading dancers also appear with the Kremlin Ballet and the Moscow Classical Ballet Theatre, both of which perform in the ***State Kremlin Palace*** *(Map 6; ☎ 928 5232, ulitsa Vozdvizhenka 1)*. The Kremlin Ballet is now the home of the ex-Bolshoi honcho Yuri Grigorovich.

In addition, there's the ***Stanislavsky & Nemirovich-Danchenko Musical Theatre*** *(Map 2; ☎ 229 8388, Bolshaya Dmitrovka ulitsa 17)*, another opera and ballet theatre, with a similar classical repertoire to the Bolshoi's, and standards often as high.

Theatre

Moscow has around 20 professional and numerous amateur theatres. A wide range of plays – contemporary and classic, Russian and foreign – is staged at most of them, with most performances in Russian. Some of the best drama can be seen at these venues:

Chekhov Art Theatre *(Map 2; ☎ 229 8760, Kamergersky pereulok 3)* is also known as MKhAT. Method acting was founded here over 100 years ago and they've been emoting ever since. Watch for English-language versions of Russian classics performed here by the American Studio (☎ 292 0941).

Lenkom Theatre *(Map 2; ☎ 299 0708, ulitsa Malaya Dmitrovka 6)* has flashy productions and a lot of musicals that will keep non-Russian speakers happy.

Maly Theatre *(Map 6; ☎ 923 2621, Teatralnaya ploshchad 1/6)* is a lovely venue founded in 1824. Mainly 19th century works are performed here, often the same place where they premiered.

Circus

Moscow has two separate circuses which put on glittering shows, with Muscovites of all ages relaxing and enjoying themselves in the audience. The first half is likely to be a modern mix of dance, cabaret and rock music before animals and acrobats assert themselves.

The 3400-seat ***New Circus*** *(Outer South Moscow Map; ☎ 930 2815, prospekt Vernadskogo 7)*, near Moscow University, has the highest reputation, especially for its animal acts and clowns.

The more central ***Old Circus*** *(Map 2; ☎ 200 6889, Tsvetnoy bulvar 13)* is in a modernised 19th century building and produces shows around a central theme.

Both circuses perform at 7 pm Wednesday to Sunday, with additional daytime shows on weekends. For advice on tickets, see the boxed text 'Tickets? Anyone for tickets?'.

Exhibitions

There's always a fascinating range of short-term art, historical, cultural and other exhibitions around Moscow. Many museums have special sections for temporary exhibitions; other good shows can be found in the city's numerous art galleries which are listed in the *Moscow Times*.

One sure bet is the ***M'ARS Gallery*** *(☎ 146 2029, Malaya Filyovskaya ulitsa 32, metro: Pionerskaya)*, west of the centre. It was founded by artists banned in the Soviet era and usually has some good new works on display.

Bars & Clubs

The club scene is even more volatile in Moscow than elsewhere. Tastes are fickle, the DJ decamps, or the owner is rubbed out by a rival mob or closes shop and retires to Monaco one step ahead of the tax authorities. That said, you should be able to find any type of bar or club your heart or morals desire.

The following places mostly serve food and are found under Places to Eat, Cafes & Bars in the map keys. They are listed in roughly ascending order of decadence.

Romance in Moscow and you're not paying for it? That's the likely result of time at the bar at ***Le Gastronome*** *(Map 2; ☎ 255 4433, Kudrinskaya ploshchad 1)*, the elegant and lovely bar of the excellent restaurant (see Places to Eat). There's live piano music and fine views from this 'Seven Sisters' skyscraper. It's open noon to midnight.

Few other towns with a population of more than 200 don't have one, so of course Moscow has an Irish theme bar. Fortunately, ***Rosie O'Grady's*** *(Map 4; ☎ 203 9087, ulitsa Znamenka 9/12)* is a good rendition of the concept. The bar staff are chatty to a fault (most even have native Russian accents) and the Guinness, Harp, et al go down a treat. The bar menu is quite good (see Restaurants) and the place is open from noon to 1 am.

Finally a place for Canucks, eh? The ***Moosehead Canadian Bar*** *(Map 4; ☎ 230 7333, ulitsa Bolshaya Polyanka)* is as laid-back as its namesake country. Russians and expats alike hang out and enjoy the live music and decent bar food (see Places to Eat). Oddly, despite the name, there's no Moosehead on tap, but Baltika's better, anyway. It's open from noon to 5 am, until 10 am on weekends.

Bedniye Lyundi *(Map 4; ☎ 951 3342, ulitsa Bolshaya Ordynka 11/6)* is a laid-back bar with a big room out the back where local rock bands perform. This is a low-pressure place to hang for an evening (and morning) and there's an excellent beer selection. It's open from 5 pm to 5 am; there's a $4 music cover charge on weekends.

American Bar and Grill *(Map 2; ☎ 251 0150, ulitsa 1 Tverskaya-Yamskaya 2/1)* is open 24 hours and, besides good food (see Places to Eat), has a hopping bar area with relatively cheap happy hours. It's a big pick-up spot between Russians and expats.

Territoria *(Map 6; ☎ 737 8865, ulitsa Tverskaya 5/6)* is a great find in an alley behind the Intourist Hotel. The DJs are excellent and perceptive to what combination of techno and pop will charge up the friendly crowds. The unresponsive can collapse on the wonderful sofas, but they'll probably want to rise for one of the many cheap foreign beers on offer. It's open until the wee hours and until at least 6 am on Saturday.

You can alternate at ***Sixteen Tons*** *(Map 2; ☎ 253 5300, Presnensky Val 6)*. There's a delightful pub downstairs with some fine Belgian brews and an excellent house-brewed bitter ($2 a half pint). Upstairs, there's a sort of deliberately cheesy retro disco and they often have good bands as well. There's no cover for the pub; upstairs it ranges from $2 to $8 depending on the night and your gender. It's open from 11 am to 6 am.

Possibly the most stylish club in Moscow is ***Bulgakov*** *(Map 2; ☎ 209 9914, ulitsa Sadovaya Bolshaya 10)*. The decor changes to match the trendy clothes of the artists and models who hang around the many couches, listen to the cool DJs or shoot pool. The flat-head doormen enforce a tough admission policy; once through, they hit you up for a $4 cover. It's open from 7 pm to 7 am.

Let's see: open 24 hours, beer for 24 roubles (about $1) – now that's what we call synergy. ***Garage*** *(Map 2; ☎ 209 1848,* *ulitsa Tverskaya 16/2)* is a funky Soviet-theme underground bar on Pushkin Square. There's a bit of a biker overlay as one old BMW machine protrudes from over the bar. After 3 am anything goes. There's never any cover charge.

Even Bruce Willis (a part-owner of the chain) might blanche at Moscow's ***Planet Hollywood*** *(Map 2; ☎ 255 9191, ulitsa Krasnaya Presnya 23B)* where the daytime movie theme gives way to porn at night as male and female strippers perform non-stop and the audience joins in. On nights when there's no strippers they host popular expat theme parties.

If you have the money – lots and lots of it – then anything goes at ***Night Flight*** *(Map 2; ☎ 229 4165, ulitsa Tverskaya 17)*. Perhaps the source of more dubious expense account charges than anywhere else in Moscow, the $20 cover allows you to enter a land of expensive and gorgeous prostitutes that, ahem, rocks until 5 am. The lunch menu in the restaurant area is entirely – and we mean *entirely* – different (see Places to Eat).

Gay & Lesbian Venues

The Moscow gay scene is becoming more open all the time. ***Chameleon*** *(Map 2; ☎ 253 6343, Presnensky Val 14)* has a huge dance floor and a mixed and friendly crowd. Open from 8 pm to 8 am, it charges $1 to $2 for men and $2 to $4 for women. The ***Three Monkeys*** *(Map 2; ☎ 208 4637, Trubnaya ploshchad 4)* is hugely popular. The DJs play a mix of techno and Russian pop and there are frequent lesbian nights. Open from 6 pm to 9 am, there is a cover of $3 on weekends only.

Jazz & Blues

The ***Arbat Blues Club*** *(Map 4; ☎ 291 1546, Filippovsky pereulok 11)* has some excellent Russian blues bands from around 8.30 pm to the small hours on Friday and Saturday nights; the cover charge is $10. The place is closed in summer.

B B King *(Map 2; ☎ 299 8206, Samotechnaya ulitsa 4/2)* has live jazz and blues from around 9 pm Thursday and Saturday when there is a cover charge of $9. On these nights the bar closes at 5 am, other nights there are frequent jam sessions and closing time is 2 am.

Cinemas

The ***Americom House of Cinema*** *(Map 4; ☎ 941 8747, Berezhkovskaya naberezhnaya 2)*, in the Radisson Slavyanskaya Hotel, shows major Hollywood movies in English. Current release films are also shown in English at the ***Dome Theatre*** *(Map 2; ☎ 931 9873, Olimpiysky prospekt 18)*, which is in the Renaissance Moscow Hotel.

SPECTATOR SPORTS

The premier football league, Vysshaya Liga, has five teams in Moscow: Spartak, Lokomotiv, TsSKA, Torpedo and Dinamo. Each has a very loyal following and interesting history: Spartak reached the semi-finals of the 1998 UEFA cup; Lokomotiv recently joined the Vysshaya Liga; TsSKA has winning tradition that goes back to its days as the official Red Army team; Mayor Luzhkov loves Torpedo; and Dinamo was once sponsored by the KGB.

You can often buy tickets immediately before games which are played at the following venues:

Dinamo Stadium (Outer North Moscow Map; ☎ 212 7172, Leningradsky prospekt 36, metro: Dinamo) seats 51,000 and hosts namesake Dinamo and TsSKA.

Luzhniki Stadium (Outer South Moscow Map; ☎ 201 1806, metro: Sportivnaya) gleams from its rebuilding with 80,000 new seats, and hosts Torpedo and Spartak.

Lokomotiv Stadium (Outer North Moscow Map; ☎ 161 4283, Bolshaya Cherkizovskaya ulitsa 125, metro: Cherkizovskaya) has wonderful murals of trains and, you guessed it, is the home of Lokomotiv.

Moscow's main entrant in the top ice hockey league (Super Liga) is Dinamo (Outer North Moscow Map; ☎ 221 3145, Leningradsky prospekt 36, metro: Dinamo), a perennial contender for top honours.

In a comedown from the days of Olympic glory, men's basketball trails soccer and ice hockey as a distant third in popularity. The top Moscow team CSKA (Outer North Moscow Map; ☎ 213 2954, Leningradsky prospekt 39A, metro: Aeroport) does well in European league play but all too often serves as a retirement home for the NBA, which poaches the best players. In contrast, some of the best play and games comes from the CSKA women's team, which plays from September to May.

SHOPPING

You can buy whatever you want in Moscow. Foreign goods are priced the same or more than they would be in their home countries; if the item seems like a steal, it's probably a bargain-basement counterfeit.

Local items you may want to purchase are caviar, vodka, traditional craftworks like lacquered artefacts and matryoshka dolls, brightly coloured woollen shawls and Russian fashion goods (the best stuff isn't an oxymoron).

Concerning antiques and anything else more than 25 years old, see the Customs section of the European Russia Facts for the Visitor chapter for details on export restrictions.

Shopping Streets

Novy Arbat is the Moscow equivalent of London's Oxford Street or an American suburban mall in that it's the place for mid-range shops. It's also equally unattractive. From Red Square to Belorussia Station, ulitsa Tverskaya is lined with shops but still has a spartan feel left over from Soviet times. The streets around Kuznetsky Most just east of the Bolshoi and those around GUM are home to the most upmarket shops.

Malls

On the eastern side of Red Square, GUM (Gosudarstvenny Univer Mag; Map 6; ☎ 921 3211) has made the transition to a market economy in fine form. It's buffed up and the 19th century building is a sight in itself. Although often called a 'department store', this is a misnomer as it is really a huge collection of individual shops spread over several floors. You can find just about anything here and wandering around can consume hours. Fortunately, you've got 12 almost every day to do your best from 8.30 am to 8.30 pm (11 am to 7 pm on Sunday).

The new zillion-dollar Okhotny Ryad shopping mall (Map 6; ☎ 737 8409) on Manezhnaya ploshchad is everything that GUM is not – tacky, over-blown and charmless. Filled with expensive boutiques (and an expensive food court) it was a bit like a zoo after the 1998 economic collapse since it was hard to tell just who was on display: the penniless Muscovites looking forlornly in through the shop windows or the morose clerks looking out from empty stores. It's open from 10 am to 10 pm daily; feeding time is up to you.

Stores

For a real department store, try TsUM (Map 2; ☎ 292 1157) which stocks everything from perfume to clothes to electronics to sporting goods. Located on ulitsa Petrovka 2, it's open from 9 am to 8 pm (until 6 pm Sunday).

Detsky Mir (Map 2; ☎ 238 0096) or 'Children's World' was the premier toy store during Soviet times when it sat under the watchful gaze of KGB headquarters across Lubyanskaya ploshchad. It now has a fun mix of imported and Russian-produced toys. It also has a good sporting goods department for things like in-line skates as well as housewares and domestic items that practical adults may consider toys. It's open from 9 am to 8 pm (closed Sunday).

For photographic equipment, slide film, camcorder tapes and other items to help you record your Russian visit, try Focus Photoshop (Map 6) which is conveniently located at ulitsa Tverskaya 4. It's open from 8 am to 8 pm daily and develops film as well.

La Casa de Cuba (☎ 737 8409), deep in the Okhotny Ryad shopping mall (see above), sells a wide range of Cuban cigars.

One of the most authentic places to buy Russian arts and crafts is Salon Moskovskogo Fonda Kultury (Map 4) or the 'Moscow Culture Foundation Salon' at ulitsa Pyatnitskaya 16. It's open from 10 am to 8 pm (closed Sunday). There are also many antiques, but watch those export rules.

Markets

The weekend 'Vernisazh' market at Izmaylovsky Park (Outer East Moscow Map; metro: Izmaylovsky Park) is a sprawling area packed with attractive art and handmade crafts. You'll not only find Moscow's biggest original range of matryoshkas, Palekh and Khokhloma ware, and dozens of artists selling their own work, but also lots of rugs from the Caucasus and Central Asia; some very attractive pottery, antique samovars, handmade clothes, jewellery, fur hats, chess sets, toys and much more. Quality is mostly high and many of the items are truly original. Prices can be reasonable, but you have to bargain for them. The market is two minutes' walk from Izmaylovksy Park metro; follow the crowds past the big hotel complex outside the station.

Many other artists set up their stalls on ulitsa Krymsky Val opposite the entrance to Gorky Park (Map 4), particularly on Saturday and Sunday. The art here is a mite less commercial than at Izmaylovksy Park, and there are only a few crafts.

GETTING THERE & AWAY

For an overview of international air and train routes to Moscow, see the European Russia Getting There & Away chapter.

Air

Moscow has five airports, each with a range of flights to a specific set of places as detailed in the following text.

To/From Russia Sheremetevo-2 airport, 30km north-west of the city centre, handles flights to/from places outside the former Soviet Union. It has had a bad reputation over the years that is not entirely valid these days. Compared to the chaos of New York's Kennedy airport, the relentless commercialism and discomfort of London's Heathrow or the terrible over-crowding at Tokyo's Narita, Sheremetevo-2 is a relaxed and easily managed place.

The range of bars and restaurants is at least on par with the usual mediocre airport offerings the world over and there are decent stores and acceptable waiting areas. Note that the best newsstand is after immigration on the arrivals level.

For flight information, call ☎ 578 9101.

Arrivals Arriving at Sheremetevo-2, the checks of your passport and visa by the immigration officials can actually be quite speedy since windows are opened to meet demand. Checked luggage can take longer, although reports of theft have declined.

Once in arrivals, there will be mobs of taxi touts but they are easily ignored. There are car rental offices, hotel and travel agency desks, exchange windows and most of the other services you'd expect at an international airport.

Departures The only problem with departing from Sheremetevo-2 are the customs checks you must endure before departure. The checks themselves are usually quick and almost perfunctory (but don't be the exception to the rule and have your documents and luggage contents out of order); however, the waits in disorganised queues can last an hour or more. For this reason you should plan to be at Sheremetevo-2 at least two hours before your flight departs. Note also that there never seem to be any of the customs forms in English that you have to fill out before inspection, so be sure to take two on your flight in.

Immigration, however, is much improved and waits are usually no more than 15 minutes. Security is handled quickly at the individual gates.

Tickets See the Travel Agencies section earlier in the chapter for travel agents who sell international flight tickets, or you can deal directly with the airlines themselves. International airline offices in Moscow include (see Within Russia later for Aeroflot and Transaero):

Air China
 (Map 2; ☎ 292 3387) ulitsa B. Dmitrovka 8/1
Air France
 (Map 4; ☎ 937 3831) ulitsa Mytnaya 1
Austrian Airlines
 (Map 4; ☎ 578 3363) in the Golden Ring Swiss Diamond Hotel at ulitsa Smolenskaya 5

British Airways
(Map 2; ☎ 258 2492) in the World Trade Centre at Krasnopresnenskaya naberezhnaya 12, 19th floor

Czech Airlines
(Map 2; ☎ 973 1847) ulitsa 2-ya Tverskaya Yamskaya 31/35

Delta Air Lines
(☎ 258 1168)

Finnair
(Map 2; ☎ 292 8788) Kuznetsky Most 3

Japan Airlines
(Map 2; ☎ 921 6448) Kuznetsky Most 3

KLM
(Map 4; ☎ 258 3600) ulitsa Usacheva 33/2

LOT Polish Airlines
(Map 4; ☎ 238 0003) ulitsa Korovy Val 7

Lufthansa
(Map 2; ☎ 737 6400) in the Renaissance Moscow Hotel at Olimpiysky prospekt 18

Malev Hungarian Airlines
(Map 2; ☎ 202 8416) ulitsa Povarskaya 21

Sabena/Swissair
(Map 2; ☎ 258 1888) in the World Trade Centre at Krasnopresnenskaya naberezhnaya 12, 20th floor

SAS
(Map 2; ☎ 925 4747) ulitsa Kuznetsky Most 3

Turkish Airlines
(Map 2; ☎ 292 4345) ulitsa B Dmitrovka 8/1

Within Russia Moscow has four airports handling flights in Russia and the CIS. Arrive at each at least 90 minutes before your flight in order to navigate the formalities of check-in and security. Although each airport handles a set range of services, there are exceptions, so confirm which airport your flight departs from. Services at the airports are very basic; buy that magazine before you leave your hotel.

The four airports and the destinations they serve are:

Bykovo (☎ 558 4738)
A miscellany of medium-range destinations including Petrozavodsk, Nalchik and Penza; about 30km south-east.

Domodedovo (☎ 155 0922)
Most flights to/from the east (including the Volga cities and Siberia) and the Central Asian states; the airport is about 40km south of the city centre.

Sheremetevo-1 (☎ 575 5791)
Most flights to/from St Petersburg, the Baltic States, Belarus and northern European Russia, some flights to Ukraine, Armenia and Georgia and all flights by Transaero Airlines. The airport is across the runways from Sheremetevo-2 so to journey between them you have to take a bus (see Getting Around later in this chapter).

Vnukovo (☎ 436 2813)
Most flights to/from the Russian Caucasus, Moldova and Kaliningrad plus some flights to/from Ukraine, Georgia and Armenia; about 30km south-west.

Tickets You can buy domestic airline tickets at most travel agents and Aeroflot offices all over town. Our favourite Aeroflot office – because it usually has few crowds – is on Korovy Val 7 (Map 4; ☎ 156 8019) near the Oktyabrskaya metro, open from 8 am to 7 pm daily. Transaero airlines also has several ticket offices, including a very convenient one in the corner of Hotel Moskva (Map 6; ☎ 241 7676, Okhotny ryad 2), which is open from 6 am to 9 pm daily.

Train

Moscow has rail links to most parts of Russia, most former Soviet states, numerous countries in Eastern and Western Europe, and China and Mongolia. See the European Russia Getting Around chapter for general information on train travel, fares, tickets, and deciphering timetables.

One important distinction to grasp when taking trains from Moscow is the difference between long-distance and 'suburban' trains. Long-distance trains run to places at least three or four hours out of Moscow, with limited stops and a range of accommodation classes. Suburban trains, known as *prigorodnye poezdy* or *elektrichky*, run to within just 100 or 200km of Moscow, stop almost everywhere, and have a single class of hard bench seats. You simply buy your ticket before the train leaves, and there's no limit on capacity – so you may have to stand for part of the way. Most Moscow stations have a separate ticket hall for suburban trains, usually called the Prigorodny Zal and often tucked away at the side or back of the station building. Suburban trains are also usually listed on separate timetables, and may go from a separate group of platforms.

Stations Moscow's nine main stations, all with accompanying metro stations, are:

Belorussia Station (Belorussky vokzal; Map 2; metro: Belorusskaya), Tverskaya Zastava ploshchad, has trains to/from Smolensk, Kaliningrad, Belarus, Lithuania, Poland, Germany; some trains to/from the Czech Republic; suburban trains to/from the west including Mozhaysk, Borodino, Zvenigorod

Kazan Station (Kazansky vokzal; Map 3; metro: Komsomolskaya), Komsomolskaya ploshchad, has trains to/from Cheboxary, Yoshkar-Ola, Kazan, Izhevsk, Ufa, Ryazan, Penza, Ulyanovsk, Samara, Novorossiysk, Central Asia; some trains to/from Vladimir, Nizhny Novgorod, the Ural Mountains, Siberia, Saratov, Rostov-on-Don; suburban trains to/from the south-east including Bykovo Airport, Kolomna, Gzhel, Ryazan

Kursk Station (Kursky vokzal; Map 3; metro: Kurskaya), ploshchad Kurskogo Vokzala, serves Oryol, Kursk, Krasnodar, Adler, the Caucasus, eastern Ukraine, Crimea, Georgia, Azerbaijan; some trains to/from Rostov-on-Don, Vladimir, Nizhny Novgorod, Perm; suburban trains to/from the east and south including Petushki, Vladimir, Podolsk, Chekhov, Serpukhov, Tula

Kiev Station (Kievsky vokzal; Map 4; metro: Kievskaya), ploshchad Kievskogo vokzala, serves Bryansk, Kyiv (Kiev in Russian), western Ukraine, Moldova, Slovakia, Hungary, Austria, Romania, Bulgaria, Croatia, Serbia, Greece, Venice; some trains to/from the Czech Republic; suburban trains to/from the south-west including Peredelkino, Kaluga

Leningrad Station (Leningradsky vokzal; Map 3; metro: Komsomolskaya), Komsomolskaya ploshchad, has trains to/from Tver, Novgorod, Pskov, St Petersburg, Vyborg, Murmansk, Estonia, Helsinki; suburban trains to/from the north-west including Klin, Tver

Pavelets Station (Paveletsky vokzal; Map 5; metro: Paveletskaya), Paveletskaya ploshchad has trains to/from Yelets, Lipetsk, Voronezh, Tambov, Volgograd, Astrakhan; some trains to/from Saratov; suburban trains to/from the south-east including Leninskaya

Riga Station (Rizhsky vokzal; Outer North Moscow Map; metro: Rizhskaya), Rizhskaya ploshchad, serves Latvia; suburban trains to/from the north-west including Istra, Novoierusalimskaya

Savyolov Station (Savyolovsky vokzal; Outer North Moscow Map; metro: Savyolovskaya), ploshchad Savyolovskogo vokzala, has trains to/from Cherepovets; some trains to/from Kostroma, Vologda; suburban trains to/from the north

Yaroslavl Station (Yaroslavsky vokzal; Map 3; metro: Komsomolskaya), Komsomolskaya ploshchad, serves Yaroslavl, Arkhangelsk, Vorkuta, Russian Far East, Mongolia, China, North Korea; some trains to/from Vladimir, Nizhny Novgorod, Kostroma, Vologda, Perm, Urals, Siberia; suburban trains to/from the north-east including Abramtsevo, Khotkovo, Sergiev Posad, Alexandrov

Tickets For long-distance trains it's best to get your ticket as far in advance as you can. Tickets on some trains may be available on the day of departure, but this is less likely in summer. Take your passport along even if you're trying to get a Russian-price ticket, as you may need to show some identification.

Russian-Price Tickets Getting Russian-price tickets (except for suburban trains, which do not have foreigner fares) is harder in Moscow than in most Russian cities. Station ticket clerks may send you away to one of the special foreigner ticket offices where you can't avoid paying a foreigner price – or you may be lucky and get a ticket with no questions asked.

Another consideration is that on some of the trains from Moscow most used by foreigners – particularly trains to St Petersburg and the main trans-Siberian trains – there's a risk of conductors or *provodniks* demanding 'fines' from foreigners travelling on Russian-price tickets.

If you are trying for a Russian-price ticket, you have to be prepared to queue, and you also have to try to make sure you're queuing for the right ticket window. Some stations have one set of ticket windows for departures within 24 hours, and another set for advance tickets (usually available up to 30, or even 45, days before travel). Advance ticket windows are usually labelled Predvaritelnaya Kassa or something similar.

Foreigner Ticket Offices If you have been turned away from station ticket windows, or have simply decided on the more straightforward option of paying a foreigner fare, you can get the straight foreigner fare at a Central Railway Agency (Tsentralnoe Zheleznodorozhnoe Agentstvo) ticket office.

A good one is at Maly Kharitonevsky pereulok 6 (Map 3; ☎ 262 2566). Window Nos 1 to 3 in room (*zal*) No 1 of building (*korpus*) No 1 sell tickets for CIS destinations from 10 days ahead to the day of departure; window Nos 7 and 8 in the ground floor hall of building No 2 sell tickets to other countries from 30 days ahead to the day of departure. It's open from 8 am to 1 pm and 2 to 7 pm daily.

Alternatively, you can deal with a travel agent where the process will be much simpler and the price slightly higher.

Bus

Buses run to a number of towns and cities within about 700km of Moscow. There are no foreigner prices and to most destinations the fares are similar to the Russian fares for *kupeynyy* class on trains. Buses are not very comfortable and to most places they're slower and less frequent than trains.

To book a seat you have to go out to the long-distance bus terminal, the Shchyolkovsky Avtovokzal (Щёлковский автовокзал), beside Shchyolkovskaya metro station in the east of the city, where queues can be bad – and it is generally advisable to book ahead, especially for travel on Friday, Saturday or Sunday.

Places to which it's most worth considering a bus are those with poor train services such as Pereslavl-Zalessky (which is not on a railway) and Vladimir (which has few afternoon trains from Moscow).

Car & Motorcycle

See the Car & Motorcycle section in the European Russia Getting Around chapter for general advice on driving.

Ten major highways, numbered M1 to M10 (but not in any logical order), fan out from Moscow to all points of the compass. Most are in fairly good condition at first but some get pretty bad farther out. The main road from Western Europe, the M1 from Poland via Brest, Minsk and Smolensk, is straight and dull but fairly quick. The M10 to St Petersburg is dual carriageway much of the way to Tver, 145km out, but there are narrow stretches beyond. The first 110km of the M2 to Oryol and Ukraine are excellent dual carriageway – something you'll remember like a dream as you hit some of the bumpy, narrow roads farther south. The M7 east to Vladimir and the M8 north-east to Yaroslavl are in reasonable condition but are busy and slow.

Moscow has no shortage of gas stations that sell all grades of petrol. Most are open 24 hours, are affiliated with Western oil companies and can be found on the major roads in and out of town. There are parts, service and repair specialists for many Western makes of car in Moscow. See the *Moscow Business Telephone Guide* for listings.

Car Rental There's little reason for the average traveller to rent a car for getting about Moscow as public transport is quite adequate, but you might want to consider it for trips out of the city.

There are lots of car rental firms in Moscow, and most tourist hotels have a rental desk of some kind, but the scene has two special features: many firms won't let you take their cars out of the city, and others will only rent a car with a driver. Companies' policies change frequently, so the only answer is to ring round some of those in the following list to try to find what you want. Cars with drivers don't always prove to be more expensive, and they save you the trouble of coping with Russian roads.

The major international rental firms have outlets in Moscow. Generally it is best to reserve your car before you arrive as advance reservations and special offers can reduce the price by 50% or more. For instance, Hertz offered us a Ford for $95 a day at the airport counter, but prebooking the same car from abroad and quoting a frequent flier number got a rate of $40 a day.

The following companies have desks at Sheremetevo-2 airport and will usually pick up or drop off the car at your hotel:

Avis
 ☎ 915 1389
Budget
 ☎ 737 0407
Hertz
 ☎ 937 3274

Boat

In summer, passenger boats from Moscow ply the rivers and canals of Russia all the way north to St Petersburg, and south to Astrakhan on the Volga Delta near the Caspian Sea.

The St Petersburg route follows the Moscow Canal and then the Volga River to the Rybinsk Reservoir, then the Volga-Baltic Canal to Lake Onega, the Svir River to Lake Ladoga and the Neva River to St Petersburg.

The main southbound route takes the Moscow Canal north to the Volga. It then follows the Volga east before heading south all the way downstream to Astrakhan (which is nine days from Moscow), via Uglich, Yaroslavl, Kostroma, Nizhny Novgorod, Kazan, Ulyanovsk, Samara, Saratov and Volgograd.

The Moscow terminus for these sailings is the Northern River Station (Severny Rechnoy Vokzal; Outer North Moscow Map; ☎ 459 7476) at Leningradskoe shosse 51. To get there, take the metro to Rechnoy Vokzal, then walk 15 minutes due west, passing under Leningradskoe shosse and through a nice park.

The navigation season depends on the route. Sailings between Moscow and Astrakhan via Yaroslavl, Nizhny Novgorod, and Kazan leave a few times a week from early June to mid-October. These ships are operated by the Capital Shipping Company (☎/fax 277 3902). See the boxed text 'Volga River Boats' in the Volga Region chapter for more information about the ships and their schedules.

Tickets are sold at the Northern River Station. If you are having any trouble at all obtaining reliable schedule information it can be worthwhile visiting the office in person.

Capital Shipping as well as other boat and tour companies operate ships between Moscow and St Petersburg that stop at some of the Golden Ring cities. See the Boat section of the European Russia Getting Around chapter and the Organised Tours section of European Russia Getting There & Away for details.

GETTING AROUND

The central area around the Kremlin, the Kitay-Gorod and the Bolshoi Theatre are best seen on foot. To almost anywhere else, the fastest, cheapest and easiest way to get around is on the metro and on foot, though buses, trolleybuses and trams come in useful sometimes.

To/From the Airports

You can get between all five airports and the city centre cheaply by a combination of bus and metro or suburban train, but if you're in a hurry, going early in the morning or late at night, or have a lot of baggage, you'll probably need a taxi.

The easiest and surest way to get from any airport into the city is to book your transfer in advance through a travel agent. This means you'll be driven straight from the airport to your destination in the city. You may not have to pay any more than a normal taxi fare. Intourist, for instance, charges $30 for transfers to/from Sheremetevo-2. Some travel firms have airport desks where you can book transfers on the spot.

The City Air Terminal (Gorodskoy aerovokzal; Outer North Moscow Map) at Leningradsky prospekt 37 has bus services to/from all the airports. However, the terminal itself is hard to reach as it is almost 1km from Dinamo, the nearest metro. Also, the services from the terminal are infrequent and confusing.

Leaving Moscow, your hotel or accommodation will always be able to arrange a taxi for you, but you can get one cheaper yourself. See the later Taxi section for how to order one. Don't rely on flagging one down on the street as it may take a long time to find a driver who is prepared to go out that far.

You can avoid the hassle of a taxi by using the metro or suburban trains in conjunction with minivan services for all five airports. Not only do you save a huge amount of money, but during times of heavy traffic, you save a lot of time as well. The only disadvantage is that the minivans only leave when full, and don't have much room for luggage.

MOSCOW

Sheremetevo At Sheremetevo-2, the minibuses leave from a special area 200m in front of the terminal. To reach it, walk straight out of the arrivals area and to the right around a car park, staying on the inside of the auto ramp. The bus stop has a small shelter and lies between the auto ramps leading to and from the upper departures level.

Minibuses make the journey as soon as they are full, which is about every 30 minutes or less; the cost is $0.30. They begin and end their journeys at Rechnoy Vokzal and Sheremetevo-1 with Sheremetevo-2 the middle stop in either direction, so make certain you get a minibus going in the right direction from Sheremetevo-2.

At Rechnoy Vokzal, leave the metro platform by the exit at the front end of your train. Walk 100m straight ahead out of the metro station to the road where the minivans are waiting. They run from about 7 am to 9 pm. The combined metro/minivan trip to or from the Sheremetevo-2 takes about one hour; Sheremetevo-1 takes 70 minutes.

Large blue Aeroflot buses follow the same route and charge about the same amount but run less often. City bus No 551 also follows this route, but it makes many stops and takes much longer.

A taxi arranged on the spot between Sheremetevo airport and the city centre takes about 45 minutes and should cost $30 to $45, though absurd prices may be asked of tourists. A better bet is to arrange one in advance from Logus 98 (☎ 138 5433), which charges about $8 for a pre-booked car to/from the Sheremetevo airports. The operators speak good English.

Domodedovo The airport is linked to Domodedovskaya metro by minibuses from about 7 am to 9 pm. The trip takes 30 to 40 minutes and the fare is $0.40. Going out to the airport, you should allow 90 minutes for the combined metro/minibus trip.

A taxi to/from the city centre should cost $25 to $35. The trip takes one to 1½ hours, depending on traffic.

Vnukovo Minibuses link the airport with Yugo-Zapadnaya metro from about 7 am to 9 pm. The trip takes 30 minutes and costs $0.40.

A taxi to/from the city centre is about $25 and can take over an hour.

Bykovo Suburban *(prigorodnye)* trains run between Bykovo train station, 400m from the airport, and Kazan Station in the city. One of their stops en route is Vykhino, by Vykhino metro. Going out to the airport, most trains heading for Vinogradovo, Shifernaya or Golutvin stop at Bykovo (as well as those marked 'Bykovo') but just a few go straight through, so always check. The trains, which take about one hour, go about every 20 minutes from 5 am to 10 pm.

A taxi to/from the city centre is about $25 to $30 and can take 1½ hours.

Metro

The metro is the easiest, quickest and cheapest way of getting around Moscow. With elegant, graffiti-free stations – many of them marble-faced, frescoed, gilded works of art – this is one Stalinist project Muscovites are proud of, and nine million of them use it every day. The stations were meant to double as air-raid shelters, which is why the escalators seem to plunge halfway to the centre of the earth.

The 150-plus stations are marked outside with big 'M' signs. Magnetic tickets are sold at ticket booths for one or five rides. Each ride costs about $0.20. Insert your ticket into the gate and when the green light illuminates, take your ticket and walk on. If you go too soon, bars will pop across your path.

Stations have maps of the system, and signs on each platform show the stations each train goes to. Interchange stations are linked by underground passages, indicated by *'perekhod'* (crossover) signs which are usually blue with a stick figure running up the stairs. Once you've figured out which train you need you'll rarely wait more than two minutes for it. With elementary Cyrillic and by counting stops, you can manage very well. If you get lost, the kindly women who supervise the escalators can point you in the right direction.

Underground Art

The Moscow metro is justly famous for the art and design of many of its stations. The best are tourist attractions in their own right. Some of our favourites are:

Kievskaya circle line station, with vivid mosaics of Ukrainian history and delightful images of a happy and well-fed proletariat.

Komsomolskaya circle line station, with mosaics of past Russian military heroes. This is the one with the chandeliers that you often see pictures of. The Komsomolskaya station on the orange line has panels depicting heroic metro workers.

Mayakovskaya, grand prize winner at the 1938 World's Fair in New York, has a central hall that's all stainless steel and marble. It could be the station serving the Chrysler Building in New York.

Novokuznetskaya, with military bas-reliefs and industrial ceiling mosaics. The elegant marble benches came from the original Church of Christ the Saviour.

Ploshchad Revolyutsii, where life-sized bronze statues in the main hall and beside the escalators illustrate the idealised roles of common men and women. Heading up the escalators the themes are from the bottom: force to carry out and protect the revolution, industry, agriculture, hunting, education, sport and child-rearing.

A few other metro facts are: the first station opened in 1935; early work was driven on by project manager Nikita Khrushchev (and we mean driven – thousands toiled around the clock in conditions that wouldn't have passed muster with modern day health & safety inspectors); up to nine million people a day ride the system, more than London and New York City combined; and the first stations are so deep because they really were designed to double as bomb shelters (you'll notice that newer stations aren't as deep after it was realised that you just couldn't dig deep enough to escape a hail of American nuclear missiles).

The carriages now have maps inside that show the stops for that line in both Roman and Cyrillic letters. The biggest confusion you may find is that often when two or more lines meet, each line's interchange station has a different name.

Bus, Trolleybus & Tram

Buses, trolleybuses and trams run almost everywhere the metro doesn't go. They can be useful along a few radial or cross-town routes that the metro misses, and are necessary for reaching sights away from the city centre.

To ride a bus, trolleybus or tram you need a ticket to stick in one of the ticket-punchers inside the vehicle. *Talony*, which cost about $0.20 each, can be bought from drivers, from street kiosks that display them, and sometimes in metro stations. The same talony are used for all three types of vehicle. Ticket inspections are rare indeed, and people often ride buses without a ticket, for which they can theoretically be fined $5.

Taxi

The simple way to get a taxi is to stand on the street and stick your arm out. Before too long a car will stop and, if the driver fancies going to your destination, you're on your way. Many private car drivers cruise around as unofficial taxis (gypsy cabs), and other drivers will often take you if they're going in roughly the same direction.

For a five minute ride, $1 is plenty; for 10 or 15 minutes, pay around $1.50 to $2.50. You can get across town for $4 or so. Generally it's better to fix the fare before you get in – but for short rides it's usually OK just to proffer an appropriate amount when you get out. Official taxis, which carry a little chequerboard logo on the side and/or a small green light in the windscreen, charge about the same. No driver uses a meter, even if the cab has one, and few drivers ever admit to having any change. You'll have to pay more if you catch a taxi right in front of a hotel.

Don't hesitate to wave on a car whose occupant(s) you don't like the look of, or are obviously drunk – and it's better not to get in if you'd be outnumbered. Problems may be more likely to crop up if you take a street cab waiting outside a nightclub or perhaps a tourist hotel or restaurant at night.

To book a taxi in advance, call the Central Taxi Reservation Office (Tsentralnoe Byuro Zakazov Taxi; ☎ 927 0000) 24 hours daily. You should give them at least one and preferably two or more hours notice. You can book one the day before for an early start to an airport. Usually the dispatcher on the phone will speak a bit of English, though it may help if you can speak some Russian too. They'll want to ring you back a few minutes before pick up, to confirm that you still want the booking and give you the car's registration number. You should be charged about $2 for the booking, then around $0.25 per kilometre.

Around Moscow
Подмосковье

This chapter covers places within about 300km of Moscow. A few are not far beyond the city's suburbs and most can be visited on day trips from the capital, but some of the more distant places are easier with an overnight (or longer) stop. The 'Golden Ring' of historic towns and villages north-east of Moscow – some of them set on the Volga River, others amid timeless country-side – is well worth a few days of your time.

This region is in many ways the heartland of Russia, with a subtly changing landscape crossed by many winding rivers – the typical provincial scene so dear to Russian hearts and immortalised by so many artists and writers. The towns and villages are an equally typical mixture of the old and picturesque and the modern and drab.

As soon as you leave Moscow, the contrasts between the capital and the slower, more old-fashioned, less colourful and often poorer provincial world make themselves felt. Even one trip out of the big city will not only take you to some fascinating and beautiful corners of Russia, but also open your eyes to the life that the great majority of Russians lead.

HIGHLIGHTS

- Taking in the superb view over Lake Seliger from the belfry at Nilova Pustyn Monastery
- Walking along the banks of the Kamenka River in Suzdal
- Admiring the architectural perfection of the Assumption and St Dmitry cathedrals in Vladimir
- Contemplating the gorgeous 16th century frescoes of the Rostov Kremlin
- Listening to the music from the bells of the Purification Church in Yaroslavl

GETTING THERE & AWAY

Train & Bus

Many places in this chapter can be reached by suburban trains from Moscow. These are some of the easiest, if not the quickest, forms of Russian transport to use: find the suburban ticket hall (пригородный зал, prigorodnyy zal) at the appropriate Moscow station, check the timetable for a train going where you want, buy your ticket (there are no foreigner prices) and you're off. All carriages are one class and no advance bookings or compartment reservations are needed.

For some destinations, you will need to take a bus or long-distance train. For these, booking ahead is advisable, although not always necessary.

Car & Taxi

A good way to go, if you don't mind coping with Russian roads, is to drive. Either rent a car or hire a taxi and driver for a day or even longer: you'll have to negotiate a price, but for two or three people it may work out economically. See also Getting There and Away in the Moscow chapter.

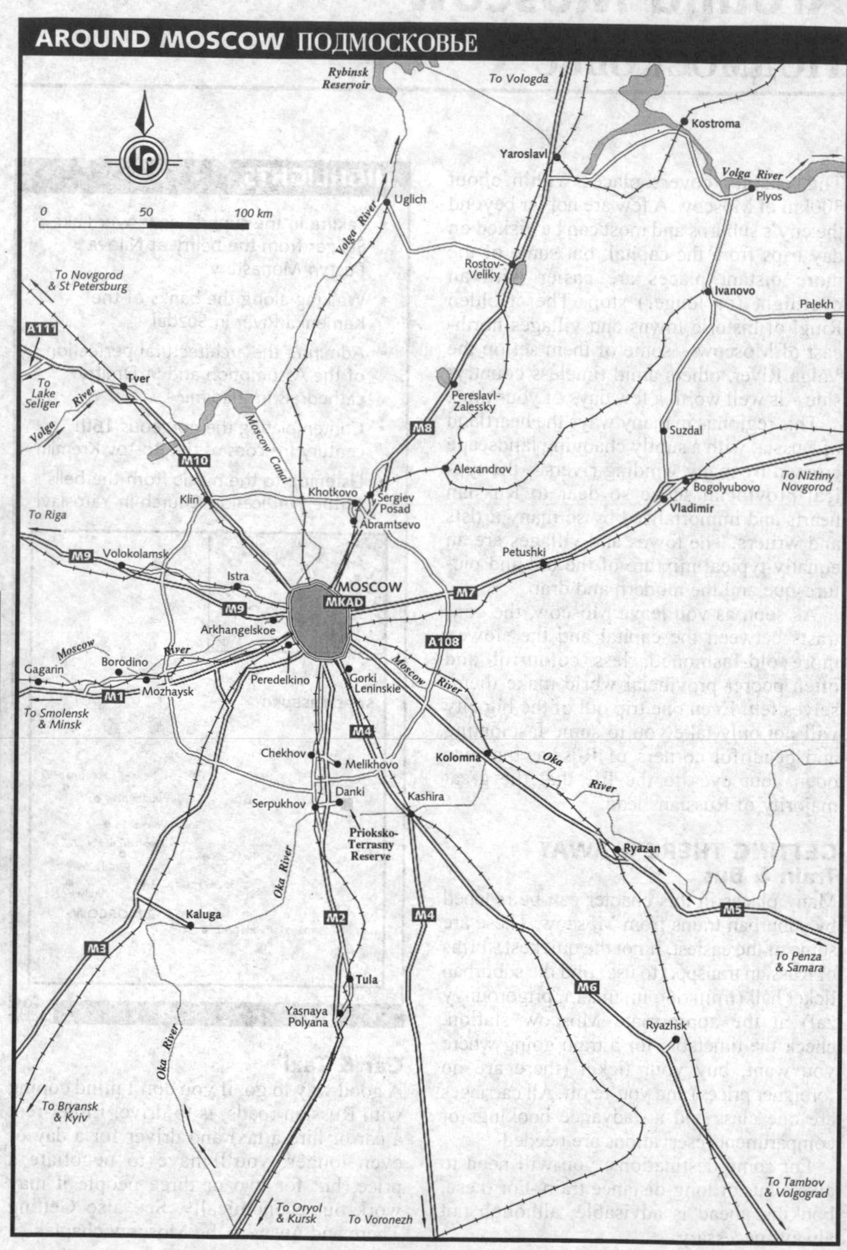

AROUND MOSCOW

Boat

Long-distance passenger services occasionally run along the Volga River and connect Moscow with Uglich, Yaroslavl, Kostroma, Plyos and cities all the way down to Astrakhan near the Caspian Sea. Cruises booked in Moscow or abroad will also take you to these places. For details, see the Getting There & Away section in the preceding Moscow chapter.

Tours

Guided tours are available from Moscow to many of the places in this chapter, and can be an interesting, informative way to go, especially if your time is limited. See the Organised Tours and Travel Agencies sections of the Moscow chapter.

North-West
Северо-запад

KLIN
КЛИН

Tchaikovsky lived in Klin, 90km north-west of central Moscow, from 1885 until 1893, the year of his death in St Petersburg. Here he wrote his *Pathetique* symphony (the Sixth), and *Nutcracker* and *Sleeping Beauty* ballets. His last residence, at ulitsa Chaykovskogo 48, has been a **museum** (now the Dom-Muzey Chaykovskogo) since his brother, Modest, bought it after his death. It's still much as it was when Tchaikovsky lived there – full of personal effects, including his Becker grand piano, now played only by top pianists on special occasions. The museum is open from 10 am to 6 pm daily except Wednesday and Thursday; admission is $3/1.80.

Getting There & Away

Klin is on the road and railway from Moscow to Tver, Novgorod and St Petersburg, and it's possible to combine it with Tver in one lengthy day trip from Moscow. Suburban trains from Moscow's Leningrad Station run to Klin two or three times an hour from 5 am, a trip of about 1½ hours.

Pyotr Ilyich Tchaikovsky

Services between Klin and Tver – a trip of just over one hour – are frequent.

TVER
ТВЕРЬ

☎ 08222 • pop 450,000

Tver, on the Volga 150km north-west of Moscow, was the capital of an unruly mini-state that was Moscow's chief rival in the 14th and 15th centuries. But its subsequent history reads like the Book of Job – punished for rising against the Mongol Tatars, conquered by Ivan III, savaged by Ivan the Terrible, seized by the Poles and completely destroyed by fire in 1763. Reborn in the 18th century after Catherine the Great made it one of her rest stops between St Petersburg and Moscow, it now looks like a little rustic St Petersburg in places.

Though Tver's baroque/classical architecture doesn't put it in the same league as some of the old Russian towns of the Golden Ring, it has just about enough attractions to make it an interesting day trip

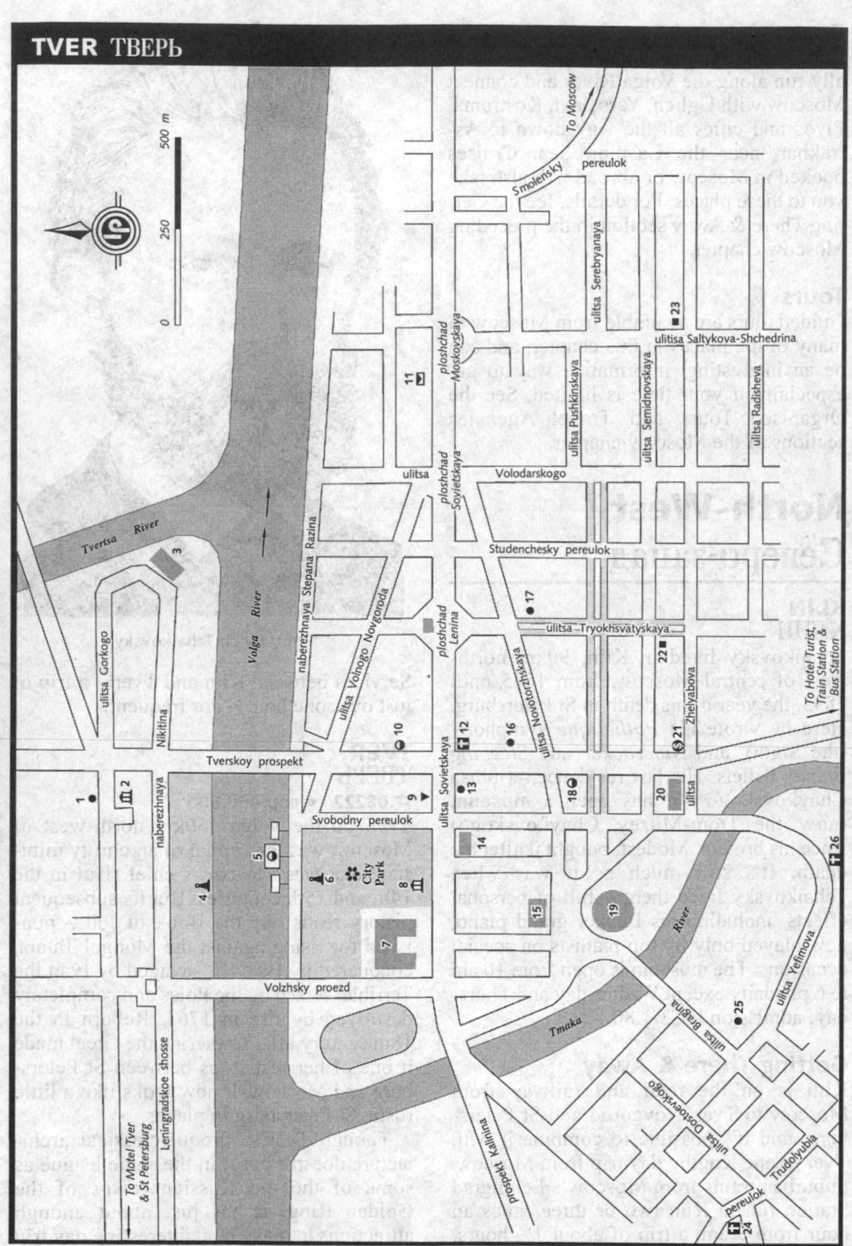
TVER ТВЕРЬ
0
250
500 m
To Moscow
Smolensky pereulok
ulitsa Serebryanaya
ulitsa Saltykova-Shchedrina
ploshchad Moskovskaya
ulitsa Pushkinskaya
ulitsa Semidnovskaya
ulitsa Radisheva
ulitsa Volodarskogo
ploshchad Sovietskaya
Tvertsa River
Studenchesky pereulok
naberezhnaya Stepana Razina
Volga River
ulitsa Volnogo Novgoroda
ploshchad Lenina
ulitsa Tryokhsvyatyskaya
ulitsa Novotorzhskaya
Zhelyabova
To Hotel Turist, Train Station & Bus Station
ulitsa Gorkogo
Nikitina
Tverskoy prospekt
ulitsa Sovietskaya
naberezhnaya
Svobodny pereulok
City Park
Volzhsky proezd
Leningradskoe shosse
To Motel Tver & St Petersburg
Tmaka River
ulitsa Bragina
ulitsa Yefimova
ulitsa Dostoevskogo
prospekt Kalinina
pereulok Trudolyubia
1
2
3
4
5
6
7
8
9
10
11
12
13
14
15
16
17
18
19
20
21
22
23
24
25
26

TVER ТВЕРЬ

PLACES TO STAY & EAT
9 Vina Stavropolya
Вина Ставрополья
15 Hotel Tsentralnaya
Гостиница Центральная
20 Hotel Volga
Гостиница Волга
22 Hotel Zarya
Гостиница Заря
23 Hotel Osnabruck
Гостиница Оснабрюк

OTHER
1 Craft Shop
2 Museum of Tver Life
Музей тверского быта
3 River Station
Речной вокзал
4 Afanasy Nikitin Statue
Памятник Афанасию Никитину
5 Excursion-Boat Landings
Пристань для речных экскурсий
6 Pushkin Statue
Памятник Пушкину
7 'Road Palace' Art Gallery
Путевой дворец
8 Regional Museum of Local Studies
Краеведческий музей
10 Tram Stop
Трамвайная остановка
11 Post and Telephone Office
Почтамт и переговорный пункт
12 Church of the Ascension
Церковь Вознесения
13 Podarki
Магазин Подарки
14 Drama Theatre
Театр драмы
16 Detsky Mir
Супермаркет Детский Мир
17 Knigi Bookshop
Магазин Книги
18 Tram Stop
Остановка трамваев
19 Circus
Цирк
21 Bank Tver
Банк Тверь
24 Church of the White Trinity
Церковь Белой Троицы
25 Market
Рынок
26 Intercession Church
Церковь Покрова Богородицы

from Moscow. You might also want to stop here for the same reason as Catherine: it's on the Moscow-St Petersburg road (and modern railway). In winter the surrounding forests are apparently good for cross-country skiing.

In 1990 Tver dumped its Soviet name, Kalinin (after Mikhail Kalinin, Stalin's puppet president during WWII, who was born here).

Orientation

The Volga runs roughly west-east through Tver, with the town centre on the southern side. Ulitsa Sovietskaya is the main east-west street. It's crossed in the central area by Tverskoy prospekt, which becomes prospekt Chaykovskogo farther south. The train station is 4km south of the centre, at the point where prospekt Chaykovskogo turns 90° east and becomes ulitsa Kominterna. The bus station is 300m east of the train station along ulitsa Kominterna.

Information

There are several currency exchange kiosks around the town centre. You can also change money, get cash advances from major credit cards and cash travellers cheques at the Bank Tver on the corner of Tverskoy prospekt and ulitsa Zhelyabova, open from 9.30 am to 4 pm daily.

The main post and telephone office at ulitsa Sovietskaya 31 is open from 8 am to 8 pm Monday to Saturday. International phone calls can be made here 24 hours daily.

A good source of maps is the Knigi bookshop (☎ 33 20 70), ulitsa Tryokhsvyatskaya 28. It's open from 10 am to 7 pm weekdays, till 5 pm on weekends.

Things to See

South of the River Classical late 1700s/early 1800s town houses and public buildings line ulitsa Sovietskaya and the riverfront naberezhnaya Stepana Razina. On the corner of ulitsa Sovietskaya and Tverskoy prospekt, the classical **Church of the Ascension** (Tserkov Voznesenia) is being restored.

At the western end of ulitsa Sovietskaya, fronted by a statue of Mikhail Kalinin, stands the town's most imposing building – Catherine the Great's 1775 'Road Palace' (Putevoy Dvorets) at ulitsa Sovietskaya 3. It houses Tver's **Art Gallery** (Tverskaya kartinnaya galereya), with Russian and Western European works. It's worth a look as it also features interiors, furniture and other items of the 18th century. Entry costs $0.30. The **Regional Museum of Local Studies** (Tverskoy kraevedchesky muzey) is at ulitsa Sovietskaya 5, and tickets cost $0.25. Both museums are open from 11 am to 6 pm Wednesday to Sunday.

The **City Park** on the river bank behind the palace has a foppish **statue** of Pushkin and, if you're lucky, live music on summer weekends. In summer, Volga excursion boats sail every hour from the piers in front of the park for an hour-long trip up or down the river ($0.70). You can chose the direction by being the first either on board or to care.

In April 1940, in Tver's NKVD headquarters somewhere on ulitsa Sovietskaya, over 6000 Polish POWs were shot one by one in a soundproof room at night. They were buried in trenches near Mednoe, 20km west of Tver. Over 8000 other Polish prisoners were massacred near Smolensk and Kharkiv, in Ukraine.

Part of ulitsa Tryokhsvyatskaya between ulitsa Zhelyabova and bulvar Radisheva is a lively pedestrian street with several cafes and shops. The sprawling **Central Market** (Tsentralny rynok) is south of the small Tmaka River. Just before the market, on ulitsa Yefimova, the old **Intercession Church** (Khram Pokroka Bogoroditsy) is being restored and is open from 7.30 am to 7 pm.

The quaintest part of town is the streets of old wooden houses with carved eaves and window frames, west of the market across ulitsa Bragina. Here, on pereulok Trudolyubia, is Tver's oldest building, the stately **Church of the White Trinity** (Tserkov Beloy Troitsy, 1564); there are daily services.

North of the River You can cross the Volga at the north end of Tverskoy prospekt or on Volzhsky proezd, which runs up beside the Road Palace. A promenade stretches along the north bank, giving a good view of the old houses on the south bank. The **statue** in the park here is of Afanasy Nikitin, a local merchant who went overland to India 30 years before Vasco da Gama sailed there, and wrote a bestseller about his trip.

The **Museum of Tver Life** (Muzey Tverskogo Byta), in a short street off ulitsa Gorkogo at ulitsa Nakhimova 3/21, is housed in an 18th century merchant's manor house. It's worth a visit for its arts, crafts, furniture and other domestic artefacts ranging over several centuries; it's open 11 am to 5 pm Wednesday to Sunday. Admission is $0.30.

Places to Stay

Hotel Tsentralnaya *(☎ 33 81 57, ulitsa Novotorzhskaya 33/8)*, opposite the circus, has plain but adequate singles/doubles for $5/7 and slightly improved rooms for $10/14. It has a bar and a restaurant next door where an average meal costs around $10, although you can't avoid the bad and loud live music. ***Hotel Volga*** *(☎ 33 81 00, fax 37 95 57, ulitsa Zhelyabova 1)*, facing the Tmaka River, has dreary doubles for $8 and a Soviet-style restaurant that offers meals for $6 to $7. Both hotels are out of the same Soviet concrete mould.

Better is ***Hotel Zarya*** *(☎ 33 21 29, ulitsa Semionovskaya 30/27)*. Its 19th century building has recently been renovated, with nice rooms for $35/60, breakfast included. The new ***Hotel Osnabruck*** *(☎ 48 84 33, fax 48 84 12, ulitsa Saltykova-Shchedrina 20)* is a three-star hotel with Western standards. Rooms are $60/80, breakfast included. This is the only hotel that accepts Visa cards.

Places to Eat

Apart from the ***hotel restaurants*** mentioned previously, the city has a lot of cafes in the centre, each having a standard selection of salads, sandwiches and drinks for under $1. The best place to eat is the air-conditioned ***Vina Stavropolya*** *(Stavropol Wines; ☎ 33 37 48, ulitsa Sovietskaya 7)*, which has a wide choice of Russian food for about $4. There is a good selection of wines from the Stavropol region in the south of Russia costing from $2 to $20.

The Detsky Mir ***supermarket***, on Tverskoy prospekt. Its opening hours are from 9 am to 9 pm daily.

Entertainment

There's a ***circus*** opposite Hotel Tsentralnaya and a ***drama theatre*** *(ulitsa Sovietskaya 16)*.

Shopping

The little crafts/souvenir shop facing the Museum of Tver Life is worth a quick look. You might find something worthwhile in the Podarki (gifts) shop on ulitsa Sovietskaya, just west of Tverskoy prospekt.

Getting There & Away

Suburban trains take 2½ to three hours to reach Tver (often still called Kalinin on timetables) from Moscow's Leningrad Station. Departures are approximately hourly. Most trains between Moscow and St Petersburg also stop at Tver.

You can also get to Tver on the bus leaving from the entrance to the Yaroslavl Station in Moscow. The buses leave every 30 minutes from 6 am to 4 pm ($1.20, three hours). The last bus leaves Tver for Moscow at 7 pm. There's a daily bus from Tver to Novgorod at 11.45 am ($5, 8½ hours).

In summer, ferries and hydrofoils sail to regional destinations from the river station at the confluence of the Volga and Tvertsa rivers. The only boats to Moscow are occasional cruise vessels. Check at the river station – if something is running you can try to buy a ticket there.

Getting Around

Tram Nos 2, 5, 6 and 11 run from the bus and train stations up prospekt Chaykovskogo and Tverskoy prospekt to the town centre, a 10 minute ride. Tram Nos 5, 6 and 11 continue over the Volga from the northern end of Tverskoy prospekt; No 2 turns west along ulitsa Sovietskaya. Tram tickets cost $0.10.

LAKE SELIGER
ОЗЕРО СЕЛИГЕР

Among pine forests 190km west of Tver, near the headwaters of the Volga, is large, island-dotted Lake Seliger, an area that has always been a cult vacation place for Russian intellectuals. It offers some of the country's best canoeing, hiking, camping and hunting.

Ostashkov
Осташков

☎ 08235 • pop 31,000

On the southern shore of the lake there is the pretty, old-fashioned town of Ostashkov, which hasn't changed much since the 1700s. From here you can take boat trips up the lake to Khachin Island, the largest of the islands.

Orientation & Information Leninsky prospekt is where the old part of Ostashkov begins.

Sberbank (☎ 2 07 02), Leninsky prospekt 119A, exchanges money and is open from 9 am to 5 pm weekdays. The post office is at pereulok Yuzhny 7A; the telephone office next door is open 24 hours. Maps are sold at Knigi bookshop at Leninsky prospekt 45. The MP Seliger travel agency (☎ 2 43 70), Leninsky prospekt 47, offers sightseeing trips in Russian.

Across the road from the bookshop, the Obretenie art gallery sells souvenirs, wood carvings and paintings by local artists.

Things to See & Do Troitsky Cathedral at the northern end of Leninsky prospekt houses the **Local Studies Museum** (Krayevedchesky muzey; open from 10 am to 5 pm daily, $0.25). You can climb the belfry for another $0.25. There are numerous other old churches along Leninsky prospekt.

Boats run all the way up the lake on even days in May and daily from June to September. Tickets range from $0.40 to $2 depending on the destination. There are one-hour tourist trips on weekends only.

About 30km north on Stolbnoy Island is the **Nilova Pustyn Monastery** (Monastyr Nilova Pustyn), built at the end of the 16th century and turned into a Stalinist labour camp before it was returned to the Church in 1995. The Polish prisoners killed at Tver in 1940 were held on Stolbnoy before they were murdered.

The magnificent **Annunciation Cathedral** (Blagoveshchensky sobor) was built in 1800s. The belfry offers a breathtaking view of the lake and the islands. Because it's an operating monastery, some restrictions apply: you are not allowed to photograph the monks or any other people on the monastery grounds. Entry to the grounds is free, but you have to receive permission from the monastery authorities to get access to the belfry.

Places to Stay and Eat The usual, rundown Soviet-style ***Hotel Seliger*** *(☎ 2 19 96)* on prospekt Kalinina has singles/

doubles for $4/6, but the hot water supply is unpredictable. However, there are several *turbazy* (rustic tourist cabins) around the lake where you can enjoy the great outdoors and lovely views. MP Seliger (see Orientation & Information earlier) can book these from about $12 per person a night, with all meals included. For extra money things get rather swank with extras such as your own toilet.

The town doesn't have much to offer in terms of restaurants. The best place is the cosy ***Neptun*** bar *(Leninsky prospekt 25)*, open from 10 am to midnight; decent meals are served for around $2 per person. You can also try the ***Khottabych*** bar at ulitsa Rabochaya (open until 10 pm daily), if you are not put off by paper plates and a quite gloomy interior. The local speciality is smoked eel, which you can also buy at the ***market*** behind Hotel Seliger.

Getting There & Away Buses run from Tver to Ostashkov (4½ hours, five daily). There is an overnight train to Ostashkov from Moscow's Leningrad Station on odd days – it's cheap and slow ($5, 11½ hours) – and an overnight bus from the Shchyolkovsky bus station ($3.50, 8½ hours), which runs on weekends only in summer.

West
Запад

ISTRA & NEW JERUSALEM MONASTERY
ИСТРА И НОВО-ИЕРУСАЛИМСКИЙ МОНАСТЫРЬ

In the 17th century, Nikon, the patriarch whose reforms drove the Old Believers from the Orthodox Church, decided to show one and all that Russia deserved to be the centre of the Christian world by building a little Holy City right at home, complete with its own Church of the Holy Sepulchre. This was the grandiose New Jerusalem Monastery (Novo-Iyerusalimsky Monastyr), founded in 1656 near the picturesque though now polluted Istra River, 50km west of central Moscow. The project was nearly stillborn when the abrasive Nikon lost his job.

Unlike other Moscow monasteries, this one had no military use, though with its perimeter walls and towers it looks like a fortress. In WWII, the retreating Germans blew it to pieces but it's gradually being reconstructed. The monastery is now in Orthodox hands again after years as a museum, and attracts a steady stream of worshippers. The nearby woods are a popular picnic spot. Another attraction is the Moscow region's Museum of Wooden Architecture, a collection of renovated 17th to 19th century buildings that show off the traditional 'gingerbread' woodwork outside and give a glimpse of old rural life inside.

Monastery

In the centre of the monastery grounds, and intended by Nikon to look like Jerusalem's Church of the Holy Sepulchre, is the **Cathedral of the Resurrection** (Voskresensky sobor). Like its prototype, it's really several churches under one roof. The huge rotunda – very ambitious in 1685 – collapsed under its own weight a few decades after it went up and had to be constructed again. One part of the cathedral where reconstruction is complete is the unusual underground **Church of SS Konstantin & Yelena** (Konstantino-Yeleninskaya Tserkov), entered via an interior staircase, with a belfry peeping up above the ground outside the cathedral. Nikon was buried in the cathedral, beneath the **Church of John the Baptist** (Tserkov Ioanna Predtechi).

At the rear of the grounds is the Moscow baroque **Nativity Church** (Rozhdestvenskaya tserkov), with chambers for the tsar on the left and the abbot on the right. It houses a museum with books, porcelain, paintings, icons, old armour and a section on the history of the monastery. The museum (☎ 560 3643) is open from 10 am to 5.30 pm Tuesday to Friday, and 11 am to 7 pm on weekends. Entrance is $1.50 and for $3 you can get a tour in English. Behind the monastery near the river is Nikon's former 'hermitage', a rather unmonastic three-storey affair.

Museum of Wooden Architecture

This collection of buildings (Architekturno-etnographichesky Otdel) just outside the monastery's north wall includes the **Epiphany Church** (Tserkov Bogoyavleniya) built in 1647, an 18th century house and inn, a 19th century peasant's home, granaries and a windmill, all from the Moscow region. It's open from 10 am to 7.30 pm; admission is $1.50.

Getting There & Away

Suburban trains run about twice an hour from Moscow's Riga Station to Istra (about one hour), from where buses run to the Muzey stop by the monastery.

By car, leave Moscow by Leningradsky prospekt and its continuation, Volokolamskoe shosse, and continue through Dedovsk to Istra. The monastery is 2km west of the town centre.

ARKHANGELSKOE АРХАНГЕЛЬСКОЕ

☎ 095

On the Moscow River a short distance west of Moscow's outer ring road, Arkhangelskoe (☎ 584 5533) is one of the grandest estates in the region. A grandson of Dmitry Golitsyn, a statesman under Peter the Great, started work on a palace in the 1780s but lost interest and sold it all to Prince Nikolay Yusupov, one of the richest Russians of that time or since.

During several ambassadorships and as Director of the Imperial Museums, Yusupov accumulated a private art collection that outclassed many European museums. After a rough start – the house was pillaged by Napoleon's troops, trashed in a serfs' revolt and nearly burned down – Yusupov fixed it up and filled it with his treasures.

The beautiful grounds and buildings are open from 10 am to 5 pm Wednesday to Sunday. Admission to the complex is $2.50.

The **main house** of the palace is mainly a series of elegant halls for showing off Yusupov's paintings, furniture, sculptures, tapestries, porcelain and glass. His paintings include an entire room devoted to the Italian master Tiepolo and – at least once upon a time, according to one source – portraits of each of his 300 mistresses.

The multilevel, Italianate **gardens** are full of 18th century copies of classical statues, plus one of Pushkin. A colonnade on the eastern side was meant to be a Yusupov family mausoleum, but was never finished.

Yusupov also organised a troupe of serf actors that eventually became one of the best known of its kind, and built them a **theatre** just west of the gardens.

Predating everything else is the little white **Church of the Archangel Michael** (Arkhangelskaya Tserkov, 1667). Yusupov smothered it with the self-important Holy Gates (Svyatie Vorota) to link it with the estate.

Places to Eat

There's a ***bufet*** in the car park and the reasonable ***Arkhangelskoe Restaurant*** *(☎ 562 03 28)* across the road, where a meal will cost around $10. For $40 you can eat at the ***Russkaya Izba*** *(Russian Cabin; ☎ 561 42 44, ulitsa Rechnaya 1)* in nearby Ilinskoe village, by the bridge. Its traditional food is very good – especially the *zakuski* (appetisers). Both places are open from noon to 10 or 11 pm.

Getting There & Away

The estate is 22km west of central Moscow. Bus No 549 to Bolnitsa (Hospital), No 62 from Moscow's Tushinskaya bus station (Avtobusnaya Stantsia Tushinskaya), alongside Tushinskaya metro station, stops at Arkhangelskoe, near the estate entrance, and Ilyinskoe. It runs about three times an hour from 6 am to 7.30 pm, with a few more services up to midnight; the fare is $0.40.

If driving, go out along Leningradsky prospekt, stay to the left as it becomes Volokolamskoe shosse, then beyond the outer ring road, fork left into Ilinskoe shosse. It's a 30 minute drive.

BORODINO БОРОДИНО

In 1812 Napoleon invaded Russia, lured by the prospect of taking Moscow. For three months the Russians retreated, until on 26 August the two armies met in a bloody, one-day battle of attrition at the village of Borodino, 130km west of Moscow. In 15 hours, more than one-third of each army was killed – over 100,000 soldiers in all. Europe would know nothing as terrible until WWI.

The French seemed to be the winners, as the Russians withdrew and abandoned Moscow. But Borodino was in fact the beginning of the end for Napoleon, who was soon in full, disastrous retreat.

The entire battlefield – more than 100 sq km – is now the **State Borodino Military-Historical Museum-Preserve** (Gosudarstvenny Borodinsky Voenno-Istorichesky Muzey-Zapovednik). It includes a museum and some three dozen monuments to generals and divisions (most erected at the battle's 1912 centenary), and further memorials to Soviet soldiers who died in a second Borodino battle during WWII.

If your interest is limited, a vivid 'snapshot' of the 1812 battle can be found at the Borodino Panorama in Moscow (see the Moscow chapter). But Borodino itself makes an easy detour if you happen to be driving between Moscow and Smolensk.

The front line was roughly along the line of the 4km road from Borodino village to the train station. The French were to its west, the Russians east. Most of the monuments are close to the road. The **museum**, about 1km south of the village, has lots of maps and an illuminated model of the battle. It's open from 10 am to 6 pm daily except Monday and the last Friday of the month; admission is $1. There's a grubby ***cafe*** by the car park.

The hilltop monument about 400m in front of the museum is the **grave** of Prince Bagration, a heroic Georgian infantry general who was mortally wounded in battle. It's surrounded by WWII trenches.

Farther south there's a concentration of monuments around Semyonovskoe village, scene of the battle's most frenzied fighting where Bagration's heroic Second Army, opposing far larger French forces, was virtually obliterated. The redoubts around Semyonovskoe changed hands eight times in the battle.

It's thought the Russian commander, Mikhail Kutuzov, deliberately sacrificed Bagration's army to save his larger First Army, opposing lighter French forces in the

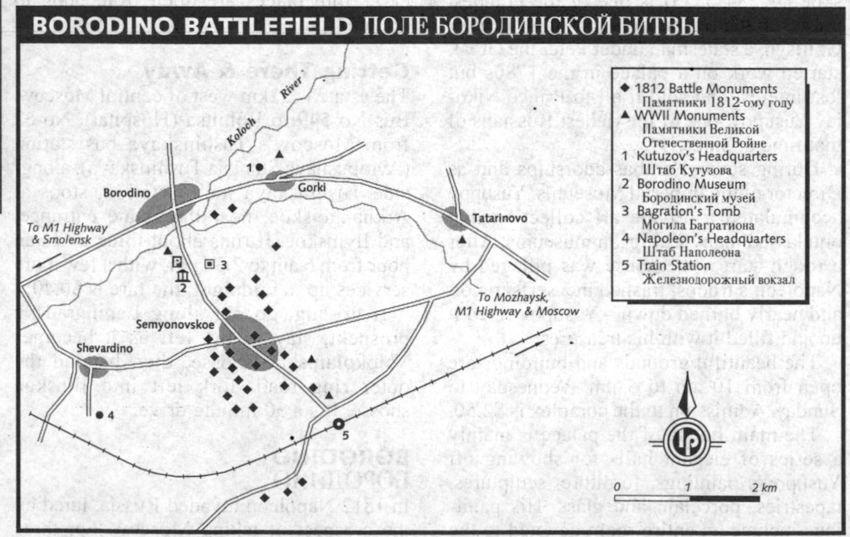

northern part of the battlefield. Kutuzov's headquarters are marked by an obelisk in the village of Gorki. Another obelisk near the Shevardinsky redoubt to the south-west – paid for in 1912 with French donations – marks Napoleon's camp. Near the train station are two WWII mass graves.

Getting There & Away

Suburban trains run every hour or so from Moscow's Belorusskaya Station to Borodino (2¼ hours). Most trains heading to Gagarin also stop at Borodino. For a day trip from Moscow, you should aim to leave by 10 am.

If driving from Moscow, stay on the M1 Minsk highway till the Mozhaysk turn-off, 95km beyond the Moscow outer ring road. It's 5km north to Mozhaysk, a sleepy old town, then 13km west to Borodino village. Drivers from Smolensk should take the 'Borodino 17' turn-off, about 9km east of the turn-off for Gagarin (where Yury grew up), then after a few kilometres turn right at the 'Muzey Borodino 12' sign.

PEREDELKINO
ПЕРЕДЕЛКИНО

☎ 095

Boris Pasternak – poet, author of *Doctor Zhivago* and winner of the 1958 Nobel Prize for literature – lived for a long time in a dacha in this now-trendy writers' colony on Moscow's south-western outskirts, just 5km beyond the city's outer ring road.

Though officially in disgrace when he died in 1960, thousands of people came to Pasternak's funeral, and even before perestroika his grave had a steady stream of visitors. The grave is in a small cemetery *(kladbishche)* near Peredelkino train station, in a little pine grove towards the rear on the right-hand side, and has a stone slab bearing Pasternak's profile.

Above the graveyard sits the tiny 15th century **Transfiguration Church** (Preobrazhenskaya Tserkov).

Pasternak's dacha is now a museum, the **Dom-Muzey Pasternaka**. Visits are by guided tour in Russian. You'll see the room where he died and the room where he finished *Dr Zhivago*. The museum (☎ 934 51 75) is open from 10 am to 4 pm Thursday to Sunday; admission is $1.40.

Villa Peredelkino *(☎ 435 14 78, 1-ya Chobotovskaya alleya 2A)*, on the same street as Peredelkino's train station, is an expensive Italian restaurant in the former dacha of Leonid Brezhnev's daughter, open from noon to midnight daily.

Getting There & Away

Frequent suburban trains take 20 minutes to reach Peredelkino, on the line to Kaluga-II station, from Moscow's Kiev Station. If you're driving, take Kutuzovsky prospekt, which becomes Mozhayskoe shosse. Beyond the outer ring road, continue on the Minskoe shosse (highway M1) and at the 21km post turn left to Peredelkino.

South
Юг

MELIKHOVO
МЕЛИХОВО

The estate south of Moscow that Anton Chekhov bought in 1892 and lived on until 1899 is open as a **museum** (Muzey A P Chekhova). Here Chekhov wrote *The Seagull* and *Uncle Vanya*, was responsible for building three local schools and a fire station, and continued to practise medicine.

Melikhovo is about 7km east of the dual carriageway that parallels the old M2 Moscow-Oryol road, signposted 50km south of the Moscow outer ring road. Suburban trains run from Moscow's Kursk Station to the town of Chekhov, 12km west of Melikhovo, from where there are occasional buses to Melikhovo.

PRIOKSKO-TERRASNY RESERVE
ПРИОКСКО-ТЕРРАСНЫЙ ЗАПОВЕДНИК

The Prioksko-Terrasny Biosphere Reserve (Prioxko-Terrasny Biosferny Zapovednik) covers 50 sq km bordering the northern flood plain of the Oka River, a tributary of the Volga. It's a meeting point of northern fir groves and marshes with typical southern meadow steppe, and its varied fauna includes a herd of European bison, brought back from near extinction since WWII.

You can't wander freely in the reserve but tours in Russian are given a couple of times a day from its excursion bureau, and foreigners who turn up alone might be given an individual tour if any English-speaking staff are on hand. The reserve is open year-round except on public holidays; tours are free.

There's a small **museum** near the office with stuffed specimens of the reserve's fauna, typical of European Russia, including beavers, elk, deer and boar. You're unlikely to see the real thing outside, except maybe elk or deer in winter.

The reserve's pride, and the focus of most visits, is its European bison nursery (pitomnik zubrov). Two pairs of bison, one of Europe's largest mammals (some weigh over a tonne), were brought from Poland in 1948. Now there are about 60 and more than 200 have been sent out to other parts of the country. The bison come into the nursery in greatest numbers at feeding time, which is 7 am and 7 pm.

Getting There & Away

Public transport is difficult. You need to take a suburban train from Moscow's Kursk Station to Serpukhov (2¼ hours), then a rare bus to the village of Danki, with some pretty wooden houses, 1km from the reserve's excursion bureau. You might also be able to negotiate a ride from the station.

For drivers, the turn-off from the Moscow-Oryol highway is 76km south of the Moscow outer ring road. Driving from Moscow, you have to turn west and then double back under the highway. Go through Danki then turn right to the reserve. It's 5km from the highway to the excursion bureau.

TULA
ТУЛА

☎ 0872 • pop 550,000

Tula, 170km south of Moscow on the M2 highway to Oryol and Ukraine, is polluted and not very pretty, but has two interesting museums devoted to its famous products – guns and samovars – that may be worth a stop if you're coming this way. If you're driving and don't want to stop, take the western bypass, since traffic in the city is heavy and the roads poor.

Tula lay in the path of Tatar armies advancing on Moscow and was fortified from the 15th century. It has long been famous for gunsmithing – a craft begun in the 16th century and confirmed when Peter the Great founded a small arms factory here in 1712 – and samovars, both industries based on local iron ore and coal deposits.

The city's economy has suffered from the fall-off in orders from the impoverished Russian army, but Tula has stayed in the forefront of military affairs through the locally stationed 106th Guards Airborne Division. They were among the troops that blasted Yeltsin's parliamentary enemies out of the Moscow White House in 1993.

Things to See

The **kremlin** is at the heart of the city on ploshchad Vosstania, through which the main north-south road through Tula passes. It was built in 1514-21 with thick limestone walls about 1km round. Inside are the **Weapons Museum** (Muzey oruzhiey), open from 10 am to 4.30 pm Wednesday to Sunday ($0.40), incongruously sited in the former **Epiphany Cathedral** (Bogoyavlensky sobor), and the five-domed **Assumption Cathedral** (Uspensky sobor). Among the conventional weapons (from muskets to kalashnikovs) in the museum are many curiosities such as the 'Velodog', a pistol designed for sale to British cyclists whom the makers imagined needed to gun down dangerous dogs in their path. The Assumption Cathedral, recently returned to Church use, was founded in the 16th century and rebuilt in the mid-18th century.

The **Samovar Museum** (Muzey samovarov), outside the kremlin entrance, has as many of these quintessentially Russian tea urns as you could wish to see – including one in the shape of Lenin's tomb! It's open from 10 am to 5 pm Tuesday to Saturday; admission is $0.40.

Places to Stay & Eat

Hotel Moskva (☎ *20 03 41*) outside Tula's Moskovsky train station seems to be the only place that considers itself good enough for foreigners. It's not really friendly, and small doubles are $28.

Babushkas around town sell a tasty local speciality called *Tulsky pryanik* – glazed gingerbread with an apricot jam filling.

Getting There & Away

Suburban trains to Tula go from Moscow's Kursk Station. The trip takes four or five hours, so it's better if you can get on a long-distance train heading for Kursk or Ukraine, many of which stop at Tula.

There are several daily buses from Moscow's Shchyolkovsky bus station, taking 4½ hours.

YASNAYA POLYANA
ЯСНАЯ ПОЛЯНА

☎ 0872

Yasnaya Polyana (Bright Glade), the estate where the great Russian writer Count Leo Tolstoy was born, spent much of his life and is buried, is 14km south of central Tula, some 240km from Moscow. Bureaucratic wrangling over control of the complex means that much of the place is in rather evocative disarray.

Tolstoy's **house**, where he died in 1910, is a simple place filled with many of his possessions. His nearby **grave** is unmarked except for the many flowers left by newlyweds, following an old tradition. The complex (☎ 33 98 32) is open from Wednesday to Sunday; the grounds from 10.30 am to 4.30 pm, and the house from 11 am to 3 pm. Admission is $2.

Leo Tolstoy, squire of Yasnaya Polyana

Getting There & Away

Bus No 114 to Shchekino from Tula's bus station stops at the Yasnaya Polyana turn-off – with a blue 'Yasnaya Polyana' sign – on the main road south from central Tula. From here it's 1km west (right) to the estate entrance.

If you're driving from Moscow, it's easier to follow Tula's western bypass all the way to its southern end and then turn back north towards Tula, than to go through central Tula, which is clogged with bad roads and heavy traffic. The Yasnaya Polyana turn-off is about 24km from the southern end of the bypass on the road back towards central Tula.

GORKI LENINSKIE
ГОРКИ ЛЕНИНСКИЕ

Lenin and his family took occasional rests at the lovely little 1830s manor house on this wooded estate, 32km south-east of the Kremlin, after he narrowly survived an assassination attempt in 1918. After suffering strokes in 1922 and 1923, Lenin spent more and more time at Gorki Leninskie, leaving only once in the eight months before he died here on 21 January 1924.

Now it's a museum, still open daily from 10 am to 4 pm except Tuesday (admission $1.25) – though numbers of visitors have plummeted from the 500,000 who flocked (or were herded) here annually in Soviet times. Some of the rooms are kept as they were, and the clocks still read 6.50 (am), the time of Lenin's death.

Getting There & Away

Bus No 439 leaves every 30 minutes for the estate from the Domodedovskaya metro station in Moscow.

By road, there are three turn-offs to the left from the M4 Kashirskoe shosse, about eight to 11km beyond the Moscow outer ring road.

North-East – The Golden Ring Северо-восток – Золотое Кольцо

The 'Golden Ring' (Zolotoe Koltso) is a modern name for a loop of very old towns north-east of Moscow that preceded the present capital as the political and cultural heart of Russia. The towns' churches, monasteries, kremlins (city forts) and museums make an incredibly picturesque portfolio of early Russian craftwork. Another attraction of the region is that some of the towns are really little more than villages, providing a peaceful glimpse of country life as it is lived all over European Russia.

Best known is little Suzdal, officially protected against industrial development and littered with so many protected buildings that it's almost one big museum. The other towns are more lived-in but are equally rich in old buildings such as churches, monasteries or kremlins. Made from stone, these buildings have outlived most wooden structures.

You do run the risk of 'old Russian church' overload here, so it pays to travel selectively. The most visited places are Sergiev Posad and Suzdal, but Vladimir and Bogolyubovo, Plyos, Kostroma, Yaroslavl, Rostov-Veliky and Pereslavl-Zalessky, in their different ways, all have big attractions too.

Most places in the Golden Ring can be visited individually on day or overnight trips from Moscow, but a better way to absorb the region's beauties and history, if you have time, is to devote a few days to taking in a combination of places. Transport and accommodation are easy enough to find as you go along. One or two-day excursions are also available from Moscow, and Golden Ring visits are a standard item on many package tours to Russia.

This section covers the Golden Ring going anticlockwise, though if you're doing a full circuit you might prefer to travel in a clockwise direction, as the distances between the first few destinations are shorter that way.

History

The Golden Ring's main towns began as outposts of the Kyivan (Kievan) Rus state and grew as people moved north as Kyiv (Kiev in Russian)) declined. At the start of the 12th century, Prince Vladimir Monomakh of Kyiv founded a fort at Vladimir and gave the Rostov-Suzdal principality in which it lay to his son Yury Dolgoruky. Yury made Suzdal his capital but concentrated his energies down south, eventually winning the title of Grand Prince of Kyiv and installing himself there. He still took the precaution of fortifying the settlements of Pereslavl-Zalessky and Kostroma in his original territory, along with a small western outpost called Moscow.

After Yury died in 1157, his son and successor, Andrey Bogolyubsky, spurned the chance of establishing himself in Kyiv and moved back to the more secure northern territories. Andrey based himself at Vladimir, which became the effective capital of Russia in 1169 when Andrey sacked Kyiv, taking the Grand Prince title north. Under these princes and their successors, Suzdal grew rich as a commercial centre and Vladimir sprouted cathedrals, monasteries and massive city walls. Rostov, Yaroslavl and other centres later split off as separate principalities.

In 1237, darkness fell as the Tatars invaded Russia, sacking and burning everything. But having made their point, they were mostly content to rule and collect taxes through local princes, which they did for the next 250 years. The region again prospered under Andrey's nephew Yaroslav, and his son Alexander Nevsky of Novgorod. But Moscow, given independence by Alexander Nevsky in 1252, grew in influence as an intermediary between the Tatars and the other Russian princes. Moscow absorbed Pereslavl-Zalessky, Vladimir and Suzdal in the 14th century; the headquarters of the Russian Orthodox Church was transferred there from Vladimir in the 1320s; and by the end of the 15th century the entire region was part of Muscovy, the Moscow state.

Architecture & Art

The majority of the Golden Ring's surviving architectural monuments date from spurts of building and rebuilding after the collapse of Tatar power. Most (particularly the fort-monasteries of Suzdal) were bankrolled in the 16th century by the Moscow princes, and from the 17th century by the Church (as happened in Rostov) and a new class of rich merchants (as in Yaroslavl).

But the buildings that gave the region a key place in the story of Russian architecture were constructed before the Tatars came. Most important are three 12th century buildings in and near Vladimir: the cathedrals of the Assumption and St Dmitry, and the Church of the Intercession on the Nerl. These are the vital link between the architecture of 11th century Kyiv and that of 15th century Moscow – early northern interpretations, in majestic, finely carved white stone, of Kyiv's Byzantine brick churches.

The Vladimir-Suzdal region was also a chief inheritor of Kyiv's Byzantine artistic traditions, though only a few fragments of 12th and 13th century frescoes survive in the Vladimir and Suzdal cathedrals and in the old church at Kidiksha. (Some icons also survive in Moscow and St Petersburg museums.) While still primarily Byzantine, these works show a bold use of colour and a range of human emotions that heralds later Russian developments.

This 'Vladimir-Suzdal school' came to an end with the Tatar invasions, and Novgorod was left to continue the development of Russian art. Art revived, prolifically, in the Golden Ring from the 15th century onwards but never regained its earlier pioneering role – though the colourful, realistic late 17th century murals by Gury Nikitin of Kostroma and his followers, which adorn several Golden Ring churches, shouldn't be missed.

Wooden Architecture Along the roads and in the villages of this region are many northern-style 'gingerbread' log houses, decorated with bright paintwork, carved doorways and window frames – and often a pensioner at the front with a bucket of vegetables for sale.

At Suzdal, Kostroma and Palekh, old wooden houses and churches are assembled in museums of wooden architecture – a convenient way to see some beautiful feats of 16th to 19th century carpentry.

Crafts The region is also famous for art on another scale. The villages of Palekh, Mstyora and Kholuy, all north-east of Vladimir, became centres of icon painting as early as the 13th century and later developed special skills at working in miniature. When the 1917 revolution destroyed the market, many painters here turned to lacquer miniatures of legendary or historical scenes on papier-mache boxes, a technique first developed in the 19th century around the village of Fedoskino, north of Moscow. Nowadays, most people know these tiny works of art as 'Palekh boxes'.

Other regional traditions include the crystal and glasswork of Gus-Khrustalny near Vladimir, the textiles of Ivanovo, and *finift*, the finely painted enamelware of Rostov-Veliky.

VLADIMIR
ВЛАДИМИР

☎ 09222 • pop 340,000

The city that gave way to Moscow as Russia's capital is now little different from a hundred other medium-sized Russian industrial towns – except that it has two of the most beautiful buildings in Russia, and a third stands a few kilometres away at Bogolyubovo. It's easy enough to take in the main sights in a few hours en route between Moscow and Suzdal.

History

Vladimir was founded by Vladimir Monomakh of Kyiv in 1108 as a fort in the Rostov-Suzdal principality that he gave to Yury Dolgoruky, one of his younger sons. Under Yury's son Andrey Bogolyubsky it became capital of the principality in 1157 or 1158, and capital of all Kyivan Rus after

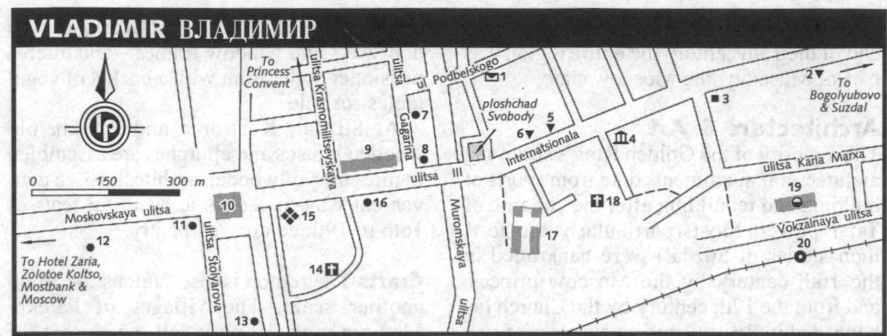

Kyiv was sacked in 1169. Andrey and his brother Vsevolod III (1176-1212) consolidated themselves as the strongest Russian princes and brought builders and artists from as far away as Western Europe to give Vladimir a Kyiv-like splendour.

Devastated by the Tatars in 1238 and 1293, the city recovered each time, but its realm disintegrated into small princedoms with Moscow increasingly dominant. The head of the Russian Church resided here from 1300 to 1326, but then moved to Moscow. Worldly power finally shifted to Moscow around this time too. Even so, the rulers remained nominally Grand Princes of Vladimir until the 15th century. In the 20th century, Vladimir prospered anew on the back of textile, mechanical engineering and chemical industries.

Orientation

The main road through the city from west to east is called successively prospekt Lenina, ulitsa Pushkina, Moskovskaya ulitsa, ulitsa III Internatsionala, ulitsa Frunze and Dobroselskaya ulitsa. Ulitsa III Internatsionala is now officially called Bolshaya Moskovskaya, but nobody seems to notice.

The Assumption and St Dmitry cathedrals are just off ulitsa III Internatsionala, standing impressively at the top of the tree-covered slope down to the Klyazma River.

The rail and bus stations are both on Vokzalnaya ulitsa at the bottom of the same slope a short distance east. The M7 Moscow-Nizhny Novgorod road makes a loop round the northern side of the city.

Information

The Vladimirsky Passage department store has a money exchange on the 3rd floor that is open from 9 am to 7 pm daily (closed on Sunday). Mostbank at prospekt Lenina 2, next to Hotel Zarya, exchanges money, gives credit card advances and is open from 9.15 am to 4 pm weekdays.

The post and telephone office on ulitsa Podbelskogo is open from 8 am to 8 pm weekdays. The Internet Place (☎ 32 30 64) is on the corner of ulitsa Gagarina and ulitsa III Internatsionala. It's open from 8.30 am to 6 pm weekdays; Internet access is $0.03 per minute.

Assumption Cathedral

Andrey Bogolyubsky announced Vladimir's succession to Kyiv as the Russian capital with a northern white-stone version of Kyiv's brick Byzantine churches. Begun in 1158, the Assumption Cathedral (Uspensky sobor) is simple but majestic in form and adorned with fine carving (innovative for the time). It was extended on all sides after a fire in the 1180s, becoming five aisles wide instead of three. The four outer domes were added then too. Since then it has changed little.

Initially, the cathedral housed a Byzantine icon of the Virgin brought from Kyiv by Andrey Bogolyubsky, which was already on its way to becoming Russia's most revered image, a national protector bestowing supreme status to the city that housed it. Moved to Moscow in 1390, it's now known as the *Vladimir Icon of the Mother of God*

VLADIMIR ВЛАДИМИР

PLACES TO STAY & EAT
2 Tri Peskarya
Три Пескаря
3 Hotel Vladimir
Гостиница Владимир
5 Bar-Restoran Stary Gorod
Бар-Ресторан Старый Город
6 Sobornaya Ploshchad
Соборная Площадь

OTHER
1 Post & Telephone Office
Почтамт и переговорный пункт
4 Vladimir Region Prerevolutionary History Museum
Музей истории дореволюционного прошлого Владимирского края
7 Sapphire
Магазин Сапфир
8 Internet Place
Интернет-салон
9 Trading Arcades
Торговые ряды
10 Golden Gate
Золотые ворота
11 Crystal, Lacquer Miniatures & Embroidery Exhibition
Выставка хрусталя, лаковой миниатюры и вышивки
12 Supermarket
Супермаркет
13 Old Vladimir Exhibition
Выставка Старый Владимир
14 St George Church
Георгиевская Церковь
15 Vladimirsky Passage
Владимиаский Пассаж
16 Khudozhestvenny Salon
Художественный Салон
17 Assumption Cathedral
Успенский собор
18 St Dmitry's Cathedral
Дмитриевский собор
19 Bus Station
Автовокзал
20 Train Station
Вокзал

and since 1930 has been kept in the Tretyakov Gallery.

A few restored 12th century murals of peacocks and prophets holding scrolls can be made out about halfway up the inner wall of the outer north aisle; this was originally an outside wall. The real treasures are the *Last Judgment* frescoes by Andrey Rublyov and Daniil Chyorny, painted in 1408 in the central nave and inner south aisle, under the choir gallery towards the west end. Among them, in the central nave, are rows of haloed evangelists and angels, with realistic, sympathetic faces, and (on the ceiling) Christ with his right arm raised.

The cathedral is a working church, and is open to visitors only from 1.30 to 5 pm daily (foreigner admission is $0.70). Adjoining the cathedral on the northern side (beside the path up from ulitsa III Internatsionala) are an 1810 **bell tower** and the 1862 **St George's Chapel**.

Cathedral of St Dmitry

Vladimir-Suzdal stone carving reached its most amazing heights on the Cathedral of St Dmitry (Dmitrievsky sobor, 1193-97), the only surviving part of Vsevolod III's palace complex. The west doorway and the upper parts of all four walls are covered in an amazing profusion of stone images – a few of them Christian but mostly animal, vegetable and mythological.

The top centre of the north, south and west walls all show King David bewitching the birds and beasts with music, which may be an oblique way of complimenting Vsevolod, who appears in person at the top left of the north wall, with a baby son on his knee and other sons kneeling on each side. Above the right-hand window of the south wall, Alexander the Great ascends into heaven, a symbol of princely might; on the west wall appear the labours of Hercules.

The cathedral is under restoration, but if you ask the people working there they will let you in. Inside, on the largêr central vault beneath the gallery on the west side, are some beautiful 12th century frescoes of apostles and angels, almost certainly by Byzantine artists.

Golden Gate

Vladimir's Golden Gate (Zolotye Vorota), part defensive tower, part triumphal arch, modelled on the very similar structure in Kyiv, was built by Andrey Bogolyubsky to guard the main, western entrance to his city about 500m west of the Assumption

Cathedral. Restored under Catherine the Great, the Golden Gate now houses a **museum** of Vladimir's military history, open from 10 am to 4 pm daily except Tuesday and the last Thursday of the month ($0.70).

To the east, on ulitsa III Internatsionala, are the late 18th century **Trading Arcades** (Torgovye ryady).

Other Attractions

The **Vladimir Region Pre-Revolutionary History Museum** (Muzey istorii dorevolyutsionnogo proshlogo Vladimirskogo kraya), at ulitsa III Internatsionala 64 close to the Cathedral of St Dmitry, includes the original coffin of Alexander Nevsky of Novgorod, the 13th century military leader who was also Prince of Vladimir. He was buried in the former Nativity Monastery farther along the street, once one of Russia's most important monasteries, but his remains were moved to St Petersburg in 1724 when Peter the Great allotted him Russian hero status. The museum is open from 10 am to 3.30 pm daily except Monday and the last Thursday of the month; admission is $0.50.

Interesting for its site as well as its contents is the **Old Vladimir Exhibition** (Vystavka Stary Vladimir), in an old water tower on Kozlov val (part of the old ramparts) and open from 10 am to 4 pm daily (closed Monday); admission is $0.50.

Near the Golden Gate, in the red-brick former Old Believers' Trinity Church (1913-16) at Moskovskaya ulitsa 2, is a **Crystal, Lacquer Miniatures & Embroidery Exhibition** (Vystavka khrustalya, lakovoy miniatyury i vyshivki) featuring the crafts of Gus-Khrustalny and other nearby towns. It's open from 10 am to 4 pm daily (closed Tuesday); admission is $0.50. In the basement to the right of the museum door is a small souvenir shop, Vladimirsky Shik. Apart from traditional souvenirs you can buy some maps and postcards of Vladimir. It's open from 10 am to 6 pm daily.

The **Princess' Convent** (Knyagnin monastyr), off ulitsa Nekrasova and founded by Vsevolod III's wife, Maria, is now a convent again after spending recent decades as a museum of orthodoxy and atheism. The only substantial surviving building is its 16th century **Assumption Cathedral** (Uspensky sobor), with many well preserved 1640s frescoes.

Some other places are worthy of attention. From ulitsa III Internatsionala 26, turn left on a narrow winding street dotted with lampposts. It'll take you to the **St George Church** (Georgievskaya tserkov) at ulitsa Georgievskaya 2A, which houses the Vladimir Theatre of Choral Music that performs on Saturday at 7 pm and Sunday throughout the year except June and July. The entrance is at the back of the street.

Places to Stay

Hotel Zolotoe Koltso *(☎ 24 88 07)*, which opened in 1992 in the west of town on the corner of ulitsa Chaykovskogo and ulitsa Balakireva, is already quite run-down. It has a good restaurant and the 350 beds are $6/8 for singles/doubles. Taking trolleybus No 8 in either direction will get you to the hotel eventually.

Nearer the centre with the same prices, but even more run-down, is ***Hotel Zarya*** *(☎ 2 34 22, ulitsa Pushkina 36)*, about 1km west of the cathedrals. The restaurant is all right and inexpensive if you don't mind the strip show.

Hotel Vladimir *(☎ 32 30 42, fax 32 73 33, ulitsa III Internatsionala 74)* is conveniently located about 500m east of the Assumption Cathedral. It charges $13/16, and has a decent restaurant where a three course meal costs $7.

Places to Eat

Apart from the ***hotel restaurants***, there are quite a few places along the main street. The inexpensive ***Bar-Restoran Stary Gorod*** *(☎ 32 51 01)*, on ulitsa III Internatsionala opposite the Cathedral of St Dmitry, has been redone. The usual selection of Russian classics could set you back $5 for a full meal; it's open until 2 am daily. Next door, ***Sobornaya Ploshchad*** *(ulitsa III Internatsionala 39)* is open from noon till 5 pm and has simple dishes for $1. The most pleasant place is ***Tri Peskarya*** *(ulitsa III Internatsionala 88)*. Turn right from the main street once you reach a tiny square with benches. A good Russian meal there would cost you $7 and it's open until 11 pm.

There is a ***supermarket*** *(Moskovskaya 10)*, open from 8 am to 10 pm daily.

Shopping

At ulitsa III Internatsionala 26, the Khudozhestvenny Salon (Art Salon) sells antiques such as old photographs, Russian medals and Roi de Paris wall clocks at a fraction of Moscow prices. It's open from 10 am to 7 pm weekdays and to 5 pm on Saturday. At Sapphire, ulitsa Gagarina 2, you can find some high quality silver jewellery made to old Russian designs for up to $10 per item. It's open from 10 am to 7 pm (closed Sunday).

Getting There & Away

Day trips to Vladimir from Moscow are easy.

Train In Moscow, Kursk Station is the terminus for all suburban and most long-distance trains to/from Vladimir. Up to 14 long-distance trains run daily in each direction between Moscow and Nizhny Novgorod, stopping at Vladimir.

Bus There are buses each way between Moscow's Shchyolkovsky bus station and Vladimir, ($1.25, 3½ hours, two daily). A further 20 daily buses to/from Moscow stop at Vladimir in transit. Buses from Vladimir run to Suzdal ($0.25, one hour, 23 daily), Nizhny Novgorod ($2, five hours, seven daily), Ivanovo ($2, three hours, eight daily) and Kostroma ($3.50, five hours, four daily).

Car Vladimir is a simple 180km drive from Moscow. This is the beginning of the road to Siberia, walked by thousands of exiles in the old days. To reach Suzdal from central Vladimir, drive about 6km east along the main street and then turn left along Suzdalsky prospekt, crossing the Vladimir bypass after 1km.

Getting Around

Trolleybus No 5 from the train and bus stations runs up to and along the main east-west street, passing Hotel Vladimir, the two main cathedrals and the town centre, Hotel Zarya, and on out to the western edge of town. Trolleybus No 1 runs from end to end of town along the main street. Trolleybus No 4 covers at least the Hotel Vladimir to Golden Gate section of the same route.

BOGOLYUBOVO
БОГОЛЮБОВО

☎ 09222 • pop 3900

When Andrey Bogolyubsky was returning north from Kyiv in the late 1150s, his horses – so the story goes – stopped where Bogolyubovo *(ba-gal-YOO-ba-va)* now stands, 11km east of Vladimir, and wouldn't go another step. This is supposedly why Andrey made nearby Vladimir, and not his father's old base of Suzdal, his capital, and why the icon of the Mother of God that he was bearing became so closely tied to Vladimir's, and ultimately Russia's, fortunes.

Whatever the legends, Andrey built a stone fortified palace that dates from 1158-65 at this strategic spot near the meeting of the Nerl and Klyazma rivers. Nearby, in 1165, he built possibly the most perfect of all old Russian buildings, the Church of the Intercession on the Nerl.

Palace & Monastery

A tower and arch from Andrey Bogolyubsky's palace survive amid a dilapidated but reopened 18th century monastery by the Vladimir-Nizhny Novgorod road in the middle of Bogolyubovo. The dominant buildings today are the monastery's 1841 **bell tower** beside the road, and its 1866 **Assumption Cathedral** (Uspensky sobor). Just east of the cathedral, Andrey's arch and tower – on whose stairs, according to a chronicle, Andrey was assassinated by hostile boyars – adjoin each other, and the arch abuts the 18th century **Church of the Virgin's Nativity** (Rozhdestvenskaya tserkov).

Church of the Intercession on the Nerl

To reach this famous little church (Tserkov Pokrova na Nerli), go back about 200m towards Vladimir from the monastery-palace

AROUND MOSCOW

complex and then turn into ulitsa Frunze that winds downhill and under a railway bridge. Under the bridge, take the path to the left along the side of a small wood. The church appears across the meadows, about 1.25km from the bridge.

Its beauty lies in its simple but perfect proportions, a brilliantly chosen waterside site and sparing use of delicate carving. If it looks a mite top-heavy, it's because the original helmet dome was replaced by a cushion dome in 1803.

Legend has it that Andrey had the church built in memory of his favourite son, Izyaslav, who was killed in battle against the Bulgars. As with the Cathedral of St Dmitry in Vladimir, King David sits at the top of three facades, the birds and beasts entranced by his music. The interior has more carving, including 20 pairs of lions. If the church is closed, try asking at the house behind.

Getting There & Away

Take trolley bus No 1 east from Vladimir and get off at Khimzavod ($0.10). Go along the main road for 100m to the taxi van stop. You need to get off at the second stop ($0.10). Taxi vans operate between 7 am and 10 pm.

Drivers from central Vladimir should head straight out east along the main road. From Suzdal, turn left when you hit Vladimir's northern bypass and go 5km.

SUZDAL
СУЗДАЛЬ

☎ 09231 • pop 12,000

Suzdal *(SOOZ-dal)*, 35km north of Vladimir, is special not just for its lovely old monasteries, convents and churches but also because they haven't been strangled by 20th century ugliness, noise and pollution.

Bypassed by industry because the Moscow-Nizhny Novgorod railway was routed 30km to the south, the town is now officially protected from unsightly development. As a result it remains the little rural settlement it always was, on low eminences above the winding Kamenka River, with green fields reaching right into the centre and its housing mostly comprised of one-storey *izbas* (wooden cottages).

Suzdal is uniquely peaceful among Russian tourist towns, and the slightly unreal 'living museum' atmosphere resulting from its protected status is a small price to pay. It's even more peaceful since the number of visitors – Russian and foreign – has fallen off dramatically due to the Russian tourism slump. It's especially picturesque in summer with its numerous churches and towers reflected on the water.

History

First mentioned in 1024, Suzdal was made the capital of the Rostov-Suzdal principality by Yury Dolgoruky in the first half of the 12th century. When Andrey Bogolyubsky returned from Kyiv in 1157 or 1158, he made Vladimir the capital, and from then on the principality was known as Vladimir-Suzdal. But, set in a fertile wheat-growing area, Suzdal remained a trade centre even after the Tatar invasions. It was an independent princedom from the early 13th to the mid-14th century, when it united with Nizhny Novgorod until both were annexed by Moscow in 1392.

Under Muscovite rule, Suzdal became a wealthy monastic centre, with particularly big building projects funded by Vasily III and Ivan the Terrible in the 16th century. In the late 17th and 18th centuries, wealthy merchants paid for 30 gorgeous little churches, which still adorn the town.

Orientation

Many places you're likely to visit are on or near the central 1.5km ulitsa Lenina, the north-south main street. The chief exceptions are the Intercession Convent and the GTK accommodation complex, just north-west of the centre.

Information

In addition to their normal weekly closing days, most Suzdal museums and monuments are closed on the last Friday of the month. A few of the minor ones close altogether from October to April.

An exchange bureau at ulitsa Lounskaya 2 is open from 10 am to 3 pm weekdays. The post and telephone office is on

Krasnaya ploshchad; the telephone office is open 24 hours.

Kremlin

The 1.4km-long earth rampart of Suzdal's kremlin (fort), founded in the 11th century, today encloses a few streets of houses and a handful of churches as well as the main cathedral group on Kremlyovskaya ulitsa.

The **Nativity of the Virgin Cathedral** (Rozhdestvensky sobor), its blue domes spangled with gold, was founded in the 1220s but only its richly carved lower section is original white stone, the rest being 16th century brick. The inside is sumptuous with 13th and 17th century frescoes (the best of the earlier ones are the figures of two elders in the upper part of the south apse) and 13th century damascene (gold on copper) west and south doors – gospel scenes on the west, angels' deeds on the south. The cathedral is under restoration and won't be open to the public until 2001 at the earliest.

The 15th to 18th century **Archbishop's Chambers** (Arkhiyereyskie palati) line the south side of the cathedral yard, with an entrance to the 18th century **Cross Hall** (Krestovaya palata) which was used for receptions. The **Suzdal History Exhibition** (Istoricheskaya Expozitsia) is reached from the tent-roofed 1635 bell tower on the east side of the yard. The old Russian painting (Drevnerusskoy zhivopisi) display, also entered from the bell tower, is well worth a visit although it concentrates on 15th to 17th century icons of the Vladimir-Suzdal school – well after its 12th to 13th century zenith, the few surviving works of which are mostly in Moscow and St Petersburg museums.

The cathedral, Cross Hall and exhibitions are all open from 10 am to 5 pm daily, except Tuesday and the last Friday of the month. Tickets are sold at Cross Hall and cost $0.75.

Just south of this group stands the 1766 wooden **St Nicholas' Church** (Nikolskaya tserkov), brought from Glatovo village near Yuriev-Polsky. Another **St Nicholas'**, one of Suzdal's own fine small churches, built in 1720-39, is on ulitsa Lebedeva just east of the cathedral group, with its pointed tower fronting the road.

Torgovaya Ploshchad

Suzdal's Torgovaya ploshchad (Trade Square) is dominated by the pillared **Trading Arcades** (1806-11) along its western side, with one pair of small churches in front of them and another pair behind, above the river. Though all these four are closed, the pretty, five-domed 1707 **Emperor Constantine Church** (Tsarevokonstantinovskaya tserkov) over in the square's north-eastern corner is a working church; the inside is ornate. The 1787 **Virgin of All Sorrows Church** (Skorbyashchenskaya tserkov) next to it is smaller but has a big bell tower.

Monastery of the Deposition

The Monastery of the Deposition of the Holy Robe (Rizopolozhensky monastyr) is said to date from 1207 but the existing buildings are 16th to 19th century. It's now a dilapidated mess but has two pretty, pyramidal entrance turrets (1688) on the south gate. Suzdal's tallest structure, a 72m **bell tower** (1813-19), rises from the east wall. The central **Deposition Cathedral** (Rizopolozhensky Sobor), with three helmet domes, dates from the first half of the 16th century; it is reminiscent of the Moscow Kremlin's Archangel Cathedral.

Alexandrovsky Convent

This little, white convent (Alexandrovsky monastyr) at the top of the river embankment stands out for its simple, quiet beauty. Reputedly founded in 1240 by Alexander Nevsky for noble women whose menfolk had been killed by the Tatars, its present **Ascension Church** (Voznesenskaya tserkov) and bell tower date from 1695.

Saviour Monastery of St Euthymius

Founded in the 14th century to protect the town's northern entrance, Suzdal's biggest monastery (Spaso-Yevfimievsky monastyr) grew mighty in the 16th and 17th centuries

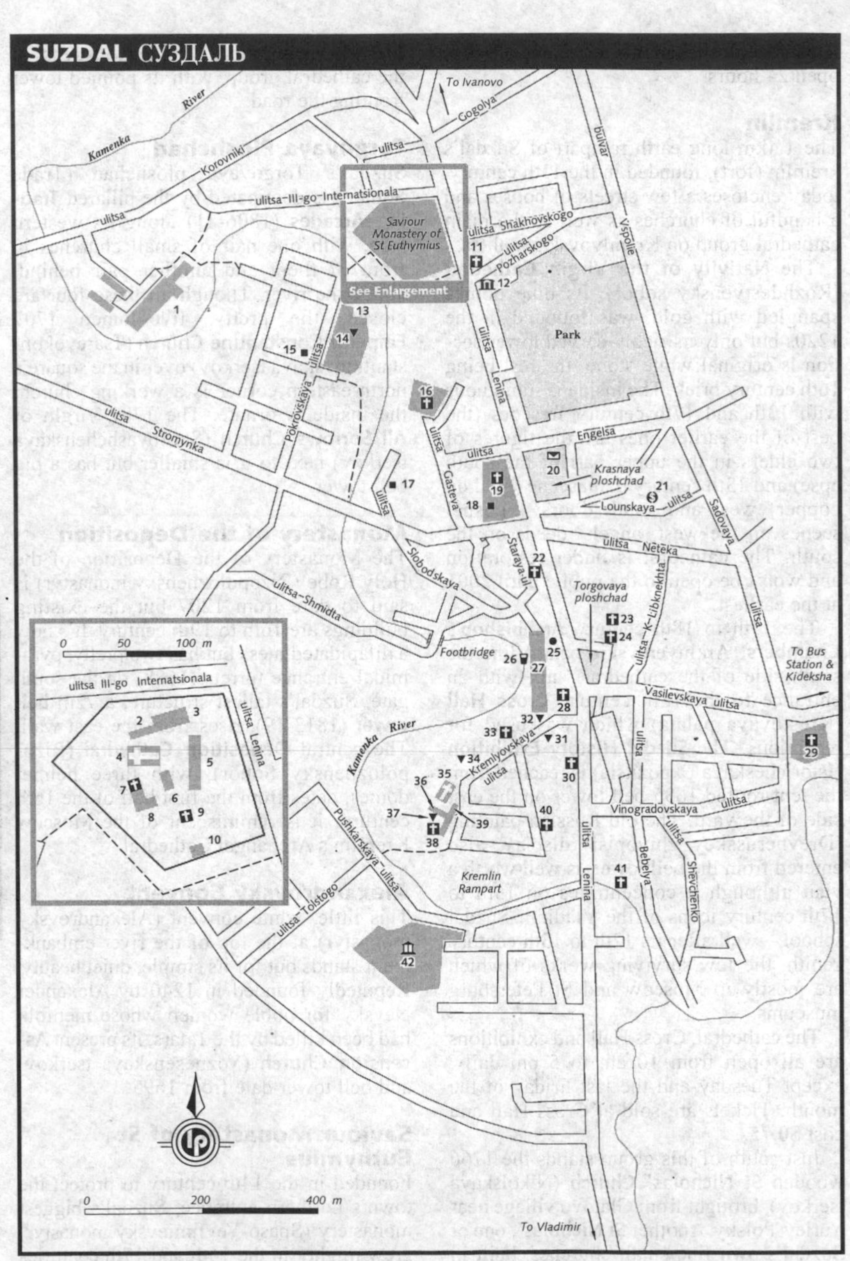
SUZDAL СУЗДАЛЬ
To Ivanovo
Gogolya
Kamenka River
Korovniki
ulitsa
ulitsa III-go Internatsionala
Saviour Monastery of St Euthymius
See Enlargement
ulitsa Shakhovskogo
ulitsa Pozharskogo
bulvar
Vspolie
Park
ulitsa Lenina
Pokrovskaya ulitsa
ulitsa Stromynka
ulitsa Engelsa
ulitsa Gasteva
Krasnaya ploshchad
Lounskaya ulitsa
Sadovaya
ulitsa Neteka
Staraya-ul
Slobodskaya
ulitsa Shmidta
Torgovaya ploshchad
ulitsa K Libknekhta
Footbridge
To Bus Station & Kideksha
Vasilevskaya ulitsa
Kamenka River
Kremlyovskaya
Vinogradovskaya
ulitsa Bebelya
Shevchenko
Pushkarskaya ulitsa
ulitsa Tolstogo
Kremlin Rampart
To Vladimir
0 50 100 m
ulitsa III-go Internatsionala
ulitsa Lenina
0 200 400 m
AROUND MOSCOW

SUZDAL СУЗДАЛЬ

PLACES TO STAY

1 Glavny Turistsky Komplex (GTK) Главный туристический комплекс (ГТК)
15 Hotel Gostevoy dom Kuchkova Гостевой Дом Кучкова
17 Likhoninsky Dom Лихонинский Дом
18 Hotel Rizopolozhenskaya Гостиница Ризоположенская

PLACES TO EAT

14 Restoran Trapeznaya Ресторан Трапезная
31 Restoran Pogrebok Ресторан Погребок
32 Restoran Gostiny Dvor Ресторан Гостиный двор
34 Slavyansky Bar Славяский Бар
37 Restoran Trapeznaya Ресторан Трапезная

SAVIOUR MONASTERY OF ST EUTHYMIUS

2 Prison Тюрьма
3 Hospital & St Nicholas' Church Больничные кельи и Никольская церковь
4 Cathedral of the Transfiguration of the Saviour Спасо-Преображенский собор
5 Monks' Quarters Братский корпус
6 Belltower Звонница
7 Assumption Church Успенская церковь
8 Father Superior's Chambers Камеры Отца-игумена
9 Annunciation Gate-Church Благовещенская надвратная церковь
10 Southern Gate-Tower Южные ворота

OTHER

11 Our Lady of Smolensk Church Смоленская церковь
12 18th Century Town House Жилой дом. XVIII в.
13 Intercession Convent Покровский монастырь
16 Alexandrovsky Convent Александровский монастырь
19 Monastery of the Deposition Ризоположенский монастырь
20 Post and Telephone Office Почтамт и переговорный пункт
21 Exchange Bureau Пункт обмена валюты
22 St Lazarus' Church (1667) Лазаревская церковь
23 Virgin of All Sorrows Church Скорбященская церковь
24 Emperor Constantine Church Царевоконстантиновская церковь
25 Produce Market Рынок
26 Bar Yakor Бар Якорь
27 Trading Arcades Торговые ряды
28 Resurrection Church Воскресенская церковь
29 St Basil's Monastery Васильевский монастырь
30 Predtechenskaya Church Предтеченская церковь
33 Assumption Church Успенская церковь
35 Nativity of the Virgin Cathedral Рождественский собор
36 Archbishop's Chambers Архиерейские палаты
38 St Nicholas' Church (Wooden) Никольская церковь (деревянная)
39 Cathedral Bell Tower Соборная колокольня
40 St Nicholas' Church Никольская церковь
41 SS Kosma & Damian Church Церковь Косьмы и Дамиана
42 Museum of Wooden Architecture & Peasant Life Музей деревянного зодчества и крестьянского быта

after Vasily III, Ivan the Terrible and the noble Pozharsky family funded impressive new stone buildings and big land and property acquisitions. It was girded with its great brick walls and towers in the 17th century.

Inside, a tall 16th to 17th century bell tower stands before the seven-domed **Cathedral of the Transfiguration of the Saviour** (Spaso-Preobrazhensky sobor). Every hour on the hour during opening times, a 10 minute concert of chimes is given on the bell tower's bells – well worth hearing. The cathedral was built in the 1590s in 12th to 13th century Vladimir-Suzdal style. Inside, some bright 1689 frescoes recounting the monastery's history, by the school of the famous Gury Nikitin from Kostroma, have been uncovered. The **tomb** of Prince Dmitry Pozharsky (1578-1642), leader of the Russian army that drove the Polish invaders from Moscow in 1612, is by the cathedral's east wall.

The 1525 **Assumption Church** (Uspenskaya tserkov) facing the bell tower adjoins the old Father Superior's chambers, which houses a display of Russian books from the 15th century on. The **monks' quarters** across the compound contain a museum of modern Russian folk art.

At the north end of the complex is the old monastery **prison**, set up in 1764 for religious dissidents, now closed to visitors, and the combined **hospital** and **St Nicholas' Church** (Bolnichnye kelyi i Nikolskaya tserkov, 1669), which contain a rich museum of 12th to 20th century Russian applied art, much of it from Suzdal itself. The entrance and ticket office are in the high gate-tower in the south wall. Foreigner entry is $1, plus $1 for each of four museums or exhibitions inside. The monastery is open from 10 am to 6 pm, except Monday and the last Thursday of the month.

Across ulitsa Lenina from the south-east corner of the monastery are the 1696-1707 **Our Lady of Smolensk Church** (Smolenskaya tserkov) and Suzdal's only surviving early 18th century **town house**; the latter is furnished in original style and open from 10 am to 4 pm daily except Monday.

Intercession Convent

The Intercession Convent (Pokrovsky monastyr), founded in 1364, has been handed back to the Church since Soviet times and a small community of black-robed nuns is in residence. The three-domed **Intercession Cathedral** (Pokrovsky sobor) in the centre, built in 1510-18, is in religious use again.

The convent was originally a place of exile for the unwanted wives of tsars – among them Solomonia Saburova, first wife of Vasily III, who was sent here in the 1520s because of her supposed infertility. The story goes that she finally became pregnant too late to avoid being divorced. A baby boy was born in Suzdal but, fearing he would be seen as a dangerous rival to any sons produced by Vasily's new wife, Yelena Glinska, Solomonia secretly had him adopted, pretended he had died and staged a mock burial. This was probably just as well for the boy since Yelena did indeed produce a son – Ivan the Terrible.

The legend received dramatic corroboration in 1934 when researchers opened a small 16th century tomb beside Solomonia's, in the crypt beneath the Intercession Cathedral. They found a silk and pearl shirt stuffed with rags – and no bones. The crypt is closed to visitors.

The **museum** of the convent's history is in a 17th century building against the west wall. It is open from 9.30 am to 3.30 or 4.30 pm daily except Tuesday and the last Friday of the month; admission is $0.60.

Museum of Wooden Architecture & Peasant Life

The highlights of this wooden 'model village' (Muzey derevyannogo zodchestva i krestyanskogo byta), illustrating old peasant life in this region of Russia, are more churches – notably the 1756 **Transfiguration Church** (Preobrazhenskaya tserkov) brought from Kozlyatievo village and the simpler 1776 **Resurrection Church** (Voskresenskaya tserkov) from Patakino. They're interesting to compare with Suzdal's brick churches from the same era. There are also log houses, windmills, a barn and lots of tools and handicrafts.

The museum is across the river south of the kremlin, open from 9.30 am to 3.30 pm daily except Tuesday and the last Friday of the month; admission is $0.60. Building interiors are open only from May to October.

Other Suzdal Buildings

Every little Suzdal church has its own charm. Our favourites include the simple **Resurrection Church** (Voskresenskaya tserkov) on Torgovaya ploshchad, built in 1719; the shabby but graceful **Predtechenskaya Church** (Pretedchenskaya tserkov, 1720) on ulitsa Lenina; and the slender tower of **St Lazarus' Church** (Lazarevskaya tserkov, 1667) with its multicoloured stonework, on Staraya ulitsa. The **SS Kosma & Damian Church** (Kosmodamianovskaya tserkov, 1725) is picturesquely placed on a bend in the river. Keep looking – you'll find more.

Suzdal's fifth monastery is **St Basil's** (Vasilevsky monastyr) on the Kideksha road. Its **cathedral** (Vasilevsky sobor) and **Purification Church** (Sretenskaya tserkov) are both 17th century.

Kideksha

The 1152 **Church of SS Boris & Gleb** (Borisoglebskaya tserkov) on the Nerl River in this quiet village 4km east of Suzdal is the oldest in the district, built for Yury Dolgoruky who had a small wooden palace here.

The palace has disappeared and the church, rebuilt many times, has lost its original vault, roof and dome and gained a 19th century porch. But the church's old floor, a metre below the modern one, gives a sense of the place's age, and drawings in the porch give an idea of what it may once have looked like. A few fragments of 12th century frescoes remain, including two figures on horseback, probably Boris and Gleb, sons of Vladimir of Kyiv, who were killed by another son, Svyatopolk, and became the first Russian saints. The church is open from 10 am to 4 or 5 pm daily except Tuesday and the last Friday of the month; admission is $0.60.

The other buildings in the compound are 18th century. The **Intercession Convent** (Pokrovsky monastyr) **Church of SS Boris & Gleb Saviour** (Borisoglebskaya tserkov) **Monastery of St Euthymius** (Spasoyefimyevsky monastyr) **Nativity of the Virgin Cathedral** (Rozhdestvensky sobor) are listed by UNESCO as World Heritage Sites.

Rides

Horse-drawn carts (sleighs in winter) in Suzdal wait for customers around the kremlin and the south end of the Trading Arcades. Bargain with the drivers (a fair price is about $10 an hour).

Places to Stay

The best value in town both by price and location is ***Hotel Rizopolozhonskaya*** *(☎ 2 07 06, fax 2 05 53)* in the decrepit Monastery of the Deposition. The hotel is in the 19th century building but has been recently renovated. The most expensive double has a living room area, decent furniture and private bathroom for just $8; basic rooms with facilities down the hall are about $5. Inexpensive but tasty meals can be arranged. Space is tight on weekends, so reserve ahead.

The nicest place to stay is ***Likhoninsky Dom*** *(☎ 2 19 01, fax 32 70 10, ulitsa Slobodskaya 34)*, on a quiet street near the town centre. Singles/doubles are $14/24 in a renovated 17th century house that once was a museum. There are only four rooms, with a pretty garden outside. The building, with a white-painted ground floor and a natural wood upper floor, is unmarked except for the number 34. This is another place where it's advisable to reserve ahead.

The main tourist hotel is the aptly titled ***Glavny Turistsky Komplex*** *(Main Tourist Complex; ☎ 2 09 08, fax 2 07 66)*, usually known by its initials GTK. Long, low, concrete and otherwise charmless, it is a far cry from the rest of the town. The only advantage is that it's far away from town on ulitsa Korovniky and doesn't spoil any view. The rooms are average size and there is a vast lobby, souvenir shop, swimming pool, a weekend disco and gloomy staff. Rooms are $36/48 including breakfast.

Hotel Gostevoy dom Kuchkova *(☎ 2 15 07, ulitsa Pokrovskaya 35)*, on an empty street not far from the Pokrovsky Convent, offers its eight doubles for $80, including breakfast. There is a small restaurant in the basement, but getting a table might not be a problem since the whole place looked deserted on our visit.

You can get thee to a nunnery at the ***Intercession Convent*** *(☎ 2 09 08)*. Though the convent has now been returned to the Church and has nuns in residence, the 30 comfortable rooms in wooden izba-style cabins installed here for Soviet visitors remain open. They have bathrooms and cost $70/90.

Places to Eat

The ***Restoran Trapeznaya*** in the Intercession Convent's Conception of St Anna Refectory Church serves good Russian food. A couple of *zakuski*, a main course and a dessert come to around $5. Save room for a dessert of bliny with honey, which is truly succulent. Ask for warming, mildly alcoholic *medovukha* (mead) to wash it all down. Hours are 9 am to 8 pm daily, though they're observed somewhat erratically.

Another ***Restoran Trapeznaya***, in the Archbishop's Chambers in the kremlin, also does decent Russian fare – like thick *pokhlyobka* soup, the ubiquitous mushrooms baked in sour cream and mead. It's open daily from 11 am to 10 pm.

Around the centre of town are a few other cafes and restaurants, less inviting but passable. One is the inexpensive ***Slavyansky Bar*** *(ulitsa Kremlyovskaya 8)* which serves snacks, sandwiches and salads for about $1 and is open from noon to 7 pm (closed

Tuesday). ***Restoran Pogrebok*** on Kremlyovskaya ulitsa has the same quality of food but higher prices (closed Monday). Another is the ***Restoran Gostiny Dvor*** at the southern end of the Trading Arcades, open daily from 11 am to 8 pm.

Meals in the main upstairs restaurant at the ***GTK*** are reasonable – about $5 – and you're inside looking out, avoiding the view of the hotel.

The town's best view is from the outside tables at ***Bar Yakor*** (Anchor) at the western side of the Trading Arcades. Make sure to pop in at sunset and stay till dark for the great vistas. Snacks and drinks cost about $1 to $2.

There's a ***produce market*** at the eastern side of the Trading Arcades near Hotel Rizopolozhenskaya. Early in the morning you're likely to find just-picked fruit and vegetables in season, and home-made dairy products like yogurt and cottage cheese.

Getting There & Away

There's no railway here. Suzdal's bus station (avtovokzal) is 1.5km east of the centre along Vasilevskaya ulitsa, at the junction of the town's eastern bypass.

If you're heading straight to Suzdal from Moscow, there's one daily bus from the Shchyolkovsky bus station at 5 pm ($3.25, 4½ hours). It returns from Suzdal to Moscow at 5.30 am. A few of the buses running between Moscow and Ivanovo also stop at Suzdal.

The common alternative is to go via Vladimir. Buses run both ways between Suzdal and Vladimir bus stations every 40 minutes between 6 am and 9 pm ($0.30, one hour). Heading north from Suzdal, you have to hope for a place on a bus coming through from Vladimir: there are two buses a day to Kostroma ($3.50, 4¼ hours from Suzdal), one or two to Yaroslavl ($5, five hours) and about five to Ivanovo ($2, two hours) where you should be able to change to a Kostroma or Yaroslavl bus.

Getting Around

The best way is on foot. There are short-cut paths in the town – like the footbridge over the river behind the GTK that cuts at least 1km off the 3km to the centre. Bus No 3 runs erratically through the day between the GTK and the bus station, via the town centre.

IVANOVO
ИВАНОВО

☎ 09322 • pop 550,000

Ivanovo, 78km north of Suzdal on the Suzdal-Kostroma road, is known for two (connected) features: its cotton textiles – it's one of Russia's biggest centres – and its women. The town's female population, swelled by the textile mills' labour needs, apparently once heavily outnumbered its male population and Ivanovo women are still – albeit apocryphally – renowned as very assertive, even aggressive, men-chasers.

Ivanovo is a very drab and dreary industrial town. You might have to change buses here if you're travelling between the northern and southern parts of the Golden Ring.

Palekh
Палех

Ivanovo is occasionally used as a base for visiting Palekh, the small village famous for icon painters and small lacquer boxes, 65km south-east on the Nizhny Novgorod road. Palekh has a good **museum** of local icons and boxes (closed Monday and the last Friday of the month; admission $0.60), fine restored 14th to 19th century icons in the **Raising of the Cross Church** (Krestovo-Sdvizhenskaya tserkov), and a few shops and exhibitions selling Palekh boxes. There are buses from Ivanovo and one daily from Vladimir via Suzdal.

Places to Stay

Wild women aside, you may end up staying in Ivanovo where the ***Tsentralnaya Hotel*** *(☎ 2 81 22, ulitsa Engelsa 1)* has singles/doubles for $10/18.

Getting There & Away

In Ivanovo, the train station is at the north end of ulitsa Engelsa; the bus station is several kilometres away in the south of town. Buses run to/from Moscow's Shchyolkovsky bus station ($5.50, 6½ hours) about eight times daily; Suzdal ($1.75, two hours) and Vladimir ($2.80, three hours) about 12 times daily; Kostroma ($2, two hours) about 12 times daily; and Yaroslavl ($2.25, two hours) two or three times daily.

Trains to Ivanovo run from Moscow's Yaroslavl Station ($3, six to eight hours).

PLYOS
ПЛЁС

☎ 09339 • pop 40,000

Plyos is a tranquil little town of trees, wooden houses and hilly streets winding down to the Volga waterfront, 62km north-east of Ivanovo and 63km south-east of Kostroma. It's a regular stop on Volga cruises, but you can also get here by bus from Ivanovo or Kostroma, and – best – in summer by hydrofoil from Kostroma or Yaroslavl (see those cities' Getting There & Away sections).

Though fortified from the 15th century and later a Volga trade centre, Pylos' renown today stems from its late 19th century role as an artists' retreat. Isaak Levitan, possibly the greatest Russian landscape artist, found inspiration here in the summers of 1888-90. The playwright Chekhov commented that Plyos 'put a smile in Levitan's paintings'.

Walk along the riverfront and take in the lovely views from the hill topped by the simple **Assumption Cathedral** (Uspensky sobor), which stands within the ramparts of the old fort. The **Levitan House Museum** (Dom-Muzey Levitana) in the eastern part of the town, across the small Shokhonka River, displays work of other artists who visited Plyos, as well as works by Levitan. It's open from 10 am to 5 pm daily except Monday; admission is $0.40.

KOSTROMA
КОСТРОМА

☎ 0942 • pop 300,000

Though founded in the 1150s and once one of the Golden Ring's most important cultural and commercial centres, Kostroma *(ka-stra-MA)*, on the Volga River 95km north of Ivanovo, now looks like it came from somewhere else. In 1773 a fire destroyed everything wooden, and the centre was rebuilt all at once, in uninspiring Russian classical style.

But the town's pride is the Monastery of St Ipaty (Ipatevsky monastyr), founded in 1332 by a Tatar ancestor of Boris Godunov and later patronised – like Kostroma in general – by the Romanov dynasty. The frescoes in its beautiful cathedral are by a school of 17th century Kostroma painters, headed by Gury Nikitin, whose work can be seen all over the Golden Ring.

Orientation

The main part of the town lies along the north bank of the Volga, with the bus and train stations out in the east end of town and the St Ipaty Monastery to the west, across Kostroma River, a Volga tributary. The central square is ploshchad Susaninskaya.

Information

You can change money at Gazprombank, ulitsa Sovietskaya 9a, from 9.30 am to 1 pm on weekdays. Cross the street from Hotel Stary Dvor and go through one of the archways. The post and telephone office is at ulitsa Sovietskaya 6, 500m east of the centre; the telephone office is open from 9 am to 8 pm daily.

Monastery of St Ipaty

The monastery's history is closely tied to the Godunov and Romanov families, fierce rivals in high-level power games before the Romanovs established their 300-year dynasty in the 17th century. The Godunovs, descended from a 14th century Tatar chief who converted to Christianity, built the monastery's **Trinity Cathedral** (Troitsky sobor) – first a wooden one, then the present white-stone building with gold domes in 1590. Inside are over 80 old frescoes by Kostroma painters (plus some 20th century additions) and a gorgeous iconostasis of gold and carved wood.

In 1600 Boris Godunov, the only member of his family to become tsar, exiled to this monastery the head of the Romanov family, Fyodor, along with other Romanovs, including Fyodor's son Mikhail. Mikhail Romanov was in Kostroma when he was

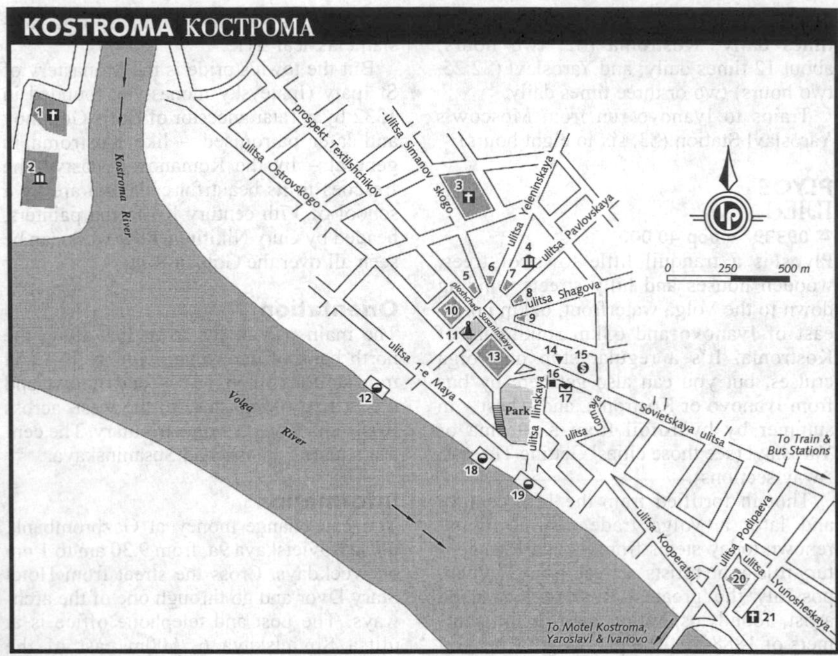

elected tsar in 1613, at the end of the Time of Troubles, and in honour of the event all his Romanov successors made a point of coming here to visit the monastery's red **Romanov Chambers** (Palaty Romanova), opposite the cathedral.

The monastery is open from 9 am to 5 pm daily from May to October, otherwise from 10 am and closed Friday. Entrance costs $1. It's 2.5km west of the town centre. Take bus No 14 from the central ploshchad Susaninskaya and get off once you cross the river, you'll see the monastery to your right.

Museum of Wooden Architecture

A group of garishly painted wooden houses behind the monastery have nothing at all to do with traditional architecture but were a set for the Russian-Italian film *Black Eyes*. But beyond them is an attractive outdoor **museum** of northern-style wooden buildings (Muzey derevyannogo zodchestva), including peasant houses, churches (one built without nails) and a windmill. The museum has the same opening hours as the monastery. Entrance here costs $0.40.

Town Centre

Ploshchad Susaninskaya was built as an ensemble under Catherine the Great's patronage after the 1773 fire and looks like a movie set. Clockwise around the northern side are: a 19th century **fire tower** (still in use, and under UNESCO protection) with a little museum on fire-fighting; a former military **jail**, an 18th century **hotel** for members of the royal family; the **palace** of an 1812 war hero, now a courthouse; and the **town hall**.

In the streets between are many merchants' town houses. Ulitsa Pavlovskaya 5 and 7 – now part of the **Art Museum** (Khudozhestvenny muzey) – were originally built in 1913 as a museum of the Romanov family, to celebrate 300 years of their rule.

KOSTROMA КОСТРОМА

PLACES TO STAY & EAT

14 Pizza Cafe
Кафе Пицца

16 Hotel Stary Dvor
Гостиница Старый Двор

20 Hotel Volga
Гостиница Волга

OTHER

1 Monastery of St Ipaty
Ипатьевский монастырь

2 Museum of Wooden Architecture
Музей деревянного зодчества

3 Monastery of the Epiphany
Богоявленско-Анастасьинский монастырь

4 Art Museum
Художественный музей

5 Fire Tower
Пожарная каланча

6 Former Military Jail
Здание бывшей гауптвахты

7 Former Hotel
Бывшая гостиница

8 Courthouse
Суд

9 Town Hall
Городская дума

10 Trading Arcades & Market
Торговые ряды и рынок

11 Susanin Monument
Памятник Сусанину

12 Pier No 1
Причал 1

13 Trading Arcades
Торговые ряды

15 Gazprombank
Газпромбанк

17 Post & Telephone Office
Почтамт и переговорный пункт

18 Pier No 2
Причал 2

19 Pier Nos 3 & 4
Причалы 3 и 4

21 Church of the Resurrection
Церковь Воскресения

The modern collection is mainly of 16th to 19th century Russian art; it's open from 10 am to 5 pm daily except Monday and Friday. Entrance costs $2 and tours in English and German can be arranged.

On the southern side of ploshchad Susaninskaya are attractive, 18th to 19th century pillared **Trading Arcades**, now housing several art and antique shops, and a food market. The **monument** in the park between the arcades is to local hero Ivan Susanin, who guided a Polish detachment hunting for Mikhail Romanov to their deaths – and his own – in a swamp.

Churches

The main functioning church in Kostroma is in the **Monastery of the Epiphany** (Bogoyavlensko-Anastasinsky monastyr) at ulitsa Simanovskogo 26. The large **cathedral** in this 14th to 19th century complex has been recently and brightly restored and is in full working order. Restoration continues on the surrounding monastery buildings.

The 17th century **Church of the Resurrection** (Tserkov Voskresenia) near Hotel Volga, with bright patterned exterior decoration, was partly financed with a load of gold coins mistakenly shipped from London.

Places to Stay

The only centrally located hotel is ***Hotel Stary Dvor*** *(☎ 31 60 39, ulitsa Sovietskaya 6)*. Dark and stuffy doubles with bathroom cost around $16. For $6 very basic rooms with facilities down the hall and a downstairs shower are available, but the latter is best avoided.

Buses approaching Kostroma from Yaroslavl or Ivanovo pass the next two hotels, and drivers may be willing to drop you off, saving you a trek back into town from the bus station.

Hotel Volga *(☎ 54 60 62, fax 54 62 62, ulitsa Yunosheskaya 1)* is 2km east of the centre just off ulitsa Podlipaeva, near the Volga bridge. The average rooms are adequately clean with private bathroom, at $15/25 for singles/doubles, including breakfast. The Volga views from the front rooms are a plus. Any city bus between the bus or train stations and the town centre (see Getting Around) will stop on the corner of ulitsa Sovietskaya and ulitsa Podlipaeva near the hotel.

The best hotel in town is the Intourist-run ***Motel Kostroma*** *(☎ 53 36 61, fax 53 23 01, Magistralnaya ulitsa 40)*, about 2km south of the Volga bridge on the road to Yaroslavl and Ivanovo. Very clean rooms at this modern place cost $30/40. There are more expensive bungalows, and a sauna too. Trolleybus No 1 runs from the train station via ulitsa Podlipaeva in front of Hotel Volga. There you have to switch to bus No 10 and ask the driver to stop at 'Motel'.

Places to Eat

Hotel Volga's ***Restoran Rus*** is reasonably good, but expensive at around $10. The ***Motel Kostroma*** has a decent restaurant that also has meals from around $10. There are several ***cafes*** along ulitsa Sovietskaya east of ploshchad Susaninskaya, but otherwise not much else. All the restaurants are Soviet style, with smells dating from that era. You can try the local variety of pizza for $1 at ***Pizza Cafe*** *(ulitsa Sovietskaya 9)*. It's open until 9.30 pm.

Getting There & Away

Train The train station is 4km east of ploshchad Susaninskaya. There are three or four daily suburban trains to/from Yaroslavl ($1.50, three hours), an overnight *skoryy* (fast) train to/from Moscow's Savyolov Station ($6, 8½ hours, daily) and a daily train to/from Khabarovsk in the Russian Far East, but there are no services to/from Ivanovo or Vladimir.

Bus The bus station is 4.5km east of ploshchad Susaninskaya on Kineshemskoe shosse, the continuation of ulitsa Sovietskaya. It has a useful advance booking window (kassa predvaritelnoy prodazhi biletov).

There are buses to/from Moscow (8½ hours, six daily), Yaroslavl (two hours, eight daily), Ivanovo (two hours, eight daily), Vladimir (5½ hours, daily) via Suzdal (4¼ hours) and Vologda (seven hours, daily). Tickets cost from $1 to $6.

Boat If you're coming from Yaroslavl in summer, the best way to get to Kostroma is by hydrofoil. Hydrofoils run twice a day. Tickets are $1 and sold 30 minutes before the scheduled time at the river station. The hydrofoils depart from Pier (Prichal) No 2 to Yaroslavl (1½ hours) and downstream to Plyos (1¼ hours). A trip by hydrofoil to Nizhni Novgorod takes eight hours with one switch along the way. Timetables are posted at the pier.

Long-distance river boats between Moscow and points down the Volga as far as Astrakhan also call at Kostroma (Pier No 3 or 4). You can get tickets ($25) on the boat.

Getting Around

Bus Nos 1, 2, 9, 9 Expres, 14K, 19 and others run between the bus station and the central ploshchad Susaninskaya, along the full length of ulitsa Sovietskaya. Trolleybus No 2 runs between the train station and ploshchad Susaninskaya.

YAROSLAVL
ЯРОСЛАВЛЬ

☎ 0852 • pop 680,000

Yaroslavl *(yee-ra-SLAV-l)*, on the Volga 250km north-east of Moscow and 70km west of Kostroma, has wide, orderly, tree-lined streets and a fascinating old heart. Being the biggest place between Moscow and Arkhangelsk, it has a much more metropolitan feel than anywhere else in the Golden Ring – yet is still a pleasantly quiet and relaxed city.

In 1010, the Kyivan prince Yaroslav the Wise took an interest in a trading post where the Kotorosl River enters the Volga. According to legend, the locals responded by setting a sacred bear on him. Yaroslav killed the bear with his axe and founded a town on the spot, putting both the bear and his weapon on its coat of arms.

Yaroslavl was the centre of an independent principality by the time the Tatars came. Developed in the 16th and 17th centuries as the Volga's first port, it grew into Russia's second-biggest city of the time, fat on trade with the Middle East and Europe.

Rich merchants competed to build churches bigger than Moscow's, with bright decoration and frescoes on contemporary themes. Though the city's pride is the Monastery of the Transfiguration of the Saviour, the merchant churches are what's special here.

Orientation

The old part of town and the modern centre are roughly between the Volga and the Pervomayskaya ulitsa inner ring road. Inside, streets radiate from Sovietskaya ploshchad to three other squares on the ring: Bogoyavlenskaya ploshchad (formerly ploshchad Podbelskogo – some old signs remain) with the landmark Transfiguration

Monastery; ploshchad Volkova with the large, 19th century classical facade of the Volkov Theatre; and Krasnaya ploshchad near the river station. Maps are readily available; see Shopping for a good source.

Information

You can change money at the Yarinterbank (☎ 32 91 07) at ulitsa Kirova 14, open from 10 am to 5 pm daily (closed Sunday). Menatep, ulitsa Svobody 28/86, changes money and gives credit card advances.

The main post and telephone office is at ulitsa Komsomolskaya 22 on Bogoyavlenskaya ploshchad (opposite the Transfiguration Monastery). It's open from 8 am to 8 pm daily (until 6 pm Sunday).

Monastery & Around

The white walls and towers of the **Monastery of the Transfiguration of the Saviour** (Spaso-Preobrazhensky monastyr) front Bogoyavlenskaya ploshchad. Founded in the 12th century, this was one of Russia's richest and best fortified monasteries by the 16th century.

The oldest surviving structures, dating from 1516 but heavily altered since then, are the **Holy Gate** (Svyatye vorota) on the river side – where the modern entrance is – and the central **Cathedral of the Transfiguration** (Preobrazhensky sobor), which is under restoration.

Entry to the grounds is free but there are charges for a number of museums and exhibitions within. The best of these, costing $0.50, is devoted to old icons and crafts (Drevnerusskoe i narodno-prikladnoe iskusstvo). The most exciting thing to do here is climb the **bell tower** (zvonnitsa) for a panorama of the city and a close-up view of the amazing spiked gold bulbs that top some of the monastery buildings. The grounds are open from 8 am to 7.30 pm daily, and the museums from 10 am to 5 pm.

Also off Bogoyavlenskaya ploshchad is the vaulted, red-brick 17th century **Church of the Epiphany** (Tserkov Bogoyavlenia). It has bright exterior ceramic tiles (a Yaroslavl speciality) and a carved iconostasis; it's open from 10 am to 5 pm daily except Tuesday ($0.40). The square's central **statue** of Yaroslav the Wise (Pamyatnik Yaroslavu Mudromu) was unveiled in 1993 by President Yeltsin of Russia and President Kravchuk of Ukraine.

TAMSIN WILSON

Church of the Epiphany, Yaroslavl

Along Pervomayskaya ulitsa, past the 19th century **Trading Arcades** (Gostiny Dvor), is the **Znamenskaya Watchtower** (Znamenskaya bashnya), built in 1658 on what was then the edge of the city.

Church of Elijah the Prophet

This church (Tserkov Ilyi Proroka), on Sovietskaya ploshchad in the centre of the old town, has some of the Golden Ring's brightest **frescoes**, by the ubiquitous Gury Nikitin of Kostroma and his school. Dating, like the church, from the 17th century, they depict religious and secular scenes in realistic style.

Closed from October to April and during wet spells, the church is otherwise open from 10 am to 1 pm and 2 to 6 pm daily. Entry is $1.25.

River Embankments

The Volga and Kotorosl embankments from the Church of Elijah the Prophet back to the Transfiguration Monastery make an

enjoyable 1.5km walk. A pedestrian promenade runs along the bank of the Volga below the level of the street, Volzhskaya naberezhnaya.

From the Church of Elijah the Prophet, head towards the river on Narodny pereulok. Here, the **Church of St Nicholas the Miracle-Worker** (Tserkov Nikoly Nadeina) was the first of Yaroslavl's stone merchant churches, built in 1622. It has a sparkling baroque iconostasis and frescoes showing the life and works of this St Nicholas, who's highly popular among Russians. It's open as a museum from 10 am to 5 pm daily, except Thursday and Friday. Entrance costs $0.35.

Just south at Volzhskaya naberezhnaya 23, facing the Volga, is the old Governor's Mansion that now houses the **Yaroslavl Art Museum** (Yaroslavsky Khudozhestvenny Muzey), with 18th to 20th century Russian art. It's open from 10 am to 6 pm daily except Monday and tickets cost $1.25. The Governor's Gardens behind the house cost $0.10 to enjoy. The **House of Matveev** (Dom Matveeva) on Sovietsky pereulok, built in the late 18th century, is one of several merchants' town houses still standing

YAROSLAVL ЯРОСЛАВЛЬ

PLACES TO STAY
10 Hotel Volga
Гостиница Волга
21 Hotel Yuta
Гостиница Юта
26 Hotel Yubileynaya
Гостиница Юбилейная

PLACES TO EAT
2 Kafe Lira
Кафе Лира
6 Café Premyera
Кафе Премьера
8 Restaurant/Café Rus
Ресторан и кафе Русь

OTHER
1 River Station
Речной вокзал
3 Church of the Nativity
Церковь Рождества Христова
4 Church of St Nicholas the Miracle-Worker
Церковь Николы Надеина
5 Yaroslavl Art Museum
Ярославский художественный музей
7 Yarinterbank
Яринтербанк
9 Rospechat
Магазин Роспечать
11 Church of Elijah the Prophet
Церковь Ильи Пророка
12 House of Matveev
Дом Матвеева
13 Volga Bastion
Волжская башня
14 Art Museum (Former Metropolitan's Palace)
Художественный музей (бывшие митрополичьи палаты)
15 Founding of Yaroslavl Monument
Памятник основанию Ярославля
16 Church of the Saviour-in-the-Town
Церковь Спаса-на-Городу
17 Church of the Archangel Michael
Церковь Михаила Архангела
18 Russian Flax
Магазин Русский Лён
19 Trading Arcades
Торговые ряды
20 Znamenskaya Watchtower
Знаменская башня
22 Post & Telephone Office
Почтамт и переговорный пункт
23 Yaroslav the Wise Statue
Памятник Ярославу Мудрому
24 Monastery of the Transfiguration of the Saviour
Спасо-Преображенский монастырь
25 Church of the Epiphany
Церковь Богоявления
27 Tram Terminal
Трамвайное кольцо

in the blocks near the embankment. A little farther along the embankment are the **Volga Bastion** (Volzhskaya bashnya), built as a watchtower in the 1660s, a fine early 19th century church, and the 17th century former Metropolitan's Chambers (Mitropolyichyi Palaty) housing the old Yaroslavl art section of the **Art Museum**, with icons and other work from the 13th to 19th centuries. The museum is open from 10 am to 5.30 pm daily except Friday; admission is $1.25.

In the leafy park behind the museum is a stone-slab **monument** marking the spot where Yaroslav founded the city in 1010. The park stretches right out onto the tip of land between the Volga and the Kotorosl. Above the Kotorosl you can discern raised embankments indicating the site of Yaroslavl's old kremlin. Also along here are three more 17th century **churches**.

South of the Kotorosl

Two 17th century churches south of the Kotorosl River are well worth searching out. In the settlement of Korovniki, picturesquely placed on the south side of the mouth of the Kotorosl, is the summer **Church of St John Chrysostom** (Tserkov Ioanna Zlatousta), an elegant conglomeration of domes, brick towers and dazzling tilework. Next to it are a winter church, and a bell tower called 'the Candle of Yaroslavl'. Take bus No 4 from Bogoyavlenskaya ploshchad for two stops, get off at Mukomolny pereulok and go along the street towards the Volga, or walk across the Kotorosl on Moskovsky prospekt and then head left for about 1.5km. The churches are under restoration but staff will let you in.

Also south of the Kotorosl is the unique, 15-domed **Church of St John the Baptist** (Tserkov Ioanna Predtechi), with intricate brick and tilework. Take tram No 3 west along Bolshaya Oktyabrskaya ulitsa to the third stop, then walk 1km south down prospekt Tolbukhina and across the bridge; the church is on the right, near the river.

River Trips

Summer services from the river station on the Volga at the north end of Pervomayskaya ulitsa include a range of slow *prigorodny* (suburban) boats to local destinations like

Nekrasovskoe (halfway to Kostroma, 2½ hours) and Konstantinovo (2¼ hours upstream), with lots of stops. The best trip is to Tolga, 35 minutes from Yaroslavl on the Konstantinovo route ($0.50), which has a convent with lovely 17th century buildings near the river. The last boat back from Tolga is at 9.30 pm. You can also get there on bus No 21 from Krasnaya ploshchad ($0.10).

Konstantinovo boats only go two or three times daily, however; the hourly service to Dolmatovo (25 minutes) might make a more convenient quick cruise. For longer-distance sailings, see Getting There & Away later in this section.

Places to Stay

Hotel Yuta *(☎ 21 87 93, fax 32 97 86, Respublikanskaya ulitsa 79)* has decent singles/doubles for $16/20 with private bathroom, TV and phone. The hotel has a bar done in tinted mirrors with snacks from around $1 to $2.

Hotel Volga *(☎ 22 91 31, ulitsa Kirova 10)* was built in the early 20th century and originally called 'Bristol'. It is located at the very centre on a small pedestrian street and has an elegant staircase and furnishings. Nicely done rooms with bathroom, TV, phone and refrigerator cost $20/30. There are also cheaper rooms with shared bath.

The more conventional ***Hotel Yubileynaya*** *(☎ 22 41 59, Kotoroslnaya naberezhnaya 11A)* overlooks the Kotorosl River close to the Transfiguration Monastery. It's the usual concrete slab building, but rooms are comfortable and cost $35/60. There's a restaurant and a bar.

Places to Eat

The cheapest and most unpretentious place to eat in town is ***Café Rus*** near Hotel Volga. It's a unique blend of a Soviet eatery with potted plants and a parrot in a cage and a posh restaurant with heavy wooden furniture and a fireplace. The prices lean towards the Soviet eatery: bliny cost only about $0.10 – cheap even by Russian standards. You have to pay first, then pass the receipt to the grumbling serving lady by the counter. It's open from 8 am to 8 pm.

McDonald's *(ulitsa Svobody 59)* is open from 8 am to 11 pm. Across the road, the nautical theme restaurant ***Pod Parusami*** *(Under the Sail; ulitsa Svobody 36)* is open from 11 am to midnight and nothing on the menu is over $2. ***Kafe Lira*** *(Volzhskaya naberezhnaya 43)* is popular with young folk and serves salads and more for under $2. It's open until 11 pm daily.

Another good eating place is the ***Café Premyera*** at ulitsa Pervomayskaya. It's in a new building in the small park in the middle of the street right behind the Volkov Theatre. Main courses of decent Russian fare average under $3, and half-litres of Baltika beer go for $0.75. The place is quite popular with young families and visiting Americans.

For a more stylish place, try ***Rus*** *(ulitsa Kirova 10)*, which is the upmarket cousin of the one with the parrot. It's located on the 2nd floor of the elegant art nouveau building and is open until midnight. The dining room is spacious, light and pleasant; a dinner of carefully prepared fresh fish can easily top $20.

Shopping

Rospechat at ulitsa Kirova 10 has a good supply of city maps, travel guides and inexpensive souvenirs. You can find pure linen table cloths, napkins and bedclothes at Russian Flax, ulitsa Pervomayskaya 51 between Bogoyavlenkaya ploshchad and ploschad Volkova. Most stores in Yaroslavl are closed Sunday.

Getting There & Away

Train The main station is Yaroslavl Glavny, 3km west of the centre along ulitsa Svobody. If your train coming into Yaroslavl happens to stop at the lesser Yaroslavl Moskovsky station, 2km south of the Kotorosl River on Moskovsky prospekt, there's no harm getting off there, since transport to the centre is no more difficult.

Around 20 trains a day run between here and Moscow's Yaroslavl Station, a trip of about five hours ($2), but most are travelling to or from places far to the north (like Arkhangelsk) or east (Yekaterinburg,

Novosibirsk, Vladivostok, Beijing in China). It may be easiest to get tickets on trains that terminate at Yaroslavl.

If you want to head on past the Ural Mountains from the Golden Ring, Yaroslavl is the place to start from. There's also daily service to/from St Petersburg and Nizhny Novgorod. For closer destinations, it's easiest to get suburban trains. For Rostov-Veliky (two hours), take any suburban train to Rostov itself, Beklemishevo or Alexandrov (about eight to 12 daily). Three or four suburban trains run daily to Kostroma (three hours).

Bus The bus station is 2km south of the Kotorosl River on Moskovsky prospekt, beside the Yaroslavl Moskovsky train station. There are one or two buses daily to/from Moscow's Shchyolkovsky bus station ($6, six hours), plus about five buses stopping in transit. Most of these stop at Pereslavl-Zalessky and Sergiev Posad. Other departures include:

Ivanovo
  $2, two hours, two daily
Kostroma
  $1.50, two hours, 10 to 11 daily
Pereslavl-Zalessky
  $2, three hours, three to four daily
Rostov-Veliky
  $0.80, 1½ hours, seven daily
Uglich
  $3.50, 4½ hours, daily
Vladimir
  $5, six hours, one or two daily
Vologda
  $6.50, five hours, two to three daily in transit

Boat In summer from the river station at the northern end of Pervomayskaya ulitsa, there's a range of passenger services on the Volga to places as distant as Astrakhan. Timetables are posted at the river station, which also has an information window.

The hydrofoils to downstream destinations will take you to Kostroma ($1, 1½ hours, two daily). Most also go to Plyos (three hours). Tickets go on sale about 30 minutes before departure.

From about early June to early October, long-distance Volga passenger ships stop every couple of days in Yaroslavl on their way between Moscow ($20, 1½ days) and cities like Nizhny Novgorod, Kazan and Astrakhan. The ships are rarely full and tickets are normally available at short notice. See the Getting There & Away section of the Moscow chapter for more details.

Getting Around

Tram No 3 goes along Bolshaya Oktyabrskaya ulitsa to the tram terminus a short walk west of Bogoyavlenskaya ploshchad (from Yaroslavl Glavny station, head 200m to the right for the stop on ulitsa Ukhtomskogo). Trolleybus No 1 runs between the station and ploshchad Volkova and Krasnaya ploshchad: you can get off at the Ploshchad Yunosti stop for the Yuta hotel.

From the bus station and Yaroslavl Moskovsky train station, trolleybus No 5 or 9 from the far side of the main road outside will get you to Bogoyavlenskaya ploshchad; No 5 goes on to Krasnaya ploshchad.

City buses, trains and trolley buses cost $0.05 per ride.

ROSTOV-VELIKY РОСТОВ-ВЕЛИКИЙ

☎ 08536 • pop 40,000

Also called Rostov-Yaroslavsky, this town *(rah-STOV vi-LEEK-i)* is one of Russia's oldest, first chronicled in 862. Today it's a sleepy, rustic little place, 57km towards Moscow from Yaroslavl, with some magnificent old buildings magically sited by a shimmering lake. Much less tourist-oriented than Suzdal (the most comparable place in the Golden Ring), Rostov lets you feel you're discovering it for yourself. And you can stay right in among those wonderful old buildings.

Perhaps to flatter its home-grown aristocracy, Yury Dolgoruky called Rostov *Veliky* (Great) in the 12th century, while making Suzdal the capital of his Rostov-Suzdal principality. By the early 13th century, the Rostov region had split first from Suzdal and then into smaller pieces. The Tatars didn't leave much of it standing, and in the late 1600s an ambitious Orthodox Metropolitan, Iona Sysoevich, cleared almost

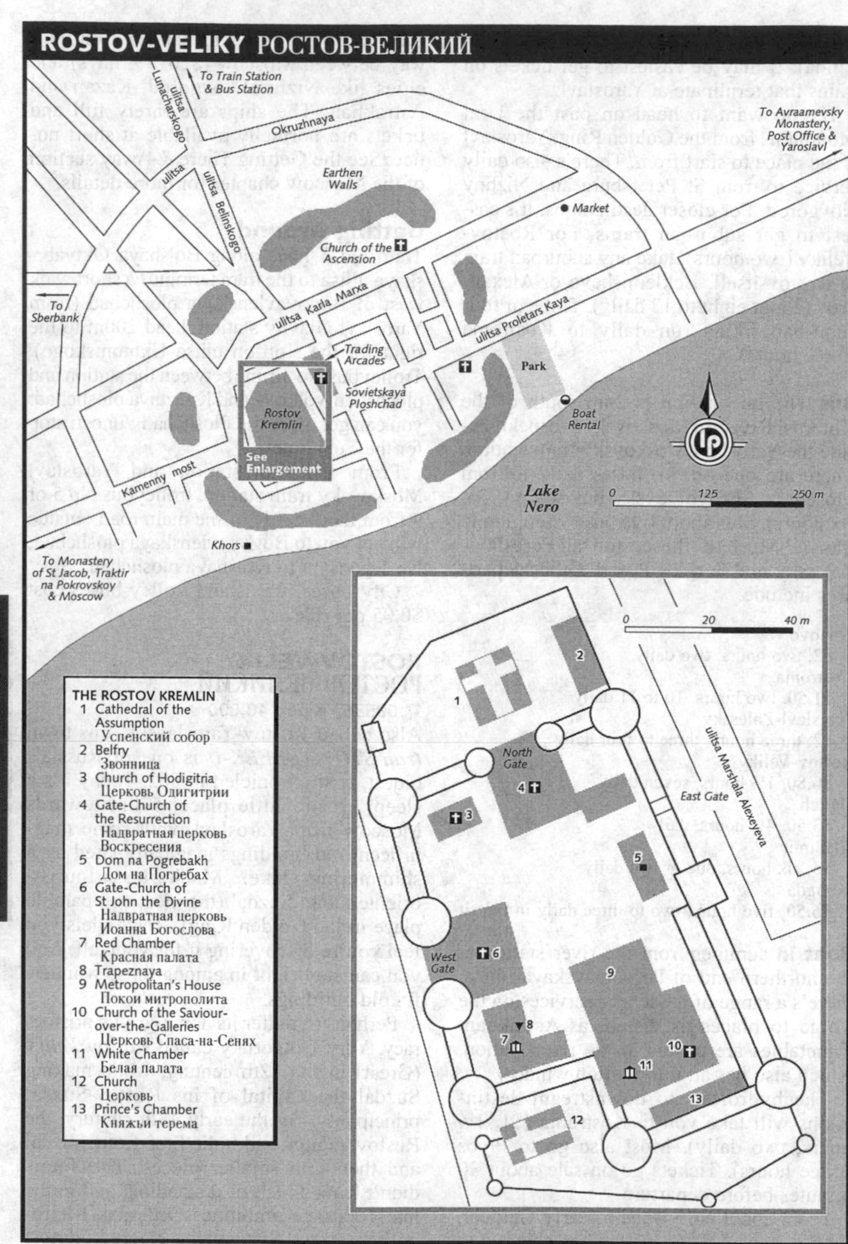
ROSTOV-VELIKY РОСТОВ-ВЕЛИКИЙ
To Train Station & Bus Station
ulitsa Lunacharskogo
Okruzhnaya
To Avraamevsky Monastery, Post Office & Yaroslavl
ulitsa
ulitsa Belinskogo
Earthen Walls
Market
Church of the Ascension
To Sberbank
ulitsa Karla Marxa
ulitsa Proletars Kaya
Trading Arcades
Park
Sovietskaya Ploshchad
Rostov Kremlin
Boat Rental
See Enlargement
Kamenny most
Lake Nero
0 125 250 m
Khors
To Monastery of St Jacob, Traktir na Pokrovskoy & Moscow
0 20 40 m
THE ROSTOV KREMLIN
1 Cathedral of the Assumption Успенский собор
2 Belfry Звонница
3 Church of Hodigitria Церковь Одигитрии
4 Gate-Church of the Resurrection Надвратная церковь Воскресения
5 Dom na Pogrebakh Дом на Погребах
6 Gate-Church of St John the Divine Надвратная церковь Иоанна Богослова
7 Red Chamber Красная палата
8 Trapeznaya
9 Metropolitan's House Покои митрополита
10 Church of the Saviour-over-the-Galleries Церковь Спаса-на-Сенях
11 White Chamber Белая палата
12 Church Церковь
13 Prince's Chamber Княжьи терема
North Gate
East Gate
West Gate
ulitsa Marshala Alexeyeva
AROUND MOSCOW

everything else away for a wonderful private kremlin on the shore of Lake Nero.

On the highway in from the south, look out for fairy-tale views across the lake to the kremlin and the Monastery of St Jacob.

Orientation & Information

The train and bus stations are together in the drab modern part of Rostov, 1.5km north of the kremlin. Nearer the kremlin, the town consists mostly of izbas, trees and empty grassy spaces, nearly enabling you to forget about the 20th century altogether. There's a small market along ulitsa Karla Marxa.

You can change money at Sberbank, Sobornaya ploshchad 2, open from 8.30 am to 4.30 pm Monday to Friday. The main post and telephone office at ulitsa Severnaya 44 is open for calls 24 hours daily. Take bus No 1 or 2 east from the kremlin.

Cathedral of the Assumption

The cathedral (Uspensky sobor) and its belfry dominate the kremlin, though they're actually outside its north wall. The cathedral, with its five magnificent onion domes, was here a century before the kremlin. The **belfry** (zvonnitsa), added in the 1680s, was famous even outside Russia; the French composer Hector Berlioz came to listen to its 13 bells. The biggest, the 32 tonne Sysoi bell, is rung only on church festivals.

Outside service hours, you can get to the cathedral through the door in the church shop at ulitsa Karla Marxa, open from 9 am to 5 pm daily. The cathedral is currently under restoration but services are held here.

Kremlin

Nearly all the kremlin buildings date from the 1670s and 1680s, Metropolitan Iona's time. The west gate and north gate (through which you can't pass) are both straddled by **gate-churches** (Tserkov Voskresenia and Tserkov Ioanna Bogoslova), rich with 17th century frescoes that you can view from May to October. Between them, the **Church of Hodigitria** (Tserkov Odigitrii) looks like it's been wallpapered on the outside. Inside is an exhibition of Orthodox Church vestments and paraphernalia.

The metropolitan's private chapel, the **Church of the Saviour-over-the-Galleries** (Tserkov Spasa-na-Senyakh), in the south-eastern corner of the kremlin, behind the **metropolitan's house** (Pokoy mitropolita or Samuilov korpus), has the most beautiful interior of all, absolutely covered in colourful 17th century frescoes. The huge **White Chamber** (Belaya palata) next door was once the kremlin's dining hall; the **Red Chamber** (Krasnaya palata), with the massive porch, was its guesthouse.

The metropolitan's house and the White Chamber both have **museums** accessed by the stairs at the rear (south) side of the White Chamber. The one in the metropolitan's house has icons, paintings and a collection of Rostov's own speciality, the luminous painted enamelware called *finift*. The one in the White Chamber, known as the otkritye fondy, displays Rostov-area glass, ceramics and furniture.

The kremlin ticket office is in the west gate: foreigners entry to the grounds is $0.15, plus $0.15 each for any of the churches or exhibitions that you want to see inside (a list of these is posted at the ticket office) or the walkway around the walls *(stenam)*. Official opening hours are from 10 am to 5 pm, but you can enter the kremlin grounds any time by the east gate, which is kept open.

Monasteries & Other Buildings

Two monasteries flank the kremlin on the lake shore. Two kilometres west (and visible like an apparition on the southern approach to Rostov) is the **Monastery of St Jacob** (Spaso-Yakovlevsky monastyr). It's under restoration but, having been returned to the Church in 1993, has a small community of monks. Its magnificent 19th century **cathedral** is worth seeing as you'd never expect to find such architectural splendour on the outskirts of a tiny town. Take bus No 1 or 2 west from the kremlin to the end of the line.

A similar distance east by bus No 1 is the dilapidated **Avraamevsky Monastery**, whose **Cathedral of the Epiphany** (Bogoyavlensky sobor), built in 1553, is probably Rostov's oldest building.

The streets around the kremlin contain several more old churches, as well as the fruit of a secular building program in the late 18th and early 19th centuries. The **Trading Arcades** (Gostiny Dvor), built in 1830, surround a 17th century **church**; there's another **church** of similar age on Sovietskaya ploshchad. The **Church of the Ascension** (Voznesenskaya tserkov) on ulitsa Karla Marxa dates from the 16th century.

Boating

The best view of the kremlin is from the lake. You can hire a row boat by the park east of the centre.

Places to Stay & Eat

A place worth seeing is the private museum and B&B ***Khors*** *(☎/fax 3 24 83, ulitsa Podozerka 30)*, named after a pagan sun god. Walk towards the lake as you exit the monastery and look for a two-storey wooden house with a garden. The museum has some household items of the last century, models of wooden churches and paintings by local artists. It's open from noon to 10 pm (free). If the door happens to be locked, knock at the house to the left. There are two very tiny but clean rooms with shower and kitchen, costing $6 and $12.

The ***Dom na Pogrebakh*** *(☎ 3 12 44)*, right inside the kremlin, is among the most atmospheric places to stay in Russia. The clean, wood-panelled rooms cost from $4 to $12, though they vary somewhat in size and view. All share clean toilets and showers.

The hotel has the ***Bufet Pogrebok***, with drinks and cakes. The ***Trapeznaya*** restaurant is also inside the kremlin to the left of the hotel. You can have a two course meal for about $3. It's open from 8 am to 8 pm. Slightly more expensive is the ***Traktir na Pokrovskoy***, down ulitsa Pokrovskaya, three blocks west of the kremlin. If you are not put off by the astonishing floral interior, a meal will cost around $5.

Getting There & Away

To/From Yaroslavl There are several suburban trains each way daily, taking two hours. Buses from Rostov to Yaroslavl go roughly every hour. These include direct ones and those stopping at Rostov in transit to Yaroslavl; any available tickets are sold when the bus arrives. The bus trip from Yaroslavl is $1.

To/From Pereslavl-Zalessky, Sergiev Posad, Uglich & Moscow By train to/from Moscow's Yaroslavl Station, you can either try for a ticket on one of the long-distance trains stopping at Rostov ($2, four hours, six daily), or go by suburban train, changing trains halfway at Alexandrov, which takes about five hours. Between Alexandrov and Rostov there are three daily trains each way.

There are transit buses to and from Moscow's Shchyolkovsky bus station, taking four to five hours, which also stop at Pereslavl-Zalessky and Sergiev Posad ($3, four to five hours, three daily). There are also three or four in-transit buses just to Pereslavl-Zalessky ($1.50, two hours) and two to Uglich ($3, three hours).

Getting Around

Rostov is a pleasant place to walk around, but bus No 6 runs between the train station and the centre if you need to save time.

UGLICH
УГЛИЧ

An old-fashioned but shabby town on the Volga 90km north-west of Rostov-Veliky, Uglich can be reached by bus from Rostov or Yaroslavl, though most tourists come to it as a stop on Volga cruises. Locals hawk Uglich-made watches to cruise passengers.

It was here that Ivan the Terrible's son Dmitry – later to be impersonated by the string of False Dmitrys in the Time of Troubles – was murdered in 1591, probably on Boris Godunov's orders.

Within the waterside kremlin, the red **Church of St Dmitry on the Blood** (Tserkov Dmitria-na-krovi), with its cluster of spangled blue domes, was built in the 1690s on the spot where the body was found. Also in the kremlin, but open erratically, are the five-domed **Transfiguration Cathedral** (Preobrazhensky sobor) and the 15th century

Prince's Chambers (Knyazhyi palaty), with turrets added in the 19th century, housing a craft exhibition (open from 10 am to 6 pm daily, closed Monday).

Opposite each other, along ulitsa Karla Marxa from the kremlin, are two other fine buildings from the 1690s: the **Church of the Nativity of John the Baptist** (Tserkov Rozhdestva Ioanna Predtechi), similar to the Church of St Dmitry on the Blood; and the large but badly dilapidated **Monastery of the Resurrection** (Voskresensky monastyr).

PERESLAVL-ZALESSKY ПЕРЕСЛАВЛЬ-ЗАЛЕССКИЙ

☎ 08535 • pop 45,000

On the shore of Lake Pleshcheevo almost exactly halfway between Moscow and Yaroslavl, Pereslavl-Zalessky's history and monuments aren't in the Golden Ring's first division, but it's a good place to visit if, like the many Muscovites who have dachas here, you want to soak up the atmosphere of a peaceful old Russian village. The southern half of the town is full of one-storey izbas, with pretty gardens in summer, and narrow dirt lanes.

Pereslavl-Zalessky – 'Pereslavl Beyond the Woods' was made a town in 1152 by Yury Dolgoruky, and Alexander Nevsky was born here. But the present town is a shadow of earlier days, having been sacked five times by the Mongol Tatars and stormed frequently by neighbouring princes and foreign armies. Its earth walls and the little Cathedral of the Transfiguration are as old as the town.

Lake Pleshcheevo takes credit as one of the birthplaces of the Russian navy, having been one of the places where Peter the Great developed his obsession with the sea, studying navigation and building a flotilla of over 100 little ships by the time he was 20.

Orientation

Pereslavl is pretty much a one-street town, with the bus station at the south-western end, 2km from the centre. Apart from the kremlin area, most of the historic sights are out past the bus station. The ticket office of the Goritsky Monastery sells town maps.

Central Area

The walls of Yury Dolgoruky's **kremlin** are now a grassy ring around the central town. You can walk along the top most of the way round. Inside, the simple **Cathedral of the Transfiguration of the Saviour** (Spaso-Preobrazhensky sobor), started in 1152, is one of the oldest standing buildings in Russia. A bust of Alexander Nevsky stands in front. Across the grassy square, the tent-roofed **Church of Peter the Metropolitan** (Tserkov Petra mitropolita), built in 1585 and renovated in 1957, looks abandoned now. Nearby are twin **churches** built in 1745.

The **Trubezh River** winds 2km from the kremlin to the lake, fringed by trees and narrow lanes. People row their narrow boats up and down until well after dark on summer evenings. You can follow the northern riverbank most of the way to the lake by a combination of paths and streets. Footbridges cross to the south bank. The **Forty Saints' Church** (Sorokosvyatskaya tserkov) sits picturesquely on the south side of the river mouth.

South Pereslavl-Zalessky

The **Goritsky Monastery** (Goritsky monastyr) was founded in the 14th century, though today the oldest buildings are the 17th century gates, gate-church and belfry. From the bus station, walk about 1.2km then turn left and it's up on the hill after 300m. The centrepiece is the baroque **Assumption Cathedral** (Uspensky sobor) with its beautiful carved iconostasis. In the refectory is a museum with icons and incredible carved wooden furnishings (open from 10 am to 5 pm, closed Tuesday and the last Monday of the month). Entrance costs $0.30, and another $0.30 for any of the museums.

Across the highway from Goritsky, the 1785 **Purification Church of Alexander Nevsky** (Tserkov Alexandra Nevskogo-Sretenskogo) is a working church. To the east, on a hillock overlooking fields and dachas, is the **Danilovsky Monastery** (Danilovsky monastyr), whose tent-roofed **Trinity Cathedral** (Troitsky sobor) was built in the 1530s. Another 16th century walled monastery is the **Fyodorovsky Monastery**

(Fyodorovsky monastyr), about 2km south on the Moscow road.

Four kilometres along the road past the Goritsky Monastery, at the south end of the lake, is the small **Botik Museum** (Muzey Botika) with assorted nautical gear and the sailboat *Fortuna*, the only one of Peter the Great's boats (except one in the St Petersburg Naval Museum) to survive fire and neglect. It's open from 10 am to 5 pm (closed Monday); admission is $0.40.

To make up for Pereslavl's lack of a mainline railway, you can reach the Botik on a tiny narrow-gauge train that rattles along its single track from the central ulitsa Kardov-skogo three times daily. The whole trip only takes about 10 minutes, costs $0.10 and is fun. Past the Botik, the train continues round to Kupan, north of the lake.

Places to Stay & Eat

Hotel Pereslavl *(☎ 2 17 88, fax 2 15 59, Rostovskaya ulitsa 7)*, 400m north of the Trubezh River, was built in 1985 but is already falling apart. However, the rooms are all right, costing from $12/17 for singles/doubles with private bathroom. There is quite a pleasant ***restaurant*** downstairs where everything is under $2.

The ***Zebra*** bar next door serves basic Russian food and is open until midnight. A place popular with the locals and Russian tourists is ***Bylina*** *(ulitsa Sovietskay 10a)*, which serves $0.20 bliny until 9 pm daily.

Getting There & Away

Pereslavl has no mainline train station, so if you don't have your own transport you must use buses. Ticket sellers at Pereslavl bus station won't usually sell tickets until shortly before departure, which causes unnecessary queuing.

To/from Moscow's Shchyolkovsky bus station there are buses starting or finishing at Pereslavl ($2, 2½ hours, three daily). There are buses to/from Sergiev Posad ($1, 1¼ hours, three daily) plus others in transit, and Yaroslavl ($2, three hours, two daily), also stopping at Rostov-Veliky (1½ hours). Other buses pass through in transit to Moscow, Yaroslavl and Kostroma.

Getting Around

Bus No 1, often very crowded, runs up and down the main street. Heading into town from the bus station, the stop is about 100m south of the bus station (away from the town centre, towards Moscow); heading out to the bus station from the centre, you can catch it just north of the river.

SERGIEV POSAD
СЕРГИЕВ ПОСАД

☎ 254 • pop 100,000

Sergiev Posad is the town around the Trinity Monastery of St Sergius (Troitse-Sergieva Lavra), one of Russia's most important religious and historical landmarks and a place of spiritual and nationalist pilgrimage. Still often referred to by its Soviet name of Zagorsk, Sergiev Posad is 60km from the edge of Moscow on the Yaroslavl road. If you find you have time for just one trip out of Moscow, this is the obvious choice.

The monastery was founded in about 1340 by Sergius of Radonezh (now patron saint of Russia), a monk with enough moral authority to unite the country against Tatar rule, blessing Dmitry Donskoy's army before it gave the Tatars their first beating in 1380. The monastery's status as defender of the motherland grew during the Time of Troubles; with Moscow occupied by the Poles, it withstood a 16 month siege and then encouraged the uprising that drove the invaders out.

As a *lavra*, or exalted monastery, and the main link in a chain of fort-monasteries defending Moscow, it grew enormously wealthy on the gifts of tsars, nobles and merchants looking for divine support. Closed by the Bolsheviks, it was reopened after WWII as the Zagorsk Historical & Art Museum and the residence of the Patriarch of the Russian Orthodox Church, again becoming a working monastery.

The patriarch, and the administrative centre of the Church, moved to the Danilovsky Monastery in Moscow in 1988, but the Trinity Monastery of St Sergius remains one of Russia's most important monasteries and spiritual sites. For concentrated wealth and artistry, beautiful churches and a sense of the interlocking history of Church and State, it shouldn't be missed. Medieval Russia still seems alive here in the incense, chanting and the armies of pilgrims and supplicants.

Orientation & Information

Prospekt Krasnoy Armii is the main street, running north-south through the town centre. The train and bus stations are on opposite corners of a wide yard to the east of prospekt Krasnoy Armii.

To reach the monastery, leave the yard along 1-ya Rybnaya ulitsa beside the bus station, with the rail tracks behind you, and turn right on prospekt Krasnoy Armii after about 250m. The monastery is about 400m along, on the left.

There are no banks or exchanges so bring enough roubles from Moscow. There's a post and telephone office outside the south-east wall of the monastery at prospekt Krasnoy Armii 127A. Stalls outside the monastery entrance sell all the usual tourist ephemera. The new bus station has remarkably clean toilets in the basement that cost $0.10 unless you're a decorated war hero, in which case you can go to your heart's content for free.

Trinity Monastery of St Sergius

The monastery grounds are open from 10 am to 6 pm daily. Entry to the grounds is free. There are additional charges to visit the museums inside or walk along the walls.

Tours of the grounds and churches (not the museums), given by English-speaking monks, cost $10 for one person, or $8 each for more than one person – ask at the kiosk next to the Gate-Church of John the Baptist (to book a tour phone ☎ 4 53 56).

Devout female visitors always wear headscarves, and all men should remove hats in the churches.

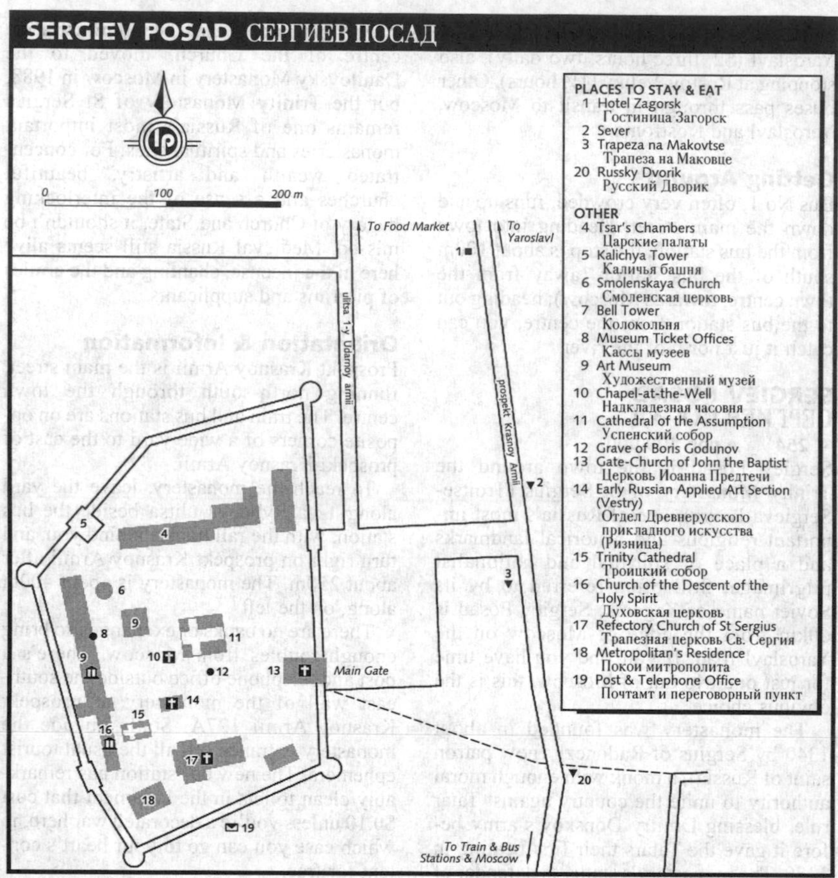

Trinity Cathedral Built in the 1420s, this squat, dark yet beautiful church (Troitsky sobor) is the heart of the Trinity monastery – and in its way the heart of Russian Orthodoxy. A memorial service for St Sergius (whose tomb stands in the south-east corner, with people lining up to light candles in front of it) goes on all day, every day, lit only by oil lamps.

Most of the icons are by the great medieval painter Andrey Rublyov and his disciples, though Rublyov's masterpiece icon of the Old Testament Trinity, to the right of the centre of the iconostasis, is a copy, the original being in Moscow's Tretyakov Gallery.

Cathedral of the Assumption This cathedral (Uspensky Sobor), with its star-spangled domes, was modelled on the cathedral of the same name in the Moscow Kremlin. It was finished in 1585 with money left by Ivan the Terrible in a fit of remorse for killing his son. Services are held here in summer but outside service times you may find it closed.

Outside the west door is the **grave** of Boris Godunov, the only tsar not buried in the Moscow Kremlin or St Petersburg's SS Peter & Paul Cathedral. Nearby, the resplendent **Chapel-at-the-Well** (Nadkladeznaya chasovnya) was built over a spring said to have appeared during the Polish siege.

Refectory Church of St Sergius The huge block with the 'wallpaper' paint job and lavish interior (Trapeznaya tserkov Sv Sergia) was once a dining hall for pilgrims. Now it's the Assumption Cathedral's winter counterpart, with morning services in cold weather. The green building next door is the metropolitan's residence.

Church of the Descent of the Holy Spirit This little 15th century church (Dukhovskaya tserkov), with the bell tower under its dome, is a graceful imitation of Trinity Cathedral. It's used only on special occasions. It contains, among other things, the grave of the first Bishop of Alaska.

Bell Tower This five tier baroque wedding cake took 30 years to build in the 18th century, and once had 40 bells.

Tsar's Chambers The 17th century royal palaces (Tsarskie palaty) at the northern end of the monastery complex are now part of an Ecclesiastical Academy.

Museums The **Old Russian Applied Art Section** (Otdel Drevnerusskogo prikladnogo iskusstva), in the vestry behind the Trinity Cathedral, is in fact the monastery's extraordinarily rich **treasury**, bulging with 600 years of donations by the rich and powerful – tapestries, jewel-encrusted vestments, solid gold chalices and more. Monthly closing days are the first Tuesday and last Friday. Your ticket ($5 for foreigners) will admit you only at a fixed time.

The **Art Museum** (Khudozhestvenny muzey) has icons and paintings from the 14th century on, and folk art (old woodcarvings, pottery, hand-printed cloth, costumes from all over Russia and some ho-hum Soviet stuff). Tickets are $4.

The museums are open from 10 am to 5 pm daily except Monday and last Friday of each month. Tickets for the three museums are sold at the *kassa* at the northern end of the Art Museum.

Walls & Tower For a walk along part of the walls (Krepostnye steny), and a climb up the 18th century **Kalichya Tower** (Kalichya bashnya) for a good view over the monastery and town, take the passage between the art and history museums. It's open from 10 am to 4 pm from June to August, closed on Tuesday and Wednesday and the last Friday of those months. Tickets are $2.

Places to Stay & Eat

Hotel Zagorsk *(☎ 4 25 16, prospekt Krasnoy Armii 171)* is about 500m north along the street from the monastery gate and has singles/doubles for $27/35, with private bathroom.

There are a few small, cheap but unexciting eateries along prospekt Krasnoy Armii north of the monastery. For lunch, try the restaurant ***Sever*** *(☎ 4 12 20, prospekt Krasnoy Armii 141)*. It's a quiet wooden building where they serve a wide selection of Russian classics. A meal will cost you around $4. It's open from 10 am to 6 pm daily.

For a more trendy place, try the ***Trapeza na Makovtse*** *(prospekt Krasnoy Armii 132)*, across the square from the monastery entrance. A meal of the nicely presented food will cost about $10. Farther down the road, the ***Russky Dvorik*** is open until 8 pm. It's done in kitsch Russian and serves traditional dishes such as bliny, pelmeni, kvas and more at tourist prices that will run to $15 a person. Both of these restaurants accept all major credit cards.

Getting There & Away

Train Suburban trains run every half-hour or so to/from Moscow's Yaroslavl Station, where the suburban ticket hall is at the rear left of the building. The trip takes a little over 1½ hours and costs $0.40; take any train bound for Sergiev Posad or Alexandrov. You can continue on to Rostov-Veliky (3½ hours) or Yaroslavl (five to 5½ hours) by taking trains to Alexandrov, and changing there to a Yaroslavl-bound suburban train.

Bus Buses to Sergiev Posad from Moscow leave from Yaroslavl train station every half-hour from 8.30 am to 7.30 pm ($0.50, 70 minutes). If you are facing the main street (Komsomolsky prospekt) with the Yaroslavsky Station behind you, the bus stop is to your left, next to the underground passage. Avoid taking Sunday afternoon buses back to Moscow – it might take much longer due to congested roads.

Buses starting at Sergiev Posad run to Pereslavl-Zalessky ($0.60, 75 minutes, three daily). About nine northbound buses a day stop here in transit to Yaroslavl, Kostroma or Rybinsk; all these will take you to Pereslavl-Zalessky, Rostov-Veliky or Yaroslavl if you can get a ticket.

ABRAMTSEVO АБРАМЦЕВО

☎ 254

The small Abramtsevo estate, 15km southwest of Sergiev Posad, was a seedbed for several 19th century movements aiming to preserve patriarchal Russian religious, social and aesthetic values. In the 1840s and 1850s it was the home of Sergey Axakov, pioneer novelist of Russian realism, and a refuge for upper-class intellectuals.

In 1870 Savva Mamontov, a railway tycoon and art patron, bought Abramtsevo and turned it into an artists' colony dedicated to a renaissance of traditional Russian art and architecture. This was to have a strong influence on painting, sculpture, applied art and even theatre. The list of resident painters alone is a who's who of 'neo-Russianism' – it includes Ilya Repin, landscape artist Isaak Levitan, portraitist Valentin Serov and the quite un-Slavonic painter and ceramicist Mikhail Vrubel.

Other projects included woodworking and ceramics workshops, Mamontov's private opera (where Fyodor Chaliapin made his debut) and several buildings designed, built and decorated in traditional style as group efforts.

All this is now the **Abramtsevo Estate Museum-Preserve** (Usadba Abramtsevo Muzey-Zapovednik), which makes a good addition to a day trip to Sergiev Posad. It's normally open from 10 am to 5 pm Wednesday to Sunday except for the last Friday each month – but may also be closed in April and October. Admission is $0.50. Call ☎ 3 24 70 to confirm the hours and ask about the English-language tours offered on some weekends.

Main House

Several rooms have been preserved intact. Axakov's dining room and study contain paintings and sculptures of family and friends, but most of the house is devoted to the Mamontov years. The main attraction is Mamontov's dining room, featuring Repin's portraits of the patron and his wife, and Serov's luminous *Girl with Peaches*. A striking majolica bench by Vrubel can be seen in the garden.

Saviour Church 'Not Made by Hand'

The prettiest building in the grounds, this small church (Tserkov Spasa Nerukotvorny) seems to symbolise Mamantov's intentions – it's a carefully researched homage by half a dozen artists to 14th century Novgorod architecture. The iconostasis is by Repin and Vasily Polenov.

Hut on Chicken Legs

This just goes to show that serious art doesn't have to be serious. The Slavophile painter Viktor Vasnetsov conjured up the fairy tale of Baba Yaga the witch with this playhouse with feet, near the church.

Convent of the Intercession

Between Abramtsevo and Sergiev Posad, in the village of Khotkovo, is the Convent of the Intercession (Pokrovsky monastyr); it was founded in 1308 though the present buildings are 18th century or later.

The parents of Sergius of Radonezh, Russia's patron saint and founder of the Trinity Monastery of St Sergius at Sergiev Posad, are buried in the convent's recently restored **Intercession Cathedral** (Pokrovsky sobor). The biggest building is the early 20th century **St Nicholas' Cathedral** (Nikolsky sobor).

Places to Eat

There is a ***restaurant*** near the museum at Abramtsevo, or if you're driving stop at the ***Restaurant Skazka*** *(Fairy Tale; ☎ 095-584 34 36)*, with its over-the-top wooden decor and excellent soups, on the highway at the 43km milestone from Moscow.

Getting There & Away

Abramtsevo is three stops and Khotkovo two before Sergiev Posad on suburban trains from Moscow's Yaroslavl Station. Most trains heading to Sergiev Posad or Alexandrov stop at both places (but a few skip Abramtsevo, so check). There are occasional buses (No 155) to Abramtsevo from the Sergiev Posad bus station.

By car, turn west off the M8 Moscow-Yaroslavl highway just north of the 61km post. Signs to Khotkovo and Abramtsevo mark the turn-off. For the Khotkovo convent, turn left just before the rail tracks in the village; for Abramtsevo, continue over the railway for a few more kilometres.

St Petersburg
Санкт Петербург

☎ 812 • pop 4.2 million

If much of Russia recalls its Eastern rather than Western roots, St Petersburg is where you'll feel Russia's European influences and aspirations. The city was founded under gruelling conditions by Peter the Great as his 'window on the West' at the only point where traditional Russian territory meets a seaway to northern Europe. Built with 18th and 19th century European pomp and orderliness, mainly by European architects, the result is a city that remains one of Europe's most beautiful. Where Moscow intimidates, St Petersburg enchants.

The vistas of elegant buildings across the wide Neva River and along the canals and avenues recall Paris, Amsterdam, Venice and Berlin. However, St Petersburg's beauty, happily little harmed by Soviet reconstruction, is of a brand all its own.

The jolly onion domes of Moscow seem almost passé here, where a more Western outlook was taken at every stage of planning and construction. Even the city's colours – the green and gold of the Winter Palace, the red beside the Anichkov most (bridge), the blue of Smolny Cathedral – reflect a closer stylistic allegiance to the courts of Europe than to the Kremlin. The buildings' playful baroque facades exude the riotous opulence of tsarist Russia.

The spirit of reform is so alive here it's palpable, though the Western-influenced shape it has assumed provides no small irony at times. Even the city itself has hopped on the money train by accepting corporate sponsorship of street signs – it's not your imagination; that street sign does say *USA Today*.

Yet as Western as you might be led to think the city is, there are reminders at every step that you are most assuredly in Russia, and that goes as much for the hustle and bustle of people with little sense of personal space, as for the bristling, romantic *joie de vivre* that informs their earnest, uncomplex friendliness in social situations. Despite their well publicised problems, residents affectionately call the city 'Piter' and swell with a pride you're unlikely to meet elsewhere in the country.

HIGHLIGHTS

- Singing along on summer nights with the guitar players along the Neva, watching the bridges rise at 2 am
- Getting lost and dazed in the glorious halls of the Hermitage
- Discovering Russian art in the Russian Museum
- Strolling down Nevsky prospekt to take in the sight of all walks of modern Russian life intermingling
- Boating along the canals and under the bridges
- Taking in a ballet at the Mariinsky Theatre

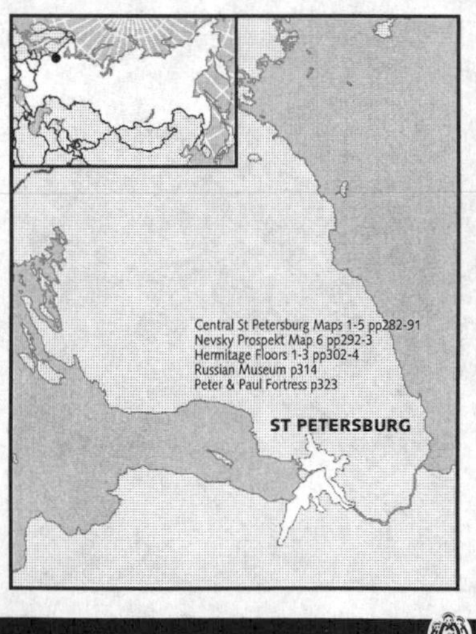

In St Petersburg, you feel history at every step; even Moscow is no match in this department. From here autocratic tsars ruled Russia for two centuries with the splendour and stubbornness that partially led to their downfall at the hands of workers and soldiers in March 1917. The city's time as Russia's capital bequeathed it an artistic and entertainment scene which is still at least equal to that of the current-day capital. Russian ballet was born in St Petersburg and the 19th century flowering of Russian music was centred here. Nijinsky, Tchaikovsky and Rimsky-Korsakov, to name but a few, spent important periods here. Pushkin was educated in, exiled from, readmitted to and killed in St Petersburg. Dostoevsky set *Crime and Punishment* here.

At one end of the cultural spectrum today are the Hermitage, one of the world's great art galleries, housed in the tsars' superb Winter Palace, and the Kirov Ballet, which has recently overshadowed Moscow's Bolshoi. At the other end, St Petersburg has produced many of Russia's top rock bands and has witnessed a rebirth of avant-garde art.

St Petersburg's latitude – level with Seward, Alaska and Cape Farewell, Greenland – keeps it bright nearly 24 hours a day in midsummer but also ensures long, grey winters. From December to March, when the Neva is ice and temperatures rarely exceed freezing, the endless nights have a twinkling magic. In summertime, the light, airy giddiness of long, warm days and a tireless festive spirit combine with an ever-present Dostoevskian heaviness to produce a magical, unforgettable effect unique to the city.

HISTORY

Peter the Great

Alexander of Novgorod defeated the Swedes near the mouth of the Neva in 1240 – earning the title Nevsky (of the Neva). Sweden took control of the region in the 17th century and it was Peter the Great's desire to crush this rival and make Russia a European power that led to the founding of the city. At the start of the Great Northern War (1700-21) he captured the Swedish outposts on the Neva, and in 1703 he founded the Peter & Paul Fortress on the Neva a few kilometres inland. After Peter trounced the Swedes at Poltava in 1709, the city he named, in Dutch style, Sankt Pieter Burkh (after his patron saint) really began to grow. Canals were dug to drain the marshy south bank and in 1712 he made the place his capital, forcing grumbling administrators, nobles and merchants to move to this northern outback and build new homes. Peasants were drafted as forced labour, many dying of disease and exhaustion; it's still known as the city built upon bones. Architects and artisans came from all over Europe. By Peter's death in 1725 his city had a population of 40,000 and 90% of Russia's foreign trade passed through it. The south bank around the Admiralty had become the city centre.

After Peter

Peter's immediate successors moved the capital back to Moscow but Empress Anna Ivanovna (1730-40) returned it to St Petersburg. Between 1741 and 1825 under Empress Elizabeth, Catherine the Great and Alexander I it became a cosmopolitan city with a royal court of famed splendour. These monarchs commissioned great series of palaces, government buildings and churches, turning it into one of Europe's grandest capitals.

The emancipation of the serfs in 1861 and industrialisation, which peaked in the 1890s, brought a flood of poor workers into the city, leading to overcrowding, poor sanitation, epidemics and festering discontent. St Petersburg became a hotbed of strikes and political violence and was the hub of the 1905 revolution, sparked by 'Bloody Sunday' on 9 January 1905, when a strikers' march to petition the tsar in the Winter Palace was fired on by troops. By 1914, when in a wave of patriotism at the start of WWI the city's name was changed to the Russian-style Petrograd, it had 2.1 million people.

The 1917 Revolution

Petrograd was again the cradle of revolution in 1917. It was here that workers' protests turned into a general strike and troops mutinied, forcing the end of the monarchy in March. The Petrograd Soviet, a socialist focus for workers' and soldiers' demands, started meeting in the city's Tauride Palace alongside the country's reformist Provisional Government. It was to Petrograd's Finland Station that Lenin travelled in April to organise the Bolshevik Party.

The actual revolution came after Bolsheviks occupied key positions in Petrograd on 24 October. The next day, the All-Russian Congress of Soviets, meeting in the Smolny, appointed a Bolshevik government. That night, after some exchanges of gunfire and a blank shot from the cruiser *Aurora* on the Neva, the Provisional Government in the Winter Palace surrendered to the Bolsheviks.

The new government moved the capital back to Moscow in March 1918, fearing a German attack on Petrograd. The privations of the Civil War caused Petrograd's population to drop to about 700,000, and in 1921 strikes in the city and a bloodily supressed revolt by the sailors of nearby Kronstadt helped to bring about Lenin's more liberal New Economic Policy.

Petrograd was renamed Leningrad after Lenin's death in 1924. It was a hub of Stalin's 1930s industrialisation program and by 1939 had 3.1 million people and 11% of Soviet industrial output. Yet Stalin feared it as a rival power base and the 1934 assassination of the local communist chief Sergey Kirov at Smolny was the start of his 1930s Communist Party purge.

900 Days

When the Germans attacked the USSR in June 1941 it took them only 2½ months to reach Leningrad. As the birthplace of Bolshevism, Hitler swore to wipe it from the face of the earth, but not before his expected New Year's victory ball in Hotel Astoria. His troops besieged the city from 8 September 1941 until 27 January 1944. Many people (and three-quarters of the industrial plants) were evacuated. Nevertheless, approximately one million died from shelling, starvation and disease in what's called the '900 Days' (actually 872). By comparison, the USA and UK suffered about 700,000 dead between them in all of WWII. Leningraders dropped dead of hunger or cold in the streets and when no cats or rats were left they ate glue off the back of wallpaper. The bodies which were not carried by exhausted relatives to the Piskaryovska cemetery were simply piled onto side streets which in the wintertime acted as temporary morgues (Repina pereulok and ulitsa Marata were noted ones). The city was saved from an even worse fate by the winter 'Road of Life' across frozen Lake Ladoga to the east, a thin supply line which remained in Soviet hands.

The Postwar Period

After the war, Leningrad was reconstructed and reborn, though it took until 1960 for its population to exceed pre-WWII levels. The city centre retains its aura of past glory and current chic, a heady mix of opulence and decay, though the outlying areas are lined with depressing, uniformly grey and chunky blocks of flats that go on forever.

The 1990s

In 1989, Anatoly Sobchak, a reform-minded candidate, was elected mayor. Almost as soon as Dzerzhinsky's statue hit the asphalt in Moscow, the Leningrad city council voted to change the city's name back to St Petersburg (though the region around the city refused to join in the fun and to this day calls itself the Leningradskaya oblast).

Sobchak's rule oversaw the 1994 Goodwill Games, which were quietly dubbed a bit of a mess, but which gave the city a needed shot in the arm and millions of roubles worth of needed cosmetic repairs to the city centre (Nevsky prospekt's fine buildings haven't looked this good since the city's heyday at the end of the 19th century).

Sobchak was succeeded as governor (a fancier term for 'mayor') by Vladimir Yakovlev, and ended up in comfortable self-exile in Paris after serious charges of corruption and fiscal mismanagement. Yakovlev hasn't earned himself a lily-white reputation, but his administration has at least spearheaded a beautification policy which has pleased the populace.

Despite a new reputation as the crime centre of Russia, mainly due to several high-profile contract killings, St Petersburg is now a tourist-friendly, cosmopolitan city with a thriving cultural and artistic core. In notable contrast to Moscow's in-fighting, dirty politics and entrenched lobbyist subculture, St Petersburg has been able to capitalise on the injection of foreign interest in Russia and business is booming. Overused as the term may be, St Petersburg has, in fact, re-established itself as Russia's window on the West.

ORIENTATION

St Petersburg sprawls across and around the delta of the Neva River, at the end of the easternmost arm of the Baltic Sea, the Gulf of Finland. Entering St Petersburg at its south-eastern corner, the Neva first flows north and then west across the middle of the city, dividing there into several branches and forming the islands making up the delta. The two biggest branches, which diverge where the Winter Palace stands on the south bank, are the Bolshaya (Big) Neva and Malaya (Small) Neva; they flow into the sea either side of Vasilevsky Island.

The heart of St Petersburg is the area spreading back from the Winter Palace and the Admiralty on the south bank, its skyline dominated by the golden dome of St Isaac's Cathedral. Nevsky prospekt, heading east-south-east from here, is the main drag, with many of the sights, shops and restaurants.

The northern side of the city is comprised of three main areas. The westernmost is Vasilevsky Island, at whose east end – the Strelka – many of the city's fine early buildings still stand. The middle area is Petrograd Side, a cluster of delta islands whose south end is marked by the tall gold spire of the SS Peter & Paul Cathedral. This is where the city began. The third, eastern, area is Vyborg Side, stretching along the north bank of the Neva.

Street Names

After 1990, many streets in Russian major cities were slowly renamed to their pre-communist names, making any map more than five years old useful only to history students. Major changes may be found in *The Traveller's Yellow Pages* (see under Information). In this chapter, we use the new names, followed in parentheses by the alternate name (except for naberezhnaya kanala Griboedova, which everyone refers to only by its old name). In practice, only a few could possibly cause confusion to tourists:

old name	new name
nab kanala Griboedova	nab kanala Yekaterinski
ulitsa Plekhanova	ulitsa Kazanskaya
ulitsa Saltykova-Shchedrin	ulitsa Kirochnaya

St Petersburg has two streets called Bolshoy prospekt: one on Petrograd Side, one on Vasilevsky Island. The two sides of some Vasilevsky Island streets are known as lines *(linii)* and opposite sides of these streets have different names – thus 4-ya linia (4th line) and 5-ya linia (5th line) are the east and west sides of the same street, which collectively is called 4-ya i 5-ya linii (4th and 5th lines).

Maps

The *St Petersburg City Map With Passenger Transport Routes* is very useful and is available at kiosks throughout the city. Karta Publishing's annually updated *Sankt Peterburg* is also very comprehensive. Try Dom Knigi and the Lensprav Information kiosk outside the Moscow Station for the best selection. If you're into old maps or need detailed maps of other regions in Russia, head directly to the bookshop (Map 2) at Bolshoy prospekt 57 on the Petrograd Side. And to make your visit a cosmically fine-tuned experience, find out which parts of the city correspond to your zodiac sign; get the *Astrologicheskaya Karta*, on sale at the Nauk bookshop, Liteyny prospekt 64.

INFORMATION

The Russian-language (and English-indexed) *Luchshee V Sankt Peterburge*, and its English-language version, *The Traveller's Yellow Pages*, are comprehensive

continued on page 294

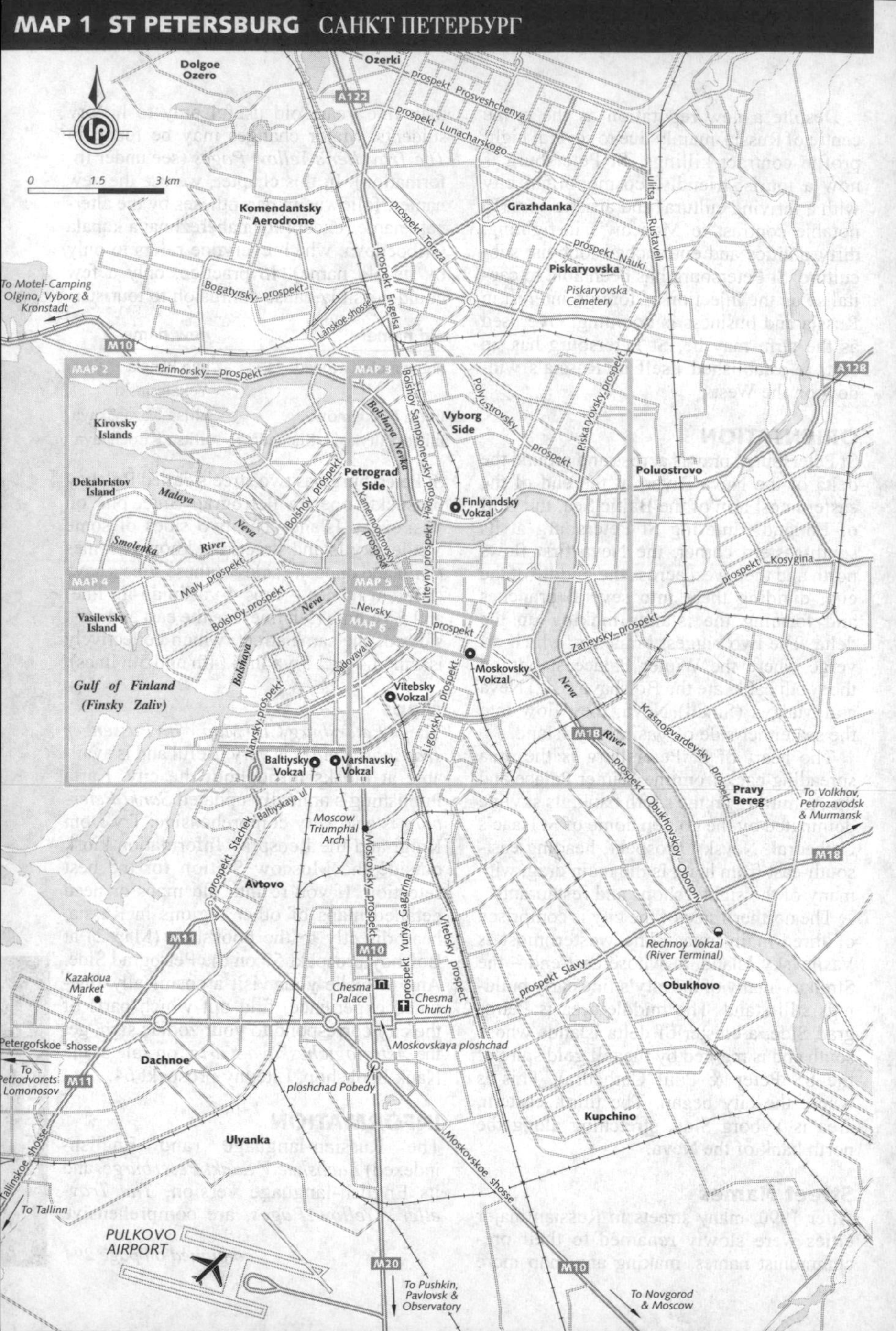

Dolgoe Ozero
Ozerki
prospekt Prosveshchenya
A122
prospekt Lunacharskogo
0 1.5 3 km
Komendantsky Aerodrome
Grazhdanka
Ulitsa Rustaveli
prospekt Toreza
prospekt Nauki
Piskaryovska
Piskaryovska Cemetery
To Motel-Camping Olgino, Vyborg & Kronstadt
Bogatyrsky prospekt
prospekt Engelsa
Lanskoe shosse
M10
MAP 2
Primorsky prospekt
MAP 3
Bolshoy Sampsonevsky prospekt
Polyustrovsky prospekt
Piskaryovsky prospekt
A128
Kirovsky Islands
Bolshaya Nevka
Vyborg Side
Dekabristov Island
Malaya Neva
Petrograd Side
Poluostrovo
Bolshoy prospekt
Kamennoostrovsky prospekt
Finlyandsky Vokzal
Smolenka River
Liteyny prospekt
prospekt Kosygina
MAP 4
Maly prospekt
MAP 5
Neva
Nevsky prospekt
MAP 6
Vasilevsky Island
Bolshoy prospekt
Zanevsky prospekt
Moskovsky Vokzal
Bolshaya
Sadovaya ul
Gulf of Finland (Finsky Zaliv)
Vitebsky Vokzal
Ligovsky prospekt
Neva
Narvsky prospekt
Krasnogvardeysky prospekt
M18 River
Baltiysky Vokzal
Varshavsky Vokzal
prospekt Obukhovskoy Oborony
Pravy Bereg
To Volkhov, Petrozavodsk & Murmansk
prospekt Stachek
Baltiyskaya ul
Moscow Triumphal Arch
Moskovsky prospekt
M18
Avtovo
M11
Rechnoy Vokzal (River Terminal)
M10
Yunya Gagarina prospekt
Vitebsky prospekt
Kazakoua Market
Chesma Palace
Chesma Church
prospekt Slavy
Obukhovo
Petergofskoe shosse
Moskovskaya ploshchad
To Petrodvorets & Lomonosov
M11
Dachnoe
ploshchad Pobedy
Kupchino
Ulyanka
Moskovskoe shosse
Tallinskoe shosse
To Tallinn
PULKOVO AIRPORT
M20
M10
To Pushkin, Pavlovsk & Observatory
To Novgorod & Moscow

MAP 2 CENTRAL ST PETERSBURG

PLACES TO STAY
23 Hotel Druzhba
Гостиница Дружба
25 Dvorets Molodyozhy Hotel
Гостиница Дворец молодёжи

PLACES TO EAT
2 Staraya Derevnya
4 Kafe Morozhenoe
24 Fujiyama
27 Red Rose
31 McDonald's
34 Laima
40 Lokanta
Локанта
45 Bistro Samson
Бистро Самсон
46 Kafe Tbilisi
Кафе Тбилиси
48 Troitsky Most
Троицкий Мост
56 Pirosmani Restaurant
Ресторан Пиросмани
57 Pirosmani Kafe
Кафе Пиросмани
64 Kalinka
Калинка
65 Orient
66 McDonald's
68 Cheburechnaya
Чебуречная

OTHER
1 London Club
3 Buddhist Datsan
Буддийский дацан
5 Boat Rental Stand
Прокат лодок
6 Amusement Park
Аттракционы
7 Ferry Landing
Пристань
8 Ferry Stop
Пристань
9 Stables
Конюшни корпус
10 Kitchen Building
Кухонный корпус
11 Yelagin Palace
Елагинский дворец
12 Water Bike Rental
Водный велосипед
13 Kamenny Island Theatre
Каменный остров театр
14 Yeltsin Dacha
Дача Ельцина
15 Polovtsev House
Дом Половцева
16 Danish Consulate
17 Peter's Tree
Дуб Петра 1
18 Sports Centre
Спортывний зал
19 Church of St John the Baptist
Церковь Иоанна Предтечи
20 Kamennoostrovsky Palace
Каменноостровский дворец
21 Sphinx Monuments
Сфинкс
22 24-Hour Food Shop
26 GAI Headquarters
ГАЙ
28 Telephone Office
Телефон
29 Post Office
Почта
30 Lensovieta Culture Palace
Дом Културы им. Ленсовета
32 Dom Mod
Дом Мод
33 Teatr Mironova
Театр Миронова
35 Paper Supply Shop
36 Photo Shop
Фото Магазин
37 Book and Map Shop
Книжный Магазин
38 Lenin Statue
Памятник В. И. Ленину
39 Babylon Super
41 Melodia
Мелодия
42 Playground
43 Kirov Museum
Музей С. М. Кирова
44 Post Office
Почта
47 Sytny Market
Сытный маркет
49 Lenfilm (Film Studios)
Ленфильм
50 Gorky Statue
Памятник А.М. Горкому
51 Planetarium
Планетариум
52 Amusement Park
Аттракционы
53 Music Hall
Мюзик Хол
54 Staraya Kniga
Старая Книга
55 Dvorets Sporta SKA (Sporting Ground)
Дворец спорта СКА
58 Petrovsky Stadium
Петровскиц Стадион
59 Yubileyny Stadium
Юбилейный Стадион
60 Jungle
61 Rostral Columns
Ростральная колонна
62 Central Naval Museum (Old Stock Exchange)
Центральный военно-морской музей
63 Institute of Russian Literature (Pushkin House)
Институт русской литературы (Пушкинский дом)
67 Konung
Конунг
69 Telephone Office

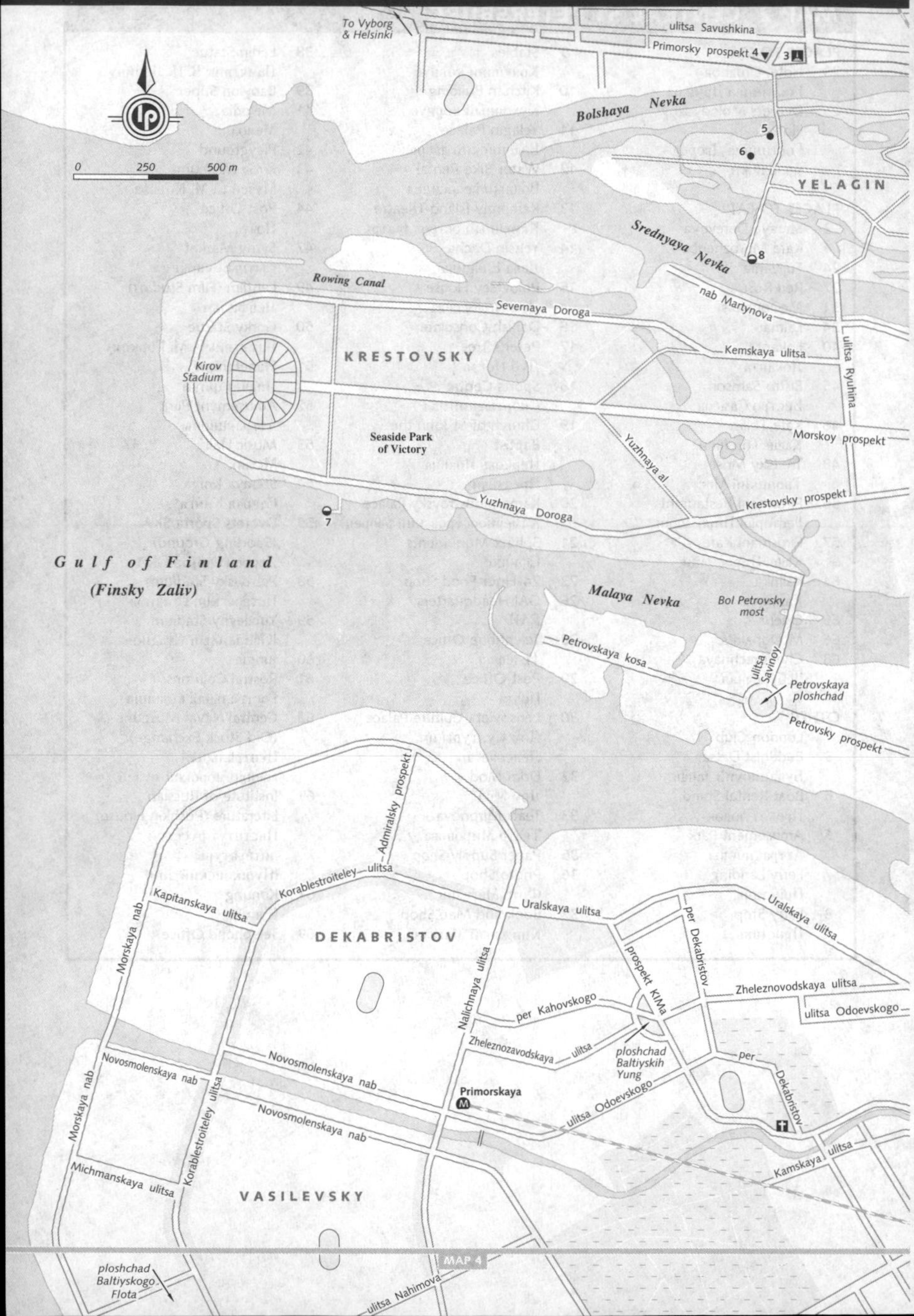

MAP 2 CENTRAL ST PETERSBURG

To Vyborg & Helsinki
ulitsa Savushkina
Primorsky prospekt
4
3
Bolshaya Nevka
5
6
YELAGIN
Srednyaya Nevka
8
0 250 500 m
Rowing Canal
nab Martynova
Severnaya Doroga
KRESTOVSKY
Kirov Stadium
Kemskaya ulitsa
ulitsa Ryuhina
Seaside Park of Victory
Morskoy prospekt
Yuzhnaya al
Yuzhnaya Doroga
Krestovsky prospekt
7
Gulf of Finland
(Finsky Zaliv)
Malaya Nevka
Bol Petrovsky most
Petrovskaya kosa
ulitsa Savinoy
Petrovskaya ploshchad
Petrovsky prospekt
Admiralsky prospekt
Korablestroiteley ulitsa
Kapitanskaya ulitsa
Uralskaya ulitsa
per Dekabristov
Uralskaya ulitsa
DEKABRISTOV
Morskaya nab
Nalichnaya ulitsa
prospekt KIMa
Zheleznovodskaya ulitsa
ulitsa Odoevskogo
per Kahovskogo
Zheleznozavodskaya ulitsa
ploshchad Baltiyskih Yung
per Dekabristov
Novosmolenskaya nab
Novosmolenskaya nab
Korablestroiteley ulitsa
Primorskaya
ulitsa Odoevskogo
Novosmolenskaya nab
Morskaya nab
Kamskaya ulitsa
Michmanskaya ulitsa
VASILEVSKY
MAP 4
ploshchad Baltiyskogo Flota
ulitsa Nahimova

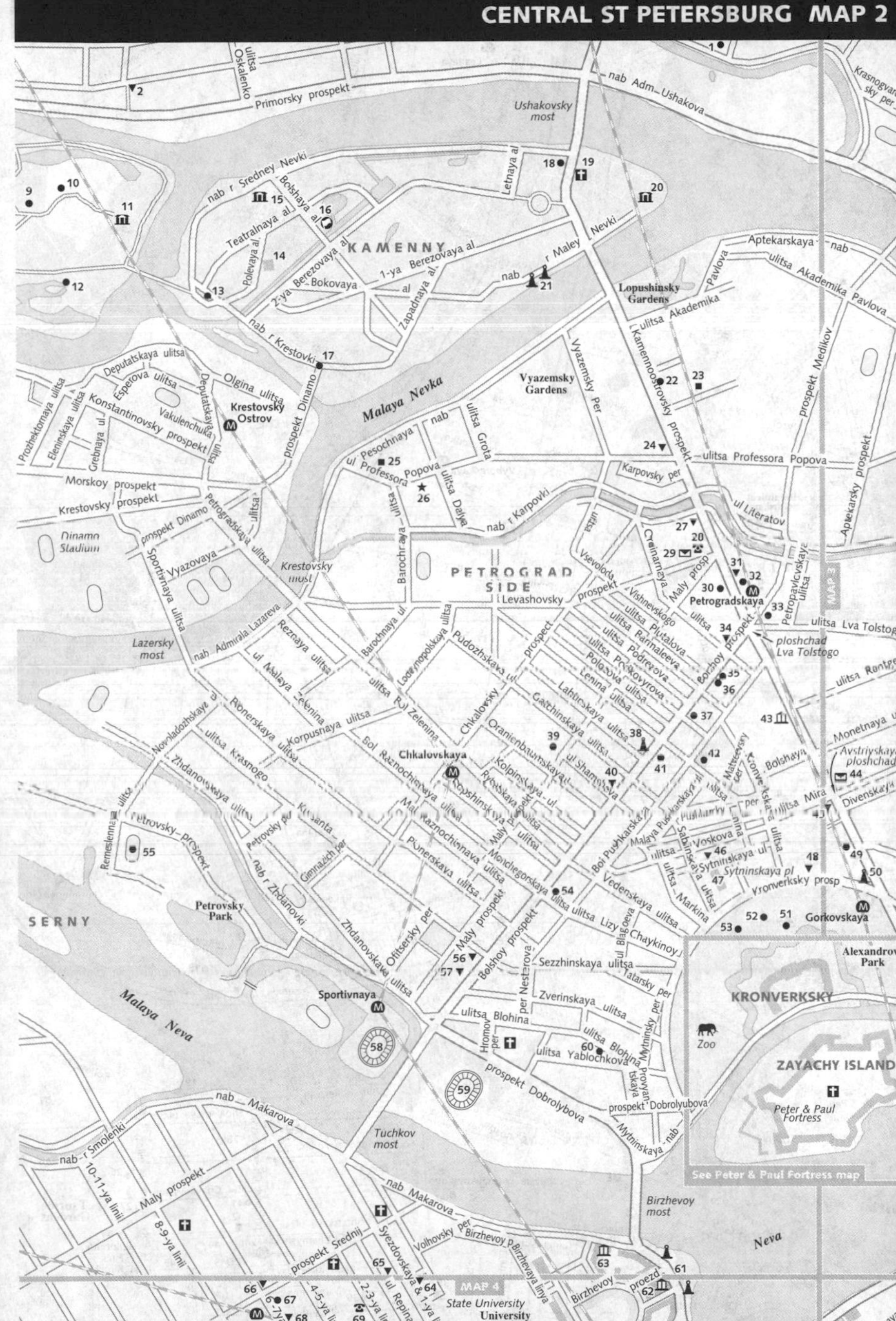

KAMENNY
PETROGRAD SIDE
SERNY
KRONVERKSKY
ZAYACHY ISLAND
Malaya Nevka
Malaya Neva
Neva
Krestovsky Ostrov
Chkalovskaya
Petrogradskaya
Gorkovskaya
Sportivnaya
Vasileostrovskaya
Lopushinsky Gardens
Vyazemsky Gardens
Petrovsky Park
Alexandrovsky Park
Peter & Paul Fortress
Zoo
Dinamo Stadium
Ushakovsky most
Krestovsky most
Lazersky most
Tuchkov most
Birzhevoy most
State University
University Botanical Gardens
Kamennoostrovsky prospekt
Bolshoy prospekt
prospekt Dobrolybova
Primorsky prospekt
Maly prospekt
See Peter & Paul Fortress map
MAP 3
MAP 4

MAP 3 CENTRAL ST PETERSBURG

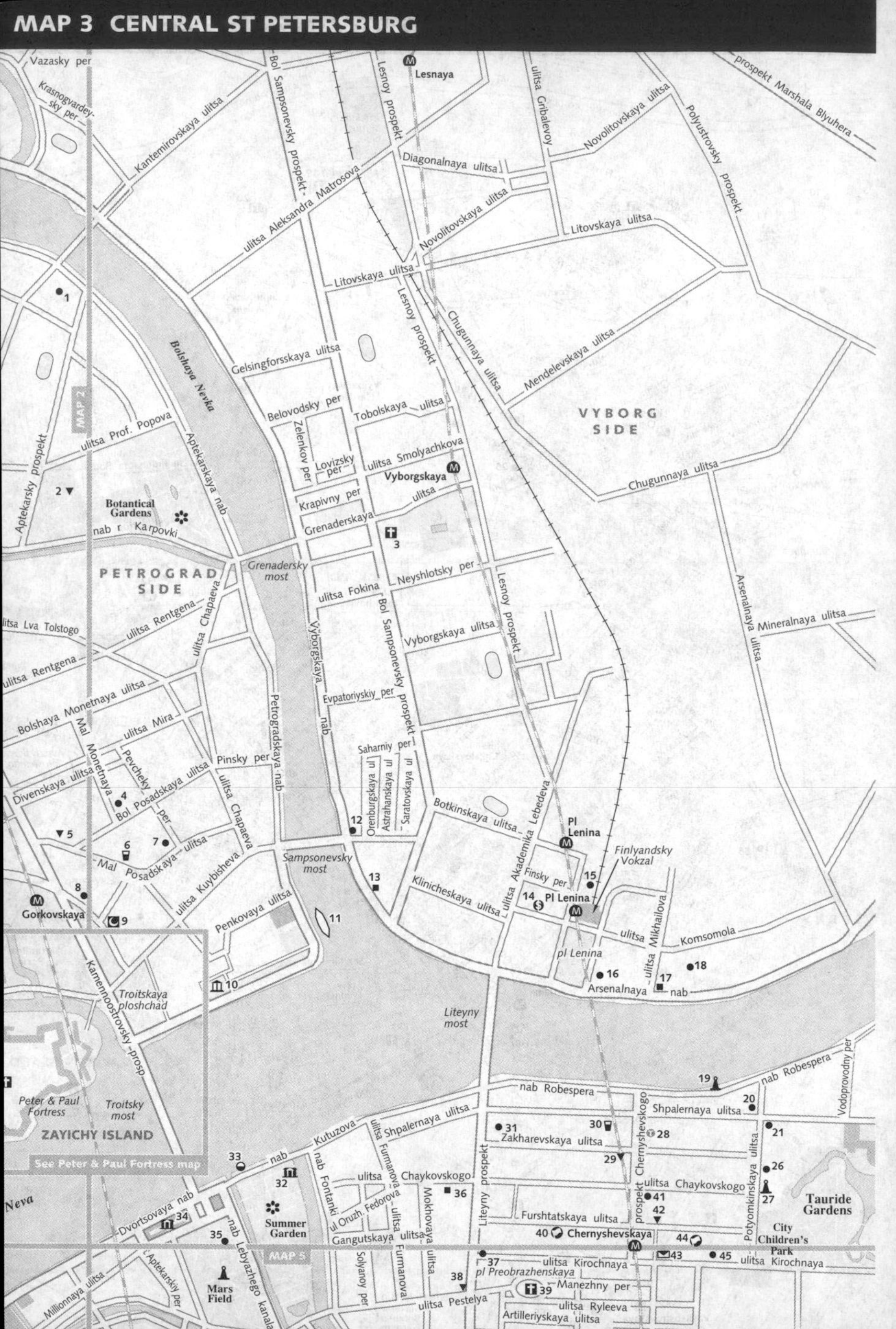

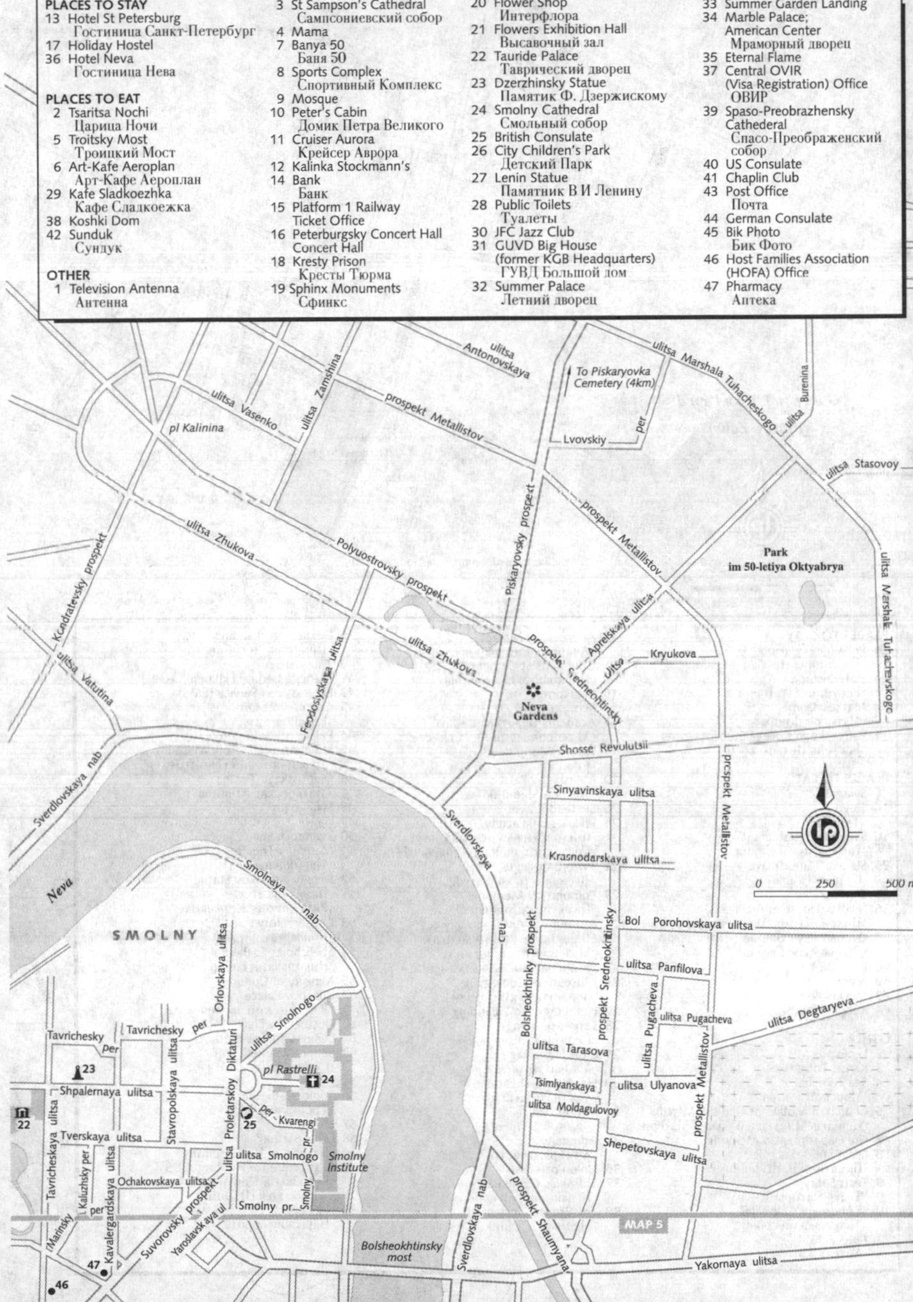

PLACES TO STAY
13 Hotel St Petersburg
Гостиница Санкт-Петербург
17 Holiday Hostel
36 Hotel Neva
Гостиница Нева
PLACES TO EAT
2 Tsaritsa Nochi
Царица Ночи
5 Troitsky Most
Троицкий Мост
6 Art-Kafe Aeroplan
Арт-Кафе Аероплан
29 Kafe Sladkoezhka
Кафе Сладкоежка
38 Koshki Dom
42 Sunduk
Сундук
OTHER
1 Television Antenna
Антенна
3 St Sampson's Cathedral
Сампсониевский собор
4 Mama
7 Banya 50
Баня 50
8 Sports Complex
Спортивный Комплекс
9 Mosque
10 Peter's Cabin
Домик Петра Великого
11 Cruiser Aurora
Крейсер Аврора
12 Kalinka Stockmann's
14 Bank
Банк
15 Platform 1 Railway
Ticket Office
16 Peterburgsky Concert Hall
Concert Hall
18 Kresty Prison
Кресты Тюрма
19 Sphinx Monuments
Сфинкс
20 Flower Shop
Интерфлора
21 Flowers Exhibition Hall
Высавочный зал
22 Tauride Palace
Таврический дворец
23 Dzerzhinsky Statue
Памятик Ф. Дзержискому
24 Smolny Cathedral
Смольный собор
25 British Consulate
26 City Children's Park
Детский Парк
27 Lenin Statue
Памятник В И Ленину
28 Public Toilets
Туалеты
30 JFC Jazz Club
31 GUVD Big House
(former KGB Headquarters)
ГУВД Большой дом
32 Summer Palace
Летний дворец
33 Summer Garden Landing
34 Marble Palace;
American Center
Мраморный дворец
35 Eternal Flame
37 Central OVIR
(Visa Registration) Office
ОВИР
39 Spaso-Preobrazhensky
Cathederal
Спасо-Преображенский
собор
40 US Consulate
41 Chaplin Club
43 Post Office
Почта
44 German Consulate
45 Bik Photo
Бик Фото
46 Host Families Association
(HOFA) Office
47 Pharmacy
Аптека
ulitsa Antonovskaya
To Piskaryovka Cemetery (4km)
ulitsa Marshala Tuhacheskogo
ulitsa Burenina
ulitsa Vasenko
ulitsa Zamshina
prospekt Metallistov
pl Kalinina
Lvovskiy per
ulitsa Stasovoy
Piskaryovsky prospekt
ulitsa Zhukova
Polyuostrovsky prospekt
Park
im 50-letiya Oktyabrya
Kondratevsky prospekt
ulitsa Vatutina
Apreiskaya ulitsa
ulitsa Kryukova
prospekt Sredneohtinsky
Feodosiyskaya ulitsa
Neva Gardens
Shosse Revolutsii
Sverdlovskaya nab
Neva
Sinyavinskaya ulitsa
Krasnodarskaya ulitsa
Smolnaya nab
SMOLNY
Bol Porohovskaya ulitsa
ulitsa Panfilova
Bolsheokhtinky prospekt
prospekt Srednekhtinsky
ulitsa Pugacheva
ulitsa Degtaryeva
Orlovskaya ulitsa
ulitsa Smolnogo
Tavrichesky per
ulitsa Tarasova
pl Rastrelli
Tsimlyanskaya
ulitsa Ulyanova
Shpalernaya ulitsa
Stavropolskaya ulitsa
Proletarskoy Diktaturi
per Kvarengi
ulitsa Moldagulovoy
Tavricheskaya ulitsa
Tverskaya ulitsa
ulitsa Smolnogo
Smolny Institute
Shepetovskaya ulitsa
Kaluzhsky per
Kavalergardskaya ulitsa
Ochakovskaya ulitsa
Suvorovsky prospekt
Smolny pr
prospekt Shaumyana
Marinsky per
Yaroslavskaya ul
MAP 5
Bolsheokhtinsky most
Yakornaya ulitsa
0 250 500 m

MAP 4 CENTRAL ST PETERSBURG

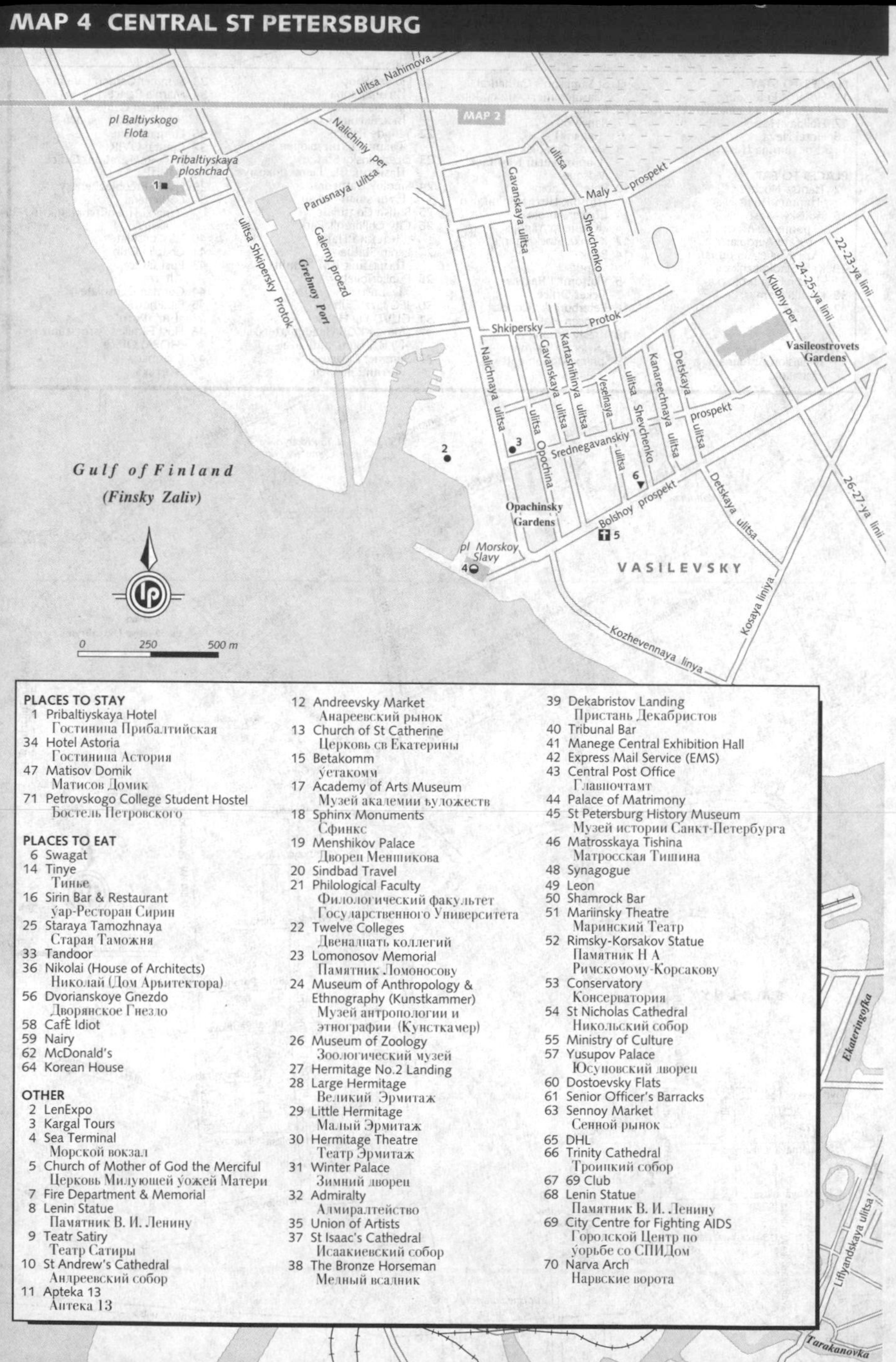

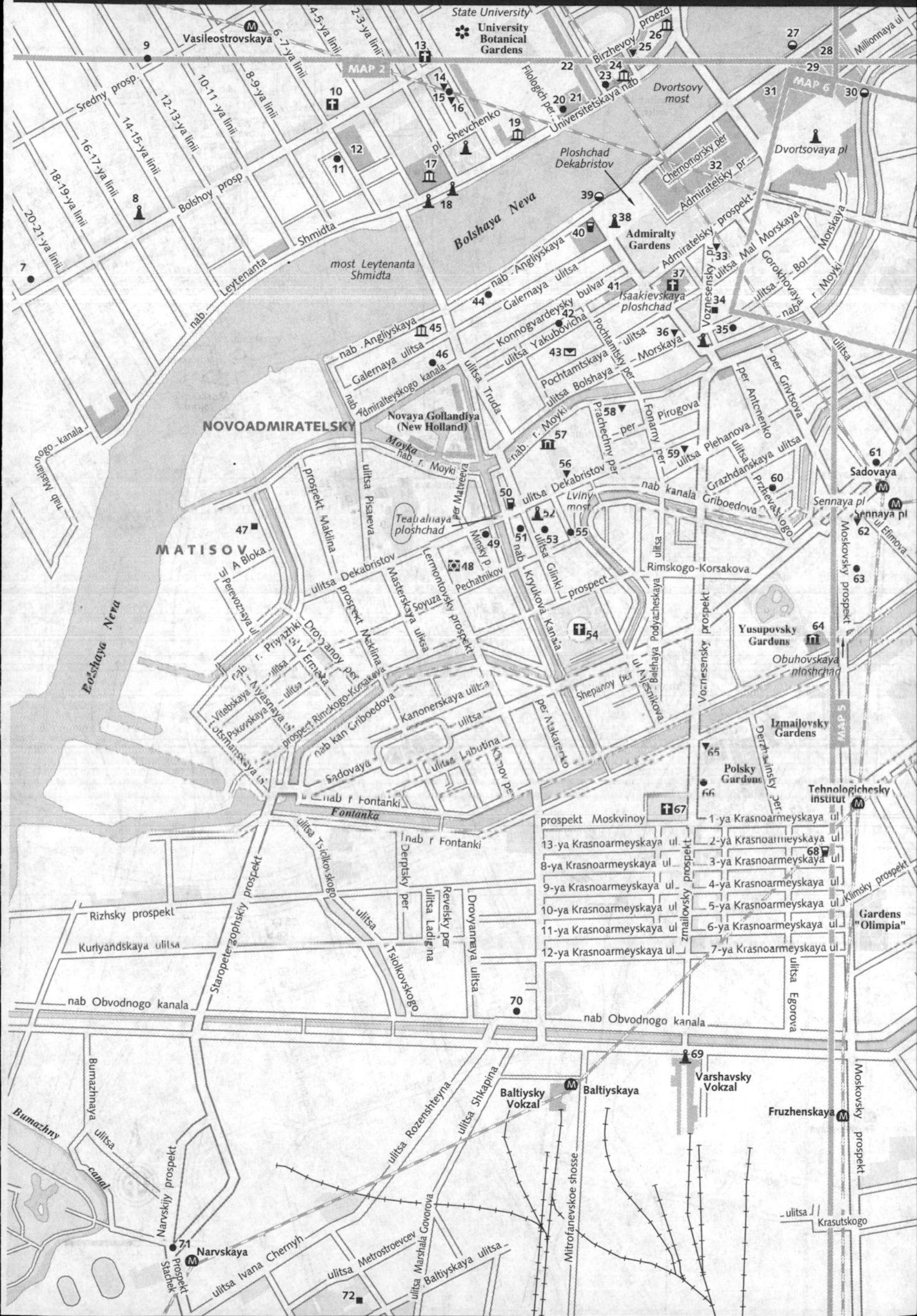
State University
University Botanical Gardens
Vasileostrovskaya
MAP 2
MAP 6
MAP 5
4-5-ya linii
2-3-ya linii
6-7-ya linii
8-9-ya linii
10-11-ya linii
12-13-ya linii
14-15-ya linii
16-17-ya linii
18-19-ya linii
20-21-ya linii
Sredny prosp
Bolshoy prosp
pl Shevchenko
Filologich per
Birzhevoy proezd
Universitetskaya nab
Dvortsovy most
Millionnaya ul
Dvortsovaya pl
Chernomorsky per
Admiratelsky pr
Admiratelsky prospekt
Ploshchad Dekabristov
Bolshaya Neva
nab Leytenanta Shmidta
most Leytenanta Shmidta
Admiralty Gardens
nab Angliyskaya
Galernaya ulitsa
Konnogvardeysky bulvar
Isaakievskaya ploshchad
Voznesensky pr
ulitsa Mal Morskaya
Gorokhovaya
ulitsa Bol Morskaya
nab r Moyki
ulitsa Yakubovicha
Pochtamtskaya ulitsa
Pochtamtsky per
ulitsa Bolshaya Morskaya
nab Admiralteyskogo kanala
ulitsa Truda
Novaya Gollandiya (New Holland)
NOVOADMIRATELSKY
Moyka
nab r Moyki
Prachechny per
per Pirogova
Fonarny per
per Antonenko
per Grivtsova
ulitsa Plehanova
Grazhdanskaya ulitsa
Przhevalskogo
nab kanala Griboedova
Sadovaya
Sennaya pl
ul Efimova
ulitsa Dekabristov
Lviny most
per Matveeva
Teatralnaya ploshchad
ulitsa Pisareva
prospekt Maklina
MATISOV
ul A Bloka
Perevoznaya ul
Minsky p
Pechatnikov
nab Kryukova Kanala
ulitsa Glinki
Rimskogo-Korsakova prospect
Soyuza
Masterskaya ulitsa
Lermontovsky prospekt
nab r Pryazhki
Drovyanoy per
Bolshaya Neva
Vitebskaya
Pskovskaya
prospect Rimskogo-Korsakova
nab kan Griboedova
Kanonerskaya ulitsa
Shepanoy per
ul Myasnikova
Bolshaya Podyacheskaya
Voznesensky prospekt
per Makarenko
ulitsa Labutina
Sadovaya
Otsmanskaya
nab r Fontanki
Fontanka
Yusupovsky Gardens
Obuhovskaya ploshchad
Moskovsky prospect
Izmailovsky Gardens
Polsky Gardens
Derzhavinsky per
Tehnologichesky Institut
prospekt Moskvinoy
1-ya Krasnoarmeyskaya ul
2-ya Krasnoarmeyskaya ul
3-ya Krasnoarmeyskaya ul
4-ya Krasnoarmeyskaya ul
5-ya Krasnoarmeyskaya ul
6-ya Krasnoarmeyskaya ul
7-ya Krasnoarmeyskaya ul
8-ya Krasnoarmeyskaya ul
9-ya Krasnoarmeyskaya ul
10-ya Krasnoarmeyskaya ul
11-ya Krasnoarmeyskaya ul
12-ya Krasnoarmeyskaya ul
13-ya Krasnoarmeyskaya ul
Izmailovsky prospekt
Klimsky prospekt
Gardens "Olimpia"
nab r Fontanki
ulitsa Tsiolkovskogo
Derptsky per
Revelsky per
ulitsa Ladigina
Drovyanaya ulitsa
Rizhsky prospekt
Kurlyandskaya ulitsa
Staropetergophsky prospekt
nab Obvodnogo kanala
ulitsa Egorova
Varshavsky Vokzal
Baltiysky Vokzal
Baltiyskaya
Fruzhenskaya
Moskovsky prospekt
Bumazhnaya ulitsa
Bumazhny canal
Narvskiy prospekt
ulitsa Rozenshteyna
ulitsa Shkapina
Mitrofanevskoe shosse
ulitsa Krasutskogo
Narvskaya
Prospekt Stachek
ulitsa Ivana Chernyh
ulitsa Metrostroevcev
ulitsa Marshala Govorova
Baltiyskaya ulitsa
Sadovaya
7
8
9
10
11
12
13
14
15
16
17
18
19
20
21
22
23
24
25
26
27
28
29
30
31
32
33
34
35
36
37
38
39
40
41
42
43
44
45
46
47
48
49
50
51
52
53
54
55
56
57
58
59
60
61
62
63
64
65
66
67
68
69
70
71
72

MAP 5 CENTRAL ST PETERSBURG

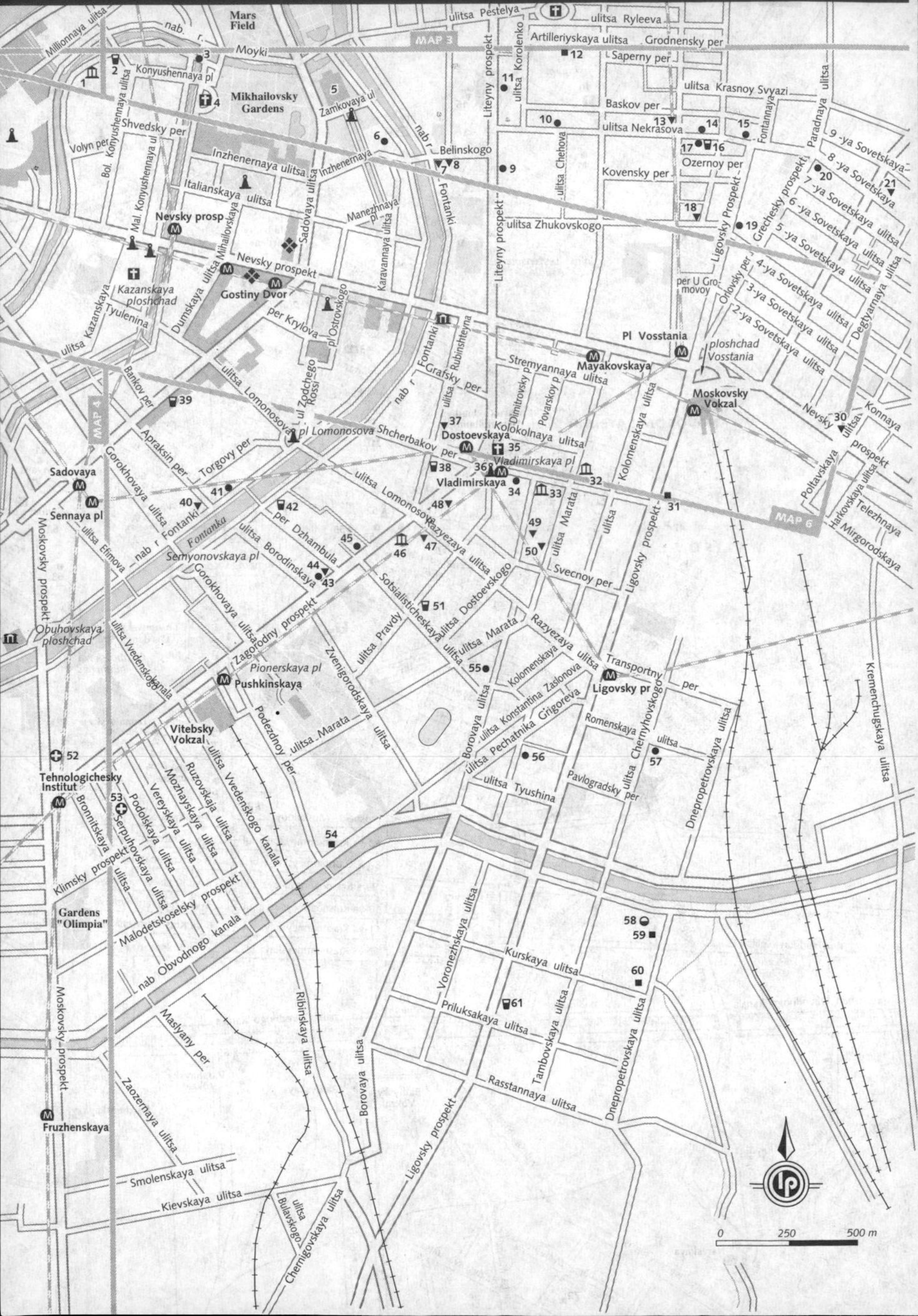

Mars Field
Mikhailovsky Gardens
Nevsky prosp
Gostiny Dvor
Kazanskaya ploshchad
Sadovaya
Sennaya pl
Mayakovskaya
Pl Vosstania
ploshchad Vosstania
Moskovsky Vokzal
Dostoevskaya
Vladimirskaya
Vladimirskaya pl
Pushkinskaya
Pionerskaya pl
Vitebsky Vokzal
Ligovsky pr
Tehnologichesky Institut
Gardens "Olimpia"
Fruzhenskaya
Semyonovskaya pl
Obuhovskaya ploshchad
Fontanka
pl Lomonosova

Millionnaya ulitsa
nab. r. Moyki
Konyushennaya pl
Bol. Konyushennaya ulitsa
Mal. Konyushennaya ul
Shvedsky per
Volyn per
Inzhenernaya ulitsa
Italianskaya ulitsa
Zamkovaya ul
Sadovaya ulitsa
Manezhnaya pl
Karavannaya ulitsa
nab r Fontanki
Belinskogo
ulitsa Pestelya
ulitsa Ryleeva
Artilleriyskaya ulitsa
Grodnensky per
Saperny per
ulitsa Krasnoy Svyazi
Baskov per
ulitsa Nekrasova
Ozernoy per
Kovensky per
ulitsa Zhukovskogo
Liteyny prospekt
ulitsa Korolenko
ulitsa Chehova
Fontannaya
Paradnaya
Grechesky prospekt
Ligovsky Prospekt
9 -ya Sovetskaya
8 -ya Sovetskaya
7 -ya Sovetskaya ulitsa
6 -ya Sovetskaya ulitsa
5 -ya Sovetskaya ulitsa
4-ya Sovetskaya ulitsa
3-ya Sovetskaya ulitsa
2-ya Sovetskaya ulitsa
Orlovsky per
per U Gromovoy
Degtyarnaya ulitsa
Nevsky prospekt
Mihailovskaya
Dumskaya ulitsa
ulitsa Kazanskaya
Tyulenina
per Krylova
pl Ostrovskogo
ul Zodchego Rossi
ulitsa Lomonosova
Bankov per
Apraksin per
Torgovy per
Gorokhovaya ulitsa
ulitsa Efimova
Moskovsky prospekt
Shcherbakov per
ulitsa Rubinshteyna
Grafsky per
Stremyannaya ulitsa
Dimitrovsky per
Povarskoy per
Kolokolnaya ulitsa
ulitsa Marata
Kolomenskaya ulitsa
Ligovsky prospekt
Konnaya
Poltavskaya
Harkovskaya ulitsa
Telezhnaya
Mirgorodskaya
per Dzhambula
ulitsa Borodinskaya
Razyezaya ulitsa
Svecnoy per
Zagorodny prospekt
Sotsialisticheskaya ulitsa
ulitsa Dostoevskogo
ulitsa Pravdy
Zvenigorodskaya ulitsa
Transportny per
Kolomenskaya
ulitsa Konstantina Zaslonova
ulitsa Pechatnika Grigoreva
Borovaya ulitsa
Romenskaya ulitsa
ulitsa Chernyhovskogo
Pavlogradsky per
ulitsa Tyushina
Podezdnoy per
ulitsa Vvedenskaya
nab kanala
ulitsa Vvedenskogo kanala
Ruzovskaja ulitsa
Mozhayskaya ulitsa
Vereyskaya ulitsa
Podolskaya ulitsa
Serpuhovskaya ulitsa
Bronnitskaya
Klimsky prospekt
Malodetskoselsky prospekt
nab Obvodnogo kanala
Dnepropetrovskaya ulitsa
Kremenchugskaya ulitsa
Voronezhskaya ulitsa
Kurskaya ulitsa
Priluksakaya ulitsa
Tambovskaya ulitsa
Rasstannaya ulitsa
Ribinskaya ulitsa
Borovaya ulitsa
Ligovsky prospekt
Maslyany per
Zaozernaya ulitsa
Smolenskaya ulitsa
Kievskaya ulitsa
ulitsa Bulavskogo
Chernigovskaya ulitsa
Moskovsky prospekt

MAP 3
MAP 4
MAP 6

1 2 3 4 5 6 7 8 9 10 11 12 13 14 15 16 17 18 19 20 21 30 31 32 33 34 35 36 37 38 39 40 41 42 43 44 45 46 47 48 49 50 51 52 53 54 55 56 57 58 59 60 61

0 250 500 m

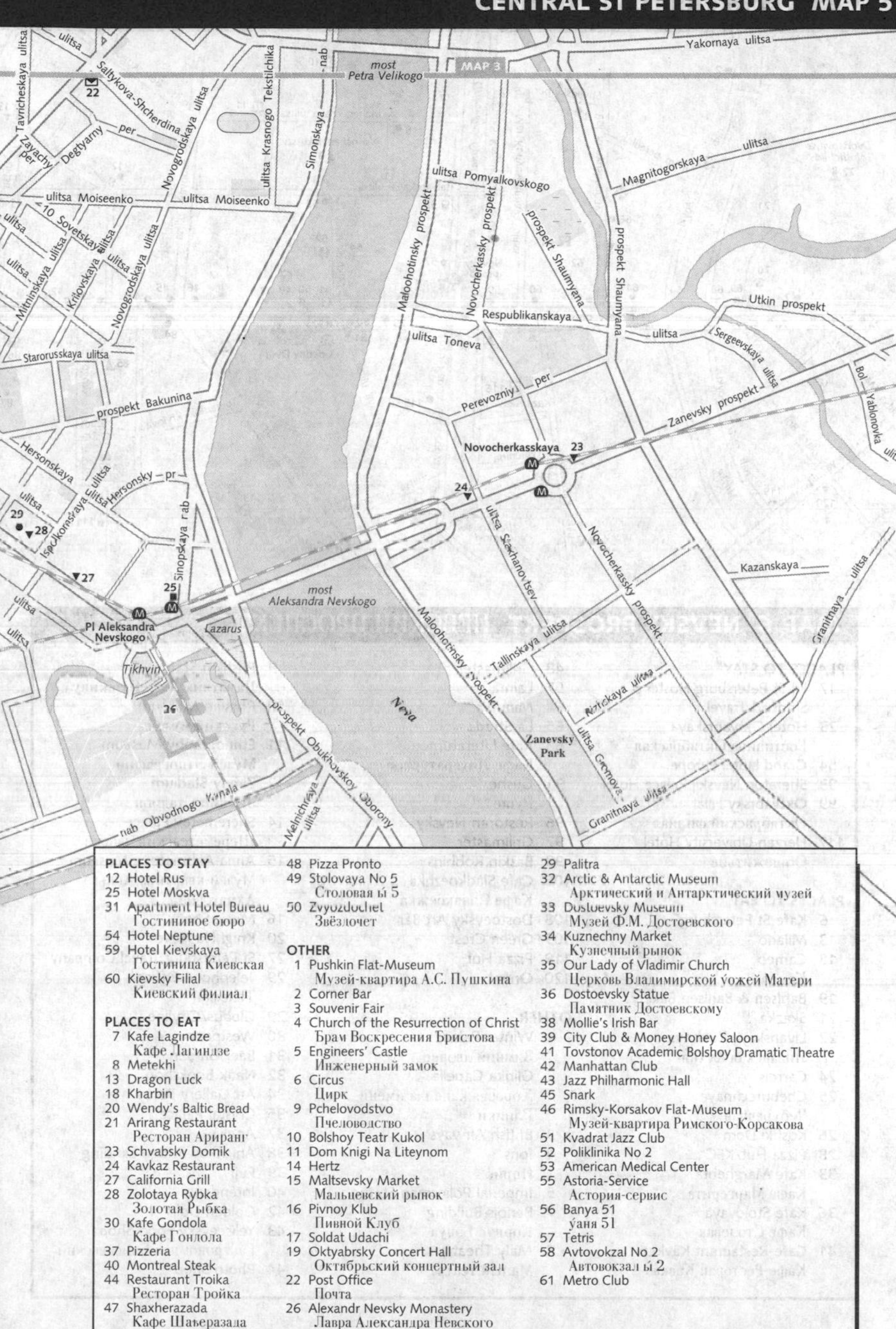

MAP 3
most Petra Velikogo
Yakornaya ulitsa
Tavricheskaya ulitsa
Saltykova-Shcherdina ulitsa
Degtyarny per
Zayachy per
Novgorodskaya ulitsa
ulitsa Krasnogo Tekstilchika
Simonskaya nab
ulitsa Moiseenko
10 Sovetskaya ulitsa
Mytninskaya ulitsa
Krilovskaya ulitsa
Starorusskaya ulitsa
prospekt Bakunina
Hersonskaya ulitsa
Hersonsky pr
Ispolkomskaya ulitsa
Sinopskaya nab
Magnitogorskaya ulitsa
ulitsa Pomyalkovskogo
Maloohotinsky prospekt
Novocherkassky prospekt
prospekt Shaumyana
Respublikanskaya ulitsa
ulitsa Toneva
Utkin prospekt
Sergeevskaya ulitsa
Perevozniy per
Zanevsky prospekt
Bol Yablonovka ulitsa
Novocherkasskaya
ulitsa Sakhanovtseva
Kazanskaya
Granitnaya ulitsa
most Aleksandra Nevskogo
Pl Aleksandra Nevskogo
Lazarus
Tikhvin
Tallinskaya ulitsa
Rizhskaya ulitsa
Neva
Zanevsky Park
ulitsa Gromova
prospekt Obukhovskoy Oborony
Melnichnaya ulitsa
nab Obvodnogo Kanala

PLACES TO STAY
12 Hotel Rus
25 Hotel Moskva
31 Apartment Hotel Bureau
Гостининое бюро
54 Hotel Neptune
59 Hotel Kievskaya
Гостиница Киевская
60 Kievsky Filial
Киевский филиал

PLACES TO EAT
7 Kafe Lagindze
Кафе Лагиндзе
8 Metekhi
13 Dragon Luck
18 Kharbin
20 Wendy's Baltic Bread
21 Arirang Restaurant
Ресторан Ариранг
23 Schvabsky Domik
24 Kavkaz Restaurant
27 California Grill
28 Zolotaya Rybka
Золотая Рыбка
30 Kafe Gondola
Кафе Гонлола
37 Pizzeria
40 Montreal Steak
44 Restaurant Troika
Ресторан Тройка
47 Shaxherazada
Кафе Шаъеразала
48 Pizza Pronto
49 Stolovaya No 5
Столовая ы 5
50 Zvyozdochet
Звёздочет

OTHER
1 Pushkin Flat-Museum
Музей-квартира А.С. Пушкина
2 Corner Bar
3 Souvenir Fair
4 Church of the Resurrection of Christ
Брам Воскресения Бристова
5 Engineers' Castle
Инженерный замок
6 Circus
Цирк
9 Pchelovodstvo
Пчеловодство
10 Bolshoy Teatr Kukol
11 Dom Knigi Na Liteynom
14 Hertz
15 Maltsevsky Market
Мальцевский рынок
16 Pivnoy Klub
Пивной Клуб
17 Soldat Udachi
19 Oktyabrsky Concert Hall
Октябрьский концертный зал
22 Post Office
Почта
26 Alexandr Nevsky Monastery
Лавра Александра Невского
29 Palitra
32 Arctic & Antarctic Museum
Арктический и Антарктический музей
33 Dostoevsky Museum
Музей Ф.М. Достоевского
34 Kuznechny Market
Кузнечный рынок
35 Our Lady of Vladimir Church
Церковь Владимирской уожей Матери
36 Dostoevsky Statue
Памятник Достоевскому
38 Mollie's Irish Bar
39 City Club & Money Honey Saloon
41 Tovstonov Academic Bolshoy Dramatic Theatre
42 Manhattan Club
43 Jazz Philharmonic Hall
45 Snark
46 Rimsky-Korsakov Flat-Museum
Музей-квартира Римского-Корсакова
51 Kvadrat Jazz Club
52 Poliklinika No 2
53 American Medical Center
55 Astoria-Service
Астория-сервис
56 Banya 51
уаня 51
57 Tetris
58 Avtovokzal No 2
Автовокзал ы 2
61 Metro Club

MAP 6 NEVSKY PROSPEKT НЕВСКИЙ ПРОСПЕКТ

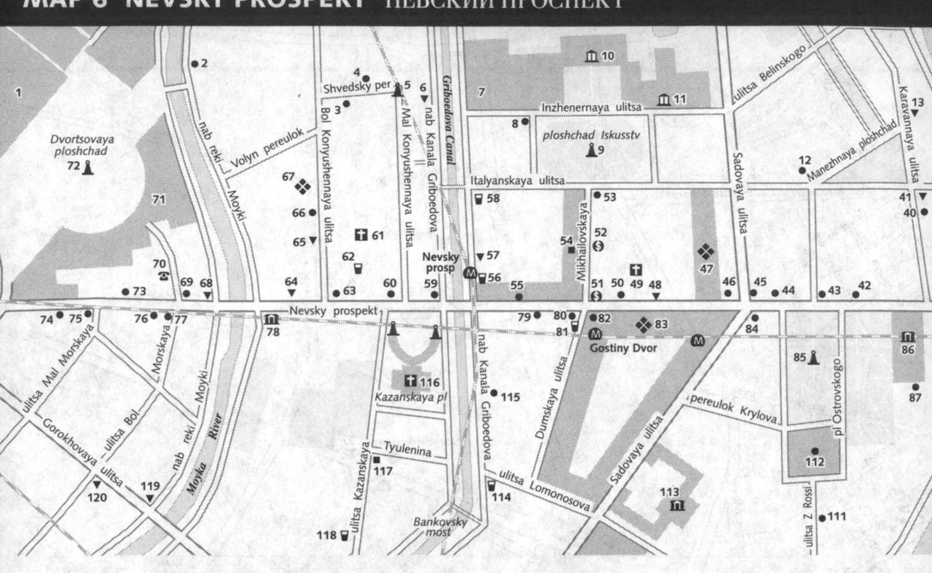

MAP 6 NEVSKY PROSPEKT НЕВСКИЙ ПРОСПЕКТ

PLACES TO STAY

17 HI St Petersburg Hostel & Sindbad Travel
23 Hotel Oktyabrskaya
Гостиница Октябрьская
54 Grand Hotel Europe
93 Sheraton Nevskij Palace Hotel
99 Oktyabrsky Filial
Октябрьский филиал
117 Herzen University Hotel
Обшежитьие

PLACES TO EAT

6 Kafe St Petersburg
13 Milano
18 Cameo
Камео
19 Bahlsen & Bahlsen Bakery
21 Skazka
22 Livanskaya Kukhnya
Ливанская Кухня
24 Carrols
25 Cheburechnaya
Чебуречная
26 Koshki Dom
28 Pizza Hut/KFC
33 Kafe Margherita
Кафе Маргерита
36 Kafe Stolovaya
Кафе Столовая
41 Cafe-Restaurant Kavkaz
Кафе-Ресторан Кавказ
48 Grillmaster
57 Laima
64 Minutka
65 La Strada
68 Kafe Literaturnoe
Кафе Литературное
91 Gushe
Гуше
96 Restoran Nevsky
97 Grillmaster
98 Baskin Robbins
105 Cafe Sladkoezhka
Кафе Сладкоежка
108 Dostoevsky Art Bar
109 Green Crest
119 Pizza Hut
120 Orient

OTHER

1 Winter Palace
Зимний дворец
2 Glinka Capella
Хоровая капелла имени Глинки
3 British Airways
4 Ipris
Иприс
5 Imperial Policeman Statue
7 Benois Building
Корпус Бэнуа
8 Maly Theatre
Малый театр
9 Pushkin Statue
Памятник А. С. Пушкину
10 Russian Museum
Русский музей
11 Ethnography Museum
Музей Этнографии
12 Zimny Stadium
Зимний Стадион
14 Sheremetev Palace
Шереметевский дворец
15 Anna Akhmatova Museum
Музей-квартира Анны Ахматовой
16 Music Shock
20 Knigi Na Neve
27 St Petersburg Travel Company
29 Telephone Office
Телефон
29 Globus/Cityline
30 Westpost
31 Beer Garden
32 Nauk Bookshop
34 Art Gallery Borey
35 Crystal Palace
37 Anglia
38 Anichkov Bridge Landing
39 Fuji
40 Intendant
42 Golden Dolls
43 Yeliseevsky Food Shop
Гастрономная Елисеевский
44 Photo Shop

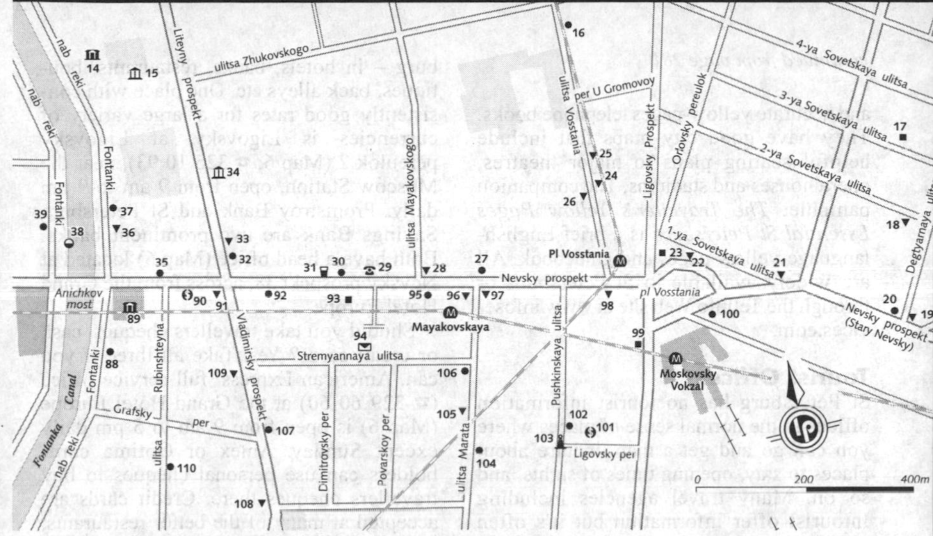

NEVSKY PROSPEKT НЕВСКИЙ ПРОСПЕКТ MAP 6

45 Teatr Kukol-Marionetok
46 Homeopathic Drug Store
47 Passazh Department Store
49 Armenian Church
50 Ticket Office
Театральная касса
51 ATM
52 Promstroy Bank &
St Petersburg Savings Bank
53 Bolshoy Zal (Big Hall)
Большой зал филармонии
55 Maly Zal imeni M. I. Glinki
(Small Hall)
Малый зал филармонии
56 Chayka
58 Club Monroe
59 Dom Knigi
Дом книги
60 Valhall
61 Lutheran Church
62 Beer Garden
63 24-Hour Pharmacy
Аптека (24-Часа)
66 Teatr Estrady
67 DLT Department Store
Д.Л.Т. Универмаг
69 Staraya Kniga
Старая книга
70 Central Telephone Office
Телефон
71 General Staff Building
Здание главного штаба
72 Alexander Column
Александровская колонна
73 Nevsky prospekt 14 (Plaque)
74 Baltic Airlines & Saigon
75 Central Airline Ticket Office
76 Bookshop
77 Iskusstv
78 Stroganov Palace
Строгановский дворец
79 Central Art Salon
80 Town Duma
81 Beer Garden
82 Excursions Ticket Booth
83 Gostiny Dvor
Department Store
Универмаг Гостиный Двор
84 National Library of Russia
Российская Националная
Библиотека
85 Catherine the Great Statue
Памятник Екатерине Второй
86 Anichkov Palace
Аничков дворец
87 Theatre of Youth Creativity
Театр юношеского творчесва
88 Cultural Centres; Libraries
89 Beloselsky-Belozersky Palace
Белосельских-Белозерских
дворец
90 ATM
92 Souvenir Shop
Сувениры
94 Post Office
Почта
95 Voyentorg
Военторг
100 24-Hour Supermarket
101 Ligovsky Currency Exchange
102 Galleries; Fish Fabrique
103 Pushkin Statue
Памятник А. С. Пушкину
104 Dzinn 24-Hour Store
Джинн
106 Nevskie Bani
107 Lensoviet Theatre
110 Maly Dramatic Theatre
111 Vaganova School of
Choreography
Хореографическое
училище имени
Вагановой
112 Pushkin Theatre
Театр драмы имени А.С.
Пушкина
113 Vorontsov Palace
Воронцовский дворец
114 Greshniki
Грешники
115 Central Train Ticket Office
Железнодорожные
билетные кассы
116 Kazan Cathedral
Казанский собор
118 Tinkoff

continued from page 281

and accurate yellow-pages telephone books. They have good city maps that include helpful seating plans to major theatres, opera houses and stadiums. The companion pamphlet *The Traveller's Yellow Pages Essential St Petersburg* is a brief English-language yellow pages and guidebook. All are widely available in St Petersburg or through the Telinfo Web site at www.infoservices.com.

Tourist Offices

St Petersburg has no tourist information offices in the normal sense of places where you can go and get a map, inquire about places to stay, opening times of sights, and so on. Many travel agencies including Intourist offer information but it's often weighted to their own interests. For more information on these agencies see the Travel Agencies section later in this chapter. If you're in a pinch, staff at the large hotels will usually help with simple requests.

Visa Registration

Though your visa should ideally be registered by the hotel or hostel you are staying in, or through the company which invited you, you may be in the situation where you must go to a local OVIR office to register it yourself. A complete list of these offices, with opening hours, is available in *Luchshee V Sankt Peterburge*, and for general inquiries, try your luck at its main office (Map 3; ☎ 278 24 81, ulitsa Kirochnaya (Saltykova-Shchedrina) 4), which is open from 9 am to 5 pm Monday to Friday. Headaches can be minimised by getting your visa registered at any hotel or hostel which can do so, even if you are not staying there, usually for a fee equivalent to the price of one night in its cheapest room. The guest reception office on the 2nd floor of Hotel Oktyabrskaya at Ligovsky prospekt 10 can do this efficiently.

Money

Exchanging Money There are exchange offices practically everywhere in St Petersburg – in hotels, banks, restaurants, boutiques, back alleys etc. One place with consistently good rates for a large variety of currencies is Ligovsky, at Ligovsky pereulok 2 (Map 6; ☎ 325 10 93), near the Moscow Station, open from 9 am to 9 pm daily. Promstroy Bank and St Petersburg Savings Bank are two prominent banks. Both have a head office (Map 6) located at Nevsky prospekt 38, across from the Grand Hotel Europe.

Should you take travellers cheques, cash or credit cards? Yes. Take all three if you can. American Express' full service office (☎ 329 60 60) at the Grand Hotel Europe (Map 6) is open from 9 am to 5 pm daily except Sunday. Amex or Optima cardholders can use personal cheques to buy travellers cheques there. Credit cards are accepted at many of the better restaurants, hotels and shops, and cash advances against Visa and MasterCard are a simple matter.

There are ATMs which accept all the major cards on the north-eastern corner of Nevsky prospekt and Mikhailovskaya ulitsa (Map 6), and inside all main metro stations, main department stores and main post offices.

Post

St Petersburg's main international and domestic post and telegraph office (*glavpochtamt;* Map 4) is at ulitsa Pochtamtskaya 9, two blocks south-west of St Isaac's Cathedral. It's open from 9 am to 8 pm Monday to Saturday and from 10 am to 6 pm on Sunday.

All nonbook parcels leaving the country must be sent from here, from Window 24 (this keeps changing though – just walk to the far left side of the main hall and look for the sign).

There are also over 400 branch offices scattered throughout the city, varying in services usually in proportion to size. A particularly friendly one is at Stremyannaya ulitsa 14 (Map 6). It is centrally located, not very busy, open from 10 am to 8 pm weekdays (until 5 pm weekends), will wrap your book or souvenir parcels (up to 5kg) and will help you fill out forms.

Express Services Express Mail Service (EMS) is provided by EMS Garantpost (☎ 311 96 71, ems@comset.net). Documents up to 2kg (500g to the USA costs $21; to Australia $30) and packages up to 31kg (5kg to the USA costs $56; to London or Paris $65; to Australia $78) take five days to reach their destination, three to European capitals. Letters and small packages can be sent from Window 15; parcels and boxes must go from their head office behind the main post office at Konnogvardeysky bulvar 4. Window 16 offers a special overnight service to Moscow and Minsk. Euroletter at Window 26 will send letters and parcels up to 2kg, charging $6 for up to 250g, $10 for 2kg. It uses express post until Sweden, then Swedish post, and swears it only takes five days to the USA and Australia.

US-managed Westpost (Map 6, ☎ 275 07 84, ☎ 327 30 92, westpost@westpost.ru, www.westpost.ru), Nevsky prospekt 86, is a privately run, international mail service for monthly and casual clients. Mail is transported daily from St Petersburg to Lappeenranta, Finland (the Switzerland of matters postal around here), and mailed from there. To the USA, a 20g letter costs $2.20, and a 1kg parcel sent express costs $55. It has a full range of delivery and courier services.

The main Western express mail services in town offer two-day delivery to Europe and the USA/Canada, and three-day delivery to Australia/New Zealand, all with services starting at $38 for letters. DHL has offices at Izmailovsky prospekt 4 (Map 4; ☎ 326 64 00) and Federal Express is at Moika 58 (Map 6; ☎ 314 40 15).

Receiving Mail The incoming state mail service is so flaky that it's rare for anyone on the move to find anything, but you can try. The most reliable option for those not staying in luxury hotels or the HI St Petersburg Hostel (which provide mail service via Finland) is limited to American Express and Optima cardholders. The wonderful folk at American Express will hold mail (letters only, no packages) and messages for cardholders and holders of travellers cheques for up to 30 days at no charge at the company's office in the Grand Hotel Europe; the mailing address is American Express, PO Box 87, SF-53501 Lappeenranta, Finland.

Westpost (see Express Services earlier) offers post boxes in Lappeenranta, with daily pick up and delivery to the Westpost office, or, for corporate clients, to their address in St Petersburg. You can become a basic Westpost client for $20 per month.

Telephone

While the city has only two million dilapidated phone lines for its four million-plus citizens, and while it may seem like your chances of winning the lottery are better than reaching the party you dialled, the situation is improving all the time. Calling from a private phone is the simplest, and, depending on the exchange rate, can be the cheapest option, especially on weekends and holidays. Calling from a hotel room is usually the most expensive option.

Payphones Payphones (таксофон, *taksofon*) are located throughout the city and are generally in working order. The green-coloured ones are the most common, and accept prepaid telephone cards (with the letters SNM – СНМ – on them), readily available from metro token booths or, at slightly higher prices, from telephone offices. There are several types of card payphones (Peterstar (☎ 329 90 90) has better prices but so far fewer phones; BCL charges the highest prices), and cards are not interchangeable.

Some older phone booths accept metro tokens (жетоны, *zhetony*) as payment. Place the token in the slot on top of the phone and dial; when the party answers, the token should drop. A series of beeps means you need to place another token in the slot or you will be disconnected.

State Telephone Offices There are several telephone offices in the centre, the most convenient being the central long-distance telephone office at ulitsa Bolshaya Morskaya 3/5 (Map 6), and the smaller, user-friendly one at Nevsky prospekt 88 (Map 6). At either place you can direct-dial calls anywhere, or order them through the operator. Prices are identical to those of private phones, but without cheap rate discounts.

Fax & Telegram

Faxes can be sent and received at the Central Telephone Office (Map 6); the incoming fax number is 314 33 60 (at Nevsky prospekt 88 the number is 314 14 80), and the cost to retrieve them is $0.40 per page. Faxes can also be sent and received at the business centres in all major hotels and in the Moscow Station, as well as at the two youth hostels, for much higher prices (to send one from the HI St Petersburg Hostel costs $10).

International telegrams can be sent from many of the larger post offices, as well as from Window 38 at the main post office.

Email & Internet Access

Hooking up to the Web is no problem here – this is Russia's cyber-window to the West. The most pleasant and least expensive place to surf or email is at the Central Telephone Office, ulitsa Bolshaya Morskaya 3/5. It has many comfy booths which you rent out at Window 6 (down the main hall and to your left) from $2 to $2.80 an hour from 9 am to 9 pm daily. There are also Internet booths at the telephone offices at Nevsky prospekt 88 (Map 6) and on 3-ya linia 8 on Vasilevsky Island (Map 2).

Tetris (Map 5; ☎ 325 48 77) is the city's first proper Internet cafe, south of metro Ligovsky Prospekt at ulitsa Charnykhovskogo 33. It charges $2.40 an hour for access from 10 am to 1 pm, $3.20 an hour from 1 pm to 9 pm, and serves good coffee and chow. You can have access to printers and get a temporary address there.

On Vasilevsky Island, you can surf the Web between 8 pm and midnight daily for $1 an hour at Betakomm (Map 4; ☎ 323 22 38), 1-ya linia 18.

There are more expensive options with no special benefits: at Westpost, Internet access is $7.20 an hour; at the HI St Petersburg Hostel $6 an hour; the hotel business centres charge even more.

To hook up to a provider, consider Cityline, located in the same offices as Globus, for some of the best prices. Peterlink (☎ 113 57 22) is another reliable company.

Internet Resources

Getting information, even the bare basics, out of Russian officials can be a frustrating, fruitless task. So it's good to know that St Pete – and Russia – has a huge presence on the Internet. There's info on everything from club dates and KGB documents to starting a business in Russia (no doubt listed under 'Risky Ventures'!).

See the European Russia Facts for the Visitor chapter for some excellent sites. Other good ones specific to St Pete are www.spb.ru (the best general starting point for St Petersburg info, including links to the St Petersburg Times and much more) and www.museum.ru (an excellent introduction to the world of Russian art, with links to many of the country's best museums, including the Hermitage).

Travel Agencies

As there is still no official, city-run tourist information office, the best sources of information are private companies. There are dozens – shop around to make sure you're getting the best deal. Here are some of the most reliable:

Sindbad Travel

Map 6; ☎ 327 83 84, fax 329 90 19, sindbad @sindbad.ru, www.sindbad.ru, 3-ya Sovetskaya ulitsa 28, inside the HI St Petersburg Hostel; its second office is inside the Philological Faculty of the St Petersburg University, at Universitetskaya naberezhnaya 11, Map 4; ☎ 324 08 80

This is a highly efficient, Western-style student (and adult) discount air ticket agency specialising in one-way or short advance tickets. The staff can also book onward youth hostel bookings through the IBN system, and book train tickets. The agency sells ISIC and ITIC cards and can make changes on student tickets issued elsewhere.

Kargal Tours

Map 4; ☎/fax 356 15 10, kangal@ mail.nevalink.ru, Nalichnaya ulitsa 3/21, Vasilevsky Island

This is another class act. The staff here can efficiently arrange tourist and business visas at reasonable rates, get discounted rates at hotels and private apartments, organise tours and language courses, and do anything else you need to have done.

American Express
Map 6; Grand Hotel Europe
Believe it or not, these people also do discounted airline tickets.

Bookshops

You'll finds books for sale everywhere – street corners, pedestrian subways, grocery shops. Anglia (Map 6; ☎ 279 82 84), Fontanka 40, is the only oasis of Western books in the city, with a dizzying collection of art, history and literature books at dizzyingly Western prices (but ISIC card holders get a 5% discount). Get your Lonely Planet guidebooks here too (the HI St Petersburg Hostel is the only other place to find them). Otherwise, English books are scarce. Try Café Idiot (see Places to Eat) for some used paperbacks (John Fowles and the like).

Snark (Map 5; ☎ 164 93 66), Zagorodny prospekt 21, was the first Russian bookstore in the city with a Western look and feel (shelves off which it's actually possible to browse!). This friendly, well stocked place gives discounts to members, features monthly themes, and has lots for the kids.

Dom Knigi (Map 6), the biggest bookshop in town, is a trip in itself. It's located in the pre-revolutionary headquarters of the Singer sewing machine company and has two newly renovated floors of mainly Russian books on every subject imaginable. While choice and availability is small compared to Western abundance, this is as good as it gets. Excellent souvenir books are on the 2nd floor. Other first-rate modern bookshops include Dom Knigi Na Liteynom (Map 5) at Liteyny prospekt 30 and Knigi Na Neve (Map 6) at Nevsky prospekt 140.

Grouped near the corner of Nevsky prospekt and ulitsa Bolshaya Morskaya (Map 6) you'll find four bookshops facing each other. Iskusstv, on the south-west corner, is tiny but has a good collection of art books. Of the four, the one next door to Iskusstv is the cheapest. Across Nevsky and west of the corner, the art bookshop is pretty much a rip-off, while on the eastern side, Staraya Kniga has a good collection of old books and great Soviet posters.

Newspapers & Magazines

The undisputed king of the hill in locally published English-language news is the excellent *St Petersburg Times*, which was begun by a Kiwi-led team in 1993, and grew so big it was bought by the *Moscow Times*. Today it's a reliable bi-weekly (Tuesday and Friday) paper packed with news and listings. It's available at hotels, restaurants and youth hostels.

Pulse is a slick colour monthly with English and Russian editions, packed with tons of entertainment listings and insightful thought-pieces, written from a young, fresh outlook. It's available free from outlets all over the city. The monthly *Neva News*, also easily found in most hotels, really tries hard but comes off as amusingly naive. But it's written with a great passion for the city and there's always something interesting in it.

Radio & TV

Aside from the BBC World Service and Voice of America on Short Wave (SW), don't expect to hear the Queen's English (or its US variant) on St Petersburg's radio waves. Some local stations worth tuning into include Radio Rossiy Sankt Peterburg at 107FM and Radio Petrograd Russky Shanson at 100.9FM. In St Petersburg you can see the two national channels plus two local ones: St Petersburg Television, with some pithy, unconventional current affairs programs that have gained a wide audience, and Channel 4, educational evening TV.

Cultural Centres

There's a whole lot o' culture going on at naberezhnaya reki Fontanki 46. On the 3rd floor sits the British Council St Petersburg (Map 6; ☎ 325 60 74), which holds classical concerts, theatre and other performances and arranges for exchanges between Russia and the UK of students, professionals and (frighteningly) economists. It has a great resource centre for foreign teachers of English.

The Goethe Institute St Petersburg (Map 6; ☎ 311 21 00) is in the same building but is hard to find: walk into the lobby, straight to the back, turn right, follow the narrow hallway and go up the flight of stairs.

The American Center (Map 3; ☎ 311 89 05), ulitsa Millionnaya 5, at the Marble Palace, disseminates American culture (snigger) when it's not too busy doing very important things. It's open from 9 am to 5.30 pm.

Laundry

Unless you're staying at a hotel, the laundrette is as close as your bathroom. Don't bother looking for any 'beautiful laundrettes' here. Most hotels and hostels offer some laundry service at varying prices. Otherwise, a few dry cleaning places offer relatively quick service (that is, three days or less!). One of the most reliable is Konung (Map 2; ☎ 323 42 97) on 6-ya linia 25, near metro Vasileostrovskaya. It charges $1.40 per 5kg load for two-day service, or $2.25 for three-hour service, and is open from 11 am until 7 pm daily.

Toilets

Public toilets – when you can find them – are better left unfound. Your best bets are large hotels, restaurants and McDonald's, of which St Petersburg has many.

Left Luggage

All the major train stations have luggage lockers and/or left-luggage services. You can also check your bags in at most of the major hotels.

Medical Services

Unless you're an uninsured US or South African resident and citizen, medical treatment in St Petersburg will be beneath the standards you're used to receiving at home. Nonetheless, within Russia, St Petersburg is second only to Moscow in medical services and offers adequate routine, and some emergency, treatment. More serious medical emergencies are best treated outside Russia; Finland is the best option.

The best bet for Western-quality treatment in St Petersburg is the American Medical Center (AMC; Map 5; ☎ 326 17 30), Serpukhovskaya ulitsa 10. This US-run facility offers a full range of medical services including gynaecological and paediatric care, dentistry, 24-hour emergency care, an emergency room, ambulance services, house calls and medical evacuations. Prices are stellar, with a basic (often required) consultation costing $215; a check-up won't be less than $100, and an HIV test will cost $75. Prices are marginally cheaper for members, but they're already paying $55 a month for the privilege.

For routine matters, a Russian *poliklinika* provides perfectly adequate care. We asked AMC doctors where they'd send their family members if the AMC weren't an option: they all said Poliklinika No 2 (Map 5; ☎ 316 62 72), Moskovsky prospekt 22, the former clinic of choice for diplomatic staff. The clinic charges $70 for house calls, $26 for in-house visits with doctors, and $31 for an HIV test. Free, anonymous HIV tests and Hepatitis B test for under $1 are available at the City Centre for Fighting AIDS (Map 4;

Warning

No matter how thirsty you are, never drink unboiled tap water in St Petersburg. In addition to heavy metal pollutants and harmful bacteria, it contains *Giardia lamblia*, a nasty parasite that causes unpleasant stomach cramps, nausea, bloated stomach, diarrhoea and frequent gas. There is no preventative drug. Metronidazole (brand name Flagyl) or Tinidazole (known as Fasigyn), are the recommended treatments. Antibiotics are of no use. Symptoms may not appear for up to several weeks after infection, and may recur for years.

To be absolutely safe, only drink water that has been boiled for 10 minutes or filtered through an antimicrobial water filter (PUR brand makes a good portable one). Treat ice with suspicion and avoid fruits and vegetables that may have been washed in the water – vegetables that peel are safest. While accepting tea or coffee at someone's house should be safe, it's best to always stick to bottled water, even for brushing your teeth. Bathing, showering and shaving, though, should cause no problems.

☎ 259 94 05) at naberezhnaya Obvodnogo kanala 179, near metro Baltiskaya. For more listings, check *Luchshee V Sankt Peterburge* or *The Traveller's Yellow Pages*.

Pharmacies Pharmacies (singular *apteka*), are located all over the city and most are well stocked with Western medications and toiletries. Apteka Petrofarm at Nevsky prospekt 22 (Map 6) is an excellent, all-night pharmacy. After hours, use the side entrance on ulitsa Bolshaya Konyushennaya (under the archway of house No 14 and to the right). There's a great homeopathic store at Nevsky prospekt 50 (Map 6).

Emergency

Emergency telephone numbers (Russian-speaking operators) are ☎ 01 for fire and ☎ 02 for police. The state-run ambulance service is still free; Russian speakers can get help by dialling ☎ 03. If you're trying to find out if someone's been in an accident and been picked up by ambulance (and where they were taken), dial ☎ 278 00 55.

Dangers & Annoyances

Every year in early spring and during winter thaws, several people die when child-sized, sword-shaped icicles fall from St Petersburg's rooftops and balconies. Walking a city block at this time can be exhausting: while stepping with trepidation on sheer ice, negotiating potholes and avoiding pedestrians, you must also crane your neck skywards to make sure one of these monsters is not dangling above your head.

Mosquitoes are another nightmare. From May through September, you may wish to leap from the very window that let the bastards in in the first place. You will want to bring along industrial-strength repellent that's at least 95% DEET. The plug-in gizmos which slowly heat repellent-saturated cardboard pads are available everywhere in the city and are pretty effective.

If you're staying in a ground-level apartment in the city centre in early autumn, just before the central heating is turned on and after it starts getting cool, you may have problems with fleas, which come up through floorboards looking for warmth. Yes, they are very happy to feed off humans if rats, their usual sup, are not around. At the first sign of these hopping devils (usually itchy ankles!), get out of the place; they can carry some of the world's worst diseases, like the bubonic plague.

THE HISTORIC HEART

Dvortsovaya Ploshchad (Map 6)

From Nevsky Prospekt or Gostiny Dvor metro, a 15 minute walk west along Nevsky prospekt brings you to Dvortsovaya ploshchad (Palace Square), where the stunning green, white and gold **Winter Palace** (Zimny dvorets) appears like a mirage (the prettiest way to view it for the first time is by entering through the grand arches at the end of Bolshaya Morskaya and see it slowly emerge), its rococo profusion of columns, windows and recesses topped by rows of larger-than-life statues. A residence of tsars from 1762 to 1917, it's now the biggest part of the Hermitage art museum.

During Bloody Sunday (9 January 1905), tsarist troops fired on workers who had peaceably gathered in the square – the shootings sparked the 1905 revolution. And it was across Dvortsovaya ploshchad that the much exaggerated storming of the Winter Palace took place during the 1917 October Revolution. There *was* gunfire before the Provisional government in the palace surrendered to the revolutionaries, but the famous charge across the square was largely invented by the film maker Eisenstein.

The 47.5m Alexander Column in the square commemorates the 1812 victory over Napoleon and is named after Alexander I. The former General Staff buildings of the Russian army (1819-29) curve round the south of the square in two great blocks joined by arches, which are topped by a chariot of victory, another monument to the Napoleonic wars.

Admiralty (Map 4)

The gilded spire of the old Admiralty at the western edge of Dvortsovaya ploshchad is an unmistakable St Petersburg landmark, currently under renovation (the spire may look like gold, but it's actually made of wood, which had begun to rot). It's visible as you walk along most of Gorokhovaya ulitsa and Vosnesensky and Nevsky prospekts. This spot was the headquarters of the Russian navy from 1711 to 1917, and today the building houses the city's largest naval college. Constructed in 1806-23 to the designs of Andreyan Zakharov, it's a foremost example of the Russian Empire style of classical architecture, with its rows of white columns and plentiful reliefs and statuary. One feature you can get a close look at is the nymphs holding giant globes flanking the main gate. Its gardens and fountain are particularly lovely in summer.

Ploshchad Dekabristov (Map 4)

West of the Admiralty, ploshchad Dekabristov (Decembrists' Square) is named after the first feeble attempt at a Russian revolution – the Decembrists' Uprising of 14 December 1825. Inspired by radical ideas from France during the Napoleonic campaigns, young officers tried to depose the new Tsar Nicholas I by drawing up troops in the square. But they allowed their opponents to argue with them and were finally dispersed with grapeshot. Most of the leaders ended up on the gallows or in Siberia.

The most famous statue of Peter the Great, the **Bronze Horseman**, with his mount rearing above the snake of treason, stands at the river end of the square. It was cast for Catherine the Great by Frenchman Etienne Falconet. The inscription reads *To Peter I from Catherine II – 1782*. This statue, along with the view of the SS Peter & Paul Fortress against raised drawbridges during summer white nights, has become the trademark image of the new spirit of St Petersburg.

Most of the west side of the square is occupied by the Central State Historical Archives in the former Senate and Synod buildings, built in 1829-34. The **Manege Central Exhibition Hall** (☎ 314 82 53) across the street used to be the Horse Guards' Riding School (constructed in 1804-07 from a design by Quarenghi). It now hosts rotating exhibitions and is open from 11 am to 7 pm daily except Thursday. Admission is $0.40.

St Isaac's Cathedral (Map 4)

The golden dome of bulky St Isaac's Cathedral (Isaakievsky sobor), looming just south of ploshchad Dekabristov, dominates the St Petersburg skyline. The Frenchman Ricard de Montferrand won a competition organised by Alexander I to design the cathedral in 1818. It took so long to build – until 1858 – that Alexander's successor Nicholas I was able to insist on a more grandiose structure than Montferrand had planned. Special ships and a railway had to be built to carry the granite for the huge pillars from Finland. There's a statue of Montferrand holding a model of the cathedral on the west facade.

Since 1990, after a 62-year gap, services have been held in the cathedral on major religious holidays.

St Isaac's obscenely lavish interior is open as a museum from 11 am to 6 pm Thursday to Monday, and to 5 pm Tuesday (closed Wednesday and the last Monday of the month). Admission is $8 ($4 for ISIC holders), and photography is not permitted.

Don't miss the sublime city views from the colonnade *(kolonnada)* around the drum of the dome, which closes an hour earlier than the cathedral. You need separate tickets for the colonnade, costing $3.20 ($1.60 for ISIC holders). Babushkas will try to prevent you from taking photos of the city skyline from up there (something intelligent about national security), but we snuck a few when they weren't looking.

Note that it's several hundred steps up the spiral staircase to the colonnade, and there are no escalators. Every printed resource on this matter seems to come up with a different number; we got bored after 180, though 262 seems a reasonable figure.

St Petersburg History Museum (Map 4)

Located about 600m west of ploshchad Dekabristov, at Angliskaya naberezhnaya 44, this interesting museum focuses on St Petersburg since the 1917 revolution. Though there's no material in English, it's good on the 1941-44 siege. It's open from 11 am to 6 pm (closed Wednesday).

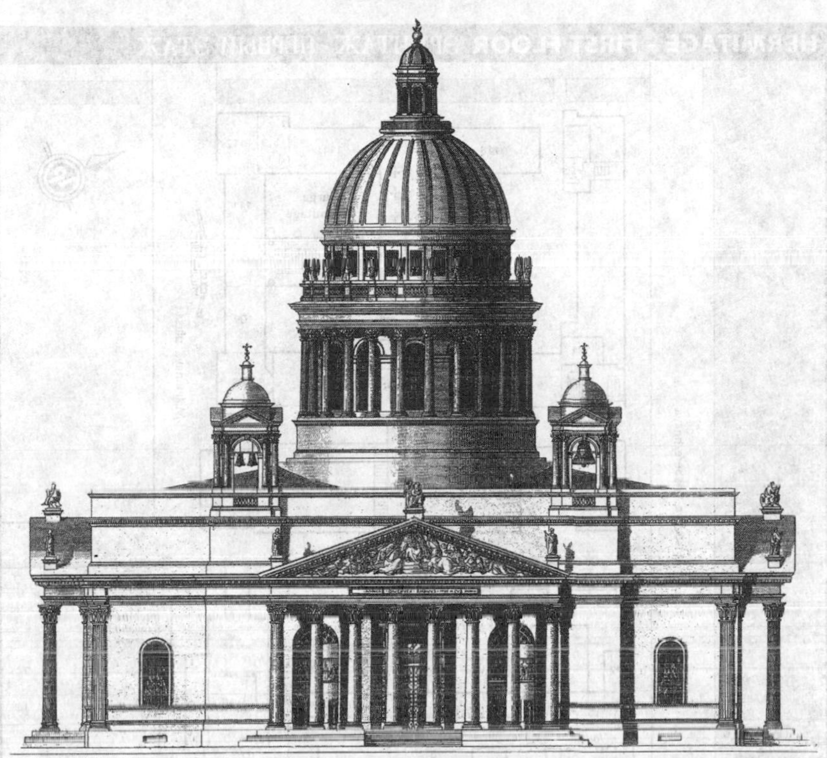

The magnificent St Isaac's Cathedral

THE HERMITAGE

Set in the magnificent palace from which tsars ruled Russia for one-and-a-half centuries, the State Hermitage (Gosudarstvenny ermitazh) fully lives up to its reputation as one of the country's chief glories. You can be absorbed for days by its treasures and still come out wishing for more.

The vastness of the place – five main buildings, of which the Winter Palace alone has 1057 rooms and 117 staircases – demands a little planning. It may be useful to make a reconnaissance tour first, then return another day to enjoy your favourite bits.

The State Hermitage consists of five linked buildings along riverside Dvortsovaya naberezhnaya. From west to east they are the Winter Palace, the Little Hermitage, the Old and New Hermitages (sometimes grouped together and called the Large Hermitage) and the Hermitage Theatre. The art collection is on all three floors of the Winter Palace and the main two floors of the Little and Large Hermitages. The Hermitage Theatre is generally not open to the public.

An excellent Web site for information about the Hermitage is www.hermitage.ru.

See the following pages for floor plans and a guide to the Hermitage's collection.

History

The present baroque/rococo Winter Palace was commissioned from Rastrelli in 1754 by Empress Elizabeth. Catherine the Great

continued on page 308

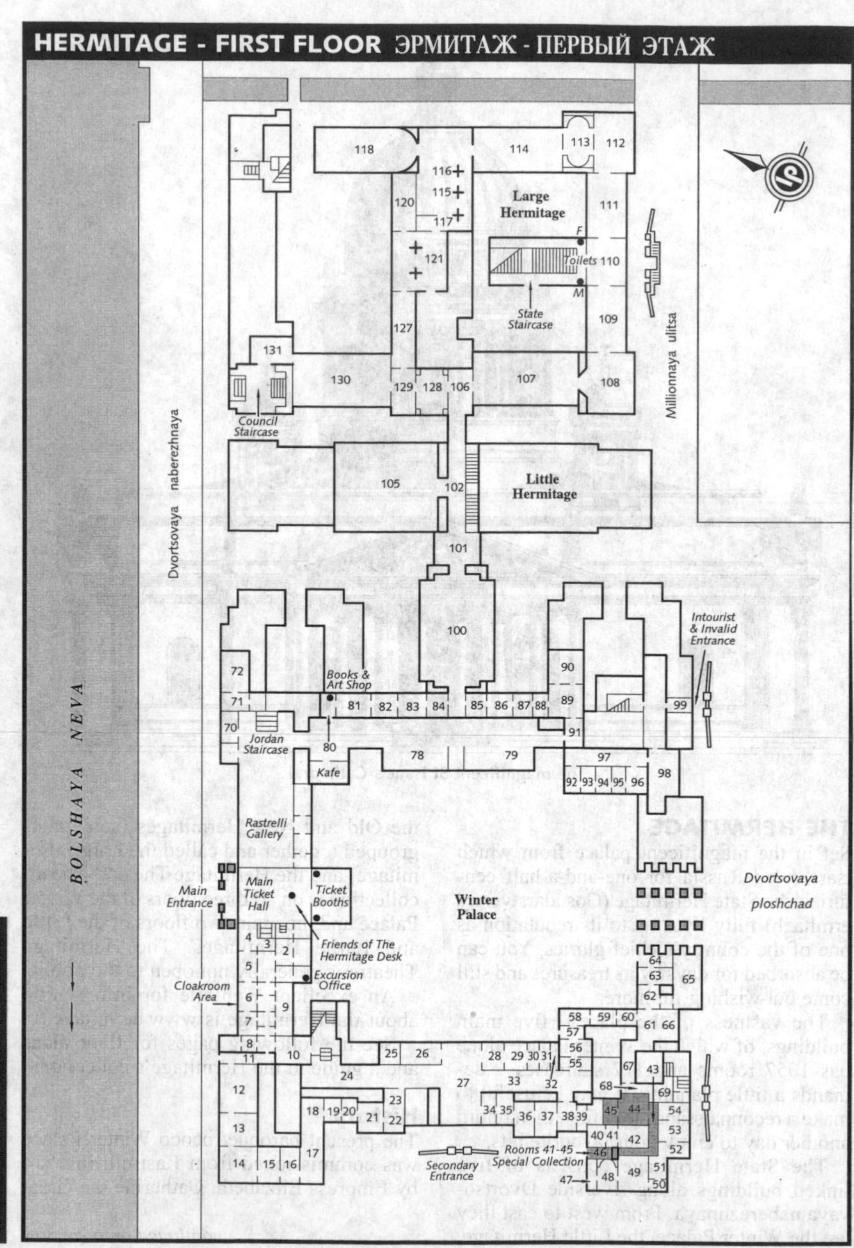
HERMITAGE - FIRST FLOOR ЭРМИТАЖ - ПЕРВЫЙ ЭТАЖ
Large Hermitage
Little Hermitage
Winter Palace
State Staircase
Council Staircase
Jordan Staircase
Toilets
Books & Art Shop
Kafe
Rastrelli Gallery
Main Entrance
Main Ticket Hall
Ticket Booths
Friends of The Hermitage Desk
Excursion Office
Cloakroom Area
Intourist & Invalid Entrance
Secondary Entrance
Rooms 41-45 Special Collection
Dvortsovaya naberezhnaya
Millionnaya ulitsa
Dvortsovaya ploshchad
BOLSHAYA NEVA

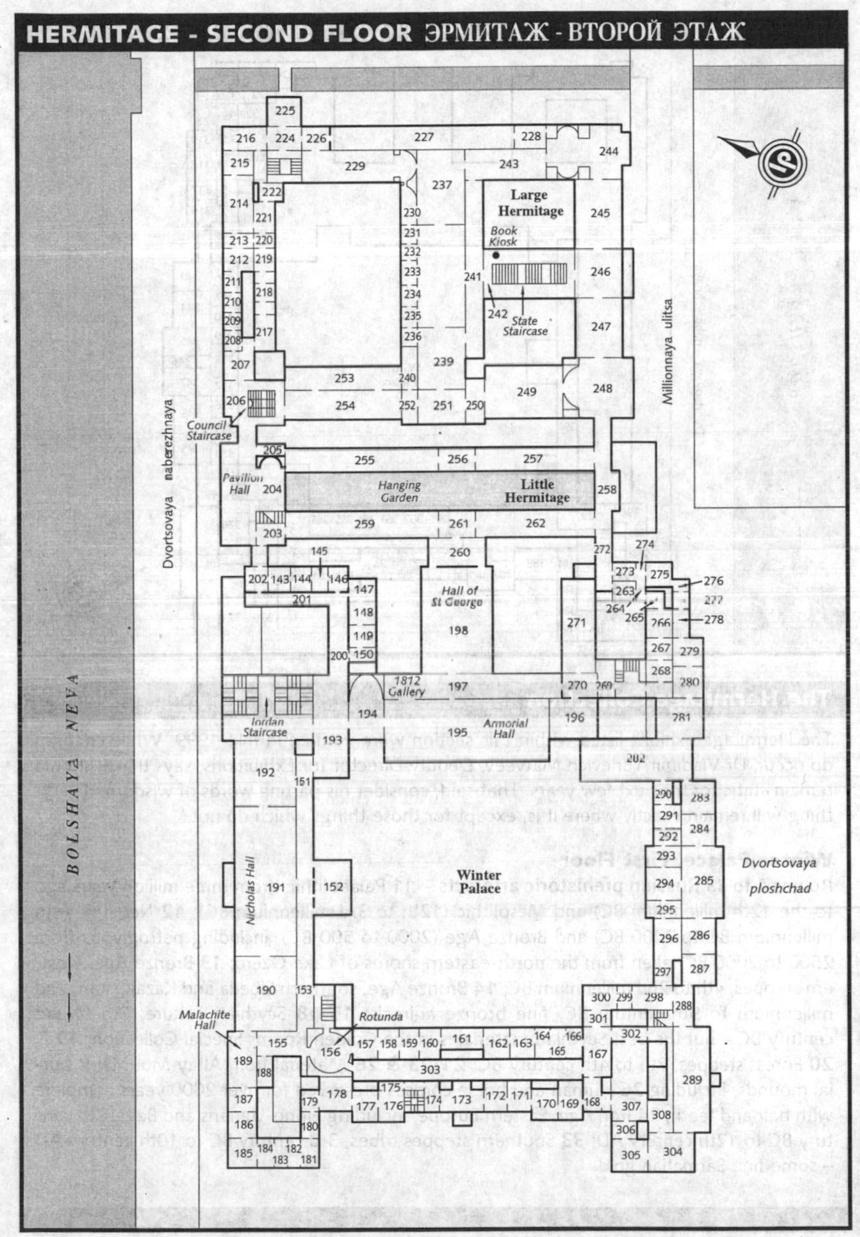
HERMITAGE - SECOND FLOOR ЭРМИТАЖ - ВТОРОЙ ЭТАЖ
Large Hermitage
Book Kiosk
State Staircase
Council Staircase
Pavilion Hall
Hanging Garden
Little Hermitage
Hall of St George
1812 Gallery
Jordan Staircase
Armorial Hall
Winter Palace
Nicholas Hall
Malachite Hall
Rotunda
Dvortsovaya naberezhnaya
Millionnaya ulitsa
Dvortsovaya ploshchad
BOLSHAYA NEVA

HERMITAGE - THIRD FLOOR ЭРМИТАЖ - ТРЕТИЙ ЭТАЖ

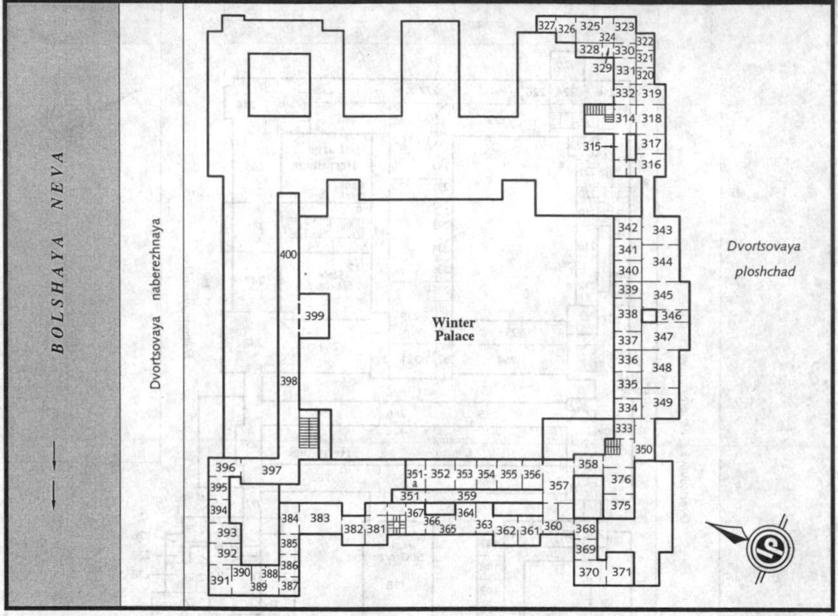

BOLSHAYA NEVA
Dvortsovaya naberezhnaya
Winter Palace
Dvortsovaya ploshchad

The Hermitage Collection

The Hermitage exhibits listed within this section were verified in mid-1999. While changes do occur, Dr Vladimir Yurievich Matveev, Deputy Director for Exhibitions, says things should remain static for the next few years. That said, consider his parting words of wisdom: 'Everything will remain exactly where it is, except for those things which do not.'

Winter Palace, First Floor

Rooms 1 to 33 Russian prehistoric artefacts – 11 Palaeolithic (from three million years ago to the 12th millennium BC) and Mesolithic (12th to 3rd millennium BC); **12** Neolithic (4th millennium BC to 2400 BC) and Bronze Age (2000 to 500 BC), including petroglyphs from 2500 to 2000 BC taken from the north-eastern shores of Lake Ozero; **13** Bronze Age, western steppes, 4th to 2nd millennium BC; **14** Bronze Age, southern Siberia and Kazakhstan, 2nd millennium to 9th century BC, fine bronze animals; **15-18** Scythian culture, 7th to 3rd century BC – but the best Scythian material is in the Golden Rooms Special Collection; **19 & 20** Forest steppes, 7th to 4th century BC; **21-23 & 26** Material from Altay Mountains burial mounds, including **26** Human and horse corpses preserved for over 2000 years complete with hair and teeth; **24** Iron Age, Eastern Europe, including Finno-Ugrians and Balts, 8th century BC to 12th century AD; **33** Southern steppes tribes, 3rd century BC to 10th century AD – some fine Sarmatian gold.

The Hermitage Collection

Rooms 34 to 40, 46 to 69 The Russian East – 34-39 Central Asia, 4th century BC to 13th century AD; **55-66** Caucasus and Transcaucasia, 10th century BC to 16th century AD, including **56** Urartu, 9th to 7th century BC, **59** Dagestan, 6th to 11th century AD, **66** 14th century Italian colonies in Crimea, **67-69** Golden Horde, 13th to 14th century.

Room 100 Ancient Egypt A fine collection, much of it uncovered by Russian archaeologists; there is no English labelling except the signs saying 'Please Do Not Touch'.

TAMSIN WILSON

The two tonne Cauldron of Tamerlane, cast in bronze in 1399 by master smith Abdal-Aziz for a mosque in present-day Kazakhstan, and now part of the Hermitage's Central Asian collection

Little Hermitage, First Floor

Rooms 101 & 102 Roman marble.
Room 105 Closed at the time of writing.

Large Hermitage, First Floor

Rooms 105 to 131 Ancient Classical culture – 106-109 & 127 Roman sculpture, 1st century BC to 4th century AD; **111-114** Ancient Greece, 8th to 2nd century BC, mostly ceramics and sculpture; **115-117 & 121** Greek colonies around northern Black Sea, 7th century BC to 3rd century AD; **128** The huge 19th century jasper Kolyvanskaya Vase from Siberia; **130 & 131** Ancient Italy, 7th to 2nd century BC, including Etruscan vases and bronze mirrors.

Winter Palace, Second Floor

Rooms 143 to 146 French paintings of the 19th and 20th century This is most of what used to be called the Hidden Treasures Revealed exhibit. It boasts oil paintings captured by the Red Army from private collections in Germany, including works by Monet, Degas, Renoir, Cézanne, Picasso and Matisse, almost all never before publicly displayed.

Rooms 147 to 189 Russian culture and art – 147-150 10th to 15th century; **151** 15th to 17th century; **152** Icons, ceramics, jewellery etc from 'Moscow baroque' period, first half of the 17th century; **153** Items relating to Peter the Great; **155-166** Late 17th and early 18th century, including **155** Moorish Dining Room; **156** Rotunda, with a bust of Peter the Great and a brass Triumphal Pillar, topped by a Rastrelli-created statue of Peter; **157 to first half of 161** Petrovskaya Gallereya, including lathing machinery used by Peter; **161** A chandelier partly built by the Great Guy; **162** Mosaic of Peter by Lomonosov; **167-173** Mid to end 18th century – spot the bizarre 1772 tapestry image of Australia (**167**); **175-187** (start at 187 and work your way back) Rooms occupied by the last imperial family, now displaying 19th century interior design, including **178** Nicholas II's Gothic library; **188 Small Dining Room** (Malaya stolovaya), where the Provisional Government was arrested by the Bolsheviks on 26 October 1917; **189 Malachite Hall** (Malakhitovy zal) with two tonnes of gorgeous green malachite columns, boxes, bowls and urns.

The Hermitage Collection

Rooms 190 to 192 Neva Enfilade One of two sets of state rooms for ceremonies and balls: **190 Concert Hall** (Kontsertny zal) for small balls, with an 18th century silver coffin for the remains of Alexandr Nevsky; **191** Great or Nicholas Hall (Bolshoy zal), scene of great winter balls, and **192** The Fore Hall; all are now used for temporary exhibitions.
Rooms 193 to 198 Great Enfilade The second series of state rooms: **193** Field Marshals' Hall; **194** Peter the Great's Hall (Petrovsky zal), with his throne; **195** Armorial Hall, bright and gilt encrusted, displaying 16th to 19th century Western European silver; **197** The 1812 Gallery, hung with portraits of Russian and allied Napoleonic war leaders; **198** Hall of St George or Great Throne Room – once a state room, now used for temporary exhibitions.
Rooms 200 to 202 Western European tapestry, 16th to 19th century.
Roms 263 to 268 German art, 15th to 18th century, including Dürer and Lucas Cranach the Elder. **Rooms 269 to 271 Western European porcelain**, 18th century (**271** was the tsars' cathedral).
Rooms 272 to 289 French art, 15th to 18th century, including **272-273** Tapestries, ceramics, metalwork; **279** Paintings by Poussin; **280** Lorrain; **284** Watteau.
Rooms 298 to 302 British art, 16th to 19th century, including **299** Reynolds; **300** Gainsborough's *Lady in Blue*.
Room 303 'Dark Corridor': Western European tapestry, 16th to 18th century, mainly from Flanders. Follow the confusing trail through 167 and 308 to get to **304** A wonderful collection of **Western European stone engravings** from the 13th to the 19th century. **305** The **Burgundy Hall**, containing English and French porcelain. **306 Maria Alexandrovna's bedroom**. **307** the **Blue Bedroom**, containing French, Austrian and German porcelain.

Little Hermitage, Second Floor

Room 204 Pavilion Hall (Pavilonny zal) A sparkling white-and-gold room with lovely chandeliers, tables, galleries, and columns. The south windows look on to Catherine the Great's hanging garden; the floor mosaic in front of them is copied from a Roman bath. Roman and Florentine mosaics from the 18th and 19th century, and the amazing Peacock Clock – a revolving dial in one of the toadstools tells the time, and on the hour (when it's working) the peacock, toadstools, owl and cock come to life.
Room 258 Flemish art, 17th century. **Room 259 Western European applied art**, 11th to 15th century. **Rooms 261 to 262 Dutch art**, 15th and 16th century.

Large Hermitage, Second Floor

Room 206 Next to the Council (Soviet) Staircase with a marble, malachite and glass triumphal arch; **Rooms 207 to 215 Florentine art**, 13th to 16th century, including: **209** 15th century paintings, including Fra Angelico; **213** 15th and early 16th century, including two small Botticellis, Filippino Lippi, Perugino; **214** Russia's only two paintings by Leonardo da Vinci – the *Benois Madonna* and the strikingly different *Madonna Litta*, both named after their last owners; **215** Art by Leonardo's pupils, including Correggio and Andrea del Sarto.
Room 216 Italian mannerist art, 16th century, and a view over the little Winter Canal to the Hermitage Theatre.
Rooms 217 to 222 Venetian art, mainly 16th century – **217** Giorgione's *Judith (Yudif)*; **219** Titian's *Portrait of a Young Woman* and *Flight into Egypt*, and more by Giorgione; **221** More Titian, including *Dana* and *St Sebastian*; **222** Paolo Veronese's *Mourning of Christ*.

The Hermitage Collection

Rooms 226 & 227 Loggia of Raphael Quarenghi's 1780s copy of a gallery in the Vatican with murals by Raphael.

Rooms 228 to 238 Italian art, 16th to 18th century – **228** 16th century ceramics; **229** Raphael and disciples, including his Madonna Conestabile and *Holy Family (Svyatoe Semeystvo)*, plus wonderful ceramics and decorations, as well as Russia's only Michelangelo, a marble statue of a crouching boy; **230-236** Usually closed, but they should contain Caravaggio and Bernini (**232**). **237** 16th century paintings, including Paolo Veronese and Tintoretto; **238** 17th and 18th century painters including Canaletto and Tiepolo; also two huge 19th century Russian malachite vases. **237 & 238** have lovely ceilings.

Rooms 239 & 240 Spanish art, 16th to 18th century – **239** Goya's *Portrait of the Actress Antonia Zarate (Antonii Sarate)*, Murillo's *Boy with a Dog*, Diego Velazquez' *Breakfast*; **240** El Greco's marvellous *St Peter and St Paul*.

Room 241 Marble sculptures, Antonio Canova and Albert Thorwaldsen. **Room 243 Giddyap Room**; Western European armour and weaponry from the 15th to 17th century, featuring four 16th century German suits of armour atop armoured (and, thankfully, stuffed) horses.

Rooms 244 to 247 Flemish art, 17th century – **245** Savage hunting and market scenes by Snyders; **246** Van Dyck portraits; **247** A large room displaying the amazing range of Rubens. It includes *Descent from the Cross (Snyatie c kresta)*, *Bacchus (Bakkh)*, *The Union of Earth and Water (Soyuz zemli i vody)*, *Portrait of a Curly-Haired Old Man (Golova starika)*, and *Roman Charity (Ottselyubie rimlyanki)*.

Rooms 248 to 252 & 254 Dutch art, 17th century – **249** Landscapes and portraits by Ruisdael, Hals, Bol and others; **250** 18th century Delft ceramics; **254** More than 20 Rembrandts ranging from lighter, more detailed early canvases like *Abraham's Sacrifice of Isaac (Zhertvoprinoshenie Avraama)* and *Dana* to *The Holy Family (Svyatoe semeystvo)* of 1645, and darker, penetrating late works like *The Return of the Prodigal Son* and two canvases entitled *Portrait of an Old Man (Portret starika)*. There's also work by Rembrandt's pupils, including Bol.

Winter Palace, Third Floor

An approximate chronological order in which to view the French art collection is 314, 332-328, 325-315 and 343-350. The staircase beside room 269 on Floor 2 brings you out by room 314.

Rooms 314 to 320, 330 to 332 French art, 19th century – **315-320 Impressionists and post-impressionists: 315** Rodin sculptures; **316** Gauguin's Tahitian works; **317** Van Gogh, Rousseau, Forain, Latour; **318** Cézanne, Pissarro; **319** Pissarro, Monet, Sisley; **320** Renoir, Degas.

Rooms 321 to 325, 328 to 329 mostly **Barbizon School**, including Corot, Courbet, Millet, though closed when we visited in 1998. **Room 331** Delacroix and Vernet

Room 334 Vincent van Gogh

Rooms 334 to 342 European art, 19th century, including landscapes by Caspar David Friedrich.

Rooms 343, 349 & 350 French art, 19th to 20th century including Bonnard, Vlaminck, Marquet, Leger and others.

Rooms 344 & 345 Picasso including his blue, Cubist and later periods.

Rooms 346 to 348 Matisse

Rooms 351 to 371 and 381 to 396 Oriental culture and art – 351-357, 359-364 Art of China and Tibet, an excellent collection; **358** Indonesia; **365-367** Mongolia; **368-371** India; **381-387** Byzantium, Near and Middle East.

Rooms 398 & 400 Coins

continued from page 301

and her successors had most of the interior remodelled in classical style by 1837. It remained an imperial home until 1917, though the last two tsars spent more time in other palaces.

The classical Little Hermitage was built for Catherine the Great as a retreat that would also house the art collection started by Peter the Great, which she significantly expanded. At the river end of the Large Hermitage is the Old Hermitage, which also dates from her time. At its south end, facing ulitsa Millionnaya, is the New Hermitage, which was built for Nicholas II to hold the still-growing art collection and was opened to the public for the first time in 1852. The Hermitage Theatre was built in the 1780s by the classicist Quarenghi, who thought it one of his finest works.

The art collection benefited when the state took over aristocrats' collections after the revolution, but Stalin sold some treasures – including about 15 Rembrandts – for foreign currency. During WWII, 324 shells fell on the palace, and bombs destroyed the original Petrovsky and Field Marshal's rooms as well as parts of the roof.

In 1995 the Hermitage ran a highly controversial exhibition, called 'Hidden Treasures Revealed', composed entirely of art captured by the Red Army in 1945. The collection, including 74 paintings, among them works by Monet, Degas, Renoir, Cézanne, Picasso and Matisse ignited a political debate about ownership, echoes of which can still be heard today. Still, the 'winners are keepers' rule has won out for now: most of the collection (only oils, no pastels) is still on display, albeit under a less conspicuous guise. The collection is in rooms 143-146 under the moniker 'French Paintings of the 19th and 20th Century'.

Admission

The Hermitage (☎ 110 90 79) is open from 10.30 am to 6 pm daily, and until 5 pm on Sunday (closed Monday). The main ticket hall is inside the main entrance on the river side of the Winter Palace. In summer only there are also ticket kiosks outside a secondary entrance at the west end of the Winter Palace, but neither kiosks nor entrances are always open. Summertime queues can be horrendous, so try to get there early.

The dual pricing system is firmly in place here. Foreigners pay $10 and Russians $0.60, while ISIC card-holders get in free. Photographs – not tripods or flashes – are permitted, though you'll have to pay a $3 charge (use of a video camera costs $10). Unless your Russian's *really* good, forget about getting in for the Russian price – these babushkas have an eagle eye for Western running shoes, bum bags, University of Whatever sweatshirts etc.

To avoid queues, you can join a tour, which whizzes round the main parts in about 1½ hours but at least provides an introduction to the place in English. It's easy to 'lose' the group and stay on until closing time. Tours can be arranged at hotels, the St Petersburg Travel Company or other travel agents, or with the Hermitage itself; the excursion tours' office is down the corridor to the right as you enter, up the stairs and the last door on the left.

You must also book with a travel agent or through the Hermitage to enter the Golden Rooms Special Collection in rooms 41-45. It'll cost another $10 to see (more if through an agent). The focus is a hoard of fabulously worked Scythian and Greek gold and silver from the Caucasus, Crimea and Ukraine, dating from the 7th to 2nd centuries BC when the Scythians, who dominated the region, and the Greeks, in colonies around the northern Black Sea, crafted the pieces to accompany the dead into the afterlife.

There is a special entrance for the physically disabled from Palace Square (the museum also has a few wheelchairs on hand).

Orientation

Rooms are numbered. There's only space to show up to 10% of the collection at any given time, so the works on view change occasionally. Only a few sections have English labelling.

From the main ticket hall, the Rastrelli Gallery leads to the white marble Jordan

Staircase, with windows and mirrors on all sides, which takes you up to the 2nd floor of the Winter Palace. The staircase is one of the few parts of the interior to maintain its original Rastrelli appearance.

See the list in the boxed text 'The Hermitage Collection' for a thorough run-down on what's in all the rooms at the time of writing. If your time is limited, the following route takes in the major highlights (room numbers are in bold type):

Winter Palace, 2nd floor **143-146** French paintings of the 19th and 20th century (aka Hidden Treasures Revealed); **189** Malachite Hall; **190-198** great state rooms.

Large Hermitage, 2nd floor **207-215** Florentine art 13th to 16th century; **217-222 & 229-237** Venetian and Italian art 16th century; **238** Italian art 17th and 18th century; **239-240** Spanish art 16th to 18th century; **244-247** Flemish art 17th century; **248-252 & 254** Dutch art 17th century.

Winter Palace, 3rd floor **315-320** Impressionists and postimpressionists; **344-348** Picasso and Matisse.

NEVSKY PROSPEKT

Though the Soviets tried renaming it 25th of October Avenue in honour of their revolution, the name never stuck. Nevsky prospekt is and always will be Russia's most famous street, running 4km from the Admiralty to the Alexander Nevsky Lavra (monastery), from which it takes its name. The inner 2.5km to Moscow Station is St Petersburg's seething main avenue, the city's shopping centre and focus of its entertainment and street life. Pushing through its crowds is an essential St Petersburg experience, and if you're there on a holiday evening (like City Day), the sight of thousands pouring like a stream down its middle is one you'll not soon forget.

Nevsky prospekt was laid out in the early years of St Petersburg as the start of the main road to Novgorod and soon became dotted with fine buildings, squares and bridges. At the beginning of the 1900s, it was one of Europe's grandest boulevards, with cobblestoned sidewalks and a track down the middle for horse-drawn trams. On either side of the tracks were wooden paving blocks to muffle the sound of horse-drawn carriages – an innovation that was apparently the first in the world and for which the prospekt was dubbed the quietest main street in Europe. Today, things are bit noisier. A walk down Nevsky is a walk into the heart of the new Russia: a buzzing, swirling mishmash of new and colourful shops, restaurants, bars, art galleries, banks and perfumeries packed to overflowing with tourists and natives, workers and beggars, people selling their pets and shoes, scamrunners, pickpockets and purse snatchers, yahoos and religious fanatics – all shoving past on their way to the action.

Admiralty End (Map 6)

Inner Nevsky, ulitsa Malaya Morskaya and ulitsa Bolshaya Morskaya were the heart of the pre-revolution financial district. Points of interest include ulitsa Malaya Morskaya 13, where Tchaikovsky died in 1893. The wall of the school at **Nevsky prospekt 14** bears a blue-and-white stencilled sign maintained since WWII starting Граждане! *(Grazhdane!)*. This sign translates as 'Citizens! At times of artillery bombardment this side of the street is most dangerous!'

Just before the Moyka River, the **Kafe Literaturnoe** is, despite being a repugnant tourist trap, worth peeping into for its Pushkin associations and ambience. Across the Moyka, Rastrelli's green **Stroganov Palace** (1752-54) has kept most of its original appearance.

Kazan Cathedral Area (Map 6)

A block beyond the Moyka, on the south side of Nevsky prospekt, the great colonnaded arms of the Kazan Cathedral (Kazansky sobor, 1801-11) reach out towards the avenue. Its design, by Andrey Voronikhin, a former serf, was influenced by St Peter's in Rome. His original plan was to build a second, mirror version of the cathedral opposite it on the northern side of Nevsky. The square in front of it has been a site for political demonstrations since before the revolution.

The cathedral now houses the Museum of the History of Religion (☎ 311 04 95, www.relig-museum.ru). Its Soviet-era suffix 'and Atheism' has long since been removed. The museum covers the history as well as the infamies of many religions. It is open 11 am to 5 pm weekdays except Wednesday, and from 12.30 pm on weekends; entrance costs $1.80 ($0.90 for ISIC holders, children and pensioners). The vastly impressive cathedral itself is free to enter. In the north transept is the grave of Field Marshal Kutuzov, the Russian commander against Napoleon in 1812.

Opposite the cathedral is St Petersburg's biggest bookshop, **Dom Knigi**, topped by the globe emblem of the Singer sewing machine company, which constructed the building in 1902-04. The building also housed the American consulate for a few years prior to WWI. Just behind the Kazan Cathedral, a bit south of the Central Train Ticket Centre, sits the **Bankovsky most**, one of St Petersburg's loveliest bridges. Suspended by cables emerging from the mouths of golden-winged griffins, the wooden bridge affords a splendid view north up the Griboedova Canal past Nevsky prospekt to the Church of the Resurrection of Christ (this is a great photo op!). In the block of Nevsky prospekt over the canal from Kazan Cathedral, pavement artists cluster in front of the **Central Art Salon** (Tsentralny khudozhestvenny salon).

Griboedova Canal to the Fontanka (Map 6)

This section of Nevsky is the busiest; a whirlwind of activity and colour of which the **Grand Hotel Europe** (the Yevropeyskaya under the Soviets) is the epicentre. The unbelievably lavish hotel was completely renovated from 1989-91, and is once again one of the city's architectural gems, boasting shameless splendour: marble and gilt, sweeping staircases and antique furnishings. If you're feeling wicked, you can lounge about in the atrium (or visit the nicest toilets in the city, the reason many strained-faced tourists come here in the first place) and you don't even have to buy one of its $4 cups of coffee.

Diagonally across Nevsky, the arcades of **Gostiny Dvor** department store stand facing the clocktower of the former **Town Duma** on ulitsa Dumskaya, seat of the pre-revolution city government. One of the world's first indoor shopping malls, the 'Merchant Yard' dates from 1757-85, stretches 230m along Nevsky (its perimeter is over 1km long) and is another Rastrelli creation. The St Petersburg equivalent of Moscow's GUM, Gostiny Dvor's facade has been completely restored, and the inside is now quite fashionable.

The wooden fence lining Nevsky prospekt is a kind of Day-Glo Hyde Park Speaker's Corner, attracting representatives of the most reprehensible lunatic-fringe political groups and religious proselytisers; in other words, get your Stalin calendars here.

On the other side of Nevsky, in the arcade at No 48, the **Passazh** department store is beautiful to look at (notice the glass ceilings) and packed with pricey goods, but has a decidedly less than exciting atmosphere. Downstairs in the basement, there's a well stocked Western supermarket.

Tucked in a recess between the banks and the cafe near ulitsa Mikhailovskaya, the **Armenian Church** (1771-80), one of two in St Petersburg, is open, though under extensive renovation. The Soviet regime deemed it reasonable to bash the place to bits and install a 2nd floor, which blocked the view of the cupola. The renovation, performed by members of the congregation, has included removal of that 2nd floor and restoration of the cupola and several icons, but there is still a long way to go. A new iconostasis is being created, as well.

The **Vorontsov Palace** on Sadovaya ulitsa, opposite the south-east side of Gostiny Dvor, is another noble town house by Rastrelli. It's now a military school for young cadets; on weekends you can watch mothers pass food parcels to their sons through the wrought-iron front gates.

Ploshchad Ostrovskogo (Map 6)

An enormous **statue of Catherine the Great** stands amid the chess, backgammon and sometimes even mahjong players that crowd the benches here. The statue depicts, according to the *Blue Guide*, 'The towering figure of the Empress standing above her close associates'. Well, *at least* three of these were her known lovers: Orlov, Potyomkin and Suvorov.

This airy square, commonly referred to as the Catherine Gardens, was created by Carlo Rossi in the 1820s and 1830s, and its west side is taken up by the lavish **National Library of Russia**, St Petersburg's biggest with some 31 million items, nearly a sixth of which is in foreign languages.

Rossi's **Pushkin Theatre** (formerly the Alexandrinsky) at the south end of the square is one of Russia's most important. In 1896 the opening night of Chekhov's *The Seagull* was so badly received here that the playwright fled to wander anonymously among the crowds on Nevsky prospekt.

Behind the theatre, on ulitsa Zodchego Rossi, is a continuation of Rossi's ensemble. It is proportion deified: it's 22m wide and high and 220m long. The **Vaganova School of Choreography** situated here is the Kirov Ballet's training school, where Pavlova, Nijinsky, Nureyev and others learned their art.

The **Anichkov Palace** (1741-50, the city's second palace), between ploshchad Ostrovskogo and the Fontanka River (its main facade faces the river and was once joined to it by a canal), was home to several Imperial favourites, including Catherine the Great's lover Grigory Potyomkin (who graciously accepted it as a gift from her). A slew of architects, including Rastrelli and Rossi, worked on it. It became the city's largest Pioneer Club headquarters after 1935 and to this day houses over 100 after school clubs for over 10,000 children.

Anichkov Bridge & Beyond (Map 6)

Nevsky prospekt crosses the Fontanka on the **Anichkov most**, with famous 1840s statues (sculpted by the German P Klodt) of rearing horses at its four corners. To witness pure artistic revenge, put prudery aside and take note of the south-western horse's genitals: unlike his anatomically correct companions, this one's are apparently in the image of the sculptor's unfaithful wife's lover (another version has it that it's Napoleon's profile).

The red 1840s **Beloselsky-Belozersky Palace**, at Nevsky 41, provides a photogenic baroque backdrop. It now houses a rather amusing **Wax Museum** (☎ 315 56 36), open from 11 pm to 7 pm daily. Between the Fontanka and Moscow Station, Nevsky prospekt has fewer historic buildings but heaps more chi-chi shops and cinemas, and in the centre of the strip is the **Sheraton Nevskij Palace Hotel**.

Marking the division of Nevsky prospekt and Stary (old) Nevsky prospekt is **ploshchad Vosstania** (Uprising Square), whose landmarks are the giant granite pillar with the Commie star, the Moscow Station, and the animation screen atop the building next to the station. Note the writing on top of Hotel Oktyabrskaya across from the station: ГОРОД ГЕРОЙ ЛЕНИНГРАД, or 'Hero City Leningrad'. Several cities were designated 'hero cities' for heroism, stoicism and losses during WWII.

Stary Nevsky juts off the north-eastern side of the square and heads south-east to the Alexandra Nevskogo bridge. Its charm is in its relative desolation and laid-back mood.

Alexander Nevsky Monastery (Map 5)

The working Alexander Nevsky Lavra (☎ 274 36 05), with the graves of some of Russia's most famous artistic figures, is entered from ploshchad Alexandra Nevskogo opposite Hotel Moskva. It was founded in 1713 by Peter the Great, who wrongly thought this was where Alexander of Novgorod had beaten the Swedes in 1240. In 1797 it became a lavra (superior monastery). Today it is open to the public and, sadly, the courtyard is filled with homeless beggars. You can wander freely around most of the grounds but for the two most important graveyards, you need to buy tickets ($1/0.50 for adults/students). They are sold outside the main gate (to your right as you enter). Opening hours are from 11 am to 6 pm, closed Monday.

The **Tikhvin Cemetery** (Tikhvinskoe kladbishche), on the right, contains the most famous graves. Tchaikovsky, Borodin, Mussorgsky, Rimsky-Korsakov and Glinka all rest here. Make a right after entering and you'll reach the tomb of Dostoevsky. The **Lazarus Cemetery** (Lazarevskoe kladbishche), facing the Tikhvin across the entrance path, contains several late great St Petersburg architects – among them Starov, Voronikhin, Quarenghi, Zakharov and Rossi.

Across the canal in the main lavra complex, the first main building on the left is the 1717-22 baroque **Annunciation Church** (Blagoveshchenskaya tserkov), now the City Sculpture Museum (Muzey gorodskoy skulptury) and closed for renovation. About 100m farther on is the monastery's 1776-90 classical **Trinity Cathedral** (Troitsky sobor). It is open daily, but services are held Saturday, Sunday and holidays from 6 am to the end of evening services (closed for cleaning between 2 and 5 pm); early liturgy from 7 am, late liturgy from 10 am and all-night vigils begin at 6 pm. Hundreds crowd in on 12 September to celebrate the feast of Saint Alexander Nevsky.

Opposite the cathedral is the St Petersburg **Metropolitan's House**. On the far right of the grounds facing the canal you'll see St Petersburg's **Orthodox Academy**, one of only a handful in Russia (another is at Sergiev Posad).

BETWEEN NEVSKY & THE NEVA

Ploshchad Iskusstv (Map 6)

Just a block north of Nevsky Prospekt metro, quiet ploshchad Iskusstv (Arts Square) is named after its cluster of museums and concert halls – notably the **Russian Museum**, one of St Petersburg's best, the **Ethnography Museum**, which has some fascinating displays of the peoples and cultures of the former Soviet Union, the **Large Hall** (Bolshoy zal) of the St Petersburg Philharmonia, venue for top classical concerts, and the **Maly Theatre**, the city's second fiddle to the Mariinsky for opera and ballet. A statue of Pushkin stands in the middle of ploshchad Iskusstv. The square, and ulitsa Mikhailovskaya which joins it to Nevsky prospekt, were designed as a unit by Rossi in the 1820s and 1830s.

Russian Museum (Map 6)

The former Mikhailovsky Palace, now the Russian Museum (Gosudarstvenny Russky muzey), houses one of the country's two finest collections of Russian art (the other is in Moscow's Tretyakov Gallery). If your time in the city is limited and you think only the Hermitage is a must-see, try your utmost to accommodate some time for this gem of a museum; your appreciation of Russian culture will be deepened by it. Its opening hours are from 10 am to 6 pm daily except Tuesday. Admission is $5.60/2.80 for adults/students.

The palace was designed by Carlo Rossi and built in 1819-29 for Grand Duke Mikhail, brother of Tsars Alexander I and Nicholas I, as a gift from his dad, Tsar Pavel I as compensation for not being able to have a chance on the throne. The museum was founded in 1895 under Alexander III, and opened three years later. The Benois building, now connected to the original palace and accessible through an entrance on naberezhnaya kanala Griboedova, was constructed in 1914-20.

Note that the facade of the palace is illuminated at night, making that the best time to photograph it. It is most impressively viewed from the back of the building, during a late-night stroll through the pleasant **Mikhailovsky Gardens** behind it.

See the following map and boxed text for a straightforward walk through the rooms.

Resurrection Church (Map 5)

The multi-domed **Church of the Resurrection of Christ** (Khram Voskresenia Khristova), partly modelled on St Basil's in Moscow, sits on the Griboedova Canal just behind the Mikhailovsky Gardens and was built in 1883-1907 on the spot where Alexander II, despite his reforms, was blown up by the People's Will terrorist group in 1881. Because of its site it's also known as the Church of the Saviour of the Spilled Blood (Khram Spasa na Krovi), and because various translations of *that* term float around you may hear it called several other names, such as 'Church of the Spilled Blood' or 'Church of the Bleeding Saviour'.

It's now most commonly known as the church that took 24 years to build and 27 to restore. In August 1997, with much fanfare, it finally opened its doors after painstaking work on the 7000 sq metres of mosaics by over 30 artists which line the walls inside. On the very spot of the assassination is a marble *Shatrovy Cen*, a monument to Alexander. The museum is open from 11 pm to 7 pm daily, and admission is $2.50/1.20 for adults/students. Most visitors agree that the church's splendour is much better appreciated from the outside.

Pushkin Flat-Museum (Map 5)

Pushkin's last home (he only lived here for a year), at naberezhnaya reki Moyki 12, is beside one of the prettiest curves of the Moyka River. This is where the poet died after his duel in 1837. His killer was a French soldier of fortune, Baron d'Anthes, who had been publicly courting Pushkin's beautiful wife, Natalia. The affair was widely seen as a put-up job on behalf of Tsar Nicholas I, who found the famed poet's radical politics inconvenient – and who, gossip said, may himself have been the one really stalking Natalia. The little house is now the Pushkin Flat-Museum (☎ 314 00 06), open from 11 am to 5 pm daily except Tuesday; admission is about $2 ($1 for ISIC holders) and includes a Russian-language tour (English tours can be arranged in advance).

Mars Field (Map 3)

The Mars Field (Marsovo pole) is the open space south of the Troitsky most. Don't take a short cut across the grass – you may be walking on graves from the 1917 revolution, the civil war, or of later communist luminaries also buried here. The field is so named because it was the scene of 19th century military parades.

Across ulitsa Millionnaya is the **Marble Palace** (☎ 312 91 96), built for Catherine the Great's lover Grigory Orlov in 1768-85, formerly housed a Lenin Museum; currently it is a branch of the Russian Museum featuring rotating exhibitions. It's open from 10 am to 5 pm daily except Tuesday; admission is $5.60/2.80 for adults/students.

Summer Garden (Map 3)

Perhaps St Petersburg's loveliest park, the Summer Garden (Letny sad) is between the Mars Field and the Fontanka River. You can enter at either the north or the south end. It's closed in April.

Laid out for Peter the Great with fountains, pavilions and a geometrical plan to resemble the park at Versailles, the garden became a strolling place for St Petersburg's 19th century leisured classes. Though changed since that era, it maintains a formal elegance, with thousands of lime trees shading its straight paths and lines of statues.

The modest, two-storey **Summer Palace** in the north-east corner was St Petersburg's first palace, built for Peter in 1710-14, and is pretty well intact. Little reliefs around the walls depict Russian naval victories. Today it's a museum (Muzey letny dvorets Petra I; ☎ 314 03 74), with opening hours from 11 am to 6 pm daily from early May to early November (closed Tuesday and the last Monday of the month). Admission is $1.80/0.60 for adults/students.

South of the Summer Garden (Map 5)

A much greater Summer Palace used to stand across the canal from the south end of the Summer Garden. But Rastrelli's fairytale wooden creation for Empress Elizabeth was knocked down in the 1790s to make way for the bulky, brick **Engineers' Castle** of Paul I, an insanely cruel tsar who lived in fear of assassination and was indeed suffocated in his bed a month after moving into the castle. Later it became a military engineering school (hence the name).

Across the Fontanka and south about half a kilometre is the yellow **Sheremetev Palace** (Map 6), built in 1750-55, which houses a lovely little museum to the great, long-persecuted poet Anna Akhmatova. The flat, on the 2nd floor, is filled with mementos of the poet, her bedroom and her study, and her correspondence with Pasternak. Downstairs, you can watch Russian-language documentaries about her life while sipping tea. The museum is open from 11 am to 5.30 pm daily except Monday, and admission is $1.

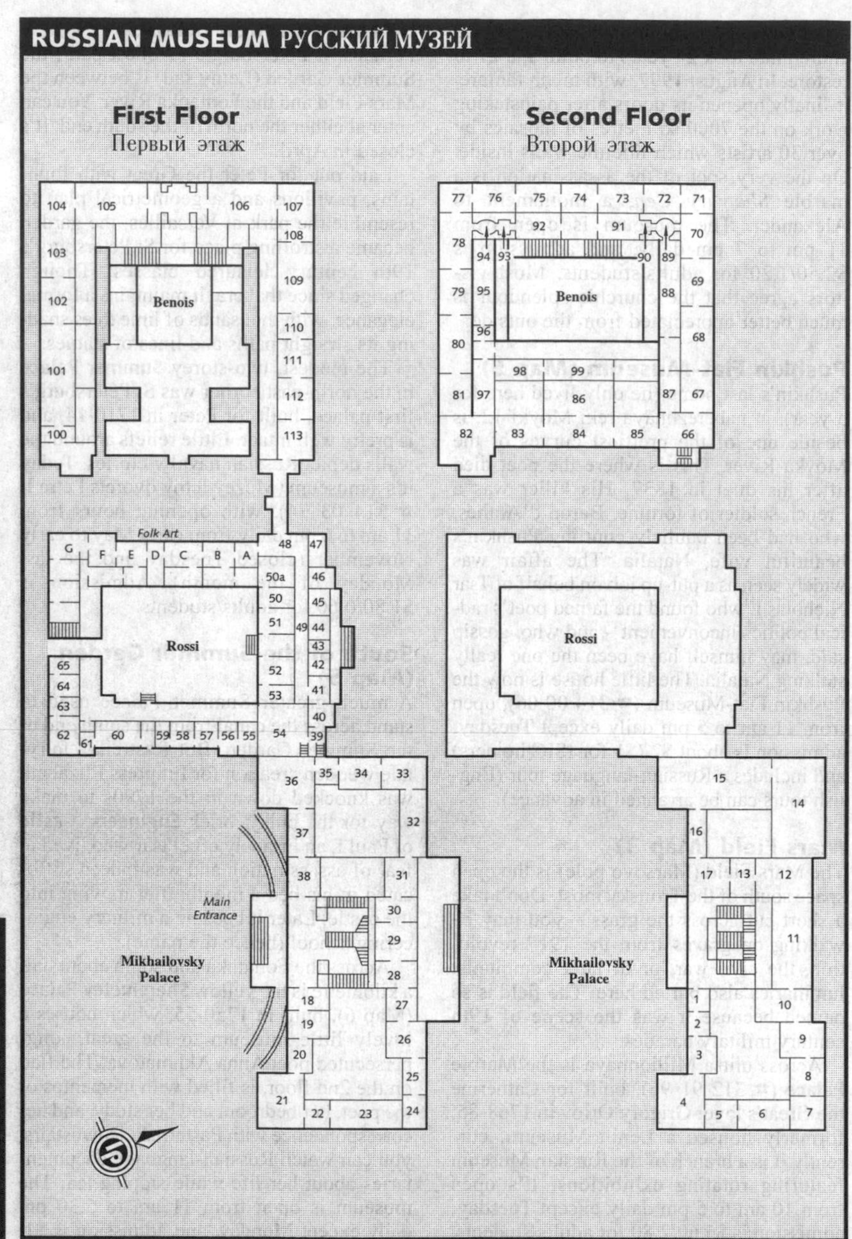

RUSSIAN MUSEUM РУССКИЙ МУЗЕЙ
First Floor
Первый этаж
Second Floor
Второй этаж
Benois
Rossi
Folk Art
Main Entrance
Mikhailovsky Palace

Russian Museum

Rooms 1 to 4 12th to 15th century icons. *Apostle Peter* and *Apostle Paul* by students of Andrey Rublyov are particularly good. **5 to 9** 17th to 18th century sculpture, portraits and tapestries, including **7** Rastrelli's pompous *Anna Joannovna and an Arab boy*. **10, 12, 13, 14, 17** Late 18th/early 19th century paintings and sculpture. **11** The White Hall, the most ornate in the palace, with period furniture by Rossi, and where Strauss and Berlioz, as guests, performed concerts. **15** Big 19th century canvases mainly by graduates of the official Academy – Aivazovsky's Crimea seascapes stand out, most frighteningly *The Wave*. Here is Ivanov's most famous work, *Christ's Appearance to the People*. (**16** is closed and used as storage.)

18 to 22 19th century works focusing on **19** the beginnings of the socially aware 'realist' tradition and including **21** spectacular works by Semiradsky and Flavitsky, including his gigantic *Christian Martyrs in Colosseum*. **23 to 38** Peredvizhniki and associated artists including **25** Kramskoy; **26** Nikolai Ge, including his fearsome *Peter I prosecuting Tsarevich Alexey in Peterhof*, **27** Shishkin and **31** KA Savitsky's *To The War*. **32** Poleneov, including his *Christ and the Sinner*. Note that in room **29**, there is an interactive computer display, in English, about the museum.

33 to 35, 54 A permanent exhibition of the work of Repin, probably Russia's best-loved artist – **33** portraits and the incomparable *Barge Haulers on the Volga*, an indictment of Russian 'social justice'; and **54** the massive *Meeting of the State Council*, Repin's rendering of the meeting at the Mariinsky Palace on 7 May 1901 (it's full of tsarist hotshots; there's a scheme in the room to help you tell who's who).

36, 37 Russian history, portraits by Surikov, a national revivalist and **36** Mikhail Mikeshin's model of the *Millennium of Russia*; **38** Historical works by Vasnetsov, including *Russian Knight at the Crossroads* and other 'sketches' for his mosaics.

39 Popular 19th century painter Malyavin's depictions of Russian mothers and maidens. **40, 41** Stunning landscapes by Kuindzhi.

42 to 47 Works by Levitan and other late 19th century painters, and **45** Ryabushkin on pre-Peter the Great 17th century Russian history, includes the very telling and humorous *Yedut*, or *They Are Coming*, depicting the perturbed-looking reception committee for the first foreigners allowed in Russia

48 Antakolski sculptures. (Exits straight ahead lead to the 10 halls of Russian folk art exhibition, including handicrafts, wood work, carvings, pottery, toys etc; exits to the right lead to the Benois building.) **49** A long corridor that houses temporary exhibitions.

50 to 53 Closed, used as storage. **55 to 59** Sculptures from the 18th to 20th century, including sensitive works by Matveev and Shubin. **60 to 65** The Furniture Fund.

66 to 79 20th century art, including **66** Vrubel, with his epic Russian *Hero* and *Venice*, and Artemiy Ober's terrifying bronze *Calamity*; **67** Nesterov's religious paintings of the history of the Orthodox Church; Konenkov sculptures and Vasnetsov's *The Entombing*; **70, 71** Serov, portraits of Russian aristocracy and other high-rollers; Trubitskoy sculptures of same including *Isaak Levitan and Children*; **72** Impressionists Korovin, Grabar and Serebryakova; Trubitskoy's *Moscow Carriage Driver* and Boris Kustodiev's *Holiday on the Volga*; **73** Kustodiev's paintings of stereotypical Russians; **74** The Rerikh Room.

75 to 79 Russian avant-garde, symbolism, neoclassical works of artists, including Saryan Kuznetsov, Petrov-Vodkin, Grigoriev, Shukhaev, Altman, Lenturov etc. Note that **79** will be home to the museum's Chagall and Malevich collection as soon as the works return from revenue producing exhibitions abroad (don't hold your breath).

83 to 113 Halls for rotating exhibitions.

From the Fontanka, enter the palace, walk through the lobby and into the courtyard, to the right, and follow the signs.

SMOLNY REGION

Tauride Gardens & Tauride Palace (Map 3)

The Tauride Gardens (Tavrichesky sad), which house the City Children's Park (Gorodskoy detsky park), are a great place for children; the kiddie rides are among the best in Russia. The view across the lake at the fine Tauride Palace (Tavrichesky dvorets), built in 1783-89 for Catherine the Great's lover Potyomkin, is a fine sight.

The palace takes its name from the Ukrainian region of Crimea (once called Tavria), which Potyomkin was responsible for conquering. Between 1906 and 1917 the State Duma, the Provisional Government and the Petrograd Soviet all met here; in the 1930s it housed the All-Union Agricultural Communist University. Today, it's home to the Parliamentary Assembly of the Member States of the CIS and you can't go in. The gardens are a block-and-a-half east of Chernyshevskaya metro.

Flowers Exhibition Hall (Map 3)

One of the finest ways to escape momentarily from a St Petersburg winter is to head for the Flowers Exhibition Hall, an indoor tropical paradise just north-west of the City Children's Park at the corner of ulitsa Potyomkinskaya and ulitsa Shpalernaya. Dig the 'monster' tree to the right of the entrance. It also has a wishing well, and there's a flower-selling stall at the front. It's open from 11 am to 7 pm daily except Monday and Thursday year-round.

Smolny (Map 3)

The **cathedral** at Smolny is one of the most fabulous of all Rastrelli's buildings, and the Smolny Institute next door was the hub of the October Revolution. Trolleybus Nos 5 and 7 via much of Nevsky prospekt end up here. The cathedral is the centrepiece of a convent built mostly to Rastrelli's designs in 1748-57. His inspiration was to combine baroque details with the forest of towers and onion domes typical of an old Russian monastery. There's special genius in the proportions of the cathedral (it gives the impression of soaring upwards), to which the convent buildings are a perfect foil.

It's possible to climb one of the 63m belfries with a guide (the views are stupendous), and the cathedral hosts temporary exhibits. It's open from 11 am to 5 pm daily except Thursday, and admission is $4/2 for adults/students.

The **Smolny Institute**, built by Quarenghi in 1806-08 as a school for aristocratic girls, had fame thrust upon it in 1917 when Trotsky and Lenin directed the October Revolution from the headquarters of the Bolshevik Central Committee and the Petrograd Soviet which had been set up here. In its Hall of Acts (Aktovy zal) on 25 October, the All-Russian Congress of Soviets conferred power on a Bolshevik government led by Lenin, which ran the country from here until March 1918.

SOUTH & WEST OF NEVSKY PROSPEKT

Sennaya Ploshchad Area (Map 4)

This teeming and rather dirty market square, interesting at any time of the day, is dominated by what seems to be a permanent exhibition of construction equipment. This is also the gateway to Dostoevskyville. The peripatetic writer, who occupied around 20 residences in his 28-year stay in the city, once spent a couple of days in debtors' prison in what is now called the Senior Officer's Barracks, just across the square from the Sennaya Ploshchad metro station. Dostoevsky had been thrown in there by his publisher, for missing a deadline ('Had we but thought of it ...' – T Wheeler). At the site of the metro station was once a large cath-edral that dominated the square.

Just west of the square and across the river, at ulitsa Kaznacheyskaya 7, is the flat where he wrote *Crime and Punishment*; Raskolnikov's route to the murder passed directly under the author's window. The old woman lived at flat 74, naberezhnaya kanala Griboedova 104; you can visit the hallway outside the flat (residents are quite used to it). Entering from the canal side, walk straight back to entrance No 5 (apartments 22-81); the flat's on the 3rd floor.

Vladimirskaya Ploshchad Area (Map 5)

Around Vladimirskaya ploshchad are the indoor **Kuznechny market** (note the 1920s worker statue on its facade), St Petersburg's biggest and best stocked. There are also a few museums and a smattering of eateries and shops, all on a backdrop to what is one of the city's liveliest areas. The onion-domed working **Our Lady of Vladimir Church** (1761-69) with its 1783 three-tiered belfry by Quarenghi dominates the square. Around it, there's an unofficial, daily market of stolen goods, clothes and jewellery. The alcoholics, thieves and genuine folks trying to make an honest rouble who gather here are dispersed regularly by the police, but always return to sell their wares; this very St Petersburg scene is worth a gander.

Dostoevsky wrote most of *The Brothers Karamazov* in a flat at Kuznechny pereulok 5, just past the market, and died there in 1881. It's now a small and worthwhile **Dostoevsky Museum** (☎ 311 18 04), open from 11 am to 6 pm daily except Monday. Every Sunday at noon there's a screening of a film version of one of the master's works. Admission is $1.20/0.60 for adults/students. A long-awaited (and gloomy) **statue** of the writer was unveiled in 1997 and now stands directly outside the Vladimirskaya metro.

The **Arctic & Antarctic Museum** (☎ 113 19 98) on ulitsa Marata focuses on Soviet polar explorations and ratty taxidermy exhibitions. Admission is $1.20/0.40 for adults/students. The museum is open from 10 am to 5 pm Wednesday to Sunday. There's a small **Rimsky-Korsakov Flat-Museum** at Zagorodny prospekt 28, open from 11 am to 6 pm daily except Monday and Tuesday, later for concerts on Wednesday and Saturday.

Just north of Zagorodny prospekt is Semyonovskaya ploshchad, where in 1849 Dostoevsky and 20 other prisoners underwent a mock execution – see the following boxed text 'Fyodor Dostoevsky' for details.

Teatralnaya Ploshchad Area (Map 4)

Teatralnaya ploshchad has been an entertainment centre since fairs were held here in the mid-18th century. Built in 1859, the **Mariinsky Theatre** (☎ 114 12 11) has played a pivotal role in Russian ballet ever since. Outside performance times you can usually wander into the Mariinsky Theatre's foyer, and maybe peep into its lovely auditorium. To organise a full tour for $10 a person, fax a request to Dr Yuri Schwartzkopf at ☎/fax 314 17 44, and call back for an answer. The St Petersburg Conservatory faces the Mariinsky. Bus Nos 3 and 22 from Nevsky prospekt serve Teatralnaya ploshchad.

One good foot route to the area is along the south side of the Moyka River from Isaakievskaya ploshchad. On the way, you'll pass the original **Yusupov Palace** (☎ 314 98 83) at naberezhnaya reki Moyki 94, where in 1916 Rasputin, as a dinner guest of Prince Felix Yusupov and friends, was fed with poisoned food, cakes, cookies and drink. Afterwards as he was happily licking his fingers, the Yusupov gang shot ol' Raspy repeatedly. But like a tsarist-era Terminator, he refused to die, and when Yusupov knelt over him, Rasputin grabbed him by the throat! At that point, Yusupov did what any sane man would do: he ran like hell. When he returned with reinforcements, they found Rasputin had dragged himself outside. They shot him a few more times, beat him with sticks for good measure, and stuffed him through the ice of the frozen river. Legend has it that Rasputin did not die until he was submerged – water was found in his lungs.

The palace's 1st and 2nd floors are open to visitors ($4/2 for adults/students) daily between noon and 3 pm but to see the basement chamber in which Raspy ate the poisoned stuff, you'll be admitted in groups of no more than three if you pay an extra $2/1. Larger groups must be arranged in advance.

North-east of Teatralnaya ploshchad, before it twists south-east, the Griboedova Canal runs under another of St Petersburg's beautiful beast-supported bridges – the **Lviny most**, with cables emerging from the mouths of golden lions.

Fyodor Dostoevsky

The St Petersburg of Fyodor Dostoevsky's *Crime and Punishment*, one of the world's greatest, most harrowing novels, is a disorderly, decaying town ravaged by the effects of early capitalism, filled with poverty and desperation, and the stench of a hot summer. The novel's alienated protagonist has become blind to St Petersburg's architectural splendours and grand vistas, inhabiting as he does a district of tradespeople, artisans, prostitutes, criminals and drunks.

Dostoevsky (1821-81) lived virtually all of his adult life in St Petersburg, and at the time of writing *Crime and Punishment* (1866) was living in exactly such a district in the central city. Having chosen the precarious career of a writer, he was always short of money (though fond of gambling) and constantly struggled to meet his publishers' deadlines. He had rejected the materialism and condescension of the intelligentsia, believing rather in the dignity and goodness of the common people, and the importance of freedom and integrity.

But who wouldn't treasure freedom and life after having stared into the face of death and narrowly escaping?

Many years earlier, in 1847, Dostoevsky had joined a secret group of revolutionary-minded socialists, the Petrashevsky Circle. Two years later, the members were all arrested, accused of harbouring criminal designs against Church and State. Dostoevsky was imprisoned for eight months in solitary confinement at the notorious Peter & Paul Fortress. Already of an unstable and depressive personality, and now suffering from epileptic attacks, he displayed a quite unexpected strength of will and courage throughout his imprisonment and interrogation.

One day, without warning, 21 of the prisoners were led to Semyonovskaya ploshchad, where a sentence of death by firing squad was announced. They were lined up, and the firing squad carefully took aim. Then suddenly the guns were lowered – a message had arrived that Tsar Nicholas I had deigned to spare their lives. Their sentences were commuted, Dostoevsky's to four years in a Siberian prison labour camp followed by a spell in the army. In this cruelly staged mock execution, Dostoevsky had no doubt he was about to die.

In his years at the Omsk prison camp, he witnessed unspeakable horrors – brutality, cruelty, filth and degradation – and at one point nearly died from a flogging. He also witnessed the existence of incredible courage, decency and humanity amid this suffering.

Moskovsky Prospekt (Map 1)

This long avenue south from Sennaya ploshchad is the start of the main road to Moscow. The iron **Moscow Triumphal Arch**, 3.5km out, looking very like Berlin's Brandenburg Gate, was built in 1838 to mark victories over Turks, Persians and Poles, demolished in 1936 then rebuilt in 1959-60. Local legend has it that the gate is built on the spot where travellers entering the city in the early days had to show that they had brought with them bricks or stones to be used in the construction of buildings.

A couple of kilometres farther south, east off Moskovsky prospekt on ulitsa Gastello, is **Chesma Palace**, built for Catherine the Great to rest en route to Tsarskoe Selo (now Pushkin). More interesting is the red-and-white 18th century Gothic **Chesma Church** (1774-80), at ulitsa Gastello 17. The church, designed by Y Feltema (who was also responsible for the Church of St Catherine on Vasilevsky Island), was built in honour of the Battle of Cesme (1770) when the Russian fleet sailed from the Baltic to the Aegean to beat the Turks.

Wide Moskovskaya ploshchad, a little way south of ulitsa Gastello, was intended under a 1930s plan to become the centre of St Petersburg, replacing the old tsarist centre. In a testament to the stubbornness of St Petersburgers during Stalin's terror, this plan was universally ignored. Moskovsky prospekt ends a few hundred metres farther

Fyodor Dostoevsky

Eventually able to return to St Petersburg 10 years later, Dostoevsky devoted himself once again to writing. His experiences in captivity had reshaped his convictions, away from the earlier radical ideas and socialism to a focus on individual freedom and responsibility, the infinite worth of the human soul, Christianity and salvation through suffering. Developing these beliefs and drawing extensively on his experiences, he created some of literature's most deep and complex characters, and some of its most powerful, tense and energetic novels.

His works display an extraordinary depth of psychological insight, with their themes of suffering, faith, the origin of evil, individual freedom, crime and the meaning of life. They include *The House of the Dead, Notes from the Underground, The Idiot, The Gambler, The Possessed, The Brothers Karamazov* and *Crime and Punishment.*

More than a century after his death, Dostoevsky has become the Russian writer most widely read in English. His novels shaped the development of the Russian novel, and his ideas influenced a host of later writers, psychologists and philosophers, and spawned new literary genres such as the dystopian novel (eg George Orwell's *1984*).

The insight he provides into the nature of evil and the importance of freedom has made him just as relevant throughout the 20th century, with its revolutions, world wars and totalitarian regimes, as the 19th.

on at ploshchad Pobedy, where the **Monument to the Heroic Defenders of Leningrad**, commemorating WWII and the siege, makes a striking first impression on entering St Petersburg.

Underground is a free exhibition, open daily except Wednesday on the blockade, highly worth the trip to metro Moskovskaya and the 10 minute walk south after it. With a mausoleum-marble interior, films about the siege, exhibits, and haunting music, it's a sobering memorial to a grief felt by many residents to this day.

Just south of the Pulkova airports, lies the **Pulkova Observatory** (☎ 106 71 63; ask for Valery Fomin). For a short time at the beginning of the century, the observatory, founded in 1839, was considered the astronomical capital of the world for the quality and scope of its research. The WWII front line was only one mile to the south so many buildings suffered damage. The hill on which the observatory stands is the region's highest elevated point; from here the Nazis used to shell the easily viewed city. Tours of the museum and arranged evening visits to star search are possible with advance arrangement. Group tours cost $2 a person (minimum $20, but they're flexible with individuals), including a peek through the telescopes (the largest being 65cm; they also have a solar telescope). Bus No 55 south from metro Moscovskaya stops right at the observatory.

VASILEVSKY ISLAND

The oldest parts of Vasilevsky Island are its eastern 'nose', the Strelka (Tongue of Land), where Peter the Great first wanted his new city's administrative and intellectual centre, and the embankment facing the Admiralty. In fact, the Strelka became the focus of St Petersburg's maritime trade, symbolised by the white colonnaded **Stock Exchange**. The two **Rostral Columns** on the point, studded with ships' prows, were oil-fired navigation beacons in the 1800s (on some holidays gas torches are still lit on them). The area remains an intellectual centre, with the St Petersburg State University, the Academy of Arts and a veritable 'museum ghetto'.

The Strelka also has one of the best views in the city: you look left to the Peter & Paul Fortress and right to the Hermitage, the Admiralty and St Isaac's Cathedral.

Museums near the Strelka

The Stock Exchange is now the **Central Naval Museum** (Tsentralny Voenno-Morskoy muzey; Map 2; ☎ 218 25 02), full of maps, excellent model ships, flags and photos relating to the Russian navy right up to the present. Also on display is the *Botik*, Peter's first boat (the granddaddy of them all); a pre-20th century submarine (it's a two-seater); and some big oars. It's open from 10.30 am to 5.30 pm except Monday, Tuesday and the last Thursday of the month. Admission for adults/students is $2/1.

To the north of the Exchange is a former maritime warehouse and former Museum of Agriculture. Beyond this the old Customs House, topped with statues and a dome, is now called Pushkin House (Pushkinsky dom), and is home to the **Institute of Russian Literature** (Map 2), and a Literary Museum with exhibits on Tolstoy, Gogol, Lermontov, Turgenev, Gorky and others. It's open from 11 am to 5 pm weekdays only.

To the south of the Exchange in another ex-warehouse is the **Museum of Zoology** (Zoologichesky Muzey; Map 4; ☎ 218 01 12), reputed to be one of the biggest and best in the world, with incredibly life-like stuffed animals from all around the world. Among the dioramas and the tens of thousands of mounted beasties is a complete woolly mammoth (!) thawed out of the Siberian ice in 1902. The museum's open from 11 am to 6 pm except Friday. Admission is just $0.60 ($0.30 for students; free Thursday). Pay at the microscopic cash window just west of the main entrance.

Museum of Anthropology & Ethnography (Map 4)

The blue-and-white building with the steeple was the city's first museum, founded in 1714 by Peter himself. This museum (Muzey Antropologii i Etnografii; ☎ 218 14 12) is about peoples outside the former USSR, with campy dioramas and displays on the cultures of Asia, Oceania, Africa and the Americas. The old anatomy theatre is the (only) big draw, with selections from Peter's original *kunstkammer*. While this translates from German to 'art chamber', the bloodthirsty crowds are really here to see Peter's collection of monstrosities, notably a ghoulish collection of preserved freaks, two-headed mutant foetuses and body parts. It's fun for the whole family.

The museum is open from 11 am to 6 pm (last entry 4.45 pm); closed Thursday. Admission for all is $1.50. The entrance is around the corner in Tamozhyonny pereulok.

Menshikov Palace (Map 4)

Alexander Menshikov was a close friend (many now say lover) of Peter the Great. In 1707 Menshikov put up one of the city's first buildings, a riverside palace (Dvorets Menshikova) just west of the Twelve Colleges. He effectively ran Russia from here for three years between Peter's death and his own exile. Later the palace was a military academy and then it went to seed until Lenin suggested it be saved. Now its lavish interiors are again filled with period art and furniture as a museum of 'Russian Culture of the First Third of the 18th Century' (☎ 213 11 22). It's open from 10.30 am to 4.30 pm except Monday; admission for foreigners is $3 ($2 for ISIC holders and children). Russian-language excursions, which start every 10 minutes, are included in the price.

JONATHAN SMITH

The Bronze Horseman statue and the Peter & Paul Fortress during the white nights of St Petersburg

GEORGI SHABLOVSKY

Engineers' Castle, built in the 1790s for Tsar Paul I

JONATHAN SMITH

Winter Palace and the Neva River at sunset

JONATHAN SMITH

A few Atlases at the New Hermitage

LEE FOSTER

The Jordan Staircase at the Hermitage

LEE FOSTER

Detail of the Jordan Staircase

LEE FOSTER

Big wheels keep on turning – royal carriage at the Hermitage, St Petersburg

Academy of Arts Museum (Map 4)

At Universitetskaya naberezhnaya 17, is the Russian Academy of Arts' Research Museum (Muzey Akademii Khudozhestv; ☎ 213 64 96, excursion desk ☎ 213 35 78), guarded by two imported Egyptian sphinxes said to be about 3500 years old. When the academy opened in 1764, boys would live in this building from the age of five until they graduated at age 15 – it was an experiment to create a new species of human: the artist. Inside are works done by Academy students and faculty since its founding, including many studies, plus temporary exhibitions. Make sure you visit the third floor, where the models for the original versions of Smolny, St Isaac's, and the Alexander Nevsky monastery are kept, and take a peek into the fabulous old library – you'd think you were in Oxford. It's open from 11 am to 6 pm except Monday and Tuesday. Admission for adults/students is $2/1; double for photography. Worthy Russian-language excursions are about $5.

A short walk away, at 7-ya linia 16, opposite the Andreevsky market, is **Apteka 13**. Built in 1902, the gorgeous interiors will blow away your notion of a drugstore; pharmaceutical tools, jars and porcelain from the 17th and 18th centuries are on display.

Twelve Colleges (Map 4)

West of the Anthropology Museum and marked by a statue of the scientist-poet Mikhail Lomonosov is Mendeleevskaya linia and the skinny, 400m-long Twelve Colleges building. Meant originally for Peter's government ministries, it's now part of the university, which stretches out behind it.

Churches (Map 4)

Vasilevsky Island has its share of churches which have odd present-day functions. The **Church of St Catherine** (Tserkov Yekateriny, 1771) at Bolshoy prospekt 1, is now a sound studio (with purportedly the best accoustics in the city) owned by the record company Melodia.

More intriguing, at the far west end of Bolshoy prospekt, on the grounds of what has always been a military training sch[ool] is the **Church of Mother of God the Merciful** (Miluyoushchi Bozhe Materi; 1889-98), designed by V Kosyakov who also did the Naval Cathedral in Kronstadt. The Soviets converted it into a surreal training base for future submariners and for life-saving exercises. The Russian Byzantine exterior is more or less intact, but the interior has been completely gutted, and there is now a 26m-high tube filled with 333 tons of water, in which young divers practise their craft. As an ironic (blasphemous?) reference to the religious purpose the space used to serve, the students have suspended an old diving suit in mid-air, looking somewhat like Christ on the cross. The church is located on a closed military base and is not open to the public; don't even hope for access.

PETROGRAD SIDE

Petrograd Side (Petrogradskaya storona) is a cluster of delta islands between the Malaya Neva and Bolshaya Nevka channels. On little Zayachy Island, Peter the Great first broke ground for St Petersburg and built the Peter & Paul Fortress.

Peter & Paul Fortress

Founded in 1703, the Peter & Paul Fortress (Petropavlovskaya krepost) is the oldest building in St Petersburg. Peter planned it as a defence against the Swedes but defeated them before it was finished. Its main use up to 1917 was as a political prison. Famous residents include Dostoevsky, Gorky, Trotsky and Lenin's older brother, Alexander. Most worth seeing are the **Cathedral of SS Peter & Paul**, with its landmark needle-thin spire, and the **Trubetskoy Bastion**.

The cathedral, though plain on the outside, was radically different from traditional Orthodox churches. If you haven't overdosed on churches, don't miss its magnificent baroque interior. All of Russia's pre-revolution rulers from Peter the Great onwards, except Peter II and Ivan VI, are buried here. Nicholas II and his family (minus Alexey and Maria – see the following boxed text 'Reburying the Past') were the latest, controversial additions.

Reburying the Past

On 17 July 1998, in a controversial ceremony partially snubbed by both the Church and the State, the remains of Tsar Nicholas II, his wife, three of his five children, their doctor and three servants were buried in the Romanov family crypt at the SS Peter & Paul Cathedral within the fortress of the same name. A 19-gun salute bid them a final farewell. The ceremony was controversial for many reasons – political, religious, scientific and financial.

While President Boris Yeltsin and then-General Alexander Lebed were in attendance, together with many Romanov family members, other politicians downplayed the event, and Patriarch Alexey II held his own, rival service in Sergiyev Posad, outside Moscow, with a few renegade Romanov descendants in attendance (those who held some pretentions to regaining the throne).

The burial, which Yeltsin called an expiation of Russia's common guilt, set off touchy debates on monarchism (to be or not to be?) as a potential solution to the country's current crisis (most of the population is against this), and on the authenticity of the royal remains (DNA analyses repeatedly 'proved' that they are indeed the royal family's).

See the boxed text 'The Riddle of the Romanov Remains' in the Yekaterinburg section of the Western Siberia chapter for details of the execution of the Romanovs.

The burial provided an at-best partial closure to an 80-year-old tragedy. Vague plans by the Orthodox Church to canonise the tsar and his family within a few years do little to alleviate the dissatisfaction felt on all sides. Yet many see the burial as a proper step towards finally settling Russia's restless soul – the next, last, and most important step is to give Lenin a proper burial. And *that* opens up yet another can of worms.

In the fort's south-west corner are reconstructions of the grim cells of the Trubetskoy Bastion; one of its first inmates was Peter's own son Alexey, whose torture Peter is said to have overseen personally. Later, they were used by tsars to keep a lid on original thinking in the empire.

In the south wall is **Nevsky Gate**, a later addition, where prisoners were loaded on boats for execution elsewhere. Notice the plaques showing water levels of famous floods. Outside are fine views of the whole central waterfront. Around to the left in summer is a fascinating collection of fishers, joggers and standing sunbathers (standing's said to give you a *proper* tan), and in winter you might see people swimming in holes cut through the ice (an activity that's said to be 'good for the health'). At noon every day a cannon is fired from the **Naryshkin Bastion**, scaring the daylights out of the tourists.

The **Commandant's House** is a Museum of the History of St Petersburg up to the 1917 revolution, and the **Engineers' Building** has a museum on the city's architecture.

Entry to the fort is free but for most buildings inside you'll need a ticket from the kiosk at the east end or the one outside the cathedral, or to make a payment at the door. Admission to all sights is $3/1.50 for adults/students, though it's frightfully easy to get the $0.40 Russian rate. The fort is open from 11 am to 6 pm (to 4 pm Tuesday) except Wednesday and the last Tuesday of the month. To get there, it's a pleasant walk across either the Troitsky or Dvortsovy most, or across Alexandrovsky Park from metro Gorkovskaya.

Behind the Fortress

Across the moat, in the fort's original arsenal, is the **Artillery Museum** (Artilleriysky Muzey; ☎ 232 02 96), open from 11 am to 5 pm daily; closed Monday and Tuesday. It's great if you like weapons. Admission is $2/1.20 for adults/students.

West of that is the **zoo** (☎ 232 28 39), which, while full of miserable animals and happy kids, has improved the condition of its exhibits despite a severe lack of funds.

PETER & PAUL FORTRESS ПЕТРОПАВЛОВСКАЯ КРЕПОСТЬ

It's open from 10 am to 5 pm daily; admission is about $1/0.20 for adults/children.

Just north of the zoo is a permanent **amusement park** (Map 2), complete with bumper cars, a couple of small roller coasters and the like. East and behind the museum is **Alexandrovsky Park**, a neat hang-out in summer and on all holidays, but too close to traffic to be peaceful. At the back, the **Planetarium** (Map 2) offers pretty cool 50-minute star shows from 10.30 am to 6 pm daily except Monday.

Museum of Political History

East of Kamennoostrovsky prospekt at ulitsa Kuybysheva 4 is the Ksheshinskaya Palace which contains the Museum of Political History in Russia (Peter & Paul Fortress Map; ☎ 233 70 48), which is way more interesting than it sounds. The Bolsheviks made it their headquarters, and Lenin often gave speeches from the balcony of this elegant Art Nouveau palace that once belonged to Matilda Kshesinskaya, famous ballet dancer and one-time lover of Tsar Nicholas II. Go in to see the house itself, the best Soviet kitsch in town (including porcelain with workers' slogans and a watch for astronauts), and some incredibly rare satirical caricatures of Lenin published in magazines between the 1917 revolutions (the same drawings a few months later would have got the artist imprisoned, or worse). It's open from 10 am to 5.30 pm; closed Thursday. Admission is $2.40/1.20 for adults/students.

Peter's Cabin (Map 3)

In a patch of trees east of the fortress at Petrovskaya naberezhnaya 6 is a little stone building. In here is preserved St Petersburg's first residence, a log cabin where Peter lived in 1703 while supervising the construction of the fortress and city. Peter's Cabin (Domik Petra; ☎ 232 45 76) is open from 10 am to 5 pm; closed Tuesday and the last Monday of the month. Admission is about $0.60/0.30 for adults/students.

Cruiser Aurora (Map 3)

In the Nevka opposite Hotel St Petersburg is the *Aurora (Avrora)*, a cruiser mothballed from the Russo-Japanese War. From a downstream mooring on the night of 25 October 1917, its crew fired a blank round from the forward gun, demoralising the

Winter Palace's defenders and marking the start of the October Revolution. During WWII, the Russians sank it to protect it from German bombs. Now, refloated, restored and painted up in awfully pretty colours, it's a museum, open from 10.30 am to 4 pm except Monday and Friday (free).

Kirov Museum (Map 2)

Sergei Minorovich Kirov, one of Stalin's henchmen after whom countless parks, plazas, squares and a town are named, spent his last days at this decidedly unproletarian apartment before being murdered and unwittingly starting a wave of deadly repression in the country, most painfully in this city. Now a museum (☎ 346 14 81), the 4th floor apartment at Kameennoostrovsky 26-28 is a quick journey back to the days of Soviet glory, including choice examples of 1920s technology and books (20,000 of them). Don't miss the Party leader's death clothes, hung out for reverence: the tiny hole in the back of his cap was where he was shot (blood stains intact!), and the torn seam on his jacket's left breast was where doctors tried to revive his heart. It's open from 11 am to 6 pm daily except Wednesday. Entrance is just $0.15.

Botanical Gardens (Map 3)

This quiet jungle in eastern Aptekarsky (Apothecary) Island, just north-east of the Petrogradskaya metro station and across the Karpova Canal, was once a garden of medicinal plants which gave the island its name. The botanical gardens (☎ 274 17 64) comprise 26 greenhouses on a 22 hectare site and are one of St Petersburg's loveliest strolling grounds and most interesting places to visit – and not just for botanists. The gardens, founded by Peter himself in 1714, offer a variety of excursions to the stunning collection, all the more impressive considering that 90% of its plants died during the war (those 'veterans' that survived have a war medal pinned onto them). In the early 1900s, these were the second biggest botanical gardens in the world, behind only London's Kew Gardens. A highlight is the 'tsaritsa nochi' (selenicereus pteranthus), a flowering cactus which blossoms only one night a year, usually in mid-June. On this night, the gardens stay open until morning for visitors to gawk at the marvel and sip champagne. If you're in town, call to find out about it. They're open from 11 am to 4 pm daily except Friday. Enter at ulitsa Professora Popova 2.

TV Antenna (Map 3)

Here's a weird one: the Leningrad Radio-Tele Broadcasting Centre's antenna (☎ 234 78 87), at the northern end of Petrograd Side, is open for excursions to its 50,000W transmitter tower. It stands 310m-high over the city, and visitors can ascend to the observation deck 200m high. It's a great place to bring kids; it offers excellent views of the entire city and environs, and you can take photos. The deck is open from 10 am to 5 pm daily except Sunday and Monday, and individual or group tours can be arranged anytime, but there's one fixed at 2 pm every Saturday. It costs $4 per person if in a group of 10 or more; $30 for a group of under six persons. To reach the TV Antenna from Petrogradskaya metro, take trolleybus No 31 (or bus No 10, 71 or 128) north for two stops. Walk down to naberezhnaya Kantemirovsky, turn right and walk to the gates facing the river.

Kirovsky Islands (Map 2)

This is the collective name for the outer delta islands of Petrograd Side – Kamenny, Yelagin and Krestovsky. Once marshy jungles, the islands were granted to 18th and 19th century court favourites and developed into elegant playgrounds. Still mostly parkland, they're huge leafy venues for picnics, river sports and white-nights cavorting.

Kamenny Island This island's charm, seclusion and century-old dachas (now inhabited by the wealthy, or by the St Petersburg Mafiagentsia), combined with winding lanes and a series of canals, lakes and ponds, make a stroll here pleasant at any time of year. At the east end of the island the **Church of St John the Baptist** (Tserkov Rozhestva Ioanna Predtechi, 1776-81) seems to have found better use as a basketball court. Behind it the big, classical **Kamennoostrovsky Palace**, built by Catherine the Great for her son, is now a weedy military sanatorium.

The island also boasts a **government retreat** (the Yeltsin dacha), used by the president when he's in town and by other bigwigs when he's not. Look for the tree, said to have been planted by Peter the Great, almost blocking naberezhnaya reki Krestovki just west of its intersection with 2-ya Beryozovaya alleya.

Kamenny Island is a short walk south of metro Chyornaya Rechka (turn right as you exit, cross the bridge and you're there).

Yelagin Island This island's centrepiece is the **Yelagin Palace** (Yelaginsky dvorets), built for his mother by Tsar Alexander I, who had architect Carlo Rossi landscape the entire island while he was at it. The palace is to your right as you cross the footbridge from Kamenny Island.

The very beautiful restored interiors of the main house include old furnishings on loan from the Europe and Astoria hotels; don't miss the stupendous 1890s carved-walnut study ensemble and the incredible inlaid wood floors. The house is open from 10 am to 6 pm (closed Monday and Tuesday). Admission is $2.40/1.20 for adults/students. Other nearby estate buildings sometimes have exhibitions, too.

The rest of the island is a lovely network of paths, greenery, lakes and channels – you can rent rowing boats at the northern end of the island – and a plaza at the west end looking out to the Gulf of Finland. It's all now the Central Park of Culture & Rest (still named after Kirov), and is 2km long and pedestrian only. Several small cafes are open in summer.

Krestovsky Island The biggest of the three islands, Krestovsky consists mostly of the vast **Seaside Park of Victory** (Primorsky Park Pobedy), dotted with sports fields and the 100,000 seat **Kirov Stadium**.

Bus No 71 from metro Petrogradskaya goes the length of Krestovsky Island to Kirov Stadium. Trolleybus No 34 from near metro Petrogradskaya terminates on Krestovsky near the footbridge to Yelagin.

VYBORG SIDE (MAP 3)

Peter the Great had no apparent interest in the far side of the Neva, and today, beyond the embankment and Finland Station, among the factories and railway lines, there are few attractions.

Finland Station

The Finlyandsky vokzal is where, in 1917, Lenin arrived from exile in Switzerland (having ridden in a sealed railway carriage through Germany, Sweden and Finland) and gave his legendary speech from the top of an armoured car, in the square where his statue now stands. After fleeing a second time he again arrived here from Finland, this time disguised as a rail fireman, and the locomotive he rode in is displayed on the platform. It's not really the same station, having been rebuilt following WWII. The Ploshchad Lenina metro station is next door.

Kresty Prison

Kresty is St Petersburg's main holding prison; if you're busted here, Kresty's where they take you to await whatever it is that awaits you. What distinguishes Kresty from, say, New York's Riker's Island, is that Kresty is on a main boulevard, and prisoners can communicate with their families and friends. On any given day you can see well wishers lining Arsenalnaya naberezhnaya until they are chased away by police patrols who try to discourage this sort of thing. Mothers, fathers and drunken friends stand crying. Wives and girlfriends move their arms in what may look like intricate dance moves, but what is in fact a crude code, known to inmates and prison guards alike.

The prisoner makes himself known by holding an article of clothing out the window (only their hands are visible, stuck through slats or holes in the steel mesh). When the friend down on the street identifies their man, they start waving their arms about, tracing Cyrillic characters in the air. The prisoner waves up and down to signal 'I understand', and side to side to signal 'repeat'. Under this method, after three or four minutes of waving, one can clearly discern the message, 'I-c-a-l-l-e-d-M-i-s-h-a'!

The process, understandably, is time consuming (a message like 'I called your lawyer but he was out to lunch' could take half an hour or so), but the family and friends on the street below (in true Russian style) bring along sausage, bread, cheese and flasks filled with hot tea. The best time to go is in the early evening; try not to be obtrusive or rude. To get a peek inside, and to help fund staff salaries and much-needed repairs, official tours have begun of the prison. Meet at 7 Arsenalnaya naberezhnaya at 11 am on Sunday. Bring $6.25 and your passport.

Piskaryovka Cemetery (Map 1)

For two and a half years during WWII the Germans besieged Leningrad and between half a million and one million people died, mostly of cold and starvation. Almost half a million were buried in mass graves in this cemetery (Piskaryovskoe memorialnoe kladbishche; ☎ 247 57 29). With acres of slightly raised mounds marked by year, it's a sobering place. At the entrance is an exhibit of photographs that need no captions. Here you'll understand the Russian obsession with that war. This is a fair way out, about a 40 minute trip from the city centre on public transport. From Ploshchad Muzhestva metro station turn left, cross prospekt Nepokoryonnykh and take bus No 123. It's the sixth stop.

ACTIVITIES

Banya

Tired? Overworked? A good beating may be all you need, and St Petersburg's public banyas (bathhouses) are as good a place as any to get one! Here are a few of the better banyas (see the boxed text in the Northern European Russia chapter for correct banya etiquette):

Banya 50 (Map 3; ☎ 233 50 92), ulitsa Malaya Posadskaya 28, metro Gorkovskaya, is a nice, clean and friendly place.

Banya 51 (Map 5; ☎ 164 31 69), ulitsa Voronezhskaya 8/10, metro Ligovsky Prospekt, has common and luxury rooms, and a cold-water pool.

Nevskie Bani (Map 6; ☎ 311 14 00), ulitsa Marata 5/7, metro Mayakovskaya, the largest in town, is smack in the city centre on the site of a cathedral torn down especially to build it. It used to be much better.

Ice Skating

There's ice skating (with skate rental) at the Yubileyny Stadium (Map 2; ☎ 119 56 01), Dobrolyubova prospekt 18, Petrograd Side, and at the Dvorets Sporta SKA (Map 2; ☎ 237 00 73), Zhdanovskaya naberezhnaya 2. Access both from metro Sportivnaya. Both charge about $5 an hour for skating and rental.

Skiing

Russians are avid cross-country skiers, and larger sporting goods shops carry skis and equipment, usually for about half the price you'd pay back home. Popular cross-country skiing destinations (for the day) are Toksovo and Tagalovo, small towns north of the city, reachable by elektrichka from Finland Station. People also head to the grounds surrounding the Pulkovo Observatorium.

Sporting Facilities

Russians don't begin casual conversations with, 'So, where do you work out?'. Gym culture here is minimal. Still, Russians are very active in recreational sports – check out *Luchshee V Sankt Peterburg* under Sports Clubs for a complete list. There are gyms at all the major hotels (prices are exorbitant), aerobic centres for women have become quite popular, and weight rooms have sprung up in many corners of the city (mainly, so far, for the likes of bodyguards and thugs).

The best sports complex in the city is called (you'll never guess) Sports Complex (Map 3; ☎ 238 16 32) at Kronverksky prospekt 9A (on the east side of Kamennoostrovsky prospekt across from metro Gorkovskaya). Its 25m pool, under a glass roof, is heavenly ($1.40 an hour, and staff will let you in without the required medical certificate if you look clean), and it has a weights room. Staff are also a good source of information for spectator sporting events in the city. The complex is open from 7 am to 11 pm daily.

St Petersburg for Children

There's heaps to do with kids in St Petersburg; there are even museums your kids will like! For starters, the Kunstkammer in the Museum of Anthropology & Ethnography is an all-time favourite with its jarred mutants display. The Botanical Gardens offers year-round, unexpected treats, and the Flowers Exhibition hall near Smolny also has great tropical plants to gawk at. Then, of course, there's the zoo and circus, the Peter & Paul Fortress and the Planetarium, all of which hold special kids' programs.

The city's parks are first rate; there's a full-scale amusement park right behind the Peter & Paul Fortress, and a smaller one in the City Children's Park in the Tauride Gardens. There's an awesome children's playground on the east side of ulitsa Bolshaya Pushkarskaya just north of ulitsa Lenina, Petrograd Side. And there are rowing boat rental outlets behind the Peter & Paul Fortress, and on Yelagin Island.

Every Sunday at noon at the bistro Orient on 1-ya linia 36, Vasilevsky Island, there's a doll show the kids can enjoy while you eat. Finally, a few theatres in town cater to kids, and these can be a real treat, even if they don't understand the language (see the Theatre section under Entertainment).

Frisbee

There are great team games of 'ultimate Frisbee' year-round, at 3 pm every Sunday at 9 pm on Monday in a field near Lesnaya metro station (Map 3), though in winter it's sometimes held inside, or sometimes out in the snow. Call George on ☎ 552 40 37 or email frisbee@neva.math.spb.ru for more information.

Hash House Harriers

A 'drinking club with a running problem', the HHH was invented by energetic British soldiers in 1938 in Malaysia, and has since spread to British consulates all over the world. The runs, in which groups go in search of hidden objects, are usually 5km or less, followed by serious 'down-down' chug-a-lug sessions and a trip to the banya. It can be great fun in a football-hooligan sort of a way. The group meets at 1 pm every second Sunday – bring running gear. Contact Sarah Powell on ☎ 325 60 36, or fax inquiries to 315 64 34.

LANGUAGE COURSES

St Petersburg Times advertises many private tutors and classes, but the Herzen State Pedagogical University (☎ 314 78 59, ssm@herzen.spb.ru, www.herzen.spb.ru) runs excellent courses for all levels, from two weeks to graduate programs several years long, 20 hours a week, for $3-5 an hour in groups of two to eight.

ORGANISED TOURS

St Petersburg Travel (Map 6; ☎ 327 31 36), at Nevsky prospekt 100, in addition to being a fully fledged travel agency, has the most reliable tour schedule – tours leave its offices several times daily, and its wide range includes city tours ($16), excursions through the Hermitage ($23), and jaunts to Pushkin and Pavlovsk (both for $40).

Peter Kozyrev runs the excellent Peter's Tours (☎ 329 80 18, pkozyrev@hotmail.com), walking tours only which leave the HI St Petersburg Hostel at 10.30 am daily. He also offers several cool variations, like a rooftops tour (you haven't *really* seen St Pete until you've seen it from above), a Dostoevsky walking tour, and you can also custom make others depending on your interest. He usually charges $8 per person for a 4-5 hour walk.

Sasha Bogdanov (☎ 356 72 06) is another affable, knowledgeable guy offering unique tours of the city. While he can guide people through the major sights at Russian prices and arrange theatre tickets, his speciality is providing visitors – from students to the elderly – with alternate experiences of the city, taking them to off-beat nooks and crannies tourists rarely see, to discover the real pulse of the city and its history. His going rate is $20 a day.

Helicopter Tours

Baltic Airlines (Map 6; ☎ 311 00 84) at Nevsky prospekt 7/9, office 12, rents out helicopters for everything from tourism to emergency hospital drop-offs. Its most economical rides are $35 flights around the city which last 10-15 minutes. These leave from the beach in front of the Peter & Paul Fortress (see Peter & Paul Fortress Map) on weekends from April through October. On summer weekends, you can fly to Petrodvorets ($35 one way), and basically fly anywhere you like if you can fork out $1100 per hour to do so (to Valaam and back should be about $3000!). Up to 20 people can fit in its copters, though.

River & Canal Trips

In summer – roughly May to September – St Petersburg makes good use of its rivers and canals. Excursion boats leave the Anichkov Bridge landing on the Fontanka River just off Nevsky prospekt (Map 6) regularly throughout the day from 10.45 am to 8 pm for a 75 minute, $4 tootle around the canals and smaller rivers, sometimes with commentary in Russian. From here, as well as at the Griboedova and Moyka canals, you can also rent your own boat (at least $24 for a half an hour for up to eight people) and go anywhere you like.

There are also 80-minute City on the Neva cruises, up the river and back from Hermitage No 2 landing every 40 minutes or so for $5. You'll generally putter into the Neva, head east, go around the horn and south to the Smolny, where you turn back and head for home. Excursions sometimes also leave from the embankment opposite the Bronze Horseman.

SPECIAL EVENTS

See the European Russia Facts for the Visitor chapter for general Russian holidays. Aside from these, there are a few specific to St Petersburg. During the last 10 days of June, when darkness hardly falls, many residents stay out all night celebrating White Nights. At that time there's a tourist-oriented White Nights Dance Festival with events ranging from folk to ballet, and the International Film Festival which hosts daily screenings and parties. The Russian Winter (25 December to 5 January) and Goodbye Russian Winter (late February to early March) festivities centre outside the city, with *troyka* (horse-drawn sleigh) rides, folk shows and performing bears.

The St Petersburg Music Spring is an international classical music festival held in April or May, and the mid-November International Jazz Festival, Osenie Ritmy (Autumn Rhythms), is centred around St Petersburg's jazz clubs.

PLACES TO STAY

Homestays & Private Flats

The Host Families Association (HOFA; Map 3; ☎/fax 275 19 92, alexei@hofak.hop.stu.neva.ru, www.spb.ru/homestays), at ulitsa Tavricheskaya 5/25, is the most established and reliable agency for finding private accommodation. It places travellers with respectable, English-speaking Russian families in apartments around town. You'll get a private room with a shared bath and breakfast included. It has four programs, starting with basic B&B ($30/50 for single/double flats in the centre). It can also rent out flats in the centre, but this can get pricey. There is a $30 charge for an invitation and registration. It has branches in other cities like Moscow, Yekaterinburg, Murmansk, Novgorod, Vladimir and Vladivostok, as well as in Riga, Tallinn and Vilnius.

The Apartment Hotel Bureau (Map 5; ☎ 106 81 07 or ☎ 290 08 25), with a tiny kiosk as an office on Ligovsky prospekt 44 a block south of the Moscow Station, can find you an empty apartment from $10 a day or a room from $4 a day. Some locations are central, but many are a fair way out. Ask lots of questions before saying yes.

It's also possible to stay in a private flat for about $10 a night by going with one of the older women who approach travellers arriving off major trains at Moscow Station. You'll have to use your judgement about who to trust (many really are genuine folks in need of extra cash) and establish how far from the city centre their place is before accompanying them (ask to see it on a map).

PLACES TO STAY – BUDGET

Camping

Not a great idea. The only camping ground is far from the centre, dangerous and poorly equipped. The ***Motel-Camping Olgino*** *(off Map 1; ☎ 238 36 71, Primorskoe shosse 59)*, about 18km north-west of the centre, is far away and full of heavy drinking clientele. It's a 20 minute ride on bus No 210 or 110 from metro Staraya Derevnya. Beds in tiny cabins are $18 per person, or $30 for a two-room 'luxury'. It does have a 24-hour banya and bowling alley, though.

Hostels & Student Accomodation

Russia's first – since 1992 – and to date only Hostelling International (HI) member hostel is the ***HI St Petersburg Hostel*** *(Map 6; ☎ 329 80 18, fax 329 90 19, ryh@ryh.ru, 3-ya Sovetskaya ulitsa)*. A place in rooms with three to six beds costs $19, and $24 per person will get you a double room; slightly cheaper in the winter and for ISIC and HI card-holders. All prices include breakfast, and there's a kitchen for guests' use. It's a five minute walk north-east of Moscow Station (metro Ploshchad Vosstania), and rooms are clean and comfortable. Staff are preternaturally friendly, and the hostel's visa support service (tourist visas only cost $35) is very reliable. Reserve by faxing, emailing, or through any HI hostel with IBN. They also reserve for Travellers Guest House in Moscow and Roza Vetrov in Novgorod. More information on the hostel can be found at www.ryh.ru.

The location of the ***Holiday Hostel*** *(Map 3; ☎ 542 73 64, fax 327 10 70, info@hostel.spb.ru, ulitsa Mikhailova 1, 3rd floor)* has its pros and cons. The pro is definitely the river view in summer – the rooftop cafe offers the classic panorama of the Peter & Paul Fortress against the backdrop of raised drawbridges. But there's not much out this way, and that incessant shouting you hear is the families of inmates calling to loved ones being held at Kresty Prison, next door (see the earlier Vyborg Side section).

The hostel is clean and fun, and staff are helpful. A bed in a double room costs $15 with breakfast ($12 for a bed in a room with three to six beds), and you'll be sent a three-month tourist visa invitation for $30. From Finland Station (metro Ploshchad Lenina) turn left, then right onto Mikhailova ulitsa; the entrance to the yard is across the street on the left.

While not close to the centre, the ***Petrovskogo College Student Hostel*** *(Map 4; ☎ 252 75 63, fax 252 40 19, ulitsa Baltiyskaya 26)* has excellent deals: a place in a double/triple is $4/6. Decent showers and toilets are shared between four rooms. There's a cafeteria on the premises, and even a sauna and weight room. From metro Narvskaya walk left (south), down prospekt Stachek away from the Narva Arch to ulitsa Baltiyskaya, where you turn left and continue another 300m.

You can't ask for a better location than that of the ***Herzen University Hotel*** *(Map 6; ☎ 314 74 72, ulitsa Kazanskaya (Plekhanova) 6)*, 120m behind the Kazan Cathedral. Getting a room can be quite a chore, though. Staff may tell you that the rooms are only for the university's students. These students may pay less, but the hotel is, in fact, open to all. Comfortable single and double rooms are $18/20, but remember that it cannot register your visa, and, if you're staying in the country for more than three days, you'll have to find alternate ways of doing this. Availability is tight, especially in summer. If the reception staff turn you away, try contacting the university staff on ☎ 14 76 76.

Hotels

City Centre, South & East of Centre

The best hotel deals in the city, hands down, belong to ***Hotel Oktyabrskaya*** (see Mid-Range) and its offshoot ***Oktyabrsky Filial*** *(Map 6; ☎ 277 72 81, fax 315 75 01, Ligovsky prospekt 43/45)*, directly opposite the Moscow Station. It may at first look like the kind of seedy place usually found opposite railway stations, but, while it is a bit run-down and not for the spoiled, it's clean, friendly, convenient and atmospheric. There are about a dozen different types of rooms to choose from, with or without bath, fridge or breakfast. Prices start at $8, and no room is more expensive than $27. If there are three or four of you, ask for its gigantic, bright triples (Nos 364 and 376 are the best). Late at night, prostitutes hang out on the street outside, but the area is safe. When reserving a room, specify your interest in the 'Filial'.

There are two budget places slightly south of the centre that aren't at all bad; the dumpy but surprisingly cheerful ***Hotel Kievskaya*** *(Map 5; Dnepropetrovskaya ulitsa 49)*, and its superior ***Kievsky Filial*** *(Map 5; Kurskaya ulitsa 40)*, a block away. Contact numbers for both are ☎ 166 58 11, fax 166 53 98. Both have singles/doubles with shared facilities for $6/10, or $14/22 with toilet and breakfast. They're in a boring neighbourhood on the Obvodny Canal near the bus station, though Moscow Station is a three-stop ride along Ligovsky prospekt on anything except Bus No 14.

Petrograd & Vyborg Sides A few pleasant minutes walk up from metro Petrogradskaya (or one stop on trolleybus 6, 31 or 34) is the run-down but perfectly adequate ***Hotel Druzhba*** *(Map 2; ☎ 234 18 44, Chapygina ulitsa 4)*. Rooms are clean, spacious, and have phones and shower/toilets. Singles/doubles/triples cost $6.50/9/11. The only drawback is that it can't register your visa (there's a nearby OVIR office, though, and the staff will give you advice on the process).

The ***Dvorets Molodyozhy Hotel*** *(Palace of Youth; Map 2; ☎ 234 32 78, ulitsa Professora Popova 47)* is in a very quiet location, but it's a 20 minute walk to metro Petrogradskaya. It's big and Soviet-modern outside, plain inside. Singles/doubles go for $14.50/13.50 per person, not including breakfast, but they have toilet and bath.

PLACES TO STAY – MID-RANGE
City Centre

The perfectly central ***Hotel Oktyabrskaya*** *(Map 6; ☎ 277 63 30, fax 315 75 01, Ligovsky prospekt 10)*, smack on ploshchad Vosstania, has done plenty of upgrading in recent years and is the best bet for your money. Euro-standard single/double rooms, depending on size, cost $26-31/31-36, with some luxury rooms going for upwards of $40. It offers a full range of services, including free visa support. Rooms are ten times cheaper than at the nearby Nevsky Palace, but the comfort level is not hugely less, if you aren't too precious.

Hotel Moskva *(Map 5; ☎ 274 30 01, fax 274 21 30, ploshchad Alexandra Nevskogo 2)*, just opposite the Alexander Nevsky Monastery, is a monstrous, three-star place not far from the centre, sitting atop the Ploshchad Alexandra Nevskogo metro. Its institutional feel, rude service, and creepy lobby makes it rather unappealing. For what you get, the rack rate of $72/94 is steep, but package tours and local travel agencies can get a cheaper rate. Try for a room at the back where it's quieter.

A newish and rather unheralded choice is the excellent ***Matisov Domik*** *(Map 4; ☎ 219 54 45, fax 219 74 19, naberezhnaya reki Pryazhki 3/1)*, about a 10 minute walk west of the Mariinsky Theatre. This family-run place has 24 super-clean rooms, all with phone, TV, free soft drinks and breakfast included. Singles/doubles/luxuries cost $38/57/84. There is also a sauna for guests' use ($14 per person). From the Mariinsky, walk west on Dekabristov ulitsa, up to the canal. Cross it, turn right and the hotel is 250m ahead.

Two hotels not far from metro Chernyshevskaya offer the finest in Soviet accommodation. ***Hotel Rus*** *(Map 5; ☎ 273 46 83, fax 279 36 00, ulitsa Artilleryskaya 1)* is a large but comfortable place with negligent staff and singles/doubles with bath for $54/78. ***Hotel Neva*** *(Map 3; ☎ 278 05 04, fax 273 25 93, ulitsa Chaykovskogo 17)*, near the former secret police and later KGB headquarters, was once a bordello (could there be a connection?). Very basic, drab rooms go for $20-65/32-75.

Vasilevsky Side

The ***Pribaltiyskaya Hotel*** *(Map 4; ☎ 356 01 58, fax 356 44 96, market@pribalt.spb.su, ulitsa Korablestroyteley 14)* is a behemoth on the Gulf of Finland – perhaps you caught its movie debut in *The Russia House*. It's very popular with package tour groups and has fair service and big, clean rooms with stunning views of the Gulf of Finland (ask). Rooms are $140/160, including breakfast and transport to and from the city centre all day on its minibuses. If you request a discount – and have a good reason for asking – you'll probably get it. There's a bowling alley, billiards hall and sauna on the premises. All in all not a bad place.

Vyborg Side

The big three-star ***Hotel St Petersburg*** *(Map 3; ☎ 542 94 11, Pyrogovskaya naberezhnaya 4)* has front rooms with amazing views over the Neva towards the Hermitage but also traffic noise if you open the windows. At $77/97 ($50 with a dull view), it's not the worst deal. It's a 15 minute walk to the nearest metro, Ploshchad Lenina.

South & East of the City Centre

Hotel Neptune *(Map 5; ☎ 210 18 11, naberezhnaya Obvodnogo kanala 93A)* is one of two hotels in Russia managed by Best Western. It's in a pretty odd location but its rooms are very nice at $95 to $140. It's about a 10 minute walk from metro Pushkinskaya.

PLACES TO STAY – TOP END

The ***Grand Hotel Europe*** *(Map 6; ☎ 329 60 00, fax 329 60 01, res@ghe.spb.ru, www.europe.hotels.spb.ru, Mikhailovskaya ulitsa 1/7)* is perhaps the finest property in town if you go by architecture and location. The rooms are lavish, some spectacular (though smaller than you'd think), and the original and breathtaking Art Nouveau interiors, along with a baroque facade designed by Rossi, have been restored to their late 19th century glory. There are shopping arcades in the lobby, several bars and restaurants, and a harpist on the mezzanine. Singles start from $295, doubles $335, and suites go from $390 to (now get this) $2350. These prices, by the way, do *not* include breakfast ($26!!) or 20% tax. There are weekend discounts, and non-smoking floors.

Hotel Astoria *(Map 4; ☎ 210 57 57, fax 210 51 33, front@astoria.spb.ru, www.astoria.spb.ru, ulitsa Bolshaya Morskaya 39)*, right in front of St Isaac's Cathedral, is the very essence of class and old-world glory, and as such tends to suit an older, rarefied clientele. Actually two hotels in one, the old wing, named the Astoria, is a five-star treat with singles/doubles starting at $300/336. Beautiful two-room apartments are $480, luxury suites $1000, and the presidential suite is $1700. Each room has its own look and feel, and most have original period antique furniture. The dining hall on the main floor is a true wonder to behold; it's easy to see why Hitler wanted to hold his victory celebration here.

The newer, adjoining wing is now actually called ***Hotel D'Angleterre***, though the administration is the same as the Astoria's. Less grand but still elegant rooms, with a four-star rating, start at $220; junior suites are $300. Romantics will like to know that poet Sergei Esenin hung himself on the 2nd floor of this hotel; it's the one whose balcony is closest to the left-hand corner when facing the hotel.

The ***Sheraton Nevskij Palace Hotel*** *(Map 6; ☎ 275 20 01, fax 301 75 24, Nevsky prospekt 57)* is a fabulously renovated place, with some of the best restaurants in town (see Places to Eat), but this is a hotel which caters to a business clientele, and its total lack of atmosphere attests to this. Corridors go on forever, like in *The Shining*, and rooms are excellent, of course, but quite forgettable. And with summer rates for singles/doubles/suites from $330/350/440 (its presidential suite, in which Prince Andrew and Ringo Starr once stayed – on separate occasions – is $1900), you'd want to remember something about your visit. It is the best equipped hotel for business conferences, though.

PLACES TO EAT

The choice of dining in St Petersburg – from cheap to very fine, from borscht to eel in orange sauce – is enormous. Telephone numbers are listed here only if you'll need to reserve a table in advance, or if the establishment offers live music or entertainment so you can check what's on.

Restaurants

Russian Most restaurants serve at least some Russian dishes, but the ones specialising in them tend to be touristy and pricey. These are some of the more worthwhile.

The ***Zvyozdochet*** *(Astrologer; Map 5; ulitsa Marata 35)* is an inexpensive place to try out some fish soup and other Russian dishes – and have your star chart read at the same time. Its subdued, almost tacky atmosphere underscores the Russian flair for mystery and drama.

For most of the following entries, don't expect to leave without paying at least $15 a person. ***Staraya Derevnaya*** *(Map 2; ☎ 431 00 00, ulitsa Savushkina 72)* is a first-rate, family-run traditional Russian restaurant (from metro Chyornaya Rechka, take tram No 2, 31 or 37). Service is great, and because it's small, it's very intimate and cosy – make reservations. On weekend evenings, there's musical entertainment in the form of traditional Russian ballads. Main courses run from $7 to $16.

For location and service, nothing in this category comes close to touching ***Austeria*** *(Peter & Paul Fortress Map; ☎ 238 42 62)*, in the Peter & Paul Fortress; dine outside and count on excellent Neva views, solid Russian food and live music nightly. Meals run from $15 to $25.

The ***Restoran Nevsky*** *(Map 6; ☎ 311 30 93, Nevsky prospekt 71)*, has been doing its best to keep up the traditions of the Communist Dining Experience for decades now. The fact that it's lasted this long means something, though just what is not clear. It has several theme rooms, some gargantuan, a great menu, and a floor show exceded in kitsch only by ***Restaurant Troika*** *(Map 5; ☎ 113 53 43, Zagorodny prospekt 27)*, whose variety show is so execrable it's worth the $50 set price. Located in a basement, this place has Russian food, pseudo-exotic dancers and big hats.

The heavily advertised ***Kalinka*** *(Map 2; ☎ 323 37 18, Syezdovskaya linia 9)*, on Vasilevsky Island, has a beautiful atmosphere, live music on original old instruments and fine food (like bear in cognac pepper and rabbit with fruits), but it can get excruciatingly packed with tourists, so weekday visits would be better. Main meals run up to $25.

For Russian meals with a twist, head to ***Cameo*** *(Map 6; 2-ya Sovetskaya 21)*. It prepares Russian food as you've never seen it before – in French style (smallish portions, colour-coordinated, lots of fruit and meat combos). It's modern and New York-stylish (there's not a Russian doll in sight), quiet, and the service is impeccable. And it's not expensive – dinner for two should be under $20.

Caucasian & Middle Eastern While ***Kavkaz Restaurant*** *(Map 5; ☎ 221 43 09, Stakhanovtsev ulitsa 5)*, near metro Novocherkasskaya, has an excellent reputation, it's only among those who like overpriced (though great) food served with an indifference unknown outside of most prison cafeterias. You're better off at its bistro next door, and better still at its new, central branch at Karavannaya ulitsa 18 (Map 6). There's both a cafe (open 10 am to 8 pm) and a pricier restaurant (open noon to 1 am) there, prices are more reasonable and service is friendly. Try its beef stuffed with pomegranate ($10).

Kafe Tbilisi *(Map 2; ☎ 230 93 91, Sytninskaya ulitsa 10)* is practically a St Petersburg institution and won't disappoint. This is a first-rate restaurant but its mouth-watering dishes are no more than $3 each. Try the home-made cheese, and its lavash and khachipuri breads.

Pirosmani Restaurant *(Map 2; ☎ 235 46 66, Bolshoy prospekt 14, Petrograd Side)* has excellent Georgian food in a unique setting. The rear wall of the restaurant is psychedelically sculpted in what's billed as a tribute to the Georgian artist's work, and there are rivers flowing through the restaurant. A three course meal will cost you $20. It's walkable from metro Sportivnaya.

If you miss hummus, tabouleh and shish-taouk, ***Livanskaya Kukhnya*** (Map 6), right on ploshchad Vosstania opposite the Moscow Station, is a Lebanese restaurant with a dreary locale and not-bad food at cheap prices. It is open from 11 am to 11 pm and closed Sundays. ***Shaxherazada*** *(Map 5; Razyezaya ulitsa 3)* sometimes has great falafel, and otherwise serves up decent cafe-style Middle Eastern dishes.

European At ***Bahlsen*** *(Map 6; Nevsky prospekt 142)* a variety of meals is served on hot marble plates in an grand, elegant setting. With main meals all under $7, this is one of the nicest mid-range places to visit. Nearby is ***Zolotaya Rybka*** *(Little Golden Fish; Map 5; ☎ 277 24 84, Nevsky prospekt 166)*, a chrome-studded place offering the best fish dishes in the city (but you're in Russia – this fish restaurant also serves meat), and maybe the best lunch deal: a full-course set menu for $3.40. At supper time, main meals are upwards of $10 but delicious.

For old-style opulence equalled only by the Astoria's dining hall, there's ***Nikolai*** *(Map 4; ☎ 311 14 02, Bolshaya Morskaya 52)*, right on St Isaac's Square in the House of Architects. This is first-class, almost regal dining – you'd think you were having lunch inside the Hermitage – and meals are $12 and up.

The ***Tsaritsa Nochi*** *(Map 3; ☎ 234 17 63, Popova 2)* beats them all for exotic locales. Situated inside the grounds of the Botanical Gardens, Petrograd Side, this is a class affair with six different styles of cooking and an impressive menu with such dishes as filet mignon stuffed with crab meat, and trout with almonds and leeks (main meals cost up to $20) The dining room is sumptuous and the table cloths are hand-sewn. There's a summer outdoor patio.

For Italian, you'll have to visit an ATM or two beforehand. ***Rossi's*** *(☎ 329 60 00)* is the Grand Hotel Europe's (Map 6) casually elegant dining option. With excellent food and service, it's good for a business lunch. Its main courses are priced from $20 to $35, starters up to $15. ***Milano*** *(Map 6; ☎ 314 73 48, Karavannaya ulitsa 8)* has dependably good Italian food, but dinner costs about $40 per person.

An impressive food emporium is the ***Schvabsky Domik*** *(Map 5; ☎ 528 22 11, Novocherkassky prospekt 28/19)*, occupying this entire block, upstairs from metro Novocherkasskaya. The Bavarian decor pushes the hokey barrier but it's fun, and the food – schnitzel, sauerkraut, lots of potatoes, sausage and roast pork – is great. So is the excellent German beer. There are three separate halls here: the cheapest is the buffet in the middle, the priciest is the restaurant to your left, and the happy medium on your right.

Asian The number and quality of St Petersburg's Asian offerings are on a par with London's. At the heavenly ***Red Rose*** *(Map 2; ☎ 346 33 43, Kamennoostrovsky prospekt 44/46)* you won't know where to start. Daily soups for $1.50, garlic eel for $6, fried Chinese bread for $1, and about a hundred other choices, all served impeccably in a traditional setting. Ask to hear its tape of Chinese versions of Russian folk songs (seriously!).

Dragon Luck *(Map 5; ulitsa Vosstania 20)* has a dreary decor and intriguing-sounding dishes like 'Ants go up a tree' and 'Pork with a fish taste'. The comfy bar at the back serves up great food 24 hours a day, and you can fill up on bar portions of excellent food very inexpensively. ***Kharbin*** *(Map 5; ☎ 272 65 08, ulitsa Zhukovskogo 34/2)* has wonderful service and dependably good Chinese food, including excellent fried eggplant in soy sauce with ginger for $4. Meals average $5, and you can cook up a storm at your table yourself for $12.

Tinye *(Map 4; 323 22 29, 1-ya linia 18)* on Vasilevsky Island has a Chinese cook and is another good bet. Its huge soups (under $2) are big enough for a meal, main dishes average $6, and the house speciality, eel on an iron plate, will cost you $10. If you feel like spending more money for less, ***Chopsticks*** *(☎ 119 60 00)*, at the Grand Hotel Europe (Map 6), is a cool place to be seen.

The best bet for Japanese is ***Fujiyama*** *(Map 2; ☎ 234 49 22, Kamennoostrovsky prospekt 54, Petrograd Side)*. It's top of the line and accordingly very expensive. It has 26 kinds of sushi, with two-piece portions from $4 to $11. Teriyaki dishes are upwards of $16 each.

Near Tekhnologichesky Institut, ***Korean House*** *(Map 4; ☎ 259 93 33, Izmailovsky* *prospekt 2)* serves up what may be the best Korean food in Eastern Europe. The food is awesome, with a decidedly heavy hand with the garlic and spices. Specialities are Korean-style beef and kim chi, with a good choice of vegetarian meals. Main courses run from $5 to $9.

Arirang *(Map 5; ☎ 274 04 66, 8-ya Sovetskaya 20)* is about double the price, but fancier, and you are given lots of free starters to keep you happy.

Indian The ***Tandoor*** *(Map 4; ☎ 312 38 86, Voznesensky prospekt 2)*, just off Isaakievskaya ploshchad, is the most central Indian place in town, with a full – albeit Russianised – Indian menu (about $7 for starters and $10 to $20 for main courses) and a limited wine list.

You'd be better off at its less convenient competitor on Vasilevsky Island, ***Swagat*** *(Map 4; ☎ 217 21 11, Bolshoy prospekt 91)*. All diners are instantly transformed into Homer Simpson-like characters, reduced to slumping in their seats as plate after plate of stupendous Indian food gets placed before them ('Mmmm tandoor chicken ...'); fabulous main courses like mixed kebabs cost $15 and murg joshina – chicken in a spicy tomato sauce – $9. Service is great and there's live sitar music nightly.

Pizza & US The ***California Grill*** *(Map 5; Nevsky prospekt 176)* is cheerful, spacious and very US in look and feel, with American food, good Cobb salads, killer burritos and fajitas (for $5), philly steak sandwiches and Reubens. It has a $5 set lunch menu and a kids menu also. It is open from 11.30 am to midnight, and has live music most nights and parties for major sporting events.

If 16oz of rare beef is your thing, ***Montreal Steak*** *(Map 5; ☎ 310 92 56, Apraksin pereulok 22)*, at the corner of naberezhnaya reki Fontanki, does excellent thick steaks at high but not outrageous prices.

The best pizza in town is at the beautiful ***La Strada*** *(Map 6; ☎ 312 47 00, Bolshoya Konyushennaya ulitsa 27)*, which has a spacious area with an enormous glass ceiling and an open kitchen area where you can watch the cooks prepare the pizzas. Portions are huge. Pizzas start at $9 but average $12, small salads are $4 and up, and there are baked potato dishes for about $8.

St Petersburg has two ***Pizza Hut*** restaurants; the original at naberezhnaya reki Moyki 71/76, and Nevsky prospekt 96 (Map 6). Both do countless varieties of pizza and have tiny salad bars. The Nevsky location also does pizza by the slice (thank you!) for under $2.

Two dependable Russian-run pizza places are ***Pizza Pronto*** *(Map 5; Zagorodny prospekt 8)* and ***Pizzeria*** *(Map 5; Rubinshteyna ulitsa 30)*.

Vegetarian This is not Russia's speciality (you'd think there was a penalty for not eating meat daily), but there are a few options. Aside from ***Cafe Idiot*** (see Cafes later), ***Troitsky Most*** is the obvious choice. It was once Hare Krishna (you can tell it was by the faded Buddha paintings still on the wall, and that it isn't by the blaring techno music), and quality was better then. Of its two locations, the original one at Malaya Posadskaya 2 (Map 3), open 24 hours, is drearier than its newer one, on nearby Kronversky prospekt 9/2 (Map 2). It serves vegie burgers, lots of salads, and dry soya meals, all quite cheap.

For the best vegetable stew in the city, head to the very pleasant ***Green Crest*** cafe *(Map 6; Vladimirsky prospekt 7)* – look for the green, pharmaceutical-looking sign. The stew is $1, and scrumptuous. It also has 10 different kinds of salads (take-aways available), and some salmon and meat dishes. It is open from 9 am to 11.30 pm. A few doors up at the corner of Nevsky, the ***Gushe*** bakery also has a neat cafe set up, serving herbal teas and soya casseroles. Otherwise, ***Minutka*** offers all-vegie sandwiches.

Top-End Offerings For the best value top-end meal in town – taking into account atmosphere, service, food and value for money – we suggest ***Staraya Tamozhnaya*** *(Old Customs House; Map 4; ☎ 327 89 80, Tamozhenny pereulok 1)* on the Strelka. The atmosphere is simply delightful, with vaulted brick ceilings, excellent live jazz, fantastic service and wonderful food. Nothing outrageous, just large portions of very well prepared Russian and European specialties from $18 to $30, and vegetarian offerings for under $18.

The rooftop ***Landskrona*** at the Sheraton Nevskij Palace Hotel (Map 6) has a reputation as the best restaurant in St Petersburg, and there's lots to back this up. The Italian specialities are served in a gorgeous setting, and there's dancing and live music; in summer, an open air terrace offers panoramic views of the city. Main courses start at $15.

At the other two luxury hotels, the restaurants are equally extravagant. The Grand Hotel Europe's flagship, ***Restaurant Europe***, and the Astoria's ***Zimny Sad*** have the most beautiful setting in town, if not the country. Both serve Sunday brunch. Expect stellar prices. But ***Dvorianskoye Gnezdo*** *(Map 4; ☎ 312 32 05, ulitsa Dekabristov 21)* is the most expensive places in town (expect to pay $60 to $80 or more per person), with a menu of European and Russian specialities. If you want to spend a packet – like Bill Clinton and Madeleine Albright did when they supped here – on good food, excellent wine and sensational service, this is the place to do it.

Cafes

These are anything from a step up from fast food to pleasant places for a hot meal with service approaching that of a restaurant. One of the coolest places is ***Cafe Idiot*** *(Map 4; ☎ 315 16 75, naberezhnaya reki Moyki 82)*, even though it's always packed with expats. All the food is vegetarian (most under $5), and the atmosphere is excellent – funky lamps and tables, and there are several rooms including one that's non-smoking. Add live jazz on weekends, bookshelves packed with used books, magazines and board games, a good Sunday brunch and delicious mugs of cappuccino and this place is *the* place to be. Check out its toilet, which is the definition of economical spacing. The cafe is open from noon to 11 pm, and even has a taxi service for those too, er, happy to make it back home alone.

Sunduk *(Map 3; ulitsa Furshtatskaya 42)* has a wonderful and eclectic atmosphere plus sandwiches, soups and full meals for under $4, excellent cappuccinos for $0.50. It's a cosy, grotto-like place with a bathroom that must be seen to be believed. ***Kafe Margherita*** *(Map 6; Liteyny prospekt 64)* is a pleasant and justly popular place for a quick lunch or dessert (it may look plastic, but it is tasty) – all placed under glass so you can point if you can't speak Russian.

Some of the best Georgian food can be had at the unassuming ***Cheburechnaya*** *(Map 6; ulitsa Vosstania 13)*. It's low-key, and its meals are first-rate – fill up on succulent *dolma*, stuffed fig leaves for $1, or any of its other Georgian dishes. It is open from 10 am to midnight daily. ***Kafe Lagindze*** *(Map 5; ulitsa Belinskogo 1)* is another excellent choice, with spicy *selyanka* for $1.50 and a huge take-away *xhachapuri* (cheese-stuffed bread) for $4. Next door is ***Metekhi*** *(Map 5; ulitsa Belinskogo 3)*, offering the same, but with inferior quality and atmosphere.

On the quiet section of Nevsky prospekt is ***Kafe Gondola*** *(Map 5, Nevsky prospekt 150)*, a cute, laid-back place that'll remind you of Brooke Shields (it's the *Blue Lagoon*-style, bamboo interiors that do it). The menu is decent, inexpensive, and it's a great place for a quiet chat.

The ***Kafe St Petersburg*** *(Map 6; kanala Griboedova 5)* used to be incredibly popular among foreigners new to town before they found other places. Very friendly Russian ladies would also be fond of the place and be oh-so-willing to strike up conversation. Nowadays, it's quieter but it still serves good food for very reasonable prices, like baked mushrooms in cream sauce for $0.60. In summer it has a shaded outdoor seating area.

We list ***Kafe Literaturnoe*** (Map 6) because it's in so many other guidebooks you might wander in thinking it's a good place. It may have had its day back in Pushkin's time (his last meal was eaten here) but today the Lit Caf is nothing more than a highly priced tourist trap. The new ***Dostoevsky Art Bar*** *(Map 6; Vladimirsky prospekt 15)* may also seem like a nice place to go (and it is, for a quick drink) – it's located in the writer's old gambling grounds and it's pretty. But once the band strikes up old Beatles songs and you wait forever for your food, the charm wears off.

Petrograd Side There are several snack places along Bolshoy prospekt, including ***Lokanta***, a great Turkish cafe on the corner of Shamsheva (Map 2). The cafe serves donners and kebabs for $1.50, soups and, of course, Turkish coffee, and is open daily from 10 am to midnight. Way down the street, next to Pirosmani Restaurant, is the ***Pirosmani Kafe*** (Map 2), a pavement cafe doing lavash bread, pastries, hamburgers and some Georgian treats.

A neat place to hang out day or night is the ***Art-Kafe Aeroplan*** *(Map 3; Malaya Posadskaya 22)* – follow the little pictures of the old bi-plane – with a saloon feel, decent food and live music at nights. ***Bistro Samson*** *(Map 2; Kamennoostrovsky prospekt 16)* has decent, large hot meals for under $3.

Vasilevsky Side A stop at ***Cheburechnaya*** *(Map 2; 6-ya linia)*, just down from metro Vasileostrovskaya, is a must, if only to try the delicious, thick Georgian soup *Chanaxhi* for $1.25, and have a gander at the colourful locals. The tiny and unassuming ***Sirin Bar & Restaurant*** *(Map 4; 1-ya linia 16)* has surprisingly good and cheap Russian food, including chicken dishes. It's open from noon to 11 pm.

Ice Cream

Russians take ice cream seriously, and even in winter blizzards, you'll see them indulging – outside, that is. St Petersburg produces some of the finest ice cream in Russia (much tastier than what you'll get on Moscow streets), and it's highly recommended to try one of the ice cream bars on sale at push-cart freezers all over the city. Baltisky and Bely Nochi are particularly good ones.

Baskin Robbins *(Map 6; Nevsky prospekt 79)* serves up its usual 31 flavours (locally produced) from 10 am to 10 pm daily. ***Cafe Sladkoezhka***, at ulitsa Marata 11 (Map 6) and on the south-western corner of Chernyshevskogo prospekt and Zakharevskaya ulitsa (Map 3), is a slick ice-cream cafe and pastry shop serving good cappuccino. There's a ***Kafe Morozhenoe*** just west of the Buddhist datsan north of Yelagin Island (Map 2).

Fast Food

Russian Outlets You may never crave a Big Mac again after sampling the Russian concept of 'fast food' – and with the great choice available, you don't need to bloat up on KFC grease just to save pennies.

The undisputed champion is ***Laima***, a few steps up from Nevsky prospekt on kanala Griboedova (Map 6), and also on the Petrograd Side at Bolshoy prospekt 88 (Map 2). The management also runs several of the city's finer restaurants, so the food quality is very high. Its huge menu includes about 20 salads, soups, stuffed peppers, chicken and fish fillets, kebabs, freshly squeezed juices and milkshakes – with no meal costing more than $3. Everything is served in spotlessly clean surroundings (and

They Deliver, Don't They?

Home delivery is a relatively new concept in Russia, but these places can turn a cosy night or day in into a culinary feast (the Places to Eat listings have more details on these establishments). ***Laima*** *(☎ 232 44 28)* will bring you some of its very fine 'fast food' (the word hardly applies to them) 24 hours a day, for about a 20% surcharge. ***Orient*** *(☎ 327 74 44)* will do the same at a 10% surcharge. ***Swagat*** *(☎ 217 21 11)* delivers its succulent Indian dishes for free. ***Fujiyama*** *(☎ 234 49 22)* will come to see you with sushi, but you'll probably want to run out to an ATM before it arrives. ***Pizza Pronto*** *(☎ 315 89 48)* will supply you with one of its finest, with a minimum order of $12, and only before 6 pm (they're scared of pranks – if you convince them you're genuine, they may deliver later).

with real cutlery!). Ask for its English menu. Oh, it is open around the clock, and yes, it delivers.

Just a small step down in quality is ***Orient*** at Bolshaya Morskaya 25 (Map 6) and on the 1-ya linia 36 on Vasilevsky Island (Map 2). Also open 24 hours, it has a large menu that includes creole turkey, fish and meat shashliks, soups and desserts for about $2-3 each. ***Koshki Dom***, a 24-hour chain with locations including ulitsa Vosstania 2 (Map 6) and Liteyny prospekt 23 (Map 3), is just another small step down and also do great, quick meals. For dessert, head to ***Skazka***, Nevsky prospekt No 27 and No 127 (Map 6), serving Russian bliny (pancakes) with a variety of fillings including mushrooms and cabbage for $0.50 and honey for $0.40.

You'd be better off avoiding the ***Fiesta*** and ***Galeo*** bistro chains, or any place named simply 'Bistro'.

For dirt-cheap fill-ups (three-course meals for about $1.50), there are several atmospheric choices. ***Stolovaya No 5*** *(Map 5; Dostoevskogo 6)* serves good meat stew *(zharkoe)* and borsch, and if you get there in the late afternoon you can sit with blood-stained female butchers from the nearby Kuznetchy market enjoying a shot of vodka. ***Kafe Stolovaya*** *(Map 6; ulitsa Sadovaya 40)* serves the same fare, with beer on tap. You don't want to use its bathroom, though. And there's great, ready-made *plov* at the ***food shop*** at Marata 1 (a heaped portion is about $0.50), to eat there or take away.

Foreign Outlets If the preceding paragraphs didn't convince you that there are places worth exploring (you paid so much to get so far from home – why act like you haven't left?), the city is full of the tried and true. There are several ***McDonald's*** restaurants, including Bolshaya Morskaya ulitsa 11; Kamennoostrovsky prospekt 39, Petrograd Side (Map 2); Sennaya ploshchad 4 (Map 4); and the nicest yet, the church-like building at Sredny prospekt 29 opposite the Vasileostrovskaya metro station (Map 2).

Other burger joints in town include the Finnish ***Carrols***, at ulitsa Vosstania 5 (Map 6) and ulitsa Marata 2. The Germans beat all *schnell*-food hamburger joints to town in 1994 when it opened the city's first ***Grillmaster*** *(Map 6; Nevsky prospekt 46)*. It does a pretty awesome roast chicken and *schweinshaxn* – oh-so-lovely roasted pig thigh. There is a second location on the south-east corner of Nevsky prospekt and ulitsa Marata, opposite ***KFC*** and the second branch of ***Pizza Hut***, both at Nevsky prospekt 96 (Map 6).

Americans from the Subway company opened a sandwich shop on Nevsky prospekt in 1994, but their Russian partners screwed them out of their investment and chased them from the country. The Russians reopened the place – with the same menu – as ***Minutka*** *(Map 6; Nevsky prospekt 20)*, which it's still called, despite a court ruling ordering it be turned back over to Subway. Either way, it does great submarine-style sandwiches with the works.

Self-Catering

Food Shops & Supermarkets Russia's most beautiful, if not most famous, food shop is ***Yeliseevsky Food Shop*** (Map 6), on Nevsky prospekt opposite ploshchad Ostrovskogo. A late 19th century rich-people's food court, the place has now been mostly restored to its pre-Soviet Art Nouveau splendour, with huge stained-glass windows and chandeliers. The left-hand entrance leads to the most impressive hall; the prices here are higher than in other shops, but the choice is good and it's worth visiting just to admire the place.

The ***supermarket***, in the basement of Passazh shopping centre (Map 6), is open from 9 am to 9 pm and will probably stock that special whatever you've been craving since you left home.

Out on the Petrograd Side, ***Babylon Super*** *(Map 2; Maly prospekt 54)* has a terrific selection of exotic (for Russia) fresh vegies, like fresh ginger root and avocado, and an awesome bakery. It takes credit cards.

Kalinka Stockmann's *(Map 3; Finlyandsky prospekt 1)*, near Hotel St Petersburg, is a good place to buy decadent Western luxuries to cook up at the nearby Holiday

Hostel. Those at the Petrovskogo College Student Hostel can try the Finnish-owned ***Spar Market*** *(Map 1; prospekt Stachek 1, metro Narvskaya)*.

There are dozens of 24-hour supermarkets dotted all over the city. Two good central ones are ***Dzinn*** (Map 6) at Marata 16, and another right on ploshchad Vosstania, just east of the Moscow Station.

Markets These are fascinating venues to visit, and not only for the choice of exotic and fresh produce (the meats are so fresh, in some cases it is still in the process of being hacked off the carcass). The market teems with life – from the mostly southern vendors trying to tip the scales in their favour (bargaining, even if the price is marked, is encouraged) to the customers being beckoned to try the honey and cream products (the only free things there).

Two of the liveliest and most central (and most expensive) are the ***Kuznechny*** on Kuznechny pereulok (Map 5), a few steps east from Vladimirskaya metro, and the ***Maltsevsky*** *(Map 5; ulitsa Nekrasova 52)*. Some others are the ***Sytny*** *(Map 2; Sytninskaya ploshchad 3/5, metro Gorkovskaya)*, behind Alexandrovsky park and up towards Kafe Tbilisi; the ***Sennoy*** *(Map 4; Moskovsky prospekt 4)*; and the more inexpensive ***Andreevsky*** *(Map 4; Bolshoy prospekt 18)*.

Bakeries ***Wendy's Baltic Bread*** (Map 5), at the corner of 8-ya Sovetskaya ulitsa and Grechesky prospekt, is nothing short of heavenly. It has by far the city's widest selection of fresh-baked breads, cakes, tortes, eclairs, croissants filled with ham and cheese, and delicious pizzas.

Gushe (Map 6) is not far behind. It's a Georgian-owned paradise on the corner of Nevsky and Vladimirsky prospekts with lots of breads, buns, and some of the most addictive pastries in town. The ***Bahlsen Bakery*** *(Map 6; Nevsky prospekt 142)* also does good bread and cakes.

ENTERTAINMENT

Check the Friday *St Petersburg Times* and especially *Pulse* for up-to-date listings.

Tickets

According to a hateful law introduced in October 1997, foreigners officially pay six times the Russian rate for entrance to the city's biggest theatres (this doesn't apply to the dozens of smaller ones), to a maximum of $48.50. This is worsened by the fact that ticket-takers in some theatres actually enforce the law – if you show up for an opera at the Maly Theatre with Russian tickets, the tickets will be confiscated and you'll only be seated after you pay the difference.

There are a couple of ways around this, none foolproof. The easiest is to buy the cheapest ticket you can and simply move down to the good seats at intermission. You can buy a Russian ticket from a tout in front of a venue an hour before performance, but if it's for one of the major theatres (Mariinsky, Maly), you still risk having to pay the difference if caught.

If you're planning a night out at the ballet, opera or theatre, see the glossary of useful theatre terms under Entertainment in the European Russia Facts for the Visitor chapter.

The best booking office at which to buy tickets is the teatralnaya kassa (Map 6; ☎ 314 93 85) at Nevsky prospekt 42, opposite Gostiny Dvor. You can get tickets for everything here, including the Kirov, but these will sell out quickly.

Concierge desks at the better hotels will be only too pleased to sell you Mariinsky tickets from $65 to $85. They do, however, get some of the best seats in the house, so if you've got a limited amount of time, you may be happy to pay their price.

Classical Music, Ballet & Opera

September to early summer is the main performing season – in summer, though there's always plenty to see and do, many companies are away on tour. An exception is the last 10 days of June, when St Petersburg stages the White Nights Dance Festival, with events ranging from folk to ballet.

The St Petersburg Philharmonica's Symphony Orchestra is particularly renowned. It has two concert halls: the ***Bolshoy Zal*** *(Big Hall; Map 6; ☎ 311 73 33)* on ploshchad Iskusstv; and the ***Maly Zal imeni M I Glinki***

(Small Hall, Map 6; ☎ 312 45 85) nearby at Nevsky prospekt 30. The ***Glinka Capella*** *(Map 6; ☎ 314 10 58, naberezhnaya reki Moyki 20)* also has high standards, focusing on choral, chamber and organ concerts. Other venues include ***Smolny Cathedral*** *(Map 3; ☎ 271 91 82)*, which usually features choral works, and the ***Peterburgsky Concert Hall*** *(Map 3; ploshchad Lenina 1)*.

St Petersburg was the birthplace of Russian ballet back in 1738: the present 1780-seat ***Mariinsky Theatre*** *(Map 4; ☎ 114 12 11, www.kirovballet.com)* was built in 1859 as the home of the Imperial Russian Opera and Ballet companies. The gilded Italianate house saw the premieres of Tchaikovsky's *Sleeping Beauty* and *The Nutcracker*. In 1935 the Soviets renamed it the Kirov Opera and Ballet Theatre, and while the theatre has reverted to its pre-revolutionary name, the company is still called the Kirov. The Kirov Ballet nurtured dance idols Nijinsky, Pavlova, Nureyev, Makarova and Baryshnikov. After hard times in the 1980s, the new Mariinsky has undergone an artistic renaissance under dynamic, workaholic artistic director Valery Gergiev, who is also guest conductor at New York's Metropolitan Opera and principal conductor of the Rotterdam Philharmonic Orchestra. New productions are paid for by Western benefactors and these days not everything is sung in Russian.

There are about five ballets and five operas performed each month. Some are stand-outs, but artistic standards vary. If the dancers and singers look overworked and underpayed, it is because they are. Orchestral playing is more muscular than refined; sets and costumes can be incredibly tacky. Despite everything, the unique flavour of the St Petersburg performing tradition is not to be missed. The ballet's home shows are nearly always sold out; ticket sales from the theatre usually start 20 days in advance. The best opera and ballet casts are often touring abroad to raise hard currency, so be sure it's the Kirov company itself, and not the Russian Ballet or a visiting ensemble.

Cheaper and easier-to-get-into ballet and opera performances, and more contemporary fare are staged at the ***Maly (Small) Theatre*** *(Map 6: ploshchad Iskusstv 1)*. Its standards are respectable. The ***Conservatory*** (Map 4), on Teatralnaya ploshchad, also stages some operas.

Theatre

There are dozens of theatrical performances each night, most of them packed: the Russian love of drama and comedy (read: emotion) is in evidence here. Tickets are available from the same ticket offices as those for classical music.

The premier drama theatre is the ***Pushkin*** *(Map 6; ☎ 110 41 03, ploshchad Ostrovskogo 2)*, which stages Russian and foreign plays, usually on a grand scale. The ***Tovstonov Academic Bolshoy Dramatic Theatre*** *(Map 5; ☎ 310 04 01, naberezhnaya reki Fontanki 65)* is another top mainstream theatre.

Even if your Russian isn't great, the plays are so good at the ***Lensoviet Theatre*** *(Map 6; ☎ 113 21 91, Vladimirsky prospekt 12)* and at the ***Maly Dramatic Theatre*** *(Map 6; ☎ 113 20 49, Rubinshteyna ulitsa 18)*, you can't go wrong. At the Lensoviet, Bruchner's *Voychek*, Beckett's *B Ozhidaniy Godo* (Waiting for Godot) and Pinter's *Lyubovnik* (The Lover) are in the repertoire and are unforgettable. There are also frequent performances for children. At the Maly, under the original direction of Lev Dodin, don't miss *Gaudeamus*, *Claustrophobia*, and Dodin's 9½ hour version of Dostoevsky's *Besy* (The Possessed). Another particularly good theatre for off-beat, excellent comedies is the ***Teatr Satiry*** *(Map 4; ☎ 213 00 12, Sredny prospekt 48)* on Vasilevsky Island.

Music-hall variety shows are staged at the ***Music Hall*** *(Map 2; ☎ 232 68 21, Alexandrovsky Park 4)* and at the ***Teatr Estrady*** *(Map 6; ☎ 314 70 60, Bolshaya Konyushennaya ulitsa 27)*. The ***Teatr Mironova*** *(Map 2; ☎ 346 16 79, Bolshoy prospekt 75, Petrograd Side)* has an excellent variety of Russian comedies and musicals.

For puppets, the main venue is the ***Bolshoy Teatr Kukol*** *(Map 5; ☎ 272 88 08, Nekrasova ulitsa 10)*, with weekend shows at 11.30 am and 2 pm; tickets for everyone cost about $1. The ***Teatr Kukol-Marionetok*** *(Map 6; ☎ 311 19 00, Nevsky prospekt 52)* has, as the name suggests, puppet and marionette shows on a varying schedule. The ***Theatre of Youth Creativity*** *(Map 6; ☎ 310 18 18)* on the grounds of the Anichkov Palace stages fairy tales and comedies good for kids of all ages and sizes.

The ***St Petersburg State Circus*** *(Map 5; ☎ 210 46 49, naberezhnaya reki Fontanki 3)* has a permanent location here, half a kilometre south of the Summer Garden. There are shows at 7 pm on Tuesday, Wednesday and Friday and at 3 and 7 pm on Saturday and Sunday. It's closed Monday and Thursday. The season runs from September to June. Tickets bought here cost from $0.40 to $3, although the foreigners price is $10.

Pubs, Bars & Beer Gardens

One of the coolest places is the ***Pivnoy Klub*** *(Beer Club; Map 5; ☎ 279 18 52, Nekrasova 37)*. This is about as good as it gets, and it's usually packed with locals (call to reserve on weekends). It manages to mix a comfy, subdued decor with a lively atmosphere. It is open until 5 am on weekends, and until 3 am weekdays.

If you need to hear your mother tongue to steady yourself while indulging, the ***Corner Bar*** (Map 5), on the south-west corner of ulitsa Bolshaya Konyushennaya and the Moyka River, is a popular expat hang-out as well as a cool local bar. There are tables outside in summer, snacks and satellite television playing sporting events. More English (and German etc) can be heard at the lively bars inside ***Cafe Idiot*** (see Cafes) and at the ***California Grill*** (see Restaurants), which has live rockabilly and sometimes jazz.

Tinkoff *(Map 6; ☎ 314 84 85, ulitsa Kazanskaya (Plekhanova) 7)* will redefine beer drinking for you. Set inside a gigantic, gorgeous brewery, it sells a large array of fresh microbrewed beers, like the succulent White Unfiltered (try it now!) for $2.25 for half a litre. It also has a full dining hall, though the (delicious) food is very pricey (there's an ATM in the entrance hall). Tinkoff opens daily at noon and keeps pouring the beer until 5 am on weekends and 2 am on weekdays.

Two Irish bars in town are always packed. ***Mollie's*** *(Map 5; Rubinshteyna ulitsa 36)* first brought the Black Stuff to the city on the Neva; draught Guinness pints are $4. It's still popular for its classic pub decor and friendly service, and serves pub food. The cool and cavernous ***Shamrock Bar*** *(Map 4; ulitsa Dekabristov 27)*, opposite the Mariinsky Theatre, has a great atmosphere (though a tad like a rowdy college pub) and similar prices to Mollies.

Fish Fabrique *(Map 6, ulitsa Pushkinskaya 10)*, in a 4th floor flat, gets an interesting crowd of artists and Berlin-loving types; pre-faded splendour, some live music and theme nights. Never a dull moment.

The ***Marine Bar*** *(☎ 274 86 89)* at the US Consulate (Map 3), ulitsa Furshtatskaya 15, isn't really open to the public, but it does have movie nights, barbecues, and every second Friday night there are get-togethers that are open to citizens of most countries if you call first. It just asks that you bring your passport and leave your weapons at home. There's dancing, pool and lots of expats and foreign students.

There are several beer gardens in the centre: one opposite the Grand Hotel Europe, between the former Town Duma and Gostiny Dvor, one in front of the Lutheran church and another at Nevsky prospekt 86, in a secluded courtyard with music, beer and snacks. ***The Bierstube*** in the Sheraton Nevskij Palace Hotel (Map 6) is pretty much what you'd expect: waitresses in dirndls, an Austrian setting, snacks and good but expensive beer. Draughts (0.5L) are $6.

If tacky sleaze is what you want, it's what you'll get at the ***Tribunal Bar*** *(Map 4; Senatskaya ploshchad 1)*, opposite the Bronze Horseman. Its ads once featured its nearly nude waitreses covered in whipped cream and chocolate sauce. On any given night, ***Chayka*** *(Map 6; naberezhnaya kanala Griboedova 14)* is filled with foreign businesspeople, German tour groups singing *Schunkellieder* and swarms of prostitutes who'll sidle up to you at the bar (if you're a male) and say something coolly seductive like, 'I want peanuts. Buy me beer.' Worth avoiding if you're picking up the tab.

Nightclubs and Discos

While most young Russians are happy wandering the streets looking for adventure or playing guitar in parks with friends, there are crowded nighclubs for all tastes and expense accounts. The Western influence has taken its toll here, though most pump out a Russian dance pop beat.

City Club *(Map 5; Apraksin Dvor 14)* is an excellent, lively place to go. Upstairs there's a dance floor and pool tables, and downstairs there's the ***Money Honey Saloon***, which has great live rock and country bands (you haven't heard *I Walk the Line* until you've heard the Russians do it!). It is open until 6 am from Wednesday to Sunday, and until 11 pm Monday and Tuesday. The crowd's randiness spills over into rowdiness sometimes, though.

Billing itself as an art bar, ***Manhattan Club*** *(Map 5; naberezhnaya reki Fontanki 90)* has good live blues and is a totally relaxed place to hang out. You can dance how you want, act how you want, but it sometimes gets a little packed with Nouveaux Bohemian wannabes. Though the slapstick comedy at the ***Chaplin Club*** *(Map 3; ulitsa Chaykovskogo 59)* is mainly in Russian, foreigners will still understand a lot of it.

The cavernous ***Metro Club*** *(Map 5; ☎ 166 02 04 for recorded announcement, Ligovsky prospekt 174)* is hugely popular with a techno-loving crowd under 25, and is a great, lively place. Admission is up to $4, cheaper the earlier you go. ISIC cardholders get a discount. There are spontaneous amateur strip shows. The energy also reaches fever pitch at ***Mama*** *(Map 3; 3B Malaya Monetnaya, Petrograd Side)* for the same crowd. Outside the centre, ***Candyman*** *(Map 1; ☎ 521 14 10, Kosygina prospekt 17)* is an astonishingly popular disco considering its location and Mafia scene. There are sometimes top Russian acts performing live. From metro Ladozhskaya take bus No 21 or trolleybus No 22 two stops.

Club Monroe *(Map 6; naberezhnaya kanala Griboedova 8)* was the first erotically themed club to open in the city, with video booths and suggestive Ancient Greek motifs. There is no sleaze here, though, just an amiable atmosphere in which to dance to your favourite Russian pop tune, drink, or chill out in its various rooms – but only until 11 pm as it's in a residential building.

Valhall *(Map 6; Nevsky prospekt 22/24)*, a Viking-theme bar, is a trip. Staff are dressed in bad opera costumes, and there's live blues, rockabilly and disco happening after midnight. It has a good beer-drinking atmosphere.

Gay & Lesbian Venues

Contact Krilija (☎ 312 31 80) for info on the latest on the city's gay scene.

69 Club *(Map 4; ☎ 259 51 63, 2-ya Krasnoarmeyskaya ulitsa 6)* is the city's premier gay nightclub, so popular it's almost been co-opted by trendies and bi-curious, thug types. Admission is up to $5, but women pay double (they can get away with that here).

Jungle *(Map 2; ulitsa Blokhina 8, Petrograd Side)* can still get wild on weekends, and the latest addition to the scene, ***Matrosskaya Tishina*** *(The Sailor's Silence; Map 4; Admiralteyskogo kanala 5)* is set in the grand Sailor's Club (don't get excited, they aren't there anymore) and features flamboyant cabaret-style shows.

For women, there's much less, but try ***Greshniki*** *(Sinners; Map 6, ☎ 219 42 91, Lomonosova 1/28)* on Friday nights.

Jazz

Check the papers for listings, or log onto www.jazz.ru.

The excellent ***JFC Jazz Club*** *(Map 3; ☎272 98 50, Shpalernaya ulitsa 33)* is probably the best in the city. A little New York-style jazz club, it's got a fun crowd, lots of expats, great atmosphere, and really good jazz bands from Russia and around the world. There's also blues on some nights.

The famous ***Jazz Philharmonic Hall*** *(Map 5; Zagorodny prospekt 27)* has two bands – a straight jazz and a Dixieland – plus guests doing mainstream and modern jazz. The more clubby ***Kvadrat Jazz Club*** *(Map 5; Pravdy ulitsa 10)*, also in that area, has traditional and mainstream jazz. From metro Vladimirskaya, go down Bolshaya Moskovskaya till it turns into Pravdy.

Cinema

The first cinema to open in the USSR, in 1929, was at the site of the present-day ***Crystal Palace*** *(Map 6; Nevsky prospekt 72)*, which was the first and so far only Western-style movie house (Dolby stereo and popcorn) in the city – and the only one to attract regular line-ups. It plays well dubbed US action and disaster flicks there. Check out *Pulse* or the *St Petersburg Times* for listings of the other cinemas which are more likely to play Russian films.

Billiards & Bowling

The city's premier pool and bowling hall is in a beautifully converted Dom Kultury. Open 24 hours a day, ***Leon*** *(Map 4; ulitsa Dekabristov 34)* has eight ten-pin lanes (under a chandelier) for between $3.60 and $13.60 an hour, and over 20 billiard tables (three sizes) in a luscious, grand space for a more reasonable $0.80-$2.80 an hour. Of course, there's a full bar with light meals.

SPECTATOR SPORTS

Zenith, St Petersburg's rather pathetic football team, loses consistently to all comers at the Petrovsky Stadium (Map 2), near metro Sportivnaya, but the team has a legion of loyal fans who deafen pedestrians all over town with rally cries on game days as they swarm past in a blue blur (blue and white are the official team colours). Zenith used to be better, though, until all the good players headed west when the Iron Curtain fell.

SHOPPING

Souvenirs

Souvenir stands set up shop around all major tourist attractions, especially at the Hermitage, in front of the Peter & Paul Fortress, and at the Souvenir Fair (Map 5), just north and across the canal from the Church of the Resurrection of Christ. At each of these places, there are *matryoshka* dolls, military gear, Russian-language T-shirts and watches galore. A certain amount of bartering is perfectly acceptable. There's a major souvenir shop at Nevsky prospekt 51 which can be pricey, but at least the selection and quality is good.

Arts & Antiques

There are dozens of art and antique shops throughout the city, but only some of them – generally the more expensive ones – will walk you through the customs clearing procedures.

Gallery Central in St Petersburg is at ulitsa Pushkinskaya 10, where heaps of galleries share a building with Timur Novikov's Museum of the New Academy of Fine Arts (Map 6; ☎ 315 28 32). The galleries have everything from paintings and sculpture to digital works, and usually you'll see lots of deep people stoned out of their brains and philosophising against a backdrop of some of the best art in Russia today.

Palitra (Map 5; ☎ 277 12 16) is a gallery owned and operated by St Petersburg artists, and is well worth a visit. It's at the end of Stary Nevsky, at No 166, and is open from 11 am to 7 pm Tuesday to Saturday.

The Center of Graphic Arts at the Union of Artists (Map 4; ☎ 224 06 22) displays some excellent artworks, though prices here are higher and the artists give a cut to the union. It's at ulitsa Bolshaya Morskaya 38, near Isaakilevskaya ploshchad, and is open from 1 to 7 pm Tuesday to Sunday.

Art Gallery Borey (Map 6; ☎ 273 36 93) at Liteyny prospekt 58 is one of the cooler art galleries in town. Its bookshop towards the back has very reasonably priced local art and some of the best art books in town.

Books

Books are everywhere in St Petersburg. For more information on where to find a bookshop to suit your needs, see the Bookshops section earlier in this chapter.

Music, Video Cassettes & CD-ROMs

Copyright? Huh? Russia is the world's largest market for bootlegged cassettes, CDs and CD-ROMs, which are available every few steps. Usually labelled in Russian or bad English, the tapes are of varying quality, but you shouldn't have any problems with CDs (for $2 a pop, it's not a huge risk). There's a rumour that 75% of all bootlegged CD-ROMs sold in Russia have a virus on them, but the $3 price tag tempts thousands every day to chance it; these are also illegal and Lonely Planet recommends people should not buy them.

Musik Shock (Map 6), ulitsa Vosstania 13, is a high-quality CD shop selling licensed copies of all kinds of music. The biggest and most crowded music shop in the city is Saigon (Map 6), Nevsky prospekt 7/9, selling bootlegged and licensed tapes, imported CDs, T-shirts and videos. Another good one is Melodia (Map 2; ☎ 232 11 39), Bolshoy prospekt 47, Petrograd Side.

Photography

One-hour drop-off places for Fuji, Kodak, Agfa and Konica are found everywhere throughout the city centre, including inside metro stations. Film is no problem to find though you may have to hunt for professional class rolls. Developing, especially at Fuji, is first-rate, and much cheaper than in the West. Main branches for Fuji include naberezhnaya reki Fontanki 23 (Map 6), for Kodak at ulitsa Bolshaya Morskaya 32, and for Agfa on the 3rd floor of Nevsky prospekt 20.

You can find good deals on truly cool Soviet photographic equipment at Bik Photo (Map 3; ☎ 272 09 35), ulitsa Kirochnaya (Saltykova-Shcherdina) 36, and in the basement photo kiosk at Nevsky prospekt 54 (Map 6). For passport photographs ($2.50 for six) try the photo studio at Nevsky prospekt 63 (follow the фото signs through the tunnels). At Nevsky prospekt 54, you can get quick black-&-whites ($1 for six the next day; $2 in two hours) in the basement, and colour ones on the 4th floor. On the Petrograd Side, try the photo shop at Bolshoy prospekt 67 (Map 2).

Soviet Memorabilia

If you want to bring some original Soviet souvenirs home, don't stop at the watches and pins available at tourist fairs. How about some truly beautiful Soviet-era commemorative stamps? They cost no more than $0.18 each and are available from the philately booth (No 11) at the central post office, ulitsa Pochtamtskaya 9 (Map 4). Or some colourful old children's games or wooden alphabet blocks (the box covers are a kitsch lover's delight)? They're under $1 each while they last, at the paper supply store at Bolshoy prospekt 69, Petrograd Side (Map 2). And if army's your thing, you'd do better to head out to the souvenir fairs at Voyentorg (Map 6; ☎ 314 62 54), Nevsky prospekt 67, under the arc and to the left. Original (as well as synthetic) articles of military clothing of all types and varieties (from soldiers' underwear – unused! – to officers' caps and parade uniforms) are sold here. Prices are very reasonable. Finally, at the 'market' around Our Lady of Vladimir Church, you'll always find some old Soviet books, records, and memorabilia.

Specialty

'I came all the way here to buy *honey*?' you ask. Yet step into Pchelovodstvo (Map 5; ☎ 279 55 70), Liteyny prospekt 42, and you won't be able to resist. There you'll find many types of fresh honey from Russia's Rostov region, dozens of products, remedies and creams made from bee pollen, as well as unique teas, which make nice gifts.

Swords, guns, knives and martial arts equipment? Head to Soldat Udachi, (Map 5), ulitsa Nekrasova 37, which sells beautiful Spanish reproductions of antique weapons. There's even a full-sized knight in shining armour for $2400, though you may have problems explaining it at the border.

If you've saved a bunch of money buying cheap CDs, you may want to splurge on a $400 bottle of Chateauneuf du Pape at St Petersburg's finest wine shop, Intendant (Map 6), ulitsa Karavannaya 18/37. It stocks everything from fine table wines for $10 to a $2280 bottle of Chateau Petrus – and the proper glasses to drink them out of.

Markets

Most of the city's markets are for food, but the best one for trinkets, clothes, leather, technical appliances, and a huge music selection is Kazakova market (Map 1), a fair way out from the centre. From metro Avtova, cross the street and hop on a special express bus (a 5-7 minute ride) straight there for $0.12. It's open from 9 am to 4 pm daily except Monday, and on the weekends there are also doll shows and street artists for the kids.

GETTING THERE & AWAY

Air

Pulkovo-1 and Pulkovo-2 are respectively the domestic and international airports that serve St Petersburg.

St Petersburg has direct air links with most major European capitals. Airline offices in St Petersburg include:

Aeroflot
(☎ 123 83 12) Pulkovo-2 airport
Air France
(☎ 325 82 52) ulitsa Bolshaya Morskaya 35
British Airways
(☎ 329 25 65) Malaya Konyushennaya ulitsa 1/3A
Czech Airlines
(☎ 315 52 59) ulitsa Bolshaya Morskaya 36
Delta Airlines
(☎ 311 58 19) ulitsa Bolshaya Morskaya 36
Finnair
(☎ 325 95 00) ulitsa Malaya Morskaya 19
KLM
(☎ 325 89 89) Zagorodny prospekt 5
LOT Polish Airlines
(☎ 273 57 21) Karavannaya ulitsa 1
Lufthansa
(☎ 314 49 79) Voznesensky prospekt 7
Scandinavian Airlines (SAS)
(☎ 325 32 55) Sheraton Nevskij Palace Hotel
Transaero
(☎ 279 64 63) Liteyny prospekt 48

Tickets for both Pulkovo and Transaero can be purchased from travel agencies such as Sindbad Travel (Map 4; ☎ 327 8384), as well as from the Central Airline Ticket Office at the corner of Nevsky prospekt and Malaya Morskaya (Map 6).

Train

The main international rail gateways to St Petersburg are Helsinki, Tallinn, Warsaw and Berlin. Trains leave daily from St Petersburg to these and, by connections, to many European capitals.

Tickets Tickets can be purchased at the Central Train Ticket Office at naberezhnaya kanala Griboedova 24 (Map 6), the Business Centre or the Intourist counters inside Moscow Station (No 40-43, in the main hall; look for the statue of Peter the Great – Intourist is on his right side), Sindbad Travel and, at a huge mark-up, from any luxury hotel. Foreigners are required to pay about six times more than the Russian rate for train tickets; many (non-Russian speaking) foreigners trying to use the cheaper tickets are told they must pay the conductor the difference between the Russian and foreigner tickets or they cannot board the train.

Moscow Most of the 12 or more daily trains to Moscow take seven to 8½ hours to complete the journey. Several are overnight sleepers, which save time and a night's accommodation costs. To Moscow, the best overnight trains are Nos 1 (11.55 pm), 3 (11.59 pm) and 5 (11.33 pm). From Moscow, Nos 2 (11.55 pm), 4 (11.59 pm) and 6 (11.10 pm) are the best. All of these trains cost from $32 to $77 each way. There's also the once-weekly, high-speed ER200, which covers the 650km between the two cities in less than five hours – it leaves from St Petersburg at 12.15 pm on Thursday, and from Moscow at 12.22 pm on Friday. Second/1st class tickets cost $56/74.

Finland There are two daily trains between St Petersburg and Helsinki. The *Repin*, a Russian-run train, departs from St Petersburg's Finland Station (Finlyandsky vokzal; Map 3) at 7.14 am, arriving at 1.18 pm. The return train leaves Helsinki at 3.34 pm and arrives in St Petersburg at 10.45 pm. The *Sibelius*, a Finnish Railways-run train, leaves St Petersburg at 4.35 pm, arriving at 10.47 pm. It leaves Helsinki at 6.30 am and arrives in St Petersburg at 1.15 pm. Tickets are $46/75 sitting/*kupe*. In St Petersburg's Finland Station, buy tickets in the Foreign Ticket Office, separate from the main hall, alongside platform 1.

You can save yourself about $12 by spending a lot of time: from St Pete's Finland Station, take any *elektrichka* to Vyborg Station, where you can meet the Helsinki-bound *Repin* at 10.16 am, or the *Sibelius* at 6.15 pm. The trip to Vyborg takes approximately 2½ hours and costs under $1.

Other Destinations There are trains at least daily to/from Novgorod, Pskov (five hours), Petrozavodsk (10 hours), Murmansk (27 to 36 hours), Vologda (12 hours), Arkangelsk (28 to 35 hours), Kaliningrad (20 hours), Tallinn (eight hours), Riga (13 hours), Vilnius (13 hours), Warsaw (28 hours) and Berlin (39 hours).

Bus

St Petersburg's bus station, Avtovokzal No 2 (Map 5; ☎ 166 57 77) – there is no No 1 – is at naberezhnaya Obvodnogo kanala 36, 1km from Ligovsky Prospekt metro. It serves Tampere, Vyborg, Pskov, Novgorod, Moscow, Novaya Ladoga, Petrozavodsk and many other smaller destinations.

For buses to and from Tallinn and Riga, Eurolines (☎ 168 27 40) at ulitsa Shkapina 10 operates several comfortable daily buses. Its offices are 50m directly west of the Baltic Station.

Stat Express (☎ 164 20 03, fax 316 24 31), located inside the Warsaw Station, has recently started a weekly service to Heidelberg, stopping in seven other German cities, with buses leaving from the Warsaw Station.

Finland There's a daily bus to Tampere from Avtovokzal No 2, leaving at 9.30 am, for $38. Finnord (☎ 314 89 51) runs buses to Helsinki via Vyborg and Lahti from its office at ulitsa Italyanskaya 37. A one-way ticket costs $40. Buses leave at 3.40 pm and 11 pm and arrive in Helsinki at 10.30 pm and 6 am respectively.

Sovavto (☎ 123 51 25) has daily coaches to Helsinki via Lappeenranta, as well as a Vyborg-Lappeenranta service. In St Petersburg, buses leave from Hotel Pulkovskaya, Hotel Moskva, Grand Hotel Europe and St Petersburg Hotel. Its two daily buses for Helsinki cost $41 and leave from the Grand Hotel Europe at 8.40 am and noon, arriving at 3.45 pm and 7 pm respectively.

Car & Motorcycle

See the European Russia Getting Around chapter for some hints on driving. Always remember to go slower than you'd like; not only are there numerous speed traps (towards Vyborg, there's one just outside the city limits, where the speed limit becomes 60km/h), but the state of the roads can easily lead you to the repair shop in no time. The road to the Estonian border can be particularly horrendous in spots.

Car Rental Renting a car here is now a pretty simple thing, though as with most simple things in Russia, it's inordinately expensive; below are some agencies offering self-drive and chauffeured vehicles. Note also that road conditions in the city are atrocious, and the GAI (traffic police) can shoot at your car if you don't pull over when they wave at your car (and, considering the number of them on the streets, they will).

Astoria-Service
: (Map 5; ☎ 112 15 83), ulitsa Borovaya 11/13
Rents out cars with drivers only for the most reasonable rates – from $3 an hour for an old Zhiguli to $8 an hour for a Mercedes (minimum three hours).

Hertz
: (Map 5; ☎ 272 50 45, rent@hertz.spb.ru), Nekrasova ulitsa 40
Has chauffer-driven cars for $186 for 10 hours, and $20 per hour after.

Svit
: (☎ 356 93 29), Pribaltiyskaya Hotel (Map 4)
Rents out Fords with drivers, for about $25 per hour.

Boat

Russian shipping services have been seriously curtailed over the past couple of years. This information can change drastically, so do check ahead. There are currently no passenger ships to and from St Petersburg, but if it starts up again, it will dock at the sea terminal (morskoy vokzal; Map 4) at the west end of Bolshoy prospekt on Vasilevsky Island.

Baltic Lines (☎ 355 16 16 or ☎ 355 61 40) has not had regular passenger cruises since 1996, but someday it may revive its route to Stockholm. Call to check the current status – staff will be happy to chat with you as they don't have much else going on. Its US agent, EuroCruises, can be contacted on ☎ 212-366 4747 or (toll-free) ☎ 800-688 3876.

River Cruises In summer, passenger boats ply the rivers and canals between Moscow and St Petersburg. The route follows the Neva River to Lake Ladoga, sometimes up to Valaam, to the Svir River and Lake Onega up to Kizhi, the Volga-Baltic canal to the Rybinskoe Reservoir and through some of the Golden Ring along the Volga to Moscow.

The river terminal (rechnoy vokzal; Map 1; ☎ 262 02 39) is at prospekt Obukhovskoy oborony 195 near metro Proletarskaya (turn right upon exiting and take any tram one stop). It is open from 9 am to 9 pm daily and has a wide variety of excellent cruises to Moscow, from five to 14 days long, taking in different routes.

Its 14-day *Rodina* cruise includes Kizhi, Valaam, Yaroslavl and many other stops. The entire trip costs only $160-360, including meals.

Its *Sankt Peterburg* takes only five days to get to Moscow (no return trip), stopping at Kizhi, for under $200. You can buy tickets directly from it – the staff are very friendly, and it will save you paying surpluses to travel agencies (who will all be glad to help you).

GETTING AROUND

St Petersburg's excellent public transport system makes getting around simple and inexpensive. The centre is best seen on foot.

To/From the Airport

St Petersburg's airport is at Pulkovo, about 17km south of the centre. This is easily and (very) cheaply accessed by metro and bus. From Moskovskaya metro (not Moskovskie Vorota), bus No 39 runs to Pulkovo-1, the domestic terminal, and bus No 13 runs to Pulkovo-2, the international terminal. The trip takes about 15 minutes. There are also numerous taxi-buses waiting at the bus stop, even faster and more convenient. Check the signs on the windows. A metro and bus combo will get you there for approximately $0.30.

Going by taxi can get expensive. From the city, hailing down a private car is your cheapest bet – they'll do it for about $5. A registered cab will ask $10.

If you're coming from the airport, you'll be introduced to what everyone calls the 'Mafia': a bunch of thugs who control who can park and wait for fares there. If there's a whiff of accent in your speech, they'll ask $40 to get you into town, then bring it down to $30 if you complain and walk away (towards the bus No 13 stop, about 20m on – be sure you get on the one heading to the metro. Ask someone, 'V metro, da?').

You can also fax in advance one of the car rental agencies (see Car Rental earlier), and it will pick you up, for about the same as the Mafia would charge you, except Astoria-Service (Map 5; ☎112 15 83), who could do this for under $20. If you're staying at any of the luxury hotels in town, or if your hotel package includes transfers, you'll be met by bus or minivan.

To/From Train Stations

Train stations are at or near metro stations, and taxis are easily found at each of them.

Metro

Though less majestic than Moscow's, the St Petersburg metro leaves most of the world's other undergrounds for dead. You'll rarely wait more than three minutes for a train (even at 6 am on a Sunday), and the clock at the end of the platform shows time elapsed since the last train departed. The grandest stations are on Line 1. Stations open around 5.30 am and close shortly after midnight.

Taking the metro is the quickest way around the wider city and, in 1999, tokens *(zhetony)* cost $0.12! Buy your tokens from the booths in the stations, place them in the entry gates, and walk through. Seven, 15 and 30-day multi-ride pass-cards with a magnetic strip are sold at all metro stations in multiples of 10, 20, 25, 40, 50, or 70 rides. All metro stations have card-reading turnstiles – place your card in the slot and when it comes back out you'll have a green light to proceed if there's sufficient credit left on the card.

Note that due to a cave-in of a section of a tunnel, there is an interuption in Line 1 service north of the city. Lesnaya and Ploshchad Muzhestva are now connected by a free shuttle-bus service (bus No 80). This situation will remain well into the next century, but should hopefully affect only those tourists interested in visiting the Piskaryovska cemetery.

Bus, Trolleybus & Tram

You buy your $0.08 ticket from a controller inside the vehicle. Bus stops are marked by 'A' signs (for avtobus), trolleybus stops by 'Ш' (representing a handwritten Russian 'T') or signs by the roadside, tram stops by a 'T' sign over the roadway, all usually indicating the line numbers too. Stops may also have roadside signs with little pictures of a bus, trolleybus or tram. Most transport runs from 5.45 am to 12.30 am.

The following are some important long routes across the city:

Along Nevsky prospekt between the Admiralty and Moscow Station: bus Nos 7 and 22; trolleybus Nos 1, 5, 7, 10 and 22. Trolleybus Nos 1 and 22 continue out to Hotel Moskva and Alexander Nevsky Monastery. Trolleybus Nos 5 and 7 continue to Smolny.

Around the Sadovaya ulitsa ring road south of Nevsky prospekt: tram Nos 3, 13 and 14. Tram No 3 continues north of Nevsky prospekt and then crosses the Troitsky Bridge into Petrograd Side.

Along Kamennoostrovsky prospekt (Petrograd Side): bus Nos 46 and 65. These cross the Neva on the Troitsky Bridge.

Bridges

Most transport shuts down between 1 and 6 am and, when the river isn't frozen, the following Neva bridges *(mosty)* are raised at night to let seagoing ships through. Exceptions to the schedule are only made during all-night festivals such as White Nights.

Alexandra Nevskogo (Map 5), 2.35 to 4.50 am
Petra Veliky (Map 5), 2.45 to 4.45 am
Liteyny (Map 3), 2.10 to 4.35 am
Troitsky (Map 3), 2 to 4.40 am
Dvortsovy (Map 4), 1.55 to 3.05 and 3.15 to 4.45 am
Leytenanta Shmidta (Map 4), 1.55 to 4.50 am
Birzhevoy (Map 2), 2.25 to 3.20 and 3.40 to 4.40 am
Tuchkov (Map 2), 2.20 to 3.10 and 3.40 to 4.40 am

Taxi

Official taxis (four-door Volga sedans with a chequerboard strip down the side and a green light in the front window) have a meter that they sometimes use, though you most often pay a negotiated price.

Unofficial taxis are anything you can stop. They're used more often than official taxis and are a legitimate form of transport in Russia. Stand at the side of the road, extend your arm and wait until something stops – it could be an ambulance, off-duty city or tour bus, army Jeep or passenger car. When something stops, you negotiate destination and price by speaking to the driver through the passenger-side window or a partially open door. If the driver asks you to *sadites* (sit down), just get in, and when you reach the destination you pay what you feel the ride was worth. But if the driver states a price, you can negotiate – your offer has been rejected if he drives off in a huff.

Telephone booking a taxi is usually a reliable way to get one. Don't call far in advance of needing the taxi; it just makes the dispatcher cranky. Several taxi services are available. Try ☎ 265 13 33 or ☎ 312 00 22.

Around St Petersburg
Окрестности Санкт Петербурга

While Moscow's Golden Ring of ancient cities is famous world-over for its exciting side-trips away from the capital, St Petersburg is no poorer in its options for day-trippers. Between 25 and 45km from central St Petersburg lie five splendid old tsarist palaces surrounded by lovely parks. Kronstadt, a once-closed naval base 29km from the city, has one of the loveliest cathedrals in northern Russia. Farther out towards the north-west is the old Finnish town of Vyborg, and eastward, near the banks of Lake Ladoga, are the Nizhnezvirsky Nature Reserve, and what very well could have been Russia's first capital, the beautiful village of Staraya Ladoga.

Though all of these are easily accessible by inexpensive public transport, if you do want a tour of the palaces, those that leave from in front of the Kazan Cathedral in St Petersburg are a good option; look for the person with the megaphone. Tours can also be booked at the excursion booths at the east and west ends of Gostiny Dvor. Both of these places charge about $3 for a tour including transport. The tours are in Russian (English-language ones can be booked in advance for an extra fee), but they are the simplest way to get there and back if you don't want to deal with public transport. The St Petersburg Travel Company offers coach tours to all of the palaces from upwards of $20 per person.

HIGHLIGHTS

- Admiring the Grand Cascade's symphony of fountains at Petrodvorets
- Getting lost in Pavlovsk's parks
- Visiting one of Russia's most ancient villages, Staraya Ladoga
- Honouring Russian naval muscle at the Naval Cathedral, Kronstadt
- Taking in the impressively restored Catherine Palace, Pushkin
- Walking through Vyborg's old and winding streets

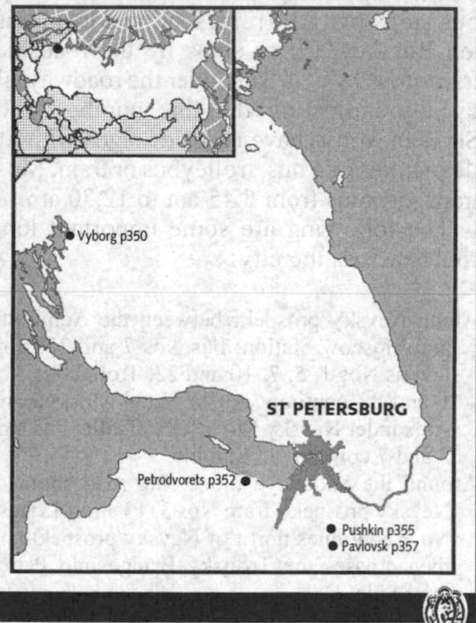

VYBORG
ВЫБОРГ

☎ 278 • pop 81,000

Vyborg *(VIH-bork)* is not seen so much as a place to go to as a place to come from – it's a Gulf of Finland port, a rail junction and the main border town on the Helsinki-St Petersburg road. It's a shame that Vyborg is not viewed as a destination in itself, as it's a lovely 13th century city filled with old buildings, winding cobblestone streets and a romantic, if dishevelled, harbour.

Vyborg, one of the oldest cities in Europe, has as a central feature the imposing medieval Vyborg Castle, built by the Swedes in 1293 when they first captured Karelia from Novgorod. Since then borders have jumped back and forth around Vyborg.

Peter the Great added the town to Russia in 1710. A century later it fell within autonomous Finland, and after the revolution

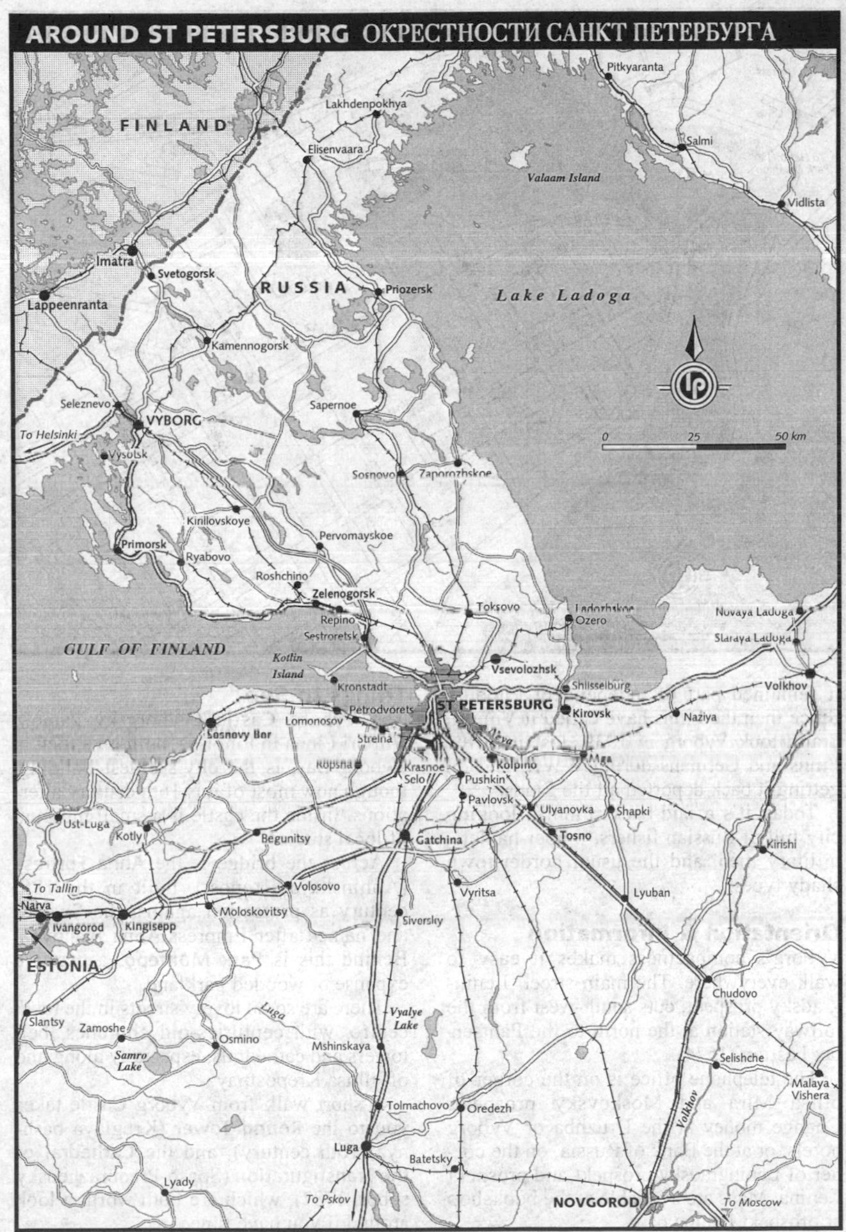
AROUND ST PETERSBURG ОКРЕСТНОСТИ САНКТ ПЕТЕРБУРГА
FINLAND
RUSSIA
ESTONIA
Lake Ladoga
GULF OF FINLAND
Valaam Island
Kotlin Island
Pitkyaranta
Lakhdenpokhya
Elisenvaara
Salmi
Vidlista
Imatra
Svetogorsk
Lappeenranta
Priozersk
Kamennogorsk
Seleznevo
VYBORG
To Helsinki
Sapernoe
Vysotsk
Sosnovo
Zaporozhskoe
Kirillovskoye
Primorsk
Ryabovo
Pervomayskoe
Roshchino
Zelenogorsk
Repino
Sestroretsk
Toksovo
Ladozhskoe Ozero
Novaya Ladoga
Staraya Ladoga
Vsevolozhsk
Kronstadt
Shlisselburg
Volkhov
ST PETERSBURG
Kirovsk
Naziya
Petrodvorets
Lomonosov
Sosnovy Bor
Strelna
Neva
Kolpino
Ropsha
Krasnoe Selo
Pushkin
Pavlovsk
Ulyanovka
Shapki
Ust-Luga
Kotly
Begunitsy
Gatchina
Tosno
Kirishi
To Tallin
Volosovo
Vyritsa
Lyuban
Narva
Ivangorod
Kingisepp
Moloskovitsy
Siversky
Luga
Vyalye Lake
Chudovo
Slantsy
Zamoshe
Osmino
Mshinskaya
Samro Lake
Selishche
Malaya Vishera
Tolmachovo
Oredezh
Volkhov
Batetsky
Lyady
To Pskov
NOVGOROD
To Moscow
0 25 50 km

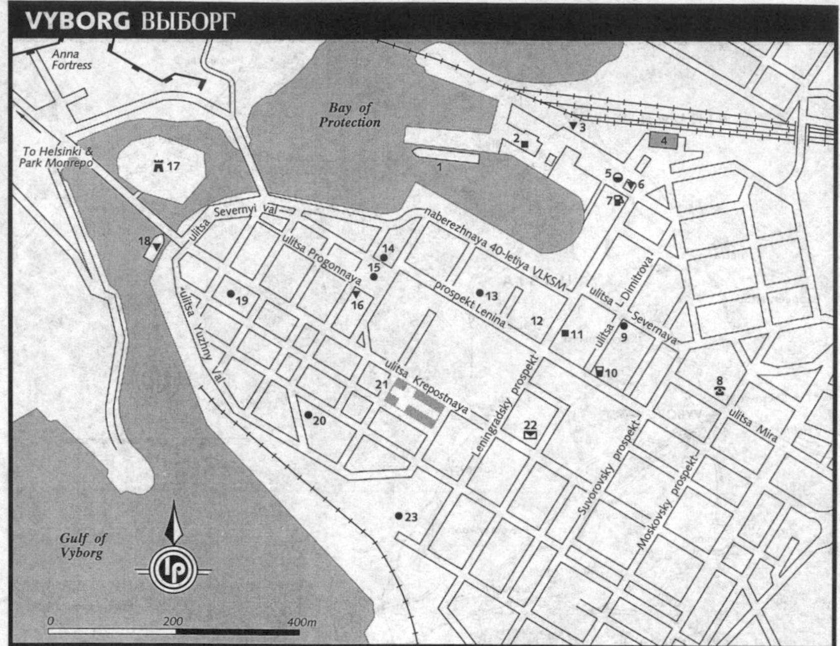

it remained part of independent Finland. Since then the Finns have called it Viipuri. Stalin took Vyborg in 1939, lost it to the Finns and Germans during WWII, and on getting it back deported all the Finns.

Today it's a laid-back, Finnish-looking city full of Russian fishers, timber-haulers, military men, and the usual border-town shady types.

Orientation & Information

Vyborg's compactness makes it easy to walk everywhere. The main street, Leningradsky prospekt, cuts south-west from the railway station at the north to the Pantserlax bastion (1574).

The telephone office is on the corner of ulitsa Mira and Moskovsky prospekt. Change money at the Druzhba or Vyborg hotels, or at the Bank of Russia, on the corner of Leningradsky prospekt and prospekt Lenina. Maps are available at the bookshop at prospekt Lenina 6.

Things to See

The **Vyborg Castle** (Vyborgsky zamok; Viipuri Linna in Finnish), built on a rock in Vyborg Bay, is the city's oldest building, though now most of it is 16th century alterations. Inside the castle is a small museum of local studies.

Across the bridge is the **Anna Fortress** (Anninskaya Krepost), built in the 18th century as protection against the Swedes and named after Empress Anna Ivanovna. Behind this is **Park Monrepo**, a massive expanse of wooded parkland.

There are some lovely streets in the town centre, with centuries-old churches, bell towers and cathedrals, especially along and off ulitsa Krepostnaya.

A short walk from Vyborg Castle takes you to the **Round Tower** (Kruglaya bashnya, 16th century), and the **Cathedral of the Transfiguration** (Spaso-Preobrazhensky sobor, 1787), which are both worth a look around if you have time.

VYBORG ВЫБОРГ

PLACES TO STAY		OTHER			
1	Korolenko Boat Hotel Гостиница Короленко	4	Train Station Железнодорожный Вокзал	14	Market Рынок
2	Hotel Druzhba Гостиница Дружба	5	Bus Station Автовокзал	15	Round Tower & Restaurant Круглая Башня и Ресторан
11	Vyborg Hotel Гостиница Выборг	7	Neste Petrol Station Несте бензоколонка	17	Vyborg Castle Выборгский замок
PLACES TO EAT		8	Telephone Office Телефон - Телеграф	19	Clock Tower Башня часов
3	Restaurant Pogrebok Ресторан Погребок	9	TTA Tours	20	City Hall Tower Башня ратуши
6	Berry Bar	10	Champion Bar Бар Чэмпион	21	Cathedral of the Transfiguration Спасо-Преображенский Собор
16	Bar-Restaurant Nordwest Бар-Ресторан Нордвест	12	Bank of Russia	22	Post Office Почта
18	Boat Café Кафе	13	Book Shop Книги	23	Pantserlax Bastion Пантсерлакс бастион

Organised Tours

TTA Tours (☎ 2 63 65, tta@vbg.ru), in a new building on the corner of ulitsa Severnaya and ulitsa Dimitrova, offers a full range of city tours and longer excursions. It even has a three-day military tour for army fetishists who don't mind paying $600 to live like a soldier in real army barracks. Continent Club (☎ 2 47 60), in the lobby of Hotel Druzhba, can also help you out.

Places to Stay

***Hotel Druzhba** (☎ 2 57 44, ulitsa Zheleznodorozhnaya 5)* has comfortable singles/doubles at $32/40, two bars, an outdoor beer garden and a decent restaurant. Just a stagger away, the ***Korolenko Boat Hotel** (☎ 3 44 78)* has clean but teensy-weensy cabins aboard a ship. It's a friendly place, and costs only $12 per person, but the 24-hour bar can get noisy. It also rents out rowing boats. The ***Vyborg Hotel** (☎ 2 23 83, Leningradsky prospekt 19)* has doubles for $18 per person.

Places to Eat

The ***market*** just north of the Round Tower has fresh produce for the self-caterer. The ***Round Tower Restaurant***, on the top floor of the tower itself, is the nicest place in town, with excellent meals for under $3. Just across the street is the ***Bar-Restaurant Nordwest***, slick and a bit tacky but with a great menu (try their salmon cream soup for $1.25) – plus they're open 24 hours. Otherwise, cellar ***Restaurant Pogrebok** (ulitsa Zheleznodorozhnaya 2)* has very good meat and chicken dishes for less than $2. Skip the ***Berry Bar*** behind the bus station. The (high) prices are all in Finmarks, and that should tell you everything. In summer, there's the ***Boat Cafe*** near the castle serving the expected.

Entertainment

The coolest bar in town is ***Champion***, on the corner of ulitsa Dimitrova and prospekt Lenina. It's open from noon to 3 am daily.

Getting There & Away

Train Vyborg is about three hours by suburban train from St Petersburg's Finland Station. Trains go nearly every hour all day; on the big board at the Finland Station they're called Vyborgskoe. If you're trying to save money on the way to Helsinki from St Petersburg catch the *elektrichka* to Vyborg and then the Helsinki train. Trains to Helsinki leave Vyborg at 9.14 am and 6.38 pm; tickets can be purchased from window No 5.

Bus All buses between St Petersburg and Helsinki stop at Vyborg. There are also eight buses a day to/from Vyborg. From St Petersburg, they leave Avtovokzal No 2 and stop in front of the western entrance/exit of the Ploshchad Lenina metro, on ulitsa Botkinskaya. These make the trip about 20 minutes faster than the train, and cost $0.80.

PETRODVORETS ПЕТРОДВОРЕЦ

Peter the Great had a cabin 29km west of St Petersburg on the Gulf of Finland, to oversee construction of his Kronstadt naval base. He liked it so much there that he built a villa, Monplaisir, and then a whole series of palaces across an estate originally called Petergof, which has been called Petrodvorets (*pet-ra-dvar-YETS*, Peter's Palace) since 1944. All are set within a spectacular ensemble of gravity-powered fountains that are now the site's main attraction. This 'Russian Versailles' is probably the most impressive of St Petersburg's suburban palaces, certainly the most popular.

While Petrodvorets was trashed by the Germans in WWII (what you see is largely a reconstruction from photos, drawings and anecdotes), it suffered heaviest damage under Soviet bombing raids in December 1941 and January 1942 (according to more recent historians). Hitler, abandoning his hopes for a New Year's victory celebration inside St Petersburg's Hotel Astoria, planned to throw a party here, and drew up pompous invitations. Stalin ordered the place heavily attacked to thwart this.

The estate is open from 9 am to 9 pm daily, while the museums are open from 10 am to 5 pm daily from the end of May to the end of September. The Lower Park and Alexandria Park are open every day. There will almost always be something closed while you are there because, inexplicably, each site has its own closing days: Grand Palace, Monday and last Tuesday of the month; Marly, Tuesday and last Wednesday; Monplaisir, Hermitage and Catherine Building, Wednesday and last Thursday; Cottage, Friday and last Thursday.

Because of the confounded opening hours, it's only possible to see everything in a single day at weekends, when the place is swarming with visitors. All the attractions charge separate admissions. Admission to

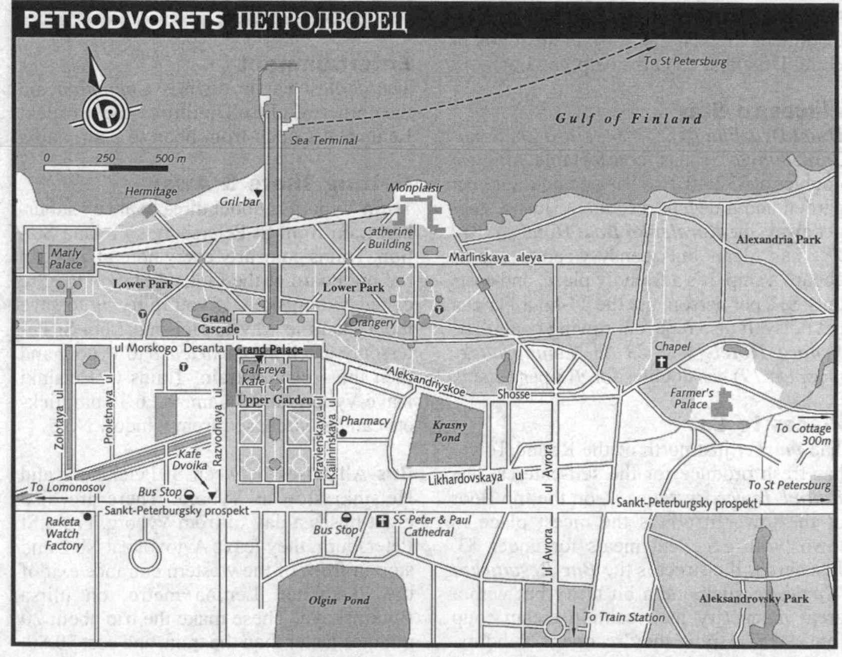

LEE FOSTER

Rostral Column, St Petersburg

MARTIN MOOS

Catherine Palace, Pushkin

JONATHAN SMITH

SS Peter & Paul Cathedral, Petrodvorets

JONATHAN SMITH

Musicians in period costume outside the Grand Palace, Petrodvorets

JONATHAN SMITH

Triumphal Arch, St Petersburg

RICHARD NEBESKY

The iconostasis of Nicholas Church, Voronezh

JONATHAN SMITH

Gothic Dom, Kaliningrad

RICHARD NEBESKY

Rostov-on-Don

JONATHAN SMITH

Apartments, Kaliningrad

COLIN HOOD

A typical timber house of Northern European Russia

the grounds is payable at the cash booths on the jetty and outside the gates leading to the Grand Cascade. If you don't care about seeing the museums, you can wait until the cash booths close at around 4 pm, then enter the grounds for free.

Things to See

Grand Cascade The uncontested centrepiece is the Grand Cascade & Water Avenue, a symphony of fountains (over 140) and canals partly engineered by Peter himself. The central statue of Samson tearing open a lion's jaws celebrates – as so many things in St Petersburg do – Peter's victory over the Swedes.

There are trick fountains – triggered by hidden switches (hidden, that is, by hordes of kids jumping on them) – designed to squirt unsuspecting passers-by. Normally the fountains play from 11 am to 7 pm daily from the last weekend in May to September.

Grand Palace Between the cascade and the formal Upper Garden is the Grand Palace (Bolshoy dvorets). Peter's modest project, finished just before his death, was grossly enlarged by Rastrelli for Empress Elizabeth and later redecorated for Catherine the Great. It's now a vast museum of lavish rooms and galleries – a monument above all to the craft of reconstruction (which is still going on). Anything not nailed down was removed before the Germans arrived, so the paintings, furniture and chandeliers are original.

Highlights include the Chesma Hall, full of huge paintings of Russia's destruction of the Turkish fleet at Çesme in 1770. Of some 20 rooms, the last, without a trace of Catherine, is the finest – Peter's simple, beautiful study, apparently the only room to survive the Germans. It has 14 fantastic carved-wood panels, of which six reconstructions (in lighter wood) are no less impressive; each took 1½ years to do. Peter the Great still looks like the tsar with the best taste.

You'll need to join a tour group to enter ($8/4 for adults/students). It's hard to get the Russian price of $1.20. Tickets are sold inside, near the lobby where you pick up your *tapochki* (slippers to wear over your shoes to avoid damaging the wooden floors).

Monplaisir Peter's outwardly more humble villa, with study and galleries facing the sea, remained his favourite and it's not hard to see why: wood-panelled, snug and elegant, peaceful even when there's a crowd – which there used to be all the time, what with Peter's mandatory partying ('misbehaving' guests were required to gulp down huge quantities of wine). The main hall has marble floors and a richly painted ceiling. At the time of researching, the villa was closed indefinitely for repairs.

Lower Park & Other Pavilions Along the Gulf shore is the Lower Park, with more fountains – big and small, elegant and silly (watch out for the trick fountains) – and more pavilions.

Near the shoreline, and finished soon after the Grand Palace, is a two-storey pink-and-white box called the **Hermitage** (literally 'retreat'), which features the ultimate in private dining on the second floor. Special elevators hoist a fully laid table into the imperial presence, thereby eliminating any hindrance by servants. The elevators are circular and directly in front of each diner, whose plate would be lowered, replenished and replaced.

Farther west is **Marly**, another of Peter's mini-palaces and guesthouses. To the east of the Grand Palace, an old orangery houses the **Historical Museum of Wax Figures**, containing 49 figures of big-wigged Russians from the 18th and 19th centuries.

Alexandria Park Even on summer weekends, the rambling, overgrown Alexandria Park is peaceful and empty. It was built for Tsar Nicholas I (and named for his tsarina) and it looks as though his heart wasn't in his royal work. Besides a mock-Gothic **chapel**, the park's diversions include the **Farmer's Palace** (1831), which vaguely resembles a stone farmstead and is currently in ruins, and the **Cottage** (1829), which is modelled on an English country cottage and is now a museum.

Petergof Palace Pharmacy This peculiar tourist attraction is an old-style apothecary shop with drawers full of medicinal plants – it looks (and smells) like the real thing. You can sip herbal teas here and, if your Russian's good enough you can ask the staff about your ingrown whatsit. It's just east of the Upper Garden and is open from 8 am to 8 pm (closed Saturday).

Petrodvorets Town Don't overlook the five-domed SS Peter & Paul Cathedral, across the road and east of the palace grounds, built in traditional style but dating only from the late 19th-early 20th century. One bus stop west of the main Grand Palace entrance, on the south side of Sankt Petersburgsky prospekt, is the Raketa watch factory, with a little boutique open weekdays until 6 pm, selling *very* cool watches.

Six kilometres east of Petrodvorets is Strelna, another estate with parklands and two palaces built for Peter (later enlarged for Empress Elizabeth by Rastrelli).

Places to Eat

There are a few cafes scattered around the Lower Park. Behind the Grand Palace is the newish ***Galereya Kafe***, doing decent snacks and light lunches for under $4.

Kafe Dvoika, on Sankt Peterburgsky prospekt at the west end of the palace grounds, is open from 11 am to midnight daily and serves decent, cheap meals. It also has a very clean toilet.

Getting There & Away

If you're not going to Petrodvorets on a tour, the easiest way to get there from St Petersburg is to take comfy double-decker Bus No 849 or 851 from outside the Baltic Station ($0.30, 40 minutes), which leave regularly throughout the day and let you off at the main entrance to the Upper Gardens, on Sankt Peterburgsky prospekt. You can also take a suburban train from the Baltic Station to Novy Petrodvorets (not Stary Petrodvorets), departing every 30 to 60 minutes until early evening, but then you'll have to take any bus but No 357 to the fifth stop, another 10 minutes.

From May to September, a fine alternative is the *Meteor* hydrofoil from the jetty in front of St Petersburg's Hermitage, which goes every 20 to 30 minutes from 9.30 am to at least 7 pm. The trip takes half an hour and costs a whopping $15 each way.

LOMONOSOV ЛОМОНОСОВ

While Peter was building Monplaisir, his right-hand man, Alexander Menshikov, began his own palace, **Oranienbaum**, 12km farther down the coast. Menshikov never saw the finished product. Following Peter's death and Menshikov's exile, the estate served briefly as a hospital and then passed to Tsar Peter III, who didn't much like ruling Russia and spent a lot of time there. After doing away with him, his wife Catherine (the Great) made it her private pleasure ground.

Oranienbaum was not occupied by the Nazis. After WWII it was renamed for the scientist-poet Mikhail Lomonosov and now doubles as a museum and public park, with boat rentals and carnival rides alongside the remaining buildings. The park itself is open all year from 9 am to 10 pm.

Biggest of all, with semicircular galleries and lower garden, is Menshikov's **Grand Palace**, *still* under renovation, though several rooms are open to the public (from 11 am to 5 pm daily except Tuesday. Admission is $1.20. Beyond the pond is **Peterstadt**, Peter III's boxy toy palace, with rich, uncomfortable-looking interiors and some Chinese-style lacquer-on-wood paintings. It's approached through the Gate of Honour, all that remains of a toy fortress where he amused himself drilling his soldiers.

Most worth seeing is Catherine's over-the-top **Chinese Palace**. It's baroque outside and extravagantly rococo inside, with a private retreat designed by Antonio Rinaldi that includes painted ceilings, fine inlaid-wood floors and walls, and decoration probably unequalled in any of the other St Petersburg palaces. The most blindingly sumptuous is the **Large Chinese Room**, designed in the 'Oriental' style of the day. It's open from 11 am to 6 pm daily except Tuesday.

Perhaps Lomonosov's best feature is the several kilometres of quiet paths through pine woods and sombre gardens, with relatively small crowds – a rarity on the Russian tourist trail.

Getting There & Away

The suburban train from St Petersburg's Baltic Station to Petrodvorets continues to Lomonosov. Get off at Oranienbaum-I (not II) Station, an hour from St Petersburg. From the station, walk past a church and then cross prospekt Yunogo Lenintsa to the park entrance. There are also taxi-buses to both Petrodvorets and Lomonosov from outside metro Avtovo.

PUSHKIN & PAVLOVSK ПУШКИН И ПАВЛОВСК

The sumptuous palaces and big, beautiful parks at Pushkin and Pavlovsk, neighbours 25km and 29km south of St Petersburg, can be combined in a day's visit – but since they're both good places to relax, you might want to take them more slowly.

Pushkin's palaces and parks were created under Empresses Elizabeth and Catherine the Great between 1744 and 1796. The

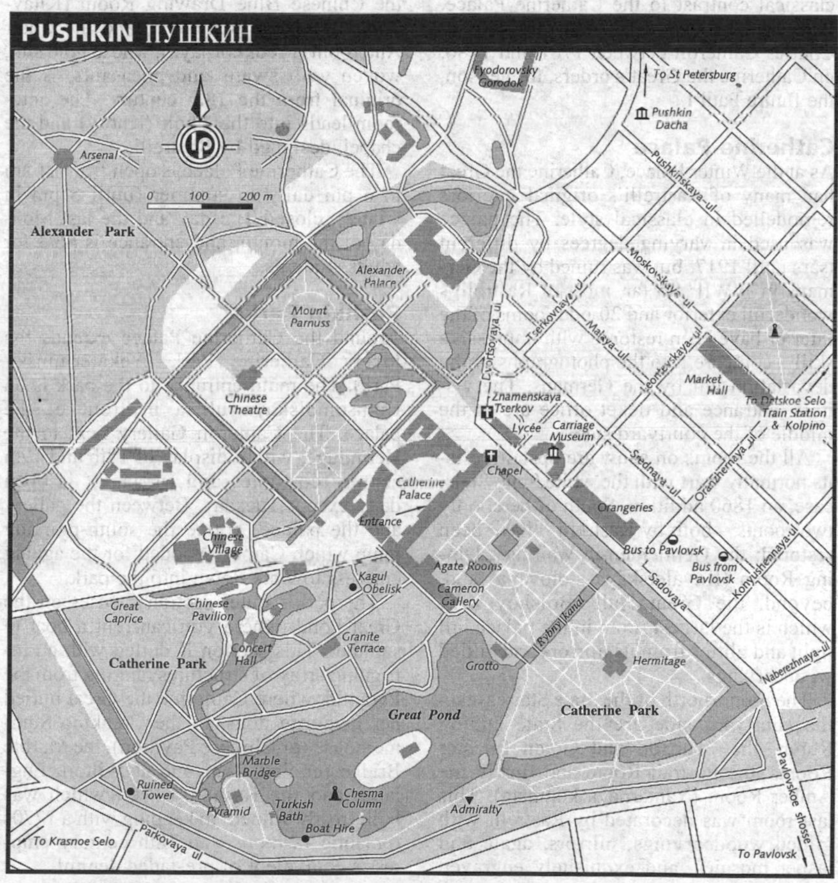

centrepiece is the vast 1752-56 baroque Catherine Palace (Yekaterininsky dvorets), designed by Rastrelli and named after Elizabeth's mother, Peter the Great's second wife. Pushkin used to be called Tsarskoe selo (Tsar's Village) but was renamed in 1937 after Russia's favourite poet, who studied here. The country's first railway opened in 1837 to carry the royal family between here and St Petersburg.

Pavlovsk's park of woodland, rivers, lakes, little valleys, avenues, classical statues and temples is one of the most exquisite in Russia, while its Great Palace is a classical contrast to the Catherine Palace. Palace and park were originally designed by Charles Cameron between 1781 and 1786, on Catherine the Great's orders, for her son, the future Paul I.

Catherine Palace

As at the Winter Palace, Catherine the Great had many of Rastrelli's original interiors remodelled in classical style. The palace was used in varying degrees by different tsars until 1917, but was ruined by the Germans in WWII. So far, most of Rastrelli's wonderful exterior and 20-odd rooms of the interior have been restored with impressive skill – compare it to the photographs of the devastation left by the Germans. The visitors' entrance and ticket office are in the middle of the courtyard side.

All the rooms on show are upstairs. Visits normally start with the white State Staircase, an 1860 addition. South of here, only two rooms – both by Rastrelli – have been restored: the Gentlemen-in-Waiting's Dining Room (Kavalerskaya stolovaya) and, beyond, the Great Hall (Bolshoy zal), which is the largest room in the palace, all light and glitter from its mirrors and gilded woodcarvings.

The rooms north of the State Staircase on the courtyard side are the State Dining Room, the Crimson and Green Pilaster Rooms, the Portrait Room and finally the Amber Room (Yantarnaya komnata). This last room was decorated by Rastrelli with gilded woodcarvings, mirrors, agate and jasper mosaics, and exquisitely engraved amber panels given to Peter the Great by the King of Prussia in 1716. But its treasures were plundered by the Nazis and went missing in Kaliningrad (then Königsberg) in 1945 (they're still looking for them!). Next along is the large, sumptuous Picture Hall (Kartinny zal).

Most of the north end is Cameron's early classical work. The elegant proportions of the Green Dining Room (Zelyonaya stolovaya) on the courtyard side are typical. Also on the courtyard side are three rooms with fabulous, patterned silk wall-coverings: the Blue Drawing Room (Golubaya gostinaya), the Chinese Blue Drawing Room (Kitayskaya golubaya gostinaya), and the Choir Anteroom (Predkhornaya), whose gold silk, woven with swans and pheasants, is the original from the 18th century. The anteroom leads into the Choir (Khory) and the chapel, designed by Rastrelli.

The Catherine Palace is open from 11 am to 6 pm daily in summer (until 5 pm in winter), closed Tuesday and the last Monday of the month, and entrance is $6/3 for adults/students.

Pushkin Parks

Around the Catherine Palace extends the lovely Catherine Park (Yekaterininsky Park). The main entrance to the park is on Komsomolskaya ulitsa in front of the palace. The Cameron Gallery next to the Hermitage, with a display of 18th and 19th century costumes and carriages, is open daily except Tuesday. Between the gallery and the palace, notice the south-pointing ramp which Cameron added for the ageing empress to walk down into the park.

The park's outer section focuses on the Great Pond, where you can rent a boat in summer. This section is dotted with an intriguing array of structures ranging from the Pyramid, where Catherine the Great buried her favourite dogs, to the Creaking Summerhouse (or Chinese Pavilion), the Marble Bridge (copied from one at Wilton, England) and the Ruined Tower, which was built 'ready-ruined' in keeping with a 1770s romantic fashion – an 18th century empress's equivalent of pre-faded denim!

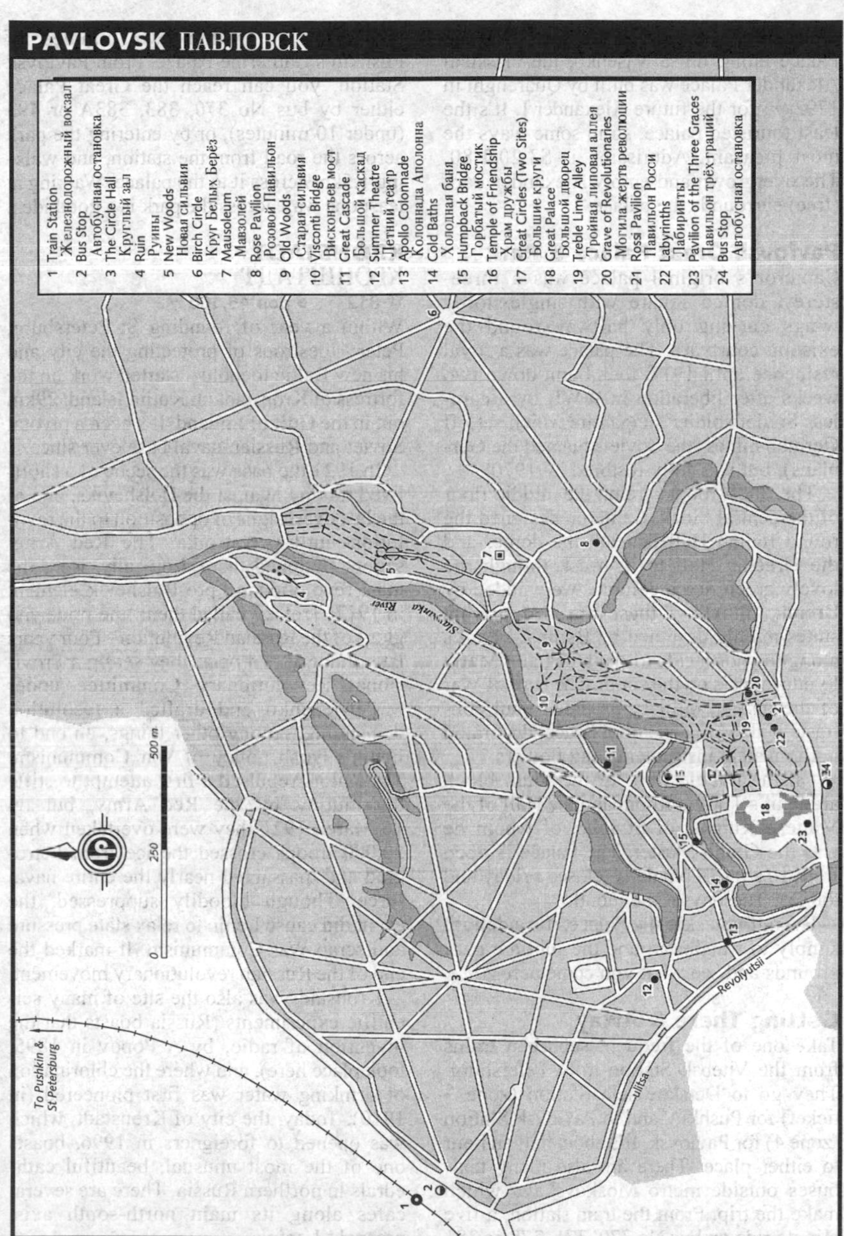
PAVLOVSK ПАВЛОВСК
1 Train Station
Железнодорожный вокзал
2 Bus Stop
Автобусная остановка
3 The Circle Hall
Круглый зал
4 Ruin
Руины
5 New Woods
Новая сильвия
6 Birch Circle
Круг Белых Берёз
7 Mausoleum
Мавзолей
8 Rose Pavilion
Розовой Павильон
9 Old Woods
Старая сильвия
10 Visconti Bridge
Висконтьев мост
11 Great Cascade
Большой каскад
12 Summer Theatre
Летний театр
13 Apollo Colonnade
Колоннада Аполлона
14 Cold Baths
Холодная баня
15 Humpback Bridge
Горбатый мостик
16 Temple of Friendship
Храм дружбы
17 Great Circles (Two Sites)
Большие круги
18 Great Palace
Большой дворец
19 Treble Lime Alley
Тройная липовая аллея
20 Grave of Revolutionaries
Могила жертв революции
21 Rossi Pavilion
Павильон Росси
22 Labyrinths
Лабиринты
23 Pavilion of the Three Graces
Павильон трёх граций
24 Bus Stop
Автобусная остановка
Slavyanka River
Ulitsa Revolyutsii
To Pushkin & St Petersburg
0 250 500 m

A short distance north of the Catherine Palace along ulitsa Vasenko, the classical Alexander Palace was built by Quarenghi in 1792-96 for the future Alexander I. It's the least touristed palace, so in some ways the most pleasant. Admission is $3.20/1.80. The overgrown and empty Alexander Park (free) surrounds the palace.

Pavlovsk Great Palace & Park

Cameron's original palace was a three-storey, domed square with single-storey wings curving only halfway round the existing courtyard. The palace was a royal residence until 1917, then burnt down two weeks after liberation in WWII by a careless Soviet soldier's cigarette which set off German mines (the Soviets blamed the Germans), but was fully restored by 1970.

The finest rooms are on the middle floor of the central block. Cameron designed the round Italian Hall beneath the dome, and the Grecian Hall to its west, though the lovely green fluted columns were added by Brenna. Flanking these are two private suites mainly designed by Brenna – Paul's along the north side of the block and Maria Fyodorovna's on the south. The Hall of War of the insane, military-obsessed Paul contrasts with Maria's Hall of Peace, decorated with musical instruments and flowers.

On the middle floor of the south block are Paul's Throne Room and the Hall of the Maltese Knights of St John, of whom he was the Grand Master. The Palace is open from 10 am to 5 pm daily, closed Friday and the last Tuesday of the month.

Even if you skip the Palace, it's a delight simply to wander around the sublime park grounds and see what you come across.

Getting There & Away

Take one of the frequent suburban trains from the Vitebsk Station in St Petersburg. They go to Detskoe selo Station (zone 3 ticket) for Pushkin, and to Pavlovsk Station (zone 4) for Pavlovsk. It's about half an hour to either place. There are also many taxi-buses outside metro Moskovskaya which make the trip. From the train station, a five minute ride on bus No 370, 371, 378 or 381 takes you to within two minutes of Pushkin's Catherine Palace. From Pavlovsk Station, you can reach the Great Palace either by bus No 370, 383, 383A or 493 (under 10 minutes), or by entering the park across the road from the station, and walking 1.5km across it to the palace. Walking at least one way across the park is a good idea.

KRONSTADT КРОНШТАДТ

☎ 812 • pop 45,100

Within a year of founding St Petersburg, Peter – desirous of protecting the city and his new Baltic toehold – started work on the fortress of Kronstadt on Kotlin Island, 29km out in the Gulf of Finland. It's been a pivotal Soviet and Russian naval base ever since.

In 1921 the base was the scene of a short-lived mutiny against the Bolsheviks, one of the last overt signs of opposition to the revolution until perestroika. The Red Army sailors stationed there, ironically, were the most revolutionary, pro-Bolshevik element in 1917; Trotsky called them 'the pride and glory of the Russian Revolution'. Four years later, hungry and poor, they set up a Provisional Revolutionary Committee under S Petrichenko and drafted a resolution demanding, among other things, an end to Lenin's harsh policy of War Communism. The sailors repulsed a first attempt to stifle the mutiny by the Red Army, but on 16 March 1921 they were overtaken when 50,000 troops crossed the ice from Petrograd and massacred nearly the entire naval force. Though bloodily suppressed, the event did cause Lenin to relax state pressure and scrap War Communism. It marked the end of the Russian revolutionary movement.

Kronstadt was also the site of many scientific experiments (Russia boasts that the invention of radio, by A Popov in 1895, took place here), and where the chlorination of drinking water was first pioneered (in 1910). Today, the city of Kronstadt, which was opened to foreigners in 1996, boasts one of the most unusual, beautiful cathedrals in northern Russia. There are several cafes along its main north-south axis, prospekt Lenina.

Things to See

The city is pleasant to stroll around, and a walk along the southern end of the island, past the port where you can easily glimpse Russian warships, is a highlight. Yet the major sight here is the **Naval Cathedral** (Morskoy Sobor, 1903-13), designed by Kosyakov and heavily influenced by the Istanbul cathedrals he visited. Built to honour Russian naval muscle, this Byzantine-styled wonder stands on Anchor Square, near an eternal flame for all of Kronstadt's sailors. It has an intricately detailed facade (anchors and all) and a haunting air of mystery. Sadly, the interior is off-limits (since 1932, it has been used as a sailor's club and cinema), but a section of it is now the **Central Naval Museum**, open from 11 am to 5 pm daily except Monday and Tuesday. Admission is $1.20.

Getting There & Away

There are numerous, daily tours leaving from in front of the Kazan Cathedral and Gostiny Dvor in St Petersburg. If you wish to go by public transport, go to metro Chyornaya Rechka in St Petersburg; exit the station to your left, cross the street and veer right towards the bus stop where bus No E510 and any number of taxi-buses or private cars will be waiting to make the half-hour trip.

In Kronstadt, the bus stop is on the corner of ulitsa Grazhdanskaya and prospekt Lenina, and from there it's about a 400m walk south-west to the Naval Cathedral. City maps are available from the bookshop at prospekt Lenina 19.

STARAYA LADOGA
СТАРАЯ ЛАДОГА

☎ 263 • pop 3000

This lovely, sleepy village, on the winding banks of the Volkhov River, is unknown to most tourists, though it's mentioned in every Russian schoolchild's history books. A three hour trip by train and bus and 125km outside St Petersburg, Staraya (Old) Ladoga acquaints visitors with one of the first – some say the first – points of settlement and trade in ancient Rus. According to some ancient texts, when the Scandinavian Viking Rurik, along with his relatives Truvor and Sineus, swept into ancient Russia in 862, he built a wooden fortress at present-day Staraya Ladoga and made this his base.

The town was known only as Ladoga until 1704 when Peter the Great founded Novaya (New) Ladoga to the north, as a transfer point for the materials arriving to build St Petersburg. Indisputably, Ladoga was more than a simple village; it was an active participant in the very birth of the Russian nation.

Archaeological expeditions continue to uncover a wealth of information about the town's past, and every summer, visitors can watch as 9th century relics are unearthed in and around the town's fortress. In 1997, a second 9th century fortress was discovered 2km outside the village, and it's known that at one time, six monasteries worked in this small region. Evidence of Byzantine cultural influences in the frescoes of the village's 12th century churches point to the town as a cultural as well as historical and commercial crossroad.

Just as the origins of Rus are continually debated, so will Staraya Ladoga's status of 'Russia's first capital'. Nevertheless, its age (historians have given 753 as the village's birthdate) and significance remains uncontested. Now protected as a national reserve, the town's basic structure and street patterns have remained virtually unchanged since the 12th century. The area boasts 132 items of archaeological and historical interest.

There are no hotels in the village – though there are several in nearby Volkhov and Novaya Ladoga – but you can contact the staff at the Historical-Architectural and Archaeological to organise accommodation in a small ***guesthouse*** *(☎ 4 93 31/70, fax 1 35 24)*. There are also no restaurants except for a ***stolovaya*** (cafeteria) on the main Volkhov road, halfway between the kremlin and the museum, so bring some food along.

Things to See

The **St George's Church** (Giorgevskaya tserkov), which was built in the second half of the 12th century, is perched atop a hill by the banks of the Volkhov River, inside the fortress grounds.

There are two permanent exhibitions here, one in the wooden **Church of Dimitri Solun** and the other inside the fortress tower. They're both open from 9 am to 6 pm daily (to 4 pm from September to May) and are closed Monday. Admission to both is $1. The church itself is open year-round, but only during dry weather, to protect the delicate 12th century frescoes still visible on the walls.

The cosy **Historical-Architectural & Archaeological Museum**, located at the far end of the park on the northern edge of town, houses a retrospective of the area's history. Centuries-old tools and stones lie alongside fragments from 12th century frescoes, clothing and detailed, recreated interiors of 19th century houses. Check out the unique works of local artist Tatiana Kozmina. Admission is $0.50, and it's open from 10 am to 5 pm daily except Monday. Staff can also organise tours of the village ($1.50 in Russian, $5 in English or French).

The **John the Baptist Church** (Ioanna-Predtechi tserkov, 1695), located atop the highest hill in the area, behind the museum, is the only church in town with a regular weekend service. On this site was a 13th century monastery. Nearby, beside the river banks, is an ancient burial mound.

Getting There & Away

An elektrichka to Volkhov (the Volkhovstroy I station) leaves the Moscow Station in St Petersburg 11 times a day and costs $1 each way. From Volkhov, take bus or minibus No 23 headed towards Novaya Ladoga from the main bus stop outside the station, just across the square. It's a 20 minute trip to Staraya Ladoga and costs $0.30. The second of the three town bus stops lets you off just past the fortress.

NIZHNEZVIRSKY NATURE RESERVE НИЖНЕЗВИРСКИЙ ГОСУДАРСТВЕННЫ ЗАПОВЕДНИК

On the south-eastern shore of Lake Ladoga, the 414 sq km Nizhnezvirsky Nature Reserve (☎ 81264-205 21, orlan@orlan.spb.su) is an important stopover for migratory birds and home to a variety of animals, among them the Lake Ladoga ringed seal *(Phoca hispida ladogensis)*, a freshwater subspecies peculiar to the area. Arrangements to visit the reserve can be made directly, or through the American Association for the Support of Ecological Initiatives. In St Petersburg call Alexander Kaprenko of the AASEI's local branch ADONIS (☎ 307 09 18, alexk@aasei.spb.su), or contact director Bill Wasch at their US headquarters (☎ 860-346 2967, fax 347 8459, wwasch@wesleyan.edu).

Western European Russia
Западно-Европейская Россия

Western European Russia, between Moscow and St Petersburg and the borders of Ukraine, Belarus, Latvia and Estonia, is an area of rolling hills, endless steppe and long-contested borders. This area saw the heaviest fighting in the country during WWII; towns in the south of the region like Kursk, Oryol, Bryansk and Smolensk have all been destroyed by war on several occasions.

By a quirk of geopolitical fate, this region also includes Kaliningrad, the strategically important wedge of Russia between Lithuania, Poland and the Baltic Sea. Not included in this chapter are European Russia's two largest cities – Moscow and St Petersburg – or the surrounding areas. These are covered in the Moscow, Around Moscow, St Petersburg and Around St Petersburg chapters.

HIGHLIGHTS

- Gazing at the centuries-old frescoes of the legendary Theophanes the Greek in Novgorod's 14th century Church of Our Saviour-at-Ilino
- Chugging mead in the Detinets restaurant within the 1000-year-old walls of Novgorod's kremlin
- Descending into the spooky burial caves of the Pechory Monastery, followed by a drive through the surrounding Pskov region
- Paying homage to 19th century Russian literature at Oryol, Mikhailovskoe, Staraya Russa and Spasskoe Lutovinovo
- Hearing the evening service at the fresco-covered St Alexey of Akatov women's monastery in Voronezh
- Admiring the zany Great Count's church in Yelets

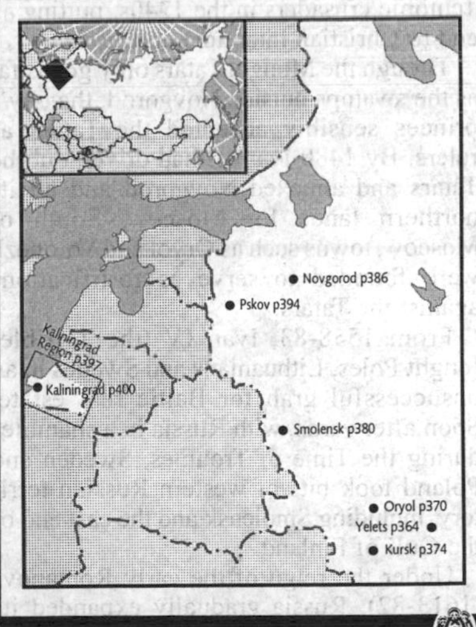

HISTORY

The region was settled by the Slavs, migrating from the west, in about the 6th to 8th centuries AD. At the same time Varangians (Vikings) from Scandinavia began trading and raiding across the region en route to the Black Sea. In 862, supposedly at the invitation of local Slavic tribes, Varangians under Prince Rurik came to rule and establish order in the land of 'Rus'. Their first permanent settlement, Novgorod, is seen by many as Russia's birthplace. Rurik's successor Oleg founded the Kyivan (Kievan) Rus state, and the upstart principalities of Vladimir and Muscovy are descended from the same line.

By the 12th century, Novgorod was a European political and commercial centre that began expanding aggressively, increasingly attracting the attention of the Swedes, who had held sway in most of present-day north-west Russia. The friction, at first economic, became ostensibly religious as Swedish crusaders tried to push back the Orthodox 'heathens'. Novgorod's Prince Alexander Nevsky is considered a Russian

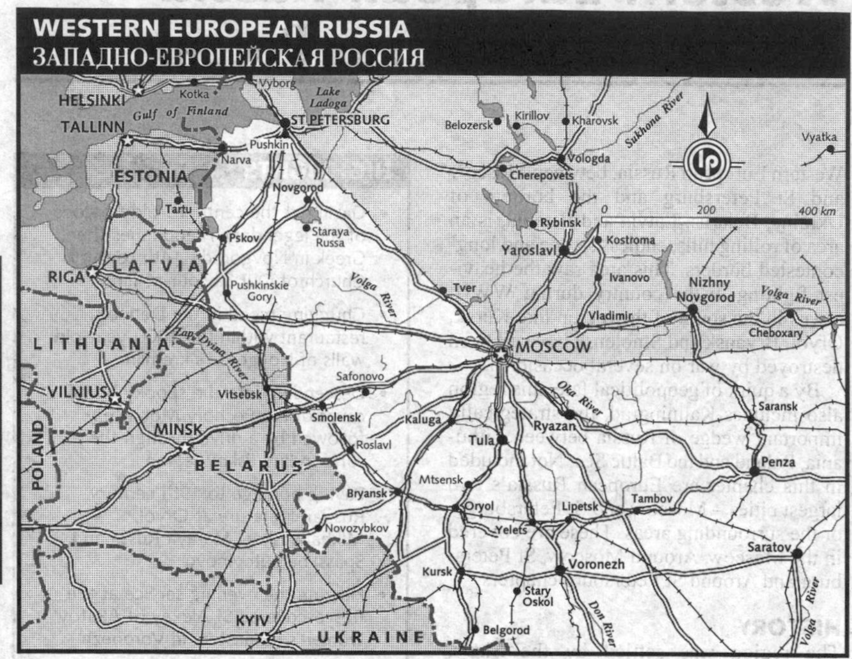

hero for thrashing both the Swedish and Teutonic crusaders in the 1240s, putting an end to Christian intentions in Russia.

Though the Mongol Tatars only got as far as the swamps outside Novgorod, the city's princes sensibly accepted the Tatars as rulers. By 1480 Ivan III had driven out the Tatars and annexed Novgorod and all its northern lands for Moscow. South of Moscow, towns such as Oryol and Voronezh were founded to serve as fortifications against the Tatars.

From 1558-83, Ivan IV (the Terrible) fought Poles, Lithuanians and Swedes in an unsuccessful grab for Baltic real estate. Soon afterwards, with Russia in a shambles during the Time of Troubles, Sweden and Poland took bits of western Russian territory, including Smolensk and the east end of the Gulf of Finland.

Under the reign of the early Romanovs (1613-82), Russia gradually expanded its territories west and south of Moscow, but experienced revolts from Cossack communities, including those from Voronezh, near the Don River.

Determined to defeat the Swedes and reach the Baltic, Peter the Great made an alliance with Poland and Denmark, and forced his way to the Gulf of Finland, pausing only to lay the foundations of St Petersburg. With his new navy, he won the Great Northern War (1700-21), gaining everything back from Sweden, plus the Baltic coastline down to Riga in Latvia. Russia's western territories expanded further – to include Lithuania, Belarus and much of Poland – with the Partitions of Poland between 1772 and 1795.

In 1920 Soviet Russia recognised the independence of Estonia, Latvia and Lithuania. During the early stages of WWII secret deals that had been struck with Nazi Germany allowed the USSR's western European border to expand again. Hitler subsequently invaded the western USSR, including the Baltic States, but lost it all (plus Kaliningrad, a previously German city) to the Red Army towards the end of the war. The tumultuous events of 1990-91 saw the new independence of the Baltic States, Belarus and Ukraine and made Russia's western boundaries into borders between countries, rather than just between republics of the Soviet Union. Since then, Belarus and Ukraine have made half-steps towards possibly rejoining Russia. However, the Baltic borders have solidified with only a minimum of economic and cultural exchange occurring between Russia and its western neighbours.

South of Moscow

Three main routes head south from the Moscow region. The eastern route, along the M4 highway, leads to Yelets and Voronezh. The central route, taken by the M2 highway and the railway heading for Kharkiv (Kharkov) in Ukraine, leads through Oryol, Kursk and Belgorod. The south-western route, heading ultimately for Kyiv (Kiev), leads to Bryansk, just off the M3 highway. All these routes take you over rolling, always-changing steppe.

YELETS
ЕЛЕЦ

☎ 07467 • pop 120,000

Yelets was founded along the Sosna River in 1146 as a fortification against the Polovtsy. It was sacked by Tatars three times and rebuilt in the 16th century, though what remains of the town today is like a perfect movie set of mid-19th century Russian life. The city is laid out in a logical grid, and the streets are lined with colonnaded buildings, wooden and brick 19th century houses and only the occasional postwar Soviet monstrosity.

The town's showpiece, visible from kilometres around, is the beautiful Ascension Cathedral, which was designed by Konstantin Ton (1794-1881), the architect who brought us St Petersburg's Moscow and Moscow's Leningrad train stations (there's a great view of it from the bridge crossing the Sosna, just east of the town). And tucked into the town's tidy streets are about half a dozen working churches and cathedrals, plus the ruins of several more.

Although it is a charming and relaxing town in the midst of some beautiful countryside, it's at best a day trip, or perhaps an overnighter, from Oryol or Voronezh. Yelets is 78km west of Lipetsk, 180km south of Tula, 170km east of Oryol and 140km north-west of Voronezh.

Orientation & Information

From the train station, walk to the east end of the platform and take bus No 1 into the city centre – a seven minute ride. The bus runs about every 10 to 15 minutes and stops just past the Hotel Yelets on ulitsa Orlovskaya (formerly ulitsa Kommunarov), the city's main street. There are no tourist offices or maps to be found. Also, bring enough roubles with you as changing money officially might be difficult.

For some reason, Yelets suffers from a disproportionately high number of Adidas-tracksuited, crew-cut men milling about the streets and kiosks. They look like Moscow thugs but are just locals with a misguided sense of style. We didn't encounter any problems in these parts, even when walking around after nightfall, but nevertheless, caution is advised.

Things to See

The town is very compact and easy to get around. The town's **City Park** (Gorodskoy park) is quite relaxing, with a Ferris wheel. There's a small **Children's Park** across the street, with basic playground equipment that is used by lots of smiling kids.

Churches are scattered throughout the town: the working **Ascension Cathedral** (Voznesensky sobor), which sits at the eastern end of ulitsa Orlovskaya, is open for services from 8 to 11 am and 5 to 7 pm. The locked and somewhat crumbling **Vvedenskaya Church** (Vvedenskaya tserkov), on Vvedensky spusk (formerly ulitsa Shevchenko), is near a cluster of photogenic late 17th and early 18th century

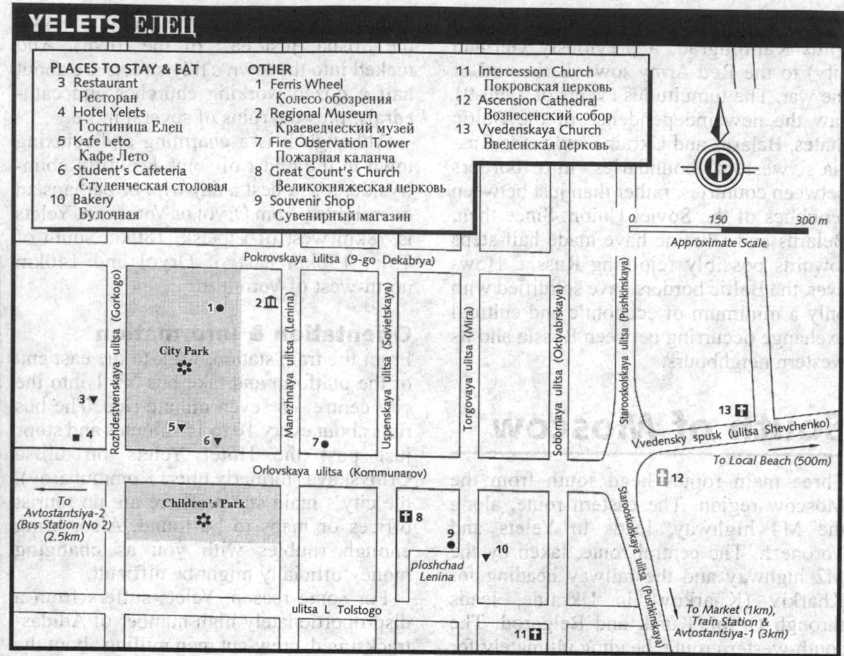

wooden houses. At the bottom of the hill, a path under the trees bearing right leads to a floating footbridge over the river to the **local beach**.

Restored on the outside but still in ruins inside, the **Intercession Church** (Pokrovskaya tserkov) is on the corner of ulitsa Sobornaya (formerly Oktyabrskaya) and ulitsa L Tolstogo. Two blocks away, the recently refurbished **Great Count's Church** (Velikoknyazheskaya tserkov) has to be one of the most unique of Russia's churches. Built during the early 1900s, it has a distinctly modernist, even Art Nouveau flair. The cross on the top is made of crystal, supposedly donated from the local glassware factory. As with most Russian Orthodox churches, you will probably be reprimanded if you start taking pictures without first asking permission from the chief priest. Also, shorts, miniskirts, bare shoulders, bare heads (for women) and covered heads (for men) are not welcome.

For a great view of the town's gilded cupolas, ask the firefighters at the antique red-brick fire house on ulitsa Orlovskaya to let you climb up their **fire observation tower**.

The town's **Regional Museum** (Kraevedchesky muzey), on ulitsa Manezhnaya (formerly Lenina) just off ulitsa Pokrovskaya (formerly ulitsa 9-go Dekabrya), houses artefacts from Yelets' colourful past. It's open from 9.30 am to 4.30 pm daily except Sunday, Monday and one cleaning day *(sanitarnyy den)* a month.

The town's main **shopping street**, ulitsa Torgovaya (formerly ulitsa Mira), is perhaps the most picturesque street in town (the kind of street where horse-drawn coal carts look perfectly appropriate). At the southern end sits the town's main square, **ploshchad Lenina**, which looks like a movie set for an Ostrovsky drama, only all the actors have gone home. On the square, opposite the direction in which Lenin is pointing, is a souvenir shop.

Places to Stay & Eat

If you speak a bit of Russian, you should be able to rent a room for the night with board (for about $5 to $10) from the postcard-perfect babushkas seemingly permanently affixed to the benches in front of their tilting, ramshackle wooden houses. Residents can be seen gathering water from the pumps on the street, so don't expect luxury.

The town's only hotel, ***Hotel Yelets*** *(☎ 2 22 35)*, is on the corner of ulitsa Orlovskaya and ulitsa Rozhdestvenskaya (formerly ulitsa Gorkogo), in the ugliest building in town. The doors to the rooms barely fill the frames, leaving space for the hotel's small cockroach population. The hot water is turned off in June and toilet paper seems to be rationed. But the rooms have nice views of the cupolas, and the staff are grateful for tourists – so grateful they charge foreigners double what they charge Russians; singles/doubles for foreigners cost $8/15.

Open from 5 pm to midnight and possibly for lunch, the hotel's ***restaurant***, located in the same building (go outside and around the left corner), is a red velvet, disco-light extravaganza. The live music starts at 8 pm. The food is very good; the house specialities *(firmennye blyuda)* include *myasnye palchiki* (finger-sized cutlets baked in a sour cream and green onion sauce) for $1.25 and *bliny* (pancakes) coated in honey ($0.35).

There's an unexciting ***market*** about 1km east of the Sosna, with fresh fruit and produce. The ***bakery*** on ulitsa Torgovaya has a few chairless tables for munching croissants and jam-filled *bulochki*. ***Kafe Leto*** in the park just off of ulitsa Orlovskaya has the standard pelmeni, shashlyk, salads and soup. Think twice before ordering the *okroshka*, a cold soup made of chopped cucumber, green onion, egg, sour cream, and *kvas* (a bubbly drink made out of mildly fermented bread). Farther along ulitsa Orlovskaya is the sinfully cheap ***Student's Cafeteria*** (Studencheskaya Stolovaya), open until 6 pm with a lunch break from 2 to 3 pm.

Getting There & Away

Yelets is on the M4 highway between Moscow and Voronezh. There are several buses a day to/from Voronezh; the fare is $1.25. Buses to/from Tula and Oryol take about six hours and leave from bus stop No 2 (Avtostantsiya-2) along the highway, about a $1 taxi ride from the Hotel Yelets, or you can take bus No 1 which stops next to the hotel. Buses to local destinations as well as some buses to Voronezh leave from the bus stop No 1 (Avtostantsiya-1) next to the train station.

On the Moscow-Donetsk railway, Yelets has daily service to Moscow (eight to 10 hours), Tula (five hours) and Oryol (four hours by train and six hours by *elektrichka*, a slower suburban train). Other trains which pass through here include the daily (during June and July) St Petersburg-Adler (near Sochi) and Moscow-Tbilisi trains, as well as the Voronezh-Riga train which departs every other day.

When at the station, peek into the picture gallery with its banner-waving collection of Soviet Realist oil paintings.

VORONEZH
ВОРОНЕЖ

☎ 0732 • pop 1 million

Voronezh is an average-sized Russian industrial city set in pleasant surroundings on the banks of the Voronezh River, about 18km from the Don River. The city and region are fondly remembered by most Russians as it has an extremely interesting folkloric history.

The black soil of the Voronezh region is as rich as the world-famous, high-yield Ukrainian soil. The potato is the major crop of the region and among the finest in all of Russia (apparently the reason is due to both the rich black soil and an ideal growing climate).

History

Voronezh was first mentioned in 12th century chronicles, but was officially founded in 1585 as a fortress against the invading Tatars. Cossack villages *(stanitsa)* were established in this frontier region, and uprisings against Russian domination were common. Some of the more legendary uprisings were led by Stenka Razin in 1670-71 and Kondraty Bulavin in 1707-08.

During the reign of Peter the Great, the first Russian warship – the *Predestinatia* – was built here in 1696; more than 200 warships from the Voronezh dockyards followed to form the new Russian fleet.

During WWII the city suffered frontline fighting for 200 days, when over 90% of the city's buildings were destroyed (especially during the most intense skirmishes in July and August 1942).

Orientation & Information

The main street is prospekt Revolyutsii; its northern tip is connected to the train station by ulitsa Bunina, while the southern tip, past ploshchad Lenina, becomes ulitsa Kirova. The other main street is ulitsa Plekhanovskaya, intersecting at ploshchad Lenina. The eastern bank of Voronezh across the reservoir was founded in 1928.

As for tourist offices, you're on your own here. There are several places to change US dollars and Deutschmarks. Voronezhsky Bank, ulitsa Plekhanovskaya 12, is one of the more convenient and is open from 9 am to 5 pm Monday to Saturday. The post office is at prospekt Revolyutsii 23, while the telephone office is at prospekt Revolyutsii 33. If it's still in business, you should be able to browse the Internet for about $3 an hour from the well equipped ground-level computer centre at the public library, ploshchad Lenina 2.

Useable but not entirely accurate maps of the city may be available from kiosks at the train station and from Dom Knigi at prospekt Revolyutsii 37, while GUM on the opposite side of the street is good for picking up some nifty souvenirs.

Museums

The **IN Kramskoy Regional Fine Arts Museum** (Khudozhestvenny muzey IN Kramskogo), prospekt Revolyutsii 18, is reached through a passage into the courtyard. The collection of Russian painting and sculpture, as well as Greek and Roman sculpture and an Egyptian sarcophagus is closed for renovations; however, the wing housing exhibitions of modern local artists is open from 10 am to 6 pm Tuesday to Sunday, and the entry fee is $0.10. As with most Russian museums, the ticket office *(kassa)* closes at least half an hour before the museum itself.

Well stocked if not well lit, the **Regional Museum** (Kraevedchesky muzey) at Plekhanovskaya 29 has permanent exhibits on Peter the Great and the history of the region from the pre-Bronze Age to the Soviet era. It is open from 10 am to 6 pm Wednesday to Sunday, excluding the first Wednesday of each month; admission is $0.10. You might find some interesting postcards of old Voronezh for sale at the kassa.

There is a large, two storey **Army Museum of the Great Patriotic War 1941-1945** (Muzey Velikoy Otechestvennoy voyny 1941-1945) at ulitsa Stepana Razina 43. It has the usual photos and weapons of destruction often found in WWII museums. One of the most interesting exhibits is a handwritten bulletin *(obyavlenie)* ordering residents to evacuate and leave everything behind except their cows and goats. Outside the museum, about 50m towards the reservoir, are a few tanks and a rocket-launching truck. The museum is open from 11 am to 6 pm daily except Monday.

There are several literary museums in Voronezh, including the **IS Nikitin House-Museum** (Dom-muzey IS Nikitina) at ulitsa Nikitinskaya 19. Nikitin was a second-rate poet born in Voronezh in the early 19th century. A better choice, if it's open, would be the curious collection of costumes and artefacts at the **AL Durov House-Museum** (Dom-muzey AL Durova), ulitsa Durova 2, near the reservoir. The Durovs were Russia's most famous circus stars. Try to call (☎ 53 03 87) in advance.

Churches & Monastery

There are a half dozen churches, cathedrals and monasteries in town. Worth visiting is the recently restored **St Alexey of Akatov women's monastery** (Svyato Alexeevo-Akatovsky monastyr) at ulitsa Osvobozhdeniya Truda 1. The interior of the church is covered entirely with frescoes. If you come at 7.30 am or 5 pm you'll hear the intensely beautiful service, sung by nuns.

The monastery, founded in 1674, is near the river, a nice walk past old and lopsided cottages and the 18th century **Vvedenskaya Church** (Vvedenskaya tserkov) at ulitsa Osvobozhdeniya Truda 20. The 19th century **Intercession Cathedral** (Pokrovsky Kafedralny sobor) is nearby at ulitsa Bekhtereva.

A pleasant walking route from the centre of town would be to start at the **Arsenal** (take any minibus from ulitsa Plekhanovskaya to the stop just before Chernyavsky bridge), then cross ulitsa Stepana Razina and take the narrow, dusty Sacco and Vanzetti ulitsa shooting north. Follow this for three blocks to ulitsa Durov; turn right and walk to the end of the cobblestone street to the Durov museum. After that, go towards the reservoir; turn right and go about 100m until you see an overgrown stone staircase; this leads to the St Alexey monastery. Follow the street away from the reservoir, past the Vvedenskaya Church and back to ulitsa Stepana Razina. From the bridge at the foot of Razin, you can see the gold dome of the Intercession Cathedral, from where it's a short walk to cafe and store-lined prospekt Revolyutsii.

Near ploshchad Lenina, the **Nicholas Church** (Nikolskaya tserkov, 1720), ulitsa Taranchenko 19-a, has an interior of fresco-covered walls and an 18th century iconostasis. From here, it's a stroll past the university and up ulitsa Plekhanovskaya to the Regional Museum.

Places to Stay

Two tier pricing is in fashion in Voronezh. The best place to stay is ***Hotel Don*** *(☎ 55 53 15, ulitsa Plekhanovskaya 8)*, one block from ploshchad Lenina. But you'll need to convince the receptionist that you were turned away from the ex-Intourist hotel and will only be in town for one night. When we checked in, the thermometer in our room was showing 30°C and a rock concert on the square was vibrating the windows. Single/double rooms, though, were large and pleasantly furnished, with bath, fridge, and phone, for $14/17. Russians pay about 30% less.

Now partly given over to offices, the ghost of Intourist is ***Hotel Brno*** *(☎ 50 92 49, ulitsa Plekhanovskaya 9)*. Its smallish and fairly clean rooms cost $12/15.

Places to Eat

Unless you just want to drink, avoid the 2nd floor ***cafe*** at the Hotel Brno. The radishes in the salad came roots and all, and the red caviar was spread on sweet bread. ***Kafe Milan*** *(prospekt Revolyutsii 44)* has coffee and gelati. Another good spot for coffee and local ice cream, as well as beer on tap and crayfish (in season), is ***Klyon***, next to the Regional Museum and open from 11 am to 11 pm daily. For yummy self-catering, try ***Anna Kafe*** *(ulitsa Plekhanovskaya 15)*, open from 10 am to 10 pm daily. ***Uventas***, a fast-food place on prospekt Revolyutsii, serves plausible burgers, chicken sandwiches ($0.75), salads and faux-quiche.

Entertainment

The ***Regional Philharmonia*** (Oblastnaya filarmoniya) is at ploshchad Lenina 11. The ***State Theatre of Opera & Ballet*** (Gosudarstvenny teatr opery i baleta) is at ploshchad Lenina 7 and the ***Regional Puppet Theatre*** (Oblastnoy teatr kukol) can be found at prospekt Revolyutsii 50.

Bands attempting jazz can sometimes be heard at ***Flamingo***, in the ground level bar of the Hotel Brno. Some of the town's fancy restaurants have night shows, including ***Pushkin*** on prospekt Revolyutsii.

Getting There & Away

Air Voronezh is so well connected by rail and bus, you probably won't be using air. However, there are several daily flights to/from Moscow (Domodedovo).

Train Trains to Moscow take about 10 hours. Trains to other destinations include: Saratov (18 hours), Kislovodsk (25 hours) and St Petersburg (24 hours).

Bus Some sample bus fares are Tambov ($3, six hours), Saratov ($6, 12 hours), Volgograd ($7, 12 hours), Oryol ($4, 10 hours) and Yelets ($1.50, three hours). You may have to pay a small fee (about $0.10) for your luggage.

Getting Around

Buses to the airport (40 minutes) depart from the train station or Hotel Brno.

The train station is at ploshchad Chernovskogo. To get to the centre of town around ploshchad Lenina, take bus No 12 or trolleybus No 2, 3 or 11 from the stop to the right as you leave the station.

The main bus station is at Moskovsky prospekt 17. To get there from the train station take tram No 12. To ulitsa Plekhanovskaya take trolleybus No 6, 7 or 12. *Marshrutki* (minibuses) also frequently make these routes; ask the driver first.

Bus, trolleybus and tram fares cost $0.03; tickets are available from ticket booths or the driver.

RAMON РАМОНЬ

The **19th century chateau** of Princess Oldenbruskoy near Ramon, 36km north of Voronezh, off the M4 highway, has a collection of antique furniture and some nice scenery. To get there, take one of the buses departing at least hourly (from 6.15 am to 7.30 pm) from the main bus station in Voronezh. The fare is $0.30. At the time of writing, there was talk of day excursions by boat from Voronezh. Check at the pier at the end of ulitsa Stepana Razina.

ORYOL ОРЁЛ

☎ 08622 for five-digit numbers, ☎ 0862 for six-digit numbers • pop 350,000

Founded in 1566 as a fortress against the Tatars, Oryol (pronounced *arr-YOL*; the name means 'eagle') is a fine provincial town with some industry and a bland but pleasant centre. The town straddles the junction of the Oka and Orlik rivers, 380km south of central Moscow.

The feeling of old provincial Russia lingers in parts of Oryol thanks to its old pastel-hued buildings, including the colonnaded shops along ulitsa Moskovskaya south of the Oka, and a few 18th and early 19th century churches.

Oryol is also the birthplace of the writer Ivan Turgenev, who was born in 1818 and often returned here from his family estate at Spasskoe-Lutovinovo, 70km north. There's a big statue of him overlooking the Oka on the sloping street, Turgenevsky spusk, off ploshchad Lenina. There's also a bust of him in the public garden named after his novel, *A Nest of the Gentry* (which mirrors life in tsarist Oryol), overlooking the Orlik at the end of Oktyabrskaya ulitsa.

Turgenev was one of a surprising number of gentry that called Oryol home (19,000 out of a population of 32,000 in 1853), and writers thrived here; 12 of them are remembered in the city's museums.

The town has held up quite well despite being devastated several times by armies, most recently in 1943 when the Red Army took it back from the Nazis (5 August, the anniversary of the liberation, is an important local holiday).

For a provincial town, it seems quite cosmopolitan; locals attribute this to Yegor Stroev, an agricultural specialist who happened to be a great chum of Gorbachev. In 1985, Stroev was appointed regional administrator and, confident of his position due to his ties to the Kremlin, he announced that the distribution of Oryol's significant agricultural output would favour Oryol rather than Moscow. Today, what Stroev's efforts have translated into is a city caught in a time warp – capitalism hasn't taken root and communism is too far gone. But at least the main streets are freshly cobbled and the cupolas newly gilded. For lovers of 19th century Russian literature, Oryol is bound to be paradise. To others, especially those who have just come from Moscow or St Petersburg, the rosy simplicity makes one realise why so many provincial Russians spent (and still spend) their days dreaming about how to leave.

Orientation

The train station is 2km north-east, and the bus station is 3km south, of ploshchad Lenina. Running between ploshchad Karla Marxa and ploshchad Lenina, the pedestrian ulitsa Lenina serves as the centre's main street, connecting the old city centre to Moskovskaya ulitsa.

Information

You can change money on the 2nd floor of the main post office or at Hotel Salyut from 9 am to 11 pm daily except Sunday, with a break from 1 to 2 pm.

The post office is on the corner of ulitsa Gorkogo and ploshchad Lenina. Email can be sent from there for a small fee. The telephone office is at ulitsa Lenina 34. Books in this literary town are everywhere, but they're mostly about crime, fad diets and how to win husbands.

Intourist, ulitsa Gorkogo 37, has a couple of English-speaking staff. The reception desk at the Hotel Rus (see Places to Stay later) is a good information source; the administrators speak some English.

Museums

Turgenev's estate Spasskoe-Lutovinovo (see later in this chapter) is the literary mecca of provincial Russia. Not to be outdone, Oryol has its own **Turgenev Museum** at ulitsa Turgeneva 11. As with all the town's literary museums, it's open from 9 am to roughly 5.30 pm daily except Friday. No one knows why, but this part of Russia has been churning out writers, poets and literary theorists since the early 1800s, starting with F Tyutchev (1803-73). The poet Afanasy Fet (1820-92), the short story writer Nikolai Leskov (1831-95), who immortalised an English jumping flea, the poet and prose writer as well as 1933 Nobel Laureate Ivan Bunin (1870-1953), and Mikhail Bakhtin (1895-1975) who did to literary theory what Lenin did to Marxism, were all from this area. Hence the plethora of literary museums, six at last count, in a town that can't boast as many good cafes.

The **Museum of Oryol Writers** is at ulitsa Turgeneva 13, next door to the Turgenev Museum. In the park behind these museums is the home of 19th century historian **TN Granovsky**, at ulitsa 7 Noyabrya 24, and the **Ivan Bunin Museum**, featuring belongings from the writer's Paris flat including the bed in which he died. At the end of the one hour excursion (the only way you're going to make sense of all the curious photos and yellowed books), the guide flips on a tape player and the man himself reads one of his last poems, a typed copy of which lays near his typewriter. Still not sated? There's a statue of Bunin (though apparently it bears no resemblance to him) in front of the **Bunin Public Library** (Biblioteka imeni Bunina) at ulitsa Gorkogo 41, opposite the Park for Rest and Culture.

The birthplace of writer and dramatist Leonid Andreev is a typical late 19th century Oryol house at 2-ya Pushkarnaya ulitsa 41. It opened as a museum in 1991 and is at the southern end of town, west of the Orlik.

Scraping for something to put on its walls, the **Regional Museum**, on the corner of ulitsa Moskovskaya and ulitsa Gagarina, is open from 10 am to 5 pm daily except Monday. It has a reptile and Pushkin exhibition, in separate halls of course, to flesh out its rather skimpy permanent collection.

The **Great Patriotic War Museum**, on the corner of ulitsa Komsomolskaya and ulitsa Normandiya Neman, is open from 10 am to 6 pm daily except Monday, and has a basic collection of weaponry, recruitment and propaganda posters and a panorama depicting the liberation of Oryol as Red Army troops advanced on Kursk.

Other Attractions

The **Park for Culture and Rest** (Park Kultury i Otdykha) is a typical small-city park, with an amusement park at the north-eastern end.

A walk down the steep embankment to the Oka, between the park and junction of the Oka and Orlik rivers, brings you to the town's **rowing boat rental stand**, open from 9 am to 9 pm in the warmer months. It rents sturdy rowing boats for $0.50 an hour. The banks of the Oka draw huge crowds of bathers and carpet washers on sunny days.

Ploshchad Mira (Peace Square), on the corner of ulitsa Moskovskaya and ulitsa Pushkina, is easily identified by its WWII tank. The fighting machine, which perches precariously atop a granite base, is a time-honoured spot for newlyweds to pose for photos on the big day. It's also the site for the city's residents to pay respects to those who fought and died in battle. There is a marble memorial, with maps, behind the tank.

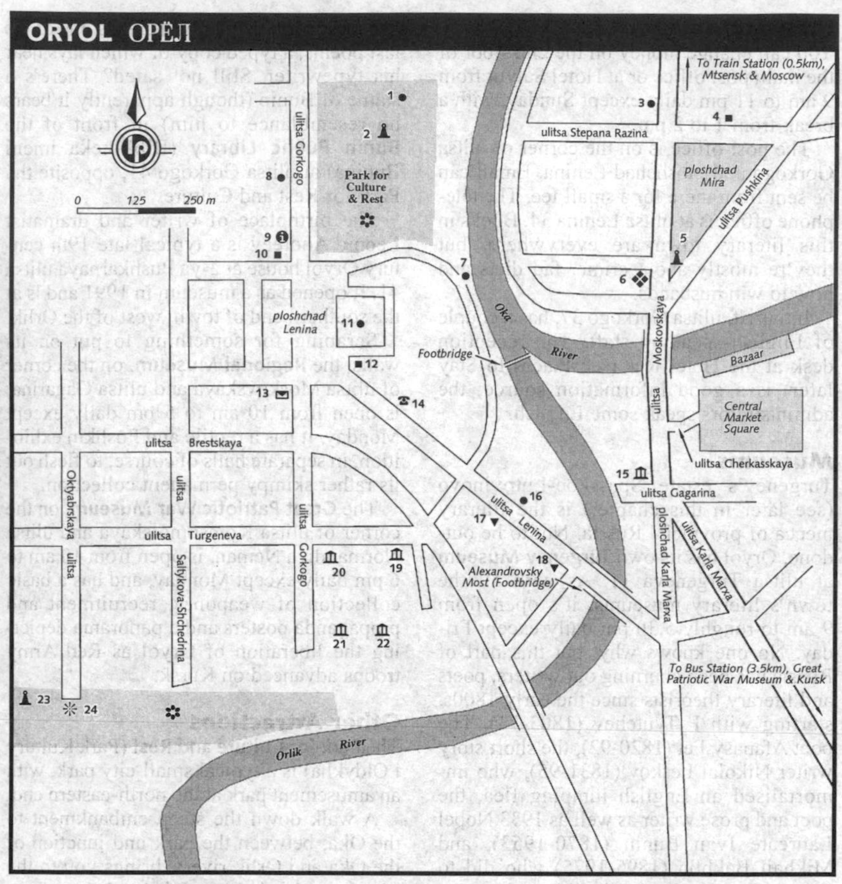

Places to Stay

Central location comes at a price; the soulless ***Hotel Salyut***, on the south-eastern corner of ploshchad Lenina, has single/double rooms for $14/21. Two tier pricing is in effect in Oryol with Russians paying half the foreigner rate.

Just across the ploshchad, ***Hotel Rus*** *(☎ 47 55 50, ulitsa Gorkogo 37)* has much nicer rooms for slightly less. There is a sign at the desk saying the hotel is 'not responsible for night calls concerning intimate services ... we kindly recommend you switch off your telephone ...'

Too cheap to attract such callers, ***Hotel Oryol*** *(☎ 5 05 25, ploshchad Mira 4)* is surprisingly pretty by Russian hotel standards with stone floors, cameo walls and canary yellow colonnades. The trick to getting a room here is to say the other hotels are booked up and/or to show up towards evening when the receptionist is least likely to send you back into the street. Though it doesn't readily accept foreigners, the foreigner price list is prominently posted at the front desk. Russians pay half the foreigner rate which is $11/20. Rooms without toilet and bath are nice and a dollar or two cheaper.

ORYOL ОРЁЛ

PLACES TO STAY
4 Hotel Oryol Гостиница Орёл
10 Hotel Rus Гостиница Русь
12 Hotel Salyut Гостиница Салют

PLACES TO EAT
17 Kafe Yagodka Кафе Ягодка
18 Beer Club at the Bridge Пивной клуб у моста

OTHER
1 Amusement Park Аттракционы
2 Turgenev Statue Памятник Тургеневу
3 Bookshop Книжный магазин
5 Tank Memorial Памятник танкистам
6 Orlovsky Univermag Орловский универмаг
7 Rowing Boat Rentals Прокат лодок
8 Bunin Public Library Библиотека Бунина
9 Intourist Интурист
11 Turgenev Theatre Театр имени Тургенева
13 Post & Telegraph Office Главный почтамт
14 Telephone Office Переговорный пункт
15 Regional Museum Краеведческий музей
16 Toy Store Магазин Игрушки
19 Turgenev Museum Музей Тургенева
20 Museum of Oryol Writers Музей писателей-орловцев
21 T N Granovsky House-Museum Дом-музей Т.Н. Грановского
22 Ivan Bunin Museum Музей Бунина
23 Turgenev Bust Бюст Тургенева
24 Garden and Lookout Point Сад и видовая площадка

Places to Eat

The *cafe* on the 3rd floor of the Orlovsky Univermag has basic meat/chicken dishes and salads for about $1. ***Kafe Yagodka*** *(ulitsa Lenina 25)* is an old Soviet watering hole where most orders are 'sto grammov vodki' (100g vodka) in a plastic cup. Along ulitsa Lenina there are a couple of cafes and beer bars, the best of which is (or was, as these establishments tend to come and go quickly) the ***Beer Club at the Bridge***, a mellow basement grotto with six wooden tables and no live music. The speciality is locally micro-brewed 'English Ale' served cold (oops) for $0.75 a mug. Appetisers include fried cheese, fried calamari, julienne (mushrooms, cheese, sour cream baked in a tin demitasse) for about $0.50 an order. As the main course, though you might have to wait 40 minutes for it, try the *kuritsa appetitnaya*, a boneless baked chicken leg stuffed with cheese and mushrooms ($1.35).

Shopping

There's a teeming daily market on the south bank of the Oka just east of ulitsa Moskovskaya. Along the river bank, a bazaar sells just about everything from toothpaste and TVs to a large selection of fresh produce from the Caucasus. This bazaar is adjacent to the market, from which tables spill out into the surrounding square. Just on the other side of the Oka, the Orlovsky Univermag, open until 8 pm daily except Sunday, has some leftover Soviet appliances, clocks and watches. There is a good grocery store on the ground level; Russian souvenirs (sometimes including lacquer boxes from the nearby town of Lipetsk) can be found on the 2nd floor.

Getting There & Away

Air There are flights to/from Moscow (Sheremetevo) several times a week ($15, 1¼ hours).

Train & Bus Oryol is on the Moscow-Kharkiv (Kharkov) railway, with numerous daily services. Buses head to Moscow several times a day (six hours), and there is a rail and bus service to Kursk (two hours by train, 3½ hours by elektrichka), Belgorod, Lipetsk, Yelets and Bryansk. There is a bus, but no direct rail service to Smolensk. If the lines at the kassa are prohibitively long, you should be able to wrangle a ticket from the conductor, especially for shorter runs.

Car & Motorcycle From Moscow the road is of varied quality – excellent dual carriageway out of Moscow, but badly surfaced and narrow for 40km either side of

Tula. South to Kursk is 152km, with the road to Kyiv (518km) branching west 55km south of Oryol.

Getting Around

The best way to see the city is on foot. From the train station, tram No 2 stops at ulitsa Karla Marxa, on the south-eastern end of the Alexandrovsky most (footbridge) leading to ulitsa Lenina. From ploshchad Karla Marxa, take trolleybus No 4 or 6 to the bus station. However, as the streets and bridges were being redone when we visited, there is the possibility that transport routes have since been altered.

A taxi to the train or bus station from ploshchad Karla Marxa should cost you about $1.

SPASSKOE-LUTOVINOVO СПАССКОЕ-ЛУТОВИНОВО

The manor of 19th century novelist Ivan Turgenev is open as a museum from 10 am to 5 pm daily except Tuesday (and the last day of each month as well as other days when it is unpredictably shut down for 'technical reasons').

Turgenev, born in Oryol in 1818, grew up at his family's estate here. The land was given to the family by Ivan the Terrible, and the local landscape and people inspired much of Turgenev's writing.

Though he spent much of his life in Moscow, St Petersburg, Germany and France, Turgenev thought of Spasskoe-Lutovinovo as his homeland and returned here many times. The beauty of the estate makes this easy to understand.

Turgenev was exiled here from St Petersburg in 1852-53 as a result of his work *The Hunter's Sketches*. He completed his most famous novel, *Fathers and Sons*, at Spasskoe-Lutovinovo.

The house, restored in the 1970s (which was when the coal stoves were installed), contains a fair-sized collection of period furniture, though the interior is almost completely devoid of personality despite the fact that some of the writer's personal items and a substantial percentage of his books still remain. There's an icon hanging in Turgenev's study that was given to the family by Ivan the Terrible. The entrance to the house was formerly the kitchen.

Several buildings remain in the grounds, including the family church, which is being restored. The big oak tree planted as a sapling by Turgenev, and the writer's 'exile house', where he lived in 1852-53, are just away from the house.

Outside the estate, descendants of the peasant serfs who once belonged to the Turgenevs still live and work on tiny farms.

Admission to the estate is $0.50 which includes a Russian-language guided tour. The foreigner rate is a steeper $1.25, though if you're overly principled about this kind of discrimination it's quite simple to pay the Russian price with minimal language skills. Photographers are charged $0.50 and 'videographers' are supposed to pay $6! Once inside the house, if you're not in a group, the caretakers might happily give you a free Russian-language tour.

There are a few small shops outside the grounds selling beer, soda, ice cream and souvenirs, including cassette recordings of the master's works.

Getting There & Away

Train Elektrichkas leave from Oryol at about 7 and 9 am for Bastyevo (1½ hours); this could change so make sure to check the schedule. From the northern end of the train station, walk east 3.5km (it's the road to the left), or catch the bus (in theory they're supposed to meet the train, but ...) which runs from Mtsensk via Bastyevo to the estate. Trains return to Oryol at 2 and 6 pm.

Bus Take the Mtsensk bus from Oryol which leaves at least once an hour from about 6 am to 9 pm ($0.60, 45 minutes), and switch at Mtsensk's bus station for an hourly Spasskoe-Lutovinovo bus ($0.25, 40 minutes). On the way back, you could try hopping onto one of the air-conditioned excursion buses.

Car & Motorcycle The estate is 6km west of the Moscow-Oryol road from a turn-off 65km north of Oryol.

KURSK
КУРСК

☎ 07100 • pop 430,000

Founded (most likely) in the 9th century, Kursk was destroyed by the Tatars in 1240. It then lay in Lithuanian territory for a couple of centuries before being annexed by Moscow and emerging as a southern frontier fort in the late 16th century. In the 18th and 19th centuries it became a grain-trade and industrial centre and an important railway junction. Much of its appearance is a result of rebuilding after severe damage during WWII.

Orientation & Information

Kursk's centre is divided by the north-south running ulitsa Lenina, with Krasnaya ploshchad at the southern end. Ulitsa Dzerzhinskogo heads quite steeply downhill from the west side of Krasnaya ploshchad to the valley of a now invisible river, where you'll find the busy central market.

A good bet for changing money is Kurskprombank (open from 10 am to 3 pm Monday to Friday, with a break from 1 to 2 pm) at ulitsa Lenina. The nearby Sberbank, at ulitsa Lenina, has surly service and hoods lurking around the exchange counter.

The post and 24 hour telephone offices are at Krasnaya ploshchad. The sign at window No 26 advertises *elektronnaya pochta* but the woman behind it had never heard of email.

Dom Knigi at ulitsa Lenina 11 has a good selection of Russian books and some maps, in Russian of course. The only book in English was a biography of Elvis Presley.

Churches

About halfway down ulitsa Lenina and a block to the east, on pleasant, tree-lined ulitsa Gorkogo, is the fine baroque **Sergievo-Kazansky Cathedral**, a working church, built in 1752-78 to a design by the Italian architect Rastrelli at the order of a wealthy merchant who sought repentance for a murder he committed (more or less in self-defence so the story goes). Turn down ulitsa Mozhayskogo opposite the Hotel Kursk to reach the church. It's green and white with blue domes. Inside are, in fact, two churches, one on top of the other, for summer and winter use.

A bit farther down ulitsa Lenina, the **Church of Ascension-Ilinsky** (Voznesensko-Ilinsky khram, 1786) was used during communism as a warehouse for Dom Knigi, a gloomy grey Stalinesque building placed smack in front of the strawberry-milk-hued, 18th century church. With the end of communism, the books were moved out and the church reopened. When a regional bank was constructed next door in 1997, tinted glass was used to reflect the church, creating the illusion that it is once again part of the main street. Inside, you can see the original frescoes of the famous icon painter Vasnetsov.

Krasnaya Ploshchad

The foot of ulitsa Lenina opens into Krasnaya ploshchad, surrounded by more imposing Stalinesque buildings – the House of Soviets on the east side, the post office on the west, the Hotel Tsentralnaya on the north-west and the matching city council building on the north-east. At the south end of the square is Kursk's most distinctive building, the domed **Assumption Cathedral** (Znamensky sobor, 1816-28), functioning again after having been zealously converted by the Soviets into a cinema.

Other Attractions

Just down the hill from the Assumption Cathedral, in the 1826-53 former bishop's palace, is the **Regional Museum**; it's open from 10.30 am to 6 pm daily except Friday and the last Thursday of the month. In the other direction from the cathedral, ulitsa Sonina runs round to the two room **Kursk Battle Museum** (Muzey Kurskoy Bitvy), in the ornate red and white former House of the Nobles which is now the Officers House (Dom Ofitserov). The museum is devoted to an important Soviet victory over the Germans in 1943. It's open from 9 am to 4 pm Wednesday to Sunday.

The **circus** on ulitsa Kolkhoznaya is unconscionable: the animals (including horses, tigers, bears and lions) are locked in tiny, filthy cages, and they all look absolutely miserable.

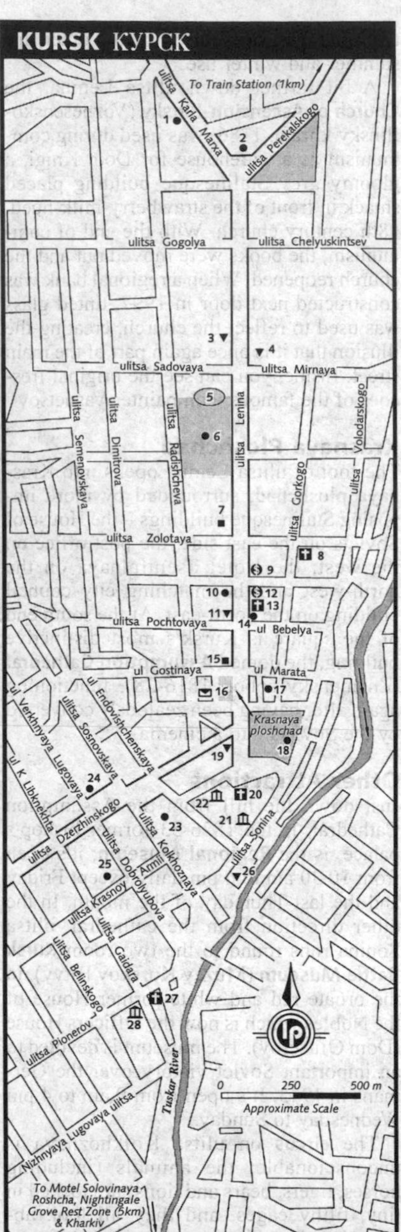

KURSK КУРСК

PLACES TO STAY

7 Hotel Kursk
Гостиница Курск
15 Hotel Tsentralnaya
Гостиница Центральная

PLACES TO EAT

3 Kafe Oktyabrskoe
Кафе Октябрьское
4 Dieticheskoe Kafe
Диетическое кафе
11 Pizzeria and Bistro
Пиццерия и Бистро
19 Bakery/Cafe
Булочная-кафе
26 Stolovaya
Столовая

OTHER

1 Northern Market
Северный рынок
2 Medical University
Медицинский университет
5 Stadium
Стадион
6 Pushkin Theatre
Театр Пушкина
8 Sergievo-Kazansky Cathedral
Сергиево-Казанский собор
9 Sberbank
Сбербанк
10 Detsky Mir
Детский мир
12 Kurskprombank
Курскпромбанк
13 Church of Ascension-Ilinsky
Вознесенско-Ильинский Храм
14 Dom Knigi
Дом книги
16 Post and 24-Hour Telephone Office
Почта и круглосуточный переговорный пункт
17 House of Soviets
Дом Советов
18 Discotheque
Дискотека
20 Assumption Cathedral
Вознесенский собор
21 Officers House
Дом офицеров
22 Regional Museum
Краеведческий музей
23 Circus
Цирк
24 Central Market
Центральный рынок
25 Banya
Баня
27 Lower Trinity Church
Свято-Троицкий Храм
28 Museum of Archaeology
Археологический музей

South of the museums, the slope up the far side holds Kursk's oldest streets, with the 1680 **Lower Trinity Church**, at ulitsa Gaidara 30, under repair after having been a planetarium. Across the street at ulitsa Pionerov 10 is an early 18th century house once belonging to a wealthy Kursk merchant and now housing the **Museum of Archaeology** (☎ 2 58 36). There is not much to see in the museum but on the 2nd floor you may find an archaeologist with whom you can arrange a walking tour ($5 to $10, depending on length) of the city. These enthusiastic scientists also give excursions to Lipovechensk, the ancient name of a 11th century fortress city 30km to the west of Kursk.

Next door to the Motel Solovinaya Roshcha, 6km out of town, is the **Nightingale Grove Rest Zone** (Zona otdykha Solovinaya roshcha), a park with a beautiful 1km tree-lined walk down to a bend of the Seym River. Trolleybus Nos 4 and 7 as well as tram No 3 run between the Solovinaya Roshcha stop on the main road outside the motel and Krasnaya ploshchad in the city centre.

Places to Stay

***Hotel Tsentralnaya** (☎ 56 90 48)*, on Krasnaya ploshchad, is a grand old place with singles/doubles for $10/13. Our double turned out to be a luxury suite with high ceilings and a black and white tiled bathroom. But don't expect the service to be luxurious.

***Hotel Kursk** (☎ 2 69 80)*, about halfway down the west side of ulitsa Lenina opposite the corner of ulitsa Mozhayskogo, is a standard Soviet place with rooms for $10/13. At the time of writing, a betting parlour was renting one of the rooms as an office, and it posted the latest international soccer scores at the front desk.

***Motel Solovinaya Roshcha** (☎ 35 92 36, ulitsa Engelsa 142A)* is 6km from Krasnaya ploshchad. Ulitsa Engelsa is the main road south, and the motel is 300m off it to the east. It's signposted, but driving from the city centre you have to go past the turn-off and then do a U-turn. The partly renovated motel is the most expensive place in town, with rooms for $30/40, including a breakfast of sausage, pelmeni and coffee.

Places to Eat

The hotel restaurants are all average. Meals generally cost $3 to $4 without liquor. The ***bufet*** at the Hotel Tsentralnaya serves edible cakes, sandwiches, 'pizza' and drinks. There is also a ***restaurant*** on the 3rd floor.

On ulitsa Lenina, next to Detsky Mir, is a very popular, smoke-filled ***pizzeria*** where everyone was drinking beer and no one was eating. In the same building, the ***bistro*** was serving stuffed peppers and eggplant on plastic plates which had partly melted in the microwave. You may have to wait for a table at ***Dieticheskoe Kafe*** on ulitsa Lenina, across from the stadium, serving fried dough stuffed with cheese ($0.25), pork Stroganov ($0.50), and *zrazy* ($1), which are gravy-smothered pork roulades stuffed with chopped liver, onions and rice. ***Kafe Oktyabrskoe***, three-quarters of the way up ulitsa Lenina, has decent *coffee po vostochnomu* (strong Oriental-style coffee), salads, fried fish and ice cream. You'll probably want to skip the restaurant in this building.

In Krasnaya ploshchad, on the corner of ulitsa Dzerzhinskogo, there's a well stocked ***bakery/pastry shop*** selling a good selection of local speciality breads including *khleb Kursky* as well as imported sausages and cheeses. It also has a small ***cafe*** with snacks and drinks. Behind the circus, in an old brick warehouse, is a ***stolovaya*** (eatery) serving up an old-fashioned Bolshevik lunch of cabbage soup, cabbage salad, beef cutlet with rice or macaroni and compote ($0.50).

The town's two main ***markets***, the Central (Tsentralny, down ulitsa Dzerzhinskogo) and the Northern (Severny, on ulitsa Karla Marxa), sell food, produce and clothes (the sort that will make you say, 'So *that*'s where they get it!').

Entertainment

The ***stadium*** on ulitsa Lenina has frequent rock concerts during June, July and August. The ***Pushkin Theatre*** next door seems to be active when the rock stars aren't. Chekhov's *The Three Sisters* was, and may still be, on their repertory.

Punks, gangs and just plain kids hang out in the park across from Krasnaya ploshchad, where there's also a teeny bopper ***disco-theque***. For the quintessential Russian experience, disrobe and scrub down in the public ***banya*** (bathhouse), a three storey ugly grey building on ulitsa Krasnoy Armii.

You might be able to stir up a game of billiards with a military man at ***Dom Ofit-serov*** (Officers House), behind the circus. The tables, for about $1 an hour, are available to the public from 1 to 9 pm daily.

Getting There & Away

Air Kursk is so well connected by bus and rail, you probably will not want to fly. However, there are flights to/from Moscow and St Petersburg.

Train Like Oryol, Kursk is on the Moscow-Kharkiv railway with trains to Moscow every half-hour, sometimes more. It's eight hours to Moscow, three to Kharkiv, and there are also daily trains to/from the Caucasus and Crimea. The station is about 3km north-east of Krasnaya ploshchad on Internatsionalnaya ulitsa.

Bus Kursk is accessible by a frequent bus service from Belgorod, Oryol, Moscow and Kharkiv. If you're arriving in Kursk by bus from the south, have the driver let you off at the Motel Solovinaya Roshcha, from where you can get a tram or trolleybus to the centre, saving an hour of doubling back.

Car & Motorcycle After a vile start through Kursk's southern industrial areas and another rough 25km or so, the 200km road to Belgorod and Kharkiv is mostly smooth and wide. Kursk has a western bypass, looping round from 12km north of the town centre to 19km south of it.

Getting Around

Bus No 19 goes up ulitsa Lenina to the train station but it's a rarity; marshrutnoe taxis ply the route more often for about $0.20.

Bus No 1 and tram No 2 go between the train station, past the corner of ulitsa Karla Marxa and ulitsa Perekalskogo (in front of the Medical University), and the bus station, north-west of the centre.

AROUND KURSK

Lipovechensk Archaeological Site

Раскопки около Липовеченска

All that's left of the wooden towers and 50 or so dirt homes, where extended Slavic families squished into a single Intourist-sized room, is a bowl-shaped hill rising over the pastures, but the excursion given by an archaeologist from the Museum of Archaeology in Kursk brings the place back to life. (Contact the museum a day ahead if you need to arrange for a translator. See Other Attractions under Kursk for the address and telephone number.)

The road to the site used to be a dodgy, bandit-thick contraband route. Not a lot unlike today, Ukrainian moonshiners smuggled vodka into Russia via Kursk. As vodka production in Russia was state-controlled, smuggling became an enormous business. About halfway to the site, you'll pass the former estate of the chief Kursk nobleman who, having lost his wife and six children to tuberculosis, asked his priest to bury him alive. Word reached Nicholas I who had the nobleman exiled until he came to his senses. Just before the site, you'll see the fields where Soviet pseudo-scientists cultivated dandelions in an attempt to use the milky substance inside the stems to manufacture rubber.

The residents of Lipovechensk were Severyane, one of the early Slavic tribes. The road to the fortress cleverly bends around the left half of the old kremlin walls so that approaching marauders would expose their unshielded sides to arrows and rocks. As Lipovechensk was on the silver road connecting Iran to the Black Sea via Derbent and the Volga, it was a wealthy, coveted city which soon outgrew its walls. In 1239, invading Mongol Tatars ransacked the fort. With the decapitated Slavic heads bouncing from their saddles, they rattled onwards to show what was in store for the rest of Rus. Nowadays, we're told, the site is used by Satan worshippers.

The only way to get out there is by taxi; call ☎ 065 to order a car. It will cost about $8, plus another $8 to $10 for the guide. The excursion takes about two hours.

Kursk Battle Memorial
Памятник Курской Битвы

The battle from 5 July to 5 August 1943, known as the Battle of the Kursk Bulge, was one of the Red Army's most important victories in WWII. German tanks attempting a pincer movement on Kursk – at the time the most forward Soviet-held town on this front – were halted by minefields and then driven back, turning Germany's 1943 counter-offensive into a retreat that saw the Red Army pass the Dnepr River by the end of September. The Kursk battle sprawled over a wide area, liberating places as far apart as Oryol and Belgorod, but the main memorial is beside the Kursk-Belgorod highway, 115km from Kursk and 40km south of Oboyan. A T-34 tank and a Yak fighter plane commemorate the part played by Soviet tankmen and airmen in the battle. Antitank guns stand on either side of a long wall sculpted with tank crew faces, beneath which is the War Glory Hall (Zal boevoy slavy), open from 10 am to 5 pm daily except Monday. At the north end of the memorial area, past the plane, a monument names the Soviet units that took part in the battle. Gun emplacements and trenches are preserved in the tree area, right of the tank.

About 8km farther south, at the south end of the village of Yakovlevo – the scene of particularly fierce fighting in the battle – there's a cannon monument.

BRYANSK
БРЯНСК

☎ 0832 • pop 475,000

Founded in 985 by Prince Vladimir, Bryansk has been transformed from an idyllic riverside town to a military and industrial behemoth. The city has been associated with things military since the days of Peter the Great, who established a shipbuilding factory here which constructed the Bryansk Flotilla between 1737-39.

From 1941-43, occupying German troops were kept maddeningly busy fighting off as many as 60,000 local partisans who took to the forests and sabotaged everything they could, which turned out to be a great deal. Partisans are credited (albeit by Soviet-era history books) with killing over 150,000 Germans. In an unsuccessful effort to flush out these pesky folks, German troops set to defoliating the forests surrounding the city.

During the Battle of the Kursk Bulge, Bryansk was decimated; today less than 10% of Bryansk's prewar buildings remain.

The accident at the Chornobyl (Chernobyl) atomic power plant in Ukraine was particularly devastating to the Bryansk region. Locals claim that the military bases at Bryansk and Oryol were ordered to fire cloud-seeding missiles to cause rain to fall over Bryansk, ostensibly to spare Moscow from the approaching radiation. Whether true – it is worth noting that during the 1994 Goodwill Games in St Petersburg, Russian scientists claimed to perform similar cloud seeding to prevent rain from washing out the event – no one argues that the Bryansk region received a huge dose of radiation from the accident. Western scientists say that short visits to Bryansk are safe.

We can't give any good reason to come here. Then again, we can't name any good reason not to come. Bryansk is a mediocre place, nothing to aah or groan about. The military base is still pretty active, and it can be glimpsed if you enter the city from the Oryol-Bryansk highway, just past the railway tracks. Surrounded by several barbed-wire fences and concrete barricades, you can see thousands of covered pieces of field artillery, anti-aircraft guns and cannons – it's probably best not to take snapshots.

Orientation & Information

Bryansk sits on four plateaus around the junction of the Snezhet, Desna and Bolva rivers. The action (and the only place of any real interest) is in the south-west. The 'centre', such as it is, hugs the 1.5km strip of prospekt Lenina, running perpendicular to ulitsa Krasnoarmeyskaya from a junction at ploshchad Krasnykh Partizan.

Even though the town has been open to visitors for nearly a decade, there's practically nothing in the way of tourist services. Maps, other than the amorphous bus route map at the central bus station, might be had at the bookshop on the main drag. The telephone office is on prospekt Lenina, and it had one computer hooked up to the Internet ($3 an hour).

The train station is about 5km west of the centre. The central bus station is just under 1km from prospekt Lenina on ulitsa Krasnoarmeyskaya.

Churches

As if you haven't seen enough of them already, Bryansk has a few restored churches. The working **Resurrection Church** (Tserkov Voskreseniya Khristova, 1739-41) is a three spired landmark with an ornate iconostasis. It's on prospekt Lenina on the corner of ulitsa Arsenalnaya. Nearby, the **Fyodorova Residence**, ulitsa Arsenalnaya 25, is a 19th century log cabin. The **Transfiguration Church** (Preobrazhensky khram) is next to the Hotel Bryansk.

Three kilometres south-east of the centre, the **Sven Monastery** (Svensky monastyr) is a nice but prosaic specimen of a 13th century working monastery. Most of the buildings inside date from the 18th century. The main gate is usually locked, so you'll need permission to get in and look around, but the monks are very friendly. Take bus No 7 from the south side of ulitsa Krasnoarmeyskaya, across the street from the bus station, to the last stop. The monastery is situated 300m up the left fork off the semi-roundabout.

Alexey Tolstoy Park

Also called 'The Park Where Trees Never Die', this is a lovely bit of green just west of ploshchad Lenina, dotted with huge but intricate and playful wooden sculptures. The sculptures are said to be made from trees in the park after they die, so that they may 'live' on. It's named after Alexey ('The Propagandist') Tolstoy, author of such unforgettable classics as *Aelita*, the touching tale of Communist revolution on Mars.

'... Gusev cut in. "Here's the layout for tomorrow ... I'll pick out a few good lads … I'll capture the electromagnetic stations and wire at once to the earth – to Moscow – for reinforcements. They'll have spaceships ready in six months" ...'

It's a favourite place to bring the kids who marvel at the fountain and run rampant through the amusement park in summer. Follow ulitsa Bolshaya Gagarina west off ploshchad Lenina and veer right past the Dinamo stadium. There are also nice parks to the east of ploshchad Lenina and ploshchad Teatralnaya.

Places to Stay & Eat

At ploshchad Lenina, ***Hotel Desna*** is a noisy dive. Rooms with dirty carpets and mildewy bathrooms cost $3/6 for a single/double. Its bufet on the 2nd floor is often closed because of 'no food supplies'.

Hotel Bryansk *(☎ 46 68 44)*, at the northern end of prospekt Lenina, has better than average rooms for $9/10. It also has an eating hall in the basement and a stuffy cafe with a nice view and 'kordon bryu' (pseudo cordon bleu) for $1.25, open noon to midnight, on the 13th floor. Across the street and open 24 hours, ***Petrovsky*** sells milk products, sausages, bread and soft drinks.

With a view of Lenin's backside, ***Kafe Luch*** is the kind of proletariat stolovaya that will make you an averred capitalist. The servers are glum and prone to yelling at the alcoholic customers. The menu of the day: ultra-salty soup, fried fish and cold groats ($0.50).

The central restaurant on prospekt Lenina has been cleverly renamed the ***Bryansk Potato***, evoking thoughts of radioactive produce. One of the house specialities is *draniki* (potato pancakes; $1). It also has trout and salmon ($2.25). The restaurant and the cafe in the same building have identical menus and prices. The cafe is more atmospheric with glass grapes hanging from the ceiling, an electric-powered fountain of plastic logs, and the clunking of billiard balls in the next room.

The ***Bryansky Karavay*** bakery, on prospekt Lenina just north of ploshchad Krasnykh Partizan, has a wide selection of bread. The city has two central ***markets***, the Tsentralny and the Nabezhetsky. Bus No 10 goes down prospekt Lenina and ulitsa Krasnoarmeyskaya to the Nabezhetsky, while bus No 10K runs the 10km between the two.

Getting There & Away

Bryansk is on the Moscow-Kyiv railway; almost every train out of Moscow's Kiev Station stops here. It's accessible by bus (three hours) and elektrichka (four hours) from Oryol, and by bus only to/from Smolensk (five hours). Bryansk is off the M3 (Moscow-Kyiv) highway from a turning 325km south-west of Moscow. Schedules for flights to Bryansk are unpredictable.

Getting Around

Between the bus and train station, take trolleybus No 2. Trolley Nos 3, 4 and 10 run past the bus station, up prospekt Lenina to the Hotel Bryansk. To the airport, take the airport bus from the bus station; there's one about every two hours.

Smolensk Region
Смоленская область

SMOLENSK
СМОЛЕНСК

☎ 08100 • pop 356,000

First mentioned in 863 as the capital of the Slavic Krivichi tribes and a major trade centre, Smolensk's position on the upper Dnepr River gave it early control over trade routes between Moscow and the West and between the Baltic and Black seas – 'from the Varangians to the Greeks'. It became part of Kyivan Rus, but after being sacked by the Tatars in about 1237, Smolensk passed to Lithuania. Moscow captured it in 1340, Lithuania in 1408, Moscow again in 1514, Poland in 1611 after a 20 month siege, and Russia in 1654.

There was a big battle between the Russians and Napoleon's army outside Smolensk in 1812 and more heavy fighting in 1941 and 1943, despite which quite a number of original or restored old buildings remain, notably churches and long sections of the city walls with fine towers reminiscent of the Moscow Kremlin.

These and the scenic slopes above the river make Smolensk worth exploring, though few visitors have spent more than a night here as they speed between Poland and Moscow. Smolensk is also the home of the successful Yak-42 airliner.

Orientation

Central Smolensk, surrounded by lengths of ancient wall, stands on a hill on the south bank of the Dnepr. The formal city centre is ploshchad Lenina with the Glinka Garden (Gorodskoy sad imeni MI Glinki) on its south side and the House of Soviets, Drama Theatre and Hotel Tsentralnaya on the north side. The train station and Kolkhoznaya ploshchad, site of the main market, are north of the river. Ulitsa Bolshaya Sovietskaya leads across the river and up the hill from Kolkhoznaya ploshchad to the centre. The Moscow-Minsk highway passes about 13km north of Smolensk.

Information

Money You can change money at any number of banks in the city, including Ska bank, at ulitsa Lenina 15 behind the Melodia music shop, or located in the foyer of the Hotel Smolensk.

Post & Communications The central post, telegraph and telephone office is at ulitsa Oktyabrskoy Revolyutsii 6. Internet access is available from two computers at the post office, to the right as you enter, from 8 am to 7 pm Monday to Friday. You'll be given a plastic card for a minimum of 30 minutes of access ($1).

You may find a curiously translated English-language map of Smolensk at Intourist. Russian-language maps are available at either of the two bookshops facing each other across ulitsa Bolshaya Sovietskaya, a block down from ulitsa Lenina.

Travel Agencies The city Intourist office (☎ 3 14 92) at ulitsa Konenkova 3, a couple of doors down from Hotel Tsentralnaya, works mostly with Cyprus-bound, shopping-crazed Russians. For foreigners, it's willing to offer a two to three hour English-language city tour at about $2 a person, as well as excursions to Novospasskaya (Mikhail Glinka's birthplace), about 100km

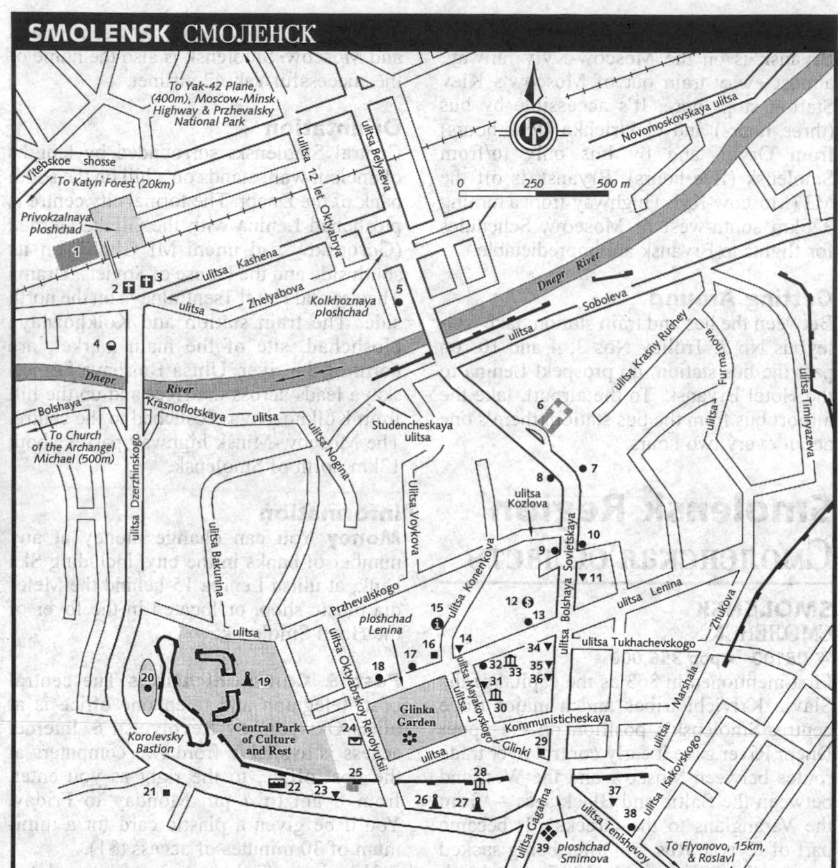

away. You'll probably need to arrange things a day in advance for the city tour and at least three days in advance for Novospasskaya. At the time of writing, there was no minimum group number; even individuals were welcome.

Fortress Walls

The 6km-long, 5.5m-thick, 15m-high walls of the Smolensk fortress were built in 1596-1602. Originally they had 38 towers, 17 of which stand today. The Central Park of Culture and Rest (Tsentralny park kultury i otdykha) backs a longish south-west stretch of the walls. Overlooking the Spartak Stadium just outside the line of the walls on the west side of the park, the Korolevsky Bastion is a high earth rampart built by the Poles who captured Smolensk in 1611. It saw heavy fighting in 1654 and 1812. The park has a 26m-high cast-iron monument to the 1812 defenders.

You can enter the Gromovaya Tower on the west side of ulitsa Oktyabrskoy Revolyutsii from 10 am to 6 pm daily except Monday. At the foot of the walls east of here you'll find an eternal flame memorial to the dead of WWII and the graves of some of

SMOLENSK СМОЛЕНСК

PLACES TO STAY
16 Hotel Tsentralnaya
Гостиница Центральная
21 Hotel Rossia
Гостиница Россия
29 Hotel Smolensk
Гостиница Смоленск

PLACES TO EAT
11 Stary Gorod
Старый город
14 Kafe Zarya
Кафе Заря
23 Pizzeria Domino
Пиццерия Домино
31 Kafe Le Bistrot
Кафе Ле Бистрот
34 Stary Rytsar
Старый рыцарь
35 Nautilus
Наутилус
36 Ladya
Ладья
37 Bar
Бар

OTHER
1 Train Station
Железнодорожный вокзал
2 St Barbara's Church
Церковь Св Варвары
3 SS Peter and Paul Church
Церковь святых Петра и Павла
4 Bus Station
Автовокзал
5 Zadneprovsky Market
Заднепровский рынок
6 Assumption Cathedral
Успенский собор
7 Smolensk Flax Exhibition
Выставка Смоленский лён
8 Trinity Monastery Bell Tower
Колокольня Троицкого монастыря
9 Bookshop
Книжный магазин
10 Bookshop
Книжный магазин
12 Ska Bank
Ска банк
13 Melodia
Магазин Мелодия
15 Intourist
Интурист
17 Drama Theatre
Драматический театр
18 House of Soviets
Дом Советов
19 Monument to the 1812 Defenders
Памятник защитникам Смоленска 1812г.
20 Spartak Stadium
Стадион Спартак
22 Wading Pool/Waterfall
Бассейн/Водопад
24 Central Post, Telegraph & Telephone Office
Главный почтамт
25 Gromovaya Tower
Громовая башня
26 Eternal Flame Memorial
Мемориал Вечный огонь
27 Monument to the Heroes of 1812
Памятник героям 1812г.
28 WWII Museum
Музей Великой Отечественной войны
30 Konenkov Sculpture Museum
Музей скульптуры Коненкова
32 Fenix Chess Club
Шахматный клуб Феникс
33 History Museum
Исторический музей
38 Art Gallery
Художественная галерея
39 Central Department Store
ЦУМ

the Soviet soldiers who died in Smolensk's defence, plus a WWII museum and another monument to the heroes of 1812.

A blessing for the traveller, except those who have rolled into town on Sunday night, all Smolensk's museums are open from 10 am to 6 pm daily except Monday. As for most Russian museums, you might not get in if you show up past 5.30 pm.

Assumption Cathedral

Smolensk's big green and white working Uspensky sobor rises at the top of a flight of steps halfway up ulitsa Bolshaya Sovietskaya. A cathedral has stood here since 1101 but this one was built in the late 17th and early 18th centuries. Topped by five domes, it has a spectacular gilded interior. Napoleon is said to have been so impressed by it that he set a guard to stop his own men from vandalising it.

To your right as you enter, you can recognise – by all the candles around it – a supposedly wonder-working icon of the Virgin. This is a 16th century copy of the original, said to be by St Luke, which had been on this site since 1103 and was stolen in 1923. The cathedral bell tower is to the left of the cathedral. There's a good view from the terrace at the eastern end of the cathedral.

Flax Exhibition

A little farther up the hill, ulitsa Bolshaya Sovietskaya cuts through the former Trinity Monastery. The bell tower is on the west side; on the east side the pink monastery church now houses the Flax Exhibition (Vystavka lyon). The latter unwittingly tells a sad tale of how the revolution and mechanisation replaced the colourful, varied, traditional textile designs with mass-produced uniformity.

History Museum & Art Gallery

Smolensk's History Museum (Muzey istorii) is at ulitsa Lenina 8. The art gallery (khudozhestvennaya galereya), at ulitsa Tenishevoy 7/1, is said to hold a curious collection of mostly Russian avant-garde paintings and trinkets collected by Princess Maria Tenisheva (see Flyonovo under Around Smolensk).

Konenkov Sculpture Museum

Smolensk's sculpture museum, ulitsa Mayakovskogo 7, has some playful woodworks by Sergey Konenkov. Upstairs, past the frightening Prorok statue, is a small but very good collection of steel, bronze and aluminium statuettes, and another room housing pure kitsch – if you've been itching to see a matryoshka doll, they have some good ones here.

Yak

Want to see a Yak-42 – in hopes you won't have to fly in one? There's a weathered specimen in front of the now nearly bankrupt Smolensk Aviation Factory on ulitsa Frunze. Take tram No 5 from the centre of town.

Places to Stay

The cheapest place in town, and you get what you pay for, is the pre-WWII ***Hotel Smolensk*** *(☎ 3 03 97, ulitsa Glinki 11/30)*. The barely comfortable single/double rooms are $8/13. At the time of writing, hot water had been turned off in the city, because the city hadn't paid its hot water bill.

Hotel Rossia *(☎ 65 56 10, ulitsa Dzerzhinskogo 23/2)* has the premier rooms in town for $8 to $12/16, including a smorgasbord breakfast of fish, hot dogs, salads, kefir etc. The only catch is the check-out time – an ungodly 8 am, and it sounds like they're strict about it. ***Hotel Tsentralnaya*** *(☎ 3 36 04)*, on the corner of ploshchad Lenina and ulitsa Konenkova, is a reasonable deal with timeworn rooms for $10/16. The check-out time here, as in most Russian hotels, is noon.

Places to Eat

There is a strip of ***bars***, open from about noon to past midnight, on Bolshaya Sovietskaya near the corner of ulitsa Lenina. The names as well as the quality change with each economic crisis so you'll have to use your best judgement. At the time of writing, ***Stary Rytsar*** (Old Knight), in the yard a few metres back from the street, was trying hard to be a slick cellar bar/cafe with expensive food and a dark dining grotto that smelled like a swimming pool.

Next door, ***Nautilus*** is just as dark, with four or five wooden booths and food that tastes like your little brother concocted it. Like most Russian restaurants, the menu has a page of strangely named salads: *Signoir Pomidor* turned out to be a chopped-up unripened tomato with some grated processed cheese and lots of mayonnaise on top ($1). The borsch had a sea of salt in it, and the escalop was a chunk of rubbery beef topped with melted cheese, relish and ketchup, and soggy fries on the side ($1). It also serves spaghetti (at your own risk) and fish, though that might not be a pleasant experience given the critters are floating around in aquariums on each table. Next door, ***Ladya*** looked to be the best bet. The atmosphere was ships ahoy.

Stary Gorod, opposite Bolshaya Sovietskaya 14, is in a maze of smoky dining rooms. Walk through the entrance tunnel, turn left, turn left again and down the stairs. It serves cheeseburgers ($0.50), omelettes ($0.10), schnitzel, *myaso po Frantsuzsky* (beef topped with cheese, mayonnaise, tomato, ketchup and relish) as well as *myaso po Smolensky* (ditto without the cheese and tomato). On ulitsa Dzerzhinskogo, near the pool, is the highly recommended ***Domino***, a pizzeria with fried chicken plus typical Smolensk fare.

Kafe Zarya, opposite the Hotel Tsentralnaya, is fine for snacks but the restaurant did not look like it has had a customer since communism collapsed. In summer, there's one of those omnipresent plastic chair and Marlboro umbrella ***cafes*** next to the Fenix Chess Club (Shakhmatny klub Fenix) at ulitsa Lenina 12. The red vinyl ***Kafe Le Bistrot*** on ulitsa Mayakovskogo, just up the street from the Konenkov Sculpture Museum, serves pizza, sandwiches, *sosiski* (boiled hot dogs), cakes, coffee and juice. There's also a popular, green and white ***bar*** serving salads, pelmeni, ice cream and coffee in the park just behind the art gallery.

Smolensk's main ***market*** is the Zadneprovsky on Kolkhoznaya ploshchad north of the river.

Getting There & Away

Air Smolensk no longer has its own airport. The nearest one with the most number of connecting flights is Moscow.

Train Smolensk is on the Moscow-Minsk-Warsaw railway with several daily trains to/from Moscow (six hours), Minsk (four hours), Brest (eight hours), Warsaw (11½ to 14 hours), Prague (26 hours) and Kaunas (10 hours), as well as trains every other day to Riga (11½ hours) and a weekly train to Berlin (41 hours). The kassa for international rail tickets, to the right as you enter the station, is open from 10 am to 6 pm (with a break from 11.30 am to 12.30 pm) Monday to Friday. If the kassa is closed and you need to travel, purchase a ticket to Brest, where the trains stop at the border for several hours, time enough to get an across-border ticket at the 24 hour kassa, so we're told.

For more information on daily rail links with Western Europe see the European Russia Getting There & Away chapter and Moscow Getting There & Away.

Bus Smolensk bus station, just south of the train station, serves most of the region's smaller towns with frequent daily services, and several times daily service to Moscow. Buses to Moscow also leave from the train station across the footbridge.

Car & Motorcycle By road it's 390km to Moscow, and 330km to Minsk. Both are among Russia's better, though duller, stretches of highway, being mostly flat, straight and empty.

Getting Around

From the train station, you'll either have to take the bus to the centre of town, from the stop on the right near the end of the car park, or cross the footbridge to the bus station and from there take a tram, unless of course the tram viaduct has been repaired and the trams are again stopping in front of the train station. A taxi from either station to any of the hotels, at the time of writing, did not cost more than $1.

AROUND SMOLENSK

Flyonovo
Флёново

In the late 19th and early 20th centuries, top Russian art and music names like Stravinsky, Shalyapin, Vrubel and Serov visited the Flyonovo estate of the artist Princess Maria Tenisheva, near Talashkino, about 15km south-east of Smolensk on the Roslavl road. The visitors joined in applied-art workshops, which the princess organised for her peasants, and helped in building projects.

The most striking result is a series of dramatic murals and mosaics on the brick Holy Spirit Church – particularly the one of Christ over the entrance. One house called Teremok, decorated with ornate peasant style carving, is now a folk-art museum, open daily except Monday. Take bus No 104 from Smolensk's bus station to Talashkino.

Katyn Forest
Катынский Лес

In 1990 the Soviet authorities finally admitted that the NKVD (predecessor of the KGB) had shot over 6000 Polish officers in the back of the head in the Katyn Forest near Smolensk in 1940. The bodies of the officers, who had been imprisoned by the Soviet occupying troops in Poland in 1939, were left in four mass graves.

Until 1990 the Soviet authorities insisted on blaming it on the Nazis. The victims were trucked from Gnezdovo, a country station, to Kozi Gory, site of the graves. The graves have not been disturbed and are now marked by memorials. About 11,000 other Polish officers almost certainly died similar deaths elsewhere in the USSR.

Less well known is the fact that the Katyn Forest was also, according to a 1989 *Moscow News* report, the site of massacres of 135,000 Soviet prisoners of war by the Nazis (out of an estimated one million Soviet POWs shot by the Germans in WWII) and of thousands of Soviet 'enemies of the state' exterminated by the NKVD in the 1930s.

Getting There & Away Getting there on your own is simple; take bus No 101 (direction: Smolensk Smetanino) from the Smolensk bus station to Kozi Gory. It's easy to miss so look for the sign saying 'Memorial Polskim ofitseram pogibshim v Katyni' about 1km past the highway flyover. If you get to Katyn, you've gone too far. The memorial is in two spots: one with a simple wood cross, and a marble headstone dedicated to Russian dead; and the more impressive Polish one farther up the path. The forest is spooky, but the memorials are moving.

Przhevalsky National Park Национальный парк имени Пржевальского

Lying 60km north of Smolensk, the birthplace of adventurer Nikolai Przhevalsky is a beautiful national park, a favourite spot for locals to spend a long weekend camping by one of the many lakes. The road to the park is asphalt and after that there are dirt roads and footpaths. A park ranger might be at the post at the entrance to the park, where you may have to pay a small fee upon entering. If no one is there, don't be surprised if one of the rangers stops by your campfire to collect the fee, which might be a shot or two of vodka.

Novgorod Region Новгородская область

NOVGOROD НОВГОРОД

☎ 8162 for six-digit numbers, ☎ 81622 for five-digit numbers • pop 240,000

The name means 'new town', but Novgorod was here by the 9th century and for 600 years was Russia's most pioneering artistic and political centre. Today it's mostly known for its history, and for some of the most diverse and beautiful architecture in the country. Methodically trashed by the Nazis, it's a sign of the city's historical importance that its old kremlin was one of the Soviet government's first reconstruction projects.

An easy and rewarding overnight stop – hence popular with foreign and Russian tourists – Novgorod is only three hours by road from St Petersburg and is just off the M10 highway connecting Moscow and St Petersburg.

History

In a sense, Russian history began here. This was the first permanent settlement of the Varangian Norsemen who established the embryonic Russian state. By the 12th century the city, called 'Lord Novgorod the Great', was Russia's biggest: an independent quasi-democracy whose princes were hired and fired by a citizens' assembly, and whose strong, spare style of church architecture, icon painting and down-to-earth *byliny* (epic songs) were to become distinct idioms.

Spared from the Mongol Tatars, who got bogged down in the surrounding swamps, Novgorod suffered most at the hands of other Russians. Ivan III of Moscow attacked and annexed it in 1477, and Ivan the Terrible, whose storm-troopers razed the city and slaughtered 60,000 people in a savage pogrom, broke its back. The founding of St Petersburg finished it off as a trading centre.

Orientation

The town has two main centres: the kremlin on the west bank of the Volkhov River, and the old market district, Yaroslav's Court, on the east bank. The kremlin side sprawls outwards like a pheasant's tail, while the east side is grid-like.

Though the Soviet street names were officially scrapped almost a decade ago, the locals still use them, therefore we've left the more important ones in parentheses. City maps in Russian and English can be found on sale at bookshops, as well as hotel and museum kiosks. The English map was out of date at the time of research; it may have since been renewed.

Information

There are many post offices around town, as well as at some of the hotels. The main telegraph and telephone office is on the corner of ulitsa Lyudogoshchaya (Sovietskaya) and ulitsa Gazon (Gorkogo), at the north end of Sofiyskaya ploshchad. If you bring your own diskette, you can send and receive email here for about a rouble per kilobyte (or roughly $0.50 for a two page letter). Internet connection might be available at the post office on the east side of town at the end of the bridge. You can change money at the hotels, or at the Sberbanks scattered about the town.

A fresh alternative to the elusive Intourist, Servis Tur (☎ 3 25 17, servtour@telecom.nov.ru), ulitsa Slavnaya 46, offers excursions of the city and kremlin (three hours; about $14 per person, or $7 if there's three or more people), museums (two hours, $5 to $6) and surrounding monasteries and churches in English, French and German. It can also arrange for homestays.

One thing Novgorod doesn't lack is souvenirs. You'll see woven birch boxes, mini wooden churches, matryoshka dolls and lacquer boxes all over the place. Keep an eye out for the locally made blue and gold china *(farfor)*.

Kremlin

Part park, part tourist attraction, part archive, this is worth seeing with a guide. Russian-language guides sometimes hang out at the Millennium monument. English-language tours can be arranged, usually a day or two in advance, through Servis Tur (see the previous Information section for contact details).

The buildings are open from 10 am to 6 pm (though it's a good idea to enter before 5 pm to be sure). The Gothic Chamber is closed on Wednesday and the last Friday of each month, and the museum on Tuesday and the last Thursday. As these schedules are subject to change – double-check the sign in English and Russian at the entrance to the museum. Tickets are $1 for foreigners, $0.20 for Russians; there's an extra charge for taking pictures.

Cathedral of St Sophia Finished in 1050, the handsome, Byzantine Cathedral of St Sophia (Sofiysky sobor) is the town's centrepiece and possibly the oldest building in Russia. The west doors, captured from the Swedes, have tiny cast-bronze biblical scenes and even portraits of the artists. The icons inside date from the 14th century, and older ones are in the museum. In comparison, the frescoes are barely dry, being less than a century old. Services usually take place between 6 and 8 pm daily. Nearby are the 15th century belfry and a leaning 17th century clock tower.

Millennium of Russia Monument Watch the crowds go round and round this bronze birthday cake, unveiled in 1862 on the 1000th anniversary of the Varangian Prince Rurik's arrival. The Nazis cut it up, intending to ship it to Germany, but the Red Army saved the day.

The women at the top are Mother Russia and the Orthodox Church. Around the middle, clockwise from the south, are Rurik, Prince Vladimir of Kyiv (who introduced Christianity), tsars Mikhail Romanov, Peter the Great and Ivan III, and Dmitry Donskoy trampling a Mongol Tatar. In the bottom band on the east side are nobles and rulers, including Catherine the Great with an armload of laurels for all her lovers. Alexander Nevsky and other military heroes are on the north side, and literary and artistic figures are on the west.

Chamber of Facets The Gothic Chamber of Facets (Granovitaya palata), part of a palace built in 1433, has a collection of icons and lavish church booty from the region.

Museum of History & Art The Muzey Istorii i Iskusstva is said to be one of the best research museums of its kind in Russia, with a huge collection of early icons, birch-bark manuscripts, paintings, early wood sculpture and applied art.

Yaroslav's Court

Across a footbridge from the kremlin is old Novgorod's market, with the remnants of a

WESTERN EUROPEAN RUSSIA

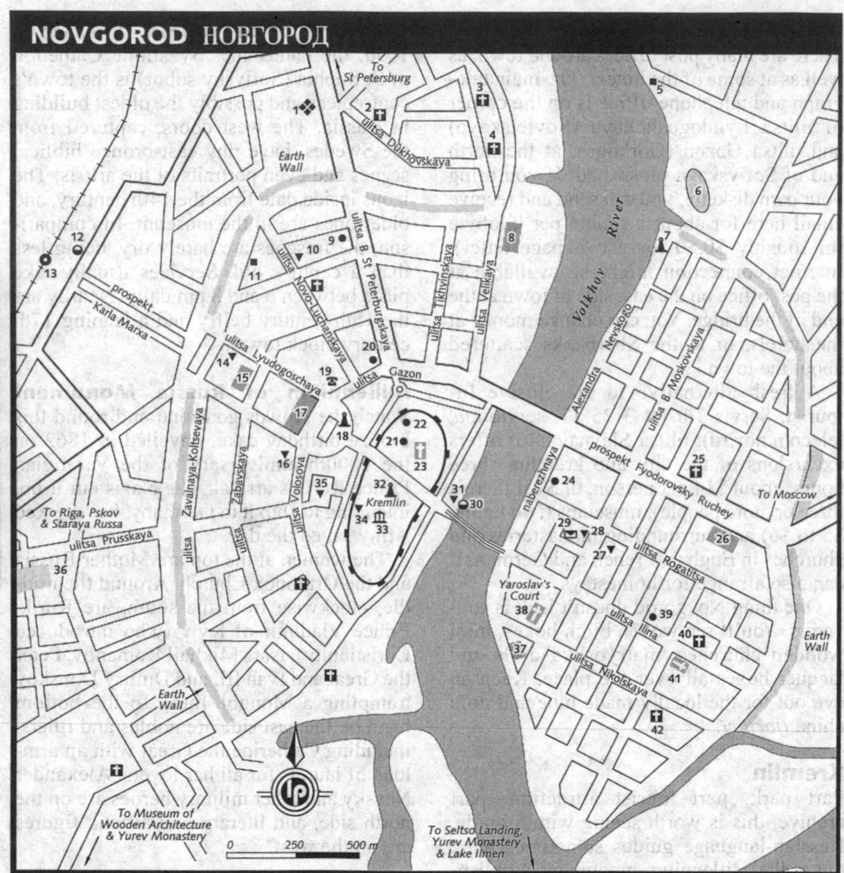

17th century arcade facing the river. Beyond that is the market gatehouse, an array of churches sponsored by 13th to 16th century merchant guilds, and a 'road palace' built in the 18th century as a rest stop for Catherine the Great.

Restored in 1995-99, the Kyiv-style Court Cathedral of St Nicholas (Nikolo-Dvorishchensky sobor, 1136) is all that remains of the early palace complex of the Novgorod princes, from which the area gets its name of Yaroslav's Court (Yaroslavovo dvorishche). Inside, fragments of 12th century frescoes include one of Job, covered in boils, with his wife passing him food on the end of a pole. The other frescoes are 19th century restorations.

Church of Our Saviour-at-Ilino

On the outside, the 14th century Church of Our Saviour-at-Ilino (Tserkov Spasa-na-Iline) has graffiti-like ornaments and lopsided gables which are almost playful. Inside are the only surviving frescoes by the legendary Byzantine painter Theophanes the Greek (and they came close to extinction when the church served as a Nazi machine-gun nest). They are barely visible

NOVGOROD НОВГОРОД

PLACES TO STAY

5 Beresta Palace Hotel
Отель Береста Палас
8 Hotel Intourist
Гостиница Интурист
11 Hotel Roza Vetrov
Гостиница Роза Ветров
15 Hotel Volkhov
Гостиница Волхов
26 Hotel Sadko
Гостиница Садко
37 Hotel Rossia
Гостиница Россия

PLACES TO EAT

10 Pivnoy Bar
Пивной бар
14 Restoran Pri Dvore; Money Bar
Ресторан При дворе
16 Kafe Charodeyka
Кафе Чародейка
27 Kafe Kolobok
Кафе Колобок
28 Kafe Yaroslavna
Кафе Ярославна
31 Summer Shashlyk Stand
Летний шашлычный киоск
34 Restoran Detinets
Ресторан Детинец
35 Gril-Bar
Гриль бар

OTHER

1 Central Department Store
ЦУМ
2 Trinity Church
Троицкая церковь
3 Church of Nikola Bely
Церковь Николы Белого
4 Church of Peter and Paul
Церковь Петра и Павла
6 Stadium
Стадион
7 Alexandr Nevsky Statue
Памятник Александру Невскому
9 Bookshop
Книжный магазин
12 Bus Station
Автовокзал
13 Train Station
Железнодорожный вокзал
17 Regional Administration Building
Областная администрация
18 Sofiyskaya Ploshchad & Lenin Statue
Софийская площадь и памятник Ленину
19 Main Telegraph and Telephone Office
Главный Телеграф и Телефон
20 Souvenir Shop
Магазин Сувениры
21 Chamber of Facets
Грановитая палата
22 Clocktower
Часозвоня
23 Cathedral of St Sophia
Софийский собор
24 Banya
Баня
25 Church of St Theodore Stratelates
Церковь Федора Стратилата
29 Post Office
Почта
30 Kremlin Landing
Причал у Кремля
32 Millennium of Russia Monument
Памятник Тысячелетие России
33 Museum of History & Art
Музей истории и искусства
36 Market
Рынок
38 Court Cathedral of St Nicholas
Николо-Дворищенский собор
39 Servis Tur
Сервис Тур
40 Church of Our Savior-at-Ilino
Церковь Спаса на Ильине
41 Cathedral of Our Lady of the Sign
Знаменский собор
42 Church of the Apostle Philip
Церковь Филиппа Апостола

but nonetheless awe-inspiring; that is if you can get in. The frescoes are under restoration, indefinitely. We pleaded with the gatekeeper and not only were let in, but also given an impromptu tour. Note Theophanes' signature use of white war-like paint around the eyes and noses of his figures, and his soul-penetrating expressions. The church itself, at ulitsa Ilina east of Yaroslav's Court, is pure Novgorod style (in contrast to the lumbering 17th century Moscow-style Cathedral of Our Lady of the Sign across the street).

Other Churches

Some other churches in the Novgorod style, which may or may not be open, are the **Church of Peter & Paul** (Tserkov Petra i Pavla, 1406) on ulitsa Zverinskaya (Bredova), behind No 14, near the Hotel Intourist, and the **Church of St Theodore Stratelates** (Tserkov Fyodora Stratilata, 1361) at ulitsa Fyodorovsky Ruchey 19 (prospekt Yuriya Gagarina). An appealing church in the angular Moscow style is **Trinity Church** (Tserkov Troitsy, 1557) at ulitsa Dukhovskaya (Musy Dzhalilya).

The **Church of Our Saviour-at-Nereditsa** (Tserkov Spasa-na-Nereditse, 1198), which has a few bits of 12th century frescoes, is in the nearby village of Seltso, a 20 minute boat ride from the kremlin landing – that is if the boats are running. At the time of research a bus left the Novgorod station at 6.35 am and returned at 7.05 pm. Double-check the schedule. You could also try to hire a car to go the 8 to 10km, though the road is quite bad.

Yurev Monastery & Museum of Wooden Architecture

In the southern marshes is this dilapidated 12th century monastery with its heavily reconstructed Cathedral of St George and a clutch of 19th century add-ons. It's not as striking as many places closer to town, though the windswept river setting makes it more appealing. The entrance is on the east (river) side. It's open from 10 am to 6 pm, and closed Wednesday. Bus No 7 from Sofiyskaya ploshchad takes 20 minutes, or you can try to catch a boat from the kremlin landing. If you get hungry while at the monastery, there's a riverside cafe with peppery shashlyk ($0.75) just south of the monastery walls.

Roughly 1km up the road is the **Vitoslavlitsy Museum of Wooden Architecture**, an open-air museum of intricate, beautiful wooden churches and peasant houses from around the region. It's open from 10 am to 6 pm daily from April to October; the rest of the year until 5 pm. Tickets are $1 for foreigners ($0.20 for Russians). As with most museums in town, there's an extra charge for photo taking. Servis Tur runs a two hour guided tour to both the monastery and the museum for about $14 per person (less if there's more than three people).

River Trips

The Volkhov River flows out of Lake Ilmen, about 10km south. On a good day, the surrounding marshes are lovely in their own way, with churches sticking up here and there. From the dock below the kremlin, you should be able to catch a boat for a two hour cruise ($1 per person). Unless the public ferries have started up again, you'll have to negotiate, probably at least a day in advance, with one of the captains to go to Yurev (expect to pay about $4) and Staraya Russa ($120, four hours each way). At the time, there were day excursions to Nikolyna-Lipne, a 13th century church on an island. There's a small beach for swimming, as well as a village-style Russian bathhouse. The guide, co-owner and host, Margarita, also serves up an old-fashioned Novgorodian meal (on birch dishes). You should be able to arrange for the excursion at the Intourist, Beresta Palace or Sadko hotels. You could also try calling Margarita (☎ 3 65 34) on Monday, when she comes into town to go grocery shopping.

Gorodki

Sometimes on summer evenings, by the kremlin's north wall, you can watch this violent species of bowling in which wood-and-iron bars are flung at elaborately stacked-up pins.

Banya

For a good sweat with a proletarian price tag, the town's mustard-coloured public banya, naberezhnaya Alexandra Nevskogo 24, is open daily. Check the schedule beside the door for bathing hours, usually from 4 to 8 pm. It costs $0.15 an hour, plus another $0.15 to rent a birch *venik* with which to whip yourself, if so inclined.

Places to Stay

Decaying is a polite way to describe ***Hotel Rossia*** *(naberezhnaya Alexandra Nevskogo 19/1)*. Its rooms are cheap ($5/10), but you'd be better off staying at the pretty, pink, former dormitory, ***Hotel Roza Vetrov*** *(☎ 7 20 33, ulitsa Zavalnaya-Koltsevaya (Chernyakhovskogo) 27A)*, which is a 15 minute walk from either the train station or the centre of town. Single/double rooms ($6/7) are clean with the bathroom/shower shared with one other room. Here you may actually have to make reservations in order to ensure accommodation during the peak months of June, July and August.

Near Sofiyskaya ploshchad, ***Hotel Volkhov*** *(☎ 11 55 01, ☎/fax 11 55 00, ulitsa Zabavskaya (ulitsa Nekrasova) 24)* has cheery, clean rooms; rooms cost $12/15 with breakfast. A half-step better, ***Hotel Sadko*** *(☎ 66 18 07, ulitsa Fyodorovsky Ruchey 16)* has spacious rooms, bright enough for heart surgery. The hotel is a bit out of the centre at the eastern end of town. Rooms are $8/12.50, including breakfast.

Overpriced, ***Hotel Intourist*** *(☎ 7 50 89, fax 7 41 57, root@intour.nov.su, ulitsa Velikaya (Dmitrievskaya) 16)*, by the river, charges $20/30 for its plain rooms plus breakfast. Though the Marco Polo chain pulled out of management, ***Beresta Palace Hotel*** *(☎ 3 47 07)*, on the east bank of the Volkhov, still has Western-style service and prices; $130/ 160 for a room with breakfast as well as use of the hotel's pool, health club, sauna and tennis courts.

The ***Savino (or Novgorodsky) camp site***, with tent sites and cabins, is 12km east of town, but everyone says to steer clear of it.

Places to Eat

West Side For good Russian dishes ($2 to $3), try ***Restoran Detinets*** (open from 11 am to 11 pm daily), partly in the kremlin wall. Down a winding two lane staircase, the bar serves strong coffee, ice cream topped with Russian balsam (a liquor flavoured with herbs) and *medovukha*, a locally brewed mead. The tables are tucked in the brick alcoves of what was the kremlin's Intercession Church.

Restoran Pri Dvore *(ulitsa Lyudogoshchaya (Sovietskaya) 3)* is a glum place but with jazzy food ($1 to $3 a dish) catering to foreign tour groups. For the same dishes, but in a slicker Russian atmosphere, try ***Money Bar*** next door; entrance is through the Kulinariya shop. Near the Hotel Roza Vetrov, there is a pretty good ***Pivnoy Bar*** with humble chicken Kyiv ($1.25) and *myaso pikantnoe*, which turned out to be a slab of beef buried in cheese, grilled onions and mayonnaise ($1.25).

In summer there's a ***shashlyk stand*** just outside the kremlin's east gate before the footbridge. A favourite with homesick foreigners, ***Kafe Charodeyka*** *(ulitsa Volosova (Meretskova) 1/1)* has Grolsch on tap ($3), Irish coffee ($2) and pizza ($2 to $3). Just outside the kremlin park's west side there is a ***Gril-Bar*** serving shashlyk and roast chicken.

East Side Quick, easy and favoured by the local working class, ***Kafe Kolobok*** *(ulitsa Bolshaya Moskovskaya 28)* has soups, salads, fresh sweet rolls, and *ponchiki* (fried dough sometimes filled with jam or meat or egg). ***Kafe Yaroslavna*** across the street offers much of the same. The sign for the dubious-looking nightclub upstairs says: 'No shorts or flip-flops allowed.'

The ***restaurant*** at the Beresta Palace Hotel has expensive cornflakes and toast for breakfast. The dinner menu strives to be simultaneously and exotically Western and Russian with Quattro Staggioni pizza, Novgorod the Great veal for $7 and pickled bear meat for $6.

Getting There & Away

Air The tiny airport on the road to the Yurev monastery has stopped passenger service indefinitely.

Train The train and bus stations are 1.5km west of the kremlin, at the end of prospekt Karla Marxa. A fast train goes daily to/from St Petersburg's Moscow Station ($2, 3½ hours) and there's a slower train to/from St Petersburg's Vitsebsk Station. There are also trains twice a week to Kyiv and three times a week to Murmansk.

Bus There are half a dozen buses to/from St Petersburg ($2, 3½ hours), 190km away. There's also a direct bus service to/from Smolensk and Pskov. For buses going to destinations within a 50km radius, including Seltso, purchase tickets at the small white building with a cupola between the bus and train stations. For long-distance buses, including those to Staraya Russa, use the kassa at the back of the bus stands.

Car & Motorcycle Novgorod is on the Moscow-St Petersburg highway, and an easy, pretty drive from Pskov.

Getting Around

From the bus and train stations, bus Nos 4 and 20 pass in range of the Hotel Volkhov (between the first and second stops from the stations, or a 10 minute walk), Intourist (Universam Kremlyovsky/Kremlyovsky Park stop, about 500m from the hotel), Sadko (the stop on the corner of ulitsa Bolshaya Moskovskaya and Fyodorovsky Ruchey right after the bus crosses the river; the hotel is 200m farther along Fyodorovsky

Ruchey); and Beresta Palace. For the Beresta, get off at the stadium, then cut through the park. Returning to the stations, you'll need to catch bus No 4 or 19 instead of No 20. A taxi at the time of writing cost $1 to $2.

STARAYA RUSSA
СТАРАЯ РУССА

☎ 81652 • pop 40,000

This small town, south beyond Lake Ilmen, about 100km from Novgorod, was a riverside trading post even in Varangian days. It's now best known as one of Dostoevsky's retreats, where he wrote *The Brothers Karamazov*, *The Possessed* and *The Adolescent*.

These days the author's house, a fine log cabin on the riverside, is open as a **museum**. Russian-language guides lead you through, pointing out every detail – family photos, books read at the time, identifying the people in photos on the walls of his study etc. They'll even tell you what the master liked for breakfast. The museum is open from 10 am to 6 pm Tuesday to Sunday, but you should have your hotel call ahead to double-check before making the trip.

In town, a model for many settings in *The Brothers Karamazov*, you can also see the **Transfiguration Cathedral** (Spaso-Preobrazhensky sobor, 1198) and the 17th century **Purification Church** (Tserkov Sreteniya).

Getting There & Away

Buses leave Novgorod's bus station about every two hours. The two hour trip costs $0.50. From the Staraya Russa bus station, buses No 1 and 7 head to the centre.

Pskov Region
Псковская область

PSKOV
ПСКОВ

☎ 8122 • pop 205,000

Pskov is as old as Russia but has always been Novgorod's 'little brother', even as the centre of an independent principality in the 14th and 15th centuries. It is, in fact, like a small, less glamorised Novgorod – built around a riverside kremlin with a beautiful cathedral inside, and bursting with churches designed by its own schools of architects and icon painters.

Pskov has many of the same kind of sights as Novgorod, but unfortunately it has not been as pampered in recent years. Many of the buildings are in complete ruin and being used as garbage dumps.

As a border town (30km from Estonia), Pskov's history is saturated with 700 years of war for control of the Baltic coast. The German Teutonic Knights captured it in 1240, but Alexander Nevsky routed them two years later in a famous battle on the ice of Lake Peipus (Chudskoe ozero to Russians). The Poles laid siege to it in the 16th century and the Swedes wrecked it the following century. Peter the Great used it as a base for his drive to the sea, and the Red Army fought its first serious battle with Nazi troops nearby.

This is also Pushkin country. The poet's grave and Mikhailovskoe, his family's estate, are a two hour drive away.

Orientation & Information

The Rizhskaya Hotel is three long blocks west of the Velikaya River, while almost everything else is on the east side. The town's axis is Oktyabrsky prospekt, ending at Oktyabrskaya ploshchad. There are several bookshops on Oktyabrsky prospekt; maps may be available there.

The main post office and central department store are on Oktyabrskaya ploshchad and the telephone office is two blocks up Oktyabrsky prospekt. To connect to the Internet, go around the corner of the telephone office, entrance from ulitsa Nekrasova. Charging $1 per hour, the two-computer office, open from 8 am to 5 pm Monday to Thursday (until 3.45 pm Friday) with a break from 12.30 to 1.30 pm, was on the 2nd floor but in the process of moving to the 1st floor. If you don't see the sign, ask, 'Gde Internet?'

You can change money at the Sberbank at Rizhsky prospekt 29, or at the main post office, to the right as you enter. The posted hours are from 9 am to 2 pm Saturday and Sunday and from 9 am to 5 pm Wednesday to Friday, with a break from 2 to 3 pm.

Old City

Pskov's walls formerly had four layers. The kremlin or *krom* was the religious and ceremonial centre. Its stone walls and the southern annexe, Dovmont Town (Dovmontov gorod), date from the 13th century. The Central Town (Sredny gorod), around ulitsa Pushkina, was the commercial centre, though little remains of it or its 14th century walls. The walls and towers of the Outer Town (Okolny gorod, 15th to 16th centuries) can still be seen along ulitsa Sverdlova, the Velikaya River embankment and across the tributary Pskova River.

Kremlin & Dovmont Town In Dovmont Town (named after an early prince), the foundations of a dozen 12th to 15th century churches are scattered around like discarded shoes. Through a passage is the kremlin, where the citizens' assembly *(veche)* elected its princes and sent them off to war, and Trinity Cathedral where many of the princes are buried. Some of the kremlin's towers and galleries are open. You can climb to the top of Vlasevskaya Tower, by the embankment outside Dovmont Town.

Trinity Cathedral The Trinity Cathedral (Troitsky sobor, 1699) is the best reason to visit Pskov. The gilded centre dome, as high as a 28 storey building, can be seen from 30km away on a clear day. It's a working church, though it was closed when we were there in the middle of the day. The daily morning and evening services are like a medieval scene – supplicants outside, black-robed, leather-booted acolytes at the door, chanting priests in heavy robes, and hymns from the gallery. All of this occurs beneath 17th century frescoes and a seven tiered iconostasis. Visitors are welcome (modestly dressed); there's no charge but donations are appreciated.

Mirozhsky Monastery

The attraction here is the UNESCO-protected, nonworking Cathedral of the Transfiguration of the Saviour (Spaso-Preobrazhensky sobor), with 12th century Byzantine frescoes considered to be one of the most complete representations of the biblical narrative to have survived the Mongols. The frescoes have suffered greatly from being flooded, whitewashed, painted over and wire brushed, all before the revolution. The cathedral has been under restoration since the 1960s. It's open from 11 am to 5.30 pm daily except Monday; admission is $1. It's across the Velikaya River; take bus No 2 from the vicinity of Hotel Rizhskaya.

Pogankin Palaces & Museum

The Pogankin Palaces (Pogankiny palaty) aren't palaces (though the walls are 2m thick) but the house and treasury of a very rich 17th century merchant. They now house the Pskov History & Art Museum.

Skip Soviet history in the new wing. In the courtyard, past an art gallery and silver works exhibit, the main house features the history of ancient Pskov, with icons and the Sword of Dovmont that passed from prince to prince. Upstairs are photos and furnishings of 19th to 20th century peasant life. Note the house's massive, tiled stove heaters. It's open from 11 am to 6 pm daily except Monday and the last Tuesday of the month. Entry is through the new wing on Komsomolsky pereulok.

More modest merchant houses include several at, and behind, ulitsa Sovietskaya 52, and at ulitsa Gogolya 42 and 43.

Churches

There are dozens of churches, of which two appealing ones are the Church of St Nicholas-of-Usokha (Tserkov Nikoly so Usokhi), on the west side of ulitsa Sovietskaya, near the main square, and the visibly crumbling Epiphany Church (Bogoyavlenskaya tserkov, 1495), with its big Pskov-style belfry, across the Pskova footbridge.

Bingo

For an antidote to gilded domes and kremlin walls – and for a glimpse of contemporary Pskovian life – peek in at Bingo, a genuine late 20th century gaming parlour complete with overweight, middle-aged smokers and aproned women in high heels running from table to table when someone yells the magic

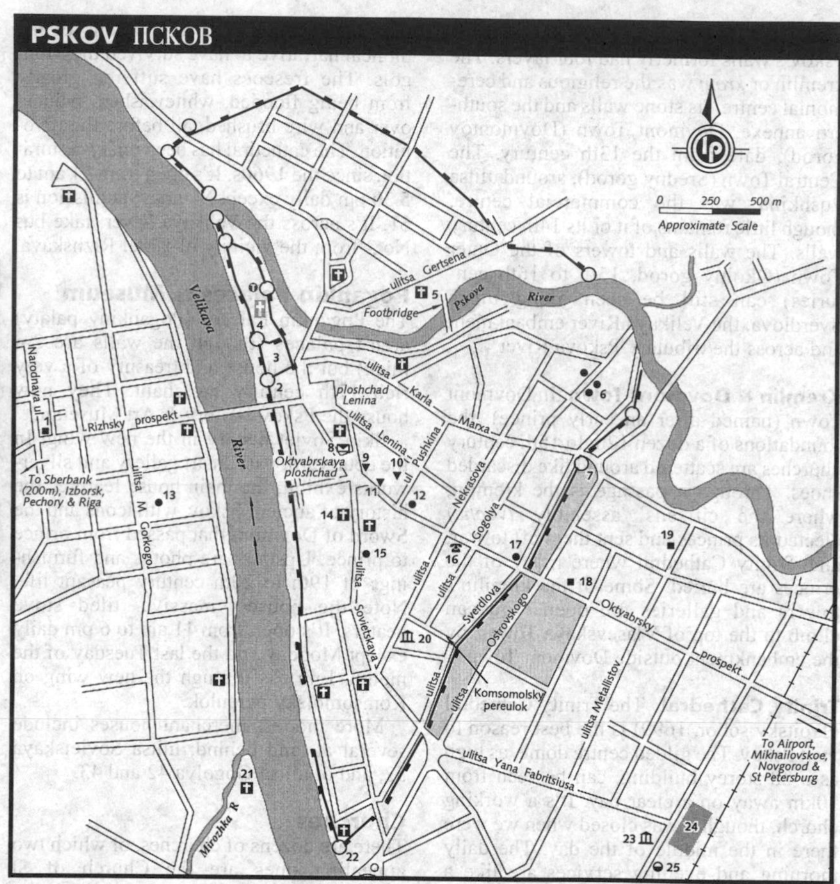

word. Bingo, at ulitsa Gorkogo 22, is open from 11 am to 5 pm daily (first game and cup of coffee free).

Places to Stay

A former dormitory, ***Hotel Krom*** on ulitsa Metallistov, has no-frills rooms with shared bath for $4. Two blocks away, the Stalinist ***Hotel Oktyabrskaya*** *(☎ 72 03 99, Oktyabrsky prospekt 36)* is conveniently located between the centre and the train station, about a 15 minute walk. The rooms facing the street are noisy, but if you don't open the windows you may be asphyxiated by the smell coming from the hot water tap (which didn't yield hot water while we were there). The rooms themselves are fine, with singles/doubles for $6/10. The bland but quiet Intourist-style ***Hotel Rizhskaya*** *(☎ 46 22 23, Rizhsky prospekt 25)*, west of the Velikaya River, has decent rooms (all with TV and phone) for $8/12.

Places to Eat

The cheap, cafeteria-style ***Kafe Cheburechnaya*** ***(Oktyabrsky prospekt 10)*** serves greasy *chebureki* (deep-fried meat dumplings), spicy Georgian soups, salads and Turkish

PSKOV ПСКОВ

PLACES TO STAY

1 Hotel Rizhskaya Гостиница Рижская
18 Hotel Oktyabrskaya Гостиница Октябрьская
19 Hotel Krom Гостиница Кром

PLACES TO EAT

9 Kafe Cheburechnaya Кафе Чебуречная
10 Kafe Uyut Кафе Уют
11 Kafe Bistro Кафе Бистро

OTHER

2 Vlasevskaya Tower Власьевская башня
3 Dovmont Town Довмонтов город
4 Kremlin & Trinity Cathedral Кремль и Троицкий собор
5 Epiphany Church Богоявленская церковь
6 Merchant Houses Торговые дома
7 Petrovskaya Tower Петровская башня
8 Main Post Office Главпочтамт
12 Gonchar Ceramics Store Магазин Гончар
13 Bingo Parlor Бинго
14 Church of St Nicholas of Usokha Церковь Николы со Усохи
15 Merchant Houses Торговые дома
16 Telephone Office Переговорный пункт
17 Souvenir Shop Сувенирный магазин
20 Pogankin Palaces & Museum Поганкины палаты и музей
21 Mirozhsky Monastery Мирожский монастырь
22 Pokrovskaya Tower Покровская башня
23 Railway Museum Железнодорожный музей
24 Train Station Железнодорожный вокзал
25 Bus Station Автовокзал

coffee. It's open from 11 am to 6 pm; the entrance is around the back.

In the same yard, ***Kafe Uyut*** has barely average food in a wooden-table, ceramic-beer-mug atmosphere, plus disco lights. The peasant cutlet *(kotleta po krestyanski)*, made of chopped pork and chicken combined, is covered in a sweet and sour mushroom sauce ($1). The *myaso po gollandski* is a beef fillet covered with cheese, mushrooms, onions, mayonnaise and an egg ($1.25).

In front of the Uyut, the 24 hour ***Kafe Bistro*** on Oktyabrsky prospekt is a minimalist, trendy cafe serving tangy cold borsch, plain meals costing about $1 to $2, a variety of desserts and espresso. The *sudak* (perch), when they have it, tastes fresh and comes sauteed or *po-polski*, boiled with an onion and egg sauce, and a side order of boiled potatoes.

The Hotel Rizhskaya has a big ***Restoran***, empty except for travellers on group tours. The ***Avrora*** at the Hotel Oktyabrskaya is a cafeteria open from 8 am to 8 pm and serving the usual salads, sandwiches, hot dogs and biscuits.

Shopping

For souvenirs, there is a shop with scarves, linen tablecloths, so-so lacquer boxes, teaware and enamelled jewellery on the corner of ulitsa Sverdlova and prospekt Oktyabrsky. Gonchar, a bit farther down on Oktyabrsky, has locally made ceramics.

Getting There & Away

Air Pskov's small, barely used airport has flights to Moscow.

Train There are several trains a day to St Petersburg's Warsaw or Vitsebsk Stations ($3 to $16, four to six hours). One train a day goes to Moscow ($9 to $16, 12 hours) and Riga ($31, seven hours). Every other day a train leaves for Vilnius ($26, five hours), and two trains a week go to Tallinn ($23, seven hours).

There are three daily elektrichki to Pechory (one hour). Some of the long-distance trains might stop here too.

Bus There are no easy connections to Novgorod by train, but there are two buses daily ($2, 4½ hours) from the central bus station, near the train station. Buses for Pushkinskie Gory via Izborsk leave every three hours ($2, 2½ hours). Buses to Pechory ($0.75, 1½ hours) also leave every three hours.

Car & Motorcycle The roads to Vitsebsk (37km), St Petersburg (265km), Novgorod

(200km), Riga (280km) and Tallinn (370km) are open to foreign drivers.

Getting Around

For the Hotel Rizhskaya a taxi (about $3) is simplest; otherwise take bus No 10 or 12 from the airport to the train station, then bus No 17 from there to the hotel (Typographya stop). Bus Nos 1, 11 and 17 from the train station pass the Hotel Oktyabrskaya.

AROUND PSKOV

Izborsk
Изборск

On a ridge with wide views over the countryside, Izborsk was once the equal of Pskov. Now it's a sleepy village by the ruins of a fortress as old as Pskov's. Inside the ruins is the 14th century **Church of St Nicholas** – the parish church – and a stone tower older than the walls. Outside is the 17th century **Church of St Sergius**, which has a little exhibit on local archaeology; some pieces date from the 8th century. A path around the back of the walls leads down to a lake. The locals you'll pass toting water bottles are coming from the 12 Springs of Happiness, Love, Health etc.

Getting There & Away It's 32km from Pskov to Izborsk on the Riga road. The Novy Izborsk train station is about 10km from Izborsk; you may have a hard time catching a ride.

Mikhailovskoe
Михаиловское

The family house of Russia's most loved writer is open as part of the **Pushkin Museum Reserve**, a three hour bus ride from Pskov. Alexander Pushkin spent two phenomenally productive years under house arrest at Mikhailovskoe, his family's estate near the settlement of Pushkinskie Gory (Pushkin Hills), 130km south of Pskov. The family first came to the area in the late 1700s, when Pushkin's great-grandfather Abram Hannibal was given the land by Empress Elizabeth. The family house was destroyed during WWII and has since been rebuilt.

The 20 hectare park is open from 9 am to 4.30 pm daily except Monday and the last Tuesday of the month; it is also closed during April and November. Entry is about $1. The attraction is Pushkin's writing room with his comfy leather chair, portraits of Byron and Zhukovsky (Pushkin's mentor, also a poet) and a mini statue of Napoleon. The big, thick religious book on his writing table he supposedly grabbed from the family book case and pretended to be reading when he saw the local priest coming for a visit.

At Pushkinskie Gory, about 800m north of the bus stop, is the **Svyatogorsk Monastery**, where Pushkin was buried.

It's lovely countryside, and it can be seen as part of a day trip.

Getting There & Away The excursion bureau at the entrance to the kremlin in Pskov runs Saturday excursions. Alternatively, you can do it yourself by catching a bus to Pushkinskie Gory from the Pskov bus station. There are several buses a day ($1, 2½ hours).

The Pushkinskie Gory bus station is 4km from the Pushkin house. There used to be a bus, but it wasn't running when we were there. The walk is pleasant. From the monastery follow the road away from monastery past the bus stop. At the fork in the road, past the shiny Western-style toilets built in celebration of Pushkin's 200th birthday (they'll probably be locked), bear left. If you bear right, you'll see the Hotel Druzhba (nice rooms with bath and shower, $4/7). At the next fork, bear right again. There will be signs.

You could also try to hitch a ride on an excursion bus leaving from the Hotel Druzhba or ask a local driver (it shouldn't cost more than $1). The last bus back to Pskov from Pushkinskie Gory leaves at around 7 pm.

Pechory Monastery
Печорский Монастырь

Founded in 1473 in a ravine full of hermits' caves, this monastery has been a working cloister ever since. With all the high ground

Duels, Fools and Poets

One does not have to be in Russia very long to realise that poets are to this country what baseball stars and presidents are to the USA, or the queen and a foamy pint to England. They're quoted constantly, their birthdays are celebrated as national holidays, and there is bound to be a bronze plaque on every house they've ever slept or sneezed in. Even their wives, nannies, mistresses and dogs are caught up and turned into the legend.

On the whole, the poets – from Pushkin and Lermontov to Pasternak and Brodsky – have been heavy drinkers, gamblers, womanisers and troublemakers. Nevertheless, school children bring flowers to their graves and can recite their poems before they know how to read. On a more sombre note, many a political prisoner sent to Siberia by Stalin has recalled in their memoirs being saved from insanity by methodically reciting all 5000-plus lines of Pushkin's *Eugene Onegin*, by rote.

For visitors to Russia, the veneration and attention enjoyed by the bards is hard to understand, and all the fuss the country makes over its wordsmiths sometimes borders on the absurd. But for Russians, their poets are an untranslatable, inexhaustible source of intrigue, sensual pleasure and spirituality which strikes at the heart of the nation. None of the poets has come as close to expressing the soul of Russia as one young dandy with a protruding jaw and high forehead backed by a mass of curly hair.

Born in 1799, the son of nobility with a dollop of African blood in his lineage, Alexander Pushkin grew up in the French-speaking high society of St Petersburg. He went to school at the Lyceum in the shadow of the royal family's summer palace. Before he reached puberty, this precocious youth was using his perfect pitch, sharp wit and flawless sense of timing to hit on court women, diplomats' wives, peasant girls and the like. He and his school friends, many of them also poets, would spend their idle hours, between balls, composing odes and love poems. A child of his time, the Romantic Age, Pushkin was obsessed with obsessions – war, male honour, beautiful and unattainable women. He is said to have had a foot fetish; his heroes were Lord Byron and Napoleon.

He wrote everything from classical odes and sonnets to short stories, plays and fairy tales. He is best loved for his poems in verse, *The Bronze Horsemen* and *Eugene Onegin*, in which he nearly answered that eternal question: why do Russians (like to) suffer so much? Politically, he was a hot potato and the tsars exiled him from St Petersburg thrice, once to his home estate in Mikhailovskoe and twice to the Caucasus, where his romping with the local beauties and war-loving men added even more fuel to his poetic fire. At home in Mikhailovskoe, he is said to have spent long evenings drinking with his childhood nanny. Pushkin himself admitted she told him many of the tales which he then turned into national legends. While on long walks, he would compose aloud. To keep his arm in good shape for duelling, he carried a cane filled with rocks.

It did not help. In 1837, Pushkin was killed in a duel over his wife, Russian beauty queen Natalia Goncharova. Even today the Russian rumour mills are producing versions of this 165-year-old scandal; only the theories about JFK's assassination come close in weirdness and speculation. During the night, Pushkin's body was carried from Chyornaya Rechka in St Petersburg and buried at the monastery near his home estate.

Four years later, another Russian bard, the 26-year-old Mikhail Lermontov, would also be killed in a duel. Eerily, soon before their quick deaths, both poets had written major works in which the highly autobiographical heroes summoned their antitheses to the field. In the poetry versions, however, the heroes lived.

outside, it's an improbable stronghold, but several tsars fortified it and depended on it. A path descends under the St Nicholas Church (Nikolskaya tserkov, 1564) into a sea of colours and architectural styles, where about 70 monks still live. Taking photos of the buildings is acceptable but not of the monks.

The central yellow church is really two buildings – at ground level is the ori-ginal Assumption Cathedral (Uspensky sobor), built into the caves, and upstairs is the 18th century baroque Intercession Church (Pokrovskaya tserkov). Below the belfry on the left is the entrance to the caves, where some 10,000 bodies – monks, benefactors and others – are bricked up in vaults, with more dying to get in.

Before WWII, this area was in independent Estonia and reportedly one-third of the people speak Estonian. The caves and churches can be visited. There are Russian-language tours of the monastery available from a booth at the entrance.

To visit the caves, you'll have to find a monk willing to lead you down through the spiderweb of dark, spooky, nearly freezing sand tunnels. Everyone carries a candle, which in places you can thrust through holes in the tunnel walls to see the wooden coffins lying lopsided on top of each other. The monks insist that there has never been the smell of decay. At the exit to the caves, you'll be shown an ancient coffin burned around the edge (supposedly this happened when some evil-doer tried to open it).

At the entrance to the grounds is the summer carriage of Peter the Great's daughter, the licentious Anna Ioannovna, who – as the story goes – came to have some fun with the monks and didn't leave until winter, on a sleigh.

It's possible for men to stay at the monastery, and eat with the monks in their modest cafeteria. Women must have head, shoulders and knees covered; wraparound skirts and shawls are provided at the monastery entrance.

There are buses and trains to the area (Pechory is an hour west of Pskov on the Riga and Tallinn lines).

Kaliningrad Region Калининградская область

A disconnected wedge of Russia too strategic to have been left in anyone else's hands, the 15,100 sq km of the Kaliningrad region lies between Lithuania, Poland and the Baltic Sea. From the 13th century until 1945, Kaliningrad was German, part of the core territory of the Teutonic Knights and their successors, the dukes and kings of Prussia. Its capital, now named Kaliningrad, was the famous German city Königsberg.

After WWI, East Prussia (the northern half of which the Kaliningrad region approximates) was separated from the rest of Germany. Hitler's desire to reunite it was one of the sparks that lit WWII. The three month campaign by which the Red Army took it in 1945 was one of the fiercest of the war, with hundreds of thousands of casualties on both sides.

Russia's Baltic Fleet is headquartered at Baltiysk, and therefore the entire region was closed to Westerners until 1991. Many areas were off limits even for locals without special permission. Though hundreds of thousands of soldiers have been moved out of the area in the 1990s, the area is still strongly militarised. Underlying its geographical vulnerability, the region's future is shrouded in unsubstantiated rumours of eventual reunification with Germany, or the establishment of a US-backed, independent, fourth Baltic State.

Kaliningrad is most frequently visited by elderly German 'nostalgia tourists', returning to what was once their homeland. Relatively few independent travellers make their way there – unfortunate as the area is unique in Russia. It's not only the country's westernmost, youngest and smallest region, but people here are faced daily with examples of what life was like before and outside the Soviet Union. All of this, plus the feeling that they live on foreign soil, gives the

population (just under 945,000) a different view of nationhood, identity and nationalism than in other parts of Russia.

The region is rich with tourism potential. Aside from the modern, urban thrills of Kaliningrad city, a number of excellent day-trip options will acquaint you with countryside Prussian castle ruins, as well as sunny beaches, the highest sand dunes in Europe, thick pine forests, clean lakes and the world's largest amber mine.

Visas

Unless you're flying, to reach the Kaliningrad region from anywhere else means you must be in possession of either a double or multiple-entry Russian visa (if you arrive from somewhere else in Russia), and/or visas for its neighbouring countries. These must be arranged in advance through their individual consulates, or through a reliable tourist agency. Be sure to know which countries your train or bus passes through and whether citizens of your country require a visa to be there (citizens of some Western nations, for example, do not require visas for the Baltic States). In Kaliningrad, the main OVIR office (☎ 22 82 74, ☎ 22 82 82) is located at Sovietsky prospekt 13, room 9.

Disabled Travellers

Inaccessible transport, lack of ramps and lifts and no centralised policy for people with physical limitations make the Kaliningrad region a challenging destination for wheelchair-bound travellers. In Kaliningrad, Hotel Kaliningrad and the Italian Café are wheelchair accessible. The staff at the Society for Invalids (☎ 21 37 98), ulitsa Kutuzova 2, are glad to provide help or information to visiting tourists.

Getting Around

Train & Bus Train services in the Kaliningrad region have been cut back over the last few years. They are less frequent and usually take longer than buses, the preferred method of transport in the area. A wide array of buses runs from Kaliningrad to neighbouring towns.

Car & Motorcycle The wide and well kept roads between cities (a rare beneficial spin-off of the region's heavy military presence) shouldn't blind you to the appalling condition of city and minor roads, as well as to the ever-present GAI, Russia's traffic police. On some roads in coastal regions you may encounter trilingual Russian-German-English signs telling you that you need special permission to enter that territory; you are unlikely to be stopped, but if you are, you may be taken to the local police station and subject to a small fine and lots of paperwork.

KALININGRAD КАЛИНИНГРАД

☎ 22 (within the region), ☎ 0122 (from elsewhere) • pop 426,300

Founded as a Teutonic Order fort in 1255, Königsberg joined the Hanseatic League in 1340 and from 1457 to 1618 was the residence of the grand masters of the Teutonic Order and their successors, the dukes of Prussia. The first king of Prussia was crowned here in 1701. The city centre was flattened by British air raids in August 1944 and the Red Army assault from 6 to 9 April 1945. Many of the surviving Germans were killed or sent to Siberia – the last 25,000 were deported to Germany in 1947-48. The city was renamed on 4 July 1946 (City Day celebrations are thus held on the first weekend in July) after Mikhail Kalinin, one of Lenin's henchmen who found favour with Stalin, and rebuilt and repeopled by Russians. Today the city – perhaps Russia's greenest, most tree-lined – feels larger than its population would suggest, and boasts a fascinating mix of historical legacies. Drab Soviet architecture stands next to some of the most picturesque avenues you'll find anywhere in Russia – all in the German sectors which survived the war.

Orientation

Leninsky prospekt, a broad north-south avenue, is Kaliningrad's main artery, running over 3km from the bus and main train station, the Yuzhny vokzal (South station), to the suburban Severny vokzal (North station). About halfway it crosses the Pregolya River and passes Kaliningrad's cathedral, the city's major landmark. Just north of the river, Leninsky prospekt passes through Tsentralnaya ploshchad, with the Kaliningrad Hotel and the unmistakable House of the Soviets. The city's real heart, though, is farther north, around the sprawling and always-busy ploshchad Pobedy. Extending north-west and north-east of this are the city's loveliest areas, with many parks and wooded areas.

Information

A free Russian/English guide to the city called *Welcome to Kaliningrad* is available in all hotel lobbies.

Money You can change money and get cash advances at branches of Investbank and other major banks. There are exchange bureaus at most hotels, with 24 hour service along Leninsky prospekt, and along the side of the State Technical University. The best rates are at the Stroivestbank, at Gendelya 10. Hotel Kaliningrad has an ATM.

Post The main post office is out of the way at Kosmonavta Leonova 22, about 700m north of prospekt Mira, but try the smaller, more convenient branch directly opposite the central market. For express mail, UPS (☎ 55 39 22) is at Chernyakhovskogo 66.

Telephone The Hotel Kaliningrad has a handy phone and fax office and an international information centre.

International phone calls can be made from card-operated public phone booths (St Petersburg cards work in these). Cards are available from post offices, kiosks and most major hotels. Only local calls can be made from the old and rarely functioning token-operated public phones (newspaper kiosks sell the *zhetons* for $0.08 a piece). International calls can be ordered at the telephone and fax centre at Teatralnaya 13/19, open 24 hours. Self-dial long-distance calls can be made one block south at its second office.

Email & Internet Access Two rooms inside the State Technical University (which housed the Gestapo headquarters until 1945) have been set up as Internet salons.

E-Type, inside a mini art gallery in room 155, is open from 9 am to 9 pm weekdays, until 7 pm Saturday. Upstairs in room 258, Amber Teleport (☎ 55 03 58) is open from 9 am to 6 pm weekdays, until 4 pm Saturday. Both places charge $0.75 an hour.

Travel Agencies The best travel agency in town is Baltma Tours (☎ 21 18 80, fax 22 88 40) at prospekt Mira 49. Staff are extremely helpful and can help with visas, accommodation and tours of all kinds, including politically incorrect bird, deer and wild boar hunting expeditions.

Things to See & Do

The outstanding German remnant is the red-brick Gothic **Dom**, or cathedral, founded in 1333, severely damaged during the war and, since 1992, under reconstruction. The **tomb of Immanuel Kant**, the 18th century philosopher who was born in, studied in and taught in Königsberg, is on the outer north side. A small **Kant museum** is on the top floor of the cathedral, which is open to tourists until 4.30 pm daily ($1.75/0.40 for adults/students). The fine blue Renaissance-style building just across the river to the south of the cathedral is the old **Stock Exchange** built in the 1870s, now a 'Sailors' Culture Palace'.

At the eastern end of wide Tsentralnaya ploshchad, on the site of the 1255 castle (whose ruins were dynamited in 1967-68), stands the upright-H-shaped **House of the Soviets** (Dom Sovietov), one of the ugliest Soviet architectural creations ever (no mean achievement). It has stood empty ever since it was discovered that the land below it was hollow, with a (now flooded) four level underground passage connecting to the Dom. Archaeological digs there every summer uncover something new. Just north of Tsentralnaya ploshchad, on ulitsa Universitetskaya near the university, is the justly popular **Bunker Museum** (Muzey Blindazh), the German command post in 1945 (open from 10 am to 6 pm daily).

North of the House of Soviets stretches the **Lower Pond** (Prud Nizhny or Schlossteich), a favourite recreation spot. Kaliningrad's outstanding **History & Art Museum** is housed in a reconstructed 1912 concert hall on the east bank. It's open from 11 am to 6 pm daily except Monday ($0.40). Ulitsa Chernyakhovskogo separates the pond's north end from the larger **Upper Pond** (Prud Verkhny). At its south-eastern corner are the fat red-brick **Bashya Dona** (Dohna Tower), a bastion of the city's old defensive ring now housing the **Amber Museum**, open from 10 am to 6 pm daily except Monday, and the **Rossgarten Gate**, one of the old German city gates. Another bastion, the rotund **Wrangel Tower**, stands near the south-west corner of the pond, surrounded by car repair garages. The **central market** on ulitsa Chernyakhovskogo is just to the south.

About 300m west along prospekt Mira is the 1927 **Kaliningrad Drama & Comedy Theatre**, restored in 1980. Another 200m farther on is the **zoo**, before the war considered the third best in the world, and 200m farther is the splendid **Cosmonaut Monument**, a gem of Soviet iconography. Immediately after the monument is **Kalinin Park**, an amusement ground and splendid, forest-like park on the grounds of an old German cemetery.

The ho-hum **Museum of the World Ocean** is moored along the Pregolya and open from 11 am to 6 pm Wednesday to Sunday ($1 for each of its three tours). The **Kaliningrad Art Gallery** at Moskovsky prospekt 62 features good exhibitions by local artists. At the city's northern border, along Sovietsky prospekt is the **Fifth Fort** (Pyaty Fort). One of the city's 15 forts constructed between 1872-92 as a second line of defence, and the only one open to the public (others are in current military 'use'), it's a heavily wooded ruin that's fun to explore for hidden passages. Take trolleybus No 1 to the Pyaty Fort stop.

Walks through the linden-scented, tree-lined old German neighbourhoods are the best way to experience old Königsberg: the entire area between prospekts Pobedy and Mira is particularly enchanting (ulitsa Kutuzova especially), as is the area to the north of the Wrangel Tower.

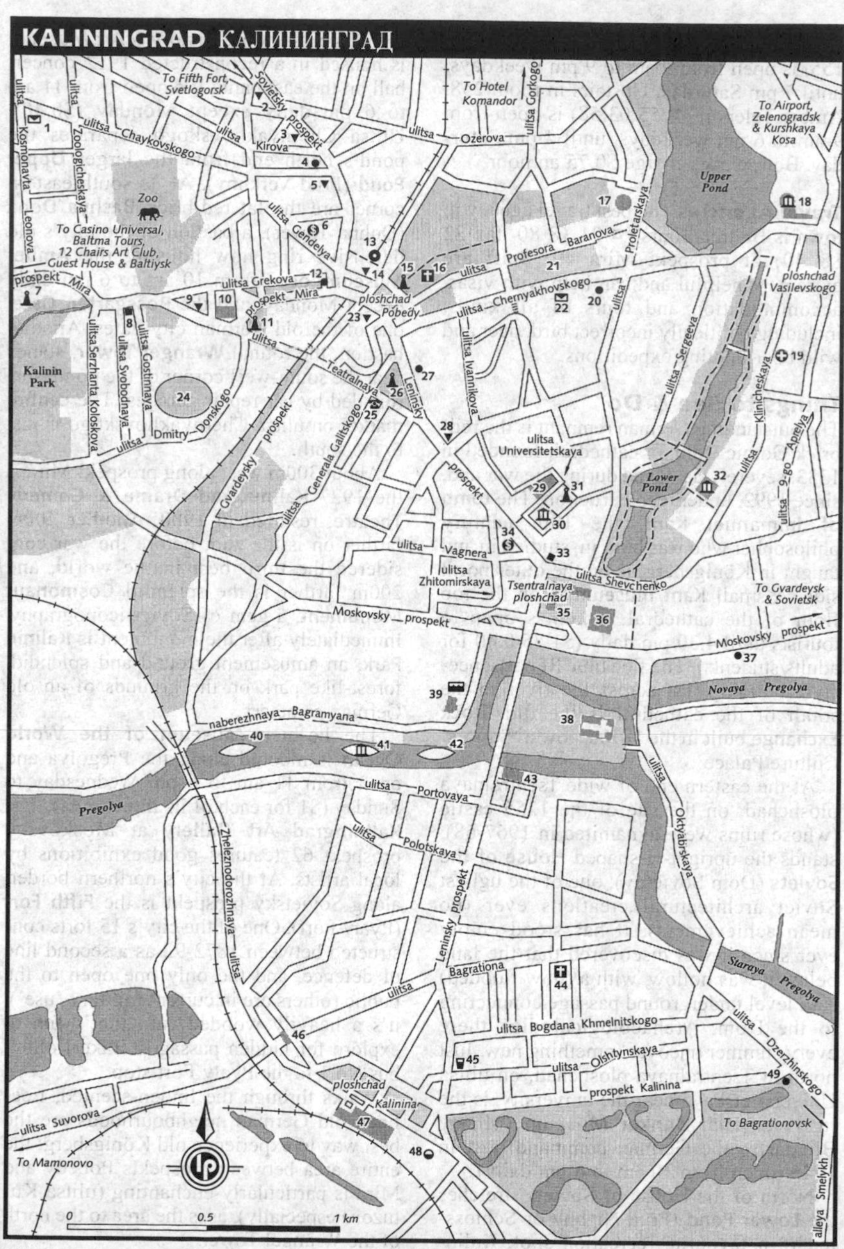
KALININGRAD КАЛИНИНГРАД
To Fifth Fort, Svetlogorsk
To Hotel Komandor
To Airport, Zelenogradsk & Kurshkaya Kosa
Upper Pond
ulitsa Kosmonavta Leonova
ulitsa Zoologicheskaya
ulitsa Chaykovskogo
ulitsa Kirova
Sovietsky prospekt
ulitsa Ozerova
ulitsa Gorkogo
ulitsa Gendelya
Zoo
To Casino Universal, Baltma Tours, 12 Chairs Art Club, Guest House & Baltiysk
ulitsa Profesora Baranova
ulitsa Proletarskaya
prospekt Mira
ulitsa Grekova
ploshchad Pobedy
ulitsa Chernyakhovskogo
ploshchad Vasilevskogo
Kalinin Park
ulitsa Serzhanta Koloskova
ulitsa Gostinnaya
ulitsa Svobodnaya
ulitsa Teatralnaya
ulitsa Ivannikova
ulitsa Sergeeva
ulitsa Klinicheskaya
ulitsa 9-go Aprelya
ulitsa Dmitry Donskogo
Gvardeysky prospekt
ulitsa Generala Galitskogo
Leninsky prospekt
ulitsa Universitetskaya
Lower Pond
ulitsa Vagnera
ulitsa Zhitomirskaya
Tsentralnaya ploshchad
ulitsa Shevchenko
To Gvardeysk & Sovietsk
Moskovsky prospekt
Novaya Pregolya
naberezhnaya Bagramyana
Pregolya
ulitsa Portovaya
ulitsa Polotskaya
ulitsa Oktyabrskaya
ulitsa Zheleznodorozhnaya
Staraya Pregolya
ulitsa Bagrationa
ulitsa Bogdana Khmelnitskogo
ulitsa Olshtynskaya
ulitsa Dzerzhinskogo
prospekt Kalinina
ploshchad Kalinina
ulitsa Suvorova
To Mamonovo
To Bagrationovsk
alleya Smelykh
0
0.5
1 km
1
2
3
4
5
6
7
8
9
10
11
12
13
14
15
16
17
18
19
20
21
22
23
24
25
26
27
28
29
30
31
32
33
34
35
36
37
38
39
40
41
42
43
44
45
46
47
48
49

KALININGRAD КАЛИНИНГРАД

PLACES TO STAY
- 8 Moskva Hotel **Гостиница Москва**
- 33 Kaliningrad Hotel **Гостиница Калининград**
- 40 Hotel Ademi **Гостиница Адеми**
- 42 Hotelschiff Hansa **Ганза**

PLACES TO EAT
- 2 Francis Drake Pub
- 3 Razgulyai **Разгуляй**
- 5 Arlenkino **Арленкино**
- 9 Gavana **Гавана**
- 14 Flagman
- 23 Valencia
- 28 Italian Gate
- 35 Kiosk Village, Oleg's, Karolina's Bar & Coffee Shop

OTHER
- 1 Main Post Office **Главпочтамт**
- 4 Main OVIR Office **ОВИР**
- 6 Stroivestbank **Стройвестбанк**
- 7 Cosmonaut Monument **Землякам Космонавтам**
- 10 Kaliningrad Drama & Comedy Theatre **Театр драмы и комедии**
- 11 Schiller Statue **Памятник Шиллеру**
- 12 State Technical University and Internet Salons **Технический Университет**
- 13 Severny Vokzal (North Station) **Северный вокзал**
- 15 Lenin Statue **Памятник В. И. Ленину**
- 16 Cathedral of Jesus the Saviour **Кафедральный собор Христа Спасителя**
- 17 Wrangel Tower **Башня Врангель**
- 18 Amber Museum, Dohna Tower & Rossgarten Gate **Музей Янтаря, Башня Дона & Варота Росгартенские**
- 19 Hospital **Больница**
- 20 UPS
- 21 Central Market **Центральный рынок**
- 22 Post Office **Почта**
- 24 Baltika Stadium **Балтика Стадион**
- 25 Telephone Office **Телефон**
- 26 Mother Russia Statue **Мать Россия**
- 27 Ostrov Sokrovishch 24-Hour store **Остров сокровищ**
- 29 University **Университет**
- 30 Bunker Museum **Музей Блиндаж**
- 31 Kant Statue **Памятник Канту**
- 32 History & Art Museum **Историко художественный музей**
- 34 Investbank
- 36 House of the Soviets **Дом Советов**
- 37 Kaliningrad Art Gallery **Художественная галерея**
- 38 Cathedral, Kant Museum & Kant's Tomb **Кафедральный собор, Музей Канта & могила Канта**
- 39 Yunost Sports Centre and Swimming Pool **Спортивный комплекс Юность и Бассейн**
- 41 Museum of the World Ocean **Музей Мирового Океана**
- 43 Former Stock Exchange **Биржа**
- 44 Church of the Holy Family **Церковь Святого семейства**
- 45 Olshtyn **Ольштын**
- 46 Brandenburg Gate **Варота Бранденбургские**
- 47 Yuzhny Vokzal (South Station) **Южный вокзал**
- 48 Bus Station **Автовокзал**
- 49 Friedland Gate **Варота Фридландские**

Places to Stay

The cheapest option is ***Hotel Ademi*** *(☎ 46 16 62)*, the westernmost floating hotel moored to the north bank of the Pregolya. Tiny singles/doubles start at $6/8. You'd be better off at ***Moskva Hotel*** *(☎ 27 20 89, prospekt Mira 19)* – locals cringe at the mention of it but its reputation is worse than it deserves. Decent single rooms cost $5-7, doubles $6.50-18. It's owned by the same team that runs the town's principal hotel, ***Kaliningrad*** *(☎ 46 94 40, fax 43 30 21, Leninsky prospekt 81)*, handily placed on Tsentralnaya ploshchad. Single rooms cost $26-54, and doubles are $38-100.

More expensive options include the second floating ship, ***Hotelschiff Hansa*** *(☎/fax 43 38 06)*. Damp rooms with breakfast cost $24/46. The best bet for your money is ***Guest House*** *(☎ 21 76 93, ulitsa Kutuzova 22)*, located in the city's prettiest district. Rooms are $26/52 with breakfast. There are only four rooms in this lovely home, so book in advance.

The fanciest place in town, with indoor pool and sauna, is ***Hotel Komandor*** *(☎ 44 18 85, fax 44 17 27, Sczastlivaya 1)*, about 5km out from the centre. Rooms with a compulsory $8 breakfast will come to a total of $76/105.

Places to Eat

The city's culinary oasis is ***Gavana*** *(prospekt Mira 10/12)*, a Cuban restaurant with a jazzy decor, open from 11 am to 11 pm daily. Exotic stuffed chicken, French juliennes and empanadas are among the many great dishes here, all costing under $5. The other absolute must-visit is ***12 Chairs Art Club*** *(prospekt Mira 67)*. Dark and ambient, this is the cosiest, most eclectic place in town. It has a full menu and lots of cocktails to keep you happy from noon to 1 am daily.

Along Sovietsky prospekt there are also a few good bets. ***Arlenkino*** at No 11 has decent but greasy meat and fish dishes and an outdoor terrace. Farther north at No 15 is the splendid ***Razgulyai***, with tasty meals (most around $4) in a cheerful, spacious, tavern-style basement, the only place like it in town. Kaliningrad's first English pub, ***Francis Drake***, at No 19a, is decidedly dull but British lagers and bitters are on tap for $2 a pint.

Within the kiosk village opposite the Hotel Kaliningrad, ***Oleg's*** at No 52 smells of the nouveau riche but serves Uzbek cuisine at reasonable prices. Try the sandwiches or the gulyash at ***Karolina's Bar***, at No 2. Nothing can beat the smell of freshly ground coffee beans inside the comfy, old-fashioned ***coffee shop*** at Kiosk No 63. It's open from 11 am to 10 pm daily and serves the best coffee and banana splits in town.

If you're after recognisable Western fare, you'll have to go to a more expensive place. A touristy spot is ***Italian Café*** *(Leninsky prospekt 27)*, serving overpriced pasta dishes. Pizza is served from 5 pm and it closes at 2 am. The stuffy ***Valencia*** *(ploshchad Pobedy 1)* has exotic Spanish dishes (yes, those are real piranhas in the aquarium). For a delicious meal and techno-tango with local Mafia types, head to the sublimely over-the-top ***Casino Universal*** *(Mira prospekt 43)*, open from noon to 6 am daily. The extensive menu includes 40 starters and 33 desserts. The ***Flagman*** restaurant on ploshchad Pobedy is also expensive but reliable.

The outdoor ***cafe*** in the park opposite ploshchad Pobedy sells excellent smoked fish and is the city's most popular all-night hang-out. The city's top club is the spectacular three storey ***Olshtyn*** *(Olshtynskaya 1)*, which also has a billiard room and restaurant.

There's an excellent ***supermarket*** *(Leninsky prospekt 16)*, open from 8 am to 11 pm daily, and a 24 hour shop inside the Ostrov Sokrovishch department store, just south of ploshchad Pobedy.

Getting There & Away

Air Kaliningrad's domestic and international airports (☎ 45 94 26) are 22km north of the city, near the village of Khrabrovo. Scandinavian Airlines (SAS; airport office ☎ 45 94 52, city office at ploshchad Pobedy 4 ☎ 55 01 32) has six weekly flights between Kaliningrad and Copenhagen. Kaliningrad Airlines (☎ 44 14 63) has two flights daily to Moscow, three flights weekly to St Petersburg (Pulkova Airlines flies an additional three to/from St Petersburg), and flights to a host of other cities in Russia and the CIS. Aeroflot (☎ 55 53 53) has daily flights to Moscow. The joint offices of Kaliningrad Airlines and Aeroflot are opposite the train station on ploshchad Kalinina.

Train There are two stations in the city: Severny vokzal (North station; ☎ 49 99 91) just off ploshchad Pobedy; and the larger Yuzhny vokzal (South station; ☎ 49 26 75), on ploshchad Kalinina. All long-distance and many local trains go from Yuzhny vokzal, passing through but not always stopping at Severny vokzal.

The daily *Königsberg Express* runs directly from Berlin to Kaliningrad. Bookings in Germany can be made through Rail Tours Mochel Reisen (☎ 7821-430 37, fax 429 98). There are also two trains daily between Kaliningrad and Brest, Kyiv (Kiev), Odesa and Warsaw. There are numerous trains from Kaunas and Vilnius, some originating from St Petersburg or Moscow.

Bus The bus station (☎ 44 36 35) is on ploshchad Kalinina at the southern end of Leninsky prospekt. There are cheap daily buses from Vilnius, Kaunas and Šiauliai, four buses daily from Smiltyne along the Neringa Spit and two from Klaipeda via

Sovietsk. Eurolines runs a daily, overnight service to/from Tallinn via Riga.

There are a number of bus services between Poland or Germany and Kaliningrad, operated by König Auto of Kaliningrad (☎ 43 04 80). The starting points in Poland are Olsztyn, Warsaw and Gdansk; in Germany, Bremen, Stuttgard, Hanover and Essen. König Auto also runs a weekly bus to and from Prague.

Car & Motorcycle From the south it is possible to enter Kaliningrad from Poland although the queues at the Lithuanian border crossings at Kybartai or on the Neringa Spit are not as monstrous. You'll find petrol is widely available.

Sea Passenger sea services have been severely cut back over the last few years, and it is highly recommended to double-check schedules. Anjuta (☎ 22 89 98) runs a daily hydrofoil service between Kaliningrad and Elblag in Poland, one-way tickets costing around $10. Inflot Ferry Agent (☎ 47 14 42, fax 46 15 91) has a weekly service to Rostock, and twice weekly to Travermünde, both in Germany. For general port information call ☎ 47 22 17.

Getting Around

Tickets for trams, trolleybuses, buses and minibuses are sold only by controllers inside. Only monthly passes are sold at the kiosks near main bus and tram stops. There are taxi stands outside all main hotels, or call ☎ 058 for a pick-up. To hire a private cab with driver for $5 per hour, call ☎ 46 59 33.

SVETLOGORSK СВЕТЛОГОРСК

☎ 2533 (within the region), ☎ 011533 (from elsewhere) • pop 13,200

Svetlogorsk (formerly Rauschen) is a pleasant, green coastal town 35km north-west of Kaliningrad. The narrow beach is backed by high, steep sandy slopes and the town is dotted with pretty wooden houses which are the main reason visitors come here; avid sunbathers head to Zelenogradsk or the Kurshkaya Kosa for heavier beach action.

On ulitsa Oktyabrskaya are the 25m **water tower** and the curious red-tile-domed Jugendstil (Art Nouveau) **bathhouse**. Around the corner is a small bufet which serves delicious, local spring water to sanatorium residents – but if you ask nicely, they'll let you have a glass. About 200m east of the main beach promenade is an impressive, colourful **sundial**, believed to be the largest in Europe.

At the eastern end of ulitsa Lenina there is a **Commemorative Chapel**, opened in 1994 on the former site of a kindergarten. It is a memorial to the 23 children and nine adults who died after an A-26 Soviet military transport plane crashed into the building. The tragedy was hushed up for almost 20 years and only came to light when the Orthodox Church built the chapel.

There are several hotel options in the town, including some very inexpensive ***ex-sanatoriums*** and a ***camping ground***, all on Kaliningradsky prospekt, about 500m west of the Svetlogorsk II train station. The top hotel in the entire Kaliningrad region is the elegant ***Hotel Rus*** *(☎/fax 3705, Vereshtschagina 8)* at the eastern end of the promenade. Sumptuous singles/doubles start at $49/59. Ask for a room with a sea view.

There are 12 trains a day from Kaliningrad to Svetlogorsk. More convenient are the 20 or so buses and taxi buses which make the trip daily, leaving from the bus station and stopping outside the Severny vokzal on prospekt Sovietsky (timetables are posted on the street at the bus stop). Svetlogorsk's bus station is 500m west of the train station, on the corner of ulitsa Lenina and Kaliningradsky prospekt.

YANTARNY ЯНТАРНЫЙ

☎ 2533 • pop 2000

Yantarny (formerly Palmnicken), 50km west of Kaliningrad and formerly a closed village, is open to tourists with special permission. This little village, whose name means 'made of amber', is (depending on your interests) worth the hassle needed to visit: its Russky Yantar amber mine (with offices in Kaliningrad city ☎ 0112-45 04 58, fax 46 67 29), around which the entire village revolves, produces over 90% of the world's amber, despite the fact that it can't find the cash to pay its employees.

Groups of 10 or more only can make advance arrangements to visit the small **amber museum** inside the mine by calling its official guide, Albert Schlosser (☎ 7353). He speaks German and Russian and works from Monday to Thursday. Museum exhibits include a hefty 2.86kg amber rock and portraits of Lenin made from amber beads.

On the beach, several hundred metres west of ulitsa Sovietskaya, is a waste water pipe outside the barbed wire surrounding the vast, lunar-like mine pit. Here, men and women, dressed in full fisherman's gear, fish for amber in the black waste water that shoots from the pipe. Some catch up to half a kilogram in just four hours and will be happy to sell you the small unpolished pieces for about $140 per kilo.

Note that the individual traveller is risking a seance with the local police without special permission to be in town, even though the police themselves aren't sure how this permission can be obtained. If you're set on going, take a bus (you won't be stopped) and ask for the necessary papers at the police station (☎ 7102) at ultisa Sovietskaya 57, where the police can levy a small fine but probably will let you go with a lecture after you fill out endless forms. In any case, the mine will not grant individual tourists permission to visit the museum. The best you can hope for is a view of the pit.

Only buses go to Yantarny. Eight per day make the trip from outside Kaliningrad's Severny vokzal ($0.55, 80 minutes).

BALTIYSK
БАЛЬТИЙСК

☎ 245 • pop 31,000

On the north side of the Kaliningrad Lagoon's narrow opening to the sea is the naval port of Baltiysk (formerly Pillau). Though it's a closed military city (it's home to Russia's Baltic Fleet headquarters), Baltiysk has been open to tourists with easily obtainable special permission since 1992. A visit is highly worth the advance planning and extra cash. The several old structures which survived the war (Pillau held on a full two weeks after Königsberg fell, surrendering to the Soviets on 26 April 1945) are what give this scenic town its charm. Facing the towering statue of Lenin in the centre of town is the impressive neogothic present-day **headquarters of the Baltic Fleet**, built in 1803. Not far away is the 16th century **Sailor's Club**, which was a casino for wartime officers.

The remains of two **castles** built by the Swedes under Gustav Adolf von Schweden during their brief period of domination are also of interest. The one diagonally opposite the Sailor's Club (1629-35) still has its walls and moat intact, though the interior now houses an off-limits military school and car park.

On the other side of the harbour in the village of Kosa, on the northern tip of the Baltiyskaya Kosa (the spit which extends to Poland and along which thousands of Germans fled on foot in the last months of the war), are the ruins of the second castle. The seaside landscape is breathtaking. Not far away are the dilapidated remnants of giant aeroplane hangars, standing eerily deserted in the spot which was once a teeming German resort and harbour.

Everyone but Kaliningrad residents must arrive in Baltiysk accompanied and in private transport (documents are rigorously checked at a border to the city). The easiest way is to go through the very friendly and flexible Golden Orchid travel agency (☎ 0122-53 85 53, or ☎ 8-245-21 098 in Baltiysk), at Frunze 6 in Kaliningrad. It can arrange permission, transport, a guide and accommodation for about $50.

KURSHKAYA KOSA
КУРШКАЯ КОСА

☎ 250

The Kurshkaya Kosa is the Russian half of the 98km-long, 2 to 4km-wide Curonian Spit, which divides the Curonian (also known as Courland) Lagoon from the Baltic Sea. It shares the same dramatic landscape as the northern Lithuanian half – high sand dunes, pine forests, an exposed western coast and a calmer eastern coast – only it's less touristy and therefore ideal for those who want to experience its beauty in isolation.

A few fishing-cum-holiday villages dot the eastern coast. The main ones, from south to north, are Lesnoy (formerly Sarkau), Rybachy (formerly Rossitten), the largest with a population of 1200, and Morskoe (formerly Pillkoppen). Admiring the dunes (the most magnificent are just south of Morskoe) and quiet walks through the pine forests, or by the sea and lagoon, are the highlights of any visit.

There are places to stay in each village. The cheapest is the ***ZRP Rest Home*** (no telephone) in Rybachy on Pogranichniy 11 (the first road to your left as you walk towards the village from the bus stop), which has sparse but comfortable rooms overlooking the lagoon for $2.25 a night. The best restaurant in the area is ***Tractor***, across from the Rybachy bus stop on the main road, serving locally caught eel and delicious fish soup.

Four buses a day from Kaliningrad (via Zelenogradsk) take the road up the peninsula to Smiltyne at its northern tip. There are about three others which run daily between Zelenogradsk and Morskoe.

Note that all but Kaliningrad residents in theory need special permission to be in the area (in theory available through any travel agency in Kaliningrad); it's considered a border zone. In practice, if you travel by bus, no one will stop you, and you can freely spend a few days there without any problems.

Northern European Russia
Северно-Европейская Россия

Northern European Russia – from the Gulf of Finland to the Arctic Barents Sea and from Finland to the Ural Mountains – is a fabric of pine and birch forest, marshes, tens of thousands of lakes and, in the far north, tundra and dwarf forests. It's a potential paradise for hikers, boaters, campers and skiers, boasting boundless, pristine wilderness. This, coupled with its recent accessibility and relatively inexpensive costs, makes it one of the world's most attractive outdoor sporting destinations.

The White Sea, cutting in deeply from the Barents, defines the geography of the far north. Sandwiched between it and Finland is Russia's Karelian Republic. Its capital, Petrozavodsk, is the base for seeing the extraordinary wooden buildings of Kizhi Island. Beyond the White Sea on the Arctic-facing Kola Peninsula – 'Russian Lapland' – is the port of Murmansk, the world's largest city inside the Arctic Circle. Farther east, the 587,000 sq km Arkhangelsk region is an adventurer's paradise. Finally, perched in the White Sea itself are the magical Solovetsky Islands, whose beauty is as breathtaking as its Gulag history is grim.

In the central north, from the Vologda region towards Arkhangelsk and Kola, lie dozens of monasteries and churches, dating from before the reign of Ivan the Terrible.

HISTORY

Early Russian incursions into the region came from Novgorod (see the History section at the start of the Western European Russia chapter). By the 12th century, Novgorod was a European political and commercial centre that began expanding aggressively up Karelia's rivers and lakes to the White Sea. Today most of the north's permanent Russians are descendants of Novgorodian merchants, adventurers, hunters and fishers, and are known as Pomory (*'po more'* means 'up to the sea').

HIGHLIGHTS

- Feeling Arctic winds nip at your face in the wild, beautiful nature of the Lapland Biosphere Reserve
- Imagining what the walls have witnessed over the centuries at the kremlin on Solovetsky Islands
- Counting the onion domes of the Cathedral of the Transfiguration, Kizhi Island
- Pretending you're part of another era at Malye Korely, Arkhangelsk
- Climbing the Bell Tower at the Archbishop's Courtyard and St Sophia's Cathedral, Vologda
- Skiing on some of Russia's best slopes in Kirovsk
- Fighting off mosquitoes on a boat trip in Karelia

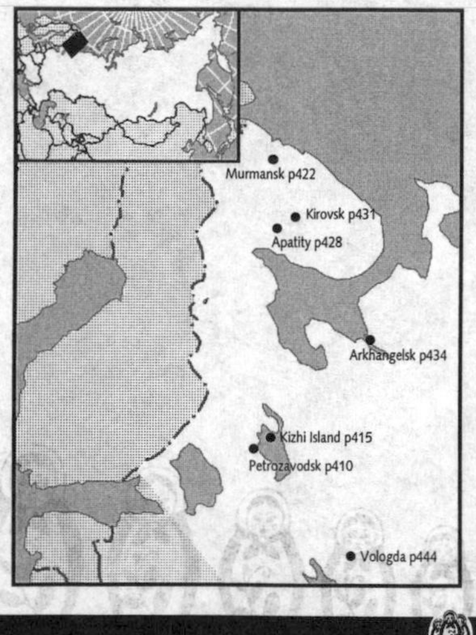

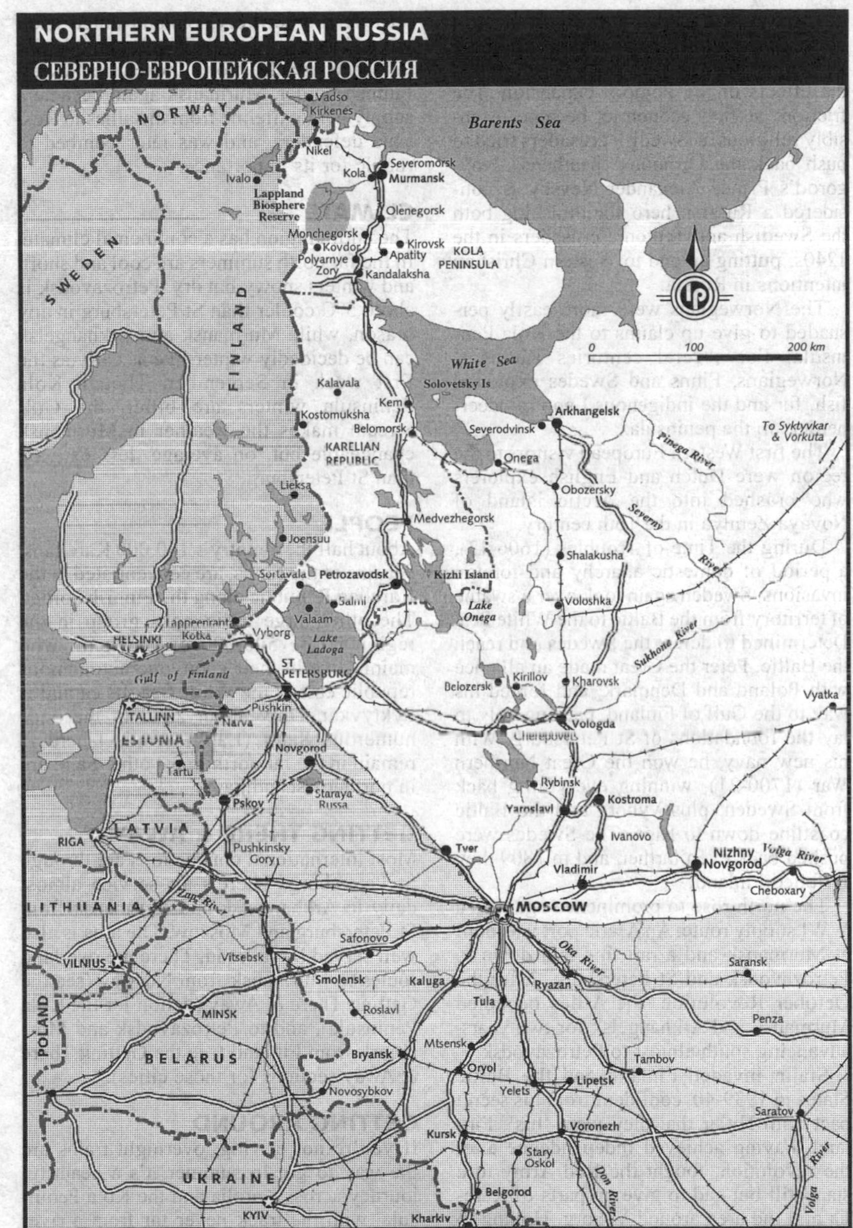
NORTHERN EUROPEAN RUSSIA
СЕВЕРНО-ЕВРОПЕЙСКАЯ РОССИЯ
Barents Sea
NORWAY
SWEDEN
FINLAND
Vadso
Kirkenes
Nikel
Ivalo
Lappland Biosphere Reserve
Severomorsk
Kola
Murmansk
Olenegorsk
Monchegorsk
Kovdor
Kirovsk
Apatity
Polyarnye Zory
Kandalaksha
KOLA PENINSULA
0
100
200 km
White Sea
Solovetsky Is
Kalavala
Kem
Kostomuksha
Belomorsk
KARELIAN REPUBLIC
Arkhangelsk
Severodvinsk
To Syktyvkar & Vorkuta
Pinega River
Onega
Obozersky
Severny
River
Lieksa
Medvezhegorsk
Joensuu
Shalakusha
Sortavala
Petrozavodsk
Kizhi Island
Salmi
Valaam
Lake Onega
Voloshka
Lappeenranta
Vyborg
Lake Ladoga
HELSINKI
Kotka
Gulf of Finland
ST PETERSBURG
Sukhone River
Kirillov
Belozersk
Kharovsk
Vyatka
TALLINN
Pushkin
Narva
ESTONIA
Cherepovets
Vologda
Novgorod
Tartu
Staraya Russa
Pskov
Rybinsk
Kostroma
Yaroslavl
Ivanovo
LATVIA
RIGA
Pushkinsky Gory
Tver
Nizhny Novgorod
Volga River
Vladimir
Cheboxary
LITHUANIA
MOSCOW
Safonovo
VILNIUS
Vitsebsk
Oka River
Saransk
Smolensk
Kaluga
Ryazan
Tula
MINSK
Roslavl
Penza
POLAND
Mtsensk
BELARUS
Bryansk
Oryol
Tambov
Lipetsk
Yelets
Novosybkov
Saratov
Kursk
Voronezh
Stary Oskol
Don River
Volga River
UKRAINE
Belgorod
KYIV
Kharkiv

The Swedes, who held sway in most of present-day north-western Russia, up to and including the Kola Peninsula, began to feel the effects of the Pomory expansion. The friction, at first economic, became ostensibly religious as Swedish crusaders tried to push back the Orthodox 'heathens'. Novgorod's Prince Alexander Nevsky is considered a Russian hero for thrashing both the Swedish and Teutonic crusaders in the 1240s, putting an end to Western Christian intentions in Russia.

The Norwegians were more easily persuaded to give up claims to the Kola Peninsula. For several centuries Russians, Norwegians, Finns and Swedes exploited fish, fur and the indigenous Lapp reindeer-herders in the peninsula.

The first Western European visitors to the region were Dutch and English explorers who crashed into the Arctic island of Novaya Zemlya in the 16th century.

During the Time of Troubles (1606-13), a period of domestic anarchy and foreign invasions, Sweden again took over a swathe of territory from the Baltic to the White Sea. Determined to defeat the Swedes and reach the Baltic, Peter the Great made an alliance with Poland and Denmark, and forced his way to the Gulf of Finland, pausing only to lay the foundations of St Petersburg. With his new navy, he won the Great Northern War (1700-21), winning everything back from Sweden, plus Vyborg and the Baltic coastline down to Riga. The Swedes were pushed back even farther, and in 1809 they forfeited Finland.

The north rose to prominence again as a WWI supply route. An Arctic port was built at Murmansk and a rail line laid down to Petrozavodsk and St Petersburg. After the October Revolution, the Allies occupied Murmansk and Arkhangelsk for two years, advancing south almost to Petrozavodsk.

Stalin invaded Finland and the Baltic States in 1939-40, confident from his secret pact with Hitler that they were 'his'. Finland, having achieved independence after the revolution, fought the Red Army to a standstill but had to give up parts of Karelia and the area around Vyborg. Hoping to retrieve this territory, Finland allied itself with Germany during WWII, and Hitler launched attacks along the entire Soviet-Finnish border. Murmansk again became a supply port, a lifeline from the allies to Russia's defenders, and was later bombed to rubble for its importance.

CLIMATE

The entire region has a continental climate. In the far north summers are cool and short, and winters snowy but dry. Petrozavodsk is about 5°C cooler than St Petersburg in any season, while Murmansk and Arkhangelsk can be decidedly winter-like as early as the first week in September. Though Kola Peninsula winters are bitter, the Gulf Stream makes the weather in Murmansk changeable but, on average, less extreme than St Petersburg.

PEOPLE

About half the country's 140,000 Karelians, cousins of the Finns, are concentrated in the Karelian Republic along the Finnish border. The other large indigenous group in the region is the 500,000 or so Komi, who mainly live in their eponymic autonomous republic east of the White Sea. Its capital is Syktyvkar. Only about 2000 of the once numerous Sami (Lapp) reindeer-herders remain in the far north; most other Sami are in northern Scandinavia.

GETTING THERE & AWAY

Most international connections are through St Petersburg. There's air service almost daily to Arkhangelsk and Murmansk from St Petersburg and Moscow. The area is also well served by railroad. There are overland routes to Murmansk from Norway (see the Getting There & Away section for the Kola Peninsula), and to Petrozavodsk and Murmansk from Finland (see the Getting There & Away sections for those cities).

GETTING AROUND

If you're not driving, overnight trains are the way to go. In summer it's a beautiful journey across Karelia and the Kola Peninsula, with the track never far from a river bank or lakeshore, endless forest and tundra stretching beyond and, industrial centres aside, crystal-clear air.

Within regions, long-distance buses provide convenient and inexpensive transport. A car can also be convenient, though break-ins are frequent in the big cities. For most stretches the St Petersburg-Murmansk highway is a fine road, though car-jacking is not unheard of around Petrozavodsk and on the southern stretch of the Kola Peninsula.

Karelia
Карелия

Karelia is a vast wilderness stretching from St Petersburg to the Arctic Circle – half is forest and much of the rest is water. Its 60,000 lakes include Ladoga and Onega lakes, the two largest in Europe.

The original Karelians are related to Finns, and western Karelia has at various times been part of Sweden, Finland and Russia. Tourism officials boast of 55 nationalities in the capital, Petrozavodsk, though 70% of the people who live here are Russian. Many are the offspring of prisoners and deportees sent by Stalin in 1931-33 to dig the White Sea Canal that links rivers and lakes into a domestic water route to the Arctic.

Karelia is a republic within Russia. Its main outputs are timber and minerals. Finnish, the closest thing outside Russian that the Karelians have to a national language, is commonly used along with Russian (though Karelian, a Finno-Ugric language, is spoken by some); bilingual signs are common.

PETROZAVODSK
ПЕТРОЗАВОДСК

☎ 8142 • pop 250,000

Tourists come here for one thing: to see the famous collection of old wooden buildings on Kizhi Island, 66km north-east of the city across Lake Onega (it's the most famous of the lake's 1368 islands). Yet it's also a starting point for adventure seekers wishing to experience the Karelian wilderness.

Petrozavodsk has a short, grim history, despite the pleasant, laid-back feel of its present-day, tree-lined avenues and extensive parklands. It was created in 1703 as an iron foundry and armaments plant for Peter the Great (its name means 'Peter's Factory'), and the town was subsequently used by both the tsars and the Bolsheviks as a place of exile for St Petersburg's troublemakers.

Orientation

The city straddles the Lososinka River where it enters Lake Onega (Onezhskoe ozero). Its axis, prospekt Marxa, runs all the way to the ferry terminal (vodnyy vokzal), and the main drag, prospekt Lenina, stretches from the train station down to the river.

City maps in Russian are on sale at most bookshops; try Ex-Libris at prospekt Lenina 23 or Karel Kniga at ulitsa Kuybysheva 22, which also has good books on local history, postcards and used books.

Information

Change money at any of the hotels or at one of the dozens of exchange bureaus competing for your dollars. There is a Sberbank at ulitsa Kuybysheva 17, and ATMs in the post office and at the train station.

The telephone/telegraph (open 24 hours) and post offices are on the corner of ulitsa Dzerzhinskogo and ulitsa Sverdlova. Though there are still a few old-style public phones which work for free, there are numerous card-operated types; your St Petersburg cards work in these as well.

The best place for Internet access is at the Internet Klub (☎ 77 47 75) at ulitsa Anokhina 20. It's open from 10 am to 7 pm Monday to Saturday and charges $0.75 an hour. The Internet Salon (☎ 77 43 27) at ulitsa Antikaynena 22 charges $1 an hour and offers provider services.

Staff at Intourist (☎ 77 47 57, fax through Finland at 358-013-677 603, intourist@onego.ru), at the Hotel Severnaya, are very friendly and can help with organising any kind of individual or group tour of the area. They can also organise transportation to Finland. Turist (☎ 77 58 65, fax 76 24 99) at ulitsa Sverdlova 30 also organises tours

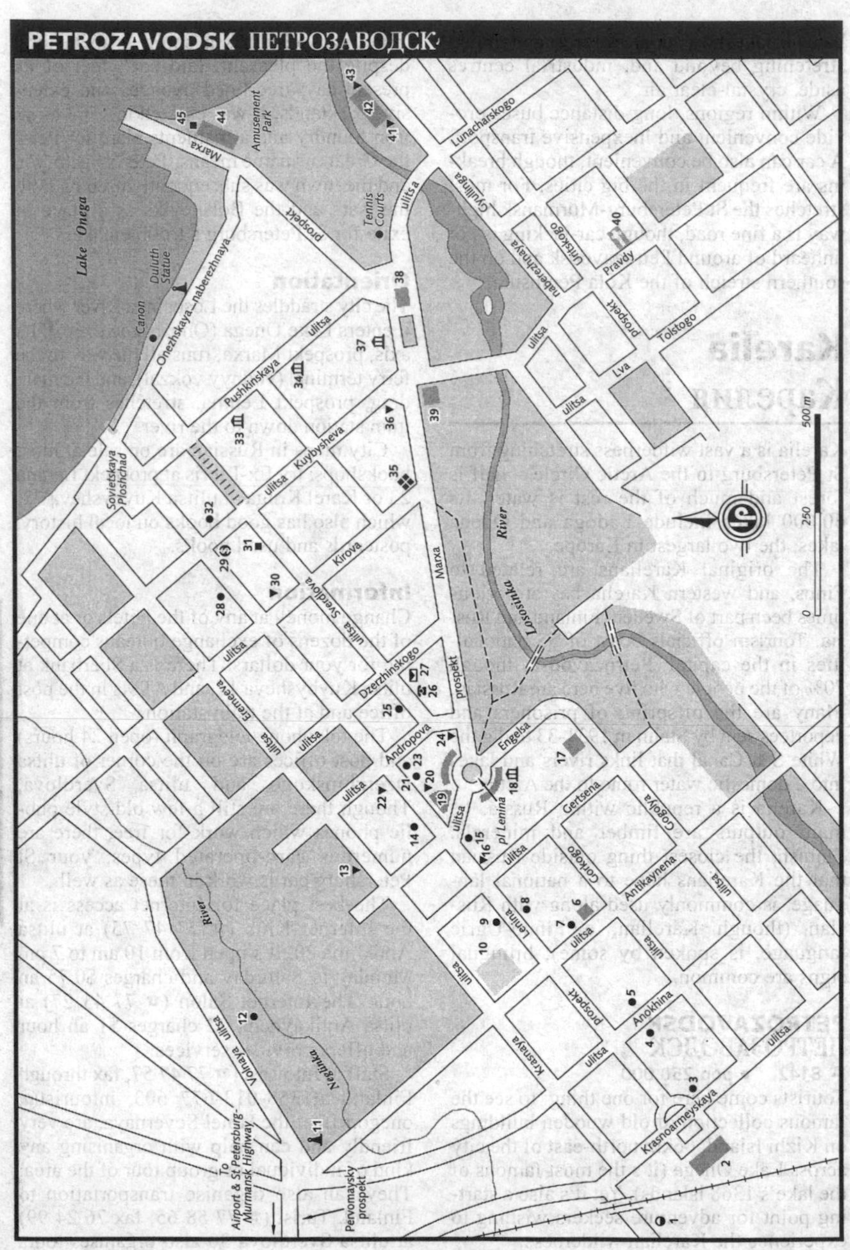
PETROZAVODSK ПЕТРОЗАВОДСК
Lake Onega
Duluth Statue
Canon
Onezhskaya naberezhnaya
Marxa
prospekt
Amusement Park
Tennis Courts
ulitsa
Lunacharskogo
Gyullinga
naberezhnaya
Uritskogo
Pravdy
prospekt
Tolstogo
Lva
Pushkinskaya
Kuybysheva
Sovietskaya Ploshchad
Kirova
Sverdlova
Dzerzhinskogo
Eremeeva
Andropova
Engelsa
pl Lenina
Gertsena
Gogolya
Gorkogo
Antikaynena
Lenina
Anokhina
Krasnaya
Krasnoarmeyskaya
Volnaya
Neglinka River
Lososinka River
Pervomaysky prospekt
To Airport & St Petersburg-Murmansk Highway
0
250
500 m
NORTHERN EUROPEAN RUSSIA

PETROZÀVODSK ПЕТРОЗАВОДСК

PLACES TO STAY

19 Hotel Severnaya Гостиница Северная
31 Karelian Government Hotel Гостиница Государства Карелии
42 Karelia Hotel Гостиница Карелия
45 Hotel Fregat & Bar Гостиница Фрегат

PLACES TO EAT

13 Ben & Jerry's Ice Cream
16 Neubrandenburg Bar & Restaurant
20 Business Klub Биснес Клуб
22 Kavkaz Кавказ
24 Petrovsky Restaurant Ресторан Петровский
30 Stolovaya Столовая
36 Kafe Morozhenoe & Tsentralny Bar Кафе Мороженое
41 Restoran Tok Ресторан Ток
43 Arirang

OTHER

1 Bus Station Автовокзал
2 Train Station Железнодорожный вокзал
3 24-Hour shop
4 Lotus Supermarket
5 Internet Klub
6 Kola-Tavs
7 Internet Salon
8 Nightclub Karmel Кармел
9 Exhibition Hall Выставочный зал
10 Central Market Центральный рынок
11 Afghan War Memorial Памятник Афганской войны
12 Drinking Well Колодец
14 Pharmacy Аптека
15 Ex-Libris Books
17 Philharmonic Hall Филармония
18 Museum of Local Studies Краеведческий музей
21 Fuji
23 Podarki Подарки
25 Turist
26 Telephone & Telegraph Office Телефон и телеграф
27 Post Office Почта
28 Finnair
29 Sberbank Сбербанк
32 Karel Books Карел Книги
33 Geological Museum Геологический музей
34 Sports Museum Дом Физкультуры
35 Department Store & Rendez-vous Bar ЦУМ
37 Fine Arts Museum Музей изобразительных искусств
38 Russian Theatre Русский театр
39 National Theatre Национальный театр
40 Cathedral of the Raising of the Cross Крестово-Воздвиженский собор
44 Ferry Terminal Водный вокзал

throughout the area and offers a pricey retreat on a tiny island near Kizhi with sauna and fishing facilities from $59 to $95 a day.

The Fuji store at prospekt Lenina 17 is open from 10 am to 8 pm daily. It sells film, and does great prints for $0.10 each. There's a well stocked pharmacy opposite the Hotel Severnaya, open from 9.30 am to 8 pm daily.

Fine Arts Museum

The Fine Arts Museum (☎ 77 37 13), prospekt Marxa 8, has a good collection of 15th to 17th century Karelian icons and some 18th to 20th century Russian paintings; it's open from 11 am to 6 pm daily except Monday. Admission for foreigners is $3 (no student price); for Russians $0.25. Tours in Russian for Russians cost $1.75; $20 in English, though discounts are available for the asking (don't be shy). Tours must be arranged in advance. This museum and the uninspiring, but pretty, classical 'crescent' of ploshchad Lenina are the oldest buildings in town.

Museum of Local Studies

Housed in this 'crescent' is the fine Museum of Local Studies (Kraevedchesky muzey; ☎ 77 27 02), which features nicely laid-out displays on the founding of the city and its environs, and everything you needed to know about the Karelian epic poem *Kalevala*. The main museum at ploshchad Lenina 1 charges adults/students $0.70/0.25 admission, and the tiny nearby wing at ploshchad Lenina 1A features changing exhibits and charges $0.25. Both are open from 10 am to 5 pm daily except Friday and offer free admission every second Sunday.

Geological Museum

Foreign geologists rave about the museum in the Geological Institute (☎ 77 34 71) at the Russian Academy of Sciences, ulitsa Pushkinskaya 11. The museum houses rocks and minerals up to three billion years old, including some indigenous to Karelia. It's open from 9 am to 5 pm weekdays, but will be happy to accept you anytime – just call in advance. You can't just waltz in off the street, though: when you enter the central building you will be intercepted by the controller ('Who knows *what* you could have in your bag!') – explain that you'd like to see the museum, and they'll get someone to accompany you up to the 5th floor.

Duluth Statue

Duluth, Minnesota, Petrozavodsk's US sister city, commissioned Rafael Consuegra to sculpt a huge metal statue that would capture the real Petrozavodskian spirit. The result is *The Fishermen*, which seems to be *The Old Man and the Sea* meets Edvard Munch's *The Scream*. It's on the lakefront just near the Geological Museum.

Amusement Park

There's a sweet amusement park behind the ferry terminal, open in summer, that's geared to smaller children. It's got a mini-Ferris wheel, plus various swing and pony rides. Closer to the lakeshore is a small roller coaster, a popular tilt-a-whirl and a 25m-high Ferris wheel for grown-ups that is slow and affords no view whatsoever of the city.

Afghan War Memorial

In the park behind Pervomaysky prospekt sits one of Russia's few memorials to veterans of the Afghanistan war. The stone monument lists local residents who died in the conflict.

Exhibition Hall

The Exhibition Hall (Vystavochny zal; ☎ 77 16 50), prospekt Lenina 26, hosts monthly art shows, and sometimes cosy chamber music concerts on Sunday afternoons. It's open from noon to 7 pm Tuesday to Sunday.

Places to Stay

Though plain, ***Hotel Severnaya*** *(☎ 76 20 80, fax 76 22 55, severnaya@onega.ru, prospekt Lenina 21)* is your best bet: it's clean, smack in the centre, and has the cheapest rooms in town. Just beware of paper cuts: it has the roughest loo paper in Russia (A4-sized writing paper cut into four!). Still, everything works and the staff are great. The cheapest singles/doubles are $4.75/6 with separate bathrooms in the hallway, $13/19 with shower in the room, and $21 for a 'eurostandard lux'. Ask for a view onto ulitsa Engelsa.

Karelia Hotel *(☎ 55 88 97, fax 55 23 06, naberezhnaya Gyullinga 2)*, a five minute walk from the ferry terminal, is a depressing monstrosity, but the rooms for $12/16 are clean. Try for a view of the lake. You'd be better off at the ***Karelian Government Hotel*** *(☎ 76 16 61, fax 76 16 82, ulitsa Sverdlova 10)*, formerly the Communist Party's recreational pad. It's been renovated by Finns and is the comfiest and safest place in town. Sparse singles/doubles/triples cost $9/15/18. There's a great sauna, and a bar open until 10 pm (but if you need alcohol after that, the front desk staff will gladly sell you some). A step down is ***Hotel Fregat*** *(☎ 77 09 16)* on the lake side of the ferry terminal. This much smaller hotel, dead in winter, has rooms on the pricier side at $20/27, including breakfast. The entrance is unmarked, next to the Bar Fregat; ring the hard-to-see bell on the left side of the door.

Places to Eat

Restaurants ***Petrovsky Restoran*** *(ulitsa Andropova 1)* has northern dishes at reasonable prices – try the local speciality, *myaso po Medvednoye* (a meat casserole with potatoes, cheese and mayo) for $2. The service is negligible, though, and the atmosphere a bit creepy. It's open from noon to 1 am daily.

Business Club, behind the Hotel Severnaya, has a small casino and is open daily from 11 am to 5 am. Its menu is extensive, with interesting meat/fruit concoctions for under $3, but the 'biznessman' (ie bandit) crowd makes it wholly unappealing.

Connected to the Karelia Hotel, next to the outside entrance of its Restaurant Karelia (skip it), is the most pleasant option in town, the Korean ***Arirang*** *(☎ 77 52 26)*. It's bright and friendly (a first in the city!) and serves up good meals like marinated eggplant with meat for under $2. It's open daily from noon until 11 pm. ***Restoran Tok***, with its entrance around back of Karelia Hotel, used to be the top place in town. It still boasts a fancy decor and extensive fish menu. All main meals are under $3, and can be enjoyed in the company of Important People and their mobile phones.

Neubrandenburg *(prospekt Lenina 23)* is a small, friendly, German-run place with tasty German dishes. It's open from 10 am to 11 pm daily, and serves up an unforgettable *sudak podzharka* (roasted perch) for $1.50.

Kavkaz *(ulitsa Andropova 13)* is the best Georgian restaurant in town – but only as there's no competition. It's popular, and open from 11 am to 10 pm daily. It serves the expected, but get there early on weekends as it runs out of half the menu by 8 pm. The trout shashlik ($1.75) is magnificent, but the curt service and depressing grey lighting leave a bad aftertaste.

Cafes ***Ben & Jerry's Ice Cream***, the American ice cream manufacturer, runs what is arguably Russia's finest scoop shop at Krasnaya ulitsa 8. It even serves up locally produced versions of Cherry Garcia and Chunky Monkey. There are sundaes and milkshakes and take-away ice cream cakes and fudge bars – is this heaven? Three scoops for $0.50! It is! It's open and jam-packed from 10 am to 8 pm daily (noon to 6 pm Monday).

While ***Kafe Morozhenoe***, on the corner of prospekt Marxa and ulitsa Kuybysheva (near the statue of Marx and Engels deciding where to eat), may not be Ben & Jerry's, its ice cream is decent, and so are the few hot meals. It's open from 10 am to 11 pm. The adjoining ***Tsentralny Bar*** stays open an extra hour serving rather plasticised pizza and cheap beer.

For a very cheap fill-up, there's always the ***stolovaya*** *(prospekt Lenina 9)*, serving up cafeteria fare for under $0.50 from 8 am to 8 pm daily. It ain't bad, but bring your own napkins – they evidently use the same A4 paper as the Hotel Severnaya!

Self-Catering There is a ***market*** on ulitsa Antikaynena, which has a good selection of fresh produce and meat (behind is a clothing and gizmo market). ***Lotus*** *(ulitsa Anokhina 37)*, the best stocked supermarket in town, is open daily from 9 am to midnight, and accepts credit cards. There are also two 24 hour shops opposite the train station, and several more lining ulitsa Lenina.

Entertainment

Concerts Kantele, a jolly Karelian folk ensemble, performs at the ***National Theatre*** *(☎ 77 95 86, prospekt Marxa 19)*, or at the ***Philharmonic Hall*** *(ulitsa Gogolya 6)*. You can buy tickets at the theatres or through Intourist. Otherwise, the ***Russian Drama Theatre*** on prospekt Marxa has nearly nightly light operas and ballets (check out the wild interior decor: a mix of Ancient Greek, Roman and Soviet, with Russian folk maidens dancing on the ceiling around an enormous chandelier).

Bars & Clubs ***Bar Fregat*** *(☎ 56 14 98)* next to Hotel Fregat gets mixed reviews for its food, but the upstairs, American-style bar isn't half bad, and the live music (especially the jazz band on Sunday night) is worth tuning in to. It closes at midnight during the week, and at 3 am on weekends. ***Bar Neubrandenburg***, adjoining its restaurant, is comfy though very smoky, and a good place to meet friendly locals. But the best place for an intimate nightcap is ***Rendezvous***, connected to the department store on prospekt Marxa. It has a few hot meals, all good, and the relaxed atmosphere, with large glass windows and indoor street lamps, is unique in the city. It's open from 11 am to midnight daily and worth a visit.

On Friday and Saturday from 11 pm to 4 am, there's something resembling a discotheque in ***Nightclub Karmel***, a palatial space on prospekt Lenina that is used as a cinema during the day. It's the kind of place where the girls dance around their purses, but there are no teeny-boppers, and the upstairs bar has reasonable prices. Entrance is $0.75.

Pool sharks will enjoy the ***billiard hall*** inside the Karelia Hotel, open from noon until 3 am weekdays, to 6 am on weekends. It's just $2 an hour for tables, and the space is roomy and pleasant.

Spectator Sports

The Sports Museum (Dom Phyzkultury; ☎ 77 53 69), ulitsa Pushkinskaya 7, is the place to check out the odd basketball or Sambo wrestling tournament. It also houses a small museum, and at the time of research a swimming pool was under construction.

Shopping

Karelian embroidery and traditional-style clothing are sometimes available at non-tourist prices in the department stores and some kiosks. If you're feeling under the weather, the local firewater Karelsky Balzam – made from 20 herbs – is said to have tremendous powers of healing. And at 45% alcohol it bloody well should! The biggest selection of handicrafts and souvenirs is at Podarki, on the corner of prospekt Lenina and ulitsa Andropova. The gift shop inside the Museum of Local Studies has a unique selection of gifts made from Karelian birch (a government-protected tree).

Getting There & Away

Air From June 1998, there have been no scheduled flights in or out of Petrozavodsk's adorable little airport. The army, which shares its runways, closed it down for repairs which are now going on indefinitely. Contact Finnair (☎ 77 61 76) at prospekt Lenina 6, or Kola-Tavs (formerly Aeroflot, ☎ 77 96 74) at ulitsa Antikaynena 20, for the latest details on whether or not flights to and from St Petersburg, Murmansk, Arkhangelsk and Helsinki via Joensuu have resumed.

Train The overnight train from St Petersburg's Moscow Station ($25) is convenient and saves the cost of a hotel. Trains leave for St Petersburg (about eight hours, four per day); Moscow (15 to 20 hours, four per day); and Murmansk (21 to 26 hours, eight per day). The train station is at the western end of prospekt Lenina.

Bus For destinations in northern Karelia, catch buses at the main bus station, behind the train station (you can walk there by crossing the tracks and following the paths, like locals do, but for safety reasons it is better to take the long way around, along ulitsa Krasnoarmeyskaya). Turistiliikenne, in Kuhmo, Finland, operates a daily bus from Kuhmo to Kostomuksha on the western border of Karelia with connecting bus service to Belomorsk for about $10. There is a daily service to St Petersburg's Avtovokzal No 2, and the nine hour ride costs only $2.50 (no foreigner prices on buses, remember). To St Petersburg, the bus leaves at 9 am; from St Petersburg at 9.30 am.

Car & Motorcycle The motorway from St Petersburg (420km) is open. Intourist in Petrozavodsk suggests that it's possible to cross at Vyartsilya (500km from Petrozavodsk via Olonets) to Tohmajrvi and on to Joensuu in Finland.

Getting Around

Bus Nos 4 and 5 will take you from the train station to Hotel Severnaya, though it's not a long walk. To order a taxi 24 hours a day, call ☎ 77 51 51 or ☎ 55 09 71.

AROUND PETROZAVODSK

To the north and west of the city lies one of the most beautiful and accessible regions for hunting, fishing, hiking and camping in Russia. Finns have been revelling in the area for some time (it used to be theirs, after all) and Finnish tourists can be found all over Karelia.

Other than in small, closed military towns along the border with Finland, you're free to roam at will. Camping and campfires are permitted almost anywhere, except where posted Не разбивать палатку ('No putting up of tents') and/or Не разжигать костов ('No campfires'), and if you're off the beaten track it is usually legal and fine

NORTHERN EUROPEAN RUSSIA

just to put up a tent and hit the hay. Check with locals if you're in doubt.

The region's lakes and rivers make for great kayaking and rubber-rafting, though there aren't many rapids. The Karelian people are keen boaters.

Intourist and Turist in Petrozavodsk run excursions to Russia's first mineral spa, founded by Peter the Great at Martsialnye Vody, and to the 10.7m waterfall and nature reserve at Kivach. The lack of a bus service makes Kivach difficult if you're without a car, as it's about 50km north of the city, but you can get to Martsialnye Vody yourself (there are several buses a day from the main bus station – ask the cashier which ones stop there). From Martsialnye Vody you can hire a taxi to Kivach for about $5.

Kizhi Island
Остров Кижи

An old pagan ritual site, Kizhi Island made a natural 'parish' for 12th century Russian colonists, though none of the earliest churches remain.

Its centrepiece is the fairy-tale **Cathedral of the Transfiguration** (Preobrazhensky sobor, 1714). With its chorus of 22 domes, gables and ingenious decorations to keep water off the walls, it is the gem of Russian wooden architecture. Even so, it's now so rickety that it's been closed, and despite UNESCO protection nobody can agree on how to restore it. Next door is the nine domed **Church of the Intercession** (Pokrovskaya tserkov, 1764). The icons from the cathedral are on display here and in the Petrozavodsk Fine Arts Museum.

The other buildings in the collection were brought from the region around Lake Onega. The nineteenth century peasant houses, some more ornate than others, are nicely restored inside. The little 14th century **Church of the Resurrection of Lazarus** may possibly be the oldest wooden building in Russia. The **Chapel of the Archangel Michael** has an exhibit on Christianity in Karelia, and music students from Petrozavodsk play its bells in summer. There are numerous other houses and windmills open to exploration.

Outside the 'museum' grounds are other churches, and a hamlet with houses like the ones inside, only occupied. The silence, fresh air and views on a sunny day are reason enough to come here (but beware of poisonous snakes in the remoter parts).

Museum entry fees are steep for foreigners at $12 (though the staff often pity students – ISIC cards aren't officially accepted, but they usually take them and charge $1.10).

Places to Eat In short, bring food. There's a ***restaurant*** near the landing and, opposite the pier, a small kiosk cluster including an overpriced 'art shop' and ***cafe***, but these open and close at will and sometimes only have yesterday's hot dogs left.

Getting There & Away Going on your own is easy – hydrofoils make the 80 minute direct trip several times a day from the Petrozavodsk ferry terminal; others stop first at Sennaya Guba, a pleasant little island full of dachas which can make a nice detour for those looking for seclusion. A return ticket is a truly outrageous $20 (but if you don't go through travel agents, it's easy to get the Russian price of $3). You can buy your return tickets early or on board. You can only go during 'navigation season', which is mid-May to mid-October.

Throughout the year, the North-Eastern Aviation Base for the Protection of Forests in Petrozavodsk (☎ 74 75 66, fax 74 24 60) runs excellent helicopter excursions to the island (three times a week in winter, and by order in summer) for just $24. In winter, you get an hour to walk around on the island, which is essentially closed (no indoor access but no entrance fees) in summer, when it all depends on the client's wishes. It will also fly anyone anywhere they wish throughout Karelia ($400 an hour for groups of up to 20). At least you know the money's going to a good cause – to feed the families of those who protect forests.

In summer the St Petersburg Travel Company runs a seven day cruise from St Petersburg via the Neva River to Valaam and Kizhi and back for between $120 to $160 per person. This can also be booked through Turist in Petrozavodsk. Similar tours, at substantially cheaper rates, can be booked through the River Terminal in St Petersburg (see the Getting There & Away section in the St Petersburg chapter, and Getting There & Away in the Valaam section for more details).

Kosalma
Косалма

One hour's bus ride north of Petrozavodsk brings you to Kosalma (pronounced *KAH-sul-ma*), a resort town for local factory workers. Boris Yeltsin still comes here now and then to stay at the former Communist Party dacha, which is now a privately owned hotel. Locals come to get away from the city and to take advantage of the Ukshizero and Kunchizero lakes, while Russian tourists use it as a starting point for river or ski tours of south-eastern Karelia.

Other than the simple pleasure of relaxation, Kosalma has little to offer. However, Hotel Kosalma can arrange for some fine Karelian adventures, like cross-country skiing and camping trips, hiking and other outdoor nature excursions (but bring your own equipment).

Places to Stay & Eat ***Hotel Kosalma*** *(☎ 73 77 89)*, 2km north of the Kosalma bus stop on the left, has singles/double rooms from $7.50/11.50, and four three-room cottages in need of repair for $18 a day. There's a sauna ($8 an hour) and a ***restaurant*** open around the clock. Just hanging around picking berries and mushrooms can be pleasant enough, but there's a nearby lake with boat rentals.

The hotel's private minibus (look for the hotel's sign) leaves from the Petrozavodsk train station every morning at 9.15 am. You can get more information or reserve places at the hotel's Petrozavodsk office (☎ 8142-55 02 32), ulitsa Pravdy 44, or try your luck and just show up.

Also in Kosalma are two ***shops*** with basic goods, open from 8 am to midnight, at the Kosalma bus stop. There is also a mediocre ***cafe***.

Getting There & Away Kosalma is on the St Petersburg-Murmansk highway, 43km north of Petrozavodsk. Buses leave Petrozavodsk's bus station at least six times a day ($1).

VALAAM
ВАЛААМ

The Valaam Archipelago, which consists of Valaam Island and about 50 smaller islands, sits in north-western Lake Ladoga (pronounced *LAH-da-ga)* south of south-western Karelia and north of St Petersburg. The main attractions here are the 14th century **Valaam Transfiguration Monastery** (Spaso-Preobrazhenskii Valaamsky monastyr), its cathedral and buildings, and the pleasant town that surrounds it.

There is some dispute about the identity of the first settlers – some sources say that they were 10th century monks – but most agree that the monastery was first settled in the late 14th century as a fortress against Swedish invaders, who managed to destroy it completely in 1611. Rebuilt with money from Peter the Great, the monastery doubled as a prison.

Many of the monks and much of the monastery's treasure were moved to Finland, which controlled the territory between 1918 and 1940. After 1940, when the territory fell back into Soviet hands, the Soviet authorities closed the monastery, took whatever was left and built what they referred to as an 'urban-type settlement' there.

Today the buildings are protected architectural landmarks, but neglect has taken its toll. Many of the buildings are decrepit and in need of repair. There are about 500 residents on the main island, including army service personnel, restoration workers, guides and clergy, most of whom get around in horse-drawn carriages or motorboats.

Getting There & Away

To/From St Petersburg Cruise ships leave the St Petersburg River Terminal (☎ 812-262 02 39) on irregular schedules (see the Getting There & Away section in the St Petersburg chapter). There are two types of boats which make the cruise, one with toilet facilities in the cabins, one without. The trip to Kizhi and back lasts three days; if you add Valaam, the trip is four days. Prices are reasonable and range from $42 to $152, including full board. Ger-Piter Tours (☎ 812-262 13 18, fax 262 55 61), located at the St Petersburg River Terminal, can assist in planning and booking.

To/From Southern Karelia From southern Karelia, the gateway to Valaam is the sleepy town of Sortavala, about 300km west of Petrozavodsk. A local bus leaves Petrozavodsk's main station at 6.30 am and arrives in Sortavala at 2.30 pm. The cost is under $3. By train from Petrozavodsk, take No 680 (whose final destination is Kostomuksha) at 7.10 pm, which gets to Sortavala at a drowsy 6.10 am. The cost for foreigners is $13 for *platskartnyy* (bunk accommodation), $19 for *kupe* (four-person couchettes). Once you get to Sortavala it's an easy 15 minute walk from the train station to the boat pier. Head north along the tracks – the direction from which the train comes into the station – until you get to the bridge, then turn right, then right again past the (probably) nude Finnish sunbathers to get to the pier.

Three boats are usually docked there: a hydrofoil, which takes 40 minutes to get to Valaam; a large boat, which takes a bit more than an hour; and a smaller boat, which takes three hours. The hydrofoil costs about $3 per person. Boats go to Valaam from about mid-May to August.

From the small pier near the main monastery where you arrive from Sortavala, it's about a 5km walk through forests and meadows to the main harbour where the boats go to and from St Petersburg. It's a blissful walk, but you can always try hitching a ride from the friendly locals along the main road.

KEM
КЕМЬ

☎ 81458 • pop 18,000

Kem (pronounced *Kyem*), founded in the 16th century, is one of European Russia's most depressing towns. Its history is as bleak as that of many others in the region: prisons

NORTHERN EUROPEAN RUSSIA

and, later, Gulags have operated in the area for centuries; during the 1920s and 1930s, prisoners on their one-way trips to the Solovetsky Islands would be herded through this town; the Nazis set up a concentration camp outside the city limits during WWII; and, during the Soviet era, police would arrest undercover monks trying to sneak their way to the monastery on Solovetsky Island.

Today, the town itself is grey and crumbling, the definition of dreary. Still, there are some lovely wooden houses on its outskirts, and the villages on the way to the port are picturesque. As a jumping-off point for the Solovetsky Islands, it is simpler, faster and cheaper than going through Arkhangelsk. The Turbaza Kem (see Places to Stay & Eat) is run by friendly people who can help arrange the three hour boat journey.

If you're stuck in Kem for a few hours, check out the wooden houses on the southeast side of town, near the lovely wooden **Assumption Cathedral** (Uspensky sobor). Just north of the eastern end of the town's main drag, prospekt Proletarskaya, is the crumbling **Annunciation Cathedral** (Blagoveshchensky sobor), which is open for services, but only just – its interior and exterior are scaffolded, and you need to walk down a plank to get to the entrance.

Don't be caught in Kem with foreign currency as exchanging it will be a problem, even at the banks; if you are stuck, discreetly ask at the kiosks in the central market – workers there will be pleased to do the trade, and at fair rates.

NORTHERN EUROPEAN RUSSIA

Places to Stay & Eat

You can stay for $2.40 a night in the pleasant stone and wood building of the ***Turbaza Kem*** *(☎ 2 03 85, fax 2 82 00, ulitsa Energetikov 22)*, or check into the newly opened ***Hotel Kem*** (no phone yet) across the street for $6 per person. The Turbaza can organise city tours and skiing/hiking expeditions, but their *raison d'être* is to send you to Solovetsky (see Getting There & Away in the Solovetsky Islands section). They can also set you up with something to eat. Otherwise, there's a ***cafe*** diagonally across from the train station that isn't bad in a fix.

Getting There & Away

Kem is a stop on the St Petersburg-Moscow-Murmansk railway. Bus No 1 runs from Kem's train station to the port, which is actually in the village of Rabocheostrovsk, a 35 minute ride away. From the bus stop, follow the road to your right, cross the train tracks and keep walking to the very end, some 500m.

Kola Peninsula
Кольский Полуостров

The Kola Peninsula (Kolsky Poluostrov), dominated by the port of Murmansk, is a 100,000 sq km knob of tundra, forest and low mountains between the White Sea and the Barents Sea. Originally populated only by Sami reindeer-herders and a few Russian trappers and fishers, the discovery of a northern sea route in the 16th century turned the tiny settlement of Kola into an Arctic trading post. In 1916, under pressure from the British to establish a supply port, Murmansk was founded (the first buildings being British-built wooden houses).

The Kola Inlet from the Barents Sea, which is ice-free year-round thanks to an eddy from the Gulf Stream, was the ideal site for the port of Murmansk, and now, at nearby Severomorsk, for the Russian Northern Fleet's home base. Thanks to the latter, the Kola Peninsula today has the somewhat dubious distinction of being home to the world's greatest concentration of military and naval forces. The discovery of ore and mineral deposits sped up growth and generated an environmental mess in many areas; thousands of square kilometres of forests are dying of sulphur dioxide poisoning from nickel smelters in the towns of Nikel and Monchegorsk.

In addition to its geological interest, the area also offers outdoor activities. The Khibiny Mountains have some fine hiking and mountaineering opportunities (new granite up to 700m high), cross-country skiing is possible anywhere, and budget skiers will love the downhill runs at Kirovsk.

North and west of the ecologically devastated city of Monchegorsk lies the relatively pristine Lapland Biosphere Reserve, a 2784 sq km natural wonderland.

GETTING THERE & AWAY

While some curious folks may wander northwards from St Petersburg, most visitors to the Kola Peninsula region are making short excursions from the northern regions of Norway.

If you're intending to enter Russia independently at Storskog, Russia's only Arctic land border, be sure to have your Russian visa (preferably from your home country) before arriving in the Norwegian border town of Kirkenes. Unless you have an official prearranged invitation, the Russian consulate in town (Norway ☎ 47-78 99 37 37), Arbeidergata 6, does not issue independent tourist visas, and no amount of charm or begging will sway the staff. Some nationalities may be issued visas at the Russian consulate in Oslo, but US citizens, in particular, shouldn't count on it.

Note that your visa must specify which Russian cities and towns you intend to visit, and without permission to visit Nikel (which is surely the most horrible spot on earth, and deserves a visit for that reason alone), Zapolyarnye, Murmansk, Pechenga or another Kola Peninsula town, you may not be allowed to cross the border.

For tour participants coming from Norway, visa fees are determined by nationality and also vary according to what sort of urgency is required; all applications require three passport photos and for the best rates, you'll have to wait a minimum of 10 days. Citizens of Canada, the UK, Italy, Japan and India pay just Nkr50 (under $7), Australians and New Zealanders pay Nkr150 ($20), while Norwegians pay Nkr245 ($32), other Scandinavians Nkr200 ($26), other EU citizens Nkr280 ($36) and US citizens Nkr350 ($45). In addition, everyone pays a service fee of Nkr50 (under $7).

If you need a visa the next day, you'll pay anywhere from Nkr1000 to Nkr2500 ($130 to $320). Naturally, this is all subject to change on a whim.

Air

The Norwegian airline Widerøe (Norway ☎ 47-67 11 60 00, fax 67 11 61 95, internetbooking@wideroe.no, www.wideroe.no) has services between Kirkenes and Murmansk on Monday and Wednesday. Braathens SAFE has twice weekly flights between Tromsø (Norway ☎ 47-77 66 00 00) and Murmansk (Russia ☎ 085-1 00 34).

Bus

Those who already have a visa can just hop on the Murmansk Shipping Company's public bus to Murmansk (seven hours, Nkr400/$51), which travels via Nikel and Zapolyarnye. It leaves Kirkenes on Wednesday, Friday and Sunday at 3 pm from the Rica Arctic Hotel and from Hotel Polyarnye Zory in Murmansk at 9 am on the same days (thanks to more-efficient border crossings, the trip back to Norway takes only four hours). Due to military exercises along the route, it's only open to foreigners – even in their own vehicles – from 7 am to 9 pm Norwegian time (9 am to 11 pm Kola time) on Monday, Wednesday, Friday and Sunday.

Organised Tours

Many visitors who have travelled as far as Kirkenes, want to visit Russia – or at least sally up to the border – and several local agencies are happy to accommodate them. If you're happy with just a quick hop across the border, you can pop over with a local travel agent who will organise your visa locally. However, your itinerary will be rather limited, and without a great deal of creativity you probably won't be permitted to continue farther into Russia.

Sovjetrejser (Norway ☎ 47-78 99 19 81, fax 78 99 11 42) organises day trips to the hell-hole, Nikel, for Nkr480 to Nkr600 ($65 to $85) per person, including lunch and a guide, and to Zapolyarnye for Nkr1100 ($147). Day trips to Murmansk run daily except Sunday and Wednesday from 1 June to 31 August, and cost Nkr1000 ($134). Weekends in Murmansk cost Nkr1650 ($220) per person plus Nkr400 ($54) per night. Straight minibus transfers between Kirkenes and Murmansk are Nkr550 ($74).

The other main player offering Russia trips is Pasvikturist (Norway ☎ 47-78 99 50 80, fax 78 99 50 57), which has adventure-oriented tours including canoeing and camping in the Pechenga wilderness, and longer tours of north-west Russia. An eight day, all-inclusive trip visiting Murmansk, the Pomor trading centre of Solovki and Arkhangelsk costs Nkr5950 ($795) per person.

MURMANSK МУРМАНСК

☎ 8152 • pop 380,000

The most novel thing about Murmansk is its location, midway between Moscow and the North Pole. It is also the largest city in the world north of the Arctic Circle, with a population of 380,000 to 400,000 (no one knows exactly because it's declining so dramatically). Temperatures range from -8° to -13°C in January, and 8° to 14°C in July.

The nearby port of Severomorsk is home to the Northern Fleet (including nuclear submarines and much of Russia's nuclear arsenal) and the city itself is the home port of Russia's nuclear icebreakers. Perhaps they're hoping the glow will light up the long polar nights!

Most of Murmansk's permanent residents are Russians, but some temporary workers are lured by good wages and other perks to work in fish processing or ship repair. The local Sami people are generally reclusive, except during the Festival of the North (see Special Events), when they come to compete in traditional games.

Orientation & Information

The city occupies three levels: the port, the centre and the surrounding heights, crowned with dozens of bland housing blocks. Dominating the centre is ploshchad Sovietskoy Konstitutsii, also known as Five-Corners (Pyat-Ugla). To the north of the centre lies Lake Semyonovskoe and an immense concrete soldier named 'Alyosha', that could only have been constructed in Russia.

One of the easiest places in town to change money is at the exchange window in the Hotel Polyarnye Zory. Less convenient is the bank on ulitsa Leningradskaya.

The main post and telephone office is just behind the Hotel Arktika. Calls on satellite phones cost about the same price as the state phones and are available to the public on the 4th floor of the Hotel Arktika. NMT-450 standard cellular phones work here, as well as in the rest of the Kola Peninsula.

Limited tourist information is available at Intourist (☎ 45 43 85), in the Hotel Polyarnye Zory (see Places to Stay later in this section), but for the best results, you'll need to speak Russian.

Things to See

St Nicholas Church (Svyato-Nikolskaya tserkov), named for the patron saint of sailors, is the Kola Peninsula's religious administrative centre, and it has a colourful history (see the boxed text 'Holy War'). You can reach it on trolleybus No 4 from the train station; after four stops, walk past

Holy War

The site of the present cathedral in Murmansk was first occupied by a wooden church, built in 1946. In 1984, the rather low-profile congregation decided they needed a new church, but thanks to the Soviet government, which allowed no other gods above itself, the work had to progress clandestinely. Not surprisingly, however, it was difficult to hide a cathedral, and when the government learned of the effort in 1985, it sent in miners with orders to dynamite the structure. This raised a holy ruckus, and demonstrators descended upon the site, blocking the miners, while simultaneous protests were held outside the Moscow city executive committee. The government eventually capitulated to some extent, allowing what remained of the building to stand, but forbidding any further work on it. However, in 1987, after perestroika allowed the exiled Christian God back into the Soviet Union, construction resumed and over the next five summers, the project was completed.

the pond and up the stairs, then along a dirt trail to the main road, and the church is to the right.

The **Fine Arts Museum** (Khudozhestvenny muzey), ulitsa Kominterna 13, was established in Murmansk's oldest stone building in 1989, and in 1994 received a permanent collection of graphic arts, paintings, decorative applied arts and bone carvings, all on an 'image-of-the-north' theme. It features seven prints by Boris Nepomnyashchy, including *Purgatory*, and biblical figures including *Cain and Abel*. The 3rd floor houses temporary exhibitions, which change monthly. Some of the works seem more than a little tragic, though (see the boxed text 'Art Imitates Life'). The museum is open from 11 am to 6 pm Wednesday to Sunday and foreigners pay $2.

In the **Museum of Regional Studies**, prospekt Lenina 90, the 2nd floor features geology, natural history and oceanography. Exhibits on anthropology, Sami and Pomor history, the Anglo-American occupation and WWII occupy the 3rd floor.

On the 2nd floor of the city administration building, ulitsa Sofi Perovskoy 3, the **Regional Centre of Crafts** holds a permanent exhibition of art by Kola Peninsula artists, including 'paintings' from coloured crushed stone powder – a technique developed in Apatity.

The hard-to-find **Military Museum of the Northern Fleet** (Muzey Militarny Severnogo Morskogo Flota), ulitsa Tortseva 15, is a must if you're a WWII or naval buff. It has six rooms on the Great Patriotic War and one on the modern fleet – torpedos, mines, model ships, and diving and chemical warfare paraphernalia. A guided tour costs around $2.50, but admission is free. To get there, take trolleybus No 4 north to the last stop, cross the street, then take bus No 10 for four stops (look for the smokestack). Walk towards the smokestack, and turn left at the shop.

Anatoly Bredov, a hero of the Great Patriotic War, is honoured with a statue on prospekt Lenina in front of the stadium. Finding himself surrounded by Nazi troops, Anatoly detonated a grenade, taking several of the bad guys with him. He's considered a hero all over the Kola Peninsula and thanks to this character, Murmansk is nicknamed Gorod Geroy (hero city).

Art Imitates Life

For an emotionally charged exposé on the modern sentiments of northern Russia, visit Murmansk's Fine Arts Museum, where much of the work brings home the sometimes tragically fatalistic perspective of most people in this neglected region. Look for the paintings by V Kumashov, such as *V Sverye* (In the North), which depicts a typical Soviet-era statue of a family rising over a huddle of forgotten pensioners on a bench, beside a sleeping stray dog. *Idut v Kino* (Going to the Cinema) shows people strolling past broken benches and mounds of garbage, concealing bottles of vodka in brown paper bags, carrying Marlboro Man shopping bags, and queuing up to catch the latest pornographic flick. Another, *Vozvrashenniye v proshloye* (Return to the Past), depicts a historic village overlooked by banks of kiosks, while *Staraya Musika* (Old Music) reveals a scene of town square musicians entertaining people queued up to buy their daily anaesthetising dose of alcohol.

In summer, you may see one of the four **atomic-powered icebreakers** of the Murmansk Shipping Company (Murmanskoye Morskoye Parokhodstvo) at the dock. Photography here, except in the port itself, is now permitted.

Lake Semyonovskoe is named after the unfortunate would-be hermit Semyon Korzhnev, an old tsarist soldier who retired at the turn of the 20th century to a cabin on the shore, and was the only resident for miles around. Imagine his disappointment when Murmansk appeared on his utopian horizon! The lake and the monumentally ludicrous statue of 'Alyosha' occupy the plateau above town. To get there, take trolleybus No 3 up prospekt Lenina.

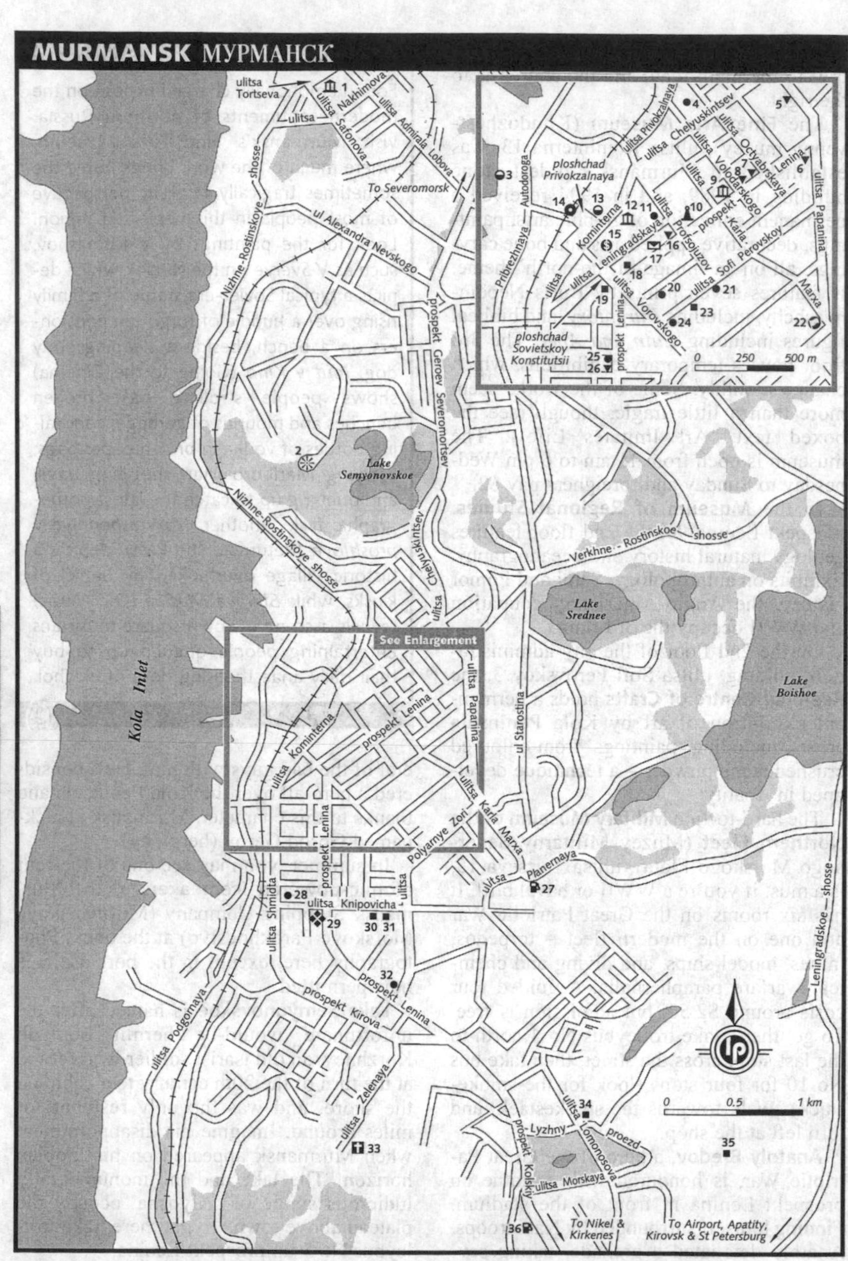

NORTHERN EUROPEAN RUSSIA

MURMANSK МУРМАНСК

PLACES TO STAY
- 18 Hotel Arktika Гостиница Арктика
- 19 Meridian Hotel Гостиница Меридиан
- 23 Obkomovsk Administratsii Hotel & Kafe Svetlana Обкомовск Гостиница Администрации и Кафе Светлана
- 30 Hotel Polyarnye Zory & Intourist Гостиница Полярные зори и Интурист
- 31 Moryak Guest House Гостиница Моряк
- 34 69th Parallel Hotel Гостиница Щестьдесять-девятая Параллел
- 35 Ogni Murmanska Hotel Гостиница Огни Мурманска

PLACES TO EAT
- 5 Harbin Харвин
- 6 Medved Медвед
- 7 Pelmennaya Restaurant Ресторан Пельменная
- 8 Pizzeria Zorachaya Пиццериа Зорачая
- 16 Kafe Yunost Кафе Юность
- 26 Burger Bar Бургер Бар

OTHER
- 1 Military Museum of the Northern Fleet Музей милитарний северного морского флото
- 2 'Alyosha' Monument & Lookout Памятник Алёша и панорама
- 3 Passenger Ferry Terminal Морской вокзал
- 4 Town Market Рынок
- 9 Museum of Regional Studies Краеведческий музей
- 10 Anatoly Bredov Monument Памятник Анатолию Бредову
- 11 Cinema Rodina & Pingvin Ice Cream Кинотеатр Родина и Пингвин
- 12 Fine Arts Museum Художественный музей
- 13 Bus Terminal Автовокзал
- 14 Train Station Железнодорожный вокзал
- 15 Bank Банк
- 17 Post Office Почтамт
- 20 Kirov Palace of Culture Дворец Культуры имени С. М. Кирова
- 21 Puppet Theatre & Regional Science Library Театр кукол и научная областная библиотека
- 22 Finnish Consulate Консульство Финляндий
- 24 City Administration, Regional Centre of Crafts & Philharmonic Concert Hall Городская Администрация и Зал Филармонии
- 25 Pharmacy Аптека
- 27 New Statoil Complex Новая автозаправочные станция 'Статоил'
- 28 Polar Research Institute Институт полярного исследования
- 29 Detsky Mir Department Store Детский мир
- 32 Aeroflot Office Агенство Аэрофлот
- 33 St Nicholas Church Свято-Миколская Церковь
- 36 Statoil Автозаправочные станция

Organised Tours

Intourist, at the Hotel Polyarnye Zory, offers several local tours, but you'll probably need a group before it will organise anything. How about a winter reindeer-sledding expedition (around $75 per person), which is met by a folk ensemble and includes an outdoor barbecue accompanied by folk dancing? Alternatively, it will arrange five-day snow-machining tours or cruises on Kola Harbour.

Special Events

The annual Festival of the North, held since 1934, takes place in the last week in March (although it often goes on longer), with each town in the area hosting its own events. Murmansk has reindeer and deer-plus-ski races (in which a reindeer pulls a contestant on skis), an international ski marathon and biathlon, ice hockey, 'polar-bear' swimming and a general carnival atmosphere. Hotels get booked up well in advance. Most events in Murmansk are held at the south end of town in Dolina Uyuta (Cosy Valley), a 25 minute ride from the train station on bus No 12. There's through-the-ice swimming at Lake Semyonovskoe, and snowmobile rides can be arranged through Intourist.

Places to Stay

The cheapest option, somewhat out of the centre, is the ***69th Parallel Hotel*** *(Gostinitsa Shestdesyat-Devyataya Parallel; ☎ 56 56 43, Lyzhny proezd 14, postal index 183042)* in Dolina Uyuta (Cosy Valley). Take trolleybus No 1 or 6 from the centre for about 10 minutes. Single/double rooms cost $23/32 with phones and TVs (some even have balconies and fridges). There's a ***cafe*** in the lobby.

At ***Gostinitsa Moryak*** *(☎ 45 55 27)*, on ulitsa Knipovicha, you'll find simple but adequate rooms for $26/30.

Hotel Polyarnye Zory *(☎ 28 95 05, fax – on the Norwegian exchange – 47-78 91 01 91, polarzor@murmansk.rosmail.com, ulitsa Knipovicha 17)*, near the Detsky Mir bus stop on prospekt Lenina, has large, clean rooms for $45/56, with cable TV. At the moment, this is considered *the* Westerners' hang-out in town, and it has a lively bar and bufet ***restaurant***.

Another option in the city centre is the ***Meridian Hotel*** *(☎ 28 86 94, ulitsa Vorovskogo 5/23)*, opposite the hulking Hotel Arktika. Run-down but clean and comfortable rooms are $53/59. It has very friendly service, and the ***bufet*** on the 4th floor serves up a great ham and egg breakfast.

An excellent, but slightly more expensive option is ***Obkomovsk Administratsii Hotel*** *(☎ 45 92 78, ulitsa Sofi Perovskoy 3)*. Decent rooms cost $64/68.

At the overpriced ***Hotel Arktika*** *(☎ 55 79 88, prospekt Lenina 82, postal index 183038)* on Five-Corners, dingy and draughty rooms with bath cost $95/100. The exception is the 4th floor, which has been renovated and furnished by a Swedish firm to Western business standards. These rooms cost $110/120 with satellite TV and a satellite phone and fax near the *dezhurnaya*'s desk. All major credit cards are accepted.

If you are determined to spend that much money, stay at the sinfully luxurious (but inconvenient) ***Ogni Murmanska*** *(☎ 55 38 62, Finnish fax 358-9-49 29 24 59)*, south of the centre off Lyzhny proezd. Rooms, with good city views, cost $100/110, including breakfast, and all are Western-standard luxury – even the bathroom floors are heated. Nicer suites cost $120/130. The security is relatively good and the restaurant is graciously short on thugs.

Places to Eat

A seasonal item is reindeer meat, and of course there is lots of fish, especially cod. Try *severyanka*, which is the local chowder.

For an upmarket feast in the company of the movers and shakers in Murmansk, go to the relatively posh ***Medved***, at the upper end of prospekt Lenina. For Chinese specialities, try ***Harbin***, around the corner on ulitsa Papanina.

Burger Bar *(prospekt Lenina 72)* has good hamburgers at an expensive $7. The cafe in front is nonsmoking, the bar and restaurant are to the rear.

If your idea of pizza is sausage and eggs on a greasy cracker, then ***Pizzeria Zorachaya***, on prospekt Lenina, north-east of ulitsa Volodarskogo, won't disappoint. The curiously aloof ***Kafe Yunost***, also on prospekt Lenina, is OK for ice cream and coffee.

Kafe Svetlana, at the Administratsii Hotel, ulitsa Sofi Perovskoy 3, is very clean and good, with stingy portions of fresh fish with vegetables for $0.50, and *plov* for about $1 – it's nonsmoking and entry is at the side of the building. There's a surprisingly clean and cheerful ***bufet*** at the passenger ferry terminal, with sandwiches, hard-boiled eggs and so forth, while ***Pingvin*** ice cream cafe at the Rodina cinema is popular and crowded.

For self-caterers there's a small ***market*** at the bottom of ulitsa Volodarskogo.

Entertainment

The ***Kirov Palace of Culture***, near the Hotel Arktika, has films and exhibits and, if you're lonely, it has weekend singles dances. The ***Regional Puppet Theatre*** *(ulitsa Sofi Perovskoy 21A)*, on the 1st floor of the Regional Science Library, holds children's puppet shows at 11 am, and 1 and 3 pm every Saturday and Sunday from September to June.

Classical concerts are held at the ***Philharmonic Concert Hall*** (Kontsertny zal filarmonii; *ulitsa Sofi Perovskoy 3)*, a newly renovated 700 seat auditorium at the city administration building. Tickets and information are available there. Murmansk also has a cinema, the Rodina, but don't expect too much of it.

Getting There & Away

For information on reaching Murmansk from Kirkenes, Norway, see Getting There & Away at the beginning of the Kola Peninsula section.

NORTHERN EUROPEAN RUSSIA

Train From the station, snail-pace trains can get you to Nikel (eight to 12 hours), Apatity (four hours), Arkhangelsk (25 hours), Petrozavodsk (21 hours), St Petersburg (eight to 27 hours, $94 on the express train), Moscow (12 to 34 hours, $134 on the express train) and beyond. Ostensibly, tickets are sold at the station from 8 am to 11 pm.

Bus From the bus station, beside the train station, you'll find bus services several times daily to other Kola Peninsula towns: Monchegorsk, Apatity, Kirovsk, Polyarnye Zory and Kandalaksha.

Car & Motorcycle The good news is that the Murmansk-St Petersburg highway is now open all the way and is relatively smooth sailing. You can also drive to or from Kirkenes, Norway, via the Storskog border crossing, but due to military exercises, the route is only open to foreigners from 9 am to 11 pm Kola time on Monday, Wednesday, Friday and Sunday. The only border crossing into Finland is between Lotta and the Finnish town of Raja Jooseppi. Although the road is open, it's used mainly by freight traffic and for independent drivers, and may well prove more difficult than the crossing at Storskog.

Getting Around

The city is well served by a relatively efficient system of trolleybuses, which connect the centre with most outlying areas, including the town of Kola. For the Hotel Arktika, get off at the train station and for the Hotel Polyarnye Zory, use the Detsky Mir bus stop.

A taxi from the airport to the centre costs around $16. Bus Nos 106 and 106Э (express) run between the airport and the train station every 20 to 30 minutes for less than $0.20; the express takes half an hour.

AROUND MURMANSK

Kola
Кола

In the Murmansk suburb of Kola, which is pretty much a city in its own right, little remains of the past but the homely **Annunciation Cathedral** (Blagoveshchensky sobor), which dates from 1809. Inside, there's a museum on Pomor life (you can see a more detailed display on this subject at the Murmansk Museum of Regional Studies). It's open from 10 am to 5.30 pm (4 pm on weekends), and is closed Monday.

From Murmansk, take bus No 106 (not No 106-γ) from the train station for 15km to the Kola stop, then walk for 10 minutes to the west from the Lotta turn-off.

Severomorsk
Североморск

☎ 8152 • pop 70,000

The headquarters of the Russian Northern Fleet is mostly closed to foreigners, but with lots of time and some stressful effort, it's possible to visit. What you need is a good reason, and there seem to be three of them. The **WWII-era submarine K-21** saw quite a bit of action and is now a museum. The **Military Aircraft Museum** in Safonovo, near Severomorsk, is said to house a spectacular exhibition of military aviation. Intourist in Murmansk can arrange tours of either place with 'lots of notice' and heavy bureaucratic intervention. The Apatity city administration can arrange a look at the **atomic cruiser *Admiral Khimov*** when it's in port at Severomorsk, but it needs at least one month's notice. For any of these trips, no one will mention prices or guarantee anything until each case is reviewed. The best help is available from Murmansk Travel & Excursions Bureau (☎ 54 15 52, fax 54 05 66 or Norway ☎ 47-78 99 16 39, fax 78 99 26 34).

NIKEL
НИКЕЛЬ

• pop 21,000

There's nothing to prepare a visitor for Nikel. Even the slums of teeming Indian cities emit some sense of hope, while this particular suburb of hell seems to be past despising its own condition. And for that – as well as for the emotional wrench you're sure to experience – Nikel is most emphatically worth visiting. If Greenpeace needs a poster child or some Hollywood director chooses to film a vision of post-nuclear apocalypse, Nikel is all prepped and ready for the cameras to roll.

Nikel was founded in the 1930s when Finns discovered rich deposits of nickel, but in 1939 the original plant was destroyed. However, it was quickly rebuilt, as nickel became essential to the Nazi war effort. In September 1944, Finland capitulated and handed the entire Pechenga region over to the Soviet Union. The following month, however, the plant was destroyed by German forces and wasn't rebuilt until 1951, when it was taken over by Pechemnikel. Over the years, strip mining operations ripped up the landscape; enormous amounts of sulphur dioxide spilled into the environment, destroying the vegetation for 50km in all directions; and the Soviet regime obviated any sort of artificial enhancements – such as pleasing architecture – that might have awakened some sense of hope.

The small **local museum** features a collection of minerals from the Kola Peninsula, as well as the historical links between Norway, Finland and north-western Russia. If for some reason you want to stay the night, prebooked rooms with shared facilities at the very simple ***Nikel Hotel*** cost $39 per person. If you just turn up, however, you're sure to pay considerably less. The town also has a small and very simple Russian ***stolovaya*** (cafeteria).

Getting There & Away

From Murmansk you can reach Nikel on the snail train, but the fastest and most comfortable option is the bus between Kirkenes (Norway) and Murmansk, which stops briefly and will drop you at the Nikel Hotel.

ZAPOLYARNYE
ЗАПОЛЯРНЫЕ

☎ 81554 • pop 23,000

The nickel-mining town of Zapolyarnye, which is only marginally more tolerable than Nikel, is the proud home of the world's deepest hole, which extends 12km beneath the surface. While there's little else to see, the town does have a decent hotel, ***Hotel Pechenga*** *(☎ 3 65 00)*, and would be a happier place than Nikel to spend the night. Single/double rooms cost $70/110. The high prices are due mainly to the fact that most of the takers are short-term Norwegian visitors (for whom these rates are a bargain!), but individual travellers are likely to get a much better deal. As well as the hotel ***dining room***, there's also a basic Russian ***stolovaya*** in town.

Getting There & Away

The easiest way to reach here is on the bus between Kirkenes, Norway, and Murmansk.

BORISOGLEBSK
БОРИСОГЛЕБСК

• pop 2000

Borisoglebsk, on the Pasvik River at the Norwegian border, was named after the 1565 church which inspired its inclusion in Russia when the boundary was drawn in 1826. The original church, named in honour of the saints Boris and Gleb, fell into disrepair in the mid-19th century and was replaced in 1872. While the original church burned down in 1944, its replacement was restored by Norwegian donors and is now a pleasant and distinctive little attraction. From 1958 to 1963, a Norwegian-Soviet joint project also created the power station and workers' housing projects at Skoltefossen, on the Pasvik River. You need special permission to visit Borisoglebsk, which – when possible at all – is best done through one of the tour agencies in Kirkenes, Norway (see Getting There & Away at the beginning of the Kola Peninsula section).

MONCHEGORSK
МОНЧЕГОРСК

☎ 81536 • pop 75,000

If you've ever had a notion to visit Hell, Monchegorsk is pretty close (perhaps not quite as close as nearby Nikel). The ground here is literally black. Ironically, the Sami name of the town translates as 'beautiful tundra'! The culprit, of course, was the glorious Soviet regime, which aimed to dominate nature with its high-blown delusions. Unfortunately, nature refused to submit without disastrous consequences. In the case of Monchegorsk, the government's brainchild was the Severonikel Kombinat plant. Between 1980 and 1993, this plant and its sister, Pechemnikel in Nikel, processed copper and nickel, and meanwhile spewed 600,000 tonnes of sulphur dioxide into the atmosphere, along with 10,000 tonnes of nickel powder and other heavy metals. In 1994 and 1995 emissions were cut roughly in half, due mainly to lower production, but given the current state of these places, it was clearly too late to make much of a difference.

The irony is, since the fall of the Soviet Union and the related decline in military orders, the plant's main clients are now subcontractors for US and Japanese auto manufacturers, who use its products to manufacture catalytic converters that reduce emissions on Western cars. If there's any good news, it's that reduced demand by the military has led to a 30% reduction in pollution. However, over 1000 sq km of forests have been utterly destroyed and it's unlikely that the damage can ever be reversed. Another irony is that the vicinity's only visitor attraction – unless you're curious about the outer limits of possible ecological devastation – is the nearby Lapland Biosphere Reserve, which is Arctic Russia's most accessible nature reserve.

Places to Stay & Eat

The town's two hotels are the ***Lapplandia*** *(☎ 2 45 26, prospekt Metallurgov 32)*, with single/double rooms from $14.25/20, and the somewhat nicer ***Sever*** *(☎ 2 26 55, prospekt Metallurgov 4)*, nearer the bus station. The latter costs $5.75/7.75. The ***restaurant*** at the Lapplandia is open from noon to 11 pm, and the Sever has a 1st floor ***bufet***.

Getting There & Away

Buses leave to/from Murmansk's bus station several times a day (three hours, $4.50).

LAPLAND BIOSPHERE RESERVE ЛАПЛАНДСКИЙ ЗАПОВЕДНИК

☎ 81536

North and west of Monchegorsk, and spanning north and west towards Norway and Finland, the UNESCO-protected Lapland Biosphere Reserve (Laplansky Zapovednik; ☎ 5 00 80, fax 5 71 99, GilyasovaEV@monch.mels.ru) consists of 2784 sq km of almost pristine wilderness; about half of it is virgin tundra, and the rest consists of alpine grasslands, marshes, rivers, lakes and five small mountain ranges (the highest peak being 1114m). The reserve was founded in 1930 to protect the area's reindeer herds; today over 1000 reindeer live on the biosphere's territory, making it one of the largest concentrations in Europe. Along with 33 species of mammals (including brown bears, elks and wolves), 201 bird species and 15 species of fish, there are more than 900 species of higher plants, mosses and lichens.

The threat to the ecological balance of the park's flora and fauna is multifaceted: on one hand, while the Khibiny mountain range manages to stave off most of the damage that Monchegorsk's nickel plant threatens to inflict, the easternmost section of the park has been decimated. Inside the park itself, poachers and careless trespassers inflict damage too (each year, fires from illegal campfires destroy hectares of forest). These miscreants, along with the usual culprits – local and regional government corruption, lack of funding – make keeping the park alive more difficult. While the Russian government provides minimal funding and the US-based Global Ecological Fund has provided support for an ecological education program, the reserve must mainly rely on itself for maintenance.

Inside, visitors can trek through the wilderness – the best times are March-April, June and August-September – or traverse it on skis, snowshoes or skidoos. The possibilities for adventure tourism are endless, ranging from hiking (the views of seemingly endless stretches of mountains are breathtaking), camping and relaxing nature walks, to winter igloo-building expeditions. There are several waterfalls on the territory, and even a German war plane resting where it fell from the skies during WWII.

Individuals or groups of less than 10 people can visit the reserve any time of the year with advance notice. There are perfectly comfortable ***guest cottages*** at the reserve's main base on the quiet banks of Chuna Lake, but visitors should expect to rough it in tents on longer expeditions. You can rest those weary bones in the base's heavenly *banya* (bathhouse) on Friday along with the friendly forest rangers who live and work there. Costs vary depending on the kind of experience you're looking for, but expect to pay $20 to $40 per day.

What to Bring

It's important to bring layers of warm clothing – the outer layer should be waterproof. You'll also need good, comfortable trekking boots, as much of this landscape is soggy muskeg, and even in the summer it can get mighty wet. Visitors are responsible for their own food and equipment – trail mix and high-protein snacks work best. Don't expect anything to be available at the reserve (one trekking group ran out of Snickers bars after two days and had to rely on the rangers' and guides' own meagre rations). Locals maintain that most of the surface water here is clean and drinkable – which is hard to believe when you consider the nuclear presence and utter devastation so near at hand – so it is a good idea to carry a means of purification. It's also wise to bring navigational equipment, although the guides are quite well equipped.

Getting There & Away

The easiest access is through Monchegorsk. Arrangements to visit the reserve must be made in advance, either directly (the most effective route), or through Eco-Nord (Apatity ☎ 81555-7 97 62, Norway ☎ 47-78 91 41 18).

APATITY
АПАТИТЫ

☎ 81555 • pop 60,000

Apatity, founded in 1966, is the world's greatest source of apatite ore and the Kola Peninsula's second largest city. While the city itself isn't that attractive to nonscientific types, Apatity makes an excellent jumping-off point for hiking, climbing and skiing expeditions in the nearby Khibiny Mountains. You may even spot the Yeti, the Big Foot-like forest loiterer (42cm-long footprints have been found) who is said to put in an occasional appearance and leave its mark. The town is also emerging as a cultural arts and crafts centre.

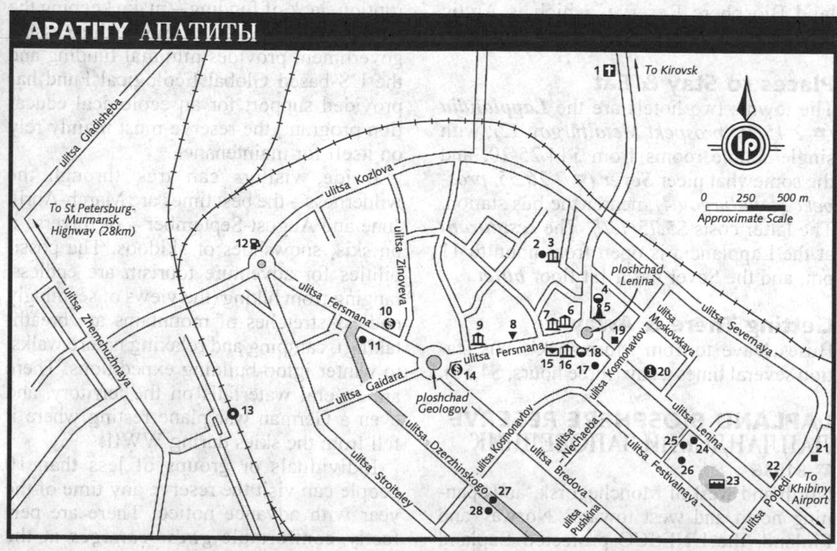

Orientation & Information

Apatity has two main sections, the Akademgorodok ('Academic Town') and the city proper. The main shopping streets are ulitsa Fersmana and ulitsa Lenina. The train station lies south-west of the centre, while the main bus stops lie on ploshchad Lenina (for Monchegorsk and Murmansk) and along ulitsa Fersmana (for Kirovsk). Maps of the region (1:1,000,000 scale) are available from Khiblny TS tour service.

You can change money at one of the two banks: Sperbank, on ulitsa Fersmana, open from 8 am to 8 pm Monday to Friday and 11 am to 5 pm Saturday; and Kommercheskiy Bank Murman, on ploshchad Geologov, open from 9.30 am to 12.30 pm Monday to Friday. The post and telephone offices are on ploshchad Lenina.

Econord (☎/fax 7 85 86, Norway fax 47-78 91 41 18, econord@inep.ksc.ru, PO Box 176, postal index 184200), formerly the Scandinavian Study Centre, is a good source of information; it's in the Akademgorodok, in the same building as the Museum of the History of the Research & Exploration of the North. The Khibiny TS tour service (☎ 3 01 16, fax 3 47 50, hts@khibiny.murmansk.ru), ulitsa Lenina 9A, operates tours around the Kola region, and can also offer town maps and limited tourist information.

Things to See & Do

The best museum in town is the **Museum of the History of the Research & Exploration of the North** (☎ 7 92 55), which was founded in the 1970s and features exhibits on Russian Arctic expeditions, both scientific and exploratory, as well as the Solovetsky Monastery, unique drawings of Novaya Zemlya and 5000-year-old Sami rock carvings, tools and other instruments. It's open from 2 to 5 pm weekdays, but will open anytime for interested visitors.

Rock fans may enjoy the user-friendly **Regional Geological Museum** at ulitsa Fersmana 16, which has fine exhibitions of local rocks and minerals, and local crafts. It's open from 9 am to 6 pm Monday to Friday. You may also want to stroll through the **Open-Air Geological Museum**, farther west on ulitsa Fersmana, which features a few paths lined with local rock samples.

The **swimming pool**, on ulitsa Festivalnaya, is open from 8 am to 10 pm daily except Monday; a 45 minute session costs

APATITY АПАТИТЫ

PLACES TO STAY

19 Hotel Ametist
Гостиница Аметист

21 Apatitstroy Health Centre
Центр Здоровя Апатитстройя

PLACES TO EAT

8 Gril-Bar
Гриль-Бар

22 Restaurant Zapolyarye
Ресторан Заполярье

OTHER

1 Church
Церковь

2 International Study Centre
Центр интернациональный Еконорд

3 Museum of the History of the Research & Exploration of the North
Музей оствоення и изученния российского серева

4 Bus Stop for Kirovsk
Остановка в Кировск

5 Lenin Statue
Памятник Ленину

6 Scientific Mineralogical Museum
Колского научного центр минералогический музей

7 Regional Geological Museum
Геологический музей

9 Open-Air Geological Museum
Геологический музей под открытым небом

10 Sberbank
СберБанк

11 Salma Arts Centre
Центр Художественный Салма

12 Petrol Station
Заправочная станция

13 Train Station
Железнодорожный вокзал

14 Commercheskiy Bank Murman
Коммерческий Банк Мурман

15 Post, Telephone & Telegraph
Почтамт, телефон и телеграф

16 Gallery M
Галлери М

17 Murmansk/Monchegorsk Bus Stop
Остановка в Мурманск/Мончегорск

18 Bus & Aeroflot Flight Ticket Office
Билетные Кассы

20 Khibiny TS Tour Service & Information
Хибины ТурСервис

23 Sports Ground & Swimming Pool
Стадион и Бассейн

24 Library
Библиотека

25 Palace of Culture
Дворец культуры

26 Skating Rink
Каток

27 Market
Рынок

28 Pharmacy
Аптека

$0.50. Staff may ask for a health certificate (which all Russians carry), but if you're clean and look healthy, you probably won't have any problems. Another building worth noting is the **library** which – yes – resembles the pages of an open book.

Apatity is an artistic centre, and a locally invented method of 'painting', using coloured dust from crushed local minerals, is now catching on all over the Russian north. The **Salma Art Salon**, at ulitsa Dzerzhinskogo 1, is a private cooperative outlet for over 200 Kola Peninsula artists. Prices are low, and the management can arrange the paperwork to expedite customs procedures. The exhibition hall to the front holds new art exhibitions and the sales outlet is at the back. The salon also holds occasional church choir presentations and piano recitals. **Gallery M**, on the 2nd floor of the Polyarnye building on ploshchad Lenina, features a changing exhibit of artworks by local artists; it's open from 2 to 6 pm Monday to Saturday.

During the third week in January, the city hosts the Stone Flower Exhibition, in which local minerals are turned into flowery works of art.

Places to Stay & Eat

Hotel Amatist** (☎ 33201, ulitsa Lenina 3)* has clean single/double rooms for $26/32. OK, there's no toilet paper or hot water and they scrub the hallways with petrol daily, but you may get lucky and have a room with a mountain view. There's a smoky bufet/bar on the 2nd floor, open until midnight, and a passable ***dining room on the main floor that's big, loud and very red.

Apatitstroy Health Centre** (Tsentr Zdorovya Apatitstroya; ☎ 3 11 81)*, at the eastern edge of town, is sometimes known as *Isobela* or the *Dom Otdikha* (rest home). It formerly served as the rest and health clinic of the Apatitsroy construction company but has now been opened to the public. This spotless resort features a nice pool and sauna/banya, winter garden and two ***restaurants. Here you'll pay $38/66 for single/double accommodation (these rates seem fairly subjective, as foreigners have reportedly paid as little as $10 per person per day), including meals and access to the pool and sauna. To get there from the centre, take bus No 8 from the train station or ploshchad Lenina.

The adjacent ***Dacha***, a four room hotel with queen-sized beds, a lounge, winter garden, sauna and cold-pool, is fine for groups and costs just $50 per person. An attendant is provided to clean the room and cook up meals using any raw materials you can provide. Contact the Health Centre for bookings and information.

If you don't mind a walk from the centre, try ***Restaurant Zapolyarye*** on ulitsa Pobedi; whenever it's open, it serves up fairly decent fare. At the ***Gril-Bar***, on ulitsa Fersmana, $1 will buy half a hot dog without a bun and for $1.50, you'll get microwaved Cup-o-Soup served in its original packaging (they even let you stir it up yourself). 'Coffee' is a spoonful of powder, a spoonful of sugar and a cup of hot water; from there, you're on your own.

If you can live by bread alone (a real plus in these parts), look for the locally made, round-loaf bread, *Pomorsky khleb* or the ubiquitous *Rom Baba* (which is notably devoid of rum and normally makes its public debut when it's several days old).

Getting There & Away

There are no flights from Murmansk, but Apatity's new Khibiny airport is served from Moscow ($124) daily except weekends, and from St Petersburg ($106) on Monday, Tuesday, Friday and Sunday.

From Murmansk, buses leave at least twice daily ($9, four hours). Most trains between Moscow, St Petersburg and Murmansk stop at Apatity; take any train headed south from Murmansk (five to eight hours). From the St Petersburg-Murmansk highway, Apatity lies 30km down a well signposted eastwards spur road, 35km south of Monchegorsk.

Bus Nos 5 and 13 (not 13K) run between the train station and the town centre. There's an hourly bus to Khibiny airport. Bus Nos 101, 102 and 105 travel between Apatity and Kirovsk.

KIROVSK
КИРОВСК

☎ 815231

The main attraction at Kirovsk is its ski hill, which offers the finest skiing in north-western Russia. In winter, the city hosts the annual All-Europe Downhill Freestyle Competition, and the city's five ski schools hold lessons in ballet skiing, ski-jumping and mogul skiing. There are also annual giant slalom and speed ski competitions. If you're unfortunate enough to break your leg while you're at it, the city's newest church boasts a 'healing' icon that will ostensibly have you fixed up in a jiffy!

The Kirovsk 'microregion', which is essentially a suburb, nestled in the Khibiny Mountains, is known not by its Russian name, Kukisvumchorr, but simply as 'Kirovsk-25'. This is in reference to its distance in kilometres from Apatity, a convention adopted by geological crews who identified dig sites by the nearest milepost.

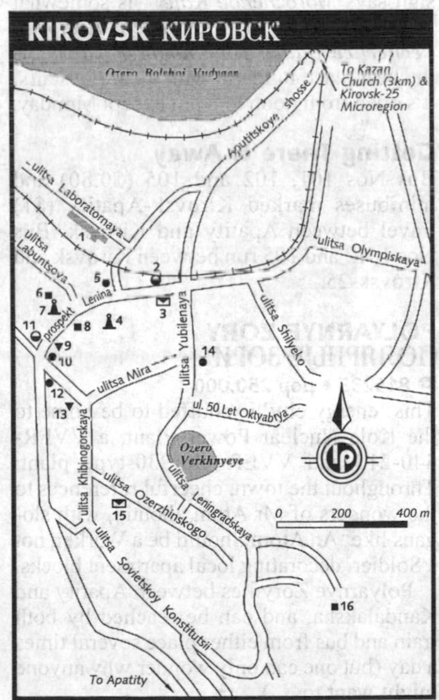

Information

You can change money at the Sberbank on prospekt Lenina. The main post office is also on prospekt Lenina, opposite the bus stop to/from Apatity. Maps are available at the city administration building.

Things to See

The new orthodox **Kazan Church** (Kazanskaya tserkov), en route to Kirovsk-25, is built on the site of another church that had been moved from Kirovsk, and is unorthodox in that it was converted from a typical north Russian wooden house. The inside is lovely, however, with an impressive iconostasis and the allegedly miraculous **Icon of St Nicholas**. On the night of 21 May 1994, the icon incredibly restored itself, and now

KIROVSK КИРОВСК

PLACES TO STAY

6 Hotel Eccos & Casino Fortuna
Гостиница Еккос и Касино Фортуна
8 Hotel Severnaya
Гостиница Северная
16 Khibiny Hotel
Гостиница Хибины

PLACES TO EAT

9 Kafe Zodiak
Кафе Зодияк
13 Restoran Vechernee
Ресторан Вечернее

OTHER

1 Kirovsk Train Station
Железнодорожный вокзал
2 Bus Stop to/from Apatity
Остановка автобуса
3 Main Post Office
Главпочтамт
4 Lenin Statue
Памятник Ленину
5 Market
Рынок
7 Kirov Statue
Памятник Кирову
10 Library
Библиотека
11 Bus Stop to/from Apatity
Остановка автобуса
12 Pharmacy
Аптека
14 Bus Tickets
Билетные Кассы
15 Post Office
Почтамт

works its miracles from 9 am to 6 pm Monday to Friday with a break between 2 and 3 pm. Take bus No 1, 12 or 105 from Kirovsk centre towards Kirovsk-25, and ask for the church. From the bus stop, walk west (back towards Kirovsk), turn south (left), then turn east (left again) and the church is 200m on the right-hand side of the road.

The most impressive building in town is the white elephant **Kirovsk train station**, which like many of the 'Potyomkin villages' that would pop up around Russia (constructed only to impress visiting officials), is an unused and ludicrous monument to Soviet anti-logic. Locals joke that its first and last passenger was Josef Stalin.

The Kirovsk-25 'microregion' has a **Regional Museum** that seems to be perpetually closed, but it's still worth a slog out there to see the surrounding mountains – or rather, the awesome gap where they used to be. A veteran geophysicist for a major Western minerals concern said that he knew of no way to accomplish such a neat removal of literally half a mountain (they look like those school-room models of a cutaway section of a volcano), other than a nuclear detonation, but local scientists insist the feat was accomplished with earth movers and heavy equipment – right. Take bus No 1, 12 or 105 from Kirovsk to the northern end of Kirovsk-25.

Activities

The 17 tow ropes up the city's ski slopes cost around $0.50 to $1 per ride, or $4.50 to $10 for a day pass. Although limited rentals are available, it's best to bring your own equipment. Ski packages can be arranged through the Apatity tour agency Khibiny TS (see Orientation & Information under Apatity earlier in this chapter). The region also offers the best hiking in north-western Russia. The most popular spot is the Khibiny Mountains, where the highest point, Judychvumchorr, rises 1200m above sea level; the Lovozero massif is just to the east.

Places to Stay & Eat

The Hungarian-built ***Hotel Severnaya*** *(☎ 2 04 42, prospekt Lenina 11)* is more or less a Western-standard hotel (except for the tiny Russian hotel beds) right in the town centre. Single or double rooms cost $30 per person, but if you're alone, you may be asked to share the room with a stranger. There's also a lobby bar and a ***restaurant*** with OK food and loud music.

The new ***Hotel Eccos & Casino Fortuna*** *(☎ 2 02 34)*, in a castle-like building in the centre, has rooms for $13/19 and luxury rooms for $55. For breakfast and dinner, you'll pay an additional $18/24 for one/two people. Construction is ongoing and it's wise to assume that when it's complete, prices will increase.

The institutional-looking ***Khibiny Hotel*** *(☎ 2 12 56)* is a large *turbaza* (tourbase) about 1km from the centre. Very basic rooms cost $11/17.

At the ***market*** on prospekt Lenina opposite the Lenin statue, you'll find imported food and drinks; it's open from 11 am to 7 pm. ***Kafe Zodiak*** *(prospekt Lenina 13)* – the sign says *Morozhenoe Kafe* – is somewhat pricey and doesn't offer much. ***Restoran Vechernee*** *(ulitsa Khibinogorskaya 29)* is the best place in town, with a cafe upstairs; it's open from noon to 8 pm except Monday.

Getting There & Away

Bus Nos 101, 102 and 105 ($0.80) and minibuses marked Kirovsk-Apatity ($1) travel between Apatity and Kirovsk. Bus Nos 1, 12 and 105 run between Kirovsk and Kirovsk-25.

POLYARNYE ZORY
ПОЛЯРНЫЕ ЗОРИ

☎ 815233 • pop 250,000

This 'energy city' is chuffed to be home to the Kola Nuclear Power Plant, a VVER-440-213 and VVER-440-230-type plant. Throughout the town, cheerful references to the wonders of Mr Atom abound, with slogans like 'An Atom Should be a Worker, not a Soldier' decorating local apartment blocks.

Polyarnye Zory lies between Apatity and Kandalaksha, and can be reached by both train and bus from either place several times a day (but one can only wonder why anyone might want to ...)

Things to See

Beside the train station is an exhibit optimistically labelled the **Museum of the Polar Partisan**, open from 10 am to 7 pm daily except Wednesday and Thursday.

For something different, the public relations director (☎ 6 81 40 or ☎ 6 39 10) at the **Kola Nuclear Power Plant** may be able to arrange a tour with five days notice. That way, you can marvel at the fish (trout, salmon and others) that swim in the tank filled with the plant's output coolant water (purportedly demonstrating the plant's safety standards).

Places to Stay & Eat

The town's hotel, ***Nevsky Berega*** *(☎ 6 41 51, ulitsa Lomonosova 1)*, is spotlessly clean, with comfortable doubles for $25. Most rooms have terraces overlooking the forest and there's a fair ***restaurant***. The ***Pivnoy Bar*** next to the market isn't bad if you feel like a snack.

KANDALAKSHA КАНДАЛАКША

☎ 81533 • pop 45,000

The Kola Peninsula's most important port after Murmansk, Kandalaksha is now a rather grim industrial city, and home to one of the military's most important aluminium plants. The Pomory fishing village, around which the town was founded and which dates from the 17th century, is still inhabited. Several daily buses from Apatity, and at least one daily from Murmansk, serve Kandalaksha. In addition, any Murmansk train will stop here. Local buses run between the train and bus stations, north-east of town, and the centre, which lies to the south-west, over the railway line.

Things to See & Do

The large **nature reserve & sea-bird sanctuary** (Kandalakshisky Gosudarstvenny Zapovednik), on the White Sea Islands, south-west of the town, is home to more than 250 species of sea birds. Most prominent are the eider ducks, gulls, murres, kittiwakes, razorbills and black guillemots, which nest in the rookeries of the Kuvshin and Kharlov islands. Summer visits can be arranged through the city administration (☎ 2 49 57), the city excursions bureau (☎ 5 03 96) or the reserve administration centre, at the southern end of town.

To reach the reserve, take bus No 1 from the train station to the last stop and walk towards the port; the administration centre will be on the left, across the river from the Pomory village. For more information, you can contact the American Association for the Support of Ecological Initiatives (☎ 1-203-347 29 67, fax 1-203-347 84 59, wwasch@eagle.wesleyan.edu), 150 Coleman Rd, Middletown, CT 06457, USA.

Places to Stay & Eat

Belomore Hotel *(☎ 2 31 00 or ☎ 2 20 13, ulitsa 50-letia Oktyabrya dom 1)* has surly staff and grotty single/double rooms for $26/35, with a ***restaurant*** that opens 'in the evening' (better opt for the ***Gril-Bar***, next door). Much better – but nevertheless quite dumpy – ***Hotel Spolokhi*** *(☎ 5 57 68, ulitsa Naberezhnaya 130)*, east of the centre, towards the riverbank, has rooms for $25/36 as well as a ***restaurant*** that's open on weekends and a bufet that operates on weekdays until 4 pm. (The desk clerk thought the author was using a compass to measure background radiation and she didn't seem surprised in the least that someone would measure radiation in the hotel lobby.)

Arkhangelsk Region Архангельская область

ARKHANGELSK АРХАНГЕЛЬСК

☎ 8182 • pop 375,400

Arkhangelsk's grim history, a product of its strategic location, has ensured that since its inception many of its residents have worn some sort of uniform.

Unfortunately, this grimness is reflected in the city's modern look; it is not a pretty city by any stretch of the imagination.

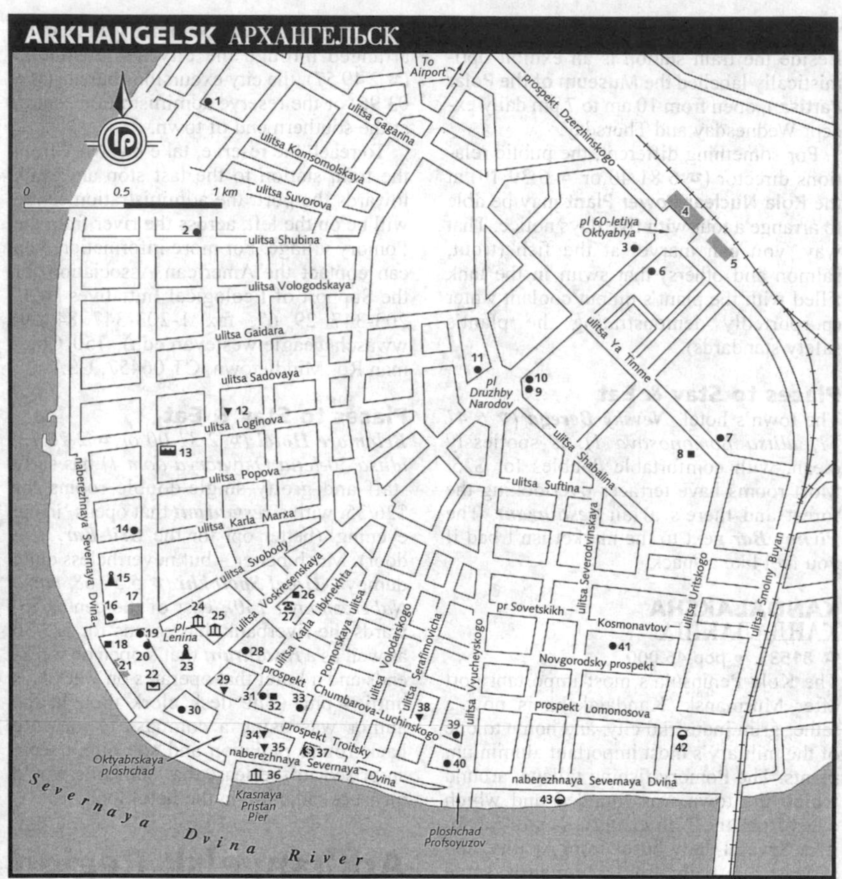

Despite a few architectural remnants from the past – which are all concentrated along the waterfront – most of Arkhangelsk is a sprawling expanse of concrete. Still, a few century-old wooden houses survive (mainly concentrated on prospekt Chumbarova-Luchinskogo), and the contrast with their next-door Soviet structures is unique.

The waterfront has a fishing village feel to it, yet a few blocks away you're face-to-face with Lenin and a view of gigantic concrete eyesores.

What it lacks in aesthetics, however, is more than made up for by a populace that is surely among the friendliest in all of Russia (even the operators don't hang up on you!), and one that is well connected with the world at large. There's a real sense of Arkhangelsk as a 'happening' city if you meet the right people (the underground scene is straining to burst), and it has a palpably magical atmosphere.

Most tourists will, however, want to use Arkhangelsk merely as a jumping-off point to one of the region's other offerings, such as the untamed northern wilderness, the open-air museum at Malye Korely, or the Solovetsky Islands.

ARKHANGELSK АРХАНГЕЛЬСК

PLACES TO STAY

8 Hotel Belamorskaya **Гостиница Беламорская**
18 Pur Navolok Hotel **Пур Наволок Отель**
26 Business Centre Hotel **Бизнес-центр Отель**
32 Hotel Dvina **Гостиница Двина**

PLACES TO EAT

12 Kafe-Bar Kardinal
29 Rendez-vous
34 Cafe Yaroslavna **Кафе Ярославна**
35 Solovetsky Podvor **Соловецкое Подворье**
38 Pof-Bun Pizzeria

OTHER

1 Snezhok **Снежок**
2 Modern
3 Bookshop **Книги**
4 Train Station **Железнодорожный вокзал**
5 Bus Station **Автовокзал**
6 Aeroflot Office **Аэрофлот**
7 Market **Рынок**
9 Sport City
10 Art Gallery
11 Cultural Centre
13 Swimming Pool **Бассейн**
14 Concert Hall **Концертный зал**
15 Great Patriotic War Monument **Памятник Великой Отечественной Войны**
16 Pomor Tur
17 State Medical Academy & Internet Salon **Государственная Медицинская Академия**
19 Detsky Mir
20 Administration Building **Административное здание**
21 Old Gostiny Dvor **Гостиный Двор**
22 Post Office **Почтамт**
23 Lenin Statue **Памятник В. И. Ленину**
24 Regional Studies Museum **Краеведческий музей**
25 Fine Arts Museum **Художественый музей**
27 Telephone Office **Телефон**
28 Dom Knigi **Дом Книги**
30 Lomonosov Drama Theatre **Драматический театр им. Ломоносова**
31 Supermarket
33 Avia Tur
36 State Naval Museum of the North **Морской Музей Севера**
37 Incombank **Инкомбанк**
39 Central Market **Центральный рынок**
40 Dvorets Sporta **Дворец спорта**
41 Club MKC **МКС**
42 Bus Stop to Malye Korely
43 Sea Terminal **Морской вокзал**

History

The construction of present-day Arkhangelsk was decreed by Ivan the Terrible in 1574, 21 years after the arrival of the first British traders who – searching for a northern access route to China – ended up in what was then a remote fishing settlement along the Severnaya Dvina River. Ivan, then still in his pre-Terrible period, enthusiastically accepted Britain's advances and established trade ties with England. The Brits, keen to discover an enormous new market for their wool, established the Muscovy Company in late 1553.

In 1693 Peter the Great, fully charged with his vision of a great Russian navy, built an admiralty and seaport at Arkhangelsk, from where he launched the Russian navy's tiny first ship, the *Svyatoy Pavel*, in 1694.

The importance of Arkhangelsk's port as a centre for trade, especially with Western Europe, led to an enormous bazaar, which reached the height of its power in the late 1700s. The 19th century and the early 20th century established Arkhangelsk as a major lumber centre, which it remains today.

Allied troops have twice played an important role in the city's history. During Russia's civil war, the allied 'interventionists' managed to land at Arkhangelsk on 2 August 1918, but otherwise accomplished nothing because of confusion and a breakdown in communication within their own multinational ranks.

During WWII, Arkhangelsk, along with Murmansk, became a key supply port bringing desperately needed foreign equipment to the Russian army, and food to supply the besieged city of Leningrad. Before and after the war, the region was home to numerous prison camps, and many of today's residents are descendants of prisoners and exiles.

Orientation

Arkhangelsk sits on a peninsula jutting into the Severnaya Dvina River. The city's streets sprawl in a rough 'V' shape with an axis formed by ulitsa Voskresenskaya, which cuts from the river at the south-west to the train and bus stations at the north-east. The most obvious landmark is the 22 storey towering skyscraper on ploshchad Lenina, an area which serves as the city's administrative centre. There is no central core as in most cities, aside from the waterfront which, in summer, is teeming with activity, and so it takes some hunting to find the city's heart and soul – this, it turns out, is spread out evenly everywhere.

City maps are available at the bookshop opposite the Aeroflot office on ulitsa Voskresenskaya and are sometimes available at the main Dom Knigi bookshop on ploshchad Lenina.

Information

Money You can change money at Incombank, on the corner of prospekt Troitsky and ulitsa Pomorskaya; or inside the post office or at any of the hotels.

Post & Communications The main post office is on the west side of ploshchad Lenina at ulitsa Voskresenskaya 5. It's open from 8 am to 7 pm weekdays, and 9 am to 5 pm on weekends. There's a DHL express courier (☎ 65 25 96) at ploshchad Lenina 4 (the 22 storey monstrosity), 5th floor.

The central telephone office is on the corner of prospekt Lomonosova and ulitsa Voskresenskaya. It is open 24 hours, and has photocopy and fax services (the number to receive a fax is ☎ 65 03 09). You can rent mobile phones for only $2 a day (plus a $24 deposit) at Artenekom (☎ 65 12 12), around the corner at ulitsa Voskresenskaya 8.

There's an Internet Salon (☎ 43 38 74) in room 424 of the State Medical Academy on prospekt Troitsky, just north of ulitsa Svobody (enter from the courtyard on the northern side). It is open from 9 am to 9 pm daily and charges $0.60 an hour.

Travel Agencies Pomor Tur (☎ 43 97 97, pomortur@atnet.ru), ulitsa Svobody 3, is the place to go. It can assist tourists with just about everything, and has the most experience in organising city and regional tours, excursions to the Solovetsky Islands and to lesser known islands in the area, as well as arranging personalised ventures out into the tundra and wilderness.

Fine Arts Museum

The city's surprisingly good Fine Arts Museum (☎ 65 35 34) on the north-east side of ploshchad Lenina boasts an impressive selection of 16th to 18th century religious artworks on the 2nd floor. Towards the rear of the 2nd floor you'll also find 19th century textiles, and some applied decorative art. There's also a good selection of paintings and portraits with 'northern' themes, and an extensive Imperial Portrait Gallery. Look for Stanislav Khlebovsky's portraits (1861) of Catherine II and the dead Prince Oranskogo.

The mezzanine level, looking very much like a tiny New York Soho loftspace, is host to classical and jazz concerts (call to find out about schedules) and temporary exhibits. In the entrance lobby, art books and very good handicrafts are for sale. Admission is $0.80; guided tours cost $2. It's open from 10 am to 5 pm daily (closed Tuesday).

Regional Studies Museum

The main reason to come to this museum (Kraevedchesky muzey; ☎ 43 66 79), also on the north-west side of ploshchad Lenina a few doors down from the Fine Arts Museum, is to see the superbly designed, sobering exhibition on the 2nd floor dedicated to local soldiers who died in the Afghanistan war. The albums, containing snapshots taken by Russian soldiers during the conflict, give a first-hand view of conditions in that country, and there is a moving display of personal effects and letters sent home from soldiers who died. Adjacent to this is a sombre account of the city's Soviet era (surprisingly few museums in Russia, to this day, portray those times in a negative light). The 1st floor houses a taxidermy collection of local sea life that's interesting in a ghoulish sort of way. Admission is $0.30. It's open from 10 am to 6 pm every day (closed Friday and the last Thursday of the month).

State Naval Museum of the North

The Naval Museum of the North (☎ 43 03 44), facing the docks at the edge of the water, just east of the Krasnaya Pristan pier, features a well laid-out exhibit on Soviet polar expeditions (there's lots on the nuclear dump that is now Novaya Zemlya), and models of 18th century ice-breakers. It even sells sea salt for your bath. It's open from 10 am to 4.45 pm daily (closed Monday); admission is $0.15.

Severnaya Dvina Embankment

Walking along the Severnaya Dvina embankment makes for a lovely stroll at any time of year. Between ulitsa Voskresenskaya and ulitsa Svobody, you'll pass the **Gostiny Dvor** (trading arcade), built at the beginning of the 18th century. This was the largest building in Russia until St Petersburg's Gostiny Dvor was built, but today only a fraction of ithe original structure remains. Have a peep inside – there's a bookshop on the 2nd floor – and don't jump as a very life-like Lenin statue greets you as you enter.

Star Trek fans will appreciate the shape of the city's **Great Patriotic War Monument** just south of ulitsa Karla Marxa. Turning up ulitsa Karla Marxa brings you to the city's **concert hall** (Kamerny kontsertny zal, ☎ 43 80 66), one of the more aesthetically successful Soviet church conversions – the acoustics are superb. Concerts are held several times a month, as are Lutheran services.

Activities

The Dvorets Sporta (☎ 43 61 49), on ploshchad Profsoyuzov at naberezhnaya Severnaya Dvina 38, has a good, 24 hour billiards hall (and bar) in the basement ($2 an hour), ice-skating from Monday to Saturday afternoons for $1/0.60 adults/children, aerobics classes and hosts sporting events.

Places to Stay

In summer, the ***State Medical University's Student Services*** *(☎ 43 75 74, kkolomentseva@asma.ru)* rents out dorm rooms in the city centre for $17, doubles or triples. The monstrous, 500 room ***Hotel Dvina*** *(☎ 26 88 88, root@dvina.sts.ru, prospekt Troitsky 52)* is the most conveniently located and is perfectly OK, with clean singles/doubles from $11. Luxury rooms cost $23. ***Hotel Belomorskaya*** *(☎ 46 53 27, belhotel@atnet.ru, ulitsa Ya Timme 3)* is slightly cheaper, and is a better choice, though in a dull area of town. It also offers hostel-like places in doubles, triples and four-bed rooms for $2 and up, and has email service in the lobby.

Most foreigners choose ***Pur Navolok Hotel*** *(☎ 43 01 26, ihotel@mail.sts.ru, naberezhnaya Severnaya Dvina 88)*. It has bay-windowed rooms with very nice river views from $27 to $72, and all the services and conveniences. There is now a true luxury hotel in town, the ***Business Centre Hotel*** *(☎ 26 91 30, fax 47-78 91 61 43, ulitsa Voskresenskaya 8)*, with kind of deluxe singles/doubles for $110/160.

Places to Eat

The town's well stocked central ***market*** is on the corner of prospekt Chumbarova-Luchinskogo and ulitsa Vyucheyskogo, near the river station. There's also an astoundingly well stocked ***supermarket*** next to Hotel Dvina, open daily from 9 am to 9 pm.

Solovetsky Podvor *(☎ 65 24 18, naberezhnaya Severnaya Dvina 78)*, located in a part of the Arkhangelsk 'branch' of the Solovetsky monastery, is an absolute must. There are two dining halls here: inside is an overpriced and stuffy restaurant, but take the first door on your left and you're into a friendly and traditional Russian *izba* (cottage), serving delicious variations of national dishes like white salmon in nut sauce and beef stewed in *kvas* for under $2.50. Try the hot honey drink, or appetiser (Western) buffet. It's open from noon to 2 am weekdays, to 4 am weekends.

Kafe-Bar Kardinal *(☎ 62 36 73, prospekt Lomonosova 206)* is the other top choice in town. In a sublimely cosy, medieval-style, cellar-like room, you can enjoy the tastiest food in the city by a roaring fire. It has mostly meat dishes (no doubt to feed the tough guys who guard the place), including 25 fish dishes, on its extensive menu, with no meal more than $5. The fanciest place in town is the restaurant inside the ***Pur Navolok Hotel***. Service here is top-rate, the food sumptuous and the decor charming, but you pay for it.

Cafe Yaroslavna *(prospekt Troitsky 37/1)* opposite the Hotel Dvina has very good Georgian food, and farther down prospekt Troitsky at No 64, ***Rendez-vous***, open 24 hours, has the longest, most complex menu in town (though only about half of it is available at any time) – and the coldest atmosphere.

The only pizzeria in town serves 25 different kinds of delicious pizza. ***Pof-Bun*** *(☎ 43 43 61, prospekt Chumbarova-Luchinskogo 8)* is in a charming house near the central market. It is open from 11 am to 11 pm daily, and they say they deliver.

You'd have to travel to Moscow to get a better cup of coffee or cappuccino than the one served in ***Magazin Coffee*** *(ulitsa Popova 14)*, inside the Dom Byta department store, a paradise for caffeine addicts. It's open from 8 am to 7 pm Monday to Saturday; it also runs the next-door ***Cafe 1999***, but it's not nearly as good.

Entertainment

There's no lack of choice for nightlife in town. The hottest, most frenetic place for an alternative (but collegiate) crowd – no pop allowed – is ***MKC*** *(prospekt Novgorodsky 34/2)*, held on Friday and Saturday from 10.30 pm to 6 am inside a cavernous student dorm. The city's coolest, hippest DJs spin here. More traditional discotheques include ***Modern*** *(☎ 29 20 74, ulitsa Shubina 9)*, open Thursday to Sunday from 11 pm, and ***Snezhok***, open Friday to Sunday after 6 pm, on the corner of prospekt Troitsky and ulitsa Komsomolskaya. Both of these host fashion shows or concerts every so often.

The city's ***Cultural Centre*** *(☎ 46 39 19)*, right on ploshchad Druzhby Narodov, also has weekend discos (not very popular) and sometimes very good jazz, cabaret or comedy shows.

Shopping

For some reason, Arkhangelsk has some of the best antiques and souvenirs in north-western Russia. Start at the Detsky Mir on prospekt Troitsky 47. On the 2nd floor you'll find Vologda lace (a better selection than you'll get in Vologda), national costumes, and handmade birch souvenirs. On the 3rd floor is an excellent antique shop, Russkaya Starina (☎ 65 18 99) which is full of surprises. Ask them to open up the old and rare book section if it's closed. There's another antique kiosk and mini art salon selling local paintings of northern landscapes inside the Dom Knigi. More original souvenirs can be found at the shop right next to the Solovetsky Podvor restaurant, and inside the Regional Studies Museum.

Getting There & Away

Air There is twice daily service to/from Moscow's Sheremetevo-1 ($54, three hours), daily to/from St Petersburg's Pulkovo-1 ($40), and five times weekly to/from Murmansk ($39) airports. There are also flights three times weekly to/from Rovaniemi in Finland and once a week to/from Tromsø in Norway.

The Aeroflot office (☎ 23 80 98) is at ulitsa Voskresenskaya 116, just west of the train and bus stations. Foreigners must use window No 9. In the centre, the central airline ticketing agent is Avia Tur (☎ 26 83 01) at ulitsa Pomorskaya 7. Arkhangelsk Airlines can be reached at ☎ 65 41 00.

The airport code for Arkhangelsk is ARH, and the airport information line is ☎ 43 94 70.

Train There is at least one direct train a day to/from Moscow's Yaroslavl Station (24 hours). Indirect trains can be taken through Vologda and then farther north. There are four trains a week to/from St Petersburg (28 to 35 hours). There is a train every second day to/from Murmansk, but there's only one wagon for the journey (32 hours). Call ☎ 23 72 41 for information.

Car & Motorcycle From Moscow, take the M8 north through Vologda, but bring extra shock absorbers. It's about 1100km.

Boat Regular passenger service has been suspended since 1994. Check with Pomor Tur for any recent changes.

Getting Around
There is an extensive network of buses, trams and taxi-buses. Bus No 54 goes from the bus station to the centre. Bus No 531 runs between the bus station and Arkhangelsk airport about once an hour from 5.55 am to 7.30 pm. Bus No 12 also runs between the bus station and the airport. Taxis can be ordered on ☎ 26 88 88.

MALYE KORELY
МАЛЫЕ КОРЕЛЫ
The open-air **Wooden Architecture Museum** (☎ 99 57 38) at Malye Korely, 25km east of Arkhangelsk, features 19th century wooden buildings, windmills and watermills, bell towers, the standout St George's Church (Georgevskaya tserkov, 1672) and the impressive five domed **Ascension Church** (Vosnesenskaya tserkov, 1669), all brought here from various places throughout the Arkhangelsk region. The architecture and construction are similar to that found in Kizhi, and the natural scenery around the reserve is quite pleasant. The Mezensky section of the museum grounds features some of the most interesting structures and the nicest views of the surrounding valleys.

Follow the large map of the grounds to your left as you enter. Most of the buildings, the churches and **chyornye izby** (or 'black cottages', so called because the lack of a full chimney resulted in smoke staining the outside walls) are open to exploration.

At the main museum area, **horse rides** are offered, though you don't get much time on the beastie. The museum is open every day from 10 am to 6 pm, in winter until 3 pm (closed Tuesday). Admission is $0.80.

Getting There & Away
Bus No 104 goes from Arkhangelsk's bus station and bus No 111 from the train station; buses run every half-hour or so until 10.30 pm. To catch either (or the faster taxi-bus No 104) wait at the bus stop on the south-western corner of prospekt Lomonosova and ulitsa Uritskogo, where they all make stops. Malye Korely is bus No 104's last stop; on No 111, ask for the museum.

SEVERODVINSK
СЕВЕРОДВИНСК
☎ 8151 • pop 236,200

The only reason to visit Severodvinsk, 40km south-west of Arkhangelsk, is to catch a glimpse of the atomic and diesel submarines parked in its harbour. Unfortunately, Severodvinsk is also a closed military city because of the atomic and diesel submarines parked in its harbour. Legal visits to the city can be arranged through Pomor Tur in Arkhangelsk if enough notice is given, but you should have a very good reason. It's easy to travel to the city (though there were rumours in 1999 that a border will soon go up again to keep out anyone, foreigner or Russian, without the proper documents), but if you are caught there without proper permission, you are risking trouble with the police, at worst deportation and possible arrest. Bear in mind that Lonely Planet does not advise illegal travel in restricted areas, and if you do decide to go independently, a day trip must suffice. You won't be permitted to stay in any hotel without the proper stamp on your visa. Pomor Tur can help you to obtain official permission and to get you there.

The city was the main base for the construction and staging of atomic materials (including subs) for use in the above ground nuclear testing range on the islands of Novaya Zemlya, 500km north-east of Arkhangelsk. Those activities have, thankfully, been brought to a halt, and with a drop-off in military orders, the factory isn't working much these days.

Despite its military nature, the town has lovely areas, with wide tree-lined streets and wooden Stalin-era houses.

Orientation & Information
Severodvinsk is laid out in a sensible grid, with the train station at the north-east end of town on ulitsa Zheleznodorozhnikov, which is due north of the harbour. The central post, telephone and telegraph office is at ulitsa Plyusina 1, off ploshchad Lenina. The town's central market is next to the train station. There are a few cafes and cafeterias in this area.

Submarines

The submarines are across the harbour from the naval base, which is at the northern end of ulitsa Portovaya. Take bus No 3, which circles the city anticlockwise from the train station, to ulitsa Trudy (in front of the statue labelled 'Geroi Truda'). Walk north on ulitsa Trudy, left on Pervomayskaya ulitsa and take the first right onto Portovaya ulitsa. (If you get lost, you could always imitate Ensign Chekhov in *Star Trek IV* and say, 'We are looking for the nuclear wessles'.)

At the end of Portovaya ulitsa you'll come to a gate; this is the entrance to the base. As soon as you cross this point (if you are lucky enough to find it unstaffed) you are irretrievably in violation of Russian law and no amount of 'But officer, I didn't see the sign' will help you.

At the water, turn left and walk along the piers. The subs are just across the harbour to the north-west. If you should happen upon someone in uniform, it's best to ask permission – in Russian – to stick around.

A much less risky (and perfectly legal) way of viewing the subs is from the long bridge to Yagry Island. From the bus station, take bus No 1, 10 or 15 to Yagry Island and get off at the Chaika stop just before the bridge, then walk across it and about midway, on your left, you'll have a view of the harbour. The black dots are the subs.

Getting There & Away

Bus No 133 and several taxi-buses from the Arkhangelsk bus station (and the sea terminal) make the 70 minute trip frequently, all day. It costs $0.30. There is no train service to Severodvinsk.

SOLOVETSKY ISLANDS СОЛОВЕЦКИЕ ОСТРОВА

• pop 1200

Perched in the forbidding waters of the White Sea's lower reaches, 165km south of the Arctic Circle, are the Solovetsky Islands (the largest of these, as well as its main village, is often referred to as Solovki). The islands have always been used for exile and retreat: here was one of the most famous monasteries in the Russian Empire, a tsarist-era penal colony, and one of the cruellest Soviet prison camps. Fate has seen to it that it's still a place from which few can leave. Though the islands have been protected as a reserve park since 1974, funding is scarce and residents are too poor to head for brighter shores. For travellers unphased by remote locations and complications in getting there, the islands offer unparalleled beauty, with frequent reminders of their troubled history to keep one's mood sober.

Expect it to be cool to cold whenever you visit. Though summer days can be as hot as 20°C, if you aren't prepared for cool evenings, or if you forget your mosquito repellent, you too will get to know something about suffering here.

History

Though reconstructed stone labyrinths on the islands, dating from the 1st and 2nd centuries BC, prove that the location was used in ancient times for worship, the modern history of the Solovetsky Islands begins in 1429 when two monks from the Kyrill-Belozersk Monastery, Savvaty and German, founded a wooden monastery in the area now called Savatevo. In the mid-16th century, another monk, Philip (who Ivan the Terrible later had murdered for his outspoken views against the tsar), founded the stone churches and thick fortress walls which still stand inside today's kremlin.

The monastery's economic prosperity from salt mines and a brisk handicrafts trade emboldened the monks to refuse the state-backed religious reforms during the 17th century Orthodox schism. These renegade Old Believers held their own in the resulting eight year battle with tsarist forces (1668-76), but were defeated when betrayed by one of their own, Feoktist.

Solovki has been used as a prison or place of forced exile for political and religious criminals since the 16th century. In 1923, a work camp for 'enemies of the people' was opened. At first, prisoners worked fairly freely, keeping up the Botanical Gardens and libraries. But in 1937, Stalin reorganised it into one of the severest Gulags in his empire. Isolated from central command, officers maintained the prisoners in intolerable conditions, torturing or killing them at will. Some of its most famous inmates were mathematician Pavel Florensky (shot there in 1937), linguist DS Likachov, poet and priest Anatoly Zhurakovsky, along with hundreds of other artists, writers and intelligentsia. The prison was closed in 1939.

During WWII, the islands became the base of a special navy youth wing and remained an important Northern Fleet base until recently. Tourism flourished in the late 1980s, when up to 40,000 people visited yearly. The number of Russian tourists has dropped off sharply due to lack of funds, and today there are only some 4000 visitors a year, mainly 'new Russians' and Finns. The monastery reopened in the early 1990s.

Orientation & Information

The Solovetsky Islands are comprised of six separate islands, with a combined land mass of 300 sq km, and over 500 lakes. Solovetsky is by far the largest (24km north to south, and 16km east to west), and all of the islands' services are in the village surrounding the kremlin.

There is a bank with mysterious operating hours, but it may not be able to change currency. A general store with similarly unpredictable opening hours, facing the monastery, has film, souvenirs, hardware and clothing. Late morning seems the best time to find these spots open. The central post office operates from 10 am to 1 pm weekdays, but from 9 am to 5 pm on Monday and Friday.

There is no way to make a direct long-distance call to the islands. Call the operator (speaking Russian is a must) and ask to be connected through an Arkhangelsk operator. Calls from the island can be made through special arrangements at the hotels.

Kremlin

You can tour many of the nonresidential kremlin buildings, either on your own or as part of a tour. The only church with regular services (8 am and 5 pm daily) is the **Annunciation Church** (Blagoveschenskaya tserkov, 1596-1601). The others have largely been under renovation for the last 30 years. It is nonetheless possible to visit the **Transfiguration Cathedral** (Preobrazhensky sobor, 1558-66), the **Assumption Church** (Uspenskaya tserkov, 1552-57), and the majestic **St Nicholas Church** (Glavny Nikolsky tserkov, 1832-34) with its adjoining **bell tower** (1777), a climb to the top of which is a must for the greatest view of the island.

State Historical-Architectural Museum

The most arresting room in the islands' sole museum focuses on the Gulag period. The walls are lined with official images of smiling workers from the Soviet period, but the detailed exhibits show the unofficial story of pain and suffering in prisons like these. The museum is open from 9 am to 5 pm daily (closed Monday). Admission is $2.

Sekirnaya Gora

Literally 'Hatchet Mountain', Sekirnaya Gora is 12km from the kremlin and is infamous thanks to the tortures Alexander Solzhenitsyn alleged took place there in his *Gulag Archipelago* (scholars now dispute many of his claims as unfounded). The unassuming **Church of the Ascension** (1857-62) at the top of the steep hill was used for solitary confinement. Many prisoners died there from cold and starvation, and their bodies were thrown down the stairs next to the church. At the bottom of the stairs lies a traditional maritime cross in memory of all who died on Solovki, placed there in the late 1980s by the Russian Patriarch. The church is perpetually closed, open only on 4 and 10 June, traditional days for memorial services on the island. There is a spectacular lookout in front of the church.

Khutor Gorka Botanical Gardens

Founded by the monastery in 1822, 5km from the kremlin, this is one of the northernmost botanical gardens in the world. Nestled in a heat-trapping valley and interlaced with an intricate system of underground hot-water pipes, the gardens boast trees and plants usually found in more southern climates.

Abandoned Prison

On the same territory as Solovki Tur (see Places to Stay & Eat) is a vacant ex-prison; roaming freely inside the ruins makes for an even creepier experience than visiting the Peter & Paul Fortress in St Petersburg. Door numbers, markings on walls, and guards' observation windows are still intact.

Places to Stay & Eat

If you're interested in experiencing the Gulag times first-hand, you can always find a place at ***Museum Hotel*** *(☎ 339, ☎ 321 or ☎ 327),* inside the kremlin at the far end of the complex. Large, damp rooms which used to accommodate prisoners offer shared space for three to eight people per room (though you're likely to get one by yourself) for only $2 a night. The spring beds seem to date from the Gulag times too. There is a kitchen of sorts, in which you can prepare meals, but no hot water, no showers, and a shared toilet (actually, a shared hole). Still, the place has helpful staff and a unique atmosphere.

Cultural-Hotel House Solovki *(☎ 246 or ☎ 283, Kovaleva 8)* has spacious, though damp and chilly rooms, and unfriendly owners. Singles or doubles with private shower and toilet are $15 per person, and shared facilities in rooms for two to four people are $8. Meals are an extra $5 for breakfast, $10 for lunch and $8 for dinner.

The best deal in the village is ***Hotel Priyout*** *(☎ 297, Primorskaya 11).* Clean, quiet rooms with modern, shared facilities for one to four people are $15 a night ($35 with three full meals; if you don't need three meals, a price can be arranged). Saunas are $5 extra, and a small car can be rented cheaply to tour the island privately. The staff are lovely and very helpful. Ask for a room facing the monastery.

The most luxurious place is worthwhile if you're planning to stay a few days and can afford $50 per person per day, including three meals. Two kilometres outside the main village, ***Solovki Tur*** *(☎ 214, Varyazheskaya 1)* boasts quiet, renovated cottages with single, double and triple rooms, and clean, shared facilities. Spacious living rooms have satellite TV and fireplaces. For $5, the friendly staff will prepare a traditional Russian *banya* (bathhouse). Pedal-boating and fishing are also possible (there's a lake on the premises), as is a laundry service, unavailable elsewhere. They can also provide transportation.

Eating out will prove a problem. There are no restaurants, but it is possible to make meal arrangements at any of the hotels without staying there. ***Produkty shops*** along ulitsa Zaozyora and ulitsa Kavaleva offer a fair selection of goods. It's still advisable to bring food from the mainland.

The only bar in town is ***Max***, on ulitsa Zaozyora, open until 1 am on Saturdays. It's a disco with an ice cream bar, where locals get into dramatic fist fights in between techno dances.

Getting There & Away

Air There is one or two 45 minute flights a week (Friday is the only certain one) to the Solovetsky Islands from Arkhangelsk, $18 each way. Schedules can be confirmed at the Vaskovo aerodrome from which flights leave Arkhangelsk (☎ 45 09 26, aoao@mail.sts.ru). Planes for up to 17 people can also be rented for $150 each way through the rather pushy Solovki Tours in Arkhangelsk (☎ 8182-44 31 19).

Boat There is no longer scheduled service to Solovki from Arkhangelsk and Belomorsk. While Turbaz Kem (☎ 81458-2 03 85), ulitsa Energetikov 22 in Kem, or Pomor Tur or Solovki Tour in Arkhangelsk will be happy to book you onto their tours of the islands, the most economical way to go is on your own, through Kem. Few individuals make their way there unaccompanied by a tour, but it is quite possible. In Kem, take bus No 1 across from the train station to the last stop, the village of Rabocheostrovsk, a 35 minute ride away. Boats leave from the tiny port there at 4 pm on Wednesday and Saturday (three hours, $11), but the only sure way to double-check these sometimes changing times is to call the Museum Hotel or one of the other hotels on the islands (the port has no number, and

Turbaz Kem may be unwilling to provide information if you are not booked on one of its tours).

Ger-Piter Tours in St Petersburg (☎ 812-262 13 18, fax 262 55 61) can organise group tours to Solovki from St Petersburg.

Getting Around

You will need people's help to see the sites outside the village. The Museum Hotel, the reserve park's headquarters and the Cultural-Hotel House Solovki all offer organised tours of Solovki, to the Anzer and Large Muksalma islands, as well as rowing boat trips through the system of canals that links several lakes. These tours cost between $4 and $20 per tour and are worthwhile, though they're often in Russian only. But the best way to see the main island is on your own. There is no official bike rental, but if your Russian is good enough, try renting one from a villager; otherwise ask at the Museum Hotel for help. The 25km round trip to Sekirnaya Gora and Savatevo makes for a nice afternoon bike excursion – that is, if you don't mind braving dirt roads and mosquitoes.

Vologda Region
Вологодская область

VOLOGDA
ВОЛОГДА

☎ 8172 • pop 304,300

'Liberated' by Novgorod from the Finns in the 12th century, Vologda thenceforth led a reasonably happy existence thumbing its nose at the Novgorodians. Taking Moscow's side against all comers seemingly from the moment of its inception, Vologda was rewarded by Ivan the Terrible, who deemed the quaint city was perhaps worthy of his living there (Vologdians are steadfast in their belief that the city was a contender for Russian capital), and a perfect site for a grand cathedral.

Vologda was an important centre of industry, commerce and arts – Vologda lace is still a coveted luxury item – up to the 17th century, but with the increasing importance of Arkhangelsk as a port and the founding of St Petersburg, Vologda's economic powerhouse status was revoked. With the construction in the late 19th century of a railway linking it to Moscow, St Petersburg and Arkhangelsk, Vologda became known more as a gateway between power centres than a force of its own. At the start of the 20th century, many political undesirables (like one Josef Stalin and philosopher Nikolai Berdyaev) were exiled there. And, for a few months in 1918, Vologda became the diplomatic capital of Russia.

Today Vologda is a pleasant provincial city with a high concentration of churches and monasteries, and many lovely parks and wooden buildings. Its surrounding areas also hold great monastic treasures.

Orientation

Vologda straddles the Vologda River, with the town's centre mainly concentrated on the southern side. The town's main axis, ulitsa Mira, runs from the train and bus station north to the junction of ulitsa Oktyabrskaya, where it juts north-east and crosses the Vologda. The Archbishop's Courtyard, which is often referred to as the Vologda Kremlin, is on the south bank of the Vologda, west of the main bridge, on Kremlyovskaya ploshchad.

Information

Money You can change money at the central department store, in the pedestrian zone, one block north of ulitsa Mira's north-east tack; there's a booth in the lobby. Or try Vologda Bank at ulitsa Mira 36, on the corner of ulitsa Oktyabrskaya. It's open from 9.30 am to 4.30 pm Monday to Friday.

Post & Communications The main post office is on ploshchad Babushkina, but there's a perfectly functional office on the corner of ulitsa Mira and ulitsa Oktyabrskaya. The main telephone office is at ulitsa Gertsena 29, on the corner of ulitsa Predtechenskaya. For Internet access, try the central library (☎ 25 18 67) on ulitsa MI Ulyanovoy just off ploshchad Revolyutsii, or the Internet Salon (☎ 72 95 71, vagor@vstu.edu.ru) of the Technical University, ulitsa Galkinskaya 3.

Travel Agencies Staff at Sputnik (☎ 25 44 81, sputnik@vologda.ru) inside the Hotel Zolotoy Yakr, room 310 (see Places to Stay later in this section) are so laid-back you'd never guess they have so much up their sleeves. They have lists and lists of different kinds of tours, including literary, children's and lace-making tours, in addition to excursions to ancient cities in the region. All are extremely reasonably priced (see how lace is made for $0.60) and quite ingenious. Intourist (☎ 72 60 63, intour@vologda.ru), ulitsa Blagoveshchenskaya 26, can also be counted on for efficiency. It offers visa support, and city and regional tours, though these are quite pricey (to Belozersk for about $90). The State Historical, Architectural and Artistic Museum Reserve (☎ 72 22 83), ulitsa Orlova 15, in the Archbishop's Courtyard administrative offices in the centre of the yard, runs most of the museums in the city and also arranges excellent tours of the kremlin, including buildings closed to the public, as well as city tours for $1.60.

Archbishop's Courtyard

Vologda's Archbishop's Courtyard is the city's historical centrepiece, a multi-towered stone fortress (1671-75) containing several noteworthy buildings, including the Treasurer's Palace (Kazenny prikaz, 1659); the house of Josef Zolotoy (Iosifovsky Korpus, 1764-69); and the baroque (but not crazily so) Resurrection Cathedral (Voskresensky sobor, 1772-76) which was built in place of the north-east tower and which (since 1952) is an art and picture gallery. The courtyard also houses the town's Museum of History & Architecture.

The courtyard was, according to the sign above the entrance, 'generously donated' by the church to the victorious Soviet atheists just after the Great October Revolution. The courtyard is open to visitors, and both the art gallery and cafe have rotating exhibitions on varying schedules.

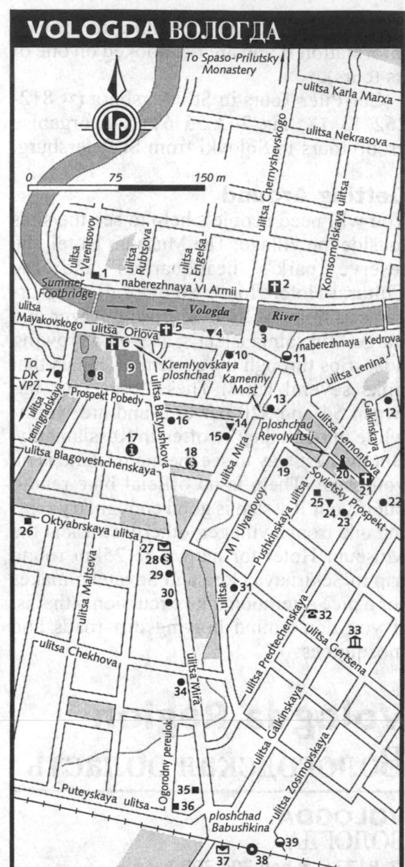

St Sofia's Cathedral & Bell Tower

Directly outside the courtyard's walls sits Vologda's most famous cathedral, St Sofia's, said to be built on the direct orders of Ivan the Terrible. Ivan's ruthlessness at Novgorod – where he sacked his own city and tortured its inhabitants, even going so far as to roast them on spits and fry them alive in enormous frying pans especially made for the occasion – was well known throughout Russia. So the workers jumped: the massive stone cathedral Ivan wanted so badly was erected in just two years (1568-70) – and they only worked in summer.

VOLOGDA ВОЛОГДА

PLACES TO STAY

1 Sretenskaya Church Dorm
Сретенская Церковь Общежитие
25 Zolotoy Yakr Hotel
Гостиница Золотой Якрь
26 Hotel Spasska
Гостиница Спасска
35 Hotel Vologda
Гостиница Вологда
36 Sputnik Hotel
Гостиница Спутник

PLACES TO EAT

4 Pizzeria
Пиццерия
14 Restaurant Mercury
24 Cafe Lesnaya Skazka
Кафе Лесная Сказка

OTHER

2 Church of St Dmitrius of Preluki
Церковь Дмитрия Прилуцкого
3 Boat Rental (summer)
Прокат лодок (летом)
5 Alexander Nevsky Church
Церковь Александра Невского
6 Saint Sofia's Cathedral
Софийский Собор
7 Regional Exhibition Hall
Выставочный зал
8 Kiddie Boat Rental
Прокат лодок для детей
9 Kremlin (Archbishop's Courtyard)
Кремль (Архиерейское подворье)
10 Spice Jam
11 Bus Stop to Spaso-Prilutsky Monastery
12 Technical University & Internet Salon
Технический Университет
13 Sport Shop
Спортивный магазин
15 Book Shop
Книжный магазин
16 Central Market
Центральный рынок
17 Intourist
Интурист
18 Central Department Store & Money Exchange
19 Central Library
Библиотека
20 Lenin Statue
Памятник В. И. Ленину
21 Church of St John the Baptist
Церковь Иоанна Предтечи
22 Drama Theatre
Драматический Театр
23 Afghanistan Hall
Афганский зал
27 Post Office
Почта
28 Vologda Bank
Вологда банк
29 Dom Knigi
Дом Книги
30 Banya
Баня
31 Stalin's Apartment
Квартира Сталина
32 Telephone Office
Телефон
33 Museum of Diplomatic Corps
Музей дипломатического корпуса
34 Souvenir Shop
Сувениры
37 Main Post Office
Главпочтамт
38 Train Station
Железнодорожный вокзал
39 Bus Station
Автовокзал

But haste, of course, makes waste. Local legend has it that Ivan, upon walking into St Sofia's for the first time, was struck on the head by a 'red tile' that had been carelessly grouted to the ceiling. Ivan angrily stormed out of the cathedral and never returned. The cathedral was finally consecrated after the feisty tsar's death. It was decorated between 1680 and 1686, but the iconostasis you'll see today was made in 1724-38 by designer Maxim Iskritsky. The frescoes were restored in 1962-78. You can gain access to the cathedral from 10 am to 5 pm daily by arrangement with the museum's administration.

Next to the cathedral, the St Sofia's Bell Tower (Kolokolnya Sofiyskogo Sobora, 1869-70) is a reconstruction of the original, which was built in 1659 and which was allegedly 78.5m tall. You can climb the much shorter reconstruction, which boasts an original clock installed in 1871 by – the sign says – the Brothers Butenop Company, from 10 am to 5 pm Monday to Friday by arrangement with the administration of the Archbishop's Courtyard (the cost is about $1.50).

Alexander Nevsky Church

Across the street from St Sofia's, this early 18th century church (Tserkov Alexandra Nevskogo) holds daily services at 8 am and 5 pm and features an excellent choir.

Museum of History & Architecture

Housed in the Archbishop's Courtyard, this museum is good fun. Vologda's commercial and military past is relived through whimsical exhibits including a 2m rifle used to defend the kremlin, huge padlocks, handcuffs and torture devices, and all sorts of taxidermy. Those with a morbid streak will appreciate the frightful female skeleton from the 2nd century BC, and the astounding anonymous painting from 1721, *Strashny Sud* (Frightful Trial). Those with an even more morbid streak will love the Soviet hammer and sickle done up in fine, delicate Vologda lace. The museum is open from 10 am to 5 pm Wednesday to Sunday. Admission is $0.20, another $0.40 for photos.

Leningradskaya Ulitsa

This peaceful, tree-lined street, which cuts southwards from the Vologda River just west of the kremlin, features stately 19th century merchant homes. At No 6, the **Regional Exhibition Hall** has art and photo exhibitions rotating monthly. It's open from 10 am to 5 pm Wednesday to Sunday. Admission is $0.20.

Church of St John the Baptist

Before the revolution, on ploshchad Revolyutsii there were three churches and one grand cathedral. All were destroyed save the disused Church of St John the Baptist (1710; the bell tower was built in 1717). You'll also find here a Great Patriotic War Memorial and eternal flame. The church makes a truly classy backdrop for the smallest **Lenin statue** around. The very first Lenin statue ever erected in the USSR, back in 1924, this is supposedly life-size (awww). His itty-bittyness stands on a big pedestal – anyone who's seen the Stonehenge scene in the film *Spinal Tap* will appreciate this.

Museum of Diplomatic Corps

This unusual museum (☎ 72 15 45, ptk@atuk.vologda.ru), ulitsa Gertsena 35, chronicles a little known blip in political history. In February 1918, when Allied ambassadors in Petrograd were ordered to evacuate (Germans were approaching), US ambassador David Francis suggested simply relocating; he studied a map and chose Vologda. The Japanese, Chinese, Siamese, Brazilian, Belgian, French, Italian and Serbian embassies followed his lead and set up shop here until they left for good in July. The eclectic and impressively researched exhibit, housed in the ex-US 'embassy', is intriguing and full of surprises.

Stalin's Apartment

You won't find this on any maps, and tour guides don't mention it, but the two storey wooden house at ulitsa MI Ulyanovoy 33 was once Stalin's home while on one of his three exiles in the city; after garnering a reputation as a carouser and woman-chaser – some say an illegitimate son still lives in Vologda – he kept escaping. The house was a museum in his honour from 1937-56, housed an exhibition on the revolution until 1967, and now serves various functions. On the 2nd floor where he lived for 2½ months (entrance from the back), there's now a legal consulting firm who are used to occasional curiosity-seekers and won't mind a polite look-see. The layout hasn't changed since Stalin's time, and the *pechka* (stove) on which he slept still works – you may even be invited to have some tea made on it!

Afghanistan Hall

Housed on the 2nd floor of a youth centre on Sovietskaya prospekt 20 (entrance on ulitsa Predtechenskaya) is the very moving Afghanistan Hall (☎ 25 55 50), commemorating locals who died in the war with that country. It's officially opened only on 15 February, a special memorial day, but staff will gladly open it to those interested if notified in advance. Letters and personal effects of the deceased contrast sharply with propaganda posters of the time.

Spaso-Prilutsky Monastery

This working monastery, dating from the 14th century, looms on the outskirts of the city. It's a bit muddy, but welcomes guests, and a visit makes for an interesting afternoon, especially if you can get inside its centrepiece, the 16th century **Cathedral of the Saviour**. The main entrance is on the northwest side of the monastery walls. If you show up alone, act interested and are polite, the monks will let you walk the grounds unescorted at no cost. Take bus No 103 to the end, or better yet, get off one stop earlier (at the Zheleznodorozhna stop, where the road forks), and cross the railway bridge, from which you can get a great photo of the place. Bus No 133 also goes to this stop.

A Russian Banya

Russians say there's a level of cleanliness that can only be attained through the rigorous action of a ritual Russian *banya*. A combination of dry sauna, steam bath, massage and plunges into ice-cold water, the banya is a weekly event that is as much a part of Russian life as, say, bowling in Bedrock. The word 'banya' has come to mean far more than its dictionary definition, which is 'bathhouse'.

Preparation often begins at home, where thermos flasks are filled to their brims with a specially brewed mixture of jams, fruits, tea and heaps of sugar. Armed with this brew, the bather heads out to the banya. (A couple of beers picked up along the way is not unheard-of either.) Based on any number of scheduling concerns, people usually go to the banya on the same day each week and, with the others there as well, a close circle is formed; the closest equivalent in the West would probably be your work-out buddies.

After stripping to your birthday suit, there's a 'warm up' in the dry sauna (the word is the same in Russian, pronounced *SA-oo-na*), where the temperature is in the low 100°s Celsius (lower 200°s Fahrenheit), and then you're ready for the *parilka* – the steam room.

The parilka will have a furnace that's heating rocks. Onto these rocks, bathers throw water, usually mixed with eucalyptus oil, with a long-handled ladle. When the room's got a good head of steam going, the bathers grab bundles of dried birch leaves *(veniki)* which they previously soaked in hot water and ... well ... beat each other with them. The beating (which feels a lot better than it sounds) is said to rid your body of toxins. This is a northern addition to the bathing tradition, one purportedly started in Novgorod; Russians in ancient Kyivan Rus would make jokes about their northern, masochistic brethren beating each other with branches – before trying it themselves ... and liking it.

After the flagellation, the air gets so unbearably hot that everyone runs out coughing. And as if the relatively cold air outside the parilka isn't enough of a shock to one's system, the next step is a plunge into the icy cold waters of the *basseyn* (pool), whose health benefits have yet to be worked out (they're probably incredibly important).

After the plunge, it's out to the changing room, where the events of the world are discussed over the tea. Then the process begins again; sessions can go on for two or three hours.

Baths are segregated by sex, and depending on the size of the place, there are either separate sections for men and women or the baths admit different sexes on different days. One more thing: alcohol affects you faster in a banya, so if you do partake, be careful and do it slowly. It's considered bad form to lose your lunch in a steam room!

Nick Selby

Boat Rental

In summer you may be able to rent rowing boats for short cruises up the Vologda. The rental station is just east of the ulitsa Chernyshevskogo bridge, across from the Church of St Dmitrius of Preluki. Kiddie boat rentals can be had in the children's playground just behind the kremlin.

Banya

The city's largest banya is at ulitsa Mira 40. It's clean, staff are friendly and it's open from noon to 8 pm Wednesday to Friday, on weekends from 9 am. Entrance is $0.65. There are also great massages available.

Places to Stay

The coolest and cheapest place in town is the converted ***Sretenskaya Church Dorm*** *(☎ 72 94 42, naberezhnaya VI Armii 85)*, directly across the Vologda from the kremlin, dating from 1731. Now a dormitory for students in the Ministry of Culture's study program, the friendly management says it will let foreigners stay there (they think you won't like it but it's fun and a crash pad as good as any). Rooms have five or more beds, and a place costs $1 (yes, $1!). There are cooking facilities but no hot water. In summer there's a floating bridge leading almost to the kremlin gate.

Right on ploshchad Revolyutsii, ***Zolotoy Yakr*** *(☎ 72 14 54, Sovietskaya prospekt 6)*, with its faded murals, has a grand, rundown feel to it and absolutely enormous rooms which are as comfy (and sometimes musty) as grandma's basement. Rooms start at $2.80. The religious philosopher Nikolai Berdyaev lived here while in exile.

It helps to bring a calculator to ***Hotel Vologda*** *(☎ 72 30 79, ulitsa Mira 92)* to work out the cost of your room. Rooms with/without shower start at $6/3 per person, but each extra you choose (black and white or colour TV, fridge, daily change of sheets etc) costs more. You'll be exhausted by the time you check in, but the rooms are clean.

Only David Lynch fans and masochists will appreciate ***Sputnik*** *(☎ 72 27 52, Puteyskaya ulitsa 14A)*, near the train and bus stations. The rudest service possible (and they try!) is followed by shabby, dreary singles/doubles from $3/2.20 per person, all in the company of local undesirables.

The town's top-end offering is ***Spasska*** *(☎ 72 01 45, ulitsa Oktyabrskaya 25)*. Rooms cost from $6/10 and are ho-hum but perfectly comfy. Luxury rooms are $27, and there's a $300-a-day apartment with a sauna if that's what you need. The very decent 2nd floor ***cafe*** serves freshly squeezed orange juice in the mornings.

Places to Eat

The town's good central ***market*** is near the corner of prospekt Pobedy and ulitsa Batyushkova.

One of the most pleasant places in town is ***Cafe Lesnaya Skazka*** *(Sovietskaya prospekt 10)*, inside the converted Chapel of the Laying of the White Robes (1911). The meat dishes are simple but delicious, and it makes great soups. A three course meal should run to about $3. It's open from 11 am to 11 pm daily.

Restaurant Mercury *(ulitsa Mira 6)* can be a blast with the right company. Very effusive women will guide you to heavily laid-out tables and lavish you with attention while a band plays Gypsy tunes (Vologda has a sizable Gypsy, or Roma, population). Good, somewhat exotic dishes start at $2.

Of the hotel restaurants, try ***Zolotoy Yakr*** (entrance around the corner on ulitsa Pushkinskaya). It has a sort-of fancy atmosphere and decent dishes for about $5 each. Skip the flashy, bombastic rip-off restaurant inside Hotel Spasska, but its 2nd floor ***cafe*** has some pleasant surprises.

Popular with the students from the university next door is the ***Pizzeria*** *(ulitsa Orlova 6)*. Its namesake is decidedly so-so, but it has other meals too. It's open from 11 am to 11 pm daily.

For late-night entertainment, there's slim pickins. ***Spice Jam*** *(Torgovaya ploshchad 8)*, 200m east of the Pizzeria, is the closest thing to a nightclub the city has (and it ain't that close). Saturdays after 11 pm most of the younger clubbers head to ***Dom Kulturny VPZ*** *(ulitsa Leningradskaya 89)* for an energetic disco. Take a taxi there (☎ 25 00 01).

Shopping

Vologda lace is the big hit; you can try the central department store (1st floor), or the great souvenir shop on the corner of ulitsa Mira and ulitsa Chekhova. Another local speciality is Vologda butter, which has a slight vanilla-nut flavour. The sports shop, at Kamenny Most 6, has rubber rafts, skis and poles, leather hunting belts and pouches, Russian weights, bicycles and motorcycles. The Dom Knigi on ulitsa Mira has, surprisingly, a large selection of Penguin classics in English.

Getting There & Away

Air Flights have been sharply curtailed recently, though there are still regular flights to St Petersburg's Pulkovo-1 and Moscow's Bykovo. Vologda's airport code is VGD and information is on ☎ 79 07 99 or ☎ 72 33 02.

Train There are at least three daily trains from Vologda to both Moscow (Yaroslavl Station; eight hours) and St Petersburg (Moscow Station; 10 hours), as well as daily service to Arkhangelsk. For information, call ☎ 79 21 36.

Bus The only long-distance bus service in and out of Vologda is a daily service to/from Yaroslavl and Ivanovo. There are also three buses a day to Cherepovets, and three a week to Rybinsk. Call ☎ 72 04 52 for details.

KIRILLOV
КИРИЛЛОВ

The **Kirilla-Belozersky Museum of History, Architecture & Fine Arts**, housed in a spectacular, but nonworking, 14th century monastery of the same name, is the reason to come here, some three hours north-west of Vologda by bus. Legend has it that the monastery's founder, Kirill, was living at the Similovsky monastery when he had a vision of the Virgin Mary showing him the towers of a new monastery. There's an icon depicting the vision inside the monastery.

The monastery's massive walls surround four main areas: the **Large Assumption Monastery**, the **Small Ivanov Monastery**, the **Stockaded Town**, and the **New Town**, all of which are open from 9 am to 5 pm daily (closed Monday). The main exhibition, which includes a tour of the churches, cathedrals and buildings, a regional history, and history of the monastery, costs $1.25. An additional $1.25 buys a tour of the catwalks and towers along the monastery's massive stone walls, built to stave off attacks from Lithuanians and Swedes. Also open for visitation (separate admissions usually apply) are the wooden chapel (the original settlement site), the Wooden Church of the Laying of the Robes, and prison cells which date from the 17th century – even Patriarch Nikon did time here, and in his boredom he is said to have turned to carpentry.

The museum also holds rotating exhibitions and sometimes demonstrates icon restoration techniques.

At **Feranpontov**, 5km west of Kirillov, is another monastery which has been converted to a branch of the Kirillov museum. Dionysius came here to paint frescoes, which can be viewed.

Getting There & Away

From Vologda's bus station, buses leave at 7.40 and 10.50 am and 1, 3.10 and 6.30 pm for the nearly three hour journey ($0.35). Several buses a day run back to Vologda, with the last leaving at 6.55 pm. When you arrive in Kirillov, ask the driver to let you off in the centre; you'll see the monastery from there.

To Feranpontov from Vologda, catch a bus or taxi to Lipinvor which stops right there.

Volga Region
Поволжье

Though the region called Povolzhye (which means Along the Volga River) meanders over a great deal of European Russia, historically and sentimentally it belongs in a chapter of its own, as it has been the main artery of the Russian heartland for over a millennium. While ancient Tver, Yaroslavl and Kostroma (see the Around Moscow chapter) decorate the upper river, many of the cities of the middle and lower Volga are industrial ports, with lots of history but limited diversions. Among the most attractive destinations are Nizhny Novgorod, Kazan, Saratov and Astrakhan, each of which warrants a day or more of sightseeing.

This chapter covers the Volga and its cities from Nizhny Novgorod to Astrakhan, plus the Perm and Ufa areas located up the eastern tributaries of the Volga, and the Rostov-on-Don area on the Sea of Azov in the south. Since 1952 the Rostov area has been linked to the Volga by the 100km-long Lenin (or Volga-Don) Ship Canal.

HISTORY

The Volga, Don and neighbouring rivers were trade routes before Russia even existed, with Slav and Norse adventurers trading along them from the Baltic Sea to Byzantium. For the Russian state the southern reaches were a perpetual headache. In the 13th century the entire region was conquered by the Tatar Golden Horde, who eventually made their capital near present-day Volgograd and hammered at Russia for two more centuries.

The Golden Horde began falling apart after being defeated by Moscow's Prince Dmitry Donskoy at Kulikovo on the Don in 1380, and a thrashing by Timur (Tamerlane) soon after. By the mid-15th century the Tatars had collapsed into separate khanates at Kazan, Astrakhan and in the Crimea. Tsar Ivan III played them off against one another and Ivan the Terrible took Kazan and Astrakhan in the 1550s, leaving only a subservient Crimean enclave.

HIGHLIGHTS

- Walking in Andrey Sakharov's footsteps in Nizhny Novgorod
- Taking in the alpine scenery on the long overnight train ride from Perm to Kazan
- Strolling the kremlin and exploring the mosques of Kazan
- People-watching from a cafe in Saratov
- Seeing the Caspian Sea from the Volga Delta below Astrakhan

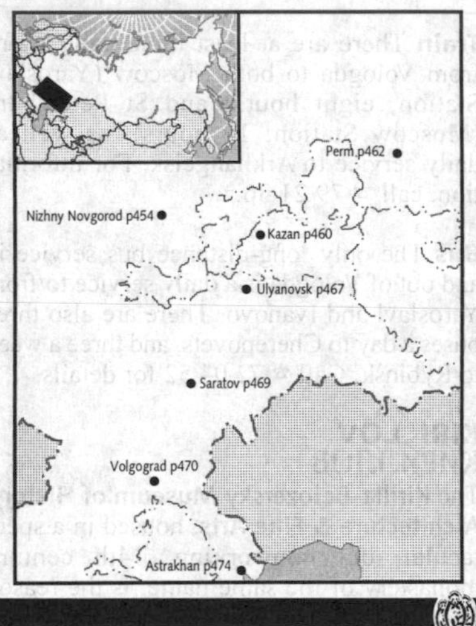

Cossacks

Serfs, paupers and dropouts began fleeing south from Russia, Poland and Lithuania in the 15th century, organising themselves into military-agricultural communities in the Dnipro (Dnepr in Russian) River area in

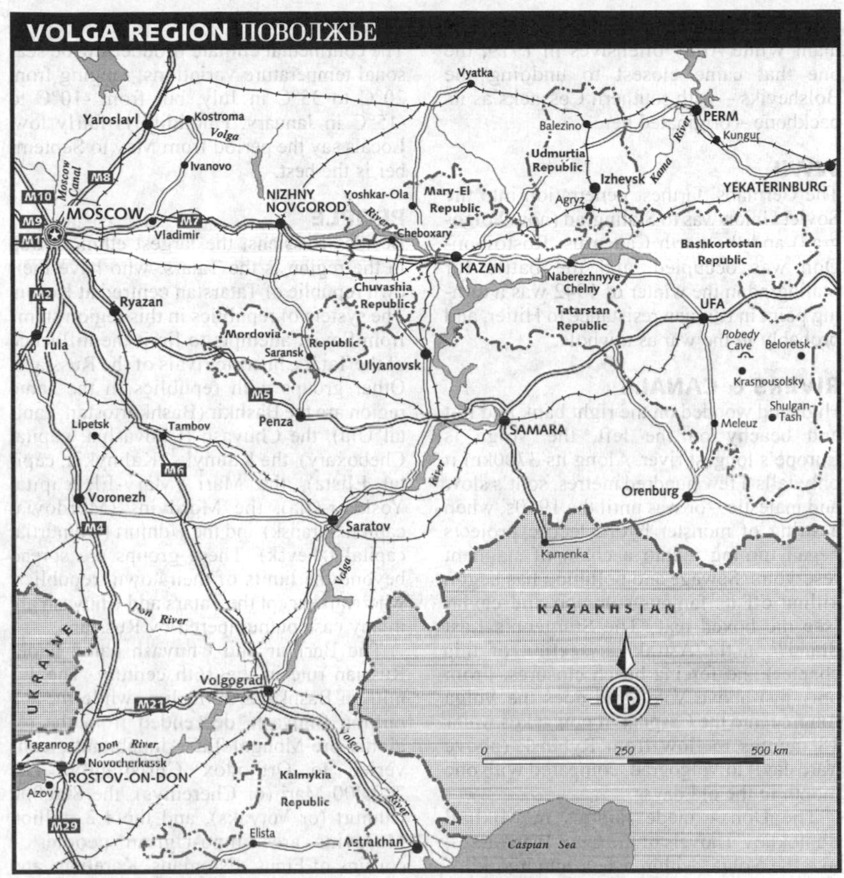

Ukraine, the Don River basin, the Caucasus and western Kazakhstan. Those in a given region, eg the Don Cossacks, also constituted an army, within which the men of each village elected their own leader *(ataman)*.

The Russian government, mindful of the trouble these people could make, later offered them autonomy in return for military services, but they made trouble anyway. Three peasant uprisings in the Volga-Don region were led by Cossacks – Stepan (Stenka) Razin in 1670, Kondraty Bulavin in 1707 and Yemelyan Pugachov in 1773. Razin's army seized the entire lower Volga basin before being routed at Simbirsk (Ulyanovsk), and Razin became a national folk hero.

After quashing Pugachov's rebellion, Catherine the Great put an end to Cossack autonomy, disbanded the Dnieper (Zaporizky) Cossacks and made the whole lower Don an administrative territory, with the capital at Novocherkassk.

Civil War

The lower Volga and Don basins put up furious resistance to the Great October Revolution. The Don Cossacks elected an anti-Bolshevik ataman in 1917. Of the three main White Army offensives in 1919, the one that came closest to undoing the Bolsheviks – with southern Cossacks as its backbone – originated here.

WWII

The Germans' farthest penetration into the Soviet Union was to Stalingrad (now Volgograd) and the north Caucasus. Rostov-on-Don was occupied, and the battle for Stalingrad in the winter of 1942 was a turning point in Russian resistance to Hitler, and probably in the war as a whole.

RIVERS & CANALS

High and wooded on the right bank and flat and beachy on the left, the Volga is Europe's longest river. Along its 3700km it only falls a few hundred metres, so it's slow and majestic – or was until the 1930s, when a string of monster hydroelectric projects began turning it into a chain of stagnant reservoirs. Sewage and pollution has begun killing off its famous sturgeon and caviar (see the boxed text 'The Sturgeon's Last Stand?' in the Astrakhan section of this chapter) and forcing beach closures. From only just above Volgograd does the Volga run free into the Caspian. It now takes water 18 months to flow from Rybinsk (above Yaroslavl) to Volgograd, compared with one month in the old days.

The Don – made famous in Mikhail Sholokhov's novels of the Civil War – rises, like the Volga, within a few hundred kilometres of Moscow, but flows to the Sea of Azov. The Lenin Ship Canal joined the two rivers near Volgograd in 1952, completing an immense network of canals, lakes and rivers linking Moscow to the White, Baltic, Caspian, Azov and Black seas; an ocean-going ship can now sail right across Russia from the Arctic to the Mediterranean.

The entire Volga region has been affected by the same economic problems as elsewhere in Russia, with the consequence being that the banks of this great river are dotted with the rusting hulks of huge industrial complexes; the legacies of long-forgotten five-year plans.

CLIMATE

The continental climate produces wide seasonal temperature variations, ranging from 20°C to 35°C in July, but from -10°C to -15°C in January. Humidity is fairly low. Locals say the period from May to September is the best.

PEOPLE

Besides Russians, the largest ethnic group in the region is the Tatars, who have their own republic of Tatarstan centred at Kazan. The system of republics in this region stems from Soviet attempts to limit the influence of the Tatars, historic rivals of the Russians. Other groups with republics in the same region are the Bashkir (Bashkortostan; capital Ufa), the Chuvash (Chuvashia; capital Cheboxary), the Kalmyks (Kalmykia; capital Elista), the Mari (Mary-El; capital Yoshkar-Ola), the Mordvins (Mordovia; capital Saransk) and the Udmurt (Udmurtia; capital Izhevsk). These groups are spread beyond the limits of their 'own' republics, where all except the Tatars and Chuvash are in any case outnumbered by Russians.

The Bashkir and Chuvash came under Russian rule in the 16th century. The 1.5 million Bashkir are Muslim, while the 1.8 million Chuvash, descended from the region's pre-Mongol-Tatar inhabitants, converted to Orthodox Christianity. The 700,000 Mari (or Cheremys), the 800,000 Udmurt (or Votyaks), and the 1.2 million Mordvins are Finno-Ugrian peoples – cousins of Finns, Estonians, Karelians and the small tribes of the far north-west.

Kalmyks are Mongolians and Tibetan Buddhists who fled feudal wars in western Mongolia in the 17th century. Stalin deported nearly all of them to Siberia in 1943, but most were allowed back in 1957. They now number only about 150,000 and constitute 45% of the population of the Kalmykia Republic, west of Astrakhan.

A large community of ethnic Germans, mostly farmers, settled along the Volga around Saratov in the 18th and 19th centuries and even got their own autonomous republic within Russia in 1924. However, this was abolished during WWII, and

Volga River Boats

From June to September boats ply the Volga River from Moscow to Astrakhan. The table below shows the average times and prices for boats used primarily by Russians for transportation. There are other services such as all-inclusive cruises aimed at Russians which cost somewhat more than those listed below. Cruises marketed to foreigners can easily cost thousands of dollars. See the Boat section of the European Russia Getting Around chapter for additional details on cruises.

River journey times can vary depending on the weather and currents. The boats used primarily for transportation like those listed below rarely stop in towns long enough for meaningful sightseeing. Simple cabins have four bunks and shared facilities. Deluxe cabins sleep two and have private bath. Food and other amenities are not lavish and cost extra. Expect a plastic deck chair and filling Russian staples. And, of course, plenty of cheap beer.

The following table shows the duration and the ascending cost of journeys from Moscow.

Moscow to:	time (hours)	simple cabin	deluxe cabin
Nizhny Novgorod	65	$23	$65
Kazan	84	$33	$73
Ulyanovsk	94	$36	$88
Saratov	130	$47	$115
Volgograd	148	$52	$131
Astrakhan	169	$59	$146

Ships travel along the route outlined above every other day (on even days in July and odd days in August) from Moscow's Severny Rechnoi Port (Northern River Station). A full one-way journey takes nine days. Tickets are sold from 1 April at Lenigradsky prospekt 1 in Moscow. It's the first building on the left after you cross the bridge next to Belorussky Vokzal and is in the same building as the Central Railway Ticket Office. The operator is the Stolichnaya Sudokhodnaya Companiya (Capitol Ship Company; ☎ 095-257 71 19/09), which runs many of the ships on Russia's inland waterways. Although you can't book these cruises from abroad the company is happy to sell space to anyone with the correct fare. The office is open from 8 am to 8 pm Monday to Saturday and to 5 pm on Sundays. Tours for the Russian cruise ships are also available. You may be able to purchase tickets for individual segments of the route at the river stations listed in this chapter.

emigration and deportation have since decreased their numbers. About 20,000 ethnic Germans remain in the region and Germany maintains a consulate in Saratov.

GETTING THERE & AROUND

The obvious way to travel between Volga region cities is on the Volga. Considering the river's historical importance, this is how the heart of Russia ought to be seen. The most interesting segments are Volgograd to Rostov-on-Don via the canal's 15 locks, and Volgograd to Astrakhan with some picturesque villages to see.

Relevant information is listed in the Getting There & Away section for each city. See also the boxed text 'Volga River Boats'. For a list of companies and contacts, see the Getting There & Away chapter for European Russia.

Transport connections between the Volga cities can be a challenge. The major cities have daily flights to Moscow but service between the towns is rare. The same can be said in part for the trains, which run on lines radiating from Moscow. Often a journey between Volga cities relatively close on the map involves circuitous routings over lines halfway back to Moscow. Buses too are slow; weaving through tiny towns where the lone daily bus may be the only link to greater Russia. Often the best way for getting from one city to another is to hire a taxi or car with a driver. Travelling the most direct route, these journeys can be completed in a quarter of the time taken by trains and buses and at reasonable prices of about $0.10 per kilometre.

NIZHNY NOVGOROD НИЖНИЙ НОВГОРОД

☎ 8312 • pop 1.5 million

Nizhny Novgorod is a pleasant city with a bustling kremlin, museums and churches under restoration, and a lively street scene. Nizhny Novgorod (not to be confused with Novgorod) belongs historically with the Golden Ring towns near Moscow. It was founded in 1221. During Soviet times the city was named Gorky after the writer Maxim Gorky (born here in 1868), who disapproved of the idea.

Nowadays, Russia's third largest city is mostly known for its pro-business government that actively encourages all manner of joint ventures with Western firms. The city has always been an economic centre; in the 19th century it was said 'St Petersburg is Russia's head; Moscow its heart; and Nizhny Novgorod, its wallet'. It is less known as the place where the late physicist, dissident and Nobel laureate Andrey Sakharov was exiled until 1986.

The town holds a popular International Trade Fair annually and some of the major local industries involve the production of MiG fighters, GAZ cars and trucks, ships and processed foods.

The district is also known for traditional crafts, including the kitschy *matryoshka* doll, and the wooden spoons, cups and dishes with their painted gold, red and black base partially covered by designs of flowers – known as Khokhloma ware after a town about 100km north of Nizhny.

Orientation & Information

The town lies on the southern bank of the Volga River and is also split by the Oka River. The western bank includes the train station and Hotel Tsentralnaya on ploshchad Lenina. The eastern bank has the museums, and the kremlin on ploshchad Minina, from which the main streets span out, including Bolshaya Pokrovskaya with many shops and restaurants. Good maps in Russian showing local transport routes are widely available for $1.

Money Alphabank (☎ 30 09 55), ulitsa Semashko 9, is open from 8 am to 8 pm weekdays. Besides the usual exchange services, it handles Western Union transfers, Visa and MasterCard cash advances and has an ATM linked to foreign networks.

Post & Communications The post office is on ulitsa Bolshaya Pokrovskaya, at ploshchad Gorkogo, and is open 24 hours. Komputerny Tsentr NN (☎ 77 33 66), ulitsa Gorkogo 152, offers Internet access at around $1.20 per hour and is open from 10 am to 8 pm daily.

Travel Agencies Intourist (☎/fax 77 54 78) is located in Hotel Tsentralnaya building and is open from 9 am to 5 pm weekdays. Besides selling airline tickets it can organise all manner of tours including boat trips and city and regional tours. A half-day excursion around town costs $30. The Team Gorky Adventure Travel Company (☎ 65 19 99, fax 63 24 44, teamgork@ray.unn.runnet.ru), ulitsa 40 Let Oktiabria 1a, organises outdoor travel in the region and throughout the rest of Russia including Siberia.

Bookshops Dom Knigi (House of Books) is in the same huge building as Hotel Tsentralnaya. Open from 10 am to 6 pm weekdays, it has a small selection of English-language classics.

Kremlin

The kremlin is perched on the hill above the Volga River but the entrances are from the other side off ploshchad Minina. The present

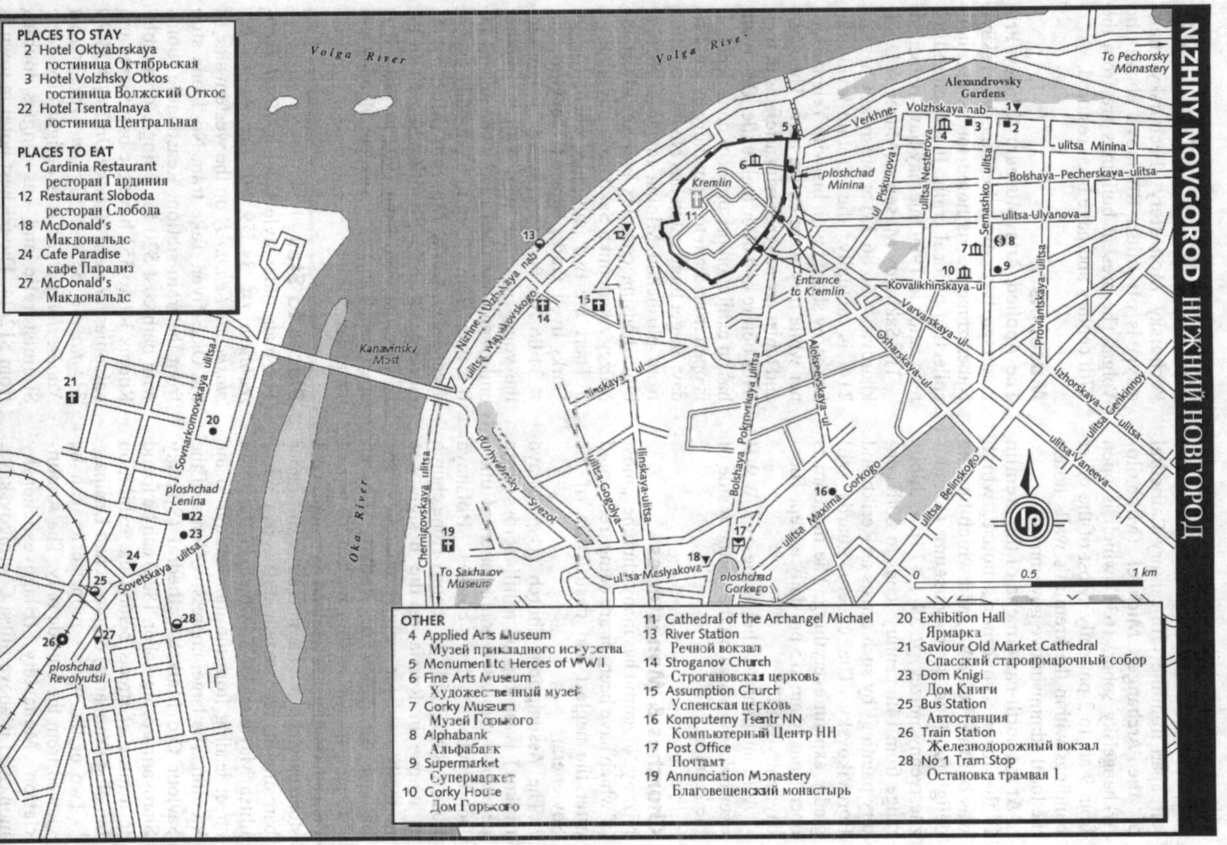

VOLGA REGION

walls, with 11 towers, are from the 16th century, but none of the original buildings are left, apart from the 17th century **Cathedral of the Archangel Michael** (Mikhailo-Arkhangelsky sobor, 1631) which is open from 9 am to 2 pm daily. Most of the other buildings within the kremlin's walls house the local administrative government.

At the north-eastern end of the kremlin is the former governor's house, which was built in the 1840s, and which has the delightful **Fine Arts Museum** (Khudozhestvenny muzey; ☎ 39 13 73). Exhibits range from 14th century icons to 20th century paintings by such artists as Rerikh and Borovikovsky. The cheery guards will gladly explain everything. The museum is open from 10 am to 5 pm daily except Tuesday; entry is $1.

A monument to the heroes of WWII overlooks the Volga on the northern side of the kremlin.

Churches & Monasteries

Nizhny Novgorod has many churches, most of which have been, or are being, renovated after the neglect and destruction of the Soviet era.

The **Assumption Church** (Uspenskaya tserkov) is on top of a hill across from pereulok Krutoy, the continuation of ulitsa Dobrolyubova that crosses Bolshaya Pokrovskaya. This 17th century stone church is unique in Russia as the design was normally used for wooden churches. The baroque **Stroganov or Nativity Church** (Stroganovskaya tserkov), built at the turn of the 18th century, has retained its magnificent stone carvings, but the interior is still rather bare after its reconstruction. It is just above ulitsa Mayakovskaya, which is the main street leading from the train station to the kremlin. The large, impressive dome of the **Saviour Old Market Cathedral** (Spassky Staroyarmarochny sobor, 1822) can be found in a maze of streets behind the exhibition building (Yarmarka) on ploshchad Lenina.

Two of the town's monasteries can be viewed from the outside only. The **Annunciation Monastery** (Blagoveshchensky monastyr) is above ulitsa Chernigovskaya. It was founded in the 13th century but most of the structures are from the 18th century. **Pechorsky Monastery** (Pechorsky monastyr) is off ulitsa Rodinova above the Volga. The present buildings are from the 17th century and have been restored.

Museums

The **Applied Arts Museum** (Muzey Prikladnogo Iskusstva), Verkhne-Volzhskaya Naberezhnaya 3, is noted for its excellent collection of local crafts. It was closed for renovation in 1999 but may have reopened.

The **Sakharov Museum** (Muzey A D Sakharova; ☎ 66 86 23) at prospekt Gagarina 214 is actually the ground-level flat Sakharov shared with his wife Yelena Bonner while they were exiled here. The walls and tables are covered with artefacts of their lives before and after their exile. One room has an exhibit on prisoners of conscience. It is open from 9 am to 6 pm daily except Friday. To get there catch bus No 43 travelling from ploshchad Minina towards Shcherbinki housing complex and get off at the Muzey Akademika Sakharova bus stop.

There are two museums where Maxim Gorky lived. **Gorky House** (Dom Gorkogo; ☎ 34 06 70), Pochtovy Syezd 21, is where the young novelist lived with his mother and grandfather until 1879 when he was 11. It is open from 10 am to 5 pm daily except Wednesday. **Gorky Museum** (Muzey A M Gorkogo; ☎ 36 15 29), ulitsa Semashko 19, is where he lived from 1902 to 1904. It is open from 9 am to 5 pm except Monday and Thursday.

Places to Stay

The main older-style hotel is ***Hotel Tsentralnaya*** *(☎ 34 59 00, fax 34 55 00, ploshchad Lenina 1)* on the western side of the Oka River. Take tram No 1 one stop from the train station. Reasonable rooms with bath cost $20 for a single or double. Rooms 340 to 351 have the best views and balconies. ***Hotel Volzhsky Otkos*** *(☎ 39 19 71, fax 36 38 94, Verkhne-Volzhskaya Naberezhnaya 2a)* is a delightfully eerie Stalinist relic and has singles/doubles from $12/24. The poshest hotel in town is

Andrey Sakharov, Conscience of the Reform Movement

Dr Andrey Dmitrievich Sakharov (1921-89) was a leading nuclear physicist who became a human rights advocate and one of the main figures opposing the Soviet regime from within. He was born in Moscow and followed in his father's footsteps as a physicist. By the age of 32 he was a full member of the Soviet Academy of Sciences, and was one of the two leading scientists involved in developing the first hydrogen bomb in the Soviet Union.

In 1961 he got in official hot water by opposing the Soviet government's intention of violating the Nuclear Test Ban Treaty. He was also vocal in opposing nuclear arms production and human rights abuses. In 1975 Sakharov was awarded the Nobel peace prize, but he never dared to go and pick it up, fearing the authorities might not let him return to the USSR. Once outside the country he would lose the ability to pressure the Communist regime through his dissident activities. His actions brought him into conflict with the government, and in 1980 he was exiled to Nizhny Novgorod (then named Gorky) after he criticised the Soviet invasion of Afghanistan. His wife, Yelena Bonner, joined him in 1984, by which time he had undertaken several hunger strikes.

Sakharov was released in 1986 by Mikhail Gorbachev, who called him with the news on a phone specially installed for that purpose. He became a member of the Congress of People's Deputies (or Parliament) in 1989, the year it was first established. He continued to criticise the Soviet leadership as a member of the congress, and by the time of his death was widely regarded as the conscience of the reform movement.

Hotel Oktyabrskaya *(☎ 32 11 24, fax 32 05 50, Verkhne-Volzhskaya Naberezhnaya 9A).* It has modern rooms for $40/55 and accepts credit cards.

Places to Eat

Ulitsa Bolshaya Pokrovskaya is the main commercial street, with many restaurants and cafes that tend to change owners and names frequently. The ***McDonald's*** across from the train station has bathrooms so clean you might want to move in. There is another on ploshchad Gorkogo by the post office.

The modern ***Gardinia Restaurant*** *(☎ 36 41 01)* overlooks the Volga from Verkhne-Volzhskaya Naberezhnaya, opposite Hotel Oktyabrskaya. For those whose appetite survives the photo of American politician Newt Gingrich by the cash register, there is a long menu of typical Russian dishes for under $2.

The ***Restaurant Sloboda*** *(☎ 34 13 15)* is on ulitsa Mayakovskogo near ulitsa Shirokaya. It is a slightly fancy place with Russian meals from $7 and is open until 9.30 pm daily. One of the best meals we had along the Volga was at the aptly named ***Cafe Paradise*** *(☎ 41 06 41, Sovetskaya 18)* which has excellent fresh Russian dishes from $2 and is open until 11 pm. Our sturgeon connoisseur gave it an A+.

Getting There & Away

Air The Aeroflot office (☎ 44 39 76) is at prospekt Lenina 7. Daily flights to Moscow (Domodedovo) cost $110. Lufthansa (☎ 54 78 44) flies three times a week to/from Frankfurt.

Train The train station is on the western bank of the Oka River at ploshchad Revolyutsii. There are several trains a day from Moscow's Yaroslavl and Kursk stations that take about seven hours and cost from $12. There is also a direct train service to/from Perm (15 hours) and Yekaterinburg (22 hours).

Bus The bus station is across from the train station. There are five daily buses to/from Moscow (Shchyolkovsky bus station) that cost $13 (nine hours). Daily buses to Ulyanovsk take 12 hours.

Boat The river station (☎ 37 33 83) is on Nizhne-Volzhskaya below the kremlin.

Getting Around

Public Transport Tickets for the trams, trolleybuses and buses cost $0.05 and can be bought on board. Tram No 1 is convenient, starting from the train station and passing Hotel Tsentralnaya, the exhibition buildings, the river station and the kremlin. From the train station, cross the street and walk past the kiosks to reach the stop.

There is a metro but it only runs south from the train station and does not go anywhere near the old part of town.

Taxi From the train station to the kremlin costs $1 if you can bargain like a local; $5 to the airport.

Car Rental Intourist will arrange a car with driver for $4 an hour.

KAZAN
КАЗАНЬ

☎ 8432 • pop 1.1 million

Kazan, founded in the 13th century, is one of the oldest Tatar cities in Russia and was the capital of part of the Golden Horde in the 15th and 16th centuries. The city was ravaged in 1552 by Ivan the Terrible, who forced the Muslim khan to become Christian and moved the Tatars to the outskirts. St Basil's Cathedral in Moscow was built to celebrate Kazan's downfall.

The city later flourished as a gateway to Siberia. Leo Tolstoy was educated in the city, some of Russia's first Marxists surfaced here, and Lenin was in fact thrown out of Kazan University for being too bolshie.

Under the Soviet Union, Kazan became the capital of a new Tatar Autonomous Republic. In autumn 1990, this oil-rich and strongly nationalist region (now renamed Tatarstan) declared its autonomy from the rest of Russia, launching several years of political warfare with the central government in Moscow. Of the 3.7 million people within the republic, only 48% are Tatars; with 43% being Russian, the dreams of an independent state might be hard to achieve and sustain.

Tatars are a Turkic people and speak a dialect of the Turkic language. Tatar nationalism is strong in Kazan – there are no Russian flags flying over the city, only the green, white and red striped Tatar flag, and all the streets are bilingually signposted.

Kazan is one of the most pleasant cities in the region and can easily occupy a day or more of your time.

Orientation & Information

Once located well up the tributary Kazanka River, Kazan is now lapped by the flat waters behind Kuybyshev Dam, 400km downstream. The main drag is ulitsa Baumana, a pedestrian street lined with cafes and shops. There is a nice beach on the north bank of the Kazanka River. A widely sold city map ($1) includes local transport information.

Ak Bars Bank (☎ 49 35 56), ulitsa Dekabristov 1, is 20 minutes from the centre by trolleybus No 1; get off at the Dekabristov stop. It will cash travellers cheques. There is an accommodating ATM inside the long-distance train station.

The post and telephone office is at ulitsa Kremlyovskaya 8. You can make calls from 7 am to 9 pm daily.

Kremlin

The city fortress, at the river end of ulitsa Kremlyovskaya, has been rebuilt a number of times over the last five centuries. Ivan the Terrible blew it up and had Pskov masons redo it in white limestone during the 16th and 17th centuries. The **Annunciation Cathedral** (Blagoveshchensky sobor, 1562) was designed by the same architect who did St Basil's Cathedral in Moscow. The leaning 17th century, 59m-high **Syuyumbike Tower** (Bashnya Syuyumbike) is named after a long-suffering princess married to three successive khans.

There are many legends associated with the tower and the Tatar queen. One of them states that the cause of the Russian siege of Kazan by Ivan IV was Syuyumbike's refusal to marry the tsar. To save her city, Syuyumbike agreed to marry the tsar only if a tower higher than any other mosque in Kazan could be built in a week. After the

VOLGA REGION

tower's completion, Syuyumbike found it impossible to leave her native city and killed herself by jumping from the upper terrace of the tower.

Some of the towers are occasionally open for viewing but even if they are closed, the kremlin grounds make for an easy stroll.

Churches & Cathedrals

Just west of the kremlin is the 16th century **St John the Baptist Cathedral & Monastery**. (Sobor i Monastyr Ionanna Krestitelya). It is often open and members of the small congregation will be happy to share their travails trying to restore the place. The colourful twin-towered **SS Peter & Paul Cathedral** (Petropavlovsky Sobor) is on Musy Dzhalilya ulitsa, between ulitsa Kremlyovskaya and ulitsa Profsoyuznaya. Built in honour of Tsar Peter I after he visited Kazan in 1722, this Russian baroque cathedral has a heavily decorated facade. It is open 7 am to 7 pm daily except from 1.30 pm to 3 pm, when the floors are scrubbed.

Tatarstan History Museum

The highlight of this small museum (Obyedinyonny muzey istorii respubliki Tatarstan), across from the kremlin at ulitsa Kremlyovskaya 2, is its ornate 18th century building. It is open 10 am to 5 pm daily except Monday and admission is $0.50.

Mosques

There are numerous mosques in Kazan, some over 100 years old. Many are on the spit of land west of Nizhny Kaban. The **Hay Market mosque** (Mechet na Sennom Rynke) on Kirova ulitsa dates from 1849; the nearby **Soltanov mosque** (Mechet Soltanov) was built in 1868.

Places to Stay & Eat

Hotel Tatarstan *(☎ 32 69 79, fax 32 65 68, ulitsa Kuybysheva 2)* is a classic 1960s Intourist hotel with a great location and ageing single/double rooms for $15/18. Skip the restaurant. From the train station take tram No 2.

Hotel Duslik *(☎ 32 61 19, ulitsa Pravo-Bulachnaya 49)* has renovated rooms for $15/24, that could have been swiped from a Holiday Inn. Unrenovated rooms cost much less and are right out of a post-apocalyptic Holiday Inn. From the train station take trolleybus No 4 to the first stop past the bridge and walk back to the hotel. To get to both hotels from the river station take trolleybus No 2.

Tatarstan's premier ***McDonald's*** *(☎ 92 16 25, ulitsa Baumana 70A)* is open from 9 am to 11 pm daily. ***Pizzeria Giuseppe*** *(☎ 32 09 38, 15 ulitsa Kremlyovskaya)* does a booming business on this tree-lined street, with its pizzas-for-one for under $1 as well as tasty items from its bakery, various ice creams and espressos. For local dishes try the little cafes along ulitsa Baumana.

Entertainment

For more than 200 years, the ***Kazan Drama Theatre*** *(☎ 92 32 00, ulitsa Baumana 48)* has presented live theatre on most nights of the year.

Getting There & Away

Air Daily one-hour flights to/from Moscow (Domodedovo) cost $120. The Aeroflot office is on the corner of Levo-Bulachnaya ulitsa and Martyna Mezhlauka ulitsa. Lufthansa (☎ 37 97 65) has twice-weekly flights to/from Frankfurt.

Train The train station is on Ukhtomskogo ulitsa and is almost an attraction in itself. The beautifully restored old building is only a waiting room. Just north, the tatty 1960s building handles suburban tickets. Farther north, long distance tickets are sold in a new building that's sleek inside and out. Foreigners buy their tickets at window No 17 on the first floor, open from 8 am to 7 pm.

Frequent trains link Kazan to Moscow's Kazansky station, they cost $38 and take about 12 hours. Many also serve Yekaterinburg, 14 hours east. Direct service to Perm takes 17 hours along a very scenic route through mountains.

Bus There are daily buses to Ulyanovsk (five hours) and Nizhny Novgorod (eight hours). The bus station is near the river

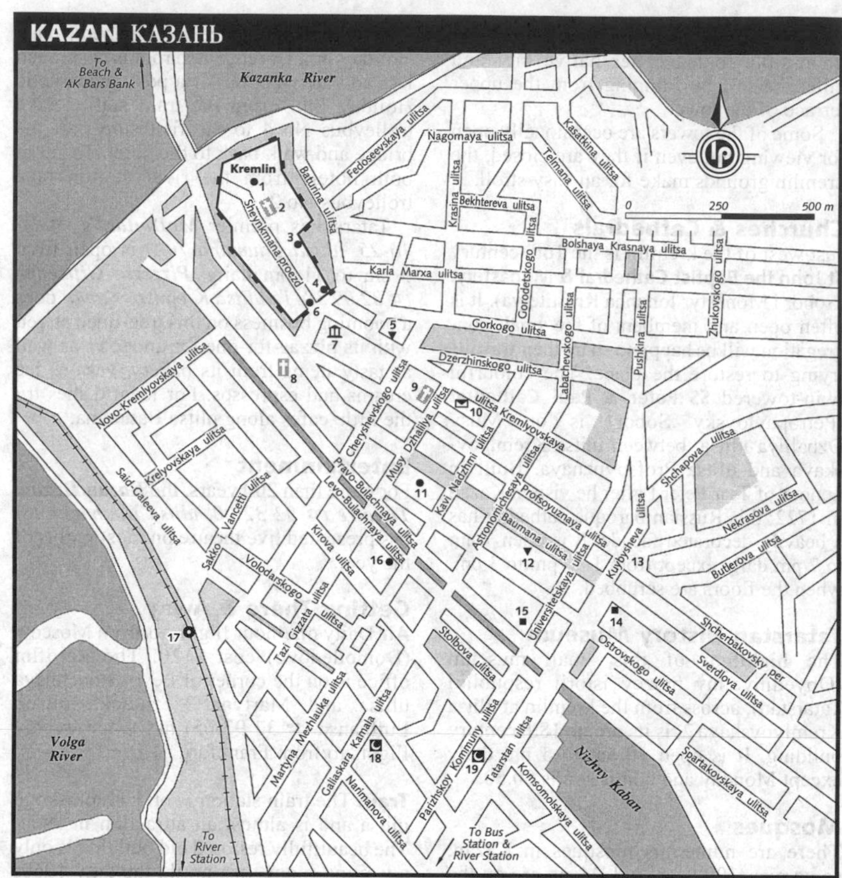

station where ulitsa Tatarstan meets ulitsa Portovaya. It is served by trolleybus No 2.

Boat The river station is at the end of ulitsa Portovaya, which is the continuation of Tatarstan ulitsa.

Getting Around

Bus, tram or trolleybus tickets cost $0.05, from the usual ticket booths or the driver. The airport bus leaves roughly hourly from 4 am to 10.30 pm. The stop is in front of the Stolichny store across from the train station. Tram No 7 links the train and river stations.

AROUND KAZAN

Raifa Monastery Раифский Монастырь

The Raifa Monastery (Raifsky Bogroditsky monastyr) was consecrated in 1665 but suffered much damage during the Soviet years, being used as a factory and reform school. Restorations continue and the church has been completed. The monastery lies about 20km west of Kazan in the village of Raifa. To get there take bus No 104 from the stop 200m to the left as you exit the long-distance train station. The trip takes about 50 minutes and the fare is $0.30.

KAZAN КАЗАНЬ

PLACES TO STAY & EAT
5 Pizzeria Giuseppe
Пиццерия Джузеппе
12 McDonald's
Макдональдс
14 Hotel Tatarstan
Гостиница Татарстан
15 Hotel Duslik
Гостиница Дуслик

OTHER
1 Syuyumbike Tower
Башня Сююмбике
2 Annunciation Cathedral
Благовещенский собор
3 Konsistorskaya Tower
Консисторская башня
4 South-Eastern Tower
Юго-восточная башня
6 Spasskaya Tower
Спасская башня
7 Tatarstan History Museum
Музей истории Татарстана
8 St John the Baptist Cathedral & Monastery
Монастырь и собор Иоанна Крестителя
9 SS Peter & Paul Cathedral
Петропавловский собор
10 Post & Telephone Office
Почта и телеграф
11 Kazan Drama Theatre
Казанский Драматический Театр
13 Kuybysheva Square
Площадь Куйбышева
16 Aeroflot Office
Агенство Аэрофлота
17 Train Station
Железнодорожный вокзал
18 Soltanov Mosque
Мечеть Солтанов
19 Hay Market Mosque
Мечеть на Сенном Рынке

PERM ПЕРМЬ

☎ 3422 • pop 1.08 million

Perm is a large industrial city located on the Trans-Siberian Railway line. It is a gateway to Siberia and Asia from Europe and its industrial development was ensured by its road and rail links. Catherine the Great decreed that Perm be made a provincial capital in 1780. Between 1940 and 1957 the town was temporarily renamed Molotov, after Vyacheslav Mikhailovich Molotov, a foreign minister during the Stalin rule who lost his post and status after a disagreement during the Khrushchev days – Molotov cocktails are also named after him.

In Chekhov's play *Three Sisters*, the main characters spend three hours desperately hoping to leave a Russian city that Chekhov said in a letter to Gorky was 'like Perm'.

Information & Orientation

Perm is a large, sprawling city, with the Kama River flowing past its northern edge. The city is centred on the intersection of ulitsa Lenina and ulitsa Komsomolsky. Most of the shops, offices and theatres are centred on this latter street, which has a dignified, tree-shaded air. Maps are easily found. Perm is two hours ahead of Moscow time.

Bank Dzerzhinskiy, ulitsa Kirova 43, is open from 9.30 am to 3.30 pm weekdays and handles Western Union transfers, cashes travellers cheques and gives credit card advances. The main post office, ulitsa Lenina 28, is open 24 hours a day. It also has an Internet service. Calls are best made from the privately run 24-Hour Phone Center, ulitsa Lenina 66.

Intourist (☎/fax 90 45 80), ulitsa Komsomolsky 54, is a friendly full-service travel agency that can issue tickets of all kinds as well as book regional tours. There is an airline ticket office in the lobby of Hotel Ural, open from 9 am to 8 pm daily.

Things to See

No one will say Perm is blessed with a lot of sights, but it has a few charms for those with reason to visit. The spire and cupola-like dome of the **art gallery** (Permskaya Gosudarstvennaya Galereya) at the top end of Komsomolsky prospekt are part of a former cathedral. The gallery was opened in 1922 and houses one of the largest icon collections in the country. It's open from 11 am to 6 pm (closed Monday); admission costs $1.

Just south of the gallery, the **Ethnographic Museum** (Permsky oblastnoy kraevedchesky muzey) has numerous stuffed local animals. It is open from 10 am to 6 pm (closed Friday) and entry is $0.25. Much livelier critters can be found just east on ulitsa Ordzhonikidze at the **zoo**, open from 10 am to 5 pm daily. Admission is $0.40.

Boris Pasternak lived and wrote *Dr Zhivago* in a blue house with white trim on ulitsa Lenina, near the corner of Gogolya. In the novel the town called Yuryatin is actually Perm.

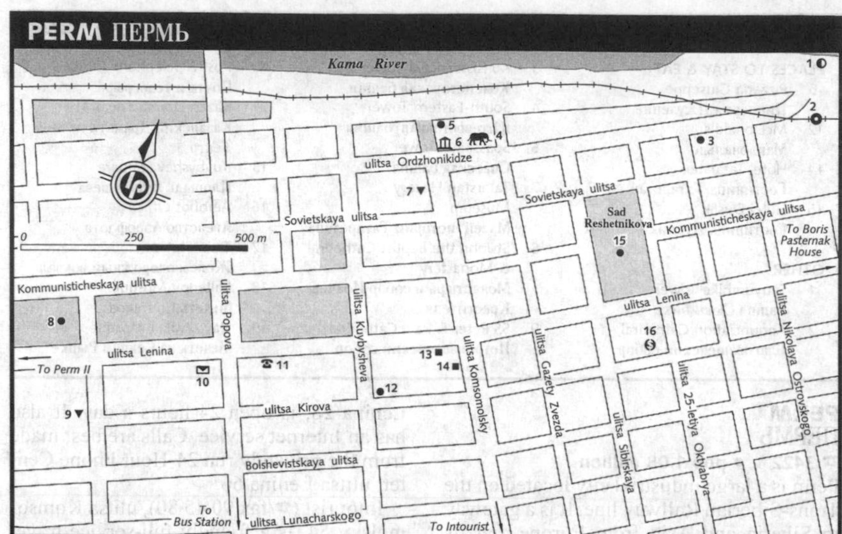

PERM ПЕРМЬ

PLACES TO STAY & EAT
7 Baskin Robbins
Баскин Роббинс
9 Yevropeysky
Европейский
13 Hotel Ural
Гостиница Урал
14 Hotel Prikamye
Гостиница Прикамье

OTHER
1 River Station
Речной вокзал
2 Perm Vokzal Railway Station (suburban trains)
Железнодорожный вокзал Пермь-2 (пригородные поезда)
3 Eurasia Travel
Евразия Трэвел
4 Zoo
Зоопарк
5 Art Gallery
Художественная галерея
6 Ethnographic Museum
Краеведческий музей
8 Perm State Drama Theatre
Пермский Государственный Драматический Театр
10 Main Post Office
Главпочтамт
11 24-Hour Phone Center
Круглосуточный переговорный пункт
12 Open-Air Market
15 Academic Theatre of Opera & Ballet
Академический Театр перы и Балета
16 Bank Dzerzhinskiy
Банк Дзержинский

Places to Stay & Eat

***Hotel Prikamye** (☎/fax 34 86 62, ulitsa Komsomolsky 27)* has shabby rooms with private bath and TV for $12/14 a single/double. There is a decent bar to the left of the entrance.

***Hotel Ural** (☎ 34 44 17, fax 90 62 20)* is on the corner of ulitsa Lenina and Komsomolsky prospekt. It is the best place to stay although its huge monolith of a structure is being built on a 50-year plan. Acceptable rooms with private bath, fridge and TV cost $13. Don't bother with the 'Eurostyle' rooms which cost double and feature an Ikea-like splendour. The hotel has a friendly pub in the basement.

An outlet of ***Baskin Robbins** (☎ 10 31 13, ulitsa Komsomolsky 7)* dishes up ice cream every day from 11 am to 10 pm. One of the best restaurants is ***Yevropeysky** (☎ 33 87 16, ulitsa Lenina 73B)*. It has carefully prepared Russian delights from $4 and, on many nights, has entertainment that ranges from flamenco dancers to lounge lizard singers. Fresh vegetables and fruit are sold at the open-air ***market*** behind Hotel Ural.

Entertainment

The ***Academic Theatre of Opera & Ballet*** *(Akademichesky teatr opery i baleta;* ☎ *12 18 48)* in Reshetnikova Garden is one of Russia's top schools and stages good traditional ballet. The Panfilov Municipal Contemporary Ballet Company performs at various locations including the ***Perm State Drama Theatre*** on ulitsa Lenina.

Getting There & Away

Air There are two daily Aeroflot flights to/from Moscow ($148). Lufthansa (☎ 28 44 42) flies to/from Frankfurt twice a week.

Train Perm is on the main trans-Siberian rail route from Moscow ($61, 20 to 22 hours, daily trains). Yekaterinburg (6 hours) is the next major city as you head east. Perm has two train stations on opposing sides of the city: Vokzal Perm in the east and Perm II Vokzal in the west. Most trains use Perm II where window No 3 serves foreigners. There are daily trains to Kazan (17 hours). To Ufa a change at Yekaterinburg is necessary and the journey can take nearly 24 hours. Remember that Perm is two hours ahead of Moscow and that most rail transport operates on Moscow time. See the following boxed text 'Amok Time'.

Bus The bus station is at the southern end of ulitsa Popova. There is a regional service to small towns in the Ural Mountains.

Boat The river station (☎ 19 93 04) is at the eastern end of ulitsa Ordzhonikidze, close to Vokzal Perm. Boats down the Kama River to the Volga and on to Astrakhan depart about once a week during summer. There is also service to Nizhny Novgorod. On summer weekends local tour boats depart every hour and cost $1.

Getting Around

Bus Nos 110, 119 and 120 serve the airport from the centre and cost $0.25 for the 35 minute ride. A taxi costs about $8. Take any bus or trolleybus, or tram No 7, for $0.10, to get from the Perm II Vokzal to Hotels Ural and Prikamye and the town centre.

AROUND PERM

There are many sights that are difficult to reach in the Perm region. Intourist operates tours to the places listed in the following text. There is also a wealth of outdoor activities such as skiing, hiking, canoeing or rafting. Eurasia Travel (☎ 90 50 81, fax 90 69 14), ulitsa Ordzhonikidze 8, Perm, operates adventure tours through the region.

Khokhlovka
Хохловка

At Khokhlovka, about 45km north of Perm, there is an open-air museum (☎ 97 01 81) of Perm's ethnographic architecture (Arkhitekturno-etnografichesky muzey Khokhlovka). There are, at present, eight wooden buildings. Two churches date back to the turn of the 18th century, while the other structures are from the 19th or early 20th century. During the first weekend of May, a folk and culture festival celebrates the coming of spring. The museum is open from 10 am to 6 pm daily from late May to October. Two to three buses a day serve Khokhlovka from Perm.

Kungur & Around
Кунгур

☎ 271 • pop 80,000

Situated 90km south-east of Perm, Kungur is one of the oldest towns in the Ural Mountains. It lies in a gigantic natural bowl where three rivers meet. It was founded in 1648 and was the centre of Perm province until 1781. In the 19th century the merchants of Kungur established trade relations with Asia and became the largest tea dealers in the country.

Things to See Kungur's attractions include the **All Saints Church** (Vsekh Svyatikh tserkov), and also a **Regional Local Studies Museum** (Krayevedchesky Muzey), ulitsa Gogolya 36, which is open from 11 am to 5 pm and costs $0.40 to enter. Other places of interest are the old **governor's house**, dating from the 17th century, and a unique row of shops called **Gostiny dvor**.

About 5km from Kungur is the **Kungur ice cave** (Ledyanaya peshchera), which is

Amok Time

Sometimes something as simple as figuring out the correct time in Russia can prove impossible. This is especially true in the Volga region where local time-keeping customs vary greatly. For instance, in Nizhny Novgorod, they set their clocks to Moscow time. But go farther east to Perm – which should be in the next time zone – and you find the clocks set two hours ahead of Moscow. This confusing situation isn't helped by the railways, which generally follow Moscow time throughout Russia (except when they don't).

Consider the following conversation we had while trying to check schedules at the Perm train station:

Us: 'Does this train leave at 14.25 Moscow time or Perm time?'
Railway employee: 'Maybe either.'
Us: 'But how can we find out?'
Railway employee (patently bored): 'Determine which time the train keeps.'
Us (trying to match the even temper of the woman behind the glass): 'But does anyone here know?'
Railway employee: 'Perhaps.'
Colonel in the Russian army standing behind us: 'Don't bother. I never know what time it is.'

famous for unique ice formations with frozen waterfalls and transparent lakes. The cave is open from 10 am to 4 pm daily and the entry fee is $1. There are daily buses between Kungur's train station and the ice cave (30 minutes).

Places to Stay & Eat In Kungur, the bare bones ***Hotel Iren*** *(☎ 3 21 57, ulitsa Lenina 30)* has rooms from $8; it also has a cafe. It is possible to stay a five minute walk from the ice cave at ***Stalagmit Hotel*** *(☎ 3 42 81)* for $15 in a decent room. There is a ***restaurant*** in the hotel.

Getting There & Away The train and bus stations in Kungur are on ulitsa Bachurina. There are five trains a day from Perm II station that take two hours and cost $0.50.

Perm 36
Пермь-36

Perm 36 (Perm tridtsat shest) is about 10km from the town of Chusovoy, which is 100km east of Perm. This was one of the infamous labour camps of the Gulag Archipelago where many dissidents were persecuted. Stalin ordered the camp built in 1946 for the detention of political prisoners, who were confined to small freezing sheds. Perm 36 closed in 1987 and the camp now has a memorial to the victims of the Gulag system and a museum and research centre.

Perm 36 is difficult to reach as there is no public transport connections with Chusovoy; however, you can hire a cab for just a few dollars. Buses and trains run between Chusovoy and Perm.

UFA
УФА

☎ 3472 • pop 1.08 million

Ufa is the capital of Bashkortostan and was founded in 1574, little more than 22 years after the Bashkirs were incorporated into the growing Russian Empire by Ivan the Terrible. The Bashkir are a Turkic people who make up less than a quarter of Bashkortostan's population of three million.

Orientation & Information

Ufa is a medium-sized, quiet and pleasant place on the bank of the Belaya River. Its wide, tree-lined streets and few high-rise buildings make it look like a town, not a city. The major shopping hub is around ploshchad Oktyabrya, also known as Tsentralny rynok (central market), through which all public transport passes on the way between ulitsa Lenina, the train station and prospekt Oktyabrya.

Sotsinvestbank at ulitsa Frunze 42 (☎ 50 29 39) changes travellers cheques, gives cash advances on credit cards and offers Western Union transfer service. It is open from 9 am to 4 pm weekdays.

The post office is on the corner of ulitsa Lenina and ulitsa Kommunisticheskaya, while the telephone office is on the opposite corner.

Intourist (☎ 23 12 04, fax 23 88 78) is in Hotel Agidel at ulitsa Lenina 14/16. Apart from standard city tours it offers white-water rafting along the Inser, Belaya and Yuryusan rivers.

Things to See

The **Lenin Memorial Centre** (Memorialny tsentr) on the corner of ulitsa Kirova and ulitsa Krupskoy has the house where Lenin stayed (No 45, which is at the ulitsa Dostoevskogo end of the museum) as well as a whole street of wooden Bashkir houses from the 1900s. The centre is open from 10 am to 6 pm (closed Monday). At ulitsa Kirova 15 there is a **historical museum** (Istorichesky muzey) with regularly changing exhibitions. It's open from 10 am to 6 pm weekdays.

Places to Stay & Eat

Hotel Agidel** (☎ 22 56 80, fax 51 04 27, ulitsa Lenina 14/16)* has basic single/double rooms with private baths for $18/28. ***Hotel Rossia** (☎ 35 89 21, fax 35 90 00, prospekt Oktyabrya 81)* has fine rooms for $25/40 as well as a currency exchange that gives Visa advances, and a ***restaurant. The new ***President-Hotel** (☎ 54 93 75, fax 54 94 75, ulitsa Avrora 2)* has Western-standard rooms for $60/70.

A good place for fresh fruit and vegetables is the ***market** (rynok)* at ulitsa Tsyurupi off ploshchad Oktyabrya. There are numerous inexpensive cafes around town serving local and Russian buffet dishes. The restaurant ***Halle** (☎ 28 65 92, ulitsa Aiskaya 93)* offers European cuisine from $2. The upmarket ***Dasko Pizza** (☎ 24 45 10, prospekt Oktyabrya 24)* offers Bashkir and European cuisine (in addition to you-know-what) and includes the president of Bashkiria among its customers.

Getting There & Away

Air Aeroflot has an office in Hotel Rossia. There are three daily flights to/from Moscow, costing $100.

Train The train station is at the northern end of ulitsa Lenina. There are daily trains to/from Moscow, taking up to 30 hours ($64), and trains to Ulyanovsk, taking anywhere between 10 and 19 hours.

Bus The bus station (☎ 24 06 08) is at the intersection of ulitsa Zorge and ulitsa Mingazheva. Buses depart from here to other towns around Bashkortostan.

Boat There is an infrequent service to/from Moscow between mid-June and early September. The river station is behind the train station.

Getting Around

Bus fans take note: public transportation in Ufa is free of charge! Special services such as bus No 101 to/from the airport cost a mere $0.20. The full journey takes 35 minutes and the route runs through the heart of the city along ulitsa Lenina and ploshchad Oktyabrya past the bus station to the train station.

All public buses, trolleybuses and trams are free (and crowded). Small private buses charge $0.15 a ride for which the spendthrift rider often gets a seat. One of these, No 2, plies the route along ulitsa Lenina through ploshchad Oktyabrya to Hotel Rossia. The ordinary bus No 106 takes a similar route.

ULYANOVSK
УЛЬЯНОВСК

☎ 84222 • pop 650,000

Founded as Simbirsk in the 17th century, Ulyanovsk (pronounced *ool-YAN-ovsk*) is a tourist stop for only one reason: it's the birthplace and boyhood home of Lenin (born Vladimir Ilich Ulyanov) and thus a former Soviet shrine. Its few Western visitors are day-tripping from Volga cruise ships. It's of interest only to see the place Lenin once occupied in the national psyche.

Ulyanovsk was initially a fortified town and Moscow's border guard post. Due to its geographic position it became a centre for trade with Asia. During the 18th century the nobles nicknamed this town 'Noble's Nest' as Russia's rich used to retire here for their holidays. The famous Russian author Ivan Goncharov was born and lived here.

Despite a new name upon Lenin's death, the city stayed a backwater until the centenary of his birth in 1970. Then, in a Brezhnevian orgy of redevelopment, the city centre became a 'memorial zone' with a museum complex, yawning plazas and the restoration of seven Ulyanov family houses and one entire neighbourhood. Today, the memorial area is a fine metaphor for the Soviet era: it's a vast, decaying monolith that nobody seems to know what to do with.

The city itself is bland, conservative and devoid of churches (Stalin knocked most of them down) or other signs of age. It's on the banks of what used to be the Volga River, now Kuybyshev Reservoir.

Orientation & Information

The main memorial zone occupies the high Volga banks from ploshchad Lenina to the giant Lenin Memorial Centre. Two blocks east is ulitsa Goncharova, which is the shopping district.

The economic crisis of the late 1990s robbed the town of its banks; however, bands of money-changers hover around the corpse of the Inkom Bank near the corner of ulitsa Goncharova and ulitsa Bebelya offering freelance exchange services. Good luck.

The main post office is located at ulitsa Goncharova 9/62 on the corner of ulitsa Tolstogo. The spiffy telephone exchange is just around the corner and is open from 8 am to 8.30 pm daily. Intourist is in Hotel Venets; however, we can't tell you what, if any, services it offers as the day we stopped by before lunch some of the staff were too drunk to talk.

Memorial Zone

Memorial Centre The megalith known as the **Big Hall** (Bolshoy Zal) is built around two Ulyanov family houses with another nearby. Upstairs are a zillion Lenin portraits, dioramas of old Simbirsk and a vast, glossy museum of the revolution, full of photos and artefacts but obscure without a guide. Off to one side a **statue** of The Man stands in a hall whose sacramental overtones would have made him squirm. The centre is open from 10 am to 6 pm.

Near the Memorial Centre Down the banks behind the centre is a string of miniparks built by the Soviet republics in 1970, which are now weedy and crumbling, rich in unintended symbolism. Above them a sometimes-functioning cable car descends to the river.

At the southern end of Kommunisticheskaya ulitsa is **Lenin's grammar school** (gimnaziya). The headmaster's son was Alexander Kerensky, later to head the provisional government Lenin overthrew. At the other end of the street are the **Regional Art and Local Studies Museums** (open from 10 am to 4 pm, closed Monday).

A non-Lenin or non-Communist sight is the **Goncharov Museum** (Muzey I A Goncharova) on the corner of ulitsa Goncharova and ulitsa Lenina. Goncharov is a well known Russian writer whose most famous work is *Oblomov*, which is about a wealthy nobleman who spent most of his life in bed. The museum is in the actual two-storey house of Goncharov's childhood, with a large collection of furniture and memorabilia from the author's life. It is open from 10 am to 6 pm (closed Monday) and admission is $0.25.

The promenade above the reservoir is a peaceful place when you've finally overdosed on Mr Lenin.

Ulyanov Family Houses Perhaps they kept skipping their rent because in addition to the three houses at the Big Hall, there are four more of the Ulyanov's houses within a block of each other on ulitsa Lenina and ulitsa Tolstogo, in a neighbourhood that has

itself been restored. Lenin aside, the area and the too-perfect **house-museum** at ulitsa Lenina 68 are worth a visit for the detailed look at upper-middle-class life of that time. A guide would be useful. Opening times are from 9 am to 4.30 pm (closed Tuesday) and the entry fee is $0.10.

Places to Stay & Eat

The only place worth spending your money at is the towering ***Hotel Venets*** *(☎ 9 45 95, ulitsa Sovietskaya 15)* which is opposite the Big Hall. Lenin tourism is way down so the bored staff will cheerfully part with rooms for $10/12 a single/double. Most have private baths and are a throw-back to an era when one had to be a hero of the production quota to get a reservation.

Cafe na Dvortsovoy *(☎ 31 25 51, ulitsa Karla Marxa 9)* is one of many cafes in the area and has a full bar and Russian standards like *bliny* for $1 and fancier fare like salmon for $1.50. ***Bistro*** is a sparkling Russian fast-food place next to the suburban bus station. Everything is under $1.

Getting There & Away

Daily flights from Moscow (Domodedovo) are $90. The Aeroflot office is at ulitsa Goncharova 4 (☎ 1 65 93).

Moscow and Volgograd are both 900km away by rail. Daily trains to both places take 15 hours or more. The fare to/from Moscow's Kazansky station is $40. Ufa is 15 hours away and Saratov is 11 hours. Ulyanovsk-Tsentralnaya is the main long-distance train station.

The long-distance bus station is 4km from the centre and is served by bus Nos 9 and 20 from the corner of ulitsa Karla Marxa and ulitsa Goncharova. Taxis cost $1. Frequent buses to Kazan take five hours.

To get to the river station take tram No 4 from Hotel Venets for five stops; from there you walk down a lane until you reach the Kuybyshev Reservoir.

Getting Around

From the airport, bus No 6 takes half an hour to the end of the line (Tsentr stop) on ulitsa Goncharova behind Hotel Venets. A taxi is about $2. Ulyanovsk-Tsentralnaya train station is 4.5km by bus No 1, 2 or 117, or tram No 4. See Getting There & Away for details on getting to/from the long-distance bus station. Trams and buses cost $0.05 per ride and tickets are available from ticket booths.

SARATOV
CAPATOB

☎ 8452 • pop 900,000

This pleasant city has a thriving commercial centre with not many sights but enjoyable, leafy streets to walk along. The tree-lined pedestrian mall of prospekt Kirova has many shops, cafes and restaurants and is a very relaxing spot to walk through or enjoy a drink or a meal. Just watching the locals promenade in their eclectic styles is matchless entertainment.

Saratov was established in 1590. It was initially a fortress forming a line of defence for the trade route along the Volga. The city was occupied during WWII by the Germans and has many monuments to its heroes.

Orientation & Information

The centre of town is the pedestrian mall on prospekt Kirova, stretching over 1km from the vast market at ulitsa Chapaeva to ulitsa Radishcheva. Three blocks west, busy prospekt Moskovsky links the train station to the river station.

Intourist (☎ 24 18 23), ulitsa Maxima Gorkogo 30, handles local tours and hotel reservations (see Places to Stay & Eat). It is open 9 am to 6 pm weekdays. There is an airline ticket office in the lobby of Hotel Volga.

Sberbank (☎ 50 32 95), prospekt Kirova 7, is open from 10 am to 6 pm weekdays and has exchange and credit card advance services. The post office is on the corner of prospekt Moskovsky and ulitsa Chapaeva. It is open from 9 am to 6 pm daily.

Saratovkniga is a fine bookstore on the corner of prospekt Kirova and ulitsa Volskaya that's open from 10 am to 7 pm (closed Sunday).

Things to See

The 17th century **Trinity Cathedral** (Troitsky sobor) at ploshchad Muzeynaya near the river station has a heavily decorated interior. Another interesting religious structure is the **Utoli Moya Pechali Church** (1903) on the corner of ulitsa Radishcheva and ulitsa Volzhskaya, the roof of which is dotted with many mini-onion domes.

The **Fine Arts Museum** (Khudozhestvenny muzey, also known as Radishchev muzey), is at ploshchad Revolyutsii and is open from 10 am to 6 pm (closed Monday); admission is $0.25.

Places to Stay & Eat

By far the best – and almost only – accommodation option is ***Hotel Volga*** *(☎ 24 36 45, fax 24 02 35, prospekt Kirova 34)*, a huge relic from the pre-revolution years that is hanging on to its faded glories and has a great location. High-ceilinged rooms with balconies average $16 and come with free breakfast. Credit cards are accepted and the staff are friendly.

In contrast, ***Hotel Slovakia*** *(☎ 26 46 92, ulitsa Lermontova 30)* is a relic of the Soviet era that is stubbornly clinging to the policies of the past. In order to secure one of the modern rooms (which admittedly have great river views), guests have to first get clearance from the Intourist travel agency. It's really not worth paying $40 for this nonsense.

The best place for fresh fruit and vegetables is the lively and thriving ***market*** on the corner of ulitsa Sakko i Vancetti and ulitsa Chapaeva.

Among the many options along prospekt Kirova is ***Pinguin bistro delikatessen***, which is in the same building as Hotel Volga and has a large choice of snacks and desserts. ***Saratov Bistro*** *(☎ 24 09 64)* at No 30 tempts customers with its grilled chicken and other meaty specialities for $1.

Entertainment

Opera and ballet performances can be seen at the ***Opera & Ballet Theatre*** (Teatr opery i baleta) near ploshchad Revolyutsii. You can take in a classical concert at the

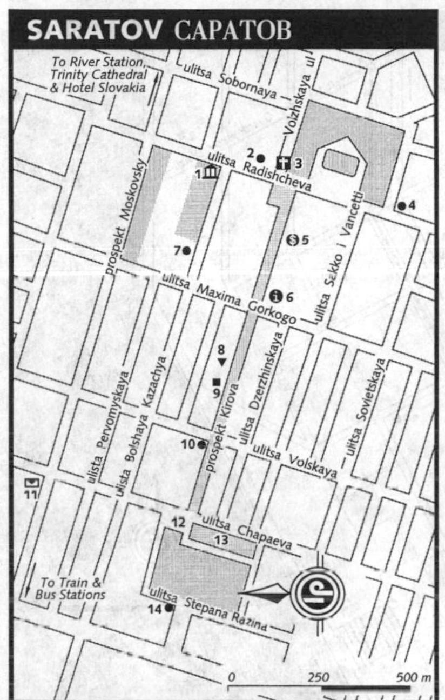

SARATOV САРАТОВ

PLACES TO STAY & EAT

8 Saratov Bistro **Саратовское бистро**
9 Hotel Volga **Гостиница Волга**

OTHER

1 Fine Arts Museum **Художественный музей**
2 Ploshchad Revolutsii **Площадь Революции**
3 Utoli Moya Pechali Church **Церковь Утоли Моя Печали**
4 Philharmonic Theatre **Филармония**
5 Sberbank **Сбербанк**
6 **Intourist**
7 Opera & Ballet Theatre **Театр Оперы и Балета**
10 Saratovkniga Bookshop **Саратовкнига**
11 Post Office **Почтамт**
12 Ploshchad Kirova **Площадь Кирова**
13 Market **Рынок**
14 Aeroflot Office **Агенство Аэрофлота**

Philharmonic Theatre (Filarmonia) on ulitsa Radishcheva.

Getting There & Away

Aeroflot (☎ 4 44 52) is at ulitsa Stepana Razina 42 and is open from 8 am to 7 pm daily. There are two daily flights to Moscow for $40.

The train station is on Privokzalnaya ploshchad, at the end of prospekt Moskovsky. Trains to/from Moscow's Paveletsky station take 16 hours and cost $41. Trains to Volgograd take nine hours, to Astrakhan 12 hours.

The regional bus station is on the south side of the train station.

The river station (☎ 26 93 24) is at naberezhnaya Kosmonavtov, the eastern end of prospekt Moskovsky. The friendly port office sells tickets and has schedule details for both long-distance and local tour boats. Look for the brown door to the left as you go down the main stairs to the river.

Getting Around

The trams, trolleybuses and buses cost $0.05; buy tickets on board. Trolleybus Nos 2 and 2A stop at the market which is a short walk from the ulitsa Kirova pedestrian zone. Trolleybus Nos 1 and 9 ply prospekt Moskovsky from the train station to the river station and pass near Hotel Volga.

VOLGOGRAD ВОЛГОГРАД

☎ 8442 • pop 1 million

The city was founded in 1589 as Tsaritsyn and was only a fortress. Volgograd is better known by its pre-1961 name, Stalingrad, the focus of one of the most decisive battles of WWII. See the following boxed text 'A Battle to the Death' for details.

Stalin organised the city's defences during the civil war and it was later renamed for him. This honour brought lots of huge Soviet building schemes before WWII and

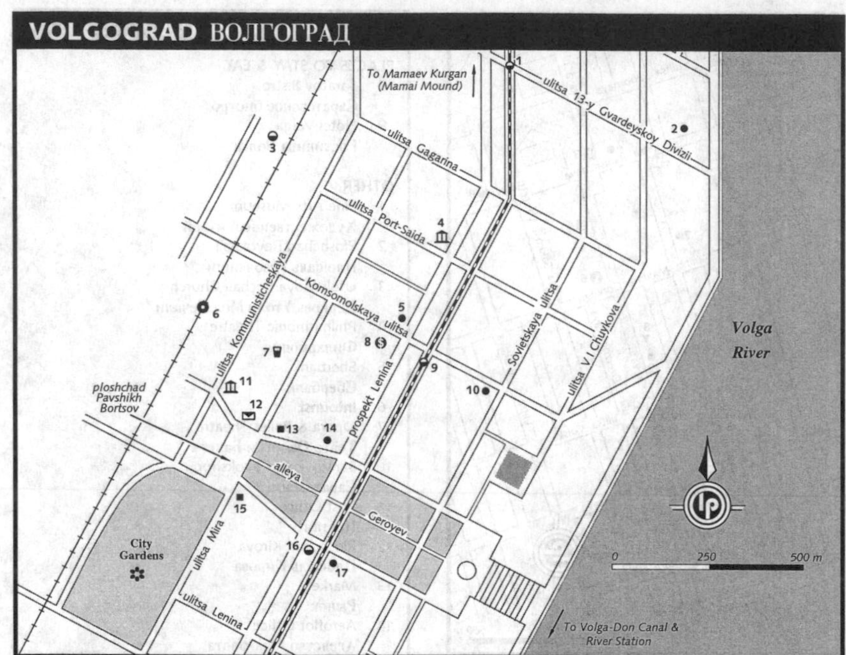

definitely helped inspire many more to repair the damage after the war. After Stalin's fall from grace in the 1950s, the city was renamed.

Today, the city shares the unfortunate honour with Ulyanovsk of no longer being a mandatory travel destination for Party members. The city is a bit sterile and although somewhat pleasant doesn't have much to offer those not interested in its many impressive battle-related sights.

Orientation & Information

Volgograd stretches 75km along the river but averages only 4km in width. Its main lengthwise artery is prospekt Lenina. From the central ploshchad Pavshikh Bortsov (Fallen Warriors' Square) a promenade, alleya Geroyev (Ave of Heroes), crosses prospekt Lenina to the river terminal.

Sberbank (☎ 33 06 34), prospekt Lenina 15, has exchange services. There is an ATM in, of all places, the L'Escale Perfume Shop, prospekt Lenina 17. The post office is on ploshchad Pavshikh Bortsov and is open 24 hours a day for telephone calls.

The friendly Intourist office, located inside Hotel Intourist, offers a multilingual all-day city tour for up to three people for $78.

Mamaev Kurgan (Mamai Mound)

This hill (known as Hill 102 during the battle) is located 3km north of the centre. It's the site of the battle's fiercest fighting for four months and is now a memorial to all who died at Stalingrad. The effect is moving – and it's hard not to be impressed with the sword-wielding statue of Mother Russia which is 72m tall and can be seen from all over town.

The area is covered with statues, memorials and ruined fortifications. The Pantheon is inscribed with 7200 names, picked at random, of soldiers who died here. To get there take the high-speed tram to the Mamaev Kurgan stop.

VOLGOGRAD ВОЛГОГРАД

PLACES TO STAY & EAT

13 Hotel Intourist
Гостиница Интурист
15 Hotel Volgograd
Гостиница Волгоград

OTHER

1 Ploshchad Lenina Tram Stop
Остановка трамвая Площадь Ленина
2 Museum of the Defence of Stalingrad & Panorama
Музей обороны Сталинграда и Панорама
3 Central Bus Station
Центральный автовокзал
4 Fine Arts Museum
Музей изобразительных искусств
5 L'Escale Perfume Shop & ATM
Парфмерный магазин Л'Эскаль
6 Train Station
Железнодорожный вокзал
7 Gallery Bar
Бар Галерея
8 Sberbank
Сбербанк
9 Komsomolskaya Tram Stop
Остновка трамвая Комсомольская
10 Central Market
Центральный рынок
11 Memorial History Museum
Мемориально-исторический музей
12 Post & Telephone Office
Главпочтамт и переговорный пункт
14 Aeroflot Office
Агенство Аэрофлота
16 Airport Bus Stop
Остановка автобуса в аэропорт
17 TABC Volga Airlines
Агенство ТАБС

Panorama & Museum of the Defence of Stalingrad

The Panorama (Panorama 'Stalingradskaya Bitva') is a 360° illustration of the battle for Stalingrad as it might have been seen from atop Mamaev Kurgan. It gruesomely captures the chaos and carnage of the battle although is located up a rather bizarre and lengthy climb. The base of the huge structure – which was the last major Soviet project in the city – holds an impressive museum (Muzey Oborony Stalingrada) complete with a massive model of the ruined centre and scores of displays.

Tours of the complex are $6 or you can take yourself around for $1. Everything is open from 10 am to 5 pm daily. The museum is built next to the ruins of a flour mill which, ironically, had been built by the Germans in 1893 and which is the only evidence of the battle left in the centre.

The complex is two blocks east of the Ploshchad Lenina high-speed tram stop but is a nice 20 minute stroll through the river park from alleya Geroyev.

Other Museums

The small **Fine Arts Museum** (Muzey Izobrazitelnykh Iskusstv; ☎ 36 39 06), is a pleasant surprise, with its collection of Russian paintings, porcelain and carved ivory. It's through a small door on ulitsa Port-Saida off prospekt Lenina, and is open from 10 am to 6 pm (closed Wednesday). The entry fee is $0.20. **The Memorial History Museum** (Memorialno-istorichesky muzey), on the corner of ulitsa Kommunisticheskaya and ploshchad Pavshikh Bortsov, has a collection of artefacts from Russian aviation and the space program, including photos and pilots uniforms. It is open from 10 am to 5 pm (closed Tuesday) and admission is $0.30.

Alleya Geroyev

In this bombastic park there is a **monument** to 3500 Red Civil War partisans who are buried beneath ploshchad Pavshikh Bortsov. At the east end, an ostentatious colonnaded stairway descends to the Volga.

River Trips

The once mighty fleet of river boats that hauled the huge tour groups on river outings is almost no more. As the ticket seller told us, 'It's very quiet around here now.' A one hour excursion boat operates on summer weekends and there is a regular service that travels 1½ hours downstream several times a day. This ride is rather scenic. Ask at the river station for boats to Tumak and expect to pay about $0.60 each way.

Places to Stay & Eat

Hotel Intourist *(☎ 36 45 53, fax 36 16 48, ulitsa Mira 14)*, on the corner of ploshchad Pavshikh Bortsov, is a treat: it has rooms of faded elegance ranging from bathless singles

A Battle to the Death

Even in a century marked by war, the Battle for Stalingrad still manages to shock with its destruction of lives and disregard for humanity. From July 1942, when the German army besieged the city on its thrust to the oil-rich Caucasus region, to February 1943, when the Soviet army captured the last remaining German soldier, the two sides fought a battle to the death with no compromise or quarter. The facts of this hell speak for themselves:

- As the two armies dug in across from each other, they made starving children carry their messages between posts. Most were killed before they received the promised food.
- The Soviets shot 13,500 of their own troops for actions such as cowardice or self-wounding to escape the front. Thousands more who had been taken captive by the Germans but then managed to escape were killed on the grounds they were possible spies.
- The Germans captured 60,000 Stalingrad civilians and shipped them back to Germany to work and die as slaves.
- After the German position became hopeless during the winter, the generals – most of whom survived – were resolute in honouring Hitler's decree against surrender. Thousands more died needlessly.
- Of the 180,000 German troops captured by the Soviets – at least 600,000 more died in battle – only 6000 survived their Siberian prisoner of war camps.
- The total number of Russian soldiers killed is unknown but is thought to approach 600,000. Even the Germans were shocked by the Soviet army's tactic of sending swarms of men to be mowed down by machine guns so that their bodies would shield the waves of troops behind.
- More than 50 years after the battle, any digging in Volgograd still turns up bodies.

to suites, and has laid-back staff and a decent ***restaurant*** and bar. Rooms cost from $30 and it accepts credit cards.

South across ploshchad Pavshikh Bortsov is ***Hotel Volgograd*** *(☎ 36 17 72, fax 33 99 29)*, another vintage gem out of a Graham Greene novel. Singles/doubles cost $12/20. The hotel has an opulent ***restaurant*** at the top of a grand staircase where the long menu of Russian dishes averages $2 a course.

Gallery Bar *(☎ 33 56 72, ulitsa Mira 11)* is an Irish-style place with pints of Guinness for an all-too-authentic $4. It's open until 11 pm. It seems that every multinational beverage company has been to Volgograd and left their multicoloured umbrellas, plastic chairs and tables behind for the scores of simple cafes that line ploshchad Pavshikh Bortsov and alleya Geroyev.

The central ***market*** is located on the corner of Komsomolskaya ulitsa and Sovietskaya ulitsa. The fragrant mountains of dill are just some of the bounty harvested from this fertile region.

Getting There & Away

Air Aeroflot Russian International Airlines (☎ 30 05 15), alleya Geroyev 6, handles international ticket sales and is open from 9 am to 7 pm daily. The old Aeroflot office is now operated by Aeroflot offshoot TABC Volga Airlines (☎ 33 62 26), alleya Geroyev 5, who handles daily flights to/from Moscow (Domodedovo) which cost $50. This office is open from 8 am to 7 pm daily.

Train Trains run to/from Moscow's Paveletsky station and cost $48 for the 20 hour journey. Other daily services link Volgograd to Kazan (10 hours), Astrakhan (nine hours) and Rostov-on-Don (16 hours).

Bus The regional bus station is a 10 minute walk across the tracks from the train station.

This is a good place to hire a car for a long-distance journey such as the one to Astrakhan that costs $50 for up to three people and takes a mere four hours.

Boat The river station, just south of the bombastic steps at the end of alleya Geroyev, was once one of the grandest on the river. Now, however, it shares the fate of many other public buildings and has much of its space given over to businesses peddling a variety of wares including some really ugly office furniture. Go around the back on the ground level to find the bit still dedicated to ticket sales.

Getting Around

It's easy to get to/from the airport. From prospekt Lenina, opposite TABC Volga Airlines, a bus does the 30 minute trip to the airport every 30 minutes or so for $0.10.

The city centre is accessible on foot, and everywhere else by the high-speed tram (skorostnoy tramvay). The tram is a kind of mini-metro along or under prospekt Lenina and costs $0.05. Stations have automatic ticket machines. There are also buses and trolleybuses that have the same fare.

ASTRAKHAN
АСТРАХАНЬ

☎ 85100 • pop 500,000

This city of canals, bridges and a mix of nationalities is situated at the upper end of the Volga River delta, about 100km from the Caspian Sea, making it both a river and a sea port. Astrakhan is pleasant with an impressive kremlin and traditional wooden Russian houses, but in summer it gets very hot and dusty.

The Golden Horde took over the area in the 13th century and it was at the end of the same century that a city was founded on the right bank of the Volga River by the Tatars. After Kazan fell to Ivan the Terrible, the rest of the Volga River region was easily taken by Ivan's troops and this original city suffered. Today's kremlin was built on the left bank of the river in 1558 by Ivan's troops, and a city was founded on the new site. It was a major trading centre for Central Asia and Caucasus and has always prospered economically. Multinational oil firms are very active in the area and the presence of free-spending Westerners has caused tourist prices to rise.

Orientation & Information

The centre of Astrakhan is on an island surrounded by the Volga River and the canals imeni 1 Maya and the Kutum. The kremlin holds a central position, with a busy commercial area just to the east. The major thoroughfare of ulitsa Pobedy cuts through the eastern part of the island and goes north to the train station. The naberezhnaya (river embankment) west of the kremlin is a great place for a stroll and in the evenings locals enjoy eating and drinking at the many stands along the river bank. Maps exist but are not sold widely.

Sberbank (☎ 22 93 81), ulitsa Trusova 11, handles exchange, credit card advances and cashes travellers cheques. It is open from 10 am to 5.30 pm weekdays. The post office is on the corner of ulitsa Kirova and ulitsa Chernishevskogo and is open from 8 am to 7 pm daily.

Intourist (☎ 22 97 30), ulitsa Ulyanovykh 6, is friendly and can help arrange trips into the remarkable Volga Delta region. In August, the red flowers of the ubiquitous floating lotus plants are not to be missed. The office is open from 10 am to 5 pm weekdays.

Kremlin

The large 16th century fortress on top of Zayachy Hill was the realisation of the architect Dorofey Myakishiev's dream. It can be entered through the main eastern **Prechistenskie Belfry Gate** (1908-12) which looks like a church tower. The **Assumption Cathedral** (Uspensky sobor, 1698-1710) is behind the gate and is being restored. In the central part of the kremlin is the yet to be restored **Trinity Cathedral** (Troitsky sobor, 18th century).

At the western end, in the **Red Gate** (Krasnye vorota, 16th century), is an exhibition of historical photos. The Red Tower is open from 11 am to 4 pm Tuesday to Sunday, and the entry fee is $0.10.

ASTRAKHAN АСТРАХАНЬ

PLACES TO STAY & EAT

3 Restoran Modern
Ресторан Модернь

9 Picnic

10 Hotel Novomoskovskaya
Гостиница Новомосковская

15 Hotel Lotos
Гостиница Лотос

OTHER

1 Intourist
Интурист

2 Sberbank
Сбербанк

4 Market
Рынок

5 Kustodiev Art Gallery
Художественная галерея имени Кустодиева

6 Shatrovaya Tower
Шатровая башня

7 History and Architecture Museum
Историко-архитектурный музей

8 Post Office
Почта

11 Prechistenskie Gate
Пречистенские ворота

12 Assumption Cathedral
Успенский собор

13 Trinity Cathedral
Троицкий собор

14 Red Gate
Красные ворота

16 River Station
Речной вокзал

17 Mosque
Мечеть

Museums

The **Kustodiev Art Gallery** (Kartinnaya galereya B M Kustodieva) at ulitsa Sverdlova 81 has an extensive art collection, with sculptures and paintings by such artists as Nesterov, Kustodiev and Levitan. It is open from 10 am to 6 pm (closed Sunday) and the entry fee is $0.30.

The interesting **History and Architecture Museum** (Istoriko-arkhitekturny muzey), located at ulitsa Sovietskaya 15, is open from 10 am to 6 pm (closed Friday) and admission is $0.70.

Religious Structures

The **Ioann Zlatoust Church** (1763) at ulitsa Magnitogorskaya is one of the few churches to survive the ravages of time and revolution and has been fully restored, including the frescoes. One that was almost ruined is the **Kazan Icon Church** (Tserkov Kazanskoy Ikony) at ulitsa Chekhova 10a, which is being restored – its frescoes are barely visible. The 16th century Spaso-preobrazhensky Monastery wasn't so lucky – only the **Shatrovaya Tower** on the corner of ulitsa Trusova and Kommunisticheskaya ulitsa remains.

There is a **mosque** (Musulman mechet No 1) at ulitsa Spartakovskaya, with a plain interior but a classical exterior.

Places to Stay

The nicely located ***Hotel Novomoskovskaya*** *(☎ 22 09 54, ulitsa Sovietskaya 40)* 'loves backpackers' according to the cheery manager. Simple rooms with shared bath are $4.

At the other end of the friendly scale is the hulking ***Hotel Lotos*** *(☎ 22 95 00, fax 22 99 12, ulitsa Kremlevskaya 4)* which has a nice river-front location. Otherwise, boisterous groups of expat oil workers, surly staff, dirty rooms and smelly food mean that it's hardly worth the inflated prices of $45/55 for a single/double.

Much better for those prices is ***Hotel Korvet*** *(☎ 34 03 78, ulitsa Boevaya 50A)*. It is a short distance off the street and reception is up a flight of stairs from the ground level of this late 19th century building. The spacious and clean rooms with private bath and TV cost $55/65. To get there from the train station, take tram Nos 1, 2 or 4 to the stop Klub TRZ.

Places to Eat

Numerous simple cafes peddle grilled meats and cold drinks along the naberezhnaya. ***Picnic*** *(ulitsa Kirova 7)* has Russian fast food for under $1 and is open from 11 am to 11 pm. The ***Restoran Modern*** *(ulitsa Trusova 35)* is actually rather old in a good, atmospheric way. It has fine Russian

The Sturgeon's Last Stand?

The delta of the lower Volga River, where the river divides into over 1000 branches, is a giant filter which cleanses the tons of pollutants from the water before it reaches the Caspian Sea. It is home to an immense treasure of flora and fauna. Among the reeds are found beavers, racoons, herons, musk rats, foxes and otters, not to mention many different species of fish, including the famous sturgeon. Unfortunately, this is the only area where the sturgeon can be found in any numbers. The dams along the Volga above Astrakhan have created an environmental disaster, with the pollution dumped into the river trapped on the bottom of the reservoirs. Restricted to the delta, and threatened by pollution and overfishing, the three main species of sturgeon – Russian, Stellate and the prized Beluga – are in danger of being destroyed. This in turn puts the caviar industry at risk.

Caviar – the salty roe, or raw eggs, of the sturgeon – is a major commodity for local consumption and export. There are five basic types of caviar, named according to the variety of sturgeon each comes from: the smallest, greenish-black type is from the 'sevruga'; the larger, greyish, grey-green or brown type is 'osetrova'; the largest, black or grey type, 'beluga'; the rarest caviar is the golden roe of the 'sterlet'; and the cheapest is the 'payusnaya', which is made from imperfect or lower grades of eggs.

Whatever the grade, caviar is rapidly becoming a rare commodity. Poaching, unregulated harvesting and pollution are causing the sturgeon stocks to crash. It is impossible to know the exact caviar production of Russia or its closest commercial competitor Iran, but combined the two admit to about 300 tons annually. However, much more is illegally harvested from the Volga Delta and Caspian Sea. The culprits include mobsters and residents desperate for cash. Although beluga caviar fetches well over $1500 a pound in Western capitals, in Astrakhan impoverished locals peddle jars for just a few dollars.

Whatever the production, it is presently far above sustainable levels. Recorded catches of Caspian sturgeon have fallen from about 25,000 tons annually in the early 1980s to under 3000 tons in 1998. The fact that the largest female sturgeons, which weigh 600kg, can carry caviar worth $250,000 makes the bounty on their scaly heads all too irresistible.

fare for $1 and is open from 10 am to midnight daily. The best place to eat is ***Restoran Korvet*** in the hotel of the same name. It has a good but small selection of dishes from $2.

There are two main ***markets***. The first is on the corner of ulitsa Pobedy and Krasnaya naberezhnaya 108 and the second is at ploshchad Svobody. At the markets ask for smoked sturgeon *(osetrina goryachego kopcheniya)*, a heavenly local speciality.

Getting There & Away

There are daily flights to/from Moscow (Domodedovo) costing $70. The Aeroflot office (☎ 25 47 49) is at ulitsa Pobedy 54. Tickets for foreigners are available from window No 2 and it is open from 8 am to 7.30 pm daily.

The train station is at Privokzalnaya ulitsa, and advance tickets are available from the Railway Ticket Office across the car park. It is open from 8 am to 6 pm (closed Sunday). Trains to Moscow take 30 hours. Daily trains also go to Volgograd (nine hours), Rostov-on-Don (24 hours) and south to Makhachkala in Dagestan (20 hours). The regional bus station is in an old cathedral on the corner of ulitsa Generala Yepisheva and naberezhnaya Privolzhskoga Zatona.

There are no regular passenger boats to the other Caspian Sea ports. It is possible to find a freighter that takes passengers, but you must have the correct visa for the country of destination. Astrakhan is the end point of cruises on the Volga and the river station is located at (naberezhnaya) Kremlevskaya ulitsa 1. The trips from Moscow take 10 days.

Getting Around

Bus No 5 and trolleybus No 3 go to/from the airport, train station and ploshchad Lenina, and can be found at any bus stop along ulitsa Pobedy, ulitsa Sverdlova or ulitsa Zhelyabova. Trolleybus Nos 1, 2, 3 and 4 run to/from the train station and ploshchad Lenina.

Bus, trolleybus and tram tickets cost $0.05 and are available on board.

ROSTOV-ON-DON
РОСТОВ-НА-ДОНУ

☎ 8632 • pop 1 million

Rostov-on-Don (Rostov-na-Donu) is the industrial centre of a farming region known for its wine, among other things. Though pleasant and relatively prosperous, it's not very exciting, but it's a base for some excursions of historical interest, including two old Don Cossack capitals, the remains of a Genoese trading centre and a 3rd century BC Greek colony. The modern town celebrated its 250th anniversary in 1999.

Orientation & Information

The city axis, ulitsa Bolshaya Sadovaya, parallels the pedestrian artery of Pushkinsky bulvar.

Mostbank (☎ 63 59 41), Voroshilovsky prospekt 12, changes currency and travellers cheques. Kredobank on the corner of Teatralny prospekt and Teatralnaya ploshchad gives cash advances on credit cards. It's open from 9.30 am to 3.30 pm weekdays and also has an ATM. The post and telegraph office is on the corner of pereulok Podbelskogo and ulitsa Serafimovicha.

Intourist (☎ 65 90 00, fax 65 90 07) is in its namesake hotel. Staff are quite helpful and can arrange regional excursions.

Rostov had one of the world's highest cholera death rates in the late 19th century and a small outbreak as recently as 1990, so stick with mineral or bottled water.

Central Market & Nativity Church

The open-air market (tsentralny rynok) sprawls around the Nativity of the Virgin Cathedral (Sobor Rozhdestva Bogoroditsy, 1884), at ulitsa Stanislavskogo 58, near pereulok Podbelskogo. The cathedral itself is being lavishly restored, including new gold-plated domes for the towers.

Museums

The **Museum of Local Studies** (Oblastnoy muzey kraevedenia; ☎ 65 55 72), ulitsa Bolshaya Sadovaya 79, features Cossack history and the peasant rebellions of Bulavin, Razin and Pugachov – good for regional info if you have a translator along.

It's open from 10 am to 6 pm (closed Mondays). The **Pushkin Fine Arts Museum** (Muzey Izobrazitelnykh Iskusstv imeni Pushkina; ☎ 66 69 07) is at Pushkinsky bulvar 115, and is open from 10 am to 5.30 pm Wednesday to Monday.

Ulitsa Bolshaya Sadovaya is lined with many heavily decorated houses dating from the late 19th century. Some of the most notable ones are Nos 27, 47, 55 and 69.

Parks

At the west end of town, **Gorky Park** has secluded gardens, men playing dominoes, a little observatory and the 19th century town hall. At the other end of ulitsa Bolshaya Sadovaya it's all Socialist grandeur: October Revolution Park, the Gorky Theatre (1936) and the Memorial to the Liberation of Rostov ('glory to Soviet tank drivers' etc). Guess where the crowds are on summer evenings?

Places to Stay & Eat

Hotel Turist *(☎ 38 42 32, ulitsa Oktyabrya)*, 2.5km north of the centre, is ageing and has basic single/double rooms for $10/18. ***Hotel Intourist*** *(☎ 65 90 65, fax 65 90 07, ulitsa Bolshaya Sadovaya)* is convenient but far from posh or even average. The rooms cost $45/50. The ***restaurant*** is best for dieters.

Some of the best food in town is at the co-op ***Kafe Alisa***, behind the cinema on the corner of Kirovsky prospekt and ulitsa Gorkogo. Dishes are around $1. Another reasonable place for Russian standards is ***Kafe Axinya*** *(ulitsa Bolshaya Sadovaya 86)*. The jolly ***Bar Glazgo*** east of Hotel Intourist and across the street has good ice cream (with fresh berries in summer) and Turkish coffee. The ***Minieuropa Supermarket*** *(ulitsa Bolshaya Sadovaya 109)* is open from 9 am to 10 pm daily and accepts credit cards.

Getting There & Away

Daily flights to Moscow (Vnukovo) are $60. The Aeroflot office (☎ 65 71 60) is at ulitsa Socialisticheskaya 144-146 and is open from 8.30 am to 6 pm daily.

At the west end of ulitsa Bolshaya Sadovaya are suburban and long-distance stations. A fast train from Moscow's Kursky station takes 23 hours. Some trains to/from Moscow go via Kharkiv (Kharkov) in Ukraine: check the Ukraine visa situation if you're thinking of taking one of these. Rostov is a rail hub and the web of daily service includes Astrakhan (24 hours), Volgograd (16 hours) and Sochi (14 hours).

The river station is at the south-eastern end of Budyonnovsky prospekt. There are occasional boats to/from Moscow via Volgograd in summer.

Getting Around

The best airport transport is a taxi, which will cost about $4 from Hotel Intourist. From the train station to Hotel Intourist the taxi mafia ask $3 but the locals pay about $0.25. Bus No 7, 12 or 13 and trolleybus No 1, 9 or 15 ply ulitsa Bolshaya Sadovaya. The public transport fare is $0.10. Boats cross the river for $0.05 from Voroshilovsky landing by the bridge.

AROUND ROSTOV-ON-DON

Starocherkassk

Старочеркасск

Founded in 1593, the stanitsa of Old Cherkassk was the Don Cossack capital for two centuries. Once a fortified town of 20,000, it's now a village of vegetable farmers with a little main street restored to its late 19th century appearance. There are remains of a fortress 3km down the River Don, called Cherkassk Krepost.

Peter the Great, visiting here, allegedly came across a drunken Cossack sitting on a barrel, wearing only a rifle. This image of a soldier who'd sooner lose his clothes than his gun so impressed the tsar that he had it drawn up as the Don Cossack army seal.

Near the west end of the main street is peasant rebellion leader **Bulavin's fortified house** (1709) where he was eventually killed. East from the plain **SS Peter & Paul Church** (1751) and the old market square are more sturdy **Cossack fort-houses.**

In a brick building beyond these is a good **museum** illustrating 16th to 20th century Cossack life and the rebellions. It is open from 10 am to 5 pm except Monday; entry costs $0.15. Next door is the **Church of Our Lady of the Don** (1761), which was the private church of a Cossack ataman, and behind it is his classical 'palace'.

At the eastern end is the square where in 1670 Razin rallied his followers and where he was later clapped in chains. In the **Resurrection Cathedral** (Voskresensky sobor, 1719) the beautiful iconostasis and baroque chandelier are a reminder that some Cossacks did pretty well for themselves.

The entry fee is $0.20 for each of these five sights.

On the last Sunday of each month in summer a 'Cossack fair' features music, dancing, crafts and horseback riding.

Getting There & Away Starocherkassk is 30km up the Don from Rostov. Hydrofoils go three times a day for $0.75, taking about 40 minutes. From the pier, head right to the cannon at the fort's south-western corner, then left and right and you're in the main street. Intourist runs a day-long tour from Rostov-on-Don by car or coach in summer. It costs $70 for up to seven individuals.

Novocherkassk
Новочеркасск

The Don Cossacks moved their capital to New Cherkassk in 1805. It's now a town of 200,000, 40km north-east of Rostov. This is supposedly the setting for Nobel laureate Mikhail Sholokhov's *And Quiet Flows the Don*. Still a hero here is Ataman Matvey Platov, a Cossack general who was part of the force that chased Napoleon back to Paris; two arches commemorate his return.

The **History of the Don Cossacks Museum** (Muzey Istorii Donskogo Kazachestva), Sovietskaya ulitsa 38, has a big collection of memorabilia including a sword presented to Platov in England; open from 10 am to 5 pm Tuesday to Sunday.

Also worth a look is the beautiful **Ascension Cathedral** (Voznesensky sobor, 1905), a working church at ploshchad Yermaka. Take bus No 1 from the train or bus station.

Intourist's half-day Novocherkassk excursion from Rostov-on-Don costs $50 for up to three individuals. From Rostov-on-Don, buses take 40 minutes and trains take 75 minutes.

Tanaïs & Azov
Танаис и Азов

From at least the 3rd century BC until the 4th century AD, the Greek colony of Tanaïs flourished on the Sea of Azov at the mouth of the Don. Genoese merchants in the 13th century established a trading settlement nearby, calling it Tana. Later the Turks built a fortress to keep the Russians out of the Black Sea. The Cossacks took it for several years and Peter the Great captured it in 1696.

The industrial city of Azov has two attractions: **Azov Fort** (Azovskaya Krepost) and an interesting **museum** containing exhibits on Cossack life and history. The museum is at ulitsa Moskovskaya 38/40, on the corner of Petrovsky prospekt, and is open from 10 am to 5 pm (closed Monday). Intourist runs half-day coach tours from Rostov-on-Don for $55. Hydrofoils travel the 45km down to Azov from Rostov every hour for $0.50.

Near the village of Nedvigovka on the road from Rostov-on-Don to Taganrog are excavations of the original Tanaïs. A **museum** is open from 9 am to 5 pm from mid-April to mid-November. Intourist tours normally stop here.

Caucasus
Кавказ

The dramatic Caucasus mountain range striding from the Black Sea to the Caspian Sea forms Russia's most southerly border. This chapter covers the northern (Russian) side of the range, the foothills and steppe to the north, and the Russian coastal strip along the Black Sea at the western end of the Caucasus. The steeper southern side of the Caucasus lies in the now independent states of Georgia and Azerbaijan.

Though parts of the Caucasus region have been tragically beset by war and ethnic conflict, its untroubled areas can make for some of the most exciting travel in Russia. It's not only different from everything to the north, but is also immensely varied. Below the mountains' jagged 3000, 4000 and 5000m peaks lie valleys that are home to dozens of peoples speaking dozens of languages, practising Christianity, Islam and Judaism, with a varied range of cultures.

The Caucasus is the most spectacular part of European Russia. Even if you're no walker or mountaineer, try to venture into the hills by visiting Dombay, or the Baxan Valley beneath Mt Elbrus (5642m), which is Europe's highest peak if you accept the traditional view that the main Caucasus watershed – just south of Elbrus – is the border between Europe and Asia. The main northern approach to the Caucasus is from Rostov-on-Don across the slowly rising Kuban Steppe and through the mineral water spa area in the foothills of the central Caucasus. Where the Caucasus meets the Black Sea is Russia's holiday coast, the main resort being Sochi. At the eastern end of the Caucasus lies Chechnya and Dagestan, a complicated ethnic jigsaw with an Asiatic atmosphere, extending from the mountains to the Caspian Sea.

An ideal itinerary would be to begin acclimatising in the mineral spa of Pyatigorsk, with a side trip to Zheleznovodsk. After two or three days, you'll be ready to bus down to Dombay for some serious hiking beneath the chiselled, snow-splattered peaks. If you're on a tight schedule, three days is enough to get a feel of the region. Afterwards you'll be ready for a soothing mineral bath at the nicest of the spa towns, Kislovodsk. From there, in a day or two, you can take a bus to Nalchik, the not so

HIGHLIGHTS

- Travelling the spaghetti-thin Georgian Military Highway that twists through the snowbound Caucasus Mountains at 2500m above sea level
- Discovering the wonders of Dombay, including waterfalls, glaciers, alpine meadows, bears, wild goats and partying with local mountain tribes
- Taking a dip in the Narzan Mineral Baths
- Visiting Russia's version of Florida & relaxing in sunny, still-Soviet Sochi

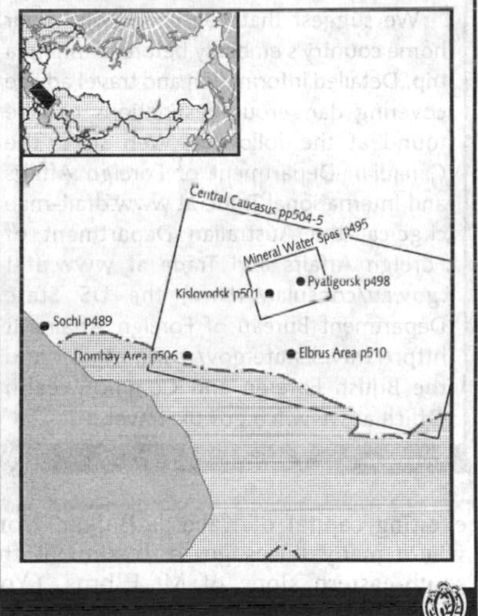

WARNING

At the time of research in 1999, it was not safe to travel to most of the Caucasus region. The areas of Chechnya, Dagestan, North Ossetia and Ingushetia were particularly dangerous. Military clashes, incidents of kidnapping of aid workers and foreigners, violent crimes and muggings had increased. As a result, we couldn't carry out first-hand research in Chechnya, Dagestan, North Ossetia or Ingushetia.

It is not enough to simply assume that it is safe to travel in these regions now. We strongly suggest you keep your eye on developments before contemplating a visit or even passing through. In the meantime, we strongly advise you to stay clear of these regions.

We suggest that you check with your home country's embassy before planning a trip. Detailed information and travel advice covering dangerous destinations can be found at the following Web sites: the Canadian Department of Foreign Affairs and International Trade at www.dfait-maeci.gc.ca; the Australian Department of Foreign Affairs and Trade at www.dfat.gov.au/consular/advice; the US State Department Bureau of Foreign Affairs at http://travel.state.gov/russia.html; and the British Foreign and Commonwealth Office at www.fco.gov.uk/travel.

exciting capital of Kabarda-Balkar, from where many buses go to Terskol at the south-eastern slope of Mt Elbrus. (You could switch Mt Elbrus and Dombay in your itinerary easily enough, but either way you must tag back to one of the mineral spas as it is not possible to cut east-west over Mt Elbrus.) After you summit Mt Elbrus, circumvent it or loll on the snowy slopes, you'll be due for a few days in Sochi on the Black Sea from where you can work your way north to Krasnodar or head south to Georgia or Turkey.

HISTORY

The northern Caucasus has been at the crossroads of Mediterranean, Central Asian, Middle Eastern and Eastern European cultures since the Bronze Age. The result is an extraordinary mix of races with three main linguistic groups: Caucasian, Indo-European and Turkic. There are also several religions represented in the region, Islam and Orthodox Christianity having the greatest numbers of adherents. The Caucasus has suffered from many invasions and occupations through the course of history. Since long before Christ, it has been squeezed between rival empires – among them the Roman, Persian, Byzantine, Arab, Ottoman and Russian.

During the most recent occupation, in the 19th century, it took the Russians several decades to subjugate the tribes of the region. This led to the 20th century Soviet policy, which was to divide and conquer in order to rule. The effects of this policy on the region's nationalities were profound, and culminated in the separatist wars of the early 1990s.

Early Days

Little is known of the prehistory of the area but there have been several prehistoric and Stone Age finds. Some of the earliest traces of human habitation are from the time of the Neolithic revolution, when hunting and gathering was being replaced with farming and the first communities were being established. These finds come from Dagestan's dry valleys and are dated to the same era as other early developments of agriculture in the Middle East and Japan, making the northern part of the Caucasus one of the cradles of civilisation.

Apart from archaeological finds, not much else is known of the early northern Caucasian people. It is known that they used copper and iron tools around 1000 BC, during the time of the so-called Koban culture. The region was connected by well established routes to the Greek civilisation, with which it had significant trading ties; this activity peaked around the 7th century BC.

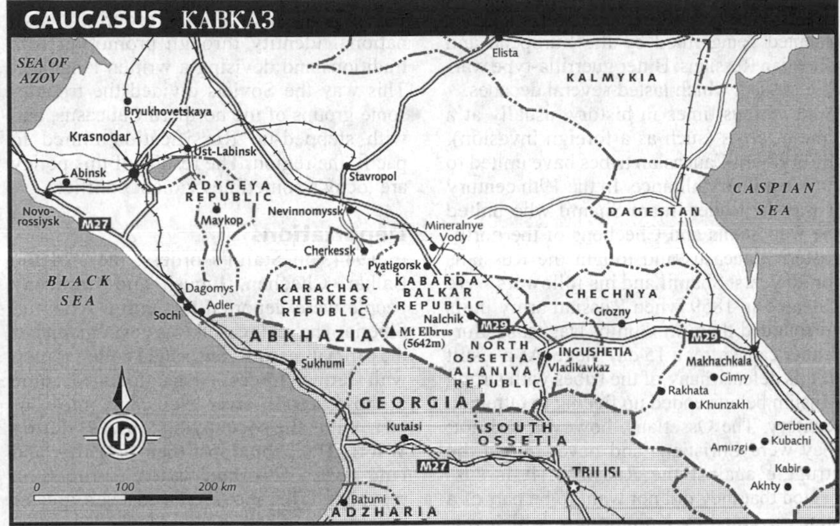

Early Invasions

The era of the great migrations brought many different peoples to the Caucasus. The Scythians arrived from the east along the northern Black Sea coast in the 8th century BC, followed by the Sarmatians, also from the east, in about the 3rd century BC. In the first millennium AD, groups such as the Kipchaks (ancestors of the present-day Balkar), the Huns, the Pechenegs and the Khazars all left their mark, some settling and mixing with the existing inhabitants.

Alans

The Alans, ancestors of the modern Ossetians, are thought to have been originally a fusion of Sarmatians, pushed into the mountains by the Huns, with local tribes. The Alan state came to prominence during the 10th century AD, and at its peak ruled most of the northern Caucasus, with established trade routes to all the major empires surrounding it. The Alans were also Christians, probably having been introduced to the religion by the Georgians.

During the 11th century, such Turkic tribes as the Kipchak, Polovtsy and Nogai constantly raided the region, and some members of these tribes ended up settling in parts of the northern Caucasus. The next major invasion was that of the Mongol Tatars in the early 13th century, which destroyed the Alan state. But a much more brutal invasion and occupation, which destroyed the last remains of the Alan state, came with Timur (Tamerlane), who also brought a new Asian terror to much of the Middle East. Many of the surviving Alans left the region or went higher up into the mountains.

Arrival of the Russians

Russian peasants and adventurers who escaped from the oppressive serf system began to settle in the lower Terek River region. It was not until the late 1550s that Russian military power reached the area as a result of a marriage between Tsar Ivan the Terrible and Maria Temryukovna, daughter of the Kabarda prince. Russian economic and military influence grew in the region, and eventually the Russians ended up pushing the Ottoman (Turkish) Empire out of the Caucasus.

The physical conquest of the Caucasus by the Russians began early in the 19th century. The resistance of the local tribes was fierce, as the predominantly Muslim populace resented being ruled by the European and Christian Russians. Bitter guerrilla-type warfare ensued, which lasted several decades.

At various times in history, usually at a time of crisis (such as a foreign invasion), the northern Caucasian tribes have united to form a military alliance. In the 19th century it was the leader Imam Shamil who united the Dagestanis and Chechens of the northeastern Caucasus and fought the Russians for 30 years. Shamil and his followers were defeated in 1859 when Russian army units surrounded them in Gunib, Dagestan. Surrender came after a 15 day siege. As a result of this defeat, many of the tribes with strong Muslim beliefs ended up fleeing to Ottoman territory. The Ossetians, however, did not; they were Christians and never joined the struggle against the Russians. It is suspected that they did not want to be part of a state governed by Koranic law, which was the aim of Shamil's proposed northern Caucasian state.

Russian Rule

At the time of the Russian Revolution in 1917, many of the northern Caucasian tribes united to form the Mountain Republic. They did not, however, manage to keep their independence for long. Once the Soviet forces had consolidated power over Russia, they also conquered most other parts of the former Tsarist Imperial Empire. The Mountain Republic was taken back in 1921 and in the same year it was given the status of an autonomous republic within the Soviet Union. The various nationalities of Dagestan were combined into a new and separate Dagestan Autonomous Republic.

The following year four new autonomous regions – Adygeya, Chechnya, Kabarda-Balkar and Karachay-Cherkess – were created from parts of the Mountain Autonomous Republic, which ceased to exist in 1924. Soviet policy was quite clear in its aim, which was to divide and rule by creating small autonomous regions that sometimes combined two totally different nationalities. The Soviet regime also used other methods to break up the unity of the mountain people – like giving each ethnic group its own national identity through promoting folk traditions and devising a written language. This way the Soviets divided the troublesome groups of the northern Caucasus, and with stepped-up Russification aimed to pacify the region. The results of this policy are today's sometimes violent conflicts.

Deportations

In 1944, on Stalin's orders, most of the Balkar, Chechen, Ingush and Karachay people were deported to Central Asia and Siberia. The real reason was never given but the official reason – suspected collaboration with German forces – was unfounded: some of those groups never even came into contact with the occupying forces during WWII. The people lost their property, and land was absorbed into surrounding republics. This move created even greater bitterness and hatred towards the Russians, but it also fuelled resentment and hatred between those nationalities that stayed and those deported. Those that stayed took the property and land of the deported groups, to whom it was never returned; nor did they receive compensation.

It was only after Stalin's death that Nikita Khrushchev, in 1957, allowed the return of the exiled groups to their former lands. During the rest of the Soviet period there seemed to be no problems between the various nationalities, mainly due to the oppressive and dictatorial nature of the Soviet regime. This changed very quickly after the failed 1991 coup in Moscow.

Post-Soviet Era

The result of the demise of the Soviet Union was the political restructuring of Russia. Many of the autonomous republics or regions were transformed into federal republics. Six of these were formed in the northern Caucasus: Karachay-Cherkess, Kabarda-Balkar, North Ossetia, Dagestan, Adygeya and Checheno-Ingushetia. The latter region later broke up into the two separate republics of Chechnya and Ingushetia. The biggest problems for the Russians came from the Ingush and the

Chechens. For a brief history of both of these groups see the section on Chechnya, and Vladikavkaz in the later Central Caucasus part of this chapter.

CLIMATE

The Black Sea coast is the mildest place in Russia in winter, rarely freezing. In summer it's warm and humid, reaching around 25°C from June to September. North of the Caucasus there's a continental climate – three or four freezing winter months but temperatures up to about 30°C from June to August.

The higher you go the cooler it gets – many Caucasus peaks are permanently snow-covered – but on a sunny summer day you'll still be sweating at 3000m. November to April/May is the wettest season, but only on the Black Sea coastal plain (where around 1200 to 1800mm of rain falls each year) does it get significantly wet.

PEOPLE & LANGUAGE

Around 15 million people inhabit the southern regions of Russia included in this chapter. Most Caucasian societies are strongly patriarchal, but the tribal nature of the mountain peoples has been diluted by Soviet education, collectivisation and urbanisation.

The region's ethnic complexity is revealed by its administrative divisions: strung across the northern side of the Caucasus are seven republics within the Russian Federation, their names indicating some of the peoples that inhabit them: from west to east, they are Adygeya, Karachay-Cherkess and Kabarda-Balkar, North Ossetia, Ingushetia, Chechnya and Dagestan.

Classified by language, of which 40 or so are spoken, the region's peoples divide into three main families. Russian is spoken just about everywhere.

Caucasians

About 2.5 million people in the region use some 30 indigenous Caucasian languages. They fall into north-western and north-eastern groups. All the written languages use the Cyrillic alphabet.

The north-western group, with about 700,000 people, includes the Kabarda, the Adygeya, the Abaza in the Karachay-Cherkess Republic (all also known as Circassians), as well as the Abkhazians of Abkhazia (who are beyond the scope of this book). Many more Circassians now live in Turkey, Syria, Jordan and Iraq.

North-eastern Caucasians divide into speakers of Nakh languages (chiefly the 800,000 Chechen and 200,000 Ingush) and speakers of the 30 or so Dagestan languages. The latter, all from Dagestan or Azerbaijan, are mostly nonwritten and have less than 10,000 speakers. All their speakers are loosely known as Lezgians – a term that still flutters Russian hearts by association with tribes whom it took Russia more than half the 19th century to tame. But Lezgi (or Kury) is also the name of one of the more important individual languages, with 200,000 speakers in Dagestan and 170,000 in Azerbaijan. Others are Avar, with about 500,000 speakers, Lakh with 100,000, and Dargwa with 300,000.

A southern group of Caucasian languages, Kartvelian, is spoken by Georgians.

Indo-Europeans

The Indo-European language family is thought to have originated in western Turkey and to have spread over most of Europe and south and south-west Asia by 1000 BC. The Slavs, mainly Russians and Ukrainians who make up 80% of the population north of the Caucasus, are Indo-European. Prominent among speakers of other Indo-European languages in the Caucasus are the Ossetians, who number around 600,000 and are thought to be descended from Sarmatians pushed south into the Caucasus by the Huns in the 4th century. Most Ossetians live on the northern (Russian) side of the Caucasus but at some stage others spilled through to the southern side into what's now South Ossetia, in Georgia.

Turks

Turkic peoples in the region include 240,000 Kumyk and 60,000 Nogay in Dagestan, and the 150,000-plus Karachay and 70,000-plus Balkar in the western and central Caucasus.

RELIGION

Most Caucasus mountain peoples like the Kabarda, Karachay, Chechens and Balkar are Muslim. There is also a small population of fewer than 10,000 Jews *(gorskie evrei)* living mostly in the cities of Nalchik, Pyatigorsk and Derbent. Russian Orthodoxy predominates in the Cossack villages *(stanitsy)* along the borders as well as in the cities.

GETTING THERE & AWAY

Air

You can fly to several places in the region including Krasnodar on the steppe, Mineralnye Vody on the northern edge of the Caucasus, Sochi on the Black Sea, Vladikavkaz and Nalchik in the Caucasus, and Makhachkala on the Caspian Sea.

Train

The main railways into the region funnel through Rostov-on-Don and then diverge – one to Mineralnye Vody, Astrakhan (a huge detour around Grozny) and Makhachkala and on to Baku (Azerbaijan), and the other to Krasnodar then down the Russian Black Sea coast as far as Sochi.

Trains along the Black Sea route used to go all the way to Tbilisi, via Abkhazia, but stopped during the Abkhazian-Georgian conflict. At the time of writing, this route had not yet reopened.

There are trains all the way from Moscow taking 1½ to two days: some go via Kharkov (Kharkiv) in Ukraine so if you're thinking of taking one of these check the Ukraine visa situation first.

Car & Motorcycle

The main route through the region runs from Rostov-on-Don to the Georgian capital Tbilisi via Mineralnye Vody, Nalchik, Vladikavkaz and the spectacular Georgian Military Highway over the Caucasus. This road was open at the time of writing but there is a constant question of safety due to the poor condition of the winding, narrow road as well as highway bandits, including local road Mafia, the police and border guards all of whom might extract a tariff *(tarify)* of anywhere from $5 to $20 and upwards for passage along 'their' sections of the highway.

The road through Chechnya, leading to Dagestan and Baku (Azerbaijan), is open but absurdly risky. The other main north-south road loops round from Rostov through Krasnodar to Sochi on the Black Sea; its continuation to Sukhumi (Abkhazia) and Batumi (western Georgia), then on to Georgia's road border with Turkey at Sarpi, is open, but again, not trouble free between Sochi and the Georgian border due to the Abkhazian-Georgian conflict.

Greedy customs officials at roadblocks in Adjaria (Georgia's southern-most republic) are extracting tarify of about $7 per person; don't bother to ask for a receipt.

Boat

Novorossiysk and Sochi are served by irregular passenger ferries and hydrofoils. It might be possible to get passage on a freighter between Makhachkala in Dagestan and Turkmenbashi (formerly Krasnovodsk) in Turkmenistan or Aqtau (formerly Shevchenko) in Kazakhstan.

For Georgian and Turkish destinations, see the Sochi section later in this chapter.

Organised Tours

Foreign companies that offer trips to the Mt Elbrus area are mentioned in those sections.

GETTING AROUND

Getting from one city to another is not difficult in the Caucasus, but finding the quickest route often requires the skills of a chess player. (To go from Teberda to Kislovodsk, a distance of only 150km, we needed to take two buses and one train.) Locals rely on a combination of bus, minibus, train and *elektrichki* (the affectionate Russian name for the slow, not very comfortable local trains). As schedules and prices flux, it's always best to consult with a local before making your move. Given the terrain, the most obvious way on the map may not be practical. It was not possible to pass through Chechnya at the time of writing.

Train

It is fairly easy to buy tickets at the station within an hour or two of departure. After the financial crisis of late 1998, train, bus and air fares became insanely cheap. No doubt that has changed.

Bus

Apart from cars and taxis, buses and mini-vans are the only available transport into the mountainous areas. Usually there are overnight buses between major destinations. As a rule, buses are faster than trains in this region.

Car & Motorcycle

Main roads are generally in a decent condition but the many animals wandering over them behave more sensibly than some of the drivers, who sometimes like to overtake in truly lunatic situations. Accidents are common.

Cable Car

One unusual form of transport you may find yourself riding in this region is the cable car. Highly exotic to northern Russians, who never see a hill from one year to the next, these are strung across any landscape with the merest hint of a slope – not just up mountains but over parks, lakes, and even along flat valleys.

Kuban Steppe
Кубанская степь

From Rostov-on-Don, the overland routes to the Caucasus and the Black Sea coast cross the intensively cultivated Kuban Steppe, named after its major river, which flows from Elbrus into the Sea of Azov. This region had a high Cossack population and its peasants were among the chief victims of the grain requisitioning and forced collectivisation of the late 1920s and early 1930s, with apparently millions of them being starved, shot or deported.

The trip from Rostov to Pyatigorsk or Kislovodsk on the northern fringe of the Caucasus can be made in a day – by road it's just under 500km. Mikhail Gorbachev, remembered bitterly by many Russians as the man responsible for perestroika and the collapse of the Soviet Union, was born near unexciting Stavropol, off the main road.

STAVROPOL
СТАВРОПОЛЬ

☎ 8652 • pop 315,000

Stavropol was the Russian military supply centre throughout the Caucasus campaigns that lasted until the 1850s. The town's on a plateau, with an economy based on the agriculture of the surrounding steppe. Mikhail Gorbachev grew up in the village of Privolnoe, 145km to the north. His academic record took him to Moscow to study, then he returned to Stavropol with his wife Raisa to begin his rise up the Party ladder while she taught at the local university.

Stavropol now has the distinction of having a large group of the combat-booted, black-clad followers of General Barkashov, leader of the Russian Unity party whose slogan is 'Russia for Russians'. The party's symbol – which you'll see spray-painted on walls – looks like a swastika, but party leaders insist the emblem has nothing to do with fascism.

As with most places in the Caucasus, people will tell you not to come here. Maybe you should heed the advice, not necessarily because of danger, but because there are more exciting places in the region to spend your time.

Orientation

The main streets are prospekt Karla Marxa, a dual carriageway going west from the train station to Hotel Stavropol, and ulitsa Dzerzhinskogo, running parallel a block south.

Things to See

The 19th century **St Andrew's Cathedral** (Andreevsky sobor) at ulitsa Dzerzhinskogo 155 is a working church. The **Regional Museum** (Kraevedchesky muzey) is at ulitsa Dzerzhinskogo 135 near Hotel Kavkaz and includes an exhibit of army uniforms from Napoleon's army, as well as many Russian and local Cossack ones. There's also an **Art Museum** at ulitsa Dzerzhinskogo 115.

KRASNODAR
КРАСНОДАР

☎ 8612 • pop 652,000

When Catherine the Great travelled south to tour the land she had won from the Turks in the Crimean War, her lover Potemkin had lively facades erected along her route to hide the mud-splattered hovels that were the extent of this newly founded city bearing her name, Yekaterinodar (Catherine's gift).

Some two centuries later, Krasnodar (the city was renamed after 1917) is resort-like with flowering parks, fountains and old Soviet-era hotels with fresh coats of paint.

One reason to come to Krasnodar is to catch a glimpse of the Kuban Cossacks whose headquarters is in the city. Sometimes they gather in uniform for meetings *(krugi)*, and if you're lucky you can even catch a folk festival in a neighbouring stanitsa. The surrounding villages of Abinsk, Bryukhovetskaya and Ust-Labinsk are worth a visit if you're interested in seeing how the Cossacks live these days.

Also near Krasnodar is the Kuban Sea (Kubanskoe More), a huge reservoir created in the 1970s. The water table rose so high, according to the Soviet press, that 3500 sq km of farmland were flooded and the foundations of 27,000 blocks of flats were waterlogged.

Orientation & Information

Krasnaya ulitsa is the 2km-long main street. The road from Rostov-on-Don feeds into its northern end, a tree-lined dual carriageway. Numbering starts from the south. Parallel, two blocks east, is ulitsa Kommunarov; one block west is ulitsa Shaumyana. Main cross streets include, in south-north order, ulitsa Mira, ulitsa Sverdlova and ulitsa Severnaya.

There are several places to change money, including in the foyer of Hotel Moskva and on the 2nd floor of the Intourist. Hotel Moskva also has a post office counter. The main post office is at ulitsa Shaumyana 6. The telephone office (open 24 hours) is at ulitsa Krasnaya 118. Internet access is available here from 8 am to 5 pm Monday to Friday for $4 per hour. The main bookshop, closed Sunday, is at ulitsa Krasnaya 82.

For trekkers, Tourist Firm Extrem (☎/fax 57 40 21, extrem@telecom.kuban.ru) offers an action-packed 15 day route over Mt Fisht (see the Around Sochi & Dagomys section later in this chapter) and onwards to the Black Sea. The guided trek, which normally runs on the first and 15th days of June, July and August, costs about $150 a person; lodging is in tents.

Things to See

The **Regional Museum** (Kraevedchesky muzey) at ulitsa Voroshilova 67 includes Scythian and ancient Greek figures. It's two blocks north and one east from Hotel Tsentralnaya. The **Art Museum** (Khudozhestvenny muzey) is at ulitsa Krasnaya 13. Both are closed Tuesday.

Places to Stay & Eat

The best place in town is the nearly quaint, very quiet ***Hotel Krasnodar*** *(☎ 53 07 97)* on ulitsa Krasnaya next to Hotel Moskva. The rooms, for $5/10 a single/double, have high ceilings, clean bathrooms; like all the hotels in Krasnodar, there is no hot water in June.

Hotel Tsentralnaya *(☎ 2 26 24, ☎ 2 90 57, ulitsa Krasnaya 25)*, on the corner of ulitsa Mira, has decent double rooms (no singles) for $6. The rooms are not as nice as those at Hotel Krasnodar but each does have a fridge and a sink; toilets and showers are down the corridor.

The looming ***Hotel Intourist*** *(☎ 55 88 97)*, about halfway along ulitsa Krasnaya, still maintains two tier pricing … need we say more? Its prices are astronomically out of whack; $40/60 for foreigners.

The best place to eat is ***Restoran Ankara*** (open from 1 pm to midnight daily). It's easy to find, just a half-block south of the telephone office. The food is quasi-Turkish, for example chicken Kapama ($2) in a baked paprika crust. The menu is in quasi-English. There are many other places to eat along ulitsa Krasnaya. The twin sidewalk ***cafes*** on either side of the entrance to Hotel

Moskva are popular. If the travel gods are with you, the beige and brown ***ice cream wagons*** selling some of Russia's best two scoops in a waffle cone ($0.25) will also be on the main drag.

The ***central market*** *(tsentralny rynok)* is opposite the circus at ulitsa Budyonnogo 129, a block west of Hotel Intourist.

Getting There & Away

Air There are daily flights to/from Moscow ($30), several flights a week to Mineralnye Vody ($14, one hour), one flight a week to Makhachkala ($30, two hours) as well as flights to the Siberian and Far East destinations of Petropavlovsk-Kamchatsky, Novosibirsk and Magadan. There are flights several times a week to Tashkent ($80, four hours) and once a week to Tbilisi ($54, three hours). Aeroflot (☎ 57 60 07), ulitsa Krasnaya 129, is just north of the Hotel Intourist. The airport is about 15km from the city; take trolleybus No 4 from the train station or the express bus from in front of Aeroflot.

Train Several trains a day pass through on the Rostov-Sochi route. Rostov is four to six hours away, Sochi five hours. There is a train every other day to Kislovodsk, with trains to Odesa, Kharkiv and Kyiv (Kiev) twice a week. Train No 338 (Adler-Tomsk) and No 328 (Adler-Krasnoyarsk) pass through Kazakhstan, for which you'll need a visa. At least one train a day goes to/from Mineralnye Vody eight hours away. The daily No 287 (Vladikavkaz-Novorossiysk) is the most convenient, leaving Mineralnye Vody at 12.20 am and arriving in Krasnodar at 8.30 am. A ticket in a *kupe* (compartment) costs $4.

Krasnodar-I station is on Privokzalnaya ploshchad at the eastern end of ulitsa Mira, next to the intercity bus station and convenient for the southern end of ulitsa Krasnaya; Krasnodar-II is at ulitsa Kommunarov 282, two blocks east of the northern end of ulitsa Krasnaya.

Bus The intercity bus station *(avtovokzal mezhdugorodnykh soobshcheny)* is opposite the train station; buses go to all destinations in the region. Sample fares and times to some destinations are Rostov-on-Don ($2, five hours and 40 minutes), Sochi ($3, eight hours), Stavropol ($2.50, six hours) and Mineralnye Vody ($3, eight hours).

Car & Motorcycle Krasnodar is 275km from Rostov-on-Don and 420km from Dagomys. The main route south goes west through Abinsk and Krymsk to the coast at Novorossiysk, but there is also the more direct road through Teuchezhsk and Goryachy Klyuch.

Black Sea Coast
Побережье Чёрного моря

The foothills of the western 400km of the Caucasus provide a scenic backdrop to a string of Black Sea resorts and ports with a fine subtropical climate – in summer, it's usually hot without being too humid, and the sea is warm. The leading resorts are Sochi and Dagomys. Besides being a fine spot to relax after hectic Caucasian travels, the region itself offers some terrific trekking, both day hikes from the resorts and longer trips through lake and waterfall-filled valleys, old Cherkess villages and alpine plateaus. From about January to April, heliskiing is popular at nearby Krasnaya Polyana and Mt Fisht.

The most direct route for motorists from the north is via Rostov-on-Don and Krasnodar. It's 420km from Krasnodar to Dagomys. South of Novorossiysk the road is scenic, touching the coast at several points but often climbing inland between towns. Trains from Rostov-on-Don reach the coast at Tuapse.

NOVOROSSIYSK
НОВОРОССИЙСК

• pop 207,000

This port on a deep, sheltered bay houses part of the Russian Black Sea Fleet displaced from Ukraine. The road from

Krasnodar comes in along Anapskoe shosse, with the Hotel Brigantina (with a restaurant) at No 18, then continues straight into the main street, ulitsa Sovietov, with the port just to its east, on the west side of the bay. The Town History Museum (Muzey istorii goroda) is on ulitsa Sovietov, a block south of the central ploshchad Geroev. Sukhumskoe shosse, which you take if you're heading for the south, leaves town along the far side of the bay.

WWII Memorials

In 1943 a small Soviet landing party held out for 225 days at the south end of the Malaya Zemlya peninsula on the western side of the bay, to form a bridgehead for the Soviet counteroffensive against the occupying Germans. Novorossiysk is peppered with WWII memorials. On Malaya Zemlya there are clusters at the southern end of prospekt Lenina, where the party landed, and farther round at Dolina Smerti (Death Valley), where it came under the fiercest bombardment.

Getting There & Away

Driving is the easiest way. There are trains from Krasnodar but not from the south, and buses from many destinations, including Krasnodar ($1, three hours) and Sochi ($2, 8¾ hours). About once a week there is a ferry service to/from Poti, Georgia ($250, two days). There were hydrofoils to/from Sochi but they've been discontinued.

NOVOROSSIYSK TO DAGOMYS

South of Novorossiysk, **Gelendzhik** is a resort of 33,000 people on an oval bay. The small beach is pebbly and the water is shallow. There is a ***camping ground***, and the possibility of private accommodation as well as ***Hotel Privetlivy Bereg*** *(☎ 86141-2 35 44)*. The road then climbs through forest to the Mikhailov Pass (Mikhailovsky pereval, 250m) and Pshad Pass (Pshadsky pereval, 550m). **Dzhubga** is a small resort with a 5km sandy beach. **Tuapse** (population 63,000) is a port and industrial town surrounded by tea plantations, which are found all the way down this coast into Georgia.

North-west of Novorossiysk and part of the Black Sea resort area is **Anapa**, well known for its sandy beaches and grape vineyards. Accommodation here is inexpensive and simple, mostly in the form of *turbaza* (tourbases) and former Young Pioneer camps.

SOCHI & DAGOMYS
СОЧИ И ДАГОМЫС

☎ 8622 • pop (Sochi) 378,000

The mountainous coast of what is now Russia's Florida, a sunny, somewhat tacky holiday land, used to belong to the Cherkess (also known as Adygey or Circassians), fierce tribes who farmed the foothills and traded with the Turks – slaves, gold and honey for salt, jewellery and wheat.

By the 1900s it was already a prestigious holiday spot. Tsar Nicholas II had a dacha built in Dagomys. Famous Russian artists and performers, including the legendary opera singer Fyodor Chaliapin, poet Vladimir Mayakovsky and writer Isaac Babel, also came here. The most prestigious resort then was the Kavkhazskaya Rivera, now in ruins near the beach below the Park Rivera.

In its Soviet heyday, the Communist elite and workers alike came here to bask on the large-pebble beaches and stroll along the cypress and palm-shaded promenades overlooking the sea. Now, army generals and the proletariat are outnumbered by kids in pirated Adidas wear, old folk nursing their ailments at one of the many sanatoria, New Russians in BMWs and yes, a few foreigners. Despite its arcades, discotheques, Zoom Flumes and beachside cafes, Sochi is a long way from Daytona Beach. It may be hard to find a room in July and August. The season starts off in late May, with a loud and messy Russian beer *(pivo)* festival.

Orientation

Sochi stretches about 7km down the coast from the Sochi River to the southern suburb of Matsesta. The train and bus stations (side by side), the harbour and the shopping centre cluster at the northern end. Kurortny prospekt, the main north-south street, runs the length of town a few blocks

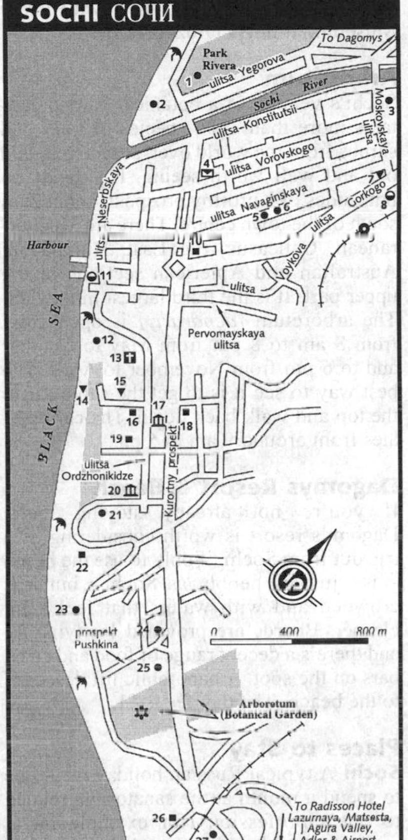

in from the sea. Dagomys is 12km north of Sochi on the main coast road. The resort stands in its own hilly grounds between the untidy town centre and the sea, and is reached by a 2km approach road.

Information

In Sochi, Hotel Zhemchuzhina has a tourist bureau (☎ 99 20 82, fax 92 87 83) open from 10 am to 6 or 7 pm daily. It runs tours around Sochi and the surrounding regions; and does theatre, plane and train bookings.

For trips to Krasnaya Polyana, Mt Fisht, Vorontsovskaya Cave, white-water rafting,

SOCHI СОЧИ

PLACES TO STAY

10 Hotel Moskva
Гостиница Москва
16 Hotel Leningrad
Гостиница Ленинград
18 Hotel Sochi-Magnolia
Гостиница Сочи-Магнолия
19 Hotel Primorskaya
Гостиница Приморская
22 Hotel Zhemchuzhina
Гостиница Жемчужина
26 Frunze Sanatorium
Санаторий имени Фрунзе

PLACES TO EAT

7 Kafe Vostok
Кафе Восток
14 Kafe Briz
Кафе Бриз
15 Stolovaya
Столовая

OTHER

1 Zelyony Teatr
Зелёный театр
2 Kavkazskaya Rivera Sanatorium
Санаторий Кавказская Ривьера
3 Markel
Рынок
4 Main Post Office
Главпочтамт
5 Bookshop
Книжный магазин
6 Aeroflot
Аэрофлот
8 Bus Station
Автовокзал
9 Train Station
Железнодорожный вокзал
11 Sea Terminal
Морской вокзал
12 Festivalny Concert Hall
Концертный зал Фестивальный
13 Church Of Michael the Archangel
Храм Михаила Архангела
17 Art Museum
Художественный музей
20 Town History Museum
Музей истории города
21 Zimny Teatr
Зимний театр
23 Letny Teatr
Летний театр
24 Circus
Цирк
25 Cable Car
Канатно-кресельная дорога
27 Stadium
Стадион

heliskiing, as well as bookings at most of Sochi's sanatoria, contact Reinfo (☎ 60 71 96, fax 62 20 42, reinfo@sochi.ru). Local mountain climbers formed the company in 1995. It caters to individual travellers and also offers 10-day expeditions including hiking, sailing and white-water rafting for $200 per person. Reinfo is in Hotel Sochi-Magnolia, office 214. An amicable, knowledgeable colleague of this firm, Sergei Shuklin, a mountain climber who speaks some English, can also be reached at home in Dagomys (☎ 30 71 96).

There are *obmennye punkty* (counters) to change roubles at the sea terminal as well as along the major streets and in most hotels. The Bank Menatep branch at the Radisson Hotel Lazurnaya gives cash advances on Visa cards at 5%. It has stopped changing travellers cheques of American Express, Thomas Cook, Visa and Citicorps.

Sochi's main post office is on Kurortny prospekt on the corner of ulitsa Vorovskogo, but some of the main hotels have their own. A bookshop selling maps in English is on ulitsa Navaginskaya 14, near Aeroflot.

A decent guide ($2) with information on the natural history of Sochi and surrounding areas, in English and Russian, is available from Reinfo.

In Dagomys, there are tourist bureaus at the Olimpiysky and Dagomys hotels. The latter has a moneychanging office.

Sochi Town Centre

Flea markets (if you've seen one in Russia, you've seen them all) line ulitsa Moskovskaya, opposite the bus station, ulitsa Voykova near the harbour, and the entire length of Navaginskaya. From the harbour, a pedestrian promenade stretches south along the jam-packed beaches, which are backed for much of their length by steep slopes with a wooded park on top.

Museums

The **Art Museum**, at Kurortny prospekt 51, has some good visiting exhibitions as well as its permanent collection – it's open from 10 am to noon and 1 to 5 pm daily except Monday. Half a kilometre farther south and a block towards the sea is the **Town History Museum**, at ulitsa Ordzhonikidze 29.

Arboretum

Sochi's version of a botanical garden contains more than 1500 species of trees and shrubs from the world over, attractively laid out and well worth seeing. It extends on both sides of Kurortny prospekt, about 2km south of the town centre. There are Mediterranean, Caucasus, Far East, Himalayan, Australian and American sections in the upper part. It is the third largest in the CIS. The arboretum *(dendrariy)* is open daily from 8 am to 8 pm from May to October and to 6 pm from November to April. The best way to see it is to get the cable car to the top and walk back down. The car operates from around 9 am to 5 pm.

Dagomys Resort & Beach

If you're not already staying there, Dagomys resort is worth considering as a trip out from Sochi, if only to use the beach – it's just as pebbly as Sochi's but less crowded and with waters that feel a lot cleaner. Boards are provided for lying on and there's a decent range of food and drink bars on the spot. A panoramic lift descends to the beach. The day fee is $1.

Places to Stay

Sochi A typical Russian holiday would be to spend a month at the sanatorium related to one's profession (for example metal workers would pack off to the stately Stalinist Metallurg Sanatory on Kurortny prospekt south of the town centre towards Adler). Now that fewer Russians can afford a trip to Sochi, these places are opening up to foreigners. You'll need reservations well in advance but it's worth a try. Built in the 1930s in Russian Imperial style, some of the sanatoria are mini Romanov palaces. The grounds are beautiful, the beaches are private, meals are included and there are pools and tennis courts. The locals say the best sanatoria (excluding the elite ones for generals etc) are the Rus (formerly imeni Lenina) and Sochi (north-west of the town centre) and the Voroshilova, Zelyonaya

Rosha (where Stalin's dacha is located) and Ordzhonikidze (all south-east).

The more central ***Frunze Sanitorium*** *(☎ 97 08 87)* on Kurortny prospekt near the stadium is also recommended. Rooms at the Frunze have private balconies; the bathrooms are shiny new with bidets and hairdryers. The grounds are lovely and reportedly the food is good. Room and board is $13/20 a single/double off season and $24/36 in July and August. You should make reservations at least three months ahead. Given advance notice, Reinfo (see Information for contact details) can help with stays at the sanatoria and Stalin's dacha.

Another popular option is to rent a room in a flat, or an entire flat. At the train station near the ticket offices *(prigorodnye kassy)* on the right end of the station when facing the tracks, the Resort Bureau (Kurortnoe byuro; ☎ 62 28 22, propan@sochi.ru) can arrange for private accommodation. Expect to pay $10 to $14 for a flat, $4 for a room or $20 to $25 for a three bedroom cottage near the water. Passengers of arriving trains are also approached for private accommodation.

Sochi also has many hotels. The large ***Hotel Moskva*** *(☎ 92 36 17, Kurortny prospekt 18)* is smack in the centre of town, noisy and run-down; rooms cost $3/12. A sprawling pale yellow hotel with a gloomy Soviet-style foyer and rooms that are cramped but clean, ***Primorskaya*** *(☎ 92 57 43, ulitsa Sokolova 1)* is a better bet, in the wooded park overlooking the sea. Rooms without phone, shower and toilet cost $3. Rooms with private shower cost about $12. From May to August, prices at most hotels increase roughly 25% every month.

Hotel Leningrad *(☎ 92 20 24, Morskoy pereulok 2)* is a step up in quality at $4/13 plus $1.50 for visa registration and a 'resort city fee', which is a tax hotel guests pay for freshly painted park benches and waste bins that aren't spilling onto the footpaths.

The 1700 bed ***Hotel Zhemchuzhina*** *(☎ 92 43 55, fax 92 87 97, Chernomorskaya ulitsa 3)* has its own beach, a pool with heated sea water and tennis courts (for a small fee). It's by the sea 2km from the centre, a 500m walk down from Kurortny prospekt past the Zimny Teatr. The comfortable standard rooms, all of which are connected to an alarm system, cost $24/44.

The western-style luxury ***Radisson Hotel Lazurnaya*** *(☎ 095-255 3800, fax 255 3804, 103 Kurortny prospekt)* is just like other Radissons around the world with similar facilities and service, including a private beach, casino, Turkish, Russian and Finnish saunas, health centre and pool that cost $20 a day to use if you're not a guest. Rooms start from $120/195 off-peak/peak and villas cost $550 a day. Airport buses go past the hotel, and from the train station take bus No 3, 4 or 17 to the Primore stop.

Dagomys Towering pyramid-like at the end of the approach road is the reportedly Mafia-ridden, four star, 1650 bed ***Hotel Dagomys***, with casino. On the way up you pass the three star ***Pansionat Olimpiysky*** and ***Motel Meridian***, where room and board in the peak season is about $36 per person. There is also ***Camping Dagomys*** whose 'cabins' are in fact caravans with the cooking fixtures removed, costing $7 for three people – they're cleaner and more comfortable than typical Russian camp sites. The caravans have their own toilets and there are separate shower blocks. All rooms in the hotels have balconies. Resort facilities include the beach, indoor and outdoor pools, the sports centre with tennis courts, a concert hall-cum-cinema, a library with several shelves of books in English, and even acupuncture facilities. All are open to anyone staying in any of the four accommodation sections, for a fee.

Places to Eat

Sochi You have your choice of the more expensive hotel restaurants or the less expensive seaside cafes, with names like Tropika, Kaliforniya and La Pizzeria. The food everywhere is about the same Russian and Caucasus mix of shashlyk, salads, grilled chicken and fish.

On a cool, 2nd floor terrace shaded by grapevines, ***Restoran Vostok*** has Central Asian fare: *plov* (a rice and meat dish) for $1, skewered beef and chicken ($2), green tea and Eastern sweets. Note that the fruit in the bowls on the tables is not free. The Vostok is on ulitsa Moskovskaya across from the train station. Despite the sign saying 24 hours, it's open from about 10 am to midnight.

On the beach front, just to the right of the stairs coming down from Hotel Leningrad, ***Kafe Briz*** is the place for those who won't make it to nearby Georgia but still want to try the food: *satsivi* (chicken in a garlic and nut sauce), *lobio* (kidney beans in a spicy sauce) and eggplant (stuffed with garlic, nuts and cilantro). The home-made wine is less than $1 a glass. The Briz also sells the standard Sochi fare, grilled trout ($2 to $3). It's open year-round.

Cheap and oddly romantic, try the ***9th floor bufet*** at Hotel Leningrad, open from 9 am to 10 pm. With plastic chairs and three tables on the balcony overlooking the sea, the bufet is the perfect place to feast on boiled eggs, *blinys* (pancakes), cucumbers and tomatoes in peace and quiet, two things that can be hard to find in Sochi restaurants in the evening. You'll have to eat and drink yourself silly to get the bill to run over $1 per person.

The ***stolovaya*** directly across from the entrance to Hotel Leningrad is a genuine Soviet-style cafeteria. From the cabbage and meat menu to the deformed aluminium forks and the inexplicable absence of knives, this is a genuine communist relic with one new twist – it actually has everything listed on the menu. The salads are fresh, the soup hot, and the dining room cockroach-free. It's open from 8 am to 8 pm daily.

Restoran Kavkazsky Aul (Caucasian Village) is in Agura Valley off the road to Adler, just inland from Matsesta. It's in an isolated and appealing spot and serves Caucasian meals from 11 am to midnight. If taking bus No 4, ask to be dropped off at the Sputnik stop, from where the restaurant is a 20 minute walk along the road. Another option is a taxi, which is better late at night because the road is unlit.

The ***Sochi market***, on ulitsa Moskovskaya, a short walk north of the bus station, has fresh fruit and vegetables.

Dagomys There are many restaurants in the Dagomys complex, the more famous being the open-air ***Restoran Dubrava*** (Russian food) and ***Kavkazskaya Kukhnya*** (Caucasian). The popular ***Restoran Saturn*** with Russian food and ***Restoran Rubin*** are both in Hotel Dagomys. ***Domashny Ochag***, near the panoramic lift to the beach, is an open-air, bamboo-and-strobe-light number that seems to sum up the Dagomys experience at one glance.

There are so many bars and cafes – with and without alcohol – in the complex that you'd need a month to find them all. The ***Bar Panorama*** on level 22 of Hotel Dagomys has the freshest of fresh air, while the bar on its main lobby floor offers air-conditioned seclusion.

Entertainment

The Dagomys complex has a cinema-cum-concert hall, a disco (in the sports centre), several nightclubs and a few restaurants with shows or live bands.

In Sochi, most of the hotels have discos, and the restaurants have shows or music. There's also a disco, called the Blonde Queen (Belaya Koroleva) but the name changes often, on ulitsa Ordzhonikidze, across from the Sanatory Morisa Toreza. Visiting rock acts as well as classical musicians and theatre troupes perform at Sochi's open-air ***Letny (summer) Teatr*** in Park Frunze or the ***Zelyony (Green) Teatr*** in Park Rivera, just north of the river. For opera, ballet and drama, check out the huge ***Zimny (winter, meaning closed-in) Teatr*** on Teatralnaya ploshchad. The tourist bureau in Hotel Zhemchuzhina sells tickets to most theatre performances, for a $0.50 fee. The glitzy, orange velvet ***Caesar Palace Casino*** at Hotel Zhemchuzhina is open from midnight to 7 am; entrance is $40 and cocktails are $4 to $5.

Getting There & Away

Air Flights to/from Sochi are much more frequent from May to October. There are six to nine daily flights to/from Moscow ($36, 2½ hours), but from November to April only a few a week. Other services include St

Petersburg ($71, three hours), Tbilisi ($51, one hour) and Yerevan ($51, 1½ hours) – several times a week in the peak season. Aeroflot also flies to/from Istanbul. Tickets can be purchased at the Tour Agency at the Aeroflot office (☎ 92 29 36), ulitsa Navaginskaya 16. For domestic flights, foreigners can buy tickets at kassa No 11, though this probably changes from season to season.

Doria (☎ 62 13 73, 62 11 67), Sovietskaya 38, flies to Istanbul (one hour, 40 minutes) twice weekly for $180 one way, $290 return (prices may differ depending on the day of the week).

Train There are several trains a day between Sochi and Moscow (36 to 38 hours) via Rostov-on-Don. Train Nos 11/12 and 79/80, though they take a few hours longer, do not pass through Ukraine, so you won't need an extra set of visas. Once a week, there's a train to Odesa (39 hours). On even-numbered days there's a train to Krasnodar (five hours), and one on odd-numbered days to Vladikavkaz (17 hours), stopping at Mineralnye Vody (13 hours). *Prigorodnye* (local) trains several times daily travel up the coast to Tuapse. The kassa for long-distance and prigorodnye trains are located on the right end of the station when facing the tracks.

Bus Services include twice-daily buses to Krasnodar ($2, eight hours), daily buses to Novorossiysk ($2, nine hours), Stavropol (14 hours, $5) and Kislovodsk (17 hours, $6).

Car & Motorcycle It's 155km from Sochi to Sukhumi, and 629km to Tbilisi – a fairly straight road, on which you could make good time if it reopens. At the time of writing, Russians and Georgians were not travelling this route, which was closed during the Georgian-Abkhazian war.

Boat Sochi is a port of call for the irregular passenger ferries and hydrofoils travelling in the peak season between Poti and Batumi, Georgia. A hydrofoil leaves Sochi for Batumi, with a stop in Poti on Monday, Wednesday and Friday ($27, four hours) and returns on Monday, Wednesday and Saturday ($45), weather permitting. Schedule changes are frequent, especially from season to season, so check at the sea terminal.

To Trabzon in Turkey a hydrofoil leaves six times a week ($66, five to six hours). A passenger ferry makes a two day sail to Istanbul once a week for $140, leaving Sochi on Monday and arriving in Istanbul on Wednesday. The ferry leaves Istanbul on Friday and returns to Sochi on Sunday, though this too could change. Tickets for the ferry and hydrofoils can be purchased in the blue building to the right of the main sea terminal.

Getting Around

To/From the Airport The airport is about 30km south of Sochi, 40km from Dagomys, on the ring road at the east side of Adler – a 30 to 40 minute drive if traffic is light.

Alternatively take express bus No 84, which runs between the airport and Sochi bus station every 40 minutes from 6 am to 4 pm, taking about 50 minutes and costing $0.30 (plus a small charge for baggage). Local bus Nos 4 and 4C also link the airport and bus station but are slower. Allow 2½ hours to reach the airport from Dagomys by bus. For a taxi, the going rate is $0.20/km.

Between Sochi & Dagomys It's a half-hour bus ride to Dagomys from Sochi on Bus No 49 which stops on the main road, about 1km from the resort. A taxi between the two shouldn't be more than $10, even late at night – much less if you bargain and aren't standing in front of the main hotels.

Sochi Bus Nos 3, 4 and 17 all travel from the bus station to Kurortny prospekt, then along Kurortny prospekt at least as far south as Matsesta. Tickets are available from conductors *(provodniki)* on the buses, but occasionally buses do not have conductors.

AROUND SOCHI & DAGOMYS

Most of the hotels offer day trips to the waterfalls, viewpoints etc in the area for about $10 per person. Both Agura Valley and Mt Bolshoy Akhun can be done in a day, without a tour. But for more dramatic

Krasnaya Polyana, Mt Fisht and the 12km-long Cave Vorontsovskaya, you should allow a couple of days. Reinfo can help with guides, cars etc.

Agura Valley
Агурское ущелье

An inland turning at Matsesta leads to a car park where you can walk to a small lake and waterfalls, one 25m high. The Orlinye Skaly (Eagle Cliffs) tower above. The Kavkazsky Aul restaurant is in the valley too. Some endangered flora here include species of cyclamen, box trees, and the Pitsunda pines growing high on the Eagle Cliffs.

Mt Bolshoy Akhun
Гора Большой Ахун

An 11km road signposted 'Akhun', shortly south of the Agura turning, leads up this hill with a lookout tower on top (admission $0.50). There are views of Sochi and Adler, Mt Fisht and Mt Chugsh (3256m), the highest in the Sochi region. The rustic ***cafe*** in the base of the tower serves excellent shashlyk, marinated *paportnik* (ferns), eggplant and other Caucasian goodies. A path to the left of the tower runs down through the Agura Valley. It's a two hour descent along the river and waterfalls, longer if you start partaking of the home-made wine sold by locals near the swimming hole. From the main road, take one of the minivans *(marshrutki)* back to the town centre; a taxi should cost about $1.

Mt Fisht
Гора Фишт

About 50km from Sochi but reachable only by helicopter or a two day trek, Mt Fisht is the start of the Caucasus mountain range. There's a hotel, ***Lunnaya Polyana***, which looks like a two storey yurt, at 1800m. Russians and foreigners heliski here (contact Reinfo). The September hiking is superb.

Krasnaya Polyana
Красная Поляна

Krasnaya Polyana (Beautiful Glade), 550m high, is a small settlement surrounded by mountains and alpine meadows, about 70km from Sochi. The spectacular road up from Adler follows the Mzymta River, passing through a deep, steep gorge after the village of Monastyrka. There are nature and minerals museums at Krasnaya Polyana, a village originally settled by Greeks migrating from Stavropol in the mid-19th century.

There is also a ski resort with a few lifts for intermediate skiing, and heliskiing for the experienced. At most hotels you can arrange for a day excursion, including a 1½ hour cable car ride. Reinfo can arrange longer overnight hikes.

From Adler's central market you can take bus No 135 that runs every two hours.

Mineral Water Spas
Минеральные Воды

The central Caucasus begin to rise from the steppe in an eerie landscape studded with mineral springs and dead volcanoes. The springs' curative powers have attracted unhealthy, hypochondriac or plain holiday-minded Russians ever since someone noticed in the late 18th century that wounded soldiers got better quicker when they bathed in them. The area had passed from Turkish to Russian hands in 1774 but still came under attack from local tribes. Early patients sometimes had to take refuge in the forts.

Today the area, known in Russian as Kavkazskie Mineralnye Vody (Caucasian Mineral Waters), is a faded holiday resort, where the healthy seem to outnumber the ailing. The atmosphere is relaxed, the air mostly fresh, and the walks lovely. The parks and elegant but decaying spa buildings recall the 19th century, when fashionable society trekked down from Moscow and St Petersburg to see, be seen, attend balls and look for a spouse.

There are five main towns – the resorts of Pyatigorsk, Kislovodsk, Yessentuki (which is more a city than a resort and probably not worth visiting if you've had enough of the others), Zheleznovodsk and the industrial and transport centre, Mineralnye Vody (Minvody for short). The whole area is

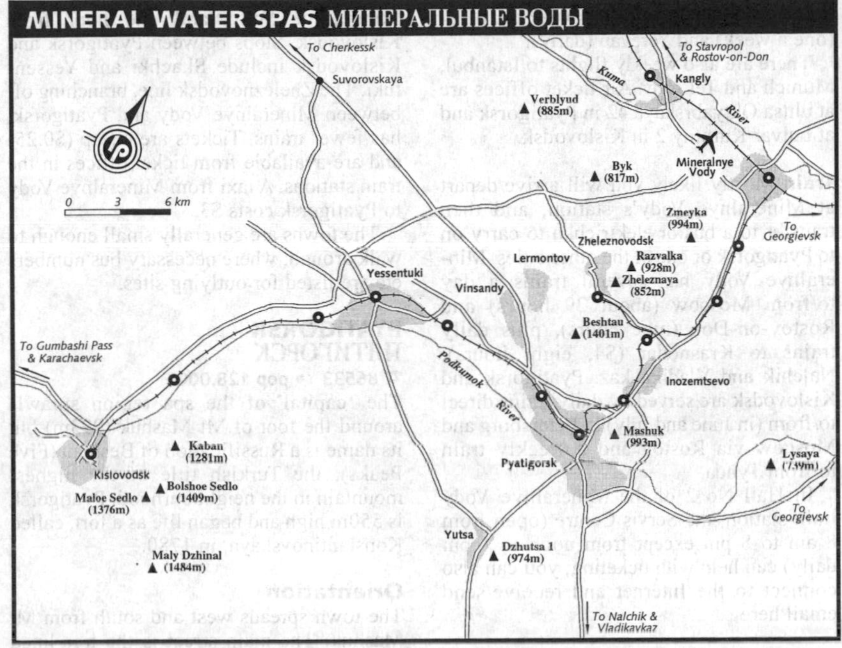

haunted by the Romantic writer Mikhail Lermontov, whose story 'Princess Mary', in his novel *A Hero of Our Time*, is set here and who, in an uncanny echo of its plot, was killed in a duel at Pyatigorsk in 1841. Many local sites crop up in the book, which also contains an episode set on the Georgian Military Highway. This short – by Russian standards very short – novel makes a great travelling companion.

Over 130 springs in the region, variously believed to benefit disorders of the muscles, bones, heart, circulation, nervous system or skin, used to gush out 60 million litres of mineral water a day. Many have since fizzled out, mainly due to lack of maintenance. Tucked in rambling verdant parks in each town, there are buildings labelled *istochnik* (spring). Many are closed, the faucets corroded and dry. But others are the highlight of the resort experience; you can simply enter the grand glass galleries and drink for free. For a fee, you can also have a dip in one of the bathhouses *(vanny)*. Don't expect Turkish luxury; the baths are strictly medicinal, 15-minute plunges monitored by a nurse. You can also subject yourself to being plastered with supposedly curative mud from Lake Bolshoy Tombukan, near Pyatigorsk.

The climate is relatively mild and September/October is considered the best season, with the leaves turning. Spring is wet.

Getting There & Away

The airport and mainline train station at Mineralnye Vody are linked to the spa towns by buses and a good local train service. In addition, a few mainline trains run along the branch line into Pyatigorsk and Kislovodsk.

Air Daily services to/from Mineralnye Vody in June, July and August include: Moscow (2¼ hours, three daily), Baku (four a week), Batumi (one a week), St Petersburg (three a week), Tashkent (twice a week), Tbilisi (one a week) and Yerevan (daily).

There are also weekly flights to Istanbul, Munich and Tel Aviv. Air ticket offices are at ulitsa Oktyabrskaya 42 in Pyatigorsk and at bulvar Kurotny 2 in Kislovodsk.

Train Mostly likely you will arrive/depart at Mineralnye Vody's station, and then transfer to a bus or elektrichka to carry on to Pyatigorsk or one of the other cities. Mineralnye Vody has several trains a day to/from Moscow (about 29 hours) and Rostov-on-Don (nine hours), plus daily trains to Krasnodar ($4, eight hours), Nalchik and Vladikavkaz. Pyatigorsk and Kislovodsk are served by daily trains direct to/from (in June and July) St Petersburg and Moscow via Rostov and a weekly train to/from Tynda.

In Hall No 2 of the Mineralnye Vody train station, the Servis Centre (open from 8 am to 8 pm except from noon to 1 pm daily) can help with ticketing; you can also connect to the Internet and receive/send email here.

Bus The Rostov-Tbilisi road goes through Mineralnye Vody and round Pyatigorsk on a bypass. Regular and frequent intercity buses and minivans (known as *mikroavtobusy* or marshrutki in these parts) serve the spa towns.

Getting Around

Frequent minivans and buses from the Mineralnye Vody airport go to the town's train station, where you can hop on a local electric train to the spas. From the train station it's more convenient to continue on by elektrichki. From the airport, you're better off going by bus to the spas. There are buses and minivans from the airport to Kislovodsk, Zheleznovodsk and Pyatigorsk ($0.20, 35 minutes). There's a taxi stand in front of the airport.

Elektrichki run hourly (more often during peak morning and afternoon hours) from about 4 am to 10 pm between Mineralnye Vody and Kislovodsk. Pyatigorsk is nearly halfway along the line, 35 minutes from Mineralnye Vody, and one hour from Kislovodsk. Stops between Pyatigorsk and Kislovodsk include Skachki and Yessentuki. The Zheleznovodsk line, branching off between Mineralnye Vody and Pyatigorsk, has fewer trains. Tickets are cheap ($0.25) and are available from ticket offices in the train stations. A taxi from Mineralnye Vody to Pyatigorsk costs $3.

The towns are generally small enough to walk around; where necessary bus numbers etc are listed for outlying sites.

PYATIGORSK ПЯТИГОРСК

☎ 86533 • pop 128,000

The 'capital' of the spa region sprawls around the foot of Mt Mashuk (993m) but its name is a Russification of Beshtau (Five Peaks), the Turkish title of the highest mountain in the neighbourhood. Pyatigorsk is 550m high and began life as a fort, called Konstantinovskaya, in 1780.

Orientation

The town spreads west and south from Mt Mashuk. The main street is the tree-lined prospekt Kirova, running west from below the Academic Gallery near the foot of Mashuk, through the town centre to the train station. The jagged crags of Beshtau (1400m) rise to the north-west, with the town's suburbs stretching to their feet. The twin snow-covered peaks of Mt Elbrus to the south can be seen from several points around town on a clear day.

Information

The Stavropolintour (☎ 4 91 76), in Hotel Intourist on ploshchad Lenina 13 (floor C), can arrange a guided tour (in English) of the city, but don't expect it to be cheap. Inexpensive (only $2 to $3) day trips, to either Dombay, Elbrus, Kislovodsk, Zheleznovodsk, the nearby Stallion Farm for a horse show, or a local wine factory for a tasting tour, are sold from stands in the city as well as at Hotel Pyatigorsk (room 205).

For longer, more serious treks to Dombay and Elbrus, contact Nikolai Oleynikov (☎ 7 20 67, elbrus@megalog.com.ru). He is a

Pyatigorsk-based mountaineer and rescuer with extensive knowledge of the off-beat treks in the Dombay/Elbrus areas, including the mountains near the village of Arkhyz.

Hotel Intourist has a kiosk open daily for money exchange. Beware of pickpockets at the Upper Market; they linger near the moneychanging stalls. The main post office is on prospekt Kirova on the corner of ulitsa Kraynego, and the telephone office is on the opposite side, just a bit farther north on ulitsa Kraynego. The post office will send email ($0.30 a message), from 9 am to 5 pm. Dom Knigi, on the corner of Dzerzhinskogo and Universitetskaya, has a good collection of maps, in Russian.

Mt Mashuk & Around

A cable car whisks you from the upper part of the town to the top of the near-perfect cone of Mt Mashuk for fresh breezes and a great panorama. It operates, weather permitting, from 10 am to 5 pm daily except Monday; a return ticket is $0.50. In the park below the lower station are a few istochnik pavilions – some of the town's sources of free mineral water. Many Pyatigorsk springs are warm – up to 60°C – and sometimes sulphurous.

From the lower cable car station the road circles round Mashuk. There is also a path, to the right of the Lechebny (Cure) Tsentr. The best views of Elbrus are from Mt Mashuk, but you're going to have to climb the mountain very early. It's a 35 minute, fairly easy climb along the edge of the cliffs; keep a watch for stray dogs.

Off the road among trees is the little domed pavilion called the **Aeolian Harp**, which has long been a favourite lookout point. It was built in 1831 to replace a real harp plucked by a weather vane. From here you can walk down via **Lermontov's Grotto**, a small cave which the writer used to visit, to the **Academic Gallery** (formerly the Elizabeth Gallery), built in 1851 by an English architect, Upton, to house one of Pyatigorsk's best known springs. It's here that Lermontov's antihero, Pechorin, first sets eyes on Princess Mary. When we were there, the spring was plugged up for repair and the cafe was closed for renovation. The small art gallery in the pavilion has a butterfly exhibition.

About a half-hour walk from the Aeolian Harp, past the **Spa Exhibition** (on Pyatigorsk's history) which was closed too but due to reopen next season, is the **Proval**, a cave open to the sky where 19th century couples would dance on a bridge over the pond of light blue sulphurous water.

The site of Lermontov's fatal duel (Mesto dueli Lermontova) is marked by a **monument** another hour or so walk round the road behind Mt Mashuk. Lermontov had been banished twice from St Petersburg to serve in the Caucasus army – first after blaming the tsarist authorities for the death of another 'troublesome' writer, Pushkin, in a duel, and second for himself duelling. In Pyatigorsk, Lermontov was challenged to a further duel for a jest about the clothes of one Major Martynov. Lermontov, firing first, aimed into the air, but was in return shot through the heart. Many saw his death, like Pushkin's, as orchestrated by the authorities.

You can reach the cable car, the Aeolian Harp and Proval by bus No 1 from the train station via prospekt Kirova and ulitsa Andzhievskogo, or bus No 15 from the Upper Market; for the duel site take bus No 113 from the Upper Market.

Park Tsvetnik

The central Flower Park – as much buildings as vegetation – contains the blue **Lermontov Gallery** (1901), a sort of glass and iron Brighton Pavilion now housing a cafe, the **Lermontov Bath** (1831), the **Yermolov Bath** (1880), now a gynaecology/fertility clinic, and spring No 2 (turned off). A path past **Diana's Grotto**, a small artificial cave, leads up to **Goryachaya (Hot) Hill**, with a much-photographed **eagle sculpture** and a **Chinese pavilion lookout**. At the modern **Drinking Gallery** (Pitevaya galereya) you can take the waters from endlessly gushing faucets (bring your own cup). It's open from 7 am to 6 pm daily, with breaks of course.

The **Spa Research Institute**, which develops mineral water treatments, is in the Classical Institut Kurortologii building at

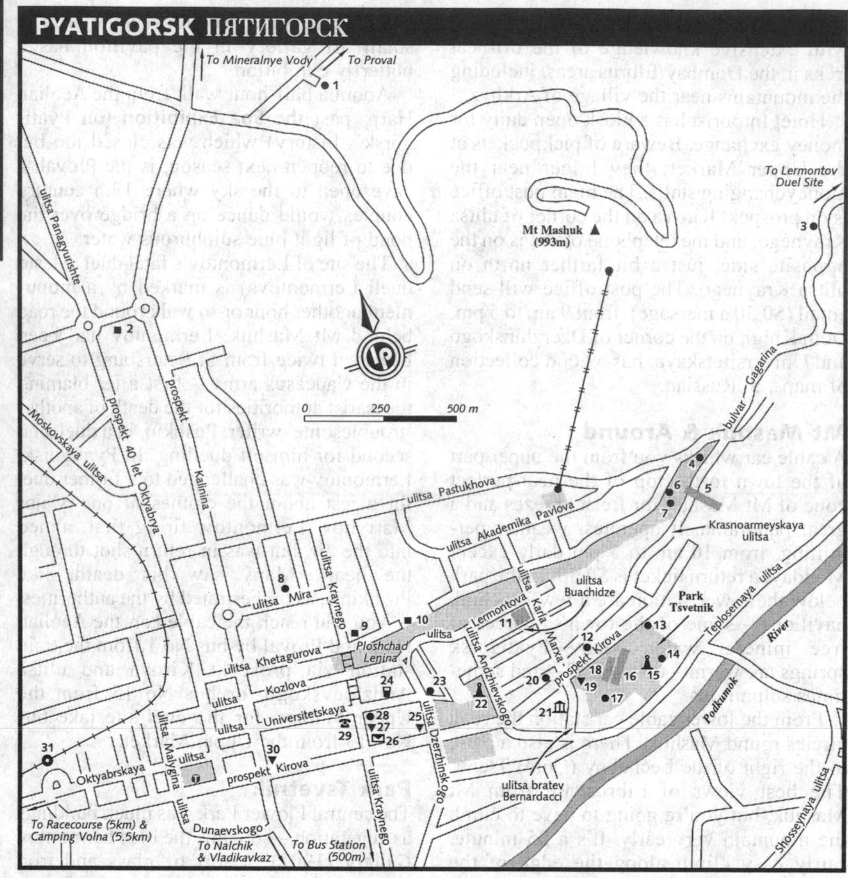

prospekt Kirova 34 near the park entrance. It was once the Restoratsiya, Pyatigorsk's first hotel and the scene of balls described in *A Hero of Our Time*. The **Regional Museum**, ulitsa bratev Bernardacci 2, is open from 10 am to 6 pm daily except Wednesday.

Lermontov Statue & Museum

The man himself stares towards Elbrus from his pedestal in the, yes, Lermontov Garden, near the foot of ulitsa Andzhievskogo. The thatched cottage where he spent his last two months in 1841 is up the hill in the Lermontov Museum-Reserve, an extended family of Lermontov-related buildings and exhibitions in a walled, off-street area. It's open from 10 am to 5 pm daily except Tuesday and the last Thursday of the month. The entrance is on ulitsa Karla Marxa.

Places to Stay

The sanatoria have the nicest rooms and are the best bargains. The catch is you'll probably need to make advance reservations. Contact Nikolai Oleynikov for help with this (see the Information section).

Not pretty, but well located and inexpensive, ***Hotel Pyatigorsk*** (☎ *3 39 31*, ☎ *5 67*

PYATIGORSK ПЯТИГОРСК

PLACES TO STAY

2 Hotel Beshtau
Гостиница Бештау
9 Hotel Pyatigorsk
Гостиница Пятигорск
10 Hotel Intourist
Гостиница Интурист

PLACES TO EAT

19 Kafe Tet-a-tet
Кафе Тет-а-тет
25 Gril Bar
Гриль бар
27 Kafe Terek
Кафе Терек
30 Kafe Gals
Кафе Галс

OTHER

1 Lermontov Duel Site
Место дуэли Лермонтова
3 Proval
Провал
4 Spa Exhibition
Курортная выставка
5 Academic Gallery
Академическая галерея
6 Aeolian Harp
Эолова арфа
7 Lermontov's Grotto
Грот Лермонтова
8 Upper Market
Верхний рынок
11 Lermontov Museum-Reserve
Музей-заповедник Лермонтова
12 Drinking Gallery
Питьевая галерея
13 Musical Comedy Theatre
Театр музыкальной комедии
14 Chinese Pavilion
Китайская беседка
15 Eagle Sculpture
Скульптура орла
16 Lermontov & Yermolov Baths
Лермонтовские и Ермоловские ванны
17 Diana's Grotto
Грот Дианы
18 Lermontov Gallery
Лермонтовская галерея
20 Spa Research Institute
Институт курортологии
21 Regional Museum
Краеведческий музей
22 Lermontov Statue
Памятник Лермонтову
23 Dom Knigi
Дом книги
24 Elen Beer Bar
Пивной бар Элен
26 Main Post Office
Главпочтамт
28 Lower Market
Нижний рынок
29 Main Telephone Office
Центральный переговорный пункт
31 Train Station
Железнодорожный вокзал

03, ulitsa Kraynego 43/1) has single/double rooms with private bath for $5/10-15.

The motel rooms at ***Motel-Camping Volna*** *(☎ 5 05 28)*, 5.5km west of the centre on Ogorodnaya ulitsa, are $3/5. The camp site cabins are self-contained and cleaner. There's little space for tents. Signposts to the place are hard to spot (it's about 500m south of ulitsa Tolyatti, which branches south off ulitsa Fevralskaya leading west from the train station). The nearest stop for tram No 2 to the train station and prospekt Kirova is on ulitsa Tolyatti.

Hotel Beshtau *(☎ 9 96 62, ulitsa Patrisa Lumumby 17)* off prospekt Kalinina has rooms for $4/7.

The three star ***Hotel Intourist*** *(☎ 4 90 18, fax 5 32 4, ploshchad Lenina 14)* is clean and comfortable with nice views from some rooms, all of which have balconies. The rooms cost from $17/19.

Places to Eat

Hotel Intourist, besides its loud and expensive Intourist ***restaurant***, has a decent ***wine bar***, which oddly closes at 7 pm. It's in the lobby, to the right of the main entrance.

There's a handful of ***cafes*** along prospekt Kirova. Many close around 6 or 7 pm. On the corner of ulitsa Dzerzhinskogo (take the stairs below the street level) is the ***Gril Bar*** with good grilled chicken ($1.50) and drinks; it's open from noon to 11 pm, and sometimes with live music (be warned) from 7 pm.

For fresh beer on tap ($0.20 a pint) and salted fish, try the blue collar ***Elen***, open from 8 am to 10 pm near the Lower Market. Also at the Lower Market, ***Kafe Terek***, open from 7 am to 9 pm, serves bliny stuffed with everything from caviar to condensed milk. The dark and loud *ratskeller* below is filled with wannabe mafiosi. At the entrance to Tsvetnik Park, ***Tet-a-tet***, on the 2nd floor balcony of the Tsvetnik Exhibition Hall, is definitely the place for people-watching, as well as good coffee and ice cream. A nice touch, though the wind usually blows them out, are the candles on the tables.

The ***restaurant*** at Hotel Pyatigorsk is favoured by the foreign students who come to play billiards. The food is decent, especially the butter-dripping chicken Kyiv ($1). A spot favoured by Russian students is

Kafe Gals, on the corner of prospekts Kirova and Kalinina. It has tea and the widest array of freshly baked sweet rolls in the Caucasus.

The ***Upper Market*** (Verkhny rynok) on ulitsa Mira functions until about 4 pm daily, and in summer until later in the evening.

Entertainment

The ***Musical Comedy Theatre*** *(Teatr muzykalnoy komedii; prospekt Kirova 17)* has several shows in repertory that are performed from June to August. There's often an evening disco in Park Tsvetnik.

KISLOVODSK КИСЛОВОДСК

☎ 86537 • pop 108,700

Kislovodsk (Sour Waters) is hillier, greener, higher (822m) and prettier than Pyatigorsk. It's probably the most popular of the resorts. 'Love affairs that begin at the foot of Mashuk reach happy endings here,' Lermontov wrote. If you're not staying here, the beautiful park alone is worth a day trip. Kislovodsk springs are mainly carbonic. The famous writer and dissident Alexander Solzhenitsyn was born here.

Orientation & Information

The train station and Narzan Gallery (Narzannaya galereya), at the eastern and western ends of ulitsa Karla Marxa, are pretty much the centre of things, with the park spreading to their south. The main post, telephone and telegraph office (open from 8 am to 8 pm daily) is on Oktyabrskaya ploshchad, at the northern end of the traffic-free bulvar Kurortny, which runs north from the Narzan Gallery. You can send email from window No 23 from 8 am until about 5 pm daily. For Internet access, try Narzan Network (open from about 9 am to 7.30 pm daily) in the post office, to the right as you enter. It charges about $1.50 per hour.

The bus station is on the Yessentuki road on the northern edge of town. Aeroflot is at bulvar Kurortny 2. Inexplicably, there is a dearth of money exchange places in town. The *obmenny punkt* at the Hotel Intourist-Narzan was mysteriously shut down after the financial crisis of late 1998. The bank at bulvar Kurortny across from the gallery has an exchange, though the rate is poor. It also has an ATM for cash advances on Visa, but don't count on it working. For maps, art albums and lewd Russian greeting cards, the Bukinist is on ulitsa Karla Marxa in the vicinity of the Narzan Gallery.

At major hotels and all along bulvar Kurortny, you should be able to arrange for an inexpensive day excursion to Dombay, Elbrus or Gora Koltso (a natural stone bridge just outside of town).

Narzan Gallery & Baths

The rich, carbonic Narzan Spring around which Kislovodsk was founded bubbles up inside its own glass dome in a graceful, well preserved gallery designed by Upton in the 1850s. It's open from 7 to 9 am, 11.30 am to 2 pm, and 4 to 6 pm. The main Narzan Baths are in a 1903 Indian temple-style building on bulvar Kurortny. Bathing in Narzan – which means Drink of Brave Warriors in Turkish – is said to prolong life and ease pain. A relaxing dunk in the brownish, tea-warm mineral water costs about $1.25. The bathhouse is open from about 9 am to 5 pm; the nurses take a break from 1 to 2 pm.

Kurortny Park

Kislovodsk's fountain and flower-filled Kurortny (Spa) Park, opening out immediately south-east of the Narzan Gallery, dates from the early 19th century. During the spa season (June to August), the main strollway is cluttered with street artists, musicians and holiday-makers toting plastic water bottles to and from the springs. There are many cafes and restaurants here too.

The main path from the gallery, initially beside the muddy Olkhovka River, passes the **Kislovodsk Resort History Exhibition** (Istoriya Kislovodskogo kurorta) and a **Lermontov statue**, both on the ulitsa Kominterna side of the park. The fiend behind bars, below the statue, is an illustration of Lermontov's famous poem, 'The Demon'.

Across the way is the **Colonnade**, with a cafe and benches where old men gather to

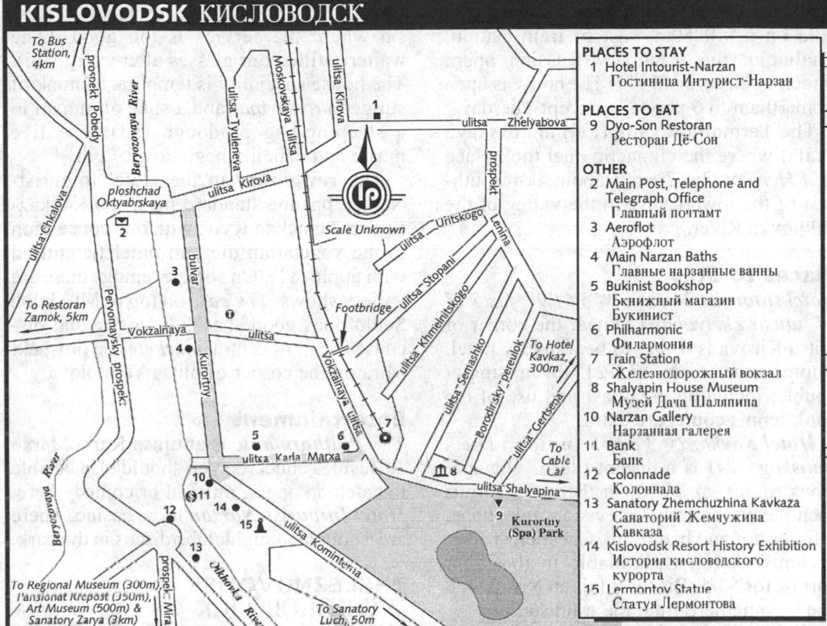

play chess and backgammon. The path heads uphill via a rose garden to the **Red Rocks** (Krasnye Kamni, coloured by their iron content), beyond which are the **Grey Rocks** (Serye Kamni), 2km from the gallery, featuring an eagle sculpture and good views. Walking routes *(marshruty)* of varying lengths are marked around the park: No 3 brings you at least this far.

A few hundred metres past the Grey Rocks you can either continue up to Krasnoe Solnyshko hill (with views of Elbrus on a good day) or turn right to the cable car that will sweep you over Krasnoe Solnyshko to the top of 1376m **Mt Maloe Sedlo** (Little Saddle). Here is a great panorama of the valleys and upland plateaus into which this end of the spa region is carved. You might be able to explore the surrounding mountaintop trails by horseback. If not, it's easy enough to walk 5km south-east along the tops to Mt Maly Dzhinal (1484m). Mt Bolshoe Sedlo (1409m) is 1km north-east. The cable car *(kanatnaya doroga)* runs from 10 am to 1 pm and 2 to 6 pm, except in fog, wind or rain. Tickets are $0.60 one way.

Other Attractions

The prospekt Lenina and prospekt Dzerzhinskogo area has some grand and curious old houses, many now sanatoria. The **Regional Museum** (Kraevedchesky muzey), which has two rooms of photographs and relics of local archaeology and history, is in an 1805 fort at Krepostnoy pereulok 3; it's open from 10 am to 6 pm daily except Monday. Admission is $0.10. To get there, walk along prospekt Mira south from the Colonnade; after about 500m you will see the small fort on the left.

Other museums include the **Culture Museum of Music & Theatre** (Muzey muzykalnoy i teatralnoy kultury) at the **Philharmoniya**, the small **Art Museum** (Khudozhestvenny muzey) at ulitsa Yaroshenko 1, and **Chaliapin's House Museum** (Dom

Shalyapina), a rickety-looking stained-glass villa on a hill 50m west of train station. Chaliapin, the legendary Russian opera singer, lived here in 1917. The house is open from 10 am to 6 pm daily except Tuesday.

The **Lermontov Cliff** (Lermontovskaya Skala) where the climactic duel took place in *A Hero of Our Time* is about 4km south-east of the town centre in the valley of the Olkhovka River.

Places to Stay

Hotel Intourist-Narzan *(☎ 3 61 97, fax 5 97 57, ulitsa Zhelyabova 5)* near the corner of ulitsa Kirova is trying to be a luxury hotel. Rooms start from $13/21 for a single/double, including breakfast and use of the pool; tennis courts are extra.

Hotel Kavkaz *(☎ 3 62 35, prospekt Dzerzhinskogo 24)* is a decent place. The spacious rooms, at $6/10, in the main corpus each have a balcony, television, telephone, refrigerator and bathroom. Cheaper, sparser accommodation is available in the other corpus for $3/5. Bus or minivan Nos 2, 4, 8 and 9 come here from the train station.

Kislovodsk also has oodles of sanatoria; the best are ***Luch***, ***Zarya***, ***Krepost*** and ***Zhemchuzhina Kavkaza***. A taxi from the train station to any of these should not cost more than $1. Local people – you'll see them standing with placards on the train platforms – also rent out rooms and apartments; prices vary.

Places to Eat

Restoran Zamok, in the Alikonovka River gorge about 7km west of the centre, used to be the most coveted spot in town. The setting is medieval, the food is mediocre Georgian, and the prices are awry. A plate of greens cost $2, as much as the shashlyk. It's on the ground floor of the Castle of Treachery & Love (Zamok kovarstva i lyubvi). Taxi is the easiest transport, costing about $1 one way. Ask the driver to wait for you, because it's a long walk back.

If you're tired of shashlyk, there is an atmospheric Korean restaurant, ***Dyo-son***, at ulitsa Shalyapina (formerly Vokzalnaya) at the north-western edge of Kurortny park. This is probably the only restaurant in Russia where the service is too good. (The waiter refilled our glasses after every sip!). The house speciality is tempura, a chunk of sturgeon *(osetrina)* and a slice of tomato in a sleeping-bag of dough ($3). The live music and dancing begin after 7 pm.

The ***restaurant*** in the Hotel Intourist-Narzan has the standard meat 'po Kavkazsky' and chicken Kyiv, with one concession to the vegetarian diet, an omelette stuffed with apple ($1). On some evenings there are variety shows. The ***cafe*** on top of Mt Maloe Sedlo does good shashlyk, coffee and biscuits. The most central ***market*** is on prospekt Mira on the corner of ulitsa Yermolova.

Entertainment

The ***Philharmonic*** is at ulitsa Karla Marxa 1. Besides concerts, you should also be able to catch an opera, musical or comedy here. ***Hotel Intourist-Narzan*** has a casino. There are a couple of nightclubs/discos in the park.

ZHELEZNOVODSK ЖЕЛЕЗНОВОДСК

• pop 15,000

The smallest of all the spa towns, Zheleznovodsk (Iron Waters) lies at the foot of Mt Zheleznaya (852m), on the northern side of Mt Beshtau. It's 6km west of the Mineralnye Vody-Pyatigorsk road and served by its own spur of the local railway. The best way to get here from Pyatigorsk is to take a bus or minivan from the Upper Market ($0.25, 25 minutes); for the park get off at the Lenin statue.

The nice park here spreads up the mountain towards the natural forest. Zheleznovodsk waters are used for digestive, kidney and metabolic problems. Several springs are in the upper reaches of the park; on the way up are the red-and-white striped **Ostrovsky Baths** (1893) which have closed, the blue and white, iron and glass **Pushkin Gallery** (1901) which was closed for renovation when we were there, and the Emir of Bukhara's late 19th century palace, now the **Sanatory Telmana**. A couple of ***cafes*** are in the park. Of the resort's 54 springs, only four are left, three of them with the same water. The others have either run dry or fallen into disrepair. To see how the place looked in the good ol' days, visit the **local museum** across from the Sanatory Telmana, open from 10 am to 5 pm daily except Monday. It has a good photograph collection.

From the park, a 3.5km ring road leads round the mountain. There's also a spiral path to the top – a climb which will take you about 1¼ hours.

Central Caucasus
Центральный Кавказ

The spectacular Caucasus mountain range, about 1000km long with peaks of more than 3000m found along three-quarters of its length, is not only a geographical but a political and ethnic barrier, its watershed forming the boundary between Russia and Georgia and Azerbaijan. The two Russian Caucasus mountain destinations most visited by foreigners are Dombay and the Baxan Valley. Towns in the foothills, like Pyatigorsk and Kislovodsk in the mineral water spas area (see the previous section) and Nalchik (see later in this chapter), are the stepping off points for these places and other mountain trips.

The main road crossing the central Caucasus is the Georgian Military Highway from Vladikavkaz to Tbilisi in Georgia.

Sometimes called the Great Caucasus to distinguish it from the separate Little Caucasus farther south around the borders of Georgia, Armenia and Azerbaijan, the Caucasus is about 25 million years old, with over 2000 glaciers, 70% of them on the north (Russian) side, some as long as 13 or 14km. The highest peaks are mostly in the middle third of the range where it's relatively narrow (farther east and west it's up to 150km wide). They include from west to east: Dombay-Yolgen (on the Russia-Abkhazia boundary), 4000m; Elbrus (Russia), 5642m; Ushba (Georgia), 4700m; Shkhara (Georgia), 5068m; Dykhtau (Russia), 5204m; and Kazbek (Georgia), 5033m. Farther east are Tebulosmta, 4493m and Bazardyuzyu, 4466m.

The name Caucasus comes from the Greek *Kaukasos*, and maybe before that from *Kazkaz*, a Hittite name for people living on the south shore of the Black Sea.

DOMBAY
ДОМБАЙ

• pop 300

The village of Dombay is 1600m high in a forested west Caucasus valley, surrounded by massive mountains needling up to snow-capped peaks. Three deep valleys watered by glacier-fed torrents – the Alibek from the west, the Amanauz from the south and the Dombay-Yolgen from the east – meet here to flow north, becoming the Teberda River a few kilometres downstream. The scenery is magnificent, and even if you're no hiker or mountaineer, chairlifts will carry you to wonderful panoramas.

Dombay is a small mountain resort directly below the main Caucasus ridge, catering for around 2000 people in hotels and camps. The hiking and climbing from June to August – when the alpine wild flowers are superb – are what attract most foreigners (though still relatively few). During the peak ski season, from late-December to April, prices double and triple, and the hotels are full. The slopes are not as steep as on Mt Cheget, and the climate is milder.

Dombay is at the heart of the Teberdinsky Nature Reserve, which stretches up to 20km either side of a line from Teberda to the crest of the Caucasus main ridge. The reserve has a herd of European bison, reintroduced after being wiped out here in the 1920s, plus lynx, bear, deer, a unique flora and bird life that includes the black griffon. Guides are genuinely essential on many routes as trails are not marked.

After the Russians, the second biggest ethnic group in the 500,000-plus population of the Karachay-Cherkess Republic, in which Dombay lies, are the 150,000-plus Karachay. They are a Muslim Turko-Tatar mountain people who, until the revolution, lived mainly on meat and milk. Their old, wooden-hut capital, Uchkulan in the upper

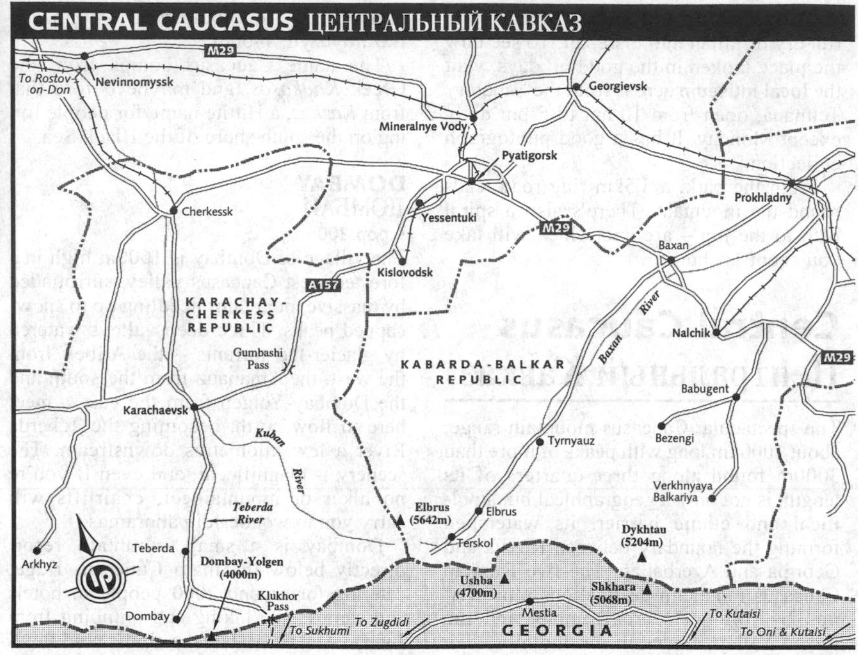

Kuban Valley east of Teberda, was replaced in 1926 by the new town of Karachaevsk.

Information

There's nowhere official to change money, so do that before you come to Dombay. There's a post and telegraph office in Hotel Dombay. Kiosks outside some of Dombay's hotels sometimes have district maps. But you are more likely to find maps in Pyatigorsk or Kislovodsk.

For the best advice on routes, guides (for $25 to $50 a day depending on the route) as well as equipment rental, check at the rescue post *(spasatelnaya sluzhba)*, a three storey cabin near Hotel Solnechnaya Dolina. You might be able to spend a night here, in true mountaineer's style, for a small fee. As most of the walks come a stone's throw from Russia's new southern border with Abkhazia, it's nearly essential to have a guide should you be stopped by the Russian border guards who keep a close watch on movement in these parts. Also, some of the most spectacular sights are tricky to get to; you need to cross glaciers, torrential rivers etc. There is also a fairly visible bear population. The hardy, friendly (somewhat English-speaking) guides at the rescue post know the terrain well. Even if you stubbornly plan on heading out on your own, at least pop into the post; remember, these guys are the ones responsible for pulling you out of the woods if you get lost.

Mussa-Achitara

The 3300m-high Mussa-Achitara (Horse Thief) ridge on the north side of the Dombay-Yolgen Valley has views around the Dombay peaks, valleys and glaciers. First, take two chairlifts – No 1 behind Hotel Krokus, then No 3 straight up the mountain to the upper cable car station (2260m). Two further chairlifts then rise to the ridge where on a clear day you can make out Elbrus to the east. The cost either way is around $3.

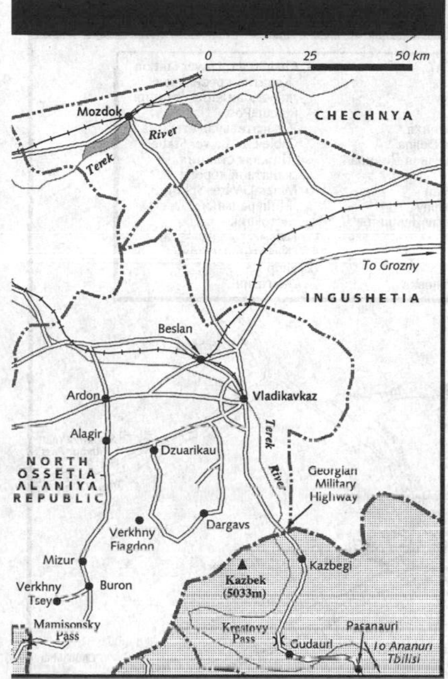

Walks

Chuchkhur Waterfalls & Ptysh Valley

It's an easy, scenic 6km from behind the start of chairlift No 1 to two fine waterfalls on the Chuchkhur River. First you follow a vehicle track, then you branch across the Russkaya Polyana clearing. It's another two hours (5km) to the first set of waterfalls. Past the waterfalls, a steep path leads towards the Chuchkhur Glacier. Twenty minutes downstream from the falls, a path forks south for a steady 2km walk up the Severny (North) Ptysh Valley and another waterfall, this one over 70m high. In the right conditions, you can actually walk on the ledge behind the falls. Continue on over the remains of avalanches that often don't melt until July, and you'll reach a small lake, about 2500m above sea level, and barely an echo from the Abkhazian border.

Amanauz Valley A marked trail, steep in parts, leads south from the end of the Dombay housing estate and goes for about 4km, up through two sets of woods to a waterfall and the Chyortova Melnitsa (Devil's Mill) viewpoint.

Alibek Glacier The track behind Hotel Solnechnaya Dolina leads about 6km up the Alibek Valley to a mountaineers' hostel, passing a climbers' cemetery after 2km. From the hostel there's a path up to little Lake Turie near the Alibek Glacier, 9km from Dombay. A strenuous variation is to fork left from the path after the hostel, and head through woods to the dramatic Alibek Falls. If you cross the dodgy bridge at the foot of the falls and then scramble up the left side you can walk on the glacier and up the scree on its right side to Lake Turie.

Klukhor Pass During the Abkhazia conflict this route was closed off, and Russian border guards are still keeping everyone out. Transport is needed for this day hike, which starts from Severny Priyut (Northern Shelter, 2040m), 17km up the Gonachkhyr Valley road.

The goal, until the way was closed, was a 2782m pass over the Caucasus watershed, which still carries remnants of the Sukhumi Military Highway, built to help the Russians subdue the west Caucasus in the 19th century. The path leads up beside a stream through glorious alpine meadows to Lake Klukhor – with ice floes even in August – then to the pass itself, on the Abkhazian border. The last part of the climb is littered with bizarre monuments to the WWII defenders of the pass.

The walk is 6km each way, takes about six hours there and back including stops, and is usually free of heavy snow from mid-June to mid-October. Over the pass, the path descends 20km or so to Yuzhny Priyut (Southern Shelter) on the Abkhazian side, a 110km drive from Sukhumi.

Other Walks Crystal Pass is a 20km, 10 to 12 hour trip up over the north side of the Alibek Valley – with more great views.

The treks to the Murudzhinskie and Azgekskie lake groups, in the ranges east

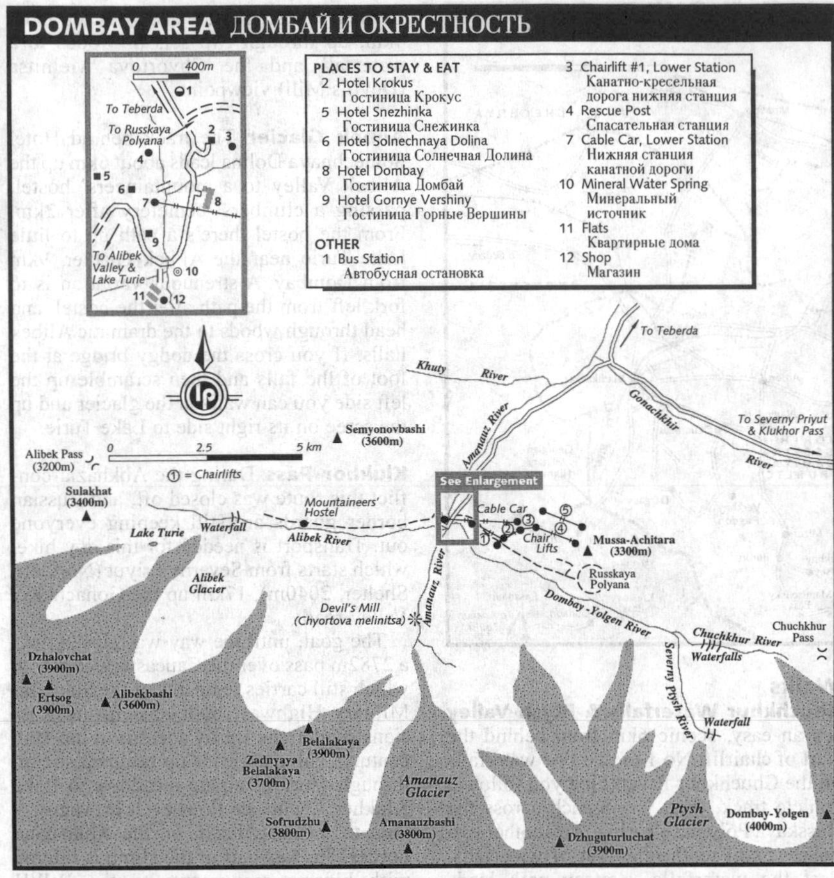

and west of the Dombay-Teberda road respectively, involve overnight camping as well as permission from the Teberdinsky Nature Reserve.

Climbs

Some peaks that can be tackled from Dombay include Sofrudzhu (3800m), Dombay-Yolgen (4000m) and Klukhor Bashi (3600m) on the main Caucasus ridge (also blocked off for the time being because it's on the Abkhazian border), and Sulakhat (3400m) and Semyonovbashi (3600m) above the Alibek Valley.

Other Activities

You can swim in the evenings in Hotel Gornye Vershiny's pool, after passing a cursory medical on floor 4. Hotel Gornye Vershiny and Hotel Solnechnaya Dolina both have decent saunas.

The skiing terrain is excellent in the form of European Alps. There are a few good long and steep runs for experienced skiers from below the Mussa-Achitara peak where chairlift No 5 ends at 3008m and down to 1620m. There is also some possibility of tree skiing. There is plenty of terrain for ski touring if you have a local guide, but beware of avalanches. Decent ski equipment and snowboards can be rented at Hotel Dombay, as well as most of the other hotels and at the rescue post. The going rate is $4 to $5 a day.

Places to Stay & Eat

Hotel Dombay *(☎ 5 81 69)* is a decent if purely functional establishment, with standard rooms costing $10 to $20 (doubles only) from June to December. The rooms are clean, with balconies, private baths and great views.

Hotel Gornye Vershiny (Mountain Peaks) is a little more spartan than the Dombay and might not be open after the snow melts. Comfortable, private, wooden ***Hotel Solnechnaya Dolina*** *(Sunny Valley; ☎ 58 269)*, 100m from the cable car, also happens to be frequented by the local mafiosi. If that bothers you, try the slightly cheaper ***Snezhinka*** just behind. From June to November, a double room (no singles) at Solnechnaya is $12; the price during the ski season is $40. Prices flex from year to year, depending on demand and economic collapses. The hotel also has a bar and restaurant. Whether it's open and when, depends on the number of tourists in town.

Locals will probably approach you to rent their flats in the village for about $2 a day (off season rate).

During the peak hiking and skiing seasons, there are several ***cafes*** and stalls selling shashlyk, sweets and drinks at the bus station, and at the top of chairlifts 1 and 3; as well as at the base of chairlift 5. If you come between peak seasons, you might want to bring some food supplies. Otherwise try your luck in the small, overpriced and scantily supplied stores in the residential area. *Ayran* – a sourish Caucasian yogurt – can usually be bought at the ***store*** in the first apartment building after the bridge.

Entertainment

In winter the convivial ***disco*** on the 1st floor of Hotel Gornye Vershiny is the nocturnal hot spot. There are a few ***billiard tables*** on the 2nd floor of Hotel Dombay. The sign on the bar entrance said in Russian: 'Closed. Don't knock.' We were told that the sign is there season-round; just go in.

Getting There & Away

The only way is by road. Coaches from Pyatigorsk usually take the 225km route through Cherkessk and Karachaevsk – which takes about five hours – but there's a shorter, more scenic route along the A157 road over the 2044m Gumbashi Pass (with good views of Elbrus) between Kislovodsk and Karachaevsk. The going price for a taxi from Mineralnye Vody to Dombay is $25.

Buses might not get you to Dombay on your appointed day: there are around three daily to Teberda from Mineralnye Vody (five hours), one from Stavropol and none from Pyatigorsk. Locals often take the more frequent bus service to Cherkessk and then switch buses there to carry on to the spa towns. You could also hitch a ride on the numerous tour buses that leave around 3 pm from the bus stop and go the way of Pyatigorsk and Kislovodsk during the peak seasons. This should cost about $2. There are road blocks and passport checks on the borders between the Karachevsky and Cherkessky regions due to political uneasiness between the Karachai and the Cherkesy spurred by local presidential elections. The Russian police monitoring the situation are polite, but insistent. They even check rucksacks for weapons.

The nearest mainline train station is Nevinnomyssk, 180km north. There is one bus daily between there and Teberda (four or five hours). Between Teberda and Dombay, the buses are not running, but it is possible to hitch a ride. It's possible to visit Dombay as a day trip from both Pyatigorsk and Kislovodsk, but you won't see much.

TEBERDA ТЕБЕРДА

Short of 20km down the valley from Dombay, Teberda is a provincial city not worth seeing in itself but useful as a base for more great hikes. Places to stay include ***Hotel Teberda*** *(☎ 5 14 25)* and ***Hotel Klukhor***, if they're open. (You might want to go to

Dombay first and while there make arrangements to stay at someone's flat in Teberda; the cost should be about $5 a night.) Many outings are common to both resorts, but the walks to the Dzhamagatskie Narzany mineral springs (west up the Dzhamagat Valley, six to seven hours round trip) and the Mukhinsky Pass (east) start here. Before setting out get permission (which includes paying a nominal fee) from the Teberdinsky Nature Reserve headquarters near the bridge. The town has a nature museum and a small zoo with animals from the reserve.

NALCHIK НАЛЬЧИК

☎ 86622 • pop 250,000

The town of Nalchik, 550m high in the foothills of the Caucasus, which rises to its west and south, began life in 1822 as a Russian fort. This is the nearest starting point for a day trip to Mt Elbrus.

Nalchik is the capital of the Kabarda-Balkar Republic within the Russian Federation. Around 400,000 of the republic's 900,000 people are Kabarda, and 70,000-plus people, most of whom live in the mountains, are Balkar. The Kabarda are the most numerous of the peoples known as Circassian or Adygey. They're famous for horse breeding. In 1557 they united with Russia in the face of a Turkish invasion, the first Caucasus people to do so. Both the Kabarda and the Balkar are Muslim and heavily patriarchal.

Orientation & Information

The main streets are prospekt Lenina, running south from the train station through the town centre, and prospekt A Shogentsukova (formerly ulitsa Respublikanskaya) two blocks east.

The Hotel Nart is on ulitsa Lermontova, just east off prospekt Shogentsukova, and the main post, telephone and telegraph office is on prospekt Shogentsukova 5 on the corner of ulitsa Lermontova. For Internet access, Dekart (open from 9 am to 6 pm daily), at Lermontov 6, charges $4 an hour. These types of private ventures tend to come and go, but hopefully this one is still around.

The only safe-looking place to change money is in Ecodom, a hardware store to the left of the post office. Knizhny Magazin Elbrus on the corner of prospekt Lenina and ulitsa Golovko has a good stock of maps. Aeroflot is at ulitsa Lenina 43.

Things to See

A large, fine park stretches over 2km south from the Hotel Nart. From its southern end a chairlift and a cable car cross lakes to wooded hills. The interesting **Kabardino-Balkar National Museum** (Natsionalny muzey) has temporary exhibits and is open from 10 am to 5.30 pm daily except Sunday and Monday. It's at ulitsa Gorkogo 52, just off ulitsa Tolstogo. The **Fine Arts Museum** at prospekt Lenina 35 is open from 10 am to 6 pm daily except Friday.

Chegem Canyon The canyon road turns west at the south end of Chegem-2 village, about 17km north of Nalchik. The spectacular part of the canyon *(ushchelie)*, about 44km up, not far past the 30m Chegem Waterfall, is 250m high but only 20m wide (through which river and road both squeeze). Around Verkhny Chegem, a farther 20 or so kilometres up, are several archaeological sites, including the Lygyt village with the remains of Muslim and Christian temples and tombs going back to the 10th century.

Golubye Ozera The Golubye Ozera (Blue Lakes) are three or four pretty lakes 39km up the Cherek Valley from Urvan, 13km east of Nalchik. Take the left fork after Babugent village in the valley. The right fork leads to Bezengi, below the Bezengi section of the Caucasus, which has several 5000m peaks, like Dykhtau and Shkhara.

Places to Stay & Eat

Though cheap and conveniently located right behind the bus station, ***Hotel Bysym*** *(☎ 1 84 09)* is probably the worst hotel in the Caucasus, and the second worst we've seen in Russia (the winner is on Sakhalin Island). Squashed mosquitoes cover the walls, the mattresses are stained, the bathroom looks like a cave and bus exhaust pours through the windows. You're better off at ***Hotel Nart*** *(☎ 2 70 26, ulitsa Lermontova 2)*, a medium-sized 1970s tower block near the park, with decent, no-frills rooms with shower for $4/7 a single/double.

At the main square, ***Hotel Rossia*** *(☎ 5 53 78)* has dogs running in the hallway and one arm bandits (to match some of the two arm types) in the foyer. The rooms with shower, however, are adequate, at $4/5-12.

Dining out is not likely to be a truly pleasant experience. Choices are limited to a few open-air cafes serving shashlyk in the park and a couple of restaurants that looked to be haunted by local hoods. ***Kafe Lakum*** to the right of the post office serves rib-sticking *khizhiny po osetinski* (flat bread stuffed with potato and cheese) for $0.60 and cold local beer. The ***market*** is just off ulitsa Gorkogo, half a block north of ulitsa Tolstogo.

Getting There & Away

Nalchik flights include Moscow daily ($49, 2½ hours), plus at least weekly service to Sochi, Yerevan and Saratov. The only direct long-distance trains seem to be the daily 39-hour services to/from Moscow, through Mineralnye Vody and Rostov-on-Don. Nalchik is served by daily buses to/from Terskol ($1, two to three hours), Astrakhan (11½ hours), Stavropol (5½ hours), Makhachkala (14 hours), as well as buses several times a day to/from Kislovodsk and Mineralnye Vody, 115km north. There is also an elektrichka to/from Mineralnye Vody though it takes longer than the bus.

Getting Around

Bus No 17, which runs between the airport and Dolinsk suburb, stops on prospekt Shogentsukova on the corner of ulitsa Lermontova (close to the centre and the Nart and Rossia hotels) and near the park chairlift. Bus No 1 covers the same stretch of prospekt Shogentsukova.

ELBRUS AREA
ПРИЭЛЬБРУСЬЕ

Elbrus rises on a northern spur of the main Caucasus ridge at the western end of the Baxan Valley. Tourist facilities littered along the valley floor make it less attractive than Dombay, but the mountains are just as majestic and there are fine walks, climbs and skiing above the human detritus. The area – known in Russian as Prielbruse (Around Elbrus Area) – pulls in a more seriously 'outward bound' crowd than Dombay, but day-trippers from Nalchik or the Caucasus mineral water spas can use chairlifts or cable cars to reach the slopes of Elbrus, or view its peaks from across the valley. The highest peak on the south side is Ushba (4700m) but several others exceed 4000m.

The upper Baxan Valley is a chief home of the Balkar, a Muslim Turko-Tatar people who, like the Karachay to their west, were exiled for supposed collaboration in WWII but returned in 1957.

Information

The village of Terskol is at the upper part of the Azau Valley along which are sprinkled several hotels. At the western end of the valley, the road ends where the Azau cable car and the Elbrus mountain trail begin.

Peak season here is December to April and June to August, with the former being the busier. In the off months, it's very likely that only one or two hotels will be open and that the chairlifts will not be working.

The vast majority of foreign tourists come here with a tour group and as there are no restaurants (except one or two cafes in Terskol) everyone takes meals in their hotel, which probably need to be ordered one day in advance if you have not payed for them with your room. In the village of Terskol there is a mountain (ski) rescue, post office and two or three sparsely stocked general stores in old train containers. There are no banks or money exchange counters, but one plus, that may not last, is that the telephone office is open 24 hours.

Mountain guides may be necessary, especially now that parts of this region are border zones with Georgia; this is more of a precaution against hassles from border guards than against marauding bands of the Svaneti who live just over the mountains. If you plan to do some high-altitude camping,

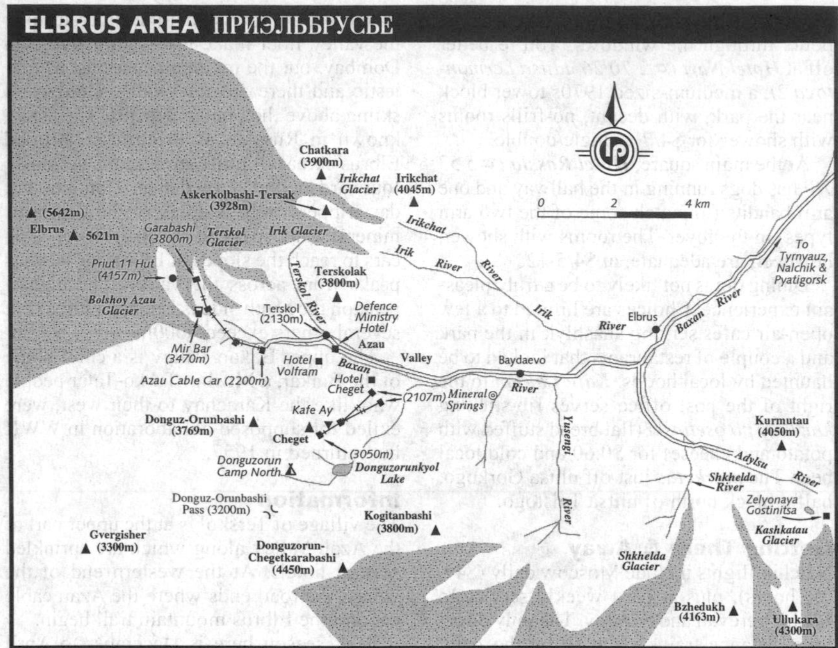

arrange for guides in advance via your tour operator or by visiting the rescue post. Guides from the rescue post charge $200 to $300 (maximum group of five) for a three day ascent of Mt Elbrus (tents and equipment extra). For the base trails, the going rate is about $25 a day.

About 300 avalanches a year occur in the 4km stretch of the valley between Terskol and the Azau cable car. The best time to catch one – from the safe distance of a chairlift – is April during mid-afternoon. As far as souvenirs go, this region is well known for its mohair and the local babushkas will be more than happy to sell you mittens, socks and maybe even a sweater if you've come unprepared for skiing.

Elbrus

Elbrus is nearly 1000m above anything else in the vicinity. It's a volcanic cone with two peaks, the western being the higher at 5642m; the eastern peak is 5621m. Though geographical purists may argue, it is the highest mountain in Europe as it lies on the Caucasus ridge that is the geographical border of Europe and Asia. The upper slopes are said to be coated in ice up to 200m thick, numerous glaciers slide down its flanks and several rivers, including the Kuban, start here. Its name, meaning Two Heads, comes from Persian. In the Balkar language it's Mingi-Tau (Thousands – ie Very Big – Mountain).

The first unconfirmed climb of Elbrus was in 1829 by a Russian expedition, but it was a lone Circassian hunter named Killar who was hired as a guide and he apparently reached the peak on his own. The lower east peak was not officially conquered until 31 July 1868 by a British expedition with DW Freshfield, AW Moore, CC Tucker, a guide François Devouassoud and two local hunters. It was not until 28 July 1874 that the higher west peak was climbed by another British expedition, consisting of F Gardiner, FC Grove, H Walker and P Knubel. The Soviet regime of course had to do things en masse, the proletarian way for propaganda purposes, and in the 1980s had groups of up to 400 climbers at one time reaching the peak. Nowadays, the ascent and descent have apparently been done in many ways just to be different: on skis, by the landing of light aircraft, hang gliding and para-gliding, but the most unusual one was apparently on a motorcycle fitted with skis.

The Azau cable car rises in two stages ($2 to $3 return) from 2350m to the Mir Bar at 3500m, which is open in the main ski season, and from where you can see both the twin peaks and the main Caucasus ridge. A chairlift continues to 3800m, which in some summers might be above the snowline, with year-round skiing – and cold! The area above the chairlift is definitely good for summer skiing but it requires walking as there are no lifts there. Hiking groups can then walk for about 1½ hours – fairly easy but slow because of the altitude and crevasses – up to the ruins of Camp 11 (Priyut odinnadtsaty) which was burnt down in 1998 and is due to be rebuilt. In its place for now are two barrels *(bochki)* housing 12 each at about 4160m and to the right of the Camp 11 site. To stay here in the peak seasons, you'll need to make arrangements in advance through a tour operator, or contact the rescuers who may be able to advise you.

The walk back down to the chairlift is around 40 minutes. Climbers heading for the top, having acclimatised, usually do the final assault in a day – about eight hours up and eight hours down. It's not technically hard.

Mt Cheget

There are fine views across to Elbrus from Mt Cheget, a spur of 3769m Mt Donguz-Orunbashi on the south side of the Baxan Valley. Two chairlifts in front of the Hotel Cheget both ascend to ***Kafe Ay*** at 2750m (usually serving cold drinks only), then another lift reaches 3005m for some stunning views. From the top, a 45 minute walk on a gravel path takes you to a small peak. The lower chairlifts ascend from roughly 9 am to 4 pm and the upper one to more or less 3 pm. You can descend until about half an hour after ascents stop. A one-way trip on one chair costs $1.

From Kafe Ay there's an easy path of about 7km round the side of Mt Cheget, passing Donguzorunkyol Lake, to Donguzorun Camp North (Severny priyut Donguzorun) at 2500m, south of Mt Donguz-Orunbashi. Mt Donguzorun-Chegetkarabashi, which is about 4450m, soars behind the lake. From Camp North it's a steep 3km up to the snow-covered Donguz-Orunbashi or Nakra Pass on the Georgian border. You'll most likely need a guide of some sort or a permit *(propusk)* from the border guards to do this route.

Other Walks

An easy walk, two to three hours one way, leads up the Terskol Valley from behind the white obelisk in Terskol village to a dramatic view of Elbrus behind the 'hanging' Terskol Glacier, which drips over a hill's edge.

From the paved road up the Adylsu Valley south of Elbrus village, it's about 1½ hours up a good, gently rising path to the impressive Shkhelda Glacier. ***Zelyonaya Gostinitsa*** (Green Hotel), a shelter (you'll need a tent) near little Bashkarinskoe Lake at the head of the Adylsu Valley, is a day walk destination. Day-walk valleys with glaciers at the top include the Irikchat west of Elbrus village, and the Yusengi, south from Baydaevo.

Skiing

Mt Cheget is one of the two main skiing locations (the other is around the Azau cable car), with skiing from December to April and with February usually being the best month. Skiing is possible year-round on the slopes below Mt Elbrus, reached via two cable cars ($2 to $3 each) – a high-altitude chairlift might be open in summer if there is enough snow. If not, then it is possible to walk up a trail alongside the chairlifts and then continue along the Garabashi Glacier to the Camp 11 site or even farther, and ski down to the top of the chairlift. At the time of writing there was no skiable snow under the chairlifts, but in summer it may, according to some locals, be possible to ski here.

It should be possible during the winter season to hire gear in the basement of the Hotel Cheget, but in summer it might be closed, especially if there is not enough snow below the chairlift. Probably the best place to rent decent gear is through the rescue post. The rate is $2.50 for quality skis, boots and pools. The lifts are pretty primitive and the accident rate for climbers and skiers is alarmingly high. Skiing on the gently sloping Garabashi Glacier is slow, but in winter skiing around and under the Azau cable car looks great, with long, steep and challenging runs.

Organised Tours

Russia's continuing conflict with Chechnya, the rash of highly publicised kidnappings and terrorist acts in the Chechen border regions have scared away many tourists from Mt Elbrus. One US firm that continues to offer climbs is Seattle-based REI Adventures (www.rei.com). It offers 13-day packages for $2400. REI works through a competent Russian tour provider, Lenalptours (☎ 812-279 07 16, fax 279 06 51, lenalptr@mail.wplus.net), ulitsa Vosstaniya 9-4, St Petersburg, which also offers Elbrus packages. It offers a 16 day ascent, a 13 day circum Elbrus trek and an 11 day ski tour.

Places to Stay & Eat

Strangely, Elbrus tends to be packed with people or ghostly empty; either way it's not easy to find lodging in hotels, so you might want to consider arranging for accommodation in advance through Lenalptours or another tour provider. If you just wander into town, you might be able to rent a flat for about $6 per person per day; check at the stores. Beneath the Azau chairlift, 4km from Terskol, you might also be able to stay in one of the rooms kept for geologists from Moscow State University; ask around.

The hotel of choice for Western groups and Russian sports teams is ***Volfram*** behind the telephone office. The spacious rooms (unheated and without hot water before 9 am, off season) are clean, with views and pink tiled bathrooms; they cost $5/10 a single/double. There are billiards and table tennis and a bar on the 3rd floor. The ***stolovaya*** (cafeteria) for guests serves hearty meals (a typical breakfast: kasha, cookies, kolbasa *and* stuffed cabbage dumplings with macaroni) for $1.25. The hotel also has a sauna, costing $12 for two hours. Next door, the Defence Ministry hotel, ***Turbaza Terskol*** has a swimming pool and a beer bar.

At the foot of Mt Cheget, ***Hotel Cheget*** has a bar, a market (only souvenirs most days) nearby and kiosks at the foot of the chairlifts, selling things like shashlyk, *pichin* (a meat-filled flat bread), *shchorpa* (a Balkar soup) and soft drinks. Small but satisfactory rooms cost from $15/25.

Getting There & Away

The way to the Elbrus area is up the Baxan River valley from the Baxan town bypass on the Pyatigorsk-Nalchik road – it's 110km to Azau Valley at the head of the valley road. The Baxan Valley is of majestic proportions but scarred by power lines and pipelines, quarries and other 20th century debris. Bits of the road are often washed away and it's under constant repair. Zhankhoteko village, near the start of the valley, has a roadside market selling colourful local woollens. Farther up, the Balkar town of Tyrnyauz, built to mine molybdenum and tungsten – used in the Soviet space effort – has a real Satanic mills feel.

During peak seasons, there is at least one bus daily to Mineralnye Vody ($2, four hours). Otherwise, you'll have to take the bus to Baxan ($1, 2½ hours) where it is possible to catch a marshrutki to many destinations, including Krasnodar, Stavropol and Pyatigorsk. A taxi to Tyrnyauz, from where you can also change to other buses, costs $6.

Getting Around

Many taxis (about $2 from Terskol to the Azau lift) and minivans operate between Cheget and Azau during peak seasons. Off season, you'll have to walk or hitch a ride from a local.

GEORGI SHABLOVSKY

Komi villager of Northern European Russia

GEORGI SHABLOVSKY

Novgorod – a barrel of fun

GEORGI SHABLOVSKY

Folk festival of Vitoslavlitsy near Novgorod – where too much embroidery is never enough

GEORGI SHABLOVSKY

The Dombay region of the Caucasus

GEORGI SHABLOVSKY

One of Northern European Russia's thousands of lakes

GEORGI SHABLOVSKY

Wild flowers in Dombay

GEORGI SHABLOVSKY

Akhun waterfalls near Sochi

VLADIKAVKAZ
ВЛАДИКАВКАЗ

☎ 86722 • pop 300,000

An untidy town, hinting that the edge of Europe isn't far away, Vladikavkaz (King of the Caucasus) was called Ordzhonikidze from 1931 to 1944 and from 1954 to 1990 after the Georgian Grigory 'Sergo' Ordzhonikidze, who led the imposition of Bolshevism on the Caucasus region in the 1920s. Some locals say he pursued his mission with near genocidal enthusiasm.

Vladikavkaz is 740m high on the swift Terek River, at the northern end of the Georgian Military Highway to Tbilisi. There have been settlements here intermittently since the 3rd millennium BC. The Russians built a fort in 1784. The Germans were stopped just a few kilometres north in WWII.

The real attractions of the area are the bizarre relics of old Ossetian settlements out in the valleys to the west. You need at least half a day, preferably more, for these.

Vladikavkaz is the capital of North Ossetia, a republic within the Russian Federation. About 700,000 of the republic's populace are Ossetians, who are thought to be descended from a group of Sarmatians, an Indo-European people from east Iran, who arrived on the steppe to the north in the last centuries BC and were pushed into the Caucasus by the Huns in the 4th century AD. They assimilated with local tribes to form a people called the Alans or Alany, whose state lasted from about the 8th to 13th centuries, when it was destroyed by the Tatars. Some escaped deep into the mountains and by the 18th century their descendants – the Ossetians – were mainly found in the valleys west of Vladikavkaz. Ossetia was incorporated into Russia, apparently peacefully, in 1774.

Most Ossetians are now Christian but maintain some animistic practices like ram sacrifice. Their main traditional festival is Jurgala, which lasts for nine days from the second last Sunday of November. South Ossetia is across the Caucasus in Georgia.

The other main group that lived in eastern South Ossetia was the Ingush, who would have preferred to be part of neighbouring Ingushetia. (Today it is the Russians who make up the largest minority in South Ossetia.) This problem, aside from the usual ethnic hatred going back hundreds of years, dates back to 1944, when under Stalin's orders most Ingush were deported to Siberia for allegedly collaborating with the German invaders. They were rehabilitated during Khrushchev's rule and allowed to return home in 1957. Another legacy of the Stalin era was the allocation of the western part of Ingushetia (known as Checheno-Ingushetia at the time) to North Ossetia. The returning Ingush found most of their property occupied by Ossetians.

Under communist rule both groups, Ossetians and Ingush, coexisted peaceably but this was an illusion. In June 1992, the Russian Duma passed a motion setting up an autonomous Ingushetia, which triggered some unfortunate events. The two groups engaged in bloody clashes from 22 October 1992, resulting in the deaths of hundreds of people. Russian forces were sent in to try to defuse the conflict. According to local accounts they sided with the Ossetians, committing atrocities in the process. The combined force of the Russians and the Ossetians eventually forced the entire Ingush population of over 50,000 into Ingushetia, to live in extremely poor conditions – most of their houses in North Ossetia were destroyed and their property confiscated.

Orientation & Information

The Hotel Vladikavkaz is on the west bank of the Terek River, a 500m walk from the main street, prospekt Mira. There are post, telephone and telegraph offices on ulitsa Vatutina on the corner of ulitsa Kuybysheva, and opposite the train station on the corner of ulitsa Markova and ulitsa Kirova. For books and maps, try Knigi at prospekt Mira 31 or Voennaya Kniga on ulitsa Kuybysheva.

Things to See

Most postcards of Vladikavkaz show the **Sunni mosque**, 100m from Hotel Vladikavkaz beside the Terek. It's the most eye-catching building in town with its blue dome, twin towers, and 300 Koranic inscriptions on the walls, but is utterly atypical. It was built in 1906-08 by a Baku oil magnate with an Ossetian wife.

The town centre is low-rise, with a number of oldish buildings on ulitsa Gorkogo, ulitsa Butyrina and prospekt Mira, a 1.25km tree-lined boulevard given over to pedestrians and trams. The **North Ossetian History, Architecture & Literature Museum** at No 11 has some amazingly deformed old Alany skulls. The **North Ossetian Art Museum** is located at No 12.

The **Khetagurov Ossetian Literature Museum** at ulitsa Botoeva 3, in an unusual old church, is named after Kosta Khetagurov (1859-1906). Khetagurov's house, at ulitsa Butyrina 19, is also a museum.

Places to Stay & Eat

Overlooking the Terek, ***Hotel Vladikavkaz*** *(☎ 75 20 28, ulitsa Kotsoeva 75)* has rooms with balconies for $17/20 a single/double.

Outside the hotel, apart from the large, well stocked fruit and vegetable market on ulitsa Kuybysheva, the food scene is grim.

Getting There & Away

Air The airport is at Beslan, 22km north. There are daily flights to/from Moscow.

Train Vladikavkaz is on a branch railway line that brings just one *skoryy* (fast) train a day from Moscow (43 hours) via Rostov-on-Don and Mineralnye Vody (3¾ hours).

Road Public buses go to/from Mineralnye Vody, Novorossiysk and Stavropol. By car it's an easy 115km from Nalchik. To the south the spectacular Georgian Military Highway winds over the Caucasus – it's 70km to Kazbegi, 220km to Tbilisi. Be warned, though, now and then buses plunge over the sides. Avalanches and falling rocks also make the way hazardous.

Aside from that, the only worries you'll have are highway bandits, border guards and police, all of whom make their living by extracting tolls at checkpoints *(shlagbaumy)* set up every 20km or so. The more you look and behave like an average local (which means using public transportation and not Benzes with tinted windows), the fewer problems you'll have.

AROUND VLADIKAVKAZ

Dargavs
Даргавс

This so-called 'village of the dead', some 40km from Vladikavkaz in the Giseldon Valley, is the cemetery of an old Ossetian village, with 44 big, stone, beehive-shaped family tombs scattered up a hillside. Skeletons are visible through holes in the bases of these tombs. Dargavs is the most spectacular of many similar cemeteries in the district, which are likely to have been established by members of an ancestor cult. Some of the tombs are partly restored. To reach Dargavs, turn left at Gizel on the Vladikavkaz-Alagir road; fork left to Karmadon when the valley divides; then cross into the next valley to the west by a dirt road over the top from Karmadon.

Kurtati Valley
Куртатинское ущелье

You can approach the glacier-watered Kurtati Valley (Kurtatinskoe ushchelie) either from Dzuarikau at its foot, on the Vladikavkaz-Alagir road, or by a dirt road over the top from a couple of kilometres above Dargavs in the next valley east. The latter comes down near the small mining town of Verkhny Fiagdon. On the slopes west of Verkhny Fiagdon are the towers and cemetery of Tsimity, the valley's old main settlement. There are more towers and defence works around Kharisdzhin, a few kilometres farther up the valley. Between Verkhny Fiagdon and Dzuarikau the valley narrows to a gorge. At Dzivgis, just above the gorge, a high stone wall across a cave above the village betrays an old refuge against invaders.

Ardon Valley & Ossetian Military Highway
Ардонское ущелье и Военно-Осетинская дорога

The Ardon Valley runs south from Alagir, 40km west of Vladikavkaz. Nuzal, above the mining village of Mizur, about 30km from Alagir, boasts an old cemetery and towers, and a frescoed 12th or 13th century chapel where David Soslan, the husband of Queen Tamara of Georgia, was buried.

The wooden **Rekom Church** at Verkhny Tsey, in the Tseyadon Valley about 15km west of Buron (which is 8km up the Ardon from Mizur), is Ossetia's most revered shrine. Probably built in the 15th to 16th century, it's dedicated to St George but may've originally been a ram cult shrine. The upper Tseyadon Valley is surrounded by glaciers.

At the top of the Ardon Valley, the road winds over the 2819m Mamisonsky Pass to Kutaisi in Georgia, following the old Ossetian Military Highway (Voenno-Osetinskaya doroga), which was built to help the Russians control the region in the 19th century. At the time of writing, buses were not using it due to the conflict in South Ossetia.

Chechnya
Чечня

Due to the unstable security situation and recent military activities in Chechnya, we were unable to carry out any first-hand research in the area. We have, however, provided some information on the people and the history of the region.

The Chechens of the northern Caucasus belong linguistically to the Nakh group and are Sunni Muslims. By reputation they are very proud, independently minded and unruly. (Chechen means 'unsubjectable' in Turkish.) They live by strict codes of honour and revenge, and clan blood feuds are well entrenched in their patriarchal culture.

As a nation they have suffered greatly at the hands of the Russians, who conquered them, along with other neighbouring nationalities, in 1859 after a 30 year war. In 1944, with great loss of life, many Chechens were deported to Siberia for allegedly collaborating with the Germans. In effect, this was Stalin's pretext for disposing of potentially troublesome nationalities. The survivors were allowed to return after Khrushchev's amnesty in 1957.

Many Russians regard the Chechens as a nation of brutal mafiosi who run a large underworld involved in extortion, drug dealing, prostitution and other organised crime. The conflict between such groups is one of the factors that makes Chechnya hard to rule. However, the gangs make up only a very small minority of the population, while the majority is still devastated by the war which began when Chechen President Dzhafar Dudaev, a former Soviet bomber pilot and air-force general, unilaterally declared independence from the Russian Federation in 1991.

Within a few days of the declaration, which was not recognised internationally, the Russian President Boris Yeltsin declared a state of emergency in Chechnya and 650 Russian troops were sent there to occupy strategic places like the airport and government buildings. The Russians were soon forced to withdraw not only because the state of emergency was rejected by the Russian parliament, but also because they realised that their positions were not defensible owing to the armed resistance of the Chechens.

On 11 December 1994, in the face of much opposition in Russia and around the world, Russian troops openly invaded Chechnya. They surrounded the capital Grozny and almost bombed it into submission, while Yeltsin tried to negotiate the total surrender of Dudaev's army. The attack on Grozny commenced on 31 December 1994, but the Chechens repulsed the attack and remained victorious for a few days. The demoralised Russian forces suffered heavy losses as a result of the poor planning of the whole operation. The Russian army's main problem was the use of untrained, raw recruits who were poorly fed and poorly dressed for the winter conflict. In 1995, after a new offensive with experienced troops, the Chechen capital fell. The hardy defenders left for the mountains of their homeland, from where they continued to fight.

In June 1995, a group of Chechens bribed their way through Russian checkpoints along the Russia-Chechnya border to a hospital in Budyonovsk, more than 100km into southern Russia. There they took about 1000 Russians hostage. During negotiations, armed confrontations between the Chechens and Russian security forces resulted in the deaths of around 120 hostages and 15 Chechen fighters. The Russian forces bungled again, and eventually the surviving Chechens negotiated their way back home. Russia provided buses to take them, and some hostages, back to rebel-held parts of Chechnya.

Both sides appeared keen to sign a peace treaty. Talks between the Russians and the Chechens were supervised by the Organisation for Security and Co-operation in Europe, and an agreement was signed in July. Its terms were a ceasefire, the release of prisoners and the demilitarisation of Chechnya. In parts of the country fighting continued. The major sticking-point – the fact that the Chechens demanded total independence, while the Russians were only willing to grant them autonomy – was barely touched upon in the July agreement.

Many Russians and Chechens viewed the war not as an ethnic conflict but a political one, concerning control over the oil pipelines that pass through Chechnya from Azerbaijan and Kazakhstan to Tuapse and Novorossiysk on Russia's Black Sea coast.

In 1999, with Dudaev dead and the more flexible and less powerful Aslan Maskhadov as president, armed gangs of Chechen fighters have been trying to overthrow the presidency and form an independent, fundamentalist Islamic state in the northern Caucasus. They are suspected of being responsible for numerous kidnappings of Russians and foreigners. It is believed that Chechen radicals planted the bomb which killed some 50 people in a Vladikavkaz marketplace in March 1999.

As this edition was going to press, Russia was again bombing the Chechen Republic in what the international community has come close to calling a ruthless and inhumane war. It began in the summer of 1999, after Chechen rebels stirred up fighting in nearby Dagestan and a series of apartment-building bombings in Moscow left many people dead and the Russian capital paralysed with fear. Yeltsin, in his umpteenth cabinet sweep that year, appointed Vladimir Putin, an ex-KGB boss, as prime minister, and gave him the task of resolving the Chechen crisis once and for all. Putin, having learned from the mistakes of his predecessors in the previous war of the mid-1990s, is taking a no-compromise stance, demanding the anihiliation of Chechen renegade forces and complete submission of the republic to Russian control. Unlike during the earlier war, when the Russian people protested against the attacks by their government on Chechnya, many Russians, fed up by terrorist acts and other criminal activities attributed to the Chechens, are supporting this war and see it as the only solution to the Chechen crisis.

Dagestan
Дагестан

At the time of writing, the word from the Russian Ministry of Foreign Affairs was that anyone travelling in Dagestan, foreigners especially, ran a high risk of being held hostage for ransom.

Dagestan means the Mountain Kingdom. This republic, stretching deep into the north-east Caucasus from its 400km Caspian coast, is the most complex and traditional part of the Caucasian ethnic jigsaw. It has about 30 languages divided into 81 nationalities, a result of its position on a great migration corridor between the Caspian and the Caucasus. Some of the largest groups are Avar, Dargin, Kumyk, Lezghin, Lakh and Tabasarans. One non-ethnic but distinctive group is the *abreks*, or the marauders, who made their living from robbery; their coup was to attack a wedding and take off with the bride.

Over two-thirds of the largely Muslim population of nearly two million live in inland villages. Most of the ethnic groups in Dagestan are fervently Muslim and apparently around 2000 mosques were destroyed on Stalin's orders. Some have been rebuilt and many more are on the drawing board.

The weather is quite hot and dry in the lowlands, where the average daily maximum July temperature is 26°C but often exceeds 30°C. It tends to be cooler in the mountains, where the sun can still get very hot. The mountain areas also have a shorter summer and the passes are only open from late June to late September. Winters are much colder with the average daily maximum temperature in the lowlands being -4°C, lower in the mountains.

The history of Dagestan reaches back into ancient times. A settlement more than 10,000 years old was found near the village of Tschoch, which can be reached on foot from another village, Gunib. Russian biologists and archaeologists have asserted that Dagestan was one of the places where cultivation and domestication first began on earth, and is thus one of the cradles of civilisation.

Dagestan has a bloodied recent history of many struggles for independence against Turks and Russians. Russia annexed Dagestan in 1813 after an arrangement with Persia. The local tribes did not take to Russian occupation easily and the fight against the Russian Imperial forces during the 19th century was led by Imam Shamil, a Lezghian, a local folk hero who led a war against the Orthodox invaders from 1845 until his surrender in 1859. He still holds a very romantic and legendary place in the nationalistic hearts of the people. The Russians still did not establish full control until 1877. It is this sort of strong nationalism and independence that made Stalin fear them and he had whole groups of villages transferred to Siberia at the end of WWII for alleged collaboration with the German invaders. The charges were false, since the local tribes could not be involved in such activities because the Germans never reached this area.

Folklore and handicraft traditions, especially in the mountainous southern half where villages cling to steep hillsides, are as rich as anywhere in Russia. Dagestan's intricately patterned carpets and textiles are the most renowned of the region's crafts. Their rug designs are quite varied depending on what nationality makes them.

TRANS-SIBERIAN RAILWAY

RICHARD NEBESKY

The Trans-Siberian Railway

The Trans-Siberian Railway and connecting routes comprise one of the most famous, romantic and potentially enjoyable of the world's great train journeys. Rolling out of Europe and into Asia, through eight time zones and over a vast 9289km of taiga, steppe and desert, the Trans-Siberian makes all other train rides seem like once around the block with Thomas the Tank Engine. The Trans-Siberian Railway extends from Moscow to the Pacific coast in the far east. It's the world's longest single-service railway, and with its European and Asian extensions it's also the world's foremost overland 'highway'.

Any attempt to find the Trans-Siberian Railway on a timetable, however, will meet with about as much success as a search through an atlas for the fabled Shangri-la. The term 'Trans-Siberian Railway' is used generically for three main lines and some of the numerous trains that run on them.

The main line runs from Moscow's Yaroslavl Station along a continuous unbroken track through Siberia to Vladivostok, in the Russian Far East. The *Rossia* departs every other day from each of the two terminuses to begin its 6½ day haul.

However, the routes traditionally referred to as the Trans-Siberian Railway are actually the two branches that veer off the main line in eastern Siberia to make a beeline for Beijing. The 7865km Trans-Mongolian Railway makes its way along the Moscow-Vladivostok line as far as Lake Baikal, where it diverts to reach the Chinese capital via Ulaan Baatar, the Mongolian capital, while the 9001km Trans-Manchurian Railway leaves the main line at Tarskaya to reach Beijing by way of Harbin and northeastern China.

The sense of passage engendered by getting on a train in European Russia and stepping off at the other end into a pungent, dusty cloud of orientalism (or vice versa) has long made these routes favourites with foreign travellers.

HIGHLIGHTS

- Raiding the station platforms for Siberian sustenance and chowing down on still-warm boiled potatoes and dill, cold beer and crayfish while the longest Russian film ever made rolls by
- Crossing the Volga River, with a glimpse of Yaroslavl
- Spotting the 1777km obelisk in the Urals, where Europe becomes Asia
- Rounding the southern tip of Lake Baikal, then chugging through the photogenic Chita region
- Surviving the Mongolian steppe and the vaudevillesque border crossing at Naushki
- Having nearly a week to do nothing

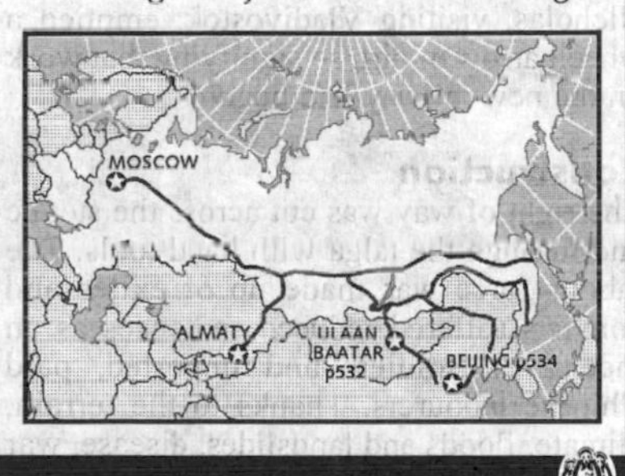

HISTORY

Beginnings

Russia's initial conquest of Siberia was by means of its rivers, with the boats dragged from one watercourse to the next. Later transport took the form of horse-drawn carriages, sledges or *tarantas* (a coach body resting on three thick poles, dragged by horses) following the Great Siberia Post Road (Veliky trakt) – little more than a trail through the snow, mud or dust. At best, to travel across Siberia was a three or four month undertaking, but for the exiles and poorer emigrants who were forced to go on foot, the journey could take a year or more – in fact, it was quicker to travel from St Petersburg to Vladivostok by crossing the Atlantic, North America and the Pacific.

With the region's burgeoning population, and both Japan and China coveting Russia's Far Eastern territories, the Russian Empire clearly needed better communication links with its extremities. Throughout the 19th century, ideas for a railway across Siberia were floated, including an 1857 proposal by the American banker Perry McDonough Collins for a rail and riverboat link from Irkutsk in eastern Siberia to the Pacific.

In 1869, the Americans completed their own coast-to-coast railway, and 1885 saw the opening of the *Canadian Pacific*. The following year, Tsar Alexander III finally authorised the building of a 7500km line from Chelyabinsk (then Russia's eastern railhead) to Vladivostok, to run along the route of the old post road and connect all its major towns. In May 1891, Tsarevich Nicholas, visiting Vladivostok, emptied a wheelbarrow of dirt, so signifying that work on the new railway had begun.

Construction

The right of way was cut across the steppe and through the taiga with hand tools. The labour force was made up of exiles and convicts (offered reduced sentences as an incentive), soldiers and imported, paid Chinese labourers. Thanks to the terrain, climate, floods and landslides, disease, war and bandit attacks, not to mention shoddy materials and bad planning, the railway took 26 years to build. But it remains the most brilliant engineering feat of its time.

The railway was divided into six sections so that construction could take place simultaneously all along the route. The first section to get under way was the Ussuri line (Vladivostok-Khabarovsk), built between 1891 and 1897, followed by the western Siberian line (Chelyabinsk-Novosibirsk), built between 1892 and 1896, and the mid-Siberian line (Novosibirsk via Irkutsk to Port Baikal), built between 1893 and 1898. Within seven years, the Trans-Siberian line stretched 5200km from Moscow to the western shore of Lake Baikal.

Baikal was initially crossed by two ice-breakers built at Newcastle-upon-Tyne in England and sent in pieces to be assembled in Irkutsk. The huge, four funnelled *Baikal* was the larger of the two, and her decks were laid with three lines of track that could accommodate an entire express train and its load. The smaller ship, the *Angara*, was used for passengers. But when the Russo-Japanese War broke out in the winter of 1904, to speed the supply of troops and munitions to the front, temporary rails were laid across the frozen lake. The first test locomotive plunged through the ice, making a hole 22km long. Undaunted, the Russians relaid the tracks, disassembled the locomotives and used teams of horses and men to pull the carriages and flat cars.

By 1904, it was finally possible to take a train all the way from St Petersburg through to Vladivostok, via the East China line across Manchuria. However, propelled by fears that they might lose control of the East China line to the Japanese, the Russians soon embarked upon the alternative Amur line, from Sretensk to Khabarovsk. Finished in 1916, with the bridge over the Amur River at Khabarovsk, it was the final link in the world's longest railway.

Early Services

Following Russia's orgy of self-publicity at the Paris Universal Exposition of 1900, the earliest Trans-Siberian travellers were lured on to the rails even before the line was fully completed. To attract overseas clientele, the *State Express* (as it was then known) was presented at the exposition as a palace on wheels with sleeping carriages, a gymnasium car, a restaurant car with a large tiled bathroom, reading lounge and piano, and even a fully functioning church car crowned with a belfry – in a mock-up landscape of stuffed seals, papier-mache icebergs and mannequins of native hunters. The same year saw the publication of the official *Guide to the Great Siberian Railway*.

The primary reason for the construction of the railway had been to further the economic and social development of Siberia, and the bulk of passengers were emigrants escaping overpopulation in European Russia. Their travelling conditions were a far cry from the sumptuousness on offer to the international set – 'stables on wheels' was one eyewitness description. But a few weeks of hardship on the rails was far preferable to crossing Siberia on foot, and in 1908 alone 750,000 peasants rode east.

Post-Revolution

Civil war interrupted the development of the railway. When the Reds finally prevailed, upgrading the Trans-Siberian was a major priority in their plans for economic rebirth by linking the iron-ore reserves of the Ural region with the Kuznetsk coalfields and the great industrial plants being developed throughout western Siberia.

In the 1920s, the railway was extended south-west from Novosibirsk via Semey (Semipalatinsk) to Almaty in Kazakhstan (the present-day Turkestan-Siberian Railway, known as the Turk Sib). In 1940, a branch line was built between Ulan Ude and Naushki, on the border with Mongolia. By 1949 it had connected with Ulaan Baatar, the Mongolian capital. The line from Ulaan Baatar to Beijing was begun four years later and completed by 1956.

In the words of one commentator, the Trans-Siberian Railway had become the iron ribbon that held the Soviet Union together. Despite the ascendancy of the aeroplane and the demise of the Soviet system, the importance of the Trans-Siberian Railway has not diminished. There is still no continuous motorable road across Siberia, and rail is still the only viable option for heavy freight. The Trans-Siberian also retains its role as a cast-iron safety cord, securing the far-flung territories to Moscow's motherly presence.

The BAM

In the 1930s, work was begun on a second Trans-Siberian line, the 3100km Baikal-Amur Mainline (Baikalo-Amurskaya Magistral, or BAM). This line was to extend from Tayshet on the existing Trans-Siberian line, around the northern tip of Lake Baikal, and on to the previously inaccessible, timber-rich Lena Basin and its coal, iron-ore and gold mines. Abandoned in WWII and stripped so its tracks could be used to lay a relief line to the besieged city of Stalingrad, it was essentially started all over again in 1974. In the meantime, the line had gained in strategic importance as an alternative to the existing Trans-Siberian, which was felt to be too vulnerable to attack by a potentially hostile China.

The BAM was called the 'Hero Project of the Century', and the youth of all the Soviet Union was called to rally to the challenge. Their response is evident in the names of some of the towns along the line – Estbam, Latbam and Litbam, named for the workers from the Baltic states who built them – and in the striking absence of elderly people in these communities today. The BAM towns grew with the new railway, which was being forced through virgin wilderness. Overcoming Siberia's swamps and mountains, its seemingly infinite number of rivers and, in particular, its vast swathe of permafrost pushed the cost of the project to a staggering $25 billion (the original Trans-Siberian is estimated to have cost the equivalent of $500 million).

Officially opened in 1991, the line still isn't finished. Although it is possible to travel the whole length of the BAM, from Tayshet to Sovietskaya Gavan on the Pacific coast, the incomplete Severomuysk tunnel is currently bypassed by a temporary line that is extremely susceptible to landslides. There is very little traffic on the line and many of its settlements have become ghost towns.

BOOKS

The *Trans-Siberian Handbook* by Bryn Thomas covers in some detail the major settlements along the line. *Russia by Rail with Belarus and Ukraine* by Athol Yates follows several major train routes radiating from Moscow. It lists sights that can be seen from trains kilometre by kilometre.

The Big Red Train Ride by Eric Newby is the travelogue to take along. His account of a couple of weeks hopping on and off the *Rossia* between Moscow and Nakhodka is a little outdated but there's still plenty of colour and detail. Sometimes he's even as funny as he thinks he is. Another great train traveller, Paul Theroux, includes an amusingly caustic account of a late-1970s Trans-Siberian journey in *The Great Rail Bazaar*. He seems in little better mood 10 years later when he boards the Trans-Mongolian as the prelude to an exhaustive rail exploration of China, recounted in *Riding the Iron Rooster*.

During the late 1980s, Brad Newsham was 'toting a bale of misery' (his words) around Japan and China and, via the Trans-Mongolian, to Moscow. He describes his woes, and little else, in *All the Right Places*. At around the same time, Mary Morris, also labouring under a cloud of self-created gloom, was following a similar self-absorbed route, related in *Wall to Wall: From Beijing to Berlin*. Both of these books will be of greater interest to psychoanalysts than to Trans-Siberian travellers.

A good antidote to modern-day whingeing is Peter Fleming's *One's Company*, in which a tumble down an embankment on board the Trans-Siberian is described with admirable sang-froid. Written in 1933, the style of the time was such that Fleming could get away with sentences such as, 'One of the most curious things about modern Russia is the startling and universal ugliness of the women'.

Fleming is just one of the dozens of writers extracted in *The Trans-Siberian Railway: A Travellers' Anthology*, edited by Deborah Manley. This is an excellent background read, now unfortunately out of print but worth tracking down. Also recommended is *Red Express* (out of print) by Michael Cordell & Peter Solness, a lavish photo album produced to accompany the Australian TV series of the same name that examined modern-day life in the ex-communist realms from East Berlin to China, following the route of the railway.

For more general reading suggestions, see Books in both the European Russia and Siberia & the Russian Far East Facts for the Visitor chapters.

ROUTES & TRAINS

For the first four days' travel out of Moscow, the Trans-Siberian, Trans-Manchurian and Trans-Mongolian routes all follow the same double-track main line, through the Urals and into western Siberia, over the Yenisey River (which marks the beginning of eastern Siberia) and on to Irkutsk. On the fifth day, after rounding the southern tip of Lake Baikal, the Trans-Mongolian route branches off, heading south for the Mongolian border 250km away. The Trans-Manchurian stays with the main line for another 12 hours past Lake Baikal, before it too peels off, heading south-east for Zabaikalsk on the Chinese border, some 368km distant.

The Trans-Manchurian takes half a day longer to reach Beijing but in doing so it avoids the need for a Mongolian visa. But it also means missing out on ever-popular Ulaan Baatar.

Every carriage has a timetable (in Cyrillic) posted in the corridor, which also notes how long the train will stop at each station. These timetables, however, are not set in stone and if the train is running late, station stops could be shortened, so ask the *provodnik* (conductor) when getting off the train. Usually, halts last from two to five minutes, but at least twice a day the train stops for 15 or 20 minutes, allowing passengers time to get off and stretch their legs or stock up from the platform kiosks. There are small white kilometre-posts on the southern side of the line marking the distance from Moscow, although these are sometimes difficult to spot because they're so close to the track.

On the Turk-Sib, there's a service at least daily between Novosibirsk and Almaty (32 to 37 hours) via Semey (Semipalatinsk) in Kazakhstan, with a branch line to Ürümqi in western China, and three or four trains weekly between Novosibirsk and Bishkek, Kyrgyzstan, (54 hours) and Tashkent, Uzbekistan (about 70 hours). See the Siberia & the Russian Far East Getting There & Away chapter for details of the Ussuriysk-Pyongyang service between Russia and North Korea.

Trans-Siberian Railway Timetable

Расписание движения поездов с Ярославского вокзала Москвы (по Транс-сибирской, Транс-монгольской и Транс-манчжурской магистралям), время московское.

Yaroslavl Station, Moscow Timetable* for Trans-Siberian, Trans-Mongolian and Trans-Manchurian Trains, Moscow Time.

НА ВОСТОК EASTBOUND

Поезд № Train No & name	Станция назначения Destination	Время отправления Departure time	Время в пути Duration of journey (hours)	Время прибытия Arrival time	Примечания Notes
2 Россия Rossia	Владивосток Vladivostok	14.00	153.49	02.45	По нечетным числам Odd-numbered dates
42	Владивосток Vladivostok	17.35	162.30	22.05	По средам и пятницам. с 12 апреля по чстным Wednesday, Friday. Even-numbered dates from April 12
140	Владивосток Vladivostok	09.40	163.48	05.28	с 2 июля - ежедневно Daily from July 2
174	Владивосток Vladivostok	09.50	164.04	05.54	с 1 по 31 августа - по нечетным Odd-numbered dates from August 1 to 31
10 Байкал Экпресс Baikal Express	Иркутск Irkutsk	21.10	81	06.40	По нечетным числам Odd-numbered dates
4	Пекин Beijing	19.55	134.38	15.33	(2) по вторникам Tuesday
20	Пекин Beijing	20.25	148.57	06.32	(5) по пятницам Friday
6	Улаан-Баатар Ulaan-Baatar	21.03	101.47	07.50	(3, 4) по средам и четвергам Wednesday, Thursday

* All train schedules are subject to change, so double-check. Trains are sometimes added during summer months. Days of the week and departure times can also change.

The Trans-Siberian

This is the Moscow-Vladivostok route, via the principal cities of Vyatka, Perm, Yekaterinburg, Omsk, Novosibirsk, Krasnoyarsk, Irkutsk, Ulan Ude, Chita and Khabarovsk.

The kilometre figures given in this section correspond to the white markers beside the railway line.

Departure is from Yaroslavl Station, **Moscow** (the 0km marker). One minute late

Detail of the Moscow-Ulaan Baatar train

onto the platform and you'll see a rapidly receding dot way down the line. That's your train – it leaves bang on time.

As the sights outside of Moscow are drab and the land mostly flat, this first leg of the journey is a good time to get acquainted with the dining car and the other passengers who will probably gravitate to the corridor, fumble with the curtains and then stand gazing out the (usually mud-spotted) windows.

As the train passes **Sergiev Posad** (73km), look to the north for the blue and gold domes. This is the Trinity St Sergius Monastery, one of Russian Orthodoxy's most important and often referred to by its Soviet-era name, Zagorsk. Four and a half hours into the journey the train makes a few minutes stop at **Yaroslavl** (282km). As the train crosses the bridge over the Volga River, the city scenes are excellent.

Also known as the dinner stop, because it usually comes sometime after sunset, there is a 15 minute halt allowing hungry travellers to raid the kiosks at **Danilov** (357km). During the night, when all you can see is your own reflection in the blackened windows, the train traverses the Volga region. At **Vyatka** (957km) there is a 15 minute breakfast stop, at around 6 am on the *Rossia* and at about noon for Trans-Manchurian and Trans-Mongolian travellers.

At **1365km**, at the approach to the Ural Mountains, local time becomes Moscow time plus one hour. By now, travellers are losing their sense of time and getting adept at passing through the screeching, violently jolting spaces between the carriages with the ground passing by at 70km/h, visible through the floor. You also begin to sense, like Dr Zhivago's wife, how significant the next station will be by how many switches you pass over as the train slows.

Now 24 hours since leaving Moscow, day two of the journey begins near **Perm** (1433km), with a much welcomed 15 minute halt. In the 1980s, Perm was best known for its UFO sightings, and until recently was closed to foreigners because of its military-industrial installations. About 110km east of Perm is the infamous Perm-36 prison. You can't see it from the tracks but some say you can feel it.

The train crosses the **Ural Mountains** for the next 1600 to 1900km. These mineral-rich wrinkles are a welcome relief after the skillet-flat terrain that fills the first leg of the journey. On the southern side of the tracks at **1777km** is a large white obelisk marking the boundary between Europe and Asia. Here also, the train is crossing into Siberia, a moment well worth noting with a beaker of champagne (warm unless you've got in with the cook in the dining car).

In the evening on the *Rossia* (night for the other trains) is a 20 minute halt at **Yekaterinburg** (1818km). Tsar Nicholas II and his family were murdered here. It's also Boris Yeltsin's home town. There are several places to get food in and just outside the station. Local time is now Moscow time plus two hours.

About four to five hours later, the train makes a brief halt in **Tyumen** (2144km), the oldest city in Siberia. A half-day later, at **2510km**, local time becomes Moscow time plus three hours.

Just in time for a morning cup of tea (or vodka for the hard-core train traveller who by now is probably experiencing a first Trans-Sib hangover), the train makes a 15 minute halt in **Omsk** (2716km), the city of Dostoevsky's exile. The train crosses the Irtysh River here.

Into day three, the train crosses the **Ob** (3332km), one of the world's longest rivers. It then makes a luxurious 20 minute halt in **Novosibirsk** (3343km), Siberia's biggest but not loveliest city, and the junction for the Turk-Sib Railway. If you're quick, you'll be able to grab something from the kiosks on the station forecourt.

Through these parts, the land on either side of the tracks is pastoral with small, isolated farmsteads in Cinemascope landscapes. Chekhov wrote in his essay 'About Siberia': 'You'll be bored from the Urals to the Yenisey. A cold valley, crooked birches, fields, once in a while a lake, snow in May on the barren, cheerless banks of the Ob tributaries ...' He was writing about the old post road, but the description holds true today. At **3488km**, local time becomes Moscow time plus four hours.

From **Tayga** (3571km) there is a branch line north to Tomsk and the closed defence-industry city of Tomsk-7. In **Mariinsk** (3719km) the train makes a 15 minute halt, arriving in the early morning for travellers on the *Rossia*.

A small white obelisk situated to the south of the tracks, at **3932km**, marks the halfway point between Moscow and Beijing (via Ulaan Baatar).

The 20 minute halt is the highlight of **Krasnoyarsk** (4104km), where there are two *bufety* in the station building. If you run through the ticket hall and out onto the station forecourt, you'll see a large mural of Lenin & co adorning the wall of the post office. Krasnoyarsk is the best place to change trains for the BAM.

Heading east out of the station the train crosses a 1km-long bridge over the **Yenisey River**, the boundary between western and eastern Siberia. At **4484km**, local time becomes Moscow time plus five hours.

In **Tayshet** (4522km), the train makes a one or two minute halt. It's at this junction that the BAM heads north to Bratsk and Severobaikalsk. This is day four of the journey, the midway point for Trans-Sib travellers, by which time you may have gone claustrophobic stir-crazy.

For the next 100km are the foothills of the **Western Sayan Mountains** (4600 to 4700km). Here the endless birch and pine forests of the taiga begin, and a real sense of wilderness sets in. The train makes a 15 minute halt in **Zima** ('winter') at 4940km.

Approaching **Irkutsk** (5191km), the skyline is dominated by the Raising of the Cross Church, on the eastern bank of the Angara River, though *Rossia* riders will have to get up awfully early to see it (you might want to enlist the help of the conductor, who's skilled at getting people up and off at the right stop). The train stops for 20 minutes at what is Siberia's liveliest station, and you may have time to buy a snack from the well stocked kiosks and *shashlyk* sellers on the street outside. North of the line, at **5228km**, an improbably cheery Lenin waves from the hillside.

But now, whatever is happening in the train – new friendships, love, massive liver abuse – stops dead, and everyone runs to the windows. The mind-numbing Siberia-scapes suddenly give way to the dramatic shores and icy blue waters of the world's deepest lake. For 200km, the line runs along the southern shore of **Lake Baikal** (5300 to 5500km) and through a series of tunnels blasted into the cliffs along the water's edge.

There's a 15 minute halt in **Slyudyanka** (5312km) which is just enough time to run down to the lake and dip in a hand. This is also where you can change for the Round-Baikal railway (see the Eastern Siberia chapter). Slyudyanka itself is an unattractive mining town. About five hours later, the train crosses the **Selenga River** (5630km). In **Ulan Ude** (5647km), there's another 15 minute halt, barely enough time to raid the kiosks on the platform and buy some *pozy*, the local Buryat-style meat dumpling.

The Trans-Mongolian junction is at **Zaudinsky** (5655km). Local time becomes Moscow time plus six hours at **5771km**.

Known as Petrovsky Zavod when some of the Decembrists were jailed here in 1830-39 – an event commemorated in a large, photogenic mural at the station – **Petrovsk-Zabaikalsky** (5790km) affords a 12 minute halt. There is a good photo opportunity of the colourful *rynok* (market) from the walk crossing the track. The river on the south side of the tracks is the Khilok, a tributary of the Selenga. The **Yablonovy Mountains** (5800 to 6300km) are blue shadows in the distance.

Bada (5884km) is a small town based around an aerodrome. Look for the MiG fighter monument and the cluster of old aircraft on the runway to the north. There is no halt here.

Entering the Chita region, the taiga gives way to rolling meadows, hills and deciduous woodland. Between the cities are log-cabin settlements, some as immaculate and brightly painted as story-book illustrations. (During the summer of 1998, this entire area was flooded, in places up to the tracks, and only the roofs of some cottages and the tops of haystacks were visible.)

You are four or five hours into day five when the train makes a 15 minute halt in **Chita** (6204km). Little of sustenance is to be found on the platform, but in the station's cavernous waiting rooms there are two good bufety.

There's a 12 minute halt in **Karymskoe** (6293km) shortly before **Tarskaya** (6312km), the Trans-Manchurian junction.

For the next 700km, starting at about **7000km**, the line runs on average only 50km north of the Amur River, the border with China. At one time, strategic sensitivity meant that carriages containing foreigners had their window blinds fastened down during this stretch.

At **Amazar** (7012km) there's a graveyard of steam locomotives, but the brief halt of eight minutes or so doesn't give much time to explore. **Yerofey Pavlovich** (7119km) was named in honour of the Siberian explorer Yerofey Pavlovich Khabarov (the remainder of his name went to the big city farther down the line). There's a 10 minute halt.

Day six begins with another 10 minute halt, at **Skovorodino** (7306km). If you get this far, and what you really wanted to do was switch trains and go north to the BAM, you've missed the junction at the city of Bam about 20km back. Get off here and hitch a ride back, or head to the next station east after Skovorodino, Bolshoy Never (Great Never), from where a desolate highway runs 1200km north to Yakutsk.

Belogorsk (7873km) is a sleepy Soviet town with a looming ex-Party headquarters, noisy restaurant and mosquito-infested riverbank, which fortunately you won't experience in the 15 minute halt unless you're changing trains to head south to Blagoveshchensk.

The train crosses the boundary between Siberia and the Russian Far East at **8185km**. Local time becomes Moscow time plus seven hours.

There is a halt of a couple of minutes in **Birobidzhan** (8358km), the capital of the Jewish Autonomous Region – note the station name in Hebrew letters. **Volochaevka** (8487km) was the site of the final battle of the civil war.

Approaching **Khabarovsk** (8531km) from the west, the train crosses a 2.5km bridge over the Amur River, the longest span on the whole line and the last stretch of the Trans-Siberian Railway to be completed. From Khabarovsk you can connect with the BAM at Komsomolsk, or take a train direct to Port Vanino for a boat to Sakhalin Island. A statue of Khabarov stands in the square outside the station, and in the ticket hall there are a couple of unsavoury snack places. There's a 25 minute halt.

This is day seven, and the last 12 hours (usually night) on the train. You'll be repacking or trying to sleep, and probably won't notice **Ussuriysk** (9177km), a 10 minute halt. Formerly named Nikolskoe in honour of the tsarevich's 1891 visit, the city was once of a greater size and importance than nearby Vladivostok. There is a twice-weekly train from here to Pyongyang.

In the morning, after nearly a week, the *Rossia* arrives at **Vladivostok** (9289km). Some people liken this to waking up in a strange bed after a long, hellish night. Make sure you have your wallet and passport before disembarking. From here you can make train connections to Harbin in north-east China or catch a boat across to the Japanese ports of Fushiki and Niigata.

The Trans-Mongolian

This branch line has been open since the mid-1950s and has become the rail route most synonymous with the 'Trans-Siberian' tag. After crossing into China's Inner Mongolia province, the train passes twice

THE TRANS-SIBERIAN RAIL ROUTES

MARTIN MOOS

And if you look out on your left you will see ... The Trans-Siberian rattling through Siberia

GEORGI SHABLOVSKY

Facade of the Vladivostok Railway Station

through the Great Wall to arrive in Beijing 5½ days after leaving Moscow. On this route, follow the Trans-Siberian landmarks until Zaudinsky. Both Mongolia and China have their own kilometre markers. In Mongolia, 0km is the border with Russia at Naushki; in China 0km is Beijing.

The train crosses the **Selenga River** at 5701km and again at 5885km before stopping for at least two hours at **Naushki** (5902/0km), a small, modern town that serves as the Russian border post.

Also known as Suhbaatar, **Sukhe Bator** (21km) is Mongolia's chief border town, and you will be subject to customs procedures here. There is little in the town to look at, and the train station is probably the building of greatest interest. Entering Mongolia brings a rapid change of scenery; the forests thin out into the lush green fields and pastures of the fertile Selenge Gol (Selenge River) basin.

With a population of just over 80,000 and a 10 minute halt, **Darhan** (123km) is Mongolia's second largest city. It was designed by the Russians in the days when grey concrete slabs and statues of Lenin were 'in'.

Ulaan Baatar (404km), the sprawling Mongolian capital, has a population of 600,000. The train stops here for 30 minutes, but as the city centre is 1km away your wanderings will be confined to the station. There's a cafeteria and the usual assortment of kiosks, plus a large number of steam engines at the northern end of the platform. See the Ulaan Baatar section under Breaking Your Journey for more details about the Mongolian capital.

Ulaan Baatar is just 311km south of the border, after which the line winds through green plains and gently swelling hills. There is a 15 minute halt at **Choyr** (649km), a small, obscure village which, prior to 1992, was home to the biggest Soviet military airbase in Mongolia. The only MiGs to be seen now are mounted on plinths.

The tracks enter the Gobi Desert and the next break is a 15 minute stop at **Saynshand** (876km), a small, dusty, dry town in the middle of the desert.

The Mongolian border post is **Dzamin-Uud** (1113km) and the Chinese border post is **Erlian (Erenhot**; 842km). The bogies (support wheels) are changed here.

There's nothing of note about the stop in **Fengzhan** (415km), but about 30km after this station you will get your first glimpse of the Great Wall as the line passes through it.

Once northern China's imperial centre, **Datong** (317km) is now one of the country's most depressing cities. The train halts for 10 minutes here and again at **Zhangjiakou** (193km).

At **Kanzuang** (82km) is a spectacular crossing of the Great Wall. About an hour later, the train pulls into **Beijing** (0km). See the later Beijing section under Breaking Your Journey for more details about the Chinese capital.

The Trans-Manchurian

The segment of this route from the junction at Tarskaya (the next stop immediately after Karymskoe) to Shenyang in China was laid by the Russians in 1897-1903 as part of the East China line to Vladivostok and Dalian (Port Arthur). It goes via Manzhouli and Harbin in north-east China, crossing steppes, the Great Khingan Mountains (Da Hinggan Ling, to the Chinese) and, after Shenyang, coastal flatlands. On this route, follow the Trans-Siberian landmarks as far as Tarskaya. Once in China, the kilometre markers show the distance from Harbin; after Harbin they show the distance to Beijing.

Zabaikalsk (6666km) is the Russian border post. You can eat in the restaurant here while the train's bogies are being changed. The Chinese border post is **Manzhouli**

TRANS-SIBERIAN RAILWAY

(935km). The train spends a further two hours or so here, so you can eat again or go shopping at the Friendship Store. One attraction is the large number of steam locomotives still at work in the shunting yards.

After leaving Manzhouli, look to the south for **Dalai Lake**, which unexpectedly pops up out of the grasslands like a great inland sea. It is Inner Mongolia's largest lake. Next come the **Great Khingan Mountains** (950 to 650km).

At **Boketu** (539km) there is a 15 minute halt and another at **Angangxi** (270km).

A large industrial city with a very visible Russian imprint, **Harbin** (0km) has lots of onion-domed Orthodox churches. Many White Russians took refuge here, fleeing the Bolsheviks. It's now famous for its ice festival, held every year from 5 January until late February. There's a 20 minute halt here.

A major industrial city with a population of six million, **Shenyang** (841km) affords a 15 minute halt.

The eastern end of the Great Wall meets the sea at **Shanhaiguan** (415km), 4km from the centre of town. It's not visible from the train, but there are lots of other great views.

Now a sprawling municipality of eight million people, in the 19th century **Tianjin** (133km) was a port city which attracted the interest of almost every European nation that had a ship to put to sea. The evidence is in the fact that Tianjin is now a living museum of early 20th century European architecture. It also possesses one of the cleanest and most modern train stations in China. There is a 15 minute halt, the last decent one before **Beijing** (0km).

The BAM

When compared with the famed Trans-Siberian and the chain of historic settlements it connects, the BAM doesn't seem to offer much. Other than a beautiful switchback route through the lake-filled mountains between Bratsk and Severobaikalsk, the scenery on the 3000km route is bleak and foreboding. It hasn't been improved by the intervention of humans, either. Almost without exception, all the towns along the BAM have grown up in the last 40 or 50 years – not a period that is ever likely to be regarded as a golden age of Russian architecture.

The possible attraction of the BAM is that it is virtually virgin territory: you're travelling across a part of Siberia that few other foreigners have ever seen. While not particularly absorbing in themselves, the towns along the line can serve as bases for exploration of the surrounding wilderness, and there are good opportunities for adventure tourism.

From its junction with the Trans-Siberian at Tayshet, the principal towns of the BAM are Bratsk, Severobaikalsk, Tynda and Komsomolsk-on-Amur. From Tynda, a short stretch of the Yakutia Railway (which was to connect Yakutsk to the BAM) runs north, but at present the line is only in use as far as Aldan. From Komsomolsk, a line also extends farther east to Sovietskaya Gavan on the Pacific coast.

BAM services include a direct Moscow-Tynda express which goes every other day, alternating with the Novosibirsk-Neryungri service. Every other day, the Moscow-Lena service connects Moscow with Ust-Kut, a city on the Lena River. There's also a Krasnoyarsk-Severobaikalsk train every other day and one or two other services to Severobaikalsk from Irkutsk via Tayshet.

BREAKING YOUR JOURNEY

Mainly due to Soviet-era restrictions, stopovers have traditionally only been made at Irkutsk and Ulaan Baatar. But now that visitors are more or less free to travel around at will, there's no reason why other towns and cities shouldn't be visited. Of the big western Siberian cities, Yekaterinburg has historic associations with the end of the Romanov dynasty, and Krasnoyarsk is well worth visiting. Of the eastern Siberian stops, Irkutsk deserves at least a few days for exploring Decembrist homes, churches, the Merchant Yard and historic, scenic sites on the way to Lake Baikal. Severobaikalsk on the BAM is a good place to enjoy the unsullied shores of Baikal, and Ulan Ude's fascinating Buryat Buddhist heritage makes it an essential stopover. Farther along the Trans-Siberian route, Khabarovsk and Vladivostok each deserve a couple of days stop.

However, no such thing as a stopover ticket exists. If you are travelling from Moscow to Beijing, and plan on spending a night or two in Irkutsk and Ulaan Baatar, you'll need three separate tickets: one for Moscow-Irkutsk, another for Irkutsk-Ulaan Baatar and a third for Ulaan Baatar-Beijing. The tickets will all be for a specific berth on a specific train on a specified day. Generally, ticket offices can only sell berths on trains leaving from that particular station – so the Irkutsk-Ulaan Baatar ticket would have to be bought in Irkutsk and the Ulaan Baatar-Beijing ticket in Ulaan Baatar – but you can also go through an agency which will be able to make all bookings in advance. For anyone flexible, independent rail travel within Russia is easy enough, and tickets for the Moscow-Vladivostok route in particular are rarely hard to get. In addition to the long-distance services, there are many daily short-haul trains on which it should be possible to get a berth without advance booking.

On the other hand, tickets to Russian or Chinese destinations are rarely easy to get in Ulaan Baatar without the help of a local tourist agent or government official. On the Trans-Manchurian route, Shanhaiguan and Tianjin are worth a couple of days stopover, and getting off at either of these cities shouldn't be a problem as they are both relatively close to Beijing and connected by frequent daily services.

All Russian train stations have prominent and reasonably decipherable timetables (see the European Russia Getting Around chapter for more information on timetables). Some larger cities have foreigners ticketing desks.

Ulaan Baatar

Visas & Embassies Visa extensions are easy to obtain at the Ministry of External Relations. Any foreigner staying in Mongolia for more than 30 days must register at the Police Registration Office in Ulaan Baatar. For more information, see the Visas entry later in the Booking section.

Tourist Information Ulaan Baatar lacks a central tourist information centre. The *Ulaan Baatar Guide*, available free around town and distributed at the airport and railway, is the best source of information. The Biz Info Centre is a travel agency, booking agency and Internet centre and can be found in the International Trade Centre.

Money The local currency is the *tögrög*. The best currency to exchange, and which may also be required for some transactions, is US dollars (cash or travellers cheques). Cash advances (in US dollars or togrogs) are available at the Trade & Development Bank (the large, modern building on the corner of Khudaldaany Gudamj and Baga Toiruu) with Visa, MasterCard and Amex cards. Chinese yuan and Russian roubles can be bought and sold at the relevant borders, and at major banks in Ulaan Baatar.

Things to See Everyone should visit the Museum of Natural History, Zanabazar Museum of Fine Arts and National Museum of Mongolian History, all within the city centre. Also worthwhile are the Winter Palace of Bogd Khaan, Gandantegchinlen (Gandan) Khiid monastery and the Monastery-Museum of Choijin Lama. And don't miss a performance of traditional music and dance at the National Academic Drama Theatre.

Places to Stay & Eat Hotel touts usually linger at the station when international trains arrive, and offer rooms in budget hotels and private homes.

UB Station Hotel *(☎ 744 169)*, next to the train station, is noisy but has decent rooms with bathroom from T13,200. ***Mandukhai Hotel*** *(☎ 322 204, Enkh Taivny Örgön Chölöö)* has dorm beds for about T5500 per person, and comfortable rooms for about T10,000 – all with shared bathroom. ***Gegee Hotel*** *(☎ 455 285)*, just off Zaluuchuudyn Örgön Chölöö, has decent rooms with bathroom for T9000 per person.

For decent, cheap food try the ***Elephant Restaurant*** *(Enkh Taivny Örgön Chölöö)* or ***Dulgunuur Tuya Restaurant***, behind the State Department Store on the same road. Western food is available at upmarket hotels such as the ***Ulaan Baatar*** and ***Bayangol*** hotels.

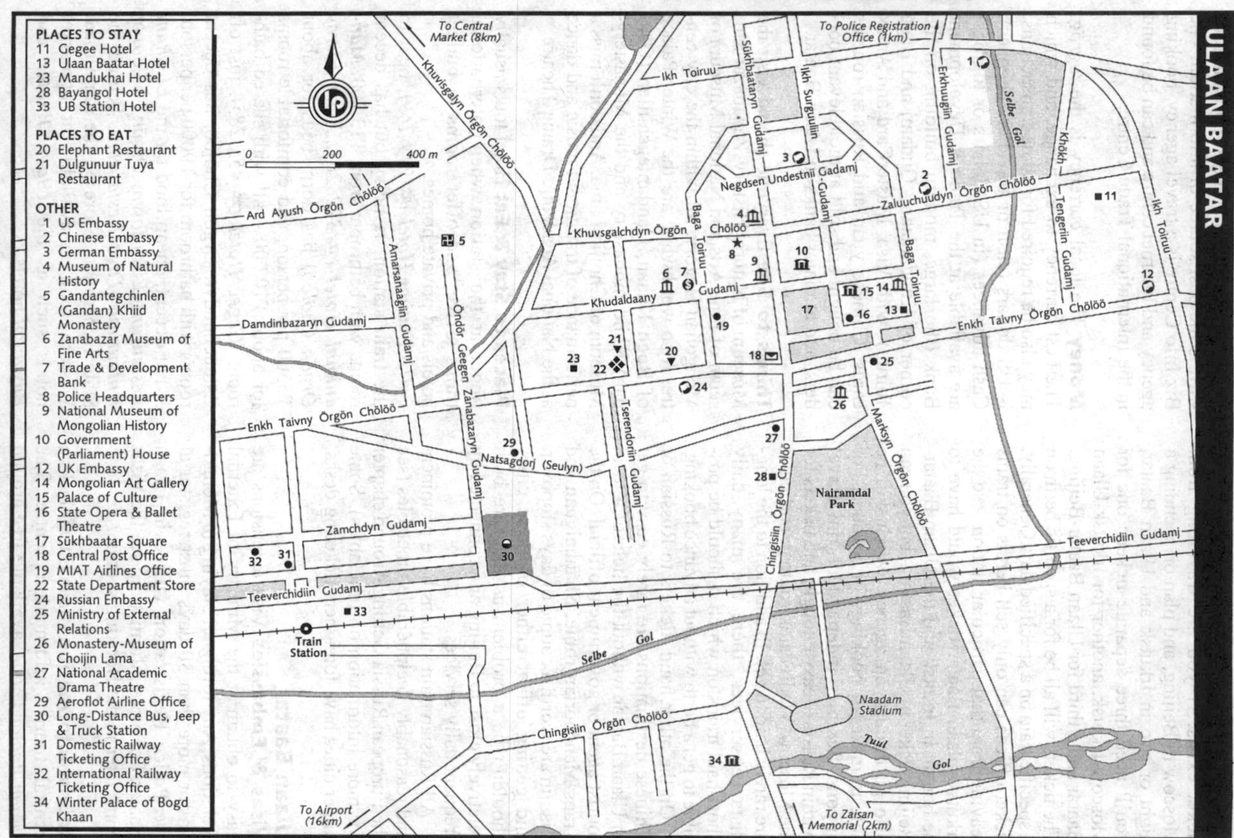
ULAAN BAATAR
PLACES TO STAY
11 Gegee Hotel
13 Ulaan Baatar Hotel
23 Mandukhai Hotel
28 Bayangol Hotel
33 UB Station Hotel
PLACES TO EAT
20 Elephant Restaurant
21 Dulguunuur Tuya Restaurant
OTHER
1 US Embassy
2 Chinese Embassy
3 German Embassy
4 Museum of Natural History
5 Gandantegchinlen (Gandan) Khiid Monastery
6 Zanabazar Museum of Fine Arts
7 Trade & Development Bank
8 Police Headquarters
9 National Museum of Mongolian History
10 Government (Parliament) House
12 UK Embassy
14 Mongolian Art Gallery
15 Palace of Culture
16 State Opera & Ballet Theatre
17 Sükhbaatar Square
18 Central Post Office
19 MIAT Airlines Office
22 State Department Store
24 Russian Embassy
25 Ministry of External Relations
26 Monastery-Museum of Choijin Lama
27 National Academic Drama Theatre
29 Aeroflot Airline Office
30 Long-Distance Bus, Jeep & Truck Station
31 Domestic Railway Ticketing Office
32 International Railway Ticketing Office
34 Winter Palace of Bogd Khaan
0 200 400 m
To Central Market (8km)
Khuvisgalyn Örgön Chölöö
To Police Registration Office (1km)
Ikh Toiruu
Sükhbaataryn Gudamj
Ikh Surguuliin Gudamj
Erkhuugiin Gudamj
Selbe Gol
Khökh Tengeriin Gudamj
Negdsen Undestnii Gadamj
Zaluuchuudyn Örgön Chölöö
Ard Ayush Örgön Chölöö
Khuvsgalchdyn Örgön Chölöö
Baga Toiruu
Amarsanaagiin Gudamj
Öndör Geegen Zanabazaryn Gudamj
Khudaldaany Gudamj
Damdinbazaryn Gudamj
Enkh Taivny Örgön Chölöö
Tserendoriin Gudamj
Natsagdorj (Seulyn)
Marksyn Örgön Chölöö
Chingisiin Örgön Chölöö
Nairamdal Park
Zamchdyn Gudamj
Teeverchidiin Gudamj
Train Station
Naadam Stadium
Tuul Gol
To Airport (16km)
To Zaisan Memorial (2km)

Getting Around From the train station, it's about 20 minutes walk to the city centre, or take a taxi. The train station has a restaurant, post office, left-luggage counter and food shops. There should also be some moneychangers.

International train tickets are available at the International Railway Ticketing Office. Tickets on international trains originating in Ulaan Baatar can be bought up to 10 days in advance, but only on the day before departure for trains between Moscow and Beijing (or vice versa). Discounts of about 20% are possible with an International Student Card.

Bus Nos 11 and 22 link the Ulaan Baatar airport with the town centre, but it's best to take a taxi.

Beijing

Visas & Embassies For information, see the Visas entry later in the Booking section.

Tourist Information The main branch of China International Travel Service (CITS) is at the Beijing Tourist Building (☎ 010-6515-8844 ext 2110, fax 6515-8260) at 28 Jianguomenwai Dajie, next to the Gloria Plaza Hotel and near Scitech Plaza. You can buy tickets for the Trans-Manchurian and Trans-Mongolian here; but it's best to call ahead to check that tickets are available.

Money Chinese currency is known as Renminbi, or 'People's Money', colloquially referred to as kuai (symbolised by 'Y'). You can withdraw money from ATMs with GlobalAccess, Cirrus, Interlink, Plus, Star, Accel, The Exchange and Explore, as well as Visa, MasterCard and American Express at the CITIC building, Scitech Plaza, Palace Hotel, Sun Dong An Plaza in Wangfujing Dajie, Capital airport and some Bank of China branches. Credit card cash advances are fairly routine at Bank of China head branches. If you have an American Express card and a bank account in US dollars, you can write a personal cheque and receive US dollars at the bank in the CITIC building.

Things to See Beijing has a number of tourist attractions worth checking out if you're stopping over for a few days. At least try to visit the Forbidden City, which was home to emperors of the Ming and Qing dynasties. Other worthwhile sights include the Natural History Museum, Tiananmen Square, Tiantan Park, plus the Lama Temple and the Confucius Temple & Imperial College.

Places to Stay & Eat The ***Jinghua Youth Hostel*** *(☎ 010-6722-2211)* is in vogue with backpackers. Dorm beds in a newly constructed wing behind the main building cost Y35 in a four-bed room. Twin rooms are Y140. Bus Nos 2 and 17 from Qianmen drop you off nearby. The hotel also has an email centre, bar and travel agent. The official address is Xiluoyuan Nanli, Yong-dingmenwai, Fengtai District, 100077 (southern part of the third ring road).

A decent budget option in the centre of the city is the ***Gong Ti Hotel*** *(☎ 010-6501-6655)*, which is located in the east side of Worker's Stadium. Doubles with shared bath start at Y140.

If you want to try that great delicacy, Beijing duck, head to ***Qianmen Quanjude Roast Duck Restaurant*** *(32 Qianmen Dajie)*, one of the oldest restaurants in the capital, dating back to 1864.

Confucian Heritage Restaurant *(3 Liulichangxi Jie)* serves the food of Shandong Province, similar to Beijing food but with more emphasis on seafood and vegetables. It has fairly long opening hours (10.30 am to 2 pm and 5.30 to 11 pm).

Another good bet for vegetarians is the brilliant ***Gongdelin Vegetarian Restaurant*** *(158 Qianmenan Dajie)*. The ***Asian Star Restaurant***, east of the Workers' Stadium on the third ring road, serves dishes from Malaysia, Singapore and India.

Getting Around The Trans-Mongolian and Trans-Manchurian trains both depart from Beijing main train station, south-east of the Forbidden City. You can get to/from the train station by subway, operating from 5.30 am to 10.30 pm. The fare is a flat Y2.

A taxi from Beijing train station to the Jinghua Youth Hostel or to the Sanlitun

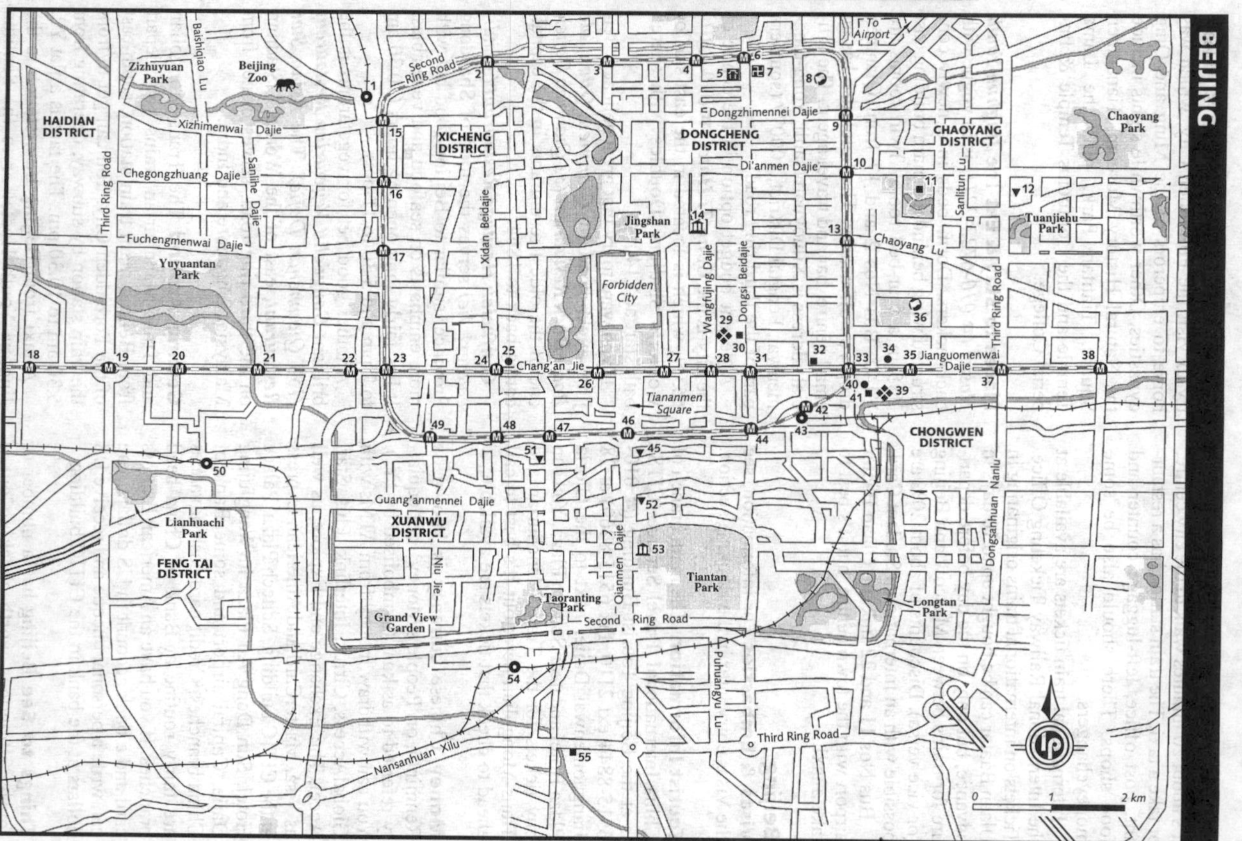
BEIJING
To Airport
Second Ring Road
Zizhuyuan Park
Baishiqiao Lu
Beijing Zoo
HAIDIAN DISTRICT
Xizhimenwai Dajie
XICHENG DISTRICT
Dongzhimennei Dajie
DONGCHENG DISTRICT
CHAOYANG DISTRICT
Chaoyang Park
Third Ring Road
Chegongzhuang Dajie
Sanlihe Dajie
Di'anmen Dajie
Sanlitun Lu
Tuanjiehu Park
Jingshan Park
Xidan Beidajie
Fuchengmenwai Dajie
Chaoyang Lu
Yuyuantan Park
Forbidden City
Wangfujing Dajie
Dongsi Beidajie
Chang'an Jie
Jianguomenwai Dajie
Tiananmen Square
CHONGWEN DISTRICT
Guang'anmennei Dajie
Lianhuachi Park
XUANWU DISTRICT
Dongsanhuan Nanlu
FENG TAI DISTRICT
Niu Jie
Qianmen Dajie
Tiantan Park
Taoranting Park
Longtan Park
Grand View Garden
Second Ring Road
Puhuangyu Lu
Third Ring Road
Nansanhuan Xilu
0
1
2 km

BEIJING

PLACES TO STAY
11 Gong Ti Hotel & Worker's Stadium
30 Palace Hotel
32 International Hotel
40 Gloria Plaza Hotel
55 Jinghua Youth Hostel

PLACES TO EAT
12 Asian Star Restaurant
45 Qianmen Quanjude Roast Duck Restaurant
51 Confucian Heritage Restaurant
52 Gongdelin Vegetarian Restaurant

METRO STATIONS
2 Jishuitan
3 Gulou
4 Andingmen
6 Yonghegong
9 Dongzhimen
10 Dongsishitiao
13 Chaoyangmen
15 Xizhimen
16 Chegongzhuang
17 Fuchengmen
18 Wanshoulu
19 Gongzhufen
20 Junshibowuguan
21 Muxidi
22 Nanlishilu
23 Fuxingmen
24 Xidan
26 Tiananmen Xi
27 Tiananmen Dong
28 Wangfujing
31 Dong Dan
33 Jianguomen
35 Yong An Li
37 Guo Mao
38 Da Wang Ziao
42 Beijing Zhan
44 Chongwenmen
46 Qianmen
47 Hepingmen
48 Xuanwumen
49 Changchunjie

OTHER
1 Beijing North (Xizhimen) Train Station
5 Confucius Temple & Imperial College
7 Lama Temple
8 Russian Embassy
14 China Art Gallery
25 Aviation Building (CAAC & Airport Bus)
29 Sun Dong An Plaza
34 CITIC Building & Friendship Store
36 Mongolian Embassy
39 Scitech Plaza
41 CITS & Beijing Tourist Building
43 Beijing Train Station
50 Beijing West Train Station
53 Natural History Museum
54 Beijing South (Yongdingmen) Train Station

area (Gong Ti Hotel) should be less than Y20; beware of taxi drivers who won't use their meter.

The airport is 27km from the Forbidden City. You can catch buses (Y16) to the airport from the International Hotel or from Xidan near the CAAC office. Buses leave every half-hour.

Inside the airport terminal is a service desk that sells tickets for buses (Y16) into town – somebody outside can direct you to the right bus. Buses leave every half-hour between 5.30 am and 7 pm, and include routes to Beijing train station, Xidan, close to the CAAC office west of the Forbidden City, and to the China Art Gallery north of Wangfujing Dajie.

A taxi (using its meter) should cost only about Y85 from the airport to the centre (including the Y10 road toll).

BOOKING

When to Go

See the Siberia & the Russian Far East Facts for the Visitor chapter for general climatic considerations. Ticket prices are the same year-round, but off-season travel agency packages may be discounted. Summer tickets for the Trans-Manchurian and Trans-Mongolian must be booked further ahead – allow a couple of months.

Classes of Travel

The standard accommodation on all long-distance, Trans-Siberian-related trains is in 2nd class *kupeyny* carriages. These carriages are divided into nine enclosed compartments, each with four reasonably comfortable berths, a fold-down table and just enough room between the bunks to turn around. On the Chinese train, 1st class *myagky* has softer beds but hardly any more space than 2nd class and is not worth the considerably higher fare. The real luxury comes with Chinese deluxe class: roomy, wood-panelled two-berth compartments with a sofa, and a shower cubicle shared with the adjacent compartment.

First class compartments on the Russian train are the same as 2nd class, except that because there are only two berths you'll have more room and more privacy, for double the cost. First class also has a slight advantage in that there are only half as many people queuing to use the toilet every morning. Other than in the deluxe class on the Chinese train, there are no showers in any category.

CLINT CURÉ

Another (lower) category of accommodation, not available on the Trans-Manchurian and Trans-Mongolian but common to all other trains in Russia, is *platskartny*. This is essentially an uncompartmentalised dormitory carriage with hard bunks that are slightly shorter than standard. Privacy is out of the question; instead of the usual maximum of three fellow travellers, you will have in effect close to 60 inquisitive companions. The scene often resembles a refugee camp, with clothing strung between bunks, a great swapping of bread, fish and jars of tea, and babies sitting on potties while their snot-nosed siblings tear up and down the corridor. That said, many travellers (women in particular) find this a better option than being cooped up with three drunken Russian men. Platskartny tickets cost half to two-thirds the price of a 2nd class berth.

Costs

In the past, the Trans-Siberian routes represented one of the cheapest ways of travelling one-third of the way around the world. But these days, with airline companies in desperate competition and slashing prices, that's no longer the case. The standard foreigner price of a Moscow-Beijing ticket is $170 for 2nd class on the Trans-Mongolian, and $191 on the Trans-Manchurian route. From Moscow to Vladivostok it's $400. A two-tier price system is often in operation and Russians sometimes pay around half these fares. While it is possible for you to get a Russian colleague to buy your ticket at the lower price, on long journeys the ticket will be checked; it's illegal for a foreigner to travel on a Russian-priced ticket, and if you are caught you're likely to be fined or threatened with being thrown off the train.

The price of the train ticket is only one expense. The other major dent in your budget is likely to be made by the cost of getting to the train's departure point and then home again at the end of the ride. In all likelihood, this will involve a flight or train to Moscow, and then a return journey from Beijing or Vladivostok (or vice versa). The number of stopovers you make should also figure in your accounting, as hotel rates in Russia are comparatively high. Depending on the level of comfort that you require, you can expect to be spending on average $30 to $50 on accommodation per night. Considering this expense, some of the packages offered by travel agencies may turn out to be good deals.

Visas

Trans-Siberian travellers will need a Russian visa of some sort, and also perhaps Chinese and Mongolian visas, depending on the route. It's safer to obtain all visas in your home country before setting out. Some tour companies arrange your visas as part of their Trans-Siberian package. Bear in mind, if you are also travelling through Belarus, Ukraine or the Baltic States, you may also need visas for some of those countries.

Russian Your safest bet when applying for a Russian visa is to think of each Russian consulate and embassy as its own fiefdom with its own set of rules, which may or may not correspond to those of the Russian border guard you eventually show your visa to. For instance, you may think when you leave the embassy that you have a Russian transit visa for 10 days (sufficient for a Moscow-Beijing trip) and then discover that the border guard tries to fine you because Russian transit visas are usually good for only three days. To try to minimise these problems, bring every official-looking document you own with you: this includes every piece of paper you gave to and received from the embassy, any vouchers from your tour company and anything else on fancy letterhead and stamped. If you're really worrying about border crossings, go on a guided tour and let the guide handle the guards.

If you pick up your Russian transit visa in China, it will usually give you three or four days in Moscow at the end of your journey. In Beijing, the Russian embassy (☎ 010-6532-2051, visa section ☎ 6532-1267) is at 4 Dongzhimennei Beizhongjie, just off Dongzhimennei Dajie. A transit or tourist visa ($50) takes one week to process; $80 for one to two day express service; or $120 for one hour service. There is a consular fee on top of the standard processing charge that varies dramatically with citizenship. You will need three photos, your passport and the exact money in dollars. For a transit visa, you will also need a valid entry visa for a third country plus a through ticket from Russia to the third country. Consular hours are Monday to Friday from 9 to 11.30 am.

In Ulaan Baatar, the Russian embassy (☎ 326 037, fax 327 018) is at Enkh Taivny Örgön Chölöö. Visas take about two days to process, and sponsors/invitations from within Russia are required. The consular section is open Monday, Wednesday and Friday from 9.30 am to 12.30 pm and 2.30 to 5.30 pm.

Mongolian If you are travelling on the Trans-Mongolian train, you will need some kind of Mongolian visa. These come in two forms: transit or tourist. A transit visa (valid for seven days) is easy enough to get (just present a through-ticket and a visa for your onward destination). Obtaining a tourist visa (usually issued for two weeks) involves the same bureaucratic somersaults as required for a Russian tourist visa, though some readers have reported obtaining visas in Irkutsk and Beijing without an invitation or prepaid hotel vouchers. (See the Consulates section in the Siberia & the Russian Far East Facts for the Visitor chapter for more information.) The visa situation changes regularly, so check with a Mongolian embassy or consulate. Currently, a 30 day tourist visa can be obtained at the airport in Ulaan Baatar only if you fly in from a country without a Mongolian embassy or consulate. Everyone else must have a visa prior to arrival. Tourist visas can be extended in Ulaan Baatar at the Ministry of Foreign Affairs at the junction of Marx and Peace Aves.

In Moscow, the Mongolian embassy (☎ 095-244 78 67) is at Spasopeskovsky pereulok 7, close to the Smolenskaya metro. It's open from 9 am to 12.30 pm and 2 to 5 pm Monday to Friday. Transit visas can be collected the same day between 4.30 and 5 pm.

In Beijing, the Mongolian embassy (☎ 010-6532-1203) is at 2 Xiushui Beilu, Jianguomenwai. The visa section is open Monday to Friday from 9 to 11.30 am and 2 to 3.30 pm.

A transit visa generally costs $30 and takes three days to issue; $60 for same-day or next-day service. Tourist visas are $40; $60 for express service. Visas are free for Finnish and Indian nationals. All Mongolian embassies shut down for the week of National Day (Naadam), which officially falls around 11 to 13 July.

Chinese Visas for individual travel in China are easy to get, though the queues and confusion at the Chinese embassy (☎ 095-143 15 40) in Moscow, at ulitsa Druzhby 6, near the Universitet metro, make this far from the best place to apply. The embassy is open from 9 am to noon Monday, Wednesday and Friday. The consulate (☎ 812-113 76 05) in St Petersburg is a better bet; it's open from 9 am to 12.30 pm Monday, Wednesday and Friday and is at naberezhnaya kanala Griboedova 134. There's also a Chinese consulate in Khabarovsk (see the Siberia & Russian Far East Facts for the Visitor chapter).

In Ulaan Baatar, the Chinese embassy (☎ 320 955, fax 311 943) is at 5 Zaluuchuudyn Örgön Chölöö. The consular section is open from 9.30 am to 12.30 pm Monday, Wednesday and Friday.

Transit visas are valid for seven days, and a standard single-entry tourist visa is usually valid for a period of one or two months and costs $70. If you want more time, ask and you may be given it; if not, it is quite easy to get visa extensions in most major cities in China.

TRANS-SIBERIAN RAILWAY

Getting to/from the Train

If you are picking up the train in Moscow, see the European Russia Getting There & Away and Moscow chapters for travel options and costs. If you are starting in Vladivostok, see the Vladivostok section in the Russian Far East chapter. See also the Siberia & the Russian Far East Getting There & Away chapter for further options.

To connect with the Trans-Manchurian or Trans-Mongolian trains at their eastern terminal, you should look into flights to Hong Kong. These are often cheaper than flying to Beijing, and connections between the two cities are straightforward.

Independent Travel

Once you get over the initial shock of Yaroslavl Station with its four or five ticket offices and Siberian-long queues, doing a Trans-Sib trip independently is easy. In Moscow, the best place currently to purchase a ticket is in the building with tinted windows next to Yaroslavl Station, to the right of the Lenin statue. The *kassa* (ticket office) is on the ground level. In Vladivostok and other major cities make sure you don't get in the line for *prigorodnye poezda* (local trains). Also, you might get dirty looks if you queue up at the kassa reserved for military. You'll know by the uniforms.

If the lines are long, you'll notice Russians saving places, going out for lunch or to shop, then jumping back in line just in time to get their ticket. You could try to do the same, but queuing is an art in Russia and you'll probably end up losing your place. Also discouraging is getting to the head of the line, to have the cashier slam the window in your face. Check the time schedules pasted in the window before getting in line. If the line is suspiciously short, it's probably because the cashier is due to go on break.

Another annoyance is being sent to a special foreigners kassa. These kassa are gradually disappearing, but if you're sent to one, expect to pay more. The trade-off is that the wait is shorter. If you're really determined to go native, you could try just standing in a different line and trying your luck with another cashier, or attempting to buy a ticket from the conductor on the platform, or enlisting the help of a sympathetic local. Whatever you do, don't let your passport or your money out of sight. And beware of buying tickets from third parties on the platform; most likely you'll be ripped off.

Once you get to the head of the line, tell the cashier your destination, what train you want, the date and class of travel. The cashier will also need your name and passport number, and to see your passport and visa. If you don't speak Russian, just write it all out. You may run into trouble if you try to buy a ticket for a destination not listed on your visa. You then have two choices: try a different kassa, or pick a new destination.

The ticket you'll be issued will be straightforward to read. From left to right will be the train number, date, month, hour and minute of departure, the carriage number and type (k for kupeyny). On the next line is the city of departure and the destination; beneath that the berth number. Your name, the price you paid and the time and date of arrival will be below that.

You'll be able to board anywhere from an hour to 20 minutes before departure. The conductor will probably check your ticket against your passport. If they grumble, they're probably looking for a bribe. Ask to see the *brigadir poezda* (train inspector).

Travel Agencies

Most travel agencies have their hands tied by Russian visa regulations, and if you're buying a Trans-Siberian ticket from them, to get the Russian visa you also have to preplan and book all accommodation and other transport. The simplest way around this is to employ the services of one of the small, independent travel companies that are registered in Russia and can issue their own invitations (a system known as visa support – see the European Russia Facts for the Visitor chapter for further details). These companies usually require that you also make use of their services, either buying train tickets or booking a couple of nights accommodation with them, but it's a fairly small price to pay for complete freedom from fixed itineraries.

It is important to note that most tour packages do not include your flights to/from the train – only your ticket, stopover accommodation, transfers and city tours and guides.

From Australasia Gateway Travel (☎ 02-9745 3333, fax 9745 3237, www.russian-gateway.com.au), 48 The Boulevarde, Strathfield, NSW 2135, Australia, offers 2nd class through-tickets on the Trans-Manchurian, Trans-Mongolian and Trans-Siberian routes for A$460, A$460 and A$1020 respectively, as well as some stopover packages.

Sundowners (☎ 03-9600 1934, fax 9642 5838), Suite 15, 600 Lonsdale St, Melbourne, Vic 3000, offers 16 to 30-day package tours on all four rail routes, as well as unescorted packages with stopovers.

The New Zealand-based operator Suntravel (☎ 09-525 3074, fax 525 3065, suntravel@suntravl.com), 407 Great South Rd, Penrose, Auckland, has 'basic express packages'. A 17 day trip from Beijing to St Petersburg, with stays along the way, costs either NZ$2573 on the Trans-Mongolian or NZ$2299 on the Trans-Manchurian. A 16 day package on the Turkestan-Siberian Railway is NZ$2086. The agency can also book straight-through tickets for NZ$868/850/1452 for the Trans-Mongolian/Trans-Manchurian/Trans-Siberian.

From Canada Exotik Tours (☎ 514-284 3324, fax 843 5493, exotiktours@exotiktours.com), 1117 Ste-Catherine O, Suite 806, Montreal, Quebec H3B 1H9, offers two nine and eight-day Moscow-Beijing packages on the Trans-Mongolian ($600) and Trans-Manchurian ($680) routes.

From Germany Lernidee Reisen (☎ 030-786 5056, fax 786 5596), Duden Strasse 78, 10965 Berlin, sells 2nd class tickets: Beijing-Moscow (DM775), Moscow-Beijing (DM735), Beijing-Ulaan Baatar (DM335), Ulaan Baatar-Beijing (DM295), Ulaan Baatar-Moscow (DM540) and Moscow-Ulaan Baatar (DM585).

Deutsches Reiseburo (☎ 069-95 8800), Emil-von-Behring Strasse 6, 6000 Frankfurt am Main 50, offers several Trans-Siberian tours, including a 15 day Moscow-Irkutsk-Khabarovsk package, returning to Moscow by air, starting from DM2645; a 16 day Moscow-Irkutsk-Ulaan Baatar-Gobi Desert package, returning to Moscow by air, for DM4395; and several tours mixing Trans-Siberian destinations with Central Asia in the DM3000 to DM4000 range. All prices include a return Germany-Moscow flight.

Travel Service Asia (☎ 7351-37 3210, fax 37 3211, TSA-Reisen@t-online.de, www.travel-service-asia.de), Schmelzweg 10, 88400 Biberach/Riss, offers package tours on the Trans-Siberian, Trans-Mongolian and Trans-Manchurian routes. A 14 day trip from Moscow via Irkutsk, Ulaan Baatar and Beijing, with two nights in Moscow, two nights in Irkutsk and two nights in Ulaan Baatar, costs DM1730. It also does Moscow-Irkutsk-Vladivostok-Japan trips for DM2850. Prices exclude air fares.

From Hong Kong & China Try Moonsky Star (also known as Monkey Business; ☎ 852-2723 1376, fax 2723 6653, MonkeyHK@compuserve.com), Flat 6, 4th floor, E-block, Chungking Mansions, 36-44 Nathan Rd, Tsim Sha Tsui, Kowloon, Hong Kong, or (☎ 8610-6356 2126, fax 6356 2127, MonkeyChina@compuserve.com), Capital Forbidden City Hotel, 48 Guanganmen Nanjie, South Building, 3rd floor, Xuanwu District, 100054 Beijing, China. The company has a lot of experience in booking Trans-Siberian trains for independent travellers. However, we've heard complaints of poor organisation, indifferent service and, in particular, inflated prices. The basic, 2nd class nonstop ticket from Beijing to Moscow, including the first night in Moscow, is $430 on the Trans-Manchurian or $395 on the Trans-Mongolian. With two-day stopovers at Lake Baikal and in Ulaan Baatar, it's $800.

Other ticket agencies in Hong Kong worth trying include Time Travel (☎ 852-2366 6222, fax 2739 5413), Block A, 16th floor, Chungking Mansions, 40 Nathan Rd, Tsim Sha Tsui, Kowloon. In Beijing, the alternative to Monkey Business is the China International Travel Service (CITS; ☎ 010-6515-8844 ext 2110, fax 6515-8260).

From Russia The Travellers Guesthouse/IRO Travel (☎ 095-971 4059, ☎ 280 8562, fax 280 7686, tgh@glasnet.ru), ulitsa Bolshaya Pereyaslavskaya 50, 10th floor, Moscow 129401, sells Trans-Mongolian tickets for Moscow-Beijing for $200, plus $20 for each stopover. Along the route, it also offers homestays in Russia and hostels in Mongolia for $15 to $25 a night.

Baikalcomplex (☎/fax 3952-38 9205, ☎/fax 43 2060, youry@travel.baikal.ru), PO Box 3598, Irkutsk 664074, offers reasonably priced tours and homestays along both the Trans-Sib and BAM railways.

From the UK The China Travel Service (☎ 020-7836 9911, fax 7836 3121, CTS@ctsuk.com), 7 Upper St Martins Lane, London WC2H 9DL, sells tickets on all routes with meals and two days lodging at the start and end of the journey for £170 to £492, depending on route, class and time of travel.

Intourist Travel (☎ 020-7538 8600, fax 7538 5967, www.intourus.demon.co.uk), Intourist House, 219 Marsh Wall, London E14 9PD, offers 2nd class Moscow-Vladivostok tickets for £405, and Trans-Manchurian and Trans Mongolian packages from £566 to £731.

Steppes East (☎ 01285-81 0267, fax 81 0693, www.steppeseast.co.uk), Castle Eaton, Swindon, Wiltshire SN6 6JU, has 13-day, individually tailored Trans-Mongolian packages for about £930.

From the USA White Nights (☎/fax 916-979 9381, wnights@concourse.net), 610 Sierra Drive, Sacramento, CA 95864, offers Moscow-Beijing tickets from $311 and Moscow-Vladivostok from $582. It also offers visa support.

WHAT TO BRING

The list of travelling essentials for a Trans-Siberian jaunt doesn't differ too much from that given in this book's Facts for the Visitor chapters, except perhaps that even greater stress should be given to bringing toilet paper. Also bring your own plug for the toilet sink, some soft, slip-on footwear like thongs (flip-flops) or Chinese cloth sandals, and loose, comfortable pants like tracksuit or shell-suit trousers. You won't need a sleeping bag, but you might want to take your own lightweight sheet because the bedding handed out on the trains is often still damp from laundering.

Boiling water is always available from a samovar at the end of each carriage, so take a plastic mug and a teaspoon (although if you forget, the *provodnitsa* has beakers), along with sachets of instant coffee or soup, hot chocolate, tea bags (sugar and creamer too, if needed). There's a dining car attached to most long-distance trains, and at every station halt you'll find clusters of kiosks and locals selling home produce, so it isn't necessary to bring too much in the way of food. Juice or water in a plastic bottle is a good idea.

How many books, games and other distractions you take along depends on whether you're travelling alone or with companions. A couple of light paperbacks should see you through, as there's plenty en route to keep you occupied. Cards or chess are a good idea both for entertainment and for breaking the ice with non-English speakers you meet.

Baggage Space If you're sensible you'll travel light, in which case you'll have no problems storing your luggage in your compartment. There is a luggage bin underneath each of the lower berths (50cm wide, 40cm high, 110cm long) and also enough space beside the bin to squeeze in another medium-sized canvas bag. Above the doorway there's a coffin-like space 160cm long, 67cm wide and 30cm high, which at a push, kick and shove will accommodate a couple of rucksacks.

There are no baggage restrictions travelling from the Moscow end, but in Beijing there is an enforced 35kg allowance. Passengers with excess baggage are supposed to present it (along with passport, ticket and customs entry declaration) the day before departure at the Luggage Shipment Office, which is on the right-hand side of the main train station in Beijing. The excess is charged at about $11 per 10kg, with a maximum excess of 40kg allowed.

THE JOURNEY

Travellers respond in different ways to being sealed in a vaguely claustrophobic carriage with a crowd of strangers for six or more days, looking out at a landscape that hardly changes, with ambiguously shifting time zones and nothing insistent but hunger and bodily functions. Paul Theroux in *The Great Railway Bazaar* likened the Trans-Siberian trip to being in bed with a high fever, with each drowsy day broken into many smaller ones by naps and dreams. But not everybody is quite as saturnine, and for some the whole point of the trip is to have one nonstop rolling party with a menagerie of new friends and experiences.

Even before the suburbs of Moscow have disappeared, passengers have begun to make themselves at home. As Laurens van der Post noted in the 1970s, Russians just take the train over, moving into a carriage as though they were there for good. The compartments these days aren't quite as homely as they were when Van der Post travelled. Then, each was equipped with tumblers, biscuits, sugar lumps, a timetable and some reading matter – typically speeches by Lenin or Marx. Still, they're fairly snug and kept warm even in deepest winter by a coal-fired boiler in each carriage.

The biggest discomfort is the sanitary arrangements. There are two toilet/wash cubicles in each carriage; however, the one next to the provodnitsas' room is often kept locked for their own private use. That means 36 people have to make use of one toilet, and one stainless steel basin for the purposes of washing. The tap water is cold, but if you have a plug you can get a cupful of hot water from the samovar to mix with it. The toilets are cleaned every morning, but prolonged exposure to them can still damage your sense of smell. There is a shaving point (220V) in the toilet cubicle, but you must ask the provodnitsa to have the electricity switched on. There's a garbage bin under the triangular seat opposite the toilet door.

Smokers are relegated to areas just before the *tambury* (platforms) that link the carriages. The windows here are the only ones that aren't screwed shut. The rest usually stay sealed throughout the journey, although during summer the provodnitsa might be persuaded to open one or two in the corridor.

Time Zones

With potentially eight time zones to choose from when riding a Trans-Siberian train, it can get a little confusing. As Mary Morris wrote in her account of a Beijing-Moscow trip, *Wall to Wall*:

> No one on the train knew what time it was. Some people said the train travelled on Moscow time but operated on local time, if you can figure that out. But half the people were on Beijing time and one diplomat said he was on Tokyo time, which was the same for some reason as Ulaan Baatar time. Our Chinese porter changed his watch 15 minutes every few hours or so but this was a system of his own devising.

The train timetables are in Moscow time but meals and lights out – and of course everything outside – are on local time. Clocks are set progressively later the farther east you are, so when it's noon in Moscow it's 3 pm in Omsk, 5 pm in Irkutsk and 7 pm in Khabarovsk, giving rise to a gently disorienting 'train lag'. After a few days, your body clock quits in disgust.

Officially, China and Mongolia only have one time zone, five hours later than Moscow time. Local time is thus unchanged from Irkutsk to Beijing, except in late April or early May and again in September, when you may find a one hour shift at the border. This is because of differences in switching to daylight-saving time.

At most stations in Russia, there are two timetables displayed: one in Moscow time *(Moskovskoe vremya)* and the other in local time *(mestnoe vremya)*.

Attendants

Your provodnitsa (most of them are women), provodnik (the male variant) or *fuwuren* (the conductor on the Chinese train) may be the main thing you remember about your trip. Each carriage has two provodnitsas who work alternate shifts from their own compartment, cleaning, stoking the boiler,

TRANS-SIBERIAN RAILWAY

making tea, handing out new linen and keeping track of passengers at stops. Some are like mothers, *babushkas* with hearts of Siberian gold beneath Wagnerian exteriors, while the other common type are peroxided postadolescents who spend most of their time flirting with the waiter in the dining car. In summer, on shorter express runs (eg Moscow-Irkutsk), many are students on holiday. It can improve your journey greatly if you get on well with the provodnitsa: you might get a window opened, be allowed to use their private and usually better cared for toilet, or even be moved to an empty compartment if one comes up.

They're unlikely to accept tips but you might leave them a small gift at the end of your trip.

Travelling Companions

If your tickets came through a company that does a lot of Trans-Siberian business, it's likely you are going to be sharing a compartment with other travellers. However, these are working trains, not tourist specials, and you have a good chance of sharing a compartment with locals. Just as there is no segregation between foreigners and natives, neither is there any division of the sexes. Who you end up with is very much a lottery. With potentially six days together sharing a space the size of a port-a-loo, and exposed to the unmitigated smells, noises and eating habits of each other, much depends on your travelling companions. If it comes to the worst and you don't feel comfortable or safe with the people sharing your compartment, then your provodnitsa may be able to engineer an exchange.

Station Halts

These are welcome respites for fresh air and exercise and to see what kind of food and drink the platform traders have to sell. Toilets are locked during stops, and that can be a long time at the border. The 'pok pok' you hear is a maintenance worker testing the bogies with a little hammer.

Stops last from one to 25 minutes; durations are given on the timetable posted in each carriage. Check this out or ask the provodnitsa, because departure comes often without a whistle and the trains slip out almost soundlessly. Also be careful about crossing tracks. It's quite common for another train to pull in between the platform and your train, in which case you will have to climb through. Much worse is if the line between you and your train happens to be carrying a slow, 3km-long freight train just at departure time. If this happens, you'll most likely be put in a taxi to catch up, or perhaps your luggage will be off-loaded down the line for you to pick up as you continue your journey on another train.

Food & Drink

On a long-haul train, the dining car can easily become the main attraction, favoured more for its makeshift role as a social centre than for any gastronomic qualities. It becomes the place to meet, hang out, drink beer and play cards.

The dining cars are changed at each border, so en route to Beijing you get Russian, Chinese and possibly Mongolian versions. Occasionally, between the Russian border and Ulaan Baatar there is no dining car, so be prepared. Everyone agrees that the food and service are best in the Chinese dining car. There's no menu and no choice, but what you normally get is a number of stir-fried dishes with rice, and this set meal costs about $6. In the Russian and Mongolian cars, the food is basic and boring but adequate – typically, grilled chicken or cutlet and rice, *gulyash* and boiled potatoes and green or tomato salads – and costs around the equivalent of $4. On Russian services other than the main line *Rossia* and *Baikal Express*, prices can get even higher. You pay in roubles in the Russian car, RMB in the Chinese and dollars in the Mongolian.

Dining cars are open from approximately 9 am to 9 pm local time, making it a constant guessing game.

In the dining car there's often a table of pot noodles, chocolate, beer, juice and the like being peddled by the staff. The prices are overinflated, though, and there's nothing that isn't available from the kiosks at the station halts.

Platform Supplies Kiosks and freelance entrepreneurs (typically babushkas squatting on upturned buckets) can unpredictably be found on station platforms. Platform kiosks are stocked with the standard Russian goods – that is, Marlboro cigarettes, Absolut vodka and Snickers bars well past their sell-by date. From Irkutsk onwards, the main staple is Chinese pot noodles (add hot water from the carriage samovar).

More interesting are the babushkas, who have farm produce such as milk, ice cream, grilled chicken or boiled potatoes, home cooking such as *pelmeni* or *pirozhki* and, depending on the season, buckets of forest berries and smoked fish. Between Moscow and Vladivostok it's possible to eat perfectly well on supplies bought solely from the babushkas; however, in Mongolia there seems to be less on offer. There's little to be had along the BAM either, except in autumn when there are huge jars of fresh caviar for sale at amazingly low prices at the stations between Tynda and Komsomolsk.

Border Formalities

Border stops can take anything between one and six hours as customs officials go through the travelling warehouses that are the Chinese traders' compartments. For foreign travellers the procedure is uncomplicated: passports, visas and currency forms are examined, and baggage searches are rare (for this reason you may be approached by a trader and asked to carry their bag across the border – this is *not* a good idea). The Trans-Mongolian crossing at Naushki can be an exciting, vaudevillesque experience, but be careful. The Russian conductors may instruct you to lock your door and windows – as you pull into the station hundreds of Mongolians start climbing through the windows to sell *pozy* (meat-filled dumplings), drinks or the duds they just stole from your neighbour's cabin.

Depending on who your carriage companions are, you also may witness the games traders play to get out of paying duties. One Mongolian businessman with whom we were travelling distributed several hundred cartons of cigarettes throughout the entire train. Once the train had crossed the border, he went back through the train reclaiming his wares and returning the stockings, candy, vodka and other chattels he had taken in exchange from fellow traders.

While the customs formalities are being carried out, passengers are free to get off the train and wander up and down the platform. This is necessary because while the train is halted, the toilets on board are locked. There are banks at the border stations, and these represent the last chance to get rid of your roubles or RMB. You'll also need to change some money to use in the dining car, as they only accept the currency of the country they belong to.

At the Chinese-Mongolian and Chinese-Russian borders, about two hours are spent hoisting the train aloft so that its bogies can be changed (the old Soviet Union used a wider gauge of track than its neighbours). If you're riding the Trans-Mongolian and want to witness this odd operation, stay on the train when it disgorges its passengers at Erlian station, on the Chinese side of the China-Mongolia border. The train then pulls into a large shed 500m away. Get off before the staff lock the doors. It's OK to walk around and take photos, then stroll back down the line to the station.

Safety

Despite the circulation of stories about people being drugged and gassed on the Trans-Siberian, safety on the rails isn't something to fret over. Common sense applies. Don't leave valuables lying about, and don't leave hand baggage unattended in a compartment during a station halt. The least safe places are those with the greatest exposure to foreign visitors: Moscow, Irkutsk, Ulaan Baatar and Beijing. A few years ago the train connecting these four cities, the Trans-Mongolian, had a bad reputation, but militia now ride the trains and matters have improved. For added safety, lock your cabins from the inside and make use of the security clip on the upper left-hand part of the door (the clip can be flipped open from the outside with a knife, but not if you stuff the hole with paper).

SIBERIA & THE RUSSIAN FAR EAST

Facts about Siberia & the Russian Far East

Gulags, snowbound exile, frozen corpses – for most foreigners the images conjured by the name Siberia are somewhat less than welcoming. For most Russians, and other peoples of the ex-Soviet republics, these and similar images are graven in a great scar on the psyche. For four centuries this immense backyard has been used, first by the tsars and then by the Soviet regime, to dispose of undesirable elements in the populace. First to go were the criminals, then the political dissenters, followed by those who had, through their labours, inched materially ahead of their neighbours. Next went the religious, the leaders and their communities dispatched east over the Ural Mountains. They were followed by an en masse exile of the stubborn citizens of troublesome nationalities. Finally, no reason at all was needed to be sent to Siberia and it became the fear of everybody.

The writer Maxim Gorky gave voice to the national dread of Siberia when he described it as 'a land of chains and ice'. But it was also – and still is – a land able to encompass the serenity of Lake Baikal, the pristine geometry of the Altay Mountains, the fiery volcanic landscapes of Kamchatka, the sparkling, blue brilliance of the Arctic and the lush semitropical forests of the Pacific coast. Of the early exiles, many chose to stay on after their sentences had ended, seduced by the wide-open spaces and, strangely enough, the sense of freedom.

Siberia ('Sibir' in Russian, from the Mongolian Altay language, meaning 'Sleeping Land') takes in essentially the entire North Asian continent, east to the Pacific and south to China and Mongolia. This means BIG – 7000 by 3500km, wrapped around a third of the northern hemisphere. Viewed from the air, the flat land goes on and on, punctuated by meandering rivers, slashes of development and long banners of

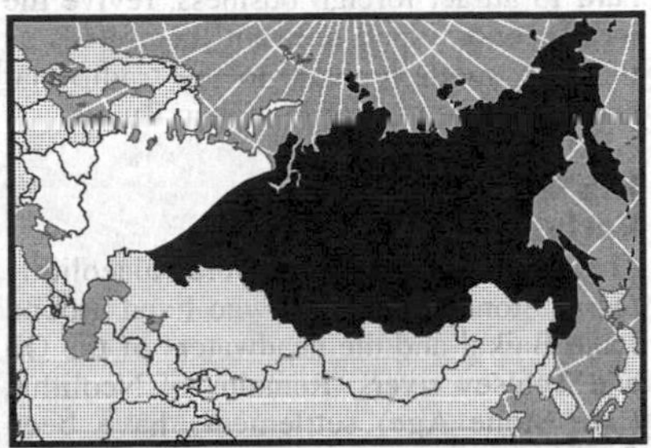

industrial smoke. The journalist George Kennan, in his 1891 *Siberia and the Exile System*, wrote:

> You can take the whole of the United States ... and set it down in the middle of Siberia without touching anywhere the boundaries of the latter's territory; you can then take Alaska and all the countries of Europe, with the exception of Russia, and fit them into the remaining margin like the pieces of a dissected map. After having thus accommodated all (this) you will still have more than 300,000 square miles of Siberian territory to spare ... an area half as large again as the Empire of Germany.

A hundred years on, with the world shrunk by air transport and satellite communications, Siberia has resisted all efforts to make it containable – or habitable: the population of this great land is only three times that of metropolitan Moscow, with most of it huddled along the railway in the south. Travellers today still write, not of trips in Siberia, but of journeys or odysseys.

For visitors, the main experience of all this size has been unending views of taiga (Siberian forest) from the cocoon of a Trans-Siberian Railway carriage, perhaps with a stop in a big city along the route. Tourist development has generally stuck close to the railway and is still sparse, but new destinations are opening up all the time.

Lake Baikal and the remote Kamchatka Peninsula are areas of outstanding natural beauty and wonder, and also classified as UNESCO World Heritage Sites, while the cities of the Russian Far East, such as Khabarovsk and Vladivostok, are working hard to attract foreign business, revive the local economy and reinvent themselves as thriving, modern rivals to the traditional centres of attention in European Russia.

HISTORY

Early History

The first known Siberians were Palaeolithic (early Stone Age) tribes who lived around Lake Baikal and the headwaters of the Ob and Yenisey rivers. Remains of Neolithic (late Stone Age) settlements have been found all over Siberia. Indeed, many northern tribes were still basically at the Neolithic stage when the Russians arrived. As late as the Iron Age, the steppes and forests from the Ural Mountains to Baikal were populated by tribes of herders whose origins lay in the Caucasus (Abakan's regional museum contains relics from burial mounds of this period). Soon afterwards the earliest Mongolians appeared.

By the 3rd century BC, the southern region of what is now Siberia was under the control of the Huns. Descendants of these nomads were later driven west, to the terror of Russia and Europe. In the first few centuries AD, Turkic tribes moved in from Central Asia. Their most prominent descendants were the Khyagas, or 'Yenisey Kyrgyz', whose 6th to 13th century empire, which took in much of Central Asia and central Siberia, was the Mongol Tatars' first big conquest. Another Turkic dynasty, the Bohai, dominated the south-east.

The first Russians in Siberia were fur traders from Novgorod who reached the northern Ob River in the late 11th century.

Mongol Tatars

Jenghis Khan got his start in the early 13th century as a warlord south-east of Lake Baikal. His confederation of armies (called Tatars, after a prominent neighbouring tribe who were among Jenghis' first conquests) pushed the Khyagas into Kyrgyzstan, went on to subdue most of Asia except far northern Siberia and, in the end, crossed Russia into Europe to create history's largest land empire. Of the empire's later fragments, the Golden Horde dominated Russia until the mid-15th century and the Golden Horde's splinters loosely controlled the Volga region and much of Siberia for another century.

The Opening of Siberia

If the Russians appreciate Ivan the Terrible for anything, it is for his seizure of the Tatar strongholds of Kazan (in 1552) and Astrakhan (in 1556), which put the entire Volga in Russian hands and swung open the door to Siberia. Seeing the writing on the wall, Yediger, the Khan of the Sibir Tatars, offered Ivan a tribute of sable pelts and became his vassal.

In 1558, the tsar authorised the powerful Stroganov family of merchants to open trading posts east of the Ural Mountains under the protection of Cossack mercenaries. When Yediger's successor, Kuchum, began plundering these settlements, a band of Cossacks and soldiers led by a convict named Yermak Timofeevich set out to teach him a lesson. In 1582, they took the Tatar capital of Kashlyk (present-day Tobolsk). In recognition of this achievement, Ivan pardoned Yermak for his past crimes and this bandit is now honoured as the 'conqueror of Siberia'. Three years later Yermak plunged into a river to escape a Tatar ambush and was drowned.

Nevertheless, the settlement of Siberia had begun and the next half-century saw one of history's most explosive expansions. Fuelled by a lust for furs, waves of Cossacks, trappers, traders and misfits had reached the Ob River by the 1580s. Until then this had represented the eastern limit of the known world. They had pushed on to the Yenisey by the end of the 16th century, the Lena by the 1620s and, in 1639, they made the Pacific coast at Okhotsk.

Behind the pioneers came the tsar's officials and soldiers to exact tributes (known as *yassak*) in the form of pelts. The export of furs became Russia's biggest moneymaker. Indigenous tribes may have found the newcomers a welcome change from the Tatars but, despite their greater numbers, with only bows and arrows against Russian muskets they had no choice in the matter anyway. Only the Tatars, the Buryats, who lived around Lake Baikal, and the Chukchi in the north-east put up much resistance. Benson Bobrick, in his history of Siberia, *East of the Sun*, likens the scenario to the push across the plains of the American West, with the Cossacks as cowboys, the Buryats etc as Indians and the tsarist army as the cavalry. Instead of a gold rush, Siberia experienced a fur frenzy.

Military stockades grew into towns – Tyumen in 1586, Tomsk in 1604, Krasnoyarsk in 1627, Yakutsk in 1632, Okhotsk in 1647, Irkutsk in 1651 and Chita in 1655. Settlement was encouraged with promises of easy land and freedom from serfdom. By the late 17th century there were as many settlers, traders, soldiers and missionaries as there were indigenous Siberians. As expeditions began to size up Siberia's huge mineral wealth, Peter the Great also sent engineers and geologists.

Edging into Manchuria

Rumours that the Amur and Ussuri river basins in the east contained desperately scarce arable land were confirmed by an exploratory expedition. In 1650, the tsar commissioned the Cossack trader Yerofey Khabarov (after whom Khabarovsk is named) to open up the region, but his rapacious barbarity was so great that the local tribes appealed to their Manchu overlords for help. Following a Chinese show of might, Khabarov withdrew to a position well north of the Amur.

Like the schoolyard game in which children creep stealthily towards one colleague facing a wall, then freeze when this 'guard' suddenly spins round, the Russians surreptitiously filtered back into Manchu territory. Even allowing for a couple of retreats, the Russians were in occupation of the north bank of the Amur by 1689. The Manchus, threatened already by the Mongols, could not afford to enter into war on another front, but nor could Russia afford to lose the Chinese market, where most of its furs were sold. The two powers came to terms in the Treaty of Nerchinsk, which sealed a peace that lasted for more than 150 years.

Russians in America

Under the Treaty of Nerchinsk, Russia had to give up all claims to the Amur valley, and instead the government began to concentrate its efforts on the largely unknown far north-eastern territories. In 1648, the Cossack Semyon Dezhnev had been the first to sail round the north-east corner of Asia, from the Pacific Ocean into the Arctic. However, the glory went to Vitus Bering, a Danish officer in the Russian navy, who discovered the strait (which now bears his name) all over again in 1728. Peter the Great called Bering to head the Great Northern Expedition which was ostensibly a scientific survey of Kamchatka (claimed for the tsar in 1697 by the explorer Atlasov) and the eastern seaboard, but in reality its aim was to expand Russia's Pacific sphere of influence as far south as Japan and across to North America.

Bering succeeded in discovering Alaska, landing in 1741. Unfortunately, on the return voyage his ship was wrecked off an island just 250km east of the Kamchatka coast. Bering died on the island, and it, too, now carries his name. (Archaeologists digging on the island in 1991 discovered his grave and the bones were flown to Moscow for scientific examination. They've since been returned to the island and reburied with full naval ceremony.)

Survivors of Bering's crew brought back reports of an abundance of foxes, fur seals and otters inhabiting the islands off the mainland, triggering a fresh wave of fur-inspired expansion. An Irkutsk trader, Grigory Shelekhov, landed on Kodiak Island (in present-day Alaska) in 1784 and, 15 years later, his successor founded Sitka (originally called New Archangel), the capital of Alaska until 1900. In 1804 the Russians reached Honolulu, and in 1806 Russian ships sailed into San Francisco Bay. Soon afterwards, a fortified outpost was established at what is now called Fort Ross, California, where the imperial flag flew and a marker was buried on which was inscribed 'Land of the Russian Empire'.

Early Exiles

From about 1650, the authorities began dumping criminals in Siberia. In the 1700s, as Siberia's natural wealth became obvious, those dumped there were put to work digging it up. As the demand for labour increased, so did the list of punishable offences: prize-fighting, prostitution, vagrancy, even fortune-telling all became grounds for banishment.

The death penalty was abolished and replaced with exile and forced labour, and people were soon being sent to Siberia without trial. POWs, religious dissenters and, more or less, anyone with an irritating opinion was soon joining the criminals on the long trail east. Exile had become big business. The Great Siberian Trakt, or Post Road, along the only route through the Ural Mountains and the taiga beyond, was developed to include a complex system of exile stations and holding prisons. By 1890, some 3400 exiles a week were marched in shackles to Irkutsk, although up to 15% failed to survive the journey.

Once in Siberia, lesser offenders were simply released into villages (exiles were permitted to comprise up to a third of the population of any settlement) though they were forbidden to return west. More serious offenders were set to work in prisons or labour camps, the most notorious of which were the silver mines at Nerchinsk, east of Chita, and the gold mines at Kara, in the Ural Mountains.

Decembrists & Other Political Exiles

The most celebrated exiles were the Dekabristy, or Decembrists, army officers and aristocrats who bungled a revolt against Tsar Nicholas I in December 1825. Five were executed, but 116 were sent to Siberia for terms of hard labour, mostly in rural parts of the Chita region. After serving their sentences, these exiles could move to towns, *personae non gratae* but allowed to carry on as best they could. Their presence had a marked effect on the educational and cultural life in their adopted towns. Pardoned by Tsar Alexander II in 1856, many chose to stay on in Irkutsk and elsewhere.

After Napoleon's defeat in 1812, Russia had taken control of Poland, and in 1863-64 an uprising nearly overthrew the puppet government. Huge numbers of Polish rebels, many well educated, were shipped to Siberia. Other famous exiles over the years included novelist Fyodor Dostoevsky, Leon Trotsky, Josef Stalin and, of course, Lenin, who spent nearly three years near Abakan.

More Expansion & the Railway

In the mid-1800s, China was racked with civil strife and the Opium Wars, and the Russians, made bold by the concessions Great Britain had wrung from the weakened Manchus, stepped up the pace of expansion in the Russian Far East. In the 1850s, ignoring old treaties, the Governor General of Eastern Siberia, Count Nikolay Muravyov, repossessed and colonised the Amur basin (for which the grateful tsar added 'Amursky' to Muravyov's name). Far from precipitating a Sino-Russian war, expansionist Russia also gained the Primorsky region (the dogleg of land between the Ussuri River and the Pacific) as a reward for its help in negotiating the lifting of an Anglo-French siege against Beijing.

Under Muravyov's direction, in 1853 Sakhalin had also been added to the Russians' grab bag of territories, though they were forced to share the island with the Japanese, who had already staked a claim to the southern half. In 1875 Japan withdrew its claim in exchange for recognition of its sovereignty over the Kuril Islands. By 1900, the Russians held all of Manchuria and had naval bases at Port Arthur and Dalny (now Lüshen and Dalian).

Siberian development was hamstrung by vast distances and poor communications. It wasn't until 1886, when Tsar Alexander III authorised the building of 7500km of railroad between Chelyabinsk (then Russia's eastern railhead) and Vladivostok, that things shifted up a few gears. Cities grew like mushrooms along the line. In less than 25 years to 1911, the immigrant population leapt above eight million. Most were peasants, who put Siberian agriculture at the head of the class in grain, stock and dairy farming (before the October Revolution, Europeans had Siberian butter on their tables). This growth was to collapse with Stalin's forced collectivisation of agriculture in the 1930s.

The Russo-Japanese War

Feeling threatened by Russian expansion across Manchuria, wary of Slavic ambitions on Korea and keenly aware that the imminent completion of the Trans-Siberian Railway would facilitate rapid troop movement into the Far East, the Japanese launched a sudden naval attack on the Russian fleet at Port Arthur in February 1904. Tsar Nicholas II ordered the Baltic fleet to sail clear around the world to join the battle, where it was immediately annihilated in the Tsushima Straits. In September 1905, a badly beaten Russia signed the Treaty of Portsmouth (Portsmouth, New Hampshire), under the terms of which it gave up Port Arthur, Dalny and southern Sakhalin and forsook any claims to Korea – but at least retained its pre-eminent position in Manchuria.

Civil War

Soviet rule was proclaimed in Siberia's major towns soon after the October Revolution, but in spite of all those exiled dissidents, this was not fertile ground for the Bolsheviks. Cossacks, merchants and a fairly contented peasantry were uneasy about Lenin's promises. Local heroes tended to be upper-class explorers, scientists or Decembrists.

A general counter-revolution swept across Siberia in May 1918, sparked by a force of 45,000 Czechoslovakian POWs. The Czechoslovaks, who had been fighting alongside the Russians against the Germans, were heading home via Vladivostok when caught out by the revolution and Russia's decision to pull out of WWI. Convinced that the new Soviet government was going to hand them over to the Germans, the fully armed Czechoslovaks seized virtually the entire Trans-Siberian Railway. The regional Bolshevik government in the Russian Far East was thrown into retreat and by mid-September all Siberia was 'White'.

Meanwhile, the tsarist Admiral Alexander Kolchak, stranded in the USA by the revolution, landed at Vladivostok and headed west at the head of a White army. His cause was boosted when the entire area from the Pacific to Lake Baikal was occupied by foreign troops – 72,000 Japanese, 7000 Americans, 6400 British, 4400 Canadians and others – all there, ostensibly, to help the Czechoslovaks.

In November 1918, Kolchak pushed into European Russia. Joining with armies from the Don basin and north-west Russia, he very nearly overthrew the Bolsheviks before being pushed back to Omsk, where his forces were decisively routed. Kolchak hastily retreated to Irkutsk. There he was captured and shot in 1920, which effectively ended the Civil War – except in the Russian Far East, where it raged on until the Red victory at Volochaevka, west of Khabarovsk, in February 1922.

Soviet Consolidation

At that point almost all the foreign troops withdrew. The Japanese, however, who rather fancied the land they had been occupying from Baikal to the Sea of Japan, stayed put. To keep things cool, the Soviet government made this area into a buffer zone, declaring it the independent Far East Republic, with its capital at Chita. When the Japanese left in 1922, it was promptly absorbed into the USSR. A Canadian expedition that in 1922 had claimed for the British Empire little Wrangel Island (ostrov Vrangelya), north of the Bering Strait, was evicted at gunpoint five years later. No more was said about it.

Siberia was never a battlefield in WWII but in virtually the closing days of the war, with Japan now on its knees, the Soviet Union occupied southern Sakhalin and the Kuril Islands. Japan accepted the loss but continues to this day to maintain a claim to the southern islands in the Kuril chain, which at their closest point are approximately 14km from Hokkaido.

The Gulag

The exile system was abolished at the turn of the 20th century, but Stalin brought it back with a vengeance, expanding it into a full-blown, home-grown slave trade. He established a vast bureaucracy of resettlement programs, labour colonies, concentration camps and special psychiatric hospitals all over Russia, commonly known as the Gulag (Glavnoe Upravlenie Lagerey, or Main Administration for Camps). Its inmates – some of whose only 'offence' was to be Jewish or a modern artist or a high-profile Buryat, or simply to have shaken the hand of such a person – cut trees, dug canals, laid railway tracks and worked in factories in remote areas, especially Siberia and the Russian Far East. A huge slice of the north-east was set aside exclusively for labour camps, and whole cities such as Komsomolsk-on-Amur and Magadan were developed as Gulag centres. It was during Stalin's rule that Siberia became synonymous with death; while Josef Stalin sat in the Kremlin, an estimated 20 million people died in the Gulag. Nadezhda Mandelstam, whose poet husband, Osip, was taken by the Cheka and sent to Siberia, where he perished, wrote that a wife considered herself a widow from the moment of her husband's arrest.

Post-Stalinist Siberia

Following Stalin's death in 1953, amnesties freed up to two-thirds of all Siberia's prisoners. Exile and labour camps remained as corrective tools of the state right up until the dissolution of the USSR, but in a vastly reduced form. For Russians, the word that replaced 'Gulag' in the Siberian word-association game was 'gigantomania'. The 1950s saw a proliferation of Olympian schemes that were variously bigger, wider, taller or more powerful than anything that had gone before (and in many cases costlier, less efficient and more environmentally disastrous, too). A series of hydroelectric power plants was constructed along the Angara and Yenisey rivers to supply power for the huge *kombinaty* (plants), such as aluminium smelters and pulp mills, that sprang up in their wake. At one point, Soviet planners even proposed building a barrage of mammoth dams along the Arctic coast to reverse the flow of the rivers and flood parts of central Siberia. Fortunately, that scheme never got off the drawing board.

Shielded from foreign attention, Siberia became a major centre of Cold War activity, with Novaya Zemlya and Kamchatka used for thermonuclear testing, nuclear weapons facilities at Lake Irtysh and Tomsk 7 and a radar station, which in the words of Eduard Shevardnadze was 'the size of the Egyptian pyramids', at Krasnoyarsk. The border with China and the Pacific seaboard bristled with antennae, tank barrels and missiles. Siberia briefly gained world attention in 1960, when a US U2 spy-plane dared these defences and was brought down over Sverdlovsk (present-day Yekaterinburg); and again in 1983, when Korean airliner KAL 007 was intercepted and destroyed just off the island of Sakhalin.

To attract the workforce to Siberia, salaries three times higher than in European Russia were offered, as well as bonus schemes, longer holidays and tax exemptions. But by the end of the 1980s, wages were failing to keep up with inflation, bonuses were cut back and, worst of all, the work was drying up. In 1989, and again in 1991, the miners of Siberia's Kuzbass region went on strike for more money and better conditions. In the history of the Soviet Union they were the first ever to employ such openly defiant tactics. The government was almost brought to its knees.

The collapse of the Soviet empire has given Siberia and Russia's Far East a greater degree of self-determination but has also left them underdeveloped, sparsely populated and short on cash. The region is rich in resources – oil, gas, coal, diamonds, bauxite, gold and other precious metals, fish and timber – and is, in fact, the potential saviour of Russia. However, most of this eldorado lies in remote regions, deep below the surface and securely locked in ice. How to get at it, and to whom the spoils (Moscow? the local inhabitants? foreign investors?) are the questions that currently dominate Siberia. They're the same questions that have always dominated. Even now, more than 350 years after the first explorations, Siberia and the Russian Far East remain untamed frontier territory.

Food and energy shortages brought on by the 1998 economic crisis have struck some outlying regions of Siberia and the Russian Far East, though conditions are not as bad as reported in the Western media, which tends to under-estimate Siberians' survival skills. Proud and self-reliant, Siberians have managed to wrench themselves from the political turmoil affecting Russians in other parts. The most famous Siberian these days is General Alexander Lebed, the governor of Krasnoyarsk, who is bidding to replace Boris Yeltsin in the Kremlin.

GEOGRAPHY

Siberia and the Russian Far East – defined for the purposes of this book as the Ural Mountains and all the land to their east, though strictly speaking Russians do not class the Ural region as part of Siberia – cover nearly 14 million sq km. The easternmost point, Big Diomede Island (ostrov Ratmanova) in the Bering Strait, is just 45km from the Alaskan mainland.

The dividing line between Siberia and the Russian Far East lies along the borders of the Khabarovsk Territory and Magadan Region. This eastern seaboard is 15,500km long – which gives Russia more 'Pacific Rim' than any other country.

The region is washed in the north by the Arctic Kara, Laptev and East Siberian seas, with the Severnaya Zemlya islands between the first two constituting its northernmost extension. In the south it has land borders with Kazakhstan, Mongolia, China and North Korea.

On a map, Siberia's dominant geographical features are its 53,000 rivers and more than one million lakes. From west to east the major rivers are the Ob, Yenisey and Lena – all of which flow north to the Arctic – and the Amur, which flows east towards the Pacific. These four drain about two-thirds of the entire area of Siberia and the Russian Far East. The Ob rises in the Altay Republic, flows through Novosibirsk and empties into the Kara Sea via the 960km-long Ob Gulf (Obskaya guba) between the Yamal and Gydansky peninsulas. If the Irtysh, which rises in China and flows through Omsk and Tobolsk, is considered the main stream of the Ob, then the Ob has a length of nearly 6000km to the Kara Sea. The Yenisey rises in Tuva and flows through Krasnoyarsk to enter the Kara Sea between the Gydansky and Taymyr peninsulas. Its tributary, the Angara, flows out of Lake Baikal and through Irkutsk and Bratsk to join the Yenisey north of Krasnoyarsk. The 4400km Lena rises in the mountains west of Lake Baikal and flows through Yakutsk to the Laptev Sea. The 4416km Amur forms a long stretch of the Russia-China border before flowing through Khabarovsk and into the Tatar Strait between the mainland and the large island of Sakhalin (which divides the seas of Japan and Okhotsk). The Amur's southern tributary, the Ussuri, which meets it at Khabarovsk, forms another long stretch of the Chinese border.

Beautiful Lake Baikal, the world's deepest lake, holds nearly one-fifth of all the world's lake water.

As you travel across Siberia, one overwhelming impression you get is of the taiga – the dense, swampy forests of birch, pine, spruce and larch that Trans-Siberian passengers watch for days on end. In parts of the south are areas of flat, dry steppe reaching southwards into Central Asia and Mongolia. To the north is tundra, or 'cold desert', with shallow, delicate vegetation. Much of it is on the permanently frozen bog called permafrost, hard as rock to a depth of hundreds of metres, with at most the top few metres thawing in summer. Under the pressure of a wheel, a railroad track or a foundation, permafrost turns to mud. To keep them from sinking, roadbeds in the tundra must be insulated and buildings erected on legs.

Another overwhelming impression – especially if you travel along the railway that runs near the southern border most of the way – is of Siberia's flatness. Between the Ural Mountains – which rarely top 1000m and are barely noticeable in their middle reaches west of Yekaterinburg – and the Yenisey River stretches the marshy West Siberian Plain, all of it below 200m. The Ob River, crossing this plain, falls only 100m in its last 2000km. Between the Yenisey and the Lena is the Central Siberian Plateau, nearly all between 200 and 1000m.

In southern regions, and from Lake Baikal and the Lena eastwards, there's more relief. South-east of Novosibirsk are the beautiful Altay Mountains, which stretch over into Kazakhstan and Mongolia and peak at 4506m-high Mt Belukha on the Kazakhstan border. A little farther east, the Western and Eastern Sayan ranges, which reach around 3000m, separate the Tuva from the rest of Russia. Mountains surround most of Lake Baikal and continue, occasionally topping 3000m, most of the way to the Sikhote-Alin range in Ussuriland, east of Khabarovsk.

In the north-east there's a tangle of ranges all the way up to the Chukotka Peninsula facing Alaska, the most dramatic – indeed, probably the most dramatic of all Russia's mountains – being the 200-odd volcanoes on the 1200km-long Kamchatka Peninsula. About 30 of these – including Siberia and the Russian Far East's highest peak, 4750m-high Klyuchevskaya – are active, some highly so. The volcanic chain continues south in the form of the Kuril Islands, strung all the way from Kamchatka to Japan, which contain a further 40 active volcanoes.

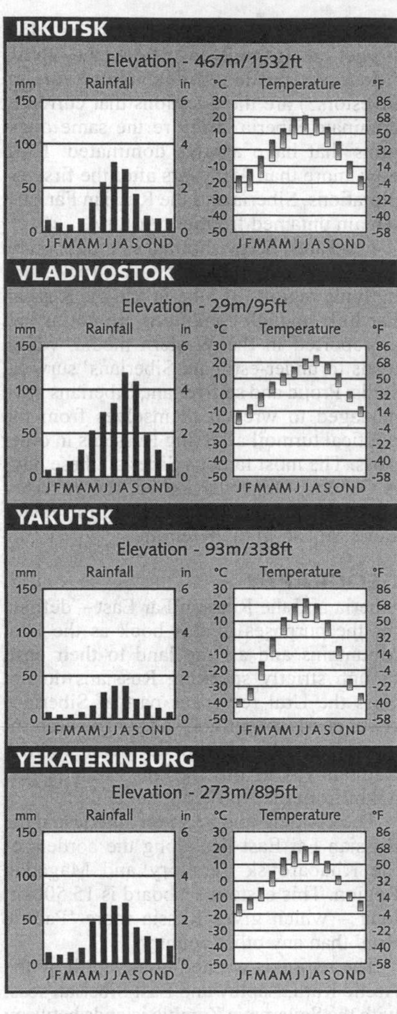

CLIMATE

Siberia's climate is sharply continental but not as fearsome as you might imagine. Winter is bitingly cold in Trans-Siberian Railway towns – average January night temperatures are -20 to -25°C, with cold snaps to -35°C – but, from January onwards, is mitigated by low humidity and lots of sun (and a sense that this is, after all, the time to see the 'genuine' Siberia). Siberians claim they feel cold if they go to St Petersburg in winter – where temperatures are a good 10°C higher – because of the humidity there. Spring comes in late April or May, later in the mountains.

July and August can be quite warm months, with temperatures averaging 15 or 20°C and reaching as high as 30°C. There are mosquitoes but, in most areas, not enough to ruin a visit. Of course, if you're trekking or doing anything else at high altitudes in summer, it can still get cold. September is the time for mushrooms, wild berries and brilliant foliage; residents claim that this is the most beautiful time of year in the Russian Far East. September and October bring unstable weather. The first frost is usually in October, and most snow falls in November and December.

You'll find it nippier if you stray northwards. In Verkhoyansk, 650km north of Yakutsk, winter temperatures have dropped to -71°C (but summers can be surprisingly warm). And south doesn't necessarily mean warm: the zone of year-round permafrost, a good indicator of nasty cold, reaches right down across the Trans-Siberian east of Lake Baikal.

Ussuriland, south-east of Khabarovsk, has a northern monsoonal climate. This means it has more rain (30 to 40% rainy days from May to September) and slightly milder winters – a balmy -13°C on a typical January day.

ECOLOGY & ENVIRONMENT

While it has undoubtedly been a great source of wealth for Russia, the oil and gas industry, through greed, inattention and a failing infrastructure, has been perhaps the country's greatest environmental desecrator. The fragile Arctic tundra has suffered massive degradation from oil spills. Environmental loss from oil exploration and production in the West Siberian Plain has reached such levels that the huge Ob River flowing across it is almost dead. Less acknowledged, though equally harmful, is the destabilisation of the delicate tundra ecosystem by the construction of buildings, roads and railways and the extraction of underground resources. Parts of the low-lying Yamal Peninsula at the mouth of the Ob, which contains some of the world's biggest gas reserves, have been literally melting into the sea as the permafrost melts near gas installations. The traditional hunting and reindeer-herding way of life of Siberian native peoples such as the Nentsy, Khanty, Mansy and Nivkhi is in danger. The tundra is also suffering the effects of acid rain, most of it the result of one smelting plant at Norilsk.

The catalogue of environmental wreckage in Siberia and the Russian Far East is as varied as it is awful. In Chukotka in the far north-east, a past nuclear testing site, the local natives have been subjected to as much radiation as they would have if they'd been at Chornobyl (Chernobyl) in 1986. But in Chukotka there were no warnings or evacuations. Now there is close to a 100% incidence of tuberculosis and a child mortality rate of 10%. Post-glasnost disclosures have revealed that the Russian Navy secretly dumped nuclear waste, including used reactors from submarines, in both the Sea of Japan, off Vladivostok, and the Arctic Ocean. Meanwhile, multinational logging concerns from the USA, South Korea and Japan, in partnership with Russia, are queuing up to clear-fell the Siberian forests, which are currently being devoured at an estimated four million hectares a year. And that's not to mention some of the northern hemisphere's worst polluted rivers, swathes of dead taiga, and air around some Siberian industrial towns that is so defiled that there'll never be any need for tinted windscreens.

The most documented instance of environmental degradation has centred around Lake Baikal. When two large pulp and cellulose plants began using the lake as a dump for waste products, it proved a rallying cause not just for locals but for concerned parties in all parts of the country. Baikal became the focus of the Soviet Union's first and most voluble environmental campaign, and the catalyst for the creation of a Russian green movement. Such was the groundswell of nationwide popular support that the government was forced to act and the offending plants were allegedly cleaned up, though scientists say there has been little actual improvement.

The limited success at Baikal was followed up with a victory for the native inhabitants of the Yamal Peninsula on the Arctic coastline of western Siberia, who managed to halt construction of a railway and gas pipeline that would have interfered with reindeer migration routes. Since 1991, international agencies have been able to add their weight to the Russian environmental cause; UNESCO is funding research around Lake Baikal; and the International Crane Foundation is involved in protecting endangered and rare crane species in the Amur and Chita regions.

FLORA & FAUNA

Siberia is divided into three distinct, broad east-west bands of vegetation type. In the northernmost extremes, fringed by the Arctic Ocean, is the icy tundra. These bleak, seemingly barren flatlands extend from 60 to 420km south from the coast. They gradually become more amicable to life and build up to taiga, the vast, dense forest that characterises and covers the greater part of Siberia. At its southern fringes, close to the borders with Kazakhstan, Mongolia and, in parts, China, the taiga peters out to become a treeless, gently undulating grassland, or steppe.

Both tundra and taiga extend across to the Pacific coast, but the Russian Far East also has two other unusual vegetative zones. Kamchatka, a peninsula in the far north-east of Russia, is an active volcanic region with, in some places, a moon-like landscape and, elsewhere, weird and wonderful gigantic plant life. Ussuriland, as a result of its lower latitude in the extreme Russian south-east, experiences tropical air and rains. The forests covering this region – and their indigenous animals and vegetation – more closely resemble those of South-East Asia than anything typically associated with Siberia.

Tundra

Falling almost completely within the Arctic Circle, the tundra is the most inhospitable of Siberian terrain. The ground is permanently frozen (in places, recorded to a depth of 1450m) like one great block of ice, with just a thin, fragile carpet of vegetation lying on top. The few trees and bushes that manage to cling tenaciously to existence are stunted dwarfs, the permafrost refusing to yield to their roots. For nine months of the year the beleaguered greenery is also buried beneath a mattress of snow. When the brief, warming summer comes, the permafrost prevents drainage and the tundra becomes a spongy wetland, pocked with lakes, pools and puddles – breeding grounds for clouds of predatory mosquitoes and gnats and a haven for wildfowl. In general, wildlife has a hard time of it on the tundra and there are few species that can survive its climate and desolation. The reindeer, however, has few problems and there are thought to be around four million of them in Russia's tundra regions. They can endure temperatures as low as -50°C and, like the camel, they can store reserves of food. The reindeer sustains itself on lichen and grasses, in winter sniffing them out and pawing away the snow cover.

A similar diet sustains the lemming, a small, round, fat rodent, fixed in the popular consciousness for its proclivity for launching itself en masse from clifftops. More amazing is its rate of reproduction. Lemmings can produce five or six litters annually, each of five or six young. The young in turn begin reproducing after only two months. With a gestation period of just three weeks, one pair could theoretically spawn close to 10,000 more lemmings in a 12 month period. In reality, predators and insufficient food supplies keep the numbers down.

Other tundra mammals include the Arctic fox, a smaller, more furry cousin of the European fox and a big lemming fan, and the wolf, which, although it prefers the taiga, will range far and wide drawn by the lure of reindeer meat.

Taiga

Siberia's taiga is the world's largest forest. It covers about five million sq km (an area big enough to blanket the whole of India) and accounts for about 25% of the world's wood reserves. Travelling on the Baikal-Amur Mainline (BAM) through the depths of Siberia, two or three days can go by with nothing but the impenetrable and foreboding dark wall of the forest visible outside the train: 'Where it ends,' wrote Chekhov, 'only the migrating birds know.' Few people choose to live in the gloomy depths of the forest, and the towns and villages cling tightly to the railways and large rivers.

Though the conditions are less severe than in the Arctic region, it's still harsh and bitterly cold in winter. The trees best suited for survival, and the main components of the taiga, are the pine, larch, spruce and firs. In the coldest (eastern) regions the deciduous larch predominates; by shedding its leaves it cuts down on water loss, and its shallow roots give it the best chance of survival in permafrost conditions. Forest-floor vegetation isn't particularly dense (though it is wiry and spring-loaded, making it difficult for humans to move through) because of the permanent shade, but there is a great variety of grasses, moss, lichens, berries and mushrooms. These provide ample nourishment for the animals at the lower end of the food chain which, in turn, become food for others. Wildlife flourishes. The indigenous cast includes squirrels and chipmunks (which dine well on pine cone seeds), voles and lemmings, as well as small carnivores such as polecats, foxes, wolverines and, less commonly, the sable, a weasel-like creature whose luxuriant pelt played such a great role in the early exploration of Siberia.

The most common species of large mammal in the taiga is the elk, a large deer that can measure over 2m at the shoulder and weighs almost as much as a bear. The brown bear itself is also extremely numerous: a farmer on the northern shores of Lake Baikal said that on any given night during summer (the bear hibernates through the colder months) he could guarantee tracking one down.

Kamchatka

The fantastic array of vegetation and wildlife on Kamchatka is a result of the geothermal bubbling, brewing and rumbling that goes on below the peninsula's surface and manifests itself periodically in the eruption of one of around 30 active volcanoes. The minerals deposited by these eruptions have produced some incredibly fertile earth, which is capable of nurturing giant plants with accelerated growth rates. John Massey Stewart, in his book *The Nature of Russia*, gives the example of the dropwort, normally a small, unremarkable plant, which in Kamchatka can grow as much as 10cm in 24 hours and reaches a height of up to 4m. This effect is at its most fantastic in the calderas (craters) of collapsed volcanoes. Here, hot springs and thermal vents maintain a high temperature year-round, creating almost greenhouse-like conditions for plants. Waterfowl and all manner of animals make their way here to shelter from the worst of winter, and Massey Stewart likens it to a 'Russian Garden of Eden'.

The volcanic ash also enriches the peninsula's rivers, leading to far greater spawnings of salmon than experienced anywhere else. And in thermally warmed pools the salmon also gain weight at a much increased rate. All of which is good news for the region's predatory mammals and large sea birds (and for local fishermen). The bears, in particular, benefit and the numerous Kamchatkan brown bears are the biggest of their species in Russia: a fully grown male stands at over 3m and weighs close to a tonne. Other well fed fish eaters are the peninsula's sea otters (a protected species), seals and the great sea eagle, one of the world's largest birds of prey, with a 2.5m wingspan. The coastline is particularly favoured by birds, with over 200 recognised species including auks, tufted puffins and swans.

Ussuriland

Completely different to the taiga, tundra or steppe, Ussuriland is largely covered by a monsoon forest filled with an exotic array of plant life and animals – from tree frogs to tigers – found nowhere else in Russia. The mix of plants and wildlife draws from the taiga to the north, and also from neighbouring China, Korea and the Himalaya. The topography is dominated by the Sikhote-Alin Mountains, which run for more than 1000km in a spine parallel to the coast. Unlike the sparsely vegetated woodland floor of the taiga, the forests of Ussuriland have a lush undergrowth, with

A New Twist to the Tiger Tale

Vladimir Shetinin is a bearded Siberian more at home in sable-lined hunting gear than his cool, grey uniform with burgundy pinstripes – the new look of the eco-police, 23 rough and hardy men whose duty it is to keep the semitropical forests, mountains and streams of Primore free from poachers and thus safe for animalkind.

When I first met Shetinin in 1993, he was a frustrated bureaucrat watching as the numbers of Siberian tigers decreased. His organisation, the Primore Ministry of Ecology, was broke, and about as close as he got to the big cats was the pelt of a poached one he'd occasionally spread out on his conference table for journalists like me.

Now he has five sparkling new jeeps and a relatively plump annual budget of $10,000, all thanks to Western grants. But the question remains: what has world attention and money really done for Primore's endangered snow leopards and tigers? Shetinin shakes his head, 'We don't have any more tigers than we did five years ago, but at least we don't have any fewer.' It's estimated that there are about 300 tigers and about 30 leopards stalking the south-east corner of Russia.

In 1996, poachers pilfered a leopard right from a nature reserve cage where it was being held for research. Since then, poachers have been slacking off, but not because they've begun to fear the eco-police, Shetinin adds gloomily, 'It's because they already have flooded the Korean market with bones and bile.'

You could say that Shetinin is pessimistic. So are a lot of other Russians who helped create the now-flailing green movement *(Zelyonoe dvizhenie)* in the late 1980s with help from the West. Nothing has quite worked out as they planned. The more profit-minded of the green bunch set up companies specialising in ecotourism but most of the environmentalists have returned to their old jobs.

Shetinin reminisces about the early days of the movement when a farming couple in Primore took in an orphaned cub and then another and then another. About the same time, the Primore environmentalists joined forces with the Hornocker Wildlife Institute, a private US foundation that had backing from the National Geographic Society, World Wildlife Fund and Exxon, the folks who provided Shetinin with his jeeps. Cute and cuddly, the farm cubs quickly

lianas and vines twined around trunks and draped from branches. However, it's the animal life that arouses most interest – not the wolves, the sable or the Asian black bear, a tree-climbing, herbivorous cousin to the more common brown bear (also found here), so much as Russia's own tiger, the Siberian or Amur tiger.

The Siberian tiger is the largest subspecies of tiger and the largest member of the cat family. Animals have been measured at up to 3.5m in length. Little wonder that the native Nanai (Nanaytsy in Russian) used to worship this incredible beast. There are estimated to be around 300 of the tigers in Ussuriland (out of a total world population of 350 to 450), which is something of a success considering that they had been hunted down to between 20 and 30 by the 1940s. The tiger was designated a protected species in 1948, and since then six reserves have been set up in the region, partly to help monitor and safeguard the cats. The tigers' favoured prey is boar, though they've been observed to hunt and kill bears, livestock and even humans.

Ussuriland is also home to the Amur leopard, a big cat significantly rarer than the tiger, though less impressive and consequently less often mentioned. Around 30 leopards roam the lands bordering China and North Korea.

A New Twist to the Tiger Tale

became the poster cats for the West's Save the Tiger campaign. They were easy to photograph and film. Tour companies began leading people to the farm. Meanwhile, the tigers got bigger and bigger, and bred successfully in captivity.

The farmer now hunts full-time to feed the animals. (An average tiger downs 10 to 20kg of meat a day.) He cannot release them because their natural instinct to avoid people has been reprogrammed, and they associate humans with their friendly food supplier. 'They'd probably just wander into some village and bang!' Shetinin exclaims. 'That would be the end.'

Shetinin says he's going nuts trying to figure out what to do. International interest has waned, he says, and the Russian green movement has gradually vanished in the face of the more pressing problem of human survival. The farmers are broke and bitter. 'The West doesn't care any more,' Shetinin says. 'They've shot their films and gone home.'

Just as Shetinin begins asking himself if the poster cats will have to be put down, into his office walks a young, well dressed man. You could say he's a New Russian, equipped with a mobile phone and big dreams. He has a large tract of land just outside of Vladivostok, near the motel-packed Sanatornaya district, and he wants to build something ...

'Not a zoo,' Shetinin says, scratching his head. 'It's more like a range, a safari-land. He thinks he can make big bucks selling tickets to tourists who want to see the tigers up close. It's a crazy idea, but I gave him permission. What else can we do with those tigers?'

So there you have it, the latest twist in the Save the Tiger saga. Stay tuned, and don't fall asleep by the pool.

Suzanne Possehl

TRUDI CANAVAN

Parks & Reserves

The following list outlines some of the major reserves *(zapovedniki)* within the area of Siberia and the Russian Far East. Some are closed to unauthorised personnel, sealed off for scientific study. Others are extremely difficult to reach, being well away from civilisation and accessible only by helicopter.

Among the exceptions are the Sikhote-Alin and Lazovsky reserves, which can be visited from Vladivostok. It is also possible to get permission to visit Kronotsky, which requires a short flight from Petropavlovsk-Kamchatsky (see the Kamchatka section in the Russian Far East chapter).

There is a book, *Nature Reserves of the USSR* by M Davydova & V Koshevoi, which may be available from specialist Russian bookshops.

Barguzin
: Covers an area of 2632 sq km on the north-east shore of Lake Baikal. It's a special reserve for the sable and also 38 other species of mammal including the Baikal seal and the flying squirrel. (See the Eastern Shore of Lake Baikal section of the Eastern Siberia chapter for details on getting there and contacts.)

Central Siberian
: A reserve of virgin taiga on the Yenisey River.

Muravyovka
: A working farm, protected marshlands and home to several species of rare and endangered

cranes, including the red-crowned crane, Muravyovka is 60km south-east of Blagoveshchensk, a literal stone's throw from the Chinese border. (See the Blagoveshchensk section in the Eastern Siberia chapter for details on getting there and contacts.)

Kronotsky
: A protected area of 10,990 sq km on Kamchatka with bears, sea lions and sea eagles. Within the reserve's boundaries are also the spectacular Valley of Geysers and Uzon Caldera. (See the Kamchatka section in the Russian Far East chapter for details on how to visit.)

Lazovsky
: A monsoon forest reserve on the Pacific coast 100km north of Vladivostok.

Sikhote-Alin
: The biggest Ussuriland reserve at 3476 sq km, stretching from the coast up into the mountains. It's home to over 340 species of bird and to the Siberian tiger. (See the introductory section to Around Vladivostok in the Russian Far East chapter for information on how to visit.)

Taymyr Peninsula
: North of Norilsk, jutting out into the Arctic Ocean, this is 13,483 sq km of protected tundra. It contains a host of wildlife including the rare red-breasted goose and muskox.

Ust-Lensky
: Russia's largest reserve covers 14,330 sq km of tundra at the mouth of the Lena River.

Wrangel Island
: Since 1976 this island, 140km off the coast of the far north-east of Russia, has been a haven for polar bears, walruses and snow geese.

GOVERNMENT & POLITICS

All of Siberia and the Russian Far East falls within the territory of the Russian Federation and is subject to rule from Moscow. To make this vast region more manageable, Siberia is split up into regions *(oblasti)*, territories *(krai)* and republics *(respubliki)*, each with its own local government and administration. The republics – Altay, Khakassia, Tuva, Buryatia and Sakha (formerly Yakutia) – have significant non-Russian populations and greater powers of self-determination. Sakha, for example, has its own presidency and constitution, both of which routinely contradict edicts issuing from the Kremlin.

Central government is responsible for defence, long-distance communications and the like, while regions are responsible for local services and privatisation. Both, in theory, are jointly responsible for foreign investment and the development of natural resources, the biggest sticking point. Products from Siberia and the Russian Far East – especially timber, minerals, petroleum, gold, diamonds and furs – still generate more than half of Russia's total hard-currency income, but the regions from which this wealth emanates are just starting to see a few of the benefits. Siberians are still worse fed, have a lower life expectancy and produce fewer and less healthy children than their counterparts in western Russia.

ECONOMY

It may well be that in terms of raw materials, Russia is the richest country on earth, and much of this natural wealth lies in Siberia and the Far Eastern territories. The gold and diamond seams there exceed those in South Africa, the oil and gas fields are as bountiful as those in the Arabian Gulf and there is more timber than in all Brazil. The region also holds a third of the world's proven coal reserves.

Traditionally, Siberian society was agrarian, although as early as 1740 its precious-metal mines were making a significant contribution to the wealth of the Russian Empire. Large-scale industrialisation began under the socialist government, facilitated by the development of the Kuznetsk coal basin, which fuelled growth along the route of the Trans-Siberian rail line. Iron foundries were established at Magnitogorsk, an enormous tractor factory at Chelyabinsk, locomotive and aircraft works at Ulan Ude, and so on. The town of Norilsk, now the largest anywhere within the Arctic Circle, was founded in 1922 to exploit the copper, nickel and other deposits of the far northern Taymyr Peninsula. WWII hastened the industrial evolution when many of European Russia's large manufacturing plants were dismantled and moved east of the Urals, well out of reach of the advancing Germans.

Oil was first discovered in Siberia in 1965. Leonid Brezhnev poured billions of roubles into extensive oilfields, principally located north of Tyumen and Omsk. In 1990 it was estimated 12 tonnes of oil every second were pumped out of the Tyumen region alone. The world's largest gas deposits lie even farther north, around Urengoy and Yamburg east of the Ob Gulf and on the Yamal Peninsula to its west. The oil and gas industries, so vital to Russia's economy, have caused untold environmental damage and threatened the existence of some northern minority peoples.

The Far East accounts for only 5% of Russia's industrial output but the region contributes in other significant ways. It has a near monopoly on diamonds and gold, as well as antimony and tungsten, and the Pacific seaboard accounts for 60% of Russia's annual fish haul. The government is tight-lipped about the quantity of precious substances the mines of Sakha might yield, but in recent years billions of dollars worth of precious stones originating in Russia have appeared on the international market, seriously challenging South Africa's long-standing primacy.

A combination of counterproductive Soviet-era central planning, daunting physical conditions and inappropriate technology has meant that some of Siberia's resources are only beginning to be tapped most recently with the help of foreign investors who have faced tremendous bureaucratic hurdles while working in some of Russia's most sensitive niches. In the summer of 1998, for example, foreign oil prospectors on Sakhalin Island woke up to Decree 352 that stipulated the Federal Security Bureau (formerly the KGB) clear all research material, which Russian companies routinely had been providing to their foreign partners. These partners – including Sodeco, Exxon, Marathon, Mitsui, Shell and Mitsubishi – have anticipated investing $25 billion, Russia's largest foreign investment, to develop Sakhalin's massive offshore oil and natural gas reserves.

POPULATION & PEOPLE

About 30 million people live in Siberia and the Russian Far East – just 22% of Russia's population in 75% of its territory. Most settlements, including all the big cities (the biggest are Novosibirsk, Yekaterinburg, Omsk and Chelyabinsk, each with between 1.1 and 1.5 million people), are strung across the south, on or near the Trans-Siberian Railway.

The population includes over 30 indigenous peoples but these only make up 4% of the total. The rest are mainly Russian but there are also Ukrainians, Tatars, Germans and most other nationalities of the ex-Soviet Union, who came as pioneers, settlers, exiles or prisoners. Of all the area's regions, territories and republics, only Tuva has a majority native population.

The indigenous population is a welter of peoples of uncertain origin, mostly small in number. They speak many languages. Most were originally shamanist and nearly all were nomadic herders (of sheep, horses and cattle in the south and of reindeer in the north); some were fishermen, trappers and hunters (of game inland and of walrus, seal and whale on the north coast). Very few had written languages until after the revolution. There are few nomads nowadays, owing to Soviet policies of forced settlement, collectivisation and industrialisation.

Few of these people have lived in great harmony with the immigrants from the west who have been arriving since the 16th century, as their territories have been exploited by Moscow for a series of economic purposes and their cultures, languages and identities have been threatened by Russification, Soviet policies and environmental damage. The very existence of some of the smaller groups is now threatened. Few indigenous peoples wield real power in 'their' republics or districts and nearly all are swamped by Russians and other non-native populations. The most numerous peoples – the Buryats, Yakuts, Tuvans, Khakass and Altay – have their 'own' republics within the Russian Federation. Eight districts *(okrugi)* within other regions or territories are named after their native inhabitants, who are, however, in nearly all cases small minorities within them. Some of the small northern minority groups are among the most disadvantaged peoples in Russia, with low life expectancy

(35 to 40 years for men), poor housing, as well as high disease and suicide rates.

Unless you venture into rural areas, you're unlikely to see (or, at any rate, recognise) any but the more numerous Buryats, Tuvans and Yakuts. Most native peoples have adopted Russian dress.

In the Soviet era there was little racial tension, probably because the indigenous population was so small and so politically powerless. Stalin sent insubordinate indigenous leaders to the Gulag in the 1930s. Since the late 1980s, however, there have been stirrings of nationalism and anti-Russian sentiment, most notably in Tuva, Buryatia and Sakha (Yakutia). Tuva saw a wave of anti-Russian violence in the early 1990s, and since then large numbers of Russians have left.

More on many of the Siberian peoples can be found in the relevant regional chapters, where they are referred to in the Russian plural, Yakuty (Yakuts), Nivkhi (Nivkh), Nanaytsy (Nanai) etc. The National Museum of Natural History, based in Washington, DC, has an Internet site at www.mnh.si.edu/arctic/features/croads that provides a virtual exhibition of the peoples of Siberia and Alaska.

Buryats

This Mongol people is the largest indigenous group, 420,000 strong in Russia. Just over half of them live in the Buryatia Republic (capital: Ulan Ude) south and east of Lake Baikal, which was Jenghis Khan's home territory. Others are in rural autonomous districts *(okrugi)* west of Irkutsk and near Chita, as well as in Mongolia and northern Xinjiang in China. Many Buryats converted to Tibetan Buddhism in the 18th century, though many Western Buryats later turned to Orthodox Christianity. The Buryats put up the strongest resistance to the early Russian presence.

Yakuts

At about 380,000, the Yakuts of the Lena River basin form the second biggest native group. They are probably the most culturally advanced group, with a vigorous arts and literature tradition. Yakuts form only about 33% of the population of the Sakha Republic (capital: Yakutsk) but hold many high governmental posts. Sakha has all Russia's diamond reserves, most of its gold, as well as rich timber and coal resources. The Yakuts are a Turkic people, skilled with horses, and thought to have migrated centuries ago from the south-west and to be related to the Kazakhs and Kyrgyz. Unlike their cousins, however, they are shamanists.

Tuvans

The 210,000 Tuvans in Russia are, like the Buryats, a Tibetan Buddhist Mongol people, but are Turkic-speaking. Nearly all of them live in the Tuva Republic (capital: Kyzyl), in the upper Yenisey basin on the Mongolian border, where they form 64% of the population. Traditionally, they have been hunters or herders of cattle, horses, sheep and yak. Tuva was part of the Chinese Empire in the 18th and 19th centuries, and later the nominally independent communist Tannu Tuva Republic from 1921 to 1944. Mongolia also has a sizable Tuvan population.

Khakass

North of the Tuvans is another Turkic people. Partly shamanist and partly Christian, the Khakass number about 80,000 but make up only about 11% of the population of the Khakassia Republic (capital: Abakan). Formerly nomad herders, they are the local remnants of the 'Yenisey Kyrgyz' Empire, which stretched from Kazakhstan to Lake Baikal from the 6th to 13th century.

Altay

This 71,000-strong Turkic-speaking people forms about 28% of the population of the mountainous Altay Republic (capital: Gorno-Altaysk) on the Kazakhstan and Mongolian borders, south-east of Novosibirsk. From the 15th to 18th century they were ruled by the fearsome Oyrats of western Mongolia, who scared the Kazakhs into joining Russia in the 18th century. The Altay came under Russian control in the 19th century.

Evenki

Probably the most ancient of the Siberian tribes are the 30,000-strong Evenki or Tungus, spread widely from the middle Yenisey River to the eastern seaboard and south to Lake Baikal, the Amur River and Manchuria. Their language is related to Chinese, though they're culturally closer to Mongolians. They form 14% of the population of the huge Evenk Autonomous District (Okrug), north of Krasnoyarsk.

Related tribes are the Evens, hunter-fishers who number 17,000 scattered around the north-east, and the 12,000 Nanai, in the lower Amur River basin.

Nentsy

The 35,000 Nentsy are the biggest of the 25 small groups known as the 'Peoples of the North'. Together with three smaller groups they are called the Samoyed (though some don't like this name because, in Russian, it sounds like 'cannibal').

Many Nentsy are still hunters and herders along the Arctic coast, east and west of the northern Ural Mountains, but they face increasing destruction of their reindeer herds' habitat by the oil and gas industries.

Khanty

Also called Ostyaks, these former hunters and fishermen are a Finno-Ugric people, related to the Finns, Estonians, Karelians and some Volga peoples. They were the first indigenous people seen by 11th century Novgorodian explorers.

The 22,000 Khanty and another small group of Finno-Ugric people, the 8000 Mansi (or Voguls), have a swampy joint autonomous district on the middle Ob River, where their share in the population has declined to just over 1% and their way of life has been shattered by the massive exploitation of the Samotlor oilfield, discovered in the 1960s.

Other Native Peoples

The six Palaeoasiatic, or Palaeosiberian, peoples are a miscellany, with languages that don't belong in any other category. Totalling about 34,000, most live in the far north-east. The most numerous are the 15,000 Chukchi and 9000 Koryaks. Their Stone Age forebears, who crossed the Bering Strait ice to America and Greenland, may also be remote ancestors of the American Indians.

Also in the far north-east are 1700 Eskimos and 700 Aleuts. Even less numerous are the Oroks of Sakhalin Island, who were counted at just 190 in the 1989 census.

Jews

In 1934 a Jewish Autonomous Region (Yevreyskaya Avtonomnaya Oblast) was created in the Russian Far East in the same spirit as other autonomous divisions, with Hebrew as its 'national' language. The exercise was a resounding failure, partly because of the incredibly harsh and remote location. Only about 0.5% of the Soviet Union's Jews went there and stayed, and today the region's 15,000 Jewish inhabitants are outnumbered by 13 to one. Most live in the capital, Birobidzhan, west of Khabarovsk.

EDUCATION

The education system in the Russian Far East and Siberia is the same as in European Russia (see Facts about European Russia for details). In practice, however, there are many differences because schools are spread over a huge, barely tamed territory where many students are not native Russian speakers. In general, education in Siberia and the Far East is poorer than in the rest of Russia. In 1998, teachers in parts of Siberia who hadn't been paid for six months or more were offered wages in the form of coffins and toilet paper. They ultimately settled for vodka.

While even the tiniest, most remote village will have a kindergarten *(detsky sad)* or even two, the system seems to break down after that, so it's not unusual to see boys and girls playing on the dirt roads on weekdays. During Soviet times, these kids would have been wrenched from their families and sent to special boarding schools *(internaty)*. It's hard to say which is better of the two evils: internaty or illiteracy.

SIBERIA & RUSSIAN FAR EAST

The Urals

History

Nentsy, Khanty and Mansi natives had traded furs, walrus ivory and other products across the Ural Mountains from the 12th century, and early Russian invaders and merchants crossed the Urals from the 1580s, but it was the region's reserves of iron ore, metals, coal and gemstones that first aroused serious Russian interest. Peter the Great sent pioneer industrialists to set up ironworks and metalworks, with mainly military purposes in mind, in the early 18th century. Industrial centres like Yekaterinburg, Chelyabinsk, Nizhny Tagil, and Perm to the west of the Ural Mountains, date from that time. At the same time indiscriminate felling of forests and pollution of lakes and rivers began. WWII brought a new industrial boom as Stalin moved over 1000 factories east of the Ural Mountains, and this growth continued after the war.

Gold and platinum were found in the Urals in the 19th century, and the element ruthenium was discovered here. Amethyst, topaz and aquamarine are among the gems mined in the region, notably in the Murzinka fields near Nizhny Tagil. Malachite is quarried at Nizhny Tagil and near Yekaterinburg.

The Ural region's arms industry tradition, meanwhile, has continued: more or less the whole region was off limits to foreigners until 1990 and some towns are still closed to outsiders for military reasons. Five of the 10 secret cities of the Soviet Union's 'nuclear archipelago' for weapons research and production were in the Ural region – Sverdlovsk-44, Sverdlovsk-45, Chelyabinsk-65, Chelyabinsk-70 and Zlatoust-36 (the numbers are their postcodes). Chelyabinsk-70 and Arzamas-16, about 100km south of Nizhny Novgorod, were the key research centres; the others were mainly uranium and plutonium production centres. Some have reportedly now gone over, at least partly, to civilian work. Chelyabinsk-65 (formerly Chelyabinsk-40) was the scene of the world's worst nuclear accident before Chornobyl, back in 1957 (though it wasn't admitted for decades). A nuclear waste tank exploded, severely contaminating an area 8km wide and 100km long, with about 10,000 people eventually moved out and 23 villages bulldozed. The 1957 explosion, along with deliberate dumping of radioactive wastes in the 1950s into the nearby Techa River and Lake Karachay (which later dried up, allowing the wind to scatter radioactive dust), have led to grave health and environmental problems in the area. Don't go poking around – radiation levels monitored on the shores of Lake Karachay give a fatal dose in one hour.

The city schools face other problems, mainly in adjusting to post-Soviet times. One Khabarovsk teacher polled her 14-year-olds on career choices. Eighty percent of the girls said they wanted to become prostitutes and as many of the boys listed 'killer' as their aspired-to profession. What's worse, the teacher admitted she was not shocked by the results, as polls of Moscow kids have yielded the same results. The proximity to Asia has also brought changes. As second languages, students are learning Japanese and Chinese, not English and German. Since 1990, narcotics have become a severe problem.

That said, the old Soviet stress on education for all is still very much in place. Seeing education as the only way the next generation will be able to enter the world market, Siberian parents are working double jobs to send their children to private academies, institutes, colleges and universities that are no longer free. How those schools are teaching Economics 101 (as opposed to Marxism-Leninism) is another story.

Geography

The Ural Mountains are divided into five sections. Yekaterinburg is on the east side of the longest, broadest and generally lowest stretch, the Middle Urals (Sredny Ural).

The highest mountain in the Southern Urals (Yuzhny Ural) is Mt Yaman Tau (1638m). The Northern Urals (Severny Ural) reach 1617m at Mt Telposiz. North of the Northern Urals (if this makes sense) come the Subarctic Urals (Pripolyarny Ural), a short stretch but with the highest peak in the whole range, 1894m Mt Narodnaya. The Arctic Urals (Polyarny Ural), whose highest peak is 1499m Mt Pay-Yer, take the range almost to the Kara Sea. The Arctic Novaya Zemlya islands, one of the Soviet Union's nuclear bomb testing grounds, are effectively a northern outcrop of the Urals.

Most of the Ural Mountains are covered in taiga, with rocky outcrops forming the peaks, but there are apparently some more dramatic rock walls on the northern peaks.

While the foothills of the Middle and Southern Urals are well populated, with several heavy industrial towns and cities (all considered to be in the Ural region, not Siberia), the more northerly Urals are very remote, with unexploited mineral riches, clear rivers and a tiny population mainly of Khanty and Nentsy hunters and reindeer herders.

Activities

Trekking in Russia & Central Asia, by Frith Maier (see Books in the Siberia & the Russian Far East Facts for the Visitor chapter), describes a two to three day hike up Konzhakovsky Kamen (1569m), the highest peak in the Middle Urals. It also details a nine to 10 day trek in the Mt Narodnaya area for those with more time and energy. July and August are the best months for such explorations. The approach to the Mt Narodnaya area is from Pechora on the Moscow-Vorkuta railway on the west side of the Urals, then by hydrofoil up the Pechora River.

Aside from hiking, cross-country skiing and rafting or kayaking are other locally popular activities. Trips on relatively easy rivers like the Chusovaya, Serga, Usva and Vilva in the Middle Urals and the Vishera in the Northern Urals can be arranged through Konstantin Brylyakov and agencies like Sputnik, both in Yekaterinburg (see the Yekaterinburg section of the Western Siberia chapter for contact details), or Eurasia Travel in Perm (see the Around Perm section of the Volga Region chapter).

ARTS

Literature

Siberia has produced generals, adventurers and even politicians of note, but there have been very few writers, artists or composers. In fact, when it comes to literature, Siberia is far more usually associated with the deaths of writers than with their genesis. The poet Osip Mandelstam, exiled for criticism of Stalin, died in 1938 in a transit camp on the outskirts of Vladivostok. The same year, Ukrainian poet Mikhaylo Draykharma failed to survive winter in a camp at Kolyma. Dostoevsky was among the writers who did survive Siberia, and his four years of hard labour in a camp near Omsk are recounted in *The House of the Dead* (1862).

The novel that etched the Siberian landscape into the hearts and minds of Westerners is *Dr Zhivago* which its author, Boris Pasternak, had smuggled to Britain where it was published in English in 1958. In latter times, Anatoly Rybakov, author of *Children of the Arbat*, was sentenced to hard labour in Siberia, an experience which, no doubt, provided much source material for his Gulag novel *Fear*, published in 1993.

One writer whose origins are in Siberia, as distinct from those who were sent there in exile, is Yuz Aleshkovsky, who was born in Krasnoyarsk on the banks of the Yenisey – though that still didn't save him from being sent farther east for a period in the camps. Aleshkovsky, who has lived in the USA since 1978, has had two books published in English, *Kangaroo* (1978) and *The Hand* (1980).

The most famed native Siberian writer is Valentin Rasputin, known for his stories decrying the destruction of the land and spirit and traditions of the Russian people. His best known work is *Farewell to Matyora* (1979), about a Siberian village flooded when a hydroelectric dam is built.

Architecture

Architecture in Siberia has scarcely evolved beyond the basic need for shelter. The original nomads' dwellings were made of poles and skins (eg the cylindrical tent-house called a *yurta*, or yurt) or, in the south, a framework of poles covered with brush and earth. Yurts are still in use in rural Tuva and Altay. Examples of these dwellings can also be found in open-air museums including those near Bratsk, Irkutsk and Ulan Ude.

The buildings of the Russian settlers are, not surprisingly, similar to those west of the Ural Mountains but fewer and more functional. Siberian variations on the traditional Russian and Ukrainian log house *(izba)* with 'wooden-lace' window frames and eaves can still be seen. The best preserved ones are in Irkutsk and the villages around Lake Baikal.

Siberia's churches were rarely anything grand, although the functional wooden structures did possess a stark beauty born of simplicity. Most of these early churches were later destroyed and the best examples which now remain are preserved in once-Russian Alaska.

Native Culture

Native art and culture has been relegated to the exhibit cases in regional museums, squeezed between the stuffed seals and the railway builders' theodolites. Outside the museums, the only other place to see native crafts is in the big city art salons, which are supplied by a small cottage industry of artisans. The Evenki keep the souvenir shops of Irkutsk stocked with small carved wooden items, while in Khabarovsk you can pick up cylindrical containers made of birch bark by local Nanai.

One art form that has survived is dance. The Buryat peoples retain their unique steps and patterns, which they put on show every summer at the Buryatia festival, but more interesting are the Koryaks of northern Kamchatka. The Koryaks use dance to tell stories, not just traditional myths and legends but also contemporary tales and anecdotes – 'the day I got my fingers trapped in the snowmobile tracks', that sort of thing – done as a fluid, ensemble mime. Dance troupes sometimes travel down to perform in Petropavlovsk-Kamchatsky, the regional capital.

Another unique example of living native Siberian culture is Tuvan throat singing. You may be lucky enough to hear this at festivals or celebrations such as weddings in Tuva. It's a kind of very deep, tuneful chanting, produced from somewhere deep down in the throat – quite startling when you first hear it. Tuvan throat singers have made international tours, and various recordings of their music are available in the West; one CD, *Voices from the Distant Steppe*, is released on the UK Realworld label.

RELIGION

Shamanism

Long before the coming of Christianity, the common religion of the indigenous tribes of Siberia was shamanism, a form of pagan earth-worship that dates back to the Stone Age, based on the observance of lunar rituals and sacred natural sites. All natural objects were believed to have a spirit and people contacted these spirits for guidance by means of a shaman: a high priest, prophet and doctor rolled into one. A few shamans still exist, particularly in Buryatia and Sakha. Some spectacular old shamans' outfits can be seen in several Siberian museums, for example the regional museums at Irkutsk and Kyzyl.

Christianity

The church made its first appearance in the 1570s in the form of a collapsible tent carried over the Ural Mountains by a mercantile-sponsored band of marauding explorers. The first permanent church structure in Siberia was built in Tyumen in 1586. Soon afterwards, as part of their methods of subjugation, the Russians began forcibly baptising the natives – in some cases, tying a couple to poles and ducking them into water through a hole cut in the ice. Unsurprisingly, Christianity was never a big hit.

The state initially backed the Church in Siberia, perceiving it as an excellent tool of colonisation. But eventually, as the wealth and influence of the Church grew, it came to be viewed as a threat to secular power and a determined attempt was made to subordinate it to the state.

After the Russian Church reforms of 1653, there were those who couldn't accept the changes and continued to worship in the old ways. These Old Believers became subject to persecution and many fled to Siberia. Their beliefs still survive in villages in the Buryatia region, particularly in the vicinity of Ulan Ude.

As well as the Old Believers, many other religious communities were exiled to Siberia or simply settled there hoping to find freedom of worship. The Skoptsy were a fanatical Christian sect exiled to Olekminsk in Yakutia during the 18th century. They believed in sexual abstinence, and to remove the threat of temptation, young males were castrated.

Many Russian Orthodox churches were destroyed in the civil war, or at least suffered some damage, which gave the Bolsheviks an excellent excuse to complete the demolition and erect patriotic statues and monuments to the Party instead. The surviving churches were usually converted to some secular use: the Church of the Trinity in Irkutsk became a planetarium; a Lutheran church in Vladivostok was commandeered for a naval museum; and the Orthodox Hodigitria Cathedral in Ulan Ude was designated a museum of atheism. The Church in Siberia has yet to exhibit any signs of recovery.

For further details on Christianity in Russia, see Facts about European Russia.

Buddhism

Buddhists in the Russian Federation number over half a million, a figure that has been growing steadily in the years since glasnost began to allow free expression of religion. All Russia's Buddhists are members of the Gelugpa or 'Yellow-Hat' sect of Tibetan Buddhism, whose spiritual leader is the Dalai Lama. All of them are descendants of peoples who originally lived on the border with Mongolia, where Buddhism reached in the 17th and early 18th centuries – Buryats near Lake Baikal and Tuvans to their west.

Contemplative and essentially atheistic, Buddhism was never a direct threat to the state and was tolerated until Stalin attempted to wipe it out in the 1930s, closing its 250 temples and 50 monasteries *(datsans)* and exiling or executing thousands of lamas, or priests. At the end of WWII, two datsans were opened, a new one at Ivolginsk near Ulan Ude and an old one at Aginsk, near Chita.

Since 1950 Buddhism has been organised under a Buddhist Religious Board at Ivolginsk. Until the era of glasnost the only approved work for Buddhist organisations was to maintain a profile in various world peace movements. Now they are free to reopen monasteries, and are doing so. The Dalai Lama has visited both Buryatia and Tuva.

Judaism

Even before the Soviet creation of the Jewish Autonomous Region centred on Birobidzhan, Siberia was home to large numbers of Jewish people. At one time they accounted for one-third of the population of Sretensk (a port town on the Shilka River, 300km east of Chita) and in the 1880s Kansk, near Krasnoyarsk, was so predominantly Jewish that it was known as the Jerusalem of Siberia.

There was also a synagogue in Verkhneudinsk (later Ulan Ude), and the one in Irkutsk is still standing and now operates as a Jewish cultural centre.

LANGUAGE

Though the minority peoples of Siberia and the Russian Far East have their own languages, Russian is the predominant tongue virtually everywhere, except in Tuva. As a result of literacy campaigns both in and outside the public school system, the Buryat and Sakha languages are also making a comeback. See the Language chapter for help with the basics.

Facts for the Visitor

Though it's something for which the old Soviet system is frequently derided, the degree of homogeneity that it installed throughout such a vast territory – one which encompasses a great variety of people, traditions and geography – is nothing short of remarkable. But it's fast disappearing. People in Vladivostok, a city east of Calcutta, and Kaliningrad, just north of Poland, are no longer driving the same curry-coloured cars of exactly the same model. The prematurely aged cement apartment blocks are giving way to one-family mansions in amazing varieties of bad taste.

Information in this chapter is largely specific to Siberia and the Russian Far East. See the European Russia Facts for the Visitor chapter for more general information on travel in Russia.

SUGGESTED ITINERARIES

Basically the only way to explore this huge chunk of the world is to move east to west or west to east, along the Trans-Siberian Railway or the Baikal-Amur Mainline (BAM). Whether and where to venture beyond the well trodden tracks depends on how much time and money you have. Certainly, you can have a great trip just by hopping from one Trans-Siberian city to the next. But the best this part of Russia has to offer is not in the cities along the Trans-Siberian, but in the vast and varied wilderness regions to the north, east and south of the tracks, namely the Altay, Lake Baikal, Taymyr, Yakutia, Kolyma, Chukotka, Sakhalin Island and Kamchatka. Ideally, you'd need a month to explore each of these huge regions. Some – Taymyr, Kolyma and Chukotka – require serious planning just to get to, never mind to survive once you get there.

If you've only got a month or less to see Siberia and the Russian Far East, you're best off sticking to the Trans-Siberian, spending a few days in some of the cities along the way and on the more easily accessible south shore of Lake Baikal. If you've got two months, that's enough to do the Trans-Siberian Railway at leisure, spend a week or so exploring Lake Baikal, and still have time to take in one other region that strikes your fancy. Don't be too rigid about your schedule; allow for the unexpected, whether that be an invitation to a dacha or a roundabout way from point A to B. This is probably the one place in the world where you can still find somewhere that nobody else has ever been.

PLANNING

When to Go

When to go depends a great deal on which Siberia you want to see and what you want to do there. In summer, getting around is easier and the bustle of street life and pavement traders adds an upbeat air to what can otherwise be some fairly charmless cities. But winter brings to life the Siberia of the imagination: starkly beautiful, sugar-frosted landscapes, and townscapes that resemble a succession of Christmas card scenes. Much of the urban grime disappears, hidden beneath a great, white cloak. Temperatures as low as -25°C, though, might not be to everybody's liking. Winter can also make overland travel other than by rail difficult, as roads become blocked.

April and May can be wet and slushy, and June and July are the worst months for biting insects. By August, the air has cleared of mosquitoes. In early October the temperature is still quite mild and the deciduous vegetation, particularly in the east, takes on a glorious russet palette. See also Climate in Facts about Siberia & the Russian Far East.

Very few hotels offer out-of-season rates; if they do it's 10 to 20%.

Maps

There aren't many good maps exclusively of Siberia; instead you should aim to pick up a good one of Russia as a whole. See Maps in the European Russia Facts for the Visitor chapter for further details.

Once in Siberia, bookshops often sell maps of neighbouring cities or regions but not necessarily of their own. If you see a map or plan of a place you may be going to, pick it up because it's quite possible you won't find one when you get there.

What to Bring

A summer or autumn trip to Siberia doesn't require you to pack anything much that's not on the list given in European Russia Facts for the Visitor. The one item you might not take out of your suitcase until the Far East is a small torch, essential for navigating hotel corridors and the night streets during power outages.

For day trips out of town, mosquito repellent is a good idea and can usually be bought in pharmacies or at kiosks. Make sure you purchase a brand containing a high concentration of DEET (diethyl-m-toluamid). To avoid acquiring a complexion like blowtorched paint while hiking or cruising, we recommend a scarf to wrap around your face or even a head net, and some thick gloves. For other health-related items to pack, see the boxed text 'Medical Kit Check List' under Health in the European Russia Facts for the Visitor chapter.

One travel survival expert working in Sakhalin suggested an inflatable tube to replace the missing toilet seats (good for people travelling with small children). In hotel rooms where hot water is lacking, the tube can also be filled with cold water and left on the radiator. When the water is warm enough, empty the tube into a can with holes in the bottom for a quickie hot shower. Of course you're going to need some way (or someone) to hold the can.

Until mid-October a jumper (sweater) and a jacket are enough to keep you warm, but from then until late May you're going to need considerably more. Thermal underwear is a must, as are thick woollen socks, gloves, a scarf, a heavy coat and a woollen hat. It's also advisable to wear thick-soled boots. Lip salve and skin-moisturising creams are also a good idea. You might also want to take a heating coil (not all hotels have a *dezhurnaya* or floor attendant to supply hot water) and some sachets of instant coffee, hot chocolate or soup.

RESPONSIBLE TOURISM

Siberians, as closely as they live with nature, don't always respect it. It's not unusual to see ship captains tossing empty bottles out their cabin windows or fish wardens moonlighting as poachers. Siberians tend to regard nature as their worst enemy, and survival is a matter of taking everything they can gather, shoot or cut. Keep that in mind when someone offers to sell you a suitcase full of frozen Kamchatkan crabs, fresh caviar, or smoked *omul*, a rare freshwater fish endemic to Lake Baikal. Also, as a responsible traveller you're probably going to be appalled by the mess some Siberian comrades leave in the forests. If you're travelling with Russians you might want to discreetly pick up your own empty vodka bottle instead of letting them smash it. Of course, you're not going to change how they live, but at least you're not making things worse.

CONSULATES

Australia
(☎ 4232-42 74 64, fax 42 69 16)
prospekt Krasnogo Znameni 42, 2nd floor, Vladivostok

China
(☎ 4212-34 85 37, ☎/fax 39 97 89)
In the north-west corner of the grounds of the Lenin Stadium in Khabarovsk
Visa applications are accepted on Monday, Wednesday and Friday from 10.30 am to 1 pm. The cost is $70 for a single-entry visa and processing takes two days.

Japan
(☎ 4232-26 75 02, fax 26 75 41)
ulitsa Verkhneportovaya 46, 6th floor, Vladivostok
Visa applications are accepted from 10 am to noon, weekdays except Wednesday.

Mongolia
(☎ 3952-34 24 47)
ulitsa Lapina 11, Irkutsk
Issues transit visas that are good for stays fewer than 10 days. For a longer stay, you'll need a tourist visa which also requires you to have a prepaid hotel voucher, unless you can convince the consul that you're a 'student type capable of fending for yourself' (the consul's

words). Transit visas cost $30 for express service or $15 if you have a few days to wait. It's open from 9 am to 1 pm, Monday to Friday, except during Naadam (usually in the second week of July).

South Korea
(☎ 4232-22 77 29, fax 22 94 71)
ulitsa Aleutskaya 45a, 5th floor, Vladivostok

UK
(☎ 3432-56 49 31, fax 59 29 01, brit@gin.global-one.ru)
ulitsa Gogolya 15A, Yekaterinburg

USA
(☎ 3432-56 46 19/91, fax 56 45 15, cgyekat@uscgyekat.mplik.ru)
ulitsa Gogolya 15A, Yekaterinburg
(☎ 4232-30 00 70, fax 30 00 91)
ulitsa Pushkinskaya 32, Vladivostok

MONEY

Unfortunately, the advice has to be to carry cash – preferably US dollars, and lots of them. Bank tellers in Siberia can be finicky about the dollars they will accept. If a bill is defaced in any way – written on, torn, dirty or badly worn – it'll be handed straight back. Some tellers won't accept any bills printed before 1990.

You might see signs saying credit cards (Visa, MasterCard, Eurocard) and travellers cheques (American Express and to a lesser extent Thomas Cook) are accepted, but any attempt to use them will probably result in a Chaplinesque scene of you pointing desperately to the sign and the stone-faced teller shaking her head no. Depending on the economic mood swing, you might be able in Yekaterinburg, Novosibirsk, Krasnoyarsk, Irkutsk, Severobaikalsk, Khabarovsk, Vladivostok and Yuzhno-Sakhalinsk to get a cash advance (in roubles and sometimes in US dollars) on a Visa card at ATMs – but don't count on it.

For those who have to carry large wads of cash, the only consolation is that security isn't the problem you might imagine. Take sensible precautions such as dividing your money into three or four stashes hidden out of view about your person (neck purse, money belt etc, all worn under your clothing), and take solace in the fact that nowadays there are a lot of Russians with gobs more money on them than you.

Costs

As a general rule of thumb, the farther east and north you go in Siberia, the more expensive it gets. For example, the cost of a loaf of black bread (the standard Russian price index) is $0.50 in Moscow, $1 in Vladivostok, $1.50 in Yakutsk and even as much as $3.50 in the northern villages of Kamchatka.

Depending on the level of comfort required, accommodation in Siberia is going to cost an average $30 to $80 per night for a double room. In the Russian Far East, the price range is $20 to $180, with the cost of a reasonably comfortable room at about $50 per night.

Dining out in Siberia, it's possible to get away at under $5 per head, but in cities such as Khabarovsk or Vladivostok the outlay for a decent meal in a restaurant is at least $10. Of course, it is possible to eat much more cheaply, maybe for just $3 or $4, but it's not guaranteed to be a pleasant experience. If you're not looking to cut corners and economise constantly, a reasonable budget would be around $50 per day, not including train fares or flights.

INTERNET RESOURCES

These days you can probably search for just about any Siberian city name and come up with a Web page, but whether it's been updated in the last year or accessible in English is another story. Here are a few sites that might be useful.

www.interknowledge.com/russia – the official site of the Russian National Tourist Office with information on Lake Baikal and the Arctic region.

www.iaito.com – provides an overview of the region's highlights, a photographic tour, tourist information and maps.

www.russianfareast.com – predominantly concerned with business travellers and investment but provides a number of useful links for tourists.

www.mnh.si.edu/arctic/features/croads – take a virtual tour of the Washington-based National Museum of Natural History's *Crossroads of Continents* exhibit, which takes a look at the peoples of Siberia and Alaska.

meteo.infospace.ru – will get you the weather forecast for most Russian cities.

BOOKS

See the European Russia Facts for the Visitor chapter for more general background reading, and the Trans-Siberian Railway chapter for books specific to that journey.

Lonely Planet

The *Russian phrasebook* has detailed language information giving invaluable help to the traveller. Lonely Planet also has guides to many neighbouring countries and regions including China, Mongolia, Central Asia, Korea and Japan. Parts of Siberia and the Russian Far East also feature in the guide to the Arctic.

Guidebooks

Though no longer in print, *Trekking in Russia & Central Asia* by Frith Maier has good coverage of the wilderness regions of the Altay and Sayan mountains, the Lake Baikal region, Ussuriland, Sakhalin, Chukotka and Kamchatka. The *Trans-Siberian Handbook* by Bryn Thomas covers in some detail the major settlements along the rail line.

Travel

Originally published in 1863, *Recollections of Tartar Steppes and their Inhabitants* by Lucy Atkinson recounts this British woman's travels through Siberia and Central Asia. During the summer of 1991, Frederick Kempe followed the Tom River north from Novokuznetsk to the Ob and on to the Arctic Sea, a journey recalled in *Siberian Odyssey: A Voyage Into the Russian Soul*. The style is journalistic (Kempe is Berlin bureau chief of the *Wall Street Journal*) and concentrates on exposing the evils of the Soviet system through interviews with some of the dozens of people he met en route. At around the same time Italian journalist Tiziano Terzani was sailing down the Amur River when he heard news of the coup in the Kremlin. *Goodnight Mr Lenin* (out of print) records the lack of immediate impact that the death of communism had in the Russian Far East and follows the writer's efforts to scramble to Moscow and get in on the story.

Cycling may not seem like the obvious way to get across Siberia, and a book describing the attempt sounds a less than thrilling prospect, but it's to the credit of two authors who undertook two different, transcontinental Russian bike rides that their books are so engrossing.

The first expedition was undertaken by a joint US-USSR team in summer 1989, setting off from Vladivostok and following roughly the route of the Trans-Siberian Railway. The resulting account, *Off the Map* by Mark Jenkins, is extremely well written but its focus on group dynamics pushes everything else into the background. In *Between the Hammer and the Sickle* (out of print), author Simon Vickers doesn't mention whether his team, which crossed Russia from west to east the following year, knew that they'd been beaten to the achievement, but he can take some consolation in the fact that his is the better book. Vickers' description of the often nightmarish journey (a recurring phrase is 'hideously ugly') provides a surprisingly absorbing, empathetic and evocative picture of Soviet suburban living and life in rural Siberia.

If the cyclists made good reading out of potentially train-spotterish material, Christina Dodwell has managed the reverse. In *Beyond Siberia* (out of print) she describes several weeks in Kamchatka, among dramatic landscapes of smouldering volcanoes and precarious snow bridges, skiing around lumbering bears and scooting up clouds of snow while riding with an aerobatically inclined helicopter pilot. But what could have been a fascinating account is rendered unflaggingly dull by some excruciatingly bad prose. Better to travel with Laurens van der Post who, in his *Journey into Russia*, never got anywhere quite as exciting as Kamchatka (he visited Bratsk, Irkutsk and Khabarovsk) but recorded what he saw with an intelligence and insight still valid more than 30 years on.

Tuva or Bust! by Californian Ralph Leighton is not so much a travelogue as a pretravelogue, describing his own and Nobel physics laureate Richard Feynman's growing obsession with Tuva, which began at a dinner-table geography guessing game in 1977, and the pair's years of trying to unravel Soviet bureaucracy in order to visit Tuva. You learn a lot about the place though Leighton doesn't actually get there till the book's epilogue. Feynman died just before the final go-ahead for their trip was received, in 1988.

General

For basic background reading, Benson Bobrick's *East of the Sun* is an excellent and very readable history of the conquest and settlement of Siberia and the Russian Far East, good on things like who mutilated whom and in what way.

A more academic treatment is given in *The Russian Far East: A History* by John J Stephan. *A History of the Peoples of Siberia* by James Forsyth covers the same ground but from the perspective of the indigenous tribes. Forsyth's book is rather heavy going and those with a more casual interest might prefer *The Forgotten Peoples of Siberia* by Fred Mayer, a beautiful photographic essay on the living conditions and traditions of groups such as the reindeer-herding Koryaks and the walrus-hunting Chukchi.

The animal and plant life of Siberia and parts east comes under scrutiny in chapters of *The Realms of the Russian Bear* (out of print) by John Sparks and *The Nature of Russia* (out of print) by John Massey Stewart, both written with the novice naturalist in mind and lavishly illustrated.

Also heavy on photographs is another natural wonders book, *Baikal, Sacred Sea of Siberia*, a pictorial tribute to the great lake with a text by travel writer and novelist Peter Matthiessen.

NEWSPAPERS & MAGAZINES

For a general overview of the Russian media see the European Russia Facts for the Visitor chapter. Every major town and city throughout Siberia and the Russian Far East has its own newspapers and periodicals. Japanese-language newspapers are available at a few hotels in the Russian Far East. The one English-language newspaper, published in Vladivostok, was available only online at vlad.tribnet.com after the economic crisis of 1998.

RADIO & TV

Each region or territory also has its own TV channel – usually a mix of local news and yet more imported soaps. Anyone who turns on the TV in some remote, unspoiled wilderness den and is confronted with *Santa Barbara*, followed by 30 minutes of whooping, high-kicking Australian aerobics, will soon start to see a grain of sense in the nationalistic rantings of Vladimir Zhirinovsky. One or two hotels in Khabarovsk and Vladivostok do have CNN and other satellite channels. If you can speak Japanese you'll benefit from the Hokkaido-based TV transmissions that can be picked up on southern Sakhalin.

PHOTOGRAPHY & VIDEO

See European Russia Facts for the Visitor for general comments. Taking photographs in Siberia only presents problems in deep winter when temperatures are way down in the minuses. At extremely low temperatures camera batteries won't function and film becomes very brittle. If cameras are exposed to cold and humidity for too long they acquire a frosty coating which can later work its way inside and cause havoc within the camera body.

There no longer appear to be any restrictions on what can or cannot be photographed, though some local people might disagree. It's always a good idea to ask permission before taking photos of people, as a courtesy.

Film stocks can be replenished in every major city and most smaller cities. In most cities, there are Fuji and Kodak photo labs which offer 24 hour processing; the quality varies, though.

TIME

The regions of Siberia and the Russian Far East spread across no fewer than eight time zones, which can have a strangely disorienting effect if you're travelling steadily across them.

When it's noon in Moscow, it's ...

2 pm in Yekaterinburg and Tyumen
3 pm in Omsk and Novosibirsk
4 pm in Barnaul, Gorno-Altaysk, Krasnoyarsk, Abakan and Kyzyl
5 pm in Bratsk, Irkutsk and Ulan Ude
6 pm in Chita, Blagoveshchensk and Yakutsk
7 pm in Khabarovsk and Vladivostok
8 pm in Sakhalin and Magadan
9 pm in Kamchatka and Providenia

Long-distance train timetables, most train station clocks and some air timetables are on Moscow time.

HEALTH

A specific local hazard in some Siberian and Russian Far East areas, from May to September, is encephalitis. Tick-borne encephalitis, a risk anywhere in rural Russia during these months, is apparently a particular danger in Ussuriland, while Japanese encephalitis (caused by mosquito bites) is a danger in rural areas bordering Mongolia, China and North Korea. Trekkers, campers and others going to rural areas should consider immunisation, which is available for both types of encephalitis. For more information on encephalitis and for overall coverage of health in Russia, see the Health section of European Russia Facts for the Visitor.

WOMEN TRAVELLERS

See the Women Travellers section in European Russia Facts for the Visitor. Anything referred to as hard to get in the better supplied, western part of the country is going to be nearly impossible to get in Siberia. East of the Urals, the idea that women are less knowledgeable and, on the whole, less capable than men still persists. It can get very irritating, but at least you don't have to live there. Siberian women relish the chance to talk alone with a foreign woman, and the first thing they'll tell you is just how hopeless their menfolk are. When journeying by train, women might consider purchasing a *platskartny* (open carriage) rather than a *kupeyny* (compartmentalised) ticket and risk getting stuck in a closed compartment with three shady characters. If you do decide to travel kupeyny and don't like your cabin mates, tell the conductor who more than likely will find you a new place.

GAY & LESBIAN TRAVELLERS

Russian society is conservative, and Siberia is even more so. See the Gay & Lesbian Travellers section in European Russia Facts for the Visitor.

DISABLED TRAVELLERS & SENIOR TRAVELLERS

Travelling in Siberia can be exhausting and at times harrowing. Scrap wood serves as makeshift planks so people can disembark from river boats. Footpaths, never mind ramps, are nonexistent. Stairs are often missing steps. But this isn't to say Siberia is off limits, especially if your guide has experience in dealing with special needs.

USEFUL ORGANISATIONS

Baikal Watch, Earth Island Institute (☎ 415-788 3666, www.earthisland.org/baikal), 300 Broadway, Suite 28, San Francisco, CA 94133, USA, is a Russian-American environmental research group active in the protection and preservation of Lake Baikal. The International Crane Foundation (☎ 608-356 9462, www.savingcranes.org), PO Box 447, Baraboo, WI 53913-0447, USA, is active in preserving crane populations in Siberia and the Russian Far East.

DANGERS & ANNOYANCES

Siberia and the Russian Far East have few dangers but they're loaded with annoyances. Some specific hazards include bears if you're trekking in Kamchatka and tick-borne encephalitis in Ussuriland (see Health), but generally speaking, you're far safer out here than in Moscow or St Petersburg. The possible exception is Irkutsk, which has long been a popular stopover for Trans-Mongolian and Trans-Manchurian passengers. Travellers have reported problems here such as the theft of bags, especially around the train station, and even the occasional mugging. This is one place to take care, especially at night.

PUBLIC HOLIDAYS & SPECIAL EVENTS

See European Russia Facts for the Visitor for general Russian holidays and events.

February-March

Tibetan Buddhist New Year (Tsagaalgan)
A moveable feast, lasting 16 days, which celebrates the lunar new year and hence advances by about 10 days a year. Mainly celebrated at family level in Buryatia and Tuva. Known as Shagaa in Tuva.

June

Tun-Payram
Khakass opening-of-summer-pastures festival. Traditional food, costumes, sports. It is celebrated in Abakan, usually on the first or second Sunday of the month, and then in villages.

July

Maitreya Buddha Festival
At Ivolginsk *datsan* (monastery) near Ulan Ude.

Buryatia Folk Festival
Celebrated at the ethnographic museum in Ulan Ude.

Ysyakh
Yakut opening-of-pastures festival. Traditional food and costumes.

August

Naadym
Tuvan summer festival, with Tuvan wrestling *(khuresh)*, throat-singing and long-distance horse races.

December-January

Russian Winter Festival
Tourist-oriented troyka rides and folklore performances at Irkutsk.

ACTIVITIES

Siberia and the Russian Far East is little more than a wilderness on which humanity has scarcely made a scratch. As such it's ideal adventure holiday terrain. Activities such as mountaineering, rafting and canoeing have always been popular with Russians and many small towns have well established outdoor clubs. One vital thing to be aware of is that you can't just turn up and expect to do things. Even if you arrive armed with addresses and phone numbers it can take two or three days to make contact with anyone – and then maybe a further couple of days for them to figure out exactly what it is that you want of them. Give people as much advance warning as possible and, even if you can't hammer out all the details, give them an idea of what you are interested in. Above all, be flexible, be patient, and don't expect things to always go smoothly.

Agencies

Foreign travel firms offer some activity-centred and adventure trips to Siberia which, at a price, take the effort out of setting it all up (see the Siberia & Russian Far East Getting There & Away chapter). Some Russian-based agencies which might be helpful:

Travel Russia
(☎ 095-290 34 39, ☎ 290 30 88, fax 956 61 85, travrus@dataforce.net)
Trubnikovsky pereulok 21, korpus 2, Moscow 121069)
Specialises in outdoor holidays, Trans-Siberian packages and tours in Altay. It also handles occasional requests from individuals and is experienced in dealing with foreigners.

Pilgrim Tours (Moskovskoe Turisticheskoe Agenstvo Piligrim)
(☎ 095-207 32 43, ☎/fax 208 10 40, pilgrimtours@glas.apc.org)
ulitsa Neglinnaya 20, korpus 2, Moscow 10301)
Another adventure-based tour outfitter, though reportedly it has become a bit rusty and its staff does not speak English.

Lenalptours
(☎ 812-279 0716, ☎ 279 0776, fax 279 0651, lenalptr@mail.wplus.net)
ulitsa Vosstania 9, kv 4, St Petersburg, 193036
Has English-speaking staff and the contacts to arrange activities in many parts of Siberia, including Altay and the northern territories.

Knowledgeable and experienced local specialists we can recommend who can fix up a wide range of activities in their regions – from rafting or skiing to trekking, riding or climbing, as appropriate – include:

Ural Mountains & Yekaterinburg Region
Konstantin Brylyakov of the Yekaterinburg Convention & Visitor Bureau
(☎ 3432-48 5451, fax 55 1664, transaer@etel.ru)
An ex-Sputnik guide with extensive knowledge of the area.

Sputnik
(☎ 3432-59 8300, ☎ 51 9157, fax 51 3483, sputnik.ekatb@gin.global-one.ru)
ulitsa Pushkina 5, Yekaterinburg
Might also be a useful first contact.

Altay

Sibalp
(☎ 3832-49 5922, ☎/fax 54 1374, sibalp@nstu.nsk.su)
ulitsa Nemirovicha-Danchenko 155/1, kv 47
A reliable firm that offers rafting, climbing and other tours in the Altay Republic.

Sputnik-Altai
(☎ 3852-36 7189, ☎ 36 7750, fax 36 7275, admin@st.alt.ru)
Sotsialistichesky prospekt 87, Barnaul
Offers hiking, horse riding and skiing.

Khakassia & Tuva

Abakan Tours
(☎ 39022-6 74 42, fax 6 37 60, morokov@dialup.comlink.khakassia.ru)
In Abakanïs Hotel Intourist in Khakassia, organises rafting and boat excursions, as well as cycling trips for the dogged on the so-called Sayan Ring through Khakassia and Tuva. One route is 1200km, includes eight mountain passes and takes in most of the important sights in both republics. There's also an easier three day route.

Lake Baikal Region

Baikalcomplex
(☎/fax 3952-38 92 05, ☎/fax 43 20 60, youry@travel.baikal.ru)
PO Box 3598, Irkutsk 664 074
Offers all kinds of adventure tours, rafting, hiking, skiing, biking, scuba diving and homestays at Lake Baikal and surrounding regions.

Igor Fedenyov
Morskaya 2A, Severobaikalsk
Charters ships for exploring the northern wonders of the lake: the Bay of Ayaya (which in the local Evenki language means very, very beautiful); the hot springs of Khakusy; the ruins of an Evenki village at the mouth of the upper Angara River, and the list goes on. It may be possible to arrange to stay at his house with his wife Valya and his English-speaking daughters, Marina and Yulya.

Magadan, Kolyma & Chukotka

Mikhail Skopets
(☎ 4132-23 29 90, ibpn@ibpn.magadan.su)
A biologist and avid fisherman whose claim to fame is that he knows the outlying regions of Magadan, including Kolyma and Chukotka, like his backyard. He also speaks English and has worked with many Westerners. Boris Levin of BOL Tours (☎/fax 4132-22 02 96, bol@online.magadan.su or bol@asianoffice.com) is reportedly another excellent northern guide.

Vladivostok & Primore

Dalintour
(☎ 4232-22 29 49, fax 26 15 44, taiga@dalint.marine.su)
ulitsa Fokina 1, Vladivostok
Organises trekking, camping and rafting in the Primorsky region. It also has experience in accommodating people with sight disabilities.

Kamchatka

Two brothers and mountain climbers, Vitaly and Sergey Malkov can fulfil most of your volcanic fantasies. They also run a camping equipment store, Alpindustriya-Kamchatka (☎/fax 41522-7 2489), Kosmichesky 4-61, Petropavlovsk-Kamchatsky, 683003 Russia. Another person highly knowledgeable of the region is Vasily Galichin (☎ 4152-11 25 44).

More companies that organise trekking, climbing and other activities are listed under Organised Tours in Siberia & the Russian Far East Getting There & Away chapter, and under Travel Agents in the regional sections.

Trekking

Much of Siberia is covered in thick taiga forest that is extremely difficult to move through and somewhat boring. The best trekking is found where the forest is broken by other physical features such as mountains or rivers. Kamchatka, with its awesome volcanic landscapes, and the very beautiful Altay Mountains are great places to explore, and some walks up the western coast of Lake Baikal, perhaps using a boat for backup, could be rewarding. Less ambitiously, many of the towns along the Baikal-Amur Mainline (BAM) are good bases for heading out into the wilds. The western part of the line passes through some quite mountainous terrain, complete with high-altitude lakes and hot springs, and abandoned Gulag camps hidden in high canyons.

Mountain Climbing

Possibilities for climbing exist in the Ural Mountains, the Altay (south of Novosibirsk on the Kazakhstan and Mongolian borders), the Kuznetsky Alatau (a range north of the Altay with less elevation but easier to reach from the Kuznetsk basin cities), the Sayan Mountains (on the Mongolian border), in the Baikalsky range (on the western shore of Lake Baikal) and among the volcanoes of the Kamchatka Peninsula. Frith Maier's book *Trekking in Russia & Central Asia* (out of print) offers information on worthwhile climbs and the difficulties they present.

Rafting & Canoeing

With its 53,000-plus rivers, Siberia has plenty of potential for waterborne adventuring. As a consequence most tour companies offer some kind of rafting, canoeing or boating program. In the Russian Far East, Alpindustriya-Kamchatka does white-water rafting along Kamchatkan rivers. Dalintour has trips in Primore.

Skiing

Almost all the skiing done in Siberia is of the cross-country variety. Any local tour agency can help out with finding a pair of skis and point you in the right direction. Alpindustriya-Kamchatka can organise skiing and snowboarding on the slopes of volcanoes as well as at a summer camp in Rodnikovoe. There are no ski resorts as such, and the closest thing is the Gorny Vozdukh (Mountain Air) tourist centre, 3km outside Yuzhno-Sakhalinsk on the island of Sakhalin. It has a couple of straight downhill runs, a slalom route and 70 and 90m ski jumps. A hotel, the Santa Resort, is conveniently located nearby. There is also a 340m ski slope with chairlifts at Solnechny Springs near Severobaikalsk.

Fishing

Siberia, and particularly the Russian Far East, are an angler's paradise with rivers swollen with grayling and various species of salmon. However, this sitting around for hours dangling a piece of string off the end of a pole and into the water can be a heart-stoppingly expensive business. While it is possible to go it alone and just head off with rod and tackle, most regions have severe restrictions on fishing.

WORK

Opportunities for work are scarce, except perhaps in large cities where native speakers of English and sometimes German or Japanese are in demand. You'll have to search high and low to find a private English-language school – the principal source of employment for English-speaking travellers worldwide – in Siberia or the Russian Far East. However, you probably will have an easy time arranging a private tutorship or setting up your own private class with the help of an advertisement in a local newspaper or by word of mouth. Being taken on as a teacher by a local state school is possible but it's an administrative nightmare and can take months to set up.

The chances of finding employment are probably best in Yekaterinburg, Novosibirsk, Khabarovsk and Vladivostok, cities that have a large number of foreign enterprises and exchanges. The semi-annual *Russian Far East Directory* has a listing of all foreign companies. It can be bought (about $17) at American Business Centers in Vladivostok, Yuzhno-Sakhalinsk and Khabarovsk, or ordered through Russian Information Services Inc (toll-free within the USA ☎ 800-639 4301, outside the USA ☎ 802-223 4955), 89 Main St, Box 2, Montpelier, Vermont, 05602 USA. You could also check the classifieds section of the English-language newspaper in Vladivostok, available on the Internet at vlad.tribnet.com.

ACCOMMODATION

Hotels in Siberia, unused to the expectations and requirements of foreign visitors, tend to be worse than those in European Russia. Paying $50 per night still does not guarantee having hot water, a functioning light in the bathroom or a seat on the toilet. Occasionally, you may experience the flip-side and find a hidden gem of a hotel, which ought to command sky-high prices but instead is dirt cheap; but such things are rare.

The Russian Far East, already visited by large numbers of Japanese and Koreans, has a number of good, upmarket hotels. These places have a high standard of amenities (in one case not just any toilet seats but thermostatically controlled, heated toilet seats) and charge correspondingly high prices.

A lot of the small, independent tourist companies are pushing homestays as a cheap alternative to hotels. The standard price is about $30, for which you should get a bed for the night, with clean sheets, and maybe breakfast. Russian-based agencies that can arrange homestays in cities along the Trans-Siberian Railway include the Travellers Guest House in Moscow, HOFA in St Petersburg, and Baikalcomplex in Irkutsk. (See Places to Stay for these cities for contact information.) Overseas, try American-International Homestays (☎ 303-642 3088 or toll-free ☎ 800-876 2048, fax 303-642 3365, www.spectravel.com/homes), PO Box 1754, Nederland, CO 80466-1754, USA, which does a 15 day Siberian homestay trip for $2199 (land only). Travel agencies in Yekaterinburg and Novosibirsk can arrange homestays in those cities (see the respective city sections in the Western Siberia chapter). See also the Accommodation section in European Russia Facts for the Visitor for further possibilities.

FOOD

Unfortunately, dining in Siberia is still stuck firmly in the Soviet era. In Russia's Far East, even the close proximity of China, Korea and Japan hasn't managed to much enliven the local cuisine. The only noticeable influence the Orient has had is to replace stodgy, grey potatoes with clots of stodgy, grey rice. In most provincial towns and cities the only restaurants generally belong to hotels, with other options being limited to a desultory handful of cafes and *stolovye* (cafeterias). In such places it's wise to arrive with provisions to relieve the tedium of potato salad and salami. There are exceptions: Irkutsk, Khabarovsk and Vladivostok are all good on the stomach. All three have a number of fine private restaurants in which, variously, it's possible to eat sushi, mu-shu pork or kangaroo. Novosibirsk has a couple of good steak bars; the food situation in the Altay Republic and Tuva is abysmal. After the 1998 economic crisis, the food supply to isolated areas in northern Siberia became critical.

Most hotel food is Russian or Ukrainian with just a 'Siberian' tacked onto the name – like *myaso po Sibirski* (meat Siberian-style), beef topped with cheese, or *vyrezka po tayozhnomu* (taiga tender loin), cubed steak cooked with herbs. The Siberian staple is *pelmeni* (steamed or boiled small, doughy packets stuffed with meat), a bit like a heavier version of ravioli. Pelmeni are usually served heaped on a plate with sour cream or butter. Farther east, pelmeni are often served in a stock soup, flavoured with fennel and sometimes with a pastry covering. In Buryatia there's a bigger, palm-sized version of pelmeni called *pozy*, sometimes spiced and commonly sold by roadside vendors at about $0.50 each – two or three make a good, greasy meal. There's a peppery version in the Russian Far East called *pyan-se*.

Fish is plentiful, especially in late summer and autumn when salmon *(losos)* or sturgeon *(osyotr)* is far more likely to grace the table than meat. Around Baikal, these fish are supplemented by *omul*, a cousin of the salmon and trout, endemic to the lake and considered a local delicacy. Russians serve it smoked, broiled or salted on a slice of bread as an appetiser, in the same manner as that most ubiquitous of Siberian appetisers, caviar. *Ikra* usually comes in two types: black (from the sturgeon), the best and most expensive caviar; and red (from the salmon), which is saltier, cheaper and far more common. Far from being the food of princes, every Siberian household has a great jar of the stuff stored somewhere cool, and on station platforms and in pavement stalls babushki sell it by the litre for about $8. (A moderate warning: several travellers have become extremely ill on fish. Russians tend to overcook it, but they don't always store it properly.)

Seafood replaces freshwater fish in the Pacific coast region, especially around

Vladivostok. Standard items on the menu include *kalmary*, *kraby* and *grebeshki* (scallops).

Few Siberians ever eat out because the meals served in restaurants could never match those dished up at home, which are prepared using ingredients fresh from the allotment, forest or river. If you are lucky enough to be invited back to a Siberian family household to eat, chances are it will be the finest meal of your trip.

Though Snickers bars seem to have monopolised the Russian sweet tooth, many cities, for example Yekaterinburg and Novosibirsk, have their own sweet factories popping out chocolates and other goodies.

DRINKS

In Siberia, as in European Russia, vodka and *shampanskoe* predominate, though they're yielding to a mind-boggling assortment of locally brewed beers and bottled waters served in plastic litre bottles. In addition to the local soft drinks *(limonady)*, Oriental sodas and juices are also popular. There isn't a village in Siberia now where you can't find a Pepsi (probably bottled in South Korea).

Getting There & Away

Moscow's airports still account for the bulk of traffic into Siberia and the Far East, but it's now also possible to go direct from the Pacific Rim region. There are international flights from China, Japan, Korea, Singapore and the USA to the Russian Far East, as well as boats from Japan and a rail route from either Pyongyang or Beijing via Harbin in north-east China.

By rail, there are three basic passages into Siberia and the Russian Far East. From the south, there are the well-travelled Trans-Mongolian and Trans-Manchurian rail routes, both of which originate in Beijing. There's also the less well known Turk-Sib Railway, which runs from Almaty in Kazakhstan, Central Asia, plus trains from Kharkiv (Kharkov) in Ukraine and, in summer only, services from Crimea, the Caucasus and the Russian Black Sea coast going at least as far as Irkutsk.

Warning

The information in this chapter is particularly vulnerable to change: Prices for international travel are volatile, routes are introduced and cancelled, schedules change, special deals come and go, and rules and visa requirements are amended. Airlines and governments seem to take a perverse pleasure in making price structures and regulations as complicated as possible. You should check directly with the airline or a travel agent to make sure you understand how a fare (and ticket you may buy) works. In addition, the travel industry is highly competitive and there are many lurks and perks.

The upshot of this is that you should get opinions, quotes and advice from as many airlines and travel agents as possible before you part with your hard-earned cash. The details given in this chapter should be regarded as pointers and are not a substitute for your own careful, up-to-date research.

AIR

Flying to Siberia probably necessitates arriving at Moscow's Sheremetevo International Airport and then facing the hassle of transferring across town to either Domodedovo or Vnukovo, the two domestic airports from which most Siberia-bound services fly out. See Moscow Getting Around section for how to travel to, from and between the Moscow airports. Every Siberian city or large town has an airport with direct Moscow flights. Usually these flights go daily; in some cases they're three times daily, as with Khabarovsk and Vladivostok. There are also flights from St Petersburg to Yekaterinburg, Novosibirsk, Krasnoyarsk, Irkutsk and Petropavlovsk-Kamchatsky.

Siberian cities can also be reached by on less frequent flights from Frankfurt (Germany), Niigata or Osaka (Japan), Shenyang and Shanghai (China), Pyongyang (North Korea), and Manila, Seoul or Singapore.

Other flights direct to Siberia or the Russian Far East are as follows.

Europe

Lufthansa (www.lufthansa.com.ru) flies from Frankfurt to Yekaterinburg, but much cheaper flights to Siberia are available through Luftbrücke (☎ 02132-9 31 60, fax 44 85), Moerser Str 100A, 40667 Meerbusch, which runs charter flights on local airlines from Hanover to Barnaul (DM1350 return), Krasnoyarsk (DM1400 return) and Omsk (DM1000 return). It can also book you on many regular flights on regional airlines from Frankfurt, Hanover or Cologne to/from Yekaterinburg, Novosibirsk and Chelyabinsk (from DM830 to DM1200).

The USA

Aeroflot (www.aeroflot.org) has nonstop flights from Anchorage to Vladivostok or Khabarovsk and offers a weekly flight from

Seattle to Vladivostok. It also offers numerous nonstop flights from Los Angeles, New York, Toronto and other major North American hubs to Moscow, with onward connections to many cities in Siberia and the Russian Far East.

The US commuter airline Bering Air (☎ 907-443 5620, info@beringair.com, www.beringair.com) runs charter flights between Nome, in Alaska, and Providenia, on the Chukotka Peninsula ($500 return), and can also help out with visas through its Russian agent.

Russia is on the other side of the International Date Line from the USA. Thus, when it's noon on Tuesday in Chukotka, it's 3 pm on Monday in Alaska (ie there's a 21 hour difference).

China, Japan & South-East Asia

From Khabarovsk, the regional airline, Dalavia Far East Airways, flies to Harbin in northern China ($150 one way), Seoul ($440 one way), Niigata ($412 one way), and once a week to Singapore ($1370 one way). Flights into Khabarovsk operated by other airlines include China Northern's Harbin connection, and a Seoul service with Asiana Airlines ($350 one way).

International connections to/from Irkutsk include weekly flights to Niigata and Shenyang (China), and twice a week to Ulaan Baatar.

Vladivostok Air flies from Vladivostok to Niigata twice a week (a two hour flight) for $363 one way, to Seoul twice a week for $300 one way and to Pusan weekly for $300 one way. Aeroflot has one flight a week from Vladivostok to Bangkok for $500 one way and Korean Air has flights twice weekly from Vladivostok to Seoul for $380. Do keep in mind, however, that with increasing competition, prices change every season.

Central Asia & Mongolia

Aeroflot or one of the numerous regional airlines can offer flights up to three times a week between Ulaan Baatar and Irkutsk and twice a week between Almaty (Kazakhstan) and Irkutsk. Almaty also has a daily connection to Khabarovsk and once or twice-weekly flights to Novosibirsk, Yekaterinburg, Barnaul and Krasnoyarsk. There may also be flights to a few Siberian cities from Tashkent (Uzbekistan), Bishkek (Kyrgyzstan) and lesser cities in Kazakhstan, but generally, since the break up of the Soviet Union, the air connections between Siberia and Central Asia have frayed.

LAND

Train

Of course, the way to do this is on the Trans-Siberian Railway from Moscow, from Japan (via ship or plane to Vladivostok), or from Beijing on branch lines through Mongolia or north-eastern China. See the Trans-Siberian Railway chapter for further details.

Other services linking Siberia with the West include trains between St Petersburg, Yekaterinburg and Omsk; a train that goes all the way from Kharkiv in Ukraine to Vladivostok every two days; and, in summer, trains from Crimea, the Caucasus and the Russian Black Sea coast, which go at least as far east as Irkutsk.

From Almaty in Kazakhstan, the Turkestan-Siberia or Turk-Sib Railway runs north via Barnaul to Novosibirsk in western Siberia. A service from Tashkent (Uzbekistan) to Barnaul and Novosibirsk also uses this line, as do trains to Krasnoyarsk from Almaty and Bishkek (Kyrgyzstan). Buses, and maybe trains, link Almaty with Ürümqi in China.

Another railway runs up the centre of Kazakhstan and carries trains between the cities of Tashkent, Almaty, Bishkek and Yekaterinburg.

A twice-weekly, two night (41 hour) train (No 41/42) runs between Ussuriysk (on the line between Khabarovsk and Vladivostok) and the North Korean capital of Pyongyang, with further connections from there to Beijing. The trip is reportedly very enjoyable: the train is frequently half empty and is composed of old carriages that date from a time when travel by rail was a much more stately affair. Steam locomotives, though not used for this service, are still in common use in North Korea.

See the Russian Far East chapter, specifically the Getting There & Away sections for Vladivostok and Khabarovsk, for more options.

SEA

The Far Eastern Shipping Company (☎ 4232 261 408), 1 Okeansky prospekt in Vladivostok, operates ferries between Vladivostok and the Japanese ports of Fushiki and Niigata irregularly from June to September. Check the Web site at www.fesco.ru for more information, or check the handwritten schedule at Biznes Intur Servis in the Vladivostok Marine Terminal. The voyage to Niigata takes 42 hours and 3rd class passage (lower deck, four berths per cabin) is $380, 2nd class (as for 3rd but on the main deck) is $400, while 1st (twin-bed cabins) is $730. All meals are included in the price, but you may be able to get cheaper fares if you negotiate. In Japan, try the Japan-Russia Travel Bureau (☎ 03-3432 6161, fax 3436 5530) in Tokyo – see Organised Tours in this chapter for the full address.

A cheaper option from Japan may be to take the ferry to Shanghai and ride the rails via Beijing. You might also be able to catch a ship from Japan to Korsakov, the southernmost port on the Russian island of Sakhalin, from where it's a $140 flight to Vladivostok or about $25 by ship to the mainland.

From Fuyuan, a small port on the Amur River in north-eastern China, a hydrofoil sails every other day to Khabarovsk, but it's not certain whether foreigners can cross the border (legally) here.

ORGANISED TOURS

The following agencies either offer complete package tours or can help with Siberian travel arrangements. Most will organise your visa, but check whether this is part of the deal. Most companies that deal with this region tend to concentrate on the Trans-Siberian rail routes; there's a comprehensive list of their addresses in the Trans-Siberian Railway chapter. See also the European Russia Getting There & Away chapter for more general Russia-oriented agents.

Australasia

Gateway Travel (☎ 02-9745 3333, fax 9745 3237, www.russian-gateway.com.au), 48 The Boulevarde, Strathfield, NSW 2135, Australia, is a Russia specialist agency, and can offer a variety of tours for groups and individuals. These include specialist packages based around hunting, fishing, mountaineering and ecotourism.

Visits to Kamchatka and Sakhalin can also be arranged via Gateway's contacts with Intourist.

Canada

Exotik Tours (☎ 514-284 3324, fax 843 5493), 1117 Ste-Catherine O, suite 806, Montreal, Quebec H3B 1H9, doesn't offer any pre-set tours but can reserve services in Siberia upon request, for groups and individuals, ranging from hotels and transportation to transfers, sightseeing and interpreters. Exotik also books flights with Aeroflot on its twice-weekly Montreal-Moscow direct service.

Germany

Hauser Exkursionen (☎ 89-2 35 00 60, fax 2 91 37 14, Hauser@Hauser-Exkursionen.de), Marienstrasse 17, 80331 Munich, offers 14-day winter tours that combine trekking and climbing in the Altay Republic near the Mongolian border for DM3715 from Frankfurt. Accommodation is in heated yurts or huts.

Another good German travel agent is Travel Service Asia (☎ 49 7351 37 32 10, fax 37 32 11, TSA-Reisen@t-online.de, www.travel-service-asia.de), Schmelzweg 10, 88400 Biberach/Riss. It puts together packages in the Baikal area that include rafting, trekking, language courses and various excursions. A typical example is a five day package with homestay that includes travel along the Angara from Irkutsk to Lake Baikal and Olkhon Island for DM585 excluding travel to/from Irkutsk. Travel Service Asia can also arrange homestays in many Siberian cities and runs tours in Khakassia and Tuva (four and seven-day tours respectively for DM565 and DM2648. All exclude to/from costs.

Japan

The Japan-Russia Travel Bureau (☎ 03-3432 6161, fax 3436 5530) at Kamiyacho Building, 3rd Floor, 5-12-12, Toranomon, Minato-ku, Tokyo 105, can arrange flights to Khabarovsk and Vladivostok. Staff there can also secure tickets for the ferry across from Niigata to Vladivostok (summer only) or for the boat to Shanghai, from where it's possible to take a train to Beijing and then on into Russia.

South-East Asia

Global Union Express Ltd (☎ 868 3231 or ☎ 845 4232, fax 845 5078 or fax 537 2605), Room 22-23, New Henry House, 10 Ice House St, Central, Hong Kong, is a general sales agent for Aeroflot and can arrange group or individual tours in Siberia including some homestays.

The UK

Exodus Discovery Holidays (☎ 8675 5550, fax 8673 0779, www.exodustravels.co.uk), 9 Weir Rd, London SW12 0LT, is planning to offer a 19 or 20-day trek in Kamchatka every second year (the next will probably be in 2001).

The 'tailor-made travel' section of Intourist Travel Ltd can book hotels almost anywhere throughout Siberia and the Russian Far East and organise transportation, transfers and sightseeing: see Organised Tours in the European Russia Getting There & Away chapter for further details.

Steppes East (☎ 01285-81 0267, fax 81 0693, www.steppeseast.co.uk), Castle Eaton, Swindon SN6 6JU, specialises in catering to offbeat requirements and has plenty of experience in the region. The company offers trekking tours to Lake Baikal and Kamchatka, and it can tailor-make trips to suit your needs.

Another specialist company is Field Studies Council Overseas (☎ 01743-85 0164, fseOverseas@bluecom.net, www.fscoverseas.mcmail.com), Montford Bridge, Shrewsbury SY4 1HW, an educational charity dedicated to environmental understanding. It runs about 50 trips abroad every year to places of special wildlife or botanical interest, including to Ussuriland in the Russian Far East.

The USA

American-International Homestays (☎ 303-642 3088 or toll-free ☎ 800-876 2048, fax 303-642 3365, www.spectravel.com/homes), PO Box 1754, Nederland, CO 80466-1754, arranges all-inclusive homestay trips, which take in Moscow, Irkutsk and Lake Baikal and last 15 days, for a cost of $2199, land only.

REI Adventures (☎ 206-891 2631 or toll-free ☎ 800-622 2236, fax 206-395 4744, www.rei.com/travel), PO Box 1938, Sumner, WA 98390-0880, offers trekking and cycling expeditions, though it doesn't go to Siberia and the Far East every year.

Nomad Travel (☎ 907-243 0313, fax 243 0333, www.nomad-travel.com), 3200 West 88th Ave, Ste 1 Anchorage, Alaska 99502, organises fishing, rafting, sledding and other excursions in the Far East.

Mountain Travel Sobek (☎ 510-527 8100, toll-free ☎ 800-227 2384, fax 510-525 7710, info@mtsobek.com, www.mtsobek.com), 6420 Fairmont Ave, El Cerrito, CA 94530, offers a 15-day cruise that begins in Petropavlovsk-Kamchatka and goes to Wrangel Island and Provedenia. Prices range from $7290 to $9590 excluding airfares.

Getting Around

Getting around in Siberia and the Russian Far East isn't so much travel as a series of expeditions. In fact, foreign visitors to the region have traditionally regarded getting around – in the form of a trip on the Trans-Siberian Railway – as constituting the whole experience. Spare a thought for those poor unfortunates who had to do it on the hoof before the first railway tracks were laid. For them the journey from A, somewhere west of the Ural Mountains, to B, somewhere in Siberia, could easily consume a year or more of their footsore lives. The distances involved are vast. From Yekaterinburg at the western limits of Siberia to Vladivostok on the Pacific coast is about the same distance as from Berlin to New York, while even a relatively short overland hop, such as the one from Irkutsk in eastern Siberia to its near neighbour Khabarovsk, is still roughly equivalent to the distance from London to Cairo. And you were wondering about taking a bus?

Information in this chapter is largely specific to Siberia & the Russian Far East. See European Russia Getting Around for more general information on travel in Russia.

AIR

Because of the vast distances involved in travelling in Siberia and the Russian Far East and the limited extent of the road and rail network, flying is sometimes the only practical way of getting around. Aircraft take on the role of buses, especially on short-haul flights. Passengers frequently have to carry their own baggage aboard and dump it at the rear before scrumming for seats, and those who lose out end up standing for the duration of the flight.

Airports and Airlines

Almost every small town has its airport (although 'airport', which tends to connote a great, high-tech temple to air transport, is perhaps a misleading term: most of these places have fewer facilities than the average bus shelter). If nothing else, it will at least have frequent flights to the nearest big town or city, and from there you'll be able to make nationwide connections. Recent years have seen the emergence of small, regional airlines, but most use old Aeroflot machines with a fresh coat of paint. The Russian Far East alone is served by some 30 domestic carriers. For the most part, these baby flots behave just like ma flot with frequent cancelled flights and price finagling.

Timetables

Flight times are always given in Moscow time *(Moskovskoe vremya)*, except when they're in local time *(mestnoe vremya)*. Check carefully, and also keep in mind that the times shown on the dusty boards in the town offices usually, but not always, correspond to the actual departure. You might want to ask your hotel administrator to call the airport and you should plan to get there earlier than the usual 30 minutes for domestic check-in.

Buying Tickets

The good news is that gone are the days when you needed to promise your first born child in order to secure a seat. Prices have shot up so high that most Russians cannot afford to fly and planes are usually half empty. You can often get a ticket just as the plane is about to leave. Another bit of good news is that some airlines, like Vladivostok-based carrier, Vlad Avia, have stopped charging foreigners double the price. But of course this does not mean they won't start again – old Soviet habits die hard.

Air tickets are bought from Aeroflot sales offices or any of the ever-growing numbers of travel agents in towns. The smaller travel agents don't always sell tickets on all flights and there doesn't seem to be any variation in prices (though that will probably change); you'll be wasting your time if you shop around. The offices are usually open six days a week, sometimes seven days,

The Joys of Travelling Without Intourist

So you're thinking about heading out on your own, braving mile-long ticket lines and surly clerks, saying goodbye to the padded prices of Intourist. You've got the key phrase down pat: *odin bilet* (one ticket) ... to – where will it be? Kamchatka, Sakhalin, you name it, some of the largest, most unexplored stretches of earth are at your call.

Take this as a quick bracer, a little advice on what awaits you, *before* you get there.

Standing in Khabarovsk airport, the biggest and most modern transportation facility in the Russian Far East, you look up at the flight board and see that six out of the 10 flights are either delayed or cancelled. Some of the reasons given: dense smoke from forest fire, bad weather, whereabouts of pilot unknown. About 20 yawning Russians, who have obviously spent the night in the lobby, are queuing. The regional director for the Sakhalin airline SAT comes out and sheepishly apologises that your plane to Sakhalin has been switched from a Boeing to a 20-seater AN-24. That means half the intended passengers must wait another day, if not longer. The question is which half?

This is when you start longing for Intourist. A well connected Intourist agent would make sure you are a 'have,' meaning some sleepless Russian is unfortunately a 'have not'.

What to do? Should you stay in line or take your chances on another route? You flip a coin, then run upstairs to find a phone. After having to wait until the operator finishes her tea break, you call the port to ask when the ship leaves from Port Vanino, only an overnight train ride away. But the dispatcher's phone has been disconnected. You run back downstairs and check the board again, and, lo and behold, flashing up there is a flight to Okha, on the north end of Sakhalin Island. And it's boarding right now!

You dash to get your luggage out of storage, then hobble to the gate. The uniformed woman takes one look at you and screams, 'Nyet!' No explanations, except that it's too much trouble to write you, a foreigner, a special ticket. (They're green instead of red, and have to be filled out, says Intourist, in English, not Cyrillic.)

As the plane, with only five passengers aboard, takes off without you, you sulk back to the first ticket line, now even longer. You forgot to ask someone to save you a place. Now as you try to butt in, the others stare malevolently at you.

Suddenly a well fed Georgian man in shiny leather shoes and a neatly ironed shirt sidles up to you and, in a combination of English, Russian and sign language, asks if you want to fly today.

Today? How can that be possible?

'Fifty, and you get on the plane now.'

You're dumbfounded. But don't be; it's simple: the director sells the tickets to this Georgian and tells the people in line there aren't any tickets. The Georgian then resells them. The two split the profits, your $50.

'Nyet,' you say and walk away. Don't worry, you'll get there; maybe not today or tomorrow, but you'll get there. And savour that feeling of victory when you finally do arrive, even if it's long after Intourist would have been sending you on to your next destination.

Suzanne Possehl

from early morning to late evening. All the airlines also have ticket offices at the airport and, as a general rule, you must buy your ticket at the airport if you plan to fly that same day.

You could also try asking an international Aeroflot agent to ticket you before you arrive in Russia. While it should be able to book you on a major flight – for example St Petersburg to Petropavlovsk-Kamchatsky

SIBERIA & RUSSIAN FAR EAST

on Pulkovskie Avialinii, the St Petersburg air carrier, it probably won't be able to book you on a short flight on one of the smaller regional airlines, for example Vladivostok to Yuzhno-Sakhalinsk on Sakhalin Avia-trassy. Still, if you're sure of your travel dates, it's worth a try.

Costs

A return fare normally costs the equivalent of twice the one-way fare. Some sample one-way foreigner airfares and flying times are:

from	to	one way ($US)	time (hours)
Moscow	Novosibirsk	137	4
Moscow	Petropavlovsk-Kamchatsky	290	9
St Petersburg	Petropavlovsk-Kamachatsky	400	9
Moscow	Khabarovsk	378	8½
Moscow	Vladivostok	300	9
Irkutsk	Vladivostok	170	3
Khabarovsk	Magadan	330	2½
Vladivostok	Yuzhno-Sakhalinsk	140	1¾

Check-In and Luggage

One thing is for certain, when flying: passports and tickets have to be presented repeatedly right up until boarding. Also, foreigners still get to wait in the separate Intourist lounge (if there is one) and will often be escorted onto the plane before everyone else. However, as the temperature on board the plane is always a good 10°C below that in the departure hall, this is a privilege you could well do without. On landing, baggage belonging to foreign passengers is usually (though not always) diverted from the proletarian baggage-claim area and delivered to the Intourist hall, but it arrives long after everybody else has collected theirs and left. This constitutes 1st class treatment.

TRAIN

The railway is the main artery of life in Siberia and the Russian Far East, sustaining and nurturing the towns and cities along its length. For the traveller, this makes the railway the ideal mode of transport because it connects almost every place of any significance. (Towns that were once wealthy and important shrivelled and all but died after the railway bypassed them.) There are no longer any restrictions on which routes travellers can go by or which trains they can take. Rail prices have been going up, especially for foreigners, but the railway remains the cheapest means of getting around. It is also, without doubt, the most comfortable and reliable.

Types of train

The same types of train run in Siberia as in European Russia (see the European Russia Getting Around chapter). The types are *skoryy poezd* (fast train) and *passazhirsky poezd* (passenger train) – with the passenger trains making many more stops. Train journeys in Siberia are measured in days rather than hours, accommodation is always in coupes *(kupeyny)*, or the open-plan, 'travelling village' version, *platskartny*. First-class compartments, with two berths as opposed to four, are available only on long-distance trains such as the Moscow-Vladivostok *(Rossia)* and the Moscow-Irkutsk *(Baikal Express)* services. Making use of overnight trains saves on hotel bills.

Timetables

In Siberia, in theory, all main-line services run on Moscow time. Local time creeps back into usage in Russia's Far East, where stations generally have two timetables, one following each system. Provided you can understand Cyrillic script, the information they give is fairly easy to decipher and purchasing a ticket is straightforward. If you don't speak Russian, simply copy down, on a piece of paper, your destination (in Cyrillic), the number of the train and the day of departure: today, (сегодня; *si-VOHD-nya*); tonight (сегодня вечером; *si-VOHD-nya VYEH-chi-rom*); tomorrow (завтра; *ZAHF-tra*); the day after tomorrow, (послезавтра; *po-sli-ZAHF-tra*) and give the paper to the ticket seller. See the boxed text 'Reading A Train Timetable' in the European Russia Getting Around chapter.

Buying Tickets

Most of the larger stations, such as Irkutsk or Vladivostok, have one ticketing hall for local *(prigorodny)* services and one for long-distance trains. Some cities also have a special office – sometimes called 'Intourist' (Интурист) – for ticket sales to foreigners, which may be staffed by someone who speaks English. At these offices you'll always be charged the full foreigner price for the ticket (whereas if you buy from the normal station windows you might get away with paying local price), but sometimes tickets may be available at these places when the other cashiers claim the train is full.

Though train inspectors might throw you off the train doing so, you'll save money and avoid having to queue at the station by buying from the conductors who stand on the platform just as the train is about to leave. Because they pocket the proceeds, they're sometimes willing to sell for about 10% off the Russian ticket price. If you're pressed for time and want to skip the ticket line but still obtain a real ticket, see the head conductor *(brigadir poezda)* who might write you a ticket on the spot, but possibly charge you a higher price.

As a general rule: the nicer the train, the harder it is to buy a ticket on the platform and the more likely it is you're going to pay more as a foreigner.

Costs

Fares vary from train to train, and also go up and down with price hikes and exchange rates. The fares given here are 2nd class fares and are current at the time of writing; 1st class, where available, is usually just less than double. Some sample fares and travelling times are:

from	to	one way ($US)	time (hours)
Moscow	Vladivostok	140	157
Khabarovsk	Komsomolsk	25	9½
Ulan Ude	Irkutsk	13	7½
Severobaikalsk	Ust-Kut	27	8½
Yuzhno-Sakhalinsk	Nogliki	50	17

Left Luggage

Every station has a left luggage room *(kamera khranenia)* and, more often than not, two – one with lockers that take items up to the size of a medium sausage-bag, and a second for bulky packs and boxes, including rucksacks. It generally costs about $0.50 to deposit hand luggage and $1 or $1.50 for the bigger items. Apart from a couple of hour-long breaks, the rooms are usually open round the clock.

BUS

The distances are too great and the roads too bad for buses to be viable as intercity transport in Siberia and the Russian Far East. Buses provide only city-airport, suburban and local links. Each region seems to have been left to scavenge for its own fleet, and the quickest way for a Russian to get rich in the Far East these days is to import a Korean minivan (called *mikriki* in jargon). They're everywhere, they're quicker and they usually don't cost more than the bus. You can flag them down at bus stops or catch them at the town's central bus station.

Baggage is usually charged for at a rate of about $0.50 per item. Travellers often get away without paying for luggage as a backpack looks like a ladies' purse compared to the mountains of boxes, burlap sacks and bags your fellow Russian travellers will be piling into the seats next to you.

CAR & MOTORCYCLE

Siberia is traversed today, as it was a century ago, by only one highway. This doesn't even merit the title 'transcontinental' because it peters out in the swamps east of Chita and doesn't re-emerge as a drivable surface for another couple of hundred kilometres. Road construction has always been far too expensive; and, compared with a railway's capacity to carry thousands of tonnes of freight, the pay-offs have always been too small.

The usual advantages of independent motoring don't exist in Siberia. There are almost no out-of-the-way places to be discovered, as the majority of settlements cling tenaciously to the lifeline of the railway. The road network plays second fiddle to the railway, follow its course closely and generally only deviate in the company of a branch line. For a motorist, the scenery is also numbingly monotonous, though the driver's eyes are better trained on the road in any case, watching for potholes. There is also the difficulty of obtaining petrol, or spares in the event of a breakdown.

People have driven from Alaska to London and, famously, from Beijing via Mongolia and Siberia to Paris. Groups have even cycled from St Petersburg to Vladivostok, and the reverse. These, though, were all full-blown expeditions, accompanied by the level of careful planning and equipping that goes into an attempt on Mt Everest or a trek across the Sahara. Motoring in Siberia can be done, but it's a challenge, and a potential source of stories for your grandchildren rather than a viable means of getting around.

There are a few exceptions. The Altay Mountains, Khakassia and Tuva, Ussuriland and Sakhalin are reasonably compact, self-contained areas with better road systems than rail, making them well suited to exploration by car. All have dramatic or at least interesting scenery, with a fair number of scattered towns and villages to provide accommodation. Car hire with driver may be possible in Khabarovsk, Vladivostok and Yuzhno-Sakhalinsk from the main desk at the major hotels but don't be surprised if your driver turns out to be the hotel receptionist's husband and the whole family has come along for the fun.

BOAT

Considering that Siberia and Russia's Far East were first opened up by boat, the region's rivers are now a very much underused means of transportation. The main reason for this, of course, is that for six to eight months of the year all the great waterways are locked solid with ice.

During summer, though, the Ob/Irtysh, Yenisey, Lena and Amur rivers are put to use as aquatic highways, and Lake Baikal is also plied by numerous ferry services. From June to September, regular services run up the Irtysh from Omsk via Tobolsk and farther north along the Ob to Salekhard. On the Yenisey, regular passenger services run between Krasnoyarsk and various points north as far as Dudinka, and upstream from Kyzyl in Tuva. The Lena provides the main supply route for Yakutsk, a city isolated in the taiga 1000km north of any railway line. During the navigation season (from late May or early June until October) there is a constant flow of river traffic between Yakutsk and Ust-Kut, a port on the Baikal-Amur Mainline (BAM). Passengers are also taken. On the Amur River there are daily hydrofoil passenger services which link Khabarovsk to Komsomolsk and Nikolaevsk near the river's mouth. Boats moving along the Irtysh and Ob rivers from Omsk via Tobolsk to Salekhard also could make for an interesting trip.

On Lake Baikal, poor maintenance and a lack of spare parts seem to cause shipping schedules to change from season to season. The only guaranteed services are those between Irkutsk and Severobaikalsk on the lake's northern shore, and, to a lesser extent, Irkutsk and Ust-Barguzin on the eastern shore, as well as the shuttles that go three or four times daily between Irkutsk and Listvyanka. Other boats do provide a ferry link up the western shore but on an erratic basis. The hydrofoil service that used to connect Irkutsk with Bratsk, downriver on the Angara, has been discontinued, though we've heard of private entrepreneurs *(chastniki)* taking passengers along the route.

On the Pacific seaboard, passage on a ship from Port Vanino provides a cheap alternative to flying across the Tatar Strait to the island of Sakhalin, and there are also irregular sailings from Korsakov, on Sakhalin, across to Yuzhno-Kurilsk in the Kuril Island chain. For the truly adventurous – with a month or so to spare – it is possible to hitch a lift on one of the supply ships that sail out of Nakhodka and Vladivostok up to the Arctic Circle towns of Anadyr and Providenia.

See the respective regional sections in the Siberia and Russian Far East chapters for more detailed information.

Western Siberia
Западная Сибирь

This chapter covers Russia from the Ural Mountains, officially just west of Siberia, to the Yenisey River, which is the natural boundary between the low-lying West Siberian Plain and the higher Central Siberian Plateau. Believe it or not, the climate west of the Yenisey is warm compared to the region east of it, allowing pine, spruce and fir to dominate the forests (the even hardier larch takes over beyond the Yenisey River).

Siberia's biggest cities are all here, chief among them Yekaterinburg, with much historical interest, and the younger Novosibirsk. The developed bits of western Siberia lie along or near the Trans-Siberian Railway, in the Ural foothills, and to a lesser extent in the oil, gas and mineral fields of the north. But the most exciting travel here is away from the railway, the cities and the industry – above all in two remote, beautiful, fascinating southern regions bordering Mongolia from which foreign visitors used to be restricted or banned. These are the Altay Republic south of Novosibirsk and the Republic of Tuva south of Krasnoyarsk.

HIGHLIGHTS

- Hiking and canoeing for a week in the Altay Republic
- Relaxing in a 1st class compartment on the flagship Ural train from Moscow to Yekaterinburg
- Exploring a section of the Irtysh, Yenisey or Ob rivers by boat
- Wandering around the kremlin in Tobolsk
- Refuelling at the Beer Mug and Pub 501 in Novosibirsk
- Travelling around remote Tuva

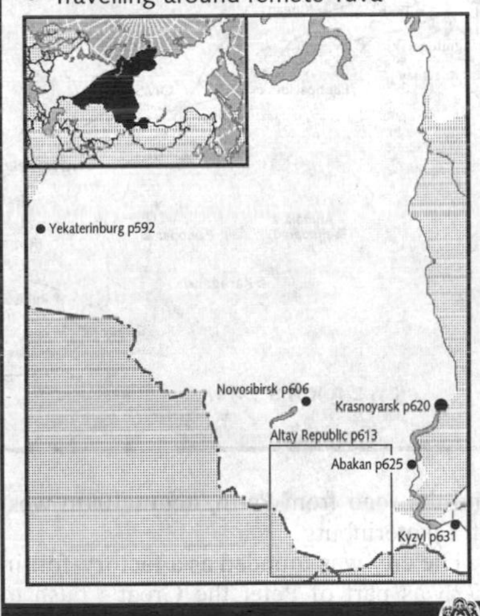

The Urals
Урал

The Ural Mountains stretch 2000km from Kazakhstan in the south to the Arctic Kara Sea in the north. They're low, as famous mountain ranges go, failing to top 2000m anywhere, and if you pass through on the train you may hardly notice them. They have been vital to Russia for almost 300 years as a major source of metals and minerals, which gave rise to a number of industrial cities on their fringes, of which Yekaterinburg, the biggest, is western Siberia's most interesting city. See the boxed text in Facts about Siberia & the Russian Far East for more information on the Urals' history.

YEKATERINBURG
ЕКАТЕРИНБУРГ

☎ 3432 • pop 1.2 million

Yekaterinburg (also sometimes written as Ekaterinburg) is 41km inside Asia but still 260km short of the official beginning of Siberia. The continental boundary is marked by obelisks beside both the railway

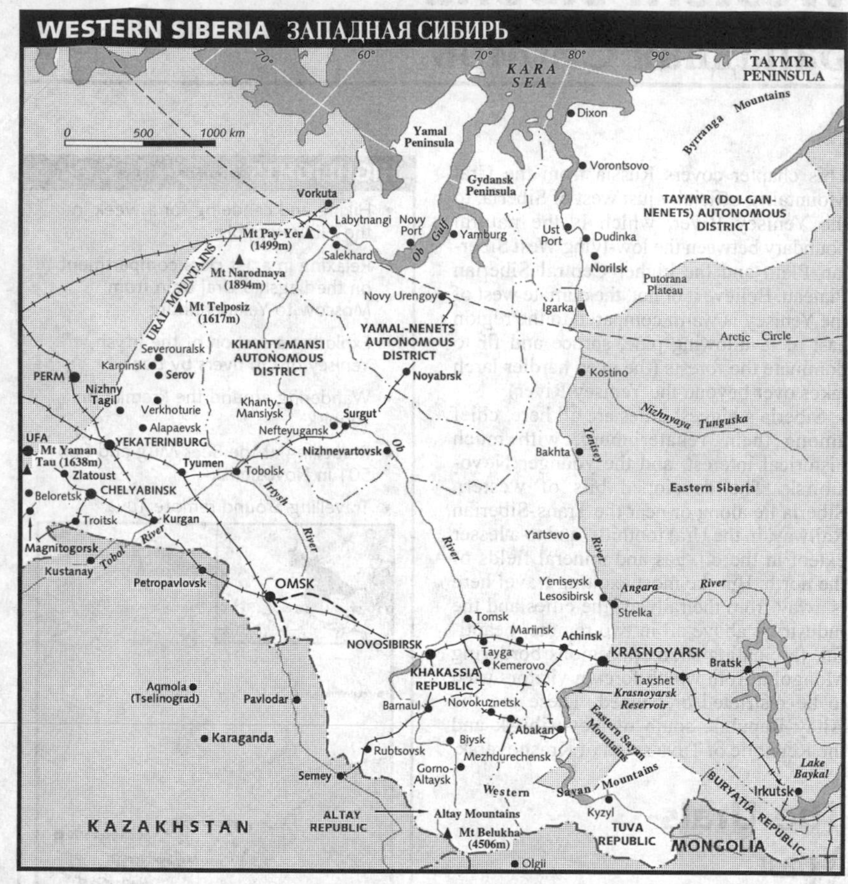

and the road from Perm, about 40km west of Yekaterinburg.

The city was founded as a factory-fort in 1723 as part of Peter the Great's push to exploit the Ural region's mineral riches, and named after two Yekaterinas – Peter's wife (later Empress Catherine I), and the Russian patron saint of mining. A year later it would have been named after only one Yekaterina, or maybe someone else altogether, for by then Peter had discovered that his wife had a lover, and had his head cut off and placed in a jar of surgical spirit in her bedroom.

By the 19th century Yekaterinburg had developed into an engineering centre supplying the Ural region's mines with machinery. It was also the centre of that century's Urals gold rush, producing some immensely rich gold barons.

In July 1918, Tsar Nicholas II and his wife and children were killed by the Bolsheviks in the basement of a house in Yekaterinburg, where they had been held. Six years later, the town was renamed Sverdlovsk, after Yakov Sverdlov, a leading Bolshevik who was thought to have arranged the murders.

WWII turned it into a major industrial centre as hundreds of factories were transferred here from vulnerable areas west of the Ural Mountains, and it was closed to foreigners until 1990 because of its many defence plants. In 1960, the US pilot Gary Powers was shot down in his U2 spy plane in this area, wrecking that year's Paris summit. (Powers, who bailed out, was exchanged for a Soviet spy in 1962.) In 1979, 64 people died of anthrax after a leak from a biological weapons plant, Sverdlovsk-17, in the city.

In 1991, Yekaterinburg took back its original name – though many people (and rail timetables) continue to call it Sverdlovsk.

It's a rather interesting place – especially, perhaps, to geologists and industrial archaeologists. Like most Russian industrial cities, Yekaterinburg has endured an economic depression since the collapse of the Soviet Union. Its industrial flagship, the Uralmash machine tool factory, once employed 40,000 workers, but this figure has now shrunk to 15,000.

Orientation

Changes to some street names may be made in the foreseeable future, including:

old name	new name
ulitsa Sverdlova	Arsenevsky prospekt
naberezhnaya Rabochey-Molodyozhi	Gimnazicheskaya naberezhnaya
prospekt Lenina	Glavny prospekt
ulitsa Malysheva	Pokrovsky prospekt
ulitsa Kuybysheva	Sibirsky prospekt
ulitsa Lunacharskogo	Vasentsovskaya ulitsa
ulitsa Karla Libknekhta	Voznesensky prospekt
ulitsa Rozy Lyuxemburg	Zlatoustovskaya ulitsa

The city centre is basically between the main boulevards, prospekt Lenina and ulitsa Malysheva, from ploshchad 1905 goda in the west to ulitsa Lunacharskogo in the east. Ulitsa Karla Libknekhta changes name to ulitsa Sverdlova as it leads 2.5km north to the train station. Prospekt Lenina crosses the Iset River three blocks west of ulitsa Karla Libknekhta.

Maps The Knigi bookshop near the train station opposite the end of ulitsa Sverdlova has a good supply of maps of the city and surrounding areas, including hiking and river maps of parts of the Ural region.

The Karta map shop at ulitsa Pervomayskaya 74 is a good source of large-scale topographical maps of many areas of the former USSR. To find it, take a tram east along prospekt Lenina to Vostochnaya ulitsa (where prospekt Lenina goes under a railway bridge), then walk 350m north on Vostochnaya ulitsa, and a block to the right along ulitsa Pervomayskaya.

Information

The English/Russian bilingual *City Guide Ekaterinburg*, which sells for around $1.50 and which can be found in the Transaero office and some hotels in town, has a good map in Russian and lots of useful information. It's updated annually.

Money Most-Bank on the corner of ulitsa Malysheva and ulitsa Mamina-Sibiryaka cashes American Express travellers cheques, changes cash, and gives cash advances on Visa, EuroCard and Cirrus credit cards. It is open from 9 am to 4.30 pm Monday to Thursday and until 3 pm on Friday (closed for lunch from 1 to 2 pm). There's a cash exchange desk at the airport.

The Uralvneshtorgbank, at ulitsa Generalskaya 7, cashes American Express travellers cheques. It's open from 9 am to 8 pm weekdays, till 6 pm weekends, and closes for lunch from 1 to 2 pm.

Post & Communications The main post office, on prospekt Lenina, has fax and EMS services. Email and Internet services operate from room 208 (turn right as you enter the building).

The Inter-City Telephone Office is nearby at ulitsa Tolmachyova 24, but it's more convenient to use one of several international telephones in room 202 of the post office. The Biznes-Servis-Byuro (☎ 53 62 48) in room 248 at Hotel Sverdlovsk offers international and domestic telephone and fax services as well as photocopying.

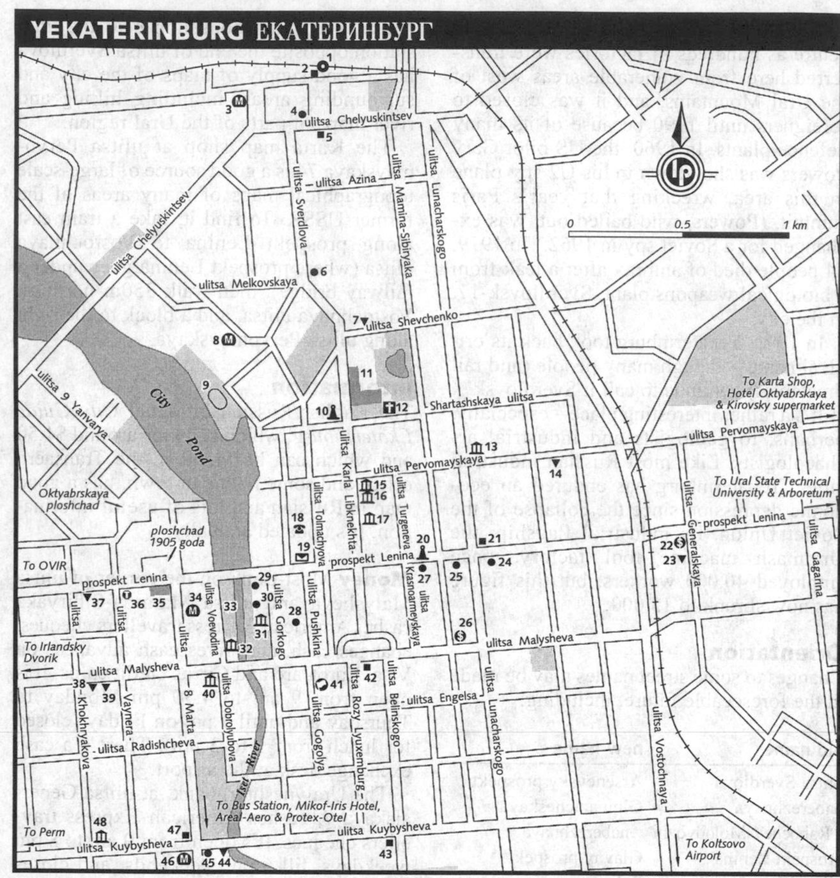

Visa Registration The OVIR office is at ulitsa Krylova 2 in a red-brick building (take tram No 2, 13 or 18 to stop Ulitsa Krylova). It's open from 10 am to 5 pm on Monday, from 9 am to 5 pm on Wednesday and from 9 am to 4 pm on Friday (closed from noon to 2 pm).

Travel Agencies Sputnik (☎ 59 83 00 or ☎ 51 91 57, fax 51 34 83, sputnik.ekatb@gin.global-one.ru), ulitsa Pushkina 5, is one reliable agency that handles bookings for the Oktyabrskaya, Ural and Magistr hotels. It has a wide range of tours, including three-hour sightseeing tours of the city in English for $65 and geology and other tours out to the Europe-Asia border lasting up to four hours at a maximum cost of $110.

For any kind of help or guidance in or around Yekaterinburg, Konstantin Brylyakov of the Ekaterinburg Convention & Visitor Bureau (☎ 48 54 51, fax 55 16 64, transaer@etel.ru) is a good person to contact. This enthusiastic ex-Sputnik guide, who works out of the Transaero office at prospekt Lenina 50, can arrange inexpensive hotel and homestay accommodation in Yekaterinburg and organise English-language city

YEKATERINBURG ЕКАТЕРИНБУРГ

PLACES TO STAY

2 Komnaty Otdykha
Комнаты Отдыха
5 Hotel Sverdlovsk
Гостиница Свердловск
21 Hotel Iset
Гостиница Исет
42 Hotel Tsentralnaya
Гостиница Центральная
43 Atrium Palace Hotel
47 Hotel Magistr
Гостиница Магистр

PLACES TO EAT

7 Vodoley
Водолей
14 Stolovaya
Столовая
23 Restoran Generalsky
Ресторан Генеральский
37 Mak Pik
Мак Пик
38 Astoria
Астория
39 La Gradara
44 Kharbin Restaurant
Ресторан Харбин

METRO STATIONS

3 Uralskaya
Уральская
8 Dinamo
Динамо
34 Ploshchad 1905 Goda
Площадь 1905 Года
46 Geologicheskaya (under construction)
Геологическая (строящаяся)

OTHER

1 Train Station
Железнодорожный вокзал
4 Knigi Shop
Магазин Книги
6 Central City Railways Office
Центральные городские железнодорожные кассы
9 Dinamo Stadium
Стадион Динамо
10 Romanov Death Site
Место убийства Романовых
11 Rastorguev-Kharitonov Mansion
Усадьба Расторгуева-Харитонова
12 Ascension Church
Вознесенская церковь
13 Military History Museum
Военно-исторический музей
15 Museum of Photography
Музей фотографии
16 Museum of Youth
Музей молодёжи
17 Yekaterinburg History Museum
Музей истории Екатеринбурга
18 Inter-City Telephone Office
Междугородный пороговорный пункт
19 Post Office
Почтамт
20 Sverdlov Statue
Памятник Я. М. Свердлову
22 Uralvneshtorgbank
Уралвнешторгбанк
24 Transaero
Трансаэро
25 Gastronom Tsentralny
Гастроном Центральный
26 Most-Bank
Мост-Банк
27 Opera & Ballet Theatre
Театр оперы и балета
28 Sputnik & Lufthansa
Спутник и Луфтганса
29 Water Tower
Водонапорная башня
30 Nature Department
Отдел природы
31 Museum of City Architecture & Urals Industrial Technology
Музей истории архитектуры города и промышленной техники Урала
32 Fine Arts Museum
Музей изобразительных искусств
33 Geological Alley & Historical Square
Геологическая аллея
35 City Hall
Городской Совет
36 Toilet
Туалет
40 Regional Local Studies Museum
Историко-краеведческий музей
41 British & US General Consulates
Генеральное консульство Великобритании и Генеральное консульство США
45 Circus
Цирк
48 Ural Geology Museum
Уральский геологический музей

tours. He also arranges rafting trips in the Urals for around $30 per person per day plus a shared $60 transportation charge.

See Around Yekaterinburg for other tours offered in the region by travel agencies.

Dangers & Annoyances Travellers should exercise 'big-city' sense when moving around Yekaterinburg, especially after dark. Also, make sure you boil the tap water before drinking it.

Time Zone The time in Yekaterinburg is Moscow time plus two hours.

Romanov Death Site

The spot where the Romanov dynasty met its final gruesome end on the night of 16 July 1918 is beside ulitsa Karla Libknekhta, 600m north of prospekt Lenina. This bleak place is marked by an iron cross and another of marble dedicated to members of the family murdered by the Bolsheviks: Nikolay (Tsar Nicholas II), Alexandra (the tsarina), and Alexey, Olga, Tatyana, Maria and Anastasia (their five children).

A church should eventually be completed behind the site, but a shortage of funds is hampering construction. To one side stands

The Riddle of the Romanov Remains

What happened to the bodies of the Romanovs after their deaths is a mixture of the macabre, the mysterious and the plain messy. After decades of rumour and speculation, expert investigations since 1991 have finally pieced the story together – almost.

When in 1991 archaeologists opened a shallow pit near Yekaterinburg, believed to be the Romanovs' grave, they found the bones of nine people. These were tentatively identified as Tsar Nicholas II, his wife Tsarina Alexandra, three of their four daughters, the royal doctor and three servants. Absent were any remains of the royal couple's one son, Tsarevich Alexey, aged 13 at the time of the killings. Also notably absent was the fourth daughter, which gave a new lease of life to theories that the youngest daughter, Anastasia (aged 17 in 1918), had somehow escaped the killings. Best known of several people who had claimed to be Anastasia was Anna Anderson, who appeared in Berlin in 1920 with convincing stories of life among the Romanovs which led many people to believe her. She died in the USA in 1984.

In 1992 bone samples from the excavated skeletons were sent to the British government's Forensic Science Service, to be tested by DNA identification techniques pioneered by British scientists. Using blood and hair samples from the Duke of Edinburgh (a grandson of the tsarina's sister) and two descendants of the tsar, the scientists had established with 'more than 98.5%' certainty by 1993 that the bones were those of the tsar, the tsarina and three of their daughters.

An official Russian inquiry team in Yekaterinburg then managed to piece together the skulls found in the pit – some badly damaged by rifle butts, hand grenades and acid – and built plaster models of the faces they had once borne. This, together with the DNA tests and dental records, satisfied them by 1994 that the three daughters found were Olga and Tatyana (the two oldest) – and Anastasia.

The missing daughter was Maria. Her and Alexey's remains were still undiscovered, but the Russians said they at least knew how they had been disposed of. And what a tale of ghoulish bungling it was. According to the Russian team, all five children had died with their parents

the little wooden Chapel of the Revered Martyr Grand Princess Yelisaveta Fyodorovna (Chasovnya vo imya Prepodobnomuchenitsy Velikoi Knyagini Yelisavety Fyodorovny). Grand Princess Yelisaveta was a great-aunt of the royal family who, soon after her relatives' murders, reportedly met an even worse end. When she survived being thrown down a mine, poisonous gas was pumped in and the shaft filled with earth. Inside the chapel are modern paintings of her and the royal family.

The Romanovs were actually killed in the cellar of a house that stood here until Boris Yeltsin had it demolished (on Politburo orders, he says) in 1977. Imprisoned by the Bolsheviks after the revolution, the royal family was moved from place to place, eventually being brought here from Tobolsk in April 1918. The Soviet government must have decided, with civil war spreading across Siberia, that the royal family was too good a potential White figurehead to leave alive. Late one night they were taken down to the cellar, told they were going to die, and shot repeatedly. The daughters, protected by 'bullet-proof vests' of jewels sewn into their underclothes, had to be finished off with bayonets.

The house was known as Dom Ipateva, after its owner, one Nikolay Ipatev. It was later used as a museum of the revolution, then as offices before being demolished.

At the back of the little park across the street from the Romanov site, the Ascension Church (Voznesenskaya Tserkov) has been restored. The ostentatious classical-fronted building lining the slope down to the north was the mansion of a rich 19th century gold family called Rastorguev-Kharitonov. A

The Riddle of the Romanov Remains

in the cellar of the Dom Ipateva. The bodies were then trucked to an abandoned mine 30km away and thrown in, followed by several grenades intended to collapse the mine shaft. The mine, however, did not collapse. The bodies were pulled out and an acids expert summoned. He brought 160 litres of acid but fell off his horse, broke a leg and couldn't help. It was then decided to distribute the bodies among various smaller mines and pour acid on them. But the lorry carrying them became bogged in a swamp, so the disposal team – by now understandably desperate – opted to bury them on the spot. They tried burning Alexey and Maria in preparation, but realised it would take days to burn all the bodies properly, so the others were just put in a pit and doused with acid. Even then, most of the acid soaked away into the ground – leaving the bones to be uncovered 73 years later.

For masterminding all this, Yakov Sverdlov got a city named after him.

In mid-1998 the royal remains were buried in St Petersburg's SS Peter & Paul Cathedral, the resting place of most of Nicholas II's predecessors back to Peter the Great. See the boxed text 'Reburying the Past' in the St Petersburg chapter for more information.

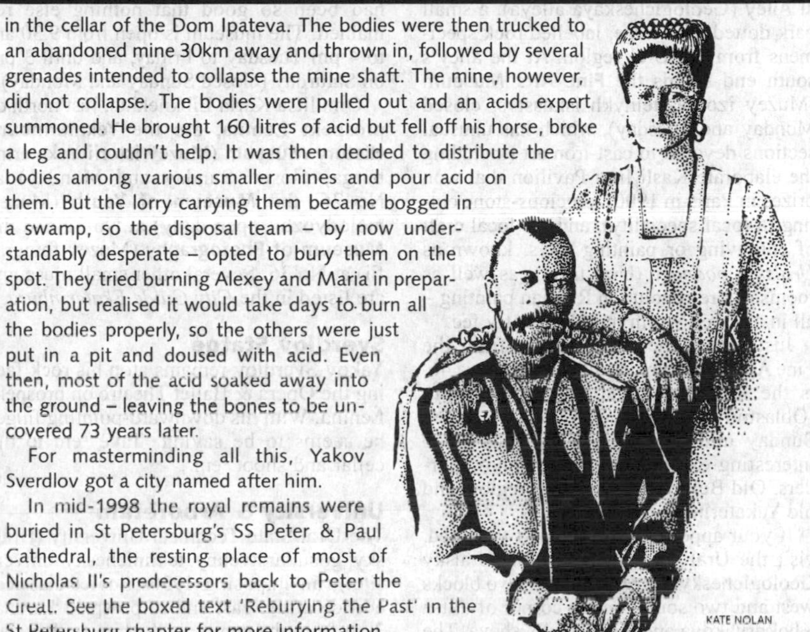

park spreads out behind the mansion. In the cellars, it's said, the Rastorguev-Kharitonovs minted their own gold coins and tortured their enemies – perhaps an inspiration for the Romanovs' guards.

Istorichesky Skver & Around

Three blocks west of ulitsa Karla Libknekhta, prospekt Lenina crosses a small dam forming the Gorodskoy prud (City Pond) on its north side, with the Iset River funnelled through a narrow channel on the south side. This was where Yekaterinburg began back in 1723. Water from the dam (reconstructed twice since that date) powered an iron forge below it. A mint and a stone-cutting works soon followed.

On either side of the river today is a plaza-cum-park called Istorichesky skver (Historical Square), which is surrounded by a clutch of old buildings and museums. Most museums are open from 11 am to 6 pm and cost less than $1 admission.

On the east side are an old **water tower**, the **Nature Department** (Otdel prirody; closed Tuesday) of the local museum, and the combined **Museum of City Architecture & Urals Industrial Technology** (Muzey istorii arkhitektury goroda i promyshlennoy tekhniki Urala; closed Tuesday and Sunday). These last two are housed in an old (though not the original) mining-equipment factory and mint buildings. The Nature Department displays minerals and precious stones from the Ural region, where emeralds, aquamarines, tourmalines, malachite, jasper and many more stones are mined. The architecture and industrial museum has antique machinery and an exhibition on the growth of the city.

WESTERN SIBERIA

On the west side of the river is **Geological Alley** (Geologicheskaya alleya), a small park dotted with large, labelled rock specimens from the Ural region. At the alley's south end stands the **Fine Arts Museum** (Muzey izobrazitelnykh iskusstvs; closed Monday and Tuesday), which has unusual sections devoted to cast-iron art (including the elaborate Kasli Iron Pavilion that won prizes in Paris in 1900), precious-stone cutting (a local speciality), and the local craft of engraving or painting trays, known as *Uralskie podnosy* (Ural trays), as well as rooms of pre-revolution Russian painting – all in all, well worth the $1.50 entry fee.

Just across the street corner from the Fine Arts Museum, at ulitsa Malysheva 46, is the **Regional Local Studies Museum** (Oblastnoy kraevedchesky muzey; closed Sunday and Monday), which has some interesting exhibits on the Romanov murders, Old Believers in the Ural region, and old Yekaterinburg.

If your appetite for rocks isn't yet sated, visit the **Ural Geology Museum** (Uralsky Geologichesky Muzey), another two blocks west and two south, on the corner of ulitsa Khokhryakova and ulitsa Kuybysheva. The museum, with over 500 Ural region minerals and a collection of meteorites, is open until 5.30 pm most days (2 to 6 pm Thursday, and closed weekends). Entry is $2.

Military History & Other Museums

The Military History Museum (Voenno-istorichesky muzey), ulitsa Pervomayskaya 27, has interesting exhibits covering the revolution, WWII and Soviet forces after WWII. In the yard behind there's a collection of tanks, planes and even a space capsule. The whereabouts of the wreckage of Gary Powers' US plane, which apparently was once in the museum, remains somewhat of a mystery. A few scraps of metal identified as Exhibit 13, upstairs in an inconspicuous glass case, are supposedly pieces taken from the plane. Next to them is a model of the land-to-air missile that brought it down. When we asked one babushka where we might find the rest of the plane, she shrugged her shoulders and suggested the hit had been so good that nothing else remained. The museum is open from 9.30 am to 4 pm Tuesday to Friday, and until 3 pm on Saturday (closed Sunday and Monday).

On ulitsa Karla Libknekhta, just north of prospekt Lenina, are the **Yekaterinburg History Museum** (Muzey istorii Yekaterinburga; closed Sunday and Monday) at No 26, the **Museum of Youth** (Muzey molodyozhi; open daily) at No 32 and the **Museum of Photography** (Muzey fotografii) at No 36. Several other small museums are listed in the *City Guide Ekaterinburg*.

Sverdlov Statue

Yakov Sverdlov remains atop his rock facing the Opera & Ballet Theatre on prospekt Lenina. With his downward-pointing finger he seems to be saying 'Take 'em to the cellar and shoot 'em'.

University & Arboretum

The Ural State Technical University (Uralsky gosudarstvenny tekhnichesky universitet), an imposing 1930s Soviet classical edifice at the east end of prospekt Lenina, 3km from the centre, is the biggest Russian university east of the Ural Mountains. It's generally known as UPI – the initials of its old name, Uralsky Politekhnichesky Institut (Ural Polytechnical Institute). In the Soviet era, despite (or maybe because of) its technological emphasis, it was renowned as a stepping stone to high political office – for Boris Yeltsin, among many others. There's a nice, quiet open-air arboretum (Dendrologichesky Park-Vystavka) a block north of the university, on the corner of ulitsa Pervomayskaya and ulitsa Mira. You can reach the university by tram No 4, 13, 15 or 18 or bus No 28 east along prospekt Lenina. Get off the tram when it turns right down ulitsa Gagarina, a block before the university.

Places to Stay

The ***Komnaty Otdykha*** (Rest Rooms), on level 4 of the west wing of the main train station, are the cheapest and most convenient option if you are just passing through. Clean and bright doubles/triples (toilets and bath-

Yeltsin & Yekaterinburg

Yekaterinburg's best known son is Boris Yeltsin, who was born of peasant parents in the village of Butka, 190km to the east. Yeltsin studied civil engineering at what is now Yekaterinburg's technical university (and met his wife Naya there), worked his way up from foreman to head of the city's house-building organisation, then moved into Communist Party work, becoming head of the Sverdlovsk regional party by 1976. He was popular as Party bosses went, as he was in the habit of riding the trams like everyone else and paying regular visits to local factories. He left after being promoted to head the Moscow Party in 1985. In 1991, during the old guard coup in Moscow, plans were drawn up for Yeltsin to run Russia's government from bunkers near Yekaterinburg if the coup succeeded. In 1992, as Russian president, he ordered the city's Sverdlovsk-17 biological weapons plant closed.

Yeltin's leadership style became more autocratic over the years. A predilection for reinforcing his own power by encouraging in-fighting in 'Tsar Boris' court' produced much political instability in the late 1990s. As a result of declining health and notorious bouts of alcoholism, Yeltsin became more and more unpredictable. In 2000, he will finally step down from office. See the Politics section in Facts about European Russia for more information on Yeltsin's influence on Russian politics.

Russians under 30, by the way, are equally likely to know of Yekaterinburg as the birthplace of the rock band Nautilus Pompilius.

room in the corridor) cost $6, while doubles with toilet go for $8. The same rooms are $2 cheaper between 8 am and 6 pm.

Konstantin Brylyakov (see Travel Agencies for contact details; book in advance) can get you into the ***Hotel of the Urals Academy of State Service***, which occupies four floors of the Academy building. Dorm beds cost around $14, while basic single rooms cost $30 (with bathroom $56). Tram No 15 going west from anywhere along prospekt Lenina will take you there (ask for stop Dekabristov). ***Hotel Tsentralnaya*** *(☎ 55 11 09, ulitsa Malysheva 74)* – the southern end of ulitsa Karla Libknekhta – has basic single/double rooms from $17/27, rising to around $40/60 with shower and toilet, and more expensive suites.

Hotel Sverdlovsk *(☎ 53 65 74, fax 53 62 48)* has little to offer except a convenient location by the train station. The corridors are so long they shimmer, paint weeps from the walls, and chunks of plaster are said to occasionally rain down from bathroom ceilings. Tired basic rooms (with bathroom) start from $34/50, while more expensive – but not more youthful – doubles cost from $92. Despite these shortcomings, it's safe and does stamp visas.

Better than any of these is ***Hotel Iset*** *(☎ 55 69 43, prospekt Lenina 69)*, in a restored Constructivist building with a ground plan in the shape of a hammer and sickle. It has bright and comfortable rooms without shower and toilet, but with TV, for $36/72, 1st class rooms with bathroom, telephone and TV for $48/96, and good two-room suites with all facilities for $53/106.

Protex-Otel *(☎ 29 70 44, fax 22 44 18, 3rd floor, ulitsa 8 Marta 70)* has overpriced singles for $60 and suites at $80/120.

Mikof-Iris Hotel *(☎ 28 38 66, fax 28 33 70, ulitsa Bardina 4A)*, 5km south-west of the centre, has comfortable two-room suites at $60/70, including breakfast.

Formerly belonging to the Communist Party, the upmarket ***Hotel Oktyabrskaya*** *(☎ 74 15 95, fax 74 50 16, ulitsa Sofyi Kovalevskoy 17)* is in a quiet, treed neighbourhood 3.5km east of the centre, north off ulitsa Pervomayskaya. Comfortable standard rooms are $101/145 the first night, $68/97 for the following nights. Suites for two people cost $183 and $155 for first and subsequent nights, and there are some cheaper small suites. The hotel has a good restaurant and a service bureau. Bus No 28 along Glavny prospekt from the city centre stops on ulitsa Pervomayskaya near the Kovalevskoy corner. The hotel is a red-brick building with only a small sign on the door to give away its name.

The small ***Hotel Magistr*** *(☎ 22 42 06, fax 22 56 74, ulitsa 8 Marta 50)* offers excellent quality, with stylishly furnished rooms for $114/130 and luxury double suites for $177, all with bathroom, telephone, television and including breakfast. You'll probably need to reserve a couple of weeks in advance as it's a favourite among businesspeople. Tram No 15 running west along prospekt Lenina goes past the door. Get off just before the circus.

The four-star ***Atrium Palace Hotel*** *(☎ 59 60 00, fax 59 60 01, ulitsa Kuibyshev 44)*, inside the World Trade Center, is top of the range, with several restaurants and bars, a nightclub, a gym with sauna and pool, and conference and office facilities. Rooms here are $198/245.

Places to Eat

Mak Pik, two blocks west of ploshchad 1905 goda on prospekt Lenina, serves a so-called 'Bik Mak' hamburger with beef, a cabbage leaf, mayonnaise, ketchup and mustard for $2.50 that goes down surprisingly well. Other burgers start from $1.50 and the toilets are usually clean.

You can eat well and cheaply at the ***Stolovaya*** *(3rd floor, ulitsa Pervomayskaya 56)* – use the middle entrance and take the stairs on the right – for about $3. The food here is basic, but filling and well prepared. ***Restoran Generalsky*** *(ulitsa Generalskaya 3)*, behind the Uralvneshtorgbank, serves similarly plain but quite good set-course dishes for $2.50, $3 and $5 in a plush, military-club atmosphere.

Irlandsky Dvorik *(ulitsa Malysheva 11)* is a pleasant restaurant and Irish pub that, among other things, does soups from around $2 to $4 and salmon pelmeni with mushrooms for $6. Half a litre of Guinness costs $6, and Kilkenny and Harp are also served. It's open from noon to midnight, and is a good place to eat and drink, especially in the evening.

More upmarket is ***Astoria***, nearby at No 28. It serves a range of pan-European dishes, although you might like to give the 'Little Frogs Legs in Sour Cream' a miss. Soups come in at around $4 to $15, and there are fish and red-meat dishes for under $15. Expect to pay over $30 though for a decent bottle of wine. ***La Gradara***, next door, serves well priced northern Italian cuisine and also has a good but expensive wine list.

The Chinese ***Kharbin*** *(ulitsa Kuybysheva 38)*, south of the centre, was once the only decent restaurant in town and is still worthwhile for meals in the middle to upper price range. You can't miss the building – it's done up like a Chinese temple outside. To get there, you can take tram No 32 from Hotel Iset.

Vodoley *(Shevchenko 9)* is a slick, new-Russian establishment with an ominous-looking bandstand; but it's the coffee-table aquarium in the entrance hall that's really a worry! Soups cost around $5 and red-meat and fish dishes are around $10 to $20. The restaurant opens at 1 pm. There's a disco and music venue upstairs that opens in the evening. It charges about $15 to $25 admission, depending on the act.

Self-caterers can take tram No 13 or 14 east from prospekt Lenina to the enormous ***Kirovsky supermarket***. It has a wide range of Western and Russian food and goods. ***Gastronom Tsentralny***, on prospekt Lenina, has quite a good range of cold meats, dairy products and the like, but no fresh vegetables.

Entertainment

City Bar, in the Atrium Palace Hotel, is an excellent place to meet Westerners, especially during its Friday evening happy hour, when fish and chips are served for the bargain price of $3 to $5 and beers are $3 to $4. ***Malakhit***, an entertainment complex on the corner of ulitsa Pervomayskaya and ulitsa Karla Libknekhta, is the place to observe New Russians in all their finery. Air hockey, feather bowling and bucking broncos are upstairs and you'll find a dance floor and stage on the 1st floor. Admission is $6.

Shopping

Locally engraved or painted trays (known as Uralskie podnosy), rings, and pictures made from ground stone are on sale in the Fine Arts Museum. Souvenirs are also sold on the small square in front of City Hall opposite ploshchad 1905 goda.

Getting There & Away

Air The main airport is Koltsovo (☎ 24 99 24), 15km south-east of the city centre. Daily Transaero and other flights go to/from Moscow ($120, 2½ hours) connecting with many international services. Lufthansa flies directly to/from Frankfurt ($1109, six hours, three times weekly). Ural Airlines has a direct service to/from Norilsk ($242, two hours, twice weekly). Other flights go daily to/from Irkutsk, several times a week to/from St Petersburg, Omsk, Novosibirsk and Vladivostok, and a few times weekly to/from Krasnoyarsk, Perm, Almaty (Kazakhstan) and Tashkent (Uzbekistan).

Another airport at Uktus in the south of the city has only a few local flights. The airline Luftbrücke (see the Siberia & the Russian Far East Getting There & Away chapter) can book weekly flights to/from Hanover and Cologne.

The Lufthansa City Center (☎ 59 83 00) operates from the Sputnik office on ulitsa Pushkina. Transaero has an office across the corridor from Lufthansa and a central office (☎ 65 91 65, transaer@etel.ru) at prospekt Lenina 50. The Areal-Aero office (☎ 29 90 51) at Bolshakova 99A, south of the city, handles bookings on all airlines. It is open from 8 am to 7.30 pm Monday to Saturday, and until 4.45 pm on Sunday.

Train Yekaterinburg is the major stop on the Trans-Siberian Railway between Perm (six hours west) and Novosibirsk (21 hours east). Apart from the Trans-Siberian, Trans-Mongolian and Trans-Manchurian trains between Moscow and Vladivostok or Beijing, there are numerous other daily trains to different cities on and off the main Trans-Siberian route. Eastbound, some go via Tyumen (five hours), others via Kurgan and Petropavlovsk (Kazakhstan); the two branches meet up again at Omsk. Westbound, some Moscow trains go via Kazan rather than Perm.

To/from Moscow (Kazan Station), the daily flagship *Ural* (No 15/16), which starts and finishes in Yekaterinburg and travels via Kazan, is a good choice (29 hours). Other services run to/from St Petersburg (35 hours, twice daily), and Tashkent, Almaty and Bishkek (every two days).

Tickets are sold to foreigners on level three, counter five, in the west wing of the main train station (closed for half an hour at 7.30 am and 7.30 pm). Rest rooms (see Places to Stay) are on level four. Toilets and left luggage are also in the west wing. Tickets for suburban services such as to Nizhny Tagil are currently sold at the ticket office *(prigorodnye kassy)* on the ground level, where there is also a suburban-train timetable. This counter may move back into the old east wing once renovations finish.

The Central City Railways Office, ulitsa Sverdlova 25, handles bookings up to 24 hours prior to departure. It's open from 8.30 am to 7.30 pm Monday to Friday, until 6 pm on Saturday (closed from 1 to 2 pm).

Bus From the bus station south of the centre at ulitsa 8 Marta 145, on the corner of ulitsa Shchorsa, there is at least one bus daily to Tyumen ($17, seven hours), 24 to Chelyabinsk ($7, four hours) and four to Nizhny Tagil ($5, three hours).

Getting Around

To/From the Airport Bus No 1 links the main train station and Koltsovo airport every 10 to 20 minutes from 5.30 am (from the station) to 11 pm. The trip takes around 45 minutes. Express bus No 167 takes almost as long, linking Koltsovo airport and the Areal-Aero air terminal. A taxi to/from the airport costs around $8/17 during the day/night.

Local Transport Many trolleybuses run up and down ulitsa Sverdlova/ulitsa Karla Libknekhta between the train station and prospekt Lenina. Tram Nos 4, 13, 15 and 18 and bus No 28 cover long stretches of prospekt Lenina, with tram Nos 4 and 15 also serving the bus station.

Bus No 23 and tram No 5 run between the train and bus stations. Tram No 5 stops near the Areal-Aero office. Many other trams run up and down ulitsa 8 Marta between ulitsa Radishcheva and the bus station.

The metro system currently runs from the Uralmash machine tool factory in the north to the train station and into the centre near ploshchad 1905 goda. A new station, Geologicheskaya, is being constructed near the circus and Hotel Magistr.

AROUND YEKATERINBURG

Nizhnyaya Sinyachikha
Нижняя Синячиха

This village, about 150km north-east of Yekaterinburg and 12km north of the town of Alapaevsk, is home to an open-air **architecture museum** of old Ural region log buildings, with displays of period furniture, tools and domestic articles. There's one stone building – a cathedral, housing a museum of Ural region art. But it's very hard to reach by public transport from Yekaterinburg – about six hours by occasional trains, four or five hours by equally rare buses.

Alapaevsk has a museum dedicated to Tchaikovsky in a house where the composer once lived. Konstantin Brylyakov can arrange day trips out there for $30 per person, plus $80 for transportation that can be shared. Sputnik offers trips with an overnight stay in a sanatorium.

Nizhny Tagil
Нижний Тагил

☎ 25 • pop 400,000

This industrial town 149km north of Yekaterinburg was once synonymous with the Demidov clan of industrialists and landowners descended from Nikita Demidovich Antufev, sent by Peter the Great to set up weapons factories in the Ural region. His dynasty ended up with mansions in St Petersburg, Moscow and abroad, only visiting their Ural empire every decade or two. Nizhny Tagil has a number of interesting museums focusing on its industrial history.

Foremost among them are the **Regional Studies Museum** (Kraevedchesky muzey), the **Nizhny Tagil Museum-Reserve of Middle Urals Mining** (Nizhny-Tagilsky muzey-zapovednik gornozavodskogo dela srednego Urala) the **Museum of the Life & Trades of the Mining Population** (Muzey byta i remesel gornozavodskogo naselenia), and the **Museum of Tray Manufacture** (Muzey podnosnogo promysla) – devoted to the well known local craft.

Hotel Tagil *(Sadovaya ulitsa 6)*, opposite the train station, is apparently reasonable. There's also ***Hotel Severny Ural*** *(prospekt Lenina 6)*, 2km west.

Several northbound long-distance trains from Yekaterinburg to places like Priobie, Nizhnyaya Tura and Kachkanar stop in Nizhny Tagil, and there are suburban trains roughly hourly. The trip from Yekaterinburg is three to four hours.

Verkhoturie
Верхотурье

This small town on the Tura River, about 170km north of Nizhny Tagil, was once the most important centre of Christianity in eastern Russia. Today it has about a dozen cathedrals, churches and monasteries. The main cathedral is second in size only to St Isaac's in St Petersburg. Konstantin Brylayakov offers two-day tours, and there's a basic ***hotel*** nearby in Aktay. A larger hotel was under construction in 1998. Suburban trains run here from Nizhny Tagil.

Tyumen & Omsk Regions
Тюменская и Омская области

The old Siberian capital of Tobolsk, north of the Trans-Siberian Railway, is the most interesting destination in these regions between Yekaterinburg and Novosibirsk.

TYUMEN
ТЮМЕНЬ

☎ 3452 • pop 496,000

Tyumen, 325km east of Yekaterinburg on the main Trans-Siberian rail line, is the capital of Russia's largest *oblast* (region), which stretches all the way to the Yamal and Gydansk peninsulas on the Arctic Kara Sea. Since the region has vast reserves of oil (produced mainly around Surgut and Nizhnevartovsk) and gas (farther north), and is Russia's largest oil-exporting area, Tyumen is something of a business capital, but there is little here to detain the casual visitor.

The first Russian fort in Siberia was founded here in 1586, near the site of Chimgi-Tura, an old capital of the Mongol-Tatar Taibuga clan that succeeded the Golden Horde in the west Siberian forests. During WWII, Lenin's corpse was kept in Tyumen, safe from the invading Germans.

Orientation & Information

The main street, running roughly east-west across town, is ulitsa Respubliki. The city centre is the area east of its intersection with ulitsa Pervomayskaya, which runs north-south for 1.5km to the train station.

There's a cash exchange desk in Hotel Kvoliti and another at Tyumenaviatrans, opposite the train station. The post office and long-distance telephone office are two and three blocks respectively east of ulitsa Pervomayskaya along ulitsa Respubliki. The OVIR office is at ulitsa Melnikayte 48 (closed Friday and Saturday).

The time in Tyumen is Moscow time plus two hours.

Things to See

Three blocks west along ulitsa Respubliki from ulitsa Pervomayskaya, then half a block north on ulitsa Semakova, is the fine, green-and-white, multidomed **Church of the Holy Sign** (Znamenskaya tserkov), built in 1786 in Russian baroque style. It's a working church. This area of town is full of **old wooden houses**, with the Tura River flowing by at the foot of a steep bank. You can walk farther west to a **monastery** in a fine position at the top of the river bank.

The **Fine Arts Museum** (Muzey izobrazitelnykh iskusstv), opposite Hotel Kvoliti, has a good collection of Russian painting and sculpture (closed on the last day of the month).

Places to Stay & Eat

There's a ***hotel (gostinitsa)*** upstairs in the train station, with singles and doubles at $10 per person, and cheaper dorms. ***Hotel Kolos*** *(☎ 22 62 24, Melnikayte 83)*, set back from the street, is cheap but nothing more. Rooms for foreigners start from $20/37 a single/double with toilet, $36/72 with bath and toilet. Two better options – both will stamp your visa – huddle together at the northern end of ulitsa Ordzhonikidze, which is just east of the post office. ***Hotel Prometey*** *(☎ 25 14 18, fax 25 14 29)* has good-value doubles for $80 with bathroom and a reasonable restaurant serving mains for around $8. The four-star ***Hotel Kvoliti*** *(☎ 39 40 40, fax 39 40 50, Ordzhonikidze 46)* has rooms for $116/136 and more expensive luxury suites. Its upmarket restaurant is well priced, with many main dishes for around $10, and there are sauna and gym facilities.

Getting There & Away

Tyumenaviatrans (☎/fax 25 05 32), opposite the train station, handles Transaero and other flight bookings. There are services to/from Moscow ($143, two hours, several times daily), Khanty-Mansiysk ($140, 2½ hours, three times a week), Salekhard ($160, three hours, daily), Irkutsk ($160, 3½ hours, twice weekly) and Tashkent ($170, two hours, daily). Other flights are to Novosibirsk and St Petersburg several times a week.

Several eastbound and westbound trains a day on the main Trans-Siberian line stop at Tyumen: Yekaterinburg is about five hours from here, Omsk eight hours, Novosibirsk 18 hours, Moscow 35 hours. At least three trains run daily to/from Tobolsk (5½ hours).

Getting Around

Any bus from the train station will take you along ulitsa Pervomayskaya to ulitsa Respubliki or ulitsa Lenina, one block before. You can pick up your bus going back in

Rasputin's Roots

The village of Pokrovskoe was the birthplace and boyhood home of Grigory Rasputin, the 'priest of sex' and cult figure of the Russian aristocracy in the early 1900s. The village can be found 50km along the road from Tyumen to Tobolsk, on the Tura River.

Born the son of a cart driver and farmer in 1869, Rasputin married locally and had three children. Though his house in Pokrovskoe has been demolished, in 1933 a BBC television crew managed to find villagers who could tell them about his time there.

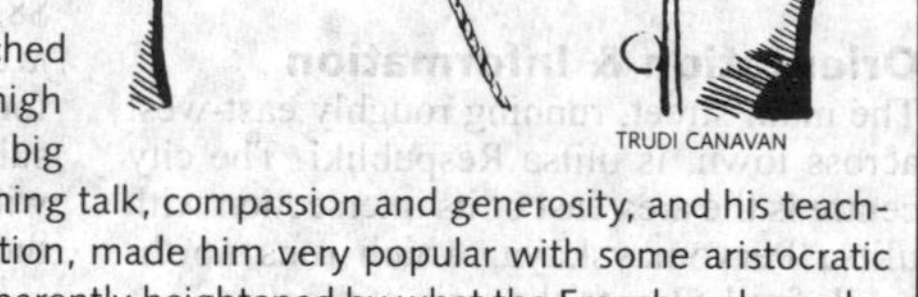

TRUDI CANAVAN

Though not a monk as is sometimes supposed, Rasputin did pray a lot. In his mid-20s, he experienced a vision of the Virgin while working in the fields, and left Pokrovskoe to seek enlightenment. On his wanderings he seemed to come to believe, as did the contemporary Khlyst (Whip) sect, that sinning (especially through sex), then repenting, could bring people close to God.

Early in the 20th century Rasputin reached St Petersburg, where some sectors of high society, with little better to do, took a big interest in holy peasants. Rasputin's soothing talk, compassion and generosity, and his teaching that promiscuity could bring redemption, made him very popular with some aristocratic women. His magnetic personality was apparently heightened by what the French ambassador called 'a strong animal smell, like that of a goat'.

Eventually Rasputin was summoned by Tsarina Alexandra and seemed able, thanks to some kind of hypnotic power, to cure the uncontrollable bleeding of her haemophiliac son, Tsarevich Alexey, the heir to the throne. As he continued his drunken, lecherous life, replete with famous orgies, Rasputin's influence on the royal family grew to the point where he could make or break the careers of ministers and generals. Naturally, this made him increasingly unpopular and many blamed him for the disasters of WWI.

His end finally came late in 1916 when Prince Felix Yusupov and others decided he had to be got rid of. This proved to be easier said than done, as Rasputin lived through being poisoned, shot repeatedly, and beaten with sticks – all in the one evening at St Petersburg's Yusupov Palace. Apparently he only died when pushed through the ice and submerged underwater.

front of the city hall (Gorodskoy Duma) on ulitsa Pervomayskaya.

TOBOLSK
ТОБОЛЬСК

☎ 34511 • pop 98,000

Tobolsk is 247km north-east of Tyumen at the confluence of the Irtysh and Tobol rivers. It was founded as a fort in 1587, near the site of Kashlyk (also called Sibir), the capital of the west Siberian khanate conquered for Russia by Yermak Timofeevich in 1582. Tobolsk's strategic location on the Irtysh made it the political, military and religious centre of Russian Siberia until the 18th century. From 1708 to 1839 the governor resided here, exercising administrative power throughout Siberia and the Far East. From 1620 it was the seat of Siberia's first bishopric – set up, incidentally, with the express purpose of stamping out incest, wife-renting and wife-stealing by sexually frustrated Cossacks.

Although Tobolsk's administrative and strategic importance waned from the 1760s, when the new Great Siberian Trakt road to the east took a more southerly route, it remained a significant centre of learning and culture right up to the early 20th century. This was reinforced by the arrival of educated Decembrists and their families in the 1830s. In 1850, Dostoevsky was brought to Tobolsk in chains and, if we can believe a letter he wrote to his brother, preferred the experience to many others he'd had.

Tobolsk's most distinguished guests, though, were Tsar Nicholas II and the royal family, who spent several months here from 1917 to 1918 before being taken to Yekaterinburg and executed.

Orientation & Information

Tobolsk has a lower town that begins at the foot of the kremlin and extends south across the valley of the Irtysh River. The main street in the upper town, ulitsa Semena Remezova, runs south-north for about 1km from the kremlin to a roundabout, where it meets Komsomolsky prospekt and continues north-west. Komsomolsky prospekt runs from the roundabout to Hotel Slavyanskaya, about 3km from the kremlin. The upper town is characterised by ugly, Soviet-era high-rise apartments.

The Sputnik offshoot, Turisticheskoe agenstvo Slavyanskaya (Slavyanskaya Tourist Agency; ☎ 9 91 14, fax 5 58 76, ric316@rosnet.rosmail.com), on level two of Hotel Slavyanskaya, has young and knowledgeable staff who, with advance notice, arrange guided tours of the city and environs in English.

You can change cash at the reception of the hotel, and next door is a post and international telephone office. OVIR is off Komsomolsky prospekt in a building behind the Drama Theatre.

The time in Tobolsk is Moscow time plus two hours.

Things to See

The centrepiece is the elegant old **kremlin**. Perched on a cliff top overlooking the Irtysh River, this was Siberia's first stone kremlin. It is dominated by the colourful blue domes of the **St Sofia Cathedral** (Sofiysky Sobor) built in 1686.

Highlights are the **Intercession Cathedral** (Pokrovsky Sobor), dating from the 1740s, the 1780 **Bishop's Chambers** (Zimny Riznitsa), the old **Trading Arcades** (Gostiny Dvor), and the **Bell tower** (Zvonnitsa) where a huge bronze imperial eagle, taken from the roof during the revolution, still lies on the floor. The **Regional Museum** (Kraevedchesky muzey) is also housed in the kremlin complex. Between the foot of the cliff and the river is the **lower town** (podgornaya chast), with many wooden houses, several churches and a sprinkling of baroque and neoclassical stone administrative buildings.

Places to Stay & Eat

The train station has excellent, but inconveniently far from town, budget rooms upstairs. ***Hotel Sibir*** *(☎ 6 23 90)*, just opposite the kremlin on ploshchad Remezova, has quite good singles with toilet for $9, and doubles with shower and toilet for $14. The quality ***Hotel Slavyanskaya*** *(☎ 9 91 00/01, fax 9 91 20, Mikrorayon 9)* is on Komsomolsky prospekt. Comfortable singles cost from $72 to $88, doubles from $120 to $200, all with bathroom facilities, breakfast and use of the sauna and swimming pool. It also has the best eating options in town, with two ***restaurants*** where main dishes cost around $10.

Getting There & Away

The train station is 14km north of the centre but connected by the regular bus No 4, which stops at Hotel Slavyanskaya and continues on to the kremlin. Several trains run daily from Tyumen, taking around 5½ hours. It's an interesting trip from Tyumen through deciduous forest and marshland, with a spectacular view of the kremlin in the distance about 30 minutes outside Tobolsk. The daily Omsk-Surgut train stops here, and there are daily trains farther north to Noyabrsk. There's at least one direct link daily with Yekaterinburg. A few buses also make the trip daily from Tyumen (four hours).

The river station (rechnoy vokzal) is a major staging post for regular boat services to Khanty-Mansiysk ($18, 28 hours). High-speed *rakety* ('rocket' boats), some of which are 30-year-old classics, provide a frequent service to/from Ust-Ishim ($8, seven hours), a village of 6000 inhabitants upriver from Tobolsk with its own regional studies museum.

From around June to September boats ply the Irtysh and Ob rivers from Omsk to Salekhard, 2714km downriver from Omsk. The journey takes around five days from Omsk, stopping at the major ports of Tobolsk (1173km), Khanty-Mansiysk (1809km) and Beryozova (2319km). It departs six or seven times per month in June, July and August, less frequently in September. The journey from Tobolsk takes about three days and costs $40.

OMSK
ОМСК

☎ 3812 • pop 1.3 million

This sprawling industrial city lies on the Trans-Siberian Railway at the point where the Om River enters the Irtysh, 900km east of Yekaterinburg and 800km west of Novosibirsk. Omsk started out in 1716 as a Cossack outpost, then in 1824 replaced Tobolsk as the seat of the governor general of Siberia.

It became a major dumping ground for exiles, the best known of whom was Fyodor Dostoevsky. In *Buried Alive in Siberia*, he wrote about his wretched years in prison here (1849-53), during which he nearly died from a flogging. In the civil war, Admiral Kolchak made Omsk the seat of his anti-Bolshevik government – until it was overrun in 1919.

Today Omsk is a resoundingly ordinary place with lots and lots of apartment blocks. Among its sights are the Stary (Old) Krepost and Novy (New) Krepost 18th century forts, a large 19th century cathedral and a park with an enormous WWII memorial. There is also a beach on the Irtysh. You can take boat excursions from the river station (see the Tobolsk Getting There & Away section for connections to Salekhard). The ***Irtysh*** *(☎ 23 27 02, fax 23 22 12)* and ***Turist*** *(☎ 31 64 14, fax 31 52 22)* are probably the two best hotels.

Getting There & Away

There are flights three or four times a day to/from Moscow (3½ hours), most days to/from Yekaterinburg and Novosibirsk, and a few times a week to places like Krasnoyarsk, Irkutsk and Abakan. There's also the ambitious Omsk Avia (☎ 30 75 21), which flies to/from Frankfurt, Stuttgart and Hanover for around $465.

By train, Yekaterinburg is about 12 hours away, Tyumen eight hours, Novosibirsk 9½ hours, and Moscow 42 hours.

Novosibirsk & Tomsk Regions
Новосибирская и Томская области

Novosibirsk, Siberia's biggest city, is a fairly common stopover on Trans-Siberian packages, being conveniently about halfway between the Ural Mountains and Lake Baikal. It is an archetypal Soviet-style place – it has grown from almost nothing since the 1920s – but perfect to get a taste of life in a largish Siberian city. South of Novosibirsk is the Altay Region and the beautiful Altay Mountains.

NOVOSIBIRSK
НОВОСИБИРСК

☎ 3832 • pop 1.3 million

Novosibirsk, a city spawned by the Trans-Siberian Railway, was founded at the rail crossing of the Ob River in 1893, which makes it the youngest of Siberia's big cities. Until 1925, it was known as Novonikolaevsk. Its mushroom-like growth began in the 1920s when it was purpose-built as an industrial and transport centre, between the coal fields of the developing Kuzbass area to the east (centred on Kemerovo and Novokuznetsk) and the mineral deposits of the Ural region to the west. In the 1930s the building of the Turk-Sib railway south from Novosibirsk to Almaty in Kazakhstan made the city a crucial transport link between Russia and Central Asia.

It is a friendly, relaxed city that boasts a measure of style. It is also one fond of dimensions: biggest city (biggest train station, biggest library) in Siberia, most sprawling after Moscow and St Petersburg, big airport, big dam. Pride of place in Omsk goes to the Opera & Ballet Theatre, 'Siberia's Bolshoi' (the biggest theatre in the country) and the home of a respected ballet company and school.

You might like to make a trip out to Akademgorodok, the purpose-built 'Academy Township' created by the Soviet Academy of Sciences south of the city, near the Ob Sea reservoir.

Orientation

The city straddles the Ob River, with the centre on its east side. The hub is ploshchad Lenina, with the Opera & Ballet Theatre, and the two main axes are Krasny prospekt, running north-south through ploshchad Lenina, and Vokzalnaya magistral, running north-west from ploshchad Lenina to the train station.

Maps Central House of Books (Tsentralny Dom Knigi), near ploshchad Lenina, has good 1:200,000 (1cm:2km) maps of some areas of Siberia, including parts of the Altay Mountains – worth looking at if you're heading for the hills. The kiosk in Hotel Sibir foyer sells a range of city maps for less than $2.

Information

Money You can change money at the post office, TsUM department store, 24 hours a day at the Vneshtorgbank in the lobby of Hotel Sibir, and at the Sibirsky Bank, ulitsa Lenina 4. These last two give cash advances on Visa cards.

Post & Communications The main post office and the long-distance telephone office are a few doors apart on ulitsa Lenina. The post office has fax, telegram, an EMS express post service, and an email service for $0.75 per handwritten page. It is open from 8 am to 7 pm weekdays and until 6 pm weekends.

Email & Internet Access Downstairs at ulitsa Trudovaya 1, Internet Klub offers visitors Web access from noon to 8 pm daily for around $1 per hour. To get there, take the lane running west behind the cylindrical, tiled kiosk on Krasny prospekt, just north of ploshchad Lenina.

Medical Services The Tsentr Farmatsevtichesky Informatsia, Krasny prospekt 31, will help you locate medications and may waiver prescription requirements on some drugs for foreigners. The staff speak Russian only.

Visa Registration The OVIR office is on the corner of ulitsa Oktyabrskaya and ulitsa Kamenskaya, behind the large Globus Theatre (enter from ulitsa Oktyabrskaya). It registers foreigners between 3 and 5 pm on Monday and between 10 am and 12 pm on Thursday.

Travel Agencies For virtually any kind of trip in the Altay, you probably can't find better help than Sibalp (☎ 49 59 22, fax 54 13 74, sibalp@online.nsk.su). Its office is west of the Ob at ulitsa Nemirovicha-Danchenko 155/1, kvartira 47, but the director, Sergey Kurgin, will meet clients at their hotel. See the Altay Republic section for more on what Sibalp can offer.

There's a helpful Intourist service bureau (☎ 23 02 03) in the Hotel Sibir lobby.

Time Zone The time in Novosibirsk is Moscow time plus three hours.

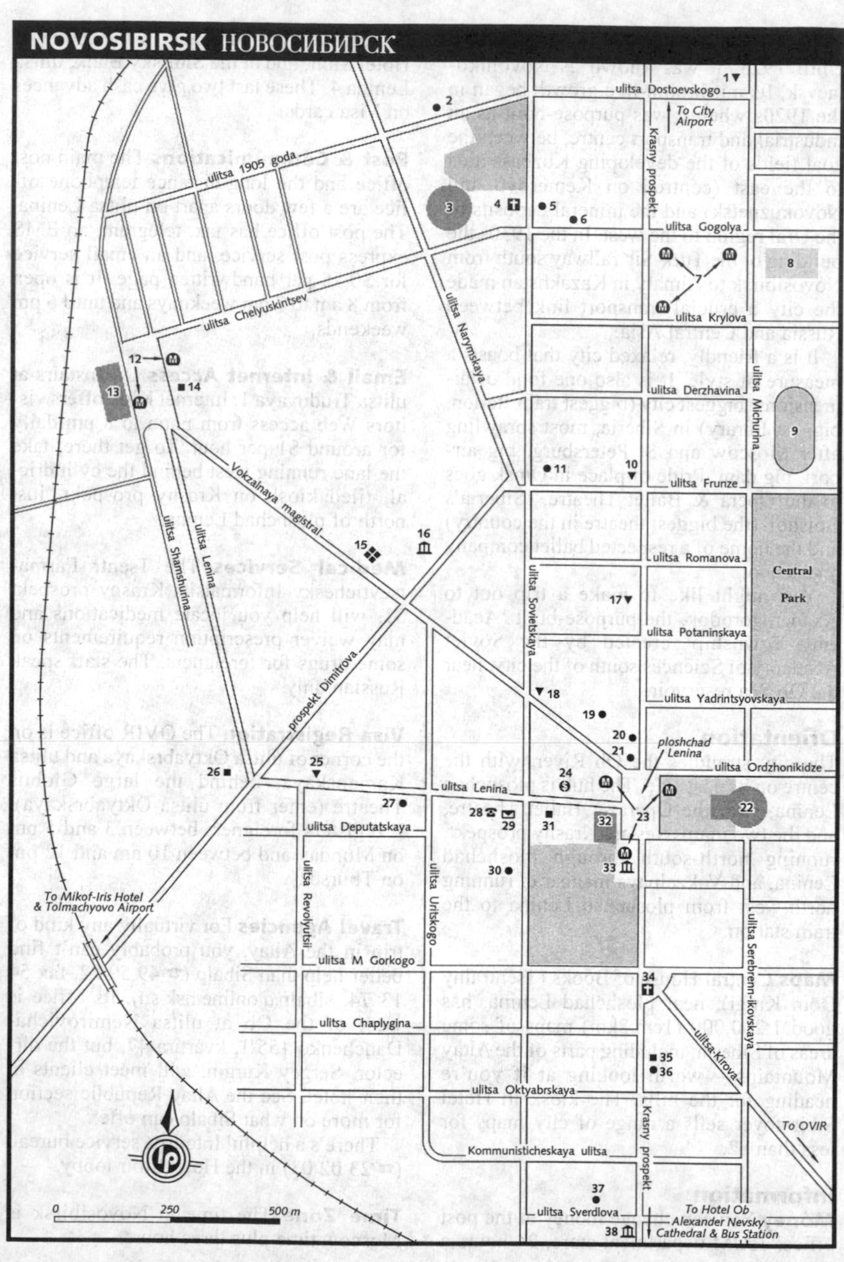
NOVOSIBIRSK НОВОСИБИРСК
ulitsa Dostoevskogo
To City Airport
Krasny prospekt
ulitsa 1905 goda
ulitsa Gogolya
ulitsa Krylova
ulitsa Chelyuskintsev
ulitsa Narymskaya
ulitsa Michurina
ulitsa Derzhavina
ulitsa Frunze
Vokzalnaya magistral
ulitsa Shamshurina
ulitsa Lenina
ulitsa Romanova
Central Park
ulitsa Sovietskaya
ulitsa Potaninskaya
prospekt Dimitrova
ulitsa Yadrintsyovskaya
ploshchad Lenina
ulitsa Ordzhonikidze
ulitsa Lenina
ulitsa Deputatskaya
ulitsa Revolyutsii
ulitsa Uritskogo
To Mikof-Iris Hotel & Tolmachyovo Airport
ulitsa Serebrenn-ikovskaya
ulitsa M Gorkogo
ulitsa Chaplygina
ulitsa Kirova
ulitsa Oktyabrskaya
To OVIR
Kommunisticheskaya ulitsa
Krasny prospekt
ulitsa Sverdlova
To Hotel Ob Alexander Nevsky Cathedral & Bus Station
0
250
500 m

NOVOSIBIRSK НОВОСИБИРСК

PLACES TO STAY

14 Hotel Novosibirsk
Гостиница Новосибирск

26 Hotel Sibir
Гостиница Сибирь

31 Hotel Tsentralnaya
Гостиница Центральная

35 Otel Tsentr Rossii
Отель Центр России

PLACES TO EAT

1 Kafe Sobek
Кафе Собек

10 New York Pizza

17 Beer Mug

18 Restoran Renessans
Ресторан Ренессанс

25 Pub 501

METRO STATIONS

7 Sibirskaya/Krasny Prospekt
Сибирская/Красный Проспект

12 Ploshchad Garina-Mikhaylovskogo
Площадь Гарина-Михайловского

23 Ploshchad Lenina
Площадь Ленина

OTHER

2 Central Flight Information Agency (main office)
Центральное агенство воздущных сообщенний (главное бюро)

3 Circus
Цирк

4 Cathedral of the Ascension
Вознесенский собор

5 City Railways Agency
Городское железнодорожное агенство

6 Central Flight Information Agency (formerly Aeroflot International Sector)
Центральное агенство воздущных сообщенний

8 Central Market
Центральный рынок

9 Stadium
Стадион

11 Baths
Баня

13 Novosibirsk Glavny Station
Новосибирск Главный вокзал

15 TsUM Department Store
ЦУМ

16 Local Studies Museum
Краеведческий музей

19 Internet Klub
Интернет Клуб

20 Tsentralny Dom Knigi
Центральный дом книги

21 Tsentr Farmatsevticheskoy Informatsii
Центр Фармацевтической Информации

22 Opera & Ballet Theatre
Театр оперы и балета

24 Sibirsky Bank
Сибирский Банк

27 U Nikolaya
У Николая

28 Telephone Office
Междугородный телефонный пункт

29 Post Office
Почтамт

30 Conservatory
Консерватория

32 Tsentralny Komplex
Центральный комплекс

33 Local Studies Museum
Краеведческий музей

34 Chapel of St Nicholas
Часовня Святителя Николая

36 Transaero
Трансаэро

37 Union of Artist's Gallery
Выставочный зал союза художников

38 Art Gallery
Картинная галерея

Opera & Ballet Theatre

With its silver dome, giant portico and rich interior, this is indeed grand; many residents consider it the city's main attraction. They also agree that the sculptural ensemble out front is pretty ugly – Lenin, the *de rigueur* peasant, soldier and worker piece, and a couple representing the socialist future but looking like they're directing traffic.

The classical ballet and opera inside are good, too, and it's easier to get to see them here than it is in Moscow or St Petersburg. It's fun to watch Russian culture-vultures on a night out here. Novosibirsk takes ballet seriously and its school is among Russia's best. Try to get tickets a day ahead.

Museums & Galleries

The **Local Studies Museum** (Kraevedchesky muzey) has two branches. The one at Vokzalnaya magistral 11 – actually a few yards up prospekt Dimitrova behind TsUM – has exhibits ranging from a mammoth skeleton and stuffed animals through Siberian rocks and minerals to the development of Novosibirsk and the 'Uralo-Kuznetsky Kombinat' (basically the supplying of iron ore from the Ural region to the Kuzbass, and coal vice-versa – which accounts for a lot of the freight traffic on the Trans-Siberian Railway). This branch is open from 10 am to 6 pm weekdays. Perhaps of greater interest is the museum's branch at Krasny prospekt 19, just off ploshchad Lenina, which focuses on applied art. Its collections from around Russia include – incongruously – a large section on military equipment. Hours vary, but it is generally open from 10 am to 4 pm weekdays. Next door is a hall for temporary exhibitions.

About 1km south, at Krasny prospekt 5 on the corner of ulitsa Sverdlova, the **Art Gallery** (Kartinnaya galereya) includes numerous works by the 19th century Russian mystical painter Nikolay Rerikh (donated by him), plus changing exhibitions. Rerikh, who now enjoys international cult status, was obsessed for a while by the beauty and mystical qualities of the Altay Mountains south of Novosibirsk. The gallery is open from 11 am to 6.20 pm daily (closed Tuesday).

Behind it, at ulitsa Sverdlova 13, the **Union of Artists' Gallery** (Vystavochny zal Soyuza khudozhnikov) shows ongoing exhibitions of local talent on the ground floor (closed Monday) – while upstairs is the commercial **Siberian Trade Bank Gallery** (Galereya Sibirskogo Torgovogo Banka).

Novosibirsk's **Russian Institute of Archaeology & Ethnography**, well known for its archaeological discoveries in the Altay Mountains, has two interesting museums: one with archaeological and ethnographic collections from throughout Siberia, the other an open-air museum of Siberian wooden architecture – Sibalp can arrange visits.

Churches

The pretty little **Chapel of St Nicholas** (Chasovnya Svyatitelya Nikolaya), in the middle of Krasny prospekt two blocks south of ploshchad Lenina, is reckoned to be at the geographical centre of Russia. Originally built in 1915 to celebrate (two years late) 300 years of the Romanov dynasty, it was knocked down in the 1930s but rebuilt in 1993 for Novosibirsk's centenary. About 700m farther down Krasny prospekt is the **Alexander Nevsky Cathedral** (Sobor Alexandra Nevskogo), one of the city's first stone buildings.

The **Cathedral of the Ascension** (Vosnesenky Sobor) at ulitsa Sovietskaya 91, near the circus, dates from the early 1900s. It has nice blue and gold domes, and is beautiful inside.

Other Attractions

Central Park (Tsentralny Park), north of the Opera & Ballet Theatre, has horse-drawn carts, a children's railway, cafes, and outdoor music on summer weekends.

Cold? A traditional Russian **banya** at ulitsa Sovietskaya 36 is open from 10 am to 9 pm daily (from 2 pm in summer). Women are only admitted on Wednesday, Friday and Sunday, men only on the other days. A massage (from September to May) costs $8. See the boxed text 'A Russian Banya' in the Northern European Russia chapter for background and etiquette.

Places to Stay

The agency Inotext (☎ 10 35 87, fax 10 04 03, inotext@online.nsk.su) can arrange inexpensive accommodation in private flats or cheap hotels. A few people standing outside the train station do the same.

The huge ***Hotel Novosibirsk*** *(☎ 20 11 20, fax 21 65 17, Vokzalnaya magistral 1)* is comfortable and conveniently located opposite the train station. Rooms start at $24/39 a single/double, $35/55 with bathroom. There are also *lyux* suites at $55/122 and some cheaper double suites. The hotel has a bar and a small supermarket.

Hotel Tsentralnaya *(☎ 22 76 60, ulitsa Lenina 3)*, in the centre, is an older place that doesn't offer as good value. The cheapest rooms, at $30/40, are 'kategoria III', with TV and washbasin and shared toilets (no showers). For rooms with private bathroom, fridge and TV (which may not work) you pay $55/77.

Hotel Ob *(☎ 66 74 01)*, on the river bank 3km south of the centre, and 750m south from Rechnoy Vokzal metro station, is an uninviting glass-and-concrete slab with rooms at $48/50, and suites from $81 to $97. All rooms have private bathroom, telephone and TV.

Intourist's glossy, upmarket ***Hotel Sibir*** *(☎ 23 12 15, fax 23 87 66, ulitsa Lenina 21)*, on the corner of prospekt Dimitrova, has pleasant, comfortable rooms for $82/136 with breakfast, $145 for a double suite. The hotel has a good restaurant and a *bufet* on floor 7. There is also a helpful Intourist service bureau (☎ 23 02 03) that will arrange rail bookings for you for a commission of around $5.

WESTERN SIBERIA

The nicest place to stay is the small, independent ***Otel Tsentr Rossii*** *(☎ 23 46 71, fax 23 49 52, Krasny prospekt 28)*, 2½ blocks south of ploshchad Lenina. Aimed mainly at foreign businesspeople and German tour groups (the German consulate is across the hall), it has about 20 very comfortable suites for up to three people at $140 per suite. This rises to $180 for enormous three-room suites. Prices include breakfast, and the hotel restaurant is fairly good.

Mikof-Iris *(☎ 41 96 88, fax 40 37 37, ulitsa Kolkhidskaya 10)*, several kilometres west of the centre, charges $40/80 for suites with breakfast. Ask a taxi driver for 'MNTK Mikrokhirurgii Glaza' (МНТК Микрохирургии Глаза).

Places to Eat

If your taste buds have almost perished in Siberia, Novosibirsk will provide welcome relief. Foremost is the Irish pub ***Beer Mug*** *(Krasny prospekt 37)* – open from noon to 11 pm – with sensational steaks from around $15 to $27, but it also does a business lunch for $11 that includes an equally good 200g steak, a large salad and a soft drink. One pint of Guinness or Kilkenny costs $5 and there's a menu in English. The salads will hearten vegetarians, and it's also a good place to drink or eat in the evening.

Pub 501 *(ulitsa Lenina 20)* is a similar place (same hours) but with a ranch theme. It is marginally more expensive than the Beer Mug. Here you'll be treated to the spectacle of a posse of young Russians roaming the spacious interior in cowboy hats. It's another good evening option.

New York Pizza *(ulitsa Lenina 12)* offers an impressive spread of sandwiches and appetisers. ***Restoran Renessans*** *(ulitsa Sovietskaya 20)* has an interesting range of pan-European dishes such as chicken stuffed with walnuts and olives for $11. There's a menu in English.

Kafe Sobek *(ulitsa Dostoevskogo 19)* is a small, good Korean cafe, though sometimes with a few too many thickset men around. A meal without drinks costs $4 or $5. The closest metro is Krasny Prospekt. A full meal with a drink or two in Hotel Sibir's excellent main 2nd floor ***restaurant*** will come to around $15 to $20.

The new ***Cafe Mexico*** on the corner of ulitsa Kirova and Krasny prospekt (next to Baskin Robbins) is the first authentic Mexican restaurant east of Moscow. The Mexican grill decor is complemented by Corona beer, musicians in sombreros and waiters in bolo ties. The food is good, but the dancing girls confuse the atmosphere.

There is a reasonable ***supermarket*** inside the Tsentralny Komplex, near ploshchad Lenina, and the large, bustling ***central market*** has an excellent range of fresh produce.

Entertainment

Aside from opera and ballet, the big theatre on ploshchad Lenina also houses the concert hall of the excellent Novosibirsk Philharmonic Society. Pop and rock concerts are sometimes held here. There are occasional recitals and chamber concerts in the Conservatory on ulitsa Sovietskaya. There's a circus on ulitsa Chelyuskintsev.

The Beer Mug, Pub 501 and New York Pizza (see Places to Eat) sometimes have live rock, blues, jazz, and even Argentinian salsa, making Novosibirsk the music capital of Siberia.

In summer, the cafe ***U Nikolaya*** on ulitsa Lenina serves coffee and soft or alcoholic drinks, as well as shashlyk, snacks and light meals, in the pleasant forecourt from 11 am to 2 pm, and in winter the action moves indoors and reportedly kicks on until very late.

Shopping

Hotel Sibir has a souvenir stall and the Krasny prospekt branch of the Local Studies Museum sells some folk art. The main department store in the city centre is TsUM on Vokzalnaya magistral. A huge flea market called the Barakholka (*barakhlo* means junk) goes on at weekends in the east of the city. Buses run from Rechnoy Vokzal metro. Hang on to your wallet.

Getting There & Away

Air Novosibirsk has two airports. Tolmachyovo, 20km west of the centre off the

Omsk road, is for most longer flights; the city airport (Gorodskoy aeroport, also called Aeroport Novosibirsk), at the north end of Krasny prospekt, 6km from ploshchad Lenina, is for shorter flights.

Luftbrücke (see the Siberia & the Russian Far East Getting There & Away chapter) can book you on regular one-way or return flights to/from Frankfurt (DM1200) and Hanover (DM1070). There are Transaero and other flights daily to/from Moscow ($137, four hours), flights most days to Yakutsk ($278, 3¼ hours), Irkutsk ($160, 2¼ hours), Almaty (Kazakhstan, $150, 2½ hours), Vladivostok ($294, 7½ hours, three times a week) and Abakan ($150, 1½ hours, at least twice weekly). From the city airport flights go to/from Krasnoyarsk ($110, two hours, four times a week).

Lufthansa flights to Novosibirsk had been cancelled at the time of writing. Transaero (☎ 23 19 17) has an office in the Otel Tsentr Rossii building at Krasny prospekt 28.

Tickets on all airlines are sold at the Central Flight Information Agency (Tsentralnoe agenstvo vozdushnykh soobshcheny), ulitsa Gogolya 3 near metro station Krasny Prospekt, open from 9 am to 6.30 pm Monday to Friday and until 5 pm on Saturday. A larger office is nearby at ulitsa 1905 goda. It is open from 8.30 am to 7 pm Monday to Friday, until 5 pm on Saturday and from 9.30 am to 4.30 pm on Sunday.

Train Numerous long-distance trains run through Novosibirsk daily. The trains go not only east and west across Siberia, but also south along the Turk-Sib line to Almaty, Bishkek and Tashkent. The station is Novosibirsk Glavny, at the west end of Vokzalnaya magistral.

The Trans-Siberian, Trans-Mongolian and Trans-Manchurian trains all come through but you're usually better off getting one of the other trains, which are less likely to be booked up. To/from Yekaterinburg and Moscow (Yaroslavl Station), one of the best is the daily 'Sibiryak', No 25/26. It takes 51 hours to Moscow. Eastbound, there are usually two or three trains a day going as far as Vladivostok (4½ days), six or seven to Irkutsk (31 to 35 hours), and nine or 10 to Krasnoyarsk (13 to 14 hours). The twice-weekly Moscow-Ulaan Baatar service (No 5/6) also comes through. Services to places off the main Trans-Siberian line include trains at least daily to Barnaul (six to 10 hours), Biysk (11 hours) and Abakan (22 hours), and most days to Severobaikalsk (42 hours) and Tynda (74 hours) on the Baikal-Amur Mainline (BAM) line.

On the Turk-Sib, there's a service at least daily to/from Almaty (32 to 37 hours) via Semey (Semipalatinsk), and trains three or four times a week to/from Bishkek (54 hours) and Tashkent (about 70 hours).

Tickets National and international tickets are sold at counter seven, upstairs at the main train station. Advance bookings can also be made at the City Railway Agency (Gorodskoe zheleznodorozhnoe agenstvo), ulitsa Sovietskaya 50, where the foreigners desk is open from 9 am to 8 pm Monday to Friday (closed weekends).

Bus The bus station is an unmarked grey building at Krasny prospekt 4, 1.5km south of ploshchad Lenina. There are 13 buses daily to Barnaul between 7 am and 8 pm ($9, five hours), one daily to Biysk ($13, 7½ hours) and nine daily to Tomsk ($10, six hours). A private-enterprise 'Kommerchesky Express' bus runs to the bus station from the train station forecourt half-hourly from 7.15 to 11.45 am and 2.15 to 8.15 pm.

Getting Around

To/From the Airport Express bus No 111Э runs to Tolmachyova (about 50 minutes) from the street in front of Hotel Novosibirsk roughly half-hourly from 5.30 am to 7 pm, but *marshrutnye taxi* are inexpensive, faster and operate most of the night. Bus No 122 runs between the station and Tolmachyovo every half an hour or so from 5.15 am to 8.40 pm. Trolleybus No 5 runs between the city airport and the Oktyabrskaya metro; trolleybus No 2 connects the train station and city airport.

A taxi to the city airport should be about $5, to Tolmachyovo less than $20.

Local Transport Buses and trolleybuses around the city centre don't seem to follow any handy routes but Novosibirsk has a useful metro system. There's one line, running beneath Krasny prospekt much of its length, with a one-stop branch to the tongue-twisting Ploshchad Garina-Mikhaylovskogo station, which is at the train station. The interchange station is Sibirskaya/Krasny Prospekt. Ploshchad Lenina is one stop south of Sibirskaya/Krasny Prospekt.

Boat From the river station by Hotel Ob (metro Rechnoy Vokzal) there are occasional excursions on the Ob River from April/May to September/October. Information can be obtained at the inquiry desk.

A long distance service runs to/from Nizhnevartovsk ($63), taking about two days altogether. Nizhnevartovsk is linked by rail with Surgut, a polluted oil drilling town and itself connected by rail with Tobolsk and Tyumen.

AROUND NOVOSIBIRSK

Akademgorodok & the Ob Sea
Академгородок и Обское Море

This 'academic township' nestled in the taiga 30km south of Novosibirsk was founded in the 1950s by the Siberian branch of the Soviet Academy of Sciences as a think-tank.

It was once an elite city with 23 highly prestigious institutes, and those who worked here enjoyed perks and a large measure of academic freedom. Tempted by lucrative salaries, many scholars and academics have now accepted positions abroad.

There isn't really much to *see* in Akademgorodok. The best part is the setting – quiet, wooded, full of birdsong, and a 15 minute walk from the 'Ob Sea' (Obskoe More), the 200km-long reservoir behind a nearby dam on the Ob. It's said to be good for swimming, and local people come in droves on summer weekends.

The main street in Akademgorodok is ulitsa Ilicha, where you'll find the post office. Some maps sold in Novosibirsk include Akademgorodok. There are many excellent museums in the institutes, but you'll need to take a guided trip – try Sibalp or Intourist in Novosibirsk.

If you want to stay overnight, ***Hotel Zolotaya Dolina*** *(☎ 35 66 09, fax 35 42 40, ulitsa Ilicha 10)* has doubles with private bathroom, fridge and TV for around $22 per person and more expensive suites.

Getting There & Away Suburban trains run from Novosibirsk Glavny Station or river station (rechnoy vokzal) to Obskoe More station 16 to 20 times daily. You need any train that's heading for Berdsk, Iskitim, Lozhok, Linevo or Cherepanovo. The trip is 50 minutes. Marshrutnoe taxi (No 15) runs to/from the bus station in Akademgorodok. In Novosibirsk it runs from the train station to ploshchad Lenina and south along Krasny prospekt.

TOMSK
ТОМСК

☎ 3822 • pop 473,000

Tomsk, 270km north-east of Novosibirsk, is perhaps Siberia's greatest might-have-been city. One of Siberia's oldest cities (founded 1604), until the Trans-Siberian Railway was built, Tomsk was also one of the most important – an administrative and commercial town on the Great Siberian Trakt at its Tom River crossing.

When it was bypassed by the railway (one story says it was a ghastly miscalculation by the city fathers, who felt that trains would just bring noise, dirt and disruption), Tomsk faded. In the Soviet era Tomsk was closed to foreigners because of Tomsk-7 (population 120,000), 16km north, part of the 'nuclear archipelago' of 10 secret weapons research and production centres. Radioactive leaks and dubious waste disposal methods – the town's water supply is threatened by radioactive wastes pumped underground – haven't exactly encouraged tourism in Tomsk, though it is apparently a stately town.

If you do come here, ***Kongress-Tsentr Rubin*** *(☎ 25 96 89, fax 25 95 59, rubin@tomsk.su, Akademichesky prospekt 16)* is one of the best hotels, with single/double rooms for $45/56.

Getting There & Away

Tomsk is 80km up a branch line from the Trans-Siberian Railway at Tayga. Through trains run from Novosibirsk and Moscow, and there are buses from Novosibirsk. From the east, you have to change trains at Tayga. There are weekly flights from Novosibirsk, and from Moscow and elsewhere.

Altay Republic & Altay Territory Республика Алтай и Алтайский Край

The Altay Mountains are one of the most beautiful and pristine parts of Siberia, and in 1998 were added to the list of natural World Heritage Sites. They rise in the Altay Republic (Respublika Altay), which begins 450km south-east of Novosibirsk, and stretch south into Kazakhstan, China and Mongolia. Siberia's highest peak, 4506m-high Mt Belukha, stands on the Kazakhstan border. To reach the Altay Republic from Novosibirsk, you must cross the separate Altay Territory (Altaysky kray) and usually make transport connections in one of its two main towns, Barnaul or Biysk.

Few foreigners get to this remote corner of Siberia but those who do – to trek, climb, raft its wild rivers or track down its archaeological sites – won't forget its haunting beauty. The 19th century Russian mystical artist Nikolay Rerikh considered it one of the world's charmed places and captured its drama in many canvases. A few foreign tour companies offer packages, but it's possible to travel here on your own – and to find good adventure guides in Novosibirsk, Barnaul or even locally. June to August are the best months here, though it can rain at any time.

The Altay Republic's highest country is in the south and east, and the mountains are divided by several river valleys, mostly running south-east to north-west. There's a great variety of landscape, from steppe to taiga to glaciers to semidesert, plus 7000 lakes, wild rivers and beautiful waterfalls. The Katun River, flowing down the centre of the republic from the Gebler glacier on Mt Belukha, and the Chulyshman River in the east, flowing into Lake Teletskoe, provide some of Russia's most challenging white-water rafting. The Katun is dotted with rapids all the way from Ust-Koxa in the south-west of the republic to Gorno-Altaysk in the north – though there are calmer stretches along the way. Altay fauna includes bears, wolves, lynx, mountain goats, elk, deer, even snow leopards, and the flora is equally varied, with glorious alpine flowers in spring and summer.

The Altay Republic is sparsely populated, with just 200,000 people. About 60% are Russians, 30% are native Altay people, and 5% are Kazakhs (mainly in the far south-east). The Altay, a Turkic-speaking people, are mostly village dwellers, but a few are still seminomadic, moving with their herds to different pastures according to the season and living in yurts in summer. Settled families still sometimes keep yurts in their gardens as an extra room or kitchen for summer use. In the remoter areas the horse is still the main means of transport. Watch out for locals who've had a bit much to drink.

The mainstays of the rural economy are sheep, goats, cattle, yaks and horses. Maral deer – whose antlers are considered to have aphrodisiac properties – and camels are bred on a few farms.

Tourists are supposed to pay $1.30 per day for the period they intend to spend in the Altay Republic. In theory, this is collected at a 'border' office when you enter the republic and checked again when you leave. But the office closes on weekends and for lunch, so enforcement is patchy. Travel companies will usually include the duty in the price of its services. See the later Gorno-Altaysk section for details on visa registration and border zone permits.

Altay Republic time is Moscow time plus four hours.

History

The Denisova Cave in the Anuy River valley, about 100km south-west of Gorno-Altaysk, was inhabited from the early

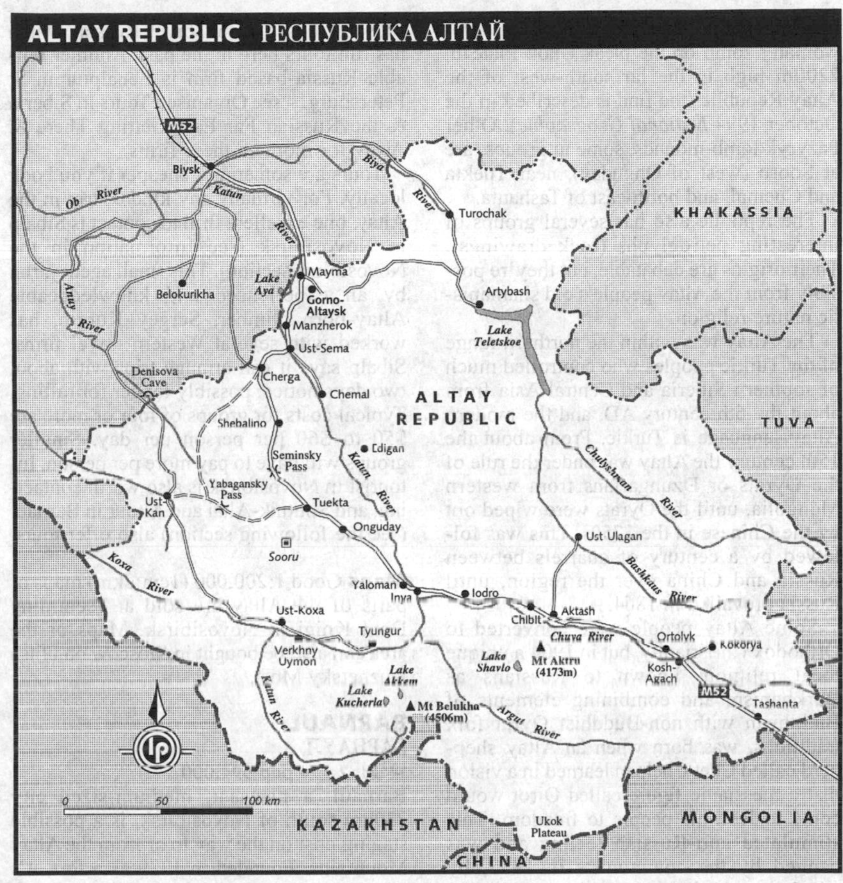

Palaeolithic (Old Stone Age) period, possibly as early as 300,000 BC, to the Middle Ages. Many important finds from different epochs have been made here.

The Altay is best known among archaeologists for its seminomadic, horse-riding, sheep-herding Pazyryk culture of the 6th to 2nd centuries BC. Pazyryk is considered part of the Scytho-Siberian cluster of cultures that stretched all the way to the steppes north of the Black Sea, which were dominated about the same time by the famous Scythians. The Pazyryks and Scythians had similar art styles.

Thanks to the Altay climate and the structure of their tombs, built underground beneath mounds *(kurgany)*, many Pazyryk burials have been wonderfully preserved. Rain or melting snow would seep into the tombs, which would then freeze and remain encased in ice for thousands of years. The Hermitage in St Petersburg displays mummified corpses, a funeral chariot, wood carvings and a wool carpet from a group of Pazyryk chieftains' tombs in the Ust-Ulagan Valley, opened in the 1940s by archaeologists from Novosibirsk's Russian Institute of Archaeology & Ethnography. In 1993 the institute's diggers uncovered a noblewoman's tomb on the bleak Ukok Plateau, 2200m high in the far south-west of the Altay Republic (the find is described in the October 1994 *National Geographic*). Other Pazyryk tomb-mounds, some in groups, are at Sooru (west of Onguday), near Tuekta and Chemal, and north-east of Tashanta.

The republic also has several groups of interesting petroglyphs (rock drawings). Their origins are debatable, but they're possibly from the Altay people's old shamanistic nature religion.

The Altay was within the northern range of the Turkic peoples who controlled much of southern Siberia and Central Asia from about the 6th century AD, and the modern Altay language is Turkic. From about the 15th century the Altay was under the rule of the Oyrats or Dzungarians from western Mongolia, until the Oyrats were wiped out by the Chinese in the 1750s. This was followed by a century of quarrels between Russia and China over the region, until Russia prevailed in 1864.

Some Altay people were converted to Orthodox Christianity, but in 1904 a unique local religion, known to Russians as Burkhanism and combining elements of Buddhism with non-Buddhist Oyrat folk traditions, was born when an Altay shepherd called Chet Chelpan learned in a vision that a messianic figure called Oirot would come to lead his people to freedom. This stimulated anti-Russian feeling and was banned by the communists in 1933, by which time the formerly seminomadic Altay people had been largely collectivised. Whether or not Burkhanism will be revived, several elements of the old nature religion, such as horse hides hung on branches or sticks, still survive.

Formerly the Gorno-Altayskaya Autonomous Region, the Altay Republic became a full republic within Russia in 1991.

Information

Travel Agencies The Munich-based Hauser Exkursionen is a reputable firm with much experience in the Altay Republic. Steppes East in Britain works with the Moscow-based firm Travel Russia, which has run tours here in the past. Another reliable Russia-based firm is Lenalptur in St Petersburg. – see Organised Tours in Siberia & the Russian Far East Getting There & Away for more on these firms.

Tours are sometimes cheaper if you book locally. For virtually any kind of trip in the Altay, one excellent firm to contact is Sibalp in Novosibirsk (see Information in the Novosibirsk section). This small agency, run by an experienced and knowledgeable Altay-born climber, Sergey Kurgin, has worked with several Western travel firms. Sibalp says it can arrange trips with about two days notice, possibly longer for rafting. Typical costs for groups of four or more are $50 to $60 per person per day. Smaller groups will have to pay more per person. Intourist in Novosibirsk is also worth contacting, and Sputnik-Altai and Altour in Barnaul (see the following section) also offer tours.

Maps Good 1:200,000 (1cm:2km) maps of parts of the Altay are sold at Tsentralny Dom Knigi in Novosibirsk. Maps of the area can also be bought in Moscow on ulitsa Kuznetsky Most.

BARNAUL
БАРНАУЛ

☎ 3852 • pop 594,000

Barnaul, a pleasant, medium-sized city 230km south of Novosibirsk, is a possible staging post on the way to or from the Altay Mountains. Founded in 1739 as a fort, it's now the capital of a region called the Altay Territory (Altaysky Kray), which is distinct from the Altay Republic, where the mountains are. Between Novosibirsk and Barnaul you enter a new time zone: Barnaul is on Moscow time plus four hours.

The 1km stretch of prospekt Lenina running between Oktyabrskaya ploshchad and ploshchad Sovietov is the main business street. To get to ploshchad Sovietov from the train and bus stations, go along ulitsa Krasnoarmeyskaya past Hotel Barnaul and turn left into ulitsa Molodezhnaya, which meets prospekt Lenina. The post and telegraph offices are opposite ploshchad

Sovietov. Inside the post office is a cash exchange desk open daily. The post office has fax and email services.

Sputnik-Altai (☎ 36 77 50, fax 36 72 75, admin@st.alt.ru, arw.dcn-asu.ru/~sputnik/), Sotsialistichesky prospekt 87, offers a range of seasonal tours and activities in the Altay Republic. Altour (☎ 23 16 98, fax 23 03 69, altmisha@alt.ru), ulitsa Chkalova 89, can arrange individual and group tour programs.

If you've got time to kill, the **Local Studies Museum** (Kraevedchesky muzey), just off ulitsa Krasnoarmeyskaya on ulitsa Polzunova, is Siberia's oldest museum (closed Monday and Tuesday).

Hotel Barnaul *(☎ 25 25 81, ulitsa Pobedy 9)* is decaying but has friendly staff. Basic rooms cost $24/50 a single/double; lyux rooms with bathroom are $60/100. ***Hotel Tsentralnaya*** *(☎ 36 84 39)*, just off ploshchad Sovietov, is slightly cheaper.

Getting There & Away

Barnaul is the place where the road to the Altay Mountains, and the railway as far as Biysk, split from the road and railway south to Kazakhstan. Leaving Barnaul, buses are generally an easier option than trains, as most trains are in transit and it can be hard to get tickets.

You can fly to/from Moscow, Novosibirsk and Krasnoyarsk. There are about 13 buses and several trains daily to/from Novosibirsk (five to six hours); 15 buses and four trains to/from Biysk (3½ hours); and five buses to/from Gorno-Altaysk (5½ hours). There are also daily trains to/from Moscow (Kazan Station, 60 hours) and every couple of days to/from Almaty in Kazakhstan (32 hours), Krasnoyarsk (around 23 hours), Irkutsk (42 hours), Bishkek (42 hours) and Tashkent (53 hours). Luftbrücke (☎ 29 93 02) has a representative in Barnaul (see the Siberia & the Russian Far East Getting There & Away chapter).

Every second day a through carriage runs to/from Abakan. It is shunted in Novokuznetsk, which usually takes four or five hours. The trip takes 24 hours and is the most direct link between Tuva or Khakassia and the Altay Republic.

BIYSK
БИЙСК

☎ 3854 • pop 239,000

Biysk, 160km south-east of Barnaul, is the nearest railhead to the Altay Mountains and, like Barnaul, is a place you may need to change transport on the way to/from the mountains. The bus and train stations are next door to each other. One or two overnight trains (11 hours) and one daytime bus (7½ hours) come daily from Novosibirsk. There are nine buses every day to/from Gorno-Altaysk (2½ hours), departing from 8.30 am to 8.30 pm, and also daily buses to Shebalino (five hours), Onguday (six hours) and Chemal (four hours), beyond Gorno-Altaysk, all leaving between 10.30 am and 4 pm. See the Barnaul section for transport to/from there.

Hotel Tsentralnaya *(☎ 22 65 88)*, a kilo metre or two east of the stations, has basic rooms from $21/37 a single/double.

GORNO-ALTAYSK
ГОРНО-АЛТАЙСК

☎ 38541 • pop 48,000

The capital of the Altay Republic is an unlovely, Soviet-style place just across the border from the Altaysky Kray, 467km from Novosibirsk. It's useful only for transport connections, visa registration and permits. The town is situated 7km south-east off the main M52 road, from a turn-off at Mayma.

If you intend to travel in the Altay Republic, be sure to name Gorno-Altaysk on your visa and register it at the militsia office on the corner of Kommunistichesky prospekt and Tipografsky pereulok, 750m east of the bus station. Kosh Agach is supposed to be on your visa if you want to enter the Mongolian border zone. Permits are issued by the militsia.

A currency exchange office inside the bus station changes cash, and a shop there sells film and processes it in about four hours. The post office is at ulitsa Gorno-Altayskaya 17, which is parallel (south) to the main street, Kommunistichesky prospekt, and still signposted by its old name, ulitsa Choros Gurkina.

The interesting **Local Studies Museum** (Kraevedchesky muzey) has a reconstructed Pazyryk burial and material on Palaeolithic sites, petroglyphs, fauna and the history of the Chuysky Trakt road to the Mongolian border. It's on ulitsa Gorno-Altayskaya, a few hundred metres east of the bus station. Opening hours are from 10 am to 4.30 pm Wednesday to Sunday.

The only hotel option is the grumpy ***Hotel Gorny Altay*** *(☎ 55 44)*, about 1km up Kommunistichesky prospekt then to the right on the short ulitsa Babushkina, facing a park with a Lenin statue. Basic rooms cost $11/16 a single/double, and it has more expensive suites.

Getting There & Away

No flights operated to/from Gorno-Altaysk at the time of research, but it's worth checking at the flight information office next door to the bus station.

By land, you have to get to Barnaul or Biysk (see those sections) then take a bus. A good way from Novosibirsk is on the overnight train to Biysk. Buses run to Gorno-Altaysk from Barnaul (5½ hours, five daily) and from Biysk (2½ hours, nine daily). A left-luggage office at the station is open from 7 am to 7 pm daily. It closes at 1 pm for one hour.

From Gorno-Altaysk, buses run 10 times daily to Manzherok (one hour), twice daily to Chemal (three hours, 1.35 pm and 6.40 pm) and daily to Shebalino (3½ hours, 4.40 pm), Onguday (six hours, 3.30 pm), Aktash (11½ hours, 9.40 am) and Kosh-Agach (12½ hours, 7.05 am). The trip to Ust-Koxa, the nearest town to Tyungur and Mt Belukha serviced by bus, involves an overnight stop in Ust-Kan (9½ hours, 1.05 pm). One possibility is to take a private taxi to Tyungur from Gorno-Altaysk (ask at the station). You may need to wait a day or so while your driver finds enough passengers. Alternatively, you can take the bus to Ust-Kan or Ust-Koxa and ask around there. The cost of the bus from Gorno-Altaysk to Ust-Koxa is $12, while a private taxi from there to Tyungur shouldn't cost you any more than $16.

CHUYSKY TRAKT
ЧУЙСКИЙ ТРАКТ

The Chuysky Trakt is the 510km stretch of the M52 from Mayma near Gorno-Altaysk to Tashanta on the Mongolian border. The border was open only to local commercial traffic at the time of research, and individual travellers are unlikely to get across unless the regulations ease. The best chance might be to get a ride in a commercial vehicle (ie a truck).

The Chuysky Trakt was built before WWII, at least partly by Gulag labour. It's said that workers who died were buried beneath the road. The road runs near the Katun River as far as Ust-Sema, about 70km from Gorno-Altaysk, briefly rejoins the Katun before Inya (375km), then follows the tributary Chuya River from Inya to Kosh-Agach. It passes through a variety of valley landscapes and reaches some pretty out-of-the-way places, with long distances between the few villages. The road is often narrow and unpaved. See the Gorno-Altaysk section for buses running from Gorno-Altaysk to various places on and off the trakt.

Lake Aya
Озеро Ая

The warm water of little Lake Aya, 25km from Gorno-Altaysk, makes it a popular local outing. Follow the 'Aya 8' sign pointing to the right (west), 14km south of Mayma, crossing a wooden suspension bridge over the Katun, and after 3km turn left at the crossroads with 'Beryozka' and 'Ozero Aya' signs. It's then less than 1km to the lake. The modern Macedonian-built ***Aya Otel*** *(☎ 3854-24 14 91, ☎ 24 69 08, fax 23 43 85)* by the lake has comfortable double, triple and quadruple rooms at $40 per person, some with balconies overlooking the lake, and a decent restaurant. Easy four-hour rafting trips on a fairly sedate stretch of the Katun can be arranged at the hotel for $16 per person. A taxi to Lake Aya from Gorno-Altaysk is about $7.50.

Manzherok
Манжерок

About 30km south of Mayma is the little ***Turkomplex Manzherok*** *(☎ 3852-44 32 18,*

WESTERN SIBERIA

☎/fax 41 77 13), beautifully sited in a pine grove on the bank of the Katun. Here you can rent a two-person tent for $3.50 or a two, three or four-bed room, with bathroom, for around $15 per person, meals included. The friendly owners can set up horse-riding or rafting trips at short notice for around $70 to $100 per day.

The site, with a bus stop outside on the main road, is located 1km north of Manzherok village, and 700m south of a black statue on a grey pedestal by the river bank. The statue is of Vyacheslav Shushkov, a Siberian engineer and writer who planned the Chuysky Trakt.

Cherga & Shebalino
Черга и Шебалино

From the village of Cherga, situated in a pretty valley about 75km from Mayma, an unsealed road runs 106km south-west through forest, emerging some 60km east of Ust-Kan. A few kilometres south of Cherga along the M52, a road leads off to the villages of Akmel, Karmay and Askat, which have maral deer farms. A maral deer farm at Shebalino (110km) is 5-6km along the road leading west up a valley from the south end of the village.

Seminsky Pass
Семинский перевал

On this pass (Seminsky pereval) over the Seminsky Range, a northern outlier of the Altay, 145km from Mayma, is the Uchebno-Trenirovochny Tsentr (UTTs), a state-run sports training centre, with the Czech-owned ***Hotel Lena*** *(☎ 32845-2 21 31)*. The hotel has two, three and four-bed rooms from $10 per person, and there are also cottages with two double rooms, a bathroom and a sitting room. For an extra $6.50 per person full board is included.

Onguday
Онгудай

There's an extremely basic little ***hotel*** behind the bus stop in the middle of this village, just down to the west of the road, 190km from Mayma. Singles/doubles cost $4/6. The toilet is out the back.

At Sooru, west of Onguday, is the 'Tsar' group of Pazyryk aristocrats' burial mounds, in a picturesque valley.

Ilgumen Rapids, Yaloman & Inya
Пороги Ильгумень, Яломан и Иня

The Chuysky Trakt rejoins the Katun for a brief stretch between the river's wild Ilgumen rapids, about 60km after Onguday, and Inya. The rapids are a starting place for white-water rafting trips down to Chemal. The bluff overlooking the start of the rapids, between the Katun and the tributary Ilgumen River, is a good place to camp.

Yaloman, the next village, has an unusual microclimate that enables its Altay people to grow cherries and apples.

Directly across the road from the 721km marker between Inya and Iodro, is Kalbak Tash, a crag with many petroglyphs. If you have no guide you'll have to look hard to find them but you should succeed. Maral deer and hunters are easily identifiable, and there's something that looks like a tiger, but one design that crops up a few times is harder to make out – it might be a shaman, it might be abstract, some Russians reckon it's a rocket.

Lake Shavlo
Озеро Шавлинское

From Chibit, about 350km from Mayma, a track leads south to beautiful Lake Shavlo (Ozero Shavlinskoe), a two day walk away at the foot of the Chuysky Range (see the later South-Western Altay Republic section).

Aktash
Акташ

A turn-off to the north here, 100km before Kosh-Agach, leads to Ust-Ulagan (60km), near the famous Pazyryk burial mounds opened in the 1940s. There's a daily bus service to Ust-Ulagan. Aktash has a depressing dump of a ***hotel*** on ulitsa Staraya Mokhova, facing the Produkty shop, which charges $3.50 per person. The rooms have nothing except beds; there's a communal washbasin in another room. You probably won't find anyone around till 8 pm. Several kilometres south of Aktash are spectacular views of snow-covered peaks.

Ortolyk
Ортолык

A few kilometres before Kosh-Agach, this is the first Kazakh village along the Chuysky Trakt.

Kosh-Agach
Кош-Агач

The 'capital' of the south-east of the Altay Republic, Kosh-Agach (population: 2700) is 471km from Gorno-Altaysk and is like the end of the world – a small town spread for no apparent reason in the middle of a wide, bleak, high, bare plain stretching in either direction to forbidding distant mountains. If you want to go somewhere that's a bit different, try it. Most of the people here are Kazakh, with a few Altay and Russians. Here, in the middle of nowhere, there is an airstrip, a few streets of one-storey houses, a town hall, a small market, a petrol station and, naturally, a Dom Kultury (House of Culture). There's even the rudimentary ***Hotel Tsentralnaya*** on the square facing the Dom Kultury, with rooms for $3.50 per person.

Kokorya, across the plain to the east, is an Altay village. Tashanta, the border post on the Russian side of the Mongolian border, is 50km down the road.

SOUTH-WESTERN ALTAY REPUBLIC
РЕСПУЛИКА АЛТАЙ, ЮГО-ЗАПАДНАЯ ЧАСТЬ

The Altay Republic's highest mountains are in the south-west – the Katunsky Range, culminating in Mt Belukha, and the Northern Chuysky Range, running east-west between the Chuya and Argut rivers, with several challenging peaks topped by 4173m-high Mt Aktru. These areas offer some of the best trekking and climbing in the Altay.

According to some Asian legends, the Belukha area is the future location of Shambhala, a paradisiac realm that will come into existence after humanity destroys itself. Others believe Shambhala is a state of heightened energy and awareness induced by supernatural phenomena or inner means – or perhaps simply by experiencing the wild beauty of Belukha!

The road to Belukha goes through some remote areas, with scattered villages. Near Ust-Kan the landscape changes from forest to beautiful upland meadows framed by hills and bluffs. There's the basic ***Hotel Chash***, a petrol station and a couple of shops, and in the nearby Altay village of Mendur-Sokkon is an **Altay Ethnographic Museum**. Verkhny Uymon has a **Nikolay Rerikh House-Museum**.

Ust-Koxa, at the confluence of the Koxa and Katun rivers, has an airstrip but no scheduled services. There's a good ***turbaza*** *(☎ 388-24 88 44)* in Ust-Koxa about 1km south of town and across the river. A bed in two-person huts costs $6. To get there by car, turn west off the main road at the 'Sooru 7' sign and petrol station. Take the first road right and cross the toll bridge, turn left immediately and follow the river for about 800m. See the Gorno-Altaysk section for transport to/from Ust-Koxa, and farther on to Tyungur, on the Katun River, the usual starting point of treks in the Belukha area.

At Tolono, on the high bank of the Katun downstream of Tyungur, are some **Turkic stone sculptures** of warriors killed in battle, dating from about 500 AD.

Trekking

One basic trek from Tyungur takes in the Kucherla River valley to beautiful Lake Kucherla, the 2800m-high Kara-Tyurek Pass to Lake Akkem, which is in the next valley east, and – if the weather plays along – great views of Belukha and its ice wall. This is described in *Trekking in Russia & Central Asia* by Frith Maier (see Books in the Siberia & the Russian Far East Facts for the Visitor chapter). There are also several extensions on this trek, including to Lake Shavlo, the base for climbs in the Northern Chuysky Range

Turbaza Vysotnik in Tyungur charges $2.50 per person in double tents, or $1 to pitch your own tent. It also has a few cabins and a great banya ($2.50). Horse riding and treks in the area can also be organised in the area. Arrangements can be made through the St Petersburg tourist agency

Lenalpturs ☎ 812-279 0716, ☎/fax 279 0651, lenalptr@ mail.wplus.net, ulitsa Vosstania 9, apartment (kv) 4, 193036 St Petersburg). The nearby ***Turbaza Kucherla*** *(☎ 29-4 17)* has cabins for two or three people at Tyungur and Lake Kucherla and also offers hiking, rafting, boating, horse-riding and climbing trips. Contact Viktor Kalanechin for further information.

EASTERN ALTAY REPUBLIC РЕСПУЛИКА АЛТАЙ, ВОСТОЧНАЯ ЧАСТЬ

Lake Teletskoe is the Altay's biggest lake, very deep at 325m and surrounded by forests. A few local tourism bases are dotted along its shores, including cabins at the north end (Zolotoe Ozero) and the south end, and ferries run along its length. Trekking is possible around here from late spring to early autumn. Treks to the south end of the lake from Edigan, about 50km south of Chemal (highest pass, 2600m), and from Balyktuyul, about 15km north of Ust-Ulagan, with passes up to 2000m, are described in *Trekking in Russia & Central Asia*. The Chulyshman River flowing into the south end of the lake is a white-water rafting favourite.

East of the lake and the Chulyshman, the **Altay Nature Reserve** (Altaysky zapovednik) stretches to the borders of Khakassia and Tuva. Buses from Gorno-Altaysk to Artybash at the north end of the lake, the only village on the lake accessible by road, leave Gorno-Altaysk at 11.05 am daily ($6.50, 8½ hours).

Krasnoyarsk Territory Красноярский край

The Krasnoyarsk Territory (Krasnoyarsky Kray) is a region of great mineral and forest wealth stretching from south of its capital, Krasnoyarsk, all the way to the Arctic coast. The dominant geographical feature is the Yenisey River, running the length of the territory. In summer, passenger boats travel the Yenisey from Krasnoyarsk almost to the Arctic Kara Sea. Krasnoyarsk is the nearest big city to the republics of Khakassia and Tuva, to its south.

Getting There & Around

Long-distance passenger boats ply the Yenisey in summer from Krasnoyarsk's river station (rechnoy vokzal) to places as far north as Vorontsovo, more than 2000km away on the Yenisey Gulf (Yeniseysky Zaliv), which opens on to the Arctic Kara Sea. The main service is to the seagoing port of Dudinka, 1989km north and well within the Arctic Circle. The voyage to Dudinka takes nearly four days (and nearly six days coming back, against the current). You can fly out of Dudinka.

Sailings to Dudinka, with 18 stops (or sometimes 13 stops on a faster service), are around twice weekly from early June to the beginning of October. Stops on the slower service include Yeniseysk (413km, 18 hours), Bakhta (1023km, 44 hours) and Igarka (1744km, 79 hours). There's a ticket office in Krasnoyarsk's river station, open from 8 am to 7 pm: the boats are not usually full, but you may not get the class you want if it's very close to departure.

One-way fares to Dudinka range from $100 to $260. The top price gets you a place in a two-person 1st class cabin with a washbasin; a four-berth 2nd class cabin is $195 per person.

It's also possible to take far more expensive 11-day cruises on the same route on the Swiss-managed *Anton Chekhov* from early June to mid-September. Intourist in Krasnoyarsk (see Information in the following Krasnoyarsk section) can book you on it from $1050 per person rising to $1400 in 1st class two-berth cabins with toilet and shower. The Moscow-based travel agent Intellektualny Fond (☎ 095-742 88 82, fax 911 22 39, infund@glasnet.ru) is more experienced in dealing with foreigners but charges between $2600 to $3040 for the same cruise.

Intourist also handles bookings for river cruises on the *Matrozov*, which mostly carries Russian tourists but is substantially cheaper, with prices ranging from $450 to $950 on similar, but less luxurious, cruises to Dudinka.

Other routes from Krasnoyarsk go to Podtesovo and Yartsevo, both north of Yeniseysk, and Vorontsovo (almost a five day trip). There are also services from Podtesovo to Boguchany on the Angara, from Boguchany to Kezhma farther up the Angara, and from Potapovo (94km south of Dudinka) to Nosok, where the Yenisey enters the Yenisey Gulf. Timetables are displayed at the Krasnoyarsk river station.

KRASNOYARSK КРАСНОЯРСК

☎ 3912 • pop 871,000

Krasnoyarsk grew from a 17th century Cossack fort to its present size thanks to the discovery of gold in the 19th century, the arrival of the Trans-Siberian Railway and the shifting of factories here during WWII. Just upstream from the city is a hydroelectric dam with a reservoir stretching 350km up the Yenisey.

It's less metropolitan but more eye-pleasing than Novosibirsk, with a sense of space imparted by outlying hills and the 2km-wide Yenisey flowing through the centre. There are quite a few 19th century buildings (though it seems nothing remains from the early days) and the centre is relatively quiet and unpolluted.

Krasnoyarsk was closed to foreigners until late in the Soviet period because of a concentration of defence-related industries.

This is also the stamping ground of Alexander Lebed, a hardline ex-army general who became the region's governor thanks to Boris Yeltsin – it's said that Yeltsin helped fund Lebed's campaign and even helped create Lebed's public image. Lebed took the image and ran, however, and has since become a political force in his own right.

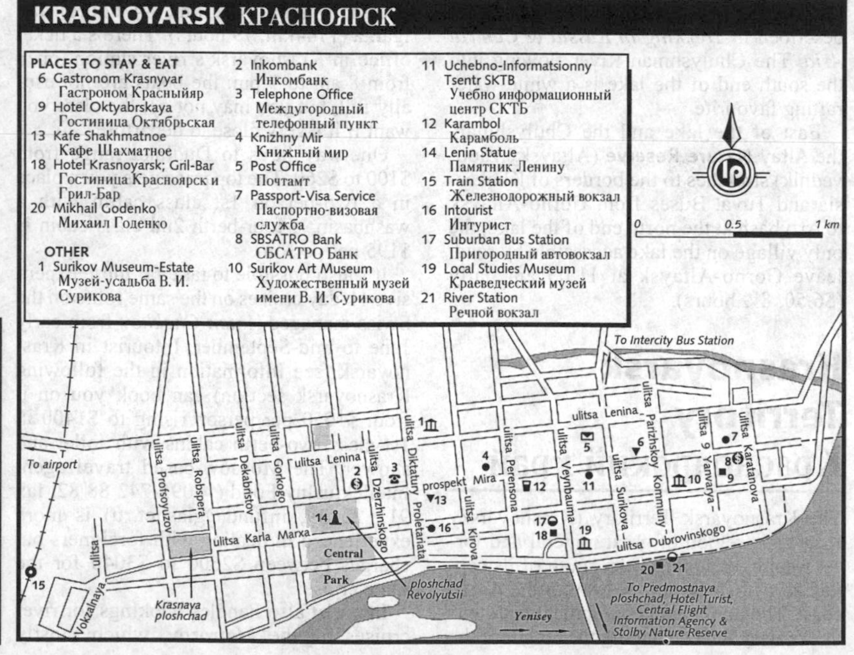

Orientation
The Yenisey flows roughly west-east through Krasnoyarsk, with the city centre a strip about four blocks wide on the north bank. The main street is east-west-oriented prospekt Mira, two blocks north of the river, and the best orientation point is Hotel Krasnoyarsk, 1½ blocks south of prospekt Mira and overlooking the bridge across the Yenisey.

Maps Knizhny Mir bookshop, prospekt Mira 86, has 1:200,000 and 1:500,000 maps of the Krasnoyarsk Territory, and city maps.

Information
There are currency exchange points at the airport (not always open). Inkombank, prospekt Mira 108, gives cash advances on Visa, American Express and EuroCard. It is open from 9.30 am to 5 pm weekdays only (closed from 1 to 2 pm). SBSATRO Bank, prospekt Mira 7A, changes American Express and Thomas Cook travellers cheques. It is open from 9 am to 7 pm Monday to Friday, and until 6 pm on Saturday.

The main post office, ulitsa Lenina 49, has EMS, fax and email services. The long distance telephone office, prospekt Mira 102, is open from 7 am to 11 pm. The Uchebno-informatsionny tsentr SKTB, prospekt Mira 53 (office 411), offers Internet access from 9 am to 10 pm weekdays. The office to contact for passport registration (Pasportno-vizovaya sluzhba) at prospekt Mira 16 is open from 10 am to 1 pm weekdays and from 2 to 5 pm. It opens from 9 am to noon on Saturday.

Travel Agencies Intourist (☎ 22 52 91, fax 23 06 74, root@intour-k.krasnoyarsk.su), ulitsa Karla Marxa 137, does a range of tours in and around Krasnoyarsk but the tours are expensive for individuals. It can arrange 12-hour helicopter tours for 10 people at $700 per person in the Sayan Mountains and might be useful for organising advance accommodation in the northern Krasnoyarsk Territory. It can also book you on inexpensive cruises north along the Yenisey River.

Time Zone The time in Krasnoyarsk is Moscow time plus four hours.

Museums
The leading 19th century Russian historical painter Vasily Surikov was born in Krasnoyarsk and lived here. His house at ulitsa Lenina 98 is now the **Surikov Museum-Estate** (Muzey-usadba V I Surikova), and is worth a visit. Don't confuse this with the **Surikov Art Museum** (Khudozhestvenny muzey imeni V I Surikova) at ulitsa Parizhskoy Kommuny 20, on the corner of ulitsa Karla Marxa, which is a wider ranging museum showing Russian art from the 18th to 20th centuries – it's open from 10 am to 6 pm daily except Monday. The **Local Studies Museum** (Kraevedchesky muzey) at ulitsa Dubrovinskogo 84, beside the Yenisey bridge, was again closed for renovation when we visited.

Stolby Nature Reserve
The best thing to do in Krasnoyarsk is to walk in the Stolby Nature Reserve (Zapovednik stolby), a hilly area of woods and strange rock pillars *(stolby)* on the southwest edge of the city. Take any tram heading towards the Yenisey bridge from in front of Hotel Krasnoyarsk, to the second stop, Predmostnaya ploshchad at the south end of the bridge, then bus No 7 from Predmostnaya ploshchad to the end of the line.

Divnogorsk
In summer (1 May to 1 September), hourly boats sail 30km up the Yenisey to Divnogorsk, site of the hydroelectric dam holding back the long Krasnoyarsk Reservoir (Krasnoyarskoe vodokhranilishche) on the Yenisey. Sailings from Krasnoyarsk (quay 4) are at noon, 2 and 4 pm, departing Divnogorsk one hour later. The trip takes around 45 minutes each way and costs $4.50 return. Buses to Divnogorsk go from the suburban bus station (prigorodny avtovokzal) behind Hotel Krasnoyarsk.

Places to Stay
The ***Mikhail Godenko*** hotel-ship moored at the river station is fair value and central,

but you should take care with security. Four-bed cabins sharing fairly clean toilets and shower cost $8 per person, two-bed cabins cost $16/26 a single/double, and two-bed lyux cabins with shower and toilet are from $34 per cabin. Cabins on the riverward side of the ship, away from the entrance and restaurant, are likely to be quieter.

Hotel Turist *(☎ 36 14 70)* on Predmostnaya ploshchad at the south end of the bridge has quite good single/double rooms from $37/58 with toilet and shower.

Hotel Oktyabrskaya *(☎ 27 05 81, ☎ 27 75 08, prospekt Mira 15)*, on the corner of ulitsa 9 Yanvarya, has very comfortable rooms with private bathroom for around $45/60, and suites are $100 to $113. Bus No 42 comes east along prospekt Mira to ulitsa 9 Yanvarya.

Best all-round value is the big ***Hotel Krasnoyarsk*** *(☎ 27 37 54, fax 27 02 36, arcad@scn.ru)* overlooking the Yenisey bridge. This comfortable and conveniently central place has rooms with private bathroom and colour TV for $45/58 and some cheaper unrenovated rooms. The upper rooms at the front have great views over the river.

Places to Eat

Hotel Krasnoyarsk has a reasonable ***restaurant***. There's also a ***Gril-Bar*** serving grilled chicken and an aubergine *(baklazhan)* hotpot for $2 or so, and soups. A ***kafe*** near the entrance serves shashlyk for $5 and salads for $1.50 to $3. It's open from 11 am to midnight and has handy, clean toilets.

Kafe Shakhmatnoe *(prospekt Mira 85)* does standard dishes like pelmeni or pork steak for $3 to $5. It's a nice spot to drink coffee, and wines are served by the glass for about $2.50 (closed from 3 to 4 pm).

In summer there are several shashlyk stands and pleasant outdoor cafes overlooking the river alongside the river station. ***Gastronom Krasnyyar*** on prospekt Mira has a wide range of foodstuffs. It's open from 10 am to 11 pm daily.

Karambol *(ulitsa Perensona 20)* is the most popular bar and nightspot that gets a youngish crowd. It's open from 2 pm to 6 am, with a one hour break at 9 pm (entry after 9 pm is $8).

Getting There & Away

Air Krasnoyarsk has two airports only 3km apart but both about 45km north-west of the city. Yemelyanovo, the main one, has flights once or more daily to/from Moscow ($155, 4½ hours), Novosibirsk ($110, two hours, four times a week), Yekaterinburg ($161, three hours, weekly), St Petersburg ($327, six hours, three times a week), Khabarovsk ($190, four hours, four times a week), Yakutsk ($317, 7½ hours, weekly) and Norilsk ($391, two hours, four times a week). Cheremshanka airport has four flights a week to Abakan ($85, one hour), Irkutsk ($133, 2½ hours) and Barnaul ($98, 1½ hours), two to Dudinka ($310, four hours) and five to Igarka ($331, 3½ hours).

Luftbrücke (☎ 23 04 94) can book direct flights to/from Hanover ($820, weekly). See the Siberia & the Russian Far East Getting There & Away chapter.

Air tickets are sold at the Central Flight Information Agency (Tsentralnoe agentstvo vozdushnykh soobshcheny) on Predmostnaya ploshchad at the south end of the Yenisey bridge. It is open from 8 am to 8 pm on weekdays and until 6 pm on weekends. Counter seven is for foreigners. To get there, take any tram heading towards the bridge from in front of Hotel Krasnoyarsk, to the second stop.

Train The station is 2.5km west of the centre on Vokzalnaya ulitsa. Several eastbound and westbound trains stop here daily and Krasnoyarsk is on the routes of the Trans-Siberian, Trans-Mongolian and Trans-Manchurian trains and the twice-weekly Moscow-Ulaan Baatar service (No 5/6).

The three-times-weekly 'Yenisey' (train No 55/56) is a good service to/from Moscow (Kazan Station), taking 64 hours, but there are six or seven other trains a day. Nine or 10 trains run daily to/from Novosibirsk (13 to 14 hours).

Eastbound, there are about six trains a day to/from Irkutsk (about 19 hours) and two as far as Vladivostok. There are trains on alternate days along the Baikal-Amur Mainline – one to Severobaikalsk, the other to Tynda and Neryungri. The Baikal-Amur Mainline splits from the main Trans-Siberian line at Tayshet, 390km east of Krasnoyarsk.

To/from Abakan, train No 23/24 (12 hours) is four or five hours quicker than Nos 657/658 and 659/660. Trains also go every couple of days in summer to/from Almaty (Kazakhstan) and Bishkek (Kyrgyzstan), and twice a week to/from Tashkent (Uzbekistan).

Bus The intercity bus station (mezhdugorodny avtovkzal) is out in the north-east of the city at Aerovokzalnaya ulitsa 22. Buses leave twice daily for Abakan (nine hours), and once daily for Shushenskoe (10½ hours) and Sayanogorsk (10½ hours). At least seven buses leave daily for Yeniseysk (7½ hours).

Boat See Getting There & Around at the start of the Krasnoyarsk Territory section for information on boat trips from Krasnoyarsk to Dudinka and other destinations.

Getting Around

To/From the Airport Bus No 135 runs between both airports and the suburban bus station behind Hotel Krasnoyarsk, about half-hourly from 5.40 am to 10.50 pm, then occasionally through the night. Advance tickets (buses fill quickly) can be bought at any counter inside the station from 6.30 am to 6.30 pm; other tickets are sold at the small booth outside from 6 am to 11 pm. The ride to Cheremshanka is about 40 minutes, to Yemelyanovo 50 minutes.

A taxi from either airport to the centre is about $20.

Local Transport Trolleybus No 7 links the train station and the Medinstitut stop at the foot of Aerovokzalnaya ulitsa. It runs via the city centre, near the intercity bus station and Hotel Oktyabrskaya.

Other services from the train station to the centre include bus No 17 and trolleybus No 14 from the station forecourt, and bus No 11 from the road out the front. Some of these come into the centre on ulitsa Karla Marxa, others on prospekt Mira. From the centre to the train station, you can pick up bus No 11 and trolleybus Nos 7 and 14 on ulitsa Lenina between ulitsa Surikova and ulitsa Perensona.

NORTHERN KRASNOYARSK TERRITORY СЕВЕРНЫЙ КРАСНОЯРСКИЙ КРАЙ

The northern part of the Krasnoyarsk Territory, beyond the Arctic Circle, offers a few possibilities if you *really* want to get off the beaten track. In summer, bring lots of mosquito repellent. Official restrictions on tourism have been imposed in some areas, notably parts of the Taymyr Peninsula, so you should try to check out the situation before coming.

Getting There & Away

You can reach the region by boat, and fly out, or vice versa. In summer, passenger boats travel from Krasnoyarsk all the way down the Yenisey to Igarka, Dudinka and Vorontsovo, on the Yenisey Gulf beyond the river's mouth (see Getting There & Around at the start of the Krasnoyarsk Territory section). There are flights from Krasnoyarsk, and elsewhere to Igarka, Dudinka and Norilsk. There are also flights between Norilsk and Moscow, including by Transaero. What's claimed to be the world's northernmost railway runs between Dudinka and Norilsk, a slow four hour trip.

Intourist in Krasnoyarsk (see Travel Agencies in the Krasnoyarsk section) is one agency that might be useful to contact if you wish to travel north.

If you want to go even further, the German-based DAV Summit Club (☎ 89-64 24 00, fax 64 24 01, E-mail@DAV-Summit-Club.de), which is affiliated with the Deutcher Alpenverein (German Alpine Association), runs an 18 day expedition to the North Pole that includes overnight stays in St Petersburg and a basic hotel in Katanga. The cost from Frankfurt is DM15,690. DAV Summit Club is at Am Perlbacher Forst 186, 81545 Munich. Lenalpturs in St Petersburg (see Organised Tours in Siberia & the Russian Far East Getting There & Away) runs a 12 day tour that includes a helicopter flight at 120m over the Taymyr Peninsula to the Russian polar scientific station on Severnaya Zemlya and beyond to the North Pole. Its 13 day ski tour to the North Pole is very similar to that offered by the DAV Summit Club and costs $6500 from St Petersburg.

Igarka & Dudinka
Игарка и Дудинка

These are seagoing ports on the lower Yenisey. Dudinka (population: 33,000) is the capital of the Taymyr (Dolgan-Nenets) Autonomous District, in which the Dolgan and Nenets peoples are far outnumbered by Russians. The living conditions of these formerly nomadic hunters and reindeer herders are apparently among the worst of all Siberian native peoples. In Dudinka the only place to stay is apparently ***Hotel Ogni Yeniseya***, with cheap but reasonable rooms.

Norilsk
Норильск

This nickel-processing city 80km east of Dudinka (population: 156,000) was founded in the 1920s to exploit big reserves of copper, nickel, cobalt and coal, and much of it was built by Gulag forced labour. Norilsk is responsible for acid rain over a wide area of the Siberian tundra. The city has a museum about its own construction and the horrors of the Gulag. ***Hotel Norilsk*** costs around $70 per night. Intourist in Krasnoyarsk can book you in.

Putorana Plateau
Плато Путорана

The Putorana Plateau is a range of glacier-worn mountains of volcanic origin beginning about 75km east of Norilsk and stretching about 350km farther east. It harbours some truly magnificent waterfalls and canyons, top-grade white-water rafting on the Kureyka River, and superb fishing. The top of the plateau is flat, barren, windswept and moonlike, with temperatures often below freezing even in summer, and wind-chill of as much as -40°C. The area is uninhabited except for a few hunters and nomads in summer. Expeditions have reached the plateau by boat along rivers and lakes from Norilsk.

Taymyr Peninsula
Полуостров Таймыр

This most northerly part of the Russian mainland has a winter 'night' two months long, with temperatures staying below freezing for eight months, and a summer 'day' lasting nearly three months. The Taymyr has over 400,000 wild reindeer, and over 13,000 sq km of the peninsula's tundra form the Taymyr Nature Reserve (Zapovednik Taymyr), Russia's second-biggest. There are also huge coal reserves up here.

Khakassia
Хакасия

The Republic of Khakassia, a patch of steppe and mountains about the size of Ireland, lies on the upper Yenisey River south-west of Krasnoyarsk. Like the neighbouring Altay and Tuva republics, it's one of the cradles of Siberian civilisation. Some of the stone idols and the thousands of burial mounds here date back at least 3000 to 5000 years. The most impressive are from the Khyagas, or 'Yenisey Kyrgyz', Empire, which spanned much of Central Asia and central Siberia in the 6th to 12th centuries.

The destruction of the Khyagas by the Mongol Tatars ended the region's golden age. Worn out by futile resistance to Jenghis Khan's son Jochi, most Khyagas finally migrated to what is now Kyrgyzstan. Those who remained – the forebears of the present-day Khakass people – were picked on by neighbours until, in 1701, they *asked* to join the Russian Empire. The Russians, who founded Abakan, modern Khakassia's capital, as a fort soon after this, offered tax incentives to encourage the Khakass to become Christians and now outnumber the indigenous population here eight to one.

Abakan is mainly of interest as a base for exploring the broad, fertile Minusinsk Basin in which it sits, and the Western Sayan Mountains along the border of Tuva to the south, a beautiful, well endowed region with dry, sunny Central Asian weather and a wide variety of scenery – steppe and taiga, fresh and salt water lakes, rivers, and mountains as high as 3000m.

Khakassia time is Moscow time plus four hours.

ABAKAN АБАКАН

☎ 39022 • pop 163,000

The clean, leafy, 20th century town of Abakan has an interesting museum and zoo – and an amazing amount of marble, of which there's a surplus from Khakassia's quarries, lining its hotel staircases, bathrooms etc.

The Yenisey north from Abakan has been converted into the Krasnoyarsk Reservoir, a flat pond stretching 350km to the Divnogorsk dam near Krasnoyarsk.

Orientation

Abakan, surrounded by suburbs of dachas and vegetable gardens, is on the west shore of the Krasnoyarsk Reservoir, where the tributary Abakan River enters the Yenisey. Most of what's important is on or near ulitsa Shchetinkina, the north-south axis.

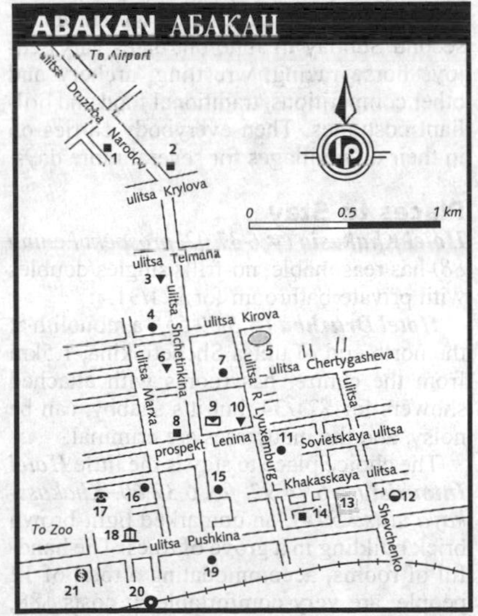

Information

You can change dollars at the airport or at the airline booking office (Aviakompania Khakassia agenstvo) on ulitsa Chertygasheva. The Sberegatelny Bank on ulitsa Pushkina changes cash and gives cash

ABAKAN АБАКАН

PLACES TO STAY

1 Hotel Sibir
Гостиница Сибирь
2 Hotel Druzhba
Гостиница Дружба
8 Hotel Khakasia
Гостиница Хакасия
14 Hotel Intourist
Гостиница Интурист

PLACES TO EAT

3 Pizzeria
Пиццерия
6 Restoran Seul
Ресторан Сеул
10 Kafe Lakomka
Кафе Лакомка

OTHER

4 Central Baths
Центральные бани
5 Stadium
Стадион
7 Aviakompania Khakassia Agenstvo (formerly Aeroflot)
Авиякомпания Хакассия агенство
9 Post Office
Главпочтамт
11 TV Tower
Телебашня
12 Bus Station
Автовокзал
13 Central Market
Центральный рынок
15 Regional Drama Theatre
Областной драматический театр
16 OVIR (for visa registration)
ОВИР
17 International Telephone Office
Междугородный телефонный пункт
18 Khakassia Local Studies Museum
Хакасский Республиканский музей краеведения
19 Department Store
Универмаг
20 Train Station
Железнодорожный вокзал
21 Sberegatelny Bank
Сберегательный Банк

advances on major credit cards. It is open from 9 am to 7 pm Monday to Friday, and from 10 am to 6 pm on Saturday.

The main post office is on ulitsa Shchetinkina near prospekt Lenina. An email service is in the room marked 'Elektronnaya Pochta', off a corridor reached from the prospekt Lenina entrance. The International Telephone Office is on ulitsa Sovietskaya.

The OVIR office, ulitsa Sovietskaya 35, is open from 9 am to 6 pm weekdays and until noon on Saturdays.

Abakan Tours (☎ 6 74 42, fax 6 37 60, morokov@dialup.comlink.khakassia.ru) has some of the most helpful and energetic staff you'll find in any travel agency in Russia. It can book you into the best rooms in Abakan's major hotels from $68 to $92 per person with full board, sells air tickets for a low commission and organises a wide range of interesting trips around Khakassia and Tuva. Its office is in the little Hotel Intourist, off Khakasskaya ulitsa, and is open from 9 am to 5 pm weekdays. It's one of the most reliable agencies in the region, and often works together with the Tuvan Ministry of Culture & Tourism to arrange general or special interest programs in Tuva.

The time in Abakan is Moscow time plus four hours.

Khakassia Local Studies Museum

The good Khakassky respublikansky muzey kraevedenia concentrates on the history and prehistory of Khakassia. In the lobby is a forest of burial totems. The earliest of these – showing a sun with a face – is at least 3000 years old. Others date from periods of matriarchal rule. On the walls are copies of striking stone paintings; the originals predate the totems by at least a millennium.

Inside, archaeology and anthropology are the best sections. The former has Stone Age implements, Bronze Age paintings, Iron Age tools, complex Khyagas jewellery, totems and burial items. The latter is mostly about the impact of Cossacks and settlers on the Khakass. A guide would be useful. The museum is at ulitsa Pushkina 96, near the train station, and is open from 10 am to 6 pm; it's closed on Monday and on the last day of each month.

Zoo

Abakan Zoo (it's owned by the local meat combine, which is where many of the animals get their food) has a collection of 70 Siberian and Russian Far East species including a rare Amur (Ussuri) tiger and camels from Tuva. It's on ulitsa Pushkina 3km west of the train station and open for most of the summer and during school holidays from 10 am to 3 pm daily (the ticket office closes at 2 pm). Take trolleybus No 2 or 4 from anywhere on ulitsa Pushkina to the Myaso Kombinat stop; you can also get No 4 southbound at the post office.

Other Attractions

The clean **Central Baths** (Tsentralnye bani), with hot and cold pools, massage and tea, are on ulitsa Kirova, off ulitsa Shchetinkina. You'll find a wooded **park** with a small beach 2km east on prospekt Lenina.

Festivals

The Khakass festival of Tun-Payram celebrates the opening of summer pastures. A gathering in Abakan (usually on the first or second Sunday in June but dates vary) enjoys horse racing, wrestling, archery and other competitions, traditional food and brilliant costumes. Then everybody carries on in their own villages for several more days.

Places to Stay

***Hotel Khakasia** (☎ 6 37 02, prospekt Lenina 88)* has reasonable, no-frills singles/doubles with private bathroom for $21/31.

***Hotel Druzhba** (☎ 5 09 55)*, a monolith at the north end of ulitsa Shchetinkina, 1.5km from the centre, has rooms with attached showers for $21/34, but it's shabby, can be noisy, and the mattresses are criminal.

The choice place to stay is the little ***Hotel Intourist** (☎ 6 74 92, fax 6 37 60, Khakasskaya ulitsa 54A)*, an unmarked light-brown brick building in a grove of trees. The handful of rooms, accommodating a total of 12 people, are very comfortable. It costs $88, but there's also one suite for $71 and four more for $80. You can book meals in the hotel's restaurant.

Despite its shabby external appearance, ***Hotel Sibir*** *(☎ 6 77 11, ulitsa Druzhba Narodov 9)*, in the north of town, has reasonable apartments for $37/59. Apartments have a kitchen with a refrigerator but no stove. Lyux suites with a living room and double beds cost $80/96. The restaurant has a band in the evening.

Places to Eat

Khakass food is Central Asian, with lots of onion, garlic and peppers, but pork is used as well as mutton. *Laghman* – fried noodles, vegetables and mutton – is common. Keep an eye out for oat biscuits called *talkan*. *Airan* is the local equivalent of yogurt and *araka* is vodka made from fermented milk!

The large and often loud ***restaurant*** at Hotel Druzhba is good value for standard Russian cuisine, and there's a bufet on the 4th floor.

There's a decent ***Pizzeria*** on ulitsa Shchetinkina north of the centre. Thick-based one-person pizzas are $1 or $2, and it also has salad and drinks. The nearby ***Restoran Seul***, also on ulitsa Shchetinkina, does quite good Korean dishes mostly from $3 to $5 with a lunch-time discount.

Kafe Lakomka, on prospekt Lenina, serves reasonable salads, *laghman* and *pelmeni* (meat dumplings) for less than $1 each.

There are a few ***shashlyk stands*** at the market and in front of the train station. The central ***market*** is on ulitsa Chkalova near ulitsa Pushkina. Local tomatoes are renowned and in autumn apples, melons and berries are good.

Getting There & Away

Air There are flights on weekdays to/from Krasnoyarsk ($85, one hour), to/from Moscow three times a week ($260, five hours), four times a week to/from Novosibirsk ($150, around two hours) and Norilsk ($220, 4½ hours).

Flights to Kyzyl had ceased at the time of research. The Aviakassa Khakassia agenstvo on ulitsa Chertygasheva sells air tickets and Abakan Tours does the same for a small commission.

Train There are at least three daily trains to/from Krasnoyarsk of which No 23/24, taking 12 hours, is easily the best. The daily 'Khakasia' runs to/from Moscow's Yaroslavl Station (75 hours) via Novosibirsk, Yekaterinburg and Perm. Trains run daily to Novosibirsk (24 hours), Yekaterinburg (46 hours) and Perm (51 hours). See the earlier Barnaul Getting There & Away section for information on a through carriage to that city. Some days of the week there's a suburban train in the afternoon to Askiz (two hours).

Bus The bus station on ulitsa Shevchenko is a rather chaotic place with minimal timetable information. There are three buses daily to Krasnoyarsk (9½ hours) and frequent buses run to Minusinsk from 6.30 am to 10.30 pm (around 40 minutes, pay on the bus) and several buses run daily to Shushenskoe, Sayanogorsk and Askiz. The trip to Shushenskoe takes around two hours and tickets can be purchased inside the bus station. Buses to Kyzyl ($12, about 10 hours) – the only means of transport there from Abakan apart from private taxi – leave from the forecourt of the train station at 7.15 am, noon and 7 pm. Private taxis (about 6 hours) will do the run for around $25 with a full load of passengers. Go to the train station around 7 am and haggle.

Getting Around

From the airport, bus No 15 or trolleybus No 3 takes 15 minutes to the town centre. The buses come down ulitsa Shchetinkina and terminate at the bus station. Trolleybus No 2 runs along ulitsa Pushkina between the bus station, train station and zoo. Taxis cost a flat-rate $1.60 per ride.

AROUND ABAKAN

Minusinsk
Минусинск

This 18th century town, 20km from Abakan on the Kyzyl road, has all the architecture Abakan lacks, all well preserved and lived-in. In the old part of Minusinsk, on an island in a branch of the Yenisey, are the original church (still in use) and wood, stone and brick houses built by 19th century Siberian gold merchants who travelled the world and built in European style.

In 1877, a pharmacist named Martyanov opened a museum in Minusinsk with his collection of rocks and bugs. It is now a big, well presented collection featuring archaeology (Bronze Age barrows, Scythian weapons), immigrants and exiles (some Decembrists served labour terms here), and the museum's library is still as it was when Lenin used it. The museum is closed to the public on Monday.

Shushenskoe
Шушенское

☎ 39139 • pop 20,000

Founded in the 18th century by immigrant peasants, Shushenskoe *(SHU-shen-ska-ya)*, 85km south of Abakan, is pleasant, shady and dead as a doornail. Its claim to fame is as the place where Lenin was exiled from St Petersburg from 1897 to 1900, and the place where he married fellow revolutionary Nadezhda Krupskaya, who had followed him here in 1898 with her mother.

On the 1970 centennial of Lenin's birth, the whole village centre was reconstructed to look as it had in 1870 (with a few houses inserted from the poor side of town for the sake of illustration).

The complex, close to the Shush River where it enters the Yenisey, is open from 10 am to 6 pm daily and admission is $1.60 (extra for photos). The cheap ***Hotel Sayany*** on ulitsa Michurina and ***Hotel Turist*** (which has a reasonable restaurant) on prospekt XXVII sezda KPSS are both within two or three blocks east of the museum area.

Sayano-Shushenskaya Dam
Саяно-Шушенская дамба

Russia's biggest hydroelectric dam, with 10 640,000kW turbines, is in the Karlovy Gorge of the upper Yenisey, 150km upstream from Abakan. Begun in 1975, construction took nearly 20 years. Don't confuse it with the little Maynskaya Dam downstream. The access road is paved with marble, the only material available from local quarries.

The trip here gives you a sample of the Siberian vegetation regions – rolling steppe (ribbed with poplars against wind erosion) near Abakan, woodland steppe at the 250-year-old mining town of Mayna, taiga around Sayanogorsk and mountains in the background everywhere.

The ***Meridian*** restaurant at Sayanogorsk is reportedly good.

SOUTH-WEST KHAKASSIA
ЮЖНО-ЗАПАДНАЯ ХАКАСИЯ

The A161 road via the iron-ore-mining town of Abaza is a possible alternative route through the Western Sayan Mountains to Tuva, for those with their own transport. It's 420km from Abakan to Ak-Dovurak in western Tuva. Askiz, 90km south-west of Abakan, is a Khakass village and a centre of Tun-Payram festivities. Abakan Tours offers trips here with the chance to see Khakass costume, sample Khakass cooking and hear and buy Khakass musical instruments. There are two good ***Kempingy*** ('Campings') along the way that Abakan Tours can tell you about and book. One, about 20 minutes from Abaza, is really a small hotel with double and triple rooms and a sauna. The other is 3km off the road, in the taiga at Stoktysh, on the Stok River near the Tuva border, and has wooden cottages.

Tuva
Тува

The Republic of Tuva (spelt **Тыва** in Tuvan), south of Khakassia across the Western Sayan Mountains, is one of the least known and most curious corners of Russia. The Tuvans are nomadic pastoralists by nature, Buddhist and shamanist by religion, Mongolian by cultural heritage, and Turkic by language.

Their republic is a transition zone between the Siberian taiga and the Mongolian steppe, with areas of rolling green hills,

WESTERN SIBERIA

plains, semidesert and forest, hemmed in by 2000m-high mountains on all sides (the Western and Eastern Sayan ranges in the north, the fringes of the Altay in the west, the Tannu Ola in the south, and a jumble of ranges in the east). The Bolshoy (big) and Maly (little) Yenisey rivers – Biy-Khem and Ka-Khem to Tuvans – flow down from the eastern mountains to meet and form the Yenisey (Ulug-Khem) at the capital, Kyzyl. White-water rafting is possible on the Maly Yenisey River.

If you intend to travel to Tuva, make sure Kyzyl appears on your visa – you'll avoid problems with police and fussy hotel staff.

History

First inhabited at least 40,000 years ago, Tuva fell under Turkic rule in the 6th century AD, was conquered by the Uyghurs from modern Xinjiang (China) in the 8th century, taken over by the Turkic 'Yenisey Kyrgyz' empire in the 9th century, then, like neighbouring regions to the east and west, ruled by Jenghis Khan's Mongolian successors from about the 13th century. When the last independent Mongolian state, that of the western Mongolian Oyrats, was wiped out by the Manchu Chinese in the 1750s, Tuva became an outpost of China but was left fairly well alone under local chiefs. It was during the Chinese period that Buddhism, of the Yellow-Hat Tibetan variety led by the Dalai Lama, came to Tuva, where it co-existed with the older shamanist nature religion. By 1929 there were 22 monasteries in Tuva, the most important being at Chadan, and about one man in 15 was a lama.

Russian traders, gold prospectors and peasants first began to settle in Tuva in the 19th century. Come the Chinese revolution of 1911, Russia stirred up a separatist movement in Tuva and took it 'under protection' in 1914 (an 'exceptionally progressive event', according to one Soviet Tuvan history). After the Bolshevik Revolution and ensuing civil war, Tuva became a nominally independent people's republic (Tannu-Tuva) in 1921. Though under Soviet supervision, prime minister Donduk's government declared Buddhism the state religion and Mongolian the official language, and favoured reunification with Mongolia.

Not surprisingly, in 1929 Moscow installed a dependable communist, Solchak Toka, as prime minister. Tuvan, the vernacular Turkic tongue, became the official language, initially written in the Latin alphabet but later converted to Cyrillic. In 1944 Stalin took away Tuva's remnants of autonomy, renamed it, with impeccable logic, the Tuvinian Autonomous Region, and incorporated it into the USSR. Russian immigration increased, Buddhism and shamanism were stamped on, and the seminomadic Tuvans were collectivised, many slaughtering their animals rather than hand them over. Limited agriculture and industry were introduced in the 1950s. However, semi-nomadism survived to some extent in the mountainous fringes and the east, where there were no roads, and so, for a while at least, did shamanism.

Poverty has fuelled ethnic tensions. After anti-Russian riots in 1990, more than 3000 skilled Russian workers left Tuva, and the drain has continued as many Russians see little future here with Tuvans now dominant in the government. Tuva proclaimed itself a full republic within Russia in 1991 and elected its first president in 1992. Some Tuvans yearn for full independence or reunification with Mongolia but such dreams seem unrealistic given Tuva's economic reliance on Moscow, which still provides most of the Tuvan budget.

Buddhism is slowly reviving and new temples have been founded in Kyzyl and elsewhere in Tuva.

People & Culture

The Tuvans form about two-thirds of the republic's 310,000 population (most of the rest are Russians).

Despite Soviet efforts at collectivisation, much of the Tuvan population is still semi-nomadic, moving their herds out from their villages to summer pastures where they live in yurts – you'll see these if you travel around rural Tuva, especially towards the mountainous fringes. The range of animals that they herd reflects Tuva's crossroads character – camels, yaks, cows, horses, goats, sheep, and even reindeer in the eastern forests.

Culturally the Tuvans go in for cross-country horse racing, a special form of wrestling called *khuresh*, carving the soft stone agalmatolite, and most famously for throat-singing – a spine-tingling, deep-down, tuneful chanting that apparently comes in four styles, called *khöömey, sygyt, kargyraa* and *borbangnadyr*.

Tuvans speak Tuvan but most of them also speak Russian. 'Hello' in Tuvan is *Ekii*.

Tuva has achieved minor cult status in California thanks to a fascination for it developed by the late Nobel physics prize-winner Richard Feynman and his friend Ralph Leighton. They set up an organisation called Friends of Tuva that has been instrumental in, among other things, taking Tuvan throat-singers and exhibitions of Tuvan artefacts to the West. The story of their obsession is told in Leighton's *Tuva or Bust!* (see Books in the Siberia & the Russian Far East Facts for the Visitor chapter). Those who are seriously interested could also seek out *Unknown Mongolia* by Douglas Carruthers, a British explorer who reached Tuva in 1911, and *Nomads of South Siberia* by Sevyan Vaynshteyn, probably the leading Russian Tuva expert (Cambridge University Press, 1980).

Festivals The main Tuvan festivals are Shagaa, the Buddhist New Year, which corresponds to the lunar new year and advances about 10 days a year, and Naadym, in July, which is an occasion for long-distance horse racing, khuresh wrestling, and throat-singing. There are similar celebrations for Republic Day (Den Respubliki), on 15 August. Constitution Day (Den Konstitutsii), on 21 October, is another holiday.

KYZYL
КЫЗЫЛ

☎ 39422 (five-digit numbers) or ☎ 3942 (six-digit numbers) • pop 95,000

The capital of Tuva sits on a broad plain, with the Bolshoy and Maly Yenisey rivers meeting on the northern edge of town. Founded as a Russian settlement in 1914, it used to be called Belotsarsk (White Tsar Town), a name that the Soviet regime couldn't help but change – though they could have displayed a little more imagination: Kyzyl is a Turkic word which simply means red.

Warning Be careful when moving about town after dark, or after 7 pm in summer, due to the problems of crime and alcohol. The police are liable to check your passport and visa thoroughly and advise you to return to your hotel.

Orientation & Information

The main street is the east-west-oriented ulitsa Kochetova, half a kilometre south of the Yenisey. A large square at its intersection with ulitsa Tuvinskikh Dobrovoltsev is the town centre.

There's a bank on ulitsa Kochetova that changes cash. Also on ulitsa Kochetova are the post and telephone offices. The post office is open from 8 am to 5 pm weekdays, and the telephone office is open until 6 pm weekdays and also until 4 pm on Saturday.

Next door is the Biznis Tsentr, which has email, copying and fax services. It is open from 8 am to 7 pm daily. An express photo service in the foyer of Hotel Kyzyl is also open daily.

OVIR is inside the Gorotdel (City Department) building on ulitsa Druzhby. It's open from 9 am to 5 pm Monday to Friday, until noon on Saturday. If you intend to travel beyond Kyzyl, make sure you are registered in Kyzyl. It is also wise to check whether a permit is required for the region you want to visit.

Inside the post office is a small pharmacy. When we visited it sold a fair range of pharmaceuticals as well as disposable syringes, condoms and toiletries.

Tsentr Asii (☎ 3 23 26, fax 3 67 22), in Hotel Odugen on ulitsa Krasnykh Partizan, is about the best travel agency in town. All faxes to them should be clearly marked 'Tsentr Asii'.

Abakan Tours is probably a better option though for tours planned in advance (see

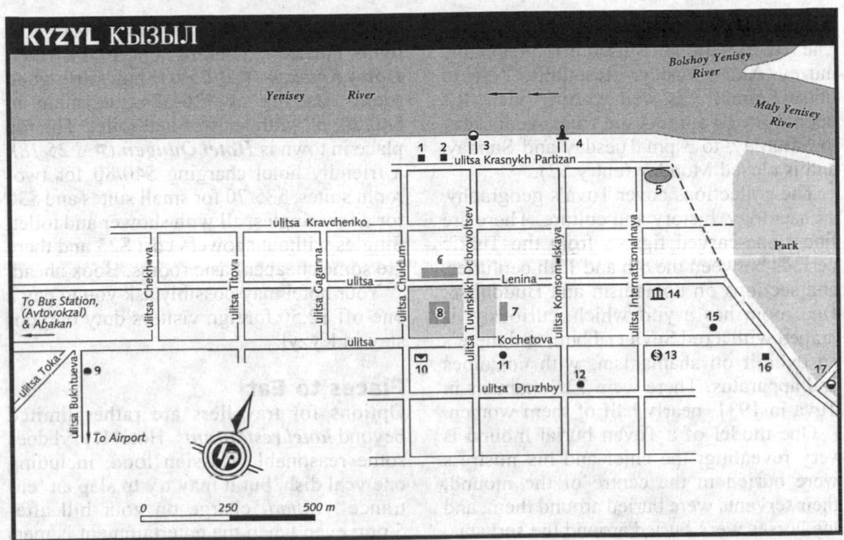

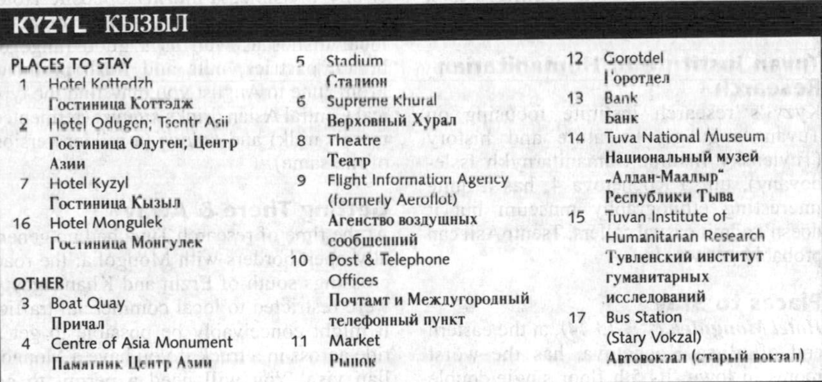

KYZYL КЫЗЫЛ

PLACES TO STAY
1 Hotel Kottedzh
Гостиница Коттэдж
2 Hotel Odugen; Tsentr Asii
Гостиница Одуген; Центр Азии
7 Hotel Kyzyl
Гостиница Кызыл
16 Hotel Mongulek
Гостиница Монгулек

OTHER
3 Boat Quay
Причал
4 Centre of Asia Monument
Памятник Центр Азии
5 Stadium
Стадион
6 Supreme Khural
Верховный Хурал
8 Theatre
Театр
9 Flight Information Agency (formerly Aeroflot)
Агенство воздушных сообщений
10 Post & Telephone Offices
Почтамт и Междугородный телефонный пункт
11 Market
Рынок
12 Gorotdel
Горотдел
13 Bank
Банк
14 Tuva National Museum
Национальный музей „Алдан-Маадыр" Республики Тыва
15 Tuvan Institute of Humanitarian Research
Тувленский институт гуманитарных исследований
17 Bus Station (Stary Vokzal)
Автовокзал (старый вокзал)

Information in the Abakan section earlier in this chapter).

The time in Kyzyl is Moscow time plus four hours.

Centre of Asia Monument

Kyzyl's focal attraction stands on the bank of the Yenisey at the end of ulitsa Komsomolskaya. Everyone says this stone globe and obelisk – or at least their forerunners – were erected here by a mysterious 19th century English adventurer to mark the geographical centre of Asia. This eccentric gent had apparently already done the same for a couple of other continents.

According to Ralph Leighton in *Tuva or Bust!*, the centre of Asia is just about here if you balance a map of Asia drawn by the obscure Gall's stereographic projection on a pin; however, it's hundreds of kilometres away from here by various other methods of calculating it.

National Museum

The Tuva National Museum (Natsionalny muzey 'Aldan-Maadyr' Respubliki Tyva) at ulitsa Lenina 7 is well worth a visit. It's open from 10 am to 4 pm from Wednesday to Saturday, to 3 pm Tuesday and Sunday, and is closed Monday (entry $2).

The collections cover Tuva's geography, archaeology, history and culture. There are fine stone-carved figures from the Turkic periods between the 6th and 12th centuries, and sections on nomadism and Buddhism. One room has a yurt which, curiously, is draped with a red Soviet ribbon, and there's an exhibit on shamanism, with costumes and apparatus. There were 725 shamans in Tuva in 1931, nearly half of them women.

One model of a Tuvan burial mound is very revealing: the chief and his mistress were buried in the centre of the mound, their servants were buried around them, and the horses were buried around the servants. Presumably not everyone willingly took part in all this burying.

Tuvan Institute of Humanitarian Research

Kyzyl's research institute focusing on Tuvan language, literature and history (Tuvlensky Institut Gumanitarnykh Issledovany), ulitsa Kochetova 4, has a quite interesting ethnography museum but it doesn't admit casual callers. Tsentr Asii can probably get you in.

Places to Stay

Hotel Mongulek *(☎ 3 13 44)*, at the eastern end of ulitsa Kochetova, has the worst rooms in town. Its 5th floor single/double suites with toilet, shower and TV cost $10/20, and one single suite goes for $8. Rooms with toilet but no shower cost $8/11, and the hotel has a basic restaurant.

The decaying but quite comfortable ***Hotel Kyzyl***, facing ulitsa Tuvinskikh Dobrovoltsev, is a far better accommodation option. Large suites cost $15/30, small suites cost $13/26, and the hotel also has some cheaper but more rudimentary singles and doubles. All the rooms have shower and toilet facilities.

The two best places are on ulitsa Krasnykh Partizan, backing on to the river. ***Hotel Kotedzh*** *(☎ 3 05 03)* has fairly good rooms starting at $26/52 and rising to $40/80, all with shower and toilet. The top place in town is ***Hotel Odugen*** *(☎ 3 25 18)*, a friendly hotel charging $40/80 for two-room suites, $35/70 for small suites and $30 for a few singles, all with shower and toilet. Singles without showers cost $25 and there are some cheaper basic rooms. Book ahead.

Your hotel may possibly ask you to pay a one-off $2.50 foreign visitors duty on your stay in Kyzyl.

Places to Eat

Options for travellers are rather limited beyond ***hotel restaurants***. Hotel Kyzyl does some reasonable Russian food, including one veal dish, but it may try to slap an 'entrance' *(vkhod)* charge on your bill after 5 pm, even when the entertainment is mercifully invisible. A ***market*** opposite Hotel Kyzyl (behind the cinema) sells home-made local dishes as well as a good range of bread, pastries, nuts and fresh produce. From June to August you may find the typical Central Asian drinks *kumyss* (fermented mare's milk) and *kaipak* (a milder version of the same).

Getting There & Away

At the time of research Tuva had no generally open borders with Mongolia: the road crossings south of Erzin and Khandagayty were restricted to local commercial traffic. It might conceivably be possible to get a ride across in a truck if you have a Mongolian visa. You will need a permit to go anywhere near the border.

Air The airport is 7km south-west of the centre. Flights are subject to cancellation for a host of reasons, including lack of fuel and bad weather. Flights are scheduled to/from Moscow ($224, six hours, weekly), Novosibirsk ($110, two hours, three or four times weekly), Irkutsk ($108, two hours, weekly), and to Kyzyl-Mazhalyk ($94, around two hours) and Mugur-Axy ($117, 1½ hours), both daily except Sunday, as well as to Kungurtug ($84, 1½ hours, daily). There are also regular services to other destinations in Tuva. It might be worth checking whether abolished services to/from Abakan have recommenced. Tickets are sold at the Flight Information Agency (Agenstvo vozdushnykh soobshcheny), ulitsa Bukhtueva, open from 8 am to 6 pm Monday to Saturday (closed from 1 to 2 pm). Bus No 6 runs from Hotel Mongulek to the office.

Bus At the time of research, Kyzyl's bus station *(stary vokzal)* was in a side-street 100m east of Hotel Mongulek. This is expected to move back eventually into its old premises (known as *avtovokzal*) on the west of town, about 3km from the centre.

Buses to/from Abakan (a bone-shattering journey over the picturesque Western Sayan Mountains) run three times daily ($12, around 10 hours). The first bus to Abakan leaves at 6.50 am. A Taks Park office near the main booking hall (stary vokzal) sells more expensive tickets on a service to Abakan taking five or six hours. Its daily bus leaves at 7 am, but you should try to book tickets in advance.

At least one Sunday bus service goes to Novosibirsk ($59, about 28 hours), and daily services run to/from Shagonar (1½ hours), Ak-Dovurak (seven hours) and Teeli (nine hours). Due to the bad condition of the road to Erzin, no scheduled service existed at the time of research. A daily bus runs from Kyzyl to the closest major town, Samagaltay, leaving mid-morning; the remaining 60km can be covered by private taxi.

Private Taxi Drivers offer rides to Abakan and other places on a vacant lot beside Hotel Mongulek, but the scene is likely to shift back to the former bus station (avtovokzal) once renovations on the building have been completed. The best time to get a ride is early in the morning. Expect to pay around $25 for the one way trip, but you may have to wait a few hours while the driver scratches together enough passengers. Choose your driver very carefully, make sure he's stone-cold sober and that he leaves Kyzyl with a full tank of petrol – supplies to petrol stations along the M54 are erratic.

Boat In summer, boats go every two or three days up the Bolshoy Yenisey to Toora-Khem near Lake Azas. The trip upstream is 12 hours, but eight hours coming back downstream. Departures are usually at 8 am – ask at the Tuvinskaya Sudokhodnaya Kompania office by the quay at the end of ulitsa Tuvinskikh Dobrovoltsev. Tickets cost $20, and are sold an hour or two before departure – take your passport.

Getting Around

Bus No 1, 'Vostok-Aeroport', from the airport enters the town along ulitsa Bukhtueva then runs along ulitsa Kochetova at least as far as Hotel Mongulek.

The 'Vostok-Avtovokzal' bus runs from the bus station along ulitsa Kochetova through the centre. A taxi to get you from the avtovokzal to the town centre will cost around $1 or $2.

EASTERN TUVA
ВОСТОЧНАЯ ТУВА

The eastern part of Tuva is mainly forested and roadless, with more rivers and lakes than the rest of Tuva.

Toora-Khem & Lake Azas
Тоора-Хем и Озеро Азас

Lake Azas (also called Lake Todzha) is big and beautiful, surrounded by forest and mountains. The way to come is by boat from Kyzyl up the Bolshoy Yenisey to Toora-Khem, about 30km west of the lake (see the Kyzyl Getting There & Away section). The river trip is beautiful, though the seating on the boat is enclosed and it's hard to see some of the views.

There's a run-down but dirt-cheap ***hotel*** at Toora-Khem with food available.

If no bus appears to take you from Toora-Khem to the lake, you should be able to find a taxi or hitch a lift. At the lake there's a cheap ***turbaza*** with four-bed cabins and basic food supplies. You can hire boats on the lake or take walks.

Erzheey
Эржеей

This is a Russian Old Believers' village reached from Sizim on the Maly Yenisey. Two kilometres from the village there's a ***camping ground*** with eight huts, a cafe and showers, where you can organise horse trips up the river to Uzhep. At Uzhep there's a ***turbaza*** with four cottages, bath house, shared kitchen and cafe. East of Uzhep, at the confluence of the Maly Yenisey and Balyktyg Khem rivers, there's a small ***turbaza*** accessible by boat in summer from Uzhep.

Kungurtug
Кунгуртуг

Kungurtug is a village in the south-east with flights from Kyzyl – though the weather is often poor and you may not be able to fly back when you want. You can visit nearby Lake Tere-Khol, with an island almost entirely covered by the ruins of an Uyghur fortress-palace of the 8th century. The man who excavated it in the 1950s, Sevyan Vaynshteyn, was baffled by how so much building material could have been carried there by water. However, he heard a local legend that the lake appeared after the fortress was built.

SOUTHERN TUVA
ЮЖНАЯ ТУВА

The village of **Samagaltay**, 165km south of Kyzyl, has a Buddhist temple. Families here carve and sell small Buddha figures made from agalmatolite.

Erzin, 220km from Kyzyl, is a town of almost entirely Tuvan people, with a ***hotel*** charging around $3 per person and a ***stolovaya*** nearby. Desert begins to the south, across the Tes-Khem River. **Bay-Dag**, north of Erzin, has camel herds.

WESTERN TUVA
ЗАПАДНАЯ ТУВА

Thirty kilometres west of Kyzyl, **Ust-Elegest** is another place with camel herds. From **Ak-Dovurak**, 300km from Kyzyl, an alternative road into Khakassia crosses the Western Sayan. **Kyzyl-Dag** near Teeli has a new Buddhist temple, bigger than the one at Kyzyl. Maps show hotels in Shagonar, Chadan, Kyzyl-Mazhalyk and Teeli.

The Mongun-Tayga district in the far south-west is a mountainous region with lakes, yak pastures and 3976m-high Mt Mongun-Tayga, the highest in Tuva. The main settlement is **Mugur-Axy** village, to which there are flights from Kyzyl.

Eastern Siberia
Восточная Сибирь

Eastern Siberia is bounded by the great Yenisey River and the maritime territories of the Russian Far East. In the north it stretches to the Arctic shoreline and in the south it is bordered by Mongolia and China. The major towns and cities are all grouped in the south along the roughly parallel routes of the Trans-Siberian and Baikal-Amur Mainline (BAM) railways. Farther north the settlements become extremely isolated and are accessible only by air.

HIGHLIGHTS

- Exploring Russia's most beautiful wonder, Lake Baikal, including the sacred, shaman-haunted Bay of Ayaya and Olkhon Island
- Riding the daredevil, breathtaking Round-Baikal Railway
- Getting your picture taken beside the world's biggest Lenin head, in Ulan Ude
- Visiting Kyakhta, the ruins of a silk and tea town on the highly militarised Mongolian border
- Discovering Yakutia: cruising the Lena River, ogling diamonds in Mirny

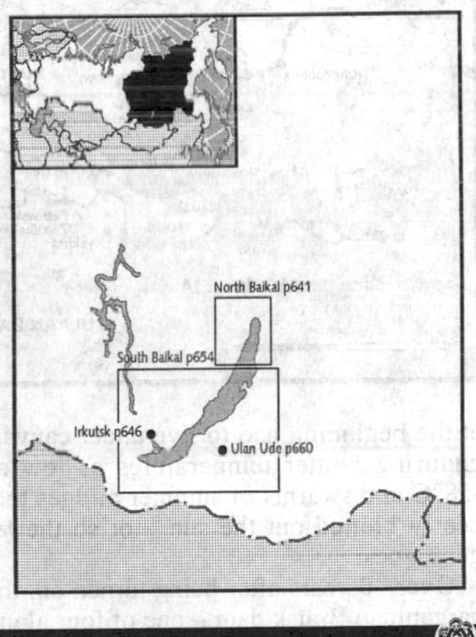

The Western BAM & Northern Lake Baikal
Западный БАМ и северный Байкал

TAYSHET
ТАЙШЕТ

• pop 70,000

About the only point of interest in Tayshet is that it's the Trans-Siberian's westernmost junction with the BAM. There's no reason to stop off here unless you're changing trains. Should you find yourself in Tayshet at that time, the train station has rest ***dormitories*** (one room for men, with about a dozen beds, plus several smaller rooms for women) for about $2 a night. Across the street is ***Hotel Birusa***.

BRATSK
БРАТСК

☎ 3953 • pop 280,000

There was a fort here on the Angara River as early as the 17th century, but it and about 40 other villages are now at the bottom of the 'Bratsk Sea', an artificial lake created in 1955 by the building of the Bratsk Hydroelectric Station (Bratskaya Gidro Elektro Stantsiya). The present-day town of Bratsk only marginally predates the dam. It rose out of virgin taiga through the labour of 1500 volunteer workers, who

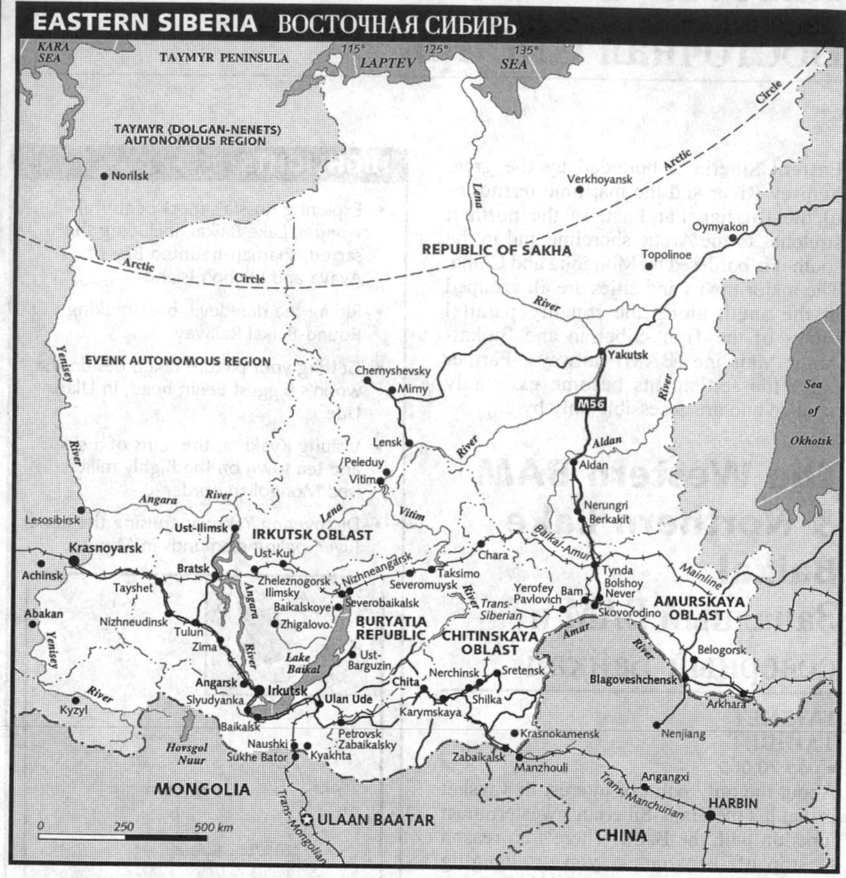

at the beginning had to live under canvas, enduring winter temperatures as low as -58°C and swarms of summer midges that nearly blotted out the sun – or so the legend goes.

Over 40 years after being turned on, the gargantuan Bratsk dam – one of four along the Angara – is still producing power at only 50% capacity, due to lack of customers. The Soviet solution was to bring customers out to the dam, and these included the world's largest aluminium-smelting plant, 20km west of the centre, and an equally big cellulose factory 5km south.

Consequently the area has become a ghetto of belching factories and the thick, grey air is among the foulest in the country. Forests are dead or dying for 100km around. So why come? The town itself, isolated in the taiga, is at least a good place to see the scale of Soviet industrial fantasies and marvel at what Russians can do when they're inspired.

Orientation & Information

The city is actually a necklace of several small settlements around the shore of the Bratsk Sea, each originally a centre for a different aspect of the dam's construction. Intourist is on the first level of Hotel Taiga, and there's an exchange bureau downstairs in the foyer. The telephone and telegraph office is just down the street at ulitsa Mira 27, and there is a post office a block east on ulitsa Kirova, with a bookshop opposite.

Bratsk is on Moscow time plus five hours.

Things to See

While the central district of Bratsk is completely without charm, neighbouring **Padun**, a 40 minute walk from the dam, has a pleasant promenade, an old log watchtower and the city's only working church.

As long as you're here, you also should have a look at the **dam and power station**. The dam itself is 1km long with a road and the BAM railway running across the top. Inside the powerhouse, you can punch 'English' on an automated display and learn all you ever wanted to know about Siberian dams.

Bratsk's other attraction is the **Angara Village**, an open-air ethnographic museum containing a reconstructed Evenki camp, another watchtower from the old fort and the obligatory 'three farmsteads of varying economic level' from the 19th century. It's 15km north of the central district, at least 4km off the road, and there's no bus to it. The museum is closed by mud in spring but it's open in summer from 10 am to 5 pm daily except Monday.

Places to Stay

The two principal hotels, both Soviet throwbacks with restaurants, bars and vodka-soused locals, are in the central district (tsentralny rayon), a forest of apartment blocks 35km south-west of the dam. The ***Taiga*** *(☎ 41 40 00, ulitsa Mira 35)* has 150 single/double rooms for $70/$120. The ***Bratsk*** *(☎ 43 84 36, ulitsa Deputatskaya 32)* has accommodation for $25/50.

Getting There & Away

Air There are flights to/from Krasnoyarsk, Irkutsk, Moscow, Novosibirsk, Omsk and Vladivostok. The Aeroflot office is at ulitsa Deputatskaya 17. At the airport the foreigners area (mezhdunarodny sektor) is at the far left end as you face the planes.

Train The strung-out town has four stations on the BAM. Anzyobi Station (also called Chekanovsky) is closest to the Taiga and Bratsk hotels; Padunskie Porogi is the next station north. The branch line into the central district is only for suburban trains. At least one daily train goes as far west as Moscow, while another goes as far as the Trans-Siberian main line at Tayshet (315km, 7½ hours). Eastbound there are daily trains to Severobaikalsk (740km, 18 hours) and Tynda/Neryungri (change here for Komsomolsk).

Boat Reportedly it's possible to catch a water taxi between Bratsk and Irkutsk, a 13 hour trip along the Angara River.

Getting Around

From the airport, buses and minivans go past Hotel Taiga to the central district bus station on ulitsa Yuzhnaya. The trip takes about 50 minutes.

ZHELEZNOGORSK-ILIMSKY ЖЕЛЕЗНОГОРСК-ИЛИМСКИЙ

☎ 39566 • pop 33,000

Though not actually on the railway, Zheleznogorsk-Ilimsky is a BAM town, created in the 1960s around an iron-ore processing plant (Zheleznogorsk means 'mountain of iron'). It is situated 150km east of Bratsk and several kilometres north of the BAM station, Korshunikha. It's notable for its exceptionally clean and well maintained appearance and for its density of museums; there's a local museum, a Museum of Russian-Japanese Friendship, the Yangel Museum and the Museum of the House of Yangel – which is a lot of history for a town barely 40 years old. The celebrated Mikhail Yangel was a leading space-race scientist who was closely involved with Yury Gagarin's epoch-making first-man-in-space flight. Yangel died in 1971.

One reason for visiting Zheleznogorsk-Ilimsky might be to use it as a base for exploring the surrounding wilderness. With its craggy mountains and lake-filled valleys, this is one of the most picturesque regions of Siberia. Ask around for Anatoly Semilet of the Kedr Tourist Club who might be able to offer experienced guides. The club might also be able to arrange ***homestays***. Alternative accommodation might be found in ***Hotel Magnetit*** *(☎ 2 17 58)*, which has single/double rooms with showers for $15/23, though the hotel administrator sometimes demands a *zayavka*, which is a scary, official piece of paper from the local government requesting that the hotel accommodate you.

UST-KUT
УСТЬ-КУТ

☎ 39565 • pop 70,000

Although now reached by the BAM railway, Ust-Kut originally grew as a port on the great Lena River. It was founded in 1631 by the explorer Yerofey Khabarov, who used it as a supply base for Yakutsk some 1988km downriver. Ust-Kut can also lay claim to one of Siberia's fabled, but in fact few, salt mines, which was operating up until the time of the revolution.

Things to See & Do

The town's points of interest include the Osetrovo **shipbuilding works**, founded in the 17th century, the nearby **museum**, and also the **mud spas**. However, the main reason for visiting would be to recreate Khabarov's route and take a **boat trip** down the Lena. During the navigation season, from late May to late September, about two boats per month make the 4½ day trip to Yakutsk. Passage is from $50 to $150 depending on the cabin. There are also hydrofoils that depart at 8 am daily heading downriver as far as Vitim and Peleduy, a 14 hour journey costing $73. From here, it's possible to get a connecting hydrofoil through Lensk on to Yakutsk, though that requires staying at least one night in Peleduy's mosquito-infested, river-port dormitory (about $5 a bed, outhouse in the yard) or taking your chances on the hospitality of the not so friendly, mostly unemployed, barely surviving locals. The dorm administrator may suggest an address; expect to pay about $8 for a room (and get more impressions about life in a Yakutia village than could ever fit in a traveller's notebook).

In the opposite direction, hydrofoils depart every day for Zhigalovo, 342km upstream, an 11 hour journey for $30. (There is a road linking Zhigalovo to Irkutsk and it may be possible to get a bus between the two.) Bookings should be made at the Osetrovo river port (☎ 2 63 94, fax 2 07 29) at ulitsa Kalinina 8, through the park across from the train station.

Places to Stay

Accommodation in Ust-Kut is at the 220-bed ***Lena Hotel*** *(☎ 2 15 07, fax 2 14 24, ulitsa Kirova 88)* across from the train station. Single/double rooms with toilet and shower are $31/40. The river port building also has fairly basic ***rest rooms***, where a place in a four-bed dormitory costs $5 and in a double room $7.50.

Getting There & Away

Ust-Kut also has a small airfield with flights to Chita ($96), Irkutsk ($93), Lensk ($91) and Mirny ($157). To get to the airfield take bus No 101 from outside the train station.

Ust-Kut is also a stop along the BAM, though on the train schedules it's called Lena. Two westbound trains a day stop here, including one (No 75 on odd-numbered days and No 91 on even days) which goes all the way to Moscow. The summer train (No 97) which goes to Kislovodsk in the Caucasus passes twice a week, on Thursday and Sunday when we were there. Eastbound, train No 76 leaves for Tynda on odd days, while No 98 does the same route on Wednesday and Sunday.

SEVEROBAIKALSK
СЕВЕРОБАЙКАЛЬСК

☎ 30139 • pop 35,000

Before the coming of the BAM railway there was no town called Severobaikalsk, just virgin taiga crowding to the edge of Lake Baikal. The town appeared almost overnight in the early 1970s. The first dwellings were temporary – railroad carriages and shacks built from scavenged railway construction materials – but a small, permanent, concrete-block town followed, built by workers from Leningrad (they're commemorated in a monument in front of Severobaikalsk's ski-slope-roofed train station). Now that their work on the BAM is finished, it's unclear how most of the town's residents are to make a living, though a lot of them are trying tourism.

Despite the fact that the best views of Baikal are those from the railway yard and the coal-fired electricity plant, Severobaikalsk is not an unattractive place. Its small size means that in minutes a hired car can have you out of the concrete and in the wilderness beside cool, clear rivers that run gurgling from rounded olive-green mountains. The town makes an excellent base from which to explore the northern end of the lake and it has some very good accommodation. The hydrofoil link with Irkutsk also makes Severobaikalsk easily accessible from the main Trans-Siberian rail route.

Orientation

Severobaikalsk is compact. The main street, Leningradsky prospekt, runs north from the train station 600m to Tsentralny ploshchad (Central Square) and that's about the extent of the town. Running east to west in front of the train station is the snappily named prospekt 60 let Soyuzu Sovietskikh Sotsialisticheskikh Respublik (60 Years of the USSR Ave). Turning right at the east end of this street will bring you to the port on Lake Baikal, 1.5km south of the train station.

Information

Most of the amenities are on or around Tsentralny ploshchad. On the east side of the square is the Torgovy tsentr, a miniature department store, and just to the south is the post office, open from 10 am to 6 pm (closed from 2 to 3 pm) on weekdays and 10 am to 5 pm on Saturday. The telephone and telegraph office is behind the trade centre, housed in a three storey block, and is open 24 hours daily. The local bank, the only place in town to change money, is next to the telephone office. It's closed on weekends.

The time in Severobaikalsk is Moscow time plus five hours.

Things to See

There is a **local museum** and an adjacent **art gallery**, both located at ulitsa Mira 2, and open from 10 am to 5 pm daily except Monday. The museum is dedicated to the building of the BAM and also has a small display of Buryat artefacts. The gallery has a limited collection of work by local artists. Neither is particularly enlightening and neither justifies the foreigners admission charge of $1.50.

Places to Stay

Severobaikalsk was never built with tourism in mind and so, blessedly, there's no Intourist presence. All the accommodation in town is the result of private initiative and it's some of the best to be found in all of eastern Siberia.

As soon as you step off the hydrofoil, the first thing you'll see is 10 attractive wooden ***cottages*** on the not-so-attractive shore of the port. They rent for $10 a night, and are made cosy with a small *samovar* and have a refrigerator. (We couldn't find the outhouse, though it looked like they were building some nice indoor facilities.) The office is at the top of the long set of steps going up a man-made hill.

Hotel Severny Baikal (*☎ 77 12*) on ulitsa Sportivnaya, in a low building reminiscent of the Wild West, has 40 spartan double rooms at $6 per person. The hotel also has two attractive single suites for $13, nicely furnished and carpeted, with fridge, phone, washbasin and a couch that could serve as a second bed. The drawback is you still have to share the one shower room and primitive hole-in-the-floor toilets with the whole hotel.

Close to the lake, in a woodland setting, are the four ***BAM guest cottages***, owned by the railway company. Each of these two-storey wooden chalets has three beautifully furnished double bedrooms, a large living room with telephone and TV, two bathrooms and an immaculate, fully equipped kitchen for residents to prepare their own meals. There's also a separate sauna building with plunge pool and party room – unfortunately, this is also a big hit with local businessmen. The cottages are 25 minutes walk from the train station, over the footbridge, then right along the road parallel to the tracks; take the first surfaced road on the left, then the first right, bearing left at the fork. Follow this road for 1km until Sibirskaya 12, a two storey yellow house on your left, which is where the cottage warden lives. At night the whole of this lonely route is unlit.

There's a similar set-up on the eastern edge of town at ***Baikal Servis***. The three small Hansel-and-Gretel-style chalets here are more upmarket, each with a fitted kitchen, living room, bathroom and just one double or triple bedroom. Again there's a separate sauna building for guests, but here with a plunge pool the size of a football field (well, maybe a tennis court) and a billiard room upstairs. The cost is $18 per cottage which sleeps three to four people. Baikal Servis can also arrange boating or fishing on Baikal and shoreline trekking. Contact Yevgeniya Kuznetsova (☎/fax 2 3912 – Russian only).

To reach the cottages from the train station it's a 20 minute walk; follow prospekt 60 let SSSR east to the T-junction, then turn left, followed by a turn at the first street on the right. The cottages are down an unsurfaced slip road 400m along on the left.

Places to Eat

There is a handful of good restaurants on the main square. The best is ***Tikhonov i Synovya***, a comfy cafe on the 2nd floor to the left of the central library. It's open from noon to midnight (closed between 4 and 7 pm). The ***Rus***, a bar/restaurant on prospekt 60 let SSSR near the train station, serves up fish, chicken (for $2 to $4) and its own brewed beer (for $1 a flagon). It's open from 9 pm to 2 am. The ***Aysberg*** is the town's disco club.

There are a half a dozen ***food shops*** plus an open-air ***market*** in the square.

Getting There & Away

Air There's no airport at Severobaikalsk but from neighbouring Nizhneangarsk, 20km to the north-east, there are six flights a week to Ulan Ude ($50, 80 minutes) and flights every other day to Irkutsk.

Train Three trains head westward: No 75 going on odd-numbered days to Moscow, No 197 which goes on even-numbered days and travels as far as Krasnoyarsk, and the summer train (No 97) to Kislovodsk in the Caucasus which passes twice a week. Eastbound, train No 76 leaves for Tynda on odd-numbered days, while No 98 does the same route on Wednesday and Sunday.

Boat From June to September a hydrofoil service runs the length of Lake Baikal between Severobaikalsk and Irkutsk. The hydrofoil departs at 6.40 am three days a week from the port at Severobaikalsk (or 6.20 am from Nizhneangarsk) and reaches Irkutsk 10 hours later after a change of craft at Port Baikal. A one-way ticket from Severo-baikalsk to Irkutsk is $46.

Getting Around

There's only one bus, and it doesn't run often. You'll probably have to flag down cars; most drivers will stop. A ride to Nizhneangarsk is about $2.

AROUND SEVEROBAIKALSK (NORTH BAIKAL)

While the southern end of Lake Baikal has been well visited since the opening of the Trans-Siberian Railway at the beginning of the 20th century, the northern end of the lake is still almost completely unknown. Consequently it is the best area to visit to enjoy the serenity of the lakeside scenery and the perfect place for camping or indulging in other wilderness pursuits such as trekking, rafting, mountaineering or, in winter, skiing.

Directly across the lake (about a three hour boat ride) is the shaman-haunted Bay of Ayaya (which in the local Evenki language means 'very, very beautiful'). Inland about 6km from Ayaya is a beautiful, high-altitude mountain lake, Frolikha. A bit down the coast are the Khakusy hot springs. The three can be combined into a glorious two day trip, with an overnight stay on the lake shore. Boats represent the main means of

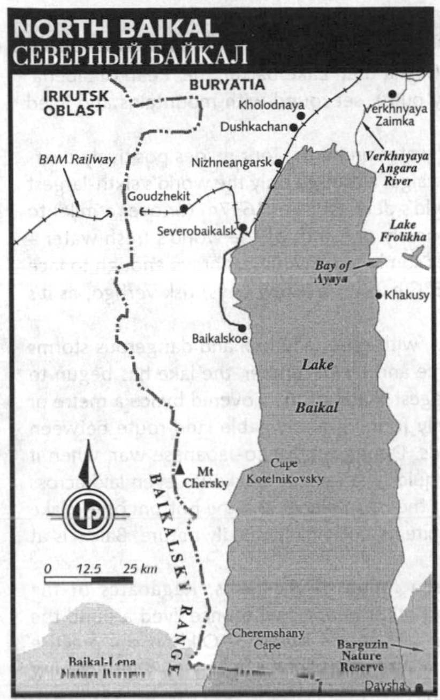

getting around Baikal's northern end, as there are no roads or railway lines along the lake shore.

A good contact is Igor Fedenyov (Morskaya 2A, Severobaikalsk), who charters ships for exploring the northern wonders of the lake: the Bay of Ayaya; the hot springs of Khakusy; the ruins of an Evenki village at the mouth of the upper Angara River, and the list goes on. The cost of chartering the ship is $100 per day, plus $15 per person per day for food, sleeping bags etc. Fedenyov, an ex-chef, makes the best *ukha* (fish soup) in Siberia, with all the ingredients pulled from his fishing nets and his own garden back in town. It's best to send him a telegram two days in advance. Indicate how many people, for how many days, the day of the week you're arriving and whether by hydrofoil or plane, so he can come and meet you.

Another useful contact is Rashit Yakhin (☎ 30139-21 560, yahin@usa.net) who worked as a guide for many foreigners until suffering a stroke. He can still arrange trips and homestays.

Nizhneangarsk Нижнеангарск

Nizhneangarsk, a small fishing village of 10,000 people about 20km north-east of Severobaikalsk, is home to the regional airstrip and a fish processing plant. Neither of these, admittedly, is a prime tourist attraction, but there is a local museum in the high school that traces the history of the settlement back to the 17th century. As well, there's a souvenir shop at ulitsa Kooperativnaya, near the airfield, which sells attractive local handicrafts – though animal lovers might just prefer to give the sealskin hats a miss. The hydrofoil for Irkutsk begins its journey in Nizhneangarsk, departing three days a week at 6.20 am.

Kholodnaya Холодная

The Evenki are one of the original indigenous peoples of the North Baikal region, although today there's little to distinguish them from the later Russian settlers. Their village of Kholodnaya, 20km north-east of Nizhneangarsk, which was originally an encampment of birch-bark yurts, is still quite attractive and offers a good insight into traditional life in deepest Siberia. Of course, the reindeer herds that the Evenki have historically tended are long gone (confiscated with forced collectivisation in the 1930s), and instead many villagers are employed at a local polar-fox farm producing fur hats and souvenirs.

About 10km from Kholodnaya are the remains of a Stalinist Gulag camp where, in the late 1930s, prisoners laboured mining mica. The camp was closed shortly before WWII but several decaying and weather-beaten buildings survive, along with towers, barbed-wire fences and three abandoned – and most likely dangerous – mine shafts. The camp is located in the Akikan Valley and the strenuous trek to reach it takes between three and four hours. Head out from Kholodnaya train station on the Kichera

Lake Baikal Озеро Байкал

There is probably no more beautiful place in all Russia than Lake Baikal, the 'Pearl of Siberia' – crystal clear (and, for the most part, drinkably pure), set round with mountains and lined with little settlements of wood cabins.

It's also one of the most interesting bodies of water on earth. Tour guides positively overflow with statistics. This 636km-long slash in the taiga, although only the world's sixth-largest lake, is still bigger than Belgium. It's also the world's deepest lake: 1637m (or over a mile) to the bottom near the western shore. It contains nearly one-fifth of the world's fresh water – more water than North America's five Great Lakes combined. Swimmers brave enough to face Baikal's icy waters (never warmer than about 15°C except in a few bays) risk vertigo, as it's possible to see down as far as 40m.

Baikal's weather is unpredictable in all seasons, with especially foul and dangerous storms in November. The first snows fall around this time and by December, the lake has begun to freeze. From February to April it's the world's biggest skating rink. Covered by ice a metre or more thick, the lake serves as a road, temporarily forming a navigable land route between the settlements at its northern and southern ends. During the Russo-Japanese war, when it was imperative that troops got to the front line quickly, a railway track was even laid across the frozen lake. However, warm currents thin out the ice in places and the bottom of the lake is said to be a graveyard of cars and trucks. Despite its potentially deadly nature, Baikal is at its most spectacularly beautiful in winter.

Some 1200 archaeological remains have been found of the Huns, Kaganates of the Zhouzhanhs, ancient Turks, Uighurs, Kidahns and other peoples who once lived around the lake. The Buryats now living on the entrancing cliff-bound island of Olkhon still practise shamanism, and woe betide if you dare to enjoy a shot of vodka on the lake without tossing a drop or two into the water, to the god Burkhan.

Ecology

From the 7km thickness of sediment at the bottom, scientists calculate that Baikal has been in existence for over 25 million years, making it by far the world's most ancient lake (almost

road, cross the river and continue up the hill until the 42km marker. A little beyond, off to the left, is an overgrown dirt track which eventually, after about an hour, becomes a path beside a stream and winds up the valley to the Gulag camp.

In the early morning, you may be able to catch a bus or a minivan to Kholodnaya. The ride takes about an hour. From Severobaikalsk, one or two eastbound local commuter trains also stop at Kholodnaya.

Baikalskoe Байкальское

Sited on a lakeside bluff at the foot of a steep, emerald-green hill, the tiny fishing village of Baikalskoe is absurdly picturesque. There's no concrete or asphalt, just a hundred or so picture-perfect weatherboard cottages with bright blue shutters and small, neat, green and flowery gardens. The first cottages were built here over a century ago but the style of life in the village has changed so little since then that they are indistinguishable from the more recent houses.

The water for all the houses is still drawn from a well and the settlement's electricity is generated by a trawler which is moored at the jetty.

It takes less than half an hour to explore the village but the surrounding area is good

Lake Baikal Озеро Байкал

all other lakes on earth are less than 20,000 years old). Like the Galapagos Islands, where animal and plant life have evolved in complete isolation from the rest of the planet, Baikal is a living museum of flora and fauna. Of over 2000 recorded plant and animal species, 70 to 80% are found nowhere else. The lake is home to varieties of fish and sponges that, elsewhere, live only in salt water. The *nerpa*, Baikal's freshwater seal, is separated by over 3000km from its nearest relative, the Arctic ringed seal, and nobody has the faintest idea how it got here.

Another curiosity is the big-eyed golomyanka fish, little more than a blob of pinkish fat with a backbone. It lives at extreme pressures at a depth of 1 to 1.5km and, when brought to the surface, dissolves into an oily spot. More edible fish include immense sturgeon and Baikal's endemic delicacy, the *omul* (a relative of the salmon and trout).

But the lake's ecosystem has proved delicate. The omul population nose-dived in the 1950s as a result of overfishing and the building of the Irkutsk dam (which raised the lake level and destroyed many of the fish's shallow-water feeding grounds). The omul has also taken a battering from the pollution carried into Baikal by the Selenga River, a vast tributary which alone supplies half the water that flows into the lake. Rising south of Russia's border, the Selenga collects pollutants from three large Mongolian cities, human and industrial waste from Ulan Ude, the Buryat capital, and effluent from a pulp mill at Selenginsk. Omul fishing is now restricted.

In the 1960s a newly built cellulose plant at Baikalsk began to dump wastes into the lake, raising a level of protest previously unheard of in the then Soviet Union. Baikal became a banner for the country's new environmental movement and the precursor of all Soviet-era environmental activism. The cellulose plant is now probably the most 'cleaned-up' factory in the whole of Russia, but despite claims to the contrary, it's believed that dumping continues.

There are three nature reserves around the lake, which total more than a million hectares. Additionally, over 250km of shoreline, including the entire western shore as far north as Olkhon Island, is now contained within two national parks. In 1996, UNESCO declared the lake and its surrounding basin to be a Natural World Heritage Site.

for walking. There's a decent path that leads up past a small hillside cemetery (filled with the graves of fishermen who died on the lake) and continues along the top of some steep cliffs.

If the fishermen aren't too busy, Baikalskoe is the place to hire a skippered boat for excursions down to Cape Kotelnikovsky or possibly, depending on the time of year, to visit the seal colonies out on the lake – although an excursion such as this needs some advance planning. Simply ask around the village whether there's anyone with a boat willing to take you out. You should expect to pay something like $10 per hour for boat hire. Again, try to get an early morning bus from the train station at Severobaikalsk. The journey takes an hour.

Cape Kotelnikovsky Мыс Котельниковский

Kotelnikovsky is a remote, uninhabited spot on the western shore of Lake Baikal 65km south of Severobaikalsk, and is known locally for its hot springs. About 10km inland from the springs are the peaks of the Baikalsky Range, a spine of mountains that stretch from the northern end of the lake to a point roughly halfway to its southern tip. The scenery around the highest peak, Mt Chersky (2588m), 40km by foot directly inland from Kotelnikovsky, is said to be some of the most spectacular in Siberia, with waterfall cascades and glacial lakes. There is a small, basic lodge at Kotelnikovsky with 16 beds at $10 per night. You can contact Baikal Servis (see Places to Stay in the Severobaikalsk section) about making reservations.

It is possible to make a day trip to Kotelnikovsky by chartering a skippered boat from Baikalskoe. The trip down the lake takes about three hours each way. For the day's hire of a boat with room aboard for four passengers you should expect to pay around $150.

TYNDA
ТЫНДА

☎ 41656 • pop 70,000

Tynda, 1320km east of Severobaikalsk, is *the* BAM town; the BAM construction company's headquarters are here, as are the editorial offices of the railway's weekly, the *BAM*. It's from Tynda that the as-yet-unfinished Yakutia Railway (or AYAM) extends north towards Yakutsk, while a branch line goes south to connect with the Trans-Siberian at the town of Bam. The town is also home to the best of the BAM museums. Housed in the city library at ulitsa Profsoyuznaya 3, the museum has not only models and photographs pertaining to the railway, but also indigenous Evenki artefacts and a small section on the Gulag.

Equally worth visiting – to shed some of the accumulated grime of your journey – is the town's public *banya* (Russian sauna). The attendant has freshly cut birch branches for sale to enable bathers to whip themselves up into a sweat-soaked state of nirvana. See the boxed text 'A Russian Banya' in the Northern European Russia chapter for background and banya etiquette. The banya is on ulitsa Amurskaya, next door to the great sledgehammer-wielding statue.

If you are overnighting in Tynda give the centrally located, prominent ***Hotel Yunost*** *(☎ 3 27 08)* on Krasnaya Presnya a miss. It charges over $100 for pokey doubles. Better value is ***Hotel Nadezhda*** *(☎ 2 96 55, ulitsa Festivalnaya 1)*, behind the Yunost. The hotel is on the 3rd floor of the building and has dormitory-style accommodation, with a few beds in each room at $10 per person. There's also ***Hotel Orbita***, which is a large guesthouse in a wooded location, 15 minutes walk from the town centre. The rooms are $16 a night and the hotel also has a very good restaurant. To get there from the train station, head for the centre of town but don't turn on to Krasnaya Presnya, the main street; carry on another 500m and turn left onto ulitsa Nadezhdy. At the end, fork left and through the hedge into the grounds of the hotel.

Getting There & Away

Trains depart west from Tynda daily for Severobaikalsk and, via Bratsk and Tayshet, for Moscow (train No 75/76). Towards the east there is a Tynda-Komsomolsk service that takes 40 hours between the two towns. Twice a week during the summer months (starting in early June) train No 97 departs from Tynda for Kislovodsk, transporting Siberians to the holiday spas of the Caucasus region of southern Russia.

Buses run from in front of the train station south to the town of Bolshoy Never, 20km east of Skovorodino on the Trans-Siberian Railway.

Irkutsk & Southern Lake Baikal
Иркутск и южный Байкал

IRKUTSK
ИРКУТСК

☎ 3952 • pop 591,000

With the cultural heritage of its aristocratic exiles, the Asiatic influences of nearby Mongolia and China, and the easy accessibility of Lake Baikal, Irkutsk is one of the most appealing cities on the Trans-Siberian trail. Irkutsk was founded in 1651 as a Cossack garrison, to bring the indigenous Buryats into line. In the 1700s, it was the springboard for expeditions to the far north and east and, under trader Grigory Shelekhov, across the Bering Strait into Alaska and California (referred to locally at that time as the 'American district of Irkutsk'). Furs and ivory were sent to Irkutsk from all over eastern Siberia and carried to Mongolia, Tibet and China in exchange for silk and tea. Mingling with the merchants were scientists, missionaries and the first cast-off convicts.

As the administrative centre of East Siberia, Irkutsk became a major junction on the exile road. Its most illustrious 19th century exiles were Decembrists and Polish rebels, many of whom chose to stay – a rough-hewn aristocracy, who kept education, the arts and political awareness at a high level. Several Decembrists' houses have been restored as museums of the time.

Disaster struck in 1879 when fire destroyed almost three-quarters of the city. However, after gold was discovered in the Lena basin in the 1880s, the city didn't simply recover, it boomed. On the charred remains of log cabins, the newly rich built brick mansions and grand public buildings. The city's Russian classical architecture dates from this period. The shops filled with luxuries and imported goods, and Irkutsk became known as 'the Paris of Siberia'.

A city of well-to-do merchants and highbrow socialites, Irkutsk did not welcome the news of the Great October Socialist Revolution. Passing power into the hands of the working people sounded like a terrible idea and the city became a centre of resistance to Bolshevism. It wasn't until 1920, with the capture in Irkutsk of Admiral Kolchak, the head of the White army, and his summary execution, that the city finally succumbed to the Red tide.

Soviet-era planning saw Irkutsk develop as an industrial and scientific centre and the face of the city was brutalised with graceless institutional architecture. Following the same blueprint, the Angara River was dammed in the 1950s, another step in the taming and modernising of Siberia.

The city still retains vestiges of its cosmopolitan and eclectic heritage. The scores of old gingerbread log houses are gradually losing out to the ugly stucco blocks loved by the Russians (understandably, since the latter come with such things as indoor plumbing) but they are still prevalent in the centre.

The single biggest attraction in Irkutsk is, of course, Lake Baikal, which is near enough for a day trip.

Orientation

The city centre is on the east bank of the Angara, above the confluence with its tributaries, the Ushakovka and the Irkut. Upstream about 5km is the Irkutsk hydroelectric station; boats to Lake Baikal leave from south of the dam.

The city's axes are ulitsa Karla Marxa (the main shopping street and once the boundary between town and garrison) and ulitsa Lenina, which runs parallel to the Angara, 500m inland. The administrative centre is ploshchad Kirova at the north end of Lenina, with its Stalin-era Party headquarters. Across the Angara are the bustling train station, university research institutes and apartment blocks.

Maps of Irkutsk can be picked up at the news kiosk in the foyer of Hotel Intourist.

Information

Money Currency-exchange places are concentrated on ulitsa Lenina, but a good one to remember is the bureau in the service department at Hotel Intourist (bulvar Gagarina 44), which works 24 hours, barring several short breaks. Cash advances on a Visa card are possible here. The Sberbank on ulitsa Karla Marxa at the southern end of ulitsa Sukhe-Batora accepts Thomas Cook and American Express travellers cheques at 3%; it also gives cash advances on MasterCard and Visa. It's open from 9 am to 4.45 pm, with a break from 1 to 2 pm.

Post & Communications The main post office, at ulitsa Stepana Razina, is open weekdays from 8 am to 8 pm, and on weekends from 9 am to 6 pm. Faxes can be sent from a desk at the post office between 8 am and 5 pm on weekdays only. The main telephone and telegraph office is on ulitsa Sverdlova, opposite the circus. Phone calls

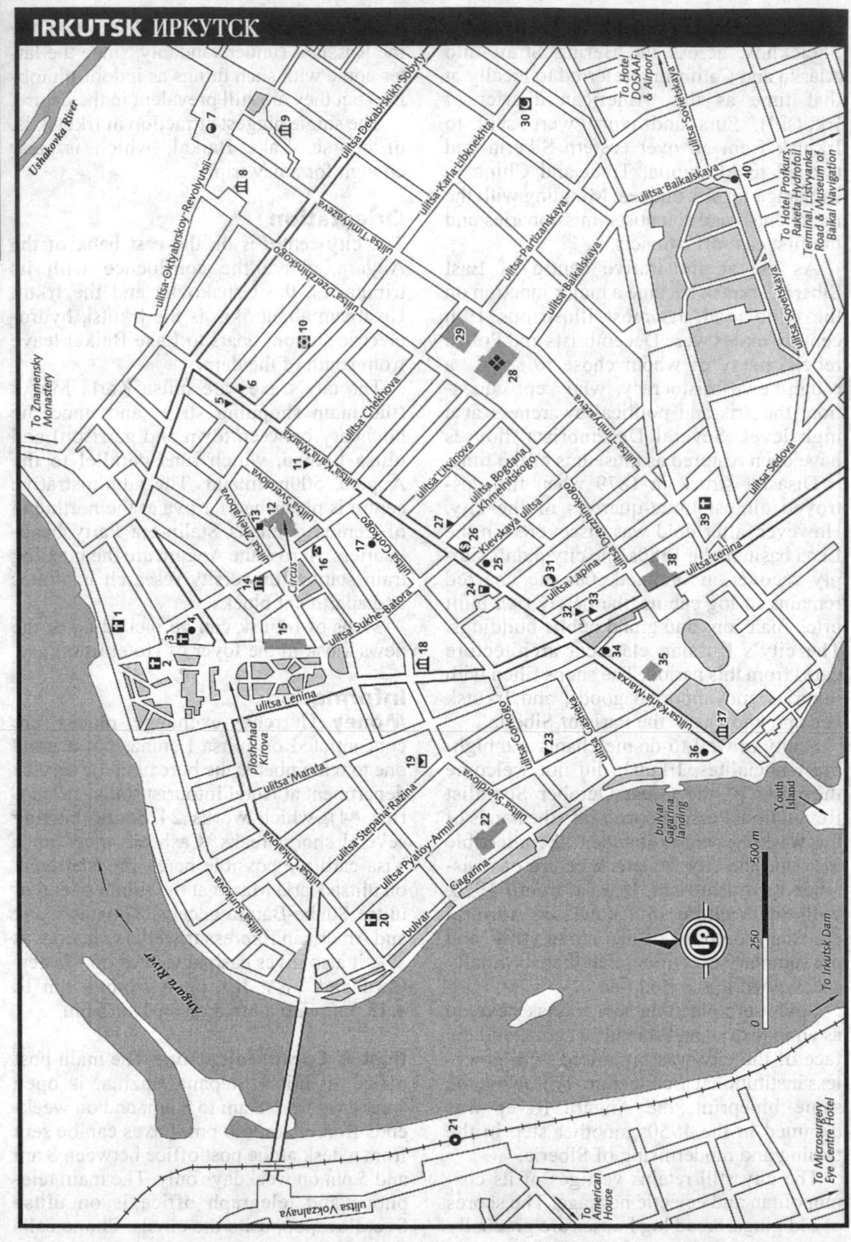
IRKUTSK ИРКУТСК
Ushakovka River
To Znamensky Monastery
ulitsa Oktyabrskoy Revolyutsii
ulitsa Dekabrskikh Sobyty
ulitsa Karla Libknekhta
ulitsa Timiryazeva
ulitsa Dzerzhinskogo
ulitsa Partizanskaya
ulitsa Baikalskaya
ulitsa Sovietskaya
To Hotel DOSAAF & Airport
To Hotel Profkurs, Raketa Hydrofoil Terminal, Listvyanka Road & Museum of Baikal Navigation
ulitsa Chekhova
ulitsa Karla Marxa
ulitsa Sverdlova
ulitsa Zhelyabova
ulitsa Litvinova
ulitsa Bogdana Khmelnitskogo
Kievskaya ulitsa
ulitsa Lapina
ulitsa Sedova
ulitsa Lenina
ulitsa Gorkogo
ulitsa Sukhe-Batora
Circus
ploshchad Kirova
ulitsa Marata
ulitsa Stepana Razina
ulitsa Chkalova
ulitsa Surikova
ulitsa Pyatoy Armii
ulitsa Gryaznova
bulvar Gagarina
bulvar Gagarina landing
Youth Island
Angara River
To Irkutsk Dam
To Microsurgery Eye Centre Hotel
To American House
ulitsa Vokzalnaya
0
250
500 m

IRKUTSK ИРКУТСК

PLACES TO STAY
- 13 Hotel Arena / Гостиница Арена
- 15 Hotel Angara / Гостиница Ангара
- 22 Hotel Intourist / Гостиница Интурист

PLACES TO EAT
- 5 Kafe Yunost / Кафе Юность
- 6 U Shveyka / У Швейка
- 11 Niva Bakery / Пекарня Нива
- 12 Restoran Aura & Kafe Peshchera / Ресторан Аура и кафе Пещера
- 23 Restoran Dragon / Ресторан Дракон
- 27 Nostalgia Kafe / Кафе Ностальгия
- 32 Bylina / Былина
- 33 Karlson Kafe / Кафе Карлсон

OTHER
- 1 Epiphany Church / Богоявленская церковь
- 2 Church of the Saviour / Спасская церковь
- 3 Catholic Church / Католическая церковь
- 4 Regional Administrative Building / Дворец пионеров
- 7 Bus Station / Автовокзал
- 8 Trubetskoy House / Дом Трубецкого
- 9 Volkonsky House / Дом Волконского
- 10 Synagogue / Синагога
- 14 Pioneers' Palace / Здание областной
- 16 Telephone & Telegraph Office / Телефон и Телеграф
- 17 Aeroflot / Аэрофлот
- 18 Art Museum / Художественный музей
- 19 Post Office / Почтамт
- 20 Trinity Church / Троицкая церковь
- 21 Train Station / Железнодорожный вокзал
- 24 Stratosphera Night Club / Ночной клуб Стратосфера
- 25 24 Hour Pharmacy / Круглосуточная аптека
- 26 Sberbank / Сбербанк
- 28 Department Store / Универмаг
- 29 Central Market / Центральный рынок
- 30 Mosque / Мечеть
- 31 Mongolian Consulate / Консульство Монголии
- 34 Antey Bookshop / Книжный магазин Антей
- 35 Okhlopkov Drama Theatre / Драматический театр имени Охлопкова
- 36 White House / Белый Дом
- 37 Regional Museum / Краеведческий музей
- 38 Philharmonic Hall / Филармония
- 39 Raising of the Cross Church / Крестовоздвиженская церковь
- 40 Puppet Theatre / Театр Кукол

to Australia and the USA cost $3 per minute, while calls to Europe are $1.10 a minute. The telephone office is open 24 hours daily, with fax service between 8 am and 8 pm. Email can be sent from both places for about $1 a message.

Travel Agencies Unless you need help with train or plane reservations, don't bother with the Irkutsk-Baikal Intourist (☎ 29 01 61), at Hotel Intourist. About all it has to offer is a city tour and some overpriced bus passages to Listvyanka. Baikalcomplex (☎/fax 38 92 05, ☎/fax 43 20 60, youry@travel.baikal.ru, PO Box 3598, Irkutsk 664 074), a small private company, offers adventure tours, rafting, hiking, skiing, biking, scuba diving and homestays on Lake Baikal and surrounding areas. It's run by an energetic mountain climber, Yury Nemirovsky, who speaks English.

Bookshops Antey, at ulitsa Karla Marxa 20 near ulitsa Lenina (behind the statue of Lenin hailing a taxi), has a selection of maps including a good one of the general Baikal region.

Time Zone Irkutsk time is Moscow time plus five hours.

Decembrist Houses

After completing their term of labour near Chita, many Decembrists settled in Irkutsk. So, too, did the wives of nine of them and the girlfriends of another two, who had followed them into exile. The first of these women was Yekaterina Trubetskaya, the wife of Prince Sergey Trubetskoy, who was allowed to go to Siberia on condition that she forfeit all titles and hereditary claims to them. She died here, and her husband subsequently returned to Moscow.

The restored houses of Trubetskoy and Count Sergey Volkonsky, with furnishings and pictures of family and friends, are now rather touching museums, although a little meaningless without the explanations of a guide. (Alternatively, get hold of *The Princess of Siberia*, Christine Sutherland's account of the life of Maria Volkonskaya.) Trubetskoy's house, with maps and paintings of exile life in the cellar, is at ulitsa Dzerzhinskogo 64, open from 10 am to 6 pm daily except Tuesday. Admission is $2.50. The Volkonsky house is one block east, just off ulitsa Timiryazeva – follow the dusty road that runs down the side of the church and it's a big bluish-grey building, unmarked. Enter through the courtyard. It's open from 10 am to 6 pm every day except Monday, and admission costs $3.50.

Irkutsk Regional Museum & Around

The red-brick piece of Victoriana at ulitsa Karla Marxa 2, near the river, was in the 1870s the museum of the Siberian Geographical Society, a club of explorers and researchers, whose names adorn the exterior. It's now the Regional Museum (kraevedchesky muzey) and is open from 10 am to 6 pm daily except Monday. Admission is $2.50, or $1.50 with student ID. The gift shop has excellent birch crafts and jewellery made from locally found semi-precious stones; maps and postcards are also available.

The best exhibitions feature indigenous tribes from the time when, under the influence of Russian settlers, they were abandoning nomadic ways: house mock-ups; shamans' robes and amazing headgear; an Evenki coat made of feathers; and fearsome Buryat idols. Upstairs, lively displays trace the history of Irkutsk through the coming of the Trans-Siberian Railway and two world wars, and bring it bang up to date with Snickers wrappers and jeans made in China. The porcelain Nubian heads and cuddly toy monkeys are, an English-speaking attendant said, thrown in for decoration.

The **obelisk** across the road from the museum was erected on the 10th anniversary of the arrival of the Trans-Siberian Railway. The faces are those of Yermak (the 'conqueror of Siberia'), Count Muravyov-Amursky (the governor general who took the Amur River back from the Chinese) and Speransky, another governor. Yury Gagarin, the first person in space, despite having no Irkutsk connections, is commemorated with a monument 300m farther north along the corniche. Almost opposite the monument is a small side street, ulitsa Gasheka, named after the Czech novelist Jaroslav Hašek, creator of the classic *The Good Soldier Švejk*. In the immediate post-Revolutionary period Hašek lived in Irkutsk, where he worked for the Bolsheviks (a move born out of expediency rather than any political conviction) as an editor and political commissar.

The small, tree-covered island just upstream of the Trans-Siberian obelisk is **Youth Island** (ostrov Yunosti). It has a small, rocky beach and what looks like a miniature Sydney Opera House but is, in fact, a dance bandstand.

Other Museums

The **Church of the Saviour** (Spasskaya tserkov), north of ploshchad Kirova, houses the Irkutsk Museum's natural-history collection of stuffed animals and early Evenki, Buryat and Yakuty clothing. Upstairs there's an exhibition hall and, ascending a claustrophobic's nightmare of a staircase, a display of local church history. It's open from 10 am to 6 pm except on Tuesday, and admission is $2. The **Irkutsk Art Museum** at ulitsa Lenina 5 has a weak collection composed of indigenous Siberian art, icons, Russian painting and Chinese porcelain, which few are going to find worth the $4 admission charge. Opening hours are from 10 am to 6 pm daily except Tuesday.

Moored within sight of the Raketa river terminal (for hydrofoils to Lake Baikal) is the icebreaker ferry *Angara*, one of two old boats, manufactured in England and shipped here in pieces, that originally ferried Trans-Siberian passengers, and the train, across the lake. It now houses the **Museum of Baikal Navigation**, and is open daily except Monday.

Other Historic Buildings

Though they're steadily disappearing, the city still has whole neighbourhoods of wooden cabins. The heaviest concentration is in the streets between ulitsa Karla Marxa and ulitsa Timiryazeva. Some of these buildings look as though they've just endured a 24 hour vodka binge (dishevelled, unsanitary and on the point of keeling over) but others are exquisite, with beautiful, lace-like, carved wood decoration. Two side by side on bulvar Gagarina, south of ulitsa Karla Marxa, illustrate the stylistic differences between early Siberian (No 14, with women's quarters upstairs facing the courtyard and few front windows) and later Russian (No 16, with 'wooden lace' decoration and many high windows facing the street).

Opposite the Irkutsk Museum on ulitsa Karla Marxa is the **White House** (Bely dom), built in 1804 as the residence of the governors general of Eastern Siberia. It's now a university science library. At ulitsa Zhelyabova 5, opposite the circus, is the huge, ornate **Pioneers' Palace** (the Pioneers were not explorers but a Soviet youth organisation), built in 1897 for a rich and eccentric gold merchant named Vtorov but commandeered by the Soviets following the revolution.

Churches

The heart of old Irkutsk was the magnificent Annunciation Cathedral, at the north end of ploshchad Kirova; but, after suffering extensive damage in the civil war, the cathedral was demolished to make way for the hulking Party headquarters, now the regional administration building (oblastnaya administratsiya). The cathedral is still visible in photos exhibited in the belfry of the **Church of the Saviour** (Spasskaya tserkov, 1706), which stands behind the Party building. The exterior of the whitewashed Saviour's church is decorated by fresco panels, one of which depicts the baptism of Buryats. Across the road is the **Epiphany Church** (Bogoyavlenskaya tserkov, 1723).

A block south of the Church of the Saviour on ulitsa Sukhe-Batora is Siberia's only Gothic building, a Catholic **Polish church** (Polskaya Kostyol) built by Polish exiles in 1881. In the 1930s it became a concert hall (it's still used for organ recitals), while around the same time the **Trinity Church** (Troitskaya tserkov) on ulitsa Chkalova, near the river, was made into a planetarium.

The baroque **Raising of the Cross Church** (Krestovozdvizhenskaya tserkov, 1758), on ulitsa Sedova near the stadium, is one of the few churches that remained open to worshippers during the Soviet era. It dominates the skyline of Irkutsk seen from the Trans-Siberian.

There is a dilapidated **synagogue** at ulitsa Karla Libknekhta 23 and a **mosque** four blocks farther south on the same street.

Znamensky Monastery

This former nunnery is the headquarters of the Orthodox diocese of Irkutsk, Chita, Buryatia and Sakha. Inside is the working Church of the Sign (Znamenskaya tserkov, 1763), restored by exiled nuns and reopened after WWII. Services are held at 10 am and 5 pm on weekends and Church holidays, and possibly at other times.

In the cemetery is the grave of the merchant-explorer Grigory Shelekhov and those of Princess Trubetskaya, wife of the exiled Decembrist, and three of her children. Another grave, marked by a stone tree with no branches, is said to be that of a merchant who had 11 daughters and no sons. The monastery is across the Ushakovka River via trolleybus No 3, or a 1.5km walk from the south end of ploshchad Kirova.

Places to Stay

There are a couple of cheap options away from the centre of town. ***Hotel Profkurs*** *(☎ 35 79 63, ulitsa Baikalskaya 263)* is a hostel attached to a technological institute, quite close to the Raketa hydrofoil terminal. Clean double rooms with shower and toilet are $12 per person. To get there from the city centre take tram No 5 from ulitsa Partizanskaya, behind the central market, and get off at the penultimate stop, Vostokenergoremont (Востокэнергоремонт) in metre-high letters on an office block to your left; the hotel is in the building directly in front as you step off the tram. To reach the hotel from the Raketa terminal, walk directly inland and pass through two housing estates. On crossing a second major road you should arrive at a car park with a chain-link fence; the hotel is beyond the car park and the small cluster of apartment blocks, beside the tram tracks. In all, it's a 15 minute walk. The catch is they may not let you in if the local OVIR hasn't registered your visa.

The ***Dosaaf*** *(☎ 27 27 40, ☎ 27 00 20, ulitsa Kultukskaya 9B)* is a dormitory *(obshchezhitie)*. Guests are given an apartment with kitchen, bathroom and living room/bedroom, which sleeps two to four persons. The place has taken a battering, but a bed is $8 to $17. Take tram No 5 from behind the market, or bus No 20 from the train station, to a stop called Pervaya Sovetskaya, at the junction of ulitsa Sovetskaya and ulitsa Dekabrskikh Sobyty. Beside the junction is a tank on a plinth; you need to go the way its barrel points (north along ulitsa Sovetskaya), taking the first left. As you reach two tall chimneys off to the right, you can see the red-brick Dosaaf building adjacent to a long, five storey apartment block. Turn right, then take the first left. You'll see the dorm on your right.

One other highly recommended option is to stay at ***American House*** *(☎ 43 26 89)*. This is a large private home 20 minutes walk from the train station, where Lida Scolocchini and her son Mark offer bed and fantastic breakfast for $20. Only six people can be accommodated so reservations must be made well in advance. The address is ulitsa Ostrovskogo 19, Irkutsk, Russia 664029. To get there, follow the tram tracks to the left as you leave the train station; when the tracks veer left up the steep hill keep going straight and cross two streets; you will see the stadium and a school on your right. Turn right and at the next crossing turn right again, then again another right at the next crossing (it sounds like you're going around in circles, but you aren't really). Then at the second crossing, take a left. Pass the brick wall on your left, and you will see the building No 19. That's it. Alternatively, take a taxi from in front of the train station and ask for Amerikansky Dom – you should pay about $2.

Hotel Arena *(☎ 34 46 42)*, on the north side of the circus, is a small, clean hotel with 18 single/double rooms for $25/42. Each room has a television and telephone, and the bathroom is shared with one other room. At ***Hotel Angara*** *(☎ 25 51 05)*, a Soviet monolith on the city's central square, most rooms have their own showers. Singles are $40 to $43, while doubles are $50 to $60, including breakfast. One thing to keep in mind is that the hotel is nearly empty of guests and some of the rooms have been let as offices, so don't be surprised to hear a fax beeping through the paper-thin walls in the middle of the night. There are also souped-up *evroremont* rooms for $70 to $113. (Evroremont is a fancy new term meaning the room or floor has been remodelled. Basically what you're paying for is a new coat of paint, cheap Italian furniture and maybe an extra light bulb.)

Across the square at ulitsa Lenina 18 are the remains of Hotel Sibir, a well known haunt of one of Irkutsk's rival Mafia gangs. When the hotel caught fire (cause unknown) in 1995, the local fire brigade happened to be 15km away attending to another mysterious blaze; by the time they raced back, the Sibir had been completely consumed.

Definitely not a hang-out of men who play with matches is the hotel attached to the ***Microsurgery Eye Centre Hotel*** *(☎ 46 25 69, ulitsa Lermontova 337)*. It's a 10 minute bus ride across to the west bank of the Angara, but the place is clean (clinically so) and modern, with bathrooms that make you feel you've just entered a 4 sq metre annexe of Sweden. The staff are friendly and there's a cafe and a sauna for guests' use. Single/double rooms are $42/46. To get there take trolleybus No 1, 7 or 10 or *mikriki* (minivan) No 3 from ploshchad Kirova and get off at the Mikrokhirurgiya glaza stop in front of the seven storey microsurgery building.

Hotel Intourist *(☎ 29 01 68, fax 29 03 14, bulvar Gagarina 44)* is no beauty, but it does benefit from a fine setting on the Angara River, and is within easy walking distance of the centre. Rooms with showers and baths are plain and clean, and there's a multitude of services including four bars, two restaurants and several cafes. Single/double rooms cost $117/133.

Baikalcomplex (see Travel Agencies earlier) can also arrange homestays in Irkutsk and the surrounding area for about $30.

Places to Eat

While not exactly a gastronomic gold mine, Irkutsk does have a number of decent places to eat. Of the two pricey restaurants at Hotel Intourist, the ***Peking*** has a good Chinese menu. Better and cheaper oriental food can be found at the ***Restoran Dragon*** *(ulitsa Pyatoy Armii (5-y Armii) 67)*, a Russian-Chinese joint venture.

With a fish tank, Christmas red and green linens and gold trimmed plates, the ***Nostalgia Kafe*** at ulitsa Bogdana Khmelnitskogo is elegant and frequented by the mobile-phone crowd. Dishes, such as beef à la Siberia or bliny with caviar, range from $2 to $7. At the ***Restoran Aura***, a tiny restaurant on the top floor of the circus building (round to the left of the main entrance), the food is fair, and (whoopee) … there's live cabaret every night. The bill will come to around $12 per person including a supplement for the entertainment.

Also in the circus building (round to the right of the main entrance) is ***Kafe Peshchera***, a good place for a daytime snack or coffee stop. The chunky playpen furniture and camouflage netting on the ceiling suggest the place was designed with kids in mind, and the racks of vodka behind the bar seem a little incongruous. However, it's the vodka that sets the tone, so much so that in the evening the Peshchera is somewhere that any safety-minded, self-preservationist individual would do well to avoid. The ***Karlson Kafe*** *(ulitsa Lenina 15)* is inspired by the character of the same name created by Swedish children's author Astrid Lindgren. In a tiny, pretty, glazed-brick interior, large pottery figures and scenes from the book adorn the walls. The food is good: mostly soup, sandwiches and beer.

The funniest place to eat at is ***U Shveyka***, near the north end of ulitsa Karla Marxa, inspired by the comic Czech soldier hero Šveyk. The sign in Russian on the wall as you enter the rathskeller below the beer garden reads: 'Beer without vodka is money to the wind.' Both go down splendidly if you begin in true soldier style by gnawing on dried fish *(vyalenaya ryba)*. Meals are small and slightly overpriced ($6), but good. The *myaso po-Sibirski* is pounded beef slathered in mayonnaise, raw onions and cheese. The Baikal sauce on the trout is ketchup and mayonnaise. Some evenings there's a strolling gypsy fiddler.

Cheap, quick cafes include ***Kafe Yunost***, on ulitsa Karla Marxa near ulitsa Karla Libknekhta, a cheery place specialising in pizza; and ***Bylina*** *(ulitsa Lenina 13)*, which serves a couple of good, basic dishes (usually macaroni and meat) for about $0.75.

Good Russian-style coffee is served at the back of the ***Niva Bakery*** *(ulitsa Karla Marxa 37)*, but there's no seating, just chest-high counters to lean against. Judging by the queues, the Niva also does the best bread in town. For Trans-Siberian food stocks, try the lively ***central market*** on ulitsa Chekhova, with fish from the barrel, berries by the bucket and kiosks serving Chinese noodles and beer.

Entertainment

The ***circus***, on ulitsa Zhelyabova just east of ploshchad Kirova, is seasonal but in the summer break the auditorium is used by other travelling shows. Check the foyer posters for details. Despite its dilapidated appearance, the 1890 ***Philharmonic Hall***, opposite the stadium on ulitsa Lenina, still has regular performances. The hot spot in town is the ***Stratosphera Night Club*** *(ulitsa Karla Marxa 15)*, a two storey disco and bowling alley extravaganza; the cover charge is $2.50 and a coffee is a whopping $3.50.

Getting There & Away

Air There are two or three flights a day to Moscow ($250, six hours) and three a week to St Petersburg ($550, 6½ hours). Siberian connections include daily flights to Novosibirsk ($133, 2½ hours), six flights a week to Bratsk ($100, one hour) and five to

Khabarovsk ($180, 2¾ hours) and Krasnoyarsk ($133). There are also flights to Petropavlovsk-Kamchatsky, Magadan and Yakutsk. International connections include weekly flights to/from Niigata in Japan, and Shenyang in China, and twice a week to Ulaan Baatar. At the airport, Intourist is in the left-hand building as you face the planes.

There is a typically dismal Aeroflot office (☎ 27 69 17) in town at ulitsa Gorkogo 29, open from 8 am to 7 pm daily.

Train Irkutsk is 88 hours from Moscow by the daily express train. A good choice is the *Baikal Express* (westbound train No 9, eastbound No 10), which departs from Moscow's Yaroslavl Station every other day at 9.05 pm. There are generally no problems getting places on this train. Another alternative is the Moscow-Vladivostok train (No 1/2), the *Rossia*. The Moscow-Irkutsk fare in a four-berth sleeper is around $110. For details of travelling on the weekly Trans-Mongolian train, or Trans-Manchurian train and breaking your journey in Irkutsk, see the Trans-Siberian Railway chapter.

There are several trains a day that will take you on to Ulan Ude (eight hours) – it's worth trying to catch an early morning train and travel what is one of the most scenic sections of the Siberian railways during daylight. You can get to Yekaterinburg (53 hours), Novosibirsk (32 hours), Krasnoyarsk (19 hours), Chita (18 hours), Khabarovsk (58 hours) and Vladivostok (72 hours) on the services mentioned above.

When facing Irkutsk train station from the front, the long-distance ticket hall is on the far left and the left-luggage office is on the far right in a separate building beyond the toilet block.

Bus Five buses a day run to Listvyanka on Lake Baikal from the bus station on ulitsa Oktyabrskoy Revolyutsii.

Boat Three times a week from June to late September, a hydrofoil makes the 10 hour trip up Lake Baikal to the northerly towns of Severobaikalsk and Nizhneangarsk. It leaves at 7 am from the Raketa terminal, south of the dam, and a one-way ticket costs $46. During the same summer months, there's also a hydrofoil service to Ust-Barguzin on the lake's eastern shore, which departs at 9 am every Monday and gets to Ust-Barguzin at 4 pm and returns on Tuesday. It's wise to check the timetables (pinned up outside the ticket office at Raketa) as services are subject to change and possibly cancellation.

See the Around Irkutsk section for details of hydrofoil services to Listvyanka and up the western shore of the lake.

Getting Around

From the airport, bus No 20 runs to the train station, stopping on ploshchad Kirova for Hotel Angara and at the Planetary stop, just before the river bridge, 10 minutes walk along the corniche from Hotel Intourist. Two trolleybuses also serve the airport: No 4 runs into town and terminates on ulitsa Sukhe-Batora near Hotel Angara; No 1 runs across the dam and passes the Microsurgery Eye Hospital.

From the train station, tram Nos 1 and 2 and bus Nos 7, 16 and 20 cross the river; all stop at Planetary, the first stop after the bridge, but only the buses stop on ploshchad Kirova.

To reach the Raketa hydrofoil terminal, take southbound bus No 16 from the train station, or trolley bus No 5 or a mikriki from the stop on the north-west corner of ploshchad Kirova. The Raketa is the fourth stop after the *Angara* steamship (look for it on the right). From ploshchad Kirova to the hydrofoil terminal is a 25 minute ride. On buses, trams and trolleybuses you pay the conductor or the driver. Tickets cost $0.25, with sometimes a small charge for luggage. A taxi from the Raketa terminal, or the airport, to ploshchad Kirova should cost no more than $5.

Local ferries make a good budget excursion, upstream to the dam and downstream to half a dozen *sadovodstva*, suburban districts with vegetable allotments and dachas. The most convenient pier is bulvar Gagarina, near Hotel Intourist. Small boats do a one hour return trip up to the dam, leaving every half-hour or so from 6.30 am to late evening. Bigger Moskva boats go about 10km downstream, a 3½ hour round trip. Buy tickets on board. The navigation season is from late April to early October.

AROUND IRKUTSK (SOUTH-WEST BAIKAL)

Baikal Road & Museum of Wooden Architecture

Автодорога Иркутск-Листвянка и музей Деревянного зодчества

The 65km Irkutsk-Listvyanka road was built in an incredible two months in 1960 after US President Eisenhower was invited to visit the great lake (some of his ancestors were allegedly Siberian gold merchants). The trip was cancelled amid the fiasco that followed the shooting down of an American U2 spy plane.

At the 47km post, the Museum of Wooden Architecture (muzey Derevyannogo zodchestva) is a collection of 17th to 19th century Siberian buildings from around the region – three farmsteads (renovated inside), two chapels and a 17th century village watchtower. The museum is open in warm weather only and is worth a visit if you're driving past en route to the lake. If you do stop, go back 100m to a turn-off on the other side of the road. A viewpoint there is full of 'wishing trees' – shrubs tied with bits of cloth by picnickers and newlyweds looking for good luck. Supposedly a shamanist hangover, it's also reminiscent of the prayer flags of Tibetan Buddhism, the religion of most Buryats. Watch out for the debris of a more recent tradition – broken glass from smashed champagne bottles.

Just past here is the biggest village on the road, Bolshaya Rechka (Big Creek). The long buildings are mink farms.

Port Baikal & the Round-Baikal Railway

Порт Байкал

It was from Port Baikal that the *Angara* and *Baikal* steamships used to ferry the whole Siberian express train and its passengers across the lake to pick up the tracks again at Mysovaya. Later, a line was built along the lake's rocky west shore, and became known as the Round-Baikal (or Circumbaikal) Railway. With a tunnel or bridge almost every kilometre, this proved the most challenging section of the Trans-Siberian. Tsar Alexander III brought in Armenian and Italian masons, and the joined ends of the Trans-Siberian soon earned the name 'the Tsar's Jewelled Buckle'. When the dam submerged the tracks between Irkutsk and Port Baikal and a short cut was laid from Irkutsk to Kultuk, the remaining 94km of the Round-Baikal Railway became a neglected branch line. Three or four times a week the train trudges to and fro with supplies for the half-dozen isolated villages along the way.

A visit to the dilapidated cabins of Port Baikal makes a melancholy trip, starting with a boat ride from Listvyanka (half a dozen boats daily each way). But the ride on the railway, with its gorgeous arches and spectacular views of the lake, is a five hour thrill, especially if the conductor is nice enough to let you stand at the head of the locomotive as the train makes its slow, treacherous way. Tickets (about $3) can be purchased on the train or at either rail terminal, Slyudyanka (which is also a Trans-Siberian stop) or Port Baikal. For the best view of the tunnels, travel from Slyudyanka to Port Baikal. Baikalcomplex (see the Travel Agencies section) can help with homestays in the villages along the railway; it also does its own tour.

Listvyanka

Листвянка

☎ 3952 • pop 2500

The small but tourist-wise village of Listvyanka is a good destination for a day trip from Irkutsk. It's centred on landings for research boats and ferries, and at the northern end of the village is its main industry, the ship repair workshops. Beyond these, a track runs along the shore and a road climbs to a solar observatory.

Many of the 2500 villagers live in the picturesque suburb of Krestovka, nestled on a valley floor just south of the landings. Little **St Nicholas Church** (Svyato-Nikolskaya tserkov) has services twice a day. The

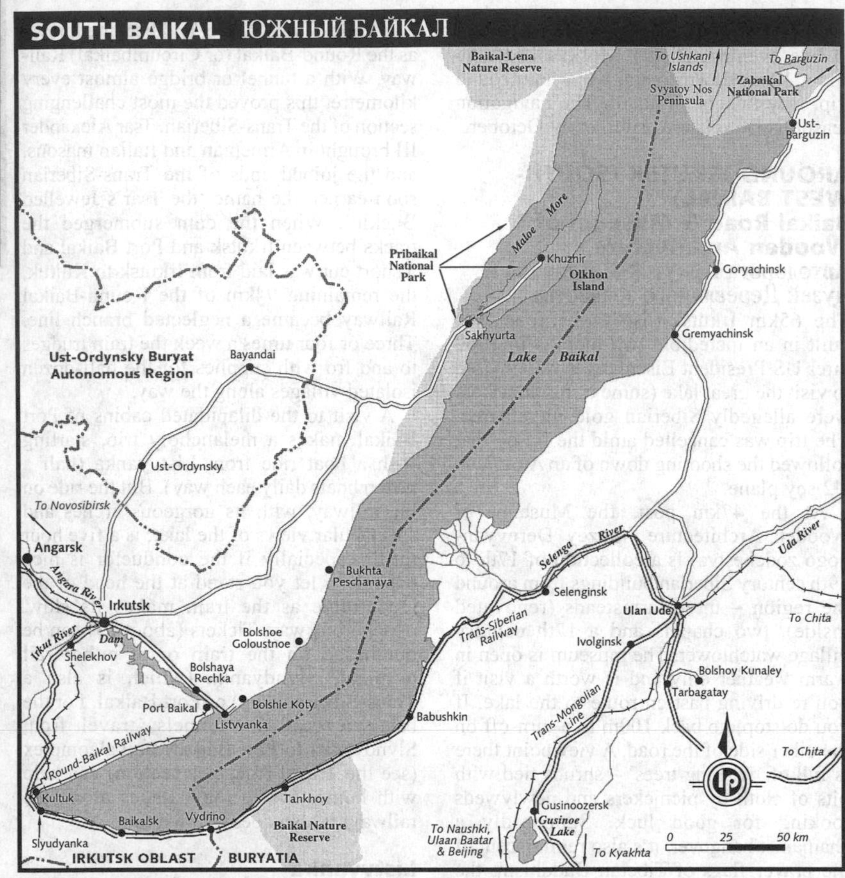

windows and naturally lit interior are unusual for a Russian Orthodox church.

Things to See South of Krestovka, 3km along the lakeside promenade, is the **Baikal Limnological Institute** (from the Greek *limne*, meaning lake). This is the headquarters for lake research by the East Siberian branch of the Russian Academy of Sciences. Inside, the cramped Baikal ecological museum has examples of some of the rare species of marine life to which Baikal is home, as well as plenty of maps, diagrams and models. Admission is $2.50. Up on the hillside behind the Limnological Institute are several guesthouses, originally built for Eisenhower's aborted visit and now part of a heart sanatorium for the privileged. Beyond them is Hotel Baikal. From the hotel, a 2.5km path climbs to an **observation point** with excellent views of the lake and mountains, Port Baikal and the Angara River.

Places to Stay The 118-bed ***Hotel Baikal*** *(☎ 29 03 91)* is a 1km climb from the highway via the access road or through the Limnological Institute grounds. Singles/doubles at $114/130 are posh by Siberian standards, and half of them have matchless views of the lake. In the village, 150m south of the hydrofoil jetty, is a green, weather-beaten, two storey ***turbaza***. It has a large dormitory and a couple of cell-like rooms (complete with filthy, bare plaster walls engraved with graffiti). Toilet facilities are basic and when we visited there was no running water – but what do you expect for less than $2 per night?

Places to Eat The Russian/Siberian food at ***Hotel Baikal*** is excellent, the service is polite and there's no band. Down in the village, opposite the hydrofoil landing, the ***Restoran Baikal*** is a little more earthy and is patronised by locals. It does basic soup, salad, meat and potatoes, edible and very cheap.

Getting There & Away Between 9 am and 4.30 pm daily there are three buses from Irkutsk bus station to Listvyanka, though it is also possible to catch a mikriki. From Listvyanka landing, the first departure is at 11 am and the last at 6 pm, though this is subject to change. You should check the timetable at Hotel Baikal or with whoever's serving in the little cafeteria beside the village bus stop. The bus also stops near the Limnological Institute. A seat one-way is $2.

The hydrofoil service between Irkutsk (leaving from the Raketa terminal) and Listvyanka has two departures from each point daily from mid-May to late September. The one-way trip takes just over an hour and costs $3. The sailings from Irkutsk leave at 8.20 am and 4 pm and from Listvyanka at 11.35 am and 7.15 pm, but double-check the schedules.

It's quite possible to hitchhike to Baikal but hard to find a good place to do it; the roundabout at the turn-off to the dam (along the route of trolleybus No 1 or bus No 16) seemed to be a good place. Bear in mind that when you hitch in Russia the driver usually expects to be paid.

Western Shore of Lake Baikal

Ferries and hydrofoils go to several landings along the west shore – but, then again, maybe they don't. Maintenance problems, lack of spare parts, financial constraints and the weather all play deciding roles in what services are running. It's very difficult to get accurate and up-to-date information, and the only sure way is to go down to the Raketa terminal in Irkutsk and ask.

One fairly reliable destination is **Bolshie Koty**, a biological research station and a worked-out 19th century gold field, 15km north of Listvyanka. The 8.30 am hydrofoil from Irkutsk, via Listvyanka, provides Bolshie Koty's sole daily transport link. It arrives at 10 am and makes the return journey two hours later. Two hours is more than enough to explore the tiny village; there's a sad, small museum, a couple of kiosks and an empty store. If you intend to eat, bring a packed lunch. A hike over the wooded hills back to Listvyanka might make a good half-day expedition.

Bukhta Peschanaya (Sandy Bay), 80km from Listvyanka, is potentially the farthest north you can go in a day trip. Three days a week, a hydrofoil makes the 3½ hour trip, with stops in Listvyanka and **Bolshoe Goloustnoe**, and returns in less than an hour, meaning you'll have to camp out if you want to explore this bay bounded by dramatic capes. At both Bolshoy Goloustnoe and Bukhta Peschanaya there's supposedly accommodation in the form of wooden cabins with saunas, double rooms and either shared or attached toilets, or in large, single-sex dormitories. Baikalcomplex may be able to help with reservations.

Olkhon, the large island off Baikal's western shore (and at 70km long, the largest of the lake's 27 islands), is accessible by bus and boat, and is probably one of the most mysteriously beautiful places on the lake.

The channel between the island and the lake shore (known as Maloe More, or 'Small Sea') is one of the few places in Baikal where the water is temperate enough for swimming.

The western shore of the island is steppe bounded by dramatic orange cliffs. Paths used by sheep and Buryat herders lead to the water. In the interior of the island are half a dozen lakes and the 1300m-high Zhima Peak on Cape Izhimey, with the only settlement of any size being the fishing village of Khuzhir, which has decent and inexpensive accommodation (ask anyone to lead you there). The northern end of Olkhon, once the domain of religious shamans, is reportedly a good place to see Baikal seals *(nerpa)*.

During summer, buses leave Irkutsk bus station for Olkhon at 8 am on Saturday, taking eight torturous hours over pot-holed roads to reach Sakhyurta, the nearest mainland village to the southern tip of the island (there's a ferry crossing point a few kilometres up the road).

The Severobaikalsk-bound hydrofoil also stops but only if a fisherman from the island rows out to meet the craft. (You'll have to ask the captain if anyone has requested the stop; if yes, then you've got about three hours on-board to find who's getting off so you can hitch a ride in their rowboat.) It's complicated and will cost you a bottle of vodka for the fisherman.

EASTERN SHORE OF LAKE BAIKAL

The eastern shore of Lake Baikal is some of Buryatia's wildest and least explored territory, not only untrodden by hiking-booted backpackers but relatively uncolonised even by local Buryats and Russians. At a certain point, all roads and tracks stop dead. Farther to the north there's not the slightest trace of civilisation for some hundreds of kilometres until the single-minded swathe of the BAM ploughs through the taiga beyond the northern end of the lake.

The most ecologically interesting parts – those which throughout history have remained free of habitation or development – now fall within the bounds of the **Barguzin National Reserve** (Barguzinsky zapovednik). Created in 1917, this is Russia's oldest national reserve. With over 263,000 hectares of protected flora and fauna, the park has long provided valuable virgin research territory for small armies of scientists hermited away in the small coastal settlement of Davsha. Davsha, linked only by boat to Ust-Barguzin 120km to the south, also acts as a reception centre for visitors, and it may be possible for travellers to get up there (see the Ust-Barguzin section) and see some of the park's unique mammal, bird and plant life.

Immediately south of the Barguzin Reserve is the **Zabaikal National Park** (Zabaikalsky Natsionalny Park), a more accessible, but still controlled, stretch of forested Baikal coastline. Within the bounds of the national park, 12km off the Svyatoy Nos Peninsula, are the Ushkani Islands, four small mountain peaks out in the lake that are the favourite basking place of Baikal's seals.

Access to Zabaikalsky is by road from Ust-Barguzin, a timber town connected by bus to Ulan Ude and by ferry to Irkutsk.

Ust-Barguzin
Усть-Баргузин

What was once a neat Siberian village on the estuary of the Barguzin River has been disfigured by prefab concrete apartment blocks, but Ust-Barguzin still has appeal as a convenient base for exploration of Baikal's wild eastern shoreline. You need to hire transport to visit the national park (admission $2.50) and it's preferable to have an idea of where you're heading. Locals can suggest good scenic spots to visit, one of which will undoubtedly be the popular hot springs (admission $5) not too far to the north. More interesting would be to take a boat over to the Svyatoy Nos Peninsula or even around its southern tip and out to the Ushkani Islands for some seal-watching.

Anyone interested in heading deeper into the reserve, or possibly visiting Davsha, should visit the national park headquarters (☎ 9 25 78) in the centre of town; ask anybody where it is.

Accommodation in Ust-Barguzin consists of the 14-room ***ski lodge*** near the cemetery. Singles/doubles are $5/10, and meals are included for an extra $5 to $10.

The hydrofoil *Barguzin* departs from Irkutsk once a week at 9 am on Monday and returns on Tuesday at 9.30 am, taking a leisurely 10 hours for the crossing. There's a daily bus south to Ulan Ude ($8.50 one way), which departs at 7.30 am and arrives six to 10 hours later depending on the weather and road conditions. Mikriki ($12 one way) also make this same trip in an hour or so less time; there's no set schedule but they usually leave in the mornings just before the bus.

Southern Buryatia Южная Бурятия

The mountainous Buryatia Republic covers an area of over 350,000 sq km, spreading around the north and east of Lake Baikal and forming an 800km 'panhandle' southwest along the Mongolian border.

For most of its history the region has been under Asiatic influence, something clearly visible in the facial features of the 250,000 indigenous Buryats. In the 1st century BC, the Huns invaded and subjugated the native tribes. Later, waves of nomadic peoples arrived, migrating north from what is present-day Mongolia. Jenghis Khan's mother is said to have come from the settlement of Barguzin, close to the eastern shore of Baikal. When her son grew to become the terror of the western world, Buryat tribes roamed as part of his horde.

The defeat of the Huns allowed for unchecked Russian expansion and in the 17th century the first Cossacks arrived among the Buryats. The Cossacks were followed by migrating peasants who introduced the natives to agriculture. While the western tribes took to this new static lifestyle, the eastern Buryats remained nomadic cattle herders and hunters. Buryatia became a great source of wealth for Russia, supplying timber, furs and gold, although the Buryats themselves, soon outnumbered by the fair-skinned squatters, benefited little. Today, Buryats make up more than 25% of the regional population. In the Soviet period, Buryatia became an autonomous republic, and then, with the USSR's demise, a republic within Russia.

The Buryats have managed to keep their language alive and it is now being taught in schools again and is heard on the streets. There is also an attempt to reintroduce the Buryatian script (written from top to bottom of the page), which they were coerced into abandoning for Cyrillic in the 1930s.

Buryats also live in two smaller 'autonomous districts' – Aginsk, south of Chita, and the very Russianised Ust-Ordynsky, west of Baikal – as well as in Mongolia and China's Inner Mongolia autonomous region.

RELIGION

Buddhism

In pre-revolutionary Russia, Buddhism was an officially recognised religion and there were 46 high monasteries *(datsans)* and 150 temples in the Buryatia, Chita and Irkutsk regions. Stalin sent thousands of lamas (priests) and others to the Gulag and destroyed all but two of the datsans – though, in recognition of wartime support from religious groups, he allowed a few to be rebuilt (the datsan at Ivolginsk, near Ulan Ude, was one of these).

Since the events of 1991 there has been a re-emergence of interest in Buddhist traditions and there are about 20 new and restored datsans in Buryatia; the datsan at Atsagat is 30km due east of Ulan Ude. The village of Atsagat is the home of Agvan Dorzhiev, Buddhist philosopher, reformer and teacher of the 13th Dalai Lama. The present incarnation of the Dalai Lama (the 14th) has visited the datsan at Ivolginsk several times.

Buddhists celebrate – openly now – six *hurals* each year. Tsagaalgan, the Buddhist New Year, carries on for 16 days at the time of the lunar new year, mostly at the family level with ceremonial food and dress. During the hural to Maitreya, Buddha of the future, held in early July, a Maitreya statue is carried in a colourful procession around the datsan grounds at Ivolginsk.

Shamanism

Despite adopting Buddhism in the 18th century, the Buryats were not inclined to give up their shamanistic beliefs and practised the two religions side by side. Many of the shamanistic sacred places *(obos)* and rock paintings are still known, and day trips to some of the closer sites can be arranged by Buryat-Intour (see Information in the Ulan Ude section).

Old Believers

As well as shamanism, Buddhism and mainstream Russian Orthodoxy, Buryatia is a home to the Semeyskie, or Old Believers. These are the descendants of conservative 17th century Russian Orthodox breakaways who fled here from persecution in northern Russia. There are still a number of Semeyskie villages, namely Desyatnikovo, Turbagatay and Bolshoy Kunaley, all within 70km south-east of Ulan Ude.

If you hop on a bus to the villages, you'll see lots of brightly painted cottages, but don't expect singing peasants in traditional dress. For that, you'll need Buryat-Intour which arranges visits to include dinner, costumes and song.

ULAN UDE
УЛАН УДЕ

☎ 3012 • pop 380,000

Despite an archetypal Stalinist centre dominated by a surreal large head of Lenin, Ulan Ude is a very un-Russian place. In fact, it's downright weird. As well as Lenin's boulderous bonce (inspired, it's said, by the outsized head of Marx on his London tomb), the visitor to Ulan Ude can also inspect a hidden hoard of Buddhist treasures and an authentically kitsch temple on the plains.

While nearby Irkutsk struts its tsarist history and traditions, Ulan Ude, capital of Buryatia, seems more conscious of the 'Asian-ness' that comes with its proximity to Mongolia and China. Founded in the 17th century as a Cossack garrison on the Selenga River and chartered as Verkhne-Udinsk in 1775, Ulan Ude grew as a trading post on the tea road route between Irkutsk and China. In the early 1900s the town's population stood at 10,000, but by 1930 this had risen tenfold with the onset of Soviet industrialisation.

The indigenous people of the region, the Buryats, put up stiff resistance to Sovietisation, as they had earlier to Russian colonisation, and grimly clung to their language, their cultural identity and the Tibetan-Buddhist faith they had adopted in the early 18th century from their cousins in Mongolia. In 1934, as part of the Soviet recognition of national minorities, the city got its present name, which is Buryat for Red Uda (the Uda River is a local tributary).

Because of Soviet installations on the Mongolian border, until 1987 the city was tightly closed and could only be visited by special permission (Eric Newby managed to spend several days here in 1977 during his big red train ride). Heavy industry was the backbone of the region with a large locomotive works, an aircraft factory and a metal-processing plant, all nearly or fully shut down, leaving the workers to find other jobs, mainly in cross-border trade.

Orientation

Tree-lined ulitsa Lenina is the city's axis, with the parade square, ploshchad Sovietov, at the north end and shopping areas around the old trading arcades towards the south. To reach ploshchad Sovietov from the train station, cross the footbridge over the tracks and walk south along ulitsa Borsoeva for 300m, then take the small side road on the right immediately after the Okean shop. Bear slightly left, toward the red-brick Hotel Geser, and the central square is a few minutes walk beyond.

The newer parts of town lie south of the river and north of the railway line. There's a fairly crude Russian-language town map available from the Buryat-Intour office at Hotel Geser; a good map of the whole republic, also in Russian and called *Respublika Buryatia*, can be found in Ulan Ude.

Information

There are exchange bureaus at Hotel Geser (open from 9 am to 6 pm) and at Hotel Buryatia (open from 9 am to 6 pm). Biznes Bank Aziya (open from 9 am to noon and 1 to 4 pm Monday to Friday) at the intersection of ulitsa Lenina and prospekt Pobedy also changes money, but the exchange rate may not be so good. The main post office is on ulitsa Sukhe-Batora, at the north-west corner of ploshchad Sovietov. It's open from 9 am to 6 pm daily. It has an international telephone desk that charges a discount rate of $1.50 per minute to Europe, $1.60 to USA and Canada, and $1.80 to Australia, after 1 pm. Email can be sent from here for about $1 a message. The telephone and telegraph office, on ulitsa Borsoeva near the railway footbridge, is open from 8 am to 10 pm.

Buryat-Intour (☎ 21 69 54, fax 21 92 67, buryatia@rex.burnet.ru) has two offices in town, the one in Hotel Geser being the easiest to find. The friendly, English-speaking staff run a variety of tours around the area including rafting, hiking, day trips to local religious and cultural sites, horse riding and winter ice fishing.

The time in Ulan Ude is Moscow time plus five hours.

Merchants' Quarter

The town's historical main artery, now renamed ulitsa Lenina, is lined with elegant, faded architecture dating from the mid-19th century. The brown mansion with statues, near ulitsa Kalandarashvili, was built in 1907 by a rich merchant. The fine, classically styled frontage along ulitsa Kuybysheva, now a clinic, was once a Merchants' Yard (Gostinny dvor, 1825).

Opposite are crumbling trading arcades (torgovye ryady), with the central department store now built into the middle of them. On the corner of ulitsa Kirova and Kommunisticheskaya is a large, pink house, home earlier this century to an American soldier, Colonel Morrow. The mercenary Morrow was aiding the Whites in the Civil War but some blatant profiteering (stealing gold from the Barguzin Valley) caused a local surge of support for the Reds and he was run out of town.

South of ulitsa Kuybysheva is the oldest quarter where you'll see some beautifully decorated log houses.

Hodigitria Cathedral & the Historical Museum

The broken-down Hodigitria Cathedral (Odigitrievsky sobor, 1785), at the southern end of ulitsa Lenina, was probably once the pride of Verkhne-Udinsk. Now it's boarded up, and its truly stupendous contents have been moved to the Historical Museum (Istorichesky muzey) on ulitsa Profsoyuznaya 29 where you can view the collected remains of pre-revolutionary Buddhism in Russia, salvaged from Buryatia's monasteries and temples on the eve of their destruction. The exhibitions include tantric sculptures, *tangkas* (icon-tapestries) and banners, vestments and masks, musical instruments and sacred volumes, along with homeless huddles of Soviet kitsch.

The artefacts found their way here when, after the revolution, a museum of Oriental art and ethnography was proposed and a serious collection was started, culled from datsans forced into more secular channels. In the 1930s, the datsans were demolished and the collection turned into an anti religious museum (its devoted curators presumably pretending to be atheists). This ironic twist is probably what saved it from destruction. The museum is open from 10 am to 5 pm daily except Monday. Admission is $6.

Ethnographical Museum

The open-air ethnographical museum (Etnografichesky muzey) of reconstructed buildings is one of the best in the country for a portrayal of indigenous and early Russian life. The exhibits begin just inside the entrance, with reconstructions of prehistoric burial mounds and stone totems, and trace the region's vernacular history through to the wooden buildings of the early 20th century.

A complex at the right rear includes yurts (nomadic tent houses, more recently used as summer outbuildings) as well as cabins adopted by the eastern Buryats when they settled down in the 19th century. Nearby, a small Buddhist temple, in a Buryat synthesis of Tibetan, Chinese and other styles, has an exhibit on temple architecture. The buildings that look like a cross between a yurt and a house are typical of the western Buryats. Note the icons inside: these people converted to Christianity. Also here are clothes and utensils for Tsagaalgan

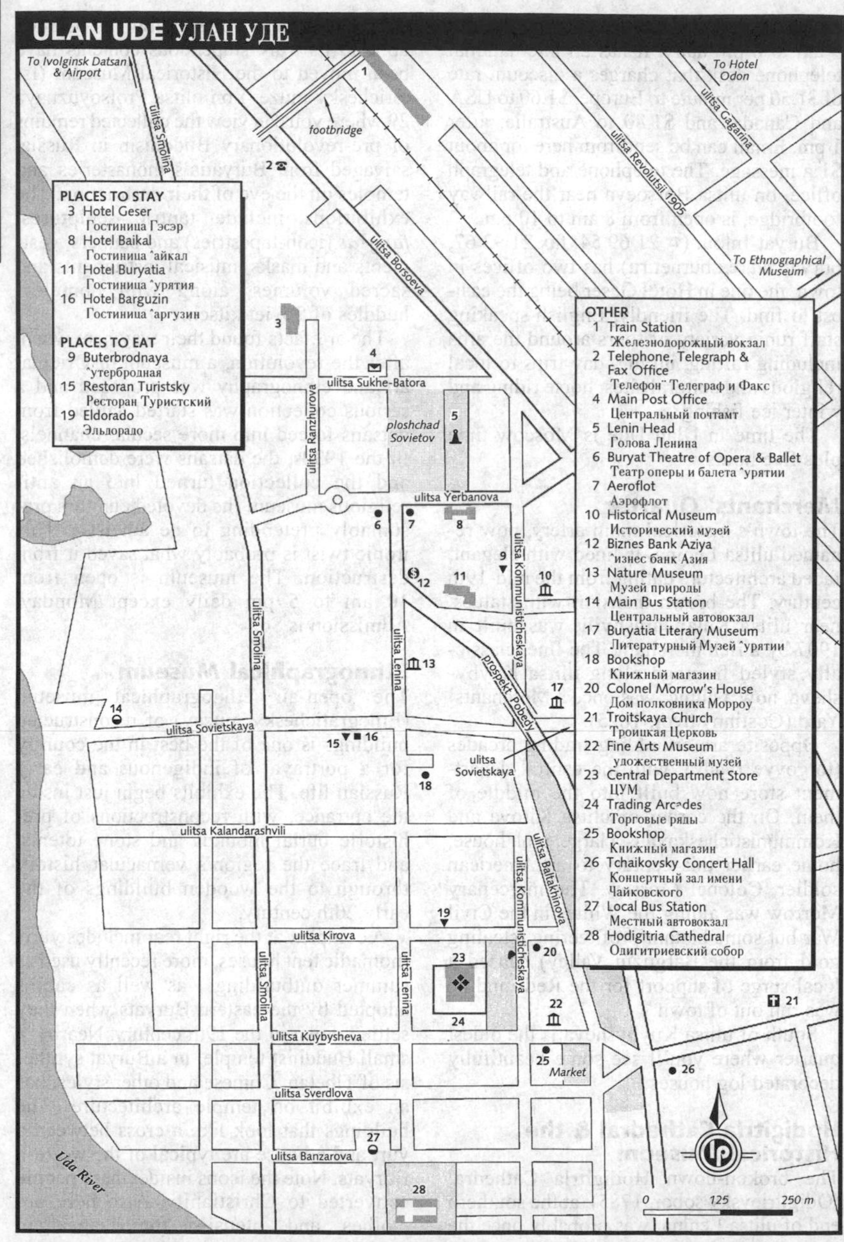
ULAN UDE УЛАН УДЕ
To Ivolginsk Datsan & Airport
To Hotel Odon
To Ethnographical Museum
footbridge
ulitsa Smolina
ulitsa Borsoeva
ulitsa Revolutsii 1905
ulitsa Gagarina
ulitsa Sukhe-Batora
ulitsa Ranzhurova
ploshchad Sovietov
ulitsa Yerbanova
ulitsa Lenina
ulitsa Kommunisticheskaya
prospekt Pobedy
ulitsa Sovietskaya
ulitsa Kalandarashvili
ulitsa Baltakhinova
ulitsa Kirova
ulitsa Kuybysheva
ulitsa Sverdlova
ulitsa Banzarova
Uda River
Market
0 125 250 m
PLACES TO STAY
3 Hotel Geser
Гостиница Гэсэр
8 Hotel Baikal
Гостиница ^айкал
11 Hotel Buryatia
Гостиница ^урятия
16 Hotel Barguzin
Гостиница ^аргузин
PLACES TO EAT
9 Buterbrodnaya
^утербродная
15 Restoran Turistsky
Ресторан Туристский
19 Eldorado
Эльдорадо
OTHER
1 Train Station
Железнодорожный вокзал
2 Telephone, Telegraph & Fax Office
Телефон Телеграф и Факс
4 Main Post Office
Центральный почтамт
5 Lenin Head
Голова Ленина
6 Buryat Theatre of Opera & Ballet
Театр оперы и балета ^урятии
7 Aeroflot
Аэрофлот
10 Historical Museum
Исторический музей
12 Biznes Bank Aziya
^изнес банк Азия
13 Nature Museum
Музей природы
14 Main Bus Station
Центральный автовокзал
17 Buryatia Literary Museum
Литературный Музей ^урятии
18 Bookshop
Книжный магазин
20 Colonel Morrow's House
Дом полковника Морроу
21 Troitskaya Church
Троицкая Церковь
22 Fine Arts Museum
удожественный музей
23 Central Department Store
ЦУМ
24 Trading Arcades
Торговые ряды
25 Bookshop
Книжный магазин
26 Tchaikovsky Concert Hall
Концертный зал имени Чайковского
27 Local Bus Station
Местный автовокзал
28 Hodigitria Cathedral
Одигитриевский собор

celebrations. A low yurt at the rear has a still for making that Central Asian standby, *kumys* (fermented mare's milk).

There are also examples of an Old Believers' settlement, including an exquisite village gate (1906) and a tiny chapel. Through the woods to the right is a complex of Evenki bark-and-skin teepees. The shaman's yard has totems of the higher world – fish, moose and bear – in front of his house and those of the lower, or dark, world at the rear, along with birds as 'guards'.

The museum is open from 10 am to 5 pm daily from June to August. It's 6km from ploshchad Sovietov on bus No 8 (which leaves you about 1km away but runs frequently). Admission is $4.50

Other Museums

Ulan Ude's other museums are small and of marginal interest. The **Fine Arts Museum** (the grey edifice on ulitsa Kuybysheva) features Buryat and other Eastern decorative and fine art. Letters, manuscripts and sepia photos make up the collection of the **Buryatia Literary Museum** at Sovetskaya 27. The **Nature Museum**, at ulitsa Lenina 46, concentrates on the wildlife of Lake Baikal and the wetlands of the Selenga Delta. Opening hours for all three museums are from 10 am to 5 pm daily except Monday.

Places to Stay

The cheapest beds in town are at ***Hotel Odon*** *(☎ 34 34 80, ulitsa Gagarina 43)*, a large, sombre establishment 2km from ploshchad Sovietov. There are 200-plus single/double rooms for $11/16. To get there from the train station, come out of the front entrance and turn right, walk to the end of the street, then head east along ulitsa Yerbanova. Ulitsa Gagarina is the third turn on your left.

Hotel Baikal *(☎ 21 37 18)*, on ploshchad Sovietov, is passable and reasonably cheap with rooms for $23/36. The best of the cheaper hotels is ***Hotel Barguzin*** *(☎ 21 57 46)* on ulitsa Sovetskaya. Like most Siberian hotels in summer, it doesn't have hot water. Rooms are $25/40.

The most comfortable place in town to stay is the old Party hang-out, ***Hotel Geser*** *(☎ 21 81 51, ulitsa Ranzhurova 11)*. This is a modern, well maintained hotel trying hard, and coming close, to achieving an international standard of service. It has an international telephone in the foyer, a sauna (for $19 an hour) and a billiard room. Rooms are $34/51 in the high season (June to September) and $31/48 during the low season, breakfast included. One annoying thing about this hotel, the phone starts ringing hourly in the evenings. It's the local escort service looking for business. They hang up if a female voice answers.

Ulan Ude's flagship hotel, ***Hotel Buryatia*** *(☎ 21 18 35, ulitsa Kommunisticheskaya 41a)*, seems keen to revive the spirit of the good old, bad old days with service that is unrepentantly Brezhnevesque, a restaurant given over to riotously partying locals, and a cafe on a par with the worst train station stolovaya. It's possible that, approached in the right frame of mind, the Buryatia could be fun; and the rooms themselves are reasonably comfortable at $46/77.

Places to Eat

The restaurant at ***Hotel Buryatia*** is popular as the town's number-one party spot. If you prefer to eat, the food is reasonable enough and includes some local specialities such as *poza*, the Buryat version of meat dumplings. The food at ***Hotel Baikal*** is cheap but near inedible. For the same price, much better is the ***Restoran Turistsky***, next door to Hotel Barguzin. Soup, a dish of meat and potatoes and tea will come to $2; it's open from 11 am to 4 pm and 6 to 11 pm.

Hotel Geser has two eating options: the cafe (open 24 hours except for breaks) serves one or two mediocre meals throughout the day for around $4, while the restaurant (open from noon to 11 pm) has a more extensive menu but higher prices. The best place in town, and popular with the business crowd, is the ***Eldorado***, also a bar and casino on ulitsa Kirova across from TsUM near the market. Meals go for $3 to $6; it's open from noon to 4 am, but sometimes closed between 4 to 7 pm.

This is Russia

We walked into the Intourist office in Ulan Ude, plopped our LP guide on the counter, and noted the director's friendly smile immediately frost over.

'You don't realise the headaches *that* book has given me', she said, launching into a tirade. 'Travellers come in here, they're in a bad mood. The conductor on the train offended them, they got accosted by a drunkard in a cafe, the cathedral they went to see was boarded up, the restaurant where they thought they'd have dinner is no longer there. And then, after all that, they open up *that* book and tell me "But it's written right here". Please, can't you add somewhere in bold that this is Russia!'

So there you have it.

For snacks, there's the ***Buterbrodnaya***, by the tram stop on ulitsa Kommunisticheskaya, a small cafe that has sandwiches, pastries and sour local beer on tap. There are also a few food stalls around the central market, east on ulitsa Kuybysheva.

Getting There & Away

Air There are direct flights almost daily to/from Irkutsk, Moscow and Vladivostok. Other Siberian connections include two a week to Chita and Omsk. There's also one flight a week to St Petersburg. The Aeroflot office is on the corner of ploshchad Sovietov and ulitsa Lenina; it's open from 10 am to 1 pm and 2 to 5 pm Monday to Saturday.

Train The *Rossia* arrives daily, bound for Moscow (train No 1), at 4.34 pm local time, and bound for Vladivostok (train No 2) at 1.30 pm. The trip to Moscow takes about four days, and about 2½ days to Vladivostok. There is one other daily service to Moscow, as well as one to Novosibirsk on even-numbered days. There are additional daily trains heading east to Chita, Blagoveshchensk and Khabarovsk.

Ulan Ude is the last major Russian city for Trans-Mongolian travellers en route from Moscow to Beijing. Train Nos 5/6, the Moscow-Ulaan Bataar express, and 263/264, Irkutsk-Ulaan Baatar (change at Naushki), also halt at Ulan Ude. For further details see the Trans-Siberian Railway chapter.

Bus There are daily buses north to Ust-Barguzin, from where it's possible to take a hydrofoil once a week across Lake Baikal to Irkutsk; and south to Kyakhta on the Russia-Mongolia border.

Getting Around

Bus No 10 goes between the airport and ploshchad Sovietov, near Hotel Baikal. East from ploshchad Sovietov, the No 10 bus goes to the train station.

IVOLGINSK DATSAN ИВОЛГИНСКИЙ ДАЦАН

This monastery at the foot of the Khamar-Daban Mountains – though Lhasa it's not – is reason enough to visit Ulan Ude. It held out as the centre of Buddhism in the USSR and today there are about 30 lamas here, mostly trained in Mongolia.

Near the front gate is the main temple, built in 1972. Its interior is a riot of colour, with hundreds of Buddha images and tangkas saved from other temples or donated from around the world. The four 'guardians' at the rear are recent paintings by Buryat artists. In the right front corner of the compound is a smaller temple, and to the left there's a round shrine to Maitreya.

To the left of the main temple is a museum containing the pride of the monastery: a beautiful 108-volume, handmade, richly illuminated Ganjur, or Buddhist scripture, in Tibetan, plus the 225-volume Danjur (commentaries) in Sanskrit, and hundreds of quaint and kitsch gifts to the monastery.

Other buildings include a library, behind the main temple, and the datsan's first building, a green temple at right rear. Nearby are sacred reliquaries called stupas and a tree said to be grown from a cutting of the original Bodhi Tree. The lamas' houses are at the back and the one with the stone lions is for the head lama, who is also head of all Buddhists in Russia.

Around the perimeter are prayer wheels. These cylinders full of prayers on scraps of paper are turned clockwise to 'activate' them. In fact, everything is done clockwise so as to keep one's right side to venerated objects. Visitors are welcome in the temples and may observe the ceremonies, which tend to start by 8 or 9 am and go on for two or three hours. The lama at the rear of the hall is the one to ask about taking photos. The temple is closed in the evening.

Buryats flock here, and on any given day they'll be lined up outside the lama houses to ask (and pay) for advice on medicine, family etc. Note the lamas' Mercedes parked around the back.

Getting There & Away

Ivolginsk is 30km west of Ulan Ude. From the bus station, bus No 104 to Kalyonaya will take you directly to the monastery, or bus No 130, which departs throughout the day, will take you as far as the village of Ivolga. From there follow the road out of the village and you'll see the datsan glinting in the distance, off to your right. It's a 4-5km walk and considerably longer if you attempt a short cut across the marshy plain with its many hidden streams.

KYAKHTA
КЯХТА

The marooned remainders of former opulence and its proximity to the Russian-Mongolian border make Kyakhta, 200km south of Ulan Ude, a fascinating excursion for the romantically minded. Although artefacts have been found in the area that date back as far as 2000 BC, the town itself was only founded in the early 18th century when the first Cossacks arrived and drove back the Mongol tribes who bred their cattle and hunted here.

As Kyakhta grew, it became a staging post on the tea route from China through Mongolia to European Russia. The shrewd townsfolk began to operate as intermediaries between merchants in Canton and Shanghai and the fur traders in the Russian cities of Siberia. By the mid-19th century, as many as 5000 cases of tea a day were arriving in Kyakhta and the town's trading links extended to Great Britain, and even North America. It became a town of millionaires. Architects from Europe designed mansions for the town's merchants, and Kyakhta's cathedral was said to hold more treasures than any other church in Siberia and reputedly had solid silver doors embedded with diamonds, rubies and emeralds.

The glorious state of affairs was brought to an end with the completion of the Trans-Siberian Railway. Almost overnight, all the tea was redirected via Vladivostok. By the time Luigi Barzini and his team drove through Kyakhta in 1907 (described in his book *Peking to Paris*), all the riches here had dried up.

Kyakhta today is like a movie-set town. Its one main street (ulitsa Lenina) is lined with stately stone buildings and behind them is almost nothing: wooden shacks clustered limpet-like on the steep valley sides, and bare hills beyond. The town's main role is as a heavily militarised border post, and the road in from the north is lined with tanks, armoured vehicles and, distant in the fields, helicopters like colonies of big black insects.

Things to See

A few indications of Kyakhta's past wealth survive in the grand colonial-style blocks on ulitsa Lenina. One of these buildings, 400m north of the bus station, houses the impressive **Regional Museum**, which is strong on geology and archaeology. Just south of the bus station, in a small green park, is the crumbling shell of what appears to have been quite an impressive church. The overgrown churchyard is home to a small fair but, like the church, the rides are long neglected and now little more than rusting skeletons. Some 800m farther south along ulitsa Lenina is the town's still-functioning, well maintained **Orthodox Church**.

If two churches of such size seems excessive in a town of such modest proportions, then the best is yet to come. A few kilometres beyond the Orthodox church, is what was once **Kyakhta Cathedral**. Designed in part by an Italian architect, with its elegant classical porticoes, central dome flanked by smaller cupolas and graceful, four-tiered bell tower, the cathedral would not look out of place in Rome or Paris. However, while externally it's fairly complete, inside the building has been gutted: there's no furniture, no decoration – nothing except a rubble-strewn hollow. To add to the incongruity, the cathedral stands almost alone on wasteland with few other buildings in the vicinity, just some tumbledown shacks and a small factory with a life-sized silver Lenin out front (he has an identical golden twin in town; both look as though they fell out of a cereal packet). This spot is in fact a crossing point on the **Russia-Mongolia border**.

Barely 50m south of the cathedral runs a chain-link fence with a guarded gate. Beyond is a customs house, then another fence, and then the plains of Mongolia. There's usually a small camp of people waiting on the Russian side to cross. It's obvious from the makeshift camps and fires that crossing here involves a long wait, and foreigners should not attempt it. With no nearby amenities, the cathedral's bell tower functions as a public toilet.

An alternative way to reach the cathedral, other than by the main road, is to climb the hill behind the bus station and follow the tank tracks. The series of huge red-brick buildings down to the right are old **tea warehouses** of the Merchants' Yard (Gostinny dvor).

Places to Stay & Eat

There are several lodgings in Kyakhta, but the only stars are the ones you'll see on your way to the bathroom. Try the ***Turist*** *(☎ 9 2431, ulitsa Lenina 21)*. There are a couple of ***cafes*** in the centre of town, as well as shops selling bread, cheese, sausage and other basic provisions.

Getting There & Away

There are daily buses to/from Ulan Ude. The journey takes five to six hours but the scenery is marvellous, if you like steppe. A one-way ticket costs about $10. A bus also runs between Kyakhta and Naushki, 25km west, from where there is a daily train to/from Irkutsk, via Ulan Ude. Naushki, a small, modern settlement, is also the last Russian station on the Trans-Mongolian rail route. There's a train once a day from here to the Mongolian town of Suhbaatar (also known as Sukhe Bator).

East from Ulan Ude

CHITA
ЧИТА

☎ 30222 • pop 315,000

Chita began life in 1653 as a Cossack stockade at the confluence of the Ingoda River and its tributary the Chita. Its status was considerably improved when in 1827 it became the residence of a group of the exiled Decembrists. After building their own prison, they went on to dig irrigation systems and cultivate the land, all initially as a means of improving their own lot but ultimately also benefiting the greater nonexile community. Under the influence of the exiles, Chita developed into a busy commercial and agricultural centre. The present-day city still has a commemorative ulitsa Dekabristov, though ulitsa Damskaya (or Ladies' Street), named in honour of the exiled Decembrists' wives and mentioned in the 1900 *Guide to the Great Siberian Railway*, seems to have disappeared.

The completion of the Trans-Baikal railway in 1900 consolidated Chita's importance, putting the town on line with both Vladivostok and Moscow. Since then, light engineering has grown to form the backbone of the regional economy. When the East Chinese Railway opened in 1901, Chita became the guardian of this route into Manchuria and home to a large military presence. For this reason the city was closed to foreign visitors until the late 1980s.

Orientation & Information

Central Chita is laid out on a grid pattern with the railway running along its southern edge. Immediately north of the train station is the sports stadium and, two blocks farther, the awesome expanse of ploshchad

Lenina. Bisecting the square, running east-west, is the wide, boulevard-like ulitsa Lenina, the city's main thoroughfare. Parallel to Lenina, three blocks south, is ulitsa Amurskaya, the main shopping street (still sometimes called by its previous name, ulitsa Kalinina).

Chita time is Moscow time plus six hours.

Things to See

The city is perhaps worth only a day's visit. There's a good **Military Museum**, housed in one of the most impressive buildings in town at ulitsa Lenina 86. There is also a fairly dull **Regional Museum** at ulitsa Babushkinskaya 113 and an **Art Museum** at ulitsa Chkalova 120.

Places to Stay

If you need to stay overnight, try ***Hotel Turist*** *(☎ 6 52 70, ulitsa Babushkinskaya 40)* or the 19th century ***Hotel Dauria*** *(☎ 6 23 65, ulitsa Amurskaya 80)*, entered round the corner on ulitsa Profsoyuznaya. The rooms are a little faded but still quite elegant with great high ceilings.

Getting There & Away

Chita is 6200km from Moscow and the last major Russian city on the route of the Trans-Manchurian (No 19/20) before the line branches off for China 100km east, at Tarskaya, crossing the border at Zabaikalsk.

BLAGOVESHCHENSK
БЛАГОВЕЩЕНСК

☎ 41622 • pop 210,000

This industrial city and regional capital is interesting mainly for its location – across the Amur River from the Chinese town of Heihe – and its stormy history. It began as a military outpost in 1644, under the name Ust-Zaysk, and was seized by the Manchurians 45 years later. The Russians, under the command of Nikolay Muravyov, took it back in 1856 and gave it its present name, which means 'Good News'.

By the end of the century Blagoveshchensk, thriving on Sino-Russian commerce, was larger and of greater importance than either Vladivostok or Khabarovsk. But in 1900, to avenge European deaths in the Chinese Boxer Rebellion, Cossacks slaughtered all of the Chinese people in the city. The dead numbered in the thousands. During the years of the Cultural Revolution, the Chinese subjected Blagoveshchensk to 24 hour propaganda blasted from loudspeakers across the river; the Soviets trained the guns of their tanks at China and fumed.

Nowadays, there is again a lively cross-border barter trade, encouraged by the free-trade zone that was declared between the Chinese and Russian cities in early 1994 (the first of its kind anywhere in Russia). There's an exchange of people also, with the shortage of labour in the Russian Amur region being remedied by importing Chinese workers. Russian and Chinese tourists cross to and fro. Westerners, however, are not allowed to cross, and the local police are quite touchy about foreigners showing up here without the city listed on their visa.

The town still retains some traces of tsarist elegance and a bust of Chekhov on the wall of one of the oldest buildings records that he spent the night there in June 1890, on his way to Sakhalin.

Blagoveshchensk time is Moscow time plus six hours.

Places to Stay

There are a number of hotels in town: ***Hotel Druzhba*** *(☎ 9 05 40 ulitsa Kuznechnaya 1)*, ***Hotel Zeya*** *(☎ 2 11 00, ulitsa Kalinina 8)* and ***Hotel Yubileynaya*** *(☎ 2 11 19, ulitsa Lenina 108)*.

Getting There & Away

The city is 110km off the Trans-Siberian on a branch line from Belogorsk, itself 660km from Khabarovsk. There is a direct overnight Khabarovsk-Blagoveshchensk fast train (No 185), a 17 hour trip.

AROUND BLAGOVESHCHENSK
Muravyovka Nature Reserve

About 60km south-east of Blagoveshchensk and reachable by bus is the Muravyovka nature reserve, a working farm and protected marsh lands where several species of rare and endangered cranes breed. The reserve, which shares its name with the nearby village, accepts guests for a reasonable fee. Your visa must have Blagoveshchensk and Muravyovka listed on it. Quarters are no-frills (a shelf in a trailer when we were there), though they're trying to put in solar panels for lights.

Contact Sergei Smirensky at amur@glas.apc.org or Elena Smirensky at elena.icf@baraboo.com.

Sakha Republic Республика Саха

YAKUTSK ЯКУТСК

☎ 41122 • pop 198,000

Yakutsk was founded in 1632 as a Cossack fort, and later served as a base for expeditions to the Pacific coast and the far northeast. The most unrepentant dissidents (including Decembrists and Bolsheviks) were exiled here. Yakutsk was, in fact, mainly a 'jail without doors'. There was no need for bars or locks: isolated amid millions of square kilometres of bug-infested, swampy forest that became one great deep-freeze for eight months of the year, no one was going anywhere. Some tried, but their bodies usually turned up in spring, uncovered by the melting snow. Hence the runaways became known by the nickname 'snowdrops'.

When it became apparent in the late 19th century that the Yakutian earth had more to give up than just corpses, the fortunes of the town underwent a dramatic change. Prospectors, adventurers and mining companies needed a base from which to exploit the newly discovered mineral wealth of the Lena River basin, and Yakutsk became a kind of 'Wild East' version of Dodge City. Supplied by Lena shipping, the town was a boozy, bawdy rest-and-recreation centre for the region's gold-miners, who rolled in to blow their wages on drink and women. The biggest building in town was the vodka factory. It supplied countless bars and a ring of brothels staffed by women from Moscow and Europe doing a little prospecting of their own. Drinking would progress to brawling and there'd be deaths, with some men murdered for their pay packets. When, one way or another, the money was gone it was back to the mines for another six months to a year of hard labour.

Today, Yakutsk – now capital of the Sakha Republic (formerly Yakutia, or the Yakut Autonomous Republic) – is a drab, ugly town of collapsing wooden houses, mud and dust in spring, grimy snow and black ice in winter. January temperatures sometimes plummet to below -60°C but usually they teeter around -30°C – still cold enough to send the town into hibernation. As if that weren't sufficient to keep dogged travellers at bay, in 1994 local authorities imposed their own visa regime and all visitors arriving at Yakutsk airport now have to pay the equivalent of around $75 admission. That's a lot of money for physical discomfort, bad food and a few small museums.

The people and landscapes of the far north, not Yakutsk, are the reason to visit this area, and there's no point coming unless you're able to spend some money on excursions – along the Lena, into the tundra or to see Yakuty or Evenki villages. And by all means, make sure you have each city or village you plan to visit on your visa so that you don't run afoul of the police. Sakha did not formally secede from Russia; but its immense wealth, size and distance from Moscow makes it a world of its own.

Orientation & Information

The main street is prospekt Lenina, most of it between ploshchad Druzhby to the west and ploshchad Ordzhonikidze to the east. The Lena River is east of Ordzhonikidze and the port is reached by following ulitsa Khabarova north from prospekt Lenina and then bearing right. The bus station is more central, just 500m north of Lenina on ulitsa Oktyabrskaya. Maps can be found in the kiosks and bookstores.

You should be able to change money at the banks or at Hotel Ontario; better yet, do it before you come. The main post and telegraph office is on ploshchad Ordzhonikidze. YakutIntour has its offices at ulitsa Arzhakova 6, which is just south of ploshchad Lenina.

The time in Yakutsk is Moscow time plus six hours.

Museum of History & Culture

This museum was founded at the beginning of the 20th century by Yemelyan Yaroslavsky, Yakutsk's favourite exile, who married a Yakut and later went west to join the Bolsheviks. It includes Esyakh festival props, the interiors of Yakut summer and winter houses, a room devoted to Yakut shamans, a kayak from the first Russian polar expedition and the skeleton of a woolly mammoth.

The museum, housed in what was once the residence of the Bishop of Yakutia (a long-defunct post), is at prospekt Lenina 5, near ploshchad Ordzho-nikidze. Also in the complex are a tower from the original Cossack fort, a whale skeleton and Yaroslavsky's house.

Other Museums

You can't miss the **Yakut Literary Museum**, shaped like a giant yurt, 1½ blocks north of prospekt Lenina on ulitsa Oktyabrskaya. Inside are exhibits on Yakut authors, musicians and playwrights and their Kazakh linguistic and literary roots. It's all quite well done, but obscure unless you have a guide.

The Academy of Sciences building, ulitsa Petrovskogo, has a starchy geological museum. There is also an **Academy of Sciences Institute of Permafrost**, which sounds about as exciting as a lump of frozen soil, but is actually worth a visit. Yakutsk is probably the only large city completely built on permafrost and, as such, it suffers some quite unique problems. Building on permafrost is like building on ice and, as the Yakutians have discovered, contact with a building's concrete or brick foundations thaws the frozen earth. The result is subsidence and there are many lopsided houses and blocks to be seen around town. Researchers have discovered that the only way to keep a building steady and upright is to sit it on stilts bored 10m into the ground. At the Permafrost Institute visitors can descend into a cavern at just such a depth, where the temperature stays constant at around -5°C.

Places to Stay

Hotel Sterkh *(☎ 24 27 01, prospekt Lenina 8)* has 44 single/double rooms for $83/131 and is 10 minutes from the airport. ***Hotel Ontario***, about a 20 minute drive from the city centre, looks like a traditional Yakut log building, but inside it's all modern Western conveniences including – the greatest luxury of all – hot water.

Hotel Yakutsk *(ulitsa Oktyabrskaya 20/1)* has thin walls, seatless toilets and chairs held together by string, but it's near the bus station.

Getting There & Away

Daily direct flights from Moscow cost about $600 and take six hours. There are also connections once a week to/from Khabarovsk and Vladivostok ($227). The unmarked check-in desk for foreigners is around the right end of the terminal (facing the planes).

During summer there are twice-monthly sailings by ship and more frequent hydrofoils between Yakutsk and the port of Ust-Kut, nearly 2000km upriver. See the earlier Ust-Kut section for further details – but note that, while it takes only 4½ days to sail to Yakutsk, the journey in the opposite direction, which is against the current, takes a whole week.

The other option, for the devotee of off-the-beaten-track travelling, is to take the bus – there is a 1200km highway between Yakutsk and the town of Bolshoy Never on the Trans-Siberian line, passing through the BAM town of Tynda. We believe there is some kind of regular service.

One reader, who made the 2000km trip between Yakutsk and Magadan on a motorbike, reports: 'It is quite difficult to pass in summer since parts of the road follow on rivers and are impassable when the rivers are not frozen. You can take a boat on the missing sections.'

When the KGB Knocks on Your Door

It was midnight and I was primed for that long-awaited bath after having travelled through half of Siberia. Soon I was up to my neck in seventh heaven, with every dusty village, screaming babushka and psycho-drunk encountered on this trip far far away. But then there was a knocking in the distance that got louder and louder.

I scrambled out of the tub and reached for a towel. It was the size of a bath mat. My clothes on the floor were drenched. 'Hold on', I shouted, pulling on last week's outfit from my backpack and opening the door.

Into my hotel room stepped a stocky, middle-aged Russian man. He wore wrinkled pants and a short-sleeved shirt, unbuttoned to show his chest had a lot more hair than his head. He said something about being from the police department and asked if the blonde girl with him could sit down. The next thing I knew, I was being asked to sign what in Russian is called a *protokol*. (It's basically an admission of guilt. After you sign it, there is little your country's embassy in Moscow can do to help.)

'I can't', I blurted. 'I don't have the legal right to.' He stood there batting his bloodshot eyes. A man like this probably doesn't get refused too often. Breathing vodka into my face, he said, 'But I thought you Americans were so free!' 'You've been misinformed', I said. 'It's you here in Russia who really are free.' This pleased him. We began to talk about his city, which I told him was truly remarkable, one of the best cities I've been in. Then I asked for his name. This was probably a mistake. He remembered the *protokol*.

'No, really, I'm not allowed to sign it.' 'OK', he answered, 'Then I'll just take your passport'. I shook my head. 'You can't have it. It's US government property.' In a way I felt sorry for him. He was drunk and just trying to do his job. 'Look', I said, 'You go home. I'll come by the police station in the morning.' As I closed the door behind him, I could see onto the square where another balding head, this one of Lenin, was bathed in moonlight.

Had I been in any other city in Russia, I probably would have packed my rucksack and left. But I was in Mirny, in the middle of the tundra, more than 5000km from Moscow. It took me two days on the Lena River through Yakutia to reach this mining city and I knew it would be near impossible to leave right now. I had come to the town because of the diamond operations in and around Mirny, which were once the USSR's most tightly held secret. In my mind, that had made Mirny a must-do.

The next morning, I get to the police station at exactly 9 am. Cramped behind a wooden school desk, a large woman in a too-tight uniform is waiting for me with another *protokol*, this one affirming that I hadn't signed the first. I refuse to sign this too. 'Get the witnesses in here', she screeches. Into this small room shuffle two more Russians, one who barely looks 18 and the other, a flighty woman in her 30s, completely clueless as to what is happening, who gives me her address and invites me to her home.

The preliminary interrogation begins. The woman officer accuses me of arriving in Mirny three days ago (I had arrived two days earlier, a critical point because I still had one day left to register with the police). She says that I refused to show the hotel administrator my passport (the administrator never asked) and that I didn't have Mirny written on my visa (this was

AROUND YAKUTSK

The territory of the Sakha Republic covers approximately 3 million sq km, almost half of which is within the Arctic Circle and almost all within the permafrost zone. It's some of the most inhospitable terrain in the whole Russian Federation. The town of Verkhoyansk, 650km north of Yakutsk, holds the record as the coldest inhabited spot on earth with temperatures recorded as

When the KGB Knocks on Your Door

true). I explain to her that Russian law does not require a tourist to have every city listed. 'But this is Yakutia', she snaps.

'As far as I know, Yakutia is a republic of Russia, so according to the Russian Constitution ...'

'Hah!! What Constitution!?' she sneers.

My heart sinks into the permafrost right beneath us. As I turn to go, I hear her say to the officers on duty, 'Don't let her leave!'

Just a week ago, when I had been in Khabarovsk, a panicking Intourist agent told me a client she had sent to Blagoveshchensk was fined as he stepped off the train because he did not have the city listed on his visa. She complained about the militsiya preying on foreign tourists to supplement miserly salaries. Maybe all I needed to do was whip out some cash (I had about $500 on me) but something told me that my situation was different. The previous day, I had held an uncut diamond worth $1 million that had been pulled from one of the dozen open pits around Mirny.

The office I'm ushered into has a large colour TV in one corner, and a basketball game is on with the volume turned off. In chairs against the wall sit the policewoman and a pudgy, beady-eyed man in a brown suit. He starts firing questions at me. Immediately it becomes clear that he has a theory why I am in Mirny. Though he doesn't use the word *spionka* (spy), it is obvious he thinks he has caught one. 'Why did you come here? Who sent you?'

I tell him I write for LP; he looks at me like I am from another planet. The police chief who is sitting behind a large desk in full view of the TV begins reading aloud from a document. Thinking it's about time I call Moscow or the insurance company that is supposed to rescue LP writers from these tricky situations, I try to interrupt him. His voice drones on. I turn to watch the game but my heart is doing rebounds. I wonder how they know so much about who I am and what I have done in my two days. Then I remember a dark-haired man who called himself Sergei. He had attached himself to me as soon as I arrived in Mirny. He followed me to the museum, to lunch, and asked lots of questions about who I knew and what my plans were. I told him that I wanted to go to the north, then to Yakutsk, the republic capital. He looked hard at me and lowered his voice, 'I don't think you'll be able to', he said. Later, someone informed me that this man was a FSB (the renamed KGB) major. Naturally, I didn't believe my source.

'So', the police chief says, finally looking up at me. 'By presidential decree ... '

He means Nikolaev, the President of Yakutia.

'The punishments are imprisonment, fine OR exile', the police chief proceeds. My only rebuttal – that having more about Yakutia in this LP guide might be good for the republic – seems a little lame.

Then, just as I begin to fathom the next six or so months in a permafrost jail cell, the telephone rings. Before I know it, the police chief is screaming at the wall for a car. I have no idea who called, but I do know miracles can happen, even in Mirny. The chief's last words to me: 'You must depart from Yakutia immediately.'

I thank him, and an hour later I am on a plane to Moscow.

Suzanne Possehl

low as -71°C (in the nearby valleys of the mountains of Oymyakon they go down to -82°C). At such times, according to Yakut lore, if you shout to a friend and they can't hear you it's because all the words have frozen in the air. But when spring comes, all the words thaw and if you go back at the right time you can hear everything that was said months ago. Summer is brief and quite uncomfortable: June, with its midsummer 'white nights', is blighted by rains and infested with mosquitoes (to such an extent that reindeer are said to have been suffocated by the midges swarming up their nostrils); July is hot and fetid; and August is perhaps the only agreeable month. On midsummer nights the sun barely sets.

The average density of the Sakha Republic's one million people (of whom 30% are Yakut) is approximately one for every 3 sq km. Most people live along the Lena River and its tributaries.

In this austere, frozen wilderness the size of India, Evenki and Chukchi still hunt for a living on the Arctic coast, Yakuty tend horses and cattle as if this were Central Asia, and Russian engineers scratch away at stupendous underground riches – oil and gas, coal and tin, gold and diamonds.

The heart of Sakha's diamond industry is the town of Mirny, 800km west of Yakutsk, while Aldan (accessible by rail from the BAM town of Tynda) is the servicing centre for the gold fields.

Lena Pillars
Ленские столбы

Sakha's main highway is the 4400km-long Lena River, which originates in the mountains to the west of Lake Baikal. It's navigable for five months of the year, but during the other months, frozen to a depth of 5m, it serves as an icy route for conventional wheeled traffic.

The Lena Pillars (Lenskie Stolby) are huge, tower-like sandstone formations that line the river for an 18km stretch, about 140km south of Yakutsk. There reportedly is a tourist hydrofoil that during summer makes regular four-hour sailings up to the rocks and allows time for picnicking or climbing before sailing back downstream to the city. The cost of the excursion is approximately $100.

MIRNY
МИРНЫЙ

☎ 41136 • pop 39,000

The first thing you'll notice in Mirny if you arrive by plane is a 1.5km-wide, 500m-deep, spiralling hole. It's a diamond mine, and diamonds are why the city was founded in 1955. After the Yakutian wilderness, Mirny – with its neat, 10-storey buildings on stilts, well laid roads and children's park with giant swings and other amusements – looks like paradise in the tundra.

But first impressions can be deceptive. While 'mirny' in Russian means peaceful, the local authorities tend to view foreigners as potential diamond thieves, spies or just unwanted free spirits in a highly controlled, strategically important area.

If you go, make absolutely sure you have the city listed on your visa, and carry some sort of official-looking paper explaining who you are and why you're there (see the previous boxed text 'When the KGB Knocks on Your Door').

Orientation & Information

It's impossible to get lost in Mirny. One road, ulitsa Lenina, runs 5km from the airport to ploshchad Lenina, on which stand the city administration building, the House of Culture and the town's only hotel.

To change money, there is a bank, about 500m north of the hotel, near the TV tower. The post and telephone office is on ulitsa Karla Marxa, near the intersection with ulitsa Lenina.

Mirny time is Moscow time plus six hours.

Things to See

There are two factories on the outskirts of the city where the diamond ore is processed. The rough *almazy* are then taken to an unmarked, highly secure building in the city centre for sorting. Both these places are strictly off limits.

The closest you can get to the diamond operations is the open 1km-deep pit which has an **observation platform**. A taxi from the hotel will cost about $5; alternatively it's about a 4km walk.

Mirny also has two good, centrally located **museums** where you'll find out more than you ever wanted to know about diamond production in Russia. For a bit of the real thing, there are two nearby shops selling the polished jewels, but the prices are high and the quality isn't that good because all the best stuff is sent to Moscow and Yakutsk.

Places to Stay & Eat

Hotel Zarnista is Mirny's only accommodation, and is a real treat with hot water and electricity. However, it's not exactly cheap, with rooms starting at $30. The Imperial-style ***restaurant*** in the lobby is good and meals are about $4.

Getting There & Away

There are only two ways to get to Mirny: by the daily 8 am bus (a five hour ride) from Lensk, on the Lena River, or by plane. Mirny has good air connections, thanks to the diamonds.

There are daily, and sometimes twice daily, flights to Moscow ($596, eight hours) as well as flights to and from Lensk, Chita and Yakutsk.

The Russian Far East
Дальний Восток

The Russian Far East is the geographical term for the territories that run along the Pacific seaboard, from Chukotka in the north, with its Arctic coastline, down to Primorsky Kray, squeezed between China, Korea and the Sea of Japan. It includes the Kamchatka Peninsula and the string of Kuril Islands which arc down to Japan, enclosing the Sea of Okhotsk and the large, fish-shaped island of Sakhalin.

HIGHLIGHTS

- Strolling along the Amur riverfront in Khabarovsk
- Checking out the naval nostalgia and sushi bars in Vladivostok
- Discovering the whistling stone beaches of the Sikhote-Alin nature reserve, home of the Siberian tigers
- Visiting Sakhalin Island for Stalinist ghost towns, still-grinning Lenins and the world's slowest railroad
- Spending a night on a live volcano, combing the black sand shores where sea lions bask, touching down in the extraterrestrial Uzon Caldera on the amazing Kamchatka Peninsula

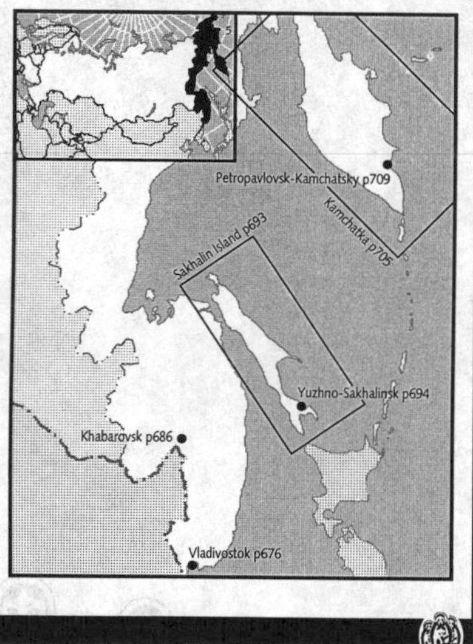

Primorsky Kray
Приморский Край

Vladivostok is the capital of Primorsky Kray (Maritime Territory) – also known as Ussuriland – the arm of land that lies bounded by China on the east and the Sea of Japan to the west.

VLADIVOSTOK
ВЛАДИВОСТОК

☎ 4232 • pop 730,000

For more than 30 years Vladivostok – meaning 'Lord of the East' – was a closed city, known only as the secrecy-shrouded home of the Russian Pacific Fleet. But these days the fleet is a rusting and disintegrating relic of a past that the city is very keen to shake off. The new Vladivostok is looking to rapidly reinvent itself as Russia's money-making, fast-spending, high-living commercial and financial centre in Asia – a role with which it's not altogether unfamiliar.

Founded in 1860 during Russia's second push across the Amur River, Vladivostok abruptly became the main Russian Pacific naval base when Port Arthur fell in the Russo-Japanese War. In 1891, Tsarevich Nicholas II made a visit to inaugurate the new Trans-Siberian rail line that was to link Vladivostok with Moscow and reinforce shaky Russian influence in the region. Korean and Chinese labourers had built the city and in the early 20th century they accounted for four out of every five of its

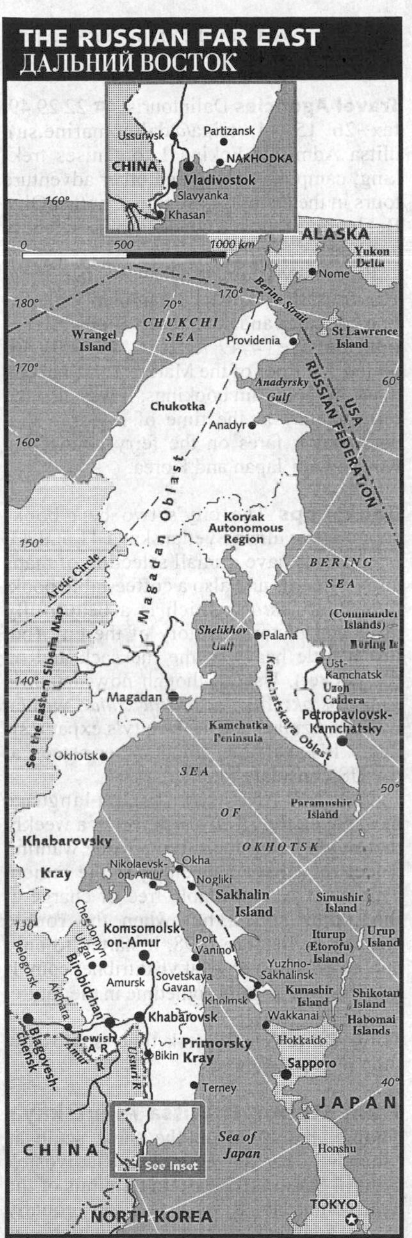

citizens. In addition, cosmopolitan Vladivostok teemed with French hoteliers, German store owners, Swiss speculators and merchants and sailors of every nation in a manner more akin to Shanghai or Hong Kong than to Moscow.

When the Reds seized power in European Russia in 1917, Japanese, Americans, French and English poured ashore here to support the tsarist counterattack. After the head of the White army, Admiral Kolchak, was defeated and executed at Irkutsk in 1920, Vladivostok held out for another two years, until Soviet forces finally marched in and drew the curtain. In the 1920s, 40% of men of working age had been Chinese, but Stalin got rid of them in 1938 by shooting several hundred accused of being spies, and deporting another 10,000. As the eastern terminus of the Trans-Siberian, Vladivostok also became the recipient of other deportees.

The northern suburb of Vtoraya Rechka became a transit centre for hundreds of thousands of prisoners waiting to be shipped up to labour, and most likely perish, in the gold fields of Kolyma. The US consulate – the only Western diplomatic office in the Soviet Far East – was forced to close in 1948 and the city was closed off entirely in 1958.

The US consulate has reopened now after 50 years, signifying the return of the outside world to Vladivostok. The difference is already visible. Four out of five motorists drive Japanese or Korean cars, while the local business personnel, who brought the vehicles over, throw around wads of roubles in the Casino Versailles. The city isn't quite on its feet; it is still looking a little pale and suffering from a nasty post-Soviet hangover, but it is recovering faster than most other places. Vladivostok is one of the very few towns or cities in Siberia and the Russian Far East that doesn't just serve as a base for wilderness exploration but is worth visiting in its own right.

Orientation

Physically, Vladivostok is one of Russia's more attractive cities. The centre is ranged in tiers on the hills surrounding the crooked finger of the Golden Horn Bay (bukhta Zolotoy Rog). South of the bay are residential and business districts, while the main commercial centre is on the north side, with its main axis ulitsa Svetlanskaya (formerly Leninskaya) running parallel to the waterfront. Near ulitsa Svetlanskaya's western end a couple of wide boulevards run off north, laboriously climbing the bayside hills; this area constitutes the city's 'downtown'. The city's main junction, site of traffic snarl-ups and congested pavements, is where ulitsa Aleutskaya (formerly ulitsa 25 Oktyabrya) intersects ulitsa Svetlanskaya. About 800m south of this crossroad, on ulitsa Aleutskaya, is the train station.

The majority of Vladivostok's hotels are west of ulitsa Aleutskaya, all within 10 minutes walk of the station. Running north, ulitsa Aleutskaya feeds into other major roads to become the main highway out of the city, passing through the Sanatornaya region, where there's a grouping of good but pricey hotels, and on to the airport.

You might want to look out for the *Vladivostok turistskaya skhema*, a reasonably accurate map of the city centre, or a 1:125,000 map, *Vladivostok and its Suburbs*, which is useful if you're planning on making any trips out of town. Most bookshops and some of the newspaper kiosks in the city centre should stock these.

Information

Money There are currency exchange desks in all the major hotels, at the Marine Terminal (Morskoy vokzal) and the Vostok Business Bank, at Verkhneportovaya 3, which also gives cash advances on Visa card at 2.5% commission.

Post & Communications The main post office is on ulitsa Aleutskaya, opposite the train station. Envelopes, stamps, post boxes etc are on the first level (the stairs are on the left immediately as you enter the building), while on the ground level is the international telephone, fax and telegraph office, open 24 hours daily.

The best place to receive and send email, for about $0.50 a message, is the business centre across from the train station, next door to the post office.

Travel Agencies Dalintourist (☎ 22 29 49, fax 26 15 44, taiga@dalint.marine.su), ulitsa Admirala Fokina 1, organises trekking, camping, rafting and other adventure tours in the Primorsky region. Contact Olga Bekhtereva who is knowledgeable, friendly and speaks English.

Primorsky Club (☎ 31 80 37, fax 32 07 10), ulitsa Russkaya 17, can help with airline bookings and hotel reservations. Biznes Intur Service (☎ 49 73 91/93, ☎ 30 01 46) on the 3rd floor of the Marine Terminal can make air and train bookings; it was also the only agency at the time of research that could book fares on the ferry connecting Russia with Japan and Korea.

Bookshops The city's two best bookshops are at ulitsa Svetlanskaya 41 and 43. Both shops have a small selection of maps and postcards and also a coffee-table book, *Old Vladivostok*, which is a beautifully produced pictorial history of the city (but just a little heavy in the rucksack and on the pocket). Useful, though now dated, is *Vladivostok: Your Essential Guide* written by Erik Azulay, one of the city's expat residents. It's available, among other places, at the US consulate for $7.

The city also has its own English-language newspaper, the *Vladivostok News*, a weekly that might be of interest to anyone wanting a feel for what's happening in the region. The paper was available free of charge at the major hotels, but when the rouble crashed in October 1998, it started to only appear on the Internet at vlad.tribnet.com. It may be back in print sometime in the future.

Time Zone Vladivostok time is Moscow time plus seven hours.

Train Station & Ulitsa Aleutskaya

Though not quite on the same scale as Moscow's Yaroslavl Station, Vladivostok Central Station (the eastern terminus of the Trans-Siberian Railway) is an equally exotic architectural concoction which was built in 1912. The ceiling in the main hall is decorated with some bold and bright socialist and pre-1917 paintings that have benefited, like the rest of the building, from renovation. The trains run in a cutting below street level and a bridge beside the station leads over the tracks to the large, characterless block of the Marine Terminal.

Across the road from the train station is a small paved terrace where the drunks gather at the feet of an unusually animated Lenin who, curiously, as if he'd known all along how things were going to turn out, stands gesticulating toward Japan, the country whose money Vladivostok now so assiduously courts.

Ulitsa Aleutskaya, formerly ulitsa 25 Oktyabrya (the date on which the Bolsheviks 'liberated' Vladivostok during the civil war), is lined with grand buildings, some of which were built by Japanese prisoners of war. The house at No 15 (the yellow building next door to the offices of the Far Eastern Shipping Company) once belonged to the family of Yul Brynner, born in Vladivostok in 1920. Brynner's grandfather, originally from Switzerland, had an import/export empire with offices throughout Manchuria and eastern Siberia. The one-day-to-be King of Siam never saw merchant service: he left Vladivostok aged four, carried to Paris by his mother, a newly abandoned wife. There's nothing to be seen at the house but there is a display devoted to Yul and the Brynner family in the Arsenev Regional Museum.

Waterfront & Ulitsa Svetlanskaya

The heart of Vladivostok is **ploshchad Bortsov za Vlast Sovietov na Dalnem Vostoke** (the Square of the Fighters for Soviet Power in the Far East) – it must be up for renaming soon – with a large **monument** to the fighters as its centrepiece. The monument acts as a focal point for musicians, orators and sloganeers of all kinds when the police, on ever-increasing alert, are not around. The square was Alexander Solzhenitsyn's first stop-off point on his internationally heralded return to Russia in 1994. On Monday and Friday, the square turns into a market where cheap Chinese and South Korean wares are sold. The monolithic slab at the western end of the paved plaza is the **White House** (Bely dom), home to the regional administration.

Before the inhabitants of the White House became responsible for shaping the city's future, the real tower of power in Vladivostok was just a few hundred metres away on the harbour road (ulitsa Korabelnaya Naberezhnaya) in the form of the headquarters of the Pacific Fleet. Next door, an S-56 submarine *(podvodnaya lodka)* lies moored on a grassy plot as a reminder of the fleet's glory days. The submarine, which sank 10 enemy ships during WWII, serves as a **museum**, and while the mainly photographic collection isn't too enthralling, clambering around inside is fun. It's open from 10 am to 1 pm and 2 to 6 pm Monday to Saturday (though sometimes the sailors on duty will let you in after hours); admission is $1.50. Opposite floats the *Krasny Vympel*, the Soviet Pacific Fleet's first ship, now also a **museum**.

Immediately north of the submarine museum, a flight of steps leads up to connect with ulitsa Svetlanskaya. Much of the architecture on this street dates from the late 19th century and bears a marked European influence. The nearby **GUM department store**, originally built by Germans towards the end of the 19th century, is now filled with domestic appliances from Japan and Italy.

Arsenev Regional Museum

The Arsenev Regional Museum (Kraevedchesky muzey Arseneva) – named for a late 19th century ethnographer/writer – at ulitsa Svetlanskaya 20 must be one of Siberia's most eccentric museums. On the ground level is the customary array of stuffed wildlife, snakes in jars etc, but the collection also includes a rare Amur leopard (unlikely to be seen anywhere else) and two Siberian tigers.

On the 2nd floor, among other things, there are Japanese ceramics, a display dedicated to the Brynner family, some interesting bits of geology and a hall housing temporary exhibitions. The museum also

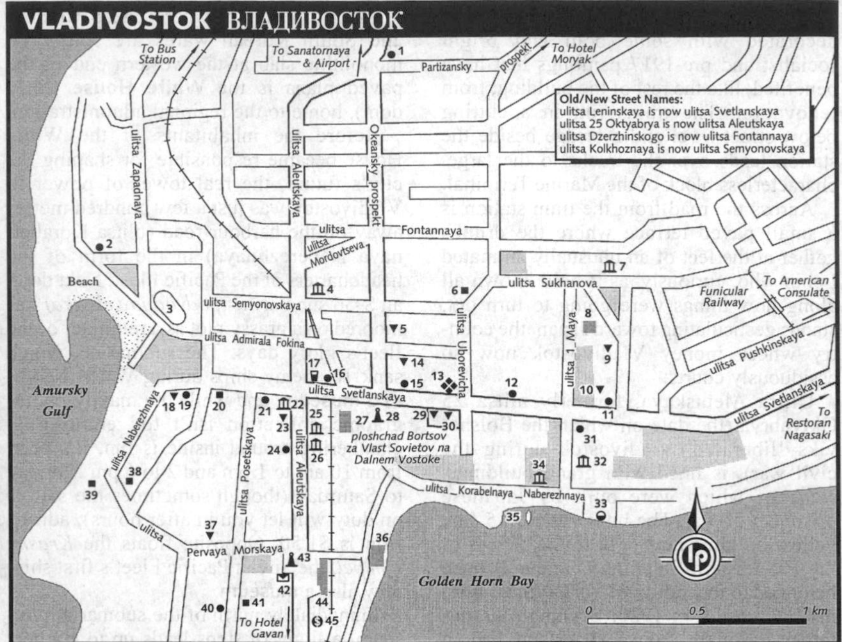

offers a chance to purchase a little bit of history, in an antique and bric-a-brac store off the lobby, full of Soviet badges, coins and tablecloth-sized flags, assorted old bank notes, icons and other memorabilia. The prices are extremely reasonable.

The museum is open daily from 10 am to 5.30 pm except Monday. The admission price is $1.50.

In a separate building of the city museum (filial muzeya Arseneva) on ulitsa 1 Maya, beside the Kino Komsomolets, is a real *Boy's Own* treat with a line-up of gleaming chrome and enamel 1930s racing bikes, a motorcycle and sidecar with a great girder-length machine gun mounted between the handlebars, and a collection of plastic model kits that as a young kid you might have disowned your parents over.

Other Museums

Hemmed in by Japan, Korea and China, this southerly protuberance of Russia has an awful lot of border to police, so it shouldn't be too surprising that the **Border Guards' Museum** (Muzey boevoy slavy pogranvoysk) is quite as large and impressive as it is. It's also now home to the **Museum of the Pacific Fleet** that, until recently, occupied the Lutheran Church near the funicular farther east. The museum is the big peach building at ulitsa Semyonovskaya 17-19. It's open from 9 am to 1 pm and 2 to 5 pm Tuesday to Saturday, except for the last Friday of each month.

A few minutes walk (downhill, mercifully) from the funicular viewpoint is the **Sukhanov Museum** (Muzey Sukhanova), ulitsa Sukhanova 9, named for the early 20th century city councillor whose home it was. The museum is simply his house preserved with its period furnishings. It's open from 10 am to 7 pm every day except Monday; admission $1.50.

The **Primorsky Art Gallery** (Primorskaya kartinnaya galereya), ulitsa Aleutskaya 12,

VLADIVOSTOK ВЛАДИВОСТОК

PLACES TO STAY

6 Hotel Hyundai
Гостиница Хундай
20 Hotel Versailles
Гостиница Версаль
38 Hotel Vladivostok
Гостиница Владивосток
39 Hotel Amursky Zaliv
Гостиница Амурский залив
41 Hotel Primore
Гостиница Приморье

PLACES TO EAT

5 Krishna Kafe
Кафе Кришна
9 Zhemchuzhina Pizzeria
Пиццерия Жемчужина
10 Zhemchuzhina
Ресторан Жемчужина
14 Edem
Элем
18 Okean
Ресторан Океан
23 Kafe Ldinka
Кафе Льдинка
29 Magic Burger
Маджик Бургер
30 Kafe Taims
Кафе Таймс
37 Nostalgia Cafe & Restaurant
Ресторан и кафе Ностальгия

OTHER

1 Market
Рынок
2 Aquarium
Аквариум
3 Stadium
Стадион
4 Border Guards' Museum
Музей боевой славы погранвойск
7 Sukhanov Museum
Музей Суханова
8 Gorky Theatre
Театр имени М. Горького
11 24 Hour Pharmacy
Круглосуточная аптека
12 Bookshops
Дом книги
13 GUM Department Store
ГУМ
15 Kino Ussuri
Кино Уссури
16 Philharmonic Hall
Филармония
17 Blue Star Cabaret
Кабаре Синяя звезда
19 Kino Okean
Кино Океан
21 Flotsky Magazin Store
Магазин Флотский
22 Arsenev Regional Museum
Объединённый краеведческий музей им. Арсенева
24 The Brynner House (No 15)
Дом Бриннера
25 Art Gallery/Art Salon
Картинная галерея/салон
26 Primorsky Art Gallery
Приморская картинная галерея
27 White House
Белый Дом
28 Monument to the Fighters for Soviet Power in the Far East
Памятник борцам за власть советов на Дальнем Востоке
31 Kino Komsomolets
Кино Комсомолец
32 (Separate building of) Regional Museum
Филиал краеведческого музея
33 Ferry Terminal
Вокзал прибрежных морских сообщений
34 Submarine Museum
Подводная лодка-музей
35 Krasny Vympel Ship Museum
Корабль-музей Красный вымпел
36 Marine Terminal
Морской вокзал
40 Aeroflot Office
Аэрофлот
42 Main Post Office
Главный почтамт
43 Statue of Lenin
Памятник Ленину
44 Central Station
Железнодорожный вокзал
45 Vostok Business Bank
Восток бизнес банк

is also something of a surprise, with a large number of 17th century Dutch works and some excellent works by Russian painters, including a piece by Kandinsky (according to Erik Azulay's guidebook – see Bookshops – it also has an early Chagall but we couldn't find it). Admission is $2 and includes entry to the contemporary gallery on the ground level. The museum is open from 10 am to 1 pm and 2 to 6.30 pm Tuesday to Saturday; 11 am to 5 pm Sunday.

Other Attractions

Directly behind the Lutheran church, a **funicular railway** (funikulyor), open from 7 am to 9 pm daily, connects ulitsa Pushkinskaya with ulitsa Sukhanova, which is about 200m farther up the steeply sloping hillside. Even if the funicular isn't working, it's worth your while tackling the adjacent steps to get to the top and a superb panorama of the bay.

At the western end of ulitsa Svetlanskaya is a small **park**, busy with photographers and their props, food sellers and the odd busker. Beyond the park, there's a narrow strip of sandy beach before the chilly waters of the Amursky Gulf (Amursky zaliv).

A few hundred metres north of the beach, past the sports stadium, is the **Okeanarium**, a large aquarium with live fish and marine creatures and stuffed birds. A little farther along the shoreline road is a pen containing some Beluga whales.

Places to Stay

One general word of caution about the budget to medium-priced hotels: Vladivostok is experiencing a severe energy shortage which means that hot water is a rarity, and even cold water disappears on occasion. Keep your bathtub full. The hotel administrator usually keeps a list where you can reserve a free 20 minute splash in the sauna room showers. It's also possible to rent the sauna; expect to pay $15 to $20 an hour.

Central Those whose optimum concern is money and not comfort or hygiene might want to check out ***Hotel Moryak*** *(Partizansky prospekt 14)*. This place is popular with visiting Russian students and the rooms are only $7. Staff were a little wary of giving a room to a foreigner but if you can speak some Russian there shouldn't be any problem. A student identity card might also help. To get there take any bus going north up Okeansky prospekt and get off at the Kartinnaya Galereya stop, right in front of the hotel – a looming, chateau-like building with a twin flight of steps up to the front door.

At ***Hotel Vladivostok*** *(☎ 41 06 10, fax 41 20 21, ulitsa Naberezhnaya 10)*, the former flagship of the Soviet era, the rooms are clean enough, with attached bathrooms, and half of them have great views over the Amursky Gulf. Singles/doubles are $33/73. The whole of the 4th floor of the Vladivostok has been leased to a private company that runs it as ***Hotel Visit*** *(☎ 41 13 00, fax 41 06 13)*. The rooms have been renovated and refurbished and come with satellite TV, direct international phone lines and fridges stocked with beer and juice. Rooms are $66/81.

There are two other concrete-hive hotels in the immediate vicinity of the Vladivostok. ***Hotel Amursky Zaliv*** *(☎ 22 55 20, ulitsa Naberezhnaya 9)*, dug into the cliff side (the top floor is at street level), has received some bad reports but we had no problems with it except for the oodles of noisy Chinese tourists chasing Russian prostitutes. The rooms were clean and comfortable and our bathroom had been newly tiled. Most rooms have balconies overlooking the bay. Rooms were from $34/80.

Close to the train station, ***Hotel Primore*** *(☎ 41 14 22, fax 41 34 05, ulitsa Posetskaya 20)* is a newly renovated establishment adjacent to a fast food restaurant. Rooms with shower are $48/53.

Though there is an insistence on pronouncing it *'ver-SAH-les'*, ***Hotel Versailles*** *(☎ 26 42 01, fax 26 51 24, ulitsa Svetlanskaya 10)* is suitably palatial, especially the long, low, vaulted reception hall which, unless you're packing a wallet full of gold American Express cards, is intimidating enough to send you scurrying back out to the gutter. The rooms are sumptuous, with every conceivable facility, but then the cost is $180/240 per night.

Just south of the city centre, ***Hotel Gavan*** *(☎ 51 24 15, fax 51 24 25, ulitsa Krygina 3)* is a quiet, proper business class hotel. Rooms are $125-135/149-159, including breakfast and use of the swimming pool. Vladivostok's grand hotel is the new, looming ***Hotel Hyundai*** *(☎ 40 74 03, ☎/fax 40 70 07, ulitsa Semyonovskaya 29)*. Rooms are $220.

Sanatornaya Sanatornaya is a wooded coastal suburb, seven stops out on the train or a 30 minute drive north of the centre. Despite being about midway between the airport and the city there's no particularly good reason to stay out here – the tranquillity of the location is countered by the nightmarish traffic that clogs the sole highway into the city. However, several of the city's most exclusive hotels are situated here. The ***Vlad Motor-Inn*** *(☎ 21 58 54, satellite phone ☎ 509-851 51 11, fax 851 51 16)*, a Canadian/Russian venture, describes itself as 'a little piece of Northern America'. The description is spot-on and the rooms are just as comfortable as any from Vancouver to Ottawa with big soft beds to sprawl on while you watch MTV or CNN and suck on a Moosehead. There's even guaranteed hot water. The adjacent restaurant has a menu full of burgers and cheesecake. The double rooms are $180 and credit cards are accepted.

In close vicinity are ***Hotel Enkay*** *(☎ 21 54 22, ulitsa Devyataya 6)*, a lavish ex-nomenklatura hang-out with rooms at $100, and the slightly cheaper ***Hotel Pansionat*** *(☎ 21 58 40, ulitsa Devyataya 14)*, originally built for the summit between Brezhnev and US President Gerald Ford that took place in 1974.

Places to Eat

It's possible to eat well in Vladivostok and it's possible to eat cheaply, but not both at the same time. The ***Vlad Motor-Inn*** (see Places to Stay) serves fantastic food, concentrating on American staples (burgers, ribs, club sandwiches) but also including some more general continental dishes – but you're looking at $15 per head for a meal without drinks. Antipodean cuisine gets a look-in at the joint Russian-Australian ***Captain Cook's*** on the ground level of Hotel Pansionat (see Places to Stay). The steaks are good (around $10), and there's kangaroo and crocodile, both of which will take a fair-sized bite out of your credit card.

Of the restaurants at the city's central hotels, the best is at ***Hotel Versailles*** but it is unwarrantedly expensive. Better value is ***Nostalgia*** *(ulitsa Pervaya Morskaya 6/25)*, a restaurant that eschews the starkness of Soviet-era eating for tsarist lavishness. The small, low-ceilinged dining room is carpeted with a plush red pile that also covers the lower half of the walls; the upper half is papered with a heavy damask, all of which combines to give the effect of sitting inside a jewellery box. The menu is Russian traditional and the food is excellent. Dishes are $5 to $8. There is also a cafe and gift shop.

The food at ***Zhemchuzhina*** (Pearl), a stylish Italian restaurant off ulitsa Svetlanskaya, is also very good. The restaurant specialises in seafood and meat in wine sauces ($4 to $5). The restaurant is 50m back from the street, just east of the junction with ulitsa 1 Maya. Around the back with a separate entrance is ***Zhemchuzhina Pizzeria***, a favourite with the rich and beautiful. The pizza is mouth-watering escapism. Close your eyes, click your knife three times and you're home.

Seafood features heavily on the menu at ***Okean*** *(ulitsa Naberezhnaya 3)*, an attractive restaurant with good service and views over the Amursky Gulf, next door to the cinema. Main courses are about $6. ***Nagasaki*** *(Svetlanskaya 115)* has Russified Japanese food for $5 to $9 a meal.

For a quick, inexpensive meal the best place is ***Kafe Taims***, on ulitsa Svetlanskaya, with creative offerings like Mexican-style cutlet (pork smothered in cheese, peppers and onions). The desserts are yummy and the cappuccino is genuine. The most popular eatery in town is next door, ***Magic Burger*** *(ulitsa Svetlanskaya 44)*, a fast-food joint that will either make you give up burgers for good or pledge your life to McDonald's. The service is speedy and the papier-mache pizzas and burgers are cheap ($0.80 each).

Certainly the most surreal eatery in this part of Russia is ***Edem*** near the corner of Okeansky prospekt and ulitsa Admirala Fokina, one block north of the fighters statue. Go down the stairs, past the wannabe rock stars and you're in a cellar with low stone arches, high wooden tables and mannequins dressed in period costumes. The main fare is sushi. The kitchen is open from noon to 2 pm and 6 to 11 pm; the bar stays open until 2 am.

Vegetarians could check out ***Krishna Kafe*** *(Okeansky prospekt 10/12)*. ***Kafe Ldinka*** *(ulitsa Aleutskaya 23)* is centrally located; it comes close to a Western-style cafe and is a good place to sit over coffee and ice cream.

For self-caterers the state department store, ***GUM*** *(ulitsa Svetlanskaya 35-37)*, is amazingly well stocked with a lot of stuff imported from Japan. It is also worth exploring if only because it's such a beautiful building. For fresh fruit and vegetables, the ***market*** is at Pervaya Rechka every day from 10 am. Take tram No 7 from in front of the train station, and go north for six stops.

Entertainment

Compared to the rest of Siberia and the Russian Far East, Vladivostok is a party city. ***The Blue Star*** *(Sinyaya zvezda; ulitsa*

Svetlanskaya 13) has erotic dancing. The bar at ***Hotel Amursky Zaliv*** is a favourite with Chinese tourists. Hotel Versailles has a ***casino***, open from 8 pm until the early hours. The hot spot at the moment is ***Crazy***, a disco on the top floor of the Marine Terminal. ***The Sky Bar***, on the 12th floor of Hotel Hyundai, is good for putting on the ritz.

Gorky Theatre (*Teatr Gorkogo; ulitsa Svetlanskaya 49)* is the city's main venue for drama, while the ***Philharmonic Hall*** *(Filarmoniya; ulitsa Svetlanskaya 15)* is next door to the Blue Star. ***Kino Okean*** *(ulitsa Naberezhnaya 3)* shows dubbed recent US releases, while ***Kino Ussuri*** on ulitsa Svetlanskaya has the latest Russian shoot 'em ups.

If you are at all interested in sport, Erik Azulay's book (see Bookshops) recommends attending a game at the ***football stadium***, where if the match leaves you less than thrilled the view from the stands across the Amursky Gulf provides fine compensation.

Shopping

Traditional handicrafts are on sale at Nostalgia, ulitsa Pervaya Morskaya 6/25. Other places to look for lacquered boxes, matryoshka dolls, painted trays and jewellery are the Art Salon down the stairs at ulitsa Aleutskaya 14 and the Art Gallery on the ground level of the same building. For souvenirs of Soviet Russia try the Regional Museum, or the Flotsky Magazin at Svetlanskaya 11, which used to be the army and navy supplies store and still has a counter selling buttons, badges and other small bits of military insignia.

Getting There & Away

Air There are flights three times daily to/from Moscow ($300, nine hours), twice daily to Khabarovsk ($85, 1¼ hours), and daily to Irkutsk ($170, four hours) and Yuzhno-Sakhalinsk ($140, 1¾ hours). Flights go three times a week to Petropavlovsk-Kamchatsky ($250, four hours) and once a week to Magadan ($308), Yakutsk ($227) and Ulan Ude ($190).

Aeroflot has direct flights at least weekly to/from Anchorage and Seattle. Vladivostok Air flies twice a week to Niigata ($363 one way, two hours) and Seoul ($300 one way), and once a week to Pusan ($300 one way). Aeroflot has one flight a week to Bangkok ($500 one way) and Korean Air has two flights a week to/from Seoul ($380).

Train Vladivostok is the eastern terminus for train No 1/2, the *Rossia*. Making the return journey to Moscow it departs every other day at a little after 1 am local time. At the time of writing, *Rossia* left on even-numbered dates as well as on the 1st, 3rd and 5th of each month. Be sure to check the schedule carefully, as this may change. Other trains west include the daily No 5 *Okean* overnight to Khabarovsk and No 7 *Sibir* to Novosibirsk; the No 53, which departs every other day (odd-numbered, and on the 2nd and the 4th) to Kharkiv, in Ukraine; and the daily No 185 to Blagoveshchensk. There is also a daily service to Sovgavan (No 251) for Port Vanino on the Pacific coast and ships to Sakhalin Island and, westbound, to Tynda and onwards along the BAM.

Twice a week an express train connects Vladivostok with Harbin in the Heilongjiang province of northern China, from where there are daily connections to Beijing. A one-way sleeper ticket to Harbin costs $46. The train crosses the border at the Chinese town of Suifenhe and also stops at Mudanjiang.

The ticket office on the 1st floor of the railway building is only for suburban services. Tickets for long-distance trains are sold on the ground floor. Go down the main stairs straight out to the tracks, turn left and go back into the building where the sign says 'Касса'.

Boat The Far Eastern Shipping Company (☎ 261 408, www.fesco.ru), 1 Okeansky prospekt, operates ferries between Vladivostok and the Japanese ports of Fushiki and Niigata during the summer months. Basically, there is no permanent schedule for these sailings from Vladivostok to

Niigata, Toyama, Fushiki and Tokyo, and also to Pusan. Check the handwritten one at Biznes Intur Servis in the Marine Terminal. The ships are said to be extremely well run with friendly cabin staff and very good food. The voyage to Niigata takes 42 hours and 3rd class passage (lower deck, four berths per cabin) is $380, 2nd class (as for 3rd but on the main deck) is $400, while 1st (twin-bed cabins) is $730. All meals are included in the price – you may be able to get cheaper fares if you negotiate.

Getting Around

To/From the Airport There is no cheap direct connection between the airport and the city centre. Instead, take any suburban train from the central station three stops to Vtoraya Rechka (Second River). There's a bus station 150m east of the railway along the main street, ulitsa Russkaya. From there take bus No 101, the express airport service. It leaves about every 20 minutes, costs $1 and takes approximately 45 minutes. Count on about two hours for the whole journey. Coming from the airport it's the reverse procedure. From the platform at Vtoraya Rechka you get a first sight of the city to the south, so you know which direction train you should catch. Alternatively, at the airport terminal and at most hotels you can catch a minivan for about $9.

Public Transport A system of buses, trolleybuses and trams makes up the city transport network but within the centre you'll probably only need to use the trams. From in front of the train station, tram Nos 4 and 5 run north then swing east onto ulitsa Svetlanskaya, to the head of the bay; tram No 7 stays on ulitsa Aleutskaya, running north past the market. Tickets, available from the conductor, are $0.35.

Ferry From the terminal on ulitsa Korabelnaya Naberezhnaya, just beyond the submarine, ferries leave every 20 minutes for the other side of the bay. There isn't much over there but the ride itself is enjoyable, chugging along past the rusting hulls of nuclear submarines.

AROUND VLADIVOSTOK

The central region of Primorsky Kray, bounded by the Ussuri and Bikin rivers and shielded from the sea by the Sikhote-Alin Mountains, is also known as Ussuriland. The Ussuriland taiga was the setting for Akira Kurosawa's 1970 film *Dersu Uzala* (based on the book of the same name by the Ussuri-born ethnographer Arsenev). The southern forests are the world's most northerly monsoon forests and home to black and brown bears, Siberian boar, the rare Siberian tiger and the virtually extinct Amur leopard, plus hundreds of species of local migratory birds.

Sikhote-Alin Nature Reserve

A most rewarding excursion would be to the Sikhote-Alin nature reserve, headquartered in Ternei. Besides tigers, the reserve, which stretches along the Pacific Coast and back into the Sikhote-Alin Mountains, has crystal-clear salmon streams, a Savannah-like oasis where the beasts come for water and dramatic beaches of large, round stones that whistle as the aloe-green waves pour over them.

You cannot just show up though. Permission to visit the reserve has to be obtained by contacting the director of the reserve, Yevgeny Smirnov (possibly reachable at dgmn@glasnet.ru). There is no guarantee that permission will be granted (it depends mostly on how busy the reserve is) and even less of a chance you'll spot a tiger, but the wilderness alone makes the trip worth it. There was one newish ***hotel*** in Ternei; it didn't have water when we were there, but the village banya next door had plenty. In the woods, accommodation is in huts; bring a sleeping bag. Dalintourist (see Travel Agencies under Vladivostok) may also be able to help you arrange a trip here.

Four times a week, a Yak-40 plane makes the one hour journey to the village of Plastun, the nearest airport to the Sikhote-Alin nature reserve. These flights are often delayed or cancelled because rains have turned Plastun's dirt runway into mud. A ticket costs about $75, and it's hit or miss whether a foreigner surcharge will be tacked on.

Slavyanka

The locals prefer pleasures of a less adventurous nature, and a popular day trip from Vladivostok is to take the ferry from the terminal on ulitsa Korabelnaya Naberezhnaya out and across the Amursky Gulf to the port of Slavyanka, 50km south toward the North Korean border. The small town is quite attractive but the surrounding beaches are the real draw, and during summer months the beaches are filled by half the populace of Vladivostok. However, if you go far enough south it is possible to find seclusion.

En route to Slavyanka some ferries stop off at Popov Island, one of the archipelago of islands south of Vladivostok, where many of the city's residents have small plots of land or dachas. The larger island to the north of Popov is Russky Island, property of the Pacific Fleet and reputed arms arsenal – one little accident there, we were told, and the whole of Vladivostok is gone. Needless to say, the island is out of bounds.

NAKHODKA НАХОДКА

☎ 42366 • pop 178,000

Nakhodka, which means 'discovery', was little more than a landing until after WWII (and was, in its infancy, called Amerikanka). Now it's a major fishing port, spread around a sheltered bay stumbled upon by a storm-tossed Russian ship in the 1850s (hence the present name).

The town prospered as a result of being the only Soviet-era Pacific port open to foreign ships. It was also the eastern terminus of the Trans-Siberian, though few foreigners ever saw more than just the road from the train station to the quay as they were quickly ushered on board the ferry for Japan. Paul Theroux managed to take a quick look round passing through one winter, and noted in *The Great Railway Bazaar* that Nakhodka 'gives the impression of being on the very edge of the world, in an atmosphere that does not quite support life … the sort of place that gives rise to the notion that the earth is flat'. With the reopening of Vladivostok, there is no reason at all to visit this place.

Khabarovsky Kray Хабаровский Край

BIROBIDZHAN БИРОБИДЖАН

☎ 42162 • pop 90,000

At Birobidzhan, a small city 180km west of Khabarovsk on the Trans-Siberian line, the sharp-eyed might spot some strange, non-Cyrillic lettering on the station building. It's only the station name but the language in which it's written is Hebrew. This is one of the scarce present-day indications of Birobidzhan's status as capital of the Jewish Autonomous Region (Yevreyskaya Avtonomnaya Oblast).

Faced with severe poverty among the Jews in European Russia, the young Soviet government proposed the creation of a rural 'homeland' to which Jews could migrate. After a search for a thinly populated area (to minimise local backlash), 36,000 sq km on the Bira and Bidzhan rivers, tributaries of the Amur, were opened to settlement in 1927. This had the extra advantage of plugging a borderland hole that was susceptible to Japanese ambitions.

But the region was unused for good reason – it was swampy and mosquito infested, with poor soil and bitterly cold winters (January average of -26°C, extremes to -40°C). About 40,000 Jews, mainly from Belarus and Ukraine, made the trek, but only a third stayed. As a further sweetener, the area was declared the Jewish Autonomous Region in 1934.

The anti-Semitism of the Stalin years killed off the project and all Jewish institutions in the region, including the schools and synagogue, were shut down. The Museum of Jewish Culture & History was razed to the ground and the use of Hebrew was banned.

Today, 15,000 Jews account for only 7% of the region's population. With the removal of Soviet-era fetters, schools are now returning to teaching Hebrew and Yiddish. Look out for the *Birobidzhaner Stern (Birobidzhan Star)*, the local Yiddish newspaper.

Orientation & Information

The city's main streets run east-west, parallel to and squeezed between the railway line and the River Bira to the south. From the station the streets are ulitsa Kalinina, ulitsa Lenina, ulitsa Sholom-Aleykhema (the main axis), ulitsa Pionerskaya and prospekt 60 let SSSR with its twin squares, ploshchad Lenina and ploshchad Sovietov.

The main post, telephone and telegraph office is at prospekt 60 let SSSR 14. There is an office of Intour-Birobidzhan at ulitsa Sholom-Aleykhema 55. Birobidzhan time is Moscow time plus seven hours. ***Hotel Vostok** (ulitsa Sholom-Aleykhema 1)* offers accommodation.

Things to See

The **Regional Museum** (Kraevedchesky muzey), ulitsa Lenina 25, has a room devoted to the Jewish history of the region, and there's a working **synagogue** at ulitsa Mayakovskogo 11 (follow ulitsa Sholom-Aleykhema east into ulitsa Komsomolskaya, on into ulitsa Sovietskaya, and Mayakovskogo is left at the end).

The town has a **Yiddish Music & Drama Theatre** (Yevreysky muzykalny i dramatichesky teatr) and several Jewish folk-music ensembles – inquire at the Intour-Birobidzhan office for details of performances and venues.

Getting There & Away

The *Rossia* and the Moscow-Khabarovsk train both make a brief halt at Birobidzhan, as do most other services. Alternatively, it's an easy day trip from Khabarovsk, just three hours by train down the line.

KHABAROVSK
ХАБАРОВСК

☎ 4212 • pop 613,500

After the monotonous taiga of eastern Siberia and its severe wilderness towns, Khabarovsk comes as a welcome relief. It is the capital of a territory, Khabarovsky Kray, that stretches 2000km north along the Sea of Okhotsk. Khabarovsk lies at the broad confluence of the Amur River and its tributary, the Ussuri, and the town almost has the air of a coastal resort. The main street, Muravyova-Amurskogo, is a leafy tree-lined boulevard with some very attractive 19th century brick architecture, and which bustles with pizza-selling street vendors and animated window-shoppers who don't seem afraid to smile. Considering that it's almost the far side of Asia from Moscow and only 25km from China, the centre of Khabarovsk has a surprisingly European feel.

The town was founded in 1858 as a military post in the campaign by the governor general of Eastern Siberia, Count Nikolay Muravyov (later Muravyov-Amursky), to take the Amur back from the Manchus. It was named for the man who got the Russians into trouble with the Manchus in the first place, the 17th century Russian explorer Yerofey Khabarov.

Until the Trans-Siberian arrived from Vladivostok in 1897, Khabarovsk was just a garrison, a fur-trading post and an Amur River landing. During the civil war, it was occupied by Japanese troops for most of 1920. The final Bolshevik victory in the Far East was at Volochaevka, 45km to the west.

In 1969, Soviet and Chinese soldiers fought a bloody hand-to-hand battle over Damansky Island in the Ussuri River. The fighting stopped just short of all-out war but it set in motion a huge military build-up. Since 1984, tensions have eased and there's now substantial cross-border trade: the Russians buy cheap clothing, junk food and trashy video games, and the Chinese buy timber and fertilisers. In mid-1991 the Russians handed Damansky and several other islands back to the Chinese. But in 1998, as the region was engulfed by forest fires, newspapers were filled with reports that Chinese lumberjacks were illegally cutting timber on the Russian-owned islands.

The Japanese are also back in occupation, not with soldiers this time but with businesses and tourists. They make up four-fifths of all foreign visitors here and their presence in town is demonstrated by the Japanese-style hotels and the restaurants that specialise in sushi. South Koreans are also arriving in large numbers, opening many businesses in Khabarovsk, including a large TV factory. As Soviet-era industries collapse, these enterprises are providing much-needed work for locals. Unsurprisingly, Khabarovsk is actively courting further foreign interest and investment.

Khabarovskians are 80% native Russian-speakers, with small Korean and Armenian communities. The only indigenous people here in any numbers are the Nanaytsy, whose capital is Troitskoe, three hours down the Amur.

Orientation

The city is on the high east bank of the Amur (which the Chinese call Heilongjiang, or Black Dragon River), just north of the confluence with the Ussuri. Topographically, the city is like a ploughed field with the three main streets running along parallel ridges. The busiest street and central attraction is ulitsa Muravyova-Amurskogo, which becomes ulitsa Karla Marxa east of the parade square, ploshchad Lenina. South of ulitsa Muravyova-Amurskogo is ulitsa Lenina, while north is bleak Amursky bulvar with the train station at its eastern end. Khabarovsk covers a large area (in fact, 400 sq km) and it's a 3.5km walk from the train station to the riverfront and Hotel Intourist.

There are numerous maps of Khabarovsk available, in English, Russian or Chinese, gathered in an atlas (for $2) – look for them in the bookshops on ulitsa Muravyova-Amurskogo.

Information

Money There is a rash of currency exchange offices across the city. The exchange bureau at Hotel Intourist is open from 9.30 am to 8.15 pm daily. The Sberbank on Amursky bulvar across from the train station had the best rates in town when we were there. It's open from 9.30 am to 6 pm weekdays and 10 am to 5 pm Saturday, with a lunch break from 2 to 3 pm.

Post & Communications The main post office is at ulitsa Muravyova-Amurskogo 28, open from 8 am to 8 pm weekdays, and from 9 am to 6 pm on weekends. A letter from here to anywhere outside Russia will cost $0.50. This post office also has an email service, but the bewildered clerk informed us she could not send to addresses outside of Russia. (Perhaps by now, the service has gone global.) The main telephone office is at ulitsa Pushkina 56, two doors along from Hotel Tsentralnaya. Calls to North America or Australia are charged at $4 per minute and to Europe $2.50 per minute; it's open from 8.30 am to 10 pm daily. There are credit-card-operated phones at Hotel Intourist but calls are charged at a blanket rate of $8 per minute.

Travel Agencies Unfortunately, Intourist-Khabarovsk (☎ 39 91 54), Amursky bulvar 2, is the main agency in town with any experience in dealing with foreigners, usually large groups with itineraries planned in advance. It will handle individual requests for tickets but not much else. The telephone directory for sale ($5) in the lobby of Hotel Intourist lists 30 tour firms. We dialled half of them, but did not get a single answer.

Bookshops Khabarovsk is the best place east of Moscow for bookshops, with the exception of Irkutsk. The Knizhny Mir at ulitsa Pushkina 56 is the best place for maps, which are all pinned up for examination. Ulitsa Muravyova-Amurskogo 17 houses two bookshops, the Knigi and the Detskaya Kniga (Children's Books).

Film & Photography You can stock up on film at the Fuji shop in the basement of Hotel Intourist, which also offers 24 hour print processing. A similar service is available at Kodak Photo Express on the corner of ulitsa Dzerzhinskogo and Muravyova-Amurskogo.

Time Zone Khabarovsk time is Moscow time plus seven hours.

Ulitsa Muravyova-Amurskogo & the Riverfront

Among those bits of **architecture** that survived the civil war are the intricate red-brick facade of the territorial public library, built in 1900-1902, and the headquarters of the

Amur Steamship Company with its round, church-like tower. Both are on Komsomolskaya ploshchad. Dating from 1858, the attractive mint-green building at ulitsa Muravyova-Amurskogo 9, now the Merkury food store, has an equally unusual interior with decorated ceilings and colourful, carved wooden figurines in the 1st floor cafeteria.

Steps from Komsomolskaya ploshchad lead to the lively **waterfront** and a small beach. South is a string of summertime food stalls and the landing stages for the suburban river boats. A **city park** stretches 1.5km downriver (north) and its leafy paths are a favourite place for locals to take an evening stroll. The giant satellite dish, not quite hidden by the trees, receives Moscow TV programs. A few hundred metres north is a cliff-top **tower**, in which, so the story goes, a troupe of WWI Austro-Hungarian POW musicians was shot dead for refusing to play the Russian Imperial anthem. Now, it contains a cafe where you can drink coffee or beer and enjoy the view across the river.

Opposite the tower is a statue of **Count Nikolay Muravyov-Amursky**, the man who secured Khabarovsk for the tsar. During Soviet times the count was displaced by the ubiquitous Lenin but has reclaimed his plinth. Muravyov's remains actually lie in Montparnasse cemetery in Paris, the city in which he died in 1881. The **monument** at the foot of the cliff below the tower marks the spot where the city's founders first stepped ashore.

Churches

The Bolsheviks succeeded in destroying almost all of Khabarovsk's churches including the grand cathedral that stood on what is now Komsomolskaya ploshchad. The result is that this city of more than half a million people has, incredibly, only three churches. Two of these, the Orthodox **Alexander Nevsky Temple** on ulitsa Yasnaya and the **Innokentievsky Temple** on ulitsa Turgeneva, are fairly unexceptional but the third, the **Church of Christ's Birth** (Khristorozhdestvenskaya tserkov) at ulitsa Leningradskaya 65, is worth a visit. Its simple wooden construction hides a kaleidoscopic interior of coloured glass and glitzy icons. It's worth turning up to hear the mesmeric, polyphonic hymn-singing. Services are held from 7 to 9 am and from 5 to 7 pm daily, though this schedule tends to change on church holidays.

Regional Museum

This very good museum (Kraevedchesky muzey), founded in 1894, looks at the natural history as well as cultural history of the indigenous peoples of the Far East. Here you can see what an Ussuri tiger looks like (there are only a few hundred left in the wild). The archaeology section includes prehistoric rock paintings. Best are photos and exhibits featuring indigenous groups (many of them extinct or nearly so) with tools, religious art and clothing – including Nivkhi clothing made of fish skin. A 360° panorama depicts the battle at Volochaevka. There is also an arresting display about the Soviet Gulag. The museum is at ulitsa Shevchenko 11, 200m north of Komsomolskaya ploshchad, and is open from 10 am to 6 pm daily except Monday.

Other Museums

Next door to the Regional Museum is the **Art Museum** (Khudozhestvenny muzey) with a patchy assortment of religious icons, Japanese porcelain and 19th century Russian painting on the upper floor, while the lower floors are given over to displays of ethnic handicrafts, a contemporary gallery and a gift shop. Admission is $2 and it's open from 10 am to 5 pm (closed Monday).

Across the road is the **Military Museum** (Voenny muzey), which is heavy on the Russo-Japanese war and the battles fought in this area. There are some striking posters and kitsch bits of Soviet regalia and also a luxury officers-only Trans-Siberian rail carriage, but beware of being too selective with your attention because the *babushka* attendants are there to ensure that every exhibit receives attention – anyone skipping displays will be sent back. The babushkas also do a good sideline in hustling military cap badges and buttons. It's open from 10 am to 8 pm weekdays and to 2 pm

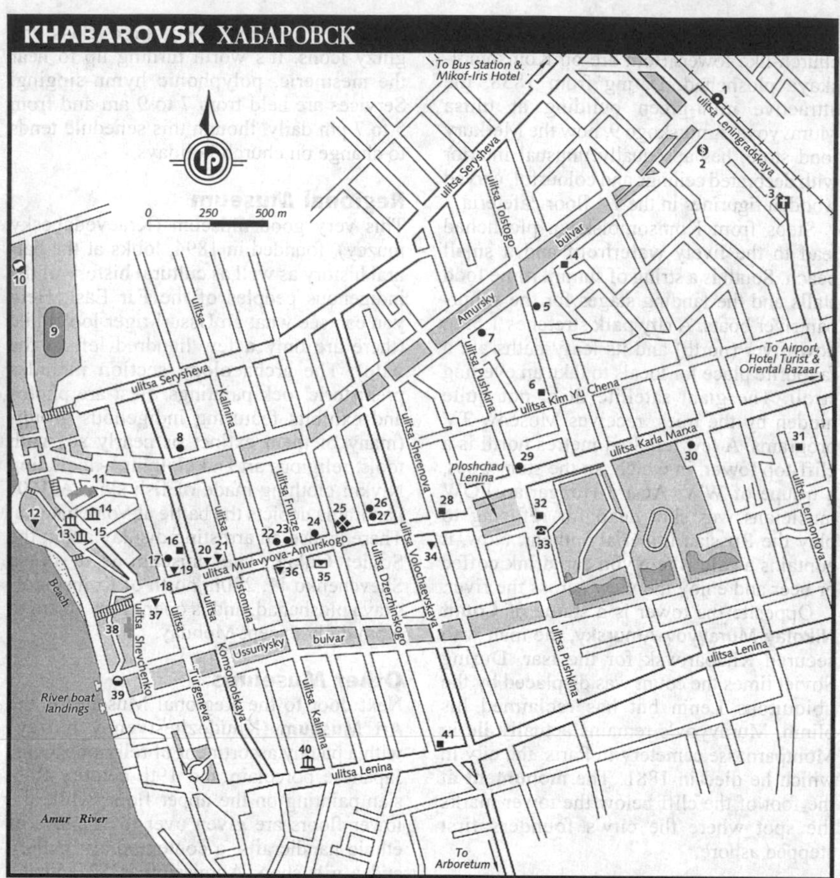

Saturday; admission is $2.50. There is also a **Museum of Geology** (Geologichesky muzey) at ulitsa Lenina 15; it's open from 10 am to 6 pm (closed Monday).

Arboretum

South on ulitsa Volochaevskaya is the Arboretum (Dendrary), a 12 hectare botanical garden. It has samples of all the trees and shrubs of the Russian Far East and is open from 9 am to 6 pm daily. Take bus No 9, 10, 25 or 29 along ulitsa Volochaevskaya to the Ussuriyskaya stop, about 3km from ulitsa Muravyova-Amurskogo.

Oriental Bazaar

This is the biggest traders market (veshchevoy rynok) in the Far East, except for maybe the one in Blagoveshchensk. From about 10 am to early afternoon, hordes of Chinese and Russian merchants fill this vacant lot with stall after stall of Russian fur hats, Turkish jeans, South Korean jackets, Chinese electronics, roller blades and shoes that dissolve in the rain. Admission is $0.15, payable at the cashiers window to the right of the main gate.

Take trolley No 1 to the ulitsa Vyborgskaya stop where cabs usually are waiting

KHABAROVSK ХАБАРОВСК

PLACES TO STAY

4 Hotel Mayak Гостиница Маяк
6 Hotel Amethyst Гостиница Аметист
11 Hotel Intourist Гостиница Интурист
16 Hotel Sapporo Гостиница Саппоро
28 Hotel of the Regional Administration Гостиница областной администрации
31 Pedagogical Institute Dormitory Общежитие педагогического института
32 Hotel Tsentralnaya Гостиница Центральная
38 Parus Business Centre Бизнес-центр Парус
41 Hotel Amur Гостиница Амур

PLACES TO EAT

12 Kafe Utyos Кафе Утес
19 Restoran Sapporo Ресторан Саппоро
20 Buterbrodnaya Бутербродная
21 Merkury Store & Cafe Магазин и кафе Меркурий
34 Kafe Bistro Кафе Бистро
36 Kafe Venetsiya Кафе Венеция
37 Restoran Zolotoy Yakor Ресторан Золотой якорь

OTHER

1 Train Station Железнодорожный вокзал
2 Sberbank Сбербанк
3 Church of Christ's Birth Христорождественская церковь
5 Circus Цирк
7 Market Рынок
8 Aeroflot Аэрофлот
9 Lenin Stadium Стадион имени В. И. Ленина
10 Chinese Consulate Китайское консульство
13 Regional Museum Краеведческий музей
14 Military Museum Военный музей
15 Art Museum Художественный музей
17 24 Hour Pharmacy Круглосуточная аптека
18 Komsomolskaya ploshchad Комсомольская площадь
22 Bookshops Книги
23 Souvenir Shop Магазин Сувениры
24 Kino Gigant Кино Гигант
25 Department Store Универмаг
26 Kodak Photo Express Фото магазин Кодак
27 Drama Theatre Драматический театр
29 Knizhny Mir Bookshop Книжный магазин
30 Theatre of Musical Comedy Театр музыкальной омедии
33 Main Telephone Office Центральный переговорный пункт
35 Main Post Office Главпочтамт
39 River Boat Ticket Office Касса речного вокзала
40 Museum of Geology Геологический музей

to take you the next 3-4km to the market for $2, or $0.50 per person if shared.

Places to Stay

Budget Several budget options exist, the cheapest of which is the ***Hotel of the Regional Administration** (☎ 32 89 57, ulitsa Muravyova-Amurskogo 33)* with a great location. The rooms are fairly spartan, with shared toilets and cockroaches, but cost only $10 per person. The hotel and reception desk are on the 1st floor (the Russian 2nd). One word of warning: the administrator on duty determines whether to admit foreigners so you might be sent away. The ***Foreign Language Department of the Pedagogical Institute*** has a student dormitory *(ulitsa Lermontova 50)* that accepts foreign visitors. The rooms are unfurnished save for beds, and are fairly grim, as are the shared toilets and showers, but it's a good opportunity to meet local English-speaking students. A bed in a single/double/triple room is $20/12/10.

To get there, follow ulitsa Leningradskaya 80m south of the junction with ulitsa Karla Marxa, then cut to the right through a gap in the buildings after the food store with the Swiss cheese on the sign; walk due west, past three apartment blocks, to reach the back of Lermontova 50. The entrance is round the front and the dormitory is on the 3rd floor.

Hotel Mayak** (☎ 32 51 31, ulitsa Kooperativnaya 11)* is conveniently close to the train station. It's housed in a fairly squalid looking apartment block but the rooms aren't too bad; singles/doubles are $23/40, all with shared toilets and showers (but no hot water in July). From the train station walk 400m along Amursky bulvar, turning left immediately after No 48. At the trolleybus No 1 stop for Maly airport, two stops before the main airport, ***Hotel Aviakompanii Vostok *(☎ 37 83 29)* is especially convenient if your flight has been postponed. There is another hotel at this stop, but it's not as nice as the Vostok which is the two storey building facing the airfield about 100m back from the main road. There was no sign on the building when we were there. The hotel administration is on the 2nd floor. Clean singles cost $20; doubles cost $33 to $40 with a private bath.

Mid-Range ***Hotel Turist*** *(☎ 37 04 17, ulitsa Karla Marxa 67)* is a typical 1970s Soviet hotel, but its boxy rooms are well maintained with TV, fridge and telephone and a clean, tiled bathroom. Rooms are $35/50. At ***Hotel Tsentralnaya*** *(☎ 32 47 59, ulitsa Pushkina 52)* you can be neighbours with Lenin, who stands just a door down at the head of his parade square. Acceptable rooms at $34/47 come with shower and toilet. The hotel is popular with Chinese and out-of-town traders. The same clientele inhabit ***Hotel Amur*** *(☎ 22 12 23, ulitsa Lenina 29)* although this hotel is considerably more grotty than the Tsentralnaya. Rooms are $24/20 per person, and a place in a three-bed room is $15.

There's a ***Mikof-Iris Hotel*** *(ulitsa Tikhookeanskaya 211)* which is a few kilometres outside the city centre. Single/double rooms are $65/40 per person. There are also some two-room suites at $94 for single occupancy, $55 each for two people, or $43 each for three. To get to the Microsurgery centre, where the hotel is located, take tram No 5 from in front of the train station and it's about a 40 minute ride.

Top End With 270 rooms on 10 floors, ***Hotel Intourist*** *(☎ 39 93 13, fax 33 87 73, Amursky bulvar 2)* accommodates almost all the packaged and prebooked tourists who hit town. The rooms all come with bathrooms and are clean, and the hotel has a plethora of bars, cafes and other amenities. However, the rooms are overpriced at $97/120.

A better alternative is ***Hotel Amethyst*** *(☎/fax 32 46 99, ulitsa Lva Tolstogo 5a)* which has 16 rooms with separate baths. Rooms are $90/130. ***Hotel Sapporo*** *(☎ 23 67 45, fax 23 60 75, ulitsa Komsomolskaya 79)* is precision-engineered to suit the requirements of Japanese business personnel, from Japanese almond soap in the sauna to the heated toilet seats. Rooms at $105/140 should be booked well in advance. The sauna with its icy pool and clean sheets to wrap yourself in while sipping strong tea afterwards makes for a good splurge at $17 per person for two hours.

As pricey and nice is the ***Parus*** *(☎ 32 72 70, fax 32 89 26, ulitsa Shevchenko 5)*, a combination hotel and business centre. The interior is a swanky version of Russian Imperial and the cosy bar on the ground floor is one of the only places in the Far East that serves a real cappuccino.

Places to Eat

Khabarovsk has some of the best restaurants in the Far East, though that's not saying much. The food is the same fare of beaten cutlets and fish smothered in cheese and onions. Gobs of Korean mayonnaise have replaced the good ol' Russian sour cream in the borsch. The stodgy, War Communism atmosphere is gone too. It has been replaced by wannabe slick: tile floors, fake plants, metallic window shades.

A prime example of this is ***Kafe Venetsiya*** on the corner of ulitsa Muravyova-Amurskogo and ulitsa Kalinina. Meals (nothing Italian) cost $4 to $8. It's open from noon to 10 pm. Slightly less expensive, ***Restoran Zolotoy Yakor*** *(ulitsa Muravyova-Amurskogo 2)*, on Komsomolskaya ploshchad, is popular with the mobile-phone crowd. This basement place is stuffy, and a keyboard looms in the corner. Your best bet for a good, quick meal is ***Kafe Bistro*** near the corner of ulitsa Muravyova-Amurskogo and ulitsa Shernova. Sandwiches are priced from $0.50, hot dishes $2 to $3, and the local beer on tap is $0.80. There's a cappuccino machine behind the counter, but don't be fooled – the stuff you get is instant.

Attracting a young, fashionable and well heeled crowd, the most popular place in town seems to be ***Restoran Sapporo*** *(ulitsa*

Muravyova-Amurskogo 3). This is really three eateries in one; it's a cafe by day and disco ($7 cover charge) after midnight on the 1st floor. On the 2nd floor, there's an old-fashioned Soviet restaurant where Russians get drunk on champagne and dance to Brezhnev-era hits. The 3rd floor sushi bar looks flashy but the menu isn't too badly priced. The Japanese trader sitting next to us rated it a 6 out of 10.

The ***Unikhab***, a swish Japanese restaurant on the top floor of Hotel Intourist, caters to Japanese business personnel. On the ground level of the same hotel, the ***Red Hall*** (Krasny Zal) is appalling. ***Korea House***, which opened in 1998, is run by a Korean-American from Los Angeles. The food is good, not great. Two main courses and three salads came to $25. The decor is Soviet, and the karaoke begins at 9 pm.

For snacks, there's lots of cheap eateries on ulitsa Muravyova-Amurskogo. In warm weather, outdoor kiosks serve shashlyk and the local version of pizza – no tomato, no meat, just a little cheese and hunks of onion. The ***Buterbrodnaya*** *(ulitsa Komsomolskaya 79)* does sandwiches and juice and is a popular hang-out for students. The nicest place for a coffee, tea, beer or ice cream is ***Kafe Utyos*** in the park overlooking the river.

The too-cute cafe at the ***Merkury store*** *(ulitsa Muravyova-Amurskogo 9)*, on the 2nd floor, will make you feel like you're seven years old again. For Trans-Siberian supplies, the Merkury store has dried fruit, nuts, cheese, biscuits etc, or for fresh fruit, try the ***market*** on Amursky bulvar near ulitsa Tolstogo.

Entertainment

There's a pitch reserved for the ***circus*** on ulitsa Tolstogo, near the market, but the show only hits town for a few months of each year, usually in early summer. There's a ***Drama Theatre*** *(ulitsa Dzerzhinskogo 44)* and a ***Theatre of Musical Comedy*** *(ulitsa Karla Marxa 64)* with a contemporary fine-arts gallery opposite.

The ***Kino Gigant*** *(ulitsa Muravyova-Amurskogo 19)* is directly across from the main post office.

Shopping

In Khabarovsk you'll find the same matryoshka dolls, painted boxes and dodgy watercolours common to all art salons and souvenir shops throughout Russia. The art salons in the Military and Art museums are pricey, and the best alternative is probably to go shopping along ulitsa Muravyova-Amurskogo. Try the souvenir shop at No 17 and the Univermag at No 23.

Getting There & Away

Air The airport at Khabarovsk is the largest in Siberia and the Russian Far East and it has direct connections with almost every other Russian airport of any size, as well as international links with several Pacific-rim countries. Domestic flights include three times a day to/from Moscow ($378, 8½ hours), twice a day to Yuzhno Sakhalinsk ($130, 1½ hours) and Vladivostok ($85, 1¼ hours), three a week to/from Magadan ($330, 2½ hours) and one a week to Yakutsk.

Internationally, Dalavia Far East Airways flies to Harbin in northern China ($150 one way), Seoul ($440 one way), Niigata ($412 one way) and once a week to Singapore ($1370 one way). Aeroflot has weekly non-stop flights to/from Anchorage ($526 return). Flights into Khabarovsk operated by other airlines include China Northern's Harbin connection, and a Seoul service with Asiana Airlines ($350 one way).

The foreign airlines all have offices on the upper floor of the airport's international terminal, a modern two storey building to the far left of the main building. The front desk at Hotel Intourist can also book seats on domestic flights and issue tickets.

All international flights are subject to a $25 departure tax, to be paid at the terminal's information desk prior to checking in. Intourist passengers making domestic flights should check in at the old international terminal, which is the odd-looking building with the portico next to the new one.

Train On the daily *Rossia* (train No 1/2), Moscow is 130 hours away, Irkutsk 60 hours and Vladivostok 13 hours. The line to Vladivostok runs only 10km from the

Chinese border in places and the *Rossia* (until the 1990s, supposedly the only train to carry foreigners in this region) has always travelled this sensitive stretch cloaked by the darkness of night. However, there are now several other services that will take you from Khabarovsk to the Pacific port.

Services westbound include the No 1 Vladivostok-Moscow train (only on odd-numbered days), the No 43 Khabarovsk-Moscow train (also on odd-numbered days) and also trains to Novosibirsk, Kharkiv (Kharkov) and Blagoveshchensk. Eastbound services include the daily No 5/6 train to Vladivostok and the train from Novosibirsk (No 8) that passes through on its way to Vladivostok on even-numbered days.

There is a daily service (No 225) to Tynda/Neryungri on the BAM. Train No 67/68 runs to/from Komsomolsk-on-Amur, another BAM station, with connections to Sovetskaya Gavan and Port Vanino for the ferry across to Sakhalin Island.

Boat There is a river connection between Fuyuan in northern China and Khabarovsk (see the following Around Khabarovsk section). Between May and October, hydrofoils run on the Amur between Khabarovsk and Komsomolsk ($14, six hours) and Nikolaevsk ($71, 15 hours). The ticket office (8 am to noon and 1 to 8 pm daily) is across from the green river boat station. When we were there the hydrofoil pulled out sharply at 6.30 am, but the schedule changes every year.

Getting Around

From the airport, 7km east of the centre, trolleybus No 1 passes Hotel Turist (Leningradskaya stop) and continues to the end of the line at Komsomolskaya ploshchad. It runs every few minutes and the trip takes half an hour. Tickets, costing $0.50, are bought from the conductor. A taxi from Hotel Intourist to the airport will cost the equivalent of $8 to $10.

The train station is at the eastern end of Amursky bulvar. From there, bus No 1 goes to Hotel Intourist. This hotel is to the left from the train station, one or two stops by any bus heading in that direction. The local bus station is on ulitsa Voronezhskaya: turn right out of the train station, follow the tram tracks round, under the railway bridge, and it's a farther 300m on the left – or take tram No 6 or bus No 11 or 6 north from the train station.

In summer, Intourist offers an open 1½ hour Amur River cruise but for considerably less you can do your own 2½ to three hour round trip by ferry to the marshy dacha suburbs from one of the landings *(prichal)* by the beach. Good choices might be the trip downstream to Green Island (Ostrov Zelyony) from landing No 5, upstream to Vladimirovka from landing No 2 or around the back channels to Priamurskaya from landing No 3. Timetables are posted beside the landings. Navigation season is May to October.

AROUND KHABAROVSK

Fuyuan (China)
Фуюань

Every other day at 8.30 am, a hydrofoil departs from the river station at Khabarovsk for Fuyuan, a small town on the Chinese bank of the Amur River, three hours sail away. If you return with the hydrofoil later the same day, supposedly no visa is required for the visit. Anyone wishing to travel on into China needs a valid visa (there's a Chinese consulate in Khabarovsk; see the Consulates section in the Siberia & the Russian Far East Facts for the Visitor chapter). From Fuyuan take a bus to Jiamusi and then on to Harbin, the transportation hub of north-east China. Several Russian tour companies advertise shopping excursions to China but at the time of research were refusing to take on foreigners; maybe this has changed.

Sikachi-Alyan
Сикачи-Алян

This is a small Nanaitsy fishing settlement of perhaps 30 or so dwellings strung along the banks of the Amur, 40km downriver of Khabarovsk. The main attractions are some 11th century BC petroglyphs – aboriginal stone carvings adorning some of the boulders on the muddy flats at the water's edge. From the village, the boulders are quite difficult to find, involving a short boat ride and a trek along the wooded shore (from June through to October, infested with swarms of mosquitoes that can easily bite through cotton, so wear something more protective, and cover your hands and face).

You need a guide, or at least someone among you who can speak Russian competently enough to ask for directions and persuade a local to row you across the small stretch of water that separates the village and the carvings.

To get to Sikachi-Alyan take bus No 205 (to Malyshevo) that runs from Khabarovsk at 7.15 am on Tuesday, Friday, Saturday and Sunday, making the return journey the same day at 7.25 pm. The trip takes two hours, and a one-way ticket is $3. Take your own food as there is no shop in the village.

KOMSOMOLSK-ON-AMUR КОМСОМОЛЬСК-НА-АМУРЕ

☎ 42172 • pop 305,000

Komsomolsk-on-Amur (usually just shortened to Komsomolsk – 'City of Youth') is the largest city on the Baikal-Amur Mainline (BAM). It's also probably the most depressing city on the BAM. Founded in 1932 in the middle of a great swamp 290km north of Khabarovsk, Komsomolsk was established to strengthen the Soviet's Far Eastern defences, and it became the site for steelworks, a secretive aircraft factory and huge shipbuilding yards, turning out icebreakers and submarines. The demise of the Soviet Union has turned Komsomolsk from a socialist dream into a communal nightmare.

Possible tourist attractions are limited to a museum of indigenous peoples and an art gallery, both on ulitsa Mira, and a museum of aviation, which is actually very good. The central, ex-Intourist ***Hotel Voskhod*** *(☎ 3 03 32, ulitsa Pervostroiteley 31)* is about the only accommodation in town, and is quite expensive at around $45 to $50 a night.

Getting There & Away

There is a daily train (No 67/68) between Komsomolsk and Khabarovsk. The journey takes 9½ hours overnight. Between early June and the end of August it's possible to travel to/from Khabarovsk by way of the Amur River, using the regular daily hydrofoil service.

SOVETSKAYA GAVAN СОВЕТСКАЯ ГАВАНЬ

☎ 42137 • pop 32,000

Sovetskaya Gavan is a port on the Pacific coast linked to Komsomolsk, 500km west, by an extension of the BAM. It was founded in 1853 and originally named Imperatorskaya Gavan (Emperor's Harbour), changing to 'Harbour of the Soviets' in 1926. After Vladivostok and Petropavlovsk-Kamchatsky, it is Russia's third largest naval base on the Pacific seaboard. Aside from a complex of concrete bunkers and gun emplacements constructed prior to WWII in anticipation of war with the Japanese, there's very little to see. Sovetskaya Gavan is often shortened to Sovgavan on rail timetables.

One train (No 251/252) connects Sovgavan and Port Vanino with Vladivostok via Khabarovsk and Komsomolsk. The journey time from Komsomolsk to Sovetskaya Gavan is 15 hours. The total journey is 24 hours.

PORT VANINO ПОРТ ВАНИНО

☎ 42137 • pop 30,000

About 20km north of Sovetskaya Gavan, and a stop before it on the railway, is Port Vanino, a civilian harbour. Vanino was only founded in 1944 and it was known primarily as a way station for prisoners being shipped up to the Kolyma Gulag camps. For visitors today, its main, and possibly only, distinction is that it's the place to board ship for Sakhalin Island.

Should you require a bed for the night in Port Vanino, there's ***Hotel Vanino*** *(☎ 59 91 40, ulitsa Pervaya Liniya 2)*.

There is no regular ferry service but about once or twice a week a freighter leaves Vanino for Kholmsk, on Sakhalin's west coast. For information on the week's sailing dates, you could try to phone Vanino harbour (☎ 5 73 00 or ☎ 5 78 57), though when we were there the phone had been temporarily disconnected because the port had not paid its bill. The ship does not sail on a set schedule. Tickets (roughly $25 per person) are bought from the counter at Vanino train station. If the ship is deemed not passenger-worthy (because it is transporting dangerous goods like oil) then you'll have to arrange for passage with the anxious sailor lingering in the doorway. Bring food provisions, as the cafeteria may only have boxed noodles. The ship arrives at Kholmsk, on Sakhalin, 16 hours later.

NIKOLAEVSK-ON-AMUR НИКОЛАЕВСК-НА-АМУРЕ

• pop 40,000

Fortress Nikolaevsk, named for the tsar, was founded in 1850 as guardian of the river mouth during Nikolay Muravyov's push down the Amur into Manchu territory. When Sakhalin Island, just 20km across the Tatar Strait, was transformed into a penal colony in 1875, Nikolaevsk became a staging post for the shiploads of convicts being sailed down the Amur. Following the trail of the prisoners, Anton Chekhov spent a night in Nikolaevsk in 1890, recording in his journal that he couldn't find a bed for the night.

Despite its remote location, by 1910 the town had become quite cosmopolitan, boasting Chinese, Japanese and British consulates, an American club set up by Californian and Bostonian traders, and a brothel staffed by French women. All of this was turned upside down when the Bolsheviks rode into town in 1920 and, as their first action, massacred every Japanese person they could find.

Nikolaevsk today still retains an enchanting tsarist character, with narrow, tree-lined streets squeezing between two-storey wooden houses. Things to see in town include a good museum and the remains of the 1850 fortress.

Getting There & Away

From June to October a hydrofoil connects Nikolaevsk with Komsomolsk, departing every morning at 6.30 am. The journey takes about 12 hours. During February and March the ice on the river is usually – though not always – thick enough for it to serve as a temporary road. The rest of the year the town is served, weather permitting, by a small airfield.

Sakhalin Island Остров Сахалин

Geographically, this island, about the size of Scotland, is an offshore extension of the Sikhote-Alin Mountains in the south-east corner of Russia, though it looks just as much a northern extension of Japan. In fact, Russia and Japan have been wrangling over it for more than a century.

The first Japanese settlers came across from Hokkaido in the early 1800s, attracted by seas that were so full of fish, whales and seals that, in the words of an early explorer, 'the water looked as though it was boiling'. The island already had occupants in the form of the Nivkhi, Oroki and Ainu peoples but, just as this didn't give pause to the Japanese, the Russians were equally heedless when they claimed Sakhalin in 1853, as part of their campaign to secure the Amur region. Japan agreed to recognise Russian sovereignty in exchange for the rights to the Kuril Islands (incidentally, also inhabited by Nivkhi, Oroki and Ainu).

Inspired by its extreme remoteness from European Russia, the tsar made the island into one huge penal colony, echoing Britain's use of Botany Bay, Australia, as a dumping ground for its unwanted human refuse. Anton Chekhov visited in 1890 and wrote up his observations in *A Journey to Sakhalin*. They can be summarised in one extract: 'I have seen Ceylon which is paradise and Sakhalin which is hell.'

Japan restaked its claim to hell, seizing the island during the Russo-Japanese War and getting to keep the southern half under the terms of the peace settlement (the Treaty of Portsmouth, 1905). The treaty was rubbished when, during the final days of WWII, the Soviet Union staged a success-

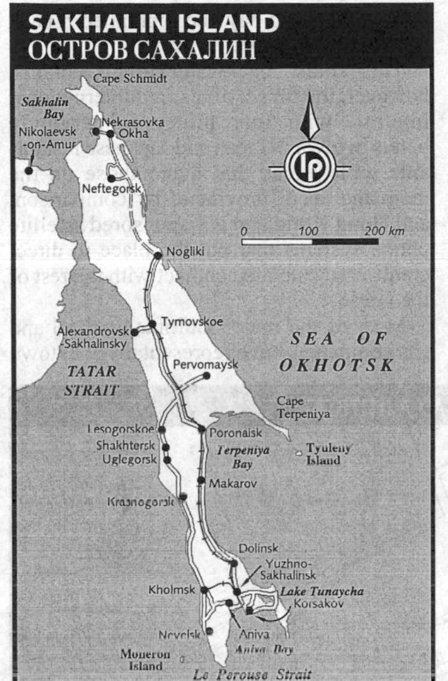

ful invasion of Sakhalin and dug in. From being the world's biggest penal colony, it became the world's biggest aircraft carrier – a highly militarised eastern outpost of the Soviet empire loaded with aircraft, missiles and guns. Just how sensitive Sakhalin had become was illustrated in 1983 when Korean Airlines flight 007 went off course over the southern part of the island and was brought down by a scrambled jet interceptor. All 267 on board were killed instantly. The Americans charged the Russians with the deliberate mass murder of innocents, while the Russians accused the USA of callously putting those lives at risk by sending flight 007 on a spying mission.

Nowadays, Russia, the USA and Japan work shoulder to shoulder extracting oil while investors from around the Pacific rim eye Sakhalin's other natural riches – gas, coal, uranium and silver, as well as timber, furs and a fine fishery. Unfortunately, Sakhalin gained world attention in May 1995 when it suffered one of the worst earthquakes in Russian history. Tremors that measured 7.5 on the Richter scale flattened the oil settlement of Neftegorsk, near the northern tip of the island, and claimed around 2000 lives.

The majority of the island's 710,000 population lives on the southern half of the island, centred mainly in the capital, Yuzhno-Sakhalinsk, and the two ports, Kholmsk and Korsakov. The Sakhalin region (Sakhalinskaya oblast) also includes the island of Moneron and the disputed Kuril chain.

YUZHNO-SAKHALINSK
ЮЖНО-САХАЛИНСК

☎ 4242, ☎ 42422 for five-digit numbers
• pop 164,000

Yuzhno-Sakhalinsk is a small town nestled sleepily among olive-green hills. While the town isn't particularly attractive, neither does it detract too much from the beauty of the surrounding landscape. There isn't much to do in Yuzhno-Sakhalinsk, but there are sufficient hotels and restaurants to make it a good starting point for further exploration of the island.

Yuzhno-Sakhalinsk was founded in 1881 as Vladimirovka, named after a major who directed the island's compulsory labour. At that time it was little more than a hamlet, composed of a few farmsteads worked by convicts. The main Russian settlements were farther north, on the coast of the Tatar Strait – places that were more accessible from the mainland. It was the Japanese who developed Vladimirovka, renaming it Toiohara and, during their 40 years of occupation, building it into a thriving township and centre of regional administration.

After the Japanese were booted out in 1945, the USSR tried to whip up enthusiasm on the mainland and get people to migrate to southern Sakhalin, with the intention that the island should be decisively and irreversibly Russified; Toiohara became Yuzhno-Sakhalinsk (literally 'Southern Sakhalin').

For 45 years the town developed in an unexceptional manner as a centre for light industry and food processing – specifically fish – before attracting widespread international attention in 1990 as the site of the 'Sakhalin experiment'.

A newly appointed governor from Moscow, Valentin Fyodorov, a former economics professor, vowed to create capitalism on the island. He privatised retail trade, distributed land and turned Yuzhno-Sakhalinsk's Communist Party headquarters into a business centre. The experiment was not an unqualified success, with the majority of people claiming to have been left poorer by the free-market reforms. Fyodorov called it a day and hightailed it back to Moscow in 1993.

This small, backwater town remains, however, the object of marked international interest, with four pricey joint-venture hotels in town, Korean and Japanese restaurants with prices that make those on the mainland seem provincial by comparison, and Hong Kong and US-sponsored satellite phone systems that put the place in direct credit-card-operated contact with the rest of the world.

Most of the major multinational oil and gas companies have representatives in town

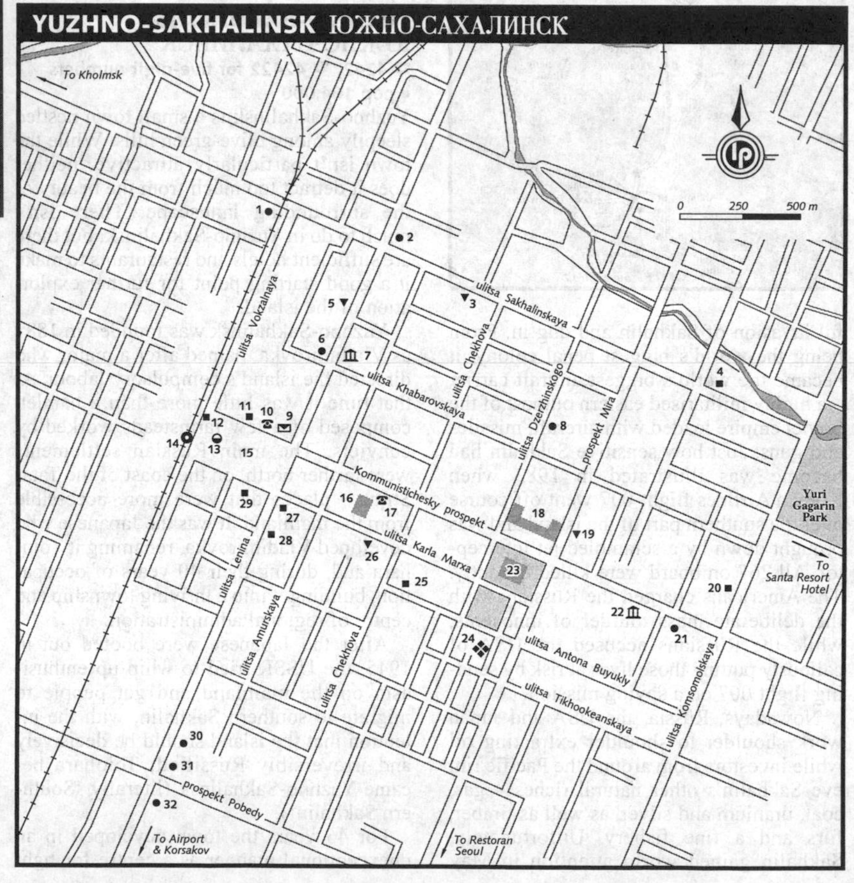

– hence the hotels, restaurants and phone systems. When the oil starts flowing (for the last few years it has been held up, waiting for the Russian parliament to pass the necessary legislation), Yuzhno-Sakhalinsk could lose some of its wild frontier charm. Maybe you ought to get there now, before it's too late.

Orientation

Yuzhno-Sakhalinsk stretches along the floor of a narrow valley 25km inland of Aniva Bay at the southern end of the island. The town's main axis, running roughly north-south, is ulitsa Lenina with ploshchad Lenina at its midpoint.

Most of the shops are along ulitsa Lenina, within 1km either side of the central square. Kommunistichesky prospekt (believe it or not, it's still called that) runs east from the square with the island's main administrative buildings strung along it.

You'll find some very good Russian-language maps of Yuzhno-Sakhalinsk and the island at many kiosks and book stores around town.

Information

The island's most centrally located post office (open 8 am to 6 pm daily) is at the north-east corner of ploshchad Lenina. The telephone office (open 8 am to 10 pm daily) where you can also send email is next door. Sakhalin is the beneficiary of the most advanced telecommunications in the whole of Russia; it's also one of the cheapest places to call abroad from the Far East. A minute to Europe, America or Australia costs \$2.75. You can send email for about \$0.20 a message, if on diskette, or \$3.60 if the email is typed for you.

There are direct-dial inter-national credit-card-operated phones at Hotel Eurasia, Hotel Sakhalin-Sapporo and in the foyer of the Sakhin Tsentr, an international business centre at Kommunistichesky prospekt 32. The phones accept American Express, JCB, MasterCard and Visa, and calls are charged at \$4 per minute. Sakhalin Telecom also has Yuzhno-Sakhalinsk linked into a satellite system with phones at the airport and their office at Kommunistichesky prospekt 43.

YUZHNO-SAKHALINSK ЮЖНО-САХАЛИНСК

PLACES TO STAY
- 4 Hotel Turist / Гостиница Турист
- 11 Hotel Moneron / Гостиница Монерон
- 12 Hotel Eurasia / Гостиница Евразия
- 20 Hotel Lada / Гостиница Лада
- 25 Hotel Natalia / Гостиница Наталия
- 27 Hotel Dalnevostochnik / Гостиница Дальневосточник
- 28 Hotel Sakhalin-Sapporo / Гостиница Сахалин-Саппоро
- 29 Hotel Rybak / Гостиница Рыбак

PLACES TO EAT
- 3 Slavyanka / Ресторан Славянка
- 5 Lunny Svet / Лунный свет
- 19 Kafe Vechernee / Кафе Вечернее
- 26 Saigon / Ресторан Сайгон

OTHER
- 1 Market / Рынок
- 2 Kino Komsomolets / Кино Комсомолец
- 6 Aeroflot / Аэрофлот
- 7 Art Museum / Художественный музей
- 8 Holiday Centre / Центр Холидей
- 9 Post Office / Почтовое отделение
- 10 Telephone Office / Телефон
- 13 Bus Station / Автовокзал
- 14 Train Station / Железнодорожный вокзал
- 15 Ploshchad Lenina / Площадь Ленина
- 16 Kino October / Кинотеатр Октябрь
- 17 Sakhalin Telecom Office / Сахалин Телеком
- 18 Sakhin Tsentr (Business Centre) / Сахинцентр (Бизнес Центр)
- 21 Officer's Club / Дом Офицеров
- 22 Regional Museum / Краеведческий музей
- 23 Chekhov Drama Theatre / Драматический театр имени Чехова
- 24 Central Department Store / ЦУМ
- 30 24-Hour Pharmacy / Круглосуточная аптека
- 31 Bookshop / Книжный магазин
- 32 Bookshop / Книжный магазин

Currency can be exchanged at the bureau in the lobby of Hotel Lada or Hotel Rybak, while the Inkombank at the Sakhin Tsentr, room 316, will give a cash advance on Visa, at 2% commission. Leave home without your travellers cheques; there wasn't any place on the island that took them when we were there.

Yuzhno-Sakhalinsk has two bookshops (at ulitsa Lenina 287 and 293), both of which are well stocked, with Russian detective novels on the shelves where the works of Dostoevsky used to be.

The time in Sakhalin is Moscow time plus eight hours.

Things to See

The pagoda-like roofs of the **Regional Museum** (Oblastnoy kraevedchesky muzey), Kommunistichesky prospekt 29, are a strong visual reminder of Sakhalin's Japanese heritage – the building was home to the Karafuto administration (Karafuto was the Japanese name for Sakhalin) before the Soviet Union regained possession of the south of the island in 1945.

On the ground level, the museum's collections deal with the island's natural and climatic features, its prehistory and some fascinating ethnography, including fish-skin robes and seal-hide tunics worn by the Ainu. The Siberian and Far Eastern penchant for taxidermy is also well in evidence, with the larger part of a whole colony of seals stuffed and on display. Upstairs is a presentation of Sakhalin's history from 1917 to 1960.

There is a very good and professionally produced English-language museum guide available at the front desk. The museum's opening hours are from 11 am to 6 pm daily except Monday, and closing at 5 pm Tuesday. Admission is $3.

In the gardens in front of the museum stand three squat pieces of ancient artillery (the sign at the front desk reading, 'To shoot please pay 30 roubles' refers, presumably, to camera-users), but for those with an interest in things that go bang, the **Officers' Club** (Dom Ofitserov), one block east, has a yard full of armoured vehicles and tanks.

The bunker-like structure at ulitsa Lenina 137 was also built by the Japanese, in this case for use as a military command centre, but the architecture gives little clue to its Oriental origins and is as dull as the meagre collection of paintings it now houses in its present role as the regional **Art Museum** (Khudozhestvenny muzey).

Places to Stay

There is a clutch of budget hotels around ploshchad Lenina: ***Hotel Moneron***, a big Wedgwood-blue building on the square's north side; ***Hotel Rybak*** *(☎ 72 37 68)*, opposite the Moneron; and ***Hotel Dalnevostochnik***, across ulitsa Lenina opposite the Rybak. All three hotels generally have sinks, television and refrigerators in the room, while toilets and showers are shared. Single/double rooms at the Moneron are $11-23/47-66; the Dalnevostochnik charges $27-37 for doubles (no singles), while the Rybak charges $27/43.

An experience in itself, ***Hotel Turist*** *(☎ 3 19 60, ulitsa Sakhalinskaya 2)* is 15 minutes walk from the town centre. When we stayed there, the electricity came on only for a couple of hours in the middle of the night and there was no hot water, which was just as well because the bathroom was missing its sink. Later, we found out the nicer rooms had been reserved for a Japanese tour group. Rooms cost $33/25-33.

The oppressive ***Hotel Lada*** *(☎ 3 31 45, ulitsa Komsomolskaya 154)*, about 1km south of the Turist, is where most of the mid-level oil workers stay. It charges $60/90 for decent accommodation, though electricity outages and water shortages are a problem.

There are no less than four upmarket hotels in Yuzhno-Sakhalinsk. Most prominent among them is ***Hotel Sakhalin-Sapporo*** *(☎ 72 15 60, fax 72 38 89, ulitsa Lenina 181)*, an old breeze-block monstrosity that has been given a refit by the Japanese. The hotel is aimed at the business traveller and offers services such as interpreters and car hire. Rooms are $70/120-140, breakfast included. The Japanese helped build ***Hotel Eurasia*** *(☎ 72 44 66, fax 46 20 03, ulitsa*

Vokzalnaya), next door to the train station, with rooms for $53/93, and the Koreans backed ***Hotel Natalia*** *(☎ 3 66 83, fax 46 27 01, ulitsa Antona Buyukly 38)*, a very private and comfortable hotel with rooms for $60/140, equipped with stoves.

The fourth joint-venture hotel is the pricey ***Santa Resort Hotel*** *(☎ 3 28 24, fax 509-856 55 55, ulitsa Venskaya 3)*, a few kilometres up on the hillside overlooking town. It's a good ski base with a downhill slope and chairlifts nearby. Rooms start at $166. The hotel supposedly rents ski equipment but the prices were not available at the time of research.

Places to Eat

Most of the cafes and restaurants are open from noon until at least 10 pm, though with an hour or two break in the middle of the day. The small and intimate ***restaurant*** at Hotel Sakhalin-Sapporo is a better-than-average hotel restaurant with good service, but it's pricey and most people prefer to congregate in the comfy bar for a drink before heading out to the city's other restaurants.

Excellent Siberian cuisine is served at the ***Slavyanka*** *(☎ 3 56 67, ulitsa Sakhalinskaya 45)*, a small, self-consciously Russian restaurant decorated with painted wooden spoons, matryoshka dolls and embroidered shawls, and with a balalaika trio on some nights. The densely typed menu is in Russian only but just take pot luck – it all looked great. Main courses are $3 to $8 and reservations are recommended. It's open from noon to 4 pm and 5 to 10 pm daily.

At ***Restoran Saigon*** *(ulitsa Karla Marxa 2)* a drab exterior disguises a very pleasant interior. In this case, the management has made a stab at evoking the Far East, with liberal use of rice-paper screens and bamboo, although the menu has about as much to do with Vietnam as Bill Clinton. The food is good, with prices similar to those at the Slavyanka. A meal ordered from the extensive menu at the Korean ***Seoul*** *(prospekt Mira 245)* will cost $30 per head; the chauffeur-driven locals say the food is good.

A good, reasonably priced cafe with excellent soups is ***Kafe Vechernee*** *(prospekt Mira 112)*, across the road from Sakhin Tsentr. For snacks, try the *pyan-se*, a spicier native version of *pirozhki*, sold on the streets. Also, there's an inexpensive ***cafeteria*** on ploshchad Lenina in the same building as Hotel Dalnevostochnik; the entrance is around the side. The small local ***market*** is on ulitsa Sakhalinskaya west of the railway.

Entertainment

Yuzhno-Sakhalinsk is hippishly decadent; places change names and genres frequently. The ***Holiday Centre*** on ulitsa Dzerzhinskogo is a restaurant, casino, sauna and hostess bar complex popular with Russian mafiosi. ***Lunny Svet*** *(ulitsa Lenina 182)* is the place to go for Sakhalin-style striptease (we won't spoil the surprise) and a decent meal. The cover charge, which you have to pay even if you eat, is $7.

RUSSIAN FAR EAST

Getting There & Away

Air There are daily flights to/from Khabarovsk ($184, 1¼ hours), Vladivostok ($140, 1¾ hours) and Moscow ($300, nine hours), as well as twice-weekly flights to Irkutsk and Novosibirsk.

Aeroflot also flies three times a week to/from Hoikodate, twice a week to Niigata, and once a week to both Harbin and Pusan. The foreigners departure hall is through a small door 15m to the left of the main entrance. There is a departure tax equivalent to $8, payable on checking in. The English-speaking Intourist desk is through a separate entrance to the left of the main entrance.

Train The farthest point north on the island reached by the railway is Nogliki on the east coast, about a quarter of the way down from the tip. It's served by two trains a day that depart from Yuzhno-Sakhalinsk at 6.40 am and 8.05 pm, arriving 13 hours later.

Bus There are numerous buses each day to Kholmsk ($3, 1½ hours). Daily buses also run north to Dolinsk and south to Korsakov.

Boat It's possible to board a ship for Port Vanino on the mainland from Kholmsk (see the earlier section on Port Vanino for further details).

From the port of Korsakov, it's possible to hitch a ride on a ship to Wakkanai, on Hokkaido, Japan's northernmost island. There are no set schedules and the port dispatcher does not always keep track of these ships. You'll have to go to the port and speak with the captains yourself; plan on spending a few days, maybe more, in Korsakov as the ship prepares to sail.

Getting Around

All buses and *mikriki* (minivans) depart from in front of the train station on ploshchad Lenina. Bus Nos 8 and 9 run to the airport, a journey of about 25 minutes for $0.50. Services begin at around 6.30 am, or one hour later on Sunday. Though you can buy tickets from the conductor, there's also a ticket office, where schedules are posted, in a small, trailer-type building to the left of the train station entrance. A taxi from the train station to the airport will cost around $6.

Cars can be hired but on an informal basis and always with a driver. Try the hotel receptionists at the Sakhalin-Sapporo who may enlist their husbands or friends; expect to pay $50 to $100 a day.

ELSEWHERE ON SAKHALIN

Almost three-quarters of the island is wild, mountain terrain, with the lower plains covered by 3m-high grasses and bamboos.

While the island is possessed of a rugged beauty, it's also very difficult to explore because of the lack of any decent transport system. Visitors will have to spend money on car hire or, alternatively, come prepared for some serious hiking and wilderness camping. There are some small airfields elsewhere on the island, including Okha and Zonalnoe, just outside of Aleksandrovsk-Sakhalinsky, which provide connections to the mainland.

For hotels outside of the capital, there is no need to book in advance, as it's likely you'll be the only guests.

Lake Tunaycha
Озеро Тунайча

One of the nicest places to go from Yuzhno-Sakhalinsk is the Lake Tunaycha region in the extreme south-east, where there's an archipelago of lakes, some only separated from the sea by narrow causeways a few metres wide. The sea coast in this area is spectacular and is favoured by seals. Amber gets washed up on the beaches of this region, and it's a favourite place for locals to go crab-hunting and camping.

To get to Tunaycha, drive south out of Yuzhno-Sakhalinsk, past the right-hand turn for the airport, and at the next crossroads turn left in the direction of Okhotskoe. It's about 45km.

Korsakov
Корсаков

☎ 42435 • pop 43,000

Thirty-five kilometres due south of Yuzhno-Sakhalinsk is the grimy port of Korsakov, centre of the island's hugely profitable fishing industry. Like most of Sakhalin's cities, it has centrally located accommodation that may become useful if you're taking the ship from here to Japan. With the Intourist seal of approval, ***Hotel Alpha*** *(☎ 4 0170, ulitsa Krasnoflotskaya 31)* is overpriced at $80/160 a single/double with breakfast included, though you might be given a less expensive room if you look poor and Russian. Try asking at the port for cheaper accommodation. It also may be possible to get a bed for a few dollars aboard a ship in port; speak with the captain.

Kholmsk
Холмск

☎ 42433 • pop 40,000

Southern Sakhalin's other major port, Kholmsk, is 40km due west of the capital. The only reason to come here is if you're taking a ferry to or from the island. In case of delays or schedule changes, a decent place to stay is ***Hotel Kholmsk*** *(☎ 2 22 48, ulitsa Sovietskaya 41)*, a clean and well kept place with single/double rooms for $36/48. The Kholmsk bus station is in front of the passenger shipping terminal.

Nevelsk
Невелск

• **pop 20,000**

From Kholmsk, you can also make bus connections to Nevelsk and other fishing towns along the south coast. The bus rattles along a dusty coastal road, past crooked cottages – some with Soviet flags hoisted and another with the roof painted with the old Soviet slogan *Miru Mir* (Peace to the World). There's a brightly coloured Lenin mural in Nevelsk's central square with the goateed hero proclaiming 'This is my city'. Soon it will be his alone. At least a third of the residents have fled to the mainland, leaving entire apartment blocks deserted.

If you're inclined to spend the night, ***Hotel Nevelskaya***, on the main street across from the bus station, is comfortable and clean. A double with toilet and shower (though not hot water) is $31, and there are also cheaper rooms.

Cape Terpeniya
Мыс Терпения

Another spectacular, way-out spot for camping and bird-watching is Cape Terpeniya (poluostrov Terpeniya). You'd have to take the mainline to Poronaysk and then a narrow gauge railroad eastward; or go by car south from Pervomaysk.

Northern Sakhalin

For those wanting an even more intense tour of the last days of communism, the north of Sakhalin is littered with decaying remnants; it's a place best visited by those with a taste for destruction.

The only public transport is the railroad that runs up the spine of the island. This unrambling ride, past rusting factories, ghost towns and long stretches of taiga more desolate than any along the Trans-Siberian, is like a horror film. About half-way, the train stops in Tymovskoe. From there, it's possible to take a bus or minivan to nearby **Alexandrovsk-Sakhalinsky**, one of the first settlements the Russians established on Sakhalin and the place in which Chekhov spent most of his time during his 1890 visit to the island.

The train then continues to **Nogliki**, a decrepit oil city. It's hard to believe, given the drabness, that $30 billion in foreign investments is being sunk just offshore, in the form of giant oil-drilling platforms anchored into the shelf to keep them from being tossed around like popcorn in the icy, fast-moving waters. If you need to stay in Nogliki, try ***Hotel Severyanka***, a former children's nursery turned into a hostel. A bed in the common room costs $10. Cross the road in front of the train station and turn left, going some 25m alongside a three-storey pink building, then turn right and cut through the park. It'll be to your left, a two storey building with a playground.

A bus or minivan will take you the next 250km north ($35, about four hours) to **Okha**, the northernmost city on the island. All northbound cars and buses leave Nogliki station at about 11.30 am, shortly after the train from Yuzhno-Sakhalinsk has arrived. You can also take the Japanese-built narrow gauge railway. At 7km/h, the locals brag it's the slowest in the world, too slow to require toilets on board since the passengers jump off, avail themselves of the bushes and then get back on. It takes an entire 24 hours to cross the sandy, never-never land of swamps, looping streams and twisted, fire-scorched scrub pine.

Okha (population: 56,000) is in the running for the title of ugliest city in Russia; the giant apple and geometrical stencils on the pre-fab buildings don't help. The threat of earthquakes and the demise of the domestic oil industry has caused the population here to dwindle to much less than its official number according to locals. If you need to stay, there's the dismal and unmarked ***Okhaneftegaz Hotel***; single/double rooms are $20/40.

From Okha, you can take a bus or minivan to **Nekrasovka**, a Nivkhi village of 1200 people 28km to the west. Transport leaves at about 7.30 am from the bus stop 500m north of the hotel, but check, as this makeshift station is likely to change location. Nekrasovka would be worth visiting during the traditional holiday festivals in early January and mid-to-late June. But at

The Nivkhi: A Culture in Decline

The Nivkhi are one of the so-called Northern Peoples, a sort of catch-all term for the ethnicities too obscure to warrant separate mention in the Soviet Red Book of Endangered Peoples. Today there are less than 2000 Nivkhi left, mostly in the north of Sakhalin Island.

Anyone interested in Nivkhi culture is directed to Rimma Petrovna, who works in the Okha administration building and can arrange a visit to the Nivkhi village of Nekrasovka.

On maps, the village is a tiny black dot about to drop into the sea. There's a single grey line leading to it and no other black dots for centimetres.

Nekrasovka was created in the 1970s as a state fish farm. Nivkhi, by tradition, are fisherfolk, who used to make clothing and boots out of pounded fish skin. Their national dish is *mos*, fish flesh mixed with wild blueberries and roots. The village has about 100 wood shacks, a couple of dirt roads, two nursery schools, a House of Culture *(dom kultury)* and a grocery store with little in it but vodka.

It is in the House of Culture, with a stereo playing Rod Stewart in the background, that a local called Zoya gave us a crash course on Nivkhi culture, revealing how times have changed. Of the 600 Nivkhi who live in the village, only 20 now speak the language. Bear hunting is now a thing of the past, the Nivkhi newspaper and radio ran out of money, and shamanism died out long ago.

SUZANNE POSEHL

Anton Chekhov, during his travels on Sakhalin a century ago, noted a high rate of alcoholism among the natives whom the Russians had introduced to vodka a few decades beforehand. I ask whether alcoholism is a problem in Nekrasovka. Zoya looks puzzled. Out of every five men, I ask, how many drink too much? 'Six', she declares.

She then puts a Nivkhi-made movie, starring local kids, into the VCR. After watching this, we are shown photo albums of Nivkhi activities.

Then Zoya, the club DJ and the director of the House of Culture put on embroidered costumes, woven from wool instead of pounded fish skin. They are preparing for the Saturday night dance. Zoya wears high-heeled pumps instead of fur boots. The DJ pulls a *buben* drum out of the closet and begins banging on it, drowning out Rod Stewart. We take some photos and call it an afternoon.

Suzanne Possehl

any other time it's depressing. See the boxed text 'The Nivkhi: A Culture in Decline'.

North of Okha is **Cape Schmidt** (poluostrov Shmidta), supposedly a subtropical paradise where the Japanese go to collect wild herbs and hunt bears. Someone who may be able to help you get there is Nikolai Pavlov (☎ 42437-2 17 76), a hunter and Okha businessman who operates a hunting lodge and runs tours of the island's north.

Getting Around

See if you can befriend someone to show you around; the people on Sakhalin are very friendly and, if you offer to foot the bill for petrol, someone is bound to take you. Alternatively, you could try to hire a car (see Getting Around in the Yuzhno-Sakhalinsk section).

Intourist Sakhalin (☎ 42422-3 43 86, fax 72 73 43, intourist@sakhalin.ru), at ulitsa Dzerzhinskogo 36, room 206, in Yuzhno-Sakhalinsk, is able to make bookings and arrange tours. At least one person there, Larisa, knows some English. There are also several semi-private tour agencies, mostly offsprings of the local government's park and environmental commissions and offering a variety of adventures. For $400 per person (minimum group of six), you can spend two days and a night on Moneron Island, 70km from Nevelsk, exploring the bird colonies, clear waters and tropical fish. Contact Mikhail Lenko (☎ 4242-72 83 80 or ☎ 72 22 36) at ulitsa Dzerzhinskogo 15, suite 140, in Yuzhno-Sakhalinsk. Khanta (☎ 4242-72 28 05), ulitsa Depovskaya 50, brings tourists on day trips to Tyuleny Island. Seal hunters also go here, so be prepared if you happen upon the grisly sights.

Kuril Islands
Курильские острова

Discovered and first charted in 1739 as part of Russia's Great Northern Expedition, the Kurils are a chain of 56 variously sized islands, arced like stepping stones between the southern tip of Kamchatka and the northern Japanese island of Hokkaido. However, if geographically the islands seem to form a link between Russia and Japan, then politically they are more of a wedge, driving the two powers apart.

A treaty of 1855 divided possession of the chain between Russia and Japan; the latter received the islands of Habomai, Shikotan, Kunashir and Etorofu. A second treaty, in 1875, gave Tokyo sovereignty over the whole lot in exchange for recognising the Russians' right to Sakhalin. But then, in the last days of WWII, with Japan collapsing under American assault, the Soviets reneged on the deal and invaded the Kurils. For three years the new Russian settlers and the existing Japanese residents lived side by side, but in 1948 Stalin ordered all the Japanese to leave. The Kurils have been a diplomatic minefield between the two nations ever since.

The islands, which form part of the Pacific 'Ring of Fire', are actually the tips of a volcanic, sea-bed mountain range. Among the peaks protruding from the sea are around 40 active volcanoes, many of which erupt frequently and violently. The islands are stunningly beautiful – the kind of places where James Bond movies are filmed, with perfectly circular azure-blue lagoons, bubbling, steaming rivers and some spectacular cliff formations (from which the bad guy gets thrown at the end).

The main centres of habitation are Severo-Kurilsk on Paramushir Island, Kurilsk on Iturup Island and Yuzhno-Kurilsk on Kunashir, the southernmost and most accessible of the island chain.

Getting There & Away

This is tricky. About the only way to reach the Kurils is to fly from Yuzhno-Sakhalinsk, a flight of just over an hour. The problem is that the islands are often wreathed in a thick fog, caused by the meeting of hot and cold streams, making airborne approaches impossible. Although in theory flights are daily, you have to be prepared to hang around for up to five days waiting for the weather to improve. An alternative does exist in sailing. Once or twice a month, a ship departs from Korsakov, Sakhalin's southern port, taking a day to reach Yuzhno-Kurilsk, on the southernmost island of Kunashir. It's not a ferry service but fare-paying passengers are taken – for inquiries contact the sea terminal information desk in Korsakov (☎ 42435-2 23 52) at pereulok Reydovy 2. A good but potentially expensive contact might be the director of the Kurilsky Reserve, Yevgeny Mikhailovich Grigorev (☎/fax 42455-2 1856, magnoliy@sakhalin.ru).

Magadan
Магадан

☎ 4132 for six-digit numbers, ☎ 41322 for five-digit numbers or ☎ 41300 where noted • pop 152,000

Magadan is barely a lifetime old but already it occupies a major place in one of the grimmest chapters of Russian history.

The origins of the town lie with the beginnings of the great terrors of the Stalin era. In 1932 gold was discovered in the Kolyma region. A new administration was brought into being, under the auspices of the NKVD, to excavate the gold and other precious metals – it was called Dalstroy. The same year, the first prisoner-laden ships arrived at a bare, swampy site on Nagaeva Bay, on the inhospitable northern shore of the Sea of Okhotsk. The prisoners were immediately set to labour, building docks and piers for the following ships, administrative blocks for their overseers and barracks for their guards. Eventually – though not before winter had come and thousands had died from working knee-deep in deathly cold waters and mud – they built their own flimsy accommodation.

Completed, the newly named town of Magadan served as a marshalling point for the human cargo destined for the hinterland gold fields of Kolyma. From the harbour, the already ragged and exhausted new arrivals were marched, shoved and prodded along the main street, ulitsa Berzina – named for the first director of Dalstroy. (Berzin was recalled to Moscow and shot in 1938 for being too lenient on his Kolyma slave force; the street became ulitsa Stalina and then, in 1956, prospekt Lenina.) The prisoners were deposited in one of the town's many transit camps, there to await selection for the different mines, 'corrective centres' and work troops out in the taiga. For many, Magadan was the last town they would ever see.

The town's trade in human lives began to end in the 1950s with the death of Stalin. The watchtowers and high, barbed-wire-topped fences came down, and the headquarters of Dalstroy were destroyed, as were the wooden barracks. All were replaced with civic brick buildings – ugly but innocuous. The town today is claustrophobic and bleak, but no more so than most other northern Siberian settlements. Its deliberate isolation, with no railway within a thousand kilometres and no easily negotiable roads heading anywhere anybody might want to go, also means that the only way in or out is by an expensive flight.

Orientation

Magadan lies in a bowl, encircled by bare hills with the west open to deep-water Nagaeva Bay. The main thoroughfare is prospekt Lenina with the central shopping district lying between Komsomolskaya ploshchad and the junction with ulitsa Proletarskaya. Immediately north of Proletarskaya are the bus station and the Aeroflot offices. Prospekt Lenina becomes Kalymskoe shosse as it climbs over the lip of the hills and runs north-east 60km to the airport.

An English-language map called *Magadan and its Surroundings* is available for about $0.50 from local bookshops (the best is on prospekt Lenina and there's another at the junction of ulitsa Dzerzhinskogo and ulitsa Portovaya).

Information

Money You can change money at the Sberbank on ulitsa Pushkina 11, and Vneshtorgbank on prospekt Karla Marxa 33, but not at hotels, at last word.

Kolyma – Russia's Auschwitz

At a conservative estimate around 20 million people were shot, starved, beaten, tortured or worked to death in Stalin's Gulag camps. That is almost as many people as live in the whole of Scandinavia and more than the entire population of Australia. Another conservative estimate has it that one-fifth of those Stalin-era victims died in the camps of the Kolyma region. There were so many corpses that their bones were used as beds for roads.

If Kolyma isn't a name as chillingly recognisable as Auschwitz, Belsen or Dachau, it is not because the horrors there were any less awful, but because they were perpetrated by a secretive government on its own citizens and because they took place in an isolated, fog-shrouded, ice-locked region, 9000km from Moscow.

At any one moment, the camps in Kolyma held about half a million occupants. Kolyma consumed prisoners – those who survived the journey there. Prisoners were shipped up, thousands at a time, from Vladivostok, where they'd been waiting in transit camps after crossing the vastness of Russia crammed into cattle cars so tightly that some died of suffocation. The sea passage took a further eight or 10 days and was, if anything, an even more deadly journey. One ship left Vladivostok too late in the year and became stuck fast in the ice, finally reaching the Kolyma coast nine months later. Not one of its thousands of prisoners survived. Those aboard another prison ship revolted and the guards held them back with hoses, filling the hold with water. It was 40°C below zero. The 3000 prisoners were delivered to Magadan entombed in ice.

The port of Magadan, capital of the Kolyma region, was the 'gateway to hell'. From its harbour the already wasted prisoners, little more than living skeletons, were marched along the infamous 'road of bones' to one of the region's 100 or more camps. Many of these were simply named by their distance from the start of the march: the 23-km camp, the 72-km camp, the 220-km camp.

Once in the camps, most of the prisoners were put to work digging for gold. They worked 14 hours a day, barely sustained by a daily diet of 700g of bread and an evening bowl of cabbage soup. Quotas were set for the amount of gold they had to recover each day. The quotas were high and in the attempt to meet them prisoners often died of exhaustion. The alternative, for anyone who failed to meet the quota, was a cut in their food ration. As hunger took its toll, the shortfall in the quota would widen and the ration would become ever smaller. Eventually the prisoner only had the strength to crawl out of sight and succumb to the cold and the release of death. It's estimated that for every kilogram of gold mined, one man died.

Post & Communications The main post, telephone and telegraph office is on the north side of the desolate ploshchad Lenina, and is open 24 hours daily.

Travel Agencies The Intourist office (fax 41300-54 176) is located at ulitsa Proletarskaya 30A.

BOL Tours (☎/fax 22 02 96, bol@online.magadan.su or bol@asianoffice.com) is an enthusiastic, one-man agency run by Boris Levin, a geologist by training. Levin has a lot of experience leading youth groups around the region and he can organise city sightseeing trips for visitors, local flora and fauna excursions, drives out to old Gulag camps, rafting expeditions, and boating trips to observe seals and, occasionally, walrus. Although BOL prefers to organise these things as seven and eight-day packages costing $750 to $850, you should be able to negotiate for individual requirements. There's a slight problem in that Levin speaks little English, but with advance notice he can find interpreters. The postal address is Box 0/77, 685000 Magadan, Russia.

Another good contact is Mikhail Skopets (☎ 23 29 90, ibpn@ibpn.magadan.su). He's a biologist and avid fisherman who says he knows the outlying regions of Magadan, including Kolyma and Chukotka, like his backyard. Another bonus is that he knows English and he has worked with many Westerners.

Time Zone Magadan time is Moscow time plus eight hours.

Things to See

At the approach to town, as prospekt Lenina crosses a small river, in the shadow of some squalid apartment blocks are what appear to be the remains of a small-scale military skirmish. Two jet fighters on sticks swoop down on the road, while behind them various other discarded war machines, including a gutted helicopter and some missile launchers, serve as a children's playground. Like the flats next to the aircraft, most of Magadan's architecture is unremittingly grim but there are some good examples of **Stalinist baroque** in the buildings that line the southern end of prospekt Lenina and the east end of ulitsa Portovaya.

More conventional sights include a **Regional Museum** (Kraevedchesky muzey) split between two homes; the building at prospekt Karla Marxa 55 has exhibits portraying life in the camps, while that at ulitsa Proletarskaya 20/A has a model of a baby mammoth recovered some years ago from a glacier in the Magadan region. There is also a **Geological & Mineralogical Museum** (Geologichesky i mineralogichesky Muzey) at ulitsa Portovaya 16.

BOL Tours knows the city well and can guide visitors to the few remains of the Dalstroy era, including the hospital where Solzhenitsyn was treated when he was marched through Magadan in the 1950s.

Places to Stay

***Hotel Severovostokzoloto** (☎ 2 35 92, ulitsa Gorkogo 14)* has the cheapest beds in town at $13/18 for single/double rooms, but the rooms are unpleasant and toilets and showers are shared.

Conveniently located across from the bus station is ***Hotel Magadan** (☎ 2 15 10, Proletarskaya 8)*. It's large and gloomy with impossibly long, unlit corridors – not recommended for anyone who has recently watched *The Shining*. The rooms, at $25/42, all have bathrooms, but are neglected and there is a chance the entire hotel will be given over to offices before you get there.

***Hotel VM-Tsentralnaya** (☎ 2 12 00, ulitsa Lenina 13)* is reportedly a decent hotel, Magadan's newest at the time of writing; rooms cost $79/96 including breakfast.

The best accommodation in town is at ***Hotel Business Center** (☎ 5 89 44, Proletarskaya 84B)*, 2km south of the bus station. It's a purpose-built business hotel with 11 clean, well furnished rooms at $78/144. The hotel, a modern, drab grey brick and glass construction, is 200m back from the road, beyond the multistorey apartment blocks.

Places to Eat

Eating options are at small ***cafes*** with ever-changing names and addresses. You are going to have to seek them out because the hotel restaurants, with the exception of the bar/cafe at VM-Tsentralnaya, are closed or should be. For imported dry foods, fresh vegetables and fruit, there is a small ***market*** at the junction of ulitsa Dzerzhinskogo and ulitsa Transportnaya, and another on Kalymskoye shosse, the road out to the airport, 800m north of the bus station.

Getting There & Away

With one exception, all roads out of Magadan go nowhere and terminate there. The one exception is the Kolyma Highway to Yakutsk, more than 1500km to the east. The 'Road of Bones' (so named for the prisoners who built it) is rough and impassable in winter, and there are no regular bus services running its length even in summer. It exists as a sometime freight route and the only way of travelling along it is to hitch. As the nearest railway runs more than 1000km south of Magadan, this means the only way in or out is by air. There are daily flights to/from

Moscow, one or two flights a week to Vladivostok and one flight a week to Khabarovsk.

The Aeroflot office (☎ 2 88 91) is behind and to the left of the bus station on prospekt Lenina, although foreigners may be sent to the airport to purchase their tickets from the international desk (as you face the main airport building, it's to your left, round the corner and through an unmarked door).

Getting Around

From early morning until late at night, two coaches run in relay between the bus station and airport forecourt. The journey takes 45 minutes and it costs the equivalent of $2.50 – pay the driver.

Kamchatka Камчатка

Dubbed 'the land of fire and ice', Kamchatka is one of Russia's least explored but most scenically spectacular regions. A 1000km-long peninsula separated from the mainland by the Sea of Okhotsk, Kamchatka is hyperactively volcanic with terrain that bubbles, spurts and spews in a manner that suggests that here, Creation hasn't quite finished yet. The region can claim 200-plus volcanoes in varying stages of activity, some long extinct, grassed over with aquamarine crater lakes, while 20 or more rank among the world's most volatile. Mt Klyuchevskaya (the highest at 4750m) last erupted in October 1994, sending so much ash into the air that international flights from North America to South-East Asia were disrupted.

The volcanoes are often surrounded by lava fields, and these lunar-like, pocked cinder landscapes served as the testing grounds for Russia's moon-walking vehicles. The thermal activity deep below the earth's surface also produces numerous hot springs, heated rivers and geysers. The most spectacular examples are to be found in the Valley of the Geysers (Dolina Geyzerov) in the Kronotsky National Park, where around 200 geothermal pressure valves sporadically blast steam, mud and water heavenwards from the canyon floor. Away from the volcanoes, Kamchatka is covered by large areas of mixed forests and plains of giant grasses, home to a vast array of wildlife including between 10,000 and 20,000 brown bears and the sable, the animal that provided much of the impetus for early Russian explorations of the peninsula.

Ironically, visitors will have a far easier time spotting once-secret military hardware like fighter planes, nuclear submarines or radar stations than they will seeing anything else in Kamchatka. The main volcanoes, the geysers, the lakes and all of the region's most breathtaking scenery is well away from the regional capital, Petropavlovsk-Kamchatsky. Helicopters have to be hired or some serious hiking has to be embarked upon, requiring nights of wilderness camping. Either way, this is one place that has to be planned for in advance – without any forward planning, you're unlikely to make it out of the capital, and while Petropavlovsk is a reasonably

attractive town, by itself it just doesn't justify the expense of getting there.

Officially, visitors still must have an invitation specifically for Kamchatka, but Aeroflot didn't ask us for any documentation before selling a ticket to Petropavlovsk and the local OVIR registered our visas even though the city was not listed. To avoid problems, include Petropavlovsk-Kamchatsky as one of your proposed destinations when applying for your Russian visa and hope it makes it onto the issued document.

HISTORY

The man credited with the discovery of Kamchatka, in 1697, was the Cossack Vladimir Atlasov who, like most explorers of the time, was out to find new lands to plunder. He established two forts on the Kamchatka River that became bases for the Russian traders who followed, looking to exact tithes of furs from the locals.

The native Koryaki, Chukchi and Itelmeni warred with their new self-appointed overlords, but fared badly and their numbers were greatly diminished. Today, the remnants of the Chukchi nation inhabit the isolated north-east of Kamchatka, while the Koryaki live on the west coast of the peninsula with their territorial capital at Palana. These peoples still maintain a traditional existence as reindeer herders and sea hunters, the animals being a source of food and raw materials for clothing. While much of their culture and language has been lost, the tradition of storytelling through mime, dance and song has survived – the writer Christina Dodwell, who spent time among the Koryaki, has described her travels with a dance troupe in *Beyond Siberia* (see the Books section in the Siberia & the Russian Far East Facts for the Visitor chapter).

Kamchatka was long regarded as the least hospitable place in the Russian Empire – a land of primeval wilderness inhabited by a few primitives, half a year's journey distant and with nothing to offer beyond a dwindling supply of furs. When the Imperial lands in Alaska were sold off in 1867, Kamchatka might also have been up for grabs if the Americans had shown enough interest. Some 53 years later there was a taker, when an American named Washington Baker Vanderlip wanted to buy the province. He was offered a 60 year concession by Lenin but the two couldn't come to terms and the deal never went through.

After WWII, in the climate of the Cold War, Kamchatka took on new strategic importance and foreign interest was definitely no longer welcome. It became a base for military airfields and early warning radar systems, while the coastline sheltered parts of the Soviet Pacific Fleet. Isolated regions of Kamchatka also served as target areas for missile testings. No foreigners, nor even nonresident Russians, were allowed anywhere near the peninsula. That all changed in 1990. These days the only hint of paranoias past is that visitors must have 'permission' to visit Kamchatka, which basically means having it listed on your visa. Touching down at Petropavlovsk-Kamchatsky airport today on a scheduled flight, there's no attempt to hide the silver pencil-snouts of fighter aircraft that protrude from the endless ranks of large grassy hummocks along the runway.

PETROPAVLOVSK-KAMCHATSKY
ПЕТРОПАВЛОВСК-КАМЧАТСКИЙ

☎ 41522 (☎ 4152 for six-digit numbers)
• pop 273,000

Petropavlovsk-Kamchatsky is the administrative centre of the Kamchatka oblast and the only settlement of any size on the whole peninsula. However, the huddles of low-rise concrete blocks that make up the town are dwarfed by Mts Avachinskaya and Koryakskaya, two brooding, active volcanoes. Both have erupted since 1990, though the town's residents, living in jerry-built Soviet structures, fear earthquakes far more than they fear the smoky mountains.

Petropavlovsk was founded in 1741 by Vitus Bering, the Danish-born Russian captain who discovered the straits that bear his name. The town was named for Bering's two ships, the *Svyatoy Pyotr* (St Peter) and *Svyatoy Pavel* (St Paul) – the suffix

Kamchatsky was added to distinguish it from all the other Petropavlovsks in Russia. It became the tsars' major Pacific sea port and was used as the base for explorations which turned up the Aleutian Islands and Alaska. The settlement was a slow developer and in 1866 it still consisted of little more than a cluster of log cabins and a small, green-domed church.

There were unlikely visitors in 1779 when a Captain Clerke sailing under the British flag entered Petropavlovsk harbour in command of the *Discovery* and the *Resolution*. These were formerly the ships of Captain James Cook, the famed explorer who had met his death in Hawaii two years previously. Clerke was continuing Cook's work with an intended expedition to the Arctic, but shortly after setting out from Petropavlovsk he was stricken with consumption and returned there to die that same year. Some 75 years later, in August 1854, more British sailed into Avacha Bay, this time accompanied by the French and intent on conquest of a less benign nature. This seaborne Crimean War invasion was successfully and unexpectedly repulsed by the small Petropavlovsk garrison.

During the Soviet era the town retained its military role and became a sizable Pacific Fleet submarine base, but its present prosperity is owed completely to the fishing industry. Rusting Petropavlovsk trawlers bring in a million tonnes of fish a year, nearly half of which is sold to Japan for hard currency. On the harbour road that jigs alongside beautiful and serene Avacha Bay, the gleamingly modernistic, reflective-glass block – the most striking building in town – revealingly, is the fisheries headquarters.

Orientation

Petropavlovsk is strung along one main axis, the road that runs in from the airport 30km east. It enters the city limits as prospekt Pobedy and changes its name no less than 11 times (prospekt Pobedy, ulitsa Tushkanova, prospekt 50 let Oktyabrya, ulitsa Vladivostokskaya, ulitsa Leningradskaya, ulitsa Ozernovskaya, ulitsa Leninskaya, ulitsa Krasnaya Sopka, ulitsa Sapun Gora, ulitsa Okeanskaya, Petropavlovskoe shosse, ulitsa Industrialnaya) before finishing up at the small fishing harbour, Rakovaya (Seashell) Bay, on the southern edge of the town. The northerly part of the road runs flat across the plain between Avacha Bay to the west and the volcanoes to the east, but below its midpoint it snakes and twists, clinging tightly to the rippling contours of the bayside hills.

Although nominally Teatralnaya ploshchad (formerly ploshchad Lenina) is the centre of town, there is no one focal point, but instead a succession of little knots strung along the main artery.

Maps of the town are available at the Regional Museum and the newspaper kiosk in the Oblast administration building on ploshchad Teatralnaya.

Information

The main post office is at ulitsa Leninskaya 56, and there's a rather ramshackle telephone and telegraph office at Vladivostokskaya 5 – don't count on making any important calls from Petropavlovsk. The Sberbank (open from 8 am to 2 pm Monday to Saturday), on the corner of ulitsa Lukashevskogo and Tushkanova, and Hotel Oktyabrskaya will exchange foreign currency. The receptionist at Hotel Petropavlovsk might also be coerced into taking your dollars but better still, bring with you all the roubles you might need.

The best bookshops, with postcards and a Russian-language guide to Kamchatka, are the Dom Knigi at prospekt 50 let Oktyabrya 7 and the Rossiyskaya Kniga also on prospekt 50 let Oktyabrya but 1km north. Another place to find postcards and maps as well as neat souvenirs and crafts made by local Eveny and Koryaki artists is the Art Salon on ulitsa Sovietskaya 30; enter from the back of the building.

The time in Petropavlovsk-Kamchatsky is Moscow time plus nine hours.

Things to See

While the town is primarily a base from which to explore the surrounding volcanic region, there are a few things to do here.

The **Regional Museum** (Kraevedchesky muzey), housed in an attractive half-timbered building overlooking the bay at Leninskaya 20, provides a beautifully presented history of the region focusing mainly on prehistory and geology, native peoples and early settlers. There's an extremely interesting section on early Russian settlers in America with reconstructions of the first settlements. It's open from 10 am to 6 pm Wednesday to Sunday; admission is $3. There is also a **Museum of Volcanology** at bulvar Piypa 9 and a **Museum of Geology** at ulitsa Beringa 117.

In front of the classically styled regional administration building at Leninskaya 14 is the **monument to Captain Clerke**, a small obelisk erected by a delegation from the British Admiralty in 1913. On Nikolskaya Hill there is a small chapel and monuments to those who fell in the failed Crimean War invasion in 1854.

Places to Stay

The choices are scant, but so are the numbers of newcomers to these parts. You shouldn't have any trouble finding a room, as most tourists use the hotels merely as places to wash up and repack their rucksacks before heading back into the wild.

The hotel favoured by tour companies is ***Hotel Petropavlovsk*** *(☎ 5 03 74, ulitsa Karla Marxa 31)*. It's a squat concrete block facing the volcanoes (and with its back to the main road, making it difficult to identify). The rooms are reasonably pleasant and have their own bathrooms; single/double rooms are $42/55. The hotel sits 100m back from ulitsa Tushkanova just north of the major road junction marked by a large obelisk.

You can try ***Hotel Edelveis*** *(☎ 5 33 24, prospekt Pobedy 27)*, though it is falling into disuse; rooms are $22/32.

Newly renovated, ***Hotel Avacha*** *(☎ 2 73 31, ulitsa Leninskaya 61)* has rooms for $50/65. It's opposite the T-34 tank monument. ***Hotel Oktyabrskaya*** *(☎ 11 26 84, ulitsa Sovietskaya 51)* is recommended for its location, close to ploshchad Teatralnaya in the prettiest part of town. The hotel has been recently upgraded. Rooms with separate bath are $76/80.

Places to Eat

The best place in town for food, atmosphere and cocktails with names like *zhurnalistochka* is the ***Press Klub*** on ulitsa Lukashevskogo in the *Argumenty i Fakty* newspaper building. It's open from 10 am to 4 pm and 4.30 pm to midnight. Despite being a little gloomy, the ***restaurant*** in the basement of Hotel Petropavlovsk serves mostly fish which is well presented and reasonably priced. Upstairs, on the ground level, there's a cheerful ***cafe-bar*** that serves decent food from an English-language menu.

The large restaurant attached to ***Hotel Avacha*** may have reopened after extensive renovation. There is also the respectable-looking ***Restoran Lonkhey*** *(prospekt 50 let Oktyabrya 24)*. It's open from noon to 5 pm and 7 to 11.30 pm.

There's a snack bar on the 1st floor of the ***Holkam supermarket*** *(ulitsa Leninskaya 62)*, with sandwiches, pastries, cakes and coffee – it's open until 7 pm. The supermarket, a sparkling Dutch-Swiss-Russian venture, is also a good place to shop for food supplies. There's also a row of 24-hour shops within walking distance of Hotel Petropavlovsk, the best of which is ***Slavyansky***. Other places include the ***traders market*** just south of Komsomolskaya ploshchad and the ***farmers market*** on ulitsa Voitsesheka.

Getting There & Away

Unless you're lucky enough to hitch a ride on a coal barge from Vladivostok, the only way to get in or out of Petropavlovsk-Kamchatsky, and indeed the rest of Kamchatka, is to fly. There are daily flights to/from Moscow ($290, nine hours) and Khabarovsk ($180, three hours), and flights three times a week to/from Vladivostok ($250, three hours).

You can book tickets at the ticket agency (open from 9 am to 1 pm and 2 to 6 pm weekdays) in Hotel Petropavlovsk. The main Aeroflot office is in the building adjacent to the hotel. There is also a half-dozen

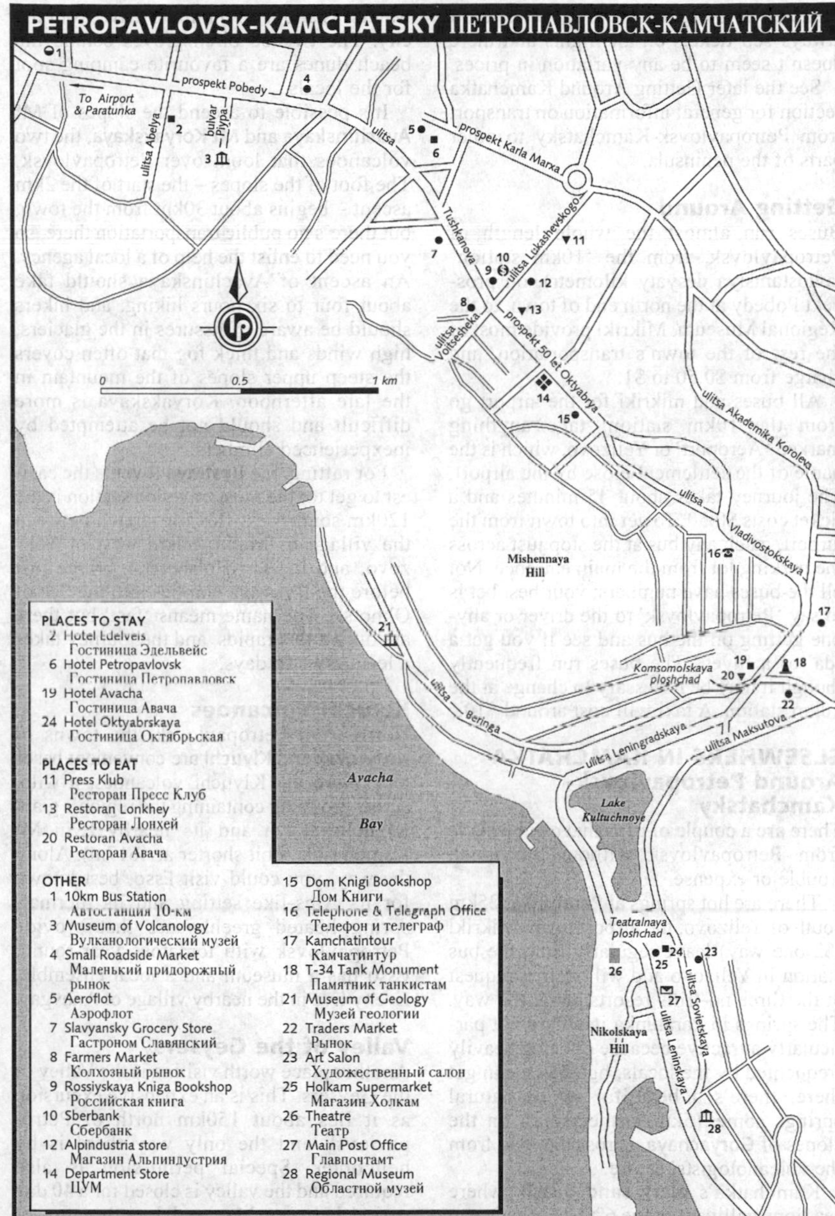
PETROPAVLOVSK-KAMCHATSKY ПЕТРОПАВЛОВСК-КАМЧАТСКИЙ
To Airport & Paratunka
prospekt Pobedy
bulvar Piypa
ulitsa Abelya
ulitsa Tushkanova
prospekt Karla Marxa
ulitsa Lukashevskogo
ulitsa Voitsesheka
prospekt 50 let Oktyabrya
ulitsa Akademika Koroleva
ulitsa Vladivostokskaya
Mishennaya Hill
Komsomolskaya ploshchad
ulitsa Beringa
ulitsa Leningradskaya
ulitsa Maksutova
Avacha Bay
Lake Kultuchnoye
Teatralnaya ploshchad
ulitsa Sovietskaya
ulitsa Leninskaya
Nikolskaya Hill
0 0.5 1 km
PLACES TO STAY
2 Hotel Edelveis
Гостиница Эдельвейс
6 Hotel Petropavlovsk
Гостиница Петропавловск
19 Hotel Avacha
Гостиница Авача
24 Hotel Oktyabrskaya
Гостиница Октябрьская
PLACES TO EAT
11 Press Klub
Ресторан Пресс Клуб
13 Restoran Lonkhey
Ресторан Лонхей
20 Restoran Avacha
Ресторан Авача
OTHER
1 10km Bus Station
Автостанция 10-км
3 Museum of Volcanology
Вулканологический музей
4 Small Roadside Market
Маленький придорожный рынок
5 Aeroflot
Аэрофлот
7 Slavyansky Grocery Store
Гастроном Славянский
8 Farmers Market
Колхозный рынок
9 Rossiyskaya Kniga Bookshop
Российская книга
10 Sberbank
Сбербанк
12 Alpindustria store
Магазин Альпиндустрия
14 Department Store
ЦУМ
15 Dom Knigi Bookshop
Дом Книги
16 Telephone & Telegraph Office
Телефон и телеграф
17 Kamchatintour
Камчатинтур
18 T-34 Tank Monument
Памятник танкистам
21 Museum of Geology
Музей геологии
22 Traders Market
Рынок
23 Art Salon
Художественный салон
25 Holkam Supermarket
Магазин Холкам
26 Theatre
Театр
27 Main Post Office
Главпочтамт
28 Regional Museum
Областной музей

agencies in town, but these agencies don't always sell tickets on all flights and there doesn't seem to be any variation in prices.

See the later Getting Around Kamchatka section for general information on transport from Petropavlovsk-Kamchatsky to other parts of the peninsula.

Getting Around

Buses run almost the whole length of Petropavlovsk, from the '10km station' (avtostantsiya desyaty kilometr), on prospekt Pobedy at the north end of town, to the Regional Museum. Mikriki provide most of the rest of the town's transportation, and charge from $0.50 to $1.

All buses and mikriki for the airport go from the 10km station; take anything marked 'Aeroport' or Yelizovo, which is the name of the settlement close by the airport. The journey takes about 45 minutes and a ticket costs $0.50. To get into town from the airport, catch any bus at the stop just across the parking lot from the main entrance. Not all the buses have numbers; your best bet is to say 'Petropavlovsk' to the driver or anyone getting on the bus and see if you get a 'da' or a 'nyet.' The buses run frequently though it may be necessary to change at the 10km station. A taxi will cost around $10.

ELSEWHERE IN KAMCHATKA

Around Petropavlovsk-Kamchatsky

There are a couple of trips that can be made from Petropavlovsk without too much trouble or expense.

There are hot springs at **Paratunka**, 25km south of Yelizovo, the airport town. Mikriki ($2 one way) leave regularly from the bus station in Yelizovo and will stop at request at the three no-frills resorts along the way. The springs in Paratunka itself are not particularly attractive because of being heavily frequented by the locals, but if you can get there, there's a beautiful set of natural springs some 15km farther south on the slopes of **Goryachaya**, across the road from the volcanologists' centre.

Kamchatka's **black-sand beach**, where sea lions gallivant in the 6°C Pacific Ocean waters, is about a 30 minute drive from the city. The twisted birch groves behind the beach dunes are a favourite camping spot for the locals.

It's possible to ascend the slopes of **Mt Avachinskaya** and **Mt Koryakskaya**, the two volcanoes that loom over Petropavlovsk. The foot of the slopes – the start of the 2km ascent – begins about 30km from the town, but there's no public transportation there, so you need to enlist the help of a local agency. An ascent of Avachinskaya should take about four to six hours hiking, and hikers should be aware of fissures in the glaciers, high winds and thick fog that often covers the steep upper slopes of the mountain in the late afternoon. Koryakskaya is more difficult and should not be attempted by inexperienced climbers.

For rafting, the **Bystraya River** is the easiest to get to; the most travelled section is the 120km south-west-flowing stretch between the village of Malki, 80km west of Yelizovo, and the Ust-Bolsheretsk bridge just before the Bystraya empties into the Sea of Okhotsk. The name means 'fast' but there are only a few rapids, and the journey takes a leisurely two days.

Klyuchi Volcanoes

North from Petropavlovsk, the towns of **Kozyrevsk** and **Klyuchi** are convenient bases to explore the Klyuchi volcanoes, a wild, active grouping containing the region's giant Klyuchevskaya and its nearby twin Mt Kamen (just a bit shorter at 4617m). Along the way, you could visit **Esso**, best known for its Alps-like setting and its thermal-spring heated greenhouses that provide Petropavlovsk with tomatoes year-round. Esso has a museum and a local ensemble. Eveny live in the nearby village of Anavgay.

Valley of the Geysers

Another place worth visiting is the Valley of the Geysers. This is an expensive excursion as it lies about 150km north of Petropavlovsk and the only way there is by helicopter. Special permission is also required and the valley is closed for a 40 day period between May and June because of migrating birds. At present the tourist agency Sogjoy (see the later Local Guides & Agencies section) is the only organisation empowered to grant access, but other tourist firms can arrange visits through Sogjoy. Make sure you also touch down in **Uzon Caldera**, the closest you'll probably ever get to feeling like you're on another planet. This is the remains of an ancient volcano, now a 10km crater with steamy lakes, enormous mushrooms and prolific berry bushes (thus well attended by the local bears). But this is not a place to go traipsing around without a guide as the ground in places is crusty and delicate over boiling mud.

Southern Volcanoes Group

Another spectacular region is the group of southern volcanoes, including **Mt Mutnovskaya** which erupted in 1994. The valleys between the peaks are filled with thermal rivers and boiling lakes. There's skiing and snowboarding from June to August in **Rodnikovoe**, about 15km north of Mt Mutnovskaya in the Vilyucha River valley. It's a three hour drive on a dirt road to Rodnikovoe, which also has hot springs.

Lake Kurilskoe

Farther south, toward the tip of the peninsula, Lake Kurilskoe in the Yuzhno-Kamchatsky reserve is the spawning ground for over a million salmon each year and, consequently, home to the Stellar sea eagle, a bird with a wingspan of around 2.5m.

GETTING AROUND KAMCHATKA

Once you've arrived at Petropavlovsk, the major problem is going to be getting around. With only one major road on the peninsula and no railways, the most common means of reaching A from B is flying. Lumbering Mi-8 helicopters operate like minibuses on Kamchatka, ferrying scientists, volcanologists and hunters between remote settlements and isolated cabins. For a one hour ride in a helicopter you're looking at a minimum of $1200 split over a maximum of 20 people. Even areas that are close enough not to necessitate helicopter transfers often, because of the lack of roads, require some kind of tracked all-terrain vehicle *(vezdekhod)*.

A few years back, scheduled short-hop flights around Kamchatka could be had for ice cream money. Now the cost is as much as a flight to Moscow and flights are mostly used by locals who have made it rich by ferrying Korean popsicles from Petropavlovsk to the isolated villages. A flight from Petropavlovsk to the west-coast Koryaki settlements of Palana and Ust-Khayryuzovo will cost $260. Flights are slightly cheaper to Ust-Kamchatsk, a small fishing town at the mouth of the Kamchatka River; Kozyrevsk, a village 40km from the volcano Klyuchevskaya; and Ozernovsky, toward the southern tip of the peninsula and just 15km from Lake Kurilskoe.

A regular bus runs from Petropavlovsk via Esso, before going on to Klyuchi. Depending on the condition of the road, it takes 12 to 15 hours to get there. A one way ticket costs $33. None of these places is set up to receive tourists and it's recommended that you take advice on accommodation before heading up there (see the following Local Guides & Agencies section). Also, take advice on your route and its possible dangers. Many locals have died exploring Kamchatka, whether overcome by sulphurous fumes on the volcanoes, crashing through thin crusts into boiling pits below, caught by winter avalanches or mauled by one of the region's large bear population.

Organised Tours

Local Guides & Agencies These local guides are usually the same ones the foreign agencies contract, so going to them directly is almost always cheaper. Do keep in mind, Russian guides work in constantly changing conditions. Between your last email and your arrival, prices may have doubled and the volcano you were planning to climb may have erupted. Be flexible. These guides know their turf and can provide unforgettable experiences even if they're not the ones you expected.

Alpindustriya-Kamchatka (☎ 41522-3 02 46, ☎/fax 7 24 89), Kosmichesky 4-61, Petropavlovsk-Kamchatsky, 683003 Russia, is run by two brothers, mountain climbers Vitaly and Sergey Malkov, out of a camping equipment store where you can also rent tents, sleeping bags, skis and other gear, a real plus if you don't want to be lugging this stuff with you across Russia. The store is located behind Restoran Lonkhey on prospekt 50 let Oktyabrya. For about $100 for transport by jeep, you'll be taken out to the ski camp in Rodnikovoe, where lodging in wooden huts is another $10 per night. For about $30, you will be dropped off in the evening at the foot of Avachinskaya and Koryakskaya volcanoes and retrieved the next day after your climb. For the same amount, camping on the beach can be arranged. A three day rafting trip along the Bystraya costs $75 per person, including transportation and food. Given ample notice, the agency can arrange and provide guides for longer expeditions, including ascents of Klyuchevskaya.

Kamchatintour (☎ 41522-7 1034, ☎ 7 3776, fax 4152-11 80 07, intur@svyaz.kamchatka.su), ulitsa Leningradskaya 124b, Petropavlovsk-Kamchatsky, handles 300 to 1000 tourists a season, mostly foreigners who come to the peninsula aboard posh cruise ships. Its tours are expensive, and the staff, though friendly and knowledgeable, may be unable to help individuals who don't give a week or two advance notice. That said, it may be able to plug last-minute travellers into an existing group or offer something on a smaller scale, like an overnight trip to Esso or Paratunka. Its offices are 150m behind the 16 storey octagonal tower (almost the only tower block in town), on the 4th floor.

Sogjoy (☎ 41522-6 14 93 or ☎ 6 29 84), ulitsa Sopochnaya 13, the tourist company that holds the key to the Valley of the Geysers, is in Yelizovo, the settlement by the airport. Some of the previously listed companies, however, should also be able to get you access to the valley, either by dealing with Sogjoy themselves or by some other means.

Vasily Galichin (☎ 4152-11 25 44) used to run a tour company. He now owns Kamchatka's first copy shop, U Pushki, directly below the Regional Museum. Though he's technically out of the guide business, he still is a good contact and will give advice on routes and maybe help make travel arrangements.

Overseas Agencies Society Expeditions (toll-free ☎ 800-548 8669, www.societyexpeditions.com), 2001 Western Ave #300, Seattle, WA 98121, has cruises of the northern Pacific rim, including Kamchatka, starting at $5820 per person.

Zeagrahm & Eco Expeditions (toll-free ☎ 800-628 8747, zoe@zeco.com, www.zeco.com), 1414 Dexter Ave N #327, Seattle, WA 98109, has similar cruises aboard the same ship, the *Clipper Odyssey*.

UKRAINE

Facts about Ukraine

Ukraine, meaning 'borderland', was the traditional crossroads between the Baltic and Black seas, the fringe between Europe and Central Asia. Settled since ancient times, Ukraine's long tradition of cultural identity stems back to Kyivan Rus, which at its peak in the 10th century was one of Europe's most powerful kingdoms. But like all borderlands, it was fated to be a battleground and coveted prize for surrounding empires – the Poles and Lithuanians to the north and north-west, the Russians from the north-east, and the Tatars and Turks from the south. Between the 14th and 19th centuries, its boundaries fluctuated during wars and broken alliances. Its population was eventually subjected to serfdom and Ukrainian culture was forcibly suppressed. In the 1930s, Stalin starved to death over six million of its people and WWII chose it as a chief battleground. At the start of the 21st century, Ukraine remains a borderland between east and west, dramatised in its struggle to reconcile its tense post-Soviet membership in the CIS with its utopian aspiration for EU and NATO membership.

Despite continuing hardships, the Ukrainian people have preserved their identities and nurtured their cultures. The country's national anthem, *Ukraine Has Not Yet Died*, summarises the national psyche – one dominated by the age-long desire for sovereignty, combined with the ingrained will to survive. Ukrainians have learned to rely on nothing but themselves, their resourcefulness and their tight, self-sufficient communities. They are tough, hard-working people, but also open and friendly, with a hospitable attitude towards foreigners, who remain a curiosity outside of the capital.

Contemporary Ukraine is a vast land, as varied and colourful as its history. In the west, the beautiful city of Lviv is stamped with a Central European elegance and is the soul of Ukrainian patriotism. Backwater villages of picket fences, duck ponds and overloaded horse carts spill across its surrounding countryside. To the south sits exotic Odesa, an intriguing port city. The ancestral Tatar homeland of Crimea, at the foot of the country, is a fabulous peninsula famed for its spectacular palaces, castles, mountains and seaside resort of Yalta. Eastern Ukraine is the country's smoggy industrial heart, pricked through with belching cities and Cossack relics. Rolling steppe sweeps across the entire country. Finally, there's Kyiv, the cosmopolitan capital. A millennium ago, it served as the centre of the first recognisable Eastern Slavic state. Today, its bustling streets and dazzling nightlife juxtapositioned against historic glittering onion domes continue to grace the city with an aura unique to the region.

HISTORY

Scythians, Greeks & Sarmatians

The Scythians, excellent horse riders who arrived from Central Asia, dominated the plains north of the Black Sea from the 7th to 4th centuries BC. The Greek Herodotus described sacrifices of 50 or more people to accompany a Scythian king's burial. He also reported that the royalty didn't wash but had vapour baths – and that for recreation they retired into tents and threw cannabis 'seeds' on heated stones, creating 'a strong aroma that no Greek burnt offering can match'. Scythians are most famed for the superb goldwork found in their tombs from the Caucasus to Hungary – often featuring highly detailed animal or

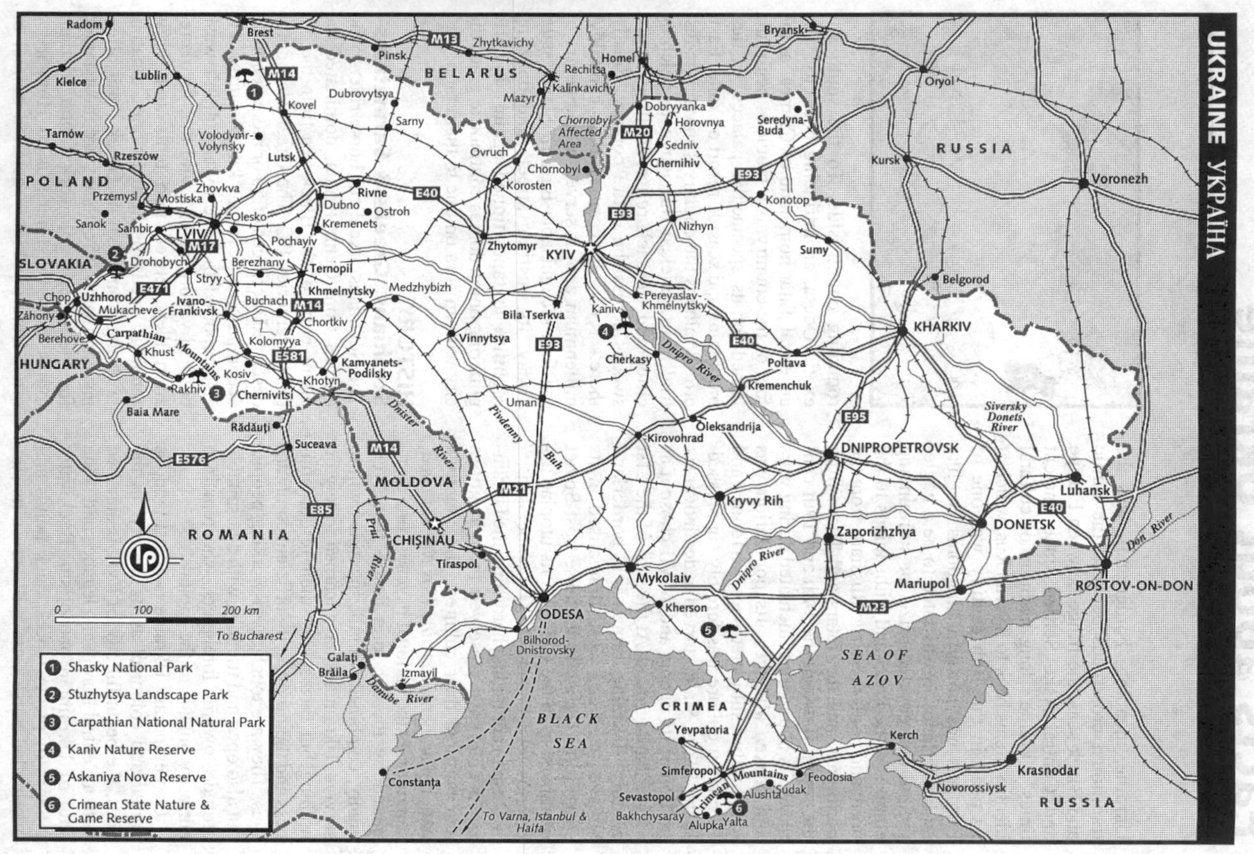
UKRAINE УКРАЇНА
RUSSIA
BELARUS
POLAND
SLOVAKIA
HUNGARY
ROMANIA
MOLDOVA
CRIMEA
SEA OF AZOV
BLACK SEA
KYIV
KHARKIV
DNIPROPETROVSK
DONETSK
ODESA
LVIV
ROSTOV-ON-DON
CHIŞINĂU
Voronezh
Oryol
Kursk
Belgorod
Bryansk
Homel
Rechitsa
Kalinkavichy
Mazyr
Zhytkavichy
Pinsk
Brest
Kovel
Lutsk
Rivne
Dubno
Ostroh
Sarny
Dubrovytsya
Kremenets
Ternopil
Pochayiv
Berezhany
Olesko
Zhovkva
Volodymyr-Volynsky
Mostiska
Przemysl
Sambir
Drohobych
Stryy
Ivano-Frankivsk
Uzhhorod
Mukacheve
Chop
Záhony
Berehove
Khust
Rakhiv
Kosiv
Kolomyya
Chernivtsi
Khotyn
Kamyanets-Podilsky
Chortkiv
Khmelnytsky
Buchach
Medzhybizh
Vinnytsya
Zhytomyr
Korosten
Ovruch
Chornobyl
Chornobyl Affected Area
Chernihiv
Sedniv
Horovnya
Dobryanka
Seredyna-Buda
Konotop
Sumy
Nizhyn
Pereyaslav-Khmelnytsky
Kaniv
Cherkasy
Bila Tserkva
Uman
Kirovohrad
Oleksandrija
Kremenchuk
Poltava
Kryvy Rih
Zaporizhzhya
Mariupol
Luhansk
Mykolaiv
Kherson
Bilhorod-Dnistrovsky
Tiraspol
Izmayil
Galaţi
Brăila
Constanţa
Yevpatoria
Simferopol
Sevastopol
Bakhchysaray
Alupka
Yalta
Alushta
Sudak
Feodosia
Kerch
Novorossiysk
Krasnodar
Lublin
Radom
Kielce
Tarnów
Rzeszów
Sanok
Baia Mare
Suceava
Rădăuţi
Crimean Mountains
Carpathian Mountains
Dnipro River
Don River
Siversky Donets River
Pivdenny Buh
Dnister River
Prut River
Danube River
To Varna, Istanbul & Haifa
To Bucharest
M13
M14
M17
M20
M21
M23
E40
E85
E93
E95
E471
E576
E581
0
100
200 km
1 Shasky National Park
2 Stuzhytsya Landscape Park
3 Carpathian National Natural Park
4 Kaniv Nature Reserve
5 Askaniya Nova Reserve
6 Crimean State Nature & Game Reserve

Ukrainian Place Names

Ironically, it is the Russified version of Ukrainian city names – indiscriminately bandied about under the USSR – that Anglophones are most familiar with. Yet since independence, Ukrainian city names have, rightly so, made something of a comeback. That is why, in this guide, we use 'Kyiv' (the English transliteration from the Ukrainian spelling) and not 'Kiev' (the English transliteration from the Russian spelling); 'Odesa' (Ukrainian) and not 'Odessa' (Russian); 'Lviv' (Ukrainian) rather than 'Lvov' (Russian); 'Uzhhorod' (Ukrainian) rather than 'Uzhgorod' (Russian); the Ukrainian 'Chornobyl' rather than the Russian 'Chernobyl', and so on ...

human representations. The finest collections are in Kyiv's Caves Monastery and the Hermitage in St Petersburg.

Around the same time as the Scythians arrived on the Ukraine steppes, Greeks, mainly from western Asia Minor, established colonies around the Black Sea coast. The two groups traded, intermarried and sometimes fought. Much of the famed Scythian goldwork was crafted by Greeks. Between the 4th and 2nd centuries BC, the Sarmatians from the east displaced the Scythians everywhere except in Crimea.

Ostrogoths, Huns, Slavs & Khazars

In the 2nd century AD, the Ostrogoths, a Germanic people from the vicinity of northern Poland, set up a state covering most of modern Ukraine. In about 370 they were subjugated by the Huns, the first of a series of nomad invaders originating in Mongolia. The Huns set up a western steppe empire and threatened the Roman Empire.

In the 6th and 7th centuries, the Slavs took advantage of the shake-up caused by the Huns to spread west, south and east – including throughout Ukraine – from the vicinity of the northern Carpathian Mountains and Vistula valley in present-day Poland. In the 8th century, most of Ukraine fell under the rule of the Khazars, originally a nomadic grouping of Turkic and Iranian tribes in the Caucasus, who built an empire combining the military advantages of nomadic horsemen with Iranian and Jewish trading skills. They adopted Judaism in the 9th century, and their capital was Itil, near the mouth of the Volga.

Kyivan Rus

From the 6th century, Scandinavians had been exploring, trading and setting up small states east of the Baltic. Known as Varyagi (Varangians) or Rus to the Slavs, they had raided Constantinople and come into conflict with the Khazars before one of them, Oleh of Novgorod, declared himself ruler of Kyiv (Kiev in Russian) in 882. Initially a southern Varangian outpost with control over only part of north-central Ukraine, Kyiv grew to be capital of a large, unified Rus state which at its biggest – under Svyatoslav (962-72) – stretched from the Volga to the Danube and to the Baltic; its prosperity was based on the control of trade from the Baltic to the Black Sea by the Dnipro and other waterways. Its Nordic lords were assimilated into their Slavic subjects' culture.

Svyatoslav crushed the Khazars, only to open the way for continual conflict with the fierce Turkic Pechenegs, who defeated and killed him in 972. Nor could he overcome Constantinople, from where his successor, Volodymyr, accepted Christianity in 988, founding what later became the Russian and Ukrainian Orthodox Church. With the new religion came Byzantine ideas of imperial authority, the beginnings of literature, systematic education and law. Byzantine art (icons, mosaics, frescoes) and architecture were also introduced, from which descended entire Eastern Slavic traditions.

Russia, Ukraine and Belarus all stemmed from this Eastern Slavic state. Present-day Russia evolved from breakaway northern princedoms centred around the Novgorod and Vladimir-Suzdal regions, and present-day Ukraine from Kyiv and breakaway western princedoms of Galicia and Volyn. Each subsequently evolved different linguistic and cultural identities. By the 11th

UKRAINE

and 12th centuries, Kyivan Rus began to splinter, dividing into some 10 rival princedoms. Vladimir Monomakh (1113-25) was the last ruler to hold it all together. When Prince Andriy Bogolyubov of Suzdal sacked Kyiv in 1169, followed by the Mongols 70 years later, the end of an empire which had ruled for 350 years was complete, and the power base moved to the north and west.

Galician-Volynian Principality

The western Galicia and Volyn regions (comprising most of present-day western, central and northern Ukraine, as well as parts of north-eastern Poland and southern Belarus) united into the Galician-Volynian Principality under Prince Roman Mstyslavych from Volyn, who in 1203 defeated his northern rivals in Suzdal and retained control of Kyiv. There was a period of relative prosperity under Prince Roman's dynamic son King Danylo, and grandson Lev, during which time the capital cities of Volodymyr (present-day Volodymyr-Volynsky), Halych and Lviv flourished along major east-west trade routes. The dynasty ended after only a few generations, with political control being absorbed by the expanding Polish and Lithuanian kingdoms in the mid-14th century. This marked the end of Ukraine's short period of self-determination, save for brief periods during the Cossack Hetmanate. During the ensuing centuries, the country chafed under the control of various external powers.

Tatars & Turks

Jenghis Khan never quite reached Ukraine, but his grandson Batu devastated Kyiv in 1240. While the Galician-Volynian Principality was controlling western Ukraine, much of eastern and southern Ukraine along with parts of European Russia and a good chunk of Siberia came under the power of the Volga-based Golden Horde.

The Golden Horde became Turkified, embraced Islam, and traded with the Mediterranean through Italian colonies in Crimea. It was weakened in the 14th century by the Black Death, the growing military strength of Moscow in the north and the expansion of Poland and Lithuania in the west. Then Timur, the last great Central Asian conqueror, invaded the region in 1395 and smashed the Golden Horde's capital, Sarai, on the Volga. The Golden Horde disintegrated in the 15th century, dividing into several still smaller khanates. One – the Crimean Khanate – became a vassal of the Constantinople-based Ottoman Turk Empire, which went on to control all coastal Ukraine by 1520. The Turks and the Crimean Tatars, as the people of the Crimean Khanate were known, were big thorns in Ukrainian, Russian and Polish sides until the 18th century.

Cossacks

The Ukraine steppe was only sparsely populated due to military devastation and plague. Initially a border region on the fringe of several expanding empires, the focus of the region's history shifted here following the fall of the Galician-Volynian Principality in the late 14th century. A century on, the area attracted runaway serfs, criminals, Orthodox refugees and other misfits from Polish and Lithuanian domains to the north-west. Along with a few semi-independent Tatar bands, the inhabitants formed self-governing militaristic communities and became known as *kazaks* (Cossacks in English), from a Turkic word meaning 'outlaw, adventurer or free person'. The people elected ruling chieftains *(hetmans)*. The most famous group of Ukrainian Cossacks, based below the rapids *(za porozhy)* on the lower Dnipro, were known as the Zaporizky, made famous by their fortified island community called Zaporizky Sich (see Zaporizhzhya in the Eastern Ukraine chapter). The Ukrainian Cossacks eventually developed the self-ruling Cossack Hetmanate, which to some degree reasserted the concept of Ukrainian self-determination, although it was 'officially' under Polish, and later Russian, rule. At the height of their power, the Cossacks waged a number of successful campaigns against the Turks, sacking the Black Sea cities of Varna and Kafa and twice assaulting Constantinople (in 1615 and 1620).

In 1596 the Union of Brest set up the Uniate Church (better known as the Ukrainian

Catholic or Greek Catholic Church) which recognised the Roman pope as leader, but followed Orthodox forms of worship involving the Old Slavonic language. This brought millions of peasants in the eastern and southern border areas of the Polish-Lithuanian state (which had once been in Kyivan Rus) into the Catholic fold of their rulers without really changing their religious practices. The Uniate Church became a binding cultural force for most Ruthenians, as these early Orthodox Ukrainians under Polish and Lithuanian control came to be known. The Cossacks remained fully Orthodox.

Polish monarchs were often at odds with the Cossacks, suppressing their autonomy while continuing to use them as mercenaries. The local peasant population also despised their Polish landlords. After a number of unsuccessful uprisings, a huge rebellion in 1648 led by the famous Cossack Hetman Bohdan Khmelnytsky (aided by Tatar cavalry) destroyed the Polish army at the battle of Pyliavtsi, near the present-day city of Khmelnytsky. Storming past Lviv, Khmelnytsky was poised for an invasion of Poland, but decided to accept an armistice and returned triumphantly to Kyiv. The following year at another battle against Polish King Casimir, near Zboriv, Khmelnytsky was betrayed by his Tatar allies and forced to sign an armistice. A further forced armistice in 1651 made Khmelnytsky finally realise that foreign support was necessary for a decisive victory over the Poles. He engaged in a formal but controversial military alliance with Muscovy in 1654. Subsequent conflicts and counteralliances with the Poles and the Swedes threw the situation into disarray. In 1660, a war broke out between Poland and Russia over control of Ukraine, ending in treaties of 1667 and 1668 granting Russia control over Kyiv and northern Ukraine east of the Dnipro. The Poles kept territory to the west of the river, laying the foundation of the divide between eastern and western Ukraine still evident today. Hetman Ivan Mazepa, aiming to unite Polish and Russian-dominated Ukraine, allied with Sweden against Russia's Peter the Great but was beaten at Poltava (1709). Following victories against the Ottomans, Catherine the Great destroyed the Cossack Sich in 1775.

The Cossacks were free peasant-warriors who served as cavalry under the tsars

Russian Control

The absorption of Ukraine was pivotal in the emergence of the Russian Empire as a world power. During the 18th century, following a series of wars with the Turks, Russia expanded into southern Ukraine. The Partitions of Poland (1772-95) saw most of western Ukraine transferred from Polish to Russian hands, except for the far west, around Lviv, which went to the Habsburg Empire. Ukrainian nationalism was born in Kyiv in the 1840s, its guru and moral leader being the prolific writer and poet Taras Shevchenko. In 1863 and 1876 tsarist authorities attempted to suppress the movement by banning the Ukrainian language in schools, journals and books. The focus of the nationalist movement shifted to

Lviv, the centre of the Uniate Church, where the Ruthenian population resented the continuing dominance of Roman Catholic Poles in this eastern corner of the Habsburg Empire.

20th Century

Civil War Following WWI and the collapse of tsarist power, Ukraine had a chance to gain independence, but none of the bewildering array of factions could win decisive support. A council *(rada)* in Kyiv, elected by mainly urban dwellers, proclaimed the autonomous Ukrainian National Republic (UNR) in 1918. Mykhailo Hrushevsky, a Ukrainian leader returned from exile, was elected the first official president of Ukraine. Meanwhile, Russian Bolsheviks, under their leader Skrypnyk, set up a rival Congress of Soviets in Kharkiv. Civil war broke out and exploded into anarchy, with six different armies vying for power and Kyiv changing hands five times within a year. The Reds, with the help of Bolsheviks, took Kyiv first, but were driven out by the UNR aided by Germans and Austrians, who in turn set up a quasi-Hetmanate state under General Skoropadsky in April 1918. Eight months later, the Directory, a rival government made up of former UNR members, took control of Kyiv, but fell into conflict between its two leaders, socialist Vynnychenko and nationalist Petlyura. At the same time, a self-proclaimed anarchist, Nestor Makhno, gained support in the south. The Bolsheviks again invaded and retook Kyiv in February 1919.

Meanwhile, in Lviv, the West Ukrainian National Republic (ZUNR) was proclaimed, beginning its own short war with Poland, which ended after seven months with an international decision to cede western Ukraine to Poland as a 'protectorate'. The remaining western Ukrainian troops joined with their eastern counterparts, and under the command of Petlyura engaged in battles against the Whites under General Denikin, and against the Red Bolshevik Army. In alliance with Poland, Petlyura launched another counterassault in April 1920, retaking Kyiv in May, only to be driven out and then cut out of another deal brokered between the two stronger powers. Ukraine was again divided under the Treaty of Riga, with Poland, along with Romania and Czechoslovakia, retaining portions of western Ukraine, while the Soviet forces were given control of the rest. Petlyura set up a government in exile, and was assassinated in Paris in 1926. During these battles, Jews were targeted by all sides – especially the Whites, who carried out numerous pogroms.

Soviet Power Ukraine was a nominally independent Soviet Socialist Republic until it became a founder member of the USSR in 1922. When Stalin took power in 1927, he looked upon Ukraine as a laboratory for testing Soviet restructuring, while stamping out 'harmful' nationalism. In 1932-33 he engineered a famine (see the boxed text 'Starved to Death'). Intellectual and political executions and deportations followed, along with the destruction of numerous Ukrainian cathedrals. Over 250 buildings, churches, cemeteries and palaces were systematically razed to the ground. During the great purges of 1937-39, an estimated one million people in the USSR were executed and a further three to 12 million sent to labour camps, a high proportion of them from Ukraine. Kyiv replaced Kharkiv as the capital of Soviet Ukraine in 1934.

WWII The Red Army rolled into Polish Ukraine in September 1939. The Germans attacked in 1941 and by the end of the year controlled virtually all of Ukraine, occupying it for over two years. Two major factions of Ukrainian partisans emerged: Soviet partisans controlled by Moscow; and the UPA (Ukrainian Insurgent Army), mainly concentrated in the west. The UPA fought both German and Russian troops with the aim of establishing an independent Ukraine. By the end of 1943 Kharkiv and Kyiv were retaken by the Soviet Red Army, which in early 1944 launched a massive offensive of 2.3 million men that pushed back the German forces and obliterated Ukraine in the process. An estimated six million Ukrainians died in the war, which left most of the country's cities in ruin.

UKRAINE

Starved to Death

The famine of 1932 to 1933 was artificially engineered and should never have happened. There was food, and plenty of it. Yet estimates put the death toll during these years at between five and seven million. It was a tragedy on an unimaginable scale that crippled the entire country.

In an experiment, Stalin collectivised the farms and ordered the production of unrealistic quotas of grain which was forcibly confiscated. No grain from a collective farm could be distributed to the peasants until all quotas had been met. Party authorities conducted house-to-house searches and confiscated all grain. Any man, woman or child caught stealing grain from a government storehouse could be executed. Internal passports were issued to prevent desperate people running off in search of food. Peasants starved to death under the gaze of gun-wielding Communist Party activists. Entire villages died of starvation. Cannibalism was commonly reported.

Soviet authorities denied for years that a famine had ever occurred. Western governments played down the atrocities as they did not want to strain ties with the new Soviet state.

After the war, the USSR kept the territory it had taken from Poland in 1939. Ukraine, like Belarus, got its own seat in the UN on the grounds of extra suffering during the war. A Ukrainian army under a government in exile led by Stepan Bandera (who was assassinated in Germany by a Soviet spy in 1959) continued a guerrilla existence up until the 1950s, while millions of Ukrainians were sent to Siberia for suspicion of 'disloyalty'. The Uniate Church, accused of collaboration with the Nazis and closely linked with Ukrainian nationalism, was banned by Stalin in 1946.

New Nationalism The focus of glasnost-era opposition to Soviet rule developed from the Uniate Church in the west and the 1986 Chornobyl disaster (see the boxed text 'Chornobyl' in Ukraine Facts for the Visitor).

With Chornobyl (called Chernobyl in Russian), discontent was provoked not only by the disaster itself but by the slow official response to it and the cover-up of its consequences. The first Kremlin announcement wasn't made until two days after the event, and May Day parades in Kyiv went ahead three days after the announcement, despite the fact that fallout was blowing over the city by that time.

The Uniate Church came out from underground in 1988, claiming four million adherents and rocking Lviv with marches and church takeovers. But the rest of Ukraine, with its large Russian and Orthodox populations, was slower off the nationalist mark. Rukh (Ukrainian People's Movement for Restructuring), the umbrella nationalist movement founded in Kyiv by prominent intellectuals and writers, won seats across the republic in the 1990 local elections, particularly in the secession-minded west, where it took control of Lviv and other city councils. But the communists still kept a majority in the republican parliament.

In July 1990, this parliament issued a sovereignty declaration which proved too little for the growing independence movement. In October, a wave of protest marches in Kyiv, inspired by hunger-striking students, forced the resignation of the old-guard prime minister. Another sign of growing nationalism was the revival of Ukraine's own autocephalous (self-governing) Orthodox Church, forcibly amalgamated with the Russian Orthodox Church in 1686.

Independent Ukraine Shortly after the failed Soviet coup in August 1991, the Communist Party of Ukraine (CPU) was banned from power and on 24 August 1991, the Verkhovna Rada (Supreme Council) adopted a declaration of independence pending a national referendum. In December some 84% of the population voted in favour of independence. Leonid Kravchuk, former chairman of the CPU, was elected president of Ukraine on 1 December 1991, and a national Armed Forces was established.

Almost immediately factions arose in the new government, disputing policy and the direction of economic reform. The leadership tended to revert to old centralist methods. Growing dissatisfaction forced the government to resign in September 1992. But difficulties likewise plagued the new government. Disagreements and tensions with Russia and the West concerning the future of Ukraine's cache of inherited nuclear weapons reached disturbing levels. In January 1994 an agreement was reached between Ukraine, Russia and the USA. In exchange for security guarantees and just compensation, Ukraine began a nuclear disarmament program which would see all Ukraine's nuclear missiles destroyed by December 2001. Complications over ownership of the Black Sea fleet harboured in the Crimean port of Sevastopol further strained Ukrainian-Russian relationships (see Government & Politics – Relations with Russia in this chapter).

Meanwhile, skyrocketing hyperinflation, fuel shortages and plummeting consumer power caused further widespread dissatisfaction, rekindling age-old differences between east and west. Western Ukrainians were concerned with achieving national independence and closer ties with the West, while the east pushed for closer economic union with Russia. The presidential election campaign in July 1994 was largely fought on these differences, with pro-Russian reformer Leonid Kuchma defeating Kravchuk; the vote was almost perfectly drawn along the line of the Dnipro River. The 1994 elections witnessed the rise of the re-established Ukrainian Communist Party, which won one-sixth of all seats in the Verkhovna Rada.

Relative economic stability was achieved by Kuchma during his years in office. Inflation fell from a spiralling 10,000% in 1993, to just under 40% in 1996 and to a record-low of 10.1% in 1997. The *hryvnia*, Ukraine's long-awaited national currency, was finally introduced in September 1996 and a process of privatisation kick-started into action. Kuchma purged the government of former communist hardliners opposed to economic restructuring, and clamped down on corrupt elements seen as paralysing Ukraine's progress towards a free market economy. In July 1997 he sacked several economic and justice ministers and, amid corruption allegations, replaced antireformist prime minister Pavlo Lazarenko with Valery Pustovoytenko, a former Dnipropetrovsk mayor and pro-reform ally. Lazarenko was consequently charged with embezzling over $2 million in state property and laundering over $4 million in Swiss bank accounts; in mid-1999 he was still awaiting trial.

Despite all this, living conditions declined and the government faced a crisis with its wage arrears, which stood at $2.3 billion at the start of 1997. In the March 1998 parliamentary elections, the Ukrainian Communist Party stormed to victory, gaining one vote in four and immediately forming a 180 seat power bloc – but not an outright majority – with its left-wing allies, the Socialists/Peasants and the Progressive Socialists. The split parliament consequently voted 19 times before successfully electing a new speaker – while the 1998 budget and over 100 bills desperately awaited parliament approval.

Strikes by miners and teachers demanding payment of wage arrears peppered 1998. In August, workers at a chemical plant in the Lviv Oblast threatened to release poisonous waste into the Dnister River if their wage arrears were not paid; while in the Poltava Oblast wives of unpaid military pilots picketed on an airfield, demanding their husbands be paid. A year of strikes climaxed in early 1999 with unpaid workers at nuclear power stations across the country threatening to cut off Ukraine's energy supply.

Any hopes Kuchma had of pulling his country out of recession were smashed by the collapse of the Russian rouble in August 1998. Despite Ukraine witnessing its first positive growth in GDP since independence during the first half of 1998, its fragile economy failed to weather the financial

To Kill or Not to Kill

Despite wanting to be part of Europe, Ukraine remains staunchly in favour of the death penalty – a legacy of the USSR which few want to see shed. Nowhere was this highlighted more than during the trial of serial killer Anatoly Onoprienko.

Dubbed the Terminator, the 39-year-old Ukrainian sailor was sentenced to death by shooting in March 1999 after murdering 52 people in Ukraine between 1989 and 1996. A nationwide search led by 2000 detectives and 3500 troops led to his eventual capture.

Onoprienko will languish on death row until the Ukrainian government decides which is the lesser of two evils: rid Ukraine of one of the world's worst mass murderers, or risk being thrown out of the Council of Europe for failing to scrap the death penalty. The last execution took place in Ukraine in March 1997; by law, the maximum jail sentence is 15 years.

storm that ripped across Russia. Consumer power in Ukraine plummeted as the hryvnia, in September alone, took a 51% tumble in value. Both the International Monetary Fund (IMF) and World Bank have since stepped in with crisis-staving loans, but it remains uncertain how quickly Ukraine will recover from this setback.

Presidential elections in October 1999 saw Kuchma run for a second five year term. The opposition (11 other candidates) represented the entire political spectrum, including green and socialist candidates. In true eastern Ukrainian style, however, 22% of punters voted for Communist Party leader Petro Symonenko, whose call for integration with Russia and Belarus, coupled with a halt to privatisation and an end to closer ties with the West, won the hearts of Ukraine's impoverished, Soviet-aspiring populace. Kuchma gained 36% of the votes but failed to win a majority, so faced Symonenko in run-off elections in mid-November. Final results saw Kuchma land almost 60% of the vote, assuring the incumbent president of another term in office. Results apart, it is clear that Ukraine's future promises to be as tempestuous and desperate as its past.

GEOGRAPHY

At 603,700 sq km, and stretching about 2000km east to west and 1000km north to south, Ukraine is the largest country wholly within Europe, scraping in just ahead of France. It is bordered by seven nations, with Russia to the east and north, Belarus to the north, Poland to the west and a large stretch of Black Sea coast to the south. It has short borders with Slovakia, Hungary, Romania and Moldova to the south-west.

The topography consists almost entirely of steppe – gently rolling, partially wooded plains – at a mean height of 175m. The horizon is broken from the north-west near Lutsk to the south-east near the central Dnipro River valley by a belt of highland, with river-valley gorges and ravines, some over 300m deep. The only serious mountains are a short stretch of the Carpathians in the west and the Crimean Mountains in the far south.

Approximately 3000 rivers flow through Ukraine. The four major rivers cross the country from west to east: the Dnister, the Pivdenny (southern) Buh, the 2201km-long Dnipro (981km of which flows through Ukraine), and the Siversky Donets. The first three flow into the Black Sea (the Dnipro making a great 90° bend south of Dnipropetrovsk to do so), but the Siversky Donets flows into the Don, which enters the Sea of Azov, part of the Black Sea.

A central 'black earth' belt of deep, thick, humus-rich soil *(chornozem)* – one of the world's most fertile regions – covers almost two-thirds of Ukraine. Regions of mineral wealth lie in the coal and iron belts of the far east and south-central regions.

CLIMATE

Inland Ukraine has a relatively moderate continental climate with little variation across the flat countryside. The hottest month is July, averaging 23°C, while the coldest, January, is freezing. During the big chill of December 1998, temperatures

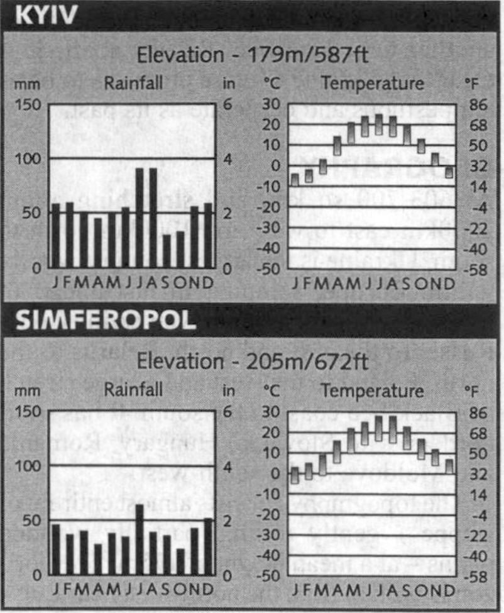

plummeted to a bone-numbing -25°C. On a brighter note, Kyiv is only frozen for two to three months of the year (December to February usually), compared to Moscow's five.

Eastern Ukraine can catch chilling Siberian breezes, while the west enjoys the tail end of the warm Mediterranean winds. The tiny corner of Transcarpathia, on the southwest side of the Carpathians, usually stays hotter and drier. On the coast, Yalta and Odesa enjoy a marginally subtropical climate and are much milder in winter, rarely dipping below freezing by day.

Inland, June and July are the wettest months. While most of the country averages 114cm of rain a year, Crimea has an annual average of only 40cm. Yalta experiences most of its limited rainfall during December and January. Come the melting snows of March and April, there is an enormous amount of natural flooding, particularly in the Carpathian region where villages become awash with mud and water and entire roads are swept away.

ECOLOGY & ENVIRONMENT

The Chornobyl disaster was but the tip of an iceberg of neglect whose continuing effects are chilling. During Soviet rule, the drive to industrialise was ruthless and exploitative, with little foresight or care given to environmental damage.

Besides the horrors of Chornobyl (increased rates of thyroid cancer, leukaemia, birth defects etc), other alarming developments occurred. In autumn 1988, 40,000 Chernivtsi children were temporarily evacuated after more than 100 of them started going bald and seeing nightmare visions. The blame was laid on thallium poisoning, although researchers were divided on the issue. Much of the Donbas and cities like Kryvy Rih and Zaporizhzhya have lingering clouds of pollution, causing increasing respiratory and other health problems. Acid rain has been reported in much of the Carpathians, around Kyiv and along the southern stretches of the Dnipro River. Many rivers have been polluted by waste runoff from industry and agriculture, due to lax restrictions and minimal controls. Much of the silt carried downstream from Chornobyl is radioactive – how far down the river and to what extent is still not fully known.

The Green Party in Ukraine is the political wing of the environmental organisation Zeleny Svit (Green World). Although small, it is a crucial voice in raising issues and encouraging politicians to clean, regulate and protect the environment. The State Committee for Environmental Protection is the official government agency assigned to deal with environmental and pollution problems.

FLORA & FAUNA

Most of Ukraine lies in a belt of steppe, primarily flat, heavily cultivated grasslands, with a few patches of forest comprised of oak, maple, linden and ash. Willow and aspen grow along the rivers. A thin belt of forest runs across the north of the country, consisting mostly of silver fir, beech, oak and spruce, with a few swamps also scattered about. The Carpathians are heavily wooded, with oaks and beech at the lower elevations and pines, junipers and alpine meadows on higher ground. A narrow strip of Mediterranean vegetation runs along the southern coast of Crimea. Vineyards thrive in Crimea and Transcarpathia.

Flora

Formerly known as the bread basket of the USSR, over half of Ukraine is covered in silvery fields of wheat, barley, rye, oats and sugar beets. Large tracts are also set aside as grazing land, and in spring explode into brilliant, swaying seas of red poppies *(maky)*, sunflowers *(sonyashnyky)* and golden mustard. Other wild flowers include daisies *(romani)*, blue *blavati*, yellow *lotysh* harvest flowers and the small, white *kashka*, which grows between the grasses and on the hills in the west. Lilac *(bozy)* is a common favourite, as is the colourful and tall hollyhock. Dozens of flowers are specially cultivated for nectar and honey *(med)* production.

Most cities have strolling areas lined with chestnut trees *(kashtany)* – the official symbol of Kyiv. The *kalina*, a deciduous bush with clusters of white flowers and red berries, was immortalised by Shevchenko and other poets as a national symbol, its fruit used for generations as a healthy juice and preserve. The linden tree *(lipa)* lines country lanes, and its fragrant flowers are used to make a sweet tea. Orchards of cherry *(vyshnya)* and apple *(yabluka)* trees have long been vivid images in songs and poems – they were a favourite of Shevchenko, and Chekhov wrote *The Cherry Orchard* while in Crimea. Birch *(bereza)* and beech *(buk)* trees grow in large groves, predominantly in the north and along rivers. With over 25 species in Ukraine, willow trees *(verba)* are traditionally used to make baskets, fences and household appliances. The largest concentration and variety of pines *(sosna)* is found in the small stretch of the Carpathian Mountains. Oak trees *(dub)* are concentrated around the Dnipro – the Zaporizky Sich was once built entirely from oak timbers. The yew tree, Carpathian rhododendron and edelweiss are protected species.

Fauna

Ukraine's animal life is diverse, with over 100 species of mammals. Millions of white geese and ducks dot the landscape and fill countless ponds across the countryside. Wolves, foxes, martens, deer, rabbits and other small furry animals are common to wooded regions and the Carpathian and Crimean mountains. The latter also has wild pigs, gazelles, mountain sheep and deer. Ukraine is home to over 350 species of birds, the secret messengers of many folk songs and fairy tales, and over 200 fish species. Species protected by law include the Carpathian wildcat and the great bustard.

National Parks

The Carpathian National Natural Park in south-western Ukraine is the largest national park *(nasionalny zapovidni parky)* and includes Hoverla (2061m), Ukraine's highest peak. The Shasky National Park in the extreme north-western corner of the country is a densely wooded lake district. Both are open to the public.

The Carpathian Mountains also shelter the Carpathian Biosphere Reserve, part of UNESCO's network of international biosphere reserves. The Carpathian Biosphere Reserve protects Europe's only remaining, virgin beech forest and was awarded the European Diploma for Protected Areas by the Council of Europe in 1998. The reserve is split into five different territories *(massifs)*, including the Stuzhytsya Landscape Park (14,665 hectares) on the Ukraine-Slovakia border. Public access is monitored.

Central Ukraine is home to a number of protected areas with controlled public access *(zapovidnyk)*. South of Kyiv, the Kaniv Nature Reserve includes 2000 hectares of pristine steppe forest and hills, with over 5000 indigenous plant species. The Askaniya Nova Reserve, 100km east of Kherson, covers 33,000 hectares of steppe, populated by wild animals introduced by a German settler in 1828, including herds of bison, zebras, wild horses, deer, Watusi cows and African ostrich. The Chornomorsky (Black Sea) Nature Reserve, about 75km south-west of Kherson, includes 57,000 hectares of estuary. It was established in 1927 to protect migratory birds. Excursions to the bird habitats are conducted in spring and autumn.

A small section of the Crimean State Nature and Game Reserve in the mountains north of Yalta is open to visitors. Covering 133,000 hectares in total, there are four such game reserves *(zapovidno-myslyvski hospodarstva)* in Ukraine.

GOVERNMENT & POLITICS

Ukraine's constitution, the final version of which was not adopted until June 1996, provides for sovereignty as a nonsocialist state. Executive power is in the hands of the president and prime minister, with legislative power vested in the 450 member Verkhovna Rada (Supreme Council). Parliamentary elections are held every four years, the most recent elections taking place in March 1998. Since 1997 member seats have been allocated by a proportional representation-type system.

The president, elected by popular vote for a five year term, appoints the prime minister and his 35 cabinet ministers; all appointments must be approved by the Verkhovna Rada. A new cabinet has to be formed every time a prime minister is appointed. President Leonid Kuchma won a second term of office in November 1999 presidential elections.

On a regional level, the country is divided into 24 administrative divisions *(oblasts)*, and one autonomous republic (Crimea). Each oblast is divided into administrative counties *(rayons)*. Oblasts and rayons are named after the principal town within their boundary.

Political Parties

Ukraine supports some 30 different political parties, eight of which overcame the 4% threshold needed to enter parliament in the 1998 parliamentary elections. The Communist Party of Ukraine (banned in 1991, re-established in May 1993) holds the most seats (119) in the Verkhovna Rada; followed by Rukh (Ukrainian People's Movement for Restructuring), the most powerful pro-reform party (47 seats). Other parties with deputies in parliament are the leftist Socialist/Peasant bloc (35 seats), the Greens (24), the pro-reform Popular Democratic Party (84), Hromada (Pavlo Lazarenko's left-centre opposition party which commands 39 seats), the leftist Progressive Socialists (17), and the centrist United Social Democratic Party (SPDU led by former president Leonid Kravchuk).

Relations with Russia

Ukraine's relations with Russia have long been controversial, serving only to exacerbate the deeply ingrained historical and ideological rift between Ukraine's east and west. While the west is opposed to closer ties and possible reunification with Russia, the east is not. During 1998 May Day celebrations, over 130,000 people took to the streets in eastern Ukrainian cities, calling for union with Russia and Belarus and for a restoration of the USSR. For these people, life under socialism, with its guaranteed housing, pensions and free medical care, remains a more rosy option than today's democracy (and accompanying economic woes).

Kuchma's cooperation with NATO is equally contentious. A member of NATO's Partnership for Peace program since 1994, Ukraine signed a new partnership accord with NATO in July 1997, prompting fears that Kuchma might eventually cede Ukraine's neutral stance in favour of fully fledged membership of the Western military alliance. These fears have been temporarily annulled by the Kosovo crisis which, in mid-1999, saw Ukraine side with Russian President Boris Yeltsin against NATO powers.

In February 1999 Russia's upper house of parliament, after months of stalling, finally ratified a historic friendship treaty signed by Kuchma and Yeltsin in May 1997. Under the treaty, Russia renounced all territorial claims on Ukraine (namely Crimea, part of Russia until 1954). In turn, Ukraine agreed to lease Sevastopol to Russia for 20 years, thereby allowing Russia to station its share of the Black Sea Fleet in the Crimean port. The Soviet Black Sea Fleet was split between the two countries in 1991 after the USSR collapsed. Under the leasing agreement, Russia will pay for its use of Sevastopol by writing off part of Ukraine's huge gas debt.

The status of Crimea's 63% ethnic Russian population is another hot topic. See the Crimea chapter for more information.

ECONOMY

The Ukrainian economy has dwindled sharply since the glory days of the USSR when it contributed 20% of Soviet production. Independence rendered virtually useless many of its ageing 'dinosaur' factories which, despite their glaring unprofitability, continue to be subsidised by the government in a bid to stave off mass unemployment. A report published by the Economic Bank for Reconstruction and Development (EBRD) in 1997 ranked the Ukrainian economy a dismal third from bottom in a survey conducted among 25 former communist countries.

Crucial measures towards privatisation have been slow, despite austere economic targets set by the IMF and World Bank. Loans promised by the latter in 1996-98 to aid Ukraine's painful transition from a centralised to a market economy were repeatedly suspended as the government dragged its feet on implementing economic reforms. In April 1998, the budget deficit for the first quarter was double the required 3% of GDP target, prompting the IMF to freeze payments on a $542 million loan and the World Bank to withdraw its aid program. Both bodies subsequently approved further funding, including a $2.2 billion IMF loan, spread over three years and conditional on the annual budget deficit in 1999 being reduced to 2% of GDP and annual inflation remaining at a steady 8% in 1999-2001.

Ukraine attracts little foreign investment compared to its more successful neighbours. Despite offering lucrative tax breaks and other financial incentives to foreign investors, Ukraine lured just $2.6 billion in foreign investment in 1991-98 (compared to Poland's $16.2 billion), and investment remains erratic. Telecommunications giant Motorola pulled out of a $500 million investment in Ukraine in April 1997, yet four months on, Ukrainian car manufacturers in Zaporizhzhya were celebrating a 10 year, $1.3 billion investment deal with Daewoo. The South Korean company produces 255,000 cars annually in its Zaporizhzhya factory, which created 150,000 new jobs when it opened.

Ukraine has enormous agricultural potential. It boasts some of the world's richest soils and largest sugar beet, grain and potato resources. Yet agricultural production is declining. Since independence, individuals have been allowed to own agricultural land (with the demise of collectivised farming), but few Ukrainians have sufficient capital to run a productive private enterprise. In 1998 crop production fell by 25.4% and sugar beet sales remained crippled by the 25% tax Russia imposed on sugar imports during the so-called 'sugar war' in May 1997. Over 90% of farms reported losses in 1998.

Purchasing power was reduced to less than zero following Russia's economic crisis in August 1998 and the consequent 51% devaluation of the Ukrainian hryvnia. In February 1999, the average monthly wage was $47, the minimum monthly wage was $16 and the average monthly pension was $30 – for the rare few who actually receive it. Wage and pension arrears, which have increased 11 and 32-fold respectively since 1995, stood at $1.95 billion and $585 million in May 1999.

Miners in eastern Ukraine are among the hardest hit by government efforts to meet IMF and World Bank requirements. Some 25 mines – out of an unprofitable 250 – were closed in 1996 but continuous strikes by miners have stopped further closure attempts. In June 1998 the government announced it would cut coal imports by 80% in a last-ditch effort to breathe new life into Ukraine's domestic coal industry.

War in Yugoslavia in 1999 dealt a further blow to Ukraine's fragile economy. Disrupted navigation on the Danube River following NATO's bombing of bridges in Novi Sad (Serbia) in April 1999 cost Ukraine $330,000 a day, according to Ukrainian government officials.

POPULATION & PEOPLE

Ukraine's population has steadily declined since independence, sitting at 50 million people in January 1999 (compared to 52 million in 1993). More than 50% of the population lives in urban areas like Kyiv, Kharkiv, Dnipropetrovsk, Odesa and Donetsk – Ukraine's largest cities, each home to over one million people. The rest of the population relies on an agricultural economy in small towns or villages.

Some 72% of the population is Ukrainian. Another 22% are ethnic Russians, mainly concentrated in the east of the country where national conviction is less intense, and most people speak Russian.

Other minority groups in Ukraine include Jews, Belarusians, Moldovans, Bulgarians, Poles, Hungarians and Romanians. The 500,000-strong Jewish minority is almost entirely urban, while the other minorities live clustered around their respective borders. Almost all of the country's Tatar population (250,000) lives in Crimea. Around 2.5 million Ukrainians live outside Ukraine, mainly in North America and in the Kuban region of Subcaucasian Russia.

EDUCATION

In the 1980s, about half of the country's pupils were taught in the Russian language, although Ukrainians constituted over 70% of the population. After independence, Ukrainian tuition was made available for all students, but choice was still individual. Small funds were also allotted to provide education in the language of minorities such as Hungarian, Polish and Romanian. Ukrainian history and literature, rather than Russian and Soviet, were given a new emphasis in the curriculum. New schools were opened, including the once-renowned Kyiv-Mohyla Akademy, the first higher education institution in Ukraine, dating from 1615. A hotbed of Ukrainian nationalism, it was closed by the tsars and only reopened in 1992 after independence.

ARTS

For decades the Western world perceived Ukraine simply as a part of Russia. Moscow's monopoly ensured that history books and cultural references placed Ukraine as an addendum to the dominant power, denying its unique and characteristic voice. Borsch, painted eggs and many of the famous Cossack song and dance traditions originated in Ukraine, not Russia.

Dance

Ballet Classical ballet was introduced to Ukraine in the 18th century, performed by serfs as entertainment for nobility. In the 19th century, Ukrainian ballet switched to an operetta style, with performances such as *Zaporizhzhets za Dunayem* (Zaporizky beyond the Danube, 1863), before turning to imitate the Russian, French and Italian counterparts of the time. The first ballets to be staged written solely by Ukrainian composers were in the 1930s, and included Verykivsky's *The Nobleman Kanovsky*, which fused classical ballet with traditional folk dance.

During the Soviet era, ballets such as Dankevych's *The Lily*, based on a Shevchenko poem, and *The Forest Song* by Skorulsky, based on a poem by Lesia Ukrainka, helped develop ballet into a genre of heroic drama and national symbolism. In the 1970s, a fleeting trend of single act, avant-garde ballets focusing on philosophical literary works by authors like Ivan Franko developed. The highlight of this movement is Maiorov's *The Dawn Poem*, based on traditional piano pieces by Korsenko.

Folk Dance Early folk dances which symbolised seasonal rituals were the inspiration for many Ukrainian ballets. They were based on the calendar feasts in peasant life: winter *(koliada)*, spring *(vesnianky)*, summer *(kupalo)* and autumn or harvest *(obzhynky)*. Combined with incantations *(zamovliannia)* and songs, dances also celebrated the rites of birth, marriage and death. The *hahilky*, famous circle dances performed by girls during Easter, combined the rituals of prayer with the celebration of spring. *Khorovody* dance games stemmed from ancient folk traditions based on courtship and social interaction.

The most famous folk dances were those of the Cossacks. Born from the drunken celebrations which followed successful campaigns, they eventually developed styles and patterns which took on special meanings within the Cossack culture. These movements (like the 'duck-kick') eventually evolved into the famous dances which today encapsulate the spirit and legend of the Cossacks.

One of the best contemporary Ukrainian folk dance groups that performs internationally is the folk ensemble Karpatsky Vizerunok from Ivano-Frankivsk.

Music

Folk Music Nostalgic fascination for oral traditions handed down between generations led to written anthologies of song and dance. *Bylyny* were lengthy epic narrative poems that told of the courageous deeds of the *bahatyri* (historic Ukrainian heroes) from Kyivan Rus. *Dumas* were lyrical ballads that glorified the exploits of the Cossacks and were performed by *kobzars* (minstrel-like bards), while *chumak* songs recounted the tales of the Cossack salt traders.

From this early oral literature stemmed Ukraine's rich folk music which incorporated elements of the ballad and bandura (see the boxed text 'The Sound of Music'). Many groups with long-standing traditions have come to the fore today – the Kyiv-based Ukrainian National Orchestra of Folk Instruments, the Volyn and Transcarpathia folk choirs, and the Hayda Ensemble from the Carpathian region.

Classical & Opera Ukrainian classical composer Mykola Diletsky's manual on music theory became the foremost music textbook in Ukraine and Russia in the late 17th century. The renowned 18th century composers Dmytro Bortniansky and Maxym Berezovsky wrote several symphonies and operas which were performed in France and Italy to wide acclaim.

The best known Ukrainian composer was the legendary Mykola Lysenko, whose late 19th century works earned him the title 'father of Ukrainian national music'. His fame lies in his analytical study of Ukrainian folk songs and their application into piano-based classical music. After his death in 1912, the music academy he founded in Kyiv produced many talented composers.

Composer and conductor Mykola Kolessa gained fame for his mid-20th century works that combine classical composition with motifs from Carpathian folk songs.

Contemporary composers such as the well respected Ukrainian-American Virko Baley have done much to promote interest in Ukrainian music. Leading Ukrainian composers today include Bibik, Hrabovsky, Karabyts, Sylvestrov, Skoryk and Stankovych. Outstanding contemporary Ukrainian classical musicians include cellist Natalie Khomo, virtuoso violinist Oleh Krysa and piano virtuosos Mykola Suk and Volodymyr Vynnytsky.

Opera legend Solomia Krushelnytska mesmerised her audiences during the early part of the 20th century with her leading roles in *Aida*, *Madam Butterfly* and the

The Sound of Music

The heart and soul of Ukrainian folk music lies in the legendary bandura or kobza player, made famous by Shevchenko's first book of poems, *Kobzar* (The Bard). Kobzar was named after 16th and 17th century wandering minstrels whose songs and ballads of heroic tales and poems were narrated to the accompaniment of the kobza, a lute-like instrument. Welcomed everywhere, the kobza player was the sacred keeper of Ukrainian folklore and Cossack legends.

In the 18th century the kobza was replaced by the unrivalled bandura, a larger instrument with up to 65 strings. Popular bandura choirs accompanied Ukrainian national songs and folk dances. Inheriting the mythical symbolism of the kobza, the bandura soon became a national symbol, with virtuosos like Ostap Verersai and F Kholodny composing many pieces whose melodies later found their way into orchestras and symphonies. *A Bandura Handbook* by Zinovii Shtokalko, a virtuoso bandurist of the 20th century, is a theoretical study of the technical and cultural aspects of the bandura.

The Ukrainian Bandura Chorus, the first professional bandurist orchestra, was founded in Kyiv in 1918 by Hnat Khotevych, a composer whose music led to his execution in Kharkiv under the Soviet regime in 1938. The Chorus (www.bandura.org) performs worldwide today.

UKRAINE

Ukrainian operetta *Zaporizhzhets za Dunayem*. Ukrainian operettas, which combine more acting and dancing than typical operas, are popular classics often performed at Ukraine's six ballet and opera theatres. Michel Volkovytsky, artistic director of the Shevchenko National Opera in Kyiv, has worked internationally and received recent acclaim for his production of Antin Rudnytsky's opera *Anna Yaroslavna*, which featured two of Ukraine's leading opera singers, V Pyvovarov and L Zabiliasta.

Literature

The origins of Ukrainian literature date to ancient Slavic chronicles. Examples include the 12th century *Slovo o polku Ihorevim* (The Tale of Ihor's Armament), considered to be a masterpiece of medieval Ukrainian literature, and the 16th century *Peresopnytsia Gospel*, which incorporated Ukrainian colloquial expressions.

Modern Ukrainian literature was propagated in the mid-18th century by Hryhorii Skovoroda, the 'Ukrainian Socrates'. A wandering philosopher and intellectual, Skovoroda wrote groups of poems and philosophical arguments in Ukrainian, directed at the common person rather than the social elite. Ivan Kotlarevsky's version of Virgil's *Aeneid* (1798), the first published work to be written in the vernacular Ukrainian language, was a reinterpretation of the Greek classic, with the heroes being replaced by robust Cossacks and peasants. He later published his famous work *Natalka Poltavka*, a classic story subsequently reproduced as a ballet, a theatrical production and a motion picture.

Kharkiv Romantics At Kharkiv University in the 1820s, several young Ukrainian intellectuals led a movement to elevate the Ukrainian language into literary respectability. Ballads, prose and poetry were published, along with two influential anthologies of Ukrainian literature, the *Zaporizky Antiquities* and *Ukrainian Anthology*. In western Ukraine, an almanac of folk songs, poems and historical articles called *Rusalka Dnistrovaia* (The Nymph of the Dnister) was published in colloquial Ukrainian, giving the common person access for the first time to an elevated form of literature in the vernacular.

Shevchenko & his Legacy Many claim that to understand Ukrainian heritage one must understand the significance of Taras Shevchenko, who was punished by exile in 1847 for his satirical poems about Russian oppression: *Son* (The Dream), *Kavkas* (Caucasus) and *Velyky i Lokh* (The Great Dungeon). See the boxed text 'Taras Shevchenko' for more on this influential poet.

After Shevchenko, many great Ukrainian authors flourished. Panteleimon Kulish, Shevchenko's contemporary, published several influential social and cultural works. National romanticism gave way to a realism that sought to further expose social injustice.

Ivan Nechui-Levytsky raised the issues of gross inequality between rich Polish landlords and poor Ukrainian peasants, a theme echoed in the work of Panas Myrnyi, whose book *Khiba revut voly?* (Do Oxen Roar?) attacked social injustice as the cause of evil within the oppressed. Stefan Rudansk was well known for his humorous wit when criticising political inequities. Leonid Hlibov wrote allegorical fables which painted Ukraine's Polish and Russian oppressors as villains, and author Pavlo Hrabovsky was exiled to Siberia because his poems openly criticised tsarist imperial policies. Volodymyr Vynnychenko, later an active politician and Ukrainian revolutionary, was a prolific and varied writer, whose early works like *Beauty and Power* portrayed class conflict in realistic terms. His later work *Beauty and Strength* expressed his concerns about the disintegration of village traditions. Novelist Mykhailo Kotsyubynsky used impressionistic writing to express social strife in rural Ukraine, often with an innovative sense of suspense. His *Shadows of Forgotten Ancestors* celebrated the strife and myth of village life in the Carpathians and was later made into a motion picture in 1965 by producer Serhii Paradzhanov.

Ivan Franko & Lesia Ukrainka Arguably the most talented and prolific writer of the

Taras Shevchenko

Taras Shevchenko (1814-61) stands unmatched as the Ukrainian writer who embodied and stirred the national consciousness – while achieving literary respectability for the Ukrainian language at a time when it was being suppressed under tsarist Russia rule. Born a serf and orphaned as a teenager, Shevchenko studied painting at the Academy of Arts in St Petersburg where he published, with great success, his first work, *Kobzar* (The Bard), a book of eight romantic poems, in 1840. His epic poem *Haidamaky* (1841) and a ballad, *Hamaliia* (1844), followed soon after.

Through his prolific work the Ukrainian language was elevated from a secondary peasant tongue to a vehicle of eloquent and poetic expression, as sophisticated as the languages used by other great writers of his time. By combining vernacular expressions and colloquial dialects with Church Slavonic, he formed a unique voice. A staunch antitsarist (once banished for 10 years to Siberia on the direct orders of Tsar Nicholas I, which led to his premature death), Shevchenko preached social justice with compelling passion, in universal terms as well as specifically to the downtrodden peasant and to the Ukrainian nation as a whole. He referred to his country as 'This land of ours that is not our own'. In 1876, 15 years after Shevchenko's death, Tsar Alexander II banned all Ukrainian books and publishing, but Shevchenko's clear and ringing message was firmly gripped in the heart of a nation. He was a national hero.

Some of Shevchenko's works – namely *Kobzar* – have been translated into Russian, German, French, Spanish and Polish. Works translated into English are all out of print, but could be found perhaps in second-hand bookshops. Titles to look for include *Poetical Works of Taras Shevchenko* by C Andrusyschen (University of Toronto Press, 1964) and *Selected Poems* by Taras Shevchenko (1945, 1979).

TAMSIN WILSON

early 20th century was Ivan Franko, whose work spanned all literary genres, including poetry, drama, fiction, social and philosophical debate, political prose and children's stories. His work was at once scholarly and moving, shedding light on the issues plaguing Ukrainian society, which eventually led to his arrest and temporary imprisonment. Some of his better known works include *The Turnip Farmer*, *The Converted Sinner* and *During Work*.

Equally distinguished and prolific was Larysa Kosach, known by her pen name Lesia Ukrainka. Born into a prestigious Ukrainian family, and well educated, her frail health inspired her to compose deeply moving poetry expressing inner strength and inspiration – symbolic beatitudes for the Ukrainian people – typified in works such as *Hope Against Hope* and *On the Wings of Songs*. The universal expression of beauty in her work *The Forest Song* inspired a ballet, an opera and a film.

Postwar & Soviet Era Olena Teliha, executed by the Gestapo in 1944, was an inspirational voice for postwar writers. Her sensitive, patriotic writings are collected in her work *The Soul on Guard*. Dokia Humenna's description of the Ukrainian peasant's plight between the wars also won her fame, while Ivan Bahrianyi portrayed life as a political prisoner in his work *Why I Refuse to Return to the USSR*. *Starfall*, by Mykola Ponedilok, portrays with wry humour the grief of 1960s Soviet life in Ukraine. A 1961 compilation of poems entitled *Journey of the Heart* propelled Lina Kostenko to international recognition. Poet and writer Vasyl Stus was eventually killed in a Soviet labour camp and most of his work was destroyed, but his *Winter Trees* (1968) and *Candle in the Mirror* (1977) are poetic legacies depicting the turmoil experienced by Soviet dissidents.

Contemporary The Union of Ukrainian Writers in Kyiv was a catalyst in the events leading up to independence, with works by writers such as Ivan Drach and Yuri Tarnavsky contributing to the public upheaval. Poet Ihor Kalyanets is a contemporary realist who relates the issues of the day using an experimental style of free verse. Other contemporary poets include Bohdan Boychuk and Maria Revakovych, and the essayist Solomea Pavlychko is also well known. The trio of poets out of Lviv who go by the title Bu-Ba-Bu, led by Yuriy Andrukhovych, are recognised by some as part of a wave of new postmodern writers. For a further listing of contemporary works, see Books in the Ukraine Facts for the Visitor chapter.

Architecture

Kyivan Rus Kyivan Rus adopted the cruciform church plan developed in Constantinople in the 9th century. At its simplest, this consisted of three parallel aisles (a small aisle on either side of the central aisle, or nave), each with an eastern apse ending in a semicircle, crossed by another aisle and a dome or cupola rising out of the intersection. Lesser domes might top the four arms of the cross or the corners of the building. The pinnacle of this achievement is displayed in St Sophia Cathedral in Kyiv, with two aisles on either side of the central nave (later doubled), five apses on its eastern side and 13 cupolas, with a pyramidal arrangement topping it all off. The Transfiguration Cathedral in Chernihiv is another example of early Byzantine architecture, with two side bell towers added later. In Kyiv, four other Byzantine cathedrals from the 11th and 12th centuries were destroyed in the 1930s by Soviet authorities, including St Michael's Monastery of the Golden Cupolas which was rebuilt in 1996-2000.

Variations on this basic design ensued, either for ornamental or functional reasons. Besides the central or twin bell towers flanking the entrance, rows of apses along the exterior north and south sides were added, which opened up into side chapels in the interior. Architectural influence from local wooden churches saw a distinct Ukrainian-Byzantine mould develop. The Trinity and All Saints churches in the Caves Monastery in Kyiv are high expressions of this style.

After the focus of Ukrainian culture moved west to the Galician-Volynian Principality, a more stoic castle-like architecture developed during the 14th century. Built of stone and with a primary function of defence, the imposing fortresses at Kamyanets-Podilsky, Khotyn and Lutsk are impressive examples.

Renaissance The Renaissance influence of the 16th century was felt predominantly in western Ukraine. Many of the castles were reworked with Renaissance detailing, including the addition of blind arcading – wall or tower ornamentation resembling a row of arches, as evident in Ostroh and Berezhany. The real hotbed of Renaissance architecture was Lviv, many of its buildings designed by Italian architects who used elements of Ukrainian-Byzantine traditions – exemplified in the Dormition Cathedral with its Kornyakt Tower and Three Saints Chapel. The majority of buildings lining the ploshcha Rynok, as well as the ornate Boyim Chapel in Lviv, are all purely proportioned Renaissance facades.

Baroque Early baroque blended with late Renaissance, adding curving lines and dynamic detailing as in the Jesuit College in Lviv. Pure baroque design was used in palaces like the Mariyinsky Palace in Kyiv, while church design developed into what is known as Ukrainian baroque, a synthesis of baroque detailing with Byzantine plan and massing. This style, with the green helmet-shaped dome as its trademark, was predominant in the 17th and 18th centuries. St Sophia and St Cyril's in Kyiv were remodelled and hundreds of new churches were designed – typified by St George's Cathedral in the Vydubytsky Monastery in Kyiv, St Nicholas' Cathedral in Nizhyn and the most stylised version of all (bordering on rococo), St Andrew's in Kyiv, designed by the great Italian architect, Rastrelli. Perhaps the most refined of all examples of Ukrainian baroque is found in the great Uspensky Cathedral of the Pochayiv Monastery.

Some Ukrainian baroque architecture also combined features of traditional wooden architecture such as a colonnaded porch and free-standing belfries. Examples include Pokrovska Cathedral in Kharkiv and many of Kyiv's churches in Podil, including the Chapel-Church of Mykola Dobry.

Classicism The severity of the classical style imposed a restraining order on the exuberance of 17th century Ukrainian baroque. Brought on by the classically minded planning of St Petersburg, city planners in Ukraine followed suit, with the Khrula ploshcha (Round Square) in Poltava an excellent example. The Podil quarter of Kyiv was redesigned according to a grid plan, and the city centres of newly developed cities like Odesa, where rational classical planning reached perfection with the grand Potemkin steps, were strongly influenced by classicism.

Revivals & 20th Century A series of architectural revivals developed at the end of the 19th century. St Volodymyr's Cathedral in Kyiv revived ancient Ukrainian Byzantine traditions, while opera houses – notably those in Kyiv, Odesa and Lviv – were designed in a Renaissance revivalist mode with the addition of heavy baroque and classical detailing – a Habsburg favourite. A modern Ukrainian style based on Art Nouveau featured in the design of the Regional Museum in Poltava and the eclectic Metropolitan Palace in Chernivtsi.

Soviet authority found expression in an inflated revivalist style called monumental classicism, where enormous temple-like edifices were erected to house the notorious committees and ministries of the State. Kyiv is full of these buildings – the Ministry of Foreign Affairs and Presidential Administration buildings are the most imposing. Over 250 churches, cathedrals, cemeteries and palaces were destroyed by the Soviets in the 1930s.

Visual Arts

Icons The icon – a small holy image painted on a limewood panel with tempera paint mixed with egg yolk and hot wax – was the key expression of religious art up to the 17th century. Brought to Ukraine by Prince Volodymyr from the Greek Byzantine settlement of Chersonesus in Crimea, icons were attributed healing and spiritual powers. Icon painters – mostly monks – developed strict codes of conformity, rarely ever signing their work, and depicting only Christ, the Virgin, angels and saints. A Kyiv school of iconography led by Alimpy and Hryhorii was set up during the 11th century at the Caves Monastery. The development of the iconostasis – a tall screen lined with symbolic rows of icons, separating the altar from the congregation – increased the production of icons. Church murals, mosaics and frescoes, as well as manuscript illuminations, developed at the same time as the icon, and played an important role in the evolution of art in Ukraine. Some of the oldest frescoes are found in Kyiv's St Sophia Cathedral.

Romanticism The first break from religious art occurred during the Cossack Hetmanate, with the beginnings of portrait painting. A secular, romantic trend of folk painting slowly developed, a common theme being the Kozak Mamay, or Cossack playing a bandura or kobza. Romanticism developed simultaneously with the national literary revival of the late 19th century. The massive output of over 1000 artistic works by the national poet Shevchenko (who was trained as an artist) began a trend towards a simplistic realism based on the romanticised themes of country life and folk traditions. Numerous artists emerged. Most remained unknown, but some, including Ukrainian-born Nikolai Ge and Ilya Repin (famous for his work *Zaporizky Cossacks Writing a Letter to the Turkish Sultan)* and others involved in the Peredvizhniki movement, gained international fame. (See Painting under Arts in the Facts about European Russia chapter for details on the Peredvizhniki movement.)

Romantic works are well represented in the art museums in Odesa and Kharkiv, the National Museum in Lviv and the Museum of Ukrainian Fine Arts in Kyiv.

Modern Styles The 1930s marked the emergence of a wide variety of styles in Ukrainian art, ranging from impressionism to futurism, cubism and constructivism. Although the techniques and interpretations of aesthetics differed with each style, the majority of Ukrainian artists stuck to similar themes of national folk culture developed by the Romantics a generation before. Fundamental to all new movements in Ukraine was the desire to develop a national consciousness and style rooted in traditions but experimental in technique. The work by M Boichuk, trained in Western Europe, stands out. His mural-style paintings, which blended modern trends with ancient Kyivan and Italian Renaissance imagery, were considered too nationalistic for the authorities. He was subsequently sent to Siberia, where he was executed with his wife in 1937. Most of his works were destroyed.

Soviet Era & Beyond Socialist Realism propagated Soviet ideals – the industrialised peasant, the muscular worker and the glories of Soviet heroes. The best and worst examples are illustrated in Kyiv's Museum of the Great Patriotic War, where towering Tin Tits is a blatant shock of bad taste, while a nearby series of sculptural relief displays a highly developed sense of expression. Ukrainian nationalism asserted itself through the age-old tradition of folk art, leading the Soviet authorities to ban folk embroidery.

Since independence, Ukrainian art has enjoyed a reawakening, with the Academy of Fine Arts in both Kyiv and Lviv producing new young artists and style revivals. Some better known contemporary artists include Hlib Visheslavsky from Kyiv and Vasyl Ryabchenko from Odesa.

Cinema

The first film studios in Ukraine were established in Kyiv and Odesa in 1915, with the original screen production of the famous novel by Kotlarevsky, *Natalka Poltavka*, acted by the beloved actress Natalia Lissenko. In 1924 one of the largest film studios in Eastern Europe, the Film Institute, was established in Kyiv, and along with the Cinema School in Odesa included 25 independent film companies. The films produced during its short heyday are considered masterpieces of the silent film era. Cinema giants included the Russian Sergey Eisenstein and the Ukrainian Alexander Dovzhenko, whose 1930 film *Zemlia* (The Earth) is considered a milestone in cinematic achievement.

During the Soviet era, Ukrainian cinema all but disappeared, until a revival in the 1950s saw the production of a number of documentary films based on historic Ukrainian themes and characters, such as Serhii Bondarchuk's *Taras Shevchenko* (1951). Slavko Novytsky, who emigrated to Canada in 1950, became the leading name during this time, producing documentaries ranging from *Pysanka: the Ukrainian Easter Egg*, a highly praised art documentary, to the moving *The Harvest of Despair* (1972), a shocking portrayal of the 1932-33 famine, which was acclaimed at the New York Film Festival.

The gifted Serhii Paradzhanov, who died in 1990, produced his first film in 1965. Called *Shadows of Forgotten Ancestors*, it was based on a Kotsyubynsky novel about feudal Carpathian Ukraine, and featured dynamic film techniques and hypersensationalism. Jailed in the 1970s, Paradzhanov emerged to continue his work. In his last film, *Ashik Kerib* (1988), his hero flees through Transcaucasia after a rash love affair with a young Turkish woman.

The annual International Film Festival held in Kyiv during the last week of October brings exposure to a swag of young,

UKRAINE

upcoming Ukrainian film directors. Yuri Illienko and I Hrabovsky are among the more established names.

Theatre

Modern dramatic theatre was introduced in Kyiv during the 17th century by students of the Caves Monastery, where the study of oratory rhetoric was obligatory. The Kyiv-Mohyla Akademy was the first to include drama and theatre as part of the secular curriculum. In 1765 Ukrainian drama was banned because it was considered to be subversive and anti-Muscovite. It moved underground and to the streets and marketplaces, where spontaneous productions became popular, usually based on Cossack and Christian legends.

In the 19th century, Ukrainian theatre resurfaced in classical and romantic modes, typified by productions like Kotlarevsky's *Natalka Poltavka*, and outstanding performances by actors such as Tetiana Danylova and Pavlo Chubynsky. In 1876 Tsar Alexander II officially banned all Ukrainian books and publications, including drama and theatre productions, so the emphasis shifted to the west of the country where the first professional Ukrainian theatre (the Besida) flourished in Lviv. In 1904 the Kyiv Music and Drama School reopened, producing many fine actors such as Maria Zankovetska and Stepan Janovych. The subsequent political turmoil, war and revolution of the first half of the 20th century almost dissolved Ukrainian theatre, but under the leadership of directors Les Kurbas and Mykola Kulish, most cities developed their theatrical companies once more.

The actor and director Lidia Krushelnytska has been prominent in theatre in the last few decades.

SOCIETY & CULTURE

While tensions between Ukrainians and Russians indisputably exist, the average traveller shouldn't be affected. Nevertheless, be sensitive to people's ethnicity – and be wary which language you speak to whom. In western Ukraine, avoid speaking Russian (English is a better alternative).

When dining in a Ukrainian home, avoid sitting at the corner of the table unless you are happy to remain unwed for the next seven years; evil spirits lurk inside the four corners. Likewise, don't shake hands across the threshold, don't spill salt on the floor (it causes a fight) and don't leave an empty bottle on the table during a meal (it also causes a fight). Never whistle unless you would like to suddenly lose all your money, and if someone gives you a knife as a gift, give them a gift in return (preferably money). And finally, when exploring the city, women should avoid sitting down on steps, walls, pavements or in fact anything built from concrete: your ovaries will freeze and you will be unable to bear children – or so any typically superstitious Ukrainian will tell you.

Treatment of Animals

Circuses in Ukraine, like those in Russia, unfortunately star bears on ice skates and hedgehog jugglers. See Circus under Arts in Facts about European Russia for details.

RELIGION

Orthodox Church

Post-Soviet Ukraine has witnessed the emergence of three different Orthodox churches. In 1686, the Orthodox Church in Ukraine – which had always paid allegiance to the Kyiv Patriarchate – was forced to recognise authority from Moscow, resulting in a long period of control by the Russian Orthodox Church. In 1921-30, in a brief flowering of Ukrainian identity, the Church in Ukraine was re-established as the Ukrainian Autocephalous Orthodox Church (UAOC). It shared identical practices with other Orthodox churches, but enjoyed allegiance to the patriarch in Kyiv rather than Moscow.

Prior to independence, all Orthodox churches in Ukraine were banned except for the official Russian Orthodox Church. In 1990, the UAOC was fully revived, while the Ukrainian section of the Russian Orthodox Church was renamed the Ukrainian Orthodox Church (UOC). Unlike the UAOC, however, the latter still paid allegiance to the Moscow Patriarchate. This prompted a further split in the Orthodox ranks in 1992 when the newly formed, breakaway Ukrainian Orthodox Church of Kyiv and All-Ukraine adopted the Kyiv patriarch as its spiritual leader.

Moscow refuses to recognise the authenticity of the UAOC or Ukrainian Orthodox Church of Kyiv and All-Ukraine. In July 1995 simmering tensions erupted in violence after the Ukrainian government – for fear of reprisals from Moscow – refused to allow Kyiv patriarch Volodymyr Romaniuk (1925-95) to be buried in Kyiv's St Sophia Cathedral. Tens of people were injured when protesters clashed with riot police during the burial service which eventually took place outside the cathedral walls. The patriarch's pavement tomb – always flower-adorned – remains a potent symbol of the split in the Orthodox Church in Ukraine today.

The Caves Monastery in Kyiv was returned to the Moscow-led UOC in 1988. Orthodox St Sofia's remains in the hands of the state, primarily because the UOC and the Ukrainian Orthodox Church of Kyiv and All-Ukraine both lay claim to it.

Uniate Church

Often referred to as Ukrainian Catholic or Greek Catholic, the Uniate Church is essentially the 'union' or combination of the Catholic and Orthodox churches which fatefully separated in 1054. The Uniate Church service follows Orthodox worship and ritual, but recognises the Roman pope as its leader and doctrinal authority. The church was formed, largely for political reasons, at the Union of Brest in 1596 (see History earlier in this chapter), and was abolished by Stalin in 1946. All of its property was confiscated or handed over to the Russian Orthodox Church. It survived underground, holding clandestine services in forests, and re-emerged in the late 1980s as a leader in the national drive for independence.

The Uniate Church – relegalised in 1991 – is heavily concentrated in the west of the country. It has an estimated 4.5 million members. Uniate priests are the only Catholic priests in the world allowed to marry.

Other Religions

The Roman Catholic Church has 1.5 million adherents in Ukraine. Small Jewish minorities exist in all cities. Muslim communities, primarily Tatars, prevail in Crimea.

LANGUAGE

During Ukraine's years as a state of the Soviet Union, Russian was the official language of the country. With the fall of the Soviet Union, Ukraine recovered its independence, and in 1990 Ukrainian was adopted as the sole official language.

The western and eastern accents differ, and there are a number of dialects spoken in the Carpathians. Russian is still used predominantly in the east and south, where over half the Ukrainians are relearning their own language. Crimea is almost entirely Russian-speaking. Russian is understood everywhere by everyone, so although it may be diplomatic and polite to speak Ukrainian (especially in the west), you'll have no problem being understood if you speak Russian.

For a brief guide to Ukrainian and a list of useful words and phrases, see the Language chapter at the back of this book. If you'd like a more in-depth guide to the language, get a copy of Lonely Planet's *Ukrainian phrasebook*.

Facts for the Visitor

HIGHLIGHTS

The adventurous escapade of navigating Ukraine aside, highlights to be found in the Ukrainian capital of Kyiv include the dimly lit but highly evocative Caves Monastery, and the sparkling St Sophia and St Michael cathedral complexes. In the west, the old town of Lviv, its central square (ploshcha Rynok) and open-air architecture museum are 'must-sees'; while down south, the exotic port city of Odesa, with its legendary architecture, Potemkin steps, museums and opera house, is an unquestionable highlight. On the Crimean coast, the Khans' Palace in Bakhchysaray, the seaside resort of Yalta and the many hikes in its cave cities are among the peninsula's most compelling treasures. Elsewhere, in Ukraine's charming backwaters, don't miss the fortified castle town of Kamyanets-Podilsky, the fabulous monastery complex of Pochayiv, and the border town of Chernivtsi, with its lively mix of cultures.

PLANNING

When to Go

Even during the high season, Ukraine's tourist spots are rarely crowded, with the exception of Kyiv's Caves Monastery (packed on Sunday year-round) and, in summer, the Odesan and Crimean beaches. The cheapest and best-value hotels in Yalta are occasionally fully booked in July and August, and Dnipro and Black Sea boats and cruises are seasonal (May to mid-October only).

Spring (late April to early June) is indisputably the best time of year to visit Ukraine. Kyiv is a perfumed cocktail of blossoming chestnut trees and spring flowers, while its people have a spring in their step as they shed their heavy winter coats and leap with joy into the bounty of colour that bursts forth. Temperatures are a few degrees cooler than in summer when it is stiflingly hot and horribly dusty. The summer months are also the wettest. Most theatres close in July and August.

In December and January it's bitingly cold inland, although there is a definite ambience to the muffled landscape lying quiet under its white blanket. Winter – from October to March – is long and can be difficult for those unaccustomed to that distinctive, murky grey wash that seems to envelope everything and everyone (imagine yourself trapped in a black and white movie for six months).

Food fluctuates with the seasons. Dishes are usually heartier in winter, fresher in spring and summer. Each holiday season has its own special foods, such as Easter breads and Christmas cakes.

Maps

Country Maps Country maps are easy to find. To ensure quality, buy one before arrival in Ukraine. The best choice is Freytag & Berndt's *Ukraine* (1:1,200,000) which includes a comprehensive index of places, larger-scale inset (1:500,000) of Crimea, and Cyrillic names for major cities. Another safe choice is Bartholomew's *Ukraine-Moldova World Travel Map* or Marco Polo's map series (1:750,000) covering Ukraine, Belarus, European Russia and the Caucasus. IGN's 3615 *Ukraine* map is less detailed (IGN 86044, 1:1,000,000), but its regional map of Crimea (IGN 86053, 1:300,000) is unbeatable for Crimea-bound travellers. It includes some hiking routes.

In Kyiv, try to find the excellent (but scarce) Topograficheskaya Karta maps. The series, based on former Soviet army mapping, covers the entire country in 286 maps (1:100,000). These are the most detailed maps available and useful to hikers (even though trails as such are not marked). The maps – printed in Russian only – cost less than $1 and are published by Topograficheskaya Karta (☎ 044-274 62 49, ☎ 274 62 69, fax 274 61 48), vulitsya Shevchenka 27/6, Kyiv.

Also available locally is *Ukraine in the Past & Today – Historic & Geographic Maps* by V Paik. This A4-sized atlas is published by

UKRAINE

Street Names

In the western regions of Ukraine, most street signs have been changed to Ukrainian and most maps have been updated. In the east, in cities such as Kharkiv, street signs are often in Russian, sometimes Ukrainian, and occasionally both. In those cities where this may cause confusion, we give both. In Crimea we use a mixture, using the street name that is predominantly used (mostly Russian), but putting the Ukrainian address term – for example, vulitsya for street, not ulitsa, and ploshcha for square, not ploshchad.

the Shevchenko Scientific Society in Edmonton-Toronto (1982) and Lviv (1998).

City Maps Kyiv is the only Ukraine city for which a map can be bought before arrival. Freytag & Berndt includes a Kyiv city map as an inset (1:35,000) on its *Ukraine* road map (see earlier); it publishes a separate city map too. Try map stockists Stanfords (☎ 020-7836 1321, fax 020-7836 0189, sales@stanfords.co.uk), 12-14 Long Acre, London WC2. Some city maps are available on Ukrainian Map Server (www.infoukes.com/ua-maps), a free, online database of Ukrainian maps.

In Ukraine, accurate city maps *(plan mista* or *plan horoda)* are readily available for all major cities. Maps covering cities in eastern and southern Ukraine are usually in Russian. Shop for maps in Kyiv before heading out elsewhere; maps for regional cities are often available in the capital but not in the respective city. Many maps include a public transport map *(skhema transporta)*.

What to Bring

The same 'what to bring' rules apply to Ukraine as to European Russia (see European Russia – Facts for the Visitor). Practically everything you could possibly need, including toiletries, is readily available in Kyiv. Exceptions include contraceptives (condoms exist, quality not guaranteed), contact lens supplies, vitamin tablets and any specific medicines or prescription drugs you require (make sure you bring your prescription with you).

Women travellers should pack a scarf to cover their head when visiting monasteries. Other day pack essentials include a torch (to assist a safe arrival home at night on unlit streets), towel or sarong, toilet paper, insect repellent (if in the countryside in summer), water bottle, Swiss army knife, universal bath plug and sunscreen.

TOURIST OFFICES

Local Tourist Offices

The notion of a well equipped tourist office staffed with friendly and knowledgeable personnel is a fairy tale in Ukraine – local tourist offices simply don't exist. At best, many hotels have a service bureau which, depending on the person behind the desk that day, can be refreshingly useful or utterly useless. Most do little more than arrange overpriced excursions for groups rather than individual travellers.

Hotel receptionists are occasionally willing to part with useful advice or answer any questions you may have. People on the street can also be extremely obliging; when asking directions to a specific place, you will more than likely be personally escorted there.

In Kyiv, there is a State Committee of Ukraine for Tourism, but its job remains a mystery. Approach a privately run travel agency instead (see Travel Agencies under Information in the Kyiv chapter). There are reasonably efficient service bureaux in Lviv and Donetsk. Quizzing the English-speaking staff who work in Ukraine's many Irish pubs (listed under Entertainment in regional chapters) or making contact with local expats are other alternatives that can yield handsome results.

Tourist Offices Abroad

Ukraine has no tourist offices abroad, but most of its consulates and embassies stock some practical country information. Foreign travel agencies specialising in Ukrainian travel are also useful (see the Ukraine Getting There & Away chapter).

VISAS & DOCUMENTS

All foreigners need a Ukrainian visa. Visas have to be obtained *before* arrival in Ukraine. No visas are issued at Kyiv's Boryspil airport or any land border.

If you are in transit, you still need a visa – unless you are a US passport holder, in which case you can transit without a visa providing you have documented proof of onward travel (a plane or train ticket and a visa, if necessary, for your country of destination).

To apply for a visa, you need to present the following to a consular office:

A valid passport, re-entry permit or refugee travel document. The expiration date of your passport should extend for at least three months beyond the date you intend leaving Ukraine.

Proof of your onward destination (for a transit visa); confirmation of a hotel booking for *every* night you intend staying in Ukraine (for a tourist visa); or an official letter of invitation from Ukraine (for a business or private visa). See the Getting the Invitation section.

A completed visa application form with affixed passport-size photograph. The form can be obtained at any Ukrainian consulate or embassy (most will fax a form) or can be printed from the Internet (www.ukremb.com). The form comprises 14 identification questions, including purpose of travel (see Types of Visa) and duration of stay. In mid-1999, it was also obligatory to state your proposed destinations – a rule that was expected to be scrapped by January 2000.

Consulates and embassies process visa applications by mail. Send the requested documentation with the required visa fee and a self-addressed stamped envelope for your passport's safe return. Visas take seven to 10 working days to process. Most consulates also offer a rush/urgent (within three days) and express (next or same-day) processing service – all for an extra fee of course.

Types of Visa

The type of visa you receive depends on what you state on your application form under 'purpose of travel' – business, private, tourist or transit.

At the time of writing, any visa (*except* a multiple-entry business visa) could be theoretically extended once in Ukraine by applying to the passport office (VVIR) of the Ministry of Internal Affairs (see Visa Extensions). This bureaucratic ordeal is best avoided; when applying for your visa, overestimate your intended length of stay.

Children under 16 and those travelling to Ukraine to study (official invitation from education body required) are entitled to $30 reduction on the visa fees listed below. Embassies and consulates in some countries (such as the UK) issue free visas to those travelling for study.

Business Visa A business visa requires an official invitation from a business contact in Ukraine. It is valid for a maximum of three months (six months for US passport holders) and can be good for one or two entries (single/double-entry). Multiple-entry business visas are valid for a maximum of six months (one year for US passport holders).

The regular processing fee for a single/double-entry visa is $30/60 (processed in seven to 10 working days), $60/120 for rush processing (three days) and $100/180 for express service (same day). Multiple-entry business visas cost $120/240 for regular/rush processing (minimum of five working days).

Private Visa A private visa is valid for a maximum of three months and allows visitors to enter Ukraine once or twice (single/double-entry). It requires an official invitation from a private party (person or organisation) in Ukraine. Single/double-entry visa prices are the same as for a business visa.

Tourist Visa A tourist visa (single or double entry) is valid for a maximum of three months (six months for US passport holders). The invitation needed to secure a tourist visa is a hotel or tour confirmation issued by a travel agency inside or outside Ukraine. Every night you stay has to be accounted for. Tourist visas issued are only valid for nights you have prebooked (and usually prepaid) hotel accommodation. Advance train reservation tickets are needed for nights spent travelling on overnight trains.

Single/double-entry prices are the same as for a business visa.

Transit Visa A transit visa can be for a single or double entry and is valid for a maximum of 72 hours per entry. This type of visa allows you to cross Ukraine by land en route to a neighbouring country – from Romania to Russia for example. To apply, you need documented proof that you are *only* transiting and do not intend staying in Ukraine, eg a train/bus/boat ticket and visa for the country of destination. Visas are issued for the duration of transit only; if you want a one or two day stopover in Ukraine, for example, apply for a tourist visa.

The fee for a single/double-entry visa is $15/30 for regular processing and $30/60 for express service.

Transit visas are *not* issued at any Ukrainian border.

Getting the Invitation

The easiest way to get an invitation *(zaproshennya)* is if you have a contact in Ukraine who can send or fax the document, which they obtain through their local visa and registration office (VVIR in Ukrainian; OVIR in Russian) of the Ministry of Internal Affairs.

For the average traveller who does not have this option, this bureaucratic task is taken care of by a travel agent who deals with travel in Ukraine (see Ukraine Getting There & Away – Travel Agencies). Some agents can provide you with an invitation for a private visa for up to one month. Most however, only offer the prebooked hotel accommodation visa support necessary for a tourist visa. Most demand that you prepay for the accommodation too. The agent then issues you with a tourist voucher confirming a hotel booking (a faxed copy is acceptable), which you present with the other necessary documents to a Ukrainian embassy or consulate. If your Ukrainian/Russian is up to scratch, you can contact a hotel in Ukraine yourself, make a booking, and ask them to send you the necessary confirmation instead.

Tourist visas are only issued for the exact number of nights you have accommodation booked: *every night* you intend spending in Ukraine *has to be accounted for*. For an extra fee (around $35), some travel agents will deal directly with the embassy for you, saving you the hassle of submitting your own visa application and – very occasionally – fiddling it so that you end up with a visa valid over and above the nights you have booked accommodation.

Visa Extensions

To extend your visa, go to the visa and registration office of the Ministry of Internal Affairs. Most offices are open from 9 or 10 am to 5 pm (closed Friday afternoon and on weekends). There is a VVIR office in every city, including Kyiv (☎ 044-225 13 54), 34 bulvar Tarasa Shevchenka (metro Universytet) and Lviv, vulitsya Rudanskoho 3, 3rd floor (behind Hotel George).

Visas can be extended for a maximum of two months; a typical 20 day extension costs around $25. The same documents are required as for any regular visa (ie invitation or proof of prebooked hotel accommodation). In return for successfully relaying to the snotty staff how long you would like to extend your visa for (see Language at the back of this book), you will be given a scrap of paper adorned with a string of numbers. Take this to a specified bank where you pay the fee necessary for your visa to be extended; include the string of numbers on the required visa payment form you fill out in the bank. Once you have stamped proof from the bank that you have paid, return to VVIR to retrieve your new visa. Most VVIR impose a $10 processing fee. This whole process takes hours rather than minutes.

HIV/AIDS Testing

Foreigners planning to stay in Ukraine longer than three months may be required to have an HIV-negative test to obtain a visa.

Medical Insurance

All foreigners entering Ukraine are required to have medical insurance valid for the duration of their stay in the country. In mid-1999, Ukraine had a reciprocal health agreement with the UK, thereby exempting British passport holders of this requirement. All other nationalities must prove they have adequate cover or purchase it at the border; in mid-1999 rates charged at Boryspil airport were $2/3/4 for up to four/seven/eight days and $7/30/45/135 for up to 15/60/90/365 days.

Registration

All foreigners are required to register their passport with VVIR within 72 hours of arrival in Ukraine. If you are staying in a hotel, registration is automatically done for you when you check in. If you are travelling on a business or private visa, you are responsible for ensuring your passport is registered by the person or organisation who invited you.

If you don't register, you can face a hefty fine when leaving the country. Most VVIR offices (see Visa Extensions earlier) charge a $10 registration fee.

Other Documents

Besides your passport with visa, you might need the following documents:

Vouchers: if you've prepaid accommodation through a travel agency prior to departure, hold on to all vouchers and receipts.

Customs declaration: this is as valuable as your visa. That small piece of paper you filled out and had stamped when you entered (see Customs later in this chapter) will be asked for when you leave – keep it safe.

Receipts: save receipts for all currency exchanges, purchases of souvenirs, and hotel payments. Officials rarely ask to see them, but it's always a good idea to have proof handy just in case.

Hotel pass: when you check in, most hotels hand you a card with your room number on it. This gets you in and out of the hotel and procures your key.

Driver's documents: if you're driving your own vehicle, keep your International Driving Permit, proof of insurance and registration handy. If renting, carry your rental agreement.

Health certificates and medical insurance: travellers coming from Asia and Africa, and possibly Latin America, may need smallpox and cholera vaccination certificates. Anyone requiring medication containing a narcotic drug should have a doctor's certificate. Everyone needs medical insurance.

Personal IDs: bring photo IDs to prove you are the person in your passport.

EMBASSIES & CONSULATES

Ukrainian Embassies & Consulates

Australia
  Consulate:
  (☎ 03-9326 0135, fax 9326 1065)
  3/902 Mount Alexander Rd,
  Essendon, Vic 3040

Belarus
  Embassy:
  (☎/fax 227 28 61) Kirova 17-306,
  Minsk 220050

Canada
  Embassy:
  (☎ 613-230 2961, fax 230 2400,
  www3.sympatico.ca/tem-ukraine)
  310 Somerset St West, Ottawa,
  Ontario K2P 0J9
  Consulate:
  (☎ 416-763 3115/4, fax 763 2323)
  2120 Bloor St West, Toronto,
  Ontario M6S IM8

Czech Republic
  Embassy:
  (☎ 02-312 20 00, fax 312 43 66)
  Charles de Gaulla 29, Prague 6

Estonia
  Embassy:
  (☎ 2 611 23 55, ☎ 631 15 55, fax 631 33 51)
  Lahe 6, Tallinn

France
  Embassy:
  (☎ 01 43 06 04 11, fax 01 43 06 02 94,
  Minitel 3615 UKRINFO)
  21 ave de Saxe, 75007 Paris

Germany
  Embassy:
  (☎ 02228-94 18 60, fax 94 18 63)
  Rheinhohenweg 101,
  53424 Remagen-Oberwinter
  Consulates:
  (☎ 030-261 41 01, fax 261 41 77)
  Kurfürstenstrasse 56, 10785 Berlin
  (☎ 089-28 20 64/5/6, fax 28 13 17)
  Oskar-von-Miller-Ring 33,
  80333 Munich

Hungary
  Embassy:
  (☎ 1-155 24 43, fax 202 22 87)
  XII Nógrádi utca 8, Budapest

Japan
  Embassy:
  (☎ 3-3445 9229, fax 3447 6768)
  6-5-26, Kita-Shinagawa, Shinagawa-ku,
  Tokyo 141

Latvia
  Embassy:
  (☎ 733 29 56, ☎ 724 30 82, ☎ 732 55 83,

UKRAINE

fax 732 55 83)
Kalpaka bulv 3, Riga

Lithuania
Embassy:
(☎ 22-22 15 36, fax 22 04 75)
Teatro 4, 2600 Vilnius
Consulate:
(☎ 22-77 84 13)
Kalvariju 159, 2600 Vilnius

Moldova
Embassy:
(☎ 2-232 560/3, fax 232 562)
Str Sfatul Tarii 55, 277004 Chisinau

Poland
Embassy:
(☎ 022-625 0127, fax 625 3230)
Al Szucha 7, Warsaw 00-580
Consulates:
(☎ 058-46 06 90, fax 46 07 07)
ul Jaskowa Dolina 44, 80-246 Gdansk
(☎ 012-656 23 36, fax 656 41 93)
ul Krakówska 41, 31-066 Kraków

Romania
Embassy:
(☎ 01-211 6986, ☎ 222 3162, fax 211 6949)
Calea Dorobantilor 16, Bucharest
Consulate:
(☎/fax 01-223 2702) Str Tuberozelor 5, Bucharest

Russia
Embassy:
(☎ 095-229 10 79, fax 924 84 69)
Leontevsky pereulok 18, Moscow

Slovakia
Embassy:
(☎ 07-533 16 72, fax 531 26 51)
Radvanská 35, 81101 Bratislava

Turkey
Embassy:
(☎ 312-439 99 73, fax 440 68 15)
Cinnah Caddesi, Alabas Sokak 3/2, Cankaya/Ankara-06690
Consulate:
(☎ 212-252 54 02, fax 252 54 03)
Gumussuyu 9294, Istanbul 80090

UK
Embassy:
(☎ 020-7727 6312, fax 7792 1708)
64 Holland Park, London W11
Consulate:
(☎ 020-7243 8923, fax 7792 1708)
78 Kensington Park Rd, London W11 2PL
(☎ 0891-515 919) visa information line charged at UK£0.36/min cheap rate or UK£0.48/min at peak times

USA
Embassy:
(☎ 202-333 7507/08/09, fax 333 7510, infolook@aol.com, www.ukremb.com)
3350 M St NW, Washington, DC 20007
Consulates:
(☎ 212-371 5690, fax 371 5547)
240 East 49th St, New York, NY 10017
(☎ 312-642 4387/88, fax 642 4385)
10 East Huron St, Chicago, IL 60611

Embassies & Consulates in Ukraine

Unless indicated otherwise, the following foreign embassies and consulates are in Kyiv (area code ☎ 044):

Australia
(☎ 225 75 86, fax 244 35 97)
vulitsya Kominternu 18, Apartment 11

Belarus
(☎ 290 02 01, ☎ 293 22 48, ☎ 295 46 67)
vulitsya Sichnevoho Povstannya 6

Bulgaria
(☎ 225 43 89, ☎ 224 53 60, fax 224 99 29)
vulitsya Hospitalna 1
Consulate:
(☎ 0482-66 60 92)
vulitsya Posmitnoho 9, Odesa

Canada
(☎ 464 11 44, fax 464 11 30)
Yaroslaviv val 31

Czech Republic
(☎ 212 04 31, fax 224 61 80)
Yaroslaviv val 34a

Estonia
(☎ 294 85 14, ☎ 296 28 86, fax 294 80 55)
vulitsya Kutuzova 8

France
(☎ 228 87 28, fax 229 08 70)
vulitsya Reyterska 37

Georgia
(☎ 246 10 67, fax 246 10 74)
vulitsya Hudryashova 9
Consulate:
(☎ 0482-22 00 75, fax 22 53 83)
vulitsya Lanzheronivska 21, Odesa

Germany
(☎ 216 74 98, fax 216 81 00)
vulitsya Honchara 84

Hungary
(☎ 212 40 04, ☎ 212 41 34)
vulitsya Reyterska 33
Consulate:
prospekt Svobody, Uzhhorod

Japan
(☎ 462 0020, fax 247 5502)
prov Museyny 4

Latvia
(☎ 462 07 08, fax 229 27 45)
vulitsya Desyatynna 4/6

Lithuania
(☎ 227 43 72)
vulitsya Antonvycha 22
Moldova
(☎ 295 26 53, ☎/fax 295 67 03, moldovak@sovamn.com)
vulitsya Kutuzova 8
Consulate:
(☎ 290 77 21, fax 229 77 22)
vulitsya Sichnevoho Povstannya 6
Netherlands
(☎ 216 1905, ☎ 216 9834, fax 216 8105)
vulitsya Turhenivska 21
Poland
(☎ 224 80 40)
Yaroslaviv val 12
Consulate:
(☎ 0322-76 05 44)
vulitsya Ivan Franko 10, Lviv
Romania
(☎ 224 52 61, ☎ 225 20 25)
vulitsya Kotsyubynskoho 8
Consulate:
(☎ 0482-23 62 98, fax 22 09 28)
vulitsya Pastera 21, Odesa
Russia
(☎ 244 09 63, fax 244 09 59)
prospekt Povitroflotsky 27
Slovakia
(☎ 212 03 10, fax 212 32 71)
Yaroslaviv val 34
Consulate:
vulitsya Tykha 8, Uzhhorod
Turkey
(☎ 294 99 64, fax 295 64 23)
vulitsya Arsenalna 18
UK
(☎ 462 00 11/12/14, fax 462 00 13, ukembinf@sovam.com)
vulitsya Desyatynna 9
Consulate:
(☎ 290 73 17, fax 290 79 47, ukembc@webber.net.ua)
vulitsya Sichnevoho Povstannya 6
USA
(☎ 246 97 50, ☎ 244 73 42/45, ☎ 216 38 05 (24 hour emergency line), fax 244 73 50, consular@usemb.33.ua, acs@usemb.kiev.ua, www.usemb.kiev.ua)
vulitsya Kotsyubynskoho 10

CUSTOMS

On arrival you are given a customs declaration form *(deklaratsia)* to fill out. These forms come in English at Boryspil airport, but not at land borders. The first six lines ask: your name, nationality, the country you are coming from, the country you are entering, purpose of visit and number of luggage items. The next seven items (numbered one to seven) ask you what you're bringing into the country. Write 'No' for the first five, which ask if you have any (1) weapons or ammunition (2) narcotics (3) poisonous or radioactive substances (4) antiques and arts objects (5) Ukrainian currency, bonds or state lottery tickets. If you have any Russian roubles on you, fill in how many in the sixth line; if not, write 'No' here too. The seventh item requires you to detail what other currencies you have (type of currency, amount in digits, then in words). Finally, the last line asks if you're carrying anything for someone else. Write 'No'. Sign and date the form.

On the form's reverse side, list all the valuables you have, including major pieces of jewellery, cameras, camcorders, laptop computers etc. If you have filled in the reverse side, or are entering Ukraine with more than 85 *hryvnia* or US$1000, walk through the red channel upon arrival at Boryspil Airport. Only walk through the green channel if you have nothing to declare.

This form is checked, stamped and handed back to you. When you leave Ukraine, you have to fill out a second identical form which, along with your original, you surrender to the customs official.

Lost Deklaratsia

If you lose your deklaratsia, your embassy can give you a letter requesting a replacement from Kyiv Customs Department (☎ 044-446 24 54), provulok Politekhnichny 4A, Kyiv.

What You Can Bring In

You can bring in any item for personal use as long as it isn't illegal drugs, weapons, ammunition, explosives, flora or fauna, a high frequency radio or radioactive material. You have to pay a duty on anything over: 1L of hard alcohol, 2L of wine, up to 100 cigarettes, 200g of tobacco, and any items or gifts exceeding a total of $5000.

What You Can Take Out

You're not allowed to take out antiques (including antique icons, books published before 1966, furniture produced before 1945), works of art (fine or applied, such as hand-woven carpets, rugs, folk art) or cultural/historical treasures (including archaeological and numismatic items, musical instruments) without special permission from the Ministry of Culture (☎ 044-226 26 45, ☎ 226 29 02), located at vulitsya Ivana Franka 19, Kyiv.

Officially, you cannot take out more money than your customs form shows you came in with. Keep all receipts for cash obtained with credit card or travellers cheques. In addition, you are not allowed to take out more than 85 Ukrainian hryvnia.

MONEY

All prices are listed in US dollars (abbreviated to $) in this book. For rules on taking money in/out of the country, see Customs earlier.

Currency

Ukraine introduced its own national currency, the hryvnia – named after the ancient coin of Kyivan Rus – on 2 September 1996. The hryvnia is divided into 100 *kopeks* and is the only legal tender in Ukraine. Coins come in denominations of one, five, 10, 25 and 50 kopeks and one hryvnia. Notes come in one, two, five, 10, 20, 50 and 100 hryvnia.

The hryvnia replaced the *karbovanets (kupon)*, a temporary currency in circulation in Ukraine from November 1992 after the Soviet rouble was scrapped. This transitional currency was intended only for use until hyperinflation was curbed – a feat that took four years to accomplish. Once introduced, the hryvnia remained stable until August 1998 when the Russian economic crisis prompted its value to tumble by 51%. The central bank has since devalued the battered hryvnia by widening its US dollar currency corridor (see Exchange Rates below).

Money Talks

After living with the Soviet rouble for more than 50 years, it is not surprising that many Ukrainians still talk roubles rather than hryvnia. Elderly pensioners who hawk sunflower seeds and cigarette sticks on street corners and many railway personnel seem particularly prone to muddling the two currencies. In short, if someone asks you for '10 roubles', they really mean '10 hryvnia'.

In the marketplace, meanwhile, numerous traders – in a less committed fashion – speak of the ubiquitous *shtukiy*. Shtukiy means 'piece' and is used to refer to the hryvnia. Others simply say *nasha denghy* (literally 'our money') when referring to the national currency.

Trust taxi drivers to realise that money talks; mention the *backsov* or *dolarov* (meaning 'dollar') and greenbacks float before their eyes.

Exchange Rates

Since February 1999 the hryvnia (hv) has traded at 3.4 to 4.6 against the US dollar – a sharp contrast to its previous 1998 trading band of 1.8 to 2.25 hryvnia to US$1 (and even higher float rate of 1.7 to 1.9 in 1997). Despite a government pledge that Ukraine won't see a further devaluation of its national currency, the hryvnia's future remains rocky. Exchange rates at the end of 1999 included:

country	unit		hryvnia (hv)
Australia	A$1	=	3.44
Canada	C$1	=	3.61
euro	€1	=	5.38
France	10FF	=	8.21
Germany	DM1	=	2.75
Hungary	100 Ft	=	2.12
Ireland	IR£1	=	6.83
Japan	¥100	=	5.25
Moldova	L10	=	4.52
Netherlands	fl	=	2.44
New Zealand	NZ$1	=	2.75
Poland	1 zl	=	1.29
Romania	L10,000	=	2.97
Russia	R10	=	1.99
Slovakia	Sk 10	=	1.27
UK	UK£1	=	8.58
USA	US$1	=	5.33

UKRAINE

Exchanging Money

Deutschmarks, US dollars and Russian roubles can be easily exchanged anywhere; other currencies such as the British pound or French franc can be hard/impossible to change in small towns. Whatever currency you bring should be in pristine condition. Banks and exchanges do not accept old, tatty bills with rips or tears, or US dollar bills issued before 1990.

Most hotels have an exchange office, usually offering a lower rate than the numerous exchange kiosks (signposted *obmin valyuty)* scattered along main streets. Exchanging on the black market is illegal. Given the dramatic fluctuation in the hryvnia, you should only change a small amount of money at any one time.

Travellers Cheques Travellers cheques can be exchanged in banks in most cities in Ukraine, but be warned: the process is a lengthy (and confusing) one, involving trips to numerous different cashiers in the bank, each responsible for a different part of the transaction.

Always take travellers cheques in US dollars (small denominations). Thomas Cook, American Express and Visa are the most widely accepted. When cashing them in, you can be issued dollars, hryvnia or a combination of the two. Expect to pay 2% commission.

Cheque-friendly establishments include branches of the nationwide bank chains Avaal or UKR Exim Bank; and Western Union/X-Change Points. The latter has its head office in Kyiv (☎ 044-221 77 31, ☎ 227 77 33, ☎ 219 14 72), ploshcha Peremohy 1, and regional offices in Lviv, Ternopil, Uzhhorod, Odesa, Yalta, Dnipropetrovsk, Donetsk, Kharkiv and Chernivtsi.

ATMs Automatic teller machines (ATMs) accepting Visa and MasterCard/EuroCard have mushroomed in Ukraine in recent years. They are known locally as *bankomats* and are found in hotel lobbies, central post offices and Irish pubs rather than on the street. ATMs are widespread in Kyiv and major cities, but the concept has yet to hit the small towns. At Boryspil airport, there is one in the arrivals hall.

Most ATMs only distribute cash in the local currency, although some do offer the choice of US dollars. Most charge 2.5% commission; the total commission you will be charged flashes on the screen for your approval at the start of the transaction.

Credit Cards & International Transfers

Avaal Bank, UKR Exim Bank and Western Union/X-Change Points all make cash advances (in dollars or hryvnia) on major credit cards (around 3% commission). The procedure is as confusing as cashing travellers cheques, and involves procuring a collection of stamps and signatures from several bank personnel.

Credit cards are accepted by most upmarket hotels, restaurants and shops both in and outside the capital. Western Union/ X-Change Points will receive money wired from anywhere in the world.

Costs

A Soviet-style, two or three tier pricing system still happily reigns in Ukraine where foreigners pay up to three times as much as Ukrainians for some goods and services. The system has been scrapped on the railways where everyone now pays the same price, but it still applies in hotels, museums and on the national airlines.

Accommodation The greatest travel expense in Ukraine is accommodation, particularly in Kyiv and cities in eastern Ukraine where it is impossible to stay for less than $50 a night; most hotels average $100 a night for a double in an ageing, concrete block. Hotel prices will certainly tumble to more realistic levels when two tier pricing is dumped – something that is inevitable.

Elsewhere in the country, prices better reflect the standard of accommodation and are reasonably low – around $15 to $20 a night with rock-bottom prices plummeting to as low as $5 in some places.

Food In Kyiv and eastern cities, count on paying Western prices – or higher. Eating

UKRAINE

out is expensive, with a full meal (not including drinks) costing anything from $25 to $50. At the other end of the scale, dining in local, cafeteria-style eateries – plentiful outside Kyiv – might not titillate your tastebuds but it won't break the bank either. In these establishment, you can eat for as little as $1. Street treats, such as ice cream, pastries and delicious cakes in small cafes, cost pennies.

Transport Transport costs are low and everyone pays the same ticket price, regardless of nationality.

Travelling 1st class *(spalny vahon)* costs approximately three times as much as 2nd class *(kupe)* and five times as much as the lowest class *(platskart)*. In March 1999, single kupe fares included Kyiv-Odesa $11, Lviv-Uzhhorod $6, Odesa-Simferopol $7 and Donetsk-Poltava $5.

Buses between cities are ridiculously cheap – approximately $1 per 100km of travel. A single ticket on the world's longest trolleybus route (85km) linking Simferopol with Yalta in Crimea also costs $1. On public transport within cities, it costs a few cents for a bus, tram or metro ride.

Taxis are the most expensive form of transport; a fair rate is $0.20 per kilometre although rates charged depend to a great extent on location, destination, time and desperation of the situation: a 40km taxi ride from Boryspil airport to central Kyiv, for example, costs up to $30 (by bus, it's $2). Kyiv and Odesa are the only cities which have modern taxis with proper meters ($0.15/km in town and $0.25/km out of town).

UKRAINE

Tipping & Bargaining

No one expects tips in local cafes and cafeteria-style eateries – unlike some upmarket restaurants which lob a hefty 10 to 15% tip on top of your already hefty bill. Bargaining only takes place at the market.

Barters & Bribes

Little blatant bribing goes on these days, although saying it with chocolates and flowers has been known to work wonders in the bureaucratic world of tourist information, ticketing, visa extensions and the like. Any sort of bribery should be handled discreetly and with caution.

POST & COMMUNICATIONS

Post

Most main post offices *(poshta* or *poshtamt)* usually open from around 8 am to 9 pm (9 am to 7 pm on Saturday, closed Sunday). Smaller post offices close earlier and are not open on Saturday.

Outward mail is slow but fairly reliable. Air-mail letters take about two weeks from Ukraine to elsewhere in Europe, and two to three weeks to America or Australia. Sending a letter or postcard up to 20g costs $0.10 within Ukraine and $0.70 to Europe and the USA. Drop your stamped letters to destinations abroad in the postbox marked *za kordon*.

Incoming post is still completely unreliable, taking anything from three weeks to an eternity. The best way to receive or have mail held for you is through a personal contact. Many hotels will hold mail if you have a reservation with them.

Express mail is faster, more reliable and substantially more expensive. The state-run International Express Mail (EMS) is available at most main post offices; letters allegedly arrive anywhere within five days. Take packages to the post office unwrapped, for their contents to be verified. DHL International, Federal Express, TNT Express Worldwide and UPS all have an office in Kyiv and cities in eastern Ukraine.

Addressing Mail Addresses are written in reverse order (Ukraina, Kyiv, 252091, vul Franko 26/8, kv 12, Yuri Orestovich Vesolovsky). The return address is written in smaller print below the main address. When addressing outgoing mail, repeat the country destination in Cyrillic before printing the addressee's name.

Common words and abbreviations included in addresses are: *budynok* or *bud.* (building), *bulvar* or *bul.* (boulevard), *dim* or *d.* (house), *etazh* (floor), *korpus* or *k.* (building within a complex), *kvartyra* or *kv.* (apartment), *maydan* (square, usually park-like), *misto* or *m.* (city), *naberezhna* or *nab.*

(embankment), *pasazh* (passage), *ploshcha* or *pl.* (square), *prospekt* or *pr.* (avenue), *provulok* or *prov.* (lane), *rayon* or *r-n* (country), *selishche* or *sel.* (settlement), *selo* or *s.* (village), *shose* (highway), *uzviz* (slope), *vkhid*, *podezd* or *pod.* (entrance number) and *vulitsya* or *vul.* (street).

Floors are numbered American-style, the ground floor being No 1. On an address, two numbers separated by a slash (/) usually indicate a corner, the second number being the address on the cross street.

See European Russia Facts for the Visitor for more details.

Telephone

Ukrainian city codes are listed in this book under the relevant section heading. Kyiv telephone numbers comprise seven digits, but most numbers elsewhere have six digits. In mid-1999, some six-digit numbers in Donetsk had changed to seven digits; when dialling the latter, drop the additional 2 from the city code (dial 062 instead of 0622). In Ivano-Frankivsk, Uzhhorod and Poltava, numbers only have five digits. If (when) these become six-digit numbers, also drop the extra 2 (dial 0342 instead of 03422 for Ivano; 0321 instead of 03122 for Uzhhorod etc).

When calling Ukraine, the country code is ☎ 380. When dialling from abroad, drop the initial 0 of the city code (eg to call Kyiv from London dial ☎ 00 380 44).

Local Calls Local calls can be made from public phones on the street. In Kyiv, Lviv, Donetsk and other big cities, most of these phones require a phonecard, sold at post and telephone offices for just a few cents. Stupidly, phones in each city require a different type of card. Some public phones are still token operated; buy a *zheton* from the post or telephone office or a street kiosk.

Intercity & International Calls Public phones on the streets are only for local calls. To make an intercity or international call you have to call from a private home or telephone office (the cheapest options), your hotel (the most expensive option) or from a Utel public card phone (the in between option).

National and international calls cannot be directly dialled from all private phones, each of which has its own idiosyncrasies regarding numbers to dial to access the respective line; check with the homeowner. The general norm, however, to make an intercity call from a private phone is to dial ☎ 8, followed by the city code (including the initial 0) and number. To call internationally, dial ☎ 8, then 10, followed by the country code, city code and number. If you can't dial directly, book a call through the international operator (☎ 079, ☎ 073) who will make the connection for you. Kyiv's international operators work in several languages (English ☎ 8-192, French ☎ 8-191, German ☎ 8-193, Spanish ☎ 8-195).

Every city has a telephone office (many open 24 hours). To make an intercity *(mizhhorodny, mizhmisky)* or international *(mizhnarodny)* call, prepay the switchboard operator who will give you a metal tag imprinted with the number of the booth *(kabina)* you have been assigned. When the booth is available, dial the number you require, following the same system as from a private phone (see earlier). If there is a black button labelled *otvet* on the booth phone, press it when the person you are calling responds; if not, you will be cut off. After your call, return to the switchboard operator who will give you a receipt plus, if necessary, change from your prepayment. In some telephone offices, the switchboard operator will dial the number for you, calling you to your assigned booth once the connection has been made.

Using a Utel card phone – located in some post offices and hotel lobbies – is the easiest way to make a national or international call. Chip cards worth 50, 100 or 200 units cost $5, $10 or $20 respectively and are sold in post offices and at hotel receptions. Instructions on how to make local, national and international calls are explained clearly in English in every Utel phone booth.

Costs Local/intercity calls cost $0.11/22 a minute (fractionally less during off-peak times between 9 pm and 6 am). International calls to Eastern/Central/Western Europe cost

$0.50/0.79/1.25 a minute; calling the USA and Canada or Australia costs $2/2.33 respectively (off-peak $1.67/1.88).

Fax

Faxes can be sent from most post offices and better hotels. Fax rates at the post office are the same as telephone rates/minute (see Costs earlier). At Kyiv's main post office, you can receive faxes for a small fee.

Email & Internet Access

A substantial number of Ukrainians are adept email and Internet users, with most business and commercial enterprises being electronically hooked up. You can send (but not receive) emails from the main post office in Kyiv and a handful of other regional post offices (Donetsk, Poltava, Simferopol and Dnipropetrovsk). The average charge is $0.20 per kilobyte; in Kyiv, you have to write the message you want to send on a piece of paper for someone else to laboriously type in to the computer.

More efficient are the numerous, privately run Internet cafes that have mushroomed in Ukraine in recent years. There are cybercafes in Kyiv, Chernivtsi, Lviv, Odesa, Simferopol, Yalta, Zaporizhzhya, and Donetsk. The average hourly charge for online access is $2.

If there is not yet a cybercafe in the town you are visiting, track down the local Internet provider who will most likely allow you to send/receive your email messages.

INTERNET RESOURCES

Most Ukrainian-related sites are short on practical survival information, but worth a surf for solid background information. This choice selection is a happy mix of both:

Brama Gateway Ukraine
 www.brama.com
 (a rich, information-based site: art and culture, business, calender of events, media and more)
Ukrainian Map Server
 www.infoukes.com/ua-maps
 (country, regional and city maps galore to be downloaded and printed)
Ukraine Factbook
 www.uazone.net/Ukraine.html
 (facts galore covering history, culture and more ...)
Kyiv University
 www.univ.kiev.ua
Ukraine
 www.physics.mcgill.ca/WWW/oleh/ukr-info.html
 (superb, hypertext site with 100+ links to Ukrainian-related Web sites; best set of Chornobyl-related links).

BOOKS

Harvard Ukrainian Institute Publications (☎ 617-495 4053, fax 495 8097, huri@fas.harvard.edu, www.sabre.org/huri), 1583 Massachusetts Ave, Cambridge, MA 02138, USA, is a publishing house which is attached to Harvard University's Ukrainian Research Institute.

In Canada, try the Canadian Institute Ukrainian Press (CIUS Press; ☎ 403-492 2972, fax 492 4967, cius@ualberta.com, www.utoronto.ca/cius), 352 Athabasca Hall, University of Alberta, Edmonton, Alberta T6G 2E8. Its catalogue can be downloaded from the Internet.

In Britain, the mail order company, Zora Books (☎ 020-7602 1691, fax 7610 4255, zorabooks@btinternet.com, www.btinternet.com/~zorabooks) specialises in the ex-USSR. It issues regularly updated book lists, and planned to open its warehouse to customers by late 1999. The Travel Bookshop (☎ 020-7229 5260), 13-15 Blenheim Crescent, London W11 2EE, is another good bet for Ukrainian travel literature.

Lonely Planet

Lonely Planet's Ukrainian and Russian phrasebooks are indispensable. There are Lonely Planet guides to Romania & Moldova, Hungary, Czech & Slovak Republics, Estonia, Latvia & Lithuania and Poland. All of Ukraine's neighbours feature in Lonely Planet's *Eastern Europe*.

Guidebooks

Hippocrene's *Language & Travel Guide to Ukraine* (1995) by Linda Hodges & George Chumak is strong on the language and conversation front, but weak on practical detail.

Hikers should invest in Bradt's 148 page *Hiking Guide to Poland & Ukraine* (1995) by Tim Burford, which details different hikes in Ukraine. Fourteen pages of *Trekking in Russia & Central Asia* (1994) by Frith Maier are devoted to trekking in Crimea.

In Ukraine, there are a couple of locally published guidebooks worth picking up. A treasure if you can track a copy down is *Cave Cities of the Crimea* (Mystetstvo, Kyiv, 1993), a pocket-size historical guide in English. Equally invaluable is *The Streets of Kyiv: Five Walks in the Centre* (1996), comprising 192 pages of detailed walking itineraries in the capital. It's published by Art Ec (☎ 044-221 52 54, fax 221 57 44), vulitsya Leonid Pervpmaysky 9, Kyiv.

The hardback *Ukraine: A Tourist Guide* (1995) by Osyp Zinkewych & Volodymyr Hula is horribly nationalistic, outdated and inaccurate in parts, but contains detailed information on destinations other guides don't touch. It's published by Smoloskyp Publishers (☎/fax 044-212 08 77), vulitsya Artema 105, R. 802, Kyiv-53.

Travel

Based upon the author's travels around Ukraine in 1993-95, *Borderland: A Journey through the History of Ukraine* (1997) by Anna Reid is a highly readable and recommended account of Ukrainian history, peppered with amusing anecdotes and insights on daily life in the post-Soviet borderland. Reid was the Kyiv correspondent for the *Economist* and London's *Daily Telegraph* from 1993-95.

Written in Moscow in the 1920s, *The White Guard* (1923; reprint 1995) by Russian novelist Mikhail Bulgakov (translated into English by Michael Gleeny) paints a brilliant picture of Kyiv during the 1918 revolution amid the city's middle-class suburbia, in which Bulgakov was raised.

History & Politics

Ukraine: A History (1993) by Orest Subtelny presents a concise and easy-to-read history, way too hefty to pack in your backpack. Despite being published more than a decade ago, *Famine in Ukraine, 1932-33* (1986) by Roman Serbyn & Bohdan Krawchenko and *The Harvest of Sorrow: Soviet Collectivisation and the Terror-Famine* (1986) by Robert Conquest remain timeless classics in their field. Both give a full historical account of the events leading up to the mass famine and its effects on the Ukrainian people and nation as a whole.

The darker side of WWII is the focus of *Collaboration in the Holocaust: Crimes of the Local Police in Belorussia and Ukraine, 1941-44* (1999) by Martin Dean. The Nazi death camp of Babyn Yar in Kyiv is the subject of DM Thomas' novel, *The White Hotel* (1993); *Babyn Yar: A Document in the form of a Novel* (1970) by A Anatoli; and *Nothing is Forgotten* by Yakov Kaper & David Budnik, which can be read on the Internet (www.peysakhov.com).

Women in Russia and Ukraine (1996), edited by Rosalind Marsh, is a collection of authoritative essays covering everything from the feminist movement to the position of gays and lesbians in post-Soviet society. For a female story from a very different perspective, read *On the Road to Stalingrad: Memoirs of a Woman Machine Gunner* (1997) by Zova M Smirnova-Medvedeva (translated by Kazimiera Cottam). Based primarily in Odesa and Sevastopol, this highly emotive autobiography describes life as a machine gunner commander in the trenches, fighting for the Soviets during WWII. War-torn Sevastopol is also depicted in *The Sebastopol Sketches* by Leo Tolstoy, who fought there in the Crimean War (1854). *The Tatars of Crimea: Return to the Homeland* (1998) edited by Edward Allworth addresses the plight of Crimea's displaced Tatars.

Dangerous Weapons, Desperate States; Russia, Belarus, Kazakstan and Ukraine (1999) addresses contemporary politics in 256 pages edited by Gary Bertsch and William Potter; as does *Ukraine: Perestroika to Independence* (1998) by Taras Kuzio & Andrew Wilson. Written by one of the country's youngest literary figures, *Letters from Kyiv* (1992) by Solomea Pavlychko is a 177 page eyewitness account of the political and economic upheavals during 1990-91. Scores of books have been written about Chornobyl.

For a total resource, the weighty five volume *Encyclopaedia of Ukraine* published by CIUS Press covers the complete A to Z of all things Ukrainian. In Ukraine, there's *All About Ukraine* (1998), a two volume encyclopaedia published by Alternativy Publishers (☎ 044-226 35 13, fax 226 35 17), vulitsya Kruglouniversytetska 20/1, Kyiv 25204.

NEWSPAPERS & MAGAZINES

A quick glance at any one of Kyiv's hundreds of street kiosks signposted in English (The Press), Ukrainian *(Presa)* and Russian *(Pressa)* is proof that the print media went wild after independence. Publications galore cover anything and everything. Most Ukrainian-language dailies publish a Russian edition too.

Demokratychna Ukraina (Democratic Ukraine) is the misnamed formal voice of the Communist Party, and it basically hasn't changed much. *Holos Ukrainy* (Voice of Ukraine) is published by the Supreme Council, hence endorsing, raising or shrouding issues as the parliament sees it. *Zerkalo Nedeli* (Mirror of the Week) is a Russian-language political weekly, while *Den* (Day) is a popularist, independent daily. *Literaturna Ukraina* (Ukrainian Literature) is the voice of the Ukrainian Union of Writers, a pro-reform, democratic, nationalist group of literary thinkers who played an important part in the push for independence in 1991.

Many English-language publications are distributed for free. The weekly *Kyiv Post* (www.thepost.kiev.ua) is scorned by local expats but read by them nonetheless. It runs local, national and international news, has special entertainment and business sections, and offers overseas subscriptions. *The Day* is an excellent weekly digest of Ukrainian news, translated from the local-language *Den*, while the weekly *Ukrainian Times* focuses on business news. Both cost $1 in news kiosks.

Whether you're inside or outside Ukraine, you can subscribe to news reports compiled by Interfax, the Ukrainian news agency (root@interfax.kiev.ua). Alternatively you can try the *Eastern Economist* (www.easterneconomist.com), an economy and investment weekly (annual subscription $550/575 for USA/elsewhere). The *Ukrainian Weekly* (www.ukrweekly.com) is published by the fraternal Ukrainian National Association (annual subscription USA/Europe $105/160) and is available in Kyiv.

Kyiv Investment Magazine (magazine@welcome.pp.kiev.ua, www.securities.com) and *The Ukrainian* are glossy A4 magazines (info@pickard.kiev.ua) that feature interesting articles. *Panorama*, published every two months, doubles as Ukraine International's inflight magazine. For cultural and entertainment news in Kyiv, pick up a copy of the free, weekly *What's On* (WhatsOn@carrier.kiev.ua).

International English-language papers are hard to find and expensive. Try lobby kiosks in top hotels; if you intend staying in Kyiv for a while, subscribe to your favourite Western newspaper via International Press Distribution & Trade (☎ 044-290 06 96, fax 290 51 49), vulitsya Suvorova 14/12, Kyiv 25210.

RADIO & TV

Top-end hotels have CNN, SkyNet and some German stations via satellite. Beyond that, you're stuck with twiddling the TV knob to see what channels you can find. The main Ukrainian channels are the state-run UT-1; and two private stations Inter and STB. In Lviv and other parts of western Ukraine, you can pick up Polish TV. Russian-language TV predominates in eastern Ukraine.

Gala Radio (100 FM; www.galaradio.com) and Hit Radio (104 FM) are two popular, DJ-led radio stations featuring the latest pop music hits. For news and views in Kyiv, tune into the Ukrainian Radio Broadcasting Corporation (106.5 FM).

The BBC World Service (☎ 044-230 20 96, ukrainian.section@bbc.co.uk) can be heard in English, Ukrainian and Russian from 6.30 to 10 am, 4 to 8 pm and 10 to 11 pm (612 AM).

VIDEO SYSTEMS

Ukraine uses SECAM L (a different system to that used in Russia), although some foreign-produced tapes are NTSC or PAL and therefore require a multisystem player.

PHOTOGRAPHY & VIDEO

Western film is widely available in most cities and large towns, although colour slide and B&W film is hard to find. Film is expensive so bring a supply with you. The same applies to camera batteries (hard to find) and films/batteries for camcorders (nearly impossible to find).

See European Russia Facts for the Visitor – Photography & Video for more details.

TIME

Ukraine is in one time zone – GMT plus two hours. During daylight saving from the first Sunday in April until the last Sunday in October, it is GMT plus three hours.

When it's noon in Kyiv, it is 2 am in San Francisco; 5 am in New York; 10 am in London; 11 am in Paris, Warsaw, Prague and Budapest; noon in Minsk, Bucharest and Cairo; and 1 pm in Moscow.

Between 1994 and 1997, Crimea clocked in on Moscow time. Today, it reluctantly adheres to Kyiv time.

ELECTRICITY

Russia and Ukraine use the same system – see European Russia Facts for the Visitor.

WEIGHTS & MEASURES

Ukraine uses the metric system – see European Russia Facts for the Visitor.

LAUNDRY

Hand-washing hot tip: pack a universal plug or block the sink (more or less) with a plastic box from a photographic film. See Laundry in European Russia Facts for the Visitor for more on the joys of life on the road without a washing machine.

TOILETS

Hotel-room toilets are passable, but public toilets are vile and nauseating, often resembling nothing more than a stinky clogged hole with foot markers on either side. You'll be more likely to find moon rock than toilet paper (even in hotels), so keep a good stash on you at all times. Sometimes in big cities and train stations there are pay toilets *(platny tualet)*, which can be marginally more bearable. In the countryside or small towns you may find yourself discreetly consulting nature – a common and sweeter-smelling practice.

Women's toilets are marked Ж *(zhinochy)*; men's are marked Ч or М *(cholovichy* or *muzhcheny)*.

HEALTH

For general information see Health in European Russia Facts for the Visitor, most of which is relevant to Ukraine – including the increase in cases of diphtheria and the incidence of tick-borne encephalitis and Lyme disease in rural areas during summer. Before departing, travellers should check with their local public health service for information on current epidemic or health risks for travellers to Ukraine. Certain immunisations, such as tetanus, typhoid and diphtheria, should be current.

Chornobyl

The risk to short-term visitors is insignificant. The areas to stay away from, at least for long-term exposure, are the northern parts of the Zhytomyr and Kyiv oblasts. Chernihiv, 80km to the east of Chornobyl, was spared by favourable winds and is completely safe to visit. Although swimming in the Dnipro around Kyiv is popular with locals, especially in summer, some authorities have advised against it – portions of silt have been contaminated by radioactive particles flowing downstream. The most absorptive foods are mushrooms and berries, two staples of the Ukrainian diet that should be avoided if their origin is uncertain. See the following boxed text for further information.

Cholera

Cholera, a disease of the intestine caused by waterborne bacteria, was in near epidemic proportions in and around Crimea in 1994 – to the point that Turkey suspended all shipping traffic arriving from Yalta and Odesa. No dangers have been reported since, but to be on the safe side, drink only bottled water (easily obtainable in most food stores) in Crimea, and in the entire country

UKRAINE

Chornobyl

On 26 April 1986, reactor No 4 at Chornobyl (Chernobyl in Russian) nuclear power station, 100km north of Kyiv, blew up during the testing of a generator. Nearly nine tonnes of radioactive material – 90 times as much as the Hiroshima bomb – were spewed into the sky. Winds over the following days, mostly blowing north and west, swept fallout into Belarus, as well as Russia, Poland and the Baltic region. Fallout affected 23% of Belarus, with 7% of Ukrainian territory and 0.5% of Russian land exposed. Thirty-one people died during the explosion, but exactly how many thousands perished due to the ensuing acute radiation sickness is unknown. A report issued by the Ukrainian Health Ministry in 1999 put the figures of those who died or suffered fatal diseases from being involved in the clean-up at 4365 and 167,653 respectively.

Immediately after the explosion, some 135,000 people were evacuated from a 30km radius around the plant. The 10km exclusion zone centred around the dead town of Prypyat remains at a high risk of exposure today. The reactor was hastily enclosed in a concrete-and-steel sarcophagus. Over the following years about 600,000 people – popularly known as 'the liquidators' – worked on clean-up operations inside the 30km zone. Although scientists agree that there is no risk of the sarcophagus exploding, the status of the estimated 180 tonnes of radioactive material still smouldering beneath the concrete is unclear. More recently, the deteriorating condition of the concrete sarcophagus which is allegedly crumbling has become a major cause for concern.

The major effects of the explosion only became clear gradually. An estimated 4.9 million people in northern Ukraine, southern Belarus and the south-western corner of Russia were affected to some degree. Many continued to live on contaminated land and produced contaminated meat, milk and vegetables, which found their way into local markets.

Today, Ukraine has evacuated most of the highly contaminated areas, although a number of resettlers, anxious to return to their villages such as Opachichi and Koupovatoye, have moved back within the forbidden zone, a practice the government mainly ignores. Workers at the Chornobyl plant today live in the new town of Slavutych, created following the 1986 disaster, and an international team of scientists has set up a 24 hour monitoring station at the plant. Over 15% of Ukraine's annual budget is consumed by Chornobyl-related clean-up and maintenance operations, an amount the government argues is nowhere close to sufficient, but all it can possibly afford. Agricultural and production losses, especially in Belarus, have also crippled the economy.

if possible. Bring a water bottle and some water-purification tablets, especially if you plan on camping or doing a lot of walking.

DANGERS & ANNOYANCES

Inherent bureaucracy and apathy are nasty hangovers from the Soviet Union that Ukraine has yet to shake off. Dumbstruck desk staff, blind waiters, paralysed shop assistants and the inevitable curtains being drawn shut to the sounds of laughter after you've waited an hour in the ticket line – these are all little annoyances which, even if you approach an establishment armed with zero expectation, are still ... darn annoying. The upside is that on the rare occasion when a service bureau employee takes an interest in your problem or question, it seems heaven-sent. Perversely, the overattention showered upon Western travellers by the hordes of pesky taxi drivers at Simferopol train station, or by black ticket marketeers at Kyiv and Odesa train stations can be equally annoying.

Annoyances that can be dangerous include anti-Semitic and racist attitudes; open

Chornobyl

Despite huge pressure from the international community, the Ukrainian government opted to reopen the remaining three reactors at Chornobyl to help solve its energy crisis. A fire in 1991 prompted the closure of reactor No 2, followed by reactor No 1 in 1996. Only reactor No 3 is on line today and has been temporarily shut down several times for urgent safety repairs to be carried out. This last reactor, the government says, will be shut down for good in 2000 providing the West drums up the financial aid for Ukraine to construct two replacement nuclear plants in Khmelnytsky and Rivne in western Ukraine. The estimated cost is US$1.2 billion. On both sides, there are increasing fears that this will not happen.

Ukraine relies on its five Chornobyl-style, nuclear power stations for more than half its energy. The Zaporizhzhya power plant in eastern Ukraine is Europe's largest.

Despite the doom and gloom, Western medical and governmental sources are unanimous that the risk to short-term visitors is insignificant.

Sam Travel Company in Kyiv (see the Kyiv chapter) organises guided ecological tours of Chornobyl. Tours can include Kyiv's Chornobyl Museum; the village of Dytyatky which borders the 30km restricted area; the dead town of Prypyat where Chornobyl workers lived before 1986 and Slavutych, its purpose-built contemporary counterpart; and lunch on-site in the power plant canteen. Tours – US$132 for one to three people or US$210 for four to nine people, including transport – have to be prepaid 15 days in advance.

manholes in the street; driving at night on unlit, unmarked, potholed roads; zigzagging drivers; inconspicuous pieces of string across the pavement to rope off crumbling buildings; and those archaic gas water heaters (called calunkers) that refuse to ignite, then bang, you've got no eyebrows left.

Crime

Organised Mafia is big-time in Ukraine. Thousands of small-scale mafiosi run rings of kiosks, supply pensioners with cigarettes to sell, and take part in the favourite pastime of the mobile elite – *kupuvati-prodati*, or buy, sell and pocket the profit. It's almost expected that all *biznesmeny* are a crooked lot and that capitalism is just controlled banditry, with you, as a Westerner, a representative of that golden capitalist dream.

Nevertheless, as a tourist you won't feel the effects of the Mafia. The biggest danger to tourists is the increasing number of mostly independent criminals who direct their attentions to ripping off naive tourists. Because you're a Westerner, you're seen as rich. Undesirables often lurk around the hotels looking for targets. Don't flash your money, stay low-key in appearance, have more than one place on your body where you stash your cash, and avoid conversations with shifty characters that approach you. At night, be careful going into and out of your hotel, especially in Kyiv. Avoid being alone late at night on the metro in Kyiv or in the parks around the centre.

In comparison to Western cities, however, Kyiv is relatively safe – nothing compared to such places as New York or Los Angeles. The usual safety and awareness precautions that all travellers normally take should be applied in Ukraine. See the Dangers & Annoyances section in European Russia Facts for the Visitor for further tips.

You can call these emergency numbers from any phone (free of charge):

Fire *(pozhezhnoyi kluzhby)*	☎ 01
Police *(militsya)*	☎ 02
Ambulance *(shvidkoyi dopomohy)*	☎ 03

BUSINESS HOURS

Official weekday working hours are 9 or 10 am to 5 or 6 pm. Most banks close for the day at 1 pm. Shops tend to be open from 8 or 9 am until 8 or 9 pm (closed Sunday), although small shops may close earlier. Most cafeteria-style eateries and cafes are open from 8 or 9 am to 6 or 7 pm, while restaurants tend to open from noon until midnight. Every establishment, whatever its trade, takes a one or two hour break either at lunchtime in the case of shops, or around 4 or 5 pm in the case of 'old school' restaurants. The concept has been scrapped by most Western-style eating places in the capital and other cities.

Museum hours are typically from 9 am to 5 or 6 pm, but they vary, and there's always one or two days a week when they're closed. In addition, museums celebrate the sanitary day *(sanitary den)*, usually during the last week of each month. Some older restaurants, shops and hotel dining rooms also adhere to this monthly scrubbing system.

PUBLIC HOLIDAYS & SPECIAL EVENTS

The main public holidays are:

New Year's Day
1 January
Orthodox Christmas
7 January
International Women's Day
8 March
Orthodox Easter (Paskha)
April
International Labour Day
1 & 2 May
Victory (1945) Day & Mother's Day
9 May
Holy Trinity Day
June
Independence (1991) Day
24 August
Great October Socialist Revolution (1917) Anniversary
7 & 8 November

Thousands of small cultural events and festivals are held throughout the country, many in celebration of the seasons and local folk traditions. Annual festivals include:

April

Humorina
In Odesa, a one day street carnival centred around humour, on the 1st of the month.

May

Kyiv Days
A colourful spring celebration and festival in honour of the capital city; last weekend of May.

June

Ivan Kupallo Day
On 6 June a celebration of Midsummer's Night is held in Kyiv, dating back to pagan origins.

August

Crimean Stars
In Yalta, special events are scheduled throughout the month to celebrate Crimean history and culture.

Independence Day
On the 24th, each city hosts festivals and parades with performances and special events.

October

Kyiv International Music Festival
In the first week of October hundreds of

international composers and musicians perform at numerous venues.

Kyiv International Film Festival Molodist
A great time to check out new cinematic talent (see the Kyiv chapter).

December

New Year
Gifts are placed under a traditional fir tree on the 31st, and special songs are sung. See out the old year with vodka and welcome in the new with champagne.

ACTIVITIES

Hiking & Trekking

Hiking, trekking and camping opportunities are richest in Crimea and the Carpathians, along with a few scattered national parks (see Facts about Ukraine – Flora & Fauna) elsewhere in the country.

Several organisations (see Ukraine Getting There & Away) organise trekking adventures in Crimea, all focusing on the spectacular Crimean mountain range along the south coast. For independent travellers, the easy hikes to the cave cities of Chufut-Kale and Manhup-Kale (see the Crimea chapter) are popular, although more remote sites exist which make many other excellent and scenic hikes. Other highlights include the Bolshoy Kanyon, the deepest canyon in Crimea, over 300m deep and 3km long; the Dzhur-Dzhur and Uchansu waterfalls; and the marmorna (marble) caves. You can also climb to the top of Crimea's highest peaks – Roman-Cosh (1545m), Demyr-Kapu (1540m) and Kemal-Yeherek (1529m).

The fabulously picturesque Carpathians occupy a broad stretch of the south-west of the country. The region is steeped in folklore and with a good map you can just about walk anywhere you like. The vast majority of these remote and highly scenic mountains are uninhabited, although most towns and villages lie along the roads. Part of the region is covered by the Carpathian National Natural Park (CNNP), with its headquarters in Rakhiv. Alongside the CNNP, several other 'green' organisations – such as the Rakhiv-based Carpathian Agency for Agro-Eco Tourism – are making small but impressive in-roads into establishing an eco-friendly, tourist infrastructure. Hiking trails are being marked, maps are becoming available and private mountain guides are available to lead you in and around the mountains (around $20 a day). Ecotours – as well as mushrooming and berrying expeditions – are also organised (see the Western Ukraine chapter for details).

Green contacts in Lviv include the Ukrainian National Eco-Centre (☎ 0322-725 792, ☎ 221 308, tschern@forest.lviv.ua), PO Box 7270, Lviv 290070; and the Carpathian School (☎ 0322-79 43 38, ksh@carpathian.uar.net), vulitsya Doroshenka 42-21, Lviv 29000.

If you intend camping or trekking, come equipped with all you're going to need; supplies are pretty nonexistent.

Skiing

The untouched slopes of the Ukrainian Carpathians offer skiers the rare opportunity to cruise along fresh, ungroomed snow, often in splendid isolation. You can ski in the Carpathian National Natural Park between November and March. Cross-country skiing is plentiful, but downhill skiing is limited to gentle, beginner-level slopes which lack any sort of 'package tour' infrastructure (read: one chairlift and a handful of ageing drag lifts). The main ski 'resort' in the national park is Yablunytsia, a small village 30km south of Yaremcha where you can hire ski equipment for no more than $5 a day.

Ice Fishing

Ice fishing is a national pastime for Ukraine's fishermen – usually vodka-fuelled – who sit for motionless hours next to a small hole drilled through the thick ice. Ice fishing is common on the Black Sea and on the country's many lakes.

Bungee Jumping

Daredevils can bungee jump amid scenic splendour (safety not guaranteed) in the fortress town of Kamyanets-Polidsky (see the Western Ukraine chapter).

Boating

Boat trips down the Dnipro are a popular way for Kyivans to cool down in summer's searing heat. In Crimea, there are plenty of opportunities to rent a small boat with pilot who will sail you around the Black Sea coastal nooks and crannies. Some spots, such as the dacha where Gorbachev was kept under house arrest in 1991, are best viewed by boat. Both scheduled and chartered boats operate between May and mid-October.

WORK

The majority of foreign workers in Ukraine are either part of large foreign joint-venture corporations such as Coca-Cola or Pac Tel, government workers such as embassy employees or political analysts, or part of some social-oriented organisation. The US Peace Corps has about 100 volunteers working in the country, either teaching English, consulting or doing social work. The Ukrainian National Association (UNA) of America regularly sends volunteers to teach at universities, as do the Soros Foundation and the associated Renaissance Foundation, which emphasise closer cultural interrelations through education. Journalists, scholars (such as Fulbright fellows) and other researchers, including archaeologists at Kamyanets-Podilsky and Khersones, are involved in only relatively small numbers. The floodgates have been opened as far as religious missionaries are concerned, and zealots are campaigning passionately.

But the freewheeling transient travellers common in other parts of Europe, who pick up seasonal work from place to place, really don't exist in Ukraine. Wages, unless you work for a foreign company, are minuscule and without the aid of some organisation or personal contact, the vast complications of setting yourself up are insurmountable.

ACCOMMODATION

Accommodation will be one of the biggest expenses of your trip, particularly if you limit your stay to Kyiv. Standards of accommodation are generally quite acceptable despite being lower than in the West.

Camping

Wild camping is permitted in the Carpathian National Natural Park – an exhilarating way to spend the night. Organised camp sites are becoming increasingly rare. For details see Accommodation in European Russia Facts for the Visitor.

Mountain Refuges

If you intend spending several days hiking in the Carpathians, contact the Carpathian National Natural Park headquarters in Rakhiv. The park authorities have keys to many of the traditional hunters' cabins in the mountains. These refuges are simple huts with no facilities beyond a roof – a welcome relief nonetheless after a long day hiking.

Hostels

Hostels of any sort have not yet hit Ukraine, not even the capital city.

Turbazas & Sanatoria

Turbazas (tourbases) are a common form of accommodation in the Carpathian region and are the cheapest places to stay. Most remain unchanged since the Soviet era, but some have been renovated with an elevated price tag to match. For more details see Accommodation in European Russia Facts for the Visitor.

Soviet-era sanatoria – holiday homes run by a number of organisations for their members – speckle the Black Sea coastline in Crimea. Since independence, many sit empty and neglected, as they are no longer filled with groups of Soviet workers on organised holidays.

Hotels

Most hotels are tall, unsightly concrete rectangles built in the 1960s and 1970s. Rooms are reasonably comfortable, despite being well worn. A double room translates as two single beds (often pushed together) and a bathroom in various degrees of cleanliness. In budget hotels, you occasionally have to make your own bed (sheets are provided) and you always have to bring your own towel, soap and toilet paper.

Some cities – like Lviv and Odesa – tout marvellous early 20th century hotels, often in a crumbling state but delightful and highly atmospheric. Other cities – Kyiv, Lviv, Ivano-Frankivsk and Dnipropetrovsk

UKRAINE

– are graced with luxurious, joint-venture hotels, well up to top Western standards but overwhelmingly expensive. The latter are the only hotels that, at the time of writing, don't sport a two tier pricing system (see Costs under Money earlier).

Western palaces aside, most hotels encounter water problems, particularly in Crimea and western Ukraine. Hot water is often only available between certain hours; the times are pinned up at reception. If not, ask the receptionist about the *voda* (water) situation. Occasionally there's no hot water (or water) at all.

In some cities there are so-called unregistered hotels that won't accept foreign tourists. This usually means the hotel is beneath acceptable norms of cleanliness, mainly in the bathrooms. Reception staff in these joints do everything to dissuade foreigners from staying, although often, if you argue hard enough, you will be given a room.

Checking In When checking in, you have to surrender your passport and fill out a general identification form which is never in English. If you have problems deciphering it, simply leave it blank and the receptionist will fill it in for you (copying the required details from your passport). Most hotels demand prepayment and keep your passport overnight to administer the necessary registration with VVIR (see Visas & Documents earlier).

In return for your cash, you're given a hotel card with your room number scrawled on it. Show this to your floor lady *(dezhurna)* who will exchange it for your key. Whenever you leave the hotel, leave your key with the dezhurna. Don't lose your hotel card.

Homestays

Homestays are becoming increasingly common in Ukraine and provide a rare and invaluable opportunity to gain a fascinating insight into how people in Ukraine really live. Your host family often acts as your personal guide, first-hand information source – and friend.

Several travel agencies abroad organise homestays. In Ukraine, the Chervona Ruta travel agency (see Information in the Kyiv chapter) arranges homestay accommodation in private homes in Kyiv, Lviv, Dnipropetrovsk, Donetsk, Poltava, Simferopol, Yalta and Sevastopol. Rural homestays are organised by the Carpathian Agency for Agro-Eco Tourism and the Carpathian National Natural Park headquarters in Rakhiv (see the Western Ukraine chapter).

In Kyiv, Odesa and other large cities, eager opportunists offer rooms for hire in their houses and flats. Great care should be made to find out what's involved; for example whether or not you have to share the double bed with snoring grandpa or need to take an hour's bus ride to get there. However, this can often be a refreshing and cheap accommodation alternative, with a great home-cooked meal thrown in. At train stations, look out for people – invariably older ladies – touting signs around their necks reading кімнати (*kimnaty*, Ukrainian) or комнаты (*komnaty*, Russian), meaning 'rooms'. Nightly rates range from $10 to $15.

FOOD

Ukrainian cuisine celebrates distinctive natural flavours and simple ingredients, rarely heavily spiced or overly complicated but always hearty and rich. Many of the country's specialities stem from peasant dishes based on grains and staple vegetables like potatoes, cabbage, beets and mushrooms, seasoned with garlic, dill and vinegar. Beef, pork, poultry and fish are widely used and most dishes are either boiled, fried or stewed. Desserts are usually laden with honey and fruit – mainly cherries and plums – and often baked into sweet breads.

Ironically, you can't always find good Ukrainian food in Ukraine. Most top-end restaurants serve trendy European cuisine, with Ukrainian fare relegated to skimpy appetisers. It's often doled out by the small cafeteria-style eateries, but the quality of their ingredients can produce a bland impression of *varenyky* (stuffed dumplings) and borsch. The best Ukrainian cooking is found in the home, and if you get invited to someone's house for a meal you'll be in for a treat. *Festive Ukrainian Cooking* (1990)

UKRAINE

by Marta Pisetska Farley and Hippocrene's *Best of Ukrainian Cuisine* (1998) by Bohdan Zahny are two books worth a nibble for those interested in concocting their own Ukrainian feast.

Many culinary dishes and drinks have much in common with those you find in Russia (see the Food & Drink section in European Russia Facts for the Visitor).

Where to Eat

Eating out in Kyiv is a world apart from eating out in the rest of Ukraine. While the dining scene in the capital has taken off recently, leaving the city with an explosive choice of ethnic cuisine, the rest of the country slumbers in a Soviet legacy of sparse menu selections, surly waiting staff and blaring pop music.

Restaurants In Kyiv, there is absolutely no need to put up with the gala ballroom overkill typical of many hotel and Soviet-era restaurants. Western-style places abound, complete with English menus and Western price tags; advance reservations are needed for many places.

Elsewhere, you can simply stroll right in and select which of the empty tables you would like to sit at, then face the delightful task of deciphering the menu – rarely in English, cheaply printed on rice paper and always stamped and signed by the chief accountant and director. Many items are not available, despite being listed. Dishes are doled out by the 100g and are almost always garnished with three neat piles of shredded carrot, beetroot and cabbage. Supposed starters and main courses are rarely served in the correct (or expected) order.

For most Ukrainians, eating out is a major (and expensive) social event, so restaurants are not geared for customers in a hurry. Bring a book or good conversation. If you want a quiet meal, come before 7 pm – by 8 pm everyone will be boogying to the obligatory band.

Cafeterias A quick meal with no hassles is served at canteen-style eateries *(yidalnya* or *stolova)*. Food here is hot, starchy, tasty and quick, served to you by a woman in a white *shmok* behind the counter who ladles out heaped portions of varenyky, scalding borsch, potatoes, meatballs, random salads and fruit-compote drinks. A *varenychna* is an eatery that only serves varenyky. A *shashlychna* is a shashlyk stand.

Kafes A *kafe* resembles a cafe in the West, where you can have a coffee or tea accompanied by a pastry or cake. Kafes abound throughout the country, obviously varying enormously in menu and ambience. Coffee is usually a frothy, grind-filled, Turkish-style beverage or alternatively a bitterly strong instant Nescafe. Tea is also black and strong usually – and both come oversweetened. If you don't want sugar say *bez tsukor* or *malo tsukor* (without or just a little sugar). A *pyrizhkova* is a cafe-bakery that specialises in cakes and sweets. Most cafes sell ice cream too, a food that most Ukrainians happily eat year-round, regardless of the outside temperature.

Snack Kiosks Sometimes called *zakusochna*, snack kiosks cluster around train and bus stations. They sell drinks and a species of snack, such as limp pieces of greasy pizza or even greasier *piroshky* – a sort of stuffed dough-bomb.

Markets Always hectic, always colourful, the *rynok*, or marketplace, is the supermarket of Ukraine, and the critical focal point of a local economy where the gardens' excess produce is sold. A daily trip, usually in the early morning, is a ritual sacred to each household, and for the tourist a reliable source of fresh vegetables, fruit, honey, nuts, cheese, eggs and various hanging chunks of meat – as well as a form of relentless entertainment. Some of the bigger markets have dairy products in a separate *molocharna* section. In small towns they're open only in the mornings, and in all markets, this is when the selection is best.

Food Stores These are the least reliable source of inspiration – often barren shelves with two unlabelled jars and a couple of dusty cans. However, there are some food stores *(hastronoms)* that stock a fair range of bottled water, bread, fruit and vegetables as well as some meats and cheeses. In some cities, Western-style supermarkets – a couple touting shopping trolleys – are springing up. In Kyiv, there are even hypermarkets.

Ukrainian Dishes

Varenyky Varenyky **(вареники)**, sometimes known as *halusky*, are the most popular Ukrainian dish. Small dumplings made with rolled dough are filled with a variety of ingredients, thrown into a huge pot of scalding water and boiled for a few minutes until they float – delicious and addictive. Most restaurants in the provinces serve them, with either cheese **(з сиром)** or meat **(з м'ясом)**, and almost always with sour cream or a grease-like sauce. *Pyrohy* refers to larger baked, pie-like varenyky filled with the same kinds of ingredients. Smaller, appetiser-sized versions of varenyky are called *pyrizhky*.

Borsch Borsch **(борщ)**, the national soup adopted by other Slavic cultures, is based on a beet and mixed-vegetable broth and comes in dozens of varieties. The most popular version is a clear broth, but cream is often added. A simple gauge of quality is the thickness of its ingredients – the best has loads of beets, beans, onions, carrots and potatoes, sometimes topped off with meat or sausage or tiny mushroom-filled varenyky and seasoned with garlic, dill, parsley and bay leaves.

The Joy of Salo

The eating of *salo* (сало), otherwise known as pig fat or lard, is a centuries-old tradition that runs deep and thick in Ukrainian blood. Any local will describe the moment the salo dissolves on the tongue in terms of sheer ecstasy. Spread thick on bread, or wrapped separately in a newspaper bundle, it's a delicacy that accompanies many humble meals. During the Soviet years, meat was often unavailable or prohibitively expensive, but salo, the faithful alternative, was always there – and still is. Conveniently stored in vats, it needs no refrigeration and has the longevity of fine wine.

Not all salo is the same. Each region takes pride in the texture and flavour of its local salo, sometimes even mixing in tiny flecks of bacon or chunks of garlic for an extra crunch. A visit to any local marketplace will reveal buyers carefully scrutinising hunks of lard before selecting the finest quality.

As for health considerations, most Ukrainians say that a little salo a day keeps the doctor away. It is even believed to absorb harmful radiation; there was a dramatic increase in salo consumption after the Chornobyl disaster. When asked whether salo clogs the arteries, most Ukrainians will argue that, on the contrary, it simply adds a protective lubricant.

Holubtsi Translated as 'little dove', *holubtsi* (голубці) are delicious cabbage rolls stuffed with seasoned rice, meat or buckwheat, and topped with a tomato-based sauce. They are time-consuming to prepare and, despite being a national dish, seem to be increasingly difficult to find.

Kotleta po-Kyivsky Known as Chicken Kyiv or Kiev to the English-speaking world, *kotleta po-Kyivsky* (котлета по-київськи) does exist, but for some reason it's not easy to find. It's a chunk of boneless chicken stuffed with butter, seasoned, floured and deep-fried – absolutely delicious if you can track down the 'elusive hen'.

Kasha An ancient dish, *kasha* (каша) is basically a grain-based gruel. The most common kind is *hrechana kasha*, a buckwheat porridge, seasoned and eaten with a sauce as a side dish or used as a stuffing. Kasha can be served as a breakfast porridge too.

Khleeb *Khleeb* (хліб) is the Ukrainian word for bread. Sweet breads and rolls *(bulochky)* are steeped with honey and tradition, often associated with holidays or ceremonies. *Babka* is a sweet egg bread popular during Easter. *Kalach* is similar to babka but denser and braided into a circular shape. *Paska* is the official Easter bread, decorated and shaped into a cross. *Korovay* is a tall, cylindrical traditional wedding bread. *Pampushki* can be fresh rolls soaked in crushed garlic and oil, or a sweet jam or fruit-filled baked roll. *Makivnik* is a sweet poppy-seed bread flavoured with honey and molasses, popular around Christmas. *Khrusty* are deep-fried strips of sweet dough coated with sugar, and *medivnyk* is a honey cake that can keep for days without going stale.

DRINKS

Drinks (напої) are usually similar to those found in European Russia. Both Crimea and Transcarpathia produce excellent wines, and champagne is produced in Kyiv and Odesa (less than $2 a bottle in supermarkets). The most popular Ukrainian brands of beer ($0.50/2 a bottle in supermarkets/bars) are Slavutych (Славутич) and Obolon (Оболонь). Kvas ($0.10 a glass) is sold on practically every Kyiv street corner in summer; look for the big vats touting a hose-pipe attachment and one glass that everyone shares.

ENTERTAINMENT

Rock & Jazz Concerts

Rock concerts are usually held in large sports complexes or cultural palaces. Once in a while a Western artist will perform, but generally domestic bands play with varying degrees of talent. Many older restaurants feature their own rock band which plays deafening, synthesiser-laden 1970s pop tunes – sometimes in its own twisted way entertaining, but usually ear-splitting.

Kyiv has a rash of bars and clubs featuring decent jazz or folk, but it's a random thing outside the capital. A number of jazz festivals do swing through. Look out for posters advertising these events.

Folk Music

Folk shows are usually geared for tourists, and are colourful and entertaining. The venues range from a reserved restaurant to a city theatre, and in summer they're staged at open-air museums of folk architecture. Hotel service bureaux and theatre ticket offices *(teatralny kasa)* may have information.

Theatre

The opera and ballet houses in Lviv, Odesa and Kyiv are spectacular and worth the $1 or so it costs to attend a performance. Kharkiv opera also has an exceptionally good troupe. Most cities have their philharmonic, puppet theatre, circus and several drama theatres – one with performances in Ukrainian and another with performances in Russian.

To buy tickets or find out what's playing, head to the teatralny kasa. These theatre ticket offices predominantly sell advance tickets, with same-day tickets available at the theatre box office, sometimes that morning but usually about one hour before the performance. If the ticket office tells you the show is sold out, go to the theatre anyway – you'll probably be able to purchase a seat beforehand. Some cities publish cultural information gazettes with listings of events: *What's On* in Kyiv is one.

SPECTATOR SPORTS

Watching Dynamo Kyiv – one of Europe's leading soccer teams – kick off at home in Kyiv is a highlight for anyone spending a few days in the capital. Tickets for matches are cheap ($0.10 to $10) and, depending on who is playing who, widely available. Most matches are held in the Respublikansky Stadium which has 100,000 seats – substantially larger than Dynamo Stadium, Dynamo Kyiv's official home ground. See also the team's (Ukrainian-language) Web site at www.dynamo.kiev.ua.

SHOPPING

Ukraine's rich folk culture is world-renowned and there's much more to buy than just *pysanky*, the beautifully painted eggs which are a Ukrainian trademark. Every region and village has hundreds of distinct pysanky patterns, each pattern symbolising a special meaning and ritual. Traditionally, eggs were drained and decorated using a lengthy heated-wax procedure, but the wooden eggs sold today are directly painted on, and produced not for the Easter ceremony but for tourists.

Ukrainian embroidery *(vyshyvka)* is steeped in tradition, with each region having traditional patterns, colours and even unique stitches. The most common is the black and red cross-stitch or *khresty*. Shirts for men *(sorochky)*, blouses for women *(blyuza)*, as well as belts, skirts and tablecloths are all attractively embroidered and sold. A hand-embroidered shirt – a labour-intensive endeavour – will cost anywhere from $10 to $40, depending on the embroidery's complexity and the quality of the material used. Also popular are long, narrow embroidered towels *(rushnyky)*. Woven rugs *(kilims)* are usually machine-made, so they don't have the attraction of the hand-made ones in the museums, but they're still a good deal.

KATE NOLAN

Ukraine is renowned for its painted eggs.

Ceramics *(keramiky)* are folksy and attractive with lots of green and yellow flowery patterns. Keep an eye out for the black ceramic (often candlesticks) with a matt finish, common in Lviv and Kyiv. Carved wooden boxes *(derevyani skrynki)*, plates *(tarilka)* and candlesticks are equally plentiful and attractive. One technique is encrustation *(enkrustasya)*, where the wood is decorated with colourful beads and metals inlaid into patterns.

Several antique shops in Kyiv sell old hand-painted wooden icons – most of which are officially illegal to take out of the country (see Customs earlier). Embroidery, ceramics, wooden boxes and every other typically Ukrainian craft can be found in every town at Ukrainsky Suvenir (a nationwide chain of gift shops), the central department store (TsUM), in the lobby shops of museums and hotels, or at one of the country's many colourful craft markets.

Getting There & Away

Travel into Ukraine is unrestricted at all border points. Land entrance or exit can be made from Russia to the north and east; Belarus to the north; Poland, Slovakia and Hungary to the west; and Romania and Moldova to the south-west. By water you can enter or exit the country via the Black Sea ports of Odesa or Yalta, or terminate a long river trip on the Danube at the port city of Izmayil. By air, most international flights arrive and depart from Kyiv's Boryspil international airport.

> **Warning**
>
> The information in this chapter is particularly vulnerable to change: Prices for international travel are volatile, routes are introduced and cancelled, schedules change, special deals come and go, and rules and visa requirements are amended. Airlines and governments seem to take a perverse pleasure in making price structures and regulations as complicated as possible. You should check directly with the airline or a travel agent to make sure you understand how a fare (and ticket you may buy) works. In addition, the travel industry is highly competitive and there are many lurks and perks.
>
> The upshot of this is that you should get opinions, quotes and advice from as many airlines and travel agents as possible before you part with your hard-earned cash. The details given in this chapter should be regarded as pointers and are not a substitute for your own careful, up-to-date research.
>
> 

AIR

For a low-down on air travel terminology, see the Air Travel Glossary in the European Russia Getting There & Away chapter.

Airports & Airlines

Most international flights enter and exit Ukraine at the Boryspil international airport, 40km south-east of Kyiv city centre. The airport is linked with most major European cities, with the main European international airlines servicing Kyiv to/from their home cities at least twice weekly. A handful of flights to/from Moscow and Eastern European countries use Kyiv's domestic Zhulyany airport, 12km west of the centre. For information on getting to/from both airports from Kyiv city centre, see the Kyiv chapter.

Outside the capital, there are weekly international flights to/from Odesa, Lviv, Chernivtsi, Dnipropetrovsk, Donetsk, Kharkiv and Simferopol.

Ukraine has two major national airlines: Ukraine International Airlines (partially owned by Swiss Air and Austrian Airlines, hence its fleet of Boeing 737s) and Air Ukraine (which flies former Aeroflot planes). These two cover most international routes to/from Kyiv. International flights in and out of Dnipropetrovsk are handled by Dniproavia, while a mind-boggling host of other domestic carriers covers flights within Ukraine (see the Ukraine Getting Around chapter). For airline addresses in Kyiv, see that chapter. International contacts include:

Air Ukraine

Canada
(☎ 416-234 1170, fax 234 1163)
4887 Dundas St West, Unit 3, Toronto, Ontario, M9A 1B2

USA
(☎ 212-599 0555, ☎ 599 0775, fax 599 0395, fax 557 3483)
551 Fifth Ave, Suite 1005, New York, NY 10176

Ukraine International Airlines

France
(☎ 01 42 93 04 36, ☎ 01 48 62 07 41, fax 01 42 93 04 52)
120 blvd Haussmann, F-75008 Paris

Germany
(☎ 030-2096 2415, fax 2096 2418) Berlin

(☎ 069-756 0790, fax 756 0791) Frankfurt
(☎ 089-2916 3118, fax 2916 3135) Munich
UK
(☎ 01293-59 66 09, fax 59 66 52, uia@ps.kiev.ua, www.uia.ukrpack.net)
USA
(☎ 1-800 876 0114, fax 736 6141, ukraine@iminet.com, www.iminet.com/SMS/Ukraine)
AMR Services, 4255 Amon Carter Blvd, MD 4234 Ft Worth, Texas 76155

Buying Tickets

Air Ukraine and Ukraine International Airlines both tout a two tier pricing system, whereby Ukrainians pay substantially less than everyone else. Neither airline offers youth or student fares. On some European routes, however, Ukraine International offers its lower Ukrainian fares to foreign students who have a Ukrainian residence permit.

Avoid purchasing tickets in Kyiv for flights departing from a regional airport; tickets are usually more expensive in the capital than in the city from which you will depart.

A $19 airport tax is included in all international fares arriving/departing from Boryspil airport.

The USA & Canada

Air Ukraine in conjunction with Uzbekistan Airways operates two scheduled weekly flights to/from Kyiv and New York. A return Kyiv-New York fare averages about $800 (minimum stay seven days; maximum a month); New York-Kyiv return fares are usually much cheaper. Air Ukraine also operates a weekly flight to/from Kyiv and Toronto ($800 return with the same restrictions).

Australia & New Zealand

There are no direct flights between Ukraine and Australia or New Zealand, but there are numerous flight combinations and options available. Low-season, return fares range from A$1550 (with Air France and Qantas) to A$1700 (with KLM).

The UK & Continental Europe

Ukraine International Airlines operates direct flights from Kyiv to over 15 countries in Europe, including daily flights to/from Amsterdam, Budapest, Frankfurt, London and Vienna; five or six flights a week to Paris, Prague and Zurich; and two flights weekly to Athens, Barcelona, Berlin, Bucharest, Brussels, Helsinki, Riga, Rome, Sofia, Tallinn and Warsaw. There are also direct daily or weekly flights with European international airlines – including Air France, Austrian Airlines, Balkan Airlines (Bulgaria), KLM-Royal Dutch Airlines, Lufthansa and Swissair – which usually carry the same fares as Ukraine International Airlines.

Outside Kyiv, European flights are limited. From Odesa airport, there are weekly flights to/from Vienna and Athens; while Dnipropetrovsk and Lviv airports both have weekly flights to/from Vienna, Frankfurt and Warsaw. There are three flights a week between Kharkiv and Vienna.

Sample return fares are: Dnipropetrovsk-Frankfurt with Dniproavia ($600 minimum one night stay/maximum three months); Odesa-Vienna with Austrian Airlines ($670 including a Saturday night stay/maximum one month); Odesa-Athens with Aerosweet ($300 including a Saturday night stay), and Kharkiv-Vienna with Austrian Airlines ($700 with a Saturday night stay/maximum one month).

Russia, Belarus, Transcaucasia & Central Asia

To/from Kyiv, there are daily flights to/from Moscow (Air Ukraine, Aeroflot, Transaero or Aerosweet), and two or three flights weekly to/from Rostov, Omsk and Novosibirsk (Ukraine International Airlines or Aerosweet). The St Petersburg-based airline, Polkavsky, flies between Kyiv and St Petersburg ($150 return). There are also weekly Moscow flights to/from Dnipropetrovsk, Donetsk, Kharkiv, Lviv and Odesa.

Belavia operates three flights a week between Kyiv and Minsk ($160 return/no restrictions). Aerosweet flies to/from Kyiv and Ashkhabad (Turkmenistan), Baku (Azerbaijan) and Tbilisi (Georgia). From Simferopol, Crimea Air flies to/from Tashkent and Samarkand (Uzbekistan) and Gyandsha (Azerbaijan).

Elsewhere

From Kyiv, there are weekly flights to/from Dubai, Cairo, Istanbul, Tel Aviv and Tunis. Outside Kyiv, there are weekly flights from Dnipropetrovsk to/from Istanbul and Tel Aviv; from Odesa to/from Dubai as well as Istanbul and Tel Aviv; and from Simferopol to Tel Aviv.

Sample return fares are: Dnipropetrovsk-Istanbul ($840 return with Dniproavia), Dnipropetrovsk-Tel Aviv ($450 return with ELAL/Aerosweet); and Odesa-Istanbul ($220 return, including a Saturday night stay/maximum one month).

LAND

Border Crossings

Ukrainian visas are *not* issued at any border crossing; travellers who arrive visa-less will be refused entry into Ukraine. Upon entry and exit at the Ukrainian border, you have to fill in a customs declaration form (see Customs in the Ukraine Facts for the Visitor chapter for details).

International trains cross into Ukraine at more than 10 different locations, coming from seven different countries. Border crossings are a straightforward but drawn-out affair, with a steady stream of customs and ticket personnel scrutinising your passport and visa.

By road, there are some 11 routes into Ukraine through frontier border stations. To avoid unsavoury complications, always stick to these official border crossings. Roads entering Ukraine often have two numbers: their international number, as well as their Ukrainian equivalent, eg the E40 (A259) between Poland and Ukraine. Place names on road signs in frontier towns are usually written in the Cyrillic and Latin alphabets. When entering Ukraine by car or motorcycle, ensure you have an Inter-national Driving Permit, the vehicle's registration papers (preferably in the form of an international motor vehicle certificate) and auto insurance that covers driving into the former USSR.

Visas

Russia Everyone requires a visa to enter Russia (see Visas in European Russia Facts for the Visitor). Avoid having to purchase your visa at the Russian embassy in Kyiv which is renowned for charging an extortionate price; visas at the Russian embassy in Warsaw are reported to be substantially cheaper.

Belarus All foreigners require a visa to enter Belarus, even those intending to do nothing more than transit the country by train. See the Belarus Facts for the Visitor chapter for more details.

Poland Americans and most Western Europeans do not require a Polish visa for stays of up to 90 days (up to six months for British passport holders), but Canadian, Australian and New Zealand passport holders do require one.

Slovakia Most Western Europeans do not require a visa to stay in Slovakia up to 90 days; 180 days for British and Irish passport holders; 30 days for Americans and Canadians. Australian and New Zealand passport holders do need a visa; check your status well before departure.

Hungary Americans, Canadians and most Western Europeans do not require a visa to enter Hungary for stays of up to 90 days. Australians and New Zealanders should check their status; at the end of 1999 they still required a visa.

Romania All Western travellers require a visa to enter Romania. Tourist visas valid for 30 days are issued at the border for around $33; alternatively buy one on the spot for $15 at the Romanian consulate in Kyiv or Odesa.

Moldova All Western travellers need a visa to enter Moldova. To secure a visa, all travellers (except US passport holders) need an official invitation from someone in Moldova or a tourist voucher confirming prebooked hotel accommodation. Single/double entry visas – *not* available at land borders – start at $30/50.

Some trains between Chernivtsi and other parts of Ukraine pass through Moldova en

UKRAINE

route. Check the visa situation before departing; you might need a Moldovan transit visa.

Train

Russia Most major Ukrainian cities have daily services to Moscow, with two border crossings: one used by trains heading to Kyiv, the other by trains passing through Kharkiv.

Trains between Kyiv and Moscow (15 hours, several daily) go via Bryansk (Russia) and Konotop (Ukraine), crossing at the Ukrainian border town of Seredyna-Buda. The best trains to take (numbers are southbound/northbound) between Moscow and Kyiv are No 1/2, the *Ukrainia*, or No 3/4, the *Kyiv*; both travel overnight. The best train between Moscow and Lviv (28 hours, daily via Kyiv) is No 73/74. Between Moscow and Odesa (28 hours, daily via Kyiv) there's the No 23/24, the *Odesa*. There are also at least two trains to/from St Petersburg to Lviv (30 hours, via Vilnius) and Kyiv (23 to 30 hours).

Trains between Kharkiv and Moscow (13 hours, about 14 daily via Kursk) cross the border just 40km north of Kharkiv. The best train is the night train, No 19/20, the *Kharkiv*. Between Moscow and Simferopol (26 hours, daily via Kharkiv) the best train is No 67/68, the *Simferopol*. Trains between Moscow and Donetsk (22 hours, three daily), Dnipropetrovsk (20 hours, twice daily), Zaporizhzhya (19 hours, twice daily) and Sevastopol (29½ hours, daily) all go through Kharkiv.

There's also a long train every other day between Kharkiv and Vladivostok and back (No 54 eastbound, No 53 westbound) via Penza, Kurgan, Novosibirsk, Chita and Khabarovsk, among other places. In summer, trains travel between Crimea and places in Siberia at least as far east as Irkutsk. Many trains travelling between Moscow and the Caucasus go through Kharkiv, including a daily service to Rostov-on-Don (12 hours), and seasonal services to Tbilisi (31 hours, once a week).

Daily international trains passing through Ukraine to/from Moscow's Kyivsky Vokzal include the *Slovakia Express*, Kyiv-Lviv-Chop-Bratislava-Vienna; No 15/16 Kyiv-Lviv-Chop-Budapest, with a carriage to Venice twice a week; and No 7/8, the *Dukla Express*, Kyiv-Lviv-Chop-Uzhhorod-Prague.

Belarus There are five main rail crossings between Belarus and Ukraine. The busiest – used by both Kyiv-Minsk trains (11 hours, daily) and Simferopol-Minsk trains (29 hours via Kharkiv, daily) – crosses the border about 40km south of Homel and about 70km north of Chernihiv, near Dobryanka on the Ukrainian side.

The Minsk-Odesa train (27 hours, every other day) goes through Kyiv, crossing the border south of Homel, or takes a more direct route to the west through Zhytomyr, crossing the border about 45km south of the Belarusian city of Mazyr at the Belarusian border village of Slavechna. The first major stop in Ukraine is in the town of Ovruch.

The Minsk-Lviv (17 hours, daily) train passes through Baravanichy (Belarus) and Rivne (Ukraine), crossing at the border village of Buchlichy, 50km south of the Belarusian town of Lunynets and 30km north of Dubrovytsya in Ukraine.

The Kyiv-Brest (14 hours), Odesa-Brest (16 hours) – both two or three times weekly – and Chernivtsi-Brest (21 hours, daily via Lviv) trains cross the border near Malaryta (Belarus), halfway between Brest and Kovel, the first major stop in Ukraine. The daily Kyiv-Berlin train (25½ hours) passes through Brest (10 hours).

Poland Trains between Lviv and the Polish cities of Warsaw (13 hours, daily), Kraków (about seven hours; change in Przemysl) and Lublin (10½ hours, daily) cross at the well used Ukrainian border stop of Mostiska, with Medyka on the Polish side, about 20km east of Przemysl (2½ hours, three times daily to/from Lviv), where trains split to Warsaw to the north and Kraków to the west. The same crossing is used for road traffic on the E40 (A259) with Shehyni the frontier town on the Ukrainian side and Medyka in Poland. Lviv, the first major city inside Ukraine for rail or road travellers from southern Poland, is 85km from the border.

The Warsaw-Kyiv line (16 to 20 hours, three times daily) passes through Lutsk, Rivne and Zhytomyr en route, crossing the border over the western Buh River just south of the Belarus border. For road travellers the Polish border town is Okopy Nowe. The daily Berlin-Kyiv train (25½ hours) also passes through Warsaw (15½ hours).

Slovakia The Prague-Kyiv (30 hours, daily) train (which stops at Košice in Slovakia and Lviv en route) crosses into Ukraine at the Slovak border post of Cierna nad Tisou and the Ukrainian border town of Chop.

Hungary The short border with Hungary has one major rail crossing, with trains running between Lviv and Budapest (12 hours, daily), crossing from Zahony on the Hungarian side to Chop on the Ukrainian side, 23km from Uzhhorod. There is a daily train to/from Kyiv and Budapest (23 hours). Daily trains linking Moscow, Kyiv and Lviv with Budapest, Prague, Bratislava and Vienna all pass through Chop.

Romania The Bucharest-Chernivtsi (11 hours, daily) rail line crosses the border about 40km south of Chernivtsi (Cernauti in Romanian) at the Romanian border town of Vadul Siret.

Moldova Trains running between Chisinau and Odesa (six hours, three daily) cross from the border town of Kuchurhan in Ukraine to Pervomaisc in Moldova, 30km from Tiraspol. The motor route E581 (M14) also crosses here, as does the Chisinau (14 hours, three a week) rail line.

Trains (12 hours, daily) and vehicles between Chisinau and Chernivtsi cross the official frontier from the border town of Mamalyha in Ukraine to Criva in Moldova, about 50km east of Chernivtsi.

Bus

Russia There are a handful of weekly buses from Kharkiv across the border into Russia on the E95 (M2) road. The official frontier crossing is 40km north of Kharkiv near the Russian border town of Zhuravlevka.

Car & Motorcycle

Russia The main auto route between Kyiv and Moscow starts as the E93 (M20) north of Kyiv, but becomes the M3 when it branches off to the east some 50km south of Chernihiv.

Driving from Ukraine to the Caucasus, the border frontier point is on the E40 (M19) road crossing just before the Russian town of Novoshakhtinsk at the Ukrainian border village of Dovzhansky, about 150km east of Donetsk.

Belarus Six roads cross between Ukraine and Belarus but only two have official frontier stations. The main M20 motor route north from Chernihiv to Homel crosses near the rail crossing, just north of the Ukrainian village of Novy Yarylovichy and south of the Belarusian village of Novaja Huta.

The main M14 motor route between Brest and Kovel crosses the border north-east of the rail crossing, just south-east of the Belarus village of Makrany.

Poland See the earlier section on train connections for Poland for details.

Slovakia The E50 motor route from Košice and Michalovce crosses at Vysne Nemecke on the Slovak side to Uzhhorod in Ukraine, becoming the M17 in Ukraine. Daily buses also cross the border. Expect long queues on weekends due to local traffic.

Hungary There are four road frontier crossings between Hungary and Ukraine. The main auto route from Debrecen and Nyiregyhaza, the E573 (M17), crosses at the same site as the rail crossing.

The other three crossings, although official, may not be open all year. The crossing near the Ukrainian village of Dzvinkove is about 20km south-east. About 35km farther south-east, Hungarian road 41 crosses at the Hungarian border village of Beregsurany, just south-west of the Ukrainian town of Berehove. Still another 30km south-east is the frontier crossing at Tiszabecs in Hungary and Vylok on the Ukrainian side (on Hungarian road 491).

Romania The E85 (A269) crosses at the same border frontier in Romania as the rail crossing, 40km south of Chernivtsi, from Vadul Siret in Romania into Porubne on the Ukrainian side. The unofficial road crossing along the picturesque border area over the Tisa River at the Ukrainian town of Tyachiv, about 30km west of Sighetu Marmatiei (Romania) and halfway between Khust and Rakhiv in Ukraine, is officially closed to foreigners.

Moldova The main M21 road heading north-east out of Chisinau, and leading eventually to Kirovohrad well into Ukraine, crosses the border frontier about 20km north-east of the Moldovan town of Duba on the Dnister River. The A272 crosses the Dnister River along the northern border of Moldova.

SEA & RIVER

Entering or leaving Ukraine by ship can only be done through the Black Sea ports of Odesa and Yalta, although services have been slashed dramatically since the collapse of the USSR. In mid-1999 there were no scheduled boats to/from Yalta and just a handful of sailings from Odesa to Istanbul (some via Constanta in Romania) and Haifa (Israel). Chartered cruise ships still use both ports.

From Odesa, there are five weekly ferries to Istanbul. Once a week, the *Captain Zaman* stops in Constanta en route on the Istanbul-Odesa-Istanbul service. Sailing time for the Istanbul-Constanta/Constanta-Odesa service is 16/15 hours. The cheapest single/return fare for an Odesa-Constanta, Constanta-Istanbul or Odesa-Istanbul passage is $50/90, while a bed in a four berth cabin with washbasin costs $75/140. Vehicles can also be taken aboard; to transport a private car under/over 1200kg costs $225/250 one way.

In Ukraine, ticketing is handled by Eugenia Travel (☎ 048-221 85 81/83, ☎/fax 222 40 47, janna@eugen.intes.odessa.ua), vulitsya Suvorov 12, 270027 Odesa.

In Turkey, you should contact Istanbul Shipping Lines (☎ 212-252 01 87, ☎ 252 02 38, fax 251 65 79, stin@atlas.net.tr), French Passage, C Block No 23, Karakoy 80030, Istanbul.

From Odesa there are one or two boats a month to Haifa (76 hours). A single/return fare for a bed in a four berth cabin aboard the *M/V D Shostakovich* is $270/400. Luxury suites start at $600/1100 one way/round trip. Eugenia Travel (see above) is a ticketing agent. Alternatively, contact Blasplan (☎ 048-25 53 56, ☎ 25 82 28, ☎/fax 25 21 13), a Ukrainian-Swiss joint venture at vulitsya Grechesky 22 in Odesa.

Between mid-June to the end of August only, the *Caledonia* sails once a week from Odesa to Varna in Bulgaria (12 hours). The Ukrainian-Bulgarian joint venture Interferry (☎ 048-23 75 76, ☎ 23 61 76, ☎ 26 68 01, eatc@paco.net), vulitsya Gogolya 17, Odesa, also operates Odesa-Varna boats.

Due to the effects of the war in Yugoslavia, all traffic along the Danube from Ukraine to Western European cities has been suspended for several years. Travel agents specialising in Ukraine (see the following Organised Tours section) can update you on the current situation.

ORGANISED TOURS

Unless noted otherwise, the following travel agencies provide a standard range of seasonal package tours to Ukraine, as well as visa services and prepaid hotel bookings, and they can sometimes arrange homestay accommodation.

Australia

Gateway Travel (☎ 02-9745 3333, fax 9745 3237), 48 The Boulevarde, Strathfield, NSW 2135 – one of the best agencies, with a wide variety of specialised tours, excursions and services, including arranging boat cruises down the Dnipro.

Canada

Caravel Tours: Travel Ltd (☎ 403-963 4575, fax 780-930 0677), Box 277, 5007 50th St, Stony Plain, Alberta T7Z IT3 – Ukrainian specialists.

RJ's Tours (☎ 780-415 5633 or ☎ 877-353 5633 (toll-free from western Canada), fax 780-415 5639, ttravel@connect.ab.ca, www.tourukraine.com), 11708 – 135A St, Edmonton, AB Canada T5M 1L5 – tours galore.

Russia

Host Families Association (HOFA; ☎/fax 812-275 1992, alexei@hofak.hop.stu.neva.ru, www.spb.ru/homestays), 5-25 Tavricheskaya, St Petersburg – arranges homestays in Kyiv, Odesa, Lviv, Chernivtsi, Chernihiv and Yalta, and offers visa support ($30). For more details see European Russia Facts for the Visitor – Accommodation.

The UK

Alpha-Omega Travel Ltd (☎ 0113-286 2121, fax 286 4964, alphaomega_uk_ops@compuserve.com), Borodin House, 6 Beaconsfield Court, Garforth, Leeds LS25 1QH – specialists in travel to the former USSR. Provides invitations ($80) in support of a single-entry, 30 day Ukrainian tourist visa and arranges business visas for a fee.

Intourist Travel (☎ 020-7538 8600, fax 7538 5967, info@intourist.co.uk, www.intourist.co.uk), 219 Marsh Wall, London E14 9FJ – one of the largest with former USSR contacts. Prebooks train tickets for within Ukraine.

Inntel Moscow (☎ 020-7937 7207, fax 7938 2912, inntelmoscow@inntel-moscow.co.uk, www.inntel-moscow.co.uk), 167-169 Kensington High St, London W8 6SH – arranges Ukrainian visas (£25 handling fee).

Prime Travel (☎ 020-7376 1700, fax 7376 1722, prime@east-west.co.uk), 15 Kensington High St, London W8 5NP – levies a £30 handling fee on visas (£20 if you book a flight/accommodation package too).

Ukrainian Travel (☎ 0161-652 5050, fax 633 0825, info@bob-sopel-travel.demon.co.uk), 27 Henshaw St, Oldham, Lancashire OL1 1NH – UK's leading Ukraine specialist, also known as Bob Sopel's.

The USA

American-International Homestays (☎ 303-642 3088, toll-free 1-800 876 2048, fax 303-642 3365, www.spectravel.com/homes), PO Box 7154, Nederland, CO 80466 – arranges homestays, individual or group trips with accommodation in the homes of host families supervised by the organisation. Has numerous Kyiv contacts.

Continent (☎ 202-232 4277), 1800 Connecticut Ave 100 NW, Washington, DC 20009 – works closely with the Ukrainian embassy in Washington; assists with visas and other sticky travel preparations.

Dunwoodie Travel (☎ 914-969 4200, fax 969 2108, dunwoodtvl@aol.com), 771A Yonkers Ave, Yonkers, NY 10704 – tours, visa services and hotel bookings.

Global Quest (☎ 516-747 8880, fax 747 8367, global@globalquesttravel.com, www.odessamerica.com/ukrainian), 170 Old Country Road, Mineola, NY 11501 – Black Sea cruises.

Scope Travel (☎ 973-378 8998, ☎ 800-242 7267, fax 973-378 7903, info@scopetravel.com, www.scopetravel.com), 1605 Springfield Ave, Maplewood, NJ 07040 – everything from rafting expeditions down the Dnister River to climbing in the Carpathians/Crimea and touring Ukraine's castles.

Getting Around

Travel within Ukraine is sufficiently unpredictable to ensure a new adventure with every journey.

AIR

Ukraine's major domestic airports are Kyiv's Zhulyany airport, Odesa, Lviv, Chernivtsi, Kharkiv, Dnipropetrovsk and Simferopol, all of which handle international as well as national flights. Other smaller, regional airports – served by just one or two flights a week to/from Kyiv – include Donetsk, Mariupol, Uzhhorod, Ivano-Frankivsk and Lutsk.

The leading domestic carriers are Air Ukraine (which flies to/from Kyiv and Chernivtsi), Ukraine International Airlines (to/from Kyiv, Lviv, Odesa, Donetsk, Dnipropetrovsk, Kharkiv and Mariupol), and the rapidly growing Dnipropetrovsk-based airline, Dniproavia. Crimea Air operates weekly flights between Simferopol and Kyiv. Two Odesa-based airlines, Odesa Airlines and Tavrey Airco, cover the Kyiv-Odesa route (also covered by the national carriers).

Air Ukraine and Ukraine International Airlines have an office in all major cities. Airline tickets for smaller airlines are sold at branches of Kiyavia travel agency (info@kiyavia.com, www.kiyavia.com). For domestic flight information call ☎ 056.

Sample return fares include Simferopol-Kyiv ($130), Kyiv-Dnipropetrovsk ($240), Kyiv-Odesa ($175 including a Saturday night stay/maximum one month) and Kharkiv-Kyiv ($160 three-month return). Quoted prices do not include the hefty 20% value added tax that is systematically applied to all domestic air fares. In addition, count on paying around $10 airport tax.

TRAIN

Trains between major cities are frequent, cheap and efficient; a train arriving or departing late is practically unheard of in Ukraine. An overnight train is the most painless and economical way to travel between cities, with most trains beautifully timed to depart at dusk and arrive at their final destination in time for breakfast.

Every train station has a left-luggage counter, signposted камери схову or камера зберігання, open 24 hours except for two or three 30-minute breaks, the times of which are pinned up outside. Prepay when you deposit your luggage and retrieve it with the receipt or metal tag you are given in exchange.

Most railway personnel in Ukraine tend to be Russian-speaking. Train tickets issued throughout the country are printed bilingually in Ukrainian and Russian.

Types of Trains

Train stations are called *zaliznychny vokzal* or simply *vokzal* (station). The regular long-distance service is a *skory poyizd* (fast train) that is not that fast; the *expres poyizd* is a faster version of the skory which makes fewer stops. A passenger train *(pasazhyrsky poyizd)* is slower still with even more stops.

Fanning out from most cities is a network of suburban trains (*prymiski poyizd*; *pryhorodny poyizd* in Russian); they're also called *elektrichka*. They link a city to its suburbs and other nearby towns and cities – often useful for day trips. These trains only have upright, hard bench seats and don't run at night.

Classes

Accommodation splits into four types:

Spalny vahon (SV) is a 1st class couchette (sleeper) with an individual compartment for two people; perfect if you're travelling as a couple, but awkward if you're alone. Not all trains offer SV, which costs approximately three times more than *kupe*.

Kupe or *kupeyny* is a 2nd class sleeper with a compartment for four people. This is the most popular class – easily comparable to a 2nd class sleeper elsewhere in Europe – and gets booked up fast on some routes. *Kupe* is approximately twice the price of *platskart*.

UKRAINE

Platskart is a 3rd class sleeper and far less desirable. The entire train car is open (no separate compartments) with groups of four bunks in each alcove along with two others in the aisle. Luggage, mattresses and blankets are stowed on additional bunks above the alcove quads. Platskart is usually overcrowded, dirty, extremely stuffy, smelly and offers passengers absolutely no privacy.

Zahalny vahon (*obshchiy* in Russian) means an upright, hard bench seat for the entire journey – torture. This is only used by people travelling short distances.

All classes have assigned places with your carriage *(vahon)* and bunk *(mesto)* numbers printed on your ticket. In SV carriages, bunks are made up, but in kupe, sheets and blankets are brought to you by the attendant. Both classes command a $1 sheet fee.

On the overnight train between Kyiv and Lviv, one carriage is run by the upmarket Grand Hotel in Lviv. Equally luxurious carriages, but with TV too, are rumoured to be in the pipeline on select trains between Kyiv and Dnipropetrovsk.

UKRAINE

Information

Sucking information out of the surly, strictly Ukrainian or Russian-speaking attendants who run the information booth – довідкове бюро *(dovidkove byuro)* – at every station is a formidable task. Most charge around $0.10/20 for each oral/written response (not necessarily the answer) to a question.

Train schedules are posted on the wall at every train station – once you have mastered some basic words, they're simple to work out. In Crimea and eastern Ukraine, schedules are written in Russian (see the boxed text 'Reading A Train Timetable' in the European Russia Getting Around chapter).

In Kyiv, an updated and comprehensive train timetable is printed in the *Kyiv Business Directory* (see the Kyiv chapter). At Kharkiv train station, you can buy pocket train timetables.

Buying Tickets

Buying tickets at the train station can be a nightmare for those without a smattering of Ukrainian or Russian. Most cities have a ticket office in the centre where you can purchase train tickets in advance (often up until a few hours before departure for trains originating from the city you are in, and up to a day before for trains originating from elsewhere). In these offices, you will encounter the same linguistic wrangles as at the train station, but at least here you can laboriously convey your message without being shoved by irate people waiting in line behind you.

At larger train stations like Kyiv and Odesa, beware of black marketeers offering tickets at a supposedly cheaper price than those on sale at the official ticketing windows. For some rail routes, these unsavoury types buy up all available tickets and resell them to desperate passengers at a higher price. Avoid any dealings with them; don't flash your wallet or part with any cash.

Rail travel is not expensive. Sample fares for a platskart/kupe/SV one-way ticket are: Kyiv-Odesa ($4/11/32), Odesa-Simferopol ($4.50/7/21), Lviv-Odesa ($6/9.50/27) and Odesa-Moscow ($19/37/60).

On the Journey

Each sleeping carriage is looked after by an attendant called a *providnik* (male) or *provodnitsa* (female), who collects your ticket and gives you wake-up calls in the morning. Most don't smile much but are generally among the best hearted service workers in the country, providing cups of tea from their samovars at the beginning and end of the journey (for a small $1 fee).

Bring plenty of food and drink with you; relying on the inadequately stocked dining car is foolish. And be prepared for some colourful encounters with locals who come fully equipped with everything from enormous vodka-fuelled picnics to slippers, wash kits and a pair of shiny tracksuit bottoms slipped on beneath their formal daywear trousers.

Plan when you want to pee. Toilets are locked some 30 minutes before/after pulling in/out of a station. Bring your own paper.

BUS

Buses serve every city and small town in the country, but are best reserved for short trips outside main cities. Between major cities it is preferable to take a night train, although for shorter distances such as Lviv-Ivano-Frankivsk or Lviv-Lutsk, buses can be quicker and more frequent.

Riding Ukraine's dirty, crowded, cranky buses displays a different, more hectic mentality than trains. Less etiquette is practised between passengers, the majority of whom are overladen with an eclectic load of luggage comprising everything from chickens and pigs to building materials and goods to trade at the market. The centre aisle is always taken up by bodies and sacks of potatoes.

Bus stations are called *avtovokzal* or *avtostantsya*. In larger cities there can be several stations – one main one used by buses travelling longer distances and a handful of smaller bus stations serving destinations within an approximate 75km radius of the city.

Buying Tickets

Tickets are sold at the bus station a few hours before departures. If the bus is passing through en route, tickets can only be bought from the driver when the bus arrives. Confusion usually ensues as would-be passengers scramble upon what is already a very full bus.

Tickets bought in advance at the originating station resemble a shop-till receipt. Your destination, and date of travel is clearly marked on these tickets, as well as your reserved seat number (місц). Don't sit in any seat other than the one reserved for you, unless you want to launch into verbal combat with a formidable babushka who will most certainly end up the victor. Tickets sold somewhere en route generally don't tout a seat number and are for standing room only. Count on paying $1 per 100km of travel.

Bus departure times and destinations are listed on pieces of paper pinned up next to the ticket windows where they're sold. Bigger bus stations have large information wall posters, and almost all stations have a schematic map on the wall featuring the cities and towns serviced. These maps are Soviet relics, however, and are not always accurate (many services have been cut since independence). The information window at the bus station is usually marked довідкове бюро. Information, either verbal or written, costs around $0.10/20 per oral/written response to a question.

Outside the bus station building, each platform is usually marked up with the destinations it serves. Long-distance buses stop every two to three hours, allowing passengers to stretch their legs and buy something to drink at a kiosk.

CAR & MOTORCYCLE

Driving in Ukraine is a unique and nerve-racking experience that any sensible motorist should avoid, especially if your car is your most precious possession. Roads tend to have no markings, are unlit at night and riddled with potholes and other unforeseen obstacles which prompt fellow motorists to drive in zigzags.

During the melting snows of spring, roads in the countryside and in smaller towns and villages are awash with water and mud. In summer, a smokescreen of dust can cloud your vision; while in winter, roads are glazed with ice or snow blocked. City roads are a combination of cobbles, potholes, trolleybuses, trams, tram lines, congestion, pollution and multiple intersections where the only apparent rule is 'first come, first served'.

Exploring Ukraine by car does guarantee an adventure, however, and an excellent way to see the country, providing you have plenty of time to spare. Hot tip: in winter, do as locals do and fill your windscreen cleaner with pure vodka (less than $1) to save it freezing.

Road Types

There are four main categories for roads in Ukraine. First are the three main highways that cut across the country – the east-west E40 (M17) from Lviv to Kharkiv via Kyiv, the E93 (M20) from Kyiv to Odesa, and the E95 (M2) from Kharkiv to Simferopol. The only sections that are dual carriageways are the first 100km or so outside of Kyiv in either direction.

Main cities and large towns are linked by secondary single carriageways that begin

UKRAINE

with the letter 'A', such as the A267 between Lviv and Ternopil.

Next are the single-lane roads that link small towns all over the country. They are narrower, often picturesque and more or less paved, have frequent potholes, and begin with the letter 'P', like the P105 between Kremenets and Pochayiv.

Then there are hundreds of smaller, mostly dirt or scantily paved tracks that link the villages.

Roads are rarely marked by their numbers; mostly, a sign states the road's destination. Ensure you have a good map and can read city names in Cyrillic. Only a handful of routes have multiple-language signs.

Road Rules

Drive on the right. Unless indicated otherwise, speed limits are 60km/h in towns, 90km/h on major roads and 110km/h on highways. Speed traps are common, but most drivers are reckless and seem oblivious to the risk of being booked by the traffic police, the State Motor Inspectorate, DAI (short for Derzhavna Avto Inspektsia, the Ukrainian equivalent of the Russian GAI). The on-the-spot fine for speeding starts at $6 although most officers are open to negotiations (meaning you pay less but don't get an official receipt). It's a criminal offence to drive after consuming alcohol or to drive without wearing a seat belt.

It is not uncommon for motorists to be stopped by a member of the DAI who will wave his baton and, once you have stopped, demand to see your *dokumenty* – have your papers ready. On major roads, at the city limits, DAI checkpoints still exist. Slow down, and pause momentarily at the raised barrier before continuing.

By law, you should always carry a fire extinguisher, first-aid kit and warning triangle in your car. In cities, a diagonal red stripe indicates temporary parking and a yellow sign, yellow-painted kerb or a red 'X' indicates no parking at all. Violators of these parking regulations risk having their car number plates removed. Retrieving your plates requires paying a hefty fine and several days of wrangling at the local DAI office.

Fuel

Petrol *(benzyn)* is widely available at octane levels of 76, 92 and 95, and occasionally in larger cities at 98. You should opt for the highest octane petrol available as the low levels can cause trouble in high-compression engines. Unleaded petrol is not widely available. Diesel is.

Always pay before filling up. Count on paying around $0.25 for a litre of A95. Never let your car get low on fuel and keep your spare can full. Kyiv is starting to sprout petrol stations that are open 24 hours.

Rental

You can only rent a car without a driver in Kyiv. Rental rates with major car rental companies such as Avis, Europcar and Hertz start at $26/day plus $0.26/km. Unlimited mileage rates start at $43/day. In Yalta, Odesa and Lviv, you can rent a car with a driver through some larger hotels. This costs substantially more.

A cheap alternative for day trips is to haggle with a taxi driver. You should hopefully pay no more than $0.25 per kilometre. Avoid negotiating with taxis which have meters; these charge waiting time too. In Kyiv and elsewhere, it is quite acceptable to stand on the roadside and flag down a private car; few private drivers will rip you off.

HITCHING

Hitching is never entirely safe in any country in the world, and we don't recommend it. Nevertheless, hitching is a very common method of getting around in Ukraine. See the European Russia Getting Around chapter.

BOAT

Dnipro River Trips

The Dnipro flows for over 800km through Russia and Belarus, gathering its main tributaries just as it begins its great 1000km journey across Ukraine, splitting the country in two with a long diagonal bend before spilling out into the Black Sea. The river is a national symbol with all sorts of poetic, cultural and historical attachments, most of its course slicing through classic areas of steppe and along the haunts of the legendary Cossacks. It's also a major transportation artery flowing past some large and important cities. Its water is harnessed by huge hydroelectric power plants and dams, at Kremenchuk, Zaporizhzhya and Dnipropetrovsk.

Passenger hydrofoil services have been drastically cut in recent years. At the time of writing, the only guaranteed service, available between May and mid-October, was the Kyiv-Cherkasy route (240km, 5¼ hours). Beyond that, river trips between Dnipro cities – such as Kremenchuk, Dnipropetrovsk, Zaporizhzhya and Kherson, as well as the Black Sea ports of Yevpatoria and Odesa – are curtailed to prearranged chartered vessels and tour packages.

Several travel agencies abroad (see the Ukraine Getting There & Away chapter) and in Ukraine (see Information under the relevant city listings) organise cruises. The most common packages are a return weekend trip from Kyiv to Kaniv, a one way cruise from Kyiv to Odesa (11 days), or a return Kyiv-Odesa cruise stopping in Kherson and Sevastopol en route (15 days). Small excursions and tours are usually arranged at each stop. Prices for an 11/15 day trip start at $1195/1435 per person.

Other River Trips

Small passenger boats *(katery)* shuttle travellers in and around the Yalta, Odesa and Feodosia areas. Infrequent boats also connect Black Sea and Crimean ports like Yalta, Feodosia, Yevpatoria, Odesa and Izmayil. None of these services are scheduled however. Agencies can charter boats for you.

LOCAL TRANSPORT

Ukrainian cities are navigable by trolleybuses, trams, city buses and – in Kyiv, Kharkiv and Dnipropetrovsk – a metro. These urban public transportation systems are overworked and underserviced, with crowds that are often unbearable. There's no room for shyness and no time to be squeamish – learn to assert yourself quickly to survive.

The upside is that public transport is dirt cheap. A ticket *(kvytok* or *bilet)* for a single ride costs no more than $0.10. Tram, trolleybus and bus tickets are sold at street kiosks close to tram or bus stops. A stands for autobus or autobus stop, T stands for a tram or tram stop, and Tp stands for a trolleybus or trolleybus stop. In many cities, you simply pay the driver or wait for the conductor to push through the crowd to sell you a ticket. Tickets have to be punched on board (or ripped by the conductor). Unclipped or untorn tickets warrant an on-the-spot fine, should you be caught.

In Kyiv, Kharkiv and Dnipropetrovsk, colourful, plastic metro tokens *(zhetony)* are sold inside metro stations. Grand plans to extend the metro lines in all three cities appear to have been permanently thwarted by lack of cash. The metro runs from around 5.30 am to midnight. M stands for metro. Plans are afoot to grace Donetsk with a 20 station metro; completion of the first phase is scheduled for 2005.

In Ukraine, as in Russia and Belarus and the entire former Soviet Union, a metro station can have several names – one for each different line that crosses at that station. Highly confusing.

In Crimea and most Ukrainian cities, zippy minibuses shadow most local bus routes. These buses are clean, unscheduled and simply depart when full. A single ride is more expensive than on a regular bus; to buy a ticket, pass your money to the passenger in front of you who will pass it on, and so on, until it reaches the driver. If you need change, it will be returned in the same amusing manner.

ORGANISED TOURS

Once you're in Ukraine, there are many travel agencies which specialise in city tours and excursions throughout the country, including Dnipro River and Black Sea cruises. Travel agencies are listed under Information in the relevant city sections.

Kyiv
Київ

☎ 044 • pop 2.6 million

Kyiv (Kiev in Russian) is the capital of Ukraine and considered the mother city for all Eastern Slavic peoples. It is the state from which neighbouring Russia and Belarus were descended (Kyivan Rus), and the Russian Orthodox Church and Eastern Slavic art and architecture were all founded here between the 9th and 11th centuries.

St Sophia Cathedral and the Caves Monastery are among the country's most fascinating sites, dating to the days of Kyivan Rus. The city's old areas stand on wooded hills above the west bank of the snaking Dnipro River. Modern Kyiv's wide boulevards and broad squares can't match the allure of the city's heritage which has somehow managed to survive Mongol invasions, devastating fires, communist urban planning and the massive destruction of WWII. Today, Kyiv has a big-city atmosphere, more cosmopolitan than any other in the country, but within its urban sprawl, gracious testaments to its tumultuous history can still be found.

HIGHLIGHTS

- Exploring bohemian Podil – don't miss the art market on Andriyivsky uzviz, St Andrew's Church or the Chornobyl Museum
- Taking a Sunday stroll down Khreshchatyk, a tunnel of blossoming chestnuts in spring
- Seeing mummified monks by candlelight in the underground passages of the Caves Monastery
- Being dazzled by St Sophia Cathedral's sparkling domes
- Shopping at Bessarabsky and Volodymyrsky markets
- Feasting on shashlyk at Kyiv's open-air Folk Architecture Museum

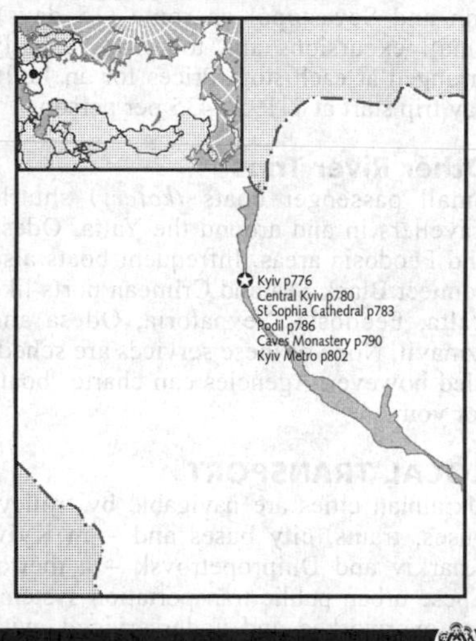

HISTORY

Archaeology suggests Kyiv has existed since 482, although traces of earlier human settlements have been discovered in the area. An 11th century chronicle written by the monks of the Caves Monastery says it was founded by the leaders of an Eastern Slav tribe – the three brothers Ky (after whom the city is said to be named), Shchek and Khoriv, and their sister Lybid, whose names today demark the topography of the city. In the 9th century, Scandinavians from Novgorod took control of Kyiv from the Magyars, Asiatic vassals of the Khazars. The story goes that in 882, a Scandinavian called Oleh killed two other Scandinavians, Askold and Dir, who had had some kind of arrangement with the Magyars, and declared himself an independent ruler, inaugurating Kyivan Rus. 'Rus' was the original name given by Eastern Slavs to the Scandinavian traders/settlers who eventually became their overlords; Kyivan Rus became the name for the great state which was eventually ruled from Kyiv by this Slavicised Scandinavian dynasty. Kyiv thrived off the river trade, sending furs, honey and slaves to pay for the luxuries of Constantinople. Under the rule of Svyatoslav (962-72), the state governed an area spreading from the Volga to the Danube and to Novgorod.

Constantinople was one rival that could not be defeated, and in 988 Svyatoslav's son Volodymyr, evidently deciding that if he couldn't beat them he might as well join them, married the emperor's sister and adopted Christianity as his state religion. Kyiv's pagan idols were destroyed and its people driven into the Dnipro for a mass baptism – an event that is commemorated each year in January during Epiphany (see Special Events).

Under Volodymyr's son Yaroslav the Wise (1017-54), Kyiv became a cultural and political centre in the Byzantine mould. St Sophia Cathedral was built to proclaim the glory of both God and city. Like all great cities, it exploited its favourable geographic location, becoming the primary trading centre and economic hub between the Baltics, Western Europe and Constantinople. By the 12th century, Kyiv reputedly had over 400 churches, but its economic prowess had already begun to wane. Power had shifted to a number of breakaway principalities, and in 1169 Andriy Bogolyubov, from the outlying north-eastern Kyivan principality of Suzdal, sacked Kyiv and took the title of Grand Prince of Rus away from the city to the north.

In 1240 Kyiv was sacked again by the Tatars. Kyiv shrank to the riverside area known as Podil – the area surrounding today's Kontraktova ploshcha – which remained its centre through centuries, first as a Lithuanian or Polish frontier town and then from 1667, following Cossack rule, as a Russian outpost. After the Second Partition of Poland, in 1793, much of Ukraine passed from Polish to Russian hands and Kyiv's importance grew as the capital of Russian Ukraine. During the next century, tsarist policies encouraged Russian emigration and Russification, while suppressing Ukrainian national identity. During the chaos following the Bolshevik Revolution, Kyiv was the site of frequent battles between Red and White Ukrainian forces.

In August 1941, the advancing Germans killed or captured over half a million Soviet troops at Kyiv. The Germans also killed about 100,000 Jews and other minorities at Babyn Yar, in the north of the city. Four in 10 buildings were destroyed and 80% of the city's inhabitants had been made homeless by the time the Red Army retook Kyiv on 6 November 1943.

The postwar years saw rapid industrialisation with the construction of unsightly suburbs. During the late 1980s, nationalistic and democratic movements from western Ukraine began to catch on in the capital city, and with the eventual collapse of the Soviet Union, the Supreme Council of Ukraine declared independence in Kyiv on 24 August 1991.

ORIENTATION

The modern centre and old city – divided into three major districts – are on the hilly west bank of the Dnipro River. The Old Town (Upper Town) is concentrated around the north end of vulitsya Volodymyrska, near St Sophia Cathedral.

Kyiv's main commercial promenade is vulitsya Khreshchatyk, running parallel to vulitsya Volodymyrska along the bottom of a valley from Bessarabska ploshcha, and heading north towards maydan Nezalezhnosti, the main square.

The area north of the Old Town from around St Andrew's Church to Kontraktova ploshcha is called Podil, or Lower Town, the historic merchants' quarter and river port.

From the northern end of Khreshchatyk, vulitsya Hrushevskoho runs south-east along a ridge to the district known as Pechersk, the historic ecclesiastical centre and site of the Caves Monastery. Woods and parks cover most of the west bank's slopes, forming an attractive 5km green belt. Across the river, on the east (left) bank are a cluster of islands hugged by beaches and parkland. Beyond lie grey housing blocks.

KYIV КИЇВ

8 Petrivka
Петрівка
14 Politekhnichny Instytut
Політехнічний Інститут
15 Vokzalna
Вокзальна
17 Palats Sportu
Палац Спорту
21 Darnytsya
Дарниця
22 Hidropark
Гідропарк
23 Palats Ukraina
Палац Україна
25 Lybidska
Либідська
27 Druzhby Narodiv
Дружби Народів

OTHER
4 Babyn Yar Monument
Пам'ятник Бабин Яр
6 St Cyril's Church
Кирилівська церква
9 Rusanivski Sady Pier
Причал Русанівські сади
10 Lokomotiv Pier
Причал Локомотив
11 American Medical Centre & Denta Lux
12 US Embassy Information Service
Інформаційний Посольства США
13 Kyiv Polytechnic Institute & British Council
16 Train Station
Залізничний вокзал
18 Dovbychka Pier
Причал Довбичка
19 Hidropark Pier
Причал Гідропарк
24 Zhulyany Airport
Аеропорт Жуляни
28 Vydubytsky Monastery
Видубицький монастир
29 Ukraine Academy of Sciences Botanical Gardens
Ботаніуний Сад Ан України
30 Long-Distance Bus Station
Автобусний вокзал
33 Ukrainian Exhibition of Economic Achievements
ВДНГ (Виставка досягнень в народному господарстві України)
34 Horse Racetrack
Парк кінських перегонів
35 Folk Architecture Museum
Музей народної архітектури
36 Sady Nyzhny Pier
Сади Нижний причал

PLACES TO STAY
1 Prolisok
Пролісок
7 Hotel Spartak
Готель Спартак
26 Hotel Druzhba
Готель Дружба
31 Hotel Mir
Готель Мир
32 Hotel Holoseevskaya
Готель Голосіївская

PLACES TO EAT
20 Mlyn
Млин

METRO STATIONS
2 Svyatoshyn
Святошин
3 Shulyavska
Шулявська
5 Lukyanivska
Лук'янівська

See Podil Map
See Central Kyiv Map
To Zhytomyr, Brest, Lviv & Vinnytsya
To Oryol & Moscow
To Boryspil Airport, Poltava & Kharkiv
To Odesa
Dnipro River
Trukhanov Island
Dolobetsky Island
Footbridge
Metro Bridge
Paton Bridge
Moskovska ploshcha
prospekt Peremohy
prospekt Chervonykh Karakiv
prospekt Heneraly Vatutina
prospekt Brovarsky
prospekt Miru
prospekt Vozziedannia
prospekt Mykoly Bazhana
prospekt 50-richchya Zhovtnya
prospekt 40-richchya Zhovtnya
prospekt Nauky
prospekt Akademika Hlushkova
bulvar Perova
bulvar Tarasa Shevchenka
bulvar Lesi Ukrainky
bulvar Druzhby Narodiv
vulitsya Khreshchatyk
vulitsya Hrushevskoho
vulitsya Volodymyrska
vulitsya Artema
vulitsya Borshchahovska
vulitsya Chervonoarmiyska
vulitsya Akademika Zabolotnoho
vulitsya Vasylkivska
Kiltseva doroha
Stolichnoe shose
0 2 4 km

Maps

Street names are correctly marked on most city maps, with the exception of vulitsya Antonvycha (formerly vulitsya Horkoho) and vulitsya Chervonoarmiyska (Krasnoarmeyskaya in Russian).

The quality *Kiev City Plan*, published by Kartografiya (☎ 573 26 84, fax 552 60 89) and available in most bookshops, includes a 1:25,000 scale map of the city, a 1:15,000 scale map of the town centre, and a handy Cyrillic-Latin street register.

Equally useful is the *Kyiv City Map* (1:35,000), distributed as an insert in the *Kyiv Business Directory* (www.business.com.ua). A more detailed map of the centre, as well as public transport route maps, is also included in the directory, which contains phonebook-style listings and is published quarterly.

Most available maps of Kyiv/Ukraine are sold at the souvenir stalls on maydan Nezalezhnosti.

INFORMATION

Tourist Offices

Kyiv lacks a tourist office but most hotels have an information bureau of sorts. The State Committee of Ukraine for Tourism (☎ 212 55 70, ☎ 224 81 49), Yaroslaviv val 36, opposite the Canadian embassy, is utterly useless.

Money

Exchange booths signposted *obmin valyut* are plentiful. Rates offered by exchange booths in hotels are not necessarily worse. The bureau de change in the arrivals hall at Boryspil airport cashes Thomas Cook and American Express travellers cheques.

There are ATMs in Boryspil airport arrivals hall; in Ukrainsky Dim at Khreshchatyk 2; in the central post office (open 24 hours); inside Kiyavia at vulitsya Horodetskoho 4; and in the lobbies of Hotel Impressa, Hotel Kozatsky, Hotel Khreshchatyk, Hotel Lybid, Hotel National, Hotel Salyut, Hotel Spartak and Hotel Ukraina.

To make cash advances on your credit card or to cash travellers cheques, go to the Western Union/X-Change Points inside Hotel Lybid, or to the telephone centre at vulitsya Bohdana Khmelnytskoho 32. Most major banks offer these services too.

European Travel Services (see Travel Agencies) is an American Express representative. It cannot replace lost travellers cheques but it assists travellers who lose their Amex credit card.

Post

The central post office is at Khreshchatyk 22 (entrance on maydan Nezalezhnosti); the complex is open 24 hours but the postal counters are only open from 8 am to 9 pm (until 7 pm on Saturday, closed Sunday). You can send/receive faxes (fax 244 72 72 or 228 35 98) from window No 3, 4 or 5. The information desk is at window No 18. DHL International (☎ 264 72 00), vulitsya Vasylkivska 1, is one of many express services in the city.

Telephone

The central telephone centre (open 24 hours) adjoins the central post office at Khreshchatyk 22; the entrance is on Khreshchatyk. You can book international calls through the operator at window No 3, or buy a Utel telephone card (window No 2) to dial direct from the Utel phone here. Phonecards are also sold here (window No 6) for the row of public card phones (local and national calls only) that line the interior of the centre.

The smaller telephone centre at vulitsya Bohdana Khmelnytskoho 32 (open from 8 am to 8 pm) is usually less crowded.

Email & Internet Access

You can send (but not receive) emails from window No 27 at the central post office (US$0.20 per kilobyte). It is more efficient to access the Internet at Kyiv's busy Cyber Kafe (☎ 228 05 48, www.cybercafe.com.ua), vulitsya Prorizna 21. Alternatively, you can try the British Council library (see Cultural Centres).

Travel Agencies

Sam Travel Company (☎ 264 11 84, fax 264 93 27, main@samcomp.kiev.ua), prospekt 40-richchya Zhovtnya 70 (metro Lybidska), adjoining Hotel Mir, is the leading inbound operator. It organises sightseeing excursions and arranges Dnipro cruises, visa support and hotel bookings. It has a second office (☎ 220 05 64, fax 227 50 19) at prospekt Chervonoarmiyska 34 (metro Ploshcha Lva Tolstoho); both are open from 9.30 am to 6.30 pm (closed Sunday). Limp (☎ 228 16 50, fax 229 79 16, laszlo@olymp-travel.kiev.ua), Khreshchatyk 21, offers similar services.

European Travel Services (☎/fax 490 59 30, ☎/fax 246 55 73/72, ets@ukrpack.net), vulitsya Ivana Franka 36, is Kyiv's only Western-run travel agency.

The Mandrivnyk Travel Company (☎ 463 76 04, fax 463 76 05, mandrivnyk@adam.kiev.ua), Poshtova ploshcha 3, at the river boat terminal and Chervona Ruta (☎/fax 293 69 09, 293 52 36, lesya@chruta.kiev.ua), vulitsya Liuteranska 24, are Dnipro and Black Sea cruise specialists.

Russia Travel (☎ 246 93 74, fax 216 42 27, info@russiatravel.kiev.ua), vulitsya Turhenivska 38, room 309/2, specialises in guess what ...

Bookshops

Naukova Dumka, vulitsya Hrushevskoho 4, next to Hotel Dnipro, has the best selection of topographical hiking maps. City maps for most Ukrainian cities are sold at Medichna Kniha, vulitsya Chervonoarmiyska 23. Mystetstvo, Khreshchatyk 24, sells guides in various languages.

The news kiosks inside Hotel National and Arizona have the best selection of foreign-language newspapers, magazines and city guides. Count on paying at least $5 for an *International Herald Tribune*.

Cultural Centres

The US embassy information service (USIS; ☎ 213 25 32, ☎ 213 91 38, fax 213 33 86, info@usis.kiev.ua, www.usis.kiev.ua), vulitsya Melnikova 63, is open from 9 am to 6 pm (closed weekends). Take trolleybus No 16 from maydan Nezalezhnosti to the first stop after vulitsya Artema becomes Melnikova. The American Library (☎ 417 31 13, www.ukma.kiev.ua/ukmalib), vulitsya Voloska 8/5, inside the Kyiv-Mohyla Akademy in Podil, is open from 2 to 5 pm (closed weekends). The Japanese Centre is located next door.

The British Council (☎ 247 72 35, fax 247 72 80, bc.ukraine@bc.kiev.ua, info@bc.kiev.ua, www.bc.kiev.ua) is at ploshcha Bessarabska 9/1. Its library (☎ 441 16 59, elc@elc.bc.kiev.ua) is inside the Kyiv Polytechnic Institute, prospekt Peremohy 37, building 1, 2nd floor, room 258.

Expatriates keen to meet other expats should contact the Hash Harriers (kievhhh@yahoo.com); it meets every second Sunday of the month.

Medical Services

The American Medical Centre (☎ 211 65 55, ☎ 213 94 11, ☎ 213 10 16), vulitsya Berdychivska 1 (metro Lukyanivska), is open 24 hours. EU nationals can seek medical care (consultation $80) at the British European Medical Clinic (☎ 573 88 73, ☎ 290 73 17), inside the British consulate, vulitsya Sichnevoho Povstannya 6 (metro Arsenalna), open from 8.45 am to 5 pm (closed weekends).

Albadent (☎ 224 49 29), Nesterovsky provulok 19/17, 2nd floor, room 239 (metro Zoloti Vorota), and Denta Lux (☎ 212 13 75), vulitsya Artema 25 (metro Lukyanivska), have English-speaking dentists.

Emergency

The American Medical Center (emergency ☎ 461 95 95) and British European Medical Clinic both offer a 24 hour emergency service. To call an ambulance dial ☎ 03.

Dangers & Annoyances

See Dangers & Annoyances in the Ukraine Facts for the Visitor chapter for information.

VULITSYA KHRESHCHATYK

Khreshchatyk, Kyiv's 1.5km commercial boulevard, is a bustling thoroughfare with wide pavements and lots of shops. It's crossable via underground passages. Between noon and 9 pm on Saturday and Sunday, the street is pedestrianised and attracts a colourful collection of buskers, street hawkers and weekend strollers. Although Khreshchatyk was completely rebuilt and more than doubled in width after the destruction of WWII, it still retains an air of cosmopolitan elegance, its long blocks lined with formal and imposing Soviet-style neoclassical facades. Its southern end is marked by **Bessarabsky Market**. Built in 1910-12, this food market was established for traders coming to Kyiv from Bessarabia.

Ploshcha Evropeyska & Around

At the northern end of Khreshchatyk is ploshcha Evropeyska, a large circular intersection. On its northern side at Khreshchatyk 2 is **Ukrainsky Dim** (☎ 228 26 40, ☎ 228 28 20), the former Lenin Museum, and now a multimedia exhibition hall with four floors of temporary exhibits and a theatre. Across Volodymyrsky uzviz, which leads down to the river bank, is the **National Philharmonic** (1882), originally the Kyiv Merchants' Assembly headquarters. The controversial **rainbow arch**, a tasteless metallic parabola rising from the park behind, is a monument to the 1654 'unification' of Russia and Ukraine. Directly behind the monument are sweeping views over the Dnipro and surrounding islands, with paths zigzagging down the hillside to the pedestrian bridge below. Hidden among trees to the left stands a **statue of Prince Volodymyr** (reachable by walking halfway down Volodymyrsky uzviz then up a flight of stairs), a monument to the ruler who in 988 brought Christianity to the Eastern Slavs.

Maydan Nezalezhnosti & Around

One long block south-west of ploshcha Evropeyska is fountain-filled maydan Nezalezhnosti (Independence Square). It is crowded with sauntering Kyivans and vendors from sunrise to sunset when, as night falls, its fountains are lit and daytime strollers are replaced by evening drinkers. Across the street, below the 1960s Hotel Moskva, is a broad marble platform where a massive red granite statue of Lenin once stood. To the right is the attractive column-lined facade of the **Tchaikovsky State Conservatory**. Khreshchatyk and Maydan Nezalezhnosti metro stations are on vulitsya Khreshchatyk, with trolleybus No 20 running its length.

Off the western side of maydan Nezalezhnosti are six streets fanning out uphill in a star-like configuration. The **Taras Shevchenko Memorial House Museum**, provulok Shevchenka No 6, is a beautifully restored, 19th century wooden house and garden where the national poet lived for a short while in 1846. The museum is open from 10 am to 6 pm (noon to 8 pm on Tuesday, closed Monday).

Upper Town

Along vulitsya Volodymyrska lie a number of Kyiv's historic landmarks. On the corner of vulitsya Bohdana Khmelnytskoho and vulitsya Volodymyrska sits the ornate **Shevchenko Opera & Ballet Theatre** (1899-1901). It's an impressive building, similar in scale and grandeur to the opera houses in Odesa and Lviv, and was the first theatre to perform classical operas translated into the Ukrainian language. Just down vulitsya Bohdana Khmelnytskoho at No 15 is the **National Science Museum**, open from 10 am

Flower Power

Summer Saturdays see white-robed brides and giddy grooms embark on a 'just married' tour of the city where, according to tradition, newlyweds lay flowers at the feet of Kyiv's most respectable heroes.

At peak times during the marrying season, queues are known to form at the six traditional spots which include Babyn Yar; the eternal flame in Glory Park; the Golden Gates; the Caves Monastery; the Foundation of Kyiv monument of Kyivan founders Ky, Shchek, Khoriv and Lybid; and the statue trio on Mykhaylivska ploshcha featuring Princess Olga, daughter of Yaroslav the Wise, with Cyril and Mephody, creators of the Slavic (Cyrillic) alphabet. Prior to independence, newlyweds would also grace Lenin's feet with a floral bouquet.

CENTRAL KYIV ЦЕНТРАЛЬНИЙ КИЇВ

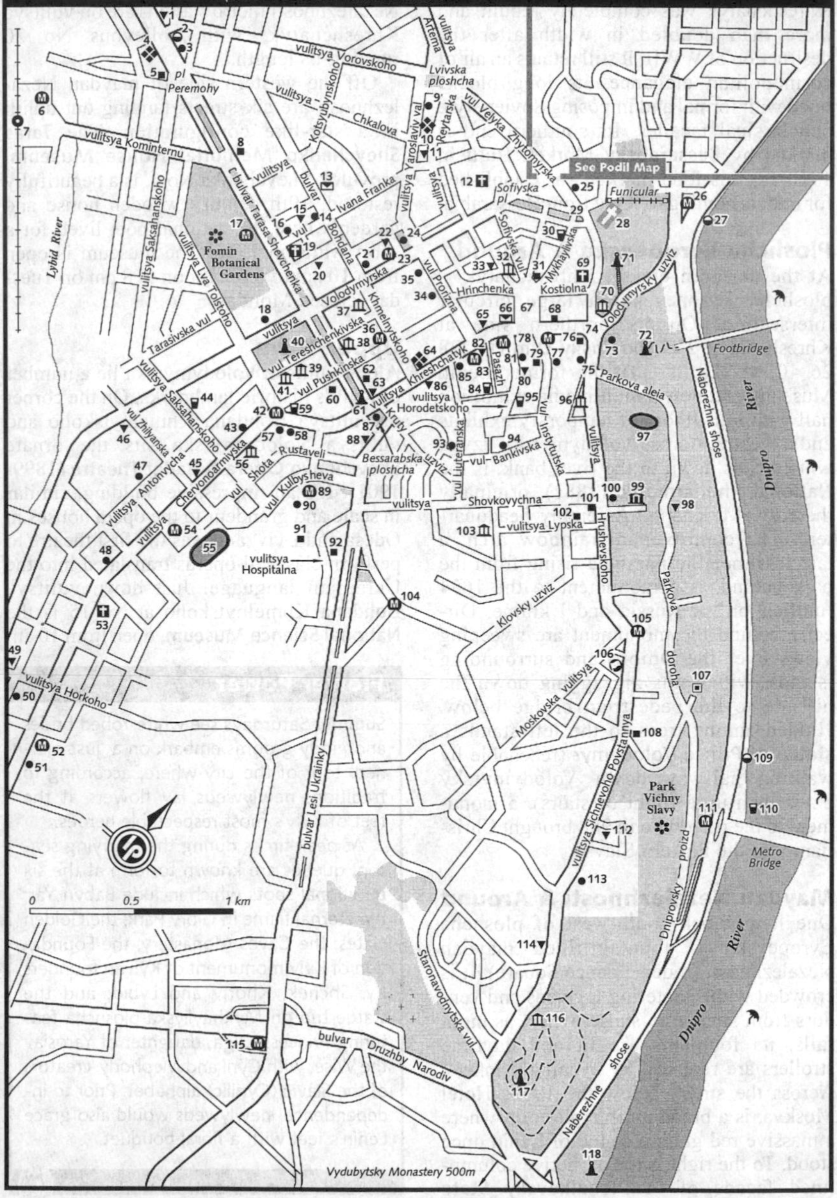

vulitsya Vorovskoho
vulitsya Artema
Lvivska ploshcha
pl Peremohy
vulitsya Chkalova
vulitsya Kotsyubynskoho
vul Velyka Zhytomyrska
vulitsya Yaroslaviv val
vul Reytarska
vulitsya Kominternu
See Podil Map
vulitsya Saksahanskoho
bulvar Tarasa Shevchenka
bulvar Bohdana
Ivana Franka
vul
Sofiyska pl
Funicular
Lybid River
Fomin Botanical Gardens
vulitsya Lva Tolstoho
Sofiyska vul
Mykhaylivska
Volodymyrska
vul Prorizna
Hrinchenka
Kostiolna
Volodymyrsky uzviz
Tarasivska vul
vulitsya Tereshchenkivska
Khmelnytskoho
vul Pushkinska
vul Khreshchatyk
Pasazh
Footbridge
Parkova aleia
vulitsya Saksahanskoho
vul Zhilyanska
Chervonoarmiyska
vulitsya Antonovycha
Horodetskoho
Kruty
Shota Rustaveli
Bessarabska ploshcha
vul Kulbysheva
uzviz
vul Luteranska
vul Bankivska
vul Instytutska
vulitsya Hrushevskoho
Naberezhna shose
Dnipro River
vulitsya Shovkovychna
vulitsya Lypska
vulitsya Hospitalna
Klovsky uzviz
Parkova doroha
vulitsya Horkoho
Moskovska vulitsya
vulitsya Sichnevoho Povstannya
Park Vichny Slavy
Dniprovsky proizd
Metro Bridge
bulvar Lesi Ukrainky
0 0.5 1 km
Staronavodnytska vul
Naberezhne shose
bulvar Druzhby Narodiv
Dnipro River
Vydubytsky Monastery 500m

1 2 3 4 5 6 7 8 9 10 11 12 13 14 15 16 17 18 19 20 21 22 23 24 25 26 27 28 29 30 31 32 33 34 35 36 37 38 39 40 41 42 43 44 45 46 47 48 49 50 51 52 53 54 55 56 57 58 59 60 61 62 63 64 65 66 67 68 69 70 71 72 73 74 75 76 77 78 79 80 81 82 83 84 85 86 87 88 89 90 91 92 93 94 95 96 97 98 99 100 101 102 103 104 105 106 107 108 109 110 111 112 113 114 115 116 117 118

KYIV

CENTRAL KYIV ЦЕНТРАЛЬНИЙ КИЇВ

PLACES TO STAY

5 Hotel Lybid
Готель Либідь
8 Hotel Ekspres & Train Ticket Office
Готель Експрес та Центральні Залізничні Каса
31 Hotel Kozatsky
Готель Козацький
60 Hotel Ukraina
Готель Україна
62 Hotel Saint Petersburg
Готель Сант Петербург
68 Hotel Khreshchatyk
Готель Хрещатик
76 Hotel Dnipro
Готель Дніпро
79 Hotel Moskva
Готель Москва
91 Hotel Rus
Готель Русь
92 President Hotel Kyivsky
Президент Готель Київський
101 Hotel Kyiv
Готель Київ
102 Hotel National
Готель Національна
108 Hotel Salyut
Готель Салют

PLACES TO EAT

1 Non-Stop
Нон Стоп
11 Vesuvio Pizza
Везувіо Піцца
15 Surpriz
Сюрприз
20 Bon-Bon Kafe
Кафе Бон Бон
22 Pantagruel
Пантагрюель
33 Kaffa
Каффа
45 Atlanta
Атланта
46 Uncle Sam
Анкл Сем
49 Maximal
Максималь
63 Nika
Кафе Ніка
65 Château de Fleur
Шато де Флєр
80 Mr Snack
Містер Снек
82 Shelter
Шелтер
86 Himalay
Гималаи
88 Bombay Palace
Бомбей Палац
98 Kureni
Курені
112 Vernisazh
Вернисаж
114 Tsarske Selo & SSSR
Царське Сєло та СССР

MUSEUMS

32 Taras Shevchenko Memorial House Museum
Літературно-меморіальний дім Т. Г. Шевченка
38 Taras Shevchenko Museum
Музей Тараса Шевченка
39 Russian Art Museum
Музей Російського мистецтва
41 Western & Oriental Art Museum
Музей західного та східного мистецтва
96 Museum of Ukrainian Fine Arts
Музей Українського обра-зотворчого мистецтва
103 Kyiv History Museum
Музей історії міста
116 Afghan War Museum
117 Defence of Motherland Monument & Museum of the Great Patriotic War
Монумент Захисту Вітчизни та Музей Великої вітчизняної війни

METRO STATIONS

6 Vokzalna
Вокзальна
17 Universytet
Університет
23 Zoloti Vorota
Золоті Ворота
26 Poshtova Ploshcha
Поштова Площа
36 Teatralna
Театральна
42 Ploshcha Lva Tolstoho
Площа Льва Толстого
52 Palats Ukraina
Палац Україна
54 Respublikansky Stadion
Республіканський Стадіон
78 Maydan Nezalezhnosti
Майдан Незалежності
83 Khreshchatyk
Хрещатик
89 Palats Sportu
Палац Спорту
104 Klovska
Кловська
105 Arsenalna
Арсенальна
111 Dnipro
Дніпро
115 Druzhby Narodiv
Дружби народів

OTHER

2 Airport Bus Stop
3 Circus
Цирк
4 Ukraina (Department Store)
Україна
7 Main Train Station
Залізничний вокзал
9 State Committe of Ukraine for Tourism
Державний Комітет України по Туризму
10 Bistro Gastronom (Supermaket)
Бістро Гастроном
12 St Sophia Cathedral
Софійський собор
13 Post Office (Branch) & Telephone Centre
Пошта
14 Vino (Wine Shop)
Вино
16 European Travel Services
18 Kyiv University
Київський Університет ім. Т. Г. Щевченка
19 St Volodymyr's Cathedral
Володимирський собор
21 Shevchenko Opera & Ballet Theatre
Театр опери та балету ім. Т. Г. Шевченка
24 Golden Gate
Золоті ворота
25 Svitoch (Sweet Shop)
Світоч
27 Main River Terminal & Mandrivnyk (Travel Agency)
Річковий вокзал ; Мандрівник
28 Saint Mykhaylivska Zolo-toverkhyi Monastery
Свято Михайлівський Золотоверхий Монастир
29 Mykhaylivska ploshcha
Михайлівська площа
30 O'Brien's
О'Брайанс
34 Teatralna Kasa
Театральна каса

continued on next page

CENTRAL KYIV ЦЕНТРАЛЬНИЙ КИЇВ

continued from previous page

35 Cyber Kafe
Кібер Кафе
37 Museum of Natural Sciences
Природознавчий музей України
40 Shevchenko Statue & Park
Пам'ятник Тарасу Шевченку та парк
43 Sam (Travel Company)
Сам
44 John Bull Pub
Джон Бул Паб
47 Europcar
Европкар
48 Dynamo Kyiv Club Shop
Магазин Динамо Київ
50 Volodymyrsky Market
Володимирський ринок
51 Ukraina Palace
Лалац Україна
53 St Nicholas' Church
Церква Св. Николая
55 Respublikansky Stadium
Республіканський Стадіон
56 Galeria Olimp
57 Medichna Kniha (Book Shop)
Медична Книга
58 Ukrainsky Suvenir
Український сувенір
59 Eric's
Ерікс
61 Lenin
Ленін
64 TsUM
ЦУМ
66 Main Post Office
Главпоштамт
67 Maydan Nezalezhnosti
Майдан Незалежності
69 Church of St Alexander
Костьол Св. Олександра
70 Ukrainsky Dim
Український дім
71 Prince Volodymyr Statue
Пам'ятник князю Володимиру
72 Monument to Unification of Russia & Ukraine
Монумент в ознаменування возз'єднання України з Росією
73 Philharmonia
Філармонія
74 Ploshcha Evropeyska
Европейська площа
75 Naukova Dumka (Book Shop)
Наукова Думка
77 Palace of Culture & Arts, Kino Palace
81 Kiyavia
84 Cowboy
Ковбой
85 Teatralna Kasa
Театральна каса
87 Bessarabsky Market
Бессарабський ринок
90 Sports Palace
Лалац Слорту
93 Chervona Ruta
Червона Рута
94 House of Monsters
Дім страхіть (будинок Городецького)
95 Rock Cafe
Рок Кафе
97 Dynamo Stadium
Стадіон Динамо
99 Mariyinsky Palace
Маріїнський палац
100 Parliament Building
Верховна Рада
106 British Consulate
Консульство Брітанский
107 Askold's Grave Rotunda
Аскольдова могила ротонда
109 Metro Pier
Метро Причал
110 River Palace
Річковий Палац
113 Caves Monastery Main Entrance
Печерська Лавра, головний вхід
118 Foundation of Kyiv Monument
Пам'ятник засновникам Києва

to 4.30 pm (closed Wednesday and Thursday). Its extensive exhibits are spread between four separate museums, which cover archaeology, geology, botany and zoology.

A block north, on the corner of vulitsya Volodymyrska and Yaroslaviv val, stands the **Golden Gate** (Zoloti Vorota), the historic main gateway into the ancient city during Yaroslav's rule, supposedly inspired by Constantinople's Golden Gate. Originally built in 1037, it was a strong link in Kyiv's extensive fortification system, with ramparts once stretching out from both sides of the gate. The gate was destroyed in a 1240 Mongol-Tatar raid, then covered with earth in 1750. What you see is a 1982 reconstruction of the original. Inside is a small museum, open from May to November (closed Thursday).

Two long blocks north, Volodymyrska vulitsya opens up to **Sofiyska ploshcha**, the historic site where Kyiv citizens triumphantly welcomed a victorious Bohdan Khmelnytsky after his battles with the Poles in the mid-17th century. A statue of the Cossack leader rises from the middle of the square.

ST SOPHIA CATHEDRAL

The western side of Sofiyska ploshcha is taken up by the St Sophia Cathedral and Monastery complex. Sofiysky Sobor, the city's oldest standing church, was built in 1017-31 in honour of Prince Yaroslav's victory over the Pechenegs, a rival tribe from the east. Named after Hagia Sofia (Holy Wisdom) Cathedral in Istanbul, Christendom's greatest church from 548 to 1453, its

Byzantine plan and decoration announced the new religious and political authority of Kyiv. St Sophia was also a centre of learning and culture, housing the first school and library in Kyivan Rus. Being adjacent to the Royal Palace and the seat of the metropolitan (a leading religious figure), the cathedral was where all royal ceremonies including coronations were staged, treaties were signed and foreign dignitaries received.

St Sophia's basic structure and several of the interior mosaics and frescoes are original, but the building's outward appearance owes most to the helmet-domed Ukrainian baroque style of the late 17th and early 18th centuries. St Sophia originally had a central nave with two aisles on each side, all with semicircular apses at the eastern end. By the end of the 11th century two arcades had been added on the northern side, two on the south – almost doubling the width – and one on the west. The walls were of patterned pink brick, some of which can be seen on the exterior of the apses, and the roof was topped by 13 semicircular cupolas on drums (the number stands for Christ and the Disciples). The harmonious pyramidal outline and the sequences of semicircles in arches, roofs, windows and walls were characteristic features of later Ukrainian and Russian churches.

The two stair towers on the west side were probably added in the 12th century and the narthex (entrance hall), between them, in the 19th century. Partly ruined by the Tatars in 1240 and further damaged during the period of Lithuanian-Polish rule, St Sophia lay abandoned until 1685-1707, when extensive repairs were made. The 18th century, 76m-tall bell tower at the entrance to the grounds from Sofiyska ploshcha, built during the reconstruction, is embellished with wedding-cake Ukrainian baroque plasterwork. The ornate tomb that lies in front of the bell tower, outside the complex walls, is the grave of Kyiv patriarch Volodymyr Romaniuk (1925-95) who was buried here, amid much controversy, in 1995 (see Religion in Facts About Ukraine).

The main entrance into the complex, which was included on UNESCO's World Heritage list in 1990, is through the bell tower. Trolleybus Nos 16 and 18 from the back of maydan Nezalezhnosti will drop you off a block north, on vulitsya Volodymyrska. The complex is open from 10 am to 6 pm (until 5 pm on Wednesday,

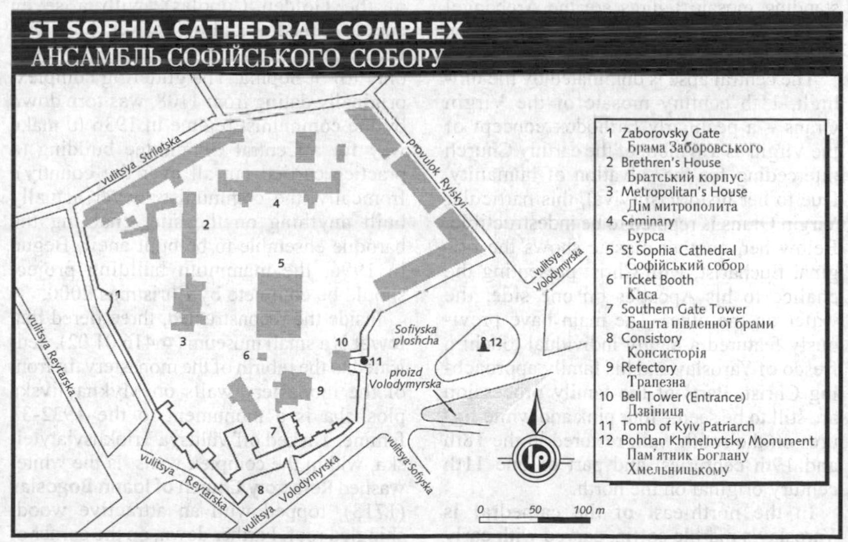

closed Thursday). Admission costs $2.50 and there is a $2.50/5 camera/camcorder fee.

Interior

The original Byzantine decorative scheme was followed by Eastern Slavic Orthodox churches for 900 years. Each figure or scene had its allotted position and together they had the effect of making the church into a giant three-dimensional symbol of the Orthodox world order. What we see today dates partly from the 11th century (some of it uncovered by 20th century restorers), partly from the 17th to 19th centuries.

Start with the central dome, where the 11th century mosaic of Christ Pantokrator (All Ruler) stares disarmingly down. This is a Byzantine Christ, embodying God the Father as well as God the Son and holding the Book of Judgement. Of the four archangels around him, only one is original. Below them, between the windows of the drum, are the Apostles (only half of one, Paul, is original). Next in the hierarchy are the four Evangelists, in the corners between the arches below the drum. Mark is original. Farther down, on the western sides of the pillars facing down the nave, the two highest-standing mosaic figures are the Archangel Gabriel and the Virgin of the Annunciation, together signifying the Incarnation.

The central apse is dominated by the 6m-high, 11th century mosaic of the Virgin Orans – a peculiarly Orthodox concept of the Virgin as a symbol of the earthly Church interceding for the salvation of humanity. Due to her historic survival, this particular Virgin Orans is reputed to be indestructible. Below her, another mosaic shows the original Eucharist, with Christ presenting the chalice to his Apostles on one side, the wafer on the other. The main nave previously featured a highly individual touch: a fresco of Yaroslav and his family approaching Christ. Parts of the family procession are still to be seen – four pink and white figures on the south wall, restored in the 18th and 19th centuries, and part of one 11th century original on the north.

In the north-east of the cathedral is Yaroslav's marble coffin, carved with early Christian symbols in the Near East in the 5th or 6th century and later brought to Kyiv. The far northern arcade has a number of exhibits concerning the history of the cathedral. The far southern arcade is closed off, but peek through the iron gate into the south-western stair tower for a glimpse of some rare secular frescoes of Byzantine court life, including musicians, chariot races and hunting scenes.

MYKHAYLIVSKA PLOSHCHA & AROUND

Stretching east from Sofiyska ploshcha to Mykhaylivska ploshcha is a long green strip of park called proizd Volodymyrsky, with a few scattered statues of pagan gods among the trees. The entire north-western side of Mykhaylivska ploshcha is dominated by the massive and imposing 1937 neoclassical **Ministry of Foreign Affairs building**, the former headquarters of the Central Committee of the Ukraine Communist Party. Just east is the top of the funicular (1905) which runs down the steep hillside to the river terminal.

The west corner of the square features the magnificent **Saint Mykhaylivska Zolotoverkhyi Monastery** (St Michael's Monastery of the Golden Cupolas), with a seven cupola cathedral and bell tower, built in a vertical axis with (and second in importance only to) St Sophia. The glittering complex, originally dating from 1108, was torn down by the communist regime in 1936 to make way for a Central Committee building (a practice carried out all over the country). Ironically, the communists never actually built anything on the site, enabling the baroque ensemble to be built anew. Begun in 1996, the mammoth building project should be complete by Christmas 2000.

Inside the reconstructed, three tiered **bell tower** is a small museum (☎ 416 01 02), dedicated to the rebirth of the monastery. In front of the monastery walls on Mykhaylivska ploshcha is a monument to the 1932-33 famine. Tucked off vulitsya Triokhsviatytelska, within the complex walls, is the whitewashed **Refectory Church of Ioann Bogoslav** (1713), topped with an attractive wood-shingled roof. Farther down, on the corner of vulitsya Kostiolna, is the 19th century Polish Catholic **St Alexander Church** (1817-42), recognisable by its large central dome and twin bell towers. Sunday mass is celebrated in English at 6 pm.

ST ANDREW'S CHURCH & AROUND

Northern vulitsya Volodymyrska, beyond St Sophia, follows the line of the main street of Yaroslav's Kyiv. **St Andrew's Church** (1746-61), poised at the northern end of the street and at the top of the charming Andriyivsky uzviz, is an inspired baroque interpretation of the traditional Ukrainian five domed, cross-shaped church by Rastrelli, the Italian architect who designed many of St Petersburg's great buildings. The slender curves of its blue, white, gold and green exterior stand out against the skyline, perched high above the Podil district at the crest of the historic Upper Town, at the supposed site where the Apostle Andrew erected a cross. Its richly decorated interior features a three tiered iconostasis and several paintings from the 18th century. The church, closed for restoration for some five years, should reopen in 2000.

Before reaching St Andrew's on vulitsya Volodymyrska, a small set of steps to your left leads to a flat-topped hillock and the reconstructed foundations of Kyiv's first cathedral, known as the **Desyatynna** (Church of the One-Tenth) because its founder Volodymyr dedicated 10% of his income to it. Founded in 989, the church collapsed under the weight of the people who had taken refuge on its roof during the 1240 Tatar siege. Farther west is the **Ukraine History Museum**, open from 10 am to 6 pm (closed Wednesday and the last Thursday of the month).

Andriyivsky Uzviz

Andriyivsky uzviz, Kyiv's most charming street, curves its way down from St Andrew's to the base of the Podil district. This steep lane is the artists' headquarters of the city and is one of the most popular places to hang out. Galleries, gift shops, restaurants and cafes line the cobbled street.

About halfway down at No 22 is a small **history museum**, dedicated to the history of Andriyivsky uzviz and the Podil district (closed Monday and Tuesday). Another staircase past the museum leads to the top of a hillock with excellent views towards St Andrew's and down over the Podil. Continuing downhill to No 13 is the **Mikhail Bulgakov House Museum**, dedicated to the 20th century Russian satirical writer whose work was heavily censored by Soviet authorities (closed Wednesday). The **One Street Museum** at No 2b hosts excellent, contemporary art exhibitions (closed Monday).

PODIL

Andriyivsky uzviz spills out into Podil, the historic mercantile quarter and trading district of Kyiv. Dating back to the earliest settlements, this flat area tucked beneath a row of hills quickly grew around the main port on the riverfront. Destroyed by Mongol-Tatar invasions in the 13th century, it was rebuilt, only to be devastated again by fire in 1811. However, it survived WWII better than most of the city, hence its relaxed, small-scale atmosphere and 19th century grid of streets.

The heart of the Podil district is **Kontraktova ploshcha**, a square named after the large, white arcaded **Kontraktova Dim** (House of Contracts) occupying the centre. Built in 1817 to house the legal headquarters for the negotiating and signing of contracts between port merchants, it houses several galleries and businesses today. Off its northern side is the **Samson Fountain**, a baroque cupola rising above a sculpture of a rather wimpy Samson wrestling a lion. On the opposite side of the square is a **statue of Hryhorii Skovoroda**, an 18th century scholar who abandoned his formal education for the life of a wandering philosopher.

Around vulitsya Spaska and vulitsya Skovoroda is an ensemble of buildings comprising the **Kyiv-Mohyla Akademy**, the first higher education institution in Ukraine established in 1615. The main building is the yellow curving facade with the large classical portico, although the oldest structure is the white building on the far northern corner

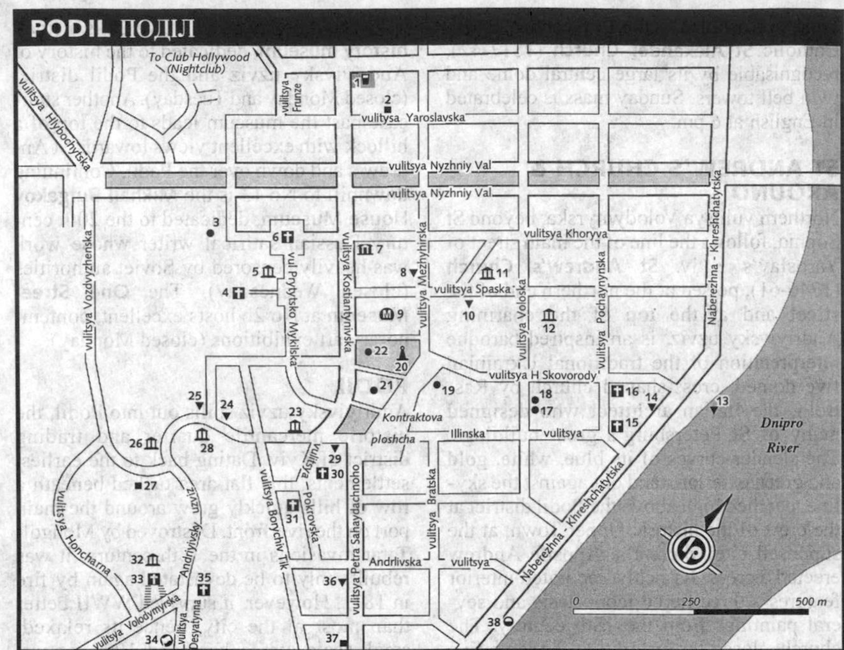

of Kontraktova ploshcha with the dome of the **Holy Spirit Church** (1703) rising from its far eastern end.

Vulitsya Spaska runs north-east to the waterfront. The **Chornobyl Museum** (☎ 417 54 22, ☎ 416 16 38), housed in a former fire tower at provulok Zhoreviy 1, contains a fascinating exhibition on the worst nuclear accident in history to date. Numerous photographs document the work of the early clean-up crews exposed to severe radiation, the six firemen who died on May 1986 immediately after the disaster, and the harrowing repercussions years on. The museum is open from 10 am to 6 pm (until 5 pm on Saturday, closed Sunday and the last Monday of the month). Admission is free; guided tours (book in advance, $5) are available in Russian or Ukrainian, but you don't need any linguistic skills to comprehend the disturbing video footage shot during the clean-up. The museum attendants will let you watch it for a $2.50 donation.

Set back from the street at vulitsya Spaska 16B is a 17th century house with a classical portico. Inside is the **Museum Hetmanstva**, dedicated to the hetmans, the Cossack chieftains of Ukraine. The house, budynok Mazepa, is named after the last great Ukrainian Cossack leader to rise up against Russian domination. Allied with the Swedes, Hetman Mazepa was wiped out by Russian troops in the battle of Poltava (1709). A block south-east is **Naberezhno-Mykilska Church**, two separate churches topped with green domes. The beige church in front dates from the 1860s, while the fanciful white baroque church behind is 100 years older. Farther down vulitsya Pochaynynska, at No 2, is the attractive **Illinska Church** (1692).

Nestled to the west of Kontraktova ploshcha are a tight pack of ecclesiastical and historic buildings. Vulitsya Prytytsko Mykilska curves north-west to the **Florivsky Monastery**, a 15th century women's con-

PODIL ПОДІЛ

PLACES TO STAY
- 2 Hotel Domus Домус Готель
- 27 Andrew's Hotel & Hotel Vozdvyzhensky Готель Андріївський та Готель Воздвиженський
- 37 Hotel Impressa Готель Імпреса

PLACES TO EAT
- 8 Gavroche Гаврош
- 10 Tequila House Текіла Хаус
- 13 Huturok Хуторок
- 14 Arizona Арізона
- 24 Kafe-Theatre Koleso Кафе-театр Колесо
- 25 Art Kafe Арт Кафе
- 29 San Tori Сан Торі
- 36 Zaporozje Запоріжжя

METRO STATIONS
- 9 Kontraktova Ploshcha Контрактова площа

OTHER
- 1 Club Al Capone Клуб Ал Капон
- 3 Podil Market Поділ ринок
- 4 Florivsky Monastery Флорівський монастир
- 5 Apteka Museum Аптека-музей
- 6 Church of Mykola Prytysko Церква Микола Притиска
- 7 House of Peter I Дім Петра
- 11 Chornobyl Museum Музей Чорнобиль
- 12 Museum Hetmanstva Музей Гетьманцтва
- 15 Illinska Church Іллінська церква
- 16 Naberezhno-Mykilska Church Набережно-Микільська церква
- 17 Kyiv-Mohyla Akademy & American Library Київ-Могилянська Академія та Американська Бібліотека
- 18 Japanese Centre Японський Центр
- 19 Kyiv-Mohyla Akademy Київ-Могилянська Академія
- 20 H Skovoroda Statue Пам'ятник Григорію Сковороді
- 21 Kontraktova Dim Контрактовий дім
- 22 Samson Fountain Фонтан Самсона
- 23 One Street Museum Музей Однієї Вулиш
- 26 Local History Museum Обласний історичний музей
- 28 Mikhail Bulgakov House Museum Музей М. О. Булгакова
- 30 Chapel Church of Mykola Dobry Церква Микола Доброго
- 31 Pokrovska Church & Bell Tower Покровська церква і дзвініниця
- 32 Ukraine History Museum Музей історії України
- 33 Desyatynna Church Десятинна церква
- 34 British Embassy Брітанский Посольства
- 35 St Andrew's Church Андріївська церква
- 38 Pier 5 Причал 5

vent, one of the few to defiantly remain open during communist times. It's entered through a unique 1740 bell tower with four classical pediments and a Renaissance cupola rising from the middle, designed by the same architect who designed the Kontraktova Dim.

The first building in the complex is the three cupola **Voznesenka Church** (1732), with a traditional Orthodox interior. Behind it is the 17th century **Trapezna Church & Refectory**. The **Voskresenska Krystovna Church** (1824), built up against the hill at the eastern end of the complex, has a unique colonnaded rotunda facade. To the right of Florivsky Monastery is Kyiv's first public pharmacy (1728), still open today and housing the fascinating **Apteka Museum** (closed Monday).

A short distance north, the street ends at the oldest standing structure in the Podil, the **Church of Mykola Prytysko** (1631), its design based on an earlier wooden church which previously stood on the site. Its whitewashed, green-roofed exterior is a lovely example of early Ukrainian baroque. Inside, past the long dark entrance narthex, are some angelic remains of an original 17th century fresco above the apse.

South of Kontraktova ploshcha off vulitsya Pokrovska at No 6 is the **Chapel Church of Mykola Dobry** (1716) with a beautiful, colonnaded upper gallery, and **Pokrovska Church & Bell Tower** (1766) at No 7. At vulitsya Pokrovska 14 is a palace dating from 1808, now the residence of the American ambassador.

Farther south, vulitsya Petra Sahaydachnoho runs into Poshtova ploshcha and the main river terminal. Opposite is a funicular (1905) which climbs the wooded slope to Mykhaylivska ploshcha.

SHEVCHENKO PARK & AROUND

Interesting museums ring Shevchenko Park. In the park is a statue of the man half of Ukraine is named after – Taras Shevchenko, the multitalented 19th century nationalist poet-artist (see the boxed text 'Taras Shevchenko' in the Facts about Ukraine chapter).

The **Taras Shevchenko Museum** (☎ 224 25 56), bulvar Tarasa Shevchenka 12, has a collection of over 4000 of his own and his contemporaries' artistic and literary works, displayed in sumptuous settings to the sounds of classical music. It's open from 10 am to 6 pm (closed Monday and the last Friday of the month). Admission costs $0.25. Kyiv's last remaining **Lenin** peers across at Shevchenko from his perch at the east end of bulvar Tarasa Shevchenka.

On the eastern side of the park are the **Russian Art Museum**, vulitsya Tereshchenkivska 9, and the **Western & Oriental Art Museum**, vulitsya Tereshchenkivska 15. The Russian collection is one of the best outside the museums of Moscow and St Petersburg, and is open from 10 am to 6 pm (until 8 pm on Friday, closed Thursday). There are 35 rooms, with over 2000 paintings, including early Novgorod, Rostov-Suzdal and Moscow icons and a fine collection from the second half of the 19th century, including Repin, Levitan, Ayvazovsky, Vrubel, plus Vasily Vereshchagin's powerful antiwar canvas, *The Conquerors*. The Western & Oriental collection has many Byzantine icons and impressive artefacts from ancient Egypt, China and Japan.

The red classical building along the western side of the park is **Kyiv University** (1837-43). In 1901 Tsar Nicholas I ordered the building to be painted blood red in response to student protests against mandatory conscription into his army. After its destruction in WWII it was rebuilt.

Surrounded by a small park, **St Volodymyr's Cathedral** (1862-96), bulvar Taras Shevchenka 20, has a seven cupola neo-Bzyantine exterior with baroque elements mixed into the three-dimensional facade. The cathedral has a spectacular interior, which is dark yet highlighted with Art Nouveau wall paintings emblazoned with gold accents.

Directly behind the Universytet metro station, a block west down bulvar Tarasa Shevchenka, are the spacious **Fomin Botanical Gardens**, laid out in 1841 and named after the prominent 1920s botanist Alexander Fomin.

FROM KHRESHCHATYK TO THE CAVES MONASTERY

The 2.5km from the northern end of Khreshchatyk to the Caves Monastery is a pleasant route, with several possible stops along the way. Trolleybus No 20 running north on Khreshchatyk will take you all the way, running south-east along vulitsya Hrushevskoho, the main road stretching along the ridge high above the Dnipro. Arsenalna metro station is midway along the route.

The few quiet backstreets branching south-east uphill from the northern end of vulitsya Khreshchatyk have numerous interesting buildings mingled in, so it's a worthwhile and pleasant stroll. Across from Hotel Moskva up a staircase high above vulitsya Instytutska is the 1840s **Palace of Culture & Arts**. Farther uphill, at No 9A, is the whimsical early 20th century pseudo-Renaissance **National Bank of Ukraine Headquarters**, with several snarling lion heads staring down from the facade. Around the corner at vulitsya Bankivska 2 is the former palace residence of a sugar merchant, now the **Union of Ukrainian Writers**, home of a group of influential literary and intellectual dissidents. Farther down, at No 10, is a building affectionately known as the **House of Monsters**. Designed by the local architect Horodetsky, the facade is covered with sculptural motifs of the animal kingdom – deer, rhinoceros and elephant heads, perched giant frogs and some mythical aquatic creatures adorning the top corners. Other monsters reside in the massive and imposing **Presidential Administration Building** opposite.

The Doric temple front of the **Museum of Ukrainian Fine Arts**, vulitsya Hrushevskoho 6, is guarded by two large lions. Inside, 21 rooms on two floors give a comprehensive view of seven centuries of fine art in Ukraine. The portraits of Lenin in various guises displayed in the 1950s and 1960s halls are particularly fun. About 500m farther, behind the **Parliament** (1939) building, the facade of which is still adorned with hammer and sickles, is the blue-and-white baroque **Mariyinsky Palace** (1747-55). The palace, based on a Rastrelli design, is used by the president to receive foreign dignitaries, but can be visited with a Russian or Ukrainian-speaking guide on Wednesday and Saturday between 2 and 5 pm. Tours (☎ 293 49 09) have to be booked in advance at Kyiv History Museum.

To reach **Kyiv History Museum**, a former palace, turn right into the next street to the west, vulitsya Lypska. Open from 10 am to 5 pm (closed Friday), its 14 rooms and two floors take you on an excellent historical journey with numerous wall paintings, old maps, models of the city and hundreds of artefacts.

Beyond Arsenalna metro, vulitsya Hrushevskoho becomes vulitsya Sichnevoho Povstannya. In parkland to the left of Dniprovsky proizd, which forks down towards the river, is a small 1810 church-rotunda – on the supposed site of **Askold's grave**. In Eternal Glory Park (Park Vichny Slavy) alongside vulitsya Sichnevoho Povstannya is an eternal flame and the graves of WWII heroes.

CAVES MONASTERY

Founded 3km south of where Kyiv stood in 1051, the Caves Monastery (Pechersk Lavra) was Kyivan Rus' first monastery. Spread across wooded slopes above the Dnipro, it's a unique array of gold domed churches, underground labyrinths lined with mummified monks, and elegant monastic buildings turned museums, one of which has a hoard of Scythian gold to rival that of the Hermitage in St Petersburg. It's the single most fascinating and extensive tourist site in the city. You need a full day to get a half-decent introduction to the whole place, although you can visit the caves and a couple of highlights in about three hours. The caves are not for the seriously claustrophobic, since their underground passages are narrow, low and often crowded. Avoid visiting on Sunday.

The monks dug out and lived in the caves where their preserved bodies now are. But the monastery so prospered that the Dormition Cathedral was built in 1073-89. This was Kyiv's second great Byzantine-inspired church, which in turn inspired the 12th century churches of Russia's Golden Ring. The monastery became Kyivan Rus' intellectual centre, producing chronicles and icons and training builders and artists. Wrecked by the Tatars in 1240, it went through a series of revivals and disastrous fires before being mostly rebuilt. The monastery was made into a museum in 1926, but part of it – the Farther Caves and their buildings – was returned to the Orthodox Church in 1988 and is inhabited by some 70 monks today.

Pechersk means 'of the caves'; a *lavra* is a senior monastery. The complex is divided into the Upper Lavra and, south, the Lower Lavra. The latter contains the caves, divided into the Nearer and Farther.

Getting There & Admission

Trolleybus No 20 east along Khreshchatyk, or south along vulitsya Hrushevskoho and vulitsya Sichnevoho Povstannya, goes to the monastery. The monastery complex (☎ 290 66 46) is open from 9.30 am to 6 pm (closed Tuesday). The two ticket booths, either side of Trinity Gate Church, the main entrance, close at 5 pm. Admission costs $2/1 for adults/children (plus a $3 camera fee) and allows access to all the museums *except* the Great Belfry, Historical Treasures Museum and Museum of Microminiature, which command a separate admission fee.

To visit the caves, you need to buy a candle ($0.15) from the kiosks next to the cave entrance; both sets of caves are open from 8 am to 4.30 pm. Women have to cover their head with a scarf and men are obliged to remove their hats. Wearing shorts is forbidden.

The excursion bureau, on the left inside the main entrance, arranges guided tours in English, French, Ukrainian and Russian; a private guide costs $20 for two hours.

Trinity Gate Church

The main entrance is through the striking Trinity Gate Church, a well preserved piece of early 12th century Rus architecture. Rebuilt in the 18th century, it once doubled as a watchtower and as part of the original monastery fortifications. Note the scorpions, fish and animals below the holy types in the entrance passage. The exterior and tiny interior were elaborately painted by leading Kyiv artists in 1734-44. Look up to see the dramatic scene of Christ upsetting the temple marketplace, above the interior doorway. The carved and gilded wooden iconostasis is 17th century, and the wooden benches are 200 years old, reserved for the elderly monks who could not take the standing-only Orthodox rituals. Two lines of **monks' dormitories** dating from the 18th century stretch out from the Gate Church.

St Nicholas' Church

Just north of Trinity Gate Church is the small, late 17th century St Nicholas' Church, with its blue dome adorned with golden stars. Inside is a temporary exhibit hall. Farther around is the Museum of Theatre, Music & Cinematic Art. Modern dramatic theatre was actually first introduced in Kyiv during the 17th century by students of the Caves Monastery.

Dormition Cathedral & Great Belfry

In the centre of the Upper Lavra are the ruins of the once-magnificent Orthodox Dormition Cathedral. By the year 2000, the cathedral should be rebuilt. Its destruction was originally blamed on the Germans; it was later proven to have been intentionally mined by the Red Army, supposedly to 'slow' the advance of German forces (as if the cathedral was a major obstacle). Only one of the cathedral's gold domes still stands. The vaulted space beneath the dome still has fragments of frescoes.

Towering to the left rises the cathedral's 96.5m-tall **Great Belfry** (1731-44). To climb the bell tower's 174 steps, purchase a separate ticket ($1.20) at the kiosk inside. The view from the top offers 360 degree panoramas over the entire complex.

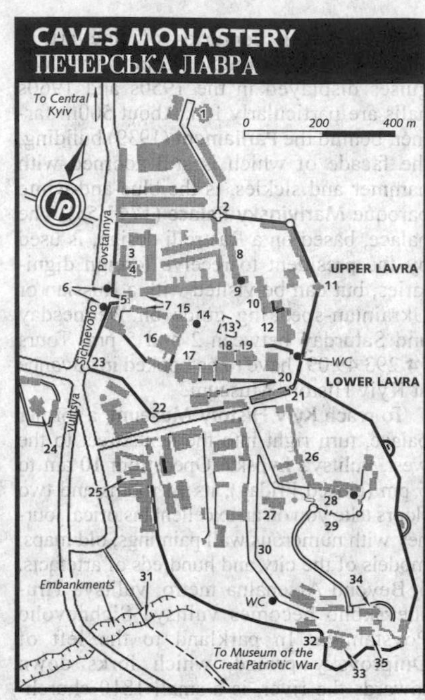

Refectory & Church

Directly south of Dormition Cathedral are the refectory and the Refectory Church of St Anthony & Theodosius, sporting the monastery's most famous gold-striped dome (1885-1905). Now a working church, the main domed space is slightly reminiscent of Istanbul's Hagia Sophia, with its ring of small narrow windows along the base of the drum. The adjacent former refectory has two elegant rows of narrow columns. Both interiors are beautifully painted with biblical scenes, saints and Art Nouveau patterns.

Historical Treasures Museum

North of Dormition Cathedral, this museum is devoted mainly to historic items and precious stones or metal found or made in Ukraine. The highlight is the upstairs

CAVES MONASTERY ПЕЧЕРСЬКА ЛАВРА

1 Church of the Saviour at Berestovo
Церква Спаса на Берестові
2 All Saints' Church
Церква Усіх Св'ятих
3 Museum of Theatre, Music & Cinematic Art
Музей театрального, музичного та кіномистецтва України
4 St Nicholas' Church & Exhibition Hall
Церква Св. Миколая та галя вистав
5 Trinity Gate Church & Main Entrance
Троїцька Надбрамна церква та головного вхід
6 Ticket Booths
Каси
7 Monks' Dormitories & Exhibition Galleries
Монаш спальні та виставка-галерія
8 Husbandry Building
Економический корпус
9 Ticket Booth for Historical Treasures Museum
Каса історичних коштовностей музей
10 Historical Treasures Museum
Музей історичних коштовностей України
11 Onufry Tower (1696-1701)
Онуфрійська вежа
12 Ukrainian Museum of Books & Printing
Музей книги та друкарства України
13 Dormition Cathedral
Успенського собора
14 Former Monastery Well & Ticket Booth for Bell Tower & Museum of Microminiature
Бувша монастирська студня, каса на дзвінниця та музей мікромініатюри
15 Bell Tower
Дзвінниця
16 Museum of Microminiature
Музей Мікромініатюри
17 Ukrainian Folk Decorative Art Museum
Музей Українського народного декоративного мистецтва
18 Refectory
Трапезна палата
19 Refectory Church of St Anthony & Theodosius
Трапезна церква Св. Антонія та Феодосія
20 Lookout Point
Видова площадка
21 Southern Gate of Upper Lavra
Південна брама верхньої лаври
22 Clock Tower (1696-1701)
Годинникова вежа
23 Ivan Kushnyk Tower (1696-1701)
Вежа Івана Кушника
24 Church of St Theodosius
Церква Св. Феодосія
25 Church of the Resurrection (1701-05)
Церква Воскресіння
26 Bell Tower of Nearer Caves
Дзвінниця блищчих печер
27 History of Religion & Culture Museum
Музей історії релігії та культури
28 Church of the Raising of the Cross
Хрестовоздвиженська церква
29 Entrance to Nearer Caves
Вхід до ближчих печер
30 Path to Farther Caves
Перехід до дальших печер
31 Moskovska Gate (18th century)
Московська брама
32 Bell Tower of Farther Caves
Дзвінниця для дальших печер
33 Church of the Nativity of the Virgin
Церква Різдва Богородиці
34 Church of the Conception of St Ann & Entrance to Farther Caves
Аннозачатвська церква вхід до дальших печер
35 Exit from Farther Caves
Вихід з дальших печер

display of a fabulous hoard of gold jewellery worked for the Scythians by Greek Black Sea colonists, much of which comes from two, 4th century BC burial mounds – the Tolstaya grave in the Dnipropetrovsk region and the Gaimana grave in the Zaporizhzhya region. The jewellery is unbelievably well crafted, especially when one grasps how old it really is (around 2500 years old). From the Tolstaya grave comes possibly the most magnificent Scythian piece of all – a large mid-4th century BC gold pectoral (a sort of large necklace) covered with superbly detailed animals and everyday scenes. Next to it is a detailed golden scabbard. Downstairs, past the 12th century model of Kyiv, are exhibits of richly ornamented goblets, crosses, chalices and icons, crafted by Ukrainian, Russian, Polish and Lithuanian masters. The Historical Treasures Museum requires a separate entrance ticket, purchased at the kiosk in the building north of the museum.

Ukrainian Museum of Books & Printing

Housed in the 18th century printshop, exhibits include a large display of books, printing presses, wood blocks, etchings and exhibits on famous Ukrainian authors.

Ukrainian Folk Decorative Art Museum

In the former Metropolitan's House (1727), this is one of the city's most fascinating museums. Among the exhibits is an excellent display of different folk dress from each oblast within Ukraine.

Museum of Microminiature

Housed in the former library, this unusual and popular exhibition displays various tiny complex creations, so small that microscopes are needed to view them. The work of Russian artist Nikolai Siadristy, the creations include the world's smallest electric motor, smallest book (with some verses of Shevchenko), smallest complete chess set (placed on the head of a nail) and a flea fitted with golden horseshoes.

All Saints' Church & the Church of the Saviour at Berestovo

The All Saints' Church (1696-98) over the monastery's northernmost service gate is a beautifully composed example of early Ukrainian baroque architecture. Its narrow and lofty interior has fine, early 20th century murals with a youthful-looking Christ glaring down from the central dome.

Farther north outside the service gate lies the Church of the Saviour at Berestovo, built by Volodymyr Monomakh as a burial church for his dynasty. Of the original church, only the western narthex stands, now forming the central crossing and transepts. Much of an original 12th century fresco, *Christ Appearing to His Disciples at the Sea of Tiberias*, was uncovered during the 1970s above the arch on the western wall of the crossing.

Nearer Caves

The Nearer Caves are reached by walking east under a short series of buttressed arches flying off the southern facade of the Museum of Books & Printing. Follow the path between the perimeter walls, and through the Southern Gate (1795) to enter the Lower Lavra. Before turning into the Nearer Caves, the path veers to the right and leads down past the **History of Religion & Culture Museum**. Across the path is the Bell Tower (1763) of the Nearer Caves. The **Church of the Raising of the Cross** (1700), with its colourful 1769 iconostasis, is beside the caves' entrance.

There's no fee to visit the caves, but it's courteous (and illuminating) to buy a candle from the stall before you enter, to carry with you throughout the passages. You follow a fixed route through about 200m of the Nearer Caves' reputed 500m of passages. Dozens of niches contain open, glass-topped coffins with mummified monks' bodies, all tastefully covered apart from the occasional protruding toe or finger. There's also an underground dining hall and three subterranean churches, decorated during the 18th and 19th centuries. The tomb of Nestor, the presumed author of the 11th century *Tales of Bygone Years*, the oldest Eastern Slavic chronicle, is on the right some way after St Varlaam's, the second church, just before the main concentration of burial niches. Also look for Antony, the monastery's first monk; the chroniclers Nikon the Great, Simon and Polikarp; the early Rus icon painters Alimpy and Hryhorii; and the 12th century healers Damian and Agapit. Many of those entombed here are saints, making the caves a sacred site and a visit akin to a pilgrimage for Orthodox believers. Visiting the caves when they're not crowded can be a very moving experience.

Farther Caves

The Farther Caves were the originals and belong to the church today. The entrance is in the **Church of the Conception of St Ann** (1679). Uphill is the seven domed **Church of the Nativity of the Virgin** (1696). Rising to the right is the unusual high-baroque **Bell Tower of Farther Caves** (1761). The Farther Caves have about 280m of passages, but the visitors' route is shorter than in the Nearer Caves. The passages are also lined with ornamented mummified monks (spot the exposed hand) and contain three underground churches.

Beyond the Caves Monastery

She Who Must Be Obeyed, Mother Russia or Tin Tits are some of the many names coined for the giant 72m-high, metallic statue of a woman brandishing a sword and shield. Formally known as the **Defence of the Motherland Monument**, she dominates any view of Kyiv from the opposite bank of the Dnipro. Her original height had to be lowered so as not to rise above the Caves Monastery's bell tower.

Before reaching the statue, you pass the **Afghan War Museum** (☎ 295 88 62), offering a rather one-sided glimpse into the horrors of the nine year conflict. Outside the museum is an open-air museum of WWII-era Soviet military, including tanks, artillery, planes and armoured personnel carriers. The **Ukrainian Museum of the Great Patriotic War** (☎ 295 94 52), vulitsya Sichnevoho Povstannya 44, directly beneath the statue, hosts an extensive and excellent display well worth the $0.50 admission fee. Both museums are open from 10 am to 5 pm (closed Monday). In the grounds is an elevated walkway, beneath which are several sculptural bas-reliefs representing the genre of Socialist Realism at its best.

Lovely **Vydubytsky Monastery**, vulitsya Vydubytsky 40, is about 1km south of the motherland monument, on a small loop road off Na Dnepryanske shose, south of the busy Paton Bridge intersection. The walk is mostly downhill. Alternatively, tram Nos 27 and 35 from Arsenalna metro, or Nos 21, 31, 32 and 34 from Dnipro metro go to Paton Bridge. Vydubytsky was founded in the 11th century, but was mostly rebuilt in the 17th and 18th centuries. Enter next to the blue and gold-roofed **bell tower** (1727-33). To your right is the centrepiece, the five domed **St George's Cathedral** (1696-1701). Its detailing is exquisite, rising straight from a simple cruciform plan. Past the refectory buildings and at the foot of the grounds is the oldest building of the complex, **St Michael's Church** (1070-88). The church is only partial, as the bulk of the structure fell into the river in the 16th century, then was rebuilt in the 1760s. To the right as you enter is the only original fresco, a dark 11th century Last Judgement scene. Uphill and behind the monastery are the **Ukraine Academy of Sciences Botanical Gardens**, especially fragrant in spring and with attractive views of the Dnipro.

EAST BANK & RIVER TRIPS

The low-lying islands and promontories on the Dnipro's east bank are mainly woods and parkland, much of which is taken up by **Hidropark**, an outdoor fun park. The white sandy beaches straddling the river are packed with sunbathers and swimmers in summer; those closer to Hidropark pier are used by winter bathers too. To get to the islands, take the metro to Hidropark, or cross the Dnipro footbridge directly below the rainbow arch. Between May and mid-October, there are boats from the river terminal to Lokomotiv pier. On the east side, boats link several spots such as Hidropark (near the metro), Spartak (south of the footbridge), Dovbychka and Rusanovsky Sady.

Kyiv panorama boats – great for cooling down amid the scorching heat – also sail in summer. Boats (☎ 416 12 68, ☎ 416 55 33) depart every hour between 8 am and 11 pm from the river terminal; tickets are sold at the kiosk at pier No 11 ($1.25/2.50 for a one/two hour trip). Alternatively, hire a nippy speedboat ($100 per hour) or a more sedate yacht to sail along the river; contact the Mandrivnyk Travel Company (see Travel Agencies earlier).

ST CYRIL'S & BABYN YAR

St Cyril's Church (☎ 435 21 23), close to the corner of vulitsya Oleny Telihi and vulitsya Frunze, about 5km north-west of the centre, has five pea-green cupolas of varying sizes which rise out of a wooded hillside. Dating to the 12th century, when it was part of a larger monastery, its present exterior is an 18th century Ukrainian baroque reconstruction. The striking interior bears numerous murals covering over 800 sq metres; those in the choir, accessible via a steep stone staircase, feature the descending of the Holy Spirit and date from 1888. St Cyril's is open from 10 am to 5.30 pm (until 4.30 pm on Thursday, closed Friday). Admission costs $1.50. Take trolleybus No 27 from Shulyavska or Petrivka metro to the Kyrylivska Tserkva stop on vulitsya Oleny Telihi, from where steps lead up to St Cyril's green domes.

Killing Fields

On 29-31 September 1941, Nazi troops rounded up Kyiv's Jewish population and marched them to the Babyn Yar ravine where an estimated 34,000 Jews were massacred in 48 hours. They were shot and buried in the ravine. Between 1941 and 1943, the Nazis used Babyn Yar as a concentration camp, called Syrets after the Kyivan suburb it was in. During the Soviet regime, the ravine was filled and topped in parts with concrete apartment blocks.

The first memorial to the estimated 100,000 people – including Jews, Roma (Gypsies) and partisans – killed at Babyn Yar was erected in 1976. Children play football in the green gullies surrounding the dramatic sculptural ensemble and weekend strollers happily picnic in the surrounding park today. It was not until 1991 that a special memorial to the Jewish victims – a seven armed Hanukkah – was unveiled. A path leads from vulitsya Melnikova 44, past a TV station, to the secluded spot where the statue was erected.

About 1.5km south-west of St Cyril's across the parkland, between vulitsya Oleny Telihi, vulitsya Melnikova and vulitsya Dorohozhitska, is **Babyn Yar** – the site of Nazi WWII killing fields (see the boxed text 'Killing Fields'). Take trolleybus No 27 from Shulyavska or Petrivka metro to the Babyn Yar stop on vulitsya Oleny Telihi or trolleybus No 16 from maydan Nezalezhnosti to vulitsya Melnikova.

FOLK ARCHITECTURE MUSEUM

The Museum of Folk Architecture and Everyday Life in Ukraine is 12km south of the centre, between the villages of Pyrohovo and Feofania. Spread out over scenic rolling hills dotted with groves of trees are a large number of quaint 17th to 20th century wooden cottages, churches, farmsteads and windmills, many with manicured flower and vegetable gardens and interiors furnished with fascinating old textiles, traditional furniture and tools. The museum is divided into seven villages representing the regional areas of eastern Ukraine, Poltava and Slobeda, Polesia, Podelia, the Carpathian region and southern Ukraine. Highlights include St Paraskeva Church from the village of Zarubyntsi (eastern Ukraine) and the Church of Mother Protectress from Kanora (Carpathia).

Summer long, the museum is filled with people strolling, sunbathing or sprawled out around a picnic hamper. Barbecued shashlyk is sold around the park and there are a couple of restaurants where you can feast on traditional Ukrainian delights. There is a large sunken restaurant in the Sloboda village; and in eastern Ukraine, not far from the main entrance, is a 19th century *shynok* (Cossack pub). Ukrainian musicians play here at weekends. In a whitewashed cottage nearby is a small gift shop (with extortionate prices). Throughout the year the museum (☎ 266 24 16, ☎ 266 14 69) hosts various festivals. It is open from 10 am to 5 pm (until 4 pm in winter). Admission costs $0.50 (plus $0.50 camera fee).

To get to the museum, take trolleybus No 4 or 11 from Lybidska metro to VDNKh stop (the Ukrainian Exhibition of Economic Achievements), then bus No 24 to the end of the line; or take a taxi ($10 each way).

SPECIAL EVENTS

The most important events in Kyiv are:

January

Epiphany

Scores of the (more hardy) faithful leap into the Dnipro to celebrate the arrival of Christianity in Kyivan Rus. Those not into swimming in the ice-cold river bring buckets of water to the islands off Hidropark to be blessed by the Kyiv patriarch.

May

The Kyiv Days

Centred around Andriyivsky uzviz, this takes place the last weekend in May.

October

Kyiv International Music Festival

Kicks off during the first week in October.

Kyiv International Film Festival Molodist

An annual event (www.uis.kiev.ua/~molodist) which takes place during the last week in October.

KYIV

PLACES TO STAY – BUDGET

Kyiv lacks budget accommodation, so don't contemplate staying in the capital unless you are prepared to fork out $50 for a room in a horribly overpriced establishment.

It is about 10% cheaper to book (and pay) for your hotel accommodation in advance through a travel agency (see Information – Travel Agencies).

Camping

Prolisok Tourist Complex *(☎ 451 80 38, ☎ 451 90 37, fax 451 90 39, prospekt Peremohy 139)* is 12km west of the centre and a hassle to reach by public transport. You can pitch your tent among quiet pine trees for $5 per person. The complex's sauna and traditional Ukrainian restaurants are open to campers. From Svyatoshyn metro station, take bus No 37 westwards down prospekt Peremohy, or trolleybus No 7 which turns off prospekt Peremohy halfway.

Apartments & Homestays

At the train station, look for babushkas brandishing signs advertising *kimnaty* (rooms to rent). Check exactly where the room is on a map before agreeing on a price.

You can rent a furnished apartment through Hotel Service (☎/fax 295 88 32, hotel@hotel.kiev.ua, http://hotel.kiev.ua). A one/two/three room apartment in the centre starts at $65/110/130. Hotel Service has an office in the arrivals hall at Boryspil airport (open from 9 am to 8 pm).

Chervona Ruta (see Information – Travel Agencies earlier) arranges homestays in the city for $45/65/90 for one/two/three people a night, including breakfast.

Hotels

Hotel Ekspres *(☎ 221 89 95, fax 221 89 47, bulvar Taras Shevchenka 38/40, metro Vokzalna or Universytet)*, adjoining the advance train ticket office, is a five minute walk uphill from the station. Basic singles/doubles start at $30/46; breakfast is $4.

Kyiv's other 'cheap' hotels are all within walking distance of Lybidska metro. ***Hotel Holoseevskaya*** *(☎ 261 41 16, fax 263 78 35, prospekt 40-richchya Zhovtnya 93)* has rooms for $15/28, not including breakfast. Nearby ***Hotel Mir*** *(☎ 264 96 46, fax 264 96 51, prospekt 40-richchya Zhovtnya 70)* has made some renovation attempts, hence the hefty $66/77 it charges for ageing rooms. Breakfast is $2. To get to either of these hotels, take trolleybus No 4, 11 or 12 from Lybidska metro.

Another budget joint is the rough-and-tumble ***Hotel Druzhba*** *(☎ 268 34 06, ☎ 268 33 00, fax 268 90 38, bulvar Druzhby Narodiv 5)*, ironically adjoining Kyiv's most exclusive sports club. The 1970s block has rooms for an astonishing $41/70. From Lybidska metro, walk towards the overpass along vulitsya Chervonoarmiyska for 200m, then turn left along bulvar Druzhby Narodiv.

Hotel Saint Petersburg *(☎ 229 73 67, ☎ 229 74 72, ☎ 229 74 17, bulvar Taras Shevchenka 4, metro Teatralna)* is not bad value, given its central location. Rooms with shared bathroom cost $30 and rooms with private bath start at $50. The reception staff speak absolutely no English.

At the top of this price range is ***Hotel Kozatsky*** *(☎ 229 27 09, fax 229 49 25, vulitsya Mykhaylivska 1/3, metro Maydan Nezalezhnosti)*, well placed overlooking Independence Square. A double with one/two beds costs $66/77 and luxury rooms start at $78. Breakfast is $8.

PLACES TO STAY – MID-RANGE

Kyiv's mid-range hotels clock in at around $100/130 a night for a single/double room with all the perks. Exceptional value are the few unrenovated rooms at upmarket ***Hotel Rus*** (see Places to Stay – Top End).

For a small and cosy option, try the charming ***Andrew's Hotel*** *(☎ 416 04 11, ☎ 463 77 89, fax 416 41 40, andrey@economix.kiev.ua, vulitsya Vozdvyzhenska 60, metro Poshtova Ploshcha)*, spitting distance from St Andrew's Church in the bohemian neighbourhood of Podil. Unfortunately, its 41 rooms starting at $80/111 for a single/double are often booked out. If so, try the lesser known ***Hotel Vozdvyzhensky*** *(☎ 462 58 43, fax 462 57 48)* which has 18 rooms from $120/165 on the 4th floor of the same building.

Overlooking central Khreshchatyk is ***Hotel Khreshchatyk*** *(☎ 229 71 93, ☎ 229 73 39, fax 229 85 44, Khreshchatyk 14, metro Maydan Nezalezhnosti)* which has $100/120 rooms. Opposite, set back off the busy boulevard, is the Stalinist ***Hotel Moskva*** *(☎ 229 03 47, vulitsya Instytutska 4, metro Maydan Nezalezhnosti)*, a 1960s Soviet-style replica of the original in the Russian capital. Some rooms on the 13th floor have a view of St Sophia Cathedral. Sleazy kiosks, slot machines and bars adorn the ground level reception area. Room prices are $128/144.

Opposite the circus is the 'better-value' ***Hotel Lybid*** *(☎ 274 00 63, fax 224 05 78, ploshcha Peremohy 1, metro Vokzalna or Universytet)*. Indisputably ugly from the outside, its renovated interior houses numerous facilities. Rooms here cost $115/125, including breakfast.

Hotel Ukraina *(☎ 229 28 07, ☎ 229 28 14, ☎ 229 28 18, fax 229 87 72, bulvar Tarasa Shevchenka 5, metro Teatralna)* is the only hotel housed in an elegant prewar building (1908). It has old-world charm and a striking central staircase. Rooms with high ceilings cost $137/164. Facilities include a couple of restaurants and bars, a post office, laundry, sauna, hairdressers and a handy shop in the lobby.

Heading westward, the ***Prolisok Tourist Complex*** (see Camping earlier) has modern doubles, refurbished in 1998, for $90/110 in winter/summer. Sports enthusiasts keen to run a few laps of the track each morning should try ***Hotel Spartak*** *(☎ 435 69 64, ☎ 435 69 77, fax 435 63 16, vulitsya Frunze 105)*, around the corner from St Cyril's Church. Singles/doubles start at $100 (20% discount if you pay in cash). Rates include free use of its swimming pool, running track and other sports facilities.

PLACES TO STAY – TOP END

Count on paying *at least* $150/200 a night in the capital's topnotch hotels.

Locals claim that ***Hotel Dnipro*** *(☎ 229 82 87, ☎ 228 09 89, fax 229 82 13, dnipro@ukrpack.net, Khreshchatyk 1/2, metro Maydan Nezalezhnosti)* is the only hotel to have been properly debugged – the reason diplomats stay at this unbelievably overpriced, but still busy, Intourist-style hotel. Unrenovated singles/doubles cost $137/150 and renovated ones start at $187/222; prices include breakfast.

Kyiv's leading 'package group' hotels are a short distance from the city heart (metro Palats Sportu or Klovska). First in line is the former Intourist ***President Hotel Kyivsky*** *(☎ 220 19 34, ☎ 220 41 44, fax 220 45 68, vulitsya Hospitalna 12)*. Within the complex, there is a nightclub, business centre, conference facilities and the Stara Fortetsya (Old Fortress) taverna-cum-restaurant (☎ 294 39 91) which brews its own beer. Rooms cost $185/210 ($150/175 at weekends). Next door is ***Hotel Rus*** *(☎ 220 56 46, ☎ 220 42 55, fax 220 43 96, bcentrerus@hotelrus.kiev.ua, vulitsya Hospitalna 4)* which, despite its bland facade, buzzes with activity inside. Its unrenovated rooms cost $63/75 and are exceptionally good value. Renovated rooms up to Western norms start at $153/165.

Podil's quaint ***Hotel Domus*** *(☎ 416 25 68, ☎ 462 51 20, fax 462 51 45, vulitsya Yaroslavska 19, metro Kontraktova Ploshcha)* is the closest you'll find to a cosy, family-run hotel. Luxuriously clad, Italian-inspired rooms are $140/190 and breakfast is $10. Also in Podil, close to the river and funicular station, is ***Hotel Impressa*** *(☎ 417 00 27, ☎ 463 79 03, fax 463 79 02, vulitsya Petra Sahaydachnoho 21, metro Poshtova Ploshcha)*. Spacious five-star double rooms are $240.

In the upmarket Pecherskiy neighbourhood, near Parliament and Mariyinsky Palace, is ***Hotel Kyiv*** *(☎ 253 49 70, fax 253 64 32, vulitsya Hrushevskoho 26/1, metro Arsenalna)*, a renovated concrete block with rooms for $138/160 (entrance on vulitsya Lypska). Nearby, is the exclusive ***Hotel National*** *(☎ 291 88 88, ☎ 291 89 90, fax 291 54 68, vulitsya Lypska 5, metro Arsenalna)*, a grandiose place which makes no bones about its strict, foreigners-only policy. The richer you are, the better chance you have of passing face control at reception. Exceedingly luxurious rooms start at

$250. Continuing southwards towards Pechersk Lavra, you come to the extraordinarily ugly ***Hotel Salyut*** *(☎ 290 61 30, vulitsya Sichnevoho Povstannya 11, metro Arsenalna)*, built like a concrete space station. Despite the Lavra's golden domes sneaking into view from rooms on the top floor, rooms are still overpriced at $150/203, plus $10 per person for breakfast.

The five star ***Hotel Saint Sophia***, part of the Inter-Continental chain, primely placed overlooking Sofiyska ploshcha, promises to raise Kyiv's hotel scene to new heights when it opens in 2000. A ***Hilton*** hotel is also due to open, rumoured to be located in one of the prewar buildings under renovation opposite the Opera & Ballet Theatre or overlooking the Golden Gate.

PLACES TO EAT

Kyiv's dining prospects match any other European city – in choice and price. Exhaustive restaurant listings feature in the quarterly *Kyiv Business Directory* and the annual *Dining Out in Kyiv*, two free, bilingual publications.

Ukrainian Restaurants

Tsarske Selo *(☎ 290 30 66, ☎ 573 97 75, Sichnevoho Povstannya 42/1, metro Arsenalna)* is Kyiv's quintessential Ukrainian restaurant, decorated in a rustic 18th century manner. Dishes include a salted fish platter ($24) and antique cabbage soup ($7). Waiting staff wear straw hats, a waterfall trickles in the corner and complimentary garlic bread and *salo* greets you when you sit down. Adjoining Tsarske Selo is ***SSSR*** *(☎ 290 30 66)*, an inspired, open-air creation where you can sample all the culinary delights of the former Soviet Union (open in summer only).

Liver pie or herrings with green onions are some of the rustic treats served with a flourish aboard ***Huturok*** *(☎ 416 80 39, Naberezhna Khreshchatytska, berth 1, metro Kontraktova Ploshcha)*, a floating Ukrainian restaurant housed in a wooden boat.

Another riverside restaurant is the unique ***Kureni*** *(☎ 293 40 62, Parkova Doroha 4)*, an open-air place with traditional Cossack *kureni* (thatched huts), located just below Mariyinsky Palace; a trail leads from here down the hillside to Parkova aleia (open from noon to midnight).

Panoramic views of the Dnipro and its beach activities can be enjoyed from the balcony terrace of the waterfront ***Mlyn*** *(☎ 516 57 28, metro Hidropark)*, housed in an old wooden mill in Hidropark. Its KGB cocktail is a house speciality.

Ethnic Restaurants

Tucked by the side of the Golden Gate is the cosy, Italianate ***Pantagruel*** *(☎ 228 81 42, vulitsya Lysenka 1, metro Zoloti Vorota)*, housed in the whitewashed cellar of a 19th century townhouse. Main dishes average $10. Summer sees its tables and chairs spill onto the square outside.

Hunger pangs can be staved off at ***Uncle Sam*** *(☎ 227 20 00, vulitsya Zhilyanska 37, metro Ploshcha Lva Tolstoho)*, an American bistro bar serving everything from brownies, waffles and hot fudge sundaes to steaks, burgers and all-day breakfasts. It is open from 11.30 to 1 am. Equally American is the jam-packed ***Arizona*** *(☎ 416 24 38, Naberezhna Khreshchatytska 25, metro Kontraktova Ploshcha)*, overlooking the Dnipro. Despite its hefty prices, rich locals and expats alike come here in droves to sink their teeth into a New York steak ($25), washed down with a jug of margarita.

In Podil, giant-sized portions of nachos, tacos and enchiladas ensure the ***Tequila House*** *(☎ 417 03 58, vulitsya Spaska 8, metro Kontraktova Ploshcha)*, Kyiv's most authentic Mexican restaurant, is always packed. The frozen margaritas are divine, although the 'smelling sex' cocktail is less convincing. Count on paying $10 a head. It is open from 11 to 1 am (until 2 am at weekends).

Among Kyiv's most expensive joints is the Japanese ***San Tori*** *(☎ 462 49 94, vulitsya Petra Sahaydachnoho 41, metro Kontraktova Ploshcha)*, worth a trip for sushi fiends (open from 11 to 1 am).

For French cuisine in Podil, try the Alsatian ***Gavroche*** *(☎ 416 55 24, vulitsya Mezhyhirska 3/7, metro Kontraktova Ploshcha)* or ***Zaporozje*** *(☎ 417 42 83, vulitsya Petra Sahaydachnoho 27, metro Poshtova Ploshcha)* which has a different *degustation* menu ($50) each month. ***Château de Fleur*** *(☎ 228 78 00, Khreshchatyk 24, metro Maydan Nezalezhnosti)* is not particularly French, despite its name.

The outside terrace of ***Himalay*** *(☎ 462 04 37, Khreshchatyk 23)*, above Kievskoe Kafe, is one of the hottest places to people-watch in summer, although its curries are far from hot. Its vast menu is a good bet for vegetarians. Starters/mains cost around $2/6. For authentic Indian food, ***Bombay Palace*** *(☎ 224 44 05, vulitsya Kruty Uzviz)*, behind Bessarabsky Market, is reputed to be the best.

Farther afield is the refreshingly cheap ***Maximal*** *(☎ 268 37 68, vulitsya Horkoho, metro Palats Ukraina)*, serving Greek cuisine in a cosy atmosphere; it has live music most nights.

Cafes

Hot spots to hang out in the sun in summer include Pantagruel's outside cafe (see Ethnic Restaurants) that mushrooms around the fountain in front of the Golden Gate on vulitsya Volodymyrska; or the Andriyivsky uzviz cafes in Podil. ***Kafe-Theatre Koleso*** at No 8a and the roof terrace atop ***Art Kafe***, a couple of doors uphill, are particularly fine.

Trendy cafes dot the length of Khreshchatyk pasazh, a hip street accessed through an ornate archway at vulitsya Khreshchatyk 15. ***Smak*** and ***Nira***, the two balcony cafes either side of the archway, are hugely popular in summer. Just off Khreshchatyk, at Lenin's feet, sits ***Nika*** *(bulvar Taras Shevchenka 2)*, a simple cafe serving cheap and hearty fodder; the toilets are squeaky clean too.

Close to the Caves Monastery is the fun and funky ***Kafe Bar Vernisazh*** *(☎ 290 52 89, vulitsya Sichnevoho Povstannya 17a)*. Its grim exterior shelters a modern, industrial-style interior strewn with a collection of contemporary art. Live bands play here at weekends. It is open until 11 pm (3 am at weekends).

Atlanta *(☎ 220 00 91, vulitsya Chervonoarmiyska 56-58, metro Ploshcha Lva Tolstoho)* serves delicious salads in two sizes for no more than $1. Its bar – which sports Kyiv's most fabulous cocktail list – and the adjoining pool hall are popular evening venues.

Kaffa *(☎ 464 05 05, provulok Taras Shevchenka 3, metro Maydan Nezalezhnosti)* is an African-inspired coffee house, serving nothing but coffee ($2 a pot) in a strictly nosmoking atmosphere. Choose from traditional or aromatic beans; banana, orange and chocolate are all good.

Bon-Bon Kafe *(vulitsya Leontovycha 3, metro Universytet)*, a red and white steel edifice in front of the flashy Budapest Club, has a pleasant summer terrace and serves expensive cakes and cocktails. Equally pricey is ***Surpriz*** *(☎ 246 48 28, vulitsya Pirogova 3, metro Universytet)*, a Parisian-style patisserie sporting a fabulous terrace and genuine *pain au chocolat*, croissants and the like. Another pleasing option for the sweet-toothed is the cafe adjoining the Svitoch sweet shop (see Self-Catering).

Non-Stop *(☎ 216 40 73, prospekt Peremohy 6, metro Vokzalna or Universytet)*, spitting distance from the bus stop for Boryspil airport, has a delightful terrace and serves a good selection of salads, mains and crepes at $2 a throw. It is open 24 hours.

Pizza & Fast Food

Vesuvio Pizza *(☎ 228 30 28, vulitsya Reytarska 25, metro Zoloti Vorota)* is reputed to serve the best pizza in town. For a quick bite standing up, try busy ***Mr Snack*** *(vulitsya Horodetskoho 4, metro Maydan Nezalezhnosti)*. Alternatively head for ***Shelter***, in Khreshchatyk pasazh, where tacos, sweet and sour pork and donuts are doled out in a space with a station-style atmosphere.

Self-Catering

Bessarabsky Market is a bright and beautiful market hall with piles of fresh fruit, vegetables, nuts and hanging hunks of different meats (identifiable by the head displayed nearby). Imported products are also sold here. Locals frequent ***Volodymyrsky Market***, a cheaper market a block west of Palats Ukraina metro station. ***Podil Market***, at the west end of vulitsya Khoryva, is one of the cleanest and least harrowing markets for first-time shoppers in Kyiv.

Stock up on local wine at ***Vino*** *(bulvar Bohdana Khmelnytskoho 33, metro Universytet or Teatralna)*. Sweets galore are sold at ***Svitoch*** *(vulitsya Velyka Zhytomyrska 10)*, a sweet shop dating from 1882.

Bistro Gastronom Gril *(Yaroslaviv val 21/20, metro Zoloti Vorota)* is a small supermarket touting proper shopping trolleys; it is open from 8.30 am to 8 pm (9 am to 6 pm on Saturday and 9 am to 8 pm on Sunday). On the left bank, ***Bravo*** *(☎ 544 05 41, vulitsya Malishka 4a, metro Darnytsya)* serves an excellent array of fresh salads, cooked meats and Ukrainian *holubsti* at its delicatessen counter (open from 10 am to 11 pm). Farther afield is ***Euromart Cash & Carry*** *(☎ 568 99 61, vulitsya Alma-Atinska 12)* where you can shop in bulk cheaply.

ENTERTAINMENT

Kyiv's unofficial 'people's corner' is on maydan Nezalezhnosti and in the subway beneath Khreshchatyk.

Weekly entertainment listings are included in *What's On* (WhatsOn@carrier.kiev.ua) and the *Kyiv Post* (editor@thepost.kiev.ua, www.thepost.kiev.ua); both are free in major hotels and restaurants. Venue and seating plan details are faithfully listed in the *Kyiv Business Directory*.

Pubs & Bars

Friday night sees ***O'Brien's Irish Pub*** *(☎ 229 15 84, vulitsya Mykhaylivska 17a, metro Maydan Nezalezhnosti)* heaving with Kyiv's young and fun expatriate population. Open from 8 to 2 am, it serves local Slavutych beer ($2 a pint) and Guinness ($4.50 a pint), as well as an all-day breakfast and other wholesome 'Irish' dishes.

The ***John Bull Pub*** *(☎ 220 13 69, vulitsya Saksahanskoho 36)*, open from noon to the early hours, is as British as they get, with live jazz or blues bands playing most weekday evenings. The underground ***The Wall***, housed in the defunct fish chutes of Bessarabsky Market, is another expat and student hot spot, complete with digital TV showing most sporting events, a bilingual menu and a fun, fun, fun atmosphere.

Inside Khreshchatyk pasazh, in the basement of Shelter, is the ***Buddy Guy Blues Club*** where you can listen to jazz or blues. A couple of doors up is ***Cowboy Club***, a busy bar-cum-music club. Excellent bands play here at weekends, drawing a predominantly local crowd. In summer, the nearby ***Rock Cafe*** *(☎ 228 28 83, vulitsya Horodetskoho 10, metro Maydan Nezalezhnosti)*, open 11 to 3 am, is *the* place to drink in the sun.

Equally buzzing is ***Eric's*** *(vulitsya Chervonoarmiyska 20, metro Respublikansky Stadion or Ploshcha Lva Tolstoho)*, a heaving cellar bar run by an endearing East German called Eric who always wears dungarees, hence the dungaree-clad bar staff. Traditional German dishes like *bockwurst* feature on the bar menu and there is live music most nights. The bar (not signposted) is through an archway off the main street.

Discos & Clubs

Eric (a hybrid of 'Eckhardt' which no one locally could pronounce, hence the change in name) is famed in town for opening (and closing six months later) the city's top clubs. The clubs never have a sign outside, making them hard to find. ***Club Al Capone*** *(☎ 235 9472, vulitsya Kostiantynivska 26, metro Kontraktova Ploshcha)*, housed in a former cinema, is allegedly there to stay (open from 8 pm to 6 am; admission $1 to $3).

Mainstream clubs (read: featuring strip shows) include the floating ***River Palace*** *(☎ 416 82 04, Naberezhna Shose, metro Dnipro)*, open from 9 pm to 6 am (admission $10); ***Club Hollywood*** *(☎ 435 40 68, vulitsya Frunze 134, metro Kontraktova Ploshcha)*, open from 10 pm to 5 am; and ***Chicago*** *(☎ 517 41 48, vulitsya Raisy Okyonoyl 3, metro Livoberezhyna)*.

Big Boy Club *(☎ 441 44 32, Harmatna 26/2, metro Shulyavska)* is a gay club.

Rock

The ***Ukraina Palace*** *(☎ 247 23 76, ☎ 247 24 4, vulitsya Chervonoarmiyska 103, metro Respublikansky Stadion or Palats Ukraina)* is the top venue for rock and pop concerts.

Classical Music

Concerts are held at the ***National Philharmonic*** *(☎ 228 62 91, Volodymyrsky Uzviz 2)*. The ticket kasa (☎ 228 16 97) is open daily from noon to 3 pm and 4 to 7 pm (closed on Sunday).

Organ and chamber music recitals are hosted at ***St Nicholas' Church***, *(☎ 268 31 86, vulitsya Chervono-armiyska 75, metro Respublikansky Stadion or Palats Ukraina)*, the only piece of truly Gothic architecture in the city.

Cinemas

English-language films are screened at ***Kino Palace*** *(☎ 228 72 23, vulitsya Instytutska 2, metro Maydan Nezalezhnosti)*, inside the Palace of Culture & Arts opposite Hotel Moskva; and at ***Kinopanorama*** *(☎ 227 30 41, Rustaveli Shota 9, metro Palats Sportu)*.

Theatre

Kyiv has over 20 theatres presenting a wide range of performances in Ukrainian or Russian. Advance tickets and schedules are available at the ***Teatralna Kasa*** at Khreshchatyk 21; vulitsya Prorizna 9 (next to the State Youth Theatre); or Maydan Nezalezhnosti (on the north-western side of the square). Tickets are available at the theatres about an hour before the curtain rises.

The ***Koleso Kafe-Theatre*** *(☎ 416 04 22, Andriyivsky uzviz 8a, metro Kontraktova Ploshcha)* in Podil is a semi-avant garde comedy/drama theatre.

Opera & Ballet

A performance at the lavish ***Shevchenko Opera & Ballet Theatre*** *(☎ 224 71 65, vulitsya Volodymyrska 50, metro Teatralna)* is a grandiose affair. The box office (☎ 229 11 69) inside is open from 11 am to 2 pm and 3 to 7.30 pm (Sunday from 3 to 7 pm only).

Circus

The ***Circus*** *(☎ 274 82 56, ☎ 221 73 19, ☎ 221 73 20, ploshcha Peremohy)* is a traditional Kyiv attraction featuring live music, loads of acrobats and, sadly, bears on rollerskates. Shows start at 7 pm (1 and 5 pm on Saturday and Sunday). Tickets costing $2 to $3 are best bought in advance from the *kasa*, inside the circus building, open from noon to 3 pm and 4 to 7 pm (from 10 am at weekends).

SPECTATOR SPORTS

Dynamo Stadium, just off vulitsya Kirova, is home to Dynamo Kyiv, one of Europe's leading soccer teams. The stadium is small, so most matches kick off at the larger Respublikansky Stadium (☎ 246 70 30, ☎ 246 70 07), vulitsya Chervonoarmiyska 55 (metro Respublikansky Stadion or Palats Ukraina). Tickets ($0.10 to $10) for its 100,000 seats are sold at kiosks in front of the entrance gates on vulitsya Chervonoarmiyska; there is another ticket kasa in the underpass of Maydan Nezalezhnosti metro station. Dynamo Kyiv paraphernalia is sold at the club shop (☎ 227 05 76), vulitsya Chervonoarmiyska 86.

Other sporting events take place at the Sports Palace (☎ 246 72 53, ☎ 246 74 06), ploshcha Sportyvna 1 (metro Palats Sportu).

SHOPPING

Souvenir stalls line the north-western side of maydan Nezalezhnosti. The best spot for Russian dolls and hats, hand-embroidered tablecloths, McLenin T-shirts, paintings, ceramics and other traditional Ukrainian crafts is cobbled Andriyivsky uzviz, where local artisans set up shop. The Union of Ukrainian Artists has its studio at Andriyivsky uzviz 11. L'Art, a fine contemporary art studio, is at No 2a.

Ukrainsky Suvenir, vulitsya Chervonoarmiyska 23, and the small but good souvenir shop at Khreshchatyk 32 are both worth a peek. For beautiful but expensive contemporary art and antiques, shop at the exclusive Galeria Olimp (☎ 235 93 18), vulitsya Chervonoarmiyska 37.

TsUM department store straddles the corner of Khreshchatyk and bulvar Bohdana Khmelnytskoho. The Ukraina department store, opposite the circus on ploshcha Peremohy, sits beneath what the Ukrainian press claims is the world's largest billboard.

COLIN HOOD

Lake Baikal, the world's deepest lake, holds nearly one-fifth of all the world's lake water

GEORGI SHABLOVSKY

One of many markets along the Trans-Siberian

GEORGI SHABLOVSKY

Among the locals

GEORGI SHABLOVSKY

Sunset in Peleduy on Lake Baikal's northern shore, Eastern Siberia

GETTING THERE & AWAY

Air

All international flights (except a handful to/from Moscow and Eastern European countries) use Boryspil international airport (☎ 296 72 43, ☎ 296 72 44), about 40km east of Kyiv. Some domestic flights use Zhulyany airport (☎ 242 23 08), which is 12km west of the centre. For details on international and domestic flights, see the Ukraine Getting There & Away and Getting Around chapters.

Ukraine International Airlines (☎ 221 83 80, fax 216 82 25, mau@ps.kiev.ua, www.uia.ukrpack.net) and Air Ukraine (☎ 216 70 40, fax 216 99 54) share offices located at prospekt Peremohy 14 and vulitsya Lysenka 4. Plane tickets are also sold at Kiyavia (☎ 056, ☎ 274 90 81/82/83, info@kiyavia.com, www.kiyavia.com), at either prospekt Peremohy 2 or vulitsya Horodetskoho 4.

Most major airlines have an airport and city centre office. These are listed in the *Kyiv Business Directory*, *Kyiv Post* and numerous other English-language publications which are free and widely available.

Train

Kyiv train station (☎ 223 11 11, ☎ 005), ploshcha Vokzalna 2, is next to Vokzalna metro station. International train information is included in the Ukraine Getting There & Away chapter.

There are at least four daily trains to/from Lviv (12 hours), Odesa (12 hours), Poltava (seven hours) and Kharkiv (11 hours); twice daily to/from Uzhhorod (20 to 21 hours) and Ivano-Frankivsk (13 to 14 hours); one or more a day to/from Simferopol (18 to 19 hours), Sevastopol (20 hours) and Chernivtsi (14 hours).

The advance train ticket office, a five minute walk from the station at bulvar Taras Shevchenka 38/40 (next to Hotel Ekspres), is open from 8 am to 7 pm (9 am to 6 pm on Saturday and Sunday).

You can also buy train tickets from desk No 6 or 7 inside the Kiyavia office at vulitsya Horodetskoho 4. Reservations can be made by telephone on ☎ 050.

Bus

There are seven bus terminals in Kyiv; most buses run from the central bus station (tsentralny avtobus vokzal; ☎ 265 04 30), ploshcha Moskovska 3, one stop from Lybidska metro station on trolleybus No 4, 11 or 12, or tram No 9 or 10.

The private Autolux bus company (☎ 442 85 83, fax 443 84 39) operates buses from Boryspil airport to Odesa via Uman (three a day); Kharkiv via Poltava (three daily) and Cherkasy (twice daily). Tickets are sold at Kiyavia or Autolux at the airport.

Car

Car rental without a driver is only available in Kyiv. The major car rental companies are:

Avis

Reservations:
Hotel Rus (☎ 294 21 03/04, fax 294 21 92, rus@avis.relc.com) vulitsya Hospitalna 4
Head office:
(☎ 294 77 07, fax 294 98 73) vulitsya Komyshinska 4
24 hour emergency
(☎ 8 050-469 62 65, ☎ 459 29 37)

Europcar

(☎ 274 99 77, ☎ 227 21 42, ☎/fax 216 60 34, ua@europcar.relc.com) vulitsya Antonovicha 48a; (☎/fax 296 77 37) Boryspil airport

Hertz

(☎ 296 73 18, ☎ 296 76 17, ☎ 296 76 14, fax 296 77 15, hertzkv@public.ua.net) Boryspil airport

Boat

Kyiv is the most northerly hydrofoil and passenger boat port on the Dnipro and the usual starting or finishing point of Dnipro River cruises. The boat terminal *(rechnoy vokzal)* is at Poshtova ploshcha 3 (metro Poshtova Ploshcha). Boats sail between May and mid-October.

In 1998 there was one southbound boat daily to Cherkasy (5¼ hours), stopping at Kaniv (3¾ hours) en route, and not making the return trip to Kyiv until the following day. Tickets are sold at the kasa inside the river terminal building; the Mandrivnyk Travel Company (see Travel Agencies earlier) also has details. For trips farther than

Cherkasy, service is limited to occasional cruises and specially chartered vessels (see the Ukraine Getting Around chapter).

GETTING AROUND

To/From the Airport

The cheapest way to get to Boryspil airport is on a Polit bus (☎ 296 73 67). Buses depart from the bus stop in front of Kiyavia, prospekt Peremohy 2, every 20 minutes between 7.30 am and 10.10 pm. Journey time is 45 minutes to one hour and a single ticket is $2. At Boryspil, Polit buses arrive/depart from in front of the international terminal.

A pricier option is the express shuttle bus (☎ 246 75 64, ☎ 224 82 51) that departs from outside Hotel Kyiv, Hotel Rus and Hotel Dnipro several times a day (40 minutes, $10 one-way); check departure times at reception. A taxi costs between $30 and $40, depending on negotiations.

To get to Zhulyany airport, take trolleybus No 9 from ploshcha Peremohy (40 minutes).

Public Transport

Kyiv's metro is clean, efficient, reliable and easy to use if you read Cyrillic (see the metro map). Trains run frequently between around 5.30 am and midnight on all three lines. Sky-blue plastic tokens *(zhetony)* costing $0.10 (good for one ride) are sold at kiosks at metro station entrances. During the first week of the month you can buy a monthly pass ($5), good for all forms of transportation.

Buses, trolleybuses and trams serve most routes. Many are shadowed by minibuses that nip along the same routes at a friskier pace. Tickets for buses, trams and trolleybuses cost $0.10 and are sold at street kiosks or directly from the driver/conductor.

A funicular links the main river terminal on Naberezhna Khreshchatytska with Mykhaylivska ploshcha; it runs between 6.30 am and 11 pm. Tickets costing $0.10 for a single journey are sold at the funicular entrance.

Taxi

Taxis congregate at the train station, on ploshcha Peremohy and outside the major hotels. To save being ripped off, avoid the dinosaur Volgas that lumber round town and opt instead for a new, canary-yellow Daewoo with a chequered black-and-white stripe down its side. The latter have meters

and charge $0.15/km in town and $0.25/km out of town.

It is still common practice in Kyiv to flag down a private car on the street; don't pay more than $2 for a short trip within the centre.

Around Kyiv

Several day trips from the cosmopolitan capital plunge you into central Ukraine, the country's traditional bread-basket region and agricultural heart where rural villages and simple farming towns neighbour endless stretches of prairie-like land and steppe.

The folk architecture museum in Pereyaslav-Khmelnytsky and Taras Shevchenko's hilltop grave in Kaniv are both accessible from Kyiv by river boat. Numerous travel agencies organise tours to Chernihiv's ecclesiastical relics of 11th century Kyivan Rus, while Uman is an excellent stepping stone for Odesa-bound travellers.

PEREYASLAV-KHMELNYTSKY ПЕРЕЯСЛАВ-ХМЕЛЬНИЦЬКИЙ

☎ 04467 • pop 24,000

Pereyaslav-Khmelnytsky is roughly 90km downriver from Kyiv. Dating from the 10th century, this sleepy provincial town was a fortress under Kyivan Rus and later a strategic Cossack military base. It was here that the great Cossack leader Bohdan Khmelnytsky signed the infamous Pereyaslav agreement on 18 January 1654, which accepted the tsar's overlordship of Ukraine, irrevocably tying its fate with Russia. A second agreement hastily signed in Pereyaslav five years later, after Khmelnytsky's death, by his son, Iruii, gave Russia political control over much of Ukraine.

The town's highlight is its **Folk Architecture Museum**. Along shaded paths set among picket fences and flower gardens are clusters of beautiful wooden churches, windmills and farmhouses, several decked out inside with original furnishings and others set up as small museums. Bring a picnic and settle in for a relaxing afternoon.

The river boat station, at the end of a long inlet off the main Dnipro, is about 1km from the museum; it's 1km farther to the town centre. From the dock turn right onto the main road, then turn left down a tree-lined road that leads to the museum entrance. From Pereyaslav-Khmelnytsky bus station, head south-east for 1.5km to the centre, continue down vulitsya Khmelnytsky and out of town for 1km, then turn right down the road to the museum entrance. The museum is open from 10 am to 5 pm (from noon on Friday, closed Wednesday). Admission is $0.50.

Most sights in the town centre are clustered on central ploshcha Vozyednannya, which lies off the main street, vulitsya Khmelnytsky. The square's south-western side is dominated by the **Ascension Monastery**. The **Kobzar Museum** (closed Wednesday and Thursday), vulitsya Khmelnytsky 20, houses exhibits on the legendary kobzar and bandura players, Ukraine's wandering, lute-toting bards who travelled between villages playing songs and reciting stories.

Getting There & Away

The most enjoyable way to get there is by boat (2¾ hours). In 1998, no seasonal hydrofoils ran to/from Kyiv to Pereyaslav-Khmelnytsky, but this could change. Check at Kyiv's main river boat terminal.

Most buses between Kyiv's main bus station and Cherkasy (about six daily) stop at Pereyaslav-Khmelnytsky.

KANIV КАНІВ

☎ 04736

When Taras Shevchenko died in 1861, he left his famous poem *Zapovit* (Testament) requesting his countrymen to bury him on a hill overlooking the great Dnipro River where, after rising up and liberating the land, they could 'freely, and with good intent, speak quietly of him'.

Kaniv, four hours and 162km down the Dnipro from Kyiv, is the spot. In 1925 the steep and scenic bluff overlooking the river called Taras' Hill (Tarasova Hora) was designated a State Cultural Preserve. The magnet and homage site for tourists is the

Shevchenko Monument & Literary Memorial Museum (☎ 2 23 65). Climb the 400 steps from near Tarasova Hora pier and ascend past a fountain on the wooded hillside to get to the museum. The tomb is beneath the towering obelisk, which is crowned with a statue of the poet. There is an observation point in front and a grove of memorial oak and chestnut trees off to the side, making it a peaceful and reflective place. Behind the neoclassical Memorial Museum a path leads to the tomb of Yadlovsky, the man who guarded Shevchenko's body from 1883 to 1933. The Tarasova Hora hotel is nearby.

About 15km south of the city is the **Kaniv Nature Reserve**, some 2000 hectares of pristine forest and hills with over 5000 species of plants indigenous to the area.

Getting There & Away

Many Kyiv-based travel agencies offer weekend cruises to Kaniv. Between May and mid-October there are three or four boats a week to/from Kyiv (3¾ hours). The nearest train station is in Lipylava, 7km away. Some Cherkasy buses from Kyiv also stop in Kaniv.

CHERNIHIV
ЧЕРНІГІВ

☎ 04622 • pop 313,000

Chernihiv (Chernigov in Russian), 140km north of Kyiv on the Desna River, was the capital of one of the most important princedoms within Kyivan Rus. Of Ukraine's 25 architectural landmarks from the 11th to 12th centuries, five are in Chernihiv, making it well worth a day trip.

The city dates from the early 8th century, but didn't become significant until 100 years later as a Kyivan Rus princedom and an important fortified crossroads. After being sacked by Tatars in 1239, the city was rebuilt and several new Byzantine churches and monasteries were added, a few of which survive today. The city subsequently fell to the Lithuanians, who built up the fortress in the 14th century, and then to Poland in the early 17th century, before eventually coming under Russian rule.

Dytynets

The city's historic core is two blocks south-east along vulitsya Lenina from central, brick-paved ploshcha Chervona. Known as Dytynets (Ramparts), it served as a strategic fortress from the 10th century, commanding trade routes south to Kyiv. Today it's a leafy park featuring a remarkable group of early religious buildings which overlook the five beautiful golden domes of the baroque **St Catherine's Church**.

The most striking of the ensemble is **Spaso-Preobrazhensky Cathedral** (1017). Its two distinctive, missile-like corner bell towers sit atop a dark and mysterious interior which houses an 18th century iconostasis and the tombs of several Kyivan Rus royalty, including Prince Mstyslav Khorobry, younger brother of Yaroslav the Wise. A history museum is housed in its north-west neighbour, the 12th century **Boryso-Hlibsky Cathedral**. The artefacts include 18th century **Royal Doors**, commissioned by the famous Cossack leader Ivan Mazepa. Farther north-west is the former **collegium** (1710), the exterior ornamentation of which is a strange combination of Byzantine and baroque motifs. Inside, icons from the 17th to 19th centuries are on display.

North-east of Boryso-Hlibsky Cathedral is the former **Archbishop's residence** (1780), which has a classical portico. South-east is **Chernihiv History Museum** (☎ 7 31 67), vulitsya Horkoho 4, inside the neoclassical Governor's house (1804). Don't miss the copy of the 1581 Ostroh Bible, the first Bible to be printed in the old Slavonic language (closed Thursday).

Lining the southern edge of Dytynets is a row of 18th century **cannons** overlooking the embankments and once protecting the fortified southern entrance to the city. South on the river bank is the **boat terminal**. In summer, you might be able to hire a boat to take you along the Desna River.

Illinsky Church & Troyitsko Monastery

From Dytynets, it's about a 3km walk to Troyitsko Monastery; alternatively take trolleybus No 8 from Dytynets to vulitsya Lva

Tolstoho. At the **Hill of Glory Monument** (dedicated to the unknown soldier) on the corner of vulitsya Uspenskoho and vulitsya Lva Tolstoho, walk up the flight of stairs past the obelisk to the monastery. A better approach is to turn left along vulitsya Uspenskoho which runs along the base of the ridge to Illinsky Church at No 33. From here, a dirt path leads uphill to the monastery.

Illinsky Church (1069) is part of the monastery complex despite being tucked into the hillside below. The highlight is **Antoniy Caves**, 315m of underground passageways, galleries and chapels constructed from the 11th to 13th centuries. Many chapels are vaulted and decorated with plasterwork, including the 16.5m-long and 8.4m-high **Church of Saint Theodosis of the Totma** which is the largest cave chapel in Ukraine. Several monks killed during the Tatar-Mongol sacking of the church in 1239 are buried in the **Chapel of the Tomb**; a pile of their bones is encased behind glass. The church and caves are open from 9 am to 5 pm (closed Thursday); admission is $0.50. The ticket kasa is in the bell tower.

Uphill, the magnificent, 58m bell tower of the **Troyitsko Monastery** is high-baroque. Beyond, amid the well maintained grounds, is the multi-cupola **Trinity Cathedral** (1679).

Places to Stay

Chernihiv has one hotel, the mandatory crumbling, Intourist-style ***Hotel Hradetsky*** *(☎ 4 50 25, vulitsya Lenina 68)*, 2km northwest of ploshcha Chervona. Singles/doubles with bathroom cost $12/18.

Getting There & Away

The train and bus stations are 2km west of ploshcha Chervona, on ploshcha Vokzalna. Trolleybus No 1 runs between the stations and the centre, stopping a block north of ploshcha Chervona.

Between Kyiv and Chernihiv there are more buses than trains. Six to eight buses run daily (four hours from Kyiv's main bus station), as opposed to some two daily trains (four to five hours).

Chernihiv is on the Kyiv-St Petersburg train line, the Kyiv-Minsk line, the Minsk-Simferopol line and on the Minsk-Odesa rail route. Each has a train passing through once a day in each direction. There is also a daily train from Chernihiv to Kharkiv, Lviv and Moscow.

UMAN
УМАНЬ

☎ 04744 • pop 95,000

With its lush green grounds and exquisitely landscaped gardens, Uman, midway between Kyiv (210km) and Odesa (280km) is a popular day trip from the capital. In 1796 Polish Count Felix Pototsky, with the help of a Belgian engineer, laid out the 150 hectare **Sofiyivka Park** for his wife Sofia, a former Turkish slave whom he had bought for two million zloty. It's a fine piece of landscaping, with grottoes, lakes, waterfalls, fountains, pavilions and 500 species of trees. Most sights are strung along the Kamenka River, particularly around the upper and lower ponds, the former having the Island of Love with a Renaissance-style rose pavilion (1850-52) on it. Tradition demands that when stepping foot on the island you shout the name of your loved one. Other sites include the Grotto of Fear and Doubts, the Fountain of Three Tears, the Grotto of Venus (1760-1800) and the fabulous Dead

Hassidic Pilgrims

Ever since the death of Rabbi Nakhman (1772-1810), Jewish pilgrims have flocked to his graveside in Uman to pay homage to this 18th century sage who founded the Breslov trend of Hassidism. The rabbi was born in Medzhybizh, 120km east of Ternopil in western Ukraine, but later moved to Uman where he died of tuberculosis.

The pilgrimage – strictly male only – takes place each year in September or October during Jewish New Year (Rosh Hashana). In 1994 a 2000 seat synagogue and Jewish centre (www.breslov.net/uman) was built to accommodate the estimated 5000 pilgrims that journey to Uman each year.

Lake and Underground River Styx. In summer, you can hire boats here.

To get to the park, head towards the centre (signposted 'vulitsya Kyivskaya'), past the bus station (on the right) and park headquarters (on the left), then follow the 'Sofiyivka' signs. The park entrance is at vulitsya Sadova 53. The modern ***Hotel Muzey*** *(☎ 5 62 75, fax 5 05 50)* next to the entrance has comfortable doubles from $26; its well lit, conservatory-style lobby houses a small collection of statues and relics.

Kafe Sofiyivka *(☎ 5 41 00)*, next to the park headquarters (opposite Uman bus station) at vulitsya Kyivskaya 129, is a cheap eating spot serving hearty salads and beef stroganoffs.

Uman is also an important Jewish pilgrimage site (see the previous boxed text 'Hassidic Pilgrims').

Western Ukraine
Західна Україна

Western Ukraine has had the unfortunate luck of being a border country, battled over and tossed back and forth between rival states for as long as anyone can remember. Its history is littered with sieges, ruin, fires and plagues. Despite this mayhem, its people have always banded together, working to protect their identity and culture as a sacred icon.

Western Ukraine was not under the repressive Russian sphere until WWII, and more liberty was allowed under Polish and Habsburg rule. As a result it has a less Russified identity, as well as an air of Central European flair to some of its cities. Whereas you'll hear mostly Russian spoken in the east and in Crimea, only Ukrainian is generally spoken here.

HIGHLIGHTS

- Living like royalty in Lviv's early 20th century hotels; don't miss a night at the opera
- Strolling the cobbled streets and fortress of Kamyanets-Podilsky
- Driving along the banks of the Tisa River on a scenic trail along the Ukrainian-Romanian border
- Discovering Europe's only virgin beech forest at the Carpathian Biosphere Reserve
- Dining à la Hutzul in a traditional rural home in the mountains
- Hiking to the top of the Ukrainian Carpathians' highest peaks

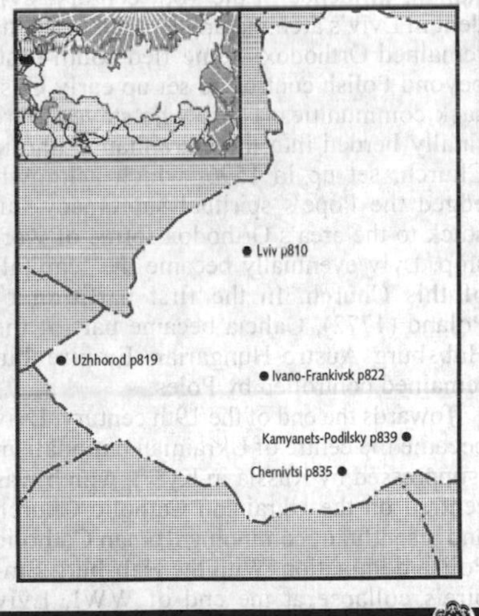

Lviv Region
Львівська область

LVIV
ЛЬВІВ

☎ 0322 • pop 830,000

Lviv (Lvov in Russian), the capital of western Ukraine, is a Central European city. Until 1939 it had never been ruled from Moscow and it was here that Ukrainian nationalism and the Ukrainian Catholic Church re-emerged in the late 1980s. Escaping the urban destruction of WWII, Lviv's skyline of towers, spires and roofs against a hilly backdrop exudes history. There are buildings in most of the main Western styles: Gothic, Renaissance, baroque, rococo and neoclassical. Lviv is also a busy industrial and commercial centre with its share of decrepit communist-era industry and housing estates on the outskirts. Yet the narrow old streets and colourful historic core make it one of the best places in the country to visit.

History

Lviv was founded as a hilltop fort in the mid-13th century by Danylo Halytsky, prince of Galicia and Volyn, a former western principality of Kyivan Rus. It was supposedly named after his son Lev, which means lion, hence the historic symbol of the city. The history of Lviv (Lemberg under the Austrians and Germans) goes hand in hand with the history of Galicia, the historic region centred around western Ukraine. For centuries it's been the region's chief city, sited on the strategic east-west trade routes and controlling Carpathian passes.

In the early 14th century, Galician forces under nobleman Dmytro Detko warded off a Polish invasion led by Prince Casimir the Great. But soon after, the Poles, aided by Hungarians, defeated the Ukrainians and began a long and bitter rule over Galicia. Over the centuries intense religious, social and ethnic conflicts between the resident Ukrainians and the ruling Poles developed. Most of the Galician nobility (many sent over from Poland, Germany and Hungary) eventually adopted the Polish language and religion – Roman Catholicism – which introduced a Western European, particularly Italian, influence in the 16th century, evident in Lviv's architecture. But the peasants remained Orthodox. Some fled south-east, beyond Polish control, to set up early Cossack communities. Those who stayed were finally herded into the Ukrainian Catholic Church, set up in 1596, which acknowledged the Pope's spiritual supremacy but stuck to the area's Orthodox forms of worship. Lviv eventually became the 'capital' of this Church. In the first partition of Poland (1772), Galicia became part of the Habsburg Austro-Hungarian Empire but remained controlled by Poles.

Towards the end of the 19th century, Lviv became the centre of Ukrainian nationalism (suppressed by Russia in Kyiv), which was centred on the Ukrainian Catholic Church and resentful of continuing Roman Catholic Polish domination. With the Habsburg Empire's collapse at the end of WWI, Lviv was, for a few days, the seat of an independent government of what was known variously as Ruthenia, western Ukraine or East Galicia. But the troops of re-emergent Poland expelled the government and Lviv returned to Polish rule (apart from a brief Soviet takeover in 1920), until September 1939 when the Red Army walked in, asserting Moscow's control over the city for the first time in its long history.

Lviv was occupied by Germany from 1941 to 1944. Soviet sources say 136,000 people died in its Jewish ghetto and nearly 350,000 in its concentration camps. After the war, Soviet forces reoccupied Lviv and most of Galicia, repressing the nationally conscious western Ukrainian people. The Ukrainian Catholic Church, forced underground by Stalin in 1946, re-emerged with glasnost in the late 1980s to play a big part in a new Ukrainian independence movement, centred in Lviv. Nationalists were voted into power unanimously in western Ukraine in 1990, and with many dissident movements centred in Lviv, the stage was set for Ukrainian independence the following year.

Orientation

Lviv's main street is the 600m-long prospekt Svobody (Freedom) which runs north from ploshcha Mitskevycha to the Ivan Franko Opera & Ballet Theatre. Directly east are the narrow, old-quarter streets centred around ploshcha Rynok. Westwards, 19th century streets lead to Ivan Franko Park. Most of what you'll want is within this roughly 1.25 sq km area, overlooked from the north-east by Castle Hill (Zamkova Hora) where Lviv was founded.

Maps *Lviv City Plan* (Klenolyst, 1993) is a quality city map, complete with an English street index on its reverse side. It costs $1 and is sold at Lviv-Inturyst inside Hotel George. A decent map of the centre is also included in the *Lviv Architectural Guide Book* (Malti-M, 1997), a glossy, 37 page guidebook with parallel texts in English and Ukrainian.

Information

Tourist Office Lviv-Inturyst (☎ 72 67 51, ☎/fax 97 12 87, genag@lviv.gu.net, www.lviv.ua/inturyst), inside Hotel George, is open from 9 am to 5 pm (closed at weekends). It organises two-hour city tours with an English-speaking guide for $30/40 per individual/group.

Money UKR Exim Bank, inside the lobby of Hotel George, is one of the best places to change money, cash travellers cheques or get a cash advance on Visa/MasterCard. It's generally open from 8 am to 8 pm daily except Sunday.

Credit card cash advances are also available at Western Union/X-Change Points inside the central train ticket office or in the main post office.

Post & Telephone The central post office, vulitsya Slovatskoho 1, is open from 6 am to 8 pm (8 am to 6 pm on Saturday, 8 am to 2 pm on Sunday). The central telephone office, around the corner at vulitsya Doroshenka 39, is open 24 hours; telegraph and fax services are available between 8 am and 10 pm.

Email & Internet Access Internet Kafe (☎ 72 45 23, mailbox@cybercafe.lviv.ua, www.cybercafe.lviv.ua), inside the Dzuga Cultural Centre, prospekt Shevchenka 3, charges $1.30/1.90 for 30 minutes/one hour online and is open from 10 am to 8 pm. The entrance (not signposted) is through a clothes shop.

Travel Agencies Mandry (☎/fax 97 16 61, mandry@ukrpack.net), ploshcha Rynok 44, is an efficient travel agency run by friendly, English-speaking staff. As well as selling international bus tickets and arranging hotel bookings, it also organises city tours (2½ hours) with an English-speaking guide for $6.50 per person. Mandry is open from 10 am to 6 pm (until 2 pm on Saturday, closed Sunday).

Bookshop An excellent array of maps and guidebooks is sold at Ukratiska, prospekt Shevchenka 8, open from 9 am to 2 pm and 3 to 6 pm (until 3 pm on Saturday, closed Sunday).

Cultural Centre The British Council (☎/fax 76 29 15, bc@bc.lviv.ua) has an office inside Lviv State University, vulitsya Universytetska 1, room 237.

Prospekt Svobody

This wide boulevard, affectionately known as the Planta by older locals, acts as a central promenade, park and gathering place. Its northern end is occupied by the voluptuous **Ivan Franko Opera & Ballet Theatre** (1897-1900). In front of the theatre is a recessed flowerbed where once stood a massive Lenin statue; the area is currently being landscaped. The 1904 palace at prospekt Svobody 20, now housing the **National Museum** (☎ 74 22 82), was once the Lenin Museum. The grand interior is almost completely occupied by a colossal central staircase. Upstairs are displays of 15th to 19th century icons and the Ukrainian section of the Lviv Picture Gallery. Each exhibit requires a separate ticket. The museum opens 11 am to 6 pm (closed Thursday and Friday).

In the middle of the tree-lined prospekt is a statue of Ukraine's national poet, Taras Shevchenko – a historic site for Ukrainian nationalist gatherings. At prospekt Svobody 15 is the **Museum of Ethnography, Arts & Crafts** (☎ 72 78 08), with a seated Statue of Liberty atop its parapet. The sumptuous interior features an excellent collection of farm culture and folk art from western Ukraine, including embroidery, ethnic dress, woodcarvings, ceramics and *pysanky* (painted eggs). The museum is open 10 am to 6 pm (closed Monday and Tuesday); admission costs $0.15. Prospekt Svobody terminates in the south at **ploshcha Mitskevycha**, a busy intersection with a tall column topped with a statue of Polish poet Adam Mickiewicz. A bubbling baroque fish fountain sits between Shevchenko and Mickiewicz.

Ploshcha Rynok

This old market square was the hub of Lviv life from the 14th to 19th centuries and today is the best preserved urban square in Ukraine. It's a wide square plaza with a large 19th century **town hall**, rebuilt with a neo-Renaissance tower after a fire destroyed the original building, at its centre. The buildings around its perimeter date from the 16th

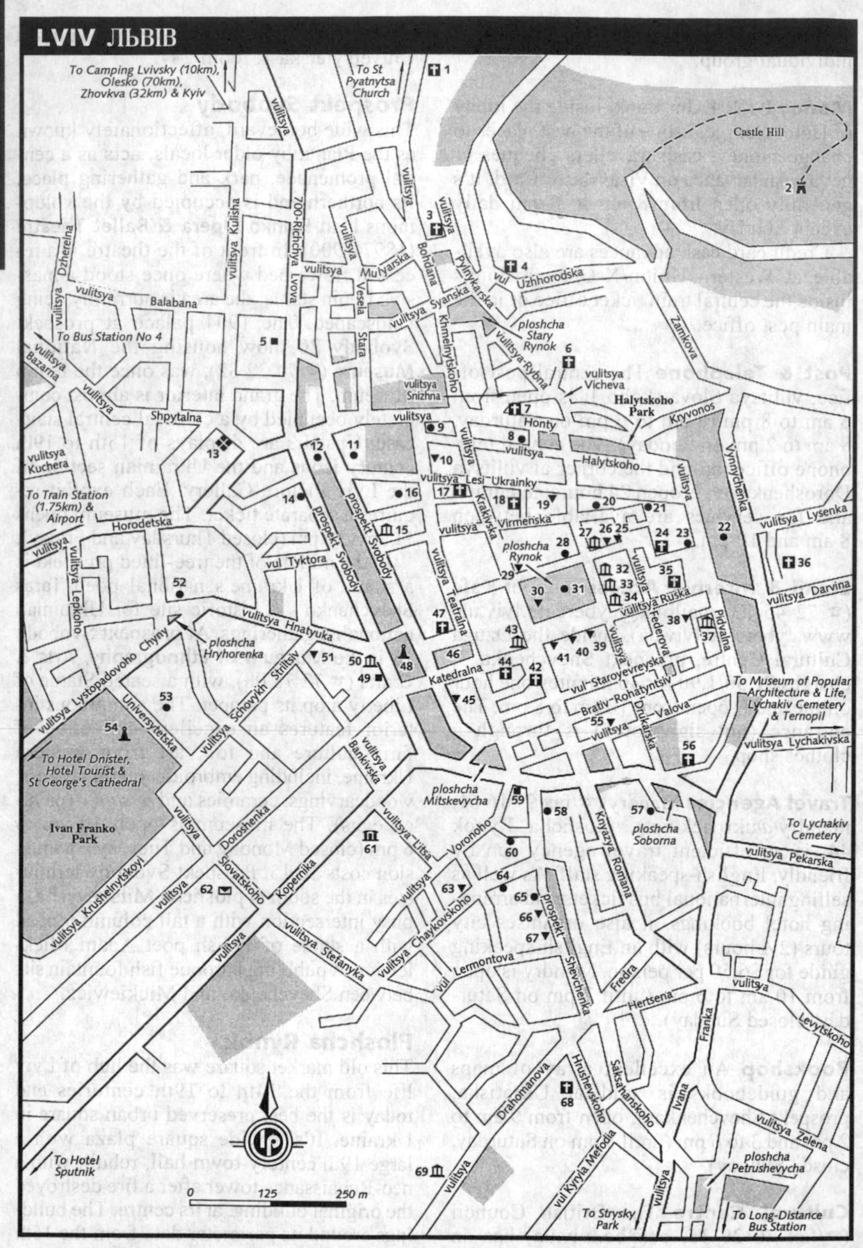

LVIV ЛЬВІВ
To Camping Lvivsky (10km), Olesko (70km), Zhovkva (32km) & Kyiv
To St Pyatnytsa Church
Castle Hill
To Bus Station No 4
To Train Station (1.75km) & Airport
To Hotel Dnister, Hotel Tourist & St George's Cathedral
Ivan Franko Park
To Hotel Sputnik
To Museum of Popular Architecture & Life, Lychakiv Cemetery & Ternopil
To Lychakiv Cemetery
To Strysky Park
To Long-Distance Bus Station
Halytskoho Park
ploshcha Stary Rynok
ploshcha Rynok
ploshcha Hryhorenka
ploshcha Mitskevycha
ploshcha Soborna
ploshcha Petrushevycha
prospekt Svobody
prospekt Shevchenka
vulitsya Kulisha
vulitsya Dzherelna
Balabana
vulitsya Bazarna
Shpytalna
vulitsya Kuchera
Horodetska
vulitsya Lepkoho
vulitsya Hnatyuka
vul Tyktora
vulitsya Teatralna
vulitsya Krakivska
vulitsya Lesi Ukrainky
Virmenska
Halytskoho
Kryvonos
Zamkova
vulitsya Vynnychenka
vulitsya Lysenka
vulitsya Darvina
vulitsya Ruska
Federova
Pidvalna
vul Staroyevreyska
Brativ Rohatyntsiv
Drukarska
Valova
vulitsya Lychakivska
vulitsya Pekarska
Katedralna
Lystopadovoho Chyny
Universytetska
Schovykh Striltsiv
Bankivska
Doroshenka
Slovatskoho
Kopernika
Krushelnytskoyi
Stefanyka
Chaykovskoho
Voronoho
Lytsa
vul Lermontova
Knyazya Romana
Fredra
Hertsena
Franka
Levytskoho
vulitsya Zelena
Ivana
Saksahanskoho
Hrushevskoho
Drahomanova
vul Kyryla Mefodia
Mulyarska
Bohdana
Khmelnytskoho
Syanska
Pylnykarska
vul Uzhhorodska
vulitsya-Rybna
vulitsya Vicheva
vulitsya Snizhna
Honty
700-Richchya Lvova
Vesela
Stara
0 125 250 m

LVIV ЛЬВІВ

PLACES TO STAY

5 Hotel Lviv
Готель Львів
49 Grand Hotel
Гранд Готель
59 Hotel George & UKR Exim Bank
Готель Жорж и УКР Ексім Баик

PLACES TO EAT

10 Jazz Fun Club
Джас Фан Клуб
19 Raphael
Рафаель
25 Noiv Kovuet
Ноїв Ковует
26 Stari Royal
Старий Рояль
29 Na Rinku
На Ринку
30 Ratusha
Ратуша
38 Kafe-Bar Vedmid
Кафе-Бар Ведмідь
39 Kvitka
Квітка
40 Zolotii Vepr
Золотий Вепр
41 Pid Levom
Під Левом
45 U Pani Steftsi
У Рані Стефці
51 Lisova Pisnya
Лісова Пісня
55 Sonata
Соната
63 Kafe Chervona Kalyna
Кафе Червона Калина
66 Svitou & Grand Club-Sofia
Світоу и Софія-Гранд Клуб
67 Europe Trident
Европа Трайдент

OTHER

1 Church of St Onefry
Церква Св. Онуфря
2 High Castle
Високий замок
3 St Nicholas Church
Миколаївська церква
4 Church of St John the Baptist
Костел Св. Іоанахрестителя
6 Benedictine Church & Monastery
Костьол Бенедиктинів і монастир
7 Church of Maria Snizhnoi
Костьол Марії Сніжної
8 Marionette Theatre
Марионетковий театр
9 Bus Ticket & Information Office
Продажу автобусних квитків та інформації
11 Ukrainian Drama Theatre
Український драматичний театр
12 Ivan Franko Opera & Ballet Theatre
Івана Франка театр опери та балету
13 TsUM Department Store
ЦУМ
14 Teatralna Kasa
Театральні каси
15 National Museum
Національний музей
16 Outdoor Arts & Crafts Market
Відкритий базар по продажу виробів мистецтва та художнього
17 Transfiguration Church
Храм Преображенийя церква
18 Armenian Cathedral
Вірменьський собор
20 House of Seasons
Дім всіх сезонів
21 Art Gallery
Арт Галерія
22 Gunpowder Tower
Порохова башта
23 King's Arsenal
Королівский арсенал
24 Dominican Church & Monastery
Костьол та монастир Домініканв
27 Apteka Museum
Аптека музей
28 Mandry (Travel Agency)
Мандри
31 Town Hall
Ратуша
32 History Museum
Історичний музей
33 History Museum & Gothic Hall Shop
Історичний музей
34 Museum of Ethnography, Arts & Crafts (furniture & porcelain)
Музей етнографії та художнього промислу
35 Uspensky Church with Three Saints Chapel & Kornyakt Bell Tower
Успенська церква і каплиця Трьох Святителів і вежа Корнякта
36 St Mary Carmelite Monastery
Монастир Кармеліток
37 Town Arsenal & Museum of Old Arms
Міський арсенал та музей старовинної зброї
42 Boyim Chapel
Боїмів каплиця
43 History Museum
Історичний музей
44 Roman Catholic Cathedral
Католицький собор
46 Ploshcha Pidkovy
Площа Підкови
47 Jesuit Church
Костьол Єзуїтів
48 Taras Shevchenko Statue
Пам'ятник Тарасові Шевченку
50 Museum of Ethnography, Arts & Crafts
Музей етнографії художнього промислу та мистецтва
52 Train Ticket Office, Air Ukraine & Lviv Airlines
Центральні Залізничні Каса и Авіалінії України и Авіалінії Львів
53 University & British Council
Уиіерситет
54 Ivan Franko Monument
Пам'ятник Івана Франка
56 Bernardine Church & Monastery
Церква і монастир Бернадинів
57 Halitsky Market
Галицький ринок
58 Dzuga Cultural Centre & Internet Kafe
Джуга Култури Центр и Інтернет Кафе
60 VVIR (Visa Office)
ВВІР
61 Pototsky Palace & Lviv Picture Gallery
Палата Потоцького
62 Central Post Office
Главпоштамт
64 Philharmonia
Філармонія
65 Ukratiska (Book Shop)
Укратнська
68 St Nicholas Church
Церква Св. Миколи
69 Museum of Old Ukrainian Culture
Музей давнього Українського мистецтва

to 18th centuries and their highly individual stone carvings are worth a close look. Traditionally, any building with more than three windows overlooking the square was heavily taxed, thus the uniformity, broken by only a few of the obviously wealthier citizens. Off each corner stand fountains with sculptures depicting Greek gods, all executed by the same sculptor in 1793.

Lviv History Museum Nos 4 and 6 in the north-eastern corner of ploshcha Rynok, and No 24 in the south-western corner, house the Lviv History Museum (☎ 72 06 71). Nos 4 and 6 have 16th century, Renaissance facades and 17th century carvings. No 4, the Black Stone House, built for an Italian merchant in 1588-89, features St Martin on a horse, and along with Nos 2 and 3 to the left, makes an impressive strip of Renaissance facades. No 6 was built for and named after the Greek merchant Kornyakt. There is an interesting sculptural row, with knights and dolphins lining the rooftop cornice. The lovely inner courtyard with a three tiered gallery is completely Italian Renaissance. The ground floor has mostly 20th century exhibits; upstairs (which requires a separate ticket) is the former palace, with one room having a 200-year-old parquet floor made of 14 wood types. The displays are of 16th to 18th century furnishings. It was here that the treaty was signed between Poland and Russia that partitioned Ukraine on 22 December 1686. Inside No 24, exhibits on three floors cover Lviv history from prehistory up to the 18th century with some good Cossack displays. All three buildings are open from 10 am to 6 pm (closed Wednesday).

Other Buildings No 10, with cannon and cannonballs on its lower corner and a faceless Roman legionnaire looming high above the parapet, owes its grandiose 18th century appearance to the Polish Lubomirsky family, its former owners. It houses the impressive furniture and porcelain sections of Lviv's **Museum of Ethnography, Arts & Crafts**, open from 10 am to 5.30 pm (closed Monday and Tuesday). The lion carving at No 14 is a symbol of Venice, whose consul lived here in the 17th century. On the north side of the square, where the buildings are mostly 18th century, spot the human faces wrapped in lion skins on No 36 and the grinning Asiatic face on No 41. Next door at No 40, the sickly Atlantes holding up a balcony are similar to those at No 3.

Around Ploshcha Rynok

The small grid of attractive streets around ploshcha Rynok comprises the historic old quarter and offers far more than just its diminutive charm. The **Roman Catholic Cathedral** (1370-1480) opposite the south-western corner of the square is a busy working church. Despite changes and chapel additions it has kept its European Gothic feel, notably at the eastern end with its tall, thin buttresses. The western tower, a Lviv landmark, was added later. On the north side of the ornate interior, the westernmost chapel near the entrance was built in black, white and pink marble in 1619 by a notoriously ruthless Lviv mayor called Kampian. Its exterior has fine stone carvings of biblical scenes. The **Boyim Chapel** (1617) near the south-eastern corner of the cathedral is the burial chapel of a wealthy Hungarian merchant family. Its west entrance facade is covered in magnificent carvings – including SS Peter and Paul at either end of the lower level, and the passions of Christ on the level above. Below the columns are carved lion heads, and high above, on top of the cupola, is a suffering Christ glaring down. The interior's carvings are equally lavish, most notably on its sculpted corbelled dome. Above the door are portraits of Georgi Boyim, who had the chapel built, and his son Pawiel.

A block west of ploshcha Rynok on the corner of ploshcha Pidkovy and vulitsya Teatralna is the 1610-35 **Jesuit Church**. Its facade reflects the transition from Renaissance to baroque, incorporating features of each style.

Occupying a 16th century building opposite the north-east corner of the square is the city's oldest functioning pharmacy (1735), known as the Black Eagle. It houses the **Apteka Museum** (☎ 72 28 86), vulitsya Drukarska 1. For $0.50, you can buy a bottle of iron-rich, medicinal wine to cure your ills, but beware of temporary tooth discolouration. Ask for 'vino'.

Vulitsya Virmenska & Around Nearby at vulitsya Virmenska 23 is the **House of Seasons**, named after the allegorical scenes on its facade and to a band of zodiac symbols running above the pilasters. Farther west at vulitsya Virmenska No 7/9 is the **Armenian Cathedral** (1363). On the corner of vulitsya Lesi Ukrainky and vulitsya Krakivska is the late 17th century twin-bell towered **Transfiguration Church**, the first church in the city to revert to Ukrainian Catholic after independence. Its interior is a lofty parade of colours with painted walls and vaults.

Vulitsya Pidvalna & Around A block north-east of ploshcha Rynok, down vulitsya Stavropihiyska, is the large dome of the **Dominican Church & Monastery** (1745-64), Lviv's finest bit of rococo with definite baroque and classical features. The lofty oval-shaped interior of the church has impressive gold-covered wooden sculptures and leads to the entrance of the monastery. East of the Dominican Church is the arched facade of the Renaissance **King's Arsenal** (1630), now housing the city's historical archives. Sitting in a park directly east of the arsenal and across vulitsya Pidvalna, is the **Gunpowder Tower** (1554-56), part of the old system of walls and bastions which once ran along vulitsya Pidvalna.

Immediately south is the three domed **Uspensky Church** (1591-1629), at the corner of vulitsya Ruska and vulitsya Pidvalna, easily distinguished by the 65m-tall, triple tiered **Kornyakt Bell Tower** (1572-78) rising beside it, named after the Greek merchant who funded its construction (see Lviv History Museum earlier). A door to the right of the tower leads into the churchyard and the small three domed **Three Saints Chapel** (1578-91). Nestled beneath the tower and built into the north side of the church, the chapel completes Lviv's finest piece of Renaissance architecture. It is the historic centre of the city's Orthodox community.

Across vulitsya Ruska at vulitsya Pidvalna 7 is a fine secessionist (early Art Nouveau) building, the former Dnister Insurance Building (1905). Farther south at vulitsya Pidvalna 5 is the 1554-56 **Town Arsenal**, part of the city's original fortification system but rebuilt after being destroyed by Swedish armies in 1704. Inside is the **Museum of Old Arms** (☎ 72 19 01), with an impressive display of cannons and armour, and a wide variety of weaponry from over 30 countries. It's open from 10 am to 5 pm (closed Wednesday).

Occupying the south-eastern section of the old town is the former **Bernardine Church & Monastery** complex, built in the early, 17th century mannerist style, now the Ukrainian Catholic Church of St Andrew. Its tower is another Lviv landmark. The dark and ambient interior features rows of ornate, carved wooden altars beneath a long, painted barrel-vaulted nave. In front of the main facade lies a small park with a 1736 baroque column. A path to the right of the entrance leads around the church to the monastery complex, past a 1761 rotunda-covered well and along the longest section of medieval defensive walls. South of the church, across the street and beyond the flower vendors, is the colourful and hectic **Halitsky Market**.

West of the Old Town

Lviv's main **University Building** (1877-81) is an attractive neoclassical edifice, a few blocks west of prospekt Svobody on vulitsya Universytetska. Across the street sits a massive monument to the western Ukrainian poet Ivan Franko, fronting the pleasant tree-filled **Ivan Franko Park**.

To the west of the park and rising from a small hilltop is the splendid **St George's Cathedral** (Sobor Yura), the historic and sacred centre of the Ukrainian Catholic Church, handed back in 1990 with great pomp and ceremony after 44 years of compulsory Orthodox control. Constructed in 1774-90 in stylised Ukrainian baroque, the complex includes an 1865 bell tower and the 1772 Metropolitan's Palace across from the church.

North of the Old Town

The small cluster of streets sandwiched between Castle Hill to the north-east and the old town to the south comprise the former **Old Rus Quarter**. The first settlement to form beneath the castle, it predates the present old town, but diminished in importance when the city centre was moved to ploshcha Rynok in the 14th century. Although few of the original structures remain, the quiet streets are still peppered with some of the city's oldest and smallest churches, making it worth an afternoon's stroll.

Tiny **St Nicholas Church**, dating from the 13th century and remodelled in the 16th century, is the oldest remainder of the Old Rus Quarter. The cruciform plan with three apses surrounding a central nave is original: an excellent example of early Byzantine architecture. The green domed church is north of ploshcha Stary Rynok on vulitsya Pylnykarska.

Continuing north on vulitsya Bohdana Khmelnytskoho for five minutes takes you to some steps and a gateway, on your right of which lies the 13th century **Church of St Onefry**. Its interior boasts a fine 19th century iconostasis. More impressive is the 17th century, wooden iconostasis inside the silver onion-domed **Church of St Pyatnytsa**, farther north on the same street.

For a sweeping 360° panorama of the city, head for **High Castle** (Vysoky Zamok), the 14th century remains of a stone castle that languish atop Castle Hill, amid a manicured hillside park.

East of the Old Town

Just to the east and uphill from the old town at Vynnychenka 30 is the former late-Renaissance 1644 **St Mary Carmelite Monastery**, now an exhibition hall.

About 2.5km east of the centre in the huge Shevchenkivsky Hayye Park is Lviv's enjoyable open-air **Museum of Popular Architecture & Life** (Muzey Narodnoyi Arkhitektury i Pobutu), vulitsya Chernecha Hora 1, well worth the visit. About 100 wooden buildings – farmsteads, smithies, windmills, churches, schools – are dotted over 60 hectares, divided into and representing the many ethnographic groups of western Ukraine. A highlight is the 1763 St Nicholas Church from Kryvky, in the Boyko region south of Lviv. The museum is open from 11 am to 6 pm (closed Monday). Take tram No 2 or 7 from the centre, or bus No 7 or 10 from near the end of vulitsya Valova north of the Bernardine monastery, to the 'vulitsya Mechnikova' stop on vulitsya Lychakivska. From here, it's a 1.25km walk; follow the signs.

About 1.5km south of the outdoor museum on vulitsya Mechnikova is the **Lychakiv Cemetery** (Lychakivska Kladovyshche), one of the most beautiful in Eastern Europe. Among its 40 hectares of tree-lined paths are 3600 monuments, including those of famous Ukrainians, such as poet Ivan Franko, many of which are topped with impressive sculpture designed by prominent artists. To reach the cemetery, stay on tram No 7 one stop past the open-air museum stop, to the Lychakivska Kladovyshche tram stop.

South of the Old Town

A block south of ploshcha Mitskevycha runs Lviv's lesser grand boulevard, **prospekt Shevchenka**, adorned with rows of attractive early 20th century buildings. At its far southern end is a statue of a seated Mykhailo Hrushevsky, Ukraine's most famous historian and the country's first president in 1918. Beyond, vulitsya Drahomanova leads to the **Museum of Old Ukrainian Culture** at No 42. Housed in a fanciful, 19th century Polish palace, it later became the residence of the head of the Ukrainian Catholic Church before being turned into a branch of the National Museum. It is open from 11 am to 5 pm (closed Friday).

From the top end of prospekt Shevchenka, vulitsya Chaykovskoho runs south-west a few blocks past the Philharmonia to the **Lviv Picture Gallery**, vulitsya Stefanyka 3. Housed in a 19th century palace, this is one of Ukraine's largest collections of European paintings dating from the 17th to 20th centuries. It's open from 10 am to 5 pm (closed Monday). **Strysky Park**, 2.5km south of the centre, was laid out in the 19th century with formal gardens and landscaped woodland.

Places to Stay

Camping ***Camping Lvivsky*** *(☎ 72 13 73, ☎ 72 14 73)*, some 10km north-east of the centre on the Kyiv road near the village of Dublyany, has tent and caravan sites. It's closed in winter.

Hotels The fabulous (and fabulously cheap) ***Hotel George*** *(☎ 72 59 52, ☎/fax 72 29 25, ploshcha Mitskevycha 1)* is the best deal in town. It's an elegant, neo-Renaissance building (1901), complete with grand staircase and the feel of faded grandeur. Rooms with private bath are fairly costly, but those with shared facilities are astonishing value. Singles/doubles with shared bathroom cost a mere $15/19; rooms with private bath start at $55/75. All prices include the best breakfast in Ukraine – a feast of cheese, sausage, *kasha* (buckwheat porridge), *bliny* (pancakes) with sour cream, bread and apple sauce. To get to the hotel, take tram No 1 five stops from the train station to the centre; tram No 9 travels from the centre to the hotel.

Hotel Lviv *(☎ 79 22 70, vulitsya 700-richchya Lvova 7)* is a tall, ugly 1970s structure with spartan but cheap rooms starting at $15/30. The concrete ***Hotel Dnister*** *(☎ 79 85 70, ☎ 72 07 83, fax 27 10 21, vulitsya Mateyko 6)* is pricey. Rooms cost $66/114.

Two more Soviet hotels lurk in Lviv's bleak suburbs. To get to ***Hotel Tourist*** *(☎ 35 10 65, vulitsya Konovaltsa 103)*, take tram No 2 from prospekt Svobody to the end of the line. ***Hotel Sputnik*** *(☎ 64 58 22, Knyahyni Olhy 116)* is at the end of the tram No 3 line. Rooms at both cost around $30/40.

Lviv's topnotch hotel is the central ***Grand Hotel*** *(☎ 72 76 65, ☎ 72 70 42, fax 76 90 60, grands@icmp.lviv.ua, prospekt Svobody 13)*. It's an elegant, fully restored 1898 Habsburg-era building and is completely up to Western standards with professional staff and superb rooms at a high price: singles/doubles/triples start at $105/135/170. Prices include breakfast and unlimited use of the fitness centre, swimming pool, sauna, jacuzzi and aerobics studio in the Grand Club-Sofia (☎ 72 90 00), run by the hotel at prospekt Shevchenka 10.

Out of Town Those seeking a touch of peace and tranquillity should head straight for the ***Grand Resort*** *(☎ 97 16 06, fax 97 16 05, grands@icmp.lviv.ua)*, a cluster of luxurious, lakeside country cottages managed by the Grand Hotel team in Basivka, some 20km south-west of Lviv in the Pustomyty district. In summer, you can fish, sunbathe, swim and munch on barbecued shashlyk. Winter guests can enjoy free use of the sauna and jacuzzi. Count on paying at least $100 for a double.

Places to Eat

Restaurants It's certainly a beautiful world at ***Beau Monde*** *(☎ 72 50 41, prospekt Shevchenka 10)* where topnotch cuisine is served with a grandiose flourish at topnotch prices. Chicken Kyiv notches up $6, squid in wine is $10 and king shrimps, a fabulous $49.

Less extravagant diners can head a couple of doors down to ***Europe Trident*** *(☎ 72 58 62, ☎/fax 97 11 73, prospekt Shevchenka 14)*. Imaginative dishes such as fiery steak, sea-gifts salad or pork ribs in whisky cost no more than $3.50. Europe also accepts credit cards and is open from 8 am to 11 pm.

Glamorous, B&W photographs of local models adorn the bare brick interior of ***Noiv Kovuet*** *(vulitsya Stavropihiyska 9)*, a trendy restaurant-cum-cafe off ploshcha Rynok. Delicious, Ukrainian cuisine is served here, against a backdrop of fine jazz and country and western hits. A couple of doors down is ***Stari Royal***, an outdated establishment by contrast, whose cosy interior is ruined by a blaring speaker and a Soviet-style cloakroom attendant.

An old-school spot which has succeeded in retaining its charm is ***Pid Levom*** *(☎ 72 68 13, ploshcha Rynok 20)*, a neck-craning, admire-the-ceiling type of place in a large medievalesque hall and cellar. Beneath, the Lion is open from noon to midnight and has live music most evenings. Similar dishes at similar prices (around $3) are served at ***Zolotii Vepr*** *(ploshcha Rynok 17)*, another cellar spot with smiling staff, typical Ukrainian cuisine, and stuffed animal heads adorning the red-brick walls. The Golden Viper is open from noon to 9 pm.

U Pani Steftsi *(☎ 79 84 35, prospekt Svobody 10)* serves a good selection of light dishes for no more than $1. Try a black caviar sandwich for $0.75 or a plate of steaming *varenyky* (stuffed dumplings) for $0.50. The menu is translated into English (quote '... alkogolik drinks ...'), the waiting staff is dressed in traditional costume and the interior is adorned with strings of red onions. Another good-value eating joint, just off the Planta, is ***Lisova Pisnya*** *(☎ 72 47 16, vulitsya Schovykh Striltsiv 5)*, which serves delicious fare such as lemon chicken shashlyk for around $2.

Two blocks north of the central square is ***Raphael*** *(☎ 79 70 33, vulitsya Lesi Ukrainky 18)*, another Ukrainian restaurant complete with an overdressed waiting staff decked out in garish blue and glittery-gold costumes.

The ***Jazz Fun Club*** *(vulitsya Teatralna 24)*, spitting distance from the opera and ballet theatre, is a glittery spot with chrome tables and chairs, a TV, and menu pinned up outside.

Cafes Sweet-toothed fiends should look no farther than ***Svitou*** *(prospekt Shevchenka 10)*, a deliciously well stocked candy shop with three small tables where you can sip coffee, eat cakes and admire the regal interior of this historic establishment. The stretch of pavement outside Svitou is lined with street stalls selling locally produced biscuits and sweets.

Ploshcha Rynok offers a number of light-bite options, the cheapest being ***Ratusha***, entered up the steps on the western side of the town hall. A starch-filled selection of Ukrainian dishes for no more than $1 are doled out at the canteen-style cafe to the left, while coffee and cakes are served in the more upmarket bar to the right. ***Na Rinku*** *(ploshcha Rynok 34)*, with its large, open doors and seating spilling onto the cobbled square, is another hot spot. For a snack standing up, try ***Kvitka***, a one room cafe at No 4 on the square.

Filling Middle Eastern fare like plov and manti is served at the five tabled ***Kafe-Bar Vedmid*** *(☎ 75 33 25, vulitsya Arsenalnya 7)*. Again, count on paying $1 a dish. In summer, terrace cafes adorn the square in front of the armoury.

Sonata, midway along vulitsya Valova, is a great people-watching spot with an elegant wooden interior and large windows overlooking the street. This modern coffee house is open from 10 am to 11 pm. ***Kafe Chervona Kalyna*** is a quaint corner cafe with a ceramic tiled ceiling, just down from the Philharmonia at vulitsya Chaykovskoho 16.

Self-Catering Your raw meat and fibre needs can be met at ***Halitsky Market***, a heaving mass of colourful market mayhem, off ploshcha Soborna, with piles of fresh fruit, vegetables, nuts and honey; it's open daily during daylight hours.

Entertainment

Bars & Discos ***Dzuga Cultural Centre***, accessed through a clothes shop at prospekt Shevchenka 3, is the hip place to hang out. By day, it serves as a bar and Internet cafe until 8 pm, when a disco takes over until 2 am. Avoid the paying toilets – a rip-off given their filthy state.

Opera, Theatre & Classical Music A walk through the old town streets at dusk will reveal the hum of local life shuffling to a close. For a perfect evening, combine a leisurely evening stroll down the Planta with a performance at the lavish ***Ivano-Franko Opera & Ballet Theatre*** *(☎ 72 85 62, prospekt Svobody 28)*, where you can be entertained in gilded surroundings for $2 to $20 depending on seating. Advance tickets are sold at the Teatralna Kasa (☎ 74 20 80, ☎ 72 88 60, fax 72 85 65), prospekt Svobody 37, open from 11 am to 2 pm and 5 to 7 pm. Schedules and advance tickets for most cultural events are available here.

The ***Philharmonia*** *(vulitsya Chaykovskoho 7)* performs in its swan-crested building off prospekt Shevchenka. The ***Ukrainian Drama Theatre*** *(☎ 72 05 90, vulitsya Lesi Ukrainky 1)* is immediately east of the opera theatre, and the ***Marionette Theatre*** is on the western end of ploshcha Danyla Halytskoho. Folklore shows are sometimes held in the ***outdoor theatre*** at the

Museum of Popular Architecture, vulitsya Chernecha Hora 1.

Shopping

The colourful outdoor arts and crafts market, a block east from the top end of prospekt Svobody, between vulitsya Lesi Ukrainky and vulitsya Zamok Kornyakta, is the place to shop for everything from pottery and ceramics to wood craft and embroidered blouses. Alternatively try the smaller outdoor crafts market on the corner of vulitsya Shpytalna and vulitsya Kulisha, next to the TsUM department store.

A good selection of pysanky, traditional Ukrainian costumes, *matryoshkas* (Russian dolls), spoons and table runners can also be found in the gift shop inside the Museum of Ethnography, Arts & Crafts. The Gothic Hall shop, inside the History Museum at ploshcha Rynok 6, sells quality antiques and art pieces. Chudozhink, ploshcha Mitskevycha 2 (open from 10 am to 2 pm and 3 to 6 pm), and Ukrainsky Suvenir, vulitsya Horodetska 35, are two art and crafts shops with plenty of wicker baskets, embroidery etc.

More unusual, contemporary buys can be had at the funky art gallery at vulitsya Virmenska 35; don't miss the fun street art which adorns the crumbling facades of the nearby courtyard.

Getting There & Away

Air The airport information desk (☎ 69 21 12) has schedule information. There are a handful of international as well as domestic flights (see the Ukraine Getting There & Away chapter). Air Ukraine (☎ 72 78 18) and Lviv Airlines both have their offices inside the train ticket office, vulitsya Hnatyuka 20-22.

Train Railway lines from nine directions converge at Lviv's main 1904 train station, 3km west of the centre at the end of vulitsya Chernivetska, north-west off vulitsya Horodetska. Tram Nos 1 and 9 go from the tram terminus in front of the train station to prospekt Svobody and ploshcha Rynok in the centre.

Domestic services include Uzhhorod (seven hours), Chernivtsi (six hours), Ivano-Frankivsk (three to four hours), Ternopil (three hours), Rivne (4½ hours) and Lutsk (four hours), twice or more a day; Odesa (13 hours) and Simferopol (30 hours) at least daily. For local trains to surrounding towns within the Lviv region, like Sambir, Drohobych, Stry and Chervonohrad, there is a daily electric train service.

Trains to/from Kyiv (10 to 12 hours) run about four times daily. Those wanting to travel in style can opt for a cabin aboard the *Grand Tour*, a luxurious carriage run by the Grand Hotel on the express night trains (Nos 91 and 92) to/from Kyiv and Lviv. Linen, tea, coffee and mineral water are included in the price. Tickets can be reserved through the Grand Hotel in Lviv (☎ 76 91 70, fax 76 90 60, grands@icmp.lviv.ua) or in Kyiv (☎ 44-223 51 06).

The most painless way to acquire a train ticket is to buy it in advance from the train ticket office (☎ 39 00 51, ☎ 39 00 52, ☎ 39 00 53), vulitsya Hnatyuka 20-22. It is open from 8 am to 2 pm and 3 to 8 pm (until 6 pm on weekends). For all train information call ☎ 005 (open 24 hours).

Bus Eight small bus stations are scattered across the city. They service outlying destinations within a 75km radius. Buses to Zhovkva depart from bus station No 4, next to Krakivsky market at vulitsya Bazarna 11 (a 10 minute walk north-west from the opera theatre). Buses to Olesko depart from bus station No 2, about 3km north of the centre at the end of tram line No 6.

The long-distance bus station, vulitsya Stryska 271, is 8km south of the centre. Buses to Ivano-Frankivsk (four daily), Chernivtsi (one daily) and buses to Poland (see Ukraine Getting There & Away) use the bus station on vulitsya Stryska. One bus a day departs from in front of the train station to Kyiv; Belarus-bound buses depart from the bulvar Khmelnychkogo bus station. Trolleybus No 5 from ploshcha Petrushevycha and bus No 18 run between the train station and this bus station.

Tickets are sold in advance at the bus ticket office (☎ 72 19 91), vulitsya Teatralna

26. It is open from 9 am to 7 pm (closed from 11.30 to 11.45 am, and from 2 to 3 and 5 to 5.15 pm). Timetables (☎ 97 11 08 for schedule information) are also posted here. For all bus information, call ☎ 004 (until 8 pm).

Tickets for buses to Western Europe are sold at Eastern European Travel (☎ 51 06 40, ☎/fax 97 17 86, sptravel@ukrpack.net), prospekt Shevchenko 13.

Getting Around

To/From the Airport The airport is about 8km west of the centre, a 20 minute ride on trolleybus No 9 from a stop in front of the main university building.

AROUND LVIV

An enjoyable day trip from Lviv is a visit to the historical town of **Zhovkva** (Жовква), 32km north. During the late 17th century, it was an important cultural and educational centre, home to a thriving colony of influential artists. Today its sprawling, central ploshcha Vicheva is lined with unkempt 17th to 18th century buildings, serving as a stark reminder of Zhovkva's gradual fall from glory. The simplistic Renaissance **palace** on the south side of the square originally served as a defensive castle (1594). From here, walls lead to the 17th century **Zvirynetska Gate**, through which Khmelnytsky and his Cossacks supposedly marched when liberating the town from the Poles in 1648. Beyond, lies **Vidpochynku Park**. There are about eight buses daily to Zhovkva (45 minutes) from Lviv's bus station No 4.

The French chateau-style hilltop castle at **Olesko** (Олесько), 70km east of Lviv, dates from the 17th and 18th centuries. It was built on the site of a 13th century fortress, destroyed by Tatar attacks in the 15th century, and finally restored in 1960-75. Opposite castle hill is the 18th century **Capuchin Church & Monastery**, now housing an **art museum**. Particularly interesting is the canvas (1692) in the portrait gallery which features the 1683 Battle of Vienna against the Turks. To get to Olesko, take a bus from bus station No 2 in Lviv (1½ hours, eight daily).

Lviv-Inturyst (see Lviv – Information earlier in the chapter) inside Hotel George organises excursions to Zovkva and Olesko ($90 for one to three individuals including transport and an English-speaking guide).

Transcarpathia Закарпатська область

UZHHOROD УЖГОРОД

☎ 01322 • pop 125,000

Uzhhorod (formerly Ungvar), 4km from the Slovak border and 25km from the Hungarian border, is the southern gateway to the Ukraine section of the Carpathian Mountains, and the main town of the Transcarpathian (Zakarpatska) region of Ukraine, which covers the south side of the mountains. It's a relaxed town with a large Hungarian and Romanian minority giving it a Balkan feel. The old centre has a quiet, old-fashioned air to its streets, while the river embankment west of pedestrian-only ploshcha Teatralna is dotted with cypress trees and protected from the north winds by the Carpathians. In summer, the Transcarpathian Folk Choir sporadically performs at a theatre in the region – an unmissable occasion.

The long autumn is reckoned to be the best season to visit the region, with the beeches turning and the grape harvest coming in. Troyanda Zakarpatie (a red dessert wine), Beregivske (a riesling) and Serednyanske are among the best known Transcarpathian wines.

History

Uzhhorod has existed since at least 903 AD. Transcarpathia was in Hungary or the Austro-Hungarian Empire from the 10th or 11th century to the end of WWI, apart from periods in the 16th and 17th centuries when parts were subject to Transylvanian and Cossack revolts. One hundred and fifty years after its founding in 1596, the Ukrainian Catholic (or Uniate) Church, combining Orthodox ritual with Roman Catholic doctrine, was established in Uzhhorod. It persuaded the peasants – traditionally Orthodox as the area had been on the fringe of Kyivan

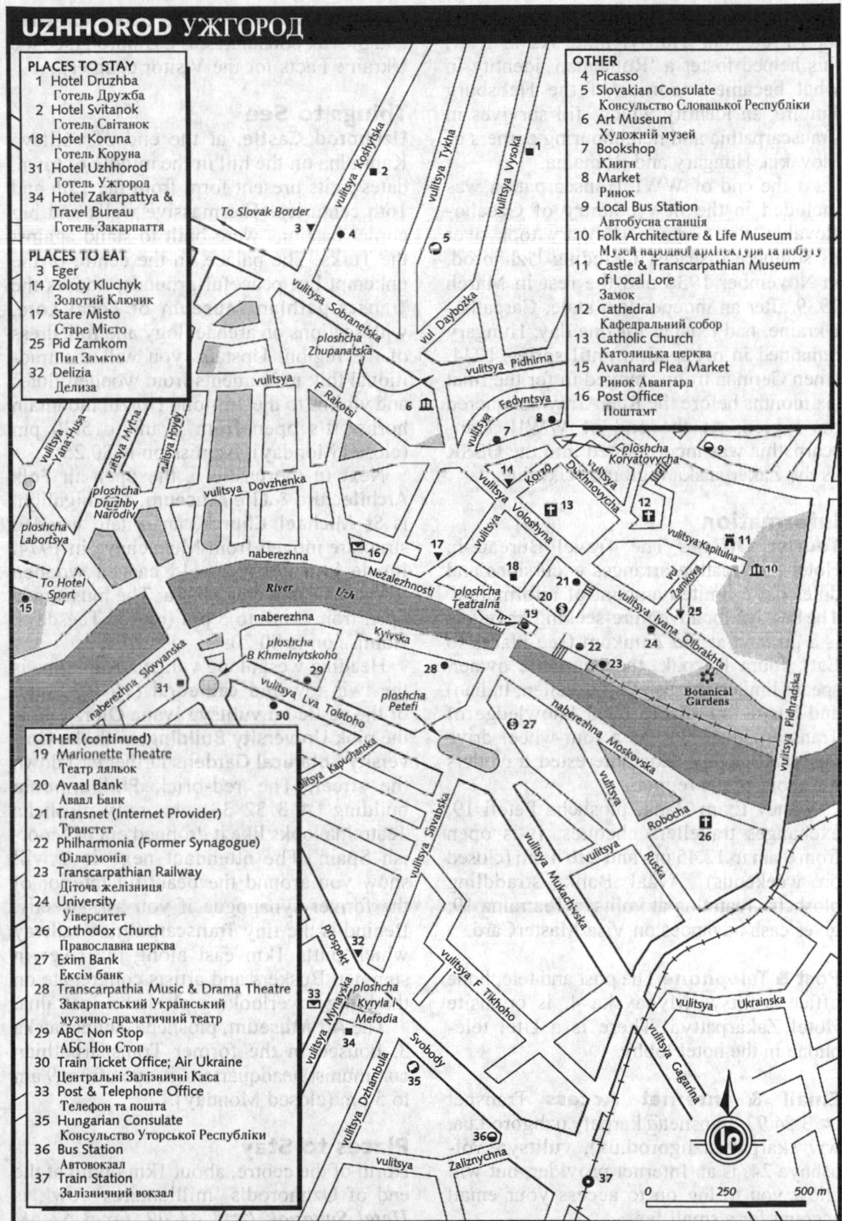
UZHHOROD УЖГОРОД
PLACES TO STAY
1 Hotel Druzhba
Готель Дружба
2 Hotel Svitanok
Готель Світанок
18 Hotel Koruna
Готель Коруна
31 Hotel Uzhhorod
Готель Ужгород
34 Hotel Zakarpattya & Travel Bureau
Готель Закарпаття
PLACES TO EAT
3 Eger
14 Zoloty Kluchyk
Золотий Ключик
17 Stare Misto
Старе Місто
25 Pid Zamkom
Пид Замком
32 Delizia
Делиза
OTHER
4 Picasso
5 Slovakian Consulate
Консульство Словацької Республіки
6 Art Museum
Художній музей
7 Bookshop
Книги
8 Market
Ринок
9 Local Bus Station
Автобусна станція
10 Folk Architecture & Life Museum
Музей народної архітектури та побуту
11 Castle & Transcarpathian Museum of Local Lore
Замок
12 Cathedral
Кафедральний собор
13 Catholic Church
Католицька церква
15 Avanhard Flea Market
Ринок Авангард
16 Post Office
Поштамт
OTHER (continued)
19 Marionette Theatre
Театр ляльок
20 Avaal Bank
Авал Банк
21 Transnet (Internet Provider)
Транстет
22 Philharmonia (Former Synagogue)
Філармонія
23 Transcarpathian Railway
Діточа желізниця
24 University
Уверситет
26 Orthodox Church
Православна церква
27 Exim Bank
Ексім банк
28 Transcarpathia Music & Drama Theatre
Закарпатський Український музично-драматичний театр
29 ABC Non Stop
АБС Нон Стоп
30 Train Ticket Office; Air Ukraine
Центральні Залізничні Каса
33 Post & Telephone Office
Телефон та пошта
35 Hungarian Consulate
Консульство Угорської Республіки
36 Bus Station
Автовокзал
37 Train Station
Залізничний вокзал
To Slovak Border
To Hotel Sport
vulitsya Koshytska
vulitsya Tykha
vulitsya Vysoka
vulitsya Sobranetska
ploshcha Zhupanatska
vul Daybozka
vulitsya Pidhirna
vulitsya F Rakotsi
vulitsya Fedyntsya
vulitsya Yana Husa
vulitsya Mytna
vulitsya Hoydy
ploshcha Druzhby Narodiv
vulitsya Dovzhenka
ploshcha Labortsya
ploshcha Koryatovycha
Korzo
vulitsya Dukhnovycha
vulitsya Voloshyna
vulitsya Kapitulna
vul Zamkova
vulitsya Ivana Olbrakhta
naberezhna
Nezalezhnosti
River Uzh
ploshcha Teatralna
naberezhna Kyivska
ploshcha B Khmelnytskoho
naberezhna Slovyanska
vulitsya Lva Tolstoho
ploshcha Petefi
Botanical Gardens
naberezhna Moskovska
vulitsya Pidhradska
vulitsya Kapuchanska
vulitsya Sváboska
vulitsya Robocha
vulitsya Ruska
vulitsya Mukachivska
prospekt
vulitsya F Tikhoho
ploshcha Kyryla i Mefodia
vulitsya Mynayska
Svobody
vulitsya Dzhambula
vulitsya Ukrainska
vulitsya Gagarina
vulitsya Zaliznychna
0 250 500 m

Rus – to look to Catholic Hungary rather than Protestant Transylvania. As in Lviv, this helped foster a 'Ruthenian' identity in what became a corner of the Habsburg Empire, an identity which still survives in Transcarpathia and neighbouring corners of Slovakia, Hungary and Romania.

At the end of WWI Transcarpathia was included in the new country of Czechoslovakia. Pro-German Hungary took over its southern districts, including Uzhhorod, in November 1938 and the rest in March 1939 after an independent state, Carpatho-Ukraine, had existed for one day. Hungary remained in occupation until spring 1944, when German troops moved in for the final six months before the Red Army conquered the region. At the end of WWII Transcarpathia was incorporated into the USSR as the Zakarpatska region of Ukraine.

Information

Tourist Offices The Travel Bureau in Hotel Zakarpattya arranges excursions and doles out a limited amount of information. The best bet for adventure-seeking travellers is a pit stop at Pid Zamkom (see Places to Eat). Ioura Ruznak, the energetic owner, speaks limited English (but excellent Italian) and has a formidable local knowledge of Transcarpathia. He has a four-wheel drive jeep and happily takes interested travellers for a tour of the region.

Money Exim Bank, ploshcha Petefi 19, exchanges travellers cheques. It is open from 9 am to 12.45 pm and 2 to 4 pm (closed on weekends). Avaal Bank, straddling ploshcha Teatralna at vulitsya Teatralna 19, gives cash advances on Visa/MasterCard.

Post & Telephone The post and telephone office, vulitsya Mynayska 4, is opposite Hotel Zakarpattya. There is a Utel telephone in the hotel lobby.

Email & Internet Access Transnet (☎ 3 54 97, transnet@karpaty.uzhgorod.ua, www.karpaty.uzhgorod.ua), vulitsya Voloshnya 24, is an Internet provider, but will allow you to log on to access your email account for a small fee.

Foreign Consulates There are Hungarian and Slovak consulates in Uzhhorod (see the Ukraine Facts for the Visitor chapter).

Things to See

Uzhhorod Castle, at the end of vulitsya Kapitulna on the hill in the middle of town, dates in its present form from the 15th and 16th centuries. The massive walls and big corner bastions were built to stand against the Turks. The palace, in the centre of the unkempt but peaceful grounds, houses the **Transcarpathian Museum of Local Lore**, with sections on archaeology and folk dress of the region. Upstairs you will see traditional folk instruments from wooden flutes and violins to the 4m-long Hutzul mountain horns. It's open from 9 am to 5.30 pm (closed Monday). Admission is $0.25.

Next to the castle is the open-air **Folk Architecture & Life Museum**. The highlight is **St Michael Church**, an ornate wooden structure moved from Mukacheve in 1974. Inside is a 200-year-old carved wooden iconostasis and candelabra. The museum is open from 9 am to 5 pm (closed Tuesday). Admission is $0.20.

Heading west along vulitsya Kapitulna is the twin-towered **cathedral** (1640). South of the castle on vulitsya Ivana Olbrakhta is the pink **University Building**, with the **University Botanical Gardens** farther east down the street. The red-brick **Philharmonia** building (☎ 3 32 38) on pretty ploshcha Teatralna looks like it dropped out of Moorish Spain. The attendant next door will show you around the beautiful interior of the former synagogue if you ask sweetly. Behind is the tiny **Transcarpathian railway** which putts 1km east along the river in summer. Buskers and artists congregate on the bridge overlooking ploshcha Teatralna.

The **Art Museum**, ploshcha Zhupanatska 3, housed in the former Transcarpathian communist headquarters, is open from 9 am to 5 pm (closed Monday).

Places to Stay

North of the centre, about 1km uphill at the end of Uzhhorod's 'millionaires' row', is ***Hotel Svitanok*** *(☎ 3 43 09, fax 3 52 68,* *vulitsya Koshytska 30)*. It is friendly with singles/doubles warranting few complaints for $5/10. Breakfast in the restaurant across the street is $0.50.

The 200 bed ***Hotel Uzhhorod*** *(☎ 3 50 60, fax 1 20 70, ploshcha B Khmelnytskoho 2)*, south of the river about 1km west of the centre, is bland and off a busy intersection but with decent rooms, most with balconies, for $15/26/35 a single/double/triple.

Hotel Zakarpattya *(☎ 9 75 10, fax 9 73 04, ploshcha Kyryla i Mefodia 5)*, 1km south of the city centre, is an agreeable effort, with well kept but overpriced rooms at $37/50 for singles/doubles. Breakfast – cold, rubber-like Frankfurter sausages, shredded cabbage, and cold lumpy mashed potato – costs an additional $2.

The charming, weather-beaten ***Hotel Koruna*** *(ploshcha Teatralna 5)* was closed for restoration at the time of writing. Locals are adamant that it will reopen.

Places to Eat

Don't leave Uzhhorod without a visit to ***Pid Zamkom*** *(Under the Castle; ☎ 3 69 83, ☎ 3 68 83, vulitsya Ivana Olbrakhta 3)*, one of Ukraine's best cafes-cum-hang-outs. The place is run by a highly energetic and entrepreneurial couple; Ioura Ruznak speaks some five languages and dreams of opening a small hotel above his cafe. The kitchen specialises in old Transcarpathian recipes, classic B&W films are screened every evening at 8 pm, and the pasta is said to be the country's best. The cosy, crowded interior is a treasure trove of Transcarpathian knick-knacks. Under the Castle is open from 7.30 am to 11 pm.

Eger, down the hill from Hotel Svitanok on vulitsya Koshytska, is a hunters'-style, grill bar and cafe. The colourful, graffiti-adorned shed opposite houses ***Picasso***, a lively bar (open from 9 am to 11 pm) and disco (8 pm to 2 am; until 5 am at weekends).

Old-timers include the uninspiring but dirt-cheap ***Stare Misto*** *(vulitsya Korzo 9)* and ***Zoloty Kluchyk*** (Golden Key), corner of vulitsya Korzo and vulitsya Voloshyna. ***Delizia***, conveniently close to Hotel Zakarpattya at prospekt Svobody 45, is a sparkling, modern pizza and ice-cream joint.

Self-caterers should aim for ***ABC Non Stop*** *(vulitsya Lva Tolstoho 42)*, a 24 hour grocery store. The ***market*** off ploshcha Koryatovycha sells fresh fruit and vegetables.

Getting There & Away

Train There are daily trains to Lviv (seven hours) and Kyiv (20 to 21 hours), and a train every other day to Ivano-Frankivsk (10 hours). The scenic train ride from Uzhhorod, along the southern base of the Carpathians to Chernivtsi (via Khust and Rakhiv) only runs on even days.

The left-luggage room at the train station is open 24 hours (closed from 11.30 am to 12.30 pm and midnight to 1 am). The information desk is open from 8 am to 8 pm ($0.01 per question). Advance tickets are sold at the train ticket office, next door to Air Ukraine at vulitsya Lva Tolstoho 33. The office is open from 8 am to 1 pm and 2 to 6 pm (until 3 pm on Saturday, closed Sunday).

Bus Uzhhorod's bus station, vulitsya Zaliznychna 2, is opposite the train station at the south-eastern end of prospekt Svobody. Daily cross-border buses link Uzhhorod with Michalovce and Košice in Slovakia and Miskolc in Hungary, and link Chop with Nyiregyhaza in Hungary.

There are four to six daily buses, via Mukacheve (45 minutes), to Rakhiv (6½ hours).

MUKACHEVE
МУКАЧЕВО

☎ 03131 • pop 90,000

Often the first train stop past the border into Ukraine from Slovakia or Hungary, Mukacheve is the unassuming secondary city of Transcarpathia. First settled in the 9th century by White Croatians, it was subsequently seized and settled by Kyivan Rus, Hungarians, Tatars, Transylvanians, Ukrainians, and Hungarians again. Today's population is a true Transcarpathian mix, and Mukacheve reflects this with an unpretentious small-town atmosphere.

Mukacheve's 14th century **Palanok Castle**, which crests the top of Zamkova

Hora (Castle Hill), is Transcarpathia's best hilltop castle, home to the famous Hungarian princess Ilona Zrini in the 17th century. Today, it peers down on a large military base at its foot.

The fairly new ***Hotel Barva***, adjoining a pharmacy and shop at vulitsya Miru 66, is the best place to stay in town. It is a two minute walk from the bus station.

Getting There & Away

The train station is 1.5km south-west of central ploshcha Miru, along vulitsya Lenina. Plenty of trains pass through with daily services to Lviv, Kyiv, Ivano-Frankivsk and Chernivtsi. The trains to Uzhhorod (about two hours) have to go back through Chop, so it's faster to take the bus.

The bus station is 1.5km east of the centre off vulitsya Miru, the street extending south-east from ploshcha Miru. From Mukacheve there are four to six buses daily to/from Rakhiv and Uzhhorod (6½ hours).

From Mukacheve the eastbound A265 runs along the Romanian border to Rakhiv, the southern gateway to the Carpathian National Natural Park. The last stretch of road, from just west of Hust onwards, skirts the Tisa River and is particularly scenic.

Ivano-Frankivsk Region
Івано-Франківська область

IVANO-FRANKIVSK
ІВАНО-ФРАНКІВСЬК

☎ 03422 • pop 234,000

Lviv's lesser partner in Galicia, Ivano-Frankivsk has traditionally been the cultural and economic capital of the Carpathian region, the hilly lands on the north-eastern side of the mountains from Transcarpathia. The city centre is a lively mix of open spaces, crowded streets and parks, and there's a teeming marketplace with a few fine churches mixed in.

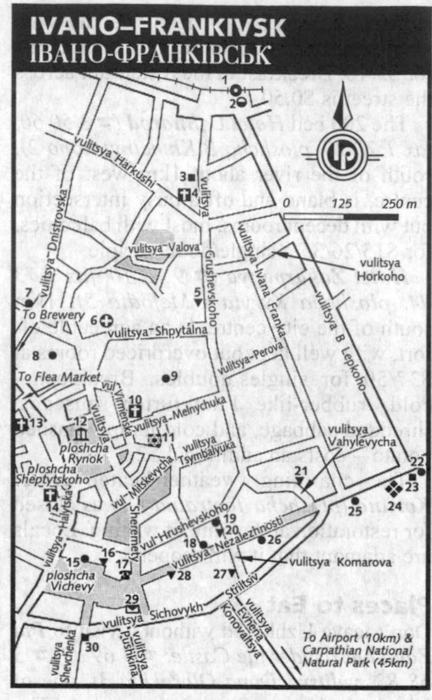

Founded in the mid-17th century on Cossack trade routes between the southern Danube and Lviv, it quickly fell under Polish rule and then to the Habsburgs a century later. The city was the second capital of the temporary Ukrainian National Republic, established in Lviv during the war for independence against Poland in 1919. During WWII the city was a centre for UPA partisans who fought against both the Germans and the Russians. Until 1962, the city was known as Stanyslaviv.

Information

The central post office is on the southern side of ploshcha Vichevy. On the opposite side of the square at vulitsya Nezalezhnosti 9 is the central telephone centre (open from 7 am to 11 pm). Avaal Bank, vulitsya Saharova 32, gives cash advances on Visa/MasterCard and cashes travellers cheques.

Quality city/regional maps and the *Ivano-Frankivsk Oblast* English-language tourist

IVANO-FRANKIVSK ІВАНО-ФРАНКІВСЬК

PLACES TO STAY

3 Hotel Roxolana
Готель Роксоляна
23 Hotel Ukraina
Готель Україна
30 Hotel Dnister
Готель Дністер

PLACES TO EAT

5 Trian Kafe
Тріан Кафе
16 Restaurant Continental
Ресторан Континентал
20 Slovan
Слован
21 Pegas
Пегас
27 Kafe & Bar Svitlitsya
Кафе та Бар Світлиця
28 Kafe Bily Kamin
Кафе Білий Камінь

OTHER

1 Train Station
Залізничний вокзал
2 Bus Station
Автобусний вокзал
4 Ukrainian Orthodox Church
Свято Троїцький Кафедральний Собор
6 Pototsky Palace Complex
Комплекс палацу Потоцького
7 Covered Market
Закритий ринок
8 Main Outdoor Market
Центральний ринок
9 Regional Government Administration
Державна обласна Адміністрація
10 Ukrainian Catholic Church (former Armenian Church)
Українська католицька церква
11 Synagogue
Синагога
12 Regional Museum
Краєзнавчий музей
13 Roman Catholic Church
Католицький церква
14 Ukrainian Greco-Catholic Cathedral
Український Греко-католицький собор
15 Passazh
Пасаж
17 Central Telephone Centre
Центральний переговорний пункт
18 Bukanist
Букініст
19 Ukrainsky Suvenir
Український сувенір
22 Ivan Franko Music & Drama Theatre
Музично-драматичний театр ім. Івана Франка
24 Magazin-Delikates
Магазин Делікатес
25 Central Flower Market
Центральний квітковий ринок
26 Book Shop
Книги
29 Post Office
Поштамт

guide ($0.50) are sold at the bookshop at vulitsya Nezalezhnosti 18 or at Bukanist, vulitsya Wezel 19. Hotel Roxolana organises city tours, excursions in Transcarpathia and car rentals with driver ($0.50/km). Hotel Ukraina can arrange a city guide for $10/hour.

City Centre

The traditional city heart is **ploshcha Rynok**, surrounded by a mix of colourful buildings with the angular 1929 star-shaped town hall in the centre. Today the building houses the **Regional Museum**, featuring the 12th century sarcophagus of King Yaroslav Osmomsyl. It's open from 10 am to 5 pm (closed Monday). East of the square is the former **Armenian church** (1742) with an attractive, undulating baroque facade and twin, rounded bell towers. A block south is a working **synagogue** (1897); the Rabbi (☎ 3 48 94) is in between noon and 2 pm.

Just west of ploshcha Rynok is the elongated ploshcha Sheptytskoho with two impressive churches at either end. South is the baroque, former **Jesuit church** (1729), since converted into a Ukrainian Catholic cathedral. At the opposite end is the **Roman Catholic church** (1672), its design reflecting the transition from the Renaissance to the baroque with rows of stubby buttresses along its sides. West of the church is a **flea market**. On vulitsya Novhorodska is an abandoned **brewery** (1767).

North of ploshcha Rynok is a large outdoor market with plenty of activity and heaps of fresh produce. Popular, pleasant and reserved for pedestrians along its western side, **vulitsya Nezalezhnosti** has several refined early 20th century buildings, culminating at its western end with spacious **ploshcha Vichevy**, which is another bustling combination of old and new architecture.

Places to Stay

Homestays The Green Tourism Development Association (☎ 2 68 24, fax 2 57 10, vulitsya Mazepa 135) arranges rural homestays in the region for around $4 a night; home-cooked meals cost extra.

Hotels The cheapest joint is ***Hotel Dnister*** *(☎ 2 35 33, vulitsya Schovykh Striltsiv 12)*. Singles/doubles/triples with shared bathroom cost $12/19/21.

A breath of fresh air has swept through ***Hotel Ukraina*** *(☎ 2 26 09, fax 2 47 71, firm@nadiya.if.ua, vulitsya Nezalezhnosti 40)* in recent years. Ugly from the outside, the standard 1970s block sports pleasant rooms adorned with traditional Ukrainian woven carpets and embroidery. Simple singles/doubles with fridge and TV cost $25/40 and renovated semi-lux/lux rooms are $40/50. Breakfast is $4.

The luxurious, 25 room ***Hotel Roxolana*** *(☎ 2 52 21, fax 2 47 69, vulitsya Grushevskoho 7-9)* is an Austrian-Ukrainian-American joint venture, professionally run in a fully restored 1907 secessionist building. It is completely Western in comfort (soft, fluffy white towels etc). Rooms with breakfast cost $75/90 for singles/doubles.

Places to Eat

Pegas *(☎ 5 25 05, vulitsya Vahylevvycha 3)* is an ageing spot, complete with menu spelt by the 100g and duly signed by the chief accountant and director. All mains (around $2) are spiced up with fries (100g), shredded cabbage (30g), shredded beetroot (20g) and shredded carrot (20g).

The Hotel Roxolana restaurant is comfortably affordable (around $0.50/$1 for a starter/main), and dishes up wholesome and tasty Ukrainian cuisine. It has a good wine list too; don't miss the Moldovan Codru for $4 a bottle. ***Slovan*** *(☎ 2 25 94, vulitsya Komarova 4)* is a flash Harry place, complete with ubiquitous doorman and suffocatingly formal waiters (open from 11 am to 11 pm).

The pedestrian part of vulitsya Nezalezhnosti is loaded with cafes. At No 2 is ***Kafe Bily Kamin*** (White Chimney Cafe) whose white rock interior dishes out ice cream and sweet cakes. Midway along vulitsya Komarova at No 3 is the spacious and exceedingly smoky ***Kafe & Bar Svitlitsya*** (open from 9 am to 10 pm). The south-eastern edge of ploshcha Rynok is another hot cafe spot. The ***Trian Kafe*** *(vulitsya Grushevskoho 31)* is a refreshingly modern cellar cafe and boasts the cleanest toilets in town. The best coffee is served in style at ***Restaurant Continental*** *(ploshcha Vichevy)*.

Magazin-Delikates adjoining Hotel Ukraina is the closest thing you'll find to a genuine, Western-style supermarket (open from 8 am to midnight).

Getting There & Away

Air A small airport, 10km south at vulitsya Evhena Konovaltsya 264A, has weekly flights with Air Ukraine to Lviv, Kyiv and other major domestic locations, and a handful of international flights (see Ukraine Getting There & Away). Bus No 1 or 1A from the train station goes to the airport in about 25 minutes.

Train There are two or more trains daily to/from Lviv (three hours), Chernivtsi (three to four hours) and Kyiv (13 to 14 hours); and a train every other day to/from Uzhhorod (10 hours). Daily services include to/from Odesa (21 hours), Moscow (15 hours), Sofia (27 hours), Brest (15 hours) and St Petersburg (36 hours).

Local train services serve Kolomyya (five daily), Rohatyn (one a day) and Rakhiv (twice daily).

Bus The bus station is directly east of the train station with several daily buses to Lviv, Kolomyya (1½ hours), Kosiv, Chernivtsi (four hours), Rakhiv (two a day) and Ternopil. Most Chernivtsi buses continue to Chisinau in neighbouring Moldova.

CARPATHIAN NATIONAL NATURAL PARK

About 45km south of Ivano-Frankivsk lies the country's largest national park, with some of the highest peaks in the Ukrainian Carpathians and lots of alpine vegetation. Protected since 1980, the 503 sq km park shelters wolves, brown bears, lynx, bison, deer and a host of other fauna and flora species – including the pretty, little, protected edelweiss. A maze of hiking trails crisscrosses the park which, come

Ukrainian Trivia

- Awesome Ukrainian pole vaulter Sergey Bubka (born 1964) is a record breaker 35 times over. The world champion has broken the outdoor pole vaulting world record 17 times and the indoor equivalent 18 times. Bubka has his own pole vaulting club in Donetsk.
- English novelist Joseph Conrad (1857-1924), best known for his short novel *Heart of Darkness* (1902), was born in the Ukrainian village of Terekhiv, Zhytomyrskoyi oblast, in north-western Ukraine. His parents were Polish.
- Kyiv was the third city in the USSR to be graced with a metro (1960), then called Lenin Metropolitan Railway. Its central stations boast the world's longest escalators (65m vertical drop).
- The geographical centre of Europe is in Ukraine according to signs posted 15km south of Rakhiv, western Ukraine. Unfortunately for Ukraine, Lithuania also claims to be home to Europe's geographical centre. Tricky.
- Home for the child musical prodigy, Sergey Prokofiev (1891-1953), was Sontsivka village, near Krasne in the Donetsk oblast. In 1904 Prokofiev left Ukraine to study at St Petersburg's Conservatory. He died the same day as Stalin.
- The period of Habsburg rule in Lemberg (present-day Lviv in western Ukraine) gave birth to Leopold von Sacher-Masoch (1835-95), an Austrian novelist whose scandalously sexy, semi-autobiographical novel entitled *Venus in Furs* (1869) gave rise to a new word: masochism.

the winter snows, becomes a playground for skiers. Hoverla (2061m), Ukraine's highest peak, sits on the park's western boundary.

The principal village in the park is **Vorokhta (Ворохта)**, but you're more likely to find accommodation to the north in the mountain resort of **Yaremcha (Яремча**; area phone code ☎ 03434) – home to the national park office and the starting point for most hikers – or in **Yasinya (Ясиня)**, a pretty alpine village just south of the Yablunytsia pass. In summer, the **Yablunytsia mountain pass** (931m), snow-blocked most of the winter, is cluttered with craft stalls. Artisans display their wares on the bonnets of their cars and the mountain air is filled with the smell of shashlyk, barbecued by the roadside. **Kvasi**, 29km farther south, is known for its mineral-rich springs.

The southern approach into the park, through charming **Rakhiv (Рахів**; population 16,400; area phone code ☎ 03132), is particularly rewarding. From Rakhiv, just 34km north of the Romanian border, the scenic (but perilously narrow) A265 snakes its way westwards for some 70km along the banks of the Tisa River and the Ukrainian-Romanian border. Some 15km south of Rakhiv towards **Dilove** is a roadside monument which, according to Ukrainians, marks the geographical centre of Europe.

Exploring the park by public transport can be trying. Given the rarity with which motorised or horse-drawn vehicles pass by, hitching can be equally hellish. If you don't have your own set of wheels or hiking boots, the only sane option is to befriend a local taxi driver who will happily drive you around for a prenegotiated fee.

Orientation

The Carpathian National Natural Park (CNNP) straddles the border between the Ivano-Frankivska and Zakarpatska regions *(oblasti)*, with parts of the park falling in either region. From the city of Ivano-Frankivsk, the A265 cuts southwards into the heart of the park. Yaremcha, 60km south of Ivano-Frankivsk, straddles the park's northern boundary. Yasinya, 55km farther south along the A265, marks the park's westernmost point.

Rakhiv, 65km south of Yaremcha on the A265 outside the park's south-western boundary, serves as a good gateway into the park. Kolomyya and Kosiv, about 28km and 60km respectively east of the park, are likewise good stepping stones into the mountains.

Maps The few maps that are available are not 100% accurate. Nos 165 and 184 in the Topograficheskaya Karta map series (see Ukraine Facts for the Visitor) cover the park and surrounding area (1:100,000 scale), but feature few hiking trails. In Yaremcha, the bookshop next to the post office stocks an occasional copy. Alternatively, try the CNNP office.

Information

The CNNP office (☎ 2 11 55, ☎ 2 11 57, ☎ 2 11 59, ecoplay@phantom.pu.if.ua) is in Yaremcha at vulitsya Stussa 6. There is usually someone in the recreation department (1st floor, room 20) who speaks English. From the main street in the village (A265), cross the railway tracks; the park office is recognisable by the stained-glass window that adorns its facade.

An equally invaluable information source is the Carpathian Agency for Agro-Eco Tourism (☎/fax 2 14 06, office@card.uzhgorod.ua) in Rakhiv at vulitsya Myru 1. The eco-tourism organisation falls under the umbrella of the Carpathian Agency for Regional Development (CARD) and arranges accommodation in *turbazas* (tourbases) and private homes, and eco-tours.

Avaal Bank, inside Turbaza Tisa in Rakhiv, gives cash advances on Visa/MasterCard.

Hutzuls

Indigenous to the Carpathians, Hutzuls are best known for their traditional folk crafts and wooden churches. The village of **Dora**, about 3km north of Yaremcha, has a particularly impressive church, built by regional ethnic Ukrainians in the 17th century.

The traditional centre of the Hutzuls is **Kolomyya** (Коломия; population 70,000; area phone code ☎ 03433), 50km east of the park and 65km south of Ivano-Frankivsk on the Prut River. Hutzul carved wooden tools, boxes, furniture, traditional embroidered folk dress and ceramic tableware are displayed in the town's **Museum of Hutzul Folk Art**, vulitsya Teatralna, 500m north of ploshcha Vidrodzhennya, the central square and marketplace. Bus No 12 goes to the centre from Kolomyya train or bus station.

Farther south, **Kosiv** (Косів; population 9000) is famed for its Saturday morning **craft market** which sees artisans from the hills roll down in their carts in the early morning to set up shop. Rooted firmly in its traditions, Kosiv was a bastion of Ukrainian identity during the years of Polish occupation and is home to the Hutsul Technical Art Institute. The market is open on Saturday from 6 am to 2 pm, although the best buys are snatched up by 8 am.

Carpathian Biosphere Reserve

The Carpathian Biosphere Reserve shelters Europe's only remaining virgin beech forest. It is part of UNESCO's network of international biosphere reserves and was awarded the European Diploma for Protected Areas by the Council of Europe in 1998.

The reserve is split into five *massifs* (territories), the largest being in the Rakhiv district. Eco-tours in the reserve can be organised in Rakhiv, at the Carpathian Biosphere Reserve headquarters (☎/fax 2 21 93, cbr@mail.uzhgorod.ua), Krasny Pleso 77, 3km from the town centre. Tours can also be arranged through CARD (see Information earlier).

Other interesting sections of the reserve farther afield include the **Valley of Narcissis** near Khoost, midway between Rakhiv and Mukacheve on the A265; and the 14,665 hectare **Stuzhytsya Landscape Park**, 30km north of Uzhhorod on the Ukrainian-Slovakian border.

Activities

Between November and March, skiers descend upon the park. The primary downhill **skiing** area is in **Yablunytsia**, a pretty village 30km south of Yaremcha. There are several drag lifts here. Skis/boots/poles can be hired in Yaremcha from the Karpaty Resort Complex for $2.50/1.50/1 per day. Downhill and cross-country skiing is also possible around Bogdan (1500m), 20km east of Rakhiv; the Turbaza Tisa in Rakhiv hires out gear.

Some 10km north of Yablunytsia along the A265 and then 8km south-east along a smaller road is **Vorokhta**. Here there are a couple of **ski jumps** and a **skiing biathlon** course, served by several drag lifts and the region's only chairlift.

In summer, the Carpathian park is transformed into a busy **hiking** area. Some trails are marked, but most are impossible to follow without the help of a local guide. The CNNP office arranges private guides for around $20 a day. From Yaremcha, a bus runs to the foot of Hoverla mountain, from where a hiking trail (four hours) leads to the top; the CNNP has details.

Places to Stay

Camping Wild camping is allowed in the park. Hikers can also spend the night in one of the wooden hunters' ***cabins*** that pepper the park. You have to provide your own food and bedding. Ask for a key from the recreation department (1st floor, room 20) at the CNNP headquarters in Yaremcha.

Homestays Staying in a private home offers travellers the chance to sample traditional Hutzul dishes such as *kulish* and *banoush*, national dishes made from corn. The CNNP recreation department arranges homestay accommodation for around $2.50 per person a night with optional home-cooked meals, mushrooming and berry picking for a small fee.

In Rakhiv, CARD (see Information earlier) arranges homestays in 50 local homes in the area under the umbrella of its Green Village Tourism Association. A night's accommodation costs $3 to $4; each meal is no more than $2.

Turbazas In Rakhiv, ***Turbaza Tisa*** *(☎ 2 10 27, ☎ 2 11 65, vulitsya Ivana Franka 4)* offers moth-eaten doubles with grubby sheets and a smelly private bathroom for $8 a night. Miraculously, the place has hot water. The reception is open from 9 am to 1 pm and 5 pm to midnight. A taxi (☎ 2 31 31) from Rakhiv bus/train station to the turbaza costs $1. Hardy travellers can also stay in the ***dorm*** used by bus drivers above the bus station (not advised for lone females).

Turbaza Syniogeriha *(Blue Mountain; ☎ 2 24 13)*, 8km from Rakhiv, is considered one of the best tourist complexes in the region. The 45 bed hotel, on the top of a mountain, has hot water year-round, a deluxe sauna, exercise and game room, and a traditional wooden *koleba* (house) where shashlyk is cooked. A bed for the night in a standard/deluxe room is $4/7, and meals are an additional $2. A taxi from Rakhiv costs around $5. Advance bookings can be made through CARD (see Homestays earlier).

The modern and luxurious ***Karpaty Resort Complex*** *(☎ 2 23 89, ☎/fax 2 21 34, vulitsya Dachna 30)* sprawls across the hillside above Yaremcha village. It has tennis courts, a swimming pool, sauna, solarium and is open year-round. Full board in a single/double/triple/quad starts at $40/50/90/100.

Getting There & Away

Train Two electric trains chug their way daily across the park from Rakhiv in the south-west to Kolomyya in the north-east. Stops along the tunnel-clad rail route include Yasinya, Vorokhta and Yaremcha.

From Kolomyya, trains head south to Chernivtsi or north to Ivano-Frankivsk (five a day); two Ivano-Frankivsk trains daily are direct from Rakhiv. There is one daily train to/from Lviv and Rakhiv; and one to three a day from Kolomyya to/from Lviv and Odesa.

Heading south into Romania, there is a sporadic local train service between Rakhiv and Sighetu Marmatiei.

Bus From Rakhiv, there are daily buses to/from Kolomyya (three daily); Chernivtsi, Ivano-Frankivsk and Mukacheve (twice daily); and Uzhhorod (seven a day). From Kolomyya, there are at least five buses daily to/from Ivano-Frankivsk, with a few less to/from Chernivtsi. At least three daily buses go to/from Kosiv.

Volyn & Rivne Regions Волиньська та Ровенська області

LUTSK ЛУЦЬК

☎ 03322 • pop 216,000

Lutsk, the chief city of the Volyn region, is preferable to Rivne, 67km down the road, as a stop between Brest and Lviv or Kyiv. Probably founded about 1000 AD by Volodymyr of Kyiv, it became part of the Galician-Volynian Principality when Kyivan Rus broke up. Taken over by Lithuania in the 14th century, it grew in trade importance despite occasional Tatar attacks. It passed to Poland in 1569, Russia in 1795, and between WWI and WWII was back under Poland.

Orientation & Information

The most interesting parts of town are south of Teatralna ploshcha, at the western end of the main street, prospekt Voli. The traffic-free section of vulitsya Lesi Ukrainky is the city's main pedestrian artery. It leads south-west from Teatralna ploshcha across busy vulitsya Kovelska, a former moat, down into the old town in a bend of the Styr River, from where parkland stretches east along the northern bank of the river.

Change money at Exim Bank inside Hotel Ukraina. The telephone and telegraph centre, 14 prospekt Voli, is open 24 hours.

Things to See

Known as Lubart's Castle after the Lithuanian prince who had it built in the 14th century, **Lutsk Castle** is the centrepiece of the old town. Its 13m-high brick walls atop earth ramparts are surmounted by three tall towers. Near the wood-roofed **Vladycha Tower** is a stairway leading up to the elevated wooden walkway with views down over the patchwork of gardens below. In the courtyard, the remains of the 12th century **Church of St John the Divine** (Ioanna Boslova), around which the castle was built, are being lazily excavated. The castle is open from 10 am to 6 pm.

The **old town** is dotted with monastic buildings from Lutsk's Polish period. The most imposing building is the **Jesuits' complex** on vulitsya Kafedralna, just west of the castle. The stately facade of its Roman Catholic **Saint Peter's & Paul's Cathedral** was originally built in 1610. Its recently renovated interior – painted in pink and yellow tones – resembles the inside of a massive Easter egg; the edifice served as a warehouse from 1948-70, a museum from 1970-76, and a church again from 1991. Opposite is an odd triple-arched 1536 **bell tower**. The austere, main Jesuit monastery building behind the cathedral – also early 17th century – was a prison in the 19th century.

Between the church and the castle is the wide-open cobbled **Zamkova ploshcha**. Down vulitsya Kafedralna to the south is the plain, 17th century **Birgittine monastery**, converted into a prison in 1846; it's now Lutsk's music academy. Across the street is a tiny park and **memorial** to Pasha Saveleva, a WWII partisan burnt alive in the prison yard by the Nazis. Stroll around the base of the castle on cottage-lined vulitsya Zamkova for nice views up to the formidable walls.

Pleasant, tree-covered **Lesi Ukrainky Park** stretches along the river east of the castle and market. The **Eternal Glory Memorial Complex** on vulitsya Nekrasova is a small park commemorating Volynian WWII heroes and victims. Numerous army statistics adorn the marble ring which surrounds the trophy. On the wall to its right (north) are the names of 107 villages destroyed by the Nazis, and a poem in memory of the 165,339 Volynians tortured and executed, and the 47,960 lost in prison camps.

The **Volyn Regional Museum** with a large classical entrance is nearby at vulitsya Shopena 20, open from 10 am to 6 pm (closed Sunday and Monday).

Places to Stay & Eat

Die-hard backpackers can spend the night in a disused ***train carriage*** at the train station; walk through the main station building and turn right along the platform. A bunk in *kupe* (2nd) class costs $0.75; as on a regular train, there is a stinky shared toilet in the corridor but no shower facilities. Reception, at the intersection of the two green carriages, is closed between 1 and 2 pm.

Hotel Ukraina *(☎ 4 33 51, fax 4 33 12, vulitsya Slovatskoho 2)* offers pleasant service with some English-speaking staff. Relatively large single/double/triple rooms cost $18/28/35.

Kafe Krai, straddling the corner of vulitsya Suvorova and vulitsya Striletska, draws a local crowd with its traditional Ukrainian dishes served in a rustic, wood interior. Another popular choice is upmarket ***Stary Zamok*** *(Old Castle; vulitsya Lesi Ukrainky 24)*. Its red borsch is accompanied by a twin set of delicious garlic-laced buns and, at $1, is worth every cent.

Dedicated budget travellers can always opt for a plateful of soggy but sodding-cheap varenyky for a bargain $0.33 at ***Pelmenna*** *(vulitsya Lesi Ukrainky 40)*. Failing that, the ***central market*** – a block away on the corner of vulitsya Zamkova and vulitsya Molodizhna – guarantees colourful, fruit-filled chaos.

Warm summer days should be whiled away in leisure, beer in hand, under the pagoda at ***Restoran Korona Vitovta***, a lovely local cafe-bar housed in a former 15th to 17th century monastery overlooking pretty Zamkova ploshcha.

Getting There & Away

The train station is 2km north-east of the centre; bus No 8 and trolleybus Nos 4 and 7 go from the station to Teatralna ploshcha. Trains go daily to/from Lviv, Rivne, Kyiv, Moscow, St Petersburg and Minsk.

The bus ticket and information office is at vulitsya Striletska 23. There are three to four buses a day to/from Lviv (four hours), six a day to/from Rivne (1½ hours) and to all surrounding destinations.

RIVNE
PIBHE

☎ 0362 • pop 250,000

In the 18th and 19th centuries, Rivne was the 'capital' of what was virtually the private kingdom of the Polish Lubomirsky family even though it was officially in Russia at the time. During WWII the Germans used the city as their administrative capital in Ukraine, and it was thoroughly destroyed as a result of fierce fighting.

Rivne today is a city of little interest or aesthetic value. Pleasant parkland sprawls along both banks of the Ustie River which snakes through the city from south to north. The main street, vulitsya Soborna, is crowned by the seven golden onion domes and five cupolas of the pretty **Resurrection Cathedral** (1895) at No 39.

A few kilometres west of the centre on vulitsya Belaya is the site of a concentration camp – marked with a **Victims of Fascism monument** – where some 80,000 were killed by the Nazis. In summer, locals flock to Gilcha Lake, about 20km south of Rivne on the road to Ostroh, to swim and sunbathe. There is a small lakeside bar and restaurant here, and a natural spring where locals fill their water bottles.

Places to Stay & Eat

Hotel Mir *(☎ 22 13 35, intour@intour.vt.rovno.ua, vulitsya Mitskevycha 32)*, off the north-eastern end of maydan Nezalezhnosti, is a central, concrete block. Its run-down doubles with shabby bathrooms go for $36, not including breakfast. Equally dated is ***Hotel Tourist*** *(☎ 26 74 13, vulitsya Kyivska 36)* next to the bus station. Singles/doubles/apartments cost $15/28/39.

Between the train station and Hotel Mir at prospekt Mira 19 is flashy ***Pharoah*** *(☎ 22 12 47)*, an upmarket restaurant with a dance floor, live music shows and a 15 page drinks menu. Next door is ***Paris***, an American-style, 1970s place where techno blares and the young order bottles of ice-cold vodka and jugs of tomato juice.

Getting There & Away

Rivne is on some major north-south train lines, with daily trains to/from Kyiv (7½ hours), Lviv (four to six hours), Odesa (16 hours), Simferopol (22 hours), Ivano-Frankivsk (nine hours), St Petersburg (20 to

23 hours), Chernivtsi (11 hours) and Minsk (10 hours).

There are frequent bus services to most outlying towns and larger cities, including six daily buses to Lutsk (1½ hours), Ostroh (1½ hours) and Ternopil (four hours via Kremenets).

OSTROH
ОСТРОГ

☎ 03654

Some 46km south from Rivne, Ostroh is one of the oldest settlements in Ukraine, dating from 1100. The town's main claim to fame is its cultural and educational heyday in the 16th century when a Greek/Latin/Slavic collegium and printing centre was established here to rival the Polish/Roman establishments in the West.

Things to See

Known as Zamkova Hora (Castle Hill), the present 14th to 19th century **fortress** complex, uphill from the centre off vulitsya Akademichna, was built on the hilltop site of an older 11th to 12th century settlement. The gracious 15th century **Bohayevayenska Church**, rebuilt in the lofty Ukrainian Byzantine style 300 years later, dominates the peaceful grounds. The north-western corner of the complex is occupied by a small 14th century **palace**. Its formidable buttresses spill over the hillside below. Inside (entrance at the top of the wooden staircase) is the regional **Ethnographic & Historic Museum** (☎ 2 25 93, ☎ 2 32 71), open from 9 am to 4.30 pm (closed Monday).

Very little is left of the formidable fortification system that once surrounded the town. Across the park, west of the fortress, is the 15th century **Uspensky Church**. A block north, the 15th to 16th century **Lutsk Gate Tower**, up some steps from near the corner of vulitsya Lutska and vulitsya Nezalezhnosti, is now the **History of Books & Printing Museum** (closed Monday). Among many lavish old books is a tiny old Slavonic alphabet book from 1578 and a copy of the famous 1581 Ostroh Bible, the first bible to be printed in the old Slavic language by Ivan Federov, as well as the 17th century *Ostrov Chronicles*, a book of Volyn and Galicia history between the 16th and 17th centuries.

Mezhyrich

Roughly 4km south of Ostroh on the road to Kremenets is the village of Mezhyrich with the impressive and formidable **Holy Trinity Monastery Fortress**, home to an Orthodox seminary. The complex, off the main road and behind a duck pond, is surrounded by walls with four octagonal towers. The inner church has Gothic detailing with Byzantine domes and dates from the 15th century. The two adjacent monastic wings with their four pointed towers and Renaissance portals are 200 years older.

Places to Stay & Eat

Hotel Viliya *(☎ 3 04 56, vulitsya Nezalezhnosti 5)* has spartan singles/doubles for $6/8. Eating options are limited to the ***Kafe Zatychok*** inside Hotel Viliya; the tiny, red-brick ***Kafe Hrot*** across the street; or the mosaic-clad ***Restoran Ostroh*** a block east.

Getting There & Away

The nearest train station is 14km north so opt for a bus. There are a handful of daily buses to Rivne (1½ hours), Ternopil, Kremenets, Shepetivka, Izyaslav and Dubno. Vulitsya Nezalezhnosti runs from the small bus station 2km east to the centre.

Ternopil Region
Тернопільська область

KREMENETS
КРЕМЕНЕЦЬ

☎ 03546 • pop 25,000

The small town of Kremenets kisses a picturesque and narrow wooded valley and, with its proximity to the fabulous Pochayiv Monastery 25km south-west, is among Ukraine's sweetest towns.

Ever since a stone castle was built in the 12th century, high up on a hill overlooking the town, there have been continual fights over who controls it. In 1795 the town became part of Russia.

Things to See

The bulk of the old town is uphill and a block west from vulitsya Shevchenko, the main road through town. The centrepiece is a former **Jesuit Cathedral** (1731-43), built by the Poles when they regained control of the town from the Cossacks, and converted into a lyceum in 1805. Peaceful botanical gardens (1809) stretch up from the former **Jesuit collegium** which sits a block south along vulitsya Drahomanova.

The town's history – from the Cossack and Polish battles to the Nazi massacre of 300 villagers in Shpykolisy, 6km south of Kremenets, on 14 July 1943 – comes to life in the **Kremenets Regional Museum** (☎ 2 20 20, ☎ 2 27 38), located 1km north along vulitsya Shevchenko. Next door is **Bohoyavlensky Monastery** (1760), an Orthodox convent.

On the small hill overlooking Bohoyavlensky Monastery is the Pyatnytske Cemetery, better known as **Kozatske Kladovyshche** (Cossack Cemetery). The 100 or so small, weathered stone crosses scattered about, some bearing faint Slavonic inscriptions, mark the graves of Cossacks who died in 1648 while liberating Kremenets from the Poles. Walking north (towards the bus station) from the centre, take the first right off vulitsya Shevchenko past the town market. Bear left when the road forks and walk for some 10 minutes uphill (north-east).

A fine panoramic view of the old town (and ungainly TV antenna erected on the site) can be had from Kremenets' hilltop **castle**. The original wooden, 12th century construction was replaced by stone 150 years later. Today all that remains is a ring of walls and a gate tower.

Places to Stay

Hotel Kyiv (☎ 2 23 72, vulitsya Shevchenko 37) has no heating, no hot water, is very dirty and – as far as foreigners are concerned – claims to be closed.

Getting There & Away

Kremenets is served by some 10 daily buses to/from Ternopil (1½ hours), six a day to/from Rivne (2½ hours) and seven daily to/from Pochayiv (30 minutes), with one bus a day to Lutsk, Lviv, Kyiv and Ivano-Frankivsk. The bus station is about 2.5km north of the centre on vulitsya Shevchenko.

POCHAYIV
ПОЧАЇВ

Pochayiv Monastery (Pochayivska Lavra), 25km south-west of Kremenets and 75km north of Ternopil, is Ukraine's second largest Orthodox pilgrimage monastery complex. It was founded by monks who escaped the monastery in Kyiv after a Tatar raid in 1240. The Mother of God icon (1597) is thought to have miraculous powers and is attributed with having saved the monastery from a Turkish attack in 1675. In 1730 control of the monastery switched to the Ukrainian Catholics, then Russian Orthodox in 1831. Today the 40 monks inhabiting the monastery adhere to the Ukrainian Orthodox Church.

The site is flooded with pilgrims during religious festivals, most notably during the Feast of the Assumption on 28 August, and the Feast of St Job on 10 September. It's a peaceful place evoking the strange mixture of mystery and ambience associated with holy sites. The main garden area has plenty of benches, trees and a spigot that offers cool refreshing water – all of which are enjoyed by the numerous pilgrims who mumble, pray and camp out.

Visitors are free to wander around Pochayiv Monastery (☎ 6 12 44) at any time. The excursion bureau, immediately on the right after you walk through the main entrance gate, organises guided tours; it is open from 11 am to 4 pm. Dress codes are strict: men are not allowed to wear hats or shorts, and women must cover their head, knees and hands (no trousers, shorts or skirts above the knee). Trouser-clad, bare-headed women can borrow a wrap-around skirt and head scarf from the excursion bureau. Compact discs ($3.50) featuring fine recordings of the monks' choir are also sold here.

Uspensky & Holy Trinity Cathedrals

The main **Uspensky Cathedral** (1771-83), west of the main entrance gate at the end of the central driveway, is an overwhelming baroque affair. Its interior, able to hold over 6000 people, is one endless expression of Orthodox iconography. The side aisles have interesting oculi which look up into the upper galleries. Several relics and icons – including the famed 'footprint of Mary' – and 'healing waters' (on the right-hand side of the central nave) attract lines of faithful. Wave after wave of old and young line up to kiss the imprint and gulp a cup of water poured by a bored-looking priest. The relics of St Job and the miraculous icon of the Mother of God are at the far end of the right-hand aisle.

Immediately north of the main entrance gate is the simple, gold-domed **Holy Trinity Cathedral** (1649). Its interior is dark and evocative with massive pillars and thick vaults beneath a deep cupola. While the Uspensky Cathedral attempts to portray the splendour of God, the Holy Trinity Cathedral evokes the mystery of the Orthodox divinity. Note the large candelabra.

Directly west of the Holy Trinity Cathedral is the 65m-tall baroque **bell tower** (1861-71). Sneak in with a tour group or a monk and climb to the top for the view and a look at the massive 100-year-old bell. Its central knocker weighs over 315kg.

South of the main entrance gate sits the **Bishop's Palace** (1825).

Places to Stay & Eat

You can stay for $0.50 a night in ***Pochayiv Monastery Hotel***, at the far western end of the monastery complex. The hotel offers rooms with six to seven beds. There are two rooms for men downstairs and rooms for women upstairs. Guests are woken between 5 and 6 am by nonobligatory morning prayer, conducted in front of the icon hanging in the corner of each room. Hot and tasty meals, served in the monastery refectory, are included in the price. To get to the hotel from the main entrance, walk straight ahead past the excursion bureau, turn right at the bell tower, and follow the road westwards (left) down the hill to the rear gate entrance. At the bottom of the hill, bear left along a small path to the hotel.

Getting There & Away

The bus station is just west of the monastery grounds, not far from the hotel. There are at least seven daily buses to/from Kremenets (40 minutes), three daily to/from Ternopil (two hours), six daily to Brody (from where you can transfer to Rivne or Lutsk), and one daily to Lviv.

TERNOPIL
ТЕРНОПІЛЬ

☎ 0352 • pop 230,000

Dating from 1549, and founded on the site of an earlier 14th century fortress, Ternopil was always a historic crossroads. Despite being destroyed many times throughout its history, taking an especially heavy toll in WWII, a few nice churches and a small but pleasant centre still remain.

On your approach into town, try not to be too perturbed by Ternopil's ugly, concrete-block suburbs that sprawl for eternity. Once in the centre, the city's pretty location at the foot of a chain of lakes becomes more evident.

Orientation & Information

Vulitsya Hetmana Sagaydachnoho is Ternopil's pedestrian artery running east-west, connecting Hotel Ternopil and maydan Voli, a park to the west, with bulvar Taras Shevchenko to the east near the train station. Vulitsya Ruska is the city's main thoroughfare and runs parallel with vulitsya Hetmana Sahayoachnoha, 200m south.

The post and telephone office is 200m west of the train station, straight down vulitsya Zaliznychna on the corner with vulitsya Kopernika.

City Centre

The **Dominican Church & Monastery** off the north-east corner of maydan Voli is the city's finest silhouette. Built in the mid-18th century, its twin towers rise from a baroque facade. Halfway down vulitsya Hetmana Sagaydachnoho, opposite a fountain vulitsya

JOHN NOBLE

St Sophia Cathedral, Kyiv

NICOLA WILLIAMS

Church at the Museum of Folk Architecture & Everyday Life, Kyiv

NICOLA WILLIAMS

Matryoshka dolls and Dinamo scarves for sale at Andriyivsky uzviz craft market, Podil region, Kyiv

JONATHAN SMITH

St Sophia Cathedral, Polatsk, Belarus

JONATHAN SMITH

War Memorial, Vitsebsk, Belarus

JONATHAN SMITH

Statue outside the Drama Theatre, Hrodna, Belarus

Valova leads south through a vaulted gateway onto vulitsya Ruska and the 17th century **Rizdva Khrystovoho Church**. The small interior is an explosion of gilded colour. From here, walk 100m south along vulitsya Zatserkovna to Ternopil's **Regional Museum** (closed Monday and Wednesday). Skip the stuffed animals on the ground floor and ascend to the upper two floors which are full of impressive historic and ethnographic displays.

Bulvar Taras Shevchenko, the town's leafy showpiece and popular hang-out, is a nice venue for a stroll, with landscaping and fountains. At its northern end is the neoclassical **Shevchenko Theatre**.

Behind Hotel Ternopil is a bit of parkland on the lakeside with views across the water to bland postwar development. South-west, near the water's edge, is the small 450-year-old **Zavyzhenska Church**, the city's oldest church reconstructed after being shut for over 45 years. It is referred to as the 'Church on the Pond', as it's supposedly where Khmelnytsky prayed with his gang of Cossacks before his infamous battle against the Polish king Casimir II near Zboriv in 1649, 35km north-west of Ternopil.

Places to Stay & Eat

Hotel Ternopil *(☎ 22 42 63, fax 43 00 21, vulitsya Zamkova 14)* is friendly with comfortable singles/doubles costing $9/18. Breakfast is $1. ***Hotel Halychyna*** *(☎ 33 53 94, vulitsya Zaozerna 3)*, on the opposite side of the lake, 1km west of the centre, is run by the same team as the Ternopil and charges similar prices.

Cafes, kiosks and street vendors adorn vulitsya Hetmana Sagaydachnoho. ***Europa*** *(☎ 25 87 41)*, at its east end, is a delightful spot without any airs and graces. Salads/soups start at $0.50/1 and mains clock in at $1.50; the steak fillet with plums is particularly tasty. In summer, Europa's tables and chairs spill across the pavement outside.

Getting There & Away

Daily domestic services include several trains to/from Lviv (three hours) and Kyiv (nine hours); once daily to/from Odesa (13 hours), Simferopol (17 hours), Kharkiv (11 hours) and Chernivtsi (four to five hours). From the train station, which is more organised and cleaner than most, walk west on vulitsya Zaliznychna for two blocks until you get to bulvar Taras Shevchenko and the centre of town.

Destinations reached by bus from Ternopil include Kremenets (seven a day), Ivano-Frankivsk (five), Pochayiv (three), Kamyanets-Podilsky (three) and Chernivtsi (four). The bus station is about 1km south of the centre; trolleybus No 9 or bus No 20 go to the centre.

Chernivtsi Region
Чернівецька область

CHERNIVTSI
ЧЕРНІВЦІ

☎ 03722 • pop 260,000

Chernivtsi, like most of western Ukraine, wasn't drawn into the Russian sphere until WWII. It was the chief city of Bucovina (Beech Tree Land), the northernmost part of old Moldavia, and boasts a Central European appearance – it was an outpost of the Habsburg Empire from 1775 through to the end of WWI, then was tossed into an enlarged Romania. In 1940, northern Bucovina including Chernivtsi was taken over by the USSR.

This mixed history has bestowed upon it a wide variety of architectural styles, from Byzantine to baroque, and the elegant streets of its old quarter are lined with grand facades. Before WWII, the city was cosmopolitan with large Jewish, Armenian and German minorities, giving it an atmosphere that remains to some degree today, a more southern and relaxed feel than most Ukrainian cities.

Orientation & Information

Chernivtsi is on the Prut River but the centre is a good 3km south of it. The old core surrounds Tsentralna ploshcha. Hotel Cheremosh has a currency exchange office and Utel telephone. You can change travellers cheques at PromInvest Bank, just north of the bus station at vulitsya Holovna 205.

The post office is at vulitsya Khydyakova 6, a block north of Tsentralna ploshcha. The telephone centre is a block south on vulitsya Universytetska. The Komputerny Svit Internet cafe (ruslan@ite.cv.ua) at vulitsya Ivana Franka 12 charges $1.50/hour for online access.

City Centre

The tree-lined **vulitsya Olha Kobylyanska**, named after the 19th to 20th century writer and civil activist Olha Kobylyanska, is the city's main pedestrian venue. Many of the Habsburg facades are vine-covered, giving the street an attractive and aged look. Peek into a number of courtyards (Nos 22, 23, 27), and a different, very Ottoman world opens up before you with wooden balconies and covered staircases. A branch of the **Regional Museum** is at No 28, open from 9 am to 5 pm (closed Wednesday).

A block east of vulitsya Olha Kobylyanska at vulitsya Ukrainska 30 is the former **Armenian Cathedral** (1869-75). Its design is based on ancient Armenian architecture featuring beautiful masonry detailing. Its meticulously painted interior has excellent acoustics and has housed an organ and concert hall since 1922.

The northern end of vulitsya Olha Kobylyanska and vulitsya Holovna converges at the bustling Tsentralna ploshcha, the historic town centre. The **City Hall** (1847) stands on the southern side. At Tsentralna ploshcha 10 is the main **Regional Museum** (closed Monday), housed in an Art Nouveau building with a unique central staircase.

North, on vulitsya Holovna, is a **Polish church** and, a block north on a narrow corner, **Parasvevya Church** (1862). A block west in the centre of ploshcha Filharmonyl is an attractive **old market hall**, a bustling hive of buying, selling and yelling. West of the Polish church is the **Philharmonia** building, attractive but closed (indefinitely) for renovation.

West of vulitsya Ivana Franka, smaller streets snake their way around **Teatralna ploshcha**, a perfect place to sit and watch the world go by. At the western end of the square is the **Music & Drama Theatre** (1904-5), a gift from the Habsburgs. It was designed in the De Stijl style by the same Viennese architects who designed the Opera House in Odesa. Tickets for theatrical events are sold at the Teatralna Kasa (☎ 22 50 85, ☎ 2 65 25) at vulitsya Lisenka 2, open from 11 am to 2 pm and 4 to 6 pm.

The former **synagogue** on the square's northern side (corner of vulitsya Lisenka) houses a Jewish Cultural and Information Centre. Four perky Atlantes support its ornate balcony.

Chernivtsi University

The architectural complex housing the former palatial residence of the Metropolitans of Bucovina is now Chernivtsi University. It's a fantastic brick ensemble with pseudo-Byzantine, pseudo-Moorish and pseudo-Teutonic-looking palaces surrounding a small landscaped court. Designed in 1864-82 by Hlavka, the Czech architect who created the Armenian Cathedral on the other side of the city, it was heavily damaged and looted in WWII. It's about 1.5km north-west of the centre; any trolleybus heading down vulitsya Universytetska will take you there.

Immediately to your left as you enter the gateway is **Seminarska Church** and the former theological seminary, with an attractive arcaded garden courtyard. The church, with its elongated central cupola, is now used for concerts and ceremonies. The interior is strikingly ornamented in Byzantine fashion. On the opposite side of the complex is the main **University Building**, its central clock tower composed of a unique, staggering cluster of forms rising up to a central cupola. The building straight ahead as you first enter is the former main **palace** residence of the Metropolitans. Two remarkable staircases are located in the far back corners. Walk up the one to the left and ask someone if you can see the **Marmurovy Zal**, a fantastic salon surrounded by rows of two tiered arcades with an intricately painted wooden ceiling.

Other Attractions

On vulitsya Ruska, about 1.5km east of Tsentralna ploshcha past Uspenska Ukrainian Catholic Church, is **St Nicholas Cathedral**.

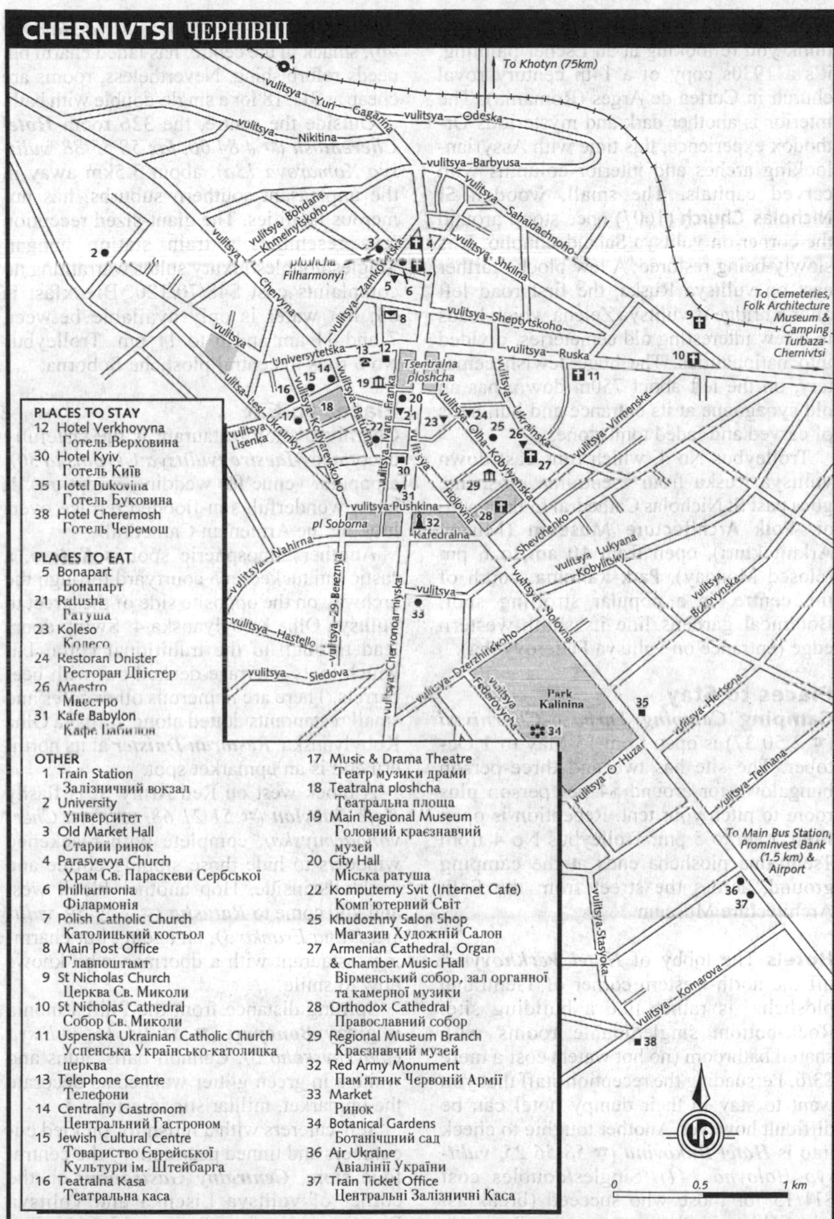
CHERNIVTSI ЧЕРНІВЦІ
To Khotyn (75km)
vulitsya–Yuri–Gagarina
vulitsya–Odeska
vulitsya–Nikitina
vulitsya–Barbyusa
vulitsya–Sahaidachnoho
vulitsya Bohdana Khmelnytskoho
vulitsya–Zamkovetska
ploshcha Filharmonyi
vulitsya–Chervyna
vulitsya–Shkilna
To Cemeteries, Folk Architecture Museum & Camping Turbaza-Chernivtsi
vulitsya–Sheptytskoho
vulitsya–Ruska
Universytetska
Tsentralna ploshcha
ulitsa–Lesi–Ukrainky
vulitsya–Lisenka
vulitsya–Kotlyarevskoho
vulitsya–Ivana–Franka
vulitsya–Olha–Kobylyanska
vulitsya–Ukrainska
vulitsya–Virmenska
vulitsya–Pushkina
pl Soborna
Kafedralna
vulitsya–Holovna
vulitsya–Nahirna
Shevchenko
vulitsya Lukyana Kobylytsia
vulitsya–29–Berezniya
vulitsya–Chervonoarmiyska
vulitsya
vulitsya–Bukovynska
vulitsya–Hastello
vulitsya–Siedova
vulitsya–Dzerzhinskoho
vulitsya Federovycha
Park Kalinina
vulitsya–Hertsena
vulitsya–O–Huzar
vulitsya–Telmana
To Main Bus Station, PromInvest Bank (1.5 km) & Airport
vulitsya–Stasyoka
vulitsya–Komarova
0
0.5
1 km
PLACES TO STAY
12 Hotel Verkhovyna
Готель Верховина
30 Hotel Kyiv
Готель Київ
35 Hotel Bukovina
Готель Буковина
38 Hotel Cheremosh
Готель Черемош
PLACES TO EAT
5 Bonapart
Бонапарт
21 Ratusha
Ратуша
23 Koleso
Колесо
24 Restoran Dnister
Ресторан Дністер
26 Maestro
Маестро
31 Kafe Babylon
Кафе Бабилон
OTHER
1 Train Station
Залізничний вокзал
2 University
Університет
3 Old Market Hall
Старий ринок
4 Parasvevya Church
Храм Св. Параскеви Сербської
6 Philharmonia
Філармонія
7 Polish Catholic Church
Католицький костьол
8 Main Post Office
Главпоштамт
9 St Nicholas Church
Церква Св. Миколи
10 St Nicholas Cathedral
Собор Св. Миколи
11 Uspenska Ukrainian Catholic Church
Успенська Українсько-католицька церква
13 Telephone Centre
Телефони
14 Centralny Gastronom
Центральний Гастроном
15 Jewish Cultural Centre
Товариство Єврейської Культури ім. Штейбарга
16 Teatralna Kasa
Театральна каса
17 Music & Drama Theatre
Театр музики драми
18 Teatralna ploshcha
Театральна площа
19 Main Regional Museum
Головний краєнавчий музей
20 City Hall
Міська ратуша
22 Komputerny Svit (Internet Cafe)
Комп'ютерний Світ
25 Khudozhny Salon Shop
Магазин Художній Салон
27 Armenian Cathedral, Organ & Chamber Music Hall
Вірменський собор, зал органної та камерної музики
28 Orthodox Cathedral
Православний собор
29 Regional Museum Branch
Краєнавчий музей
32 Red Army Monument
Пам'ятник Червоній Армії
33 Market
Ринок
34 Botanical Gardens
Ботанічний сад
36 Air Ukraine
Авіалінії України
37 Train Ticket Office
Центральні Залізничні Каса

With four twisted cupolas that make you think you're looking at an Escher painting, it's a 1930s copy of a 14th century royal church in Curtea de Arges (Romania). The interior is another dark and mysterious Orthodox experience, this time with Assyrian-looking arches and interior columns with carved capitals. The small, wooden **St Nicholas Church** (1607) once stood around the corner on vulitsya Sahaidachnoho. It is slowly being restored. A few blocks farther east on vulitsya Ruska, the first road left after a bridge is vulitsya Zelena which leads to a few interesting old cemeteries, divided into nationalities. The huge Jewish cemetery, on the left about 750m down, has an old synagogue at its entrance and hundreds of carved and faded tombstones.

Trolleybus No 4, which runs east down vulitsya Ruska from Tsentralna ploshcha, goes past St Nicholas Cathedral to the open-air **Folk Architecture Museum** (Muzey Arkhitekturi), open from 10 am to 6 pm (closed Monday). **Park Kalinina**, south of the centre, is a popular strolling spot. Botanical gardens line its south-western edge (entrance on vulitsya Federovycha).

Places to Stay

Camping ***Camping Turbaza-Chernivtsi*** (☎ 2 50 37) is open from 15 May to 1 October. The site has two and three-person bungalows for around $4 per person plus room to pitch your tent. Reception is open from 9 am to 5 pm. Trolleybus No 4 from Tsentralna ploshcha ends at the camping ground, across the street from the Folk Architecture Museum.

Hotels The lobby of ***Hotel Verkhovyna***, off the north-western corner of Tsentralna ploshcha, is rather like a building site. Rock-bottom single/double rooms with shared bathroom (no hot water) cost a mere $3/6. Persuading the reception staff that you want to stay in their dumpy hotel can be difficult however. Another toughie to check into is ***Hotel Bukovina*** *(☎ 58 56 25, vulitsya Holovna 141)*. Singles/doubles cost $11/15 for those who succeed (breakfast negotiable with the restaurant staff).

Hotel Kyiv *(☎ 2 24 83, vulitsya Holovna 46)*, smack in the centre, has faded charm but needs refurbishing. Nevertheless, rooms are cheap at $11/18 for a single/double with bath.

Outside the centre, the 326 room ***Hotel Cheremosh*** *(☎ 4 84 00, fax 58 55 88, vulitsya Komarova 13a)*, about 3.5km away in the unpleasant southern suburbs, has numerous facilities. The giant-sized reception area resembles a train station hangar. Singles/doubles/luxury suites warranting no complaints cost $48/70/120. Breakfast is $3; hot water is only available between 7 and 11 am and 6 to 11 pm. Trolleybus No 6 runs to central ploshcha Soborna.

Places to Eat

Chernivtsi's top restaurant is the tastefully decorated ***Maestro*** *(vulitsya Ukrainska 30)*, a popular venue for wedding receptions. It has a wonderful, sun-flooded terrace overlooking the Armenian Cathedral.

Another atmospheric spot is ***Koleso***, a rustic inn tucked in a courtyard through the archway on the opposite side of the street to vulitsya Olha Kobylyanska 4. Swing doors lead through to the traditional cellar bar which touts a terrace decked out with beer barrels. There are numerous other cafes and small restaurants dotted along vulitsya Olha Kobylyanska. ***Restoran Dnister*** at its northern end is an upmarket spot.

A block west on Red Army St is flashy ***Kafe Babylon*** *(☎ 51 21 68, vulitsya Chervonoarmiyska)*, complete with blackened windows to hide those sipping coffee and cocktails inside. Hop another block west and you come to ***Ratusha*** *(☎ 2 57 59, vulitsya Ivana Franka 3)*, an ageing but charming restaurant with a doorman who knows how to smile.

Spitting distance from the Philharmonia is glitzy ***Bonapart*** *(☎ 51 04 16, vulitsya Chaykovskoho 5)*. Cannon balls, guns and waiters in green glitter waistcoats decorate the upmarket, militaristic interior.

Self-caterers with a fetish for pickled cucumbers and tinned peas can try the central food store, ***Centralny Gastronom*** on the corner of vulitsya Lisenka and vulitsya Batutina (open from 8 am to 10 pm).

Getting There & Away

Train The train station (☎ 005, ☎ 9 21 90), vulitsya Gagarina 38, is 1.5km north of the centre. Advance train tickets are sold at the train ticket office (☎ 4 29 24, ☎ 055), vulitsya Holovna 128. It is open from 9 am to 7 pm.

Chernivtsi is close to the rail border at Vadul-Siret (Romania). All trains heading to Ukrainian destinations to the east, north-east or south-east pass briefly through Moldova (see Ukraine Getting There & Away).

Domestic services include three or four trains a day to/from Kyiv (14 hours), stopping at Vinnytsya or Khmelnytsky along the way; two or three daily to/from Lviv (six hours), via Ivano-Frankivsk (three to four hours); Odesa (12½ hours) and St Petersburg (40 hours). To Kamyanets-Podilsky, the bus is more frequent.

Bus The bus station (☎ 4 16 35), vulitsya Holovna 219, is some 4km south-east of the centre. At least two buses a day run between Chernivtsi and all the major western Ukrainian cities. Four to six daily buses run to/from Ivano-Frankivsk (four hours) and Ternopil (three hours via Chortkiv), and at least eight daily run to/from Kamyanets-Podilsky (two hours), including the ones which go to Khmelnytsky.

Getting Around

Trolleybus No 3 runs along vulitsya Holovna from the bus station, through the centre, to the train station.

KHOTYN
ХОТИН

About 75km north-east of Chernivtsi, halfway along the road to Kamyanets-Podilsky, lies the small town of Khotyn. Its large, picturesque **fortress**, whose massive walls loom high above the smooth water of the Dnister River, is worth the stop if you have time. Its strategic location was critical in ensuring trade routes along the river, thus making it a sought-after prize over the centuries.

Built out of wood in the 12th century, Khotyn fortress was strengthened over the years and replaced by stone in the 15th century. First an outpost of the Galician-Volynian Principality, it was under the control of the Cossacks before the Poles took it over in the 15th century, only to be kicked out by the Turks the following century. The Russians finally took it over and partially destroyed it in the 19th century.

The fortress and its grounds are open. Within its impregnable walls are a keep, a chapel with carved tracery windows and a vaulted porch overlooking a courtyard, four towers, several ruined walls which once formed part of a commandant's palace, and some underground cellars. While walking, beware of holes in the ground that drop down to the cellars.

Getting There & Around

Very few trains stop in Khotyn, so you'll probably arrive by bus. The fortress is about 4km north of the bus station – a 45 minute walk north along vulitsya Shevchenko, across the market square and beyond, following the occasional sign that says 'Fortetsya' (Фортеця). Turn right after the road curves and head towards a statue in the distance. Walk past the statue, through the first set of walls and through to the other side for a spectacular view down a grassy hillside towards the fortress, perched above the river.

There are at least five or six buses a day running between Chernivtsi and Kamyanets-Podilsky that stop in Khotyn. There is no hotel in town.

Khmelnytsky Region
Хмельницька область

KAMYANETS-PODILSKY
КАМЯНЕЦЬ-ПОДІЛЬСЬКИЙ

☎ 03849 • pop 108,000

The old town of Kamyanets-Podilsky, 85km north-east of Chernivtsi on the Khmelnytsky road, has stood since at least the 11th century on a sheer-walled rock 'island' carved out of the steppe by a sharp loop in the Smotrych River. The south-western bridge, which for centuries was the only link between the old town and the 'mainland', is guarded by a highly picturesque castle. In 1977, the old town was designated an architectural and historical reserve, with slow restoration taking place ever since. The combination of historic architecture and dramatic landscape is well worth a stop on your way to/from Chernivtsi.

History

In the mid-11th century, Kamyanets-Podilsky was an important Kyivan Rus settlement, on the main trade routes from Kyiv south into the Balkans. Controlled by the Galician-Volynian Principality from the 12th to 14th centuries, it briefly fell into Lithuanian hands before the Poles took it over in 1430. As it was a key southern border post of Poland for over two centuries, it was subjected to numerous attacks by Tatars, Moldavians and Ottoman Turks. It fell to a Turkish siege in 1672. In 1699 it was returned to Poland, but only after its churches had been looted. It then fell to the Russians in 1793, who used the castle as a prison for Ukrainian nationalists in the 19th century. It became the temporary capital of the brief Ukrainian National Republic in 1919. During WWII the Germans used the old town as an isolated 'ghetto', where an estimated 85,000 people died. Intensive fighting and air raids destroyed some 70% of the old town.

Orientation & Information

The fortified old town – a rock island lassoed by a tight loop of the Smotrych River – is accessed by two main bridges. One bridge to the west leads to the castle; another bridge to the east leads to the 'new town', in a Soviet-style street grid. Central vulitsya Koriatovychiv runs for some 2km east-west through the new town, from the bus station in the far east, to the old town in the far west. The train station is 1km north of the bus station on vulitsya Pryvokzalna.

Decent city maps ($0.50) are sold at the castle ticket kiosk. Change money and get credit card cash advances at Avaal Bank, vulitsya Starobulvarna 10. The central post and telephone office is on the northern side of ploshcha Soborna; a smaller branch is at vulitsya Troitska 2.

Old Town

The main settlers of the old town were Ukrainians, Poles, Armenians and Jews. Each traditionally occupied a different quarter. In the town's heyday during the interwar period, there were five Roman Catholic churches, 18 Orthodox churches, and a Jewish community of 23,500 served by 31 prayer houses. This diversity was wiped out in WWII: only 13 churches survive (in various degrees).

Churches & Other Buildings In the centre of the old town you'll find the 16th century **Dominican Monastery & Church** with its tall, ornately moulded bell tower. It was founded in the 14th century but remodelled and expanded in baroque style in the 18th century. Its gilded interior is currently being renovated. North of the monastery is a park-like area, once the Ukrainian and Polish market square.

In the park centre is the former, 14th century **town hall**. Once you have paid the $0.25 entrance fee to view the eclectic collection of local art on the ground floor, the formidable door attendant will invite you to scale the **18th century clock tower** ($0.25). There is a fantastic panorama from the top, but the climb up is perilous. The complex is open from 8.30 am to 5 pm. Nearby is an enclosed **Armenian well** (1638) with a wood-tile roof.

The 1580 **Cathedral of SS Peter & Paul** (Petropavlovska) is off what was the north-western corner of the market square. It is entered through a **Triumphal Gate**, erected in 1781 in honour of a visit by Polish King Stanislas II Augustus. The Turks used the cathedral as a mosque in the late 17th century, adding a 42m-high **minaret**, topped by the Poles with a 3.5m-tall golden Virgin Mary statue in 1756. The attractive and solemn interior was reconsecrated by the Roman Catholic Church in 1991.

Armenian Quarter South of the Dominican monastery is the long and narrow former

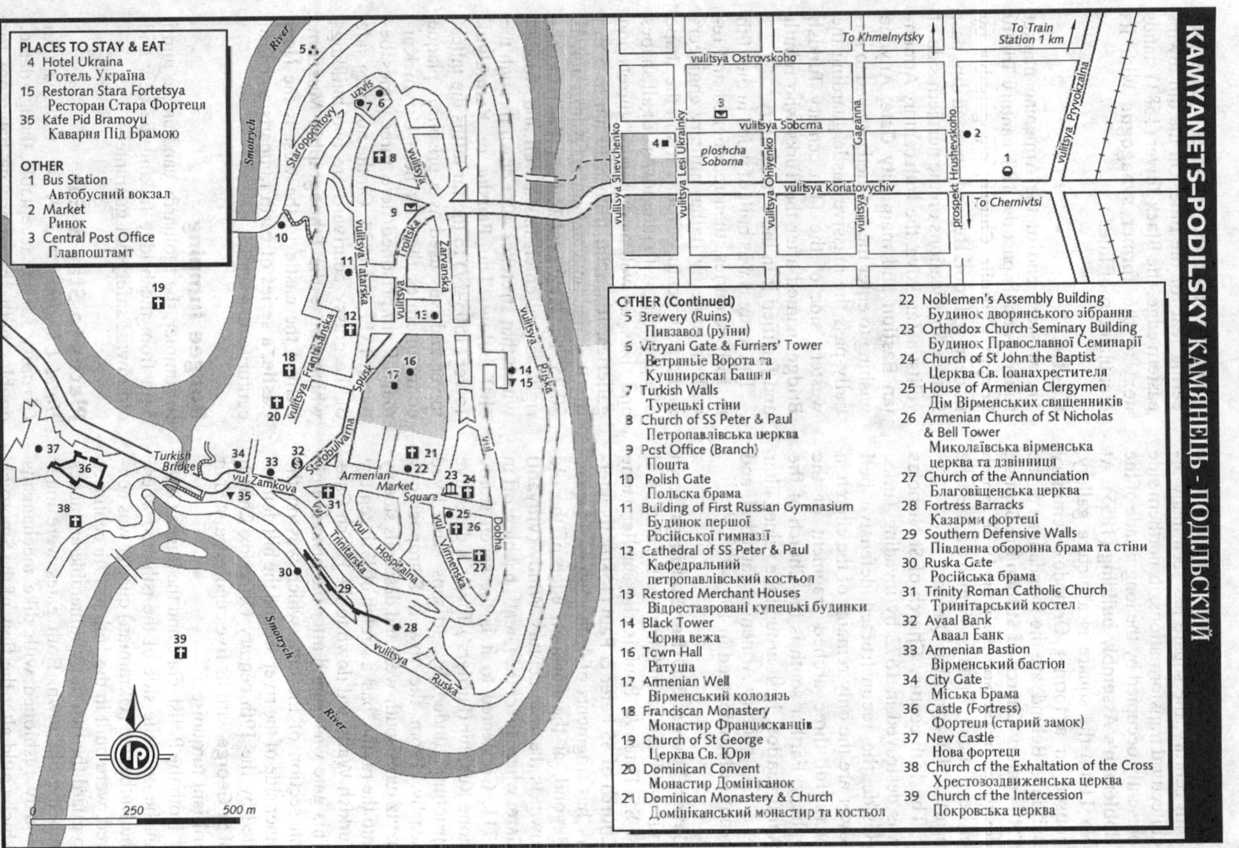
KAMYANETS–PODILSKY КАМЯНЕЦЬ - ПОДІЛЬСКИЙ
PLACES TO STAY & EAT
4 Hotel Ukraina
Готель Україна
15 Restoran Stara Fortetsya
Ресторан Стара Фортеця
35 Kafe Pid Bramoyu
Каварня Під Брамою
OTHER
1 Bus Station
Автобусний вокзал
2 Market
Ринок
3 Central Post Office
Главпоштамт
OTHER (Continued)
5 Brewery (Ruins)
Пивзавод (руїни)
6 Vitryani Gate & Furriers' Tower
Ветряные Ворота та
Кушнирская Башня
7 Turkish Walls
Турецькі стіни
8 Church of SS Peter & Paul
Петропавлівська церква
9 Post Office (Branch)
Пошта
10 Polish Gate
Польська брама
11 Building of First Russian Gymnasium
Будинок першої
Російської гимназії
12 Cathedral of SS Peter & Paul
Кафедральний
петропавлівський костьол
13 Restored Merchant Houses
Відреставровані купецькі будинки
14 Black Tower
Чорна вежа
16 Town Hall
Ратуша
17 Armenian Well
Вірменський колодязь
18 Franciscan Monastery
Монастир Францисканців
19 Church of St George
Церква Св. Юря
20 Dominican Convent
Монастир Домініканок
21 Dominican Monastery & Church
Домініканський монастир та костьол
22 Noblemen's Assembly Building
Будинок дворянського зібрання
23 Orthodox Church Seminary Building
Будинок Православної Семинарії
24 Church of St John the Baptist
Церква Св. Іоанахрестителя
25 House of Armenian Clergymen
Дім Вірменських священників
26 Armenian Church of St Nicholas
& Bell Tower
Миколаївська вірменська
церква та дзвінниця
27 Church of the Annunciation
Благовіщенська церква
28 Fortress Barracks
Казарми фортеці
29 Southern Defensive Walls
Південна оборонна брама та стіни
30 Ruska Gate
Російська брама
31 Trinity Roman Catholic Church
Тринітарський костел
32 Avaal Bank
Аваал Банк
33 Armenian Bastion
Вірменський бастіон
34 City Gate
Міська Брама
36 Castle (Fortress)
Фортеця (старий замок)
37 New Castle
Нова фортеця
38 Church of the Exhaltation of the Cross
Хрестовоздвиженська церква
39 Church of the Intercession
Покровська церква
To Khmelnytsky
To Train Station 1 km
vulitsya Ostrovskoho
vulitsya Soborna
vulitsya Pryvokzalna
ploshcha Soborna
vulitsya Shevchenko
vulitsya Lesi Ukrainky
vulitsya Ohiyenko
Gagarina
prospekt Hrushevskoho
vulitsya Koriatovychiv
To Chernivtsi
Smotrych River
Staroposhtovy uzviz
vulitsya Tatarska
vulitsya Troitska
Zarvanska
vulitsya Ruska
vulitsya Frantsyskanska
Spusk
Starobulvarna
Turkish Bridge
vul Zamkova
Armenian Market Square
vul Trinitarska
vul Hospitalna
vul Virmenska
Dobha
vulitsya Ruska
Smotrych River
0 250 500 m

Armenian market square. Founded in the 14th century, the square has seen many architectural transformations, its northern side presently occupied by the long facade of the **Noblemen's Assembly building** (1855). At No 11 on the square is a **picture gallery**, housed in a former Orthodox seminary building. Behind, are the foundations of the 15th century **Church of St John the Baptist**, destroyed by the Soviets in the 1930s. South of here, along vulitsya Virmenska, lies the heart of the Armenian Quarter.

The 15th century **Church of St Nicholas** was destroyed in 1672 by invading Turks. Beside the reconstructed defensive bell tower are the only remains of the church, a beautiful three arched fragment of the gallery. Farther south is the **Church of the Annunciation**, built around the ruined altar of a 13th century Armenian cathedral, and beautifully renovated in 1991-97.

Gates, Towers & Other Buildings Down vulitsya Tatarska and north of the Cathedral of SS Peter & Paul is the smaller stone **Church of SS Peter & Paul** (1580). Its interior has fragments of 16th century frescoes. Beyond, at the northern edge of the old town, is the 16th century **Windy (Vitryani) Gate**, where Peter the Great's hat blew off in 1711. Connected to it is the seven storey stone **Kushnir (Furriers') Tower**, a defensive structure funded by artisans who lived nearby. From the tower, Staropochtovy uzviz turns south-west and descends steeply into the ravine, past a stretch of 17th century **Turkish Walls** and down to the **Polish Gate**. This gate was named after the historic Polish section of the city, which was on the other side of the river around the hill dominated by the 19th century Orthodox **Church of St George** with its five cupolas painted in brilliant turquoise.

Both the Polish Gate and the **Ruska Gate**, on the opposite side of the isthmus, where the Ruthenian (Ukrainian) quarter was centred, were built in the 16th to 17th centuries to guard the two most vulnerable entrances into the old town. Both gates were ingeniously fashioned with dike mechanisms which could alter the flow of the Smotrych River and flood the entrances – an engineering feat for the time. On the old town's eastern edge, the **Black Tower** (1583) stands next to the former **synagogue** with its crenulated roof line.

Castle

The western end of the Armenian market square funnels past the 18th century **Trinity Roman Catholic Church**, recognisable by its deep-red roof. Beyond, the road dips past further fortifications on the northern side of vulitsya Zamkova, the 16th century **Armenian Bastion** and main **City Gate**. Anyone wishing to enter the fortified city had to initially pass the massive castle guarding the western side of the 11th century **Turkish Bridge**, named after the Turks who rebuilt and fortified it in the 17th century.

The fortress was built of wood in the 10th to 13th centuries, then redesigned and rebuilt in stone by Italian military engineers in the 16th century. Today it's in the shape of a polygon, with nine towers of all shapes and sizes, as well as dungeons, turrets and galleries. It's open from 8.30 am to 5 pm (until 6 pm on weekends). Admission is \$0.25. The **New East Tower** (1544), to your right as you enter, has a well and wooden winch that stretches 40m down through the cliff below. The **Papska** or **Karmalyuk Tower** (1503-17) to the far left is the tallest tower and was used as a prison. A plaque commemorates the folk hero Ustym Karmalyuk, imprisoned here three times between 1817 and 1823. On the northern side of the grassy courtyard are two buildings which house the **Ethnographic Museum**. Behind the castle to the west is the **New Castle**, a series of earth ramparts and 17th century stone walls.

Bungee Jumping

In summer, the foolhardy can bungee jump 54m from the bridge linking the new and old towns; safety not guaranteed.

Places to Stay & Eat

Hotel Ukraina *(☎ 3 91 48, vulitsya Lesi Ukrainky 32)* has acceptable, though dated, doubles with shared/private bathroom for

$10/19. Foreigners are immediately offered the $30 two room luxury suite.

Flashing lights and loud music are a trait of ***Restoran Stara Fortetsya***, a restaurant-cum-disco housed in a former synagogue, next to the Black Tower at bulvar Schidny 1. Just before you cross the Turkish Bridge on the south side in the old town is the ***Kafe Pid Bramoyu***, a beer and shashlyk place set inside part of the bridge fortifications.

Getting There & Away

Kamyanets-Podilsky is on the railway line between Chernivtsi and Khmelnytsky; some trains continue past Khmelnytsky to Kyiv (12 hours).

Between Chernivtsi and Kamyanets-Podilsky there are more buses than trains. At least eight daily buses run to/from Khmelnytsky (three hours) and Chernivtsi (two hours), with about four or five of the Chernivtsi buses stopping at Khotyn (one hour) on the way. There are also daily buses to Ternopil and Kyiv.

Getting Around

Bus No 9 runs from the bus station to the new town and ploshcha Soborna. From ploshcha Soborna bus No 5 runs to the west end of the Armenian market square in the old town. From the train station, bus No 1 runs to the new and old towns.

Southern Ukraine
Південна Україна

For hundreds of years southern Ukraine, bordering the lands of the Ukrainian Cossacks and those of the Crimean Tatars, resembled a 'wild-west' no-man's land. Military outposts, and settlements of renegades and runaway peasants, sprang up along the banks of the Dnipro. After Russia's victory in the Russo-Ottoman War of 1768-75, Catherine II deemed the Ukrainian 'buffer zone' unnecessary and ordered the disbandment and destruction of the quasi-independent Cossack Hetmanate State. With the Cossacks and Tatars defeated, much of the land was distributed among Russian, Serbian and German colonists, and the doors opened for massive Russian expansion, which led to the annexation of not only southern Ukraine, but Crimea as well.

The landscape of southern Ukraine is predominantly rich, fertile steppe, sucking nutrients from its many estuaries and rivers. About 100km east of Kherson is the Askaniya Nova Reserve, 33,000 hectares of virgin steppe land populated with feral animals whose ancestors were brought to the site by a German settler in 1828.

HIGHLIGHTS

- Splashing out on a night at Odesa's Viennese-inspired Ballet & Opera Theatre
- Strolling the streets of the Black Sea port, taking in its fabulous baroque architecture
- Enjoying a champagne picnic on the beach (strictly Odesan champagne only)
- Mooching around museums all morning then lunching in the sun on busy vulitsya Derybasivska
- Becoming a night owl and discovering Odesan nightlife

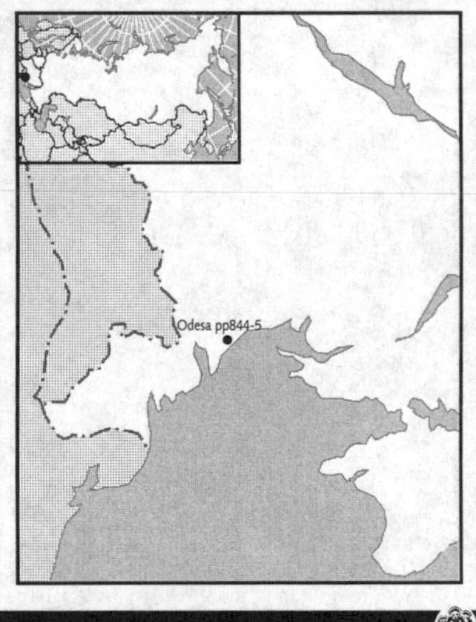

ODESA
ОДЕСА

☎ 0482 • pop 1.1 million

Odesa (Odessa in Russian), the Black Sea's gateway to Ukraine, is a potent brew of diverse ingredients yielding a strange southern magic. It is the country's biggest commercial Black Sea port, a hectic industrial city with polluted seas, and an enticing holiday centre where people flock to laze on beaches and stroll through leafy streets. Odesa is a crossroads of cultures, languages and trade, and a leading centre of capitalist and black market activity. Past associations make it dear to both Russian and Ukrainian hearts: Alexander Pushkin lived here in exile during the 1820s and it was home to writer and film director Alexander Dovzhenko.

The Dnister estuary is 40km south-west of Odesa, and the Dnipro estuary 60km to the east. Inland from this coast are several *limany* (estuaries now cut off from the sea) with mud which supposedly has curative powers, drawing thousands to Odesa's sanatoria. May to September are the best months, with maximum temperatures averaging between 20 and 27°C. In winter the sea may freeze for a few days, but ships still get through. In short, when in Ukraine, Odesa is a city that should *not* be missed.

History

The site of Odesa, useful as both port and fort, was controlled from 1526 to 1789 by the Ottoman Turks. During its expansionist campaign in the 18th century, Russia took this coastal region and constructed, with slave labour, a new port at Odesa, rebuilding the town and naming it after the ancient Greek colony Odessos, thought to be nearby but later identified in modern Bulgaria.

Armand-Emmanuel du Plessis, Duc de Richelieu, a nobleman who had fled to Russia from the guillotine of the French Revolution, governed the Odesa region from 1803 to 1814 and it grew quickly. By the 1880s it was the second biggest Russian port, Ukrainian grain being the main export, and an important industrial city. Unemployment in years of bad harvest led to unrest and Odesa was a hotbed of the 1905 revolution, when the workers were supported by the mutinous battleship *Potemkin Tavrichesky*. Afterwards there were severe reprisals and 80,000 residents, out of a total population of 600,000, fled.

Between 1917 and 1920 Odesa was variously controlled or occupied by Ukrainian nationalists, Bolsheviks, Germans and Austrians, French and Allied forces, Bolsheviks again, Whites and finally Bolsheviks once more. This was followed by famine in 1921 and 1922. In 1941 Odesa was besieged for over two months by the Germans.

Russian is the predominant language in Odesa. Most street signs are bilingual (Russian/Ukrainian).

Orientation

Central Odesa is laid out in an easy grid format, stretching south from Prymorsky bulvar overlooking the passenger port. The port is in the middle part of a 35km S-bend in the coast, with the city stretching several kilometres back from the seafront to the north and south. Most activity occurs on and around vulitsya Derybasivska, part of which is pedestrianised.

Maps City maps have street names written in Russian; those printed before 1995 feature old street names. The *Pearls of Odesa City Map* ($1) includes a street index in Cyrillic/Latin transliterations and useful tram and trolleybus schemes. The Russian-language *Pearls of Odesa City-Guide* ($0.50) includes a list of old/new street names.

Information

Tourist Offices The establishment at vulitsya Derybasivska 13 pertains to be a Tourist Information Centre (☎ 22 39 83). Beyond selling a scanty array of city and regional maps, its staff is utterly useless to English-speaking travellers. Russian speakers can enjoy a city tour with a Russian-speaking guide for $10. The large map on the street outside the centre highlighting key sights is quite handy.

Money There is a 24 hour currency exchange machine outside Marine Transport Bank at the passenger port. Bank Pivdennyi, in the main terminal, cashes travellers cheques and gives credit card cash advances. There is an ATM inside Hotelship Shevchenko, moored at the port.

In town, there is an ATM inside Mick O'Neills Irish Bar (see Bars in the Entertainment section later) and a 24 hour currency exchange next to Hotel Grand Moscow. Cash travellers cheques, wire money and get cash advances on Visa/MasterCard at Western Union/X-Change Points, inside the central theatre ticket office on the corner of vulitsya Rishelevska and vulitsya Derybasivska.

Post & Telephone The central post office is at vulitsya Sadova 10. The International Telephone Point, vulitsya Derybasivska 12, is open 24 hours.

DHL Worldwide Express has an office at the passenger port. In town, the Hotel Londonskaya Business Centre (☎/fax 25 53 70) is its agent.

SOUTHERN UKRAINE

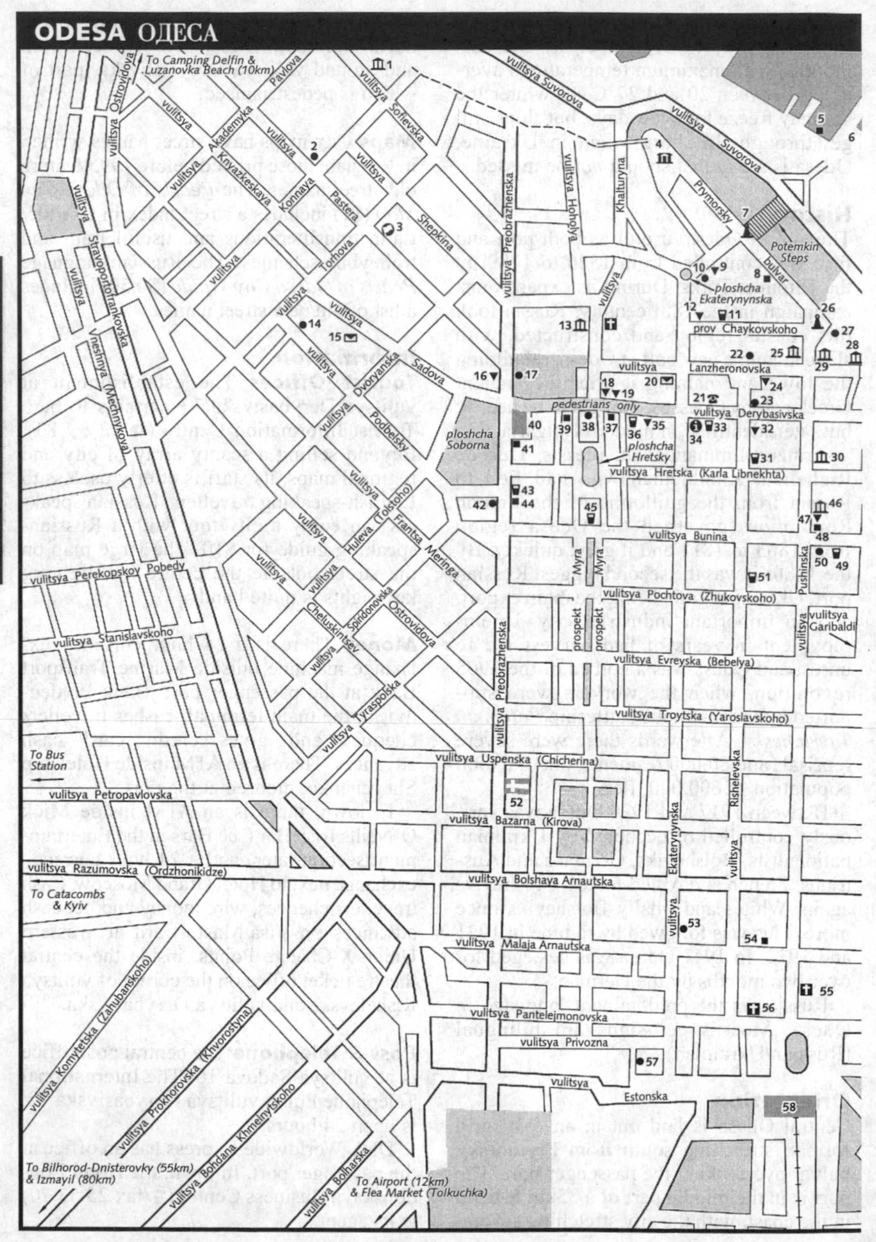
ODESA ОДЕСА
To Camping Delfin & Luzanovka Beach (10km)
vulitsya Suvorova
Potemkin Steps
ploshcha Ekaterynynska
prov Chaykovskoho
vulitsya Lanzheronovska
vulitsya Derybasivska
pedestrians only
ploshcha Soborna
ploshcha Hretsky
vulitsya Hretska (Karla Libnekhta)
vulitsya Bunina
vulitsya Pochtova (Zhukovskoho)
vulitsya Garibaldi
vulitsya Evreyska (Bebelya)
vulitsya Troytska (Yaroslavskoho)
vulitsya Uspenska (Chicherina)
vulitsya Bazarna (Kirova)
vulitsya Bolshaya Arnautska
vulitsya Malaja Arnautska
vulitsya Pantelejmonovska
vulitsya Privozna
vulitsya Estonska
vulitsya Perekopskoy Pobedy
vulitsya Stanislavskoho
vulitsya Petropavlovska
vulitsya Razumovska (Ordzhonikidze)
To Bus Station
To Catacombs & Kyiv
To Bilhorod-Dnisterovky (55km) & Izmayil (80km)
To Airport (12km) & Flea Market (Tolkuchka)
vulitsya Komytetska (Zahubanskoho)
vulitsya Prokhorovska (Khvorostyna)
vulitsya Bohdana Khmelnytskoho
vulitsya Bolharska
vulitsya Ostrovidova
vulitsya Akademyka Pavlova
vulitsya Sofievska
vulitsya Knyazkeskaya
vulitsya Konnaya
vulitsya Pastera
vulitsya Shepkina
vulitsya Torhova
vulitsya Stavropotrotrankovska
vulitsya Vneshnya (Mechnykova)
vulitsya Dvoryanska
vulitsya Sadova
vulitsya Podbelsky
vulitsya Huleva (Tolstoho)
vulitsya Frantsa Meringa
vulitsya Cheluskintsev
vulitsya Spiridonovska
vulitsya Ostrovidova
vulitsya Tyraspolska
vulitsya Preobrazhenska
vulitsya Hoholya
vulitsya Khalturyna
Prymorsky bulvar
prospekt Myra
Ekaterynynska
Rishelevska
Pushkinska
1 2 3 4 5 6 7 8 9 10 11 12 13 14 15 16 17 18 19 20 21 22 23 24 25 26 27 28 29 30 31 32 33 34 35 36 37 38 39 40 41 42 43 44 45 46 47 48 49 50 51 52 53 54 55 56 57 58

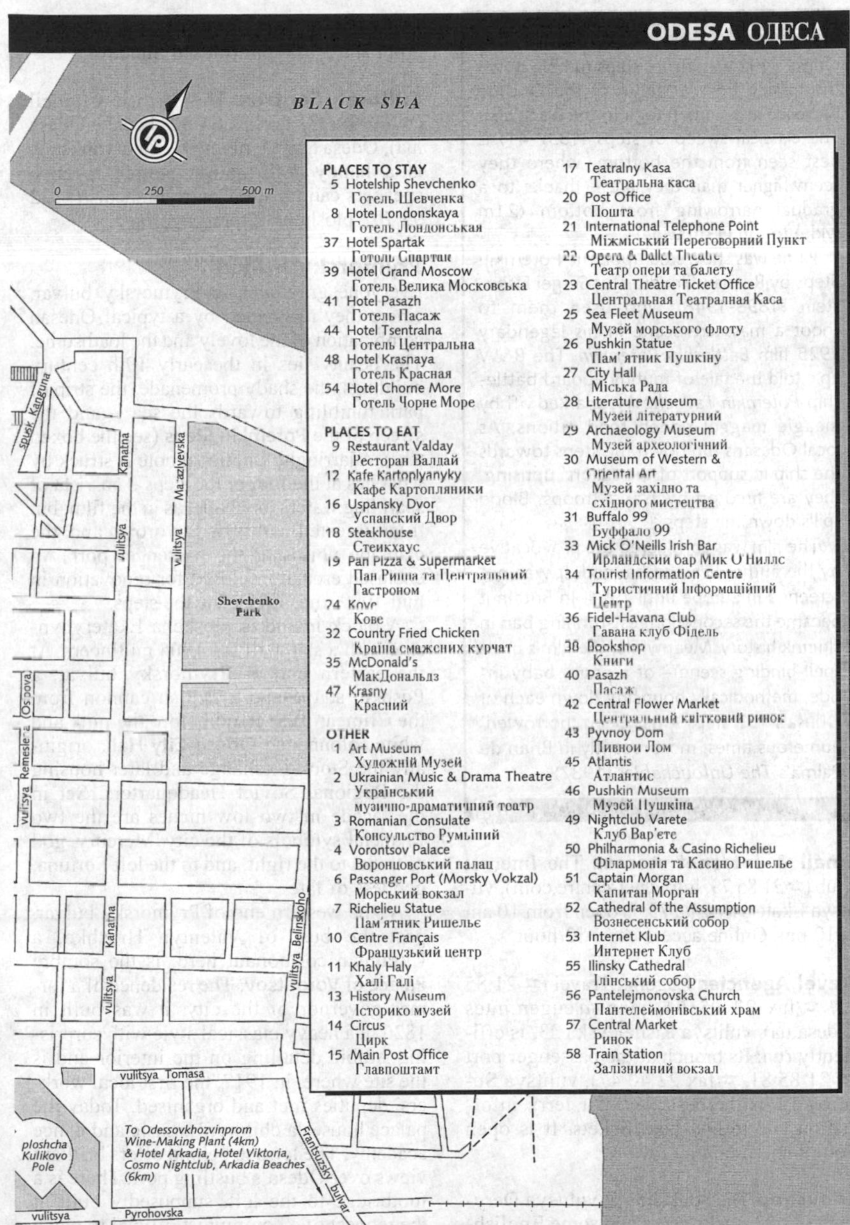
ODESA ОДЕСА
BLACK SEA
0 250 500 m
PLACES TO STAY
5 Hotelship Shevchenko
Готель Шевченка
8 Hotel Londonskaya
Готель Лондонська
37 Hotel Spartak
Готель Спартак
39 Hotel Grand Moscow
Готель Велика Московська
41 Hotel Pasazh
Готель Пасаж
44 Hotel Tsentralna
Готель Центральна
48 Hotel Krasnaya
Готель Красная
54 Hotel Chorne More
Готель Чорне Море
PLACES TO EAT
9 Restaurant Valday
Ресторан Валдай
12 Kafe Kartoplyanyky
Кафе Картопляники
16 Uspansky Dvor
Успанский Двор
18 Steakhouse
Стейкхаус
19 Pan Pizza & Supermarket
Пан Рицца та Центральний Гастроном
74 Kove
Кове
32 Country Fried Chicken
Країна смажених курчат
35 McDonald's
МакДональдз
47 Krasny
Красний
OTHER
1 Art Museum
Художній Музей
2 Ukrainian Music & Drama Theatre
Український музично-драматичний театр
3 Romanian Consulate
Консульство Румыніі
4 Vorontsov Palace
Воронцовський палац
6 Passanger Port (Morsky Vokzal)
Морський вокзал
7 Richelieu Statue
Пам'ятник Ришельє
10 Centre Français
Французький центр
11 Khaly Haly
Халі Галі
13 History Museum
Історико музей
14 Circus
Цирк
15 Main Post Office
Главпоштамт
17 Teatralny Kasa
Театральна каса
20 Post Office
Пошта
21 International Telephone Point
Міжміський Переговорний Пункт
22 Opera & Ballet Theatre
Театр опери та балету
23 Central Theatre Ticket Office
Центральная Театралная Каса
25 Sea Fleet Museum
Музей морського флоту
26 Pushkin Statue
Пам'ятник Пушкіну
27 City Hall
Міська Рада
28 Literature Museum
Музей літературний
29 Archaeology Museum
Музей археологічний
30 Museum of Western & Oriental Art
Музей західно та східного мистецтва
31 Buffalo 99
Буффало 99
33 Mick O'Neills Irish Bar
Ирландскии бар Мик О'Ниллс
34 Tourist Information Centre
Туристичний Інформаційний Центр
36 Fidel-Havana Club
Гавана клуб Фідель
38 Bookshop
Книги
40 Pasazh
Пасаж
42 Central Flower Market
Центральний квітковий ринок
43 Pyvnoy Dom
Пивнои Дом
45 Atlantis
Атлантис
46 Pushkin Museum
Музей Пушкіна
49 Nightclub Varete
Клуб Вар'єте
50 Philharmonia & Casino Richelieu
Філармонія та Касино Ришельє
51 Captain Morgan
Капитан Морган
52 Cathedral of the Assumption
Вознесенський собор
53 Internet Klub
Интернет Клуб
55 Ilinsky Cathedral
Ілінський собор
56 Pantelejmonovska Church
Пантелеймонівський храм
57 Central Market
Ринок
58 Train Station
Залізничний вокзал
spusk Kanguna
vulitsya Kanatna
vulitsya Mazazlyevska
Shevchenko Park
vulitsya Remeslena
Ospova
vulitsya Kanatna
vulitsya Belinskoho
vulitsya Tomasa
ploshcha Kulikovo Pole
Frantsuzsky bulvar
vulitsya Pyrohovska
To Odessovkhozvinprom Wine-Making Plant (4km) & Hotel Arkadia, Hotel Viktoria, Cosmo Nightclub, Arkadia Beaches (6km)

192 Steps

Odesa's 192 waterfront steps tumble down the hillside from a statue of the Duc de Richelieu in a Roman toga to the Black Sea. The classical sweep of steps (1837-41) is best seen from the bottom, where they seem higher than they are – thanks to a gradual narrowing from bottom (21m wide) to top (13m wide).

Fame was showered upon the Potemkin Steps by Russian film director Sergei Eisenstein (1898-1948) who used them to shoot a massacre scene in his legendary 1925 film *Battleship Potemkin*. The B&W epic told the tale of mutiny aboard battleship *Potemkin Tavrichesky*, sparked off by meagre maggot-ridden food rations. As local Odesans run down the steps towards the ship in support of the sailors' uprising, they are fired on by Tsarist troops. Blood spills down the steps.

The film was considered too provocative by the authorities and banned. It was not screened in Europe until 1954. In Britain it became the second longest-running ban in cinema history. Meanwhile, the film's most spell-binding scene – of a pram, baby inside, methodically bouncing down each of Odesa's 192 steps – has been 'borrowed' numerous times, most recently in Brian de Palma's *The Untouchables* (1987).

Email & Internet Access The Internet Klub (☎ 21 85 79, info@net-centre.com), vulitsya Ekaterynynska 75, is open from 10 am to 10 pm. Online access costs $2/hour.

Travel Agencies Eugenia Travel (☎ 21 85 83, ☎/fax 22 05 54, janna@eugen.intes .Odesa.ua), vulitsya Rishelevska 23, is efficiently run. Its branch at the passenger port (☎ 21 85 81, ☎/fax 22 40 47), vulitsya Suvorov 12, is the best place for ferry information and to buy boat tickets. It is open from 9 am to 6 pm.

Bookshop The bookshop at vulitsya Derybasivska 27 stocks maps and some English-language books. It is open from 10 am to 2 pm and 3 to 6 pm (closed Sunday).

Cultural Centres The British Council (☎ 49 68 33, fax 49 64 52, bc@bc.Odesa .ua), Odesa State University, Dvoryanksa 2, is a handy information source. French speakers can try the Centre Français (☎ 22 92 70), ploshcha Ekaterynynska 5.

Prymorsky Bulvar

Everyone gravitates to Prymorsky bulvar, where they're greeted by a typical Odesan combination of the lovely and the loathsome. The beauty lies in the early 19th century buildings, the shady promenade, the strip of park tumbling towards the sea – and the sweep of the **Potemkin Steps** (see the boxed text). A jarringly functional note is struck by what lies at the foot of the steps – no vista of sparkling waters, or chapel as in the film, but truck-infested vulitsya Suvorova and the clanking noises of the passenger port. An enclosed escalator, closed for renovation in mid-1999, runs up beside the steps.

A block inland is ploshcha Ekaterynynska, with a statue of the 1905 mutineers. At the eastern end of Prymorsky bulvar, a Pushkin statue and a British cannon from the Crimean War stand before the pink and white colonnaded **Odesa City Hall**, originally the Stock Exchange and later housing the Regional Soviet Headquarters. Set in the facade in two low niches are the two financial symbols of the city, Mercury, god of trade, to the right, and to the left Fortuna, goddess of fate.

At the western end of Prymorsky bulvar, past the bust of Valentyn Hrushko, a Ukrainian cosmonaut hero, is the sombre **Palace of Vorontsov**. The residence of a former governor of the city, it was built in 1826 in a heavy classical style with surprising Arabic detailing on the interior and is the site where, in 1917, the first local workers' deputies met and organised. Today the palace houses a children's music and dance academy. The terrace behind offers brilliant views over Odesa's bustling port. There is a footbridge to the left, supposedly built at the request of a communist official to make it easier for his mother to visit him, which leads to a park and the pleasing pedestrian extension of the promenade.

City Centre

The low-rise blocks south of Prymorsky bulvar are tree-lined, and at their liveliest and most intriguing on warm summer evenings. On vulitsya Lanzheronovska, facing down vulitsya Rishelevska, sits the elaborate and famous **Opera & Ballet Theatre**. It was designed in the 1880s by Viennese architects Felner & Gelmer in the Habsburg baroque of the day, with a number of Italian Renaissance features thrown in to liven up the ensemble. A block south is Odesa's main commercial street, vulitsya Derybasivska, named after a Frenchman, De Ribas, who led the capture of Odesa from the Turks in 1789. Two pleasant tree-filled parks lie at its western end, including ploshcha Soborna (Cathedral Square) on the corner of vulitsya Preobrazhenska, named after a large cathedral which stood on the site before it was torn down by the Soviet regime in the 1930s. Stroll through the **Pasazh**, a lavishly ornate shopping mall built in 1897-98 which boasts rows of baroque sculptures. At vulitsya Preobrazhenska 70 is the **Cathedral of the Assumption**, an impressive blue/white ensemble of five swooping domes and a tall bell tower rising over the entrance.

On the south-east side of the city centre, on vulitsya Pantelejmonovska, are the five bulbous silver domes and pointed bell tower of the neo-Byzantine **Pantelejmonovska Church**. Just down Pushkinska is the blue **Ilinsky Cathedral** (1886), richly adorned beneath a large central dome.

Museums & Galleries

Odesa has an excellent collection of museums, mostly housed in sumptuous former palaces. One of the most interesting is the **Archaeology Museum** (☎ 22 63 02), vulitsya Lanzheronovska 4, open from 10 am to 5 pm (closed Monday). Established in 1875, it was the first museum of its kind in the former Russian Empire. It houses archaeological finds from the Black Sea region

The Tryzub

That ubiquitous symbol stamped on everything from flags and buildings to cars, trains, money, and all kinds of official documents is, in fact, the *tryzub* (тризуб) – meaning 'three-toothed' or 'trident' in English. The tryzub is Ukraine's national symbol, with a history harking back 1000 years.

The exact origins of the symbol are unknown, but there are several theories. Some historians believe it to be derived from the classic mythological symbol of Neptune's trident spear. The most widely accepted theory, however, claims the design of the tryzub is based on the Cyrillic letters B, Я and O, which represent the three most celebrated rulers of ancient Kyivan Rus – Prince Volodymyr, King Yaroslav and Queen Olha. Variations on this theory suggest the design is patterned on the word *volya* (воля), meaning 'freedom'; or simply derived from the letter B and its mirror image, an acronym for Volodymyr Velyky (Volodymyr the Great), the Slav ruler who converted Kyivan Rus to Christianity in 988.

Throughout Ukrainian history the tryzub has symbolised Ukrainian identity and sovereignty. When Ukraine declared its independence from the Russian Empire in 1917, the fledgling government was quick to adopt the mark as its national emblem. Forbidden under the Soviet regime, the symbol was again adopted during the 1980s by the Ukrainian independence movement, Rukh. After the break-up of the USSR and the coming of independence in 1991, the Ukrainian Verkhovna Rada (Supreme Council) officially readopted the tryzub, set against a heraldic shield, as the country's coat of arms. The tryzub often appears on the Ukrainian flag, centred between its bands of blue and gold – the blue representing the sky, the gold representing wheat.

predominantly, including a replica statue of a Slavic pagan god. The highlight is the Gold Room (Zolota Kladova), which has jewellery and coins from early Black Sea civilisations, including the first Slavic coins of St Volodymyr (10th century AD) with the *tryzub* symbol on them. The prize item is a simple 14th century BC gold vase from the Crete Mycenaean civilisation.

Across the road at vulitsya Lanzheronovska 6 is the **Sea Fleet Museum** (☎ 24 05 09), also known as the Museum of the Ukrainian Black Sea Fleet (despite the fleet being in Russian hands).

At No 2, the **Literature Museum** (☎ 22 32 13) has excellent exhibits on the lives and works of Pushkin, Gogol, Chekhov, Tolstoy, Gorky, Shevchenko, Franko and Dovzhenko. It's open from 10 am to 6 pm (closed Sunday). Pushkin buffs should also take a stroll around the nearby **Pushkin Museum**, vulitsya Pushkinska 13. On the corner of Pushkinska and vulitsya Bunina sits the breathtaking **Odesa Philharmonia**, designed by Italian architect Bernardazzi who designed Hotel Krasnaya.

The **Museum of Western & Oriental Art** (☎ 24 66 48), housed in a gilded palace at vulitsya Pushkinska 9, is open from 10.30 am to 6 pm (closed Wednesday). Upstairs are 14 rooms full of works by European masters such as Hals, Caravaggio and Canaletto. Russian and Ukrainian art are well covered in the **Art Museum** (☎ 23 72 87), vulitsya Sofievska 5a, open from 10 am to 5 pm (closed Thursday). The **Regional History Museum** (☎ 25 52 02), vulitsya Gavannaya 4, is open daily from 10 am to 4.30 pm except Monday.

Catacombs

The sandstone on which Odesa stands is riddled with some 1000km of tunnels, quarried out for building in the 19th century. One network of tunnels in Nerubayske village, 12km north-west of Odesa centre, which sheltered a group of partisans in WWII, has been turned into the **Museum of Partisan Glory**, open from 9 am to 4 pm (until 2 pm on Saturday, closed Sunday). Russian/Ukrainian guided tours are available.

The very infrequent bus No 87 from the stop at the end of prospekt Myra stops outside the catacombs. Alternatively, take a taxi ($6 one-way).

Beaches & Ferries

Odesa's beaches are unbelievably crowded in summer, and the water is none too clean, but they're still fun to visit. Luzanovka beach in the north, about 6km across the bay from the passenger port, is very busy and has a funfair, an open-air disco and so on. The southern beaches are less crowded and more picturesque, with rocky headlands breaking up the coastline, and parkland stretching back up from the beach. In order, going from the centre of Odesa, they are: Lanzheron (3km), Otrada, Delfin, Arkadia (the most popular), Chayka, Kurortny, Zoloty Plyazh (Zolotoy Bereg in Russian, and sometimes called Bolshoy Fontan) and Chernomorka (18km). Two of the best are Zoloty Plyazh and Chernomorka, while Arkadia has the most restaurants, open-air discos, seaside kiosks etc. There is a cable car at Lanzheron.

Trams, buses or trolleybuses go within walking distance of all the beaches. Take tram No 5 to the end of the line to get to Arkadia beach. The boats and hydrofoils that used to plough the waters summer-long appear to have dried up, but it is worth asking at the passenger port to see if any *katery* (motorboats) are running.

Champagne

Crisp, sparkling white bubbly has been produced in Odesa at the Odessovkhozvinprom wine-making plant since 1857. Best known for its signature Sovietskaya champagne produced under the Soviet Union, its cellars today include more expensive vintages such as French Bulevard. The plant produces five million bottles of wine and 1.5 million bottles of champagne annually, reaped from grapes harvested from 23 collective farms in the Odesa oblast. Sovietskaya champagne sells for a bargain $2 in shops and kiosks.

It is possible to tour the Odessovkhozvinprom factory outlet (☎ 22 17 74, ☎/fax 22 35 78, wineprom@farlep.net) at bulvar

Frantsuzky 10, open from 8 am to 3 pm (closed on weekends). The hotel travel bureaux also arrange excursions here. Tram No 5 stops near the outlet.

Special Events

Odesa's annual Carnival Humourina, celebrated on 1 April, is no joke. The festival (☎/fax 25 22 73, org@humor.odessa.ua, www.humor.odessa.ua) fills the streets with carnival floats and processions and is the biggest party of the year for most Odesans.

Places to Stay

Camping ***Camping Delfin*** *(☎ 55 52 50, doroha Kotovsky 307)* is about 10km north of the centre, near Luzanovka beach. Wooden cabins and bungalows housing two to five people are available for around $8 per person. You can also pitch your own tent here. Bus Nos 130, 160 and 170 from ploshcha Hretsky (Martynovskoho) stop at the busy intersection about 300m north of Delfin.

Homestays The train station area is always busy with ageing babushkas with signs reading *kimnaty* (rooms) hung around their necks or pinned to their breasts. A bed for the night in a private home should cost no more than $5 to $10 a night.

Hotels Odesa is blessed with some central, deliciously low-rise, 19th century hotels with grand staircases, wide corridors and big rooms. Bottom of the pile is ***Hotel Spartak*** *(☎ 26 89 24, vulitsya Derybasivska 25)* where the reception staff do everything possible to dissuade guests from staying. Those that do, pay $7 for a bed in a single/double/triple with shared bathroom. Hot water is available from 6 am to midnight.

The best of the bunch is ***Hotel Tsentralna*** *(☎ 26 84 06, fax 26 84 07, vulitsya Preobrazhenska 40)*, opposite the flower market. Singles/doubles/triples with shared bathroom cost $10/11/14 and rooms with private bath are $19/37/55.

A block north-west is the decrepit but charming ***Hotel Pasazh*** *(☎ 22 48 49, ☎ 26 97 36, fax 26 84 07, vulitsya Preobrazhenska 34)*, above a beautiful shopping arcade (1897-98). Spacious rooms with private bath are $19/26/32. Around the corner, crumbling ***Hotel Grand Moscow*** *(☎ 22 40 16, vulitsya Derybasivska 29)* has rooms with bathrooms for $18/25/32. It also has a handful of cheaper rooms with shared bathroom and a bed for $4 per person.

An increasingly popular option with discerning travellers is the floating ***Hotelship Shevchenko*** *(☎ 24 51 12, fax 22 33 60, shevchenko@paco.net)*, a 222 bed cruise ship moored at the passenger port. Under Swiss management, it gets excellent reports, even though the cabins are small. Singles/doubles start at $73/92 (50% discount for children aged two to 12). Half/full board is available.

Close to the train station, the former Intourist joint, ***Hotel Chernoye More*** *(☎ 24 20 28, ☎ 24 10 31, fax 24 00 31, vulitsya Rishelevska 59)* is a 1970s concrete block with disgruntled staff who charge $1 to answer any question which involves a telephone call (such as train information). Overpriced rooms start at $85/120. Travellers who get here early enough should snag one of the unrenovated $35/40 rooms.

Near the beach 6km south-east of the centre is ***Hotel Arkadia*** *(☎ 63 75 27, fax 63 87 76, vulitsya Henuezska 24)*. Rooms cost $18/24 and hot water is available from 7 to 10 am and 8 to 11 pm. Next door but one, ***Hotel Viktoria*** *(☎ 61 89 03)* has nicer but pricier rooms for $42/50. Take tram No 5 from ploshcha Hretsky (Martynovskoho) in town to the end of the line to get to Arkadia beach and its nearby hotels. Bus No 129 from the airport/train station will take you to ploshcha Shevchenko (with the tall obelisk).

Near the sea, ***Hotel Londonskaya*** *(☎ 22 50 19, fax 25 53 70, londred@paco.net, Prymorsky bulvar 11)* is a restored gem dating from 1867 with a beautiful courtyard and ridiculously high price tags. Its 53 rooms start at $149/215 and peak at an awesome $297/381.

Odesa's top-notch hotels include the historic ***Hotel Krasnaya*** *(☎ 22 72 20, ☎ 25 85 20, fax 25 53 09, RedLond@paco.net, vulitsya Pushkinska 15)*, the front door of which is flanked by grandiose, half-naked classical figures. The beautiful Renaissance exterior (1898) shelters 72 rooms, costing $110/153. Luxury suites are $194/258. Trolleybus Nos 4 and 10 and bus Nos 109 and 155 heading south to the train station and north to the passenger port stop one block east of the hotel.

Places to Eat

Most bars listed in the Entertainment section tout mouth-watering menus. The ***Steakhouse** (☎ 28 77 75, vulitsya Derybasivska 20)* makes it into Ukraine's top 10 restaurants. Delicious steaks topped with an imaginative sauce (such as whisky, honey and peach) are served in a traditional rustic interior. Mains average $5, the menu is in English and there is a Georgian wine list. The toilets are behind the bar and past the kitchen.

***Uspansky Dvor** (☎ 26 67 88, vulitsya Preobrazhenska 23)* is a calm and tranquil Spanish restaurant with a fantastic grill room out back where shashlyk is cooked over an open fire. More traditional dishes like paella ($10 for 300g) are served in the room overlooking the street. It is open 24 hours.

Kove** (☎ 26 98 06, vulitsya Lanzheronovska)* is a pricey but fabulous sushi bar. Service is impeccable and the complex sushi platter ($25) for two people is a true treat (open from noon to midnight). ***Krasny, a Chinese restaurant next door to Hotel Krasnaya, has a carpeted terrace and is also better suited to the corporate bank account.

Less modern places include ***Restaurant Valday** (☎ 22 67 37, ploshcha Ekaterynynska 3)*, an old-school spot with heavy, ornately carved doors leading into its upmarket interior. Friendly ***Kafe Kartoplyanyky** (vulitsya Ekaterynynska 2)* is one of a handful of small, cheap cafeteria-style eateries in the centre where strange salads and plates heaped with mystery meat and potato dishes cost no more than $2.

In summer, pedestrianised vulitsya Derybasivska is transformed into one huge outside cafe, abuzz with chatter well into the early hours. ***McDonald's** (vulitsya Derybasivska 23)* is also in front of the train station on vulitsya Pantelejmonovska. Rivalling the latter in the cleanliness and smiling staff stakes is ***Country Fried Chicken** (vulitsya Rishelevska 5)*. You can get pizza to take away at the ***Pan Pizza*** outlet inside the well stocked ***supermarket*** *(☎ 28 77 75, vulitsya Derybasivska 20)*.

The central market is on vulitsya Privozna at the south-eastern end of prospekt Myra.

Entertainment

Odesa's nightlife is fun, funky and eclectic.

Bars, Clubs & Casinos ***Mick O'Neills Irish Bar** (☎ 26 84 37, vulitsya Derybasivska 13)* stocks oodles of ale and Guinness, and touts a mighty-long menu which leaves you spoilt for choice. Highlights include brown bread ice cream with whisky sauce, Irish apple pie and an all-day mixed grill breakfast ($6). O'Neills is open 24 hours.

Nearby, ***Fidel-Havana Club** (vulitsya Derybasivska 23)* is an American-style joint with a boat-shaped bar at one end, an extensive breakfast/lunch/dinner and drink menu, and – unfortunately – female strippers at weekends. It is open from 11 to 1 am. ***Buffalo 99** (vulitsya Rishelevska 5)* gets equally packed. Marginally more sedate is ***Captain Morgan** (vulitsya Rishelevska 15)*, a pirate-style bar with a fine wooden summer terrace, delicious freshly squeezed juices and 30% discount during happy hour (7 to 8 pm). ***Pyvnoy Dom** (vulitsya Preobrazhenska 38)* is a traditional beer house on two floors.

Live bands take to the stage at ***Khaly Haly** (☎ 25 74 64, provulok Chaykovskoho 18)*, an Elvis-inspired, rock 'n' roll bar with a psychedelic interior and garishly dressed waiting staff. The hottest nightclubs in town include ***Atlantis** (☎ 25 72 05, ploshcha Hretsky 1)* which practises face control and costs $4; and ***Cosmo** (☎ 60 59 61, ☎ 68 82 03, Gagarinska plato 5)* near Arcadia beach.

An old Russian tchaika and a flashy new limousine adorn the exterior of the upmarket ***Casino Richelieu** (☎ 24 94 16, vulitsya Bunina 15)*, worth a visit to peek at the fabulous Moorish-style building in which it is housed.

Classical Music & Opera You can buy advance theatre tickets from the ***Centralnya Teatralny Kasa***, on the corner of vulitsya

Rishelevska and vulitsya Derybasivska; or the ticket office (☎ 22 02 45), vulitsya Preobrazhenska 28.

Classical music buffs should head for the stunning ***Philharmonia*** *(☎ 25 01 89, 25 69 03, vulitsya Bunina 15)*. Equally irresistible is a performance at the lavish ***Opera & Ballet Theatre*** *(☎ 29 13 29, provulok Chaykovskoho 3)*, closed Monday. Its interior is decorated in Louis XVI style and its ceiling is painted with Shakespearean scenes. Tickets for same-day operas are sold in the *kasa* (ticket office), on the theatre's western side.

Other options include the ***Ukrainian Music & Drama Theatre*** *(☎ 23 55 66, vulitsya Pastera 15)*; the ***Russian Drama Theatre*** *(☎ 22 72 50, vulitsya Hretsky 48)*; or, for the young-at-heart, the ***circus*** *(☎ 22 19 73, vulitsya Podbelsky 25)*.

Shopping

Odesa's weekend *tovkuchka* or *tovchok* (both meaning 'crush' or 'push') is one of the country's biggest flea markets – a wonderland of every kind of imitation-Western junk imaginable. The market, on the city's western edge, is just south of Ovidiopilska doroha, shortly before the ring road. By public transport, take south-west bound tram No 4 from vulitsya Uspenska to the end of the line, then bus No 160.

Getting There & Away

Air Odesa is linked by daily flights to Kyiv, as well as several international destinations (see the Ukraine Getting There & Away chapter).

Train The Soviet slogan 'Welcome to Hero City' greets passengers when they step off the train at Odesa train station on ploshcha Pryvokzalna. Most signs at the station are in English. The left-luggage room is on platform 1 (open 24 hours).

From Odesa there are five trains a day to/from Kyiv (12 hours); three trains daily to Chisinau (five to seven hours) and Moscow (23 to 29 hours); two trains daily to/from Chernivtsi (12½ hours), Lviv (13 hours), Simferopol (13 hours), and Kharkiv (16 to 20 hours); and one train daily to Izmayil (eight hours), Minsk (26 hours), St Petersburg (29 hours, in summer only) and Rostov (27 hours). There is a train every other day to/from Warsaw (27 hours).

Most trains heading to western Ukraine pass through Moldova, for which a visa is required (see the Ukraine Getting There & Away chapter).

Bus Odesa's long-distance bus station (☎ 004), vulitsya Kolontaevskaya 58, is 3km west of the train station.

Boat From the passenger port *(morsky vokzal*; ☎ 22 32 11), vulitsya Suvorova, there are regular ferry services to Istanbul, Constanta and Haifa (see the Ukraine Getting There & Away chapter). Schedule information and tickets are available at the passenger port from Eugenia Travel (see Travel Agencies earlier).

Odesa is also a terminus for the Dnipro River hydrofoils and passenger boats (see the Ukraine Getting Around chapter)

Getting Around

To/From the Airport Odesa airport (☎ 65 81 86, ☎ 21 35 76, ☎ 006) is about 12km south-west of the city centre, off Ovidiopilska doroha. Bus No 129 goes to/from the train station; bus No 101 runs to/from ploshcha Hretsky in the city centre.

Public Transport Odesa has a comprehensive public transport network with a central terminus at ploshcha Hretsky and the circular roundabout in front of the train station.

To get to the centre from the train station (a 20 minute walk), there are several options: bus Nos 137 and 146 pass the train station en route to ploshcha Hretsky. Bus Nos 155 and 109, and trolleybus Nos 4 and 10, go up vulitsya Pushkinska before curving around to vulitsya Suvorova past the passenger port and the foot of the Potemkin Steps. Tram No 5 travels between the train and bus stations.

Taxi The central taxi rank (☎ 077) is on ploshcha Hretsky. Yellow-coloured taxis with a chequered stripe down the sides have a meter and are less likely to rip you off than the unmetered Volgas that labour round town.

BILHOROD-DNISTROVSKY БІЛГОРОД-ДНІСТРОВСЬКИЙ

☎ 04849 • pop 59,000

The White City on the Dnister, 55km from Odesa, is an ordinary industrial port town but has an impressive fortress on the banks of the river. First settled by Greeks, then Romans, the site was subsequently controlled by Cossacks, Tatars, Russians and Romanians.

The 13th century fortress, founded by Stefan II of Moldavia on a strategic spur of land overlooking the Dnister estuary, is among Ukraine's largest. Its walls stretch nearly 2km and its moat, once filled by an artificial tributary of the river, is 6m deep. The large and unkempt grounds inside the walls are separated into two main sections – one for merchants, the other for soldiers – by a tall internal wall with two gateways. You can walk along most of the walls, accessed by several stairways, for views of the complex. Artefacts excavated from Greek Tyras and the fortress are displayed in Bilhorod-Dnistrovky's **Regional Museum**, vulitsya Pushkinska 19 (closed Monday).

Getting There & Away

There are eight electric trains daily between Odesa and Bilhorod-Dnistrovsky, taking 2½ hours. Trains between Odesa and Izmayil also stop in Bilhorod-Dnistrovsky. To get to the fortress from the train station, walk along vulitsya Vokzalna and, after the park, turn right onto vulitsya Dzerzhinskoho. From here, the fortress is a 1.5km walk.

IZMAYIL ІЗМАЇЛ

☎ 04841 • pop 95,000

The Danube River port of Izmayil, 80km from the Black Sea, provides a rarely used back door into the country. It is a pleasant city, but not worth a special trip.

The city's hub is prospekt Suvorova, named after the war hero who helped take the city from the Turks during the Russian-Turkish War in 1790. From the regional museum in the north, it leads south past **Pokrovsky Cathedral** (1822-36) to the passenger port from where seasonal boats set sail up and down the Danube and to other Black Sea destinations (see the Ukraine Getting There & Away chapter). Two kilometres west of prospekt Suvorova is the 16th century **Mala Mechet** (Minor Mosque), the final remnant of a once-magnificent fortress built by the Turks after they conquered Izmayil.

Getting There & Away

There is one train daily to/from Odesa (eight hours), via Bilhorod-Dnistrovsky. From the train station, bus No 10 goes to the centre.

The Ukrainian Danube Shipping Company (☎ 90 210), prospekt Suvorova 2, used to operate boats along the Danube to Western European cities. Due to war in Yugoslavia, this service has been stopped for several years now, and is unlikely to be resumed.

Crimea
Крим

Hanging off mainland Ukraine into the Black Sea, the Crimean peninsula is a golden prize that has always been difficult to control. A land bridge merging East and West, it was fought over for hundreds of years by numerous nations, but it was Russia that eventually wielded the firmest fist. After expelling ethnic Tatars, Stalin sent Russians in droves, and today's population of 2.7 million is 63% Russian, 25% Ukrainian, and only 9% Tatar, with Russian being the predominant language on the peninsula.

Crimea first became a chic leisure spot in the 1860s when Russia's imperial family built a summer pad at Livadia. During the Soviet era, millions followed each year for warmth and beauty, sea and mountain air. While actual numbers of visitors have declined since independence, the peninsula continues to be a star attraction. In early spring, cherry blossoms burst forth in Crimea when it is still grey and grizzly elsewhere in Ukraine; while summer-long, pine and palm trees lend a tropical fragrance to the air.

Crimea is linked to the mainland only by the Perekop Isthmus in the north-west. In the north-east, the Arabatskaya Strelka, a 110km-long sandspit, almost encloses the very shallow Sivash Lagoon, which is crossed by the main road and railway from the north. Yalta, with its varied string of resorts and historic sites along a narrow coastal strip, is the main magnet. Behind soar the forested Crimean Mountains – the highest mountains between the Caucasus and the Carpathians.

HIGHLIGHTS

- Riding the world's longest trolleybus line from Simferopol to Yalta
- Discovering Crimea's underworld in the cave cities of Chufut-Kale and Manhup-Kale
- Hiking along the coastal 'Sunny Path' from Livadia Palace to Swallow's Nest
- Seeing how the Crimean khans lived in the Tatar capital of Bakhchysaray
- Sipping sweet wines and lazing in the sun on the beach at Yalta
- Exploring the exotic, 19th century seaside palace and gardens of Alupka

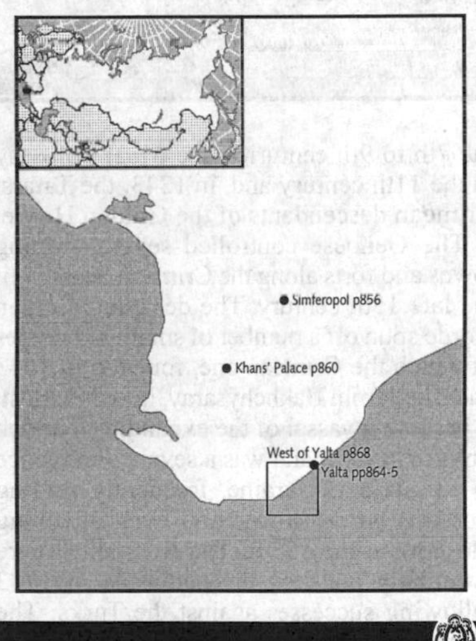

HISTORY

Greeks set up colonies on Crimea's coast at roughly the same time as the Scythians arrived from the east, during the 8th to 6th centuries BC. Panticapaeum, a Greek city at Crimea's eastern tip, ruled the Bosporan kingdom which held sway round the Sea of Azov and over much of Crimea until at least the 4th century AD. Another Greek settlement, Chersonesus near Sevastopol, became the seat of a bishop and, until the 13th century, an outpost of the Byzantine Empire. But most of Crimea fell to new arrivals from the East, such as the Khazar Empire of

CRIMEA

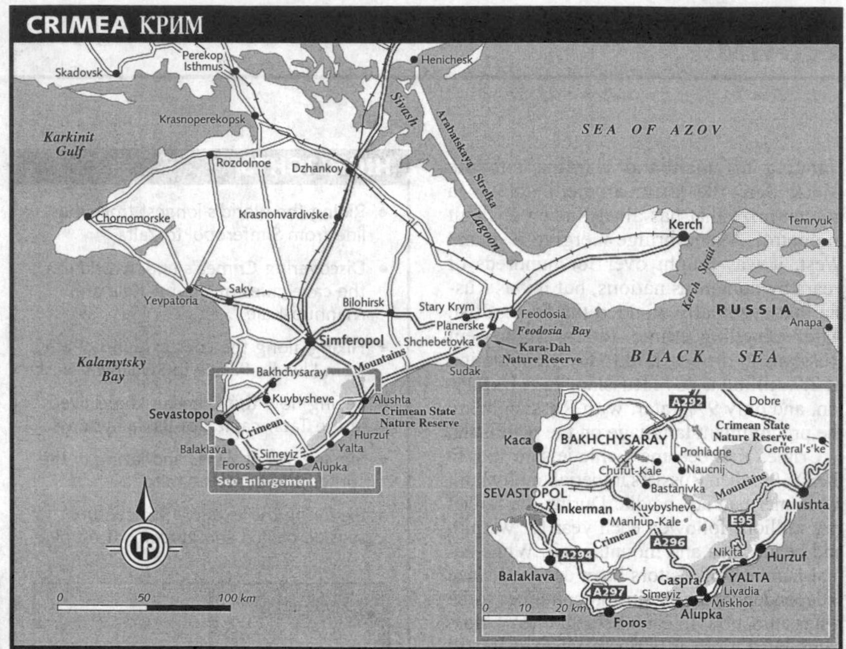

the 7th to 9th centuries, the tribal Polovtsy in the 11th century and, in 1243, the Tatars, Crimean descendants of the Golden Horde.

The Genoese controlled several trading towns and forts along the Crimean coast until the late 15th century. The decaying Golden Horde spun off a number of smaller khanates of which the Crimean one, founded in 1443 and ruled from Bakhchysaray, lasted longest. It became a vassal of the expanding Turkish Empire in 1475 and was a severe annoyance to Russia and Ukraine, frequently raiding Cossack border towns and even attacking Moscow in the 1550s. The Russian Empire eventually annexed the peninsula in 1783 following successes against the Turks. The takeover prompted an exodus of Crimean Tatars to the Ottoman Empire. Russians, Ukrainians and some Bulgarians and Germans resettled the peninsula.

The blunder-strewn Crimean War of 1854-56 was a classic clash of imperial ambitions. Russia wanted to take over the decaying Turkish Empire, while Britain and France wanted to stop this. So when in 1853 Russia occupied some Turkish provinces north of the Danube, the British and French assembled a big force at Varna, in what's now Bulgaria, to defend Istanbul. The Russians withdrew, but the allies were now committed to a fight, so together with the Turks they decided to invade Crimea. They took Sevastopol, Russia's main Black Sea port, in September 1855 after a year's siege.

The charge of the British Light Cavalry Brigade at Russian artillery resulted from misunderstood commands at the battle of Balaklava (October 1854), one of two Russian attempts to break the siege. Each side lost an estimated 250,000 in the war – many of those on the allied side dying from disease, bad hospitals and poor supplies, to which British nurse Florence Nightingale drew attention. After the war, Russian warships were banned from the Black Sea for 15 years.

In the civil war that followed the Russian Revolution, Crimea was one of the last White bastions, holding out till November 1920. In WWII it suffered a three year German occupation and lost nearly half of its entire population. Stalin then deported the remaining Crimean Tatars, about 200,000, mainly to Uzbekistan, and at least a third died en route. In 1954 Khrushchev transferred legislative control of Crimea to Ukraine.

Since Ukrainian independence, many political complications have arisen. The Russian majority in Crimea has been anxious for more autonomy, even possible reunification with Russia. In December 1998 the parliament of the autonomous republic succeeded in amending its constitution – the fifth attempt since 1992 – to allow it greater autonomy. But Crimea still remains firmly under central government control. Attempts by the Crimean parliament to make Russian the official language on the peninsula, to switch its time zone to Moscow time, to gain economic independence from Kyiv, and to hold a referendum on whether Crimea should return to Russian rule, have all been systematically overruled by Ukraine's Verkhovna Rada (Supreme Council).

SIMFEROPOL
СІМФЕРОПОЛЬ

☎ 0652 • pop 358,000

Simferopol is the Crimean crossroads where the northern plains end and the southern mountains start. The city is surprisingly developed and, as the seat of the 96 deputy Crimean Rada, is considered the 'capital' of the republic. Most visitors to Crimea arrive in Simferopol first.

Founded in the 18th century beside the 15th century Crimean Tatar town of Ak-Mechet (White Mosque), Simferopol was the last Russian stop before the front line during the Crimean War, and a giant hospital for the wounded. Long ago the Scythian town of Neapolis, whose site can be visited, stood here. In summer, a holiday atmosphere washes up from the coast as sailors come in from the Crimean naval bases to hang out around central vulitsya Karla Marxa, vulitsya Pushkina and vulitsya Horkoho. Most of the city centre is pleasantly pedestrianised.

Information

Simferopol has no tourist office. You can cash travellers cheques and get cash advances on Visa/MasterCard at Avaal Bank, Naberezhnaya 32.

The central post office is at vulitsya Rozy Lyuxemburg 1. You can send/receive emails (syppop@sc.pout.crimea.ua) at desk No 23, hall No 2 (US$0.10 per message plus $0.002 per kilobyte). Alternatively, try Sky-Net Internet Kafe (☎ 25 31 64), vulitsya Karla Marxa 7, open from 9 am to 10 pm ($2/hour online access); or Dom Cafe Club (see Places to Eat). DHL Worldwide Express (☎/fax 51 06 15) has an office in Hotel Ukraina (room No 126/7). There is a telephone centre in the central bus station.

The excellent *Simferopol* city map, published in 1999, is sold at the kiosk inside Hotel Moskva.

Things to See

The **Crimean Regional Museum** (☎ 27 63 64), vulitsya Pushkina 8, is open from 9 am to 5 pm (closed Tuesday). The Crimean War with maps, tombstones, weaponry and a series of English lithographs is covered on the 1st floor. A block north-west on vulitsya Hoholya is the five domed **Three Saints Church**. The small **Art Museum**, vulitsya Lybknekhta 35, is open from 10 am to 4.30 pm (closed Monday).

Two blocks north along vulitsya Zhukovskoho is the seat of the **Crimean Rada**, a concrete pentagon-shaped monstrosity. The exterior is kitted out with loudspeakers, so strollers in the park opposite can listen to the boring parliamentary sessions. The Council of Ministers to the Crimean Republic meets in the former House of Soviets, guarded by a statue of Lenin, on ploshcha Lenina.

Just east of the centre is the swooping-domed **Church of SS Peter & Paul** and the **Holy Trinity Cathedral**. A bit farther east up quaint vulitsya Kurchatova is a restored

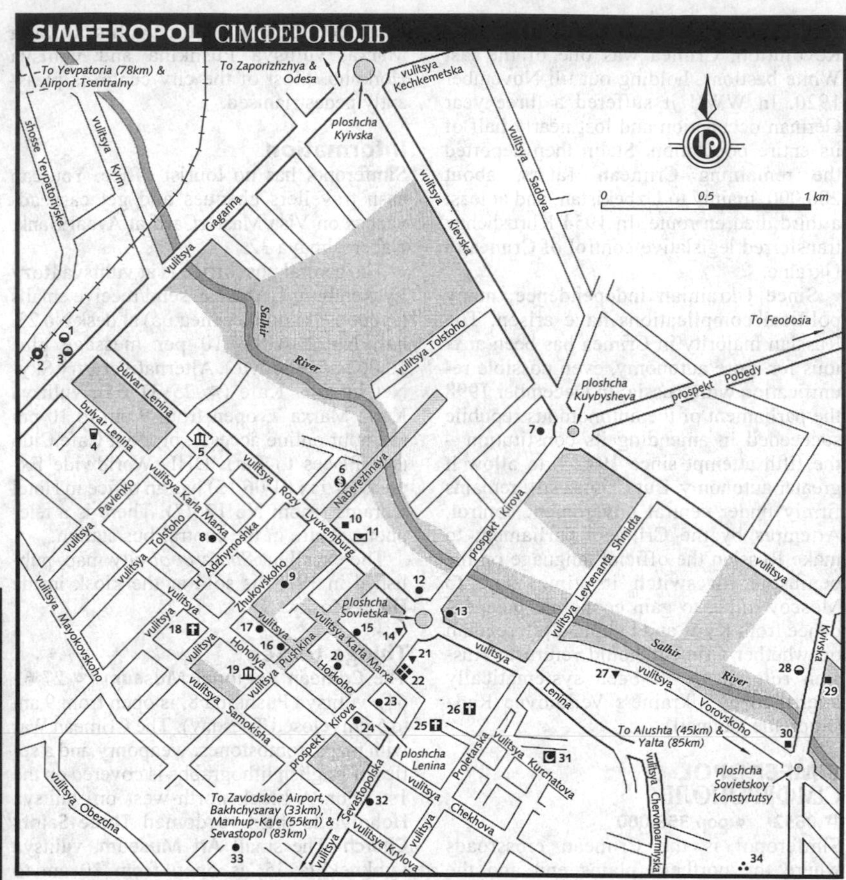

mosque in a small colourful neighbourhood repopulated by returning Crimean Tatars.

Farther east, 2km from the centre between vulitsya Vorovskoho and vulitsya Chervonoarmiyska (Krasnoarmeyskaya), is **Neapolis**, probably the capital of the late Scythian state in Crimea from the 3rd century BC to the 3rd or 4th century AD. There's little to see on the hilltop site beyond some scattered excavations, mounds, humps and an untidy stone reconstruction of a 2nd century BC **royal mausoleum.** Locals use the 20 hectare area as grazing ground for their goats.

Places to Stay

Hotel Ukraina *(☎ 51 01 65, fax 27 65 65, vulitsya Rozy Lyuxemburg 9)* is attractive and central with friendly floor staff. Well worn singles/doubles with shared bathroom cost $11/16; those with private bathroom are $25/32. From the train station take trolleybus Nos 5 and 2 to the Ukraina stop on vulitsya Rozy Lyuxemburg or trolleybus Nos 1, 4 and 6 to ploshcha Lenina.

Hotel Moskva *(☎/fax 23 97 95, vulitsya Kyivska 2)* is 2km east of the centre, near the bus station. Singles/doubles with private bath cost $17/27 and luxury suites for

SIMFEROPOL СІМФЕРОПОЛЬ

PLACES TO STAY
10 Hotel Ukraina
Готель Україна
29 Hotel Auto
Готель Авто
30 Hotel Moskva
Готель Москва

PLACES TO EAT
14 Eva Fast Food
Єва фаст фуд
21 Falstaff; Pink Flamingo
Фалстаф та Пинк Фламинго
27 Kafe Marakande
Кафе Мараканд

OTHER
1 Trolleybus terminal for Alushta & Yalta
Троллейбусная станция до Алушта та Ялта
2 Train Station
Залізничний вокзал
3 Bus Station
Автобусна вокзал
4 Dom Cafe Club
Дом Кафе Клуб
5 Art Museum
Художній музей
6 Avaal Bank
Аваал Банк
7 Market
Ринок
8 Crimean Wines (Shop)
Вина Крыма
9 Crimean Parliament
Верховна Рада
11 Post & Telephone Office
Пошта та телефон
12 Russian Drama Theatre
Театр Юного Глядача
13 Simferopol Cinema
Кіно театр Симферополь
15 Sky-Net Internet Kafe
Скій-Нет Интернет Кафе
16 Horkoho Theatre
Театр ім. Горького
17 Biblioteka
Бібліотека
18 Three Saints Church
Церква Трьох Святих
19 Crimean Regional Museum
Кримский краєведцеский музей
20 Circus
Цирк
22 TsUM (Department Store)
ЦУМ
23 Ukrainian Music & Drama Theatre
Український театр музики та драми
24 Council of Ministers (former House of Soviets)
Рада Міністрів
25 Holy Trinity Cathedral
Святотроїцька катедра
26 Church of SS Peter & Paul
Петропавлівська церква
28 Central Bus Station
Центральний автобусний вокзал
31 Mosque
Мечеть
32 Train & Airline Ticket Office
Каса продажу залізничних та авіаційних квитків
33 Central Market
Центральний ринок
34 Neapolis
Скіфський неаполь

three people are $82. Opposite the bus station is ***Hotel Auto*** *(vulitsya Kyivska 5)* which, if you can persuade the staff to let you stay, has dirt-cheap doubles for $10. To get to both hotels take trolleybus No 1, 2 or 6 from the train station, or No 4 from the city centre, to the *avtovokzal* (bus station).

Places to Eat

Kafe Marakande *(vulitsya Vorovskoho 17)* is an excellent Uzbek restaurant with a sunny terrace overlooking a small park. Sit at small, upright tables or on cushions on the floor and munch on delicious plov and other spicy dishes. It is open from 8 am to 11 pm (closed Sunday).

There's a cluster of eating joints around the TsUM department store on prospekt Kirova. The half-sunken ship sticking out of the paved square here is the entrance to ***Falstaff***, a cellar bar-cum-restaurant decked out like a boat. Its menu sports 14 vodka types. The snazzy ***Pink Flamingo*** *(☎ 27 89 98, vulitsya Odeskaya 2)* has an upmarket cabaret show. Nearby, ***Eva Fast Food*** *(☎ 27 04 34, vulitsya Ushinskoho 2/46)* is spotlessly clean and doles out soups, shashlyk, hot dogs and *bliny* (pancakes).

Dom Cafe Club *(bulvar Lenina 12)* is a funky art cafe-cum-club with huge sofas, live bands most weekends, Internet access and an adjoining art gallery. Ring the bell to enter.

Don't leave Simferopol without a visit to ***Crimean Wines*** *(vulitsya Karla Marxa 42)*, open from 8 am to 8 pm. Sweet Crimean wines and champagne start at $2 a bottle.

Getting There & Away

Air Simferopol airport (☎ 29 55 16, sairpo rt@pop.cris.net), called Aeroport Tsentralny, is north of the centre. Crimea Air operates flights to Kyiv (two to three a day) and Kharkiv (one a day). There is also a handful of international flights (see the Ukraine Getting There & Away chapter).

Crimea Air has an office at the airport (☎ 29 56 04, ☎ 24 80 79) and in the lobby of Hotel Ukraina (☎ 27 10 76, ☎ 27 23 14,

CRIMEA

☎/fax 25 51 34). Kiyavia (☎ 27 23 77, ☎ 27 21 16), ploshcha Moskovska, also sells airline tickets.

Train Simferopol is Crimea's main railway junction. Portraits of Lenin, Engels, Karl Marx and various Russian greats adorn the station's plush interior. Local trains run along the Crimean peninsula to/from Yevpatoria (two hours, six daily), Bakhchysaray (40 minutes, one daily) and Sevastopol (two hours, six daily). Farther afield, there are two trains daily to/from Kyiv (14 to 15 hours) and Moscow (21 to 26 hours via Kharkiv and Zaporizhzhya); and a daily service at least to/from Donetsk (12 hours), Dnipropetrovsk (10¾ hours), Lviv (30 hours), Kharkiv (10 hours) and Odesa (13 hours). Other destinations include Kerch (seven hours, six daily), Minsk (29 hours, every other day) and St Petersburg (35 hours, every other day). There are seasonal services to/from Rostov-on-Don (14 to 15 hours) and even Siberia.

Advance tickets are sold from window No 9 at the train station or from the train ticket office (☎ 27 33 16), vulitsya Sevastopolska 22, open from 8 am to 5.45 pm (closed on weekends).

Bus & Trolleybus Apart from Sevastopol (best served by train), other sites in Crimea are better reached from Simferopol by trolleybus or bus.

To/From Yalta & Alushta There are no direct trains to Yalta so from Simferopol catch the world's longest trolleybus line, which crosses a mountain pass (752m) on its 85km journey. Trolleybus No 52 serves Yalta (2½ hours, every 20 minutes between 5.30 am and 8.20 pm); and No 51 goes to/from Alushta (1½ hours, every 20 minutes between 6.40 am and 8.10 pm). Trolleybuses depart from the terminal next to the train station clock tower (to your left when exiting the train station). The time of the next departure is posted in the ticket office window. A single ticket for Yalta/Alushta costs $1/0.50. Small/large bags theoretically need a separate ticket ($0.10/1).

A speedier option is to take one of the nippy express minibuses that plough to/from Yalta (one hour), departing from the bus stop between the train and trolleybus stations. Buses depart when full. Alternatively, take a regular Yalta-bound public bus (two hours, hourly departures) from the small bus station opposite the trolleybus terminal.

Taxi drivers will hound you from the moment you get off the train. Be prepared to negotiate – and still be ripped off. A fare to Yalta should cost no more than $25.

To/From Other Places From the small bus station opposite the train and trolleybus stations, there are daily services to Sudak (2½ hours, eight daily) and Yevpatoria (1¾ hours, 11 daily).

Buses to other destinations use the central bus station, vulitsya Kyivska 4. There are regular services to/from Odesa (10 hours, two daily), Sevastopol (two hours, nine daily), Sudak (2½ hours, seven a day), Feodosia (2½ hours, eight a day) and Rostov (14 hours, once daily).

YEVPATORIA
ЄВПАТОРІЯ

☎ 06569 • pop 115,000

Completely off the beaten track, Yevpatoria, 78km north-west of Simferopol, is an ancient city holding a crumbling array of relics reflecting the rich and diverse cultures in Crimean history. Once a thriving coastal resort, the old town and adjoining waterfront area overlooking Yevpatoria Bay are miserably quiet today.

Settled by Greeks in the 6th to 5th centuries BC, the town was inhabited by immigrant Slavs in the 10th to 12th centuries, then renamed Hezlev by the Turks who fortified it and turned it into a slave-trading market in the 15th century. The surrounding walls have long gone, but traces of the past remain along vulitsya Matveeva, a rough-and-tumble street once dotted with 18th century Karaite prayer houses.

Yevpatoria's Turkish-style **Dzhuma-Dzhami Mosque** (1552), in a park near ploshcha Prymorska on the seafront, was designed by famous architect Khodzhy Synan. It is Crimea's largest mosque with tall minarets and the twin mihrabs (prayer niches) either side of the entrance that were restored in 1976. The two ornate marble tombs, left of the entrance, belong to Turkish generals killed during the Crimean War. Some 30 worshippers use the mosque today, cared for by a Crimean Tatar who has lived in a rusting caravan next to the mosque since returning 'home' in the early 1990s.

Accommodation in Yevpatoria is limited. ***Hotel Yuzhnaya*** *(☎ 3 03 39, vulitsya Kirova 50)* is the only hotel open in winter; doubles with sink and cold water cost $5. ***Hotel Krym*** *(☎ 2 34 12, vulitsya Revolyutsy 46)*, close to the waterfront, has rooms for $10 per person in summer.

There are 11 buses daily from Simferopol to Yevpatoria bus station (1¾ hours). To get from the bus station, 1.5km north-west of the old town, to the seafront, take tram No 3 to ploshcha Teatralna then tram No 1 along the waterfront to the old town.

BAKHCHYSARAY БАХЧИСАРАЙ

☎ 06554 • pop 20,000

The small town of Bakhchysaray, 33km south-west of Simferopol, and the abandoned cave cities in its surrounding limestone hills, bring you face to face with the Tatar era and other remnants of Crimea's past. From the 15th century until 1783, Bakhchysaray (Turkish for 'garden palace') was the seat of the Crimean khans, the last westwards bastion of the descendants of Jenghis Khan's hordes. From 1475, these Crimean Tatars were vassals of the Ottoman Empire; and as the embodiment of both the terrible Tatar hordes and the 'depraved infidel' Turks, they are the cruel bogeymen of many a Slavic fairy tale.

An excellent choice of hiking maps and the English-language *Cave Cities of the Crimea* (see Books in Ukraine Facts for the Visitor), both indispensable to anyone intending to explore the region's cave cities, are sold at the souvenir stalls outside the entrance to the Khans' Palace.

Lost Homeland

On 18 May 1944, the entire Crimean Tatar population, which peaked at five million during Crimean Khanate rule, was deported by Stalin to Kazakhstan, Uzbekistan and Siberia. Collaboration with the Nazis during WWII was the alleged crime. The Tatar language, written in Cyrillic since 1940, was banned and all Tatar traces obliterated by Stalin who repopulated the area with Ukrainians, Russians, Bulgarians and Germans. An estimated 46.2% of the total Crimean Tatar population died during this forced deportation.

Since the late 1980s, about 260,000 Tatars have returned to Crimea in search of a lost homeland. An estimated 100,000 are disenfranchised and not entitled to Ukrainian citizenship. Few speak their Turkic mother tongue, an endangered language that readopted the Latin alphabet in 1997. Home for 40% of returned Tatars is a makeshift camp with no electricity or running water supply in shantytowns on the Crimean peninsula, mainly around Simferopol.

Traditionally, the Crimean Tatar community is self-governed by its own Kurultay (Parliament) and 33 member Mejlis (Cabinet), headed by Mustafa Dzhemilev. Dzhemilev and his deputy, Refat Chubarv, both hold seats in Ukraine's Supreme Council. March 1998 elections to the 96 deputy Crimean Parliament however saw the Crimean Tatars lose all 14 seats they had held since 1994.

Khans' Palace

The Tatar rulers' palace (Khansky Palats) was built by Russian and Ukrainian slaves in the 16th century under the direction of Persian, Ottoman and Italian master builders. Despite being rebuilt several times since, it still resembles its original state.

Inside the main **mosque** (1740) is the khans' private prayer room, with an original carved wooden ceiling. The mosque's carved wooden balcony *(mafil)* was for

CRIMEA

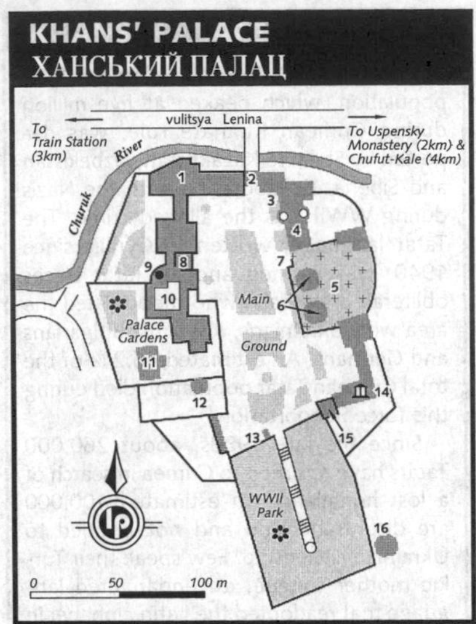

KHANS' PALACE
ХАНСЬКИЙ ПАЛАЦ

1 Main Exhibition Hall
Головні виставки кімнати
2 Entrance Gateway
Вхід
3 Ticket Kasa
Каса
4 Mosque
Мечеть
5 Khans' Cemetery
Ханський цвинтар
6 Mausoleums
Гробівниці Ханоб
7 Entrance to the Cemetery
Вхід на цвинтар
8 Entrance to Khans' Palace & Museum
Вхід до Ханського Палацу та музею
9 Ambassador's Gate
Амбасадорська брама
10 Courtyard & Fountain of Tears
Гаремний город і Фонтан Сліз
11 Harem & Summer House
Гаремовий
12 Tower
Башта
13 Alexander I Fountain
Фонтан Александра
14 Art Museum
Бувші стайні
15 Gateway
Брама
16 Tower
Башта

women only. Past the mosque, among finely carved tombstones in the **cemetery,** are two octagonal rotunda tombs *(dyurbe)*, miniature mausoleums for the khans. Next to the cemetery, the former stables have been converted into an **art museum** featuring 18th to 20th century art.

Opposite is the main palace and museum complex – a series of courtyards and Ottoman-style buildings where indoor and outdoor spaces blend together. Passing through the finely carved **Ambassador's Gate** (also called Portal Aleviza after its Italian creator Alevisio Novi), you come to the beautiful inner courtyard. Its highlight is the **Fountain of Tears** (1764), glorified by Russian poet Alexander Pushkin in his poem *The Bakhchysaray Fountain* (1820). The fountain is said to have been made by a captive Persian, Omer, for the last Crimean khan, Giri, who was so ruthless that people said he had a lump of wool for a heart. Eventually Giri fell in love with a captive Polish girl in his harem who, when she died, caused him to weep, proving he had a heart after all. He ordered Omer to make a rock weep too, to perpetuate his grief. The **Golden Fountain** (1733), its white marble ornately inscribed in gold leaf, tinkles in the tranquil courtyard too.

Behind the palace is the **harem**, which traditionally belonged to the khan's oldest wife (rather than his mother). A fountain forms the centrepiece of the **summerhouse** which has an early 18th century, carved wood ceiling.

The palace's north wing houses the fascinating **main exhibition hall**, 12 rooms featuring various historical exhibits on Tatar culture (nothing on the deportations) and the life of the khans.

The palace, vulitsya Lenina 129, is open from 9 am to 5 pm (closed Tuesday, Wednesday and the last day of the month). In winter it closes at 4 pm. Admission to the palace and museum is $1.50 (ticket kasa is to the left as you enter). Captions are in English and Russian.

Uspensky Monastery

East of the Khans' Palace the main road becomes vulitsya Gasprinkchov Prinskoho (formerly Lyuxemburg). About 500m down this road is the small **Mosque of Tokhtala-Dzhama** with a 16 sided minaret. Another 1km on, past cottages on the right and sheer rock walls on the left, is the hamlet of **Starosele**. From here, just past the bus stop and small car park, a paved path branches up to the right to Uspensky Monastery (five minutes walk) and Chufut-Kale beyond. From the end of the path, steps lead up to the gold-domed **bell tower** and on to the church, built inside the limestone rock. There are excellent views of the canyon from outside the church entrance. Across the canyon there are more trails and some smaller caves – good for hiking.

The monastery was probably founded by Byzantine monks in the 8th or 9th century. From the church, a footpath leads along the rock face, past a series of former shallow caves carved out of the rock. Since 1993, following the return of some eight monks to the isolated complex, many are inhabited again. Numerous additional cells, white-washed and with blue window frames, have also been built in the rock face.

Chufut-Kale

The biggest and most accessible of several cave cities in the limestone hills of south-west Crimea is on top of a long bluff, a pleasant 2km hike down the track past Uspensky Monastery, then up the steep hillside to the left. Originally called Kyrk-Or Forty Fortifications, the city was settled between the 6th and 12th centuries. Around 1400, Tokhtamysh, the last powerful ruler of the Golden Horde, used it as a refuge after his empire was smashed by Timur in the 1390s. In the 17th century Crimean khans imprisoned eminent Poles, Russians and Ukrainians here. The last inhabitants – who had left by the mid-19th century – were the Karaites, a dissident Jewish sect founded in Baghdad in 770 AD. They renamed the city Chufut-Kale (Jewish Fortress).

Approaching from Uspensky, you enter by the 14th century **South Gate** which leads to a Swiss-cheese composition of carved-out rooms and steps. To the right on the clifftop are two *kenassas* (Karaites' prayer houses), locked and impossible to enter, in a walled courtyard. Beyond are a series of foundations and low stone walls. A stone path leads to the red-tile roofed **Muslim mausoleum** (1437) of Dzhanike-Khanym, daughter of Tokhtamysh. Beyond, the cliff drops dramatically and there is an expansive view over the next valley. Farther along, the grooved, stone path leads through an archway. This archway is a section of the **Middle Defensive wall**, part of an impressive system of defensive walls built in the 6th century and reinforced in the 15th century. At its prime, the Middle Defensive wall was 8m high and 10m thick. To the left after the archway, a track leads to two **burial chambers** with a view right over the cliff's edge. Continuing along the main stone path, the century-old, cartwheel grooves in the road become very prominent. Past the inhabited homestead on the right, you reach the locked **East Gate**.

About 2km farther east of Chufut-Kale is another smaller cave city called **Tepe-Kermen**.

Places to Stay

Wild camping is allowed near Chufut-Kale; water is available from a fountain at the chapel next to the Uspensky Monastery. Bring your own food and supplies.

The small and basic ***Turbaza Prival*** is a 1km walk from the Khans' Palace (follow the red arrows painted on the walls from vulitsya Lenina).

Getting There & Away

There are six trains daily between Simferopol and Sevastopol, stopping in Bakhchysaray (40 minutes from Simferopol), and an additional one a day that terminates in Bakhchysaray. There are also buses between Bakhchysaray and Simferopol; the train is faster and more frequent.

Getting Around

Bakhchysaray train station is 3km west of the Khans' Palace, and the bus station is

1.5km north-east of the train station. Bus No 4 runs between the two. From the train station, bus No 2 (11 a day between 6 am and 9 pm) stops in front of the palace and, in Starosele, at the foot of the track leading up to Uspensky Monastery.

To get to the palace on foot from the train station (a 45 minute walk), walk 300m east of the train station to the large intersection, then continue straight ahead (third road from left).

MANHUP-KALE
МАНГУП-КАЛЕ

Manhup-Kale, 22km south of Bakhchysaray and 3km from the village of Zalesnoe, is another famous and fascinating cave city. It dates from the 6th century and, like Chufut-Kale, was settled by various peoples – pagan to Christian to Tatar to Karaite – and finally abandoned in the 15th century.

Exploring the Caves

From the southern end of Zalesnoe walk about 1km until you see, on your left, four rock peaks rising in a row out of wooded ravines. They're actually four fingers of land stretching out from the same long ridge. Turn off the road towards the small hamlet at the base of the ridge. On the farthest fingertip east you'll see small holes and some cave openings – that's where the biggest concentration of caves is. The other three fingers have only a few scattered walls. The best way up is between the first two fingers; a trail leads up to your right just as you approach the small group of cottages. At the top of the ridge follow the trail to the farthest finger of land until you see a large stone gateway and long wall. Beyond are the carved-out chambers and caves. Explore especially along the far eastern edge of the cliff; many chambers have windows looking out over the vast vista. The most impressive is the final cave room carved out of the very tip of the cliff with stairs leading down the west side to a burial chamber with tiny cells.

Getting There & Away

The closest village to Manhup-Kale, Zalesnoe, is reached from Bakhchysaray bus station by two daily buses. The easiest way to reach the village is to hitch or take a taxi (about $6).

YALTA
ЯЛТА

☎ 0654 • pop 90,000

In the late 18th century, when Crimea fell under Russian control, Yalta became the empire's classiest Black Sea resort with Tsar Alexander II making nearby Livadia his summer residence. Prior to the revolution the coast was peppered with aristocratic estates, and artistic figures such as Tolstoy, Chekhov and Rachmaninov spent much time here. Afterwards, these estates were turned into sanatoria for the workers, but once again new generations of high and mighty soon established themselves, building lavish dachas and continuing the area's tradition as the exclusive hideaway of the rich and powerful.

Yalta's setting is spectacular – a narrow cypress-strewn strip between the Crimean Mountains and the Black Sea. Shielded from north winds, temperatures only just dip below freezing in winter and are several degrees warmer than Kyiv in summer. People bathe from June to October – by which time they can usually look up to snow on the peaks above.

The famous Yalta Conference of 1945 was in fact held in Livadia (see Livadia later).

Orientation

Yalta lies between the gently curving shore of Yalta Bay (Yaltinsky Zaliv) and Yuzhnoberezhnoe shose, the highway forming a ring road round the edge of town, about 1km from the bay. The bus station is 1.5km north of the centre, just before the ring road. The commercial centre is around and back from the mouth of the little Bystra (Bystraya) River. Tourists congregate on naberezhna Lenina, the waterfront promenade which stretches west from the Bystra River to the Vodopadna (Vodopadnaya) River on the east side of town.

Maps NPP Kartografiya publishes the excellent *Yalta* city map (1998). Unfortu-

CRIMEA

nately, the map only seems to be available in Kyiv.

Information

Money Exchange travellers cheques at Bank Ukraini, naberezhna Lenina 3, or Exim Bank, inside Hotel Yalta. There is an ATM in the hotel lobby too. In town, exchange kiosks dot the waterfront.

Post & Telephone The central post office, ploshcha Lenina, is open from 8 am to 8 pm. The telephone centre is at vulitsya Moskovska 9.

Email & Internet Access The Internet Club (☎ 35 17 22, book@yalita.yalta.iuf.net), inside Spartak Cinema at vulitsya Marshaka 9a, is open from 10 am to 5 pm and 7 to 11 pm. The Internet Centre inside Hotel Oreanda (see Places to Stay) is usually hogged by square-eyed kids playing computer killer games. Both charge $2/hour.

Travel Agencies The annoyingly bureaucratic service bureau (☎ 35 01 42) inside Hotel Yalta supposedly assists tourists between 9 am and 5 pm (8 am to 8 pm in summer). It arranges car rental (with driver) and organises numerous excursions, including helicopter rides and caving expeditions.

Around the Waterfront

Everyone gravitates to **naberezhna Lenina**, the vehicle-free waterfront promenade with jetties, palms, beaches, snack bars, photographers, gardens and art markets. The naberezhna stretches south-west to **Prymorsky Park**, where there's a monument inscribed with part of Lenin's 1920 Crimea decree 'On the Use of the Crimea for the Medical Treatment of the Working People'. In front are some of Yalta's shingle beaches. At the western end of the naberezhna, before Hotel Oreanda, vulitsya Pushkinska is a pretty promenade stretching west along the small Vodopadna River past stately sanatoria and mansions. An informal art market sets up in the garden behind naberezhna Lenina.

The boarding point for the **chairlift** which swings above the rooftops to Darsan, a temple-like lookout on the hill, is behind naberezhna Lenina 17. It operates between 9 am and 5 pm. **Alexandr Nevsky Cathedral** off vulitsya Sadova is a beautiful piece of neo-Byzantine architecture with fantastic detailing.

Way up the hill off vulitsya Zahorodna is the **Armenian church** (1909-17), built in traditional Armenian style. Concerts are held here.

Chekhov House-Museum

Anton Chekhov (1860-1904), who suffered from tuberculosis almost half his life, spent much of his last five years in Yalta where he wrote *The Cherry Orchard* and *Three Sisters* and met Tolstoy. Chaliapin and Rachmaninov played the piano in the white cottage he had built at vulitsya Kirova 112. Today, the dacha houses the Chekhov House-Museum (☎ 39 49 47), open from 10 am to 5 pm (closed Monday, Tuesday and the last day of the month).

All nine rooms in the cosy cottage are pretty much as Chekhov left them upon his departure from Yalta for Germany in May 1904. His piano still sits in the 1st floor sitting room. Admission is $2/1 for adults/students.

Take bus No 8 from the Spartak bus terminus to the Dom Muzey A P Chekhova stop. Trolleybus No 1 from ploshcha Radyanska (Sovietskaya) will drop you a few blocks downhill to the south.

Polyana Skazok

Yalta's Polyana Skazok (Fairy-Tale Glade) is an open-air museum featuring characters from Ukrainian and Russian children's stories cast in iron, concrete and wood. Winnie the Pooh and Mowgli also lurk here.

Polyana Skazok is 5km from the centre – almost 1km up from the Polyana Skazok bus stop on Yuzhnoberezhnoe shose where vulitsya Kirova crosses over. It's open from 8 am to 8 pm from 15 May to 15 September (9 am to 5 pm and closed Wednesday the rest of the year). Take bus No 26, 27, 28 or 11 from Yalta bus station to the Polyana Skazok bus stop or bus No 8 from the Spartak bus terminus to the end of the line.

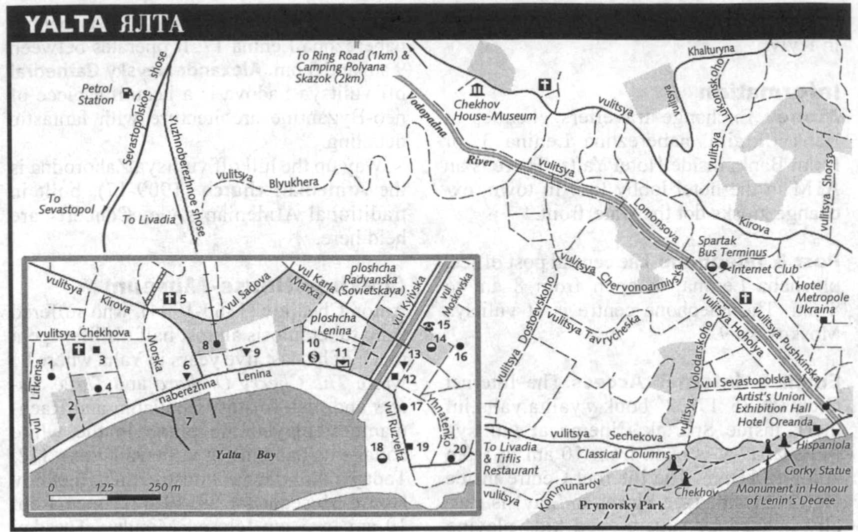

Wine Tasting

Much of the Crimean coast has been covered in vines for 150 years, particularly at **Massandra** where grapes have been harvested for the region's predominantly sweet wines since 1785. Livadia white Muscat, red Kamin Alushta and others can be tried and tested at the Massandra wine tasting complex, near Alupka (see Around Yalta). In Yalta, head for the Massandra wine shop (☎ 72 11 98, ☎ 35 26 79), vulitsya Svetkva 6, open from 9 am to 7 pm. As well as $2 bottles of regular table wine, it stocks older collection vintages, including white and pink Muscats from 1950 ($150 a bottle) and 1936 ($210 a bottle). Count on paying $20 for a 10-year-old red.

The Crimean Wines shop, naberezhna Lenina, has a bar and cafe where you can taste different wines; unfortunately its selection is fairly limited.

Places to Stay

Camping ***Camping Polyana Skazok*** *(☎ 39 52 19, ☎ 39 74 39)*, 5km from the centre on a wooded hillside beneath majestic cliffs, has two-person cabins for about $3 per person. Take the bus to the Polyana Skazok stop (see Polyana Skazok earlier), from where it is a 1.5km walk uphill.

Homestays At Yalta bus station, look out for middle-aged women with a placard reading *komnati* (Russian) or *kimnaty* (Ukrainian) strung around their neck. Don't pay more than $15 a night.

Hotels Heating in Yalta's hotels is not guaranteed in winter, while hot water can be scarce in summer. In July and August (when most hotels hike up their prices), advance reservations are recommended.

On the edge of town, heading towards the enormous Hotel Yalta, is the small, 60 bed ***Hotel Otdich*** *(☎ 35 50 79, vulitsya Drazhynskoho 14)*. It has good-value singles/doubles/triples with TV, toilet, shower and hot water for $7/16/20 and is one of the few places which does not increase its prices in the summer months.

A couple of old but central hotels which provide quaint and cheapish lodging include ***Hotel Krym*** *(☎ 32 60 01, fax 32 20 01, vulitsya Moskovska 1)*, near ploshcha Lenina. It has singles/doubles/triples for $6/18/24, with single rooms sharing a toilet

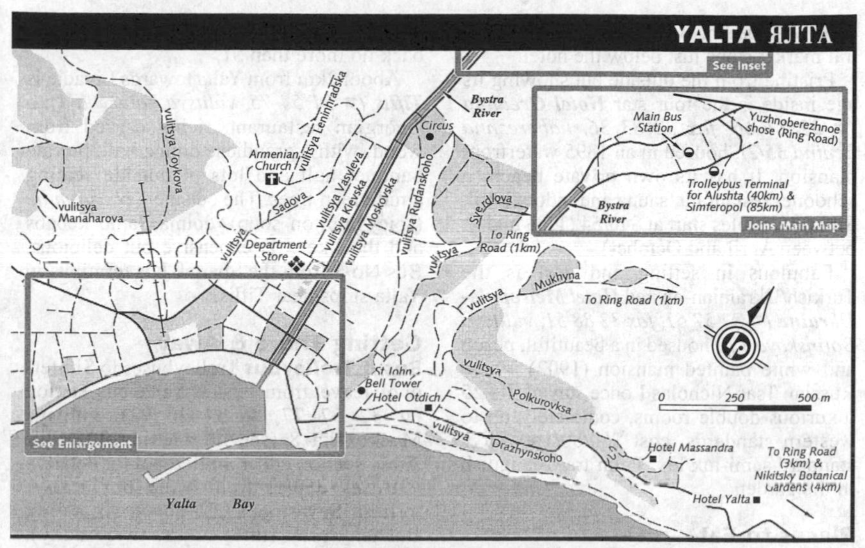

YALTA ЯЛТА

PLACES TO STAY

3 Hotel Palats
Готель Палац
12 Hotel Krym
Готель Крим
19 Hotel Yuzhnaya
Готель Южная

PLACES TO EAT

2 Bely Lev (White Lion)
Белый Левь
6 Crimean Wines
Вина Крыма
9 Restoran Gurman
Ресторан Гурман
13 Kafe Krym
Кафе Крим

OTHER

1 Chekhov Theatre
Театр Ім. Чехова
4 Concert Hall (Summer Stage)
Концертный зал
5 Alexander Nevsky Cathedral
Катедра Александра Невського
7 Piers 6, 7 & 8
Причаил 6 7 та 8
8 Chair Lift
Ліфт
10 Bank Ukraini
Банк України
11 Post Office
Пошта
14 Bus Terminal
Автобусний кінцевий
15 Telephone Centre
Переговорний Пункт
16 Central Market
Центральний ринок
17 Bookshop
Книги
18 Passenger Port
Морський вокзал
20 Crimean Wines (Shop)
Вина Крыма

in the corridor; and ***Hotel Palats*** *(☎ 32 43 80, fax 32 18 62, vulitsya Chekhova 8)*, in a pretty block behind the summer stage theatre. It has spacious, clean and comfortable doubles/triples with private bathroom for $30/40. There is no hot water at night.

Two other cheapies near the seafront are ***Hotel Yuzhnaya*** *(☎ 32 58 60, vulitsya Ruzvelta 10)*, opposite the passenger port; and ***Hotel Massandra*** *(☎ 32 78 00, vulitsya Drazhynskoho 48)*, just west of Hotel Yalta. Both are closed in winter, and charge similar prices to the Krym when open.

Continuing along the street, you eventually come to the ridiculously mammoth, 2230 bed ***Hotel Yalta*** *(☎ 35 01 50, fax 35 33 93, vulitsya Drazhynskoho 50)*, about 1.5km east of the centre. Singles/doubles cost $24/30 (two to three times more expensive in summer). The Yalta sports 16 floors, 10 bars, seven restaurants, an outdoor pool, a sauna, massage parlour and a lift up/down to its private beach. Bus No 34 from the central market stops just below the hotel.

Pristine from the outside but showing its age inside is the four star ***Hotel Oreanda*** *(☎ 32 81 66, fax 32 83 36, naberezhna Lenina 35/2)*, housed in an 1895 waterfront mansion. It has its own private beach, a schooner restaurant, sauna and indoor pool. Singles/doubles start at $40/54 (15% higher between April and October).

Fabulous in setting and cost is the Turkish/Ukrainian-owned ***Hotel Metropole-Ukraina*** *(☎ 32 57 61, fax 32 88 51, vulitsya Botinskaya 13)*, housed in a beautiful, peach and white painted mansion (1902) where Russian Tsar Nicholas I once stayed. Its 25 luxurious double rooms, completely up to western standards, cost $60/80/100 for a standard/semi-lux/lux. Palm trees languish in the garden.

Places to Eat

Come summer, naberezhna Lenina buzzes with open-air cafes, kiosks and bars that sprawl across the wide promenade. Numerous restaurants also line the waterfront.

Set a little back from the sea on the promenade is the grandiose ***Bely Lev*** *(☎ 32 77 36, naberezhna Lenina 31a)*, housed in a turreted building with a marble terrace, fountain and horribly loud music blasting from speakers outside. Inside its chandelier-clad interior, the White Lion plays classical music (open from noon to 3 am). Pay an extra $1 to dine by candlelight. An entire suckling pig costs $100.

Nearby is ***Hispaniola*** *(☎ 31 08 31)*, an ex-movie galleon beached opposite Hotel Oreanda with tables below in the cabins and up top on deck too. Meals tend to be fish-based.

A smiling, English-speaking staff and quiet music are the trademarks of ***Gurman*** *(☎ 32 03 06, naberezhna Lenina 11)*, a popular spot with lots of seafood on its menu. The fish shashlyk and mussels (each $4) are both excellent.

Dirt-cheap Ukrainian dishes are served without a flourish at the cafeteria-style ***Kafe Krym*** next to Hotel Krym. A full meal comprising shredded carrot salad, mashed potatoes, meatballs and soup will set you back no more than $1.

About 2km from Yalta towards Livadia is ***Tiflis*** *(☎ 31 54 75, vulitsya Vaturyna 1)*, a Georgian restaurant, richly carved from wood, with a grandiose dining hall, private banquet hall and lots of outside seating amid green trees. The cuisine – *chaka pulie* (spicy mutton soup), dolma, lamb kebabs and the like – is expensive but delicious. Bus No 5 from the Spartak bus terminus in Yalta stops near Tiflis.

Getting There & Away

Bus & Trolleybus Trolleybuses to Simferopol leave from beside Yalta bus station (☎ 32 57 77, ☎ 34 20 92), vulitsya Moskovska 8 (see the Getting There & Away section under Simferopol for details).

Buses depart from Yalta bus station to/from Sevastopol (2½ hours, six daily), Bakhchysaray (three hours, twice daily), Feodosia (six hours, one a day), Kerch (eight hours, once daily) and Odesa (12½ hours, once daily).

Boat Few boats sail in and out of the passenger port *(morskoy vokzal)*, at the end of vulitsya Ruzvelta. From July to September the *Caledonia* sails once weekly to/from Yalta and Odesa (see the Ukraine Getting There & Away chapter). There is an information desk (☎ 32 00 94) in the terminal building.

Getting Around

Buses and trolleybuses run around town, along the coast and into the hills. The Yalta bus and trolleybus stations are between vulitsya Moskovska and vulitsya Kyivska, about 1.5km from the waterfront. Many routes use ploshcha Radyanska (Sovietskaya) or the bus terminus next to the central market. Some depart from the Spartak terminus, west of Hotel Oreanda, where vulitsya Marshaka and Pushkinska join.

From the central bus station, trolleybus No 1, 2, or 3 goes to the town centre.

Most local bus routes are also ploughed by zippier minibuses which simply depart when full. These buses are about three times more expensive than the slower, scheduled buses. Pay the bus driver when on board, respecting the ritual of passing your fare to the passenger in front who will, in turn, pass it to the next passenger until it eventually reaches the driver. Your change will be returned in the same way. Avoid the seat next to the door unless you want to be responsible for opening/closing it at each stop.

AROUND YALTA

Nikitsky Botanical Gardens

Even if you're no gardener or botanist, the Nikitsky Botanical Gardens, tumbling down 3 sq km of hillside to the sea, 5km east of Yalta, are worth a visit for their beauty and views. Founded in 1812, they are home to 28,000 species, including 2000 rose types, a 500-year-old yew tree and a 1000-year-old pistachio tree.

The gardens are split into four sections: the Upper Park (Verkhny Park) and Lower Park (Nizhny Park), together called the Arboretum; Prymorsky Park; and Cape Montedor Park (Mys-Montedor Park). The Upper Park has the rose garden and a fine observation area. Prymorsky Park has delicate subtropical plants. The gardens are open from 8 am to 7 pm (8 pm in summer); admission is $2/1 for adults/children.

From the bus terminus next to Yalta central market, take bus No 34 to the Upper Gate bus stop. Stroll through the gardens down to the sea, then walk a short distance back up the hill to get the return bus to Yalta from the Lower Gate bus stop. If you want to add 2km to your walk, take the more frequent Hurzuf bus No 31 to the NBS bus stop on the Yalta-Alushta highway. The gardens are signposted from there.

Hrusheva Polyana
Грушева Поляна

Native animals of the Crimean Mountains – deer, bears, boar and wild sheep – can be viewed in enclosures at Hrusheva Polyana (Pear Tree Glade), high above the Nikitsky Gardens, 11km east of Yalta within the Crimean Game Reserve. This is the only part of the reserve open to visitors. The road leads up from Massandra on the eastern side of the Yalta ring road. Bus No 33 from Yalta bus station goes here three times daily.

Hurzuf
Гурзуф

Hurzuf's steep, winding streets and old wooden houses, backed by Mt Roman-Kosh (1545m), are a magnet for artists and writers. The village, 18km north-east of Yalta, is built around a picturesque bay with the rocky Genoese Cliff (Skala Dzhenevez) at its eastern end. Bear Mountain (Gora Medved or Ayudag, 565m) looms along the coast to the east, protruding into the sea.

Overhanging wooden balconies, a few cafes and the odd shop adorn vulitsya Leningradska, the curving, picturesque main street. The beach just west of the town centre is backed by **Hurzufsky Park**, home to some elegant wooden, 19th century sanatoria and lots of red squirrels. The dacha of the Duc de Richelieu, governor of Odesa (1803-14), today houses the **Pushkin in Crimea Museum**, a history museum open from 10 am to 5 pm (closed Monday and Tuesday).

Chekhov's dacha at vulitsya Chekhova 22, also a museum (closed Monday), sits close to the foot of Genoese Cliff. From the east side of the cliff, a vast children's holiday camp called Artek Pioneer Camp stretches most of the way to Bear Mountain. Next to the camp entrance on the eastern end of vulitsya Leningradska are the remains of a 6th to 15th century **clifftop fortress**, founded by the Byzantines and rebuilt by the Genoese. A path round to the left leads through a rock tunnel to the sea-cliff edge. Beyond is a handsome swathe of beach.

Bus No 31 (every 30 to 45 minutes) links Hurzuf with Yalta bus station.

Alushta
Алушта

Yalta's poor sibling, 40km north-east, is a sea of high-rise concrete towers and offers little of interest to see or do. From the bus station roundabout, where the Simferopol-Yalta road touches north-west Alushta, vulitsya Horkoho runs down to the harbour

CRIMEA

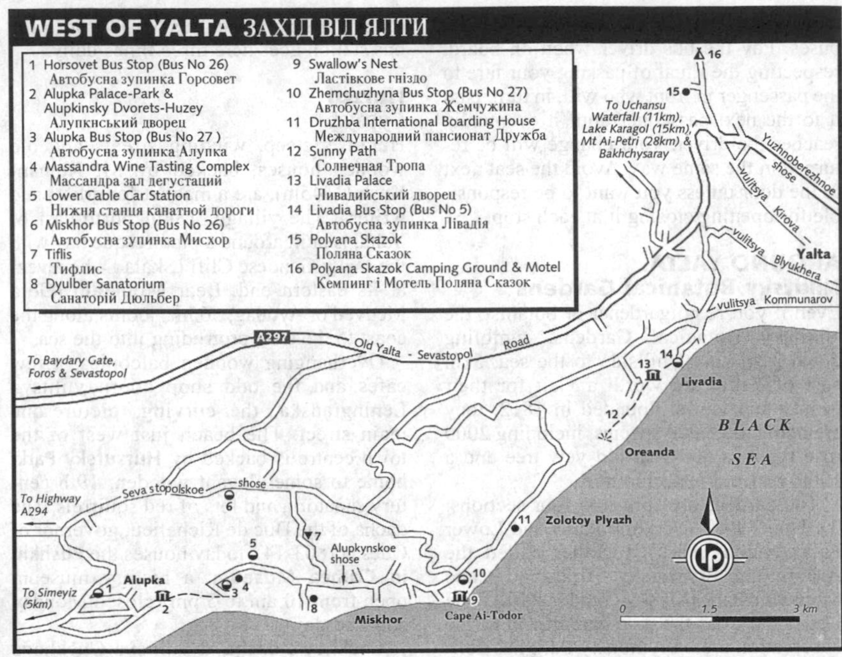

1km away. Bus Nos 2 and 4 follow this seabound route.

East of the harbour is the promenade, with a few small subdivided beaches and a larger nonpaying half-sand, half-rock beach at the far end. Westwards are some parks and paths leading towards the Rabochy Uholok (Workers' Corner) where most sanatoria are concentrated. Behind the resort, the road to Simferopol passes between Mt Chatyrdag (1527m) to the west, and Mt Demerdzhi (1239m) and Mt Severnaya Demerdzhi to the east. Mt Demerdzhi has some spectacular rock pillars.

Hotel Alushta *(☎ 5 50 62, ☎ 5 52 78, vulitsya Oktyabrska 50)*, the tall unsightly building next to Alushta bus station, is only open in summer. Grotty singles/doubles cost $14/29.

Trolleybus No 52 (Yalta-Simferopol train station) trundles from Yalta through Alushta (one hour, every 20 minutes), while No 51 runs between Alushta and Simferopol train station (1½ hours, every 20 minutes).

Uchansu Waterfall, Lake Karagol & Mt Ai-Petri

Heading north-west from Yalta, bus No 30 (four times daily) from Yalta bus station takes you within walking distance of two beauty spots in the mountains off the Bakhchysaray road. From the Vodopad (Waterfall) stop about 11km out, you can walk to a platform beside the 100m-high Uchansu Waterfall. From the Karagol stop, 3km farther up the road, a track leads to forest-ringed Lake Karagol. Both spots have a restaurant.

Continuing past the Karagol stop, the road winds spectacularly up to the top of the range 13km on; the summit of Mt Ai-Petri (St Peter, 1233m) sits to the left. A cable car from a peak north of Ai-Petri whisks passengers down to Mishkor, near Alupka, 16km west of Yalta.

Livadia
Лівадія

It was Livadia, 3km west of Yalta, that marked Yalta on the world map – first in 1860 when the imperial family built here, then in February 1945 when Stalin, Roosevelt and Churchill held their Yalta Conference in **Livadia Palace**. The royal, Italian Renaissance-style palace (1911) was built as a summer residence for Tsar Nicholas II. It used local white Crimean granite and touted pretty Florentine and Arabic courtyards. After the revolution, it became a peasants' sanatorium.

The 1945 conference was mainly a matter of the three WWII victors confirming earlier decisions on the carve-up of Europe. The UK and the USA couldn't stop Stalin keeping the eastern third of Poland, conquered by the Red Army, but Poland got part of Germany as compensation. Stalin agreed to allow free elections in Poland, which never happened, and to declare war on Japan, which he did only after the atom bomb had been dropped on Hiroshima. A reproduction of the round table at which they reached these agreements stands in the conference room, along with photos and other memorabilia. The rest of the palace is dedicated to an exhibition on Nicholas II and his family. Some captions are in English. The numerous B&W photographs of the royal family and their entourage traipsing stylishly around the area are fun to see.

The palace (☎ 31 55 79, ☎ 31 55 81) is open from 8 am to 7.30 pm (closed Wednesday and the last day of the month). From October to May, hours are 10 am to 4.30 pm. You can stroll through the lovely park and gardens at any time. A highlight is the **Sunny Path** (Solnechnaya Tropa), a footpath amid trees which leads 1.5km west to a lookout point over Oreanda. From here you can continue for several more kilometres westwards along the coast. To get to Swallow's Nest (a 1½ hour walk from Livadia), cut down the mountainside, following the signs for 'Turbaza Kitkynz & Sanatoria Parus'.

From Yalta, bus No 5 from the Spartak bus terminal goes to the Livadia stop, a five minute walk from the palace.

Swallow's Nest

Swallow's Nest (Ласточкіно Гніздо, Lastochkino Gnizdo) – the glory of a million postcards – is a fairy-tale castle perched at the top of a sheer cliff on Cape Ai-Todor, 10km west of Yalta. It was built in 1912 for Baron Steingel, a German oil magnate, and was heavily reconstructed in 1970. Today it houses a pompous Italian restaurant (☎ 24 75 71) which charges a ridiculous price for unauthentic Italian dishes ($7 for a carbonara). Admittedly, the sea view is magnificent. Artisans, crafts people and hawkers flog their wares in front.

In summer, Hotel Yalta runs boat excursions from Yalta to Swallow's Nest, but bus No 27 from Yalta bus station (Yalta-Alupka) to the Zhemchuzhyna stop is cheaper. From the bus stop walk 200m down the hill to the roadside Yacht Kafe, from where steps (entrance $1) lead to the jetty and castle.

Alupka
Алупка

Crimea's most exotic palace-park complex is at Alupka, 16km west of Yalta. Its coastal setting is stunning. Designed and built in 1828-46 by English architects for the English-educated Count Mikhail Vorontsov, the immensely rich regional governor, the palace is a bizarre combination of Scottish castle on its landward side, and Arabic fantasy facing the sea. Vorontsov brought serfs from his estates all over Russia to create the palace and park. Churchill stayed here during the 1945 Yalta Conference.

Six gorgeous Italian-marble lions flank the staircase outside the palace's seaward front. Entry into the landscaped park is free year-round, but the palace's luxuriant interior, now the **Alupkinsky Palace Museum** (☎ 7 22 81), is only open from 8 am to 9 pm (closed Monday and on days of high humidity). Hours between 1 October and 1 June are 10 am to 4 pm. Admission is $1.50/0.75 for adults/children. Highlights include an 1860 Becker piano, a beautiful sunroom and a main dining room with impressive woodwork and a balcony for musicians.

Alupka is also home to the **Massandra wine tasting complex** (☎ 72 11 98) where you can taste Crimean wines as part of a tour. Between May and November, tours kick off at 11.30 am, and 12.30, 3.30 and 4.30 pm (closed Sunday and Monday). The rest of the year it is open on Tuesday and Thursday (tours at 11.30 am and 3.30 pm), and Saturday (11.30 am).

Simeyiz (Сімеїз), 5km west, is a small resort with a few interesting Moorish-looking buildings poking up among the trees above its pebbly beach. Sheer cliffs provide a dramatic backdrop.

Getting There & Away Bus No 27 runs hourly from Yalta bus station to the Alupka stop, from where you can walk across the park to the palace. The wine tasting complex is 50m up the hill from the bus stop. The lower station for the cable car *(kanatnoye dorohy)* up the cliff just north to Mt Ai-Petri is about 1km east, between Alupka and Dyulber sanatorium (painted blue and white).

If you're going to Simeyiz, walk up to Alupka town above the western end of Alupka palace. Turn left along vulitsya Lyuxemburg for some 300m until it meets the main road and the Horsovet bus stop. Bus No 26 goes to Simeyiz (every 45 minutes), No 39 to Foros (three times a day); both serve Yalta.

Baydary Gate & Foros Church

Baydary Gate is a stone arch over the old Yalta-Sevastopol road (A297) where it crests the coastal escarpment at 527m, 51km west of Yalta. It was built in 1848 to mark the completion of this road, most of which is now superseded by the highway (A294) lower down. About 45km west of Yalta, turn right off the A294 at the crossroads where 'Foros' is signposted down the hill (left), and 'Baydarskie Vorota 6.5km' up the hill (right). The way up is beneath towering rock walls.

About 4km west of the crossroads is the picturesque Foros Church, with its nine golden domes of various sizes, dramatically overlooking the sea from the top of a precipitous crag. The story goes that a runaway horse bearing the daughter of 19th century tea tycoon Alexander Kuznetsov suddenly reared up and stopped on this spot, saving her from certain death. Kuznetsov built the church in thanks.

Far below the cliffs is **Foros**, an unattractive modern development. Some 2km west, nestled near the waterfront, is Gorbachev's dacha where he was put under house arrest during the 1991 coup attempt. An aerial view of its terracotta roof can be enjoyed from the highway – a scenic road that offers splendid mountain and sea views for much of its way to Sevastopol.

SEVASTOPOL СЕВАСТОПОЛЬ

☎ 0692 • pop 375,000

Sevastopol was the focus of the Crimean War, besieged and bombarded for 349 days by the British, French and Turks in 1854-55, devastating the city so badly that Mark Twain, when visiting the city a decade later, wrote 'In whatsoever direction you please, your eye encounters scarcely anything but ruin, ruin, ruin!'. In 1942 the same catastrophe repeated itself when the city fell to the Germans after a brutal 250 day siege.

Until 1996, Sevastopol was a closed city; the entire city and a large area around it were off limits to visitors. The official military checkpoint (still manned today) on the Yalta-Sevastopol highway, 13km south of the city limits and 22km from the centre, marks the boundary of the formerly closed zone.

In town, Russia's ageing and rusty Black Sea Fleet slumbers in the harbour. The ownership of the former Soviet fleet, split between Russia and Ukraine following the collapse of the USSR, remained a hot topic until early 1999 when Ukraine agreed to lease the port to Russia for 20 years in lieu of its increasing oil debt to the big bear. Consequently, Sevastopol's surprisingly bright and cheerful streets and squares buzz with the comings and goings of military personnel in uniforms: Russian soldiers sport black; Ukrainian soldiers, camouflage green.

Orientation & Information

Prospekt Nakhimova, the main street, crosses town east-west from ploshcha Lazareva, to ploshcha Nakhimova on the water's edge. From this large waterfront square, vulitsya Lenina runs the length of the harbour eastwards to ploshcha Ushakova, another busy hub. The train station is north of the harbour; from vulitsya Lenina bear left along vulitsya Vokzalnya.

The excursion office (☎ 52 51 10, ☎ 59 15 41) at the port, off ploshcha Nakhimova, is only useful if you speak Russian. There is an ATM in the lobby of Hotel Sevastopol.

Things to See

Waterfront ploshcha Nakhimova sits on the city's southernmost tip, at the mouth of the harbour where Russia's Black Sea Fleet nestles. Walk under the **classical arches** (1846) on the square to reach the water's edge. From here, small ferries make daily crossings to the northern side of the harbour.

Larger-than-life classical structures adorn prospekt Nakhimova. From the small park in front of the **Russian Drama Theatre** (☎ 52 43 28) at No 6 cut onto bulvar Prymorsky to view the **Eagle Column** (1904), an eagle-topped column on a rock in the sea which commemorates Russian ships sunk in the harbour mouth in 1854 to stop enemy ships entering. The city **Art Museum** is at No 9 and there's a **dolphinarium** at No 2.

Opposite Hotel Sevastopol at No 8, steps lead to **Lenin**. The golden dome of **Vladimirsky Cathedral** glistens behind the chiselled silhouette of the communist leader. From the statue, bear left through the park along vulitsya Voronyna to the elegant **Russian headquarters of the Black Sea Fleet**, control centre for the 460 vessels in the fleet that Russia owns; since 1991, Ukraine has owned 162 ships. The history of the controversial fleet from its foundation in 1783 to 1945 is colourfully illustrated in the **Black Sea Fleet Museum**, vulitsya Lenina 11, next to the Russian Officers' House. It is open from 10 am to 5 pm (closed Monday and Tuesday). Admission is $1.

The defence of Sevastopol during the Crimean War is the focus of the **painted panorama**, inside a circular edifice built at the centre of the gun emplacements and redoubts at a defensive bastion used during the war. Street hawkers sell a handy English-language brochure and Black Sea Fleet uniforms outside, and from the grounds there's a great view of Russian submarines lurking in the port. The panorama, on a hillock above the train station at bulvar Istorichesky, is open from 9.30 am to 5 pm (closed Monday). Admission is $1.

On a peninsula 3km south-west of Sevastopol are the excavated ruins of the **ancient Greek city of Chersonesus** (Kherson to Ukrainians, Khersones to Russians), founded in 422 BC and ruined by Tatars in the late 14th century. In between, Chersonesus went through wars, trade-based prosperity, absorption into the Roman then Byzantine empires, nomad attacks, and capture in 988 AD by Volodymyr of Kyiv. In return for marriage to the Byzantine emperor's sister, Volodymyr returned the city to Byzantine control and agreed to be baptised as a Christian on the spot, thus launching what eventually became the Russian Orthodox Church. Much of the site has been excavated, the highlight being a row of marble columns from an early Christian church a few metres from the shore.

Places to Stay

***Hotel Sevastopol** (☎ 52 36 82, fax 52 36 71, prospekt Nakhimova 8)*, dating from 1952, has an attractive, columned facade which shelters dimly lit singles/doubles for $19/38. Similar prices are charged at ***Hotel Ukraina** (☎ 52 21 27, vulitsya Gogolya 2)*, a typical Soviet concrete block opposite Big Ben Nightclub, overlooking ploshcha Ushakova, in the city's commercial heart.

Getting There & Away

There are six trains daily to Sevastopol from Simferopol (two hours).

SUDAK
СУДАК

☎ 06566 • pop 15,000

Sudak, at the base of a shallow bay, is some 125km north-east of Yalta along a twisted and narrow coastal road which affords a glimpse of Crimea at its most wild and untouched. About 55km east of Alushta, near the black-shingle beach resort of **Rybach**, the lush palm trees and cypresses of warm western Crimea are replaced by stark steppe as the climate cools.

As one of the main Genoese trading centres on the Great Silk Road, Sudak was graced with a giant **Genoese Fortress** (Sudakska Krepost) in the 14th and 15th centuries. It was built by a predominantly Tatar workforce on a massive cliff perched out over the sea. Ten of its 18 original defensive towers still stand so its silhouette of towers and crenulated walls remains spectacular. To the west rises Mt Perchem (576m), its face dramatically dropping into a sheer cliff; and to the far east is Mt Urmani-Ustu (352m), its two peninsular points protruding into the sea. Below and stretching east is a strip of sandy beach.

Most of the towers still bear their original Italian names. The main fortress entrance is via a forecourt which leads through the Holovna (Main) Gate between the **Tower of Torcello** (right) and the **Tower of Di Franco Di Pagano** (left). Inside, the walls encircle over 30 hectares of desolate sloping terrain with a few overgrown ruins and foundations lying about. The largest tower on the dramatically sloping south side along the coastline is the 14th century, twin towered **Consul's Tower**. The next tower up, the 14th to 15th century **Tower of St George** leads out to a viewpoint and a stepped path on the seaward side of the long crenulated wall that eventually leads to the apex, the remains of the 14th century **Dozornaya Tower**.

The fortress is open from 9 am to 8 pm (until 5 pm from October to May). There is a sporadic bus between the bus station, north of town, and the fortress.

Places to Stay & Eat

The large ***Hotel Horyzont*** *(☎ 2 22 83, fax 2 11 83, vulitsya Turistikoyu 8)*, near the foot of the fortress, has decent rooms, and some have fortress views. A bed in a single or double starts at $17, and prices include full board (obligatory).

Getting There & Away

From Sudak there are buses to/from Simferopol (2½ hours, seven daily), Yalta (four hours, once daily) and Feodosia (two hours, twice daily).

KARA-DAH NATURE RESERVE КАРА-ДАГ ЗАПОВІДНИК

☎ 06562

The road between Sudak and Feodosia is dry, rugged and mountainous with weathered old vineyards on sloping patches of terrain. About halfway along the coast just east of the village of **Shchebetovka** is the Kara-Dah Nature Reserve, with a number of dramatic rock formations boasting names such as 'The Devil's Finger' and 'The King and the Earth', all situated around Mt Svyataya (575m). From the northern end of Shchebetovka, hike to the seaside hamlet of **Kurortnoe** about 3.5km away. From here trek north-east about 6km through the Kara-Dah reserve, eventually reaching the village of **Koktebel** (formerly Planerske). From here you can catch a bus to Feodosia, 35 minutes away (twice daily).

Bring water, food and a good map, as supplies are rare. Accommodation options in Koktebel include the dirt-cheap ***Hotel Karahol*** *(☎ 3 63 35, vulitsya Lenina 102)*, on the main road through town; or the upmarket ***Turbaza Prymore*** *(☎ 3 63 22, ☎ 3 62 75)* at the east end of the village. Walk around the back of the shabby building on vulitsya Lenina to its modern, sparkling building overlooking a long, pebble beach. Full board costs $11/14/18 in May and September/June/July and August.

FEODOSIA ФЕОДОСІЯ

☎ 06562 • pop 87,000

Tucked in a coastal corner of Crimea about 60km east of Sudak, the city of Feodosia is a conglomeration of clanking industry, crooked cottages, elegant old mansions, several museums, some 13th century Genoese stone walls, and a handful of Armenian churches. Between 1475-1616, it was the largest slave-trading centre on the Black Sea coast and was known as 'the vampire that drinks the blood of Rus' by the Slavs. Today, its serene streets and sandy beaches overlooking crescent-shaped Feodosia Bay are pleasant to stroll along if you happen to be in the area.

On the main road to Simferopol, 23km west of Feodosia is the farming town of **Stary Krym** (**Старий Крим**), 3km south of which is the 14th century Armenian **Surp-Khach Monastery** (**Сурп-Хач Монастирь**). The complex, surrounded by dense woods, includes original monks' cells, a refectory and a beautiful church with a series of vaulted chambers.

Things to See

The city centre is north-west of the waterfront train station on prospekt Lenina. Elegant mansions line the section of prospekt Lenina on the seafront behind **Kameshky Beach**; exit the train station and turn right (north) to get here. The influence of numerous diverse cultures on Crimean history is explored in the **Regional Museum** (closed Tuesday), at the south end of vulitsya Halereyna.

The old town is south-east along the curve of the bay, behind the now-defunct **port**. The 14th century Armenian **Serhiya Church**, south of the train station along prospekt Lenina and vulitsya Horkoho, has exquisitely carved marble tablets embedded in its facade. Adjoining it is the **Tomb of Ayvazovsky** (1817-1900), a 19th century Armenian seascape artist who was born, lived and worked in Feodosia. Two blocks east is the **Mufty-Dzhamy Mosque** (1623), vulitsya Lenina, with an elegant 12 sided white minaret.

Continue east on vulitsya Lenina then turn right (south) on vulitsya Krupskoy to get to the ruined **Tower of St Giovanni di Scaffa** (1342) and **Tower of St Fomi** (1373), part of the city's Genoese fortification system. Bearing left (north) from vulitsya Lenina along vulitsya Karantynna (Karantynnaya) takes you to Feodosia's **citadel**, built by the Genoese on a bluff overlooking the bay after they took control of the city from the Golden Horde in the 13th century. Its rubbled ruins are today littered with ramshackle cottages and vegetable patches, goats grazing and chickens scratching for fodder; while one of the few remaining sections of wall still standing has been graffitied with the Russian slogan 'Stop or we'll shoot!'. Down the hillside towards the sea, there's a crumbling ensemble of 14th century **Armenian churches**.

Places to Stay & Eat

Feodosia's rock-bottom option is the ***Komnati Otdikha*** (rest rooms) at the train station, adjoining the left-luggage office on the platform. A bed in a double/triple/quad costs $1. Opposite the train station, ***Hotel Astoria*** *(☎ 3 23 27, ☎ 3 23 16, prospekt Lenina 9)* charges $2/4 for a bed in a double with shared/private bathroom.

Hotel Moryak *(☎ 3 24 14, vulitsya Lenina 8)* belongs to the port. A bed in a room with shared bathroom (ask for the shower key at reception) is $6 and singles/doubles with bath are $13/24. Note the Soviet postcard dispenser inside the entrance.

Kafe Assol, on the corner of vulitsya Lybknekhta and vulitsya Halereyna, serves giant-sized portions of excellent *holubsti* (stuffed cabbage leaves), *zharkovya* (beef stew) and other traditional Ukrainian dishes – for less than $1.

Kafe-Bar Istanbul *(prospekt Lenina 12)* is inside the exquisite Dacha Stamboly, an Ottoman-style palace (1911) built by a rich Turkish magnate who reputedly had his own private harem. During WWII, the mansion was used as a Nazi headquarters and people were executed in the back garden. Its interior has been beautifully restored and is a joy to dine in.

Getting There & Away

Feodosia's train service is limited to Vladislavovka (30 minutes, four daily) from where you can catch a train to Kerch (two hours); and to Moscow (22 to 26 hours, every other day) via Zaporizhzhya and Kharkiv.

The bus station is 2km north of the centre. Buses go to/from Simferopol (2½ hours, eight a day), Sudak (two hours, two a day) and Kerch (two hours, one a day).

Bus No 2 links the station with town.

KERCH
КЕРЧ

☎ 06561 • pop 182,000

At the eastern tip of the Crimean peninsula, Kerch is both an industrial port and military base. Its sights include the ruins of ancient Panticapaeum, a history and archaeology museum, and some old tombs which have yielded fine ancient Greek art. There are six daily trains to/from Simferopol (seven hours). In the summer months, you might be able to catch a ferry to Russia, north to Temryuk (83km) or south to Anapa (96km).

Eastern Ukraine
Східна Україна

Eastern Ukraine is mostly sprawling steppe, punctuated by swathes of forest and cultivated fields, highlighted by stretches of undulating grassland. Over 80% of Ukraine's Russian population (of 22%) lives in the east's major cities, all of which are heavy industrial centres.

Although Ukrainians constitute the majority of the population, the Russian language predominates. Many street signs are written in Russian (listed in parentheses in this chapter) as well as Ukrainian, while some city councils have declared Russian to be their official city language. In April 1999, Russian was declared the official business language of Lysychansk, near the Russian border, after 81.5% of its 120,000-strong population acknowledged Russian as their mother tongue.

Cities in eastern Ukraine are noticeably more developed than those in the west of the country. They attract mainly business travellers, hence most hotels are painfully expensive.

HIGHLIGHTS

- Discovering Socialist Realism: riding a trolleybus down the length of Zaporizhzhya's 10km-long prospekt Lenina
- Strolling through Kharkiv's streets and parks, not missing Blahoveshchensky Cathedral or the central market
- Seeing where Peter the Great defeated Sweden's Charles XII at the Poltava battlefield
- Exploring Cossack culture on Khortytsya Island, 16th century sich of the Zaporizky Cossacks

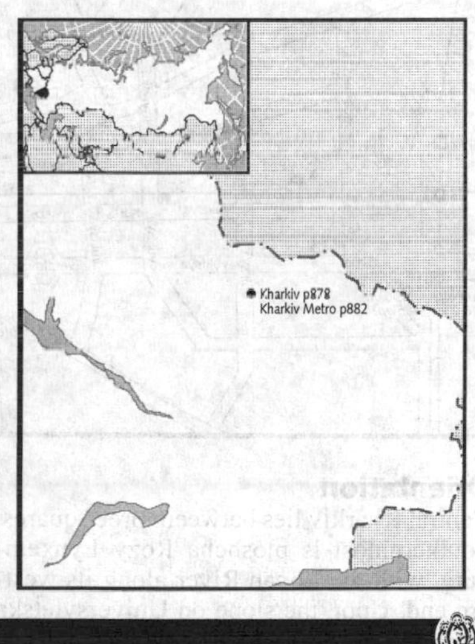

KHARKIV
ХАРКІВ

☎ 0572 • pop 1.6 million

Ukraine's second major city is an unpretentious working place, but with a curious history and an active cultural life. It is a surprisingly likeable combination of old and new, narrow and spacious, grey and green, with numerous parks to stroll and a distinctive student feel to its lively streets.

Founded in 1654 as a Cossack outpost, Kharkiv – 40km from the Russian border – was one of the first Ukrainian cities to be absorbed into the Russian sphere of influence, supporting Moscow's tsars consistently through Cossack uprisings and campaigns against the Crimean Tatars. It grew into an important fort on the Tatar frontier, and became the administrative and cultural centre of Russian Ukraine in the 1760s. Kharkiv (Kharkov in Russian) was the capital of Soviet Ukraine from 1917 to 1934, and was the site of the first wave of repression against Ukrainian nationalists and intelligentsia. The city was heavily damaged in WWII, and has since become a centre for the manufacturing of machines such as tractors, turbines and engines.

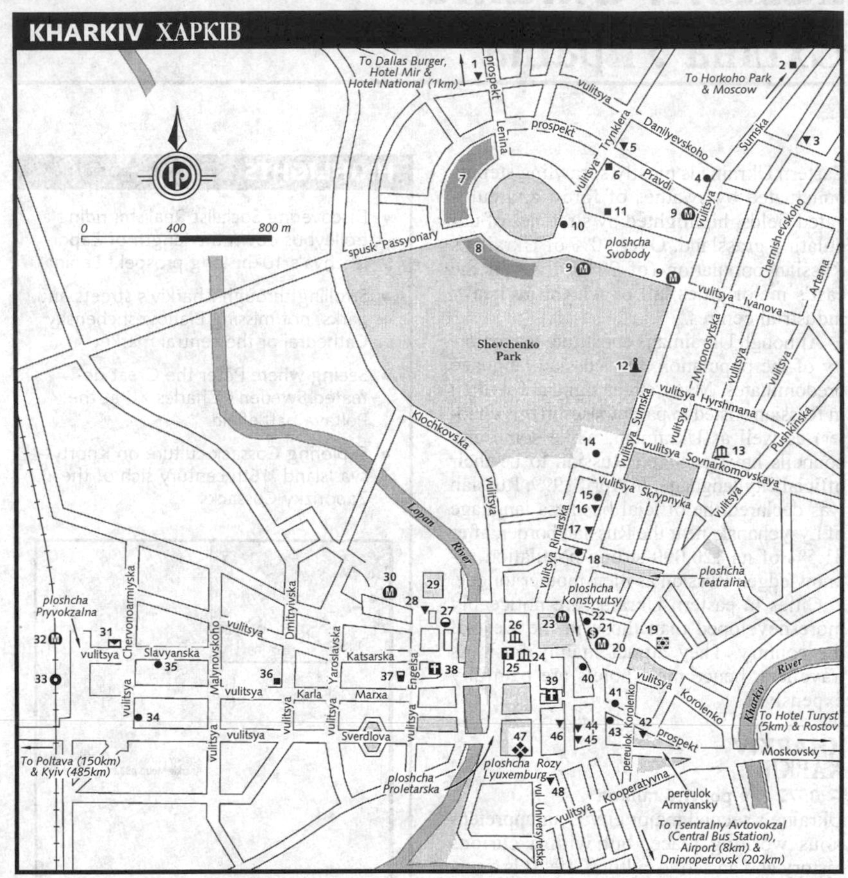

Orientation

Central Kharkiv lies between three squares. Southernmost is ploshcha Rozy Lyuxemburg, with the Lopan River along its western end. Upon the slope on Universytetska Hora (University Hill) is ploshcha Konstytutsy (formerly ploshcha Radyansky Ukrainy). From here, vulitsya Sumska (Sumskaya) heads north in the direction of Moscow, past vast ploshcha Svobody.

Maps The useful *Kharkiv-Carta Schema* (1:30,000) can be picked up for $1 from a babushka at the train station, or from Knizhkovy Svit, a bookshop on the corner of ploshcha Konstytutsy and prospekt Moskovsky. Both sell oblast and country maps too, as well as printed train timetables ($0.20).

Information

Kharkiv has no tourist information office, but French speakers should visit the Centre Français, ploshcha Konstytutsy 26, 4th floor, room 44/45.

There are numerous exchange kiosks on ploshcha Konstytutsy; the one at No 11 is open 24 hours, and the bank at No 22

KHARKIV ХАРКІВ

PLACES TO STAY
2 Hotel Kyivskaya
Готель Київськая
6 Hotel Kharkiv
(Rich Man's Entrance)
Готель Харків
11 Hotel Kharkiv
(Poor Man's Entrance)
Готель Харків
36 Hotel Pivdenny
Готель Південний

PLACES TO EAT
1 Baskin Robbins
Баскин Роббінс
3 Restoran Dom
Chaya
Ресторан Дом Чая
5 Versailles Kafe
Версай Кафе
16 Kafe Varenyky
Кафе Вареники
17 Zanzi Bar
Занзі Бар
28 McDonald's
МакДональдз
42 Pekin
Пекин
44 Kafe Arlekino
Кафе Арлекино
45 Il Monte
Іл Монте
46 Stare Misto
Старе Місто
48 McDonald's
МакДональдз

METRO STATIONS
9 Universytet
Університет
20 Radyanska
Радянська
23 Istorychny Muzey
Історичний музей
30 Tsentralny Rynok
Центральний ринок
32 Pivdenny (Yuzhny) Vokzal
Південний вокзал

OTHER
4 Crimean Wines
Вина Крима
7 Hosprom Building
Дім Госпрому
8 University
Університет
10 Lenin
Ленін
12 Shevchenko Monument
Пам'ятник Шевченку
13 Art Museum
Художній музей
14 Opera & Ballet Theatre
Театр опери та балет
15 Teatralna Kasa
Театральна каса
18 Shevchenko Ukrainian Drama Theatre
Український театр драми імені Шевченка
19 Synagogue
Синагога
21 Bank
Банк
22 Centre Français
Французький центр
24 History Museum
(Old Section)
Історичний музей
25 Pokrovska Church
Покровська церква
26 History Museum
(Modern Section)
Історичний музей
27 Bus Station No 2
Автобусна станція 2
29 Central Market
Центральний ринок
31 Post & Telephone Office
Пошта та телефон
33 Pivdenny (Southern)
Train Station
Південний вокзал
34 Supermarket
35 Train Ticket Office
Центральні Залізничні Каса
37 Klub DNK & Kafe Stil
Клуб ДНК та Кафе Стіл
38 Blahoveshchensky Cathedral
Благовещенський собор
39 Uspensky Cathedral
Успенський собор
40 Vedmedik (Sweet Shop)
Ведмедик
41 Ukrainsky Suvenir
Український сувенір
43 Knizhkovy Svit (Bookshop)
Книжковий Світ
47 TsUM (Department Store)
ЦУМ

changes travellers cheques and gives cash advances on Visa/MasterCard. Western Union/X-Change Points has an office inside Hotel Mir. There is an ATM inside Hotel Kyivskaya.

The post office on the corner of vulitsya Slavyanska and vulitsya Chervonoarmiyska (Krasnoarmeiskaya) has an exchange office which offers good rates.

The British Council (☎/fax 47 16 50, bc@bc.univer.kharkov.ua) is inside Kharkiv State University, maydan Svobody 4, 8th floor, room 23.

Ploshcha Svobody

Traffic-free ploshcha Svobody is almost 750m long and covered in cobblestones. It's probably the only large square in the world designed as a unit in the constructivist style, although it was never entirely completed. Planned as an ensemble of Ukraine government buildings when Kharkiv was the republican capital, it was built between 1925 and 1935. The complex was damaged during WWII, and largely rebuilt using German POW labour. The late 1920s **House of State Industry** (Hosprom) at its western end was the first Soviet skyscraper – a geometric series of concrete and glass blocks and bridges. Its symmetry is now ruined by the TV pylon on one tower. On the southern side of the square is the **university**, formerly the House of Planning that displays classic Soviet aesthetics. The university and **Hotel**

Kharkiv on the opposite side of ploshcha Svobody date from the early 1930s. Lenin still proudly stands in the midst of it all, his hand outstretched across the vast open space. The pleasant **Shevchenko Park** and zoological gardens line the southern side of the square.

Vulitsya Universytetska & Around

Vulitsya Universytetska runs south from the western side of ploshcha Konstytutsy (formerly Radyansky Ukrainy), Kharkiv's original marketplace. In the centre of the square is a large granite sculptural ensemble commemorating Kharkiv's designation as the first capital of Soviet Ukraine on 24 December 1917. Across the square at vulitsya Universytetska 8 are the 1820s **Bishop's Palace** and the fine 1689 **Pokrovska Church** (Intercession of the Virgin).

The church is the oldest building in the city and its brick detailing is still superb. The Bishop's Palace houses the 19th and 20th century section of the **Kharkiv History Museum**, open from 9 am to 5 pm (closed Tuesday). The upstairs section is devoted to 20th century warfare, while downstairs features historic sacred and folk art. The pre-industrial section of the museum, vulitsya Universytetska 10, is open from 10 am to 7 pm (closed Monday).

Farther down the street, the golden-domed 1770s **Uspensky (Assumption) Cathedral** has been transformed into a concert hall since the 1950s. Its eclectic, 19th century bell tower (89.5m tall) is a landmark, with neoclassical pediments and detailing capped by a Byzantine dome. Tickets for organ concerts are sold at the kiosk (☎ 47 18 33, ☎ 23 21 79) at vulitsya Universytetska 11. On the opposite side of the street, the WWII **eternal flame** burns.

The striking red-and-cream striped brickwork on **Blahoveshchensky Cathedral** (1881-1901), across the Lopan River on ploshcha Karla Marxa, was based on Istanbul's Hagia Sophia. The bell tower is beautifully proportioned Eastern baroque sugar-candy cane.

Vulitsya Sumska

Kharkiv's main drag is lively and hectic, lined with an elegant mix of theatres, cafes, stores and restaurants. The pretty **Shevchenko Ukrainian Drama Theatre** at No 9 is across the street from ploshcha Teatralna, and is flanked by the busts of two writers, Gogol (an ethnic Ukrainian) and Pushkin.

Farther north up vulitsya Sumska at No 25 is the large granite **Opera & Ballet Theatre**. The building was designed in the brutalist style, but the interior is softer and more aesthetically pleasing than its harsh exterior suggests.

Vulitsya Radnarkomivska (Sovnarkomovskaya) runs along the northern edge of a park; an **Art Museum** is at No 11. Just before the museum, on the corner of vulitsya Myronosytska, is the former KGB building. A bust of Felyx Yandmundovych, a high-ranking member, sits outside. The Art Museum (open daily from 10 am to 5.30 pm) has a couple of paintings by Repin, including a version of his famous *Zaporizky Cossacks Writing a Letter to the Turkish Sultan* which took the artist 11 years to paint.

Still farther north on vulitsya Sumska on the eastern edge of Shevchenko Park, halfway between the opera theatre and ploshcha Svobody, is a tall statue of Shevchenko. Dramatic enough to rival nearby Lenin, the hero-poet is encircled by an ensemble of Cossacks and peasants. About 2km north of ploshcha Svobody, vulitsya Sumska runs along **Horkoho Park**, where you'll find plenty of tree-lined paths, a funfair, cinema, a summertime chairlift and children's locomotive, as well as hills for wintertime sledding.

Places to Stay

For budget accommodation, try ***Hotel Ekspres*** *(☎ 20 24 14, ☎ 12 52 76)* above the train station. An ominous sign above reception reads 'express hotel for transit passengers'. Rooms of various categories are on offer but the cheapest bed is $6. About 300m east of the train station is the downtrodden ***Hotel Pivdenny*** *(vulitsya Karla Marxa 30)* where the reception staff make no bones about the fact that they (direct quote) '... have a bad hotel'. The truly desperate seeking nothing more than a bed pay $4 a night.

Out of town, ***Hotel Turyst*** *(☎ 92 10 46, ☎/fax 92 30 10, prospekt Moskovsky 144)*, 5km south-east of the centre on the Rostov road (metro: Marshala Zhukova) is a Soviet-looking concrete block. When you enter, the doorman is quite likely to screech (direct quote) 'What do you want?'. Rooms cost $15/24 a single/double; breakfast is $1.

The only central hotel is ***Hotel Kharkiv***, a 1930s edifice with a 'rich man's entrance' on the corner of vulitsya Trynklera and prospekt Pravdi, and a 'poor man's entrance' on ploshcha Svobody (metro: Universytet). The first entrance leads to the more expensive, renovated part of the hotel (☎ 45 68 89) where doubles start at $30; the latter leads to the unrenovated section (☎ 45 60 68) where a single/double with shared bathroom in the corridor costs $4/8 and rooms with private bathroom cost $11/15. Non-Russian speakers might have a hard time checking into the cheaper section.

North of ploshcha Svobody, friendly ***Hotel Mir*** *(☎ 30 55 43, fax 32 44 07, prospekt Lenina 27A)* has the misfortune to overlook the spot where building work started (then stopped) on a metro station. Rooms cost $31/42, including breakfast. The former Intourist ***Hotel National*** *(☎ 32 05 08, fax 32 05 12, prospekt Lenina 21)* has snotty staff and singles/doubles for $47/78. Breakfast is $9. To get to either hotel take trolleybus No 18 or 39 along prospekt Lenina or bus No 45, 285 or 287.

A cut above the rest is ***Hotel Kyivskaya*** *(☎ 14 31 01/04/07, fax 14 31 00, vulitsya Kultury 4)*, by the side of Kharkiv's baroque Wedding Palace. Singles/doubles with private bathroom are $63/87.

Places to Eat

Vulitsya Sumska is a gold mine of eating establishments. The hippest place to wine, dine and be seen is ***Zanzi Bar*** *(☎ 12 66 21, vulitsya Sumska 11)* where animal footprints adorn bright orange walls. Highlights on its tempting menu include seafood lasagne ($5) and frothy cappuccinos. Those on a tighter budget should head to the cafeteria-style ***Kafe Varenyky*** *(vulitsya Sumska 21)* where $1 buys a steaming plate of filling varenyky.

Another satisfying spot is ***Il Monte*** *(☎ 12 75 59, ploshcha Rozy Lyuxemburg)*, an Italian-inspired restaurant on two floors; ring the bell to attract the waiter's attention if you are dining up top. Pizza/pasta starts at $2/7. A brave attempt at Chinese cuisine is made at ***Pekin*** *(☎ 12 76 02, vulitsya Moskovsky 10/12)*.

Among the more pleasant, old-school establishments is the charmingly aged ***Restoran Dom Chaya*** (House of Tea), on the north-eastern corner of vulitsya Karazina and vulitsya Myronosytska (open from noon to midnight). Shashlyk? Excellent. Service? Snail-slow. Traditional Ukrainian dishes are served in a modern environment at ***Kafe Arlekino*** *(vulitsya Kvitki-Osnovyanenko 7)*. Just opposite, the cellar restaurant ***Stare Misto*** is decorated like a medieval hall. Once upon a time it used to be popular ...

Versailles Kafe, set in a small park off ploshcha Pravdi, is not quite France but is popular nonetheless. Its breaded cheese-balls, or dolma with oodles of smatana – each for $1 – are delicious.

The American ice-cream chain ***Baskin Robbins*** *(prospekt Lenina 3)* is open from 10 am to 10 pm. ***Dallas Burger*** at No 25 is equally squeaky clean.

The ***Klub DNK & Kafe Stil*** *(☎ 12 00 33, vulitsya Engelsa 17)* is a bohemian spot overlooking Blahoveshchensky Cathedral; techno DJs take to the turntable here most weekends.

Self-Catering The vast ***central market*** *(vulitsya Engelsa 33)*, west of the Lopan River (metro: Tsentralny Rynok), is a small city in itself. In and around the covered hall are piles of fresh vegetables, pumpkins, honey, nuts, meat and fish. Behind is a sea of vendors selling everything from cheap booze and expensive fur hats to used car parts.

The modern ***supermarket*** opposite the train station is open 24 hours a day. You can stock up on wine at ***Vyna Kryma***, a Crimean wine shop at vulitsya Sumska 51.

***Vedmedik** (ploshcha Konstytutsy 11)* is an old-fashioned sweet shop.

Getting There & Away

Air Kharkiv airport is served by domestic and international flights (see Ukraine Getting There & Away). Aerosweet Airlines (☎ 19 53 70, fax 19 53 71) has its office inside Hotel Kharkiv (entrance on ploshcha Svobody). Ukraine International and Air Ukraine are inside Hotel National. Austrian Airlines (☎ 14 89 51/52) only has an office at the airport.

Train Life-size statues of Lenin and Marx greet passengers in the main hall, lit with glass chandeliers, as they enter the grandiose train station building, dominating ploshcha Pryvokzalna (metro: Pivdenny Vokzal) 2km west of ploshcha Rozy Lyuxemburg. Printed, pocket-size train timetables for local and national trains are sold by babushkas who set up stalls here.

Several lines meet at Kharkiv, with numerous trains travelling to/from Moscow daily (12 to 13 hours). Other services, at least daily, include: Kyiv (10 hours), Odesa (20 hours), Rostov-on-Don (12 hours), Simferopol (10 hours), Tbilisi (31 hours), Zaporizhzhya (4½ hours) and Minsk (17 hours, via Sumy). There are trains to/from Lviv (24 hours) every other day.

Train tickets can be bought in advance at the nearby ticket office, vulitsya Slavyanska 6 (open from 8 am to 7 pm).

Bus Tsentralny Avtovokzal (☎ 21 65 02), the central bus station, is at prospekt Gagarina 22 (metro: Prospekt Gagarina).

Getting Around

To/From the Airport The airport is 8km south of the centre, off prospekt Gagarina. Trolleybus No 5 from the Prospekt Gagarina metro stop terminates at the airport. Bus No 119T runs from prospekt Lenina, and along vulitsya Sumska and prospekt Gagarina, to the airport.

Public Transport Kharkiv has an efficient three line metro. Buy a plastic token *(zheton)* for $0.10 before descending to the tracks. The Pivdenny Vokzal metro stop is in front of the train station. When, and if, the cash-strapped municipality ever finds the funds to complete the north-south line, there will be a metro stop in front of Hotel Mir on prospekt Lenina.

POLTAVA ПОЛТАВА

☎ 05322 • pop 325,000

The 480km stretch from Kharkiv to Kyiv is classic Ukraine steppe, partially wooded, and sweeping expanses of flat terrain broken only by Poltava, which is set on three hills on the Vorskla River. Here, in 1709, Peter the Great decisively defeated the combined forces of Sweden's Charles XII and the Ukrainian Cossack leader Ivan Mazepa, ending both Sweden's expansionist ambitions and Ukraine's hopes for an independent Cossack state, and paving the way for Russian domination in Ukraine and beyond.

Orientation & Information

The town centre, 3km north-west of the train station, straddles the 1.5km stretch of vulitsya Zhovtneva, from Kruhla ploshcha in the north-west to maydan Soborna Park in the south-east. The battle site is about 7km north of the centre.

Access your email account at the central post office (pochta@pi.net.ua), Kruhla ploshcha 33, open from 8 am to 7 pm (9 am to 5 pm on Sunday).

Things to See

The focal point is the circular plaza **Kruhla ploshcha** (round square), laid out in the early 19th century in an attempt to emulate the grand planning ideals of St Petersburg. In its centre is the **Iron Column of Glory**, surrounded by miniature cannons and topped by a golden eagle, erected on the 100th anniversary of Peter the Great's battle.

South-east of Kruhla ploshcha, vulitsya Zhovtneva becomes a pedestrian precinct for a few blocks. Farther down is the leafy Zhovtnevy Park, with the **Poltava Regional Museum** along its south-eastern edge, in front of a 1926 cubist Taras Shevchenko monument. The Art Nouveau building (1903-08) is ornamented with the ceramic crests of each district capital in the Poltava oblast. Inside are historic and ethnographic exhibits (closed Wednesday).

Overlooking the north-eastern corner of the park is the **memorial cross to the Cossacks**. Bear east down vulitsya Parizkoi Komuny for one block to **Spaska Church** (1705), a small, squat building set on the corner of vulitsya Spaska. A block north (left) at vulitsya Spaska 11, past the monument to Tsar Peter I, is the **Poltava Art Museum** (1919).

From the lookout point beside the museum, there is a good view of **Khrestovozdvyzhensky Monastery** (Elevation of the Cross), 3km north-east of the centre. The complex was built in the early 18th century in the Ukrainian baroque style and the main cathedral is the only one still standing in the country with seven cupolas, rather than the usual five. To walk to the monastery (30 minutes), head east on vulitsya Radyanska from Kruhla ploshcha.

Battlefield You may want to hire a taxi ($2) to take you out to the battle site, 7km north. It can also be reached on the very rare No 5 bus from the *rynok* (market) on vulitsya Shevchenko, two blocks south-west of Kruhla ploshcha. The battle was fought over a large area around what's now vulitsya Zinkivska. The best starting point is the **Poltava Battle Museum**, Shvedska mohyla 32, by the Peter the Great statue; open from 9.30 am to 5 pm (closed Monday). Inside are displays concerning the battle including maps, paintings and military diagrams. Obviously glorifying Peter the Great's tremendous victory, the displays are short on Sweden's viewpoint and there's nothing (beyond one paltry portrait) to document the Cossack forces under Hetman Ivan Mazepa.

In front of the museum on a hill is a memorial cross to the Russian troops killed, behind which lies a pretty brick Orthodox church (1895). Farther down the road is a memorial cross to the 9000 Swedes who died in the battle.

Places to Stay & Eat

The standard ***Hotel Turyst*** *(☎ 2 09 21, vulitsya Miru 2)* is about 500m west of the train station, across the bridge and to the left.

Back in the USSR

Independence declarations aside, there are 11 good reasons why travelling in Ukraine makes you almost believe you're back in the Soviet Union.

- Hotels, museums and national airlines impose two or three tier pricing.
- Manned militia checkpoints lurk at the entrances to every oblast/city.
- You are obliged to register your presence with VVIR within 72 hours of arrival.
- At train station information booths, you have to pay for each oral/written response (not necessarily the answer) you get to each question.
- Hotel floors tout a formidable *dezhurna* (don't upset her).
- Tea on overnight trains is served in glass cups; glasses with digits stamped underneath are USSR relics (post-Soviet production has no uniform price stamp).
- When buying bus or train tickets, you are shunted from kasa to kasa, only for the kasa to close for a technical break when you finally succeed in finding the kasa which sells tickets to your destination or reach the front of the queue.
- You walk into a hotel and the doorman hollers, 'What do you want?'.
- Lenin stands on city squares and street corners.
- Despite being born and bred in Ukraine and holding a Ukrainian passport, numerous Russian speakers believe their country to have died with the USSR; for them, their nationality is Soviet.
- Thousands of people have not been paid for months, yet they still work for fear of losing their jobs.

Singles/doubles cost $16/25. In town, tatty ***Hotel Teatralny*** *(☎ 2 43 21, vulitsya Zhovtneva 19)* has bare-bone rooms costing $8/22 for a single without/with private shower; doubles are twice the price.

Potsylunok Fortuny, on the corner of vulitsya Lenina and vulitsya Frunze, is a clean and modern fast-food place serving ice cream, burgers and battered fried chicken (open from 11 to 2 am). The ***Kafe Kholodok*** *(vulitsya Zhovtneva 27)* has excellent sweet and savoury *bliny* (pancakes) for less than $1 (open from 10 am to 11 pm). Its toilet is the cleanest in town.

Getting There & Away

There are two train stations in Poltava; the main one is Poltava-Pivdenna (south). From here, there are 10 trains to/from Kyiv (seven hours) and 11 a day to Kharkiv (three to four hours). Two a day run to/from Odesa (13 hours); and one a day to Uzhhorod (15 hours) and Lviv (21 hours). There is a train every other day to/from Simferopol (17 hours) and Moscow (20 hours).

To get to the centre from the train station, take trolleybus Nos 1, 2, 4, 6 and 11.

DNIPROPETROVSK
ДНІПРОПЕТРОВСЬК

☎ 0562 • pop 1.2 million

Dnipropetrovsk, 202km south of Kharkiv on the west bank of the Dnipro River, is Ukraine's industrial giant.

A closed city which produced missiles under the USSR, it is the country's leading metallurgy centre. Its other known product is Leonid Kuchma, director of the missile factory in his hometown (Europe's largest) before becoming president. Former Soviet first secretary, Leonid Brezhnev, also kicked off his political career here.

Dnipropetrovsk was settled in 1787 on the site of a former Zaporizhzhyan village, although absolutely nothing remains of its Cossack heritage today. It was called Sicheslav until 1918 and Katerynoslav until 1926. Today, it is known as DP by the city's substantial expatriate population. Dnipropetrovsk is abbreviated to DN-SK (ДН-СК) on most train timetables.

Things to See

Tree-lined prospekt Karla Marxa – the city's central, two lane boulevard – runs for several kilometres from the train station at its western end to ploshcha Karla Marxa at its eastern end. Parallel is naberezhna Lenina which snakes along the banks of the Dnipro River.

The **History Museum** (☎ 46 34 22, prospekt Karla Marxa 16) is open from 10 am to 6 pm (closed Monday). Neoliths adorn its courtyard. Adjoining the museum is a **diorama**, an 840 sq metre painted canvas featuring WWII. The terrace behind is lined with WWII anti-aircraft batteries, the centrepiece of which is a fighter plane. Its nose is aimed directly at the glistening gold spire and dome of **Preobrazhensky Cathedral** (Transfiguration of Our Saviour), a classical structure dating from 1830-35 which languishes amid parkland.

The western end of prospekt Karla Marxa is dominated by the **Gorky Russian Drama Theatre** (☎ 45 34 92) at No 97. The classical arches next to it mark the entrance to **Hloba Park**, a city park featuring a lake encircled by a **miniature railway**.

Places to Stay & Eat

DP's cheapest joint is ***Hotel Rassvet*** *(☎ 46 00 37, vulitsya Fudzhuka)* which has ugly singles/doubles with bathroom and cockroaches running wild for $10/20.

Hotel Central *(☎ 45 03 47, prospekt Karla Marxa 50)* has simple singles/doubles from $20/31.

Good value is ***Hotel Astoria*** *(☎/fax 44 23 04, prospekt Karla Marxa 66)* which has comfortable doubles for $33. Next door is ***Hotel Astoria*** *(☎ 37 42 70, ☎ 37 42 71)*, bearing the same name as its cheaper neighbour but run by a different company. Luxurious doubles cost from $55 to $124.

Fabulous ***Grand Hotel Ukraine*** *(☎ 34 10 10, fax 34 02 00, vulitsya Korolenko 2, admin@grand-hotel-ukraine.dp.ua)* overlooks prospekt Karla Marxa. Housed in a renovated 1904 building, it is Ukraine's most Western hotel with price tags to match: singles/doubles start at $150/175.

Flashy restaurants, casinos and strip clubs line prospekt Karla Marxa. The simple but sweet ***Kafe Varenyky*** at No 90 is a budget place to eat, with folkloric Cossack murals on its walls and handsome helpings of varenyky for $0.50. For a touch of the Wild West, head for ***Western*** *(☎ 46 52 36, vulitsya Dzerzhinskoho 1/3)*, adjoining the Triumph shopping mall at prospekt Karla Marxa 34.

Ranford supermarket *(prospekt Karla Marxa 54)* touts trolleys, as does ***Astoria supermarket*** *(prospekt Karla Marxa 66)*, open 24 hours and home to an ATM.

Getting There & Away

Air Dniproavia has direct flights to Kyiv (twice weekly) and to a handful of international destinations (see Ukraine Getting There & Away). Its office is at Dnipropetrovsk airport (☎ 651 818, ☎ 995 311, fax 650 496).

Train From the central train station (☎ 004, ☎ 50 39 53), prospekt Karla Marxa 108, there are rail services once daily to/from Zaporizhzhya (two hours), Kharkiv (5½ hours) and St Petersburg (16 hours); twice daily to/from Donetsk (five hours), Odesa (15 hours), Lviv (22 hours) and Moscow (20 hours); and four a day to/from Simferopol (10¾ hours).

A handful of trains use the southern train station (Dnipropetrovsk Pivdenny). Trains go to/from Donetsk and Simferopol (twice daily), and Odesa (one a day).

Bus Buses to destinations within a 90km radius leave from the small bus station, close to the train station at vulitsya Kurchatova 1. The long-distance bus station (☎ 001, ☎ 42 66 18) is farther up the same street at vulitsya Kurchatova 10. Major bus services include to/from Donetsk (7½ hours, twice daily) and Kharkiv (5½ hours, nine daily).

Getting Around

The Dnipropetrovsk metro, which opened in 1995, comprises one line which crosses the city from east to west (open from 5.30 am to midnight). The Vokzal stop – currently the westernmost stop – is in front of the central train station; construction sites mark the places on prospekt Karla Marxa where new stations will be built, when there is sufficient cash to complete the line extension.

Trolleybus б and tram No 1 run from the train station, along the length of prospekt Karla Marxa, to ploshcha Octobryskaya (behind Preobrazhensky Cathedral).

ZAPORIZHZHYA ЗАПОРІЖЖЯ

☎ 0612 • pop 900,000

Zaporizhzhya (Beyond the Rapids), 106km south of Dnipropetrovsk on the east bank of the Dnipro River, is one of the smoggiest places on earth. Its only draw is its colourful Cossack heritage which can be explored on Khortytsya Island, the 16th century *sich* (fortified base) of the famous Zaporizky Cossacks.

Cossack culture aside, Zaporizhzhya is a place to be avoided. The 40km series of rapids which the city used to overlook (and which previously made navigation on the Dnipro near impossible), are now submerged by the lake behind Zaporizhzhya's Dniproges Hydroelectric Dam. The USSR's first dam was built under US supervision to much fanfare in 1927-32 and transformed Zaporizhzhya into a major industrial centre. The city has been choked by smoke and fumes ever since.

Orientation & Information

The entire city branches off Zaporizhzhya's one main artery, prospekt Lenina, which stretches for 10km from Zaporizhzhya-1 train station at its south-eastern end, to ploshcha Lenina overlooking Dniproges Dam. Khortytsya Island lies in the Dnipro, parallel and 2km south-west of prospekt Lenina.

There is a post and telephone office on prospekt Lenina at Nos 186 and 230. There is an ATM in the lobby of Hotel Zaporizhzhya; and a currency exchange and email service (common@intour.packet.zp.ua) in its service bureau.

The service bureau (☎ 39 96 12, ☎ 33 31 84) inside Hotel Zaporizhzhya arranges guided tours ($25/hour including car/driver) of the city, Khortytsya Island and of the west-bank powerhouse of the Dniproges Dam; it organises folkloric evenings in summer.

Dniproges Dam

You can look down on the 760m curve of the Dniproges Dam (Dniprovska Hidroelektrostantsiya) from ploshcha Lenina. A road runs across the top and boats pass by two channels along the east bank. The dam's early promoters didn't emphasise the fact that it was built under US supervision with mainly US equipment. Partly wrecked in WWII, it was rebuilt and a second powerhouse was later added on the east bank, more than doubling the capacity to 1500 MW. Today, the Zaporizhzhya region also has nuclear and thermal power, so Dniproges' capacity is rarely used.

Khortytsya Island

Sometime around 1553-54, the Cossack hero-leader Baida united scattered groups of Cossacks to build a fort on what was then a remote but strategically located island below the Dnipro rapids. Beyond the control of Polish or Russian authority, the famous Zaporizky Sich was the cradle of Ukrainian Cossackdom, the 'free base' where any man, irrespective of social background, could come to join the Cossack brotherhood.

Since 1965 the island has been a reserve (2690 hectares), although it's tough to imagine the Cossack revelry of the past with electrical cables and a massive bridge crossing over to the island, and the dam and industrial facilities in plain view. Nevertheless, you can visit the **Historical Museum of Zaporizky Cossacks**, open from 10 am to 4.30 pm (closed Monday), which includes a couple of painted dioramas and numerous Cossack artefacts excavated from the island. Neoliths adorn its grounds which sprawl across the island's rocky northern end. Admission costs $0.50. Other Cossack haunts on the island include the Sechebny Vorota, the Cossacks' jetty, and the Hadyucha Peshchera (Snake Cave). Also here is the Chyorna Skala (Black Rock), where the Kyivan Rus King Svyatoslav is said to have been killed by the Pechenegs in 972.

Westbound trolleybus No 2 or 16 from Hotel Zaporizhzhya go to the northern end of Khortytsya. Get off at the Muzey stop, and head right before the road leaves the island again. In summer, there are occasional cruises around the island, departing from the mainland jetty at the foot of bulvar Tarasa Shevchenka.

Zaporizhzhya Oak

West of the Dnipro River in the Verkhnya Khortytsya area is a 600 to 700-year-old oak from which you can dangle any Cossack legend you choose. Did Bohdan Khmelnytsky address his troops beneath it before they marched against the Poles in 1648? Or was this where the Cossacks wrote their insulting letter to the Turkish sultan immortalised (or just imagined?) in Repin's painting? We may never know, but we can certainly admire the oak's girth of 6.5m. You can find the tree down vulitsya Hoholya off vulitsya Istomina, reached by the very rare No 19 bus from ploshcha Lenina, at the far north-western end of prospekt Lenina near the dam.

Places to Stay

Zaporizhzhya's dirt-cheap option is miserable ***Hotel Dnipro*** *(☎ 33 04 45, prospekt Lenina 202)*, spitting distance from the WWII memorial park. Singles with shared/private bathroom cost $10/17; doubles clock in at $17/30. Turn left when you enter the building to get to the sour-faced receptionist.

Hotel Teatralny *(☎ 64 24 34, prospekt Lenina 39)* is a dying establishment with a very kitsch Cossack mural adorning its reception walls. Singles/doubles with shower and toilet cost $30/56.

At the other extreme is three star ***Hotel Intourist-Zaporizhzhya*** *(☎ 34 12 92, prospekt Lenina 135)*, a 1970s block so overpriced it's amazing it gets any business at all. Singles/doubles with age-old furnishings go for an exorbitant $80/95.

Places to Eat

O'Brien's Irish Bar *(☎ 32 56 04, prospekt Lenina 169)* serves everything from steaks and shashlyk ($8) to shepherds pie, filled potato skins and an English breakfast ($5). Live bands play here most weekends; there are a couple of pool tables and TV screens; and the service sucks. Adventurous drinkers can sample an O'Brien's Rainbow (a Fanta, Guinness and vodka cocktail). Opening hours are from 10 to 2 am.

Loony Blues *(prospekt Lenina 166)* is a fun, upmarket jazz bar-cum-restaurant with blues, sax and food (open from noon until the early hours).

The ***Citi supermarket*** is on the side street that runs east off prospekt Lenina (between Loony Blues and the regional administration building). It is open from 8 am to 11 pm (until 9 pm on Monday).

On Khortytsya Island, near the Muzey bus stop, is ***Zaporizka Sich***, a touristy place with banquet-style dining and a sunny terrace (open from 11 am to 5 pm and 6 to 11 pm).

Getting There & Away

Zaporizhzhya-1 train station (☎ 005, ☎ 64 39 17) is at the south-eastern end of prospekt Lenina. From here, there are trains to/from Dnipropetrovsk (two hours), Kyiv (14 hours), Moscow (16 to 20 hours), Kharkiv (4½ hours), Lviv (27 hours), Odesa (17 hours) and Simferopol (five hours). Few trains use Zaporizhzhya-2 station (☎ 64 21 67), 4km north-west down vulitsya Lenina and north-east on vulitsya Leppika.

The bus station (☎ 64 26 57) is at prospekt Lenina 22, near Zaporizhzhya-1 train station.

Trolleybus Nos 3 and 23 travel the 10km length of prospekt Lenina between Zaporizhzhya-1 train station and ploshcha Lenina; No 3 crosses Dniproges Dam.

There are no scheduled boat services from Zaporizhzhya richkovy vokzal (☎ 64 15 30), vulitsya Hlitserna, at the southern end of vulitsya Leppika. The service bureau in Hotel Zaporizhzhya has up-to-date information.

DONETSK
ДОНЕЦЬК

☎ 0622 • pop 1.1 million

About 240km east of Zaporizhzhya and 280km south-east of Kharkiv, Donetsk is the capital of the Donbas (Donetsky Basin) – eastern Ukraine's great mining and industrial belt, whose coal miners are one of the most powerful labour groups in the country.

Since the collapse of the Soviet Union, government attempts to close some of Donetsk's 40-odd mines – many unprofitable – have been thwarted by striking miners calling for wage arrears to be paid and safety conditions in the mines to be improved. In May 1999, an explosion in one of the city mines killed 39 miners and injured 48; a methane explosion the previous year in another Donetsk mine left 63 dead.

Until 1924, Donetsk was called Yuzovka after a Welshman, John Hughes, who set up the first metallurgical plant here in 1872 to exploit the region's coal. From 1924 until 1961, the industrial hub was called Stalino after Stalin.

Today, beyond seeing a model Soviet city, there's little to lure tourists. In true *Full Monty* style, the city of Donetsk is twinned with Sheffield in the UK.

Orientation

Vulitsya Artema is 10km long and links the train station, at its northern end, with the centre. Central Donetsk is laid out in a Soviet grid system; most restaurants are clustered on bulvar Pushkina, the street running parallel (north-south) with Artema. Another block east is vulitsya Universytetska. Bulvar Shevchenka crosses these three streets from east to west.

Information

For local news, views, restaurant reviews and inside gossip, pick up a copy of *The Dejurnaya* (dejurnaya@iname.com), a witty monthly bulletin published by a group of die-hard expats.

Money You can cash travellers cheques, get cash advances on credit cards and change money at Avaal Bank, adjoining Hotel Ukraina.

Post & Telephone There is an ATM inside the post office on vulitsya Artema. The telephone office is around the corner on vulitsya Komsomolsky; to call a new, seven digit telephone number in Donetsk from another city, drop the second 2 from the city code.

Email & Internet Access You can send emails from Aist Net (☎ 332 84 79, info@aist.net, www.aist.net), vulitsya Artema, room No 309 (entrance via the red metal door).

Travel Agencies Intourist (☎ 93 40 78, ☎/fax 92 72 00, info@tours.donetsk.ua), inside Hotel Druzhba, organises excursions, including a coal mine tour ($100 for up to three people). It arranges car rental ($10/hour with driver).

Things to See & Do

Despite there being about 50 mines in the city itself, it doesn't seem too dirty. In fact, the city once won a UNESCO prize for being one of the cleanest industrial centres with a population of over one million. Locals graze their goats on the city slag heaps studding the horizon, while enterprising expatriates picnic on them.

The **Opera & Ballet Theatre** (☎ 92 23 48) sits midway along vulitsya Artema at No 82. The **Art Museum** is just behind at vulitsya Pushkina 35. The **regional museum** on four floors, about 2km north-east at vulitsya Cheluskintsiv 189A, is one of the few museums in Ukraine to have exhibits up to the present day (closed Tuesday). Tram No 1 runs along the length of vulitsya Cheluskintsiv from bulvar Shevchenka.

A colourful open-air **craft fair** transforms vulitsya Pushkina into a bustling market on Saturday.

Places to Stay

Hotel Ukraina *(☎ 91 19 50, vulitsya Artema 88)* does not always have hot water despite its claims otherwise. As a foreigner you will be automatically offered a luxury double for $70; insist on one of the cheaper $40 rooms (with private bathroom). Singles/doubles at ***Hotel Druzhba*** *(☎ 337 30 36, fax 337 33 31, vulitsya Universytetska 48)* are good value at $35/46.

Hotel Donbas *(☎ 93 13 66, vulitsya Artema 80)* is considered the city's leading hotel with facilities and a price tag to match.

Places to Eat

Donetsk is blessed with the very cheap and cheerful ***Kafe Al-Bakup*** *(bulvar Shevchenko 17)*, a Syrian place where visitors can dine on delicious spicy soups, plov, kebabs and the like for just a few dollars (closed Sunday).

Scrumptious cakes and honey-laden baklava can be eaten in (or taken away) at the small but sweet ***Kafe Napoleon*** *(vulitsya Artema 50)*. Other fun places to dine such as ***Galleria***, ***Picasso*** and ***Narn*** are on vulitsya Pushkina.

The pricey ***Arizona*** *(☎ 32 47 91, vulitsya Universytetska 2)*, inside the International Business Centre, is an American hang-out run by the same team that runs Arizona in Kyiv (open from 8 to 3 am).

Getting There & Away

From Donetsk airport (☎ 51 53 22), north of the centre, Air Ukraine operates four daily flights to/from Kyiv and a daily flight to Moscow. The airline ticket office (☎ 57 44 22) is at vulitsya Artema 167.

The advance train ticket office, vulitsya Universytetska 35, is open from 8 am to 6 pm (closed Sunday). Train services include to/from Moscow (17 hours, three daily) via Kharkiv (5½ hours); and Kyiv (15 hours). There is a train daily to/from Dnipropetrovsk (seven hours), Odesa via Zaporizhzhya, Poltava (odd days only), Simferopol (12 hours, one a day), Sevastopol (15 hours, once daily), St Petersburg and Minsk.

Trolleybus No 2 links the train station with the centre; it runs the length of vulitsya Artema.

BELARUS

Facts about Belarus

For many travellers, Belarus is a lot like that carton of spoiled milk at the back of the fridge – everyone knows it's bad, but they want to smell it for themselves. The country's reputation as an island of dictatorship amid Europe's democratic sea precedes it – heightened in recent years by the authoritarian-style presidency of Alexander Lukashenko. Its human rights record is dubious at best, and the standard of living here makes that of Russia – a country with which is has strived to strengthen ties in recent years – seem downright average. If for no other reason than stepping back in time to an era and form of leadership all but lost in the modern world, Belarus is well worth a visit.

But ask anyone who has actually visited this Slavic state and you'll get a rather different picture. Despite the massive media coverage of Lukashenko's iron rule, most visitors will be undisturbed by any of his government's machinations. Business and enterprise in the capital of Minsk break through the stiff controls imposed by the state like so many capitalist weeds. The city itself is a shining testament to classic Soviet urban planning, rebuilt from scratch after WWII. Brest is a lively and hectic border town with a Western air about it, Hrodna a cocktail of historical legacies, and Polatsk a sleepy legacy of past glory. The countryside is virtually empty of tourists, and historic towns such as Njasvizh and the castle at nearby Mir make a relaxing day's excursion from the capital.

Geographically, Belarus has been described as a flat, dull piece of land straddling the shortest route between Moscow and the Polish border. Flat it is, but dull is a subjective term. Wide stretches of unbroken birch groves, vast, forested marshlands and gently sloping green fields may not be exciting, but they retain a haunting beauty – especially when interspersed with wooden villages that seem frozen in 18th century isolation. Given its location, this swathe of terrain was obviously of great interest to

many people, including the Russians, Poles, Lithuanians, Germans and others who fought savagely over it for centuries. The real victims of these power struggles were the Belarusians. The country suffered grievously in both world wars – WWII took a quarter of its population and laid waste most of its cities. In 1986, the Chornobyl disaster in Ukraine dumped most of its devastating fallout on Belarus soil, and the nation is still dealing with the aftermath.

HISTORY

Arrival of the Slavs

Evidence of human occupation in Belarus goes back to the early Stone Age. Eastern Slavs were certainly here in the 6th to 8th centuries AD during the Slav expansion, and those who settled on the territory of modern Belarus formed a number of principalities including Polatsk (first mentioned in 862), Pinsk, Turov and Minsk. These fell under the general control of Kyivan Rus, the Slavic state founded at Kyiv in the 9th century which brought Orthodox Christianity to the Slavs. The economy was based on slash-and-burn agriculture and a certain amount of river trade, particularly on the Dnjapro.

Lithuanian & Polish Control

When Kyivan Rus was smashed by the Mongol Tatars in 1240, many Belarusian towns became Tatar vassals. In the 14th century, Belarus was gradually taken over by Lithuania, a growing power on Belarus' north-western border. It was to be 400 years before Belarus came under Russian control, a period in which Belarusians became linguistically and culturally differentiated from the Russians to their east and the Ukrainians to their south. Belarus means 'White Russia', a term of obscure origin said, among other things, to be derived from the people's pale complexion or their white dress.

Lithuania permitted its subject peoples a fair degree of autonomy – even using Belarusian as its own state language during the early years. Even after Lithuania became Roman Catholic following the uniting of its crown with Poland's in 1386, the Belarusian peasantry remained Orthodox. However, they were effectively reduced to serf status by agricultural reforms in the 16th century. Lithuania sank into a junior role in its partnership with Poland, especially after the two states' formal union in 1569, and across Lithuanian territory (including Belarus) the nobility adopted Polish culture and language and the Catholic religion.

In 1596, the Polish authorities arranged the Union of Brest, which set up the Uniate Church (also known as Ukrainian Catholic or Greek Catholic) and brought much of the Orthodox Church in Belarus under the authority of the Vatican. The Uniate Church insisted on the pope's supremacy and Catholic doctrine but permitted Orthodox forms of ritual.

For the next two centuries of Polish rule, Belarus largely stagnated. Trade was controlled by Poles and Jews and most Belarusians remained peasants. Poland became steadily weaker, and towards the end of the 18th century it and its dominions were carved up between Russia, Prussia and Austria in the three Partitions of Poland (1772, 1793 and 1795-96). All of Belarus was absorbed into Russia.

Tsarist Rule

Under Russian rule a policy of cultural Russification was pursued, and in 1839 the Uniate Church was abolished, with most Belarusians turning to Orthodoxy. The Russian rulers and the Orthodox Church regarded Belarus as 'western Russia' and tried to obliterate any sense of a separate Belarusian nationality. Publishing in the Belarusian language was banned.

The economy slowly developed in the 19th century with the emergence of small industries such as timber milling, glass-making and boat-building, the freeing of the serfs in the 1860s, and the building of railways in the 1880s. However, poverty in the countryside remained at such a high level that 1.5 million people – largely the more wealthy or educated – emigrated in the 50 years before 1917, mostly to Siberia or the USA, causing a sizable diaspora that hails from this period.

During the 19th century Belarus was part of the Pale of Settlement, the area where Jews in the Russian Empire were required to settle, and a large Jewish population developed. The majority of Belarusians remained on the land – poor and illiterate – and they were outnumbered in towns by Russians as well as Jews. Due to their cultural stagnation, their absence from positions of influence and their historical domination by Poles and Russians, any sense among Belarusian speakers that they were a distinct nationality was very slow to emerge.

World Wars & Soviet Rule

During WWI there was considerable fighting between Russia and Germany on Belarusian soil, and consequently much destruction. In 1918, under German occupation, an independent Belarusian Democratic Republic was declared, before Polish and Bolshevik forces took up the cudgels over Belarus in 1919. The 1921 Treaty of Riga allotted roughly the western third of modern Belarus to Poland, which launched a program of Polonisation that provoked armed resistance by Belarusians.

The Bolshevik-controlled area, the Belorusian Soviet Socialist Republic (SSR), became a founding member of the USSR in 1922. This small area, centred on Minsk, was enlarged a few years later with the transfer from the USSR's Russian Republic of the eastern Polatsk, Vitsebsk, Orsha, Mahileu and Homel areas, all with large Belarusian populations.

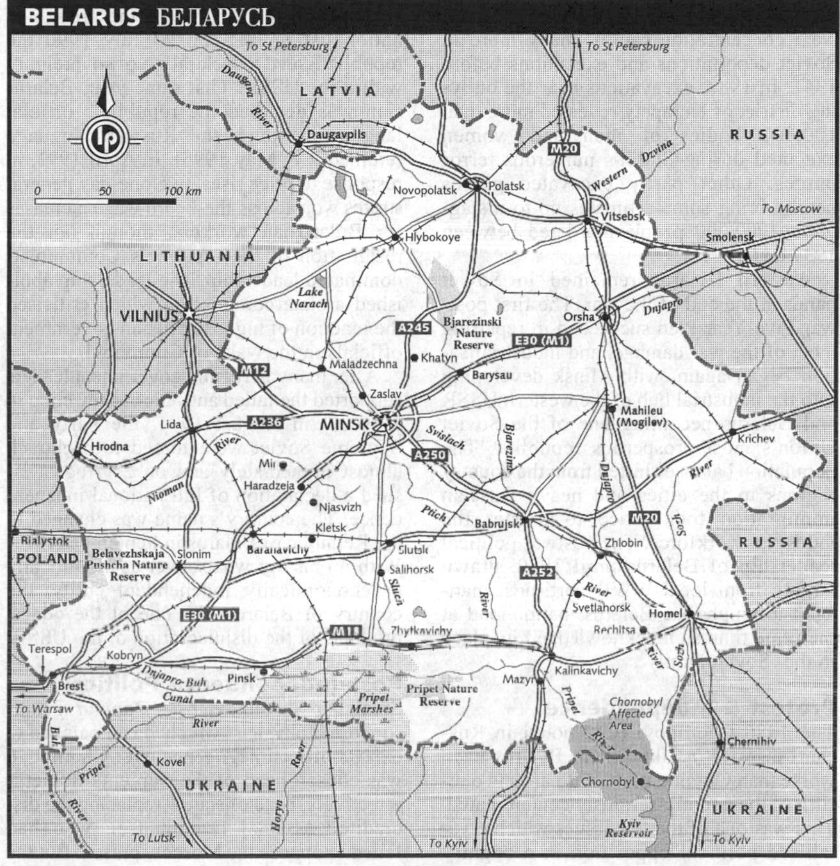

The Soviet regime in the 1920s encouraged Belarusian literature and culture, but in the 1930s, as happened throughout the USSR, nationalism and the Belarusian language were discouraged and their proponents persecuted. The 1930s also saw industrialisation, agricultural collectivisation, and purges in which hundreds of thousands were executed – most in the Kurapaty Forest, outside Minsk.

When the USSR and Nazi Germany began WWII by invading opposite sides of Poland in September 1939, western Belarus was seized from Poland by the Red Army – only to find itself on the front line again when the Nazis turned around and invaded the USSR in 1941. Belarus was quickly overrun by the Germans despite a heroic stand by the Soviet garrison at Brest. The German occupation was savage and partisan resistance widespread until the Red Army drove the Germans out, with massive destruction on both sides, in 1944. There were big battles around Vitsebsk, Barysau and Minsk, and barely a stone was left standing in Minsk. At least 25% of Belarus' population (more than two million people) died between 1939 and 1945. Many of them, Jews and others, died in 200-plus Nazi concentration camps, many more in Soviet deportations and executions before 1941. In 1988, excavations near the outlying district of Kurapaty revealed more than 100,000 bodies of men and women executed during Stalin's numerous terror purges. Other partly excavated graves nearby bring some estimates up to a staggering 900,000 people murdered between 1937 and 1941.

Western Belarus remained in Soviet hands at the end of the war. The first postwar Five-Year Plan succeeded in repairing most of the war damage, and industrialisation began again, with Minsk developing into the industrial hub of the western USSR and Belarus becoming one of the Soviet Union's most prosperous republics. The population balance shifted from the country regions to the cities and heavy Russian immigration took place to bolster the industrial workforce. The postwar political leadership of Belarus until 1980, drawn largely from local WWII partisans, managed to emphasise Belarus' nationhood at the same time as it acknowledged its place in the 'Soviet family'.

Protest & Independence

The 1986 Chornobyl (Chernobyl in Russian) disaster in Ukraine hit Belarus even worse than Ukraine itself, with around one-fifth of the country seriously contaminated. This was one of the few issues which crystallised political opposition in a country considered to be among the most rigidly communist of the Soviet republics.

In 1988 the Belarusian Popular Front was formed to address the issues raised by the Chornobyl disaster and the declining use of the Belarusian language. The leader of the Popular Front since its inception has been the archaeologist Zjanon Paznjak, who first revealed the existence of mass graves in the Kurapaty Forest. The Popular Front staged some well attended demonstrations but the Communist authorities employed various devices to reduce its representation in the new republican Supreme Soviet (parliament), elected in 1990.

However, in response to the growth of nationalist feeling, on 27 July 1990 the republic issued a declaration of sovereignty within the USSR. That same year, Belarusian was declared the republic's official language (though the Russian language rejoined it in May 1995). In April 1991, in response to price rises, two one-day general strikes won across-the-board wage increases for Belarusian workers, though not the resignation of the republic's Communist-dominated leadership. The leadership abolished a state commission which criticised the inaction of high Belarusian government officials in the wake of Chornobyl.

After many Party and government leaders supported the failed anti-Gorbachev coup in Moscow in August 1991, the Party and Supreme Soviet were forced to backtrack almost immediately and on 25 August issued a declaration of full national independence. The country's name was changed to the Republic of Belarus in September 1991. With no history whatsoever as a politically or economically independent entity, the country of Belarus was one of the oddest products of the disintegration of the USSR.

Post-Independence Politics

Stanislau Shushkevich, a Popular Front-supported physicist who had campaigned to expose official negligence over Chornobyl, was chosen head of the Supreme Soviet – effectively, head of state – replacing the discredited Mikalaj Dzemjantsei, who had failed to oppose the Moscow putsch. But the Supreme Soviet remained dominated by the Communist old guard. In December 1991 Belarus became a founding member of the Commonwealth of Independent States (CIS) with Minsk the group's headquarters.

Shushkevich pursued a centrist line between the old guard and the reformist Popular Front block in the Supreme Soviet. The Communist Party was suspended after the 1991 Moscow coup, but was reinstated in 1993 and gradually reasserted its power. The KGB remained in existence. Economic reform was slow, with the old guard opposing privatisation of state enterprises or state-run farms.

Symbols of Belarus: The More They Change ...

Beleaguered Belarus' national symbols have gone through a fair amount of upheaval in the past 10 years. Although the hammer and sickle of the USSR have been largely dispensed with, other symbols of the Soviet era re-emerged after 1995.

During the 1990-95 period of nationalist reawakening in Belarus, the country brought from retirement the silver knight on his rearing horse, sword drawn, which dates from medieval times. The symbol (called *Pahonia*, or 'the chase') represents the call to arms in defence of the homeland. But the rule of the knight's six ended golden cross – the ancient symbol of Jarillo, the pagan Slavic sun god – was limited, and in 1995 the knight was banished to the closet once again, to be replaced by the Soviet-era symbol of the rising sun and half-circle of wheat, capped by a neat five point red star, missing only the logo 'Workers of the World Unite'.

The national flag – two stripes of white, which represent freedom and purity, split by a swath of red, a symbol of valour and courage – was also replaced by the banner used when Belarus was just a republic of the USSR: a large red stripe covering the top two-thirds, with a green stripe at the bottom (the only change was the removal of a small hammer and sickle). The interim symbols of Pahonia and the white-red-white flag are now considered illegal by the current regime and people have been arrested for displaying them.

With the Communists advocating closer ties with Russia and regaining popularity during these economically difficult times, Shushkevich came into increasing conflict with them. Against his will, Belarus signed a CIS collective-security agreement subordinating Belarus' military policy to Russia's, and plans were laid for monetary union with Russia in exchange for a transfer of resources. Finally, Shushkevich was dismissed in January 1994, having lost a Supreme Soviet vote of confidence over corruption charges. He was replaced by a former senior police officer, Mechislau Gryb.

In July 1994, in Belarus' first direct presidential elections, Alexander Lukashenko, a quirky, non-Party former collective-farm director, heavily defeated Vjacheslav Kebich, a Communist who had served as prime minister since 1990. Lukashenko, who had supported the 1991 anti-Gorbachev coup in Moscow and led the anticorruption investigation which unseated Shushkevich, had campaigned on promises to reverse price rises, stop privatisation and corruption, break the Mafia and move closer to Russia. In 1997, Moscow and Minsk made their first formal pact, and several more have followed. The goal of a common currency and closer political ties still develops apace.

Lukashenko's style of presidency was individualistic and authoritarian and he clashed frequently with the Supreme Soviet. Finally, in a bid to increase his powers in 1996, he held what the West still regards as an illegitimate referendum. This referendum – through the dubious support of the populace – effectively stripped the authority of the parliament, now to be appointed by Lukashenko, and made the entire government subservient to the president (see the Government & Politics section for details).

Since then, the opposition has been reduced to a few groups that hold moderately successful rallies in the capital but have been unable to galvanise popular support into one unified whole. Also, Belarus' always-tenuous ranking among Eastern Europe's emerging democracies has plummeted: in April 1997, Lukashenko ordered the Soros Foundation – a nonprofit organisation created by billionaire financier George Soros to encourage a free society – to pay $3 million in supposed back taxes despite the fact that it had donated $13 million to schools and hospitals (instead of paying, the foundation closed and left the country). In August that same year Lukashenko had a Russian TV journalist arrested for supposedly violating the border with Lithuania, holding him in prison without trial for two months. He aimed higher in June 1998, when ambassadors from a number of European Union nations and the USA were abruptly and ignominiously locked out of their residence complex at Drozby, a suburb of Minsk. Lukashenko said the building was in need of repairs; foreign officials believe his actions were simply one more attempt to antagonise the West without actually provoking a major dispute. Nonetheless, EU ambassadors left en masse – although the embassies themselves remained open – and only returned to their postings in Minsk in January 1999.

In May 1999, the opposition held a presidential 'election' at what would have been the expiration of Lukashenko's original five year term. They hoped it would be a turning point, finally showing Lukashenko that the country as a whole was against him, but because the opposition was split among itself and the poll was filled with improprieties, even the head of the opposition electoral commission admitted it would have to be held again. The fact that one of the presidential candidates, Zjanon Paznjak, lives in exile and the other, former prime minister Mikhail Chigir, is in prison did not help.

GEOGRAPHY

Belarus has an area of 207,600 sq km, slightly smaller than the UK or Romania. It borders Russia in the north and east, Latvia and Lithuania in the north-west, Poland in the west and Ukraine in the south.

It's a low-lying country, with the highest hill, Dzerzhinskaja in the central west, reaching only 345m. The terrain consists of low ridges dividing broad, often marshy lowlands with many small lakes. One of the two main upland ridges runs in an arc across the country from the Polish border to the Russian border in the east, passing north of Minsk; the other runs north-west from central Belarus towards Vilnius in Lithuania. In the south are the Pripet Marshes, Europe's largest marsh area, though they have largely been drained for agriculture.

Belarus' major river is the Dnjapro, which flows into eastern Belarus from Smolensk in Russia (where it's known as the Dnepr), then turns south to cross into Ukraine (where they call it the Dnipro). Since the Buh flows into the Vistula, which empties into the Baltic Sea, and the Pripet joins the Dnjapro, which flows into the Black Sea, this canal provides a shipping link between the two seas. The north of Belarus is drained by the Dzvina River which flows from Russia to Latvia, while the Nioman flows north through Hrodna into Lithuania.

CLIMATE

Belarus has a continental climate, which becomes marginally more severe as you move from south-west to north-east. Average January temperatures are between -4 and -8°C, with frosts experienced for seven to eight months of the year. The warmest month is July, when temperatures normally reach 17 to 19°C. Rainfall is moderate at 500 to 700mm a year, with June to August the wettest months. There's snow cover continuously from December/January to March/April.

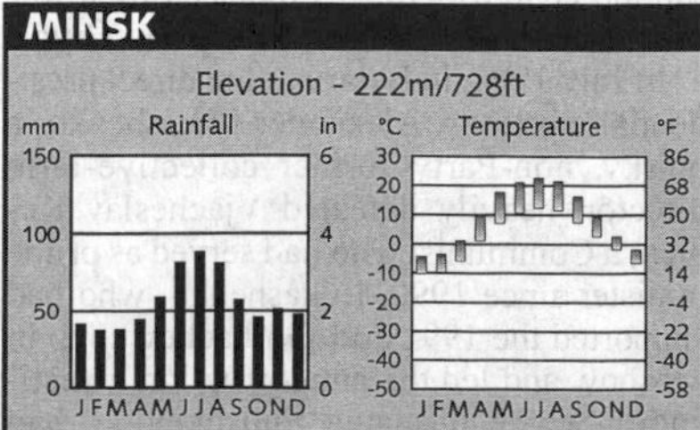

ECOLOGY & ENVIRONMENT

The disaster over a decade ago at Chornobyl has been the defining event for the Belarusian environment, despite its limited scope to the south-eastern corner of the country. But several decades of Soviet rule were not much better for the nation as a whole, with notoriously environmentally unfriendly factories springing up everywhere in the rush to industrialise. The result is cities often half-blackened by air pollution from old factories and outdated cars still puttering around. The flipside is that most of the countryside is unspoilt, and old farmsteads have slowly been reclaimed by new forests.

FLORA & FAUNA

Belarus was once completely covered in forest. By the 16th century a majority was removed for farming but great plots have regrown, especially in the south around the Pripet Marshes, where hundreds of species of swamp flora thrive. The forests are a mixture of coniferous and deciduous trees, with conifers such as pine and spruce dominating in the north, and deciduous trees such as oak and beech in the south. Silver birch is most common everywhere, growing in dense groves that break up the otherwise monotonous landscape.

The Belavezhskaja Pushcha Nature Reserve, north of Brest on the western border with Poland, is Europe's largest piece of surviving primeval mixed forest, with about 1300 sq km of the rich vegetation that once covered most of the continent. Once used as private hunting grounds for Polish and Russian royalty, the forest is now known for its European bison (wisent), Europe's largest mammal. Other significant reserves in Belarus include the Bjarezinski Nature Reserve, south of Polatsk, and the Pripet Nature Reserve, west of Mazyr. The famed Blue Lakes (Blakitnye Ozera), north of the town of Lake Narach off the Vilnius-Polatsk road, are renowned for their natural beauty.

Other animal species found in the nature reserves as well as throughout the wooded areas of the country include the elk, deer, boar, wolf, fox, squirrel, marten and hare. Beaver, otter, mink and badger can be found in and around the 20,000 streams and 10,000 small lakes of Belarus, with the largest populations in the isolated southern swamp regions and along the northern marshes of the Dzvina River, near Polatsk. The main fowl populations consist of ducks, grouse, woodcock and partridge.

GOVERNMENT & POLITICS

In theory, Belarus has an executive president, chosen in direct popular elections. The president chooses a prime minister, who is responsible for many of the day-to-day affairs of government. The country's parliament is the Supreme Soviet. In practice, however, the country is run by the sitting president, Alexander Lukashenko.

On 24 November 1996, 70% of Belarus gave Lukashenko the power he had always wanted. In a nationwide referendum that has never been officially recognised by the West, Belarusians said yes to a new constitution, effectively extending Lukashenko's five year term by two years. The new rules allowed Lukashenko to dissolve the Supreme Soviet and fill it with nodding donkeys. (The referendum also voted down measures that would abolish capital punishment and set up a free market system, and gave approval to switching the national Independence Day from 27 July – when the first Constitution was passed in 1991 – to 3 July, the day of Soviet liberation of Minsk in WWII.) Opposition parliamentarians, who were already being booted from their rostrums the following day, called the vote a farce, claiming that Lukashenko had monopolised the media and was not legally able to amend the constitution through a referendum.

Be that as it may, the result of that vote has guided life in Belarus since. With his new powers in hand, Lukashenko cracked down on media, halted or reversed economic reforms, stifled political opposition and played chicken with the West – harshly condemning it while at the same time trying to make moderate reforms in order to attract the funding he needs to keep the country running. Politically, Belarus is one of the most isolated countries in Europe.

The country is divided into six administrative regions centred on the cities of Minsk, Brest, Hrodna, Vitsebsk, Homel and Mahileu.

ECONOMY

Belarus, despite attempts at reform in the early 1990s, has devolved back into a largely planned economy, able to show some positive growth only as a result of soft state loans to key industries. In 1997 and 1998, Lukashenko spent much time crowing about the 'Belarusian Economic Miracle', but analysts say official figures are inflated and reflect nothing more than heavy dependence on Russia and the state sectors. According to the official statistics, Belarus' gross domestic product (GDP) grew 8% in 1998 after an 8.5% rise in 1997; without easy loans, say local officials, GDP would have fallen some 10% in 1998.

Agriculture accounts for about 20% of the country's GDP and occupies more than half the land, with livestock (chiefly cattle and pigs) responsible for 60% of agricultural produce; potatoes, grain, sugar beet and flax are the main crops. Industry contributes over 40% of the GDP, with heavy industry concentrated mainly in Minsk. More important are the mineral and chemical processing industries such as the fertiliser plants at Salihorsk and Hrodna and the oil refineries at Novopolatsk and Mazyr.

The country has few mineral resources and is almost totally dependent on Russia for oil and gas supplies, and at least in part on Lithuania for electricity. It is, however, rich in peat, which is used as fuel for power stations and in the manufacture of chemicals. It also has substantial deposits of potassium salts, used in fertiliser.

Despite its relative prosperity in Soviet times Belarus, like other ex-Soviet states, suffered severe economic problems during and after the break-up of the USSR. Problems included falling output, massive inflation, falling average wages ($31 a month by 1999), the abandonment of agricultural land because of Chornobyl fallout, and the closure of many enterprises due to inefficiency or declining demand for military equipment. Belarus was hit particularly hard, since the specialised nature of many of its industries made them dependent on raw materials and customers from all over the Soviet Union.

The central bank has actively printed money on a large scale which, combined with Russia's August 1998 devaluation, helped push inflation into the triple digits by early 1999. These economic policies have also turned Western lending agencies, such as the IMF and the World Bank, against the country, leaving it even more heavily dependent on Russia. Although Lukashenko has made some effort to win back much-needed international assistance, most analysts dismiss changes thus far as token gestures.

Foreign investment trickled to $18.6 million by 1998, down from $45.7 million the year before. Privatisation has ceased (with only about 10% of state-run companies sold by 1998) and Lukashenko's half-hearted attempt at 'market socialism' has led nowhere. Inflation was running at a monthly 50% in March 1999 and an astounding one-third of all Belarusian businesses were operating in the red. As a legacy of the full employment of the Soviet era, unemployment in the country is very low; however, the minimum monthly wage was barely $4 in early 1999.

POPULATION & PEOPLE

Belarus has 10.3 million people, with nearly 78% Belarusian, 13% Russian, 4% Polish and about 3% Ukrainian. There was once a huge Polish and Jewish population as well as a substantial German minority – all of whom were either killed or fled during WWII, or were sent off to Siberia in its aftermath. Prior to WWII, 10% of the national population was Jewish and in cities like Minsk, Hrodna and Brest, Jews made up between one and two-thirds of the population. A conservative estimate of the overall death toll in the war is put at 2.2 million, with close to another 900,000 'purged' by the Soviet regime before and after the war.

To bolster industry and fill the shortage in the labour force, large Russian immigration took place during the 1960s. These immigrants now form the core of the 1.3 million-strong ethnic Russian minority.

The overall population density of the country is low (an average of less than 50 persons per square kilometre), though it is higher around the cities and substantially lower in isolated regions like the Pripet Marshes and the north-western lowlands. Following WWII, the desperate economic situation forced a mass migration to urban areas, raising the urban population from 20% after 1945 to 70% in 1996.

EDUCATION

Most schools now teach exclusively in Russian, although in theory students should be able to find some classes in Belarusian. In Minsk, the number of Belarusian-language schools dwindled from 220 in 1994 to less than 20 in 1999. Higher education is almost exclusively in Russian.

ARTS

Few cultural artefacts survive from the early Slavic settlements of the 6th to 8th centuries, which were followed by long periods of foreign rule, first by Lithuania and later by the Polish and Russian empires. Without control of its own destiny, Belarusian cultural identity was, outside the rural framework, subdued and often suppressed, with only brief periods of revival in the 16th and 19th centuries.

Literature & Drama

Many 12th century Orthodox hymns and sermons can trace their origins to Belarus. The hero of early Belarusian literary achievement was Francyska Skaryny of Polatsk (after whom Minsk's main street is named). In the early 16th century he became the first person to translate the Bible into the Belarusian language. This, as well as other editions by Skaryny between 1517 and 1525, were some of the first books to be printed in all of Eastern Europe. In the late 16th century, the philosopher and humanist Simon Budny printed a number of works in the Belarusian language, including controversial editions of the day such as *Justification of a Sinner Before God*. The 17th century Belarusian poet Symeon of Polatsk was the first writer to introduce the baroque style of literature to Russia.

The 19th century saw the beginning of modern Belarusian literature with works by writers and poets such as Maxim Haradsky, Maxim Bohdanovish, Janka Kupala and Jakub Kolas. Many of these writers had been active in the influential nationalist newspaper *Nasha Niva* (Our Cornfield), which had to be published in Lithuania from 1906 to 1916. Haradsky's novel *Two Souls* (1919) and Kupala's play *The Locals* (1922) are poignant expressions of the repressed state of Belarus after WWI and during the revolution. Kolas is considered by many to be the pioneer of classical Belarusian literature.

A period of cultural revival in the 1920s and early 1930s saw the rise of many talented poets and writers, including Jazep Pushcha and satirist playwright Kandrat Krapiva. But during the subsequent occupation and Soviet rule, most writers either emigrated or were forced to follow the prescribed literary formulas dictated by the Soviets. A slight revival occurred in the 1960s with works by Vasyl Bykov and V Karatkevich.

Music

Belarusian folk music is well known and visitors to the country shouldn't miss a performance. Modern folk music originated from ritualistic ceremonies either based on peasant seasonal feasts or, more commonly, on the traditions of church music (hymns and psalms) which became highly developed in Belarus from the 16th century onwards. Classical music in the modern sense only developed in Belarus within the last 100 years, with composers such as Kulikovich Shchehlov and Yevheny Hlebov, who composed the operas *Your Spring* (1963) and *Alpine Ballad* (1967).

Architecture

Although WWII did a thorough job of destroying centuries of architectural heritage, a few examples still survive amid the typically sterile and mundane cement blocks of postwar construction.

Of the early Slavic 6th to 8th centuries settlements and the subsequent Kyivan Rus rule, all that remains today is the 10th century St Sophia Cathedral in Polatsk. It's the oldest surviving building in the country, although it was completely renovated in the 18th century. Much of the tiny Church of SS Boris & Hlib in Hrodna remains from the 12th century.

In western Belarus, Polish control in the 17th and 18th centuries left a baroque touch which later filtered to Russia through travelling Belarusian and Ukrainian artisans. Baroque examples include the reconstruction of St Sophia Cathedral, Hrodna's Farny Cathedral and Minsk's Bernardine Convent, all commissioned by the Polish crown.

The classical revival in the late 18th and early 19th centuries is exemplified in the reconstruction of the Governor's Palace in Hrodna.

SOCIETY & CONDUCT

From the popularity of President Lukashenko, you could derive that the Belarusian people like a firm (ie totalitarian) leader, and this is not far from the mark. Throughout history the Belarusian people have been the underclass in their own country, with little distinct culture or history of their own. As such, Belarusians are quiet, somewhat reserved people (with the exception of the Russian nouveau riche element). Once introductions are made, however, they can be unrelentingly generous and very friendly. As a rule Belarusians do not make eye contact on the street or say hello to strangers, although like Russians they are very fond of staring at unfamiliar tourists or foreigners.

RELIGION

Belarus, like Ukraine, has always been a crossing point between Latin and Eastern Orthodox Christianity, with the Polish Catholics to the west and the Orthodox Russians to the east. Some 80% of the populace is Eastern Orthodox. In 1990 the Belarusian Orthodox Church was officially established.

As a legacy of centuries of Polish rule, 20% of the population (about two million people) is Roman Catholic, of whom 15% are ethnic Poles. Some tension exists between the Polish Catholics, who favour services in the Polish language, and the Belarusian Catholics, who resist the Polonisation of their church.

In the early 1990s the Uniate Church – an Orthodox sect that looks to Rome, not Moscow – was re-established and now has a following of over 100,000, many of them Ukrainians living in Belarus. There's also a small Protestant minority, the remnant of a once large German population. The number of Baptist churches has grown to over 200 and there are small pockets of Tatars, who practise Islam, as well as scattered urban Jewish communities, although most of the latter are emigrating.

LANGUAGE

The centralised Soviet system subjected Belarus to a process of Russification, with the result that well over 80% of Belarusian school pupils were taught exclusively in Russian until 1988 and Russian was imposed as the official language of all business and government transactions.

In 1990, shortly before independence, Belarusian was announced as the country's only official language. The government, reacting to demand from activists and academics, began to provide the necessary provisions for education to shift emphasis back to Belarusian history and literature. Just as a resurgence of the national tongue seemed ready to blossom, Lukashenko decreed in 1995 that Russian was also to be the official language, on an equal footing with Belarusian, and most ordinary citizens heaved a sigh of relief and reverted exclusively to Russian (although Belarusian is occasionally spoken in the countryside). Today only about 11% of school children are instructed in Belarusian.

Belarusian is an Eastern Slavonic language, closely related to both Russian and Ukrainian. It's normally written in the Cyrillic alphabet (see the Language chapter at the back of the book for details), but there does exist a rarely used Belarusian language in the Latin alphabet.

Belarusian, like Ukrainian but not Russian, has the letter і, pronounced *ee*. It also has the unique letter ў, pronounced like 'w' in the word 'west'. Transliteration is also different, with й transcribed as *j*, ю as *ju*, я as *ja* and ё as *io*. Г is pronounced and transcribed *h*, as in Ukrainian. The Russian letter o often becomes a in Belarusian – making, for example, Komsomolskaja into Kamsamolskaja, which looks closer to its pronunciation in any case. The Russian Gogolya becomes Hoholja in Belarusian.

You'll see an apostrophe used in written Belarusian to separate a consonant from the syllable that follows it.

To honour the local language we use the new form of transliteration described above, however confusing it may seem. Although it may seem to you noble to try a little Belarusian, be aware you're more likely than not to be greeted with consternation and confusion.

At the time of writing, although Russian is by far more often spoken on the street, a surprising amount of signage – at bus/train stations, metro stops, streets, museums etc – remains in Belarusian.

Belarus	**Беларусь** ***beh-lah-ROOS***
Hello.	**Добры джень.** ***DOB-ree DZHEN***
Goodbye.	**Да пабачэньня.** ***DA pah-bah-CHEN-nyah***
yes	**так** ***tahk***
no	**не** ***nye***
Please.	**Калі ласка.** ***kah-LEE LAHS-kah***
Thank you.	**Дзякуй.** ***DZYAH-koo-ee***
good	**добры** ***DOHD-ree***
bad	**дрэнны** ***DREHN-nee***

Facts for the Visitor

HIGHLIGHTS

Belarus, sadly, is a country with few traditional attractions for tourists. Many who come here simply want to gawk at the utter Sovietisation of an agrarian society; they won't be disappointed. Minsk, aside from its barely charming, rebuilt old town, is impressive only because of its flatness and ties to an era now long gone, no longer evident even in Moscow. The capital is a good place to sample life under Soviet rule, but it offers little for tourists to do – although its cultural events are usually outstanding and the WWII museum is among the best of its kind.

Outside Minsk, Polatsk is a quiet retreat from the bustling metropolis and boasts two ancient churches that merit a visit. Hrodna has a pleasant old town and a stunning Polish Catholic church. No visitor should pass up the opportunity to see Brest's amazing fortress, a Soviet war monument whose scope defies words.

PLANNING

When to Go

There is no high or low season as far as tourism is concerned – in Belarus it's always low. With summer being the warmest but wettest season and with winter a grey freeze, the best time to visit is typically late summer or spring. For more details see the When to Go section in the Ukraine Facts for the Visitor chapter.

Maps

Maps, including several very new and detailed ones, are widely available in Minsk and sparingly in the other cities. Quality differs widely – be sure to check the year of print, as some are Soviet-era. There is an excellent 1:750,000 scale map of Belarus on sale for about $2 (it is a fold-out with a red cover). For a longer stay in Minsk, spend $3 on the Kvadro-Graf map entitled *Ulitsi Minska*, with detail down to every number on every structure in the entire city. At various points you may be able to find topographical maps of Belarus, but grab them when you do as you're unlikely to spy them twice. A city and regional series called *Minsk i okrestnosti* (or Hrodna, Brest, Vitsebsk or Polatsk) exists, mapping out the namesake city and surrounding region, but it's not very user-friendly.

TOURIST OFFICES

There are no tourist information offices in the formal sense in Belarus, but there are some service bureaux and excursion offices, usually in hotels, which may be willing to provide information and sell services. Outside Belarus, information is rare and hard to come by. Consult some of the travel agencies listed in the Ukraine, Russian Far East and Belarus Getting There & Away chapters as well as your local embassy (see the list later in this chapter).

The main travel agency in Belarus is Belintourist, basically a slightly updated, Belarusian version of the Soviet-era Intourist (see Travel Agencies in the Minsk chapter for more details).

VISAS & DOCUMENTS

All foreigners visiting Belarus will need a visa. Arranging one before you arrive is absolutely essential. To get it, you will need a photograph, an invitation from a private person or a business or a voucher from a hotel, and your passport. There are three types of visas: tourist, issued if you have a tourist voucher or hotel reservation; visitor, if your invitation comes from an individual; and business, if your invitation is from a business. Tourist and visitor visas are issued for 30 days, while business visas are valid for 90 days.

Once you enter the country you must be officially registered, a process most hotels will do for a small fee. Otherwise, you will need to seek out the nearest local passport office (OVIR) of the Ministry of the Interior. The main office is in Minsk (☎ 017-231 91 74) at vulitsa Francyska Skaryny 8.

Transit Visas

If you are transiting through Belarus to or from Russia – with a proper Russian visa – you will have a 48 hour period of grace in Belarus. However, there may be a problem when taking certain trains from St Petersburg or Pskov to Warsaw, as some pass through Latvia and Lithuania before crossing a tiny corner of Belarus. On these trains your Russian visa may be taken away from you as you leave Russia and enter Latvia (Russian visas are separate slips of paper). If this happens, even though your Russian visa would still have been valid when you crossed Belarus, you won't have it with you to prove that fact – so you might get hit with the cost of a Belarusian transit visa ($30).

Travellers should check up on the route of their train and, if it goes through Latvia or Lithuania, be prepared for any transit visa complications that might result. Travellers on the direct train between Warsaw and Vilnius will need to obtain a transit visa.

For a transit visa, no invitation is necessary, only a copy of your train ticket proving your destination lies beyond the border. At the time of research, transit visas were not available on the border. It's better to obtain one before you set off for Belarus.

Applying for a Visa

By far the simplest – although the most expensive – way to get a visa is to apply through a travel agency that specialises in such things.

In Poland, try near the train station in Warsaw, or ask at Orbis. In Vilnius, the most convenient jumping-off point, go to Litamicus (☎ 370 2-22 44 74, fax 61 36 37), Gedimino prospectas 24, or West Express (☎ 370 2-22 25 00), Stulginskio gatve 5, and you can get a visa in one day with nothing more than a picture of yourself and $75 to $100.

The most important component is the invitation (from a hotel, person or business) or voucher (issued by a travel agency): individuals in Belarus can get an official invitation *(izveshchenie)* from their local OVIR office and send it to you. This process can take three months and should be avoided if possible. Much simpler is to get a faxed confirmation from your hotel or call Belintourist, which can help with invitations and vouchers, or visit its Web site (www.belarustourist.minsk.by) where you can apply for a voucher online.

Most travel agencies who deal with travel to the region can help (see those listed in the Getting There & Away chapters for European Russian and Ukraine).

Make sure the expiration date of your passport extends for at least a month beyond your departure from Belarus and carry photocopies of the personal data as a backup. Taking extra passport photos with you is also a good idea.

Visa costs vary from embassy to embassy, seemingly according to the whim of that day. Typically they will cost about $30 for seven working days service and $70 for next-day service. Transit visas cost $20 for seven working days service, $30 for next-day service.

Visa Extensions

In theory, you cannot extend your transit visa inside Belarus if you decide to stay longer than the allotted 48 hours. In practice, however, this may be possible. Try at the Belintourist office or the Ministry of Foreign Affairs in Minsk (☎ 017-222 26 74) at vulitsa Lenina 19.

Nontransit visas cannot be extended beyond the 30 day limit for tourists, or the 90 day limit for holders of business visas; you will need to apply for a new visa.

EMBASSIES & CONSULATES

Belarusian Embassies & Consulates

Belarus' diplomatic representation abroad includes the following:

Canada
  Embassy:
  (☎ 613-233 9994)
  Suite 600, 130 Albert St, Ottawa, Ontario K1P 5G4
France
  Embassy:
  (☎ 01 44 14 69 79, fax 01 44 14 69 70)
  38 Boulevard Suchet, 75016 Paris

Germany
Embassy:
(☎ 0228-201 13 10, fax 201 13 19, consular department ☎ 0228-201 13 30, fax 201 13 39)
Fritz-Schäffer-Strasse 20, 53113 Bonn
Consulate:
(☎ 030-5 36 35 929, fax 5 36 35 923, consular department ☎ 030-5 36 35 934, fax 5 36 35 924)
Am Treptower Park 32, 12435 Berlin

Latvia
Embassy:
(☎ 2-732 25 50, fax 732 28 91)
Jezusbasnicas 12, Riga 1003
Consulate:
(☎ 54-37 573, fax 52 945)
18-Noyabrya 44, Daugavpils

Lithuania
Embassy:
(☎ 22-26 38 28, fax 26 34 43)
Klimo gatve 8, Vilnius
Consulate:
(☎ 22-23 06 26)
Muitines gatve 41, Vilnius

Netherlands
Embassy:
(☎ 070-363 15 66, fax 364 05 55)
Piet Heinstraat 3, 2518 CB Den Haag

Poland
Embassy:
(☎ 022-617 32 12, fax 617 84 41)
Ulica Atenska 67, 03-978 Warsaw
Consulates:
(☎ 058-41 00 26, fax 41 40 26)
Ulica Yackova Dolina 50, 80-251 Gdansk
(☎ 085-44 55 01, fax 44 66 61)
Ulica Warshiskeho 4, 15-461 Bialystok

Russia
Embassy:
(☎ 095-924 70 31, ☎ 924 70 95 for visa inquiries, fax 928 64 03)
Maroseyka ulitsa 17/6, 101000 Moscow
Consulate:
(☎ 095-924 70 31, fax 928 64 03)
Armyansky pereulok 6, 101000 Moscow

UK
Embassy:
(☎ 020-7937 3288, fax 7361 0005)
6 Kensington Court, London W8 5DL

Ukraine
Embassy:
(☎ 044-290 02 01, fax 290 34 13)
vulitsya Kutuzova 8, 252011 Kyiv

USA
Embassy:
(☎ 202-986 1604, fax 986 1805)
1619 New Hampshire Ave NW, Washington, DC 20009
Consulate:
(☎ 212-682 53 92, fax 682 54 91)
708 Third Ave, New York, NY 10017

Embassies & Consulates in Belarus

The following addresses are all in Minsk, telephone area code ☎ 017.

France
(☎ 210 28 68, fax 210 25 48)
ploshcha Peramohi 11

Germany
(☎ 233 42 17, fax 236 85 52)
vulitsa Zakharava 26

Latvia
(☎ 239 16 12, fax 250 67 84)
vulitsa Starazhouskaja 15, Hotel Belarus

Lithuania
(☎ 234 77 84, fax 276 94 71)
vulitsa Varvasheni 17

Poland
(☎ 213 41 14, fax 236 49 92)
vulitsa Rumjantsava 6

Russia
(☎ 250 36 65, fax 250 36 64)
vulitsa Staravilenskaja 48

UK
(☎ 229 23 03, fax 229 23 06)
vulitsa Karla Marxa 37

Ukraine
(☎ 227 27 96, fax 227 28 61)
vulitsa Kirava 17-306

USA
(☎ 231 50 00, fax 234 78 53)
vulitsa Staravilenskaja 46

CUSTOMS

When you arrive (or beforehand, on the train) you may be given a customs declaration form *(deklaratsia)* to fill out, most likely in Russian. For a description of this form and how to fill it out see Customs in the Ukraine Facts for the Visitor chapter. The customs form is identical for both countries.

For legalities concerning what you can bring in or take out of the country refer to Customs in the European Russia Facts for the Visitor chapter. Belarus' customs laws are basically the same as Russia's. For information, contact the State Customs Office in Minsk (☎ 017-234 43 55), vulitsa Khoruzhoy 29, or the local customs office (☎ 017-220 38 22), vulitsa Ostrovskoho 2A, Minsk.

MONEY

All prices are listed in US dollars (abbreviated to $) in this book.

Currency

The official currency is the Belarusian rouble, which replaced the Soviet rouble in May 1992. It was intended to be a transitional monetary unit, to be used only until the economy stabilised and the Belarusian *taler* could be issued.

Belarusian roubles are better known as *zaichiki* or 'rabbits', named after the completely worthless one rouble note that featured a leaping rabbit. The extinct rabbits have been replaced – thanks to inflation – by the equally worthless 1000 rouble note, featuring the Academy of Sciences building.

As of January 2000, Belarus will be revamping its currency, knocking off three zeros from all bills. This will undoubtedly cause some confusion and may encourage scoundrels and the like to rip off unwary tourists – so don't be one! It will take three years to remove all of the old currency from circulation and replace it with the new, so be aware of how many zeros are on your bill.

Also be aware that Belarus' on-again, off-again merger-in-waiting with Russia may mean a complete replacement of Belarus' currency with the Russian rouble.

Exchange Rates

In late 1999, $1 could be exchanged for upwards of one million Belarusian roubles on the street and 400,000 roubles at banks, but inflation was still high and this rate will likely be much changed. If you plan to stay for longer than a week, you may want to exchange a little at a time; otherwise, it is probably more convenient to find a good rate and exchange $100 on the spot – which may last a good five to seven days.

With the exception of top-end hotels and international transport services, it is illegal to accept payment in dollars.

Exchanging Money

Travellers should carry the usual credit cards and travellers cheques as a precaution, but charging things in Belarus can mean paying an additional 20% over the going exchange rate if your bill is not listed in dollars. A few ATMs exist in Minsk, but at the time of research were out of dollars.

To cash travellers cheques you'll need to seek out the larger banks and hotels. Outside of Minsk, it can be difficult to find places that will perform this service. For this reason, it's important to have a substantial amount of cash as well – the most widely accepted currency being US dollars. Make sure the notes are new, preferably since 1992, as exchange kiosks and most banks will not accept any with tears or markings.

Besides all hotels, there are a number of exchange kiosks (with the sign *obmin valjuty*) on the main streets as well as at all major banks. At the time of writing, there was a severe shortage of dollars in circulation, meaning most ordinary citizens would happily – if illegally – exchange their roubles at a fairly advantageous rate, certainly better than at banks and most kiosks. Caution and judgement should be used in these circumstances, but the practice is fairly widespread.

Costs

For travellers to Belarus, the major cost will be accommodation (refer to hotel prices in city chapters) but everything else is very cheap. A full meal will cost on average no more than $5, a night at the opera never more than $1, and domestic train tickets are also cheap (eg $1 for the overnight Minsk-Brest train).

You must pay for all food, entertainment and basic services in roubles, as well as cheaper lodging (payment for accommodation at more upmarket hotels will be required in US dollars). You'll have to pay in hard currency for a train ticket out of the country (eg $66 for Minsk-Prague, $15 for Brest-Warsaw).

As a Western foreigner, you will be subject to paying a higher price than locals for hotel accommodation; rates for CIS citizens are somewhere in between.

POST & COMMUNICATIONS

Post

The word for post office is *pashtamt*. Ordinary mail in and out takes about the same time as in Ukraine. Addresses are written the same way as in Ukraine – basically in the opposite direction to the West, with the country first and the name last. See the Ukraine Facts for the Visitor chapter for more information.

Sending Mail The cheapest way to mail important items which need to be delivered on time is to use the more reliable Express Mail Service (EMS), offered at most main post offices, or better – but more expensive – one of the multinational services (UPS, DHL, TNT) in Minsk.

Receiving Mail The best way to receive mail in Belarus is through a personal contact, but many hotels (especially if you've prebooked) will hold clearly marked mail for you if you let them know when you're coming. Receiving valuable items by post is inadvisable and you can forget packages altogether. Embassies and consulates won't hold mail.

Telephone

Intercity Calls The standard card phone will not allow you to dial internationally, but can handle intercity and CIS calls. To make an intercity call: dial ☎ 8, wait for a new tone, then dial the city code and number.

Useful numbers include:

- Minsk Information (☎ 09)
- Infoline (☎ 085)
- CIS & Baltics Information (☎ 053)
- International Information (☎ 233 29 84)
- AT&T Direct (☎ 8 800 101)

International Calls International phone calls can be made in one of three ways: from a private phone, from special long-distance telephone offices *(perehovorny punkt)* – often found near or in main post and telegraph offices – or through new, blue card phones called URMET, found in most hotels, some restaurants and all post offices. URMET phones accept special cards available from post offices and some kiosks. To dial any country except former USSR countries, dial ☎ 8, wait for the new tone, then dial ☎ 10, the country code, city code and the number. If you can't get through, try placing your call with an international operator (in Minsk ☎ 017-233 29 71).

For all calls within the CIS, which excludes the Baltic States, dial ☎ 8, wait for the new tone, then dial the city code and local number.

To phone Belarus from any country outside the CIS, dial ☎ 375 (Belarus' new country code) followed by the city code and local number.

Fax

The main post offices and most hotels have fax capabilities and will happily send and receive faxes for you.

INTERNET RESOURCES

There is no access to Western Internet providers in Belarus, but a few local providers do offer services. In main cities, the post or telephone office will send email for a very tiny fee, but you'll have to bring it in on disk or type it there; a few also offer live Internet access. There is one cybercafe in Minsk (see Post & Communications in the Minsk chapter).

For research before you go, the In Your Pocket people publish a very handy guide to Minsk at www.inyourpocket.com. The Virtual Guide to Belarus (www.belarusguide.com) is run by Belarusian scientists abroad. The Belarusian Chronicle (chronicle.home.by) is a handy English-language source of up-to-date current events in the country. Belintourist (www.belarustourist.minsk.by) has helpful visa information and allows you to make hotel reservations and book tours online.

BOOKS

Some of the books mentioned in European Russia Facts for the Visitor deal with the whole former USSR and include portions relating to Belarus.

Guidebooks

Minsk – A Historical Guide by Guy Picarda (1994) has detailed historical information and plenty of travel information on Minsk, including walking tours of the city and motoring tours of the surrounding region.

Minsk in Your Pocket is a handy little English-language guide. It is updated annually and should be promptly bought if you find it in any kiosk or hotel lobby newsstand in Minsk. It contains listings of restaurants, hotels and a bunch of important addresses.

History & Politics

Belarus: At a Crossroads in History by Jan Zaprudnik is probably the best history and commentary on the conditions affecting the newly independent nation, though it was published in 1993. *Belorussia: the Making of a Nation* by Nicholas Vakar covers history up to the 1950s including the origins of folk traditions. *Belorussia Under Soviet Rule: 1917-57* by Ivan Lubachko covers in detail just what it says.

Out of Fire, edited by Ales Adamovich, Janka Bryl & Vladimir Kolesnik, is a shocking collection of first-hand stories of the brutal atrocities committed during WWII, although told with a decidedly Soviet slant. *Defiance: The Bielski Partisans*, by Nechama Tec, tells the story of Jewish WWII partisans in the forests of western Belarus.

Belarus: From Soviet Rule to Nuclear Catastrophe, by David Marples, is the most recent assessment of the brutality of the Soviet regime, the Chornobyl disaster in Belarus and Lukashenko's referendum.

Kurapaty: Articles, Comments and Photographs, by opposition leader Zjanon Paznjak, is a controversial 1994 exposé of the Soviet slaughter of Belarusian citizens at Kurapaty, just outside of Minsk. For the flipside of WWII atrocities, read *Collaboration in the Holocaust: Crimes of the Local Police in Belorussia and Ukraine, 1941-44*, by Martin Dean.

NEWSPAPERS & MAGAZINES

Most widely distributed newspapers are government-controlled and freedom of the press is nonexistent. The most popular is the apolitical daily *Vecherny Minsk* (Evening Minsk), which has listings of cultural events.

The only English-language newspapers produced in Belarus are the twin *Minsk News* and *Belarus Today*, fairly independent weeklies that are sporadically available at newsstands and in most hotels; they can be contacted at minsknews@belarustoday.com (☎/fax 262 30 18). Western newspapers are extremely scarce – try in Minsk at the British Council, the United States Information Service (USIS) or the IBB Hotel.

RADIO & TV

State-owned Radio Minsk, heavy on classical concerts, can usually be picked up anywhere along the dial on the plastic radio hanging on your hotel room wall. The most popular station is FM 104.6, Radio BA, the first private radio station in the country. FM 108 is Belarus State Radio.

If your hotel TV works, you'll be able to pick up Russian TV as well as the national Belarusian TV channel.

PHOTOGRAPHY & VIDEO

Film (predominantly only colour print) can be widely purchased in Minsk and at most large department stores in other places. For further information and photo tips, refer to the Photography & Video section in the European Russia Facts for the Visitor chapter.

TIME

The entire country is on the same time zone as Ukraine, ie GMT/UMC plus two hours. At midnight on the last Sunday in March the country shifts to 'summer time', setting clocks ahead one hour, and on the last Sunday in September sets them back again.

When it's noon in Minsk, it's ...

2 am in San Francisco;
5 am in New York and Toronto;
10 am in London;
11 am in Paris, Warsaw and Prague;
noon in Vilnius, Kyiv, Helsinki, Bucharest, Ankara and Cairo;
1 pm in Moscow;
6 pm in Ulaan Baatar and Beijing;
8 pm in Sydney;
10 pm in Auckland.

ELECTRICITY

Belarus' electrical system is the same as Russia's: standard voltage is 220V, 50Hz AC. Sockets require a continental or European plug with two round pins. See the European Russia Facts for the Visitor chapter for more information.

HEALTH

Most of the information given under Health in European Russia Facts for the Visitor also applies to Belarus, including the incidence of tick encephalitis and Lyme disease in rural areas in summer. Travellers should check with their local public health service office for information on current epidemic or health risks in Belarus. Certain immunisations, such as tetanus, typhoid and diphtheria, should be current.

Chornobyl

The southern half of Belarus is a living monument to the 1986 Chornobyl disaster in neighbouring Ukraine – 70% of the fallout landed on Belarusian territory. Around one-fifth of Belarus was seriously affected and was for years off limits to travellers. By 1990, two million people, 20% of the country's forests and well over 250,000 hectares of agricultural land had been contaminated. The plight of residents in the worst-hit south-eastern areas only gradually became clear with increasing reports of cancer and related diseases, birth deformities and so on.

The risk to short-term visitors from the aftermath of the Chornobyl nuclear disaster is considered insignificant. The areas in Belarus to stay away from, at least for long-term exposure, are the south-eastern regions, the most contaminated being the very south-eastern corner of the country. The city of Homel and south of Mahileu were heavily exposed. See the boxed text on Chornobyl under Health in the Ukraine Facts for the Visitor chapter.

USEFUL ORGANISATIONS

The dynamic independent youth organisation called Next Stop – New Life, based in Minsk (☎ 017-221 27 22, fax 221 81 79, nextstop@user.unibel.by), organises festivals and youth exchanges, cultural events and ecological summer camps. Its address is Fizkulturnaja 26a.

DANGERS & ANNOYANCES

Crime levels in Belarus, though still far below those of Western countries, are on the rise. As a foreigner you have a slightly higher chance of being targeted – don't flash your money around or put yourself in a vulnerable situation. For further information and general advice see the Dangers & Annoyances sections in the earlier Ukraine and European Russia Facts for the Visitor chapters.

BUSINESS HOURS

Most shops close for lunch for an hour in the afternoon. For the typical business hours of restaurants, banks and museums, see the Business Hours section in the Ukraine Facts for the Visitor chapter.

PUBLIC HOLIDAYS & SPECIAL EVENTS

The main public holidays, which may or may not be recognised due to any presidential whim, are:

New Year's Day
  1 January
Orthodox Christmas Day
  7 January
International Women's Day
  8 March
Catholic Easter
  March/April
Orthodox Easter
  March/April
Radunitsa
  Ninth day after Orthodox Easter
International Labour Day
  1 May
Victory Day (1945)
  9 May
Independence Day
  3 July
Dzyady (Memory Day)
  2 November
Anniversary of the October Revolution
  7 November
Catholic Christmas
  25 December

ACTIVITIES

Nature lovers should visit the Belavezhskaja Pushcha Nature Reserve, north of Brest on the western border with Poland. The largest area of ancient forest in Europe, it has substantial herds of the once nearly extinct European bison (see the Around Brest section).

If you have your own vehicle, the region known as the Blue Lakes (Blakitnye Ozera), north of the town of Narach off the Vilnius-Polatsk road, is renowned for its natural beauty and is a popular camping and hiking area. The two main Blue Lakes are Lake Bolbuk and Lake Hlublja. About 20km south-east is the country's largest lake, Lake Narach (80 sq km), which is also a popular outdoor recreational area. With thousands of small lakes and streams totalling more than 90,000km in length, fishing is obviously a national pastime.

WORK

Most foreigners working in Belarus are affiliated with either an embassy, a joint venture or a university such as the Institute of Foreign Languages at vulitsa Zakharava 21, 220662 Minsk. Transient seasonal work doesn't exist.

ACCOMMODATION

As with most of the former Soviet Union, farmers and villagers are generally generous about allowing campers to pitch a tent on their lot for an evening, although they may be downright astounded to see non-natives so far out in the countryside. Outside national parks you may camp in forests and the like, provided you don't make too much of a ruckus. For camping somewhere that is obviously private property, it's always better to inquire first and perhaps offer a token sum. Camping within cities is forbidden.

Hotels

While accommodation standards in Belarus tend to be lower than those in the West, they are still generally acceptable. Prices and brief descriptions of most hotels are given in city Places to Stay sections. Unless stated otherwise, these prices include rooms with a private bathroom (toilet and shower) – the very upper end may be payable only in US dollars. Cheaper hotels usually have triple rooms, without conveniences, that cost about half as much as singles.

For descriptions of rooms and check-in procedures see the Accommodation section in Ukraine Facts for the Visitor.

Homestays

Homestays and exchanges are catching on, and more travel agencies are organising them. Usually the host family also acts as your personal guide and a source of information. Agencies dealing with homestays, usually only in the Minsk area, include:

American-International Homestays (☎ 303-642 3088, toll-free 800-876 2048, fax 303-642 3365, www.spectravel.com/homes), PO Box 7154, Nederland, CO 80466, USA

Gateway Travel (☎ 02-9745 3333, fax 9745 3237), 48 The Boulevarde, Strathfield, NSW 2135, Australia

Host Families Association (HOFA; ☎/fax 812-275 1992, alexei@hofak.hop.stu.neva.ru, www.spb.ru/homestays), 5-25 Tavricheskaya, St Petersburg, Russia

FOOD & DRINK

State-subsidised foodstuffs, particularly meats and dairy products, as well as bread, often are rationed to prevent speculative trade in them. However, in larger cities this is easily negated by simply going to one of the several large, modern grocery stores where supplies are plentiful. Open farmers markets usually carry these goods as well.

The Belarusians love their mushrooms as much as the Ukrainians love their beets and cabbage, and mushroom-gathering is a traditional expedition in Belarus. Many main dishes utilise the fungus in one way or another. *Hribnoy sup* is a mushroom and barley soup, and *kotleta pokrestyansky* is usually a pork cutlet smothered with a mushroom sauce. *Dranniki* are potato pancakes – a most traditional Belarusian dish. *Kletsky* are dumplings stuffed with either (surprise) mushrooms, cheese or potatoes.

To drink, try Belarusian *kvas*, a popular elixir made of malt, flour, sugar, mint and fruit. *Belovezhskaja* is a bitter medicinal herbal drink.

ENTERTAINMENT

Most forms of entertainment are staged in Minsk, the cultural capital of the country. The Minsk Ballet is one of the best in Eastern Europe and shouldn't be missed. Belarusian folk choirs are popular, with a long performing tradition. For listings of cultural events and activities see the Minsk Entertainment section.

SPECTATOR SPORTS

Dinamo Minsk is Belarus' top soccer club and plays frequently, but there's no denying that ice hockey is the number one spectator sport in the country. In Olympic events, Belarus has, in the past, been a major power in the biathlon, but has slumped of late and in 1998 appointed the leader of the still-functioning KGB to head the squad. The gymnastics team, led by multiple gold-medal winner Vitaly Scherbo, has also traditionally done well.

SHOPPING

Folk art is the main source of souvenirs, which include carved wooden trinkets, ceramics and woven textiles. Unique to Belarus are wooden boxes intricately ornamented with geometric patterns composed of multicoloured pieces of straw.

Getting There & Away

Travel into Belarus is unrestricted at all main border points, provided you have a valid visa. Land travel in either direction is possible between Belarus and Russia to the east, Lithuania and Latvia to the north, Poland to the west and Ukraine to the south. All international flights arrive and depart from Minsk. For more details, see the European Russia and Ukraine Getting There & Away chapters.

AIR

Most international flights entering and departing Belarus do so at the Minsk-2 international airport, about 40km east of Minsk. A few shorter international flights arrive at the smaller Minsk-1 airport, closer to town. The airport at Brest does not handle international flights.

Belavia (belavia.hypermart.net), Belarus' national airline, has direct connections to a number of European destinations, including London ($420 return), Stockholm, Warsaw, Prague, Vienna, Berlin, Frankfurt and Rome (all twice a week). It also flies to the east coast of the USA (via Shannon, Ireland), Delhi (via Tashkent) and Beijing (all once a week). Belavia also offers daily flights to Kyiv and Moscow ($250 return), and weekly flights to a number of other cities in Russia. Belavia has an office in Minsk at vulitsa Njamiha 14 (☎ 017-229 28 38). In London, you can reach it on ☎ 020-7393 1201; in Moscow on ☎ 095-923 1084; and in Berlin on ☎ 30-2023 2025.

A number of other airlines service Minsk. Airline offices in the capital include:

Austrian Airlines (☎ 017-276 89 70)
praspekt Masherava 19
Estonian Air (☎ 017-234 23 76)
vulitsa Maxima Bogdanovicha 11
LOT Polish Airlines (☎ 017-226 66 28)
praspekt Masherava 7
Lufthansa Airlines (☎ 017-284 71 30)
praspekt Francyska Skaryny 56
Transaero (☎ 017-226 91 02)
praspekt Masherava 11

Warning

The information in this chapter is particularly vulnerable to change: international travel prices are volatile, routes are introduced and cancelled, schedules change, special deals come and go, and rules and visa requirements are amended. Airlines and governments seem to take a perverse pleasure in making price structures and regulations as complicated as possible. You should check directly with the airline or a travel agent to make sure you understand how a fare (and ticket you may buy) works. In addition, the travel industry is highly competitive and there are many lurks and perks. The upshot of this is that you should get opinions, quotes and advice from as many airlines and travel agents as possible before you part with your cash. The details given in this chapter should be regarded as pointers and are not a substitute for your own careful, up-to-date research.

LAND

Border Crossings

All major land border crossings into Belarus are unrestricted provided you have a proper visa. Long queues are not uncommon. The most frequently used bus crossings are those on the quick four hour trip between Vilnius and Minsk, and the seven hour trip between Minsk and Bialystok in Poland. Buses stop at the border for customs and passport controls.

If you're driving your own vehicle, there are about 10 main road routes into Belarus through border stations. To avoid possible complications, drivers should enter by one of these official routes. For information on driving permits, insurance and other requirements, see Ukraine Getting There & Away. Roads in Belarus are predictably bad, but main highways are passable. Fuel is available on the outskirts of most major cities but may be difficult to find elsewhere.

International trains cross into/out of Belarus at more than 10 crossing points and from five different countries.

To/From Latvia

The main road and rail crossing lies between Polatsk and Daugavpils (four to five hours) along the Dzvina River valley, which is also used by some Kaliningrad-Moscow trains.

To/From Lithuania

There are two train lines converging on Vilnius from Belarus. The busiest is the Minsk-Vilnius line (four to five hours, several trains daily) which passes through Maladzechna. The Warsaw-Vilnius direct line passes through Hrodna. A few electric trains also run between Hrodna and Druskininkai, just inside the Lithuanian border.

The only road crossing foreigners are allowed to use is on the Minsk-Vilnius road.

To/From Poland

The main train route into Belarus from Poland is the Brest crossing; the Polish border station is the town of Terespol. Dozens of trains pull through each day, including the well used Warsaw-Minsk-Moscow route. For advice on taking the train from Brest to Warsaw, see the Brest Getting There & Away section.

The other rail and road crossing is between Hrodna and Bialystok, the same crossing used by some of the St Petersburg-Vilnius-Warsaw trains (road 18 in Poland). The Polish border station is at Kuznica Bialostocka. Two buses a day run between Minsk and Bialystok (seven hours).

To/From Russia

The main northern rail and road crossing from Minsk to St Petersburg (via Vitsebsk) is the Belarusian border town of Ezjaryshcha and the Russian town of Lobok. The train and main road between Minsk and Moscow cross the border between Orsha (Belarus) and Smolensk (Russia), near the Russian town of Krasnoe. Train and road traffic between Smolensk and Vitsebsk crosses the border just to the north near the Russian town of Rudnya and the Belarusian town of Lezna. Train and road traffic between Homel and Moscow crosses the border 45km east of Homel, passing through the towns of Bryansk or Orel in Russia.

To/From Ukraine

For details on major road and rail crossings between Belarus and Ukraine, see the Ukraine Getting There & Away chapter.

ORGANISED TOURS

Very few travel agencies specialise in trips to Belarus, but there are a number of agencies which handle travel to the former USSR. Several of the agencies mentioned in the Ukraine and European Russia Getting There & Away chapters can also make arrangements for Belarus. Add to the list Belintourist (☎ 017-226 98 40, fax 223 11 43, www.belarustourist.minsk.by), praspekt Masherava 19, Minsk 220078, Belarus.

Getting Around

Travel within Belarus, although not always easy, is completely unrestricted. The country is linked by a system of train lines, bus routes and roads, and the cities themselves are navigable by trolleybus, tram, city bus and, in Minsk, a metro. Local transport can often be crowded, grungy, slow and uncomfortable.

AIR

Minsk and Brest can handle domestic as well as international flights, though only the Minsk airports are operating regularly. Contact the Minsk office of the Belarusian national airline, Belavia (☎ 017-229 28 38), vulitsa Njamiha 14, for the current status of domestic flights in Belarus.

TRAIN

Trains between major cities are moderately frequent and relatively cheap. For listings of journey durations see the Getting There & Away sections for each city concerned. A typical train ticket between Minsk and Polatsk (seven to eight hours) or Minsk and Brest (four to six hours) on a 2nd class sleeper *(kupe)* costs around $1 to $2. Local electric trains are even cheaper, but much slower. Train stations are called *zhelznadarazhniy* or *vokzal* (station). All trains to and from Minsk run on Minsk time.

The train system in Belarus is identical to that of Ukraine and Russia (see the European Russia and Ukraine Getting Around chapters). The only difference is that in Belarusian, fast trains are called *khutki*, odd dates are called *nyachot* and even dates *chot*.

BUS

Using the bus system in Belarus is similar to Ukraine and Russia (see the Ukraine Getting Around chapter). Buses are often the better option for travellers on most routes, due to more convenient departure times and frequencies. Information on the duration and frequency of services to specific destinations is given in the Getting There & Away sections for each city concerned. A bus journey from Minsk to Polatsk (five hours) will cost about $1.50.

CAR & MOTORCYCLE

With spare parts rare, road conditions rugged and getting lost inevitable, driving or riding in Belarus is undeniably problematic, but is always an adventure and the best way to really see the country. Make sure you know a bit about general mechanics before setting off, and don't take a shiny, new car and expect it to stay that way; the possibility of getting carjacked by bandits on the lookout for Western cars being imported to Russia is another strike against driving anything flashy. Also be aware that truckers sometimes drive at night without headlights.

The E30 (M1) highway, dissecting the country, is the major route between Warsaw and Moscow. It's in relatively good shape, but petrol stations are still few and far between.

For more information on road conditions, rules and regulations, fuel, repairs and motorbikes, see the Getting Around chapters for Ukraine and European Russia. The road police are unforgiving, so be sure to obey all legal limits and have all the necessary documents handy.

Road Rules

You will be instructed by signs to slow down when approaching GAI (road police) stations, and not doing so is a sure-fire way to get a substantial fine. You may see GAI signs in Russian (ГАЙ) or in Belarusian (ДАЙ).

Rental

Cars can be rented in Belarus with or without a driver – but it may be cheaper to bargain with a taxi driver if you just want to go to one destination and back for a day trip. Prices for car rental range from $12 to $15 an hour or $50 to $300 a day depending on the type of car and whether or not you have a driver. Sometimes the charge is by the kilometre, sometimes by the hour, sometimes by the day.

See the Minsk Getting There & Away section for details of some car rental agencies.

HITCHING

Hitching is never entirely safe in any country in the world, and Lonely Planet doesn't recommend it. Nevertheless, it is a very common method of getting around in Belarus, especially for students (see European Russia Getting Around). Travellers who decide to hitch should understand that they are taking a potentially serious risk. Avoid hitching at night or alone. Women should exercise extreme caution.

LOCAL TRANSPORT

Local transport in Minsk is reasonably efficient, in Brest below average, and in other cities outright pathetic. In any event it will be quite crowded.

Tickets *(kvitok* or *bilet)* are very cheap. You can buy them at most kiosks around bus stops. Plastic metro tokens *(zhetony)* are sold in Minsk's metro stations. Minsk sells monthly passes ($2) during the first week of every month for all modes of transport. There are ticket inspectors but the fine for fare evasion is very small.

An A sign indicates a bus stop, T indicates a tram stop, Tp a trolleybus stop, and M a metro station.

ORGANISED TOURS

Once you're in the country and you wish to have a tour or excursion arranged for you, contact Belintourist (☎ 017-226 98 40, fax 223 11 43, www.belarustourist.minsk.by) at praspekt Masherava 19, Minsk.

Minsk
Мінск

☎ 017 • pop 1.7 million

In a land of war memorials, Minsk is the greatest of all testimonies to the horrors of WWII. It's estimated that half the city's people died in WWII, including almost the entire population of 50,000 Jews. (This was one of the handful of towns where Tsar Nicholas II had ordered Jews to congregate in 1835.) Virtually every building here has been erected since 1944, when Minsk's recapture by the Soviet army left barely a stone standing.

Minsk is probably the single best example of pure Soviet planning on a grand scale, as the masters in Moscow were given a blank slate after the war. The excess of monumental classicism was supposed to give the impression of worker utopia, but in fact offers little more than grey dreariness. The uniformity of the facades is softened only by a few pleasant parks and a decidedly mediocre re-creation of the 17th to 18th century city centre. The city's 930th anniversary was celebrated with gusto in 1997 and much public money went into a fresh coat of paint for the buildings, making the city appear a little brighter.

Over the past 50 years Minsk has watched its population triple with the pouring in of industry. Before independence, Minsk was the industrial powerhouse of the western USSR – a steel and concrete giant towering unexpectedly out of the endless plains. It has an undeniable pride in having survived innumerable disasters – coming back from the dead not just after WWII but after frequent destruction by fire throughout the centuries, sacking by Crimean Tatars in 1505, ruin by the French in 1812, and damage by the Germans in 1918 and by the Poles in 1919-20.

Although Minsk is the nominal capital of the Commonwealth of Independent States (CIS), a decision made in the hope of turning the city into a 'Brussels of the East', it is little more than a figurehead. It has developed something of a bustling, cosmopolitan atmosphere, but the wide, busy streets and imposingly ugly style of architecture offer visitors little to admire.

HIGHLIGHTS

- Reflecting upon the scope of destruction suffered here in WWII at the Museum of the Great Patriotic War
- Taking in top-quality opera or ballet for bargain prices
- Zipping into the countryside to see the impressive castle at Mir
- Filling up on tasty pizzas at Patio Pizza, one of the few bastions of Western civilisation in the city

ORIENTATION

The city of Minsk stretches about 15km from north to south and east to west, the Brest-Moscow highway crossing it from south-west to north-east. The highway is called praspekt Francyska Skaryny in the centre, and the main focus is the 2.5km stretch between ploshcha Nezalezhnastsi and ploshcha Peramohi.

Vulitsa Lenina, 750m north-east of ploshcha Nezalezhnastsi, is one of the main streets intersecting praspekt Francyska Skaryny. Just one block to the north, Lenina becomes praspekt Masherava, where you'll find the Belintourist office. Both the main train and bus stations are two blocks south-east of ploshcha Nezalezhnastsi, with the metro station (of the same name) on the spot. There's a big ring road *(koltsevaja doroha)* that runs around the city perimeter.

Maps

If you're planning a longer stay in Minsk, spend $3 on the Kvadro-Graf map called *Ulitsi Minska*, with detail down to every number on every structure of the entire city. It's available at most kiosks around the bus and train stations.

INFORMATION

Tourist Offices

There are no tourist information offices in the formal sense anywhere in Belarus, but in Minsk there are a few places which may be willing to provide information and sell services; see Travel Agencies later in this section for details.

Money

There are exchange offices in every hotel, in most big shops, lining major streets and around the bus and train stations. The one in Hotel Jubileynaja lobby exchanges travellers cheques and makes cash advances on major credit cards; it's open 24 hours. The exchange office in Hotel Kastrychnitskaja (called Hotel Oktjabrskaja in Russian) also makes cash advances and will deal with travellers cheques.

Along praspekt Francyska Skaryny you'll find a bevy of hard-currency exchange kiosks. At No 14 there is also a Belvneshekonombank ATM; a Belarus Bank ATM is across from the train station. Both were out of foreign currency cash at time of print. Ask at your hotel if any of the machines are working.

Post & Communications

Minsk's central post office *(pashtamt)* is at the eastern end of ploshcha Nezalezhnastsi at praspekt Francyska Skaryny 10. It's open from 8 am to 8 pm Monday to Saturday, 10 am to 5 pm on Sunday. It is worth visiting if only for the impressive neo-baroque domed interior. For express delivery, use the state-run Express Mail Service (☎ 227 85 12) here or couriers DHL (☎ 223 75 50), TNT (☎ 234 42 07) or UPS (☎ 259 18 11), who have offices in a few hotels around town.

The central telegraph office *(tsentralny telegraf)*, also at praspekt Francyska Skaryny 10, is open from 7 am to 11 pm daily. You can make international calls here and even send text-only email, for a tiny fee, if you bring in your own text files on floppy disk. For more information on making international calls, see the Post & Communications section in the Belarus Facts for the Visitor chapter.

Aside from email services at the central telegraph office, only one true cybercafe (☎ 232 85 30) exists in Minsk. It's in the back room of a regular cafe at vulitsa Surganova 47/5, and offers three computers with online access for $0.50 per hour (open from 3 to 11 pm). The post office at vulitsa Kujbysheva 75 offers one fairly modern computer for Web surfing.

Travel Agencies

The main travel agency, Belintourist (☎ 226 98 40, ☎ 226 90 56, ☎ 226 95 01, fax 223 11 43, www.belarustourist.minsk.by) is next door to Hotel Jubileynaja at praspekt Masherava 19. The helpful staff can arrange city or national tours for groups or simply book tickets; a few speak English. It is open from 8 am to 8 pm daily.

Smok (☎ 228 69 27, fax 210 13 62), at praspekt Francyska Skaryny 43, and Merlintour (☎ 223 51 25, fax 268 38 26), at praspekt Masherava 5, are also quite amenable places.

Bookshops

The two main bookshops are Tsentralnaja Kniharnya Mahazin at praspekt Francyska Skaryny 19, and Svetoch at praspekt Masherava 11 – both are good for maps and full-colour books on Belarusian cooking, but have only technical computer manuals in English. For recreational reading, try Lexis (☎ 233 15 12) at vulitsa Zakharava 21, near the British Council.

Cultural Centres

The following are good places to catch up on current events, swap stories with expats or just get your hands on a good book.

British Council (☎ 236 79 53), in the Institute of Foreign Languages, vulitsa Zakharava 21. Open from 11 am to 5 pm Tuesday, Thursday, Friday and Saturday, 2 to 7 pm Wednesday (closed Sunday and Monday).

United States Information Service (USIS; ☎ 217 88 29), Kaliningrasky pereulok 18B. Open from 2 to 5 pm Monday to Friday.

Goethe Institute (☎ 236 34 33), vulitsa Frunze 5. Open from 9 am to 6 pm Monday to Thursday and 8 am to 4.30 pm Friday.

Laundry

As in Russia and Ukraine, there are no laundry facilities. Upmarket hotels may provide a laundry service.

Toilets

Public toilets – when you can find them – are better left unfound. Your best bets are large hotels, restaurants and McDonald's.

Left Luggage

There are lockers at the bus station and a left-luggage desk at the train station.

Medical Services

Medical service is, predictably, well behind Western Europe and in some cases behind other parts of the CIS. No reliable, Western-run clinics operate, but the EcoMedservices (☎ 220 45 81) at vulitsa Tolstoho 4 is open around the clock and comes the closest. Or try the Medical Centre (☎ 220 04 56) inside Hotel Minsk. Also contact your embassy to see who they recommend.

Emergency

Emergency contact numbers are: fire ☎ 01, police ☎ 02, ambulance ☎ 03 and gas ☎ 04.

Dangers & Annoyances

Rallies and protests can be a concern for visitors to Minsk. Opposition demonstrations, held fairly frequently, often end in several arrests and should therefore be avoided. If caught up in one, act confused, uninterested, passive and get out as soon as possible. Speaking English is no guarantee, but it should increase your chances of not being overly hassled.

For better or worse, Minsk has a reputation as the most heavily policed city in the world. You will encounter little street crime and the danger level is low, but you will be quite eagerly fined for jaywalking.

WALKING TOUR

Minsk's main street, praspekt Francyska Skaryny (formerly Leninsky prospekt), was renamed after Skaryny, the national hero who, in the 16th century, was the first printer to utilise the printing press in the Old Slavonic and Belarusian languages. Today the thoroughfare is huge (it tripled in width when it was rebuilt after WWII) and hectic. Trolleybus Nos 1, 2 and 18 ply it and there are metro stations at either end – Ploshcha Nezalezhnastsi and Ploshcha Peramohi, with the Kupalawskaja/Kastrychnitskaja metro station interchange halfway down.

The 500m-long **ploshcha Nezalezhnastsi** (Independence Square; called ploshchad Nezavisimosti in Russian) situated at the south-western end of praspekt Francyska Skaryny is dominated by the Belarusian government building (behind the Lenin statue) on its northern side, and the equally proletarian Belarusian State University on the south side.

Breaking the theme of Soviet classicism that dominates ploshcha Nezalezhnastsi is the red-brick **Polish Catholic Church of St Simon** (1910), next to the Belarusian government building. Its tall, gabled bell tower and attractive detailing are reminiscent of many brick churches in the former Teutonic

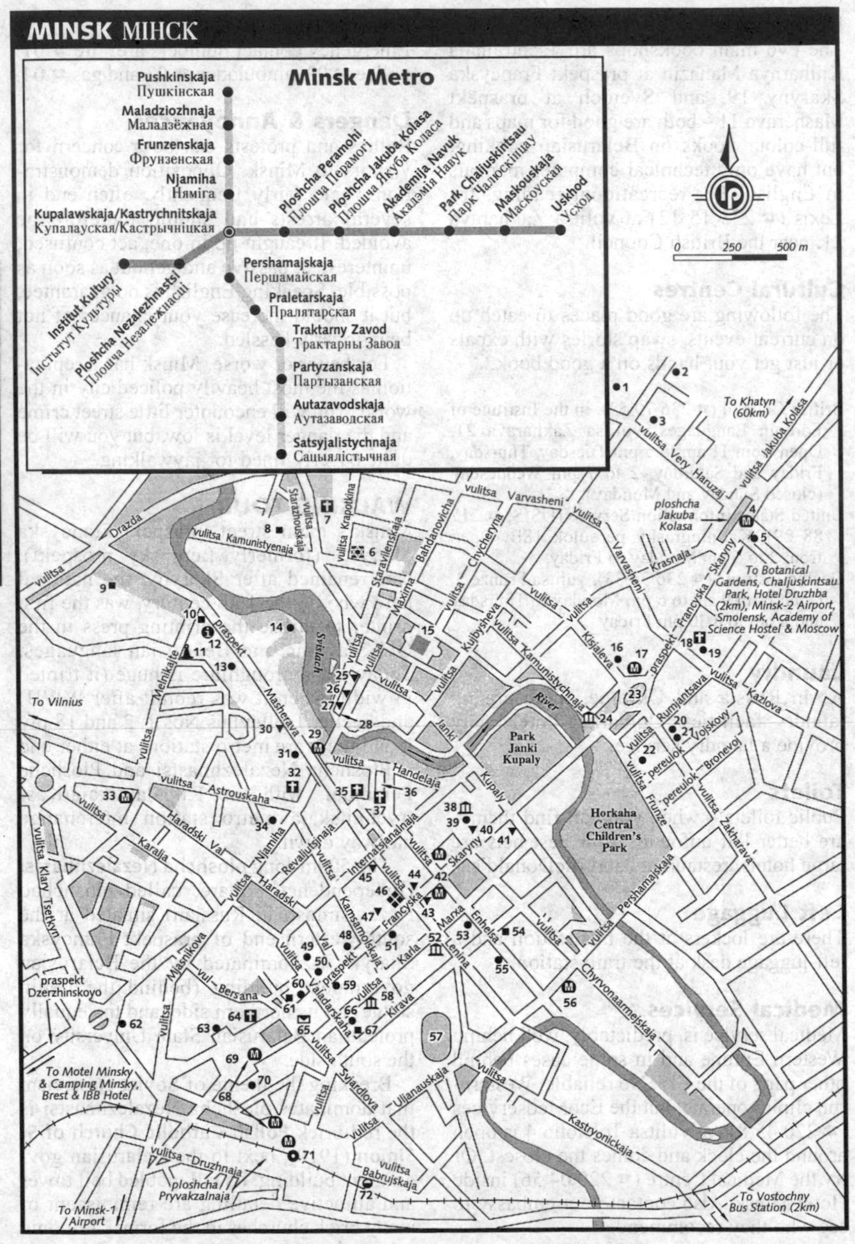
MINSK МІНСК
Minsk Metro
Pushkinskaja
Пушкінская
Maladziozhnaja
Маладзёжная
Frunzenskaja
Фрунзенская
Njamiha
Няміга
Kupalawskaja/Kastrychnitskaja
Купалаўская/Кастрычніцкая
Pershamajskaja
Першамайская
Pralетarskaja
Пралятарская
Traktarny Zavod
Трактарны Завод
Partyzanskaja
Партызанская
Autazavodskaja
Аутазаводская
Satsyjalistychnaja
Сацыялістычная
Institut Kultury
Інстытут Культуры
Ploshcha Nezalezhnastsi
Плошча Незалежнасці
Ploshcha Peramohi
Плошча Перамогі
Ploshcha Jakuba Kolasa
Плошча Якуба Коласа
Akademija Navuk
Акадэмія Навук
Park Chaljuskintsau
Парк Чалюскінцаў
Maskouskaja
Маскоўская
Uskhod
Усход
0
250
500 m
To Khatyn (60km)
To Botanical Gardens, Chaljuskintsau Park, Hotel Druzhba (2km), Minsk-2 Airport, Smolensk, Academy of Science Hostel & Moscow
To Vilnius
To Motel Minsky & Camping Minsky, Brest & IBB Hotel
To Minsk-1 Airport
To Vostochny Bus Station (2km)
ploshcha Jakuba Kolasa
ploshcha Pryvakzalnaja
Park Janki Kupaly
Horkaha Central Children's Park
Svislach
River
vulitsa Very Haruzaj
vulitsa Jakuba Kolasa
vulitsa Varvasheni
Krasnaja
praspekt Francyska Skaryny
Kisjaleva
vulitsa Kazlova
vulitsa Rumjantsava
pereulok Vojskovy
pereulok Bronevoi
vulitsa Frunze
vulitsa Zakharava
vulitsa Pershamajskaja
vulitsa Chyrvonaarmejskaja
vulitsa Kastryonickaja
vulitsa Kamunistychnaja
vulitsa Kulbysheva
vulitsa Chycheryna
Maxima Bahdanovicha
vulitsa Staravilenskaja
vulitsa Krapotkina
vulitsa Starazhouskaja
vulitsa Kamunistyenaja
Drazda
vulitsa
Melnikaite
praspekt Masherava
Janki Kupaly
vulitsa Handelaja
vulitsa Astrouskaha
Haradski Val
Karalja
vulitsa Klary Tsetkyn
vulitsa Njamiha
Revaljutsijnaja
Internatsianalnaja
Haradski
Val
Kamsamolskaja
Francyska
Skaryny
Karla Marxa
Enhelsa
Lenina
Kirava
praspekt Dzerzhinskoyo
vulitsa Mjasnikova
vul Bersana
Valadarskaha
vulitsa Sviardlova
Uljanauskaja
vulitsa Druzhnaja
vulitsa Babrujskaja
MINSK

MINSK МІНСК

PLACES TO STAY

8 Hotel Belarus
Гасцініца Беларусь
9 Hotel Planeta
Гасцініца Планета
10 Hotel Jubileynaya
Гасцініца Юбілейная
54 Hotel Kastrychnitskaja
Гасцініца Кастрычніцкая
61 Hotel Minsk
Гасцініца Мінск
67 Hotel Svislach
Гасцініца Свіслач

PLACES TO EAT

25 Kitaiskoye Pradmestsye
Китайское Прадмесце
26 Trajetskaje Pradmestsye
Троіцкае прадмесце
27 Karchma Trajetskaja
Карчма Троіцкая
30 Tractor
Трактор
40 Zio Pepe; Art Café
Зио Пэпэ
41 Kafe Uzbekistan
Кафэ Узбекістан
43 Patio Pizza; El Rincon Espanol
Патио Пицца/Испанский Куток
44 Capriccio
Капрычча
45 Restaran Krinytsa
Рэстаран Крыніца
47 Bar/Restaran Sem Pjatnits
Бар-рэстаран Сем пятніц

OTHER

1 Reactor
Реактор
2 Aquarium
Аквариум
3 Kamarowski Rynok
Камароўскі рынак
5 Belarusian State Philharmonia
Беларуская Дзяржаўная філармонія
6 Synagogue
Синагога
7 St Mary Magdeline Church
Царква св. Марыі Магдалены
11 Jewish Ghetto Monument
12 Belintourist Office
Кантора Белінтурыст
13 Kinateatr Maskva; Paradise Club; Bierhaus
Кінатэатр Масква; Парадиз
14 Sports Palace
Палац Сиорта
15 National Academic Opera & Ballet Theatre
Дзяржаўны акадэмічны вялікі тэатр оперы і балета
16 Former Residence of Lee Harvey Oswald
18 St Roha Church
Царква св. Роха
19 Art Palace
Палац мастацтва
20 Institute of Foreign Languages & British Council
Інстытут замежных моў і консулат Вялікабрытаніі
21 Lexis
Лексіс
22 Goethe Institute
23 Ploshcha Peramohi & Victory Obelisk
Плошча Перамогі і манумент Перамогі
24 Museum of the First Congress of the Russian Social Democratic Workers' Party
Дом-музей 1 з'езда Расійскай сацыял-дэмакратычнай партыі
28 Restored Area
Рэстаўрыраваная зона
31 Svetoch
Светох
32 SS Peter & Paul Church
Петрапаўлаўская царква
34 Rakovsky Brovar
Ракоускрий Бровар
35 Cathedral of St Dukhawski
Святадухаўскі царква
36 Ploshcha Svabody
Плошча Свабоды
37 Bernardine Church
Бернардзінская царква
38 Museum of the Great Patriotic War
Музей гісторыі Вялікай Айчыннай вайны
39 Trade Unions' Culture Palace
Палац культуры прафсаюзаў
46 GUM Department Store
Дзяржаўны універсальны магазін
48 KGB Building
Будынак КДБ
49 Russian Drama Theatre
Рускі драматычны тэатр
50 Tsentralnaja Knihamya Mahazin
Централное Кнігарня Магазин
51 Train Ticket Office
Чыгуначныя білетныя касы
52 Belarusian State Art Museum
Дзяржаўны мастацкі музей Беларусі
53 Janka Kupala Belarusian National Theatre
55 State Puppet Theatre
57 Dinamo Stadium
Стадыён Дынама
58 Belarus National Museum of History & Culture
Беларускі Дзяржаўны краязнаўчы музей
59 Mastatsky Salon
Мастацкі Салон
60 Theatre Ticket Office
Тэатральная каса
62 State Theatre of Musical Comedy
Тэатр музычнай камедыі
63 Belarusian Government Building
Дом ураду Беларусі
64 Polish Catholic Church of St Simon
Касцёл Сымона і Елены
65 Central Post & Telegraph Office
Главпаштамт
66 Suveniry
Крама Сувеніры
69 Ploshcha Nezalezhnastsi
Плошча Незалежнасці
70 Belarusian State University
Беларускі дзяржаўны універсітэт
71 Main Train Station
Чыгуначны вакзал і мытня
72 Bus Station
Аўтобусны вакзал

METRO STATIONS

4 Ploshcha Jakuba Kolasa
Плошча Якуба Коласа
17 Ploshcha Peramohi
Плошча Перамогі
29 Njamiha
Няміга
33 Frunzenskaja
Фрунзенская
42 Kupalawskaja/Kastrychnitskaja
Купалауская/Кастрычніцкая
56 Pershamajskaja
Першамайская
68 Ploshcha Nezalezhnastsi
Плошча Незалежнасці

north of Poland. It was used as a cinema in the Soviet era, and it became a key opposition meeting place in the last years of the USSR.

Between ploshcha Nezalezhnastsi and vulitsa Lenina are many of Minsk's main shops and cafes, including the large GUM department store at No 21. An entire block at No 17 is occupied by a yellow neoclassical building with an ominous, temple-like Corinthian portal – the headquarters of the new KGB. On the opposite side of the street is a long narrow park with a bust of Felix Dzerzhynsky, the founder of the KGB's predecessor, the Cheka, and a native of Belarus.

After praspekt Francyska Skaryny crosses the Svislach River it reaches **ploshcha Peramohi** (Victory Square; called ploshchad Pobedy in Russian), a busy intersection with a tall victory obelisk – the former symbol of Soviet Minsk – rising from its centre beside the eternal flame.

Just north, at vulitsa Kisjaleva 2, is the apartment building where Lee Harvey Oswald – the future alleged assassin of US President John F Kennedy – lived for a few years in his early 20s.

OLD TOWN

The congested overpass that now carries vulitsa Lenina over vulitsa Njamiha near the Njamiha metro station was the site of Minsk's marketplace in the 12th century, but there's no trace left today. However, in late May 1999 the metro entrance was the site of a brutal stampede in which 52 people died. The tragedy occurred when hundreds of young people ran into the pedestrian tunnel to escape a sudden thunderstorm at a beer festival.

Ploshcha Svabody to the south-east became the new city centre in the 16th century. The baroque, twin-towered Orthodox **Cathedral of St Dukhawski** off the northern end of the square stands defiantly on a small hill overlooking its rather bleak surroundings. It was once part of a Polish Bernardine convent founded in the 17th century along with the former **Bernardine Church** next door, which now houses city archives. The former monastery buildings farther to the right (east) have been restored and now house a music academy affiliated with the classical-looking conservatory building at the far south-western end of ploshcha Svabody.

Across the vulitsa Lenina overpass sits the attractively restored 17th century **SS Peter & Paul Church**, the city's oldest church, dwarfed by the imposing concrete structures that surround it.

A small area of housing on the east bank of the Svislach River, immediately north of vulitsa Maxima Bahdanovicha, has been rather halfheartedly rebuilt in 17th to 18th century style to make a small-scale, low-rise contrast with the rest of the city. There are a few cafes, bars, restaurants and the odd craft/gift shop to tempt you there for a lazy hour or two. Two blocks north-east is the **National Academic Opera & Ballet Theatre** set in a leafy park.

The nicest small church you'll find in the city is about 500m north of here near Hotel Belarus. The attractive little **St Mary Magdeline Church** and chapel was built in 1847 in the ancient Orthodox style, with a pointed octagonal bell tower over the entrance and a single sweeping dome over the cruciform plan.

JEWISH MINSK

Behind Hotel Jubileynaja on vulitsa Zaslavskaja, a small obelisk marks the site of the city's WWII Jewish ghetto, where in the summer of 1941 tens of thousands of the city's once vibrant community were murdered and buried. In 1897, some 56% of Minsk was Jewish, although that level dropped to about 40% during the interwar Soviet period, when Jewish culture was heavily persecuted.

Today the community is tiny and continues to shrink, as most Jews choose to emigrate rather than live in a society that by and large turns a blind eye to anti-Semitism. The **synagogue** at vulitsa Krapotkina 22 is one of the few active ones left in the country. For more information, contact the Israeli Cultural Centre (☎ 230 18 74) at vulitsa Uralskaja 3.

Jewish Belarus

Belarus' Jewish community dates from the 14th century, when Brest and Hrodna both grew as cultural centres, and when Jews were encouraged to settle in these areas by the liberal policies of the Lithuanian rulers. After control switched to Russia in the late 18th century, Belarus was part of the Pale of Settlement where Jews were allowed to live; however, a series of brutal pogroms in 1881 and uncontained anti-Semitism thereafter caused many to flee west.

Between the wars, Jews in the western Polish half of Belarus were oppressed and most lived in poverty. In the east, the Soviet regime crushed Jewish culture, although some individuals rose to prominence in the Communist Party.

At the beginning of WWII, there were some 670,000 Jews in western Belarus; the majority were killed by the invading Nazis, rounded up into some 164 ghettos across the country and shot, buried in pits where they fell. By 1959, only some 150,000 Jews were left in the country; where they had made up more than half the population in Minsk, Hrodna and Brest, they now accounted for no more than 5%.

But not all the tales are tragic. In the forests of western Belarus, the war's largest group of armed Jewish partisans rescued others and fought the Nazi forces under the leadership of a peasant, Tuvia Bielski, and his brothers. The group had grown to 1200 members by the time Soviet forces retook the region in 1944. Bielski later left for the USA, where he died in 1987.

MUSEUMS & ART GALLERIES

The museums listed here charge a small admission price (usually about $0.50).

Belarus National Museum of History & Culture

This museum, vulitsa Karla Marxa 12, takes you on a journey into the turbulent history of the nation. It begins with a replica of the printing press used by national hero Francyska Skaryny and ends on the top floor, usually reserved for ethnographic displays or period installations. It is open from 11 am to 7 pm daily except Wednesday.

Belarusian State Art Museum

Housed behind a formal, grey, classical facade at vulitsa Lenina 20, this museum has 17th to 20th century paintings, including some by Repin, Levitan and Vrubel, as well as an impressive collection of Belarusian art. The *Bulgarian Martyrs* by Makovsky is brilliant and moving. The museum is open from 11 am to 7 pm daily except Tuesday.

Museum of the Great Patriotic War

This sobering museum (Great Patriotic War is the Soviet name for WWII) is at praspekt Francyska Skaryny 25A, recessed off the street behind the classical-style Trade Unions' Culture Palace. The 28 rooms graphically display the horrors of WWII and go a long way towards explaining Belarus' apparent obsession with the Great Patriotic War, which claimed the life of one in four Belarusians. Most grisly are the POW displays and photos of partisans being executed. The museum also graphically depicts the Nazi atrocities against Jews during the war, giving special attention to the Maly Trostenets concentration camp where over 100,000 Jews from Minsk and surrounding cities were murdered.

The museum is open from 11 am to 6 pm daily except Monday.

Museum of the First Congress of the Russian Social Democratic Workers' Party

Just shy of ploshcha Peramohi on the far side of the river is a replica of the small green wooden house where the Russian Social Democratic Workers' Party – Russia's original Marxist party – held its illegal founding congress in 1898. The house bears the sign '133 Ul. Zakharevskaja' – the former address of this location which, in those days, was on the edge of the city. Today its address is praspekt Francyska Skaryny 31a and there is a small museum inside (open from 10 am to 5 pm daily except Monday).

PARKS & GARDENS

The **Park Janki Kupaly** is a pleasant stretch of greenery bordered on two sides by the snaking Svislach River, and has rowing boats for rent on the east side during the summer. In the centre is a small museum dedicated to the eponymous poet.

About 3km north-east of ploshcha Peramohi are two pleasant parks – the **Botanical Garden**, open Wednesday to Sunday, and the woodland **Chaljuskintsau Park**, both near the Park Chaljuskintsau metro station.

PLACES TO STAY

Hotels in Minsk follow a predictable mould – all rooms are Soviet-era, in varying states of disguise. The exception to this rule is the German-Belarusian IBB Hotel.

Budget travellers face a thin choice, as most hotels in the centre charge at least $50/65 a night for single/double rooms, while cheaper student places are a fair distance from town and decidedly dicey. The latest craze in customer abuse seems to be the permanent 'no space' signs displayed to discourage irritating overnighters – to thwart this, book at least one night before you arrive.

Camping

Motel Minsky and ***Camping Minsky*** *(☎ 299 51 40)* are 17km south-west of the city centre on the Brest highway (Brestskoe shosse; E30/M1) at the 727km marker, shortly beyond the Ptich Reservoir (Vodokhranilishche Ptich), a favourite local recreation spot. The motel, a popular truck stop, is tatty with small rooms ($11/16 for a single/double) and a restaurant, and no visible pluses. The camping area, the only formal site around the city, has cabins for $3 per person and tent sites for $1 per person. The camping ground may close soon, so be sure to call first.

To get here, take one of six buses a day to the town of Dzerzhinsk – these buses stop on the highway outside the motel on the way. Alternatively, grab one of four daily electric trains bound for Plaschevo and get off at Ptich. A taxi to/from the city should cost about $5.

Hotels – Budget

For the absolute lowest in low-budget, check into ***Hotel Druzhba*** *(☎ 266 24 81, vulitsa Tolbukhina 3)*, near the Park Chaljuskintsau metro station, where spartan quad rooms with common bath go for $3.50 per person. The hotel's usual clientele tends towards the older, seedier, only-need-the-room-for-one-hour variety, so be aware of what you're getting into.

A better choice is the ***Academy of Science Hostel*** *(☎ 268 57 01, fax 268 48 71, vulitsa Surganova 7)*, but try to book ahead as it rarely has space. It is near the Akademija Navuk metro station, one stop before Park Chaljuskintsau, half a block from Hotel Druzhba.

Hotel Svislach *(☎ 220 97 83, vulitsa Kirava 13)* is tops for budget travellers, with down-at-the-corners, unapologetically Soviet-style rooms for $10 per person. It is tidy with a schizophrenic staff – one minute surly, the next servile – and ideally located two blocks south of praspekt Francyska Skaryny and three blocks north-east of the train and bus stations.

Hotels – Mid-Range

The stately ***Hotel Minsk*** *(☎ 20 01 32, praspekt Francyska Skaryny 11)*, on the far north-eastern side of ploshcha Nezalezhnastsi, has rooms only moderately nicer than the Svislach. Decent singles/doubles cost $42/64, and the helpful service bureau in the lobby will try to assist you if the hotel is full.

The two former Intourist hotels are large and modern-looking and a few hundred metres apart on praspekt Masherava, about 1.5km north of praspekt Francyska Skaryny. The lobby of ***Hotel Jubileynaja*** *(☎ 226 90 24, fax 226 91 71, praspekt Masherava 19)* could be mistaken for a Sheraton, but there's no mistaking the lower-end rooms for $55/65 – spruced-up yuk is still yuk. Better rooms cost upwards of $222. ***Hotel Planeta*** *(☎ 226 78 55, fax 226 77 80, praspekt Masherava 31)* has slightly shabbier rooms for $55/75. For both hotels, bus Nos 36 and 69 travel between Hotel Jubileynaja and the bus stop in front of vulitsa Kirava 4, a block north of the main train station. Trolleybus Nos 21, 39 and 56 leave from in front of the GUM department store (a block south-west of the Kupalawskaja/ Kastrychnitskaja metro station) and run straight along vulitsa Lenina and praspekt Masherava to both hotels.

Hotels – Top End

Slightly better than its cousins, the towering 23 storey ***Hotel Belarus*** *(☎ 239 17 05, fax 239 12 33, belarus@hotel.minsk.by, vulitsa Starazhouskaja 15)*, on the far side of the river, has one recently renovated floor with all the trimmings. Sadly, all rooms sport a hideous orange, faux-baroque decor. Single/ double rooms here range from $80/90 up to $170/190.

Perhaps the nicest place in central Minsk is ***Hotel Kastrychnitskaja*** *(☎ 222 32 89, fax 227 33 14, vulitsa Enhelsa 13)*, recessed off the street on the corner of vulitsa Kirava, behind the President's Office. It's known as ***Hotel Oktjabrskaja*** in Russian. A favourite of visiting diplomats, rooms cost $64/75, payable in hard currency or by credit card. The Kupalawskaja/Kastrychnitskaja metro station is two blocks north-west.

The ***IBB Hotel*** *(☎ 270 39 94, fax 270 39 95, praspekt Gazety Pravda 11)* wins the grand prize as the city's sole greenfield hotel – a business-level, Western-standard oasis in the south-western corner of the city. Its location (just off the praspekt Dzerzhinskovo highway to Brest) is a drawback, but if you're ready to spend $75/100 for a room, you can probably spring for the $1 to $2 taxi ride into the centre.

PLACES TO EAT

Pleasant dining in the capital remains a challenge but is always cheap (if nothing else). Ethnic food is the most expensive, while hearty peasant meals are on offer more and more. One note of warning: breakfast is unheard of, with the exception of some mediocre warmed-up gruel served by most hotels.

Restaurants

Belarusian For a peek at what passed for fine dining 15 years ago, make your way to the underground bar/restaurant ***Sem Pjatnits*** *(praspekt Francyska Skaryny 19)*. The cafe's name (literally 'Five Fridays') is a colloquialism for indecisiveness, which is appropriate considering the lengthy Russian-Polish menu, sporting all the best of both cuisines. Obliging service and the charm of the rumbling metro below only add to the delight; the real plus is on the bill – just $1 for caviar and *bliny* (pancakes).

The 'peasant food' trend has begun to catch up with urbanite Minskovites longing for a bit of home-cooked heritage, and a number of new restaurants are serving hearty portions of good Belarusian food. Foremost among these is ***Tractor*** *(praspekt Masherava 11)*, an early 20th century country kitchen tucked behind a row of cement blocks, open from noon to 5 am daily. The outstanding ***Rakovsky Brovar*** (see Bars & Clubs under Entertainment later in this chapter) serves similar fare in an expansive but equally rustic setting.

Mediterranean The obvious place to take shelter from post-Soviet cuisine is within the cosy walls of ***Patio Pizza*** *(praspekt Francyska Skaryny 22)*, with an all-you-can-eat fresh salad bar for $1 and large, brick-oven-cooked pollo pesto or vegetable pizzas for $3 to $6. It is a favourite with expats and an excellent place to strike up some contacts with fellow English speakers. Next door is ***El Rincon Espanol***, run by the same folks, serving fine if pricey Spanish cuisine but only open sporadically.

Farther down praspekt Francyska Skaryny, ***Zio Pepe*** at No 25 has outstanding Italian pasta and pizza in a rather claustrophobic, smoky basement.

Ethnic ***Kafe Uzbekistan*** *(vulitsa Janki Kupaly 17)*, on the corner of vulitsa Kirava, is a small and enduring cafe/restaurant serving hearty portions of spicy Central Asian food in a rather tacky and dated atmosphere. The rice and meat plov is good, but far outdone by the shashlyk at $4. Vegetarians will have slim pickings.

Chinese eateries have sprouted recently, including ***Kitaiskoye Pradmestsye*** *(vulitsa Staravilenskaja 10)* in the restored area, which is as overplush as all the rest of the Chinese restaurants in town but has authentic dishes. You may feel a pinch in your pocket, however, with a meal for two easily topping $15.

Hotel Sputnik, out of town towards the airport at vulitsa Brilevskaja 2, shelters ***Taj***, a passable Indian restaurant.

Top End ***Restoran Krinytsa*** *(vulitsa Lenina 2)* is the city's top fancy restaurant, serving a rather bland mix of pseudo-European cuisine in stuffily upscale environs. Choose the $3 to $5 businessmen's lunch, a generous *prix fixe* menu. The IBB Hotel's ***Westfalia*** is as high-class as the hotel itself.

Cafes

A number of restaurants and cafes lurk within the tiny cluster of restored buildings between the river and vulitsa Maxima Bahdanovicha. ***Karchma Trajetskaja*** (Trinity Tavern; *vulitsa Staravilenskaja 4)*, along the riverfront, has outstanding cappuccino and the best aura of any coffee spot, plus a cosy upstairs dining area. The nearby ***Trajetskaje Pradmestsye*** *(vulitsa Staravilenskaja 8)* specialises in Belarusian dishes, including *dranniki s miasom*, tasty potato pancakes with bacon.

The premier meet-and-greet cafe is ***Capriccio*** *(praspekt Francyska Skaryny 23)*, a deluxe stand-up eatery serving tasty pastries and sandwiches as well as real espresso. You have to first pay at the cashier, then give the receipt to the counter staff to receive your food or drink – a thoroughly confusing system and a legacy of Soviet rule. There's a tiny deposit for the espresso cups. Upstairs is a relatively modern grocery store, and a shvarma stand sometimes operates in the entryway.

Self-Catering

Most hotels have small refrigerators, but precious few have anything to cook on; the chambermaid may let you borrow her hotplate. The immense ***Kamarowski Rynok*** on vulitsa Very Haruzaj – one very long block north-west of the Ploshcha Jakuba Kolasa metro station – is a mini-city of market mayhem. Inside the cavernous covered hall are hundreds of neat piles of nuts, spices, breads, dried fish, meat carcasses and other produce. Outside, beneath the canopies, it repeats itself in a more chaotic fashion with a smaller selection but cheaper prices. Even if you're not shopping, it gives an excellent peek into another side of the city.

There are no Western-style supermarkets, but there are a few stores on praspekt Francyska Skaryny that are well stocked. The pick of the bunch is the one upstairs from Capriccio (see above).

ENTERTAINMENT

Bars & Clubs

Discos are widespread, but as the average Belarusian may have trouble scraping together enough roubles to get from one day to the next, you're likely to face a predictable crowd – leather jackets, short skirts, wads of cash. Many clubs are also 'offices' for a growing number of prostitutes (avoid discos at the hotels, which are filled mostly with sex workers), and you're almost guaranteed an 'erotic show' at some point near midnight.

The most popular place for a slightly younger, hipper crowd is ***Yula*** *(vulitsa Surganova 26)*, open from 9 pm to 5 am. It has a high-tech, spacious interior and is run by the popular BA radio station.

Reactor *(vulitsa Very Haruzaj 29)*, which often has live music, is very well regarded and is just north-west of the Kamarowski Rynok. One block north, ***Aquarium*** *(vulitsa Kulman 14)* maintains a reputation for the city's best live shows and a fairly relaxed environment. ***Paradise Club*** *(praspekt Masherava 13)*, inside the Kinateatr Maskva, has two floors of lights and late-night dancing.

For a more relaxed beer and chat, try ***Art Cafe*** *(praspekt Francyska Skaryny 25)*, the

MINSK

large columned building, which turns disco in the evenings but still has a studenty feel.

The best place for a Belarusian pint is ***Rakovsky Brovar*** *(vulitsa Vitsebskaja 10)* and several other locales farther out. With a variety of light and dark beer brewed on site, the Brovar has quickly become the most popular place for suds-lovers of all stripes. A few expat hold-outs still prefer ***Bierhaus*** *(praspekt Masherava 13)*, in the same building as the Paradise Club.

Classical Music, Opera & Ballet

Minsk has quite a lively cultural life and its Belarusian Ballet is one of the best companies in Eastern Europe. Ballets, along with a whole host of operas, are performed at the grand, Soviet-style ***National Academic Opera & Ballet Theatre*** *(vulitsa Paskevic 23)*, set in a park.

The ***Belarusian State Philharmonia*** *(praspekt Francyska Skaryny 50)* also has a high reputation – it has folk ensembles as well as a symphony orchestra and is based next to the Ploshcha Jakuba Kolasa metro station. To buy advance tickets or to find out what's playing, head to the ticket office *(teatralnaja kasa)* at praspekt Francyska Skaryny 13. Same-day tickets are usually available only from the theatres.

Belarusian folk song and dance shows are staged periodically and are well known for their rich traditions – check the listings at the ticket office or ask at the Belintourist office. The Belarusian Musical Autumn in the last 10 days of November is a festival of folk and classical music and dance.

Other theatres include the ***Janka Kupala Belarusian National Theatre*** *(vulitsa Enhelsa 7)*, a block from Hotel Kastrychnitskaja (Oktjabrskaja), the ***State Puppet Theatre*** *(vulitsa Enhelsa 20)*, the ***State Theatre of Musical Comedy*** *(vulitsa Mjasnikova 44)*, west of ploshcha Nezalezhnastsi, and the ***Russian Drama Theatre*** *(vulitsa Valadarskaha 5)*.

SPECTATOR SPORTS

Dinamo Minsk, Belarus' top soccer club (often appearing in European competitions), has a 55,000-capacity stadium at vulitsa Kirava 8. The Sports Palace, at praspekt Masherava 4, hosts stellar ice-hockey matches.

SHOPPING

The best gift and souvenir shop is the Suveniry next to Hotel Svislach at vulitsa Valadarskaha 23, with a good selection of wooden 'straw boxes', ceramics and textiles for cheap prices. At praspekt Francyska Skaryny 12 is the Mastatsky Salon, with a good selection of porcelain and wooden souvenirs. The bookshop at praspekt Francyska Skaryny 19 also has a few trinkets. The Art Palace at vulitsa Kazlova 4, north of the river, has a small antique kiosk upstairs, and there's a selection of ceramics for sale in the lobby of the Belarusian State Art Museum.

GETTING THERE & AWAY

Air

Most international flights use Minsk-2 airport, built in 1989 about 40km east of the city off the Moscow highway. A few shorter international flights use Minsk-1 airport, at the end of vulitsa Chkalava, about 3km south of ploshcha Nezalezhnastsi (flights to Moscow and St Petersburg use both airports). See Belarus Getting There & Away for more information on international flights to/from Minsk and the contact details of airlines serving the country.

The Belarusian national airline, Belavia, has an office (☎ 229 28 38) at vulitsa Njamiha 14. For international flight information call ☎ 225 02 31, for Minsk-2 airport information call ☎ 297 31 20.

Train

Minsk is on the main Moscow-Warsaw-Berlin line, and there are around 16 trains daily to Moscow (12 hours), one daily to Warsaw (nine to 12 hours), and three per week to Berlin (19 hours). Most Moscow trains stop at Smolensk (usually four hours).

At least two trains a day go to St Petersburg (16 hours, via Vitsebsk), four a day to Vilnius (4½ hours), two to Kaliningrad (15 hours) and one daily to Kyiv (14 hours). Other international cities served include

Lviv (14 hours, on odd days), Riga (14 hours, odd days) and Prague (25 hours, four times a week). Every other day (dropping to twice weekly in winter) there are trains to Chisinau (27 hours), Odesa (27 hours), and Simferopol (22 hours, odd days); all three pass through Kyiv.

Domestic trains include about eight a day to Brest (four to six hours), some of which continue on to Warsaw. Three trains a day go to Hrodna (eight hours), two a day to Polatsk (seven to eight hours), five a day to Homel (4½ hours), and at least three a day to Vitsebsk (seven hours), including those which continue on to St Petersburg.

Local commuter trains include about six a day to Baranavichy, south-west of Minsk, and about 20 a day to Maladzechna, to the city's north-west. Times are posted on the wall on the ground floor of the main train station; the times in red are for weekends and holidays only, those in black for every day.

Buying Tickets Domestic train tickets can be purchased with roubles, while hard currency is required for non-CIS international tickets. Tickets for the slow electric trains are easily bought from the *kasy* on the ground floor of the train station, while local long-distance and CIS international tickets are sold upstairs (but only use these upstairs windows as a last resort).

For long-distance or international tickets, your best bet is to head to the ticket office in the Belintourist office (☎ 226 90 56, fax 223 11 43) at praspekt Masherava 19 (open from 8 am to 8 pm daily). Alternatively, go directly to the international ticket office (☎ 213 17 19) at vulitsa Voronyanskoho 6, open from 9 am to 8 pm daily; when it closes a window (☎ 296 33 55) across from the station at ploshcha Pryvakzalnaja 4 is said to sell international tickets from 8 pm to 8 am.

The ticket office on praspekt Francyska Skaryny 18, between vulitsa Lenina and Kamsamolskaja, sells most long-distance and CIS tickets in a clean, orderly environment. It's open from 9 am to 8 pm weekdays, 9 am to 7 pm weekends. There's also a less hectic ticket office across the street from the train station.

Bus

Minsk has two bus stations. The central long-distance bus station (tsentralny avtovokzal; ☎ 004 or ☎ 227 78 20) is at vulitsa Babrujskaja 12, about 200m east of the train station. There are three buses a day to Bialystok in Poland (seven hours) and 10 to Hrodna (five to six hours). Three cities in Lithuania are serviced: Kaunas (5½ hours, twice a day), Klaipeda (eight hours, daily) and Vilnius (four hours, five times daily); one bus a day runs to Riga, Latvia (10½ hours). Ten buses daily service the town of Navahrudak (four to six hours) stopping at Mir (two to 2½ hours) along the way. One bus daily goes to the town of Kletsk, stopping at Njasvizh (2½ to three hours) on the way.

The Vostochny (eastern) bus station is about 3km south-east of the centre. Bus No 8 and trolleybus No 13 travel between the two stations. Daily buses leaving Vostochny bus station include those to Homel (seven hours), Pinsk (seven hours), Vitsebsk (6½ hours) and Warsaw (11 hours). Polatsk (five hours) is served twice daily. There are also eight buses daily to Mahileu/Mogilev (four hours).

Car & Motorcycle

The Brestskoe shosse, the road from Minsk to Brest (E30/M1), is one of the best in the country – an excellent dual carriageway all the way. Minsk to Smolensk has a few narrow, slow stretches, though patches of forest alleviate its tedium.

Car rental agencies in Minsk include Avis (☎ 234 79 90, fax 239 16 13) upstairs at Hotel Belarus, vulitsa Starazhouskaja 15, and Eurocar (☎ 226 90 62, fax 223 87 16) at praspekt Masherava 11. Both have offices at the Minsk-2 airport as well.

GETTING AROUND

To/From the Airport

The taxi drivers who lurk around Minsk-2 airport are vultures who all want about $20 to $25 for the 40 minute ride into the city (it should cost about $10 to $15). You can try to bargain them down or else wait for one of the hourly buses that cost $1.

Metro

Minsk has two handy metro lines, intersecting at the midpoint of praspekt Francyska Skaryny. Ploshcha Nezalezhnastsi metro station has one entrance at the train station, with that metro line following praspekt Francyska Skaryny across the city, stopping in the middle and at ploshcha Peramohi.

Note that a few metro stations may still have their old names up – ones to look out for are Ploshcha Nezalezhnastsi, which may be marked as Ploshcha Lenina; Ploshcha Peramohi, which may be marked as Ploshcha Pobedy; and Kupalawskaja, which may be marked as Oktjabrskaja.

Plastic tokens called *zhetony* can be bought downstairs at all stations from the attendant. Purchase a handful (they're very cheap) so you won't be bothered later. The metro operates from 6 am to 12.30 am.

Bus & Trolleybus

Buses and trolleybuses, operating from 5.30 am to 1 am, serve those parts of the city not covered by the metro system. Trolleybus Nos 1, 2 and 18 ply praspekt Francyska Skaryny between ploshcha Nezalezhnastsi and ploshcha Peramohi.

Around Minsk

KHATYN
ХАТЫНЬ

The hamlet of Khatyn, 60km north of Minsk, was burned to the ground with all its inhabitants in a 1943 Nazi reprisal. The site is now a memorial centred around a sculpture modelled on the only survivor, Yuzif Kaminsky. Also here are the Graveyard of Villages, commemorating 185 other Belarusian villages annihilated by the Germans; the Trees of Life (actually concrete posts) commemorating a further 433 villages that were destroyed but rebuilt; and a Memory Wall listing the Nazi concentration camps in Belarus and some of their victims.

Khatyn is about 5km east of the Minsk-Vitsebsk road. The turn-off is about 15km north of Lohoysk, opposite the village of Kazyny. There's no reliable public transport out there, but a taxi will cost between $20 and $25 for the return journey from Minsk. Organised trips through Minsk's Belintourist run during the summer and cost about $10 per person if you latch onto a big group.

Don't confuse Khatyn with the Katyn Forest near Smolensk, where the NKVD (the predecessor of the KGB) murdered thousands of 'enemies of the people' and Polish officers in the 1930s and 1940.

MIR
МІР

☎ 01770

About 85km south-west of Minsk and 8km north off the Minsk-Brest road is the small town of Mir where, overlooking a pond, sits the fine 16th century Mir Castle. Built predominantly of stone and red brick, it's a walled complex with five formidable towers surrounding a courtyard and keep. The impressive exterior detailing was intended to be aesthetic as well as defensive. Today the castle is under restoration, but one tower is already open as an archaeological museum operating from 10 am to 5 pm Wednesday to Sunday. Plans are afoot to expand this to include a hotel and restaurant.

Getting There & Away

From the central bus station in Minsk there are about 10 buses a day heading to the town of Navahrudak (Novogrudok in Russian), stopping in Mir shortly after they turn off the main highway, just over two hours into the trip. (See directions for Njasvizh for an alternative way of getting to Mir.)

NJASVIZH
НЯСВІЖ

☎ 01770

Njasvizh, 120km south-west of Minsk, is one of the oldest sites in the country and dates from the 13th century. It reached its zenith in the mid-16th century while owned by the mighty Radziwill magnates, who had the town designed and rebuilt with the most advanced system of fortification known at the time. Over the centuries, war, fire and neglect diminished the town's status and today it's a random mix of painted wooden cottages and bland housing, but with enough fine pieces of 16th century architecture scattered about to happily occupy you for a few hours.

Walk south-east (to your right) down vulitsa Savetskaja from the bus station. On your right after about five minutes, in the middle of the main square, is the 16th century **town hall**, one of the oldest of its kind surviving in the country.

Facing away from the hall, cross vulitsa Savetskaja one block to vulitsa Leninskaja and the impressive **Farny Polish Roman Catholic Church**. Large and sombre, it was built between 1584 and 1593 in early baroque style and features a splendidly proportioned facade. The building facing it is a former **printing house** where, in the late 16th century, the philosopher Simon Budny printed some controversial works in the Belarusian language. Budny's statue stands in front of the printing house.

Just beyond the Farny Church is the striking red-brick arcaded **Castle Gate Tower**. Built in the 16th century, it was part of a wall and gateway controlling the passage between the palace and the town. Beyond the Farny Church a causeway leads to the 16th century **Radziwill Palace Fortress** designed by the Italian architect Bernardoni (who was also responsible for the Farny Church). The Bolshevik army marched in and looted the palace in November 1917. Today the complex houses a sanatorium for up to 200 patients with cardiac and neurological disorders.

Places to Stay & Eat

Hotel Njasvizh *(☎ 5 53 67, vulitsa Belaruskaja 9)*, off the main square, is a friendly place with a shabby baroque quality and a sleepy restaurant. Simple, decent rooms cost $5/7 for a single/double.

On the main square is ***Kafe Teremok***, serving sweets and drinks. ***Kafe Chabarok*** *(vulitsa Leninskaja 13)*, across from the post office, serves more hearty fare.

Getting There & Away

Buses to Kletsk, about 16km south of Njasvizh, stop at Njasvizh along the way, but only once or twice a day from Minsk.

Alternatively, take one of the six daily electric trains to Baranavichy and get off at the Haradzeja stop, about two hours (12 stops) from Minsk. This station is between Mir, 15km to the north, and Njasvizh, 15km to the south. At least 15 buses a day make the 30 minute trip from Haradzeja to Njasvizh. There are also two buses daily running between Njasvizh and Mir, stopping in Haradzeja en route.

Elsewhere in Belarus
Па Беларусі

Outside Minsk, Brest and Hrodna, the rest of the country sees relatively few tourists. Most cities suffered great destruction in WWII, both architecturally and culturally, as many of the multiethnic communities were killed or driven out. Yet much still remains to entice the traveller off the beaten path. In cities such as Hrodna and Polatsk many historic vestiges remain, and many of the small villages are still lost somewhere in the 18th century. The countryside is serene with great swathes of forest, clusters of lakes and kilometres of streams, drawing many campers and hikers from the cities.

HIGHLIGHTS

- Wandering around the ruins of the Brest Fortress
- Dining in splendour on the best Indian food in the CIS at Restoran Indija in Brest
- Strolling the well preserved old town of Hrodna for a taste of Belarus long past
- Squinting through the misty darkness at centuries-old frescoes in the St Efrasinnia Monastery in Polatsk

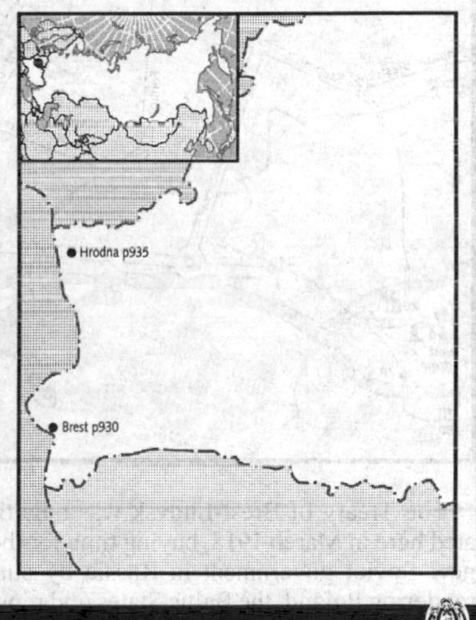

BREST
БРЭСТ

☎ 0162 • pop 350,000

Brest, located on the border with Poland, has always had a more cosmopolitan and Western feel than anywhere else in the country, Minsk included. It is on one of the busiest road and rail border points in Eastern Europe, less than 200km from Warsaw and 346km from Minsk. Although much of the once popular 'shuttle trade' – people hopping back and forth across the border to take advantage of price discrepancies – has disappeared, there is still an active hustle-and-bustle atmosphere. Brest will dazzle you with one of the true wonders of the Soviet era – Brest Fortress, a simply astounding and unrivalled example of that bizarre architectural genre, the Soviet war memorial. Those with extra time should not miss the Belavezhskaja Pushcha Nature Reserve, 60km to the north.

First mentioned in 1019 and originally known as Bereste, Brest was sacked by the Tatars in 1241 and tossed between Slavic, Lithuanian and Polish control for several decades until it finally settled under the control of the Grand Duchy of Lithuania. The Uniate Church was set up here in 1596 at the Union of Brest, forming a branch of Orthodox Christians who were faithful to Rome as a way of bridging the largely Slavic populace and the then Polish rulers. The peace was short-lived, as Russians invaded in 1654, often supported by the Slavic peasants and farmers, and a series of wars featuring a Swedish invasion levelled Brest.

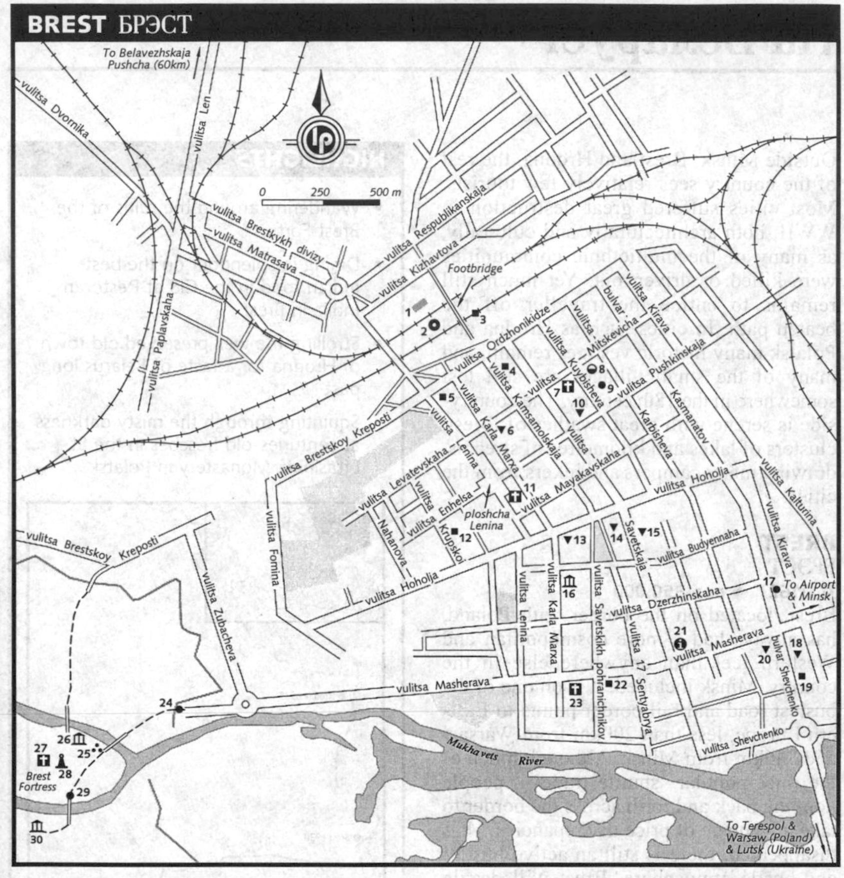

The Treaty of Brest-Litovsk was negotiated here in March 1918, buying time for the new Soviet government in Russia by surrendering Poland, the Baltic States and most of Ukraine and Belarus to German control. As a result, Brest was well inside Poland from 1919 to 1939, but when the Soviet Union and Nazi Germany again carved up Poland and the Baltic States in August 1939, the town found itself on the border, with the Buh River the dividing line between German and Soviet forces. It was therefore the front line when Germany attacked the USSR on 22 June 1941. The two hugely outnumbered regiments in its fortress held out for over a month – a heroic defence for which Brest was named one of the former Soviet Union's 11 'Hero Cities' of WWII.

Orientation & Information

Central Brest, about 2km square, fans out south-east from the main train station to the Mukhavets River. Vulitsa Savetskaja is the main drag and has several pedestrian sections. Brest Fortress lies at the confluence of the Buh and Mukhavets rivers, about 2km south-west of the centre down vulitsa Masherava, which becomes vulitsa Mask-

BREST БРЭСТ

PLACES TO STAY

3 Wagon Hotel
4 Hotel Maladzyezhnaja Гасцініца Маладзёжная
5 Hotel Buh Гасцініца Буг
12 Vesta Hotel Гасцініца Веста
19 Hotel Belarus Гасцініца Беларусь
22 Hotel Intourist Гасцініца Інтурыст

PLACES TO EAT

6 Pekin Пекин
10 Restoran Brest Рэстаран Брэст
13 Restoran Indija Рэстаран Індыя
14 Kafe Kres Кафэ Крэс
15 Vizit Bar Визит Бар
18 Zio Pepe Зио Пэпэ
20 Kafe Bulbjanaja Кафэ Бульбяная

OTHER

1 Domestic Train Ticket Terminal Чыгуначныя білетныя касы мясцовага кірунку
2 Main Train Station & International Customs Чыгуначны вакзал і мытня
7 St Nikolaiv Church Царква св. Нікалая
8 Bus Station Аўтобусны вакзал
9 Market Рынак
11 St Christopher's Polish Catholic Church
16 Regional Museum Абласны музей
17 Domestic Train & Bus Ticket Office Чыгуначныя і аўтобусныя білетныя касы мясцовага кірунку
21 Brest Intourist Інтурыст Брэста
23 St Simon Orthodox Cathedral Праваслаўны сабор св. Сымона
24 Brest Fortress Main Entrance Галоўны ўваход у Брэсткую крэпаць
25 White Palace (Ruins) Белы палац (развалiны)
26 Defence of Brest Fortress Museum Музей абароны Брэстскай крэпасці
27 Nikalaivsky Church Царква Свяціцеля Нікалая
28 Main Monument, Brest Fortress Галоўны манумент, Брэстская крэпасць
29 Kholmskie Gate Холмскія вароты
30 Bereste Archaeological Museum Археалагічны музей Бярэсце

ouskaja as you head east of town. The Brest Intourist office, at vulitsa Savetskaja 116 near Hotel Intourist, is more for outbound travellers but has some information and is very helpful and friendly; it's open from 9 am to 6 pm daily except Sunday.

Churches

From the train station, cross the footbridge that leads over the train tracks towards the town, turn left (east) for one block, and then head south down vulitsa Savetskaja. On the corner of vulitsa Mitskevicha is the breathtakingly detailed 200-year-old **St Nikolaiv Church**, with traditional Orthodox aesthetics. Head farther along vulitsa Mitskevicha and turn left (south) on vulitsa Lenina and you'll reach ploshcha Lenina, where a statue of Lenin points east towards Moscow – but, ironically, appears more to be pointing across the street to the 1882 **St Christopher's Polish Catholic Church**. Next to Hotel Intourist on vulitsa Masherava is the gold and white 17th century **St Simon Orthodox Cathedral** with a richly gilded interior.

Museums

Three blocks west of vulitsa Savetskaja on the corner of vulitsa Karla Marxa and vulitsa Budyennaha is the **Regional Museum**, which holds little of interest aside from the usual regional knick-knacks and a bit of Soviet paraphernalia. It's open from 10 am to 6 pm Tuesday to Saturday; admission is $0.50.

South of the fortress is the **Bereste Archaeological Museum**. The main exhibit is part of the artisans' quarter of 13th century Brest, which has been excavated and preserved under a protective roof. Around the central pit are a number of small, interesting exhibits. The museum is open from 10 am to 6 pm Wednesday to Sunday; admission is $0.50.

Brest Fortress

If you are going to see only one Soviet WWII memorial in your life, make it Brest Fortress (Brestskaja krepost). As if the scale of the fortress and the heroism of its defenders weren't enough, the Soviet additions of a giant stone face and glistening obelisk show everything that was wrong and right with the Soviet Union.

It's at the western end of vulitsa Masherava, about a 20 minute walk from the centre; the hourly bus No 17 travels between here and Hotel Intourist. Entrance is free.

Between 1838 and 1842 the entire town of Brest was moved east to make way for this massive fort around the confluence of the Buh and Mukhavets rivers. During the interwar period it was used mainly for housing soldiers and had lost most of its military importance. Nevertheless, two regiments bunking here at the time of the sudden German invasion in 1941 defended the aged fort for an astounding month and a half. The whole structure withstood incredible attacks, including at least 500 cannons and 600 bombs. Within five hours of launching their offensive, the Nazi forces had taken the entire city of Brest – except the fortress. When it finally fell, the front line of the war was tens of kilometres to the east. What is left of the fortress is too overwhelming to be poignant, but too emotional to be gauche.

At the main entrance (vulitsa Masherava), a looped recording of soldier songs, gunfire and a radio broadcast informing of the German attack echo from a large, star-shaped opening in a huge concrete mass on top of the old brick outer wall. Inside, the enormous central monument comes into view – a stone soldier's head projecting from a massive rock, entitled 'Valour'.

As you step into the centre, to your right are the brick ruins of the **White Palace**, where the 1918 Treaty of Brest-Litovsk was signed. Farther to the right is the **Defence of Brest Fortress Museum**, which is open from 9 am to 6 pm daily except Monday (admission $0.50). Its extensive and dramatic exhibits demonstrate aptly the plight of the defenders.

Behind the Valour rock is the partly ruined shell of the **Nikolaivsky Church**, the oldest church in the city, which dates from when the town centre occupied the fortress site. Once part of a large monastery before being turned into a soldier's garrison club, it was gutted during the 1941 siege but is undergoing restoration.

To the south is the **Kholmskie Gate**; its bricks are decorated with crenulated turrets and its outer face is riddled with hundreds of bullet and shrapnel holes.

Places to Stay

For true penny-pinchers, ***Wagon Hotel*** (no telephone) offers four-bunk train carriages for travellers who don't mind using the train station bathrooms. At less than $1 a night for a single space, who can complain? Seek out the blue, unattached train carriage just outside the international ticket building, underneath the overpass, with a sign *vagon gostinitsa*. It's not recommended for lone female travellers.

The top choice for any traveller is ***Vesta Hotel*** *(☎ 23 71 69, fax 23 78 39, vulitsa Krupskoi 16)*. A bit difficult to find, the plain-looking hotel was built in the late 1980s and remains immaculately clean and quiet. Prices are a reasonable $15/28 for a single/double room; it fills rather quickly, so call ahead.

The rest of the city breaks down into two sets: the more moderate and convenient set includes ***Hotel Buh*** *(☎ 23 64 17, vulitsa Lenina 2)*, near the corner of vulitsa Ordzhonikidze, and ***Hotel Maladzyezhnaja*** *(☎ 6 10 76, vulitsa Kamsamolskaja 6)*, just on your left as you come down the stairs of the rail overpass. At both of these popular hotels, adequate rooms with no surprises go for a moderately overpriced $25 for a single or a double. The hotels are run by the same company and have not been renovated.

The second set is the 'tourist-class' sisters: the predictably upscale ***Hotel Intourist*** *(☎ 25 20 82/3, vulitsa Masherava 15)* is a typical 1970s creation, but well staffed and comfortable. Rooms cost a pricey $27/46/74 for singles/doubles/triples, hard currency only. No better, and perhaps a bit worse for the somewhat seedy clientele, is ***Hotel Belarus*** *(☎ 22 16 46, fax 22 16 58, bulvar Shevchenko 6)*, about 1km west along the road. Slightly more run-down singles/doubles cost $18/25; a deluxe double is

$75. Both hotels can be reached by bus No 6 from the train station. For Hotel Intourist get off at the Intourist stop; for the Belarus get off at the Maskouskaja stop.

Places to Eat

All the hotels in Brest have restaurants or small cafes, but none of them is anything better than adequate.

The best restaurant in town – and for our money in the country – is ***Restoran Indija*** on the corner of vulitsa Karla Marxa and vulitsa Hoholja. Run by an Indian family, it draws expats from across the region and could stand up admirably against the finest curry houses of London or Bombay. The food is simply outstanding, with highlights including the mixed kebab plate for $5 and spot-on nan bread. A full meal costs around $8 to $10.

For heartier and cheaper sustenance, head for ***Kafe Bulbjanaja*** on the corner of vulitsa Masherava and bulvar Shevchenko, a cafeteria-style eatery (open 8 am to 8 pm) where a pile of food costs about $1. For the upscale version, with much the same food but in a formal, soulless, Soviet-style setting, try ***Restoran Brest*** (open noon to 5 am), on the corner of vulitsa Savetskaja and vulitsa Pushkinskaja.

A number of passable cafes lie along vulitsa Savetskaja, which is a popular place for an evening stroll. ***Kafe Kres*** *(vulitsa Savetskaja 63)*, just south of vulitsa Hoholja, is a relatively cosy corner cafe with German beer on tap and savoury mini-pizzas. Across the street, ***Vizit Bar*** *(vulitsa Savetskaja 50)* has a bit of a canned feel but is popular with the city's hipper youth.

Getting There & Away

The airport is about 15km east of the centre, but now only services charter flights.

Train Brest is an important border crossing on the well used Warsaw-Minsk-Moscow line. There are at least four regular trains a day to Warsaw (four to five hours) and about the same number to Moscow (12 to 15 hours), stopping at Minsk (four to five hours) and Smolensk on the way. There are also much slower electric trains to Minsk four times a day (seven hours), and just across the border to Poland, usually packed with shuttle traders. There are three trains daily to Kyiv (14 to 15 hours). Other trains go to Prague (16 hours, four per week), Berlin (12 hours, three per week), St Petersburg (22 hours, daily) and Kaliningrad (19 hours, odd days).

Domestic trains, besides those to Minsk, include four trains a day to Pinsk (three hours) and two a day to Vitsebsk (between 10 and 20 hours).

For all trains leaving Brest for Poland, you have to go through customs at the station. A new facility to ease this process has been built, but it is still hectic so get to the station at least an hour before your train's departure. Tickets for major trains are purchased from the international ticket windows *(mezhdunarodnie kassi)* in the main hall of the ticketing building; for Poland-bound trains you will need hard currency. For the shorter-distance electric trains that just cross over the border, you'll have to slog through a long line next door where even the no-smoking signs are in Polish. It makes more sense to either head east or hop on a long-distance train heading west, like the Moscow-Warsaw or Moscow-Prague train.

For the domestic electric trains (to Minsk, Pinsk or Polatsk), tickets can be purchased in the smaller building, across the tracks, away from the city and over the pedestrian bridge from the main hall, with the sign *passazhirsky pavilon* (passenger train terminal). Domestic train tickets and information can also be obtained from the ticket offices at bulvar Shevchenko 118, just up from vulitsa Masherava, open from 8 am to 7 pm.

Bus The bus station is in the centre of town, next to the market. You can only get to Hrodna by bus (three daily, seven to eight hours), as the train no longer runs. Buses also run thrice daily to Warsaw (five hours) and twice daily to Lviv (nine hours). Through-buses go on to Prague and Bremen twice a week.

Getting Around

Brest is a large city, but most of what you'll want to see is easily navigable on foot. About the farthest you'll go is the 30 to 40 minute walk to the fortress. City buses do connect most points, but are predictably crowded and don't run very frequently; fares are cheap.

AROUND BREST

Belavezhskaja Pushcha Nature Reserve

About 1300 sq km of primeval European forest survives in the Belavezhskaja Pushcha reserve, which stretches north from the town of Kamjanjuky, about 60km north of Brest. A small part of the forest – which is all that remains of a canopy that eight centuries ago stretched to the Baltic Sea – is in Poland, which administers the reserve jointly with Belarus.

Some 55 mammal species including elk, deer, lynx, boar, wild horse, wolf, badger, ermine, marten, otter, mink and beaver live here, but it is most celebrated for its 1000 or so European bison, the continent's largest land mammal. These free-range *zoobr* – slightly smaller than their American cousins – were driven to extinction after WWI and then bred back into existence from 54 animals that had survived in zoos. Now a total of 3200 exist, half of them in and around western Belarus, Lithuania, Poland and Ukraine.

There's a nature museum and enclosures where you can view bison, deer, boar and other animals. The reserve went from obscurity to the front page in late 1991, as the presidents of Belarus, Russia and Ukraine officially signed the death certificate of the USSR with a document creating the Commonwealth of Independent States (CIS) at the Viskuli dacha here.

Only five buses a day go from Brest central bus station to Kamjanjuky, the main town just inside the reserve. To visit the reserve in your own vehicle without a guide you may need a police permit, depending on current regulations. The Intourist service bureau in Brest can help you with this and can also arrange visits.

HRODNA
ГРОДНА

☎ 0152 • pop 290,000

Hrodna (called Grodno in Russian), 282km west of Minsk, may rank as the most picturesque city in all of Belarus – simply because it survived the war better than anywhere else and has more historic buildings intact to prove it. Settled since ancient times and first mentioned in 1128, it was an important town under the Polatsk princedom and became a crucial outpost on the fringes of Kyivan Rus.

Absorbed by Lithuania in the late 14th century, Hrodna fast became a major defensive fort and trading centre. Control quickly shifted to the Polish crown, which built an extensive palace and added several churches to bolster its presence.

After Poland was carved up in 1772, the city went to Russia before being taken by Napoleon on his march to Moscow in 1812. Overrun in WWI, the city was one of the first (after Brest) to be besieged by the invading Germans in 1941. Unlike Brest, it fell easily, suffering far less damage than it did when the Soviet forces came back through at the end of WWII. In the process, the once multiethnic population of Hrodna, including a large Jewish contingency, was wiped out.

Today it's an industrial and cultural centre and, with its proximity to both Lithuania (42km away) and Poland (24km), has a bit of a cosmopolitan atmosphere.

Orientation

The centre is about 2km south-west of the train station and occupies an elevated portion of land overlooking a shallow bend in the Nioman River to the south. The focus is along the commercial, pedestrian-only vulitsa Savetskaja and the spacious ploshcha Savetskaja at its southern end. The bus station is 1km south of the train station down vulitsa Chyrvonarmejskaja (bus No 18 runs between the two stations), and 1km east of the centre down vulitsa Karla Marxa. Vulitsa Azhyeshka stretches from the train station 1.5km to the centre and bus No 3 plies it.

Vulitsa Savetskaja

Vulitsa Savetskaja is a favourite strolling venue – a pleasing cobblestone strip of curious shops and cafes behind pastel facades. It is easily the most picturesque and well maintained kilometre in the country – which is saying both a lot and not much at all. The southern end spills into the wide and elongated **ploshcha Savetskaja,** which in turn ends in an extended, tree-filled park.

Churches & Museums

At vulitsa Azhyeshka 23, near the train station, is the attractive 1904-5 **Pokrovsky Cathedral**, a red and white candy house with blue and gold domes. Nearby at No 29 is the small **City History Museum**, open from 10 am to 6 pm Tuesday to Saturday. It has a few exhibits and is the best place to pick up handcrafted items and souvenirs.

At the north-eastern corner of ploshcha Savetskaja is the proud and pointy baroque **Farny Cathedral**, built during Polish rule in the 18th century. Inside is a row of ornate altars leading to a huge main altarpiece constructed of multiple columns interspersed with sculpted saints. Recently renovated, it is among the most arresting

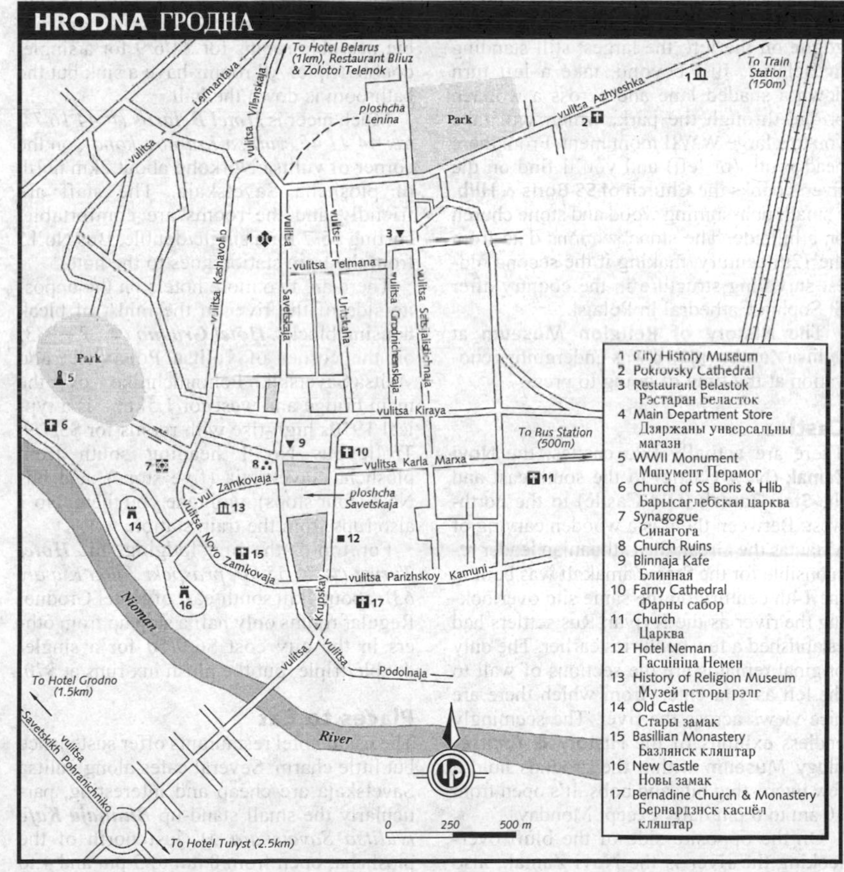

churches in Belarus and should not be missed. Another church once stood on the opposite side of the square. It was damaged in WWII and later razed by the Soviet regime; fragmented foundation ruins mark the spot.

Off the far south-eastern end of ploshcha Savetskaja is the **Bernardine Church & Monastery**. Built predominantly in Renaissance style in the 16th century, the bell tower was redone with a defiant baroque flair 250 years later, and again after damage in WWII.

Beyond the turn-off for the castle on vulitsa Novo Zamkovaja you'll see a dilapidated and abandoned 19th century **synagogue** on the left, the largest still standing in Belarus. Just beyond, take a left turn down a shaded lane and across a wooden bridge through the park, which will take you to a large WWII monument. From there head south (or left) and you'll find on the river's banks the **Church of SS Boris & Hlib**, a small, unassuming wood and stone church on a hillside. The stone sections date from the 12th century, making it the second oldest surviving structure in the country after St Sophia Cathedral in Polatsk.

The **History of Religion Museum** at vulitsa Zamkovaja 16 was undergoing renovation at the time of going to press.

Castles

There are actually two castles, the **Novi Zamak** (New Castle) to the south-east and the **Stari Zamak** (Old Castle) to the north-west. Between them is a wooden carving of Vytautas the Great, the Lithuanian leader responsible for the Stari Zamak. It was built in the 14th century on the same site overlooking the river as the Kyivan Rus settlers had established a few centuries earlier. The only original remains are the sections of wall to the left as you enter, from which there are nice views across the river. The seemingly endless exhibits of the **History & Archaeology Museum** within the grounds hold a few interesting bits and bobs. It's open from 10 am to 6 pm daily except Monday.

On the opposite side of the bluff overlooking the river is the Novi Zamak, also known as the Governor's Palace, which was built in 1737 as the royal palace for Polish King Stanislav August II. Originally built in opulent rococo, it was completely gutted by fire and rebuilt in a subdued classical style. In the early 20th century it was converted to a hospital and taken over by the Communists as their headquarters. It was recently converted into a museum, library and head office for the Ministry of Culture. Inside is another section of the History & Archaeology Museum.

Places to Stay

Hotel Neman *(☎ 44 17 53, vulitsa Krupskay 8)*, off ploshcha Savetskaja, has worn but passable rooms for $4/6/9 for a single/double/triple. All rooms have a sink but the bathroom is down the hall.

Much nicer is ***Hotel Belarus*** *(☎ 44 16 74, fax 44 41 45, vulitsa Kalinovskoho)*, on the corner of vulitsa Norkoho about 2km north of ploshcha Savetskaja. The staff are friendly and the rooms are comfortable, costing $5/7 for a single/double. Bus No 15 from the train station goes to the hotel.

There are two more hotels on the opposite side of the river in the midst of bleak housing blocks. ***Hotel Grodno*** *(☎ 22 42 33)* on the corner of vulitsa Popovicha and vulitsa Savetskikh Pohranichniko – over the main bridge and west for 1.5km – is a typical 1970s high-rise with rooms for $5/7/9. Trolleybus No 1 heading south from ploshcha Savetskaja (five stops), and bus No 3 (four stops), will take you there; No 3 also runs from the train station.

For top-of-the-line lodging, hit ***Hotel Turyst*** *(☎ 26 55 90, praspekt Janki Kupaly 63)*, about 4km south-east of Hotel Grodno. Regular rooms only half a step up from others in the city cost $6/9/10 for a single/double/triple, but the plush lux runs at $70.

Places to Eat

The usual hotel restaurants offer sustenance but little charm. Several cafes along vulitsa Savetskaja are cheap and interesting, particularly the small stand-up ***Blinnaja Kafe*** *(vulitsa Savetskaja 5)*, just north of the ploshcha, open from 8 am to 3 pm and 4 to

8 pm. It does delicious bliny with curd, fruit or meat for a fraction of a dollar.

***Restaurant Belastok** (vulitsa Gorodnichenskaja 20)* is your best bęt in the town's centre. It offers a quiet lunch of schnitzel, fries and salad for under $1 or the same thing in the evening accompanied by deafening electronic music.

About 4km north-west of the centre, beyond Hotel Belarus, are Hrodna's two best eateries within spitting distance of each other. We prefer ***Restaurant Bliuz** (vulitsa Vrublevskoho 1a)*, with a slightly jazzy atmosphere, inventive food and attentive service. Across the street and a bit more starched is ***Zolotoi Telenok***, with less experimental cuisine but a quieter atmosphere in the evenings. Trolleybus No 9 runs from the centre to both.

Getting There & Away

Train There are three trains a day to Minsk (six to eight hours), two a day to Polatsk (seven to eight hours) and one on even days to Vitsebsk (13 hours).

Hrodna lies on the main St Petersburg-Warsaw line. About two trains a day cross the border to Warsaw (seven hours), stopping in Bialystok along the way. Three trains a week go to St Petersburg (21 hours) via Minsk and Vitsebsk. One train a day runs to Moscow (19 hours) and one a day to Berlin (17 hours), from Vilnius. Trains run at least once a day to Vilnius (three hours), usually from Warsaw.

Electric trains run to a number of outlying towns and to Druskininkai in Lithuania on weekends (about 1½ hours).

Bus There are buses to Minsk (five to six hours, 11 per day) as well as Brest (seven to eight hours, three per day). To Lithuania, weekday buses run to Vilnius (five hours) and daily buses to Kaunas (four hours).

Getting Around

With the exception of several far-flung hotels and a few restaurants, you can easily walk around central Hrodna in an hour or two. Bus service is cheap but not terribly frequent, and taxis are fairly inexpensive.

POLATSK
ПОЛАЦК

☎ 02144 • pop 87,500

Polatsk, 261km north of Minsk, is a sleepy riverfront town with a rich history as the birthplace of the Belarus nation as well as of national hero Francyska Skaryny, who published the first Bible in the Slavonic language in 1517-19. Today, however, it has little to occupy more than half a day.

Polatsk goes back to the Varangians in the 6th century. The princedom of Polatsk, first mentioned in 862, was one of the earliest Slav settlements. Just out of striking range of the Mongol hordes that sacked Kyiv in 1240, it was absorbed by the Kingdom of Lithuania in 1307 and later by Poland, which introduced Catholicism and reduced the citizens to serfs under powerful Polish and German landowners. Polatsk prospered as a river port but was continually flung back and forth between the feuding Muscovy tsars and Polish crown, being reduced to rubble more than once. Battles between Napoleonic and tsarist forces were waged here in 1812. The spark of nationalist fervour that arose out of Polatsk in the late 19th century ended with WWI and was sealed with the Soviet takeover shortly after.

Orientation

The centre lies 1km south of the train and bus stations along the east-west praspekt Karla Marxa, which has ploshcha Lenina at its western end. The most interesting area is along vulitsa Lenina, parallel and one street closer to the Dzvina River from praspekt Karla Marxa.

Things to See

From the train station, cross the street and walk straight (south) down vulitsa Hoholja for about 10 minutes until it stops at ploshcha Francyska Skaryny and a statue of the eponymous printer born here in 1490. Hotel Dzvina is on your right. The main thoroughfare of praspekt Karla Marxa runs to the west (right) for about 1km to ploshcha Lenina.

Ploshcha Lenina is notable only for what was once there – a tall monument to the

French-Russian war of 1812 and, where a dismal WWII monument to the 'Liberators of Polatsk' now sits, the magnificent baroque Nikolaivsky Cathedral (until it was destroyed by the communists in 1964). To the north lie several nicely painted wooden cottages, including one at Voikova 1 that houses the new **Museum of Weaving** (Muzey Tkatsvo), showing off a modest collection of traditional weaving. It's open from 10 am to 5 pm daily except Sunday.

From ploshcha Lenina, vulitsa Krizhovaja leads south to the 18th century domed **Bohajavlensky Cathedral**, a working Orthodox church, across from the **Belarusian Museum of Historical Books & Printing**, open from 10 am to 5 pm Wednesday to Sunday. Heading west (right) down vulitsa Lenina – which runs parallel with the Dzvina River – you will find the small, brick **Regional Historic Museum** (Krajazmuchy Muzey) at No 11, a former Lutheran church from the late 18th century. The museum (open from 10 am to 5 pm Wednesday to Sunday) has pictures and artefacts from Polatsk's rich history.

St Sophia Cathedral

Farther down vulitsa Lenina is the finely moulded facade of St Sophia Cathedral, its twin baroque bell towers rising high over the Dzvina River. It's the oldest surviving monument of architecture in Belarus and one of two original 11th century Kyivan Rus cathedrals (the other is in Novgorod) which were modelled and named after the St Sophia Cathedral in Kyiv. Its original 11th century appearance, however, has long gone. Damaged by fire in the 15th century, it was turned into an armoury that was subsequently destroyed by retreating Russians in 1710. About 40 years later the Poles reconstructed it – inside and out – as a baroque Catholic cathedral.

The interior is a museum (open from 10 am to 5 pm daily except Monday) with a model inside showing the original Kyivan Rus Byzantine appearance. Original 11th century foundations can be seen in the vaulted basement. Out front is a large stone on which a cross was carved in the 12th century by Prince Boris, who scoured the region etching Christian symbols on every formerly pagan rock or stone he could find.

St Efrasinnia Monastery

The St Efrasinnia Monastery was founded in 1125 by Saint Efrasinnia (1110-73), Belarus' first saint and the first woman to be canonised by the Orthodox Church. She was the founder of the city's first library and had a strong independent streak, shunning numerous offers of marriage to establish her own convent here and to commission the **Holy Saviour Church**. Still standing, it's one of the finest examples of early 12th century religious architecture in Belarus. The wall paintings inside are being restored, but the small, dark interior is mesmerisingly beautiful. The small **Church of the Transfiguration** (Spaso-Preobrazhenski Sabor), on the right as you enter, was originally built in the 17th century, although the current facade dates from 1833. The large church in the centre was built in 1897. To get to the monastery, you can either walk due north from ploshcha Lenina on vulitsa Frunza for a brisk half-hour, watching for the complex on your right, or take bus No 4 or 17 three stops from the north end of ploshcha Lenina, on the far side of the street.

Places to Stay & Eat

The one hotel in town is ***Hotel Dzvina*** *(☎ 4 22 35, praspekt Karla Marxa 13)*, a stately piece of Soviet baroque at the north-western corner of ploshcha Francyska Skaryny. Average but adequate singles/doubles cost $3/4. The restaurant, entered off praspekt Karla Marxa around the corner, serves a mediocre meal but seems to be the best in town.

Directly across from the train station, ***Kafe Bulbyanaja***, open from 7 am to 7 pm daily, serves a choice of two dishes a day in a barely sanitary, cafeteria-like environment for under $1. ***Kafe Khvilinka*** *(praspekt Karla Marxa 11)* has mostly sweets and pastries in a rather charming, faux-fin-de-siècle interior, open from 9 am to 9 pm daily.

Getting There & Away

The modern-looking building next to (east of) the older train station sells long-distance train tickets, while the other sells tickets on the four daily electric trains connecting Polatsk and Vitsebsk (two hours). Most long-distance routes are served by through-trains.

Two to three trains a day run to Minsk (seven to eight hours). One train goes daily to Moscow (13 hours) via Smolensk (five hours). There are four trains a week to Riga (eight hours) via Daugavpils. Three trains weekly run to Warsaw (16 to 19 hours). Once or twice a week there's a train to Simferopol (29 hours) stopping in Mahileu/Mogilev (six hours). Four per week go to Homel (11 hours).

The bus station is 100m east of the train station, with at least twice-daily services to Minsk (five hours), six times a day to Vitsebsk (two hours) and once daily to Pskov (six hours), Hrodna (14 hours) and Homel (12 hours). Lockers are available.

Getting Around

This town is an easy stroll even with a moderate backpack; the half-hour walk out to the monastery will be as far as you will need to go. A few bus routes do cover the city, but you may be waiting for longer than it would take to walk there.

VITSEBSK
ВІЦЕБСК

☎ 0212 • pop 87,500

Vitsebsk (called Vitebsk in Russian), 277km north of Minsk, once boasted over 30 churches and was a cosmopolitan, cultural centre. WWII and the Soviet legacy took care of all that, replacing what was destroyed with Stalinist planning and industrial might. Yet an air of elegance still lingers in parts of the old town, and it's a lively enough place to warrant a stopover en route to or from Minsk.

Vitsebsk, like Polatsk, has a rich history going back to the 6th century Varangian explorers from Scandinavia who began to settle at strategic river junctions on their migration south. Part of the Polatsk princedom, Vitsebsk was also pulled into the sphere of Kyivan Rus, then fell under the Lithuanian and Polish umbrella before being finally pinched by Moscow. Its location at a crossroads and close to a border (only 45km from Russia) helped promote the city's cultural flair, and it became a haunt for many artists including Vasili Kandinsky, Kasimir Malevich and Marc Chagall (who was born here in 1887).

The city is also the site of the Slavyanski Bazar (Slavic Bazaar), a massive song and culture festival that draws Slavs from around the world, taking place annually in mid or late July.

Orientation

The remnants of the old town lie along a ridge about 2km north-east of the train station and across the Dzvina River. Heading due east from the station is the main thoroughfare, vulitsa Kirava, which becomes vulitsa Zamkovaja after it crosses the river, and vulitsa Frunze after it crosses vulitsa Lenina, the main north-south thoroughfare.

Things to See

From the train station, trolleybus No 3, 4 or 5 will drop you (after two stops) at the intersection of vulitsa Zamkovaja and vulitsa Lenina, just south of the old town, but it's a short and pleasant 1.5km walk. As you cross the river on the right is a pair of very different Russian Orthodox churches, reconstructions built in 1998 of 10th (wooden) and 13th century (white stone) styles.

At the intersection, turn left onto vulitsa Lenina. Immediately on the left at No 2 is the **City Art Museum**, with temporary exhibitions as well as 18th to 20th century European works, including some 18th century realism by Yudel Pyen, one of Chagall's teachers. It's open from 11 am to 6 pm Wednesday to Sunday. Continue past the museum to the old **town hall**, distinguished by its clock tower. Inside is a collection of up to five rotating exhibitions, the best of which is the permanent **Ancient Vitsebsk** (Drevnyi Vitsebsk) with two rooms full of 11th to 14th century artefacts from the city (same opening hours).

Marc Chagall

Surrealist painter and visionary Marc Chagall (1887-1985) took his first view of the world when he was born in Vitsebsk on 7 July 1887. He spent 1897 to 1910 in the small brick house at vulitsa Pokrovskaja 11, now kitted out with early 20th century Jewish knick-knacks and photos (open from 11 am to 7 pm daily except Monday).

Chagall left Vitsebsk behind to go on to greater fame in St Petersburg and Moscow, finally settling in Paris from 1923 until the end of his life, churning out fantastically poetic and often humorous murals and artwork. Many of his pieces reflect the Jewish country life of his childhood, largely influenced by his upbringing in Vitsebsk.

MICK WELDON

To see some replicas of his work, visit the Chagall Museum (open from 11 am to 7 pm daily except Monday), with two floors of his colourful, surrealist lithographs, including reproductions of the famous murals he did for the Moscow Jewish State Theatre, considered so mesmerising that they were at one point banned from the stage for distracting the audience.

The official Soviet authorities were none too thrilled with the expatriated artist, however, and turned down his offer to donate several original pieces to the city of his birth in the 1960s. Now his motherland is without a single authentic Chagall.

To the left (west) of the town hall and heading north is vulitsa Suvarova, the main street of the old town. Vulitsa Suvarova eventually leads to a pleasant park. The elegant former palace you see to the left is the still-functioning KGB headquarters, and on the right is the **Chagall Museum** (see the boxed text 'Marc Chagall').

Places to Stay & Eat

Hotel Vitsebsk *(☎ 37 28 35, fax 36 95 36, vulitsa Zamkovaja 21)* is a standard high-rise post-Soviet hotel. Perhaps a bit more drab than others, it's 1km east of the train station on the other side of the main bridge spanning the Dzvina River. Standard rooms cost $22/30 for a single/double.

Much more intimate and courteous is ***Hotel Oridan*** *(☎/fax 36 24 56, vulitsa Savetskaja 21/17)* in the old town. Rooms cost $32/50, making it the country's biggest lodging bargain and an absolute must if you're staying the night.

Off the Oridan's lobby is the city's finest ***restaurant***, even serving a decent breakfast. The popular and artsy ***Kafe Teatralnaja*** gives succour and sustenance to a varied, cheerful crowd in its dark, underground sprawl on vulitsa Pushkina, on the east side of the large theatre near the river. For a light, sweet snack, pop into ***Morozhenoje*** *(vulitsa Lenina 53)*, open from 10 am to 10 pm.

Getting There & Away

Vitsebsk is on one of the major railway lines heading south from St Petersburg into Ukraine. At least four trains a day run from Vitsebsk to Minsk (five to six hours) and St Petersburg (10 to 13 hours). Daily trains run to Kyiv (16 hours) and on even-numbered days there are trains to Lviv (25 hours) and Odesa (26 hours).

Two trains daily cross the border into Smolensk (three to four hours), with one continuing on to Moscow (10 to 11 hours). Trains run on even-numbered days to Riga (13 hours) via Daugavpils (six to seven hours). Trains to Warsaw (14 to 17 hours) run twice a week.

Domestic trains other than those to Minsk include at least one to Brest (13 hours), every odd day to Hrodna (12 hours), Mahileu/Mogilev (three hours) and Homel (seven to eight hours). Local electric trains connect Polatsk and Vitsebsk (two hours) about four times daily, but most south or westbound trains pass through Polatsk.

One daily bus runs to Minsk (five hours) and to Mahileu/Mogilev. Three to four buses daily connect the city with Polatsk (two hours), and twice a week one ventures to Prague (29 hours).

Getting Around

With Vitsebsk larger than most of the other regional centres, you will do most of your walking here on the long stroll from the train station into town, a route regularly plied by most buses. Otherwise, you can easily cover the rest of the city on foot.

Language

RUSSIAN

Cyrillic Alphabet

The Cyrillic alphabet resembles Greek with a few additional characters. Every language that uses Cyrillic has its own slightly different variant. The alphabet table on p.944 shows the letters of the Russian alphabet and the Roman-letter equivalents used to transliterate them in this language guide.

Pronunciation

The sounds of а, о, е and я are 'weaker' when the stress in the word does not fall on them – eg in вода, *voda* (water) the stress falls on the second syllable, so it's pronounced *vada*, with the 'a' representing both the unstressed pronunciation for о and the stressed pronunciation for а. The vowel й only follows other vowels in so-called diphthongs, eg ой *oy*, ей *ey, yey*. Note that Russians usually print ë without the dots, a source of confusion in pronunciation.

The 'voiced' consonants б, в, г, д, ж and з are not voiced at the end of words, eg хлеб (bread), is pronounced *khlyep* (not *khlyeb*), or before voiceless consonants. The г in the common adjective endings его and ого is pronounced 'v'.

Two letters have no sound but function by modifying other sounds. A consonant followed by the 'soft sign' ь is spoken with the tongue flat against the palate, as if followed by the faint beginnings of a 'y' – it's represented in this section by an apostrophe. The rare 'hard sign' ъ after a consonant inserts a slight pause before the next vowel.

Transliteration

There's no ideal system for going from Cyrillic to Roman letters; the more faithfully a system indicates pronunciation, the more complicated it is.

The transliteration system used in this language guide differs from that used in the rest of this book (which follows the US Library of Congress System I – good for deciphering printed words and rendering proper names); it's intended to assist you in pronouncing Russian letters and sounds, with an emphasis on practicality. Most letters are transliterated in accordance with the sounds given in the pronunciation guide. A few exceptions are listed below:

е	written as *e* (except at the beginning of words, when it's written as *ye*)
ай	written as *ay*
ей	written as *ey*
ий	written as *iy*
ой	written as *oy* (when stressed) as *ay* (when unstressed)
ый	written as *y*
ж	written as *zh*
х	written as *kh*

Books

A good teach-yourself set (a book and two tapes) is the BBC's *Get By in Russian*. Another good book-and-cassette set for beginners is *Colloquial Russian* by Svetlana le Fleming & Susan E Kay. The paperback *Penguin Russian Course* is good for more devoted learners. Before you head off, get a copy of the new edition of Lonely Planet's detailed and useful *Russian phrasebook* and a small dictionary such as the *Pocket Oxford Russian Dictionary*.

Two books are worthy of mention. The 4kg *Random House Russian-English Dictionary of Idioms* by Sophia Lubensky is a must for any serious student of Russian. Developed over 12 years, originally to help spooks speak (it was undertaken by the US National Cryptologic School, Department of Defense), it contains over 7500 idioms and set expressions not found in traditional Russian-English dictionaries. It's not much fun for beginners – all the Russian listings are in Cyrillic, and no direct (only idiomatic) translations are given. Also note that the meanings and spellings are in American English. *Russian Proverbs* by Chris Skillen & Vladimir Lubarov is a lovely little hardcover with a selection of the most charming

The Russian Cyrillic Alphabet

Cyrillic	Roman	Pronunciation
А, а	a	as the 'a' in 'path' (in stressed syllable) as the 'a' in 'about' (in unstressed syllable)
Б, б	b	as the 'b' in 'but'
В, в	v	as the 'v' in 'van'
Г, г	g	as the 'g' in 'god'
Д, д	d	as the 'd' in 'dog'
Е, е *	e	as the 'ye' in 'yet' (in stressed syllable) as the 'yi' in 'yin' (in unstressed syllable)
Ё, ё **	yo	as the 'yo' in 'yonder'
Ж, ж	zh	as the 's' in 'measure'
З, з	z	as the 'z' in 'zoo'
И, и	i	as the 'i' in 'litre'
Й, й	y	as the 'y' in 'boy'
К, к	k	as the 'k' in 'kind'
Л, л	l	as the 'l' in 'lamp'
М, м	m	as the 'm' in 'mad'
Н, н	n	as the 'n' in 'not'
О, о	o	as the 'o' in 'more' (in stessed syllable) as the 'a' in 'hard' (in unstressed syllable)
П, п	p	as the 'p' in 'pig'
Р, р	r	as the 'r' in 'rub' (rolled)
С, с	s	as the 's' in 'sing'
Т, т	t	as the 't' in 'ten'
У, у	u	as the 'u' in 'put'
Ф, ф	f	as the 'f' in 'fan'
Х, х	kh	as the 'ch' in 'Bach'
Ц, ц	ts	as the 'ts' in 'bits'
Ч, ч	ch	as the 'ch' in 'chin'
Ш, ш	sh	as the 'sh' in 'shop'
Щ, щ	shch	as 'sh-ch' in 'fresh chips'
ъ	(no symbol)	'hard sign' (see p.943)
Ы, ы	y	as the 'y' in 'busy'
ь	'	'soft sign'; (see p.943)
Э, э	e	as the 'e' in 'ten'
Ю, ю	yu	as the 'yu' in 'yule'
Я, я	ya	as the 'ya' in 'yard' (in stressed syllable) as the 'ye' in 'yearn' (in unstressed syllable)

* Е, е is transliterated *Ye*, *ye* when at the beginning of a word

** Ё, ё is often printed without dots

Russian proverbs – from 'it's madness to bring a samovar to Tula' to 'a bad peace is better than a good fight'. It lists both Russian and English and has very nice illustrations (though a couple are in the wrong place!) throughout.

Grammar

This drives even serious students crackers. Nouns have gender and six possible endings; verbs also decline, as in Latin. One result is that things named after people have odd endings – Lenin Ave is *prospekt Lenina*, Tchaikovsky Square is *ploshchad Chaykovskogo* and so on. For a beginner, the best way around this is to ignore it; you can pick up the meanings of printed words without worrying too much about endings.

Fortunately there are also simplifications. Russian has no articles ('a' and 'the' in English). The verb 'to be' is commonly omitted in simple sentences, eg 'I am an American' (male) is я американец *(ya amerikanets)*. Russians also don't normally use the verb 'to have'. Instead they use the preposition у, which means 'at' or 'by', with a special form of the pronoun: eg 'I have' is **у меня** *(u minya est')*, literally 'by me (is)'.

Questions

The easiest way to turn a statement into a question is to use a rising tone and a questioning look, or follow it with a quizzical *da?* – eg 'is this Moscow?', это **Москва**, да? *(eta maskva, da?)*.

Negation

A sentence is made negative by putting не before its main word, eg 'this is not Moscow', **это не Москва** *(eta ni maskva)*.

Pronouns

Normally, **вы** (*vy*, 'you' plural) is used in conversation. The singular ты *(ty)* is for talking to children, relatives and close friends.

I
ya я

you (singular informal)
ty ты

he, she, it
*on, **ana**, **ano*** **он, она, оно**
we
my **мы**
you (plural or singular formal)
vy **вы**
they
ani **они**

Useful Words & Phrases

Two words you're sure to use are **Здравствуйте** *(zdrastvuyte)*, the universal 'hello' (but if you say it a second time in one day to the same person, they'll think you forgot you already saw them!), and **Пожалуйста** *(pazhalsta)*, the multipurpose word for 'please' (commonly included in all polite requests), 'you're welcome', 'pardon me', 'after you' and more.

Good morning.
dobraye utra **Доброе утро.**
Good afternoon.
dobryy den' **Добрый день.**
Good evening.
dobryy vecher **Добрый вечер.**
Goodbye.
da svidaniya **До свидания.**
Goodbye (casual).
paka **Пока.**
How are you?
kak dila? **Как дела?**
Yes.
da **Да**
No.
net **Нет.**
Thank you (very much).
(bal'shoye) spasiba
(Большое) спасибо.
Pardon me.
prastite/pazhalsta
Простите/Пожалуйста.
No problem/Never mind.
nichevo (literally, 'nothing')
Ничего.
I don't speak Russian.
ya ni gavaryu pa ruski
Я не говорю по-русски.
I don't understand.
ya ni panimayu
Я не понимаю.

Do you speak English?
vy gavarite pa angliyski?
Вы говорите по-английски?
Will you write it down, please?
zapishite pazhalsta
Запишите, пожалуйста.
I like (it).
mne nravitsya
Мне нравится.
Can you help me?
pamagite pazhalsta
Помогите пожалуйста.
May I take a photo?
mozhna fatagrafiravat'?
Можно фотографировать?

I need ...
mne nuzhna ... **Мне нужно ...**
Where is ...?
gde ...? **Где ...?**
toilet
tualet **туалет**
translator
pirivotchik **переводчик**

Names & Introductions

In introducing yourself you can use your first name, or first and last. Russians often address each other by first name plus patronymic (a middle name based on their father's first name) eg Natalya Borisovna (Natalya, daughter of Boris), Pavel Nikolaevich (Pavel, son of Nikolay). This requires careful attention when someone is being introduced to you!

What's your name?
kak vas zavut? **Как вас зовут?**
My name is ...
minya zavut ... **Меня зовут ...**
Pleased to meet you.
ochen' priyatna **Очень приятно.**
my husband
moy muzh **мой муж**
my wife
maya zhina **моя жена**
my boyfriend
moy paren' **мой парень**
my girlfriend
maya devushka **моя девушка**

Countries

Where are you from?
atkuda vy? Откуда вы?
Australia
afstraliya Австралия
Canada
kanada Канада
France
frantsiya Франция
Germany
germaniya Германия
Great Britain
velikabritaniya Великобритания
Ireland
irlandiya Ирландия
New Zealand
novaya zelandiya Новая Зеландия
USA, America
se she a, amerika США, Америка

Transport – general

What town is this?
kakoy eta gorat?
Какой этот город?
map, transport map
karta, skhema transparta
карта, схема транспорта
ticket, tickets
bilet, bilety билет, билеты
baggage
bagazh багаж
arrival
pribytiye прибытие
departure
atpravleniye отправление
one-way
v adin kanets, yedinyy в один конец, единый
return, round-trip
tuda i abratna, abratnyy туда и обратно, обратный
free/occupied
svabodna/ zanyata свободно/ занято

Transport – air

airport
aeraport аэропорт
check-in
registratsiya регистрация
customs
tamozhnya таможная
When does it leave?
kagda vyletayet? Когда вылетает?

Transport – bus, trolleybus, tram, metro

The usual way to get to the exit in a crowded bus is to say to anyone in the way, Вы выходите? *vy vykhoditi?*, 'Are you getting off?'.

bus
aftobus автобус
trolleybus
traleybus троллейбус
tram
tramvay трамвай
fixed-route minibus
marshrutnaye taksi маршрутное такси
stop (bus/trolleybus/ tram)
astanofka остановка
ticket/tickets (city bus, trolleybus/tram)
talon/talony талон, талоны
metro token, tokens
zhiton, zhitony жетон, жетоны

Transport – train

railway station
zhileznadarozhnyy vagzal
железнодорожный (ж. д.) вокзал
When does it leave?
kagda atpravlyaetsya?
Когда отправляется?

train
poyezt поезд
carriage
vagon вагон
compartment
kupe купе
seat, place
mesta место
soft or 1st-class (compartment)
myahkiy мягкий

Signs

Under Repair
rimont РЕМОНТ
Men's (toilet)
muzhskoy tualet МУЖСКОЙ ТУАЛЕТ (М)
Women's (toilet)
zhenskiy tualet ЖЕНСКИЙ ТУАЛЕТ (Ж)
Entrance/Exit
fkhot/vykhat ВХОД/ВЫХОД
Pedestrian Crossing
pirikhot ПЕРЕХОД
Cashier, Ticket Office
kasa КАССА
Information Desk
spravachnaye byuro СПРАВОЧНОЕ БЮРО
No Smoking
ne kurit' НЕ КУРИТЬ
No Vacancy
mest net МЕСТ НЕТ

hard or 2nd-class (compartment)
kupeynyy купейный
reserved-place or 3rd-class (carriage)
platskartnyy плацкартный
local train
eliktrichka, prigaradnyy poyezt электричка, пригородный поезд
'fast' train (long-distance)
skoryy poyezt скорый поезд
slower intercity train (literally, 'passenger')
passazhyrskiy poyezt пассажирский поезд
carriage attendant
pravadnik (m) проводник
pravadnitsa (f) проводница

Transport – taxi & car

taxi
taksi такси
petrol/service station
zapravochnaya stanstiya заправочная станция

Transport – boat

river station
rechnoy vagzal речной вокзал
pier/quay
prichal/pristan' причал/пристань
steamship
parakhot пароход
hydrofoil (literally, 'high-speed')
skarastnaya скоростная

Around Town

House numbers are not always in step on opposite sides of the street. Russian addresses are written back-to-front; see Post & Telecommunications in the European Russia Facts for the Visitor chapter.

square/plaza
ploshchat' площадь (пл.)
street
ulitsa улица (ул.)
avenue
praspekt проспект (просп.)
lane
piriulak переулок (пер.)
descent/slope
spusk спуск
boulevard
bul'var бульвар
highway
shase шоссе
embankment
nabirizhnaya набережная (наб.)
building
korpus корпус
museum
muzey музей
theatre
teatr театр
church
tserkof' церковь
circus
tsirk цирк

money
den'gi деньги
currency exchange
abmen valyuty обмен валюты
bank
bank банк

travellers cheques
*da**rozh**nyye **che**ki* дорожные чеки
small change
*raz**men*** размен
post office
***poch**ta* почтамт
stamp
***mar**ka* марка
postcard
*at**kryt**ka* открытка
telephone
*tili**fon*** телефон
fax
faks факс/телефакс

... telephone office
*... tili**fon**yy punkt* ... телефонный пункт
intercity
*mezhdugo**rod**nyy* междугородный
international
*mezhduna**rod**nyy* международный

north
***se**ver* север
south
yuk юг
east
*vas**tok*** восток
west
***za**pad* запад
to (on) the left
*na**le**va* налево
to (on) the right
*na**pra**va* направо
straight on
***prya**ma* прямо
(go) back
*na**zat*** назад
here, there
tut, tam тут, там

I'm lost.
*ya zablu**dil**sya/zablu**di**las'* (m/f)
Я заблудился/заблудилась.

Accommodation

How much is a room?
***skol'**ka **stoit** **no**mer?*
Сколько стоит номер?
Do you have a cheaper room?
*u vas est' di**shev**le **no**mer?*
У вас дешевле номер?

floor supervisor (literally, 'on duty')
*de**zhur**naya*
дежурная

hotel
*gas**ti**nitsa* гостиница
room
***no**mer* номер
floor/storey
*e**tazh*** этаж
key
klyuch ключ
boiling water
*kipya**tok*** кипяток
soap
***my**la* мыло
toilet paper
*tua**let**naya bu**ma**ga* туалетная бумага
towel
*pala**ten**tse* полотенце
blanket
*adi**ya**la* одеяло
too hot/stuffy
***zhar**ka/**dush**na* жарко/душно

The ... isn't working.
*... ni ra**bo**tait* ... не работает.
toilet
*tua**let*** туалет
tap/faucet
kran кран
heating
*ata**ple**niye* отопление
light
svet свет
electricity
*elec**tri**chestva* электричество

Food

For a longer list of words and phrases related to ordering meals, and specific foods, dishes and drinks, see the Food & Drink special section in European Russia.

breakfast
***zaf**trak* завтрак
lunch (afternoon meal)
***a**bet* обед

dinner, supper	
*u**zhin***	ужин
restaurant	
*rista**ran***	ресторан
cafe	
*ka**fe***	кафе
canteen	
*sta**lovaya***	столовая
snack bar	
bufet	буфет
buffet/smorgasbord/ Swedish Table	
shvetskiy stol	шведский стол
to take away	
*s sa**boy***	с собой

Shopping

Please show me.	
*paka**zhiti** pu**zhal**sta*	Покажите пожалуйста.
How much is it?	
skol'ka stoit?	Сколько стоит?
Do you have ...?	
u vas est' ...?	У вас есть ...?
shop	
*maga**zin***	магазин
bookshop	
knizhnyy** maga**zin	книжный магазин
department store	
*univir**sal'nyy** maga**zin***	универсальный магазин
newsstand	
*gazetnyy **kiosk***	газетный киоск
market	
rynak	рынок
(colour) film	
*(stvet**na**ya) **plyon**ka*	(цветная) плёнка
pharmacy	
*ap**te**ka*	аптека
souvenirs	
*suvi**ni**ry*	сувениры
good/OK	
*khara**sho***	хорошо
bad	
***plo**kha*	плохо
this, that	
***eta**, to*	это, то
open/closed	
*ot**kryta**/za**kryta***	открыто/закрыто

Numbers

How many?		
skol'ka?		Сколько?
0	***nol'***	
1	***adin***	
2	***dva***	
3	***tri***	
4	***chityri***	
5	***pyat'***	
6	***shest'***	
7	***sem'***	
8	***vosim'***	
9	***devit'***	
10	***desit'***	
11	***adinatsat'***	
12	***dvinatsat'***	
13	***trinatsat'***	
20	***dvatsat'***	
21	***dvatsat' adin***	
30	***tritsat'***	
40	***sorak***	
50	***pyat'disyat***	
60	***shest'disyat***	
70	***sem'disyat***	
80	***vosimdisyat***	
90	***divyanosta***	
100	***sto***	
200	***dvesti***	
300	***trista***	
400	***chityrista***	
500	***pyat'sot***	
600	***shist'sot***	
700	***sim'sot***	
800	***vasimsot***	
900	***divyat'sot***	
1000	***tysyacha***	
2000	***dve tysyachi***	
3000	***tri tysyachi***	
4000	***chityri tysyachi***	
5000	***pyat' tysyach***	
6000	***shest' tysyach***	
10,000	***desyat' tysyach***	
20,000	***dvatsat' tysyach***	
30,000	***tritsat' tysyach***	
73,568	***sem'desyat tri tysyachi pyat'sot shesdisyat vosim***	
100,000	***sto tysyach***	
one million		
(adin) milion		(один) миллион

Emergencies

I'm sick.
*ya **bo**lin* (m) — Я болен.
*ya bal'**na*** (f) — Я больна.
I need a doctor.
*mne **nu**zhin vrach* — Мне нужен врач.
Fire!
*pa**zhar**!* — Пожар!
Help!
*na **po**mashch!/ pama**gi**ti!* — На помощь!/ Помогите!
Thief!
vor! — Вор!
hospital
*bal'**ni**tsa* — больница
police
*mi**li**tsiya* — милиция

Time, Days & Date

Round hours are fairly easy, except that there are three different ways of saying the Russian equivalent of 'o'clock', depending on the hour. Thus one o'clock is *adin chas* (or simply *chas*), two o'clock is *dva chi**sa*** (and similarly for three and four o'clock – *tri chi**sa**, chityri chi**sa***) and five o'clock is *pyat' chas**of*** (and simiiarly up to 20). For in-between times the standard formula gives brain-twisters like 'without-25-five' for 4.35. You'll be understood if you say the hour followed by the minutes: eg 9.20 is **девять двадцать** ***(devit' dvatsat')***. For minutes under 10 insert zero, **ноль** *(nol')*: eg 2.08 is **два-ноль-восемь** *(dva nol' vosim)*. Timetables use a 24-hour clock: eg 3 pm is **пятнадцать часов** *(pit**nat**sat' chi**sof**)*.

Dates are given as day-month-year, with the month usually in Roman numerals. Days of the week are often represented by numbers in timetables; Monday is 1.

hour
chas — час
minute
*mi**nu**ta* — минута
What time is it?
*ka**to**ryy chas?* — Который час?
At what time?
*f ka**to**ram chi**su**?* — В котором часу?

am/in the morning
utra — утра
pm/in the afternoon
dnya — дня
in the evening
vechira — вечера
local time
mesnaye vremya — местное время
Moscow time
*mas**kov**skaye **vremya*** — московское время

When?
*kag**da**?* — Когда?
today
*si**vod**nya* — сегодня
yesterday
*vchi**ra*** — вчера
tomorrow
***zaf**tra* — завтра
day after tomorrow
*posli**zaf**tra* — послезавтра

Monday
*pani**del'**nik* — понедельник
Tuesday
***ftor**nik* — вторник
Wednesday
*sri**da*** — среда
Thursday
*chit**verk*** — четверг
Friday
***pyat**nitsa* — пятница
Saturday
***su**bota* — суббота
Sunday
*vaskri**sen'**e* — воскресенье

Centuries are written in Roman numerals.

century, centuries
в., вв. *(v, vv)*
year, years
г., гг *(g, gg)*
beginning/middle/end
начало/середина/конец
*(na**cha**la/siri**di**na/ka**nets**)*
AD (literally, 'our era')
н.э. *(n.e – **na**sha era)*
BC (literally, 'before our era')
до н.э. *(do n.e – da **na**shey ery)*

10th century AD
  Х в. н.э. *(disyatyy vek **na**shey ery)*
7th century BC
  VII в. до н.э. *(syed'**moy** vek da **na**shey ery)*

UKRAINIAN

Ukrainian, like Russian and Belarusian, is an Eastern Slavic language. It's arguably the closest of the three to the original 9th century Slavonic used in Kyiv before the more formal Church Slavonic from Bulgaria was introduced with Christianity in the 10th century. Because of Ukraine's history of domination by outside powers, the language was often considered inferior or subservient to the dominant languages of the time – Russian in the east, Polish in the west. In 1876 Tsar Alexander II forbade schooling in Ukrainian and banned all Ukrainian books and publishing, setting a precedent of Russification which has carried through to some degree to the present day. Nonetheless, as in all communities struggling for independence and national identity, the concept of language is held sacred in Ukraine, and each successive national revival has made it a rallying point.

Today, the Ukrainian language is being revived, and in 1990 it was adopted as the official language. The western and eastern accents differ, with various dialects in the Carpathians. Russian is still spoken predominantly in the east and south, where over half the Ukrainians are relearning their own language. Crimea is almost entirely Russian-speaking. Russian is understood everywhere by everyone, so although it may be diplomatic and polite to speak Ukrainian (especially in the west), you'll have no problem being understood if you speak Russian.

If you have no knowledge of Ukrainian it's wise to bring along a dictionary or phrasebook. Lonely Planet's *Ukrainian phrasebook* is a detailed and useful aid to those who want to delve deeper into the language.

Alphabet & Pronunciation

Around 70% of the Ukrainian language is identical or similar to Russian and Belarusian. The Cyrillic chart in the Russian section of this chapter covers the majority of letters used in Ukrainian alphabet. Ukrainian has three additional letters not found in Russian – і, ї, and є – all of which are neutral vowel sounds (the Russian letter о is often replaced by a Ukrainian і). The Ukrainian г usually has a soft 'h' sound. The Ukrainian alphabet doesn't include the Russian letters ё, ы and э, and has no hard sign, ъ, although it does include the soft sign, ь. These differences between the two languages are sometimes quite simple in practice: for example, the town of Chernigov in Russian is Chernihiv in Ukrainian. Overall, Ukrainian is softer sounding and less guttural than Russian.

The -я *(-ya)* ending for nouns and names in Russian (especially street names) is dropped in Ukrainian, and the letter и is transliterated as *y* in Ukrainian, whereas in Russian it's transliterated as *i*, eg a street named *Deribasovskaya* in Russian would be *Derybasivska* in Ukrainian.

Useful Words & Phrases

Good day/Hello.
  dobryy den' — **Добрий день.**
Good morning.
  dobryy ranok — **Добрий ранок.**
Goodbye.
  do pobachennya — **До побачення.**
Good night.
  dobryy vechir — **Добрий вечір.**
How are you?
  yak zhyvesh?/ yak spravy? — **Як живеш?/ Як справи?**
Yes.
  tak — **Так.**
No.
  ni — **Ні.**
Please.
  ***pro**shu* (in the west) — **Прошу.**
  *bud' **las**ka* (in the east) — **Будь ласка.**
Thank you (very much).
  (shchyro) dyakuyu — **(Щиро) дякую.**
Pardon me.
  *pro**bach**te* — **Пробачте.**
I don't understand.
  *ya ne rozu**mi**yu* — **Я не розумію.**

I don't understand Ukrainian.
ya ne rozumiyu po-ukrayinsky — Я не розумію по-українськи.

Do you speak English?
chy vy hovoryte po-angliysky? — Чи ви говорите по-англійськи?

I wish to extend my visa.
ya khochu prodovzhyty vizu — Я хочу продовжити візу

I want (I'd like) ...
ya khochu ... — Я хочу ...

Where can I ...?
de mozhna ...? — Де можна ...?

good/OK
dobre — добре

bad
pohano — погано

when, where
koly, de — коли, де

here, there
tut, tam — тут, там

Getting Around

Where is the train station?
de vohzal? — Де вокзал?

Where is the bus station?
de avtovohzal? — Де автовокзал?

Where is the ... stop?
de zupunka ...? — Де зупинка ...?

tram
tramvayu — трамваю

trolleybus
troleybusu — тролейбуса

bus
avtobusu — автобуса

metro
metro — метро

departing trains
vidpravlenya — відправлення

arriving trains
prybutya — прибуття

odd dates
neparni — непарні

even dates
parni — парні

daily
shchodenno — щоденно

year round
postiyno, shchoroku — постійно, щороку

ticket
kvytok/bilet — квіток/білет

platform
platforma — платформа

timetable
rozklad — розклад

track
koliya — колія

entrance
vkhid — вхід

exit
vykhid — вихід

suburban
prymis'kyy, prihorodnyy — приміський, пригородний

intercity
mizhmis'kyy — міжміський

international
mizhnarodnyy — міжнародний

car
aftomobil' — автомобіль

petrol
benzyn — бензин

oil
maslo — масло

water
voda — вода

battery
batareya/akumulyator — батарея/акумулятор

tyre
shyna — шина

spark plugs
svichky — свічки

brakes
hal'ma — гальма

Accommodation & Food

Where is the hotel?
de hotel'? — Де готель?

Where is a restaurant?
de restoran? Де ресторан?
Where is the toilet?
de tualet? Де туалет?
breakfast
snidanok сніданок
lunch
obid обід
early dinner/late dinner
obid/vecherya обід/вечеря
snack
lehka zakuska легка закуска
pastry/cake shop
kondyters'ky vyroby кондитерськи вироби
appetisers
zakusky закуски
cottage cheese
syr сир
black/red caviar
chorna/chervona ikra чорна/червона ікра
soup, sauce
sup, pidlyva суп, підлива
salad
salata салата
main course
druhe друге
meat, pork
m'yaso м'ясо
pork
svynyna свинина
shashlyk
shashlyk шашлик
veal cutlet
telyacha vidbyvna теляча відбівна
chicken
kurka/kurcha курка/курча
fish
ryba риба
trout
forel' форель
pike
shchuka щука
sausage
kovbasa ковбаса
meat balls
frikadeli фрикаделі
dessert
desert десерт
ice cream
morozyvo морозиво
biscuit, cookie
pechyvo печиво
cake
tistechko/tort тістечко/торт
cheese fritters
syrnyk сирник

Drinks

juice/fruit drink
sik/kompot сік/компот
milk/yoghurt
moloko/yohurt молоко/йогурт
hot chocolate
haryachyy shokolad гарячий шоколад
coffee/tea
kava/chay кава/чай
beer/wine
pyvo/vyno пиво/вино
vodka
horilka горілка
Cossack kvas
kozuts'kyy kvas Козацький квас
Ukrainian pepper vodka
ukrayins'ka horilka z pertsem українська горілка з перцем

Shopping

Do you have ...?
chy ye u vas ...? Чи є у вас ...?
I need ...
meni treba ... Мені треба ...
How much?
skil'ky? Скільки?
How much does this cost?
skil'ky tse koshtuye? Скільки це коштує?

Numbers

Pronunciation of numbers in Ukrainian is similar to that of Russian. If you use the Numbers guide in the Russian section of this chapter you'll have no trouble being understood.

At the Market

fruit
frukty фрукти
nuts
horikhy горіхи
vegetables
ovochi овочі

almonds
mihdal' мигдаль
apples
yabluka яблука
apricots
abrykosy абрикоси
bananas
banany банани
cherries
vyshni вишні
currants
smorodyna смородина
gooseberries
ahrus агрус
grapes
vynohrad виноград
lemons
lymony лимони
oranges
apel'syny апельсини
peaches
persyky персики
plums
slyvy сливи
red currants
porichky порічки
strawberries
sunytsi суниці
watermelon
kavun кавун
wild strawberries
polunytsi полуниці

beans
kvasolya квасоля
beetroot
buryaky буряки
cabbage
kapusta капуста
carrots
morkva морква
mushrooms
hryby гриби
onions
tsibulya цибуля
peas
horokh горох
potatoes
kartoplya/ barabolya картопля/ бараболя
pumpkin
harbuz гарбуз
tomatoes
pomidory помідори

Glossary

You may encounter some of the following terms and abbreviations during your travels in Russia (R), Ukraine (U) and Belarus (B). See also the Language chapter and the Food & Drink special section in the European Russia Facts for the Visitor chapter.

aeroport – airport
aerovokzal – airline terminal
apteka – pharmacy
ataman – Cossack leader
avtobus – bus
avtomat – automatic ticket machine
avtostantsiya – bus stop
avtovokzal – bus terminal

babushka – grandmother
balalaika – traditional Russian musical instrument, usually with a triangular body and three strings
BAM – Baikal-Amur Mainline (a Trans-Siberian rail route)
bankomat – automatic teller machine (ATM)
banya – bathhouse
bashnya – tower
baza otdykha – literally, relaxation base; often used to describe lodges and sanitoria
benzin – petrol
biblioteka – library
bilet – ticket
biznesmen, biznesmenka – literally, businessman/woman, but often used to mean a small-time operator on the fringe of the law
bolnitsa – hospital
boyar – high-ranking noble
bufet – snack bar selling cheap cold meats, boiled eggs, salads, bread, pastries etc
bulochnaya – bakery
bulvar – boulevard
buterbrod – open sandwich

CIS – Commonwealth of Independent States; an alliance (proclaimed in 1991) of independent states comprising the former USSR republics, with the exception of the three Baltic States

dacha – country cottage, summer house
datsan – Buddhist monastery
deklaratsia – customs declaration
detsky – child's, children's
Detsky Mir – Children's World, name for many department stores
dezhurnaya – woman looking after a particular floor of a hotel
dolina – valley
dom – house
dorogoy – expensive
duma – parliament
dvorets – palace
dvorets kultury – literally 'culture palace'; a meeting, social, entertainment, education centre, usually for a group like railway workers, children etc

elektrichka – suburban train
etazh – floor (storey)

GAI (Gosudarstvennaya Avtomobilnaya Inspektsia) – State Automobile Inspectorate (traffic police)
gallereya – gallery
gastronom – speciality food shop (R)
gavan – harbour
gazeta – newspaper
glasnost – literally 'openness'; the free-expression aspect of the Gorbachev reforms
glavpochtamt – main post office
gril-bar – grill bar, often limited to roast chicken
gora – mountain
gorod – city, town
gostinitsa – hotel (R)
gostiny dvor – trading arcade
granitsa – border
Gulag (Glavnoe Upravlenie Lagerey) – Main Administration for Camps; the Soviet network of concentration camps
GUM (Gosudarstvenny Univermag) – State Department Store

hastronom – grocery or specialty food shop (U) – see also *gastronom*
hostinitsa – hotel (U) – see also *gostinitsa*
hryvnia – Ukrainian unit of currency

i – and
ikra – caviar
imeni – 'named after' (often used in names of theatres, libraries etc – for example Moscow's Konsertny zal imeni Chaykovskogo is the Tchaikovsky Concert Hall)
inostranets – foreigner
Intourist – the old Soviet State Committee for Tourism, now hived off, split up and in competition with hundreds of other travel agencies
istochnik – mineral spring
izba – traditional single-storey wooden cottage
izveshchenie – notification

kafe – cafe
kamera khranenia – left-luggage office
kanal – canal
karta – map
kassa (R), **kasa** (U) – ticket office, cashier's desk
kater – small ferry
Kazak – Cossack
kemping – camp site, often with small cabins as well as tent sites
KGB (Komitet Gosydarstvennoy Bezopasnosti) – Committee of State Security
khleb – bread
kholm – hill
khram – church
kino – cinema
kipyatok – boiled water
kladbishche – cemetery
klyuch – key
kniga – book (plural *knigi*)
kolkhoz – collective farm
kolonna – column, pillar
koltsevaya doroga – ring road
kombinat – complex of factories
Komsomol – Communist Youth League
kopek – kopeck; the smallest, worthless unit of Russian currency
korpus – building (ie one of several in a complex)
kray – territory
krazha – theft
kreml – kremlin, a town's fortified stronghold
kruglosutochno – around the clock
krugovoy – round trip
kulak – Stalinist name for a wealthier peasant
kupe – compartment (on a train)
kvartira – flat, apartment
kvitantsia – receipt

lavra – senior monastery
lednik – glacier
les – forest
lyux – a *lyux* room in a hotel is a kind of suite, with a sitting room in addition to the bedroom and bathroom

Mafia – anyone who has anything to do with crime, from genuine gangsters to victims of their protection rackets; also applied to anyone who's successful at anything (no-one believes they could have done it legally)
magazin – shop
manezh – riding school
marka – postage stamp or brand, trademark
marshrut – route
marshrutki, marshrutnoe taxi – minibus that runs along a fixed route
mashina – car
matryoshka – set of painted wooden dolls within dolls
mavzoley – mausoleum
mestnoe vremya – local time
mesto – place, seat
mezhdugorodnyy – intercity
mezhdunarodnyy – international
mikriki – minivan
militsia – police
mineralnaya voda – mineral water
more – sea
morskoy vokzal (R), **morsky vokzal** (U) – sea terminal
Moskovskoe vremya – Moscow time
most – bridge
muzey – museum; also some palaces, art galleries and nonworking churches
muzhskoy – men's (toilet)
naberezhnaya – embankment

nomenklatura – literally 'list of nominees'; the old government and Communist Party elite
novy – new

obed – lunch
oblast – region
obmen valyuty – currency exchange
obmenny punkt – exchange point (bureau, counter)
okrug – district
ostanovka – bus stop
ostrov – island
OVIR (Otdel Viz I Registratsii) – Department of Visas & Registration
ozero – lake

pamyatnik – monument, statue
Paskha – Easter
passazhirskiy poezd – intercity stopping train
pereryv – break (when shops, ticket offices, restaurants etc close for an hour or two during the day; this always happens just as you arrive)
perestroika – literally 'restructuring'; Mikhail Gorbachev's efforts to revive the Soviet economy
pereulok – lane
peshchera – cave
pivo – beer
plan goroda – city map
plyazh – beach
ploshcha (U, B), **ploshchad** (R) – square
pochta, pochtamt – post office
poezd – train
poliklinika – medical centre
poluostrov – peninsula
polyana – glade, clearing
posilka – parcel
posolstvo – embassy
praspekt – avenue (B) – see also *prospekt*
prichal – landing, pier
priglashenie – invitation
prigorodnyy poezd – suburban train
prodazha – sale
proezd – passage
prokat – rental
propusk – permit, pass
prospekt – avenue (R, U)
provodnik (m), **provodnitsa** (f) – carriage attendant on a train

rabochy den – working day (Monday to Friday)
rayon – district
rechnoy vokzal – river terminal
reka – river
remont, na remont – closed for repairs (a sign you see all too often)
restoran – restaurant
Rozhdestvo – Christmas
rubl – rouble
ruchnoy – handmade
rynok – market

sad – garden
samolyot – aeroplane
samovar – urn with an inner tube filled with hot charcoal used for heating water for tea
sanitarny den – literally 'sanitary day'; the monthly day on which a shop, museum, restaurant, hotel dining room etc shuts down for cleaning
schyot – bill
schyotchik – taxi meter
selo – village
sever – north
shlagbaum – checkpoint, barrier
shosse – highway
shtuka – piece (many produce items are sold by the piece)
skhema transporta – transport map
skoryy poezd – literally, fast train; a long-distance train
sneg – snow
sobor – cathedral
Sodruzhestvo Nezavisimykh Gosudarstv (SNG) – Commonwealth of Independent States (CIS)
soviet – council
spravka – certificate
spusk – descent, slope
Sputnik – former youth-travel arm of Komsomol; now just one of the bigger tourism agencies
stanitsa – Cossack village
stary – old
stolovaya – canteen, cafeteria
sutok – period of 24 hours

suvenir – souvenir

taiga – northern pine, fir, spruce and larch forest
taksofon – pay telephone
talon – bus ticket, coupon
tapochki – slippers
teatr – theatre
teatralnaya kassa – theatre ticket office
telegramma – telegram
traktir – tavern
tramvay – tram
troyka – vehicle drawn by three horses
tserkov – church
tsirk – circus
TsUM (Tsentralny Univermag) – name of department store
tualet – toilet
tuda i obratno – 'there and back', return ticket
turbaza – tourist camp
turistka stoyanka (U) – camping ground

ulitsa – street (R)
univermag, universalnyy magazin – department store
ushchelie – gorge, canyon
uzhin – supper

valyuta – foreign currency
vanna – bath
vareniki (R)**, varenyky** (U) – Ukrainian fillings, with a variety of possible fillings
velosiped – bicycle
vezdekhod – all-terrain vehicle
vkhid (U)**, vkhod** (R) – way in, entrance
voda – water
vodapad – waterfall
vodny vokzal – ferry terminal
vokzal – station
vorovstvo – theft
vostok – east
vrach – doctor
vulitsa (B)**, vulitsya** (U) – street – see also *ulitsa*
vykhid (U)**, vykhod** (R) – way out, exit
vykhodnoy den – day off (Saturday, Sunday and holidays)

yantar – amber
yezhednevno – every day
yug – south
yurt – nomad's portable, round tent-house made of felt or skins stretched over a collapsible frame of wood slats

zakaz – reservation
zakaznoe – registration (of mail)
zakuski (R)**, zakusky** (U) – appetisers
zal – hall, room
zaliv – gulf, bay
zamok – castle, fortress
zapad – west
zapovednik – (nature) reserve
zavtrak – breakfast
zheleznodorozhnyy vokzal – train station
zhenskiy – women's (toilet)
zheton – token (for metro etc)

LONELY PLANET

Phrasebooks

Lonely Planet phrasebooks are packed with essential words and phrases to help travellers communicate with the locals. With colour tabs for quick reference, an extensive vocabulary and use of script, these handy pocket-sized language guides cover day-to-day travel situations.

- handy pocket-sized books
- easy to understand Pronunciation chapter
- clear & comprehensive Grammar chapter
- romanisation alongside script to allow ease of pronunciation
- script throughout so users can point to phrases for every situation
- full of cultural information and tips for the traveller

'... vital for a real DIY spirit and attitude in language learning'

– *Backpacker*

'the phrasebooks have good cultural backgrounders and offer solid advice for challenging situations in remote locations'

– *San Francisco Examiner*

Arabic (Egyptian) • Arabic (Moroccan) • Australian *(Australian English, Aboriginal and Torres Strait languages)* • Baltic States *(Estonian, Latvian, Lithuanian)* • Bengali • Brazilian • British • Burmese • Cantonese • Central Asia (Uyghur, Uzbek, Kyrghiz, Kazak, Pashto, Tadjik • Central Europe *(Czech, French, German, Hungarian, Italian, Slovak)* • Eastern Europe *(Bulgarian, Czech, Hungarian, Polish, Romanian, Slovak)* • Ethiopian (Amharic) • Fijian • French • German • Greek • Hebrew • Hill Tribes • Hindi & Urdu • Indonesian • Italian • Japanese • Korean • Lao • Latin American Spanish • Malay • Mandarin • Mediterranean Europe *(Albanian, Croatian, Greek, Italian, Macedonian, Maltese, Serbian, Slovene)* • Mongolian • Nepali • Pidgin • Pilipino (Tagalog) • Quechua • Russian • Scandinavian Europe *(Danish, Finnish, Icelandic, Norwegian, Swedish)* • South-East Asia *(Burmese, Indonesian, Khmer, Lao, Malay, Tagalog Pilipino, Thai, Vietnamese)* • South Pacific Languages • Spanish (Castilian) *(also includes Catalan, Galician and Basque)* • Sri Lanka • Swahili • Thai • Tibetan • Turkish • Ukrainian • USA *(US English, Vernacular, Native American languages, Hawaiian)* • Vietnamese • Western Europe *(Basque, Catalan, Dutch, French, German, Greek, Irish, Italian, Portuguese, Scottish Gaelic, Spanish (Castilian), Welsh)*

LONELY PLANET

Mail Order

Lonely Planet products are distributed worldwide. They are also available by mail order from Lonely Planet, so if you have difficulty finding a title please write to us. North and South American residents should write to 150 Linden St, Oakland, CA 94607, USA; European and African residents should write to 10a Spring Place, London NW5 3BH, UK; and residents of other countries to PO Box 617, Hawthorn, Victoria 3122, Australia.

ISLANDS OF THE INDIAN OCEAN Madagascar & Comoros • Maldives • Mauritius, Réunion & Seychelles

MIDDLE EAST & CENTRAL ASIA Arab Gulf States • Central Asia • Central Asia phrasebook • Hebrew phrasebook • Iran • Israel & the Palestinian Territories • Israel & the Palestinian Territories travel atlas • Istanbul • Istanbul to Cairo • Jerusalem • Jordan & Syria • Jordan, Syria & Lebanon travel atlas • Lebanon • Middle East on a shoestring • Syria • Turkey • Turkey travel atlas • Turkish phrasebook • Yemen
Travel Literature: The Gates of Damascus • Kingdom of the Film Stars: Journey into Jordan

NORTH AMERICA Alaska • Backpacking in Alaska • Baja California • California & Nevada • Canada • Chicago • Chicago city map • Deep South • Florida • Hawaii • Honolulu • Las Vegas • Los Angeles • Miami • New England • New Orleans • New York City • New York city map • New York, New Jersey & Pennsylvania • Pacific Northwest USA • Puerto Rico • Rocky Mountain • San Francisco • San Francisco city map • Seattle • Southwest USA • Texas • USA • USA phrasebook • Vancouver • Washington, DC & the Capital Region • Washington DC city map
Travel Literature: Drive Thru America

NORTH-EAST ASIA Beijing • Cantonese phrasebook • China • Hong Kong • Hong Kong city map • Hong Kong, Macau & Guangzhou • Japan • Japanese phrasebook • Japanese audio pack • Korea • Korean phrasebook • Kyoto • Mandarin phrasebook • Mongolia • Mongolian phrasebook • North-East Asia on a shoestring • Seoul • South-West China • Taiwan • Tibet • Tibetan phrasebook • Tokyo
Travel Literature: Lost Japan

SOUTH AMERICA Argentina, Uruguay & Paraguay • Bolivia • Brazil • Brazilian phrasebook • Buenos Aires • Chile & Easter Island • Chile & Easter Island travel atlas • Colombia • Ecuador & the Galapagos Islands • Healthy Travel Central & South America • Latin American Spanish phrasebook • Peru • Quechua phrasebook • Rio de Janeiro • Rio de Janeiro city map • South America on a shoestring • Trekking in the Patagonian Andes • Venezuela
Travel Literature: Full Circle: A South American Journey

SOUTH-EAST ASIA Bali & Lombok • Bangkok • Bangkok city map • Burmese phrasebook • Cambodia • Hanoi • Healthy Travel Asia & India • Hill Tribes phrasebook • Ho Chi Minh City • Indonesia • Indonesia's Eastern Islands • Indonesian phrasebook • Indonesian audio pack • Jakarta • Java • Laos • Lao phrasebook • Laos travel atlas • Malay phrasebook • Malaysia, Singapore & Brunei • Myanmar (Burma) • Philippines • Pilipino (Tagalog) phrasebook • Singapore • South-East Asia on a shoestring • South-East Asia phrasebook • Thailand • Thailand's Islands & Beaches • Thailand travel atlas • Thai phrasebook • Thai audio pack • Vietnam • Vietnamese phrasebook • Vietnam travel atlas

ALSO AVAILABLE: Antarctica • The Arctic • Brief Encounters: Stories of Love, Sex & Travel • Chasing Rickshaws • Lonely Planet Unpacked • Not the Only Planet: Travel Stories from Science Fiction • Sacred India • Travel with Children • Traveller's Tales

Alternative Place Names

The lists show some variants you may come across for place names used in this book. The following abbreviations are used:

(B) Belarusian
(E) English
(F) Finnish
(G) German
(L) Lithuanian
(K) Kazakh
(M) Mongolian
(R) Russian
(S) Soviet name
(U) Ukrainian

RUSSIA

Black Sea – Chyornoe More (R)
Dnepr (River) – Dnipro (U), Dnjapro (B)
Izhevsk – Ustinov (S)
Kaliningrad – Königsberg (G)
Coronian or Courland Spit – Kurshskaya kosa (R), Kuršiu nerija or Neringa (L), Kurische Nehrung (G)
Lake Ladoga – Ladozhskoe ozero (R)
Lake Onega – Onezhskoe ozero (R)
Lake Peipus – Chudskoe ozero (R)
Lomonosov – Oranienbaum (pre-WWII name)
Moscow – Moskva (R)
Nizhny Novgorod – Gorky (S)
Petrodvorets – Petergof (pre-WWII name)
Rybinsk – Andropov (S)
St Petersburg – Sankt-Peterburg (R), Leningrad (S), Petrograd (1914-24)
Sakha (republic) – Yakutia (S)
Samara – Kuybyshev (S)
Sergiev Posad – Zagorsk (S)
Svetlogorsk – Rauschen (G)
Tver – Kalinin (S)
Vladikavkaz – Ordzhonikidze (S)
Volgograd – Stalingrad (pre-1961)
Vyborg – Viipuri (F)
White Sea – Beloe More (R)
Yekaterinburg – Sverdlovsk (S)
Zelenogradsk – Cranz (G)
Zemlya Frantsa-Iosifa – Franz Josef Land (E)

UKRAINE

Bilhorod-Dnistrovsky – Belgorod-Dnestrovsky (R)
Chernihiv – Chernigov (R)
Chernivtsi – Chernovtsy (R)
Chornobyl – Chernobyl (R)
Dnipro (River) – Dnepr (R), Dnjapro (B)
Dnipropetrovsk – Dnepropetrovsk (R)
Hluchiv – Glukhov (R)
Ivano-Frankivsk – Ivano-Frankovsk (R)
Izmayil – Izmail (R)
Kamyanets-Podilski – Kamenets-Podilsky (R)
Kharkiv – Kharkov (R)
Khmelnytsky – Khmelnitsky (R)
Kyiv – Kiev (R)
Kirovohrad – Kirovograd (R)
Krivy Rih – Krivoy Rog (R)
Luhansk – Lugansk (R), Voroshilovgrad (S)
Lviv – Lvov (R)
Mariupol – Zhdanov (S)
Mukacheve – Mukachevo (R)
Odesa – Odessa (R)
Ostroh – Ostrog (R)
Pochaiv – Pochaev (R)
Rivne – Rovno (R)
Ternopil – Ternopol (R)
Uzhhorod – Uzhgorod (R)
Vinnytsya – Vinnitsa (R)
Zaporizhzhya – Zaporozhie (R)
Zhytomyr – Zhitomir (R)

BELARUS

Belarus – Belorussia (S)
Baranavichy – Baranovichi (R)
Dnjapro (River) – Dnepr (R), Dnipro (U)
Ezjaryshcha – Yezerishche (R)
Homel – Gomel (R)
Horodeja – Gorodeya (R)
Hrodna – Grodno (R)
Mahileu – Mogilyov (R)
Malaryta – Malorita (R)
Maldzechna – Molodechno (R)
Mazyr – Mozir (R)
Navahrudak – Novogrudok (R)
Polatsk – Polotsk (R)
Vitsebsk – Vitebsk (R)

AUSTRIA

Vienna – Vena (R)

CHINA

Beijing – Pekin (R)
Harbin – Kharbin (R)
Manzhouli – Manchzhuria (R)
Shenyang – Shenyan (R)
Ürümqi – Urumchi (R)

CZECH REPUBLIC
Prague – Praga (R)

FINLAND
Helsinki – Khelsinki (R)

GERMANY
Hannover – Gannover (R)

GREECE
Athens – Afiny (R)

HUNGARY
Budapest – Budapesht (R)
Debrecen – Debretsen (R)
Zahony – Zakhon (R)

KAZAKHSTAN
Aktau – Shevchenko (S), Aqtau (K)
Aqmola – Tselinograd (S/R)
Aktyubinsk – Aqtöbe (K)
Almaty – Alma-Ata (R/S)
Atyrau – Gurev (R/S)
Karaganda – Qaraghandy (K)
Kustanay – Qostanay (K)
Petropavlovsk – Petropavl (K)
Semey – Semipalatinsk (R)

KYRGYZSTAN
Bishkek – Frunze (S)

LITHUANIA
Vilnius – Vilnyus (R)

MOLDOVA
Chisinau – Kishinyov (R)

MONGOLIA
Suhbaatar – Sukhe Bator (R)
Ulaan Baatar – Ulan Bator (R)

NORTH KOREA
Pyongyang – Pkhyonyan (R)

POLAND
Bialystok – Belostok (R)
Braniewo – Branevo (R)
Elblag – Elblong (R)
Gdynia – Gdynya (R)
Kraków – Krakov (R)
Kuznica Bialostocka – Kuznitsa (R)
Olsztyn – Olshtyn (R)
Przemysl – Pshemysl (R)
Warsaw – Varshava (R)

SLOVAKIA
Cierna-nad-Tisou – Chierna-nad-Tissoy (R)
Košice – Koshitse (R)

TURKMENISTAN
Ashghabat – Ashkhabad (R)
Turkmenbashi – Krasnovodsk (S/R)

Acknowledgments

THANKS

Many thanks to the travellers who used the last edition and wrote to us with helpful hints, useful advice and interesting anecdotes:

Abby Sandor, Abby Twinn, Abigail Browne, Adam Sebire, Adrian Booth, Adrian Brooks, Adrian Messmer, Aernout Nieuwekerk, Ake Dahllot, Alan Bowtell, Alan Rooney, Alec Parkin, Alexander & Stefan Haines, Alexander Akopian, Alexander Czarnobaj, Alexander Czarnobats, Alexander Zumdieck, Alexandre Akopian, Alison Ehlers, Allen Kupetz, Andrea Gregovich, Andreas Meiser, Andrew Clark, Andrew Wiseman, Andrius Rupsys, Andy Ganner, Aneta Kowal, Angela Hollingsworth, Ann Coady, Ann De Schryver, Annette Holden, Anthony Agriam, Anthony Darragh, Anthony Schlesinger, Ari Katz, Augustin Mettler, Barney Smith, Barry Blick, Barry Coombes, Barry Sachais, Bart Nemmers, Beat Buechler, Beatrice R Carnevale, Ben Bethel, Benedict Kent, Bernhard Kockoth, Bert Flower, Beth Diamond, Bev Broger, Bill Stone, Billy Leung, Birgith Sloth, Bob Cromwell, Bob Guldin, Bob Lewis, Bob Schnelle, Bonnie van der Velde, Brenda Plonis, Brian Payne, Brod Klinger, Bruno De Cordier, Bryce Collishaw, C P Cottis, Caroline Moncur, Cassie Williams, Charles Hirsch, Charlotte Pepper, Chris & Bev Bennett, Chris Jackson, Chris Webb, Christian Mathieu, Christopher Carrier, Christopher Pratt, Claire Bouchard, Claire Stephenson, Clare & Rinlay McNicol, Claude Rouget, Colette Shields, Colin Thubron, Colin Watkins, Colleen Poulter, Caroline Porcher, Caroline Spiers, Csaba Mikusi, Daan van der Schriek, Dagmar Wabel, Daniel Leach, Daniel Stone, Daniele Massazza, Dave Blood, Dave Ruchpaul, David Berner, David Cowans, David Oakley, David Reid, David Saville, David Throckmorton, David Young, David Zuckerman, Dianne & Marty Weisenfeld, Dieuwke Papma, Dina Koutcherova, Dougal Nivison, Dr Nikolaus Lutz-Dettinger, Dr P T Antonopoulos, Drew N, E Clive Rumens, Eileen Dover, Einar Andersen, Ek Suttipong Aramkun, Ekaterina Cherkasova, Eleanor M Barden, Eleanor Mathieson, Emily Finer, Emily Hoche-Mong, Emma Phillips, Emma Tidy, Eric D'Souza, Eric S Johnson, Evert van der Zweerde, F Lulli, Fabian Walling, Fergus O'Connell, Fiona Charlesson, Fiona Clarkson, Fiona Mulvay, Flouis Bylsma, Francis Wauquier, G D Jarvis, G Kane, Gareth Oubridge, Gary Lane, Gary M Lane, Geoff Bland, Geoff Cox, Geoff Meek, George Migeod, Gerard Souness, Gerry Timmermans, Gilles Cogneau, Gillian M Long, Glenn Holland, Glenn Reynolds, Graham Jackson, Graham Still, Gregor Preac, Guido M Bauer, Hans J Buhrmester, Harald Schubert, Harry Cadle, Hazlini Harun, Helen Peers, Helmut Luders, Henry Lipiec, Herman Wierenga, Howard Gethin, Ingo Holzle, Irene Hiralal-Hasler, Italo Vecchi, Ivan Jaselsky, J & A Sultanov, J F Sanderson, J Nathan, Jaana Palantera, Jacqueline & Andreas Kuoni, Jalnada Hogenkamp, James Brownlee, James E Storms, Jamie Akhavi, Jan Marzec, Jane Bloomfield, Jane Eliza, Jane Humphreys, Jason Porter, Jeanette & Christian, Jean-Francois Maion, Jean-Patrick, Jeff Rhodes, Jerome Simpson, Jill Patterson, Jim Ellison, Jo Govaerts, Joanne Brais, Joerg Glaser, John A Lee, John Frost, John Hogan, John Lough, John Neil, John Park, John Scaife, John Shay, Jolanda Hogenkamp, Jolanda Kortekaas, Joost van der Ven, Jop Van Kemper, Josh Welbaum, Judith Cristy, Julia Sultanov, Julie Dickinson, Julle Tuulianen, Justin Mason, K Schoendorf, Karen Culver, Kari Makelainen, Karl Scharbert, Karl Vik, Kate Glover, Katharine Allen, Kathleen Hancock, KD Atkinson, Ken Lawrence, Kenneth W Kemp, Kerry Just, Kevin Burden, Kim Iskyan, Kirsty Vicary, Krishna Ramaraju, Krista Nannery, Kristan Schiller, Krzysztof Rybak, Kuwakubo Megumi, Kyle Thorson, Kyril Dambuleff, L Bowers, Lars Tarald Kvam, Laura J Cinat, Laurie Schadt, Lee & Paula Roussel, Leo Falk, Leonid Ragozin, Lex Spek, Lindsay Gowland, Lindsay Image, Liza Kaplan, Lora Anne Gerard, Lucinda Haque, Lyndal Le Bas, Lynn Bramwell, M Rosseel, M W Pollock, Maarten van Baggum, Makiko Kitago, Makiko Mia Kitago, Marc Flrick, Marc Heerbrandt, Marcel Van Coile, Marcia Peerlinck, Margot Stuart, Mahir Cagri, Maria Malyk, Maria Sviatopolk-Mirski, Marianne Semmel, Marina Eskina, Marion Rimmer, Mark B Durchslag, Mark Davess, Mark Edebone, Mark Luta, Mark Nicholls, Mark Tinker, Mark Wallem, Markus Hirnsperger, Markus Senn, Martin Ragnar, Martin Tatuch, Matthias Unterburg, Max Maydanik, Megan Corrigan, Michael Angermann, Michael Eckert, Michael Hess, Michael McClean, Michael Paulsmeyer, Michael Smit, Mike Roycroft, Monique Verschuren, Morgane Rolland, Moritz von Buttlar, Moshe Porat, N Moore, Nanna Koekoek, Natalie Rusak, Nathe Lawver, Ned Hutchinson, Nicholas Sherman, Nick Fisk, Nick Hobbs, Oksana Piaseckyj, Othmar Zendron, P J Bruyniks, P Zambrzycki, Paal Skogholt, Pam Balash, Paul Floyd, Paul Futcher, Paul Hudson, Paul Longfellow, Paul Zambrzycki, Peggy Henderson, Pere-Jordi Palol, Peter Ebbutt, Peter Brechbuehler,

Peter Martinson, Peter Sluijter, Peter Wuhrer, Petr Ishkin, Phil & Emma Benton, Phil Dunnington, Phil Hayward, Phil Perrin, Piers Wood, R & J Tompkins, Rafal Turowski, Rahul Moodgal, Randy Kempa, Rashit G Yahin, Ray Bayliss, Rex Green, Rhona Badham, Ricardo A Fridman, Richard Fountain, Richard Lax, Richard Madge, Richard Naisby, Richard Sondervan, Rikard Berg, Riri S Manor, Rob de Raaij, Rob Kouwenberg, Rob van den Berg, Robert Bowles, Robert Pritchard, Roger & Jaqueline Tompkins, Roger Landau, Roland & Christian, Ron Cook, Ron Helfrich, Rosanna Fiore, Russ Preston, Ruth Lewis, Samantha Sinclair, Samantha Daniels, Sandra Bates, Sarah Cross, Sarah Dennis, Satoshi Sugihara, Shane O'Connor, Simon Bristow, Simon Britten, Simon Dadd, Stefan A Grant, Stephen Chiusano, Stephen Ireland, Stephen Kenmar, Stephen McPhillips, Stephen Miles, Steve O'Donnell, Sue Hucknall, Sue Nass, Susanne Clerkin, Suzanne Salter, Suzanne Shillaker, Tarja Kuhne, Ted Bongiovanni, Ted Sears, Terry Deague, Theodora Delville, Therry van der Burgt, Tim Macmillan, Toby Wakely, Toke Rude, Toni-Lee Capossela, Tony Brooks, Trygve Inda, Ulrich Fischer, Val Afualo, Vasiliy Shibaev, Verena Hartges, Veronica Bradley, Vincent Guiry, Vit Bartek, W Heideureich, W Van Loock, Walter Wylie, Werner Reindorf, Wesley Pullman, William Stone, Yuki Halls.

Guides by Region

Lonely Planet is known worldwide for publishing practical, reliable and no-nonsense travel information in our guides and on our Web site. The Lonely Planet list covers just about every accessible part of the world. Currently there are thirteen series: travel guides, shoestring guides, walking guides, city guides, phrasebooks, audio packs, city maps, travel atlases, diving & snorkeling guides, restaurant guides, first-time travel guides, healthy travel and travel literature.

AFRICA Africa on a shoestring • Africa – the South • Arabic (Egyptian) phrasebook • Arabic (Moroccan) phrasebook • Cairo • Cape Town • Cape Town city map• Central Africa • East Africa • Egypt • Egypt travel atlas • Ethiopian (Amharic) phrasebook • The Gambia & Senegal • Healthy Travel Africa • Kenya • Kenya travel atlas • Malawi, Mozambique & Zambia • Morocco • North Africa • South Africa, Lesotho & Swaziland • South Africa, Lesotho & Swaziland travel atlas • Swahili phrasebook • Tanzania, Zanzibar & Pemba • Trekking in East Africa • Tunisia • West Africa • Zimbabwe, Botswana & Namibia • Zimbabwe, Botswana & Namibia travel atlas
Travel Literature: The Rainbird: A Central African Journey • Songs to an African Sunset: A Zimbabwean Story • Mali Blues: Traveling to an African Beat

AUSTRALIA & THE PACIFIC Auckland • Australia • Australian phrasebook • Bushwalking in Australia • Bushwalking in Papua New Guinea • Fiji • Fijian phrasebook • Healthy Travel Australia, NZ and the Pacific • Islands of Australia's Great Barrier Reef • Melbourne • Melbourne city map • Micronesia • New Caledonia • New South Wales & the ACT • New Zealand • Northern Territory • Outback Australia • Out To Eat – Melbourne • Out to Eat – Sydney • Papua New Guinea • Pidgin phrasebook • Queensland • Rarotonga & the Cook Islands • Samoa • Solomon Islands • South Australia • South Pacific Languages phrasebook • Sydney • Sydney city map • Sydney Condensed • Tahiti & French Polynesia • Tasmania • Tonga • Tramping in New Zealand • Vanuatu • Victoria • Western Australia
Travel Literature: Islands in the Clouds • Kiwi Tracks: A New Zealand Journey • Sean & David's Long Drive

CENTRAL AMERICA & THE CARIBBEAN Bahamas, Turks & Caicos • Bermuda • Central America on a shoestring • Costa Rica • Cuba • Dominican Republic & Haiti • Eastern Caribbean • Guatemala, Belize & Yucatán: La Ruta Maya • Jamaica • Mexico • Mexico City • Panama • Puerto Rico
Travel Literature: Green Dreams: Travels in Central America

EUROPE Amsterdam • Amsterdam city map • Andalucía • Austria • Baltic States phrasebook • Barcelona • Berlin • Berlin city map • Britain • British phrasebook • Brussels, Bruges & Antwerp • Budapest city map • Canary Islands • Central Europe • Central Europe phrasebook • Corsica • Croatia • Czech & Slovak Republics • Denmark • Dublin • Eastern Europe • Eastern Europe phrasebook • Edinburgh • Estonia, Latvia & Lithuania • Europe on a shoestring • Finland • France • French phrasebook • Germany • German phrasebook • Greece • Greek Islands • Greek phrasebook • Hungary • Iceland, Greenland & the Faroe Islands • Ireland • Italian phrasebook • Italy • Krakow • Lisbon • London • London city map • London Condensed • Mediterranean Europe • Mediterranean Europe phrasebook • Norway • Paris • Paris city map • Poland • Portugal • Portugal travel atlas • Prague • Prague city map • Provence & the Côte d'Azur • Romania & Moldova • Rome • Russia, Ukraine & Belarus • Russian phrasebook • Scandinavian & Baltic Europe • Scandinavian Europe phrasebook • Scotland • Slovenia • Spain • Spanish phrasebook • St Petersburg • Switzerland • Trekking in Spain • Ukrainian phrasebook • Vienna • Walking in Britain • Walking in Ireland • Walking in Italy • Walking in Spain • Walking in Switzerland • Western Europe • Western Europe phrasebook
Travel Literature: The Olive Grove: Travels in Greece

INDIAN SUBCONTINENT Bangladesh • Bengali phrasebook • Bhutan • Delhi • Goa • Hindi & Urdu phrasebook • India • India & Bangladesh travel atlas • Indian Himalaya • Karakoram Highway • Kerala • Mumbai (Bombay) • Nepal • Nepali phrasebook • Pakistan • Rajasthan • Read This First: Asia & India • South India • Sri Lanka • Sri Lanka phrasebook • Trekking in the indian Himalaya • Trekking in the Karakoram & Hindukush • Trekking in the Nepal Himalaya
Travel Literature: In Rajasthan • Shopping for Buddhas

Lonely Planet Journeys

Journeys is a unique collection of travel writing – published by the company that understands travel better than anyone else. It is a series for anyone who has ever experienced – or dreamed of – the magical moment when they encountered a strange culture or saw a place for the first time. They are tales to read while you're planning a trip, while you're on the road or while you're in an armchair in front of a fire.

These outstanding titles explore our planet through the eyes of a diverse group of international writers. JOURNEYS books catch the spirit of a place, illuminate a culture, recount a crazy adventure or introduce a fascinating way of life. They always entertain, and always enrich the experience of travel.

MALI BLUES

Traveling to an African Beat

Lieve Joris (translated by Sam Garrett)

Drought, rebel uprisings, ethnic conflict: these are the predominant images of West Africa. But as Lieve Joris travels in Senegal, Mauritania and Mali, she meets survivors, fascinating individuals charting new ways of living between tradition and modernity. With her remarkable gift for drawing out people's stories, Joris brilliantly captures the rhythms of a world that refuses to give in.

THE GATES OF DAMASCUS

Lieve Joris (translated by Sam Garrett)

This best-selling book is a beautifully drawn portrait of day-to-day life in modern Syria. Through her intimate contact with local people, Lieve Joris draws us into the fascinating world that lies behind the gates of Damascus. Hala's husband is a political prisoner, jailed for his opposition to the Assad regime; through the author's friendship with Hala we see how Syrian politics impacts on the lives of ordinary people.

THE OLIVE GROVE

Travels in Greece

Katherine Kizilos

Katherine Kizilos travels to fabled islands, troubled border zones and her family's village deep in the mountains. She vividly evokes breathtaking landscapes, generous people and passionate politics, capturing the complexities of a country she loves.

'beautifully captures the real tensions of Greece' – *Sunday Times*

KINGDOM OF THE FILM STARS

Journey into Jordan

Annie Caulfield

Kingdom of the Film Stars is a travel book and a love story. With honesty and humour, Annie Caulfield writes of travelling in Jordan and falling in love with a Bedouin with film-star looks.

She offers fascinating insights into the country – from the tent life of traditional women to the hustle of downtown Amman – and unpicks tight-woven western myths about the Arab world.

Lonely Planet Online

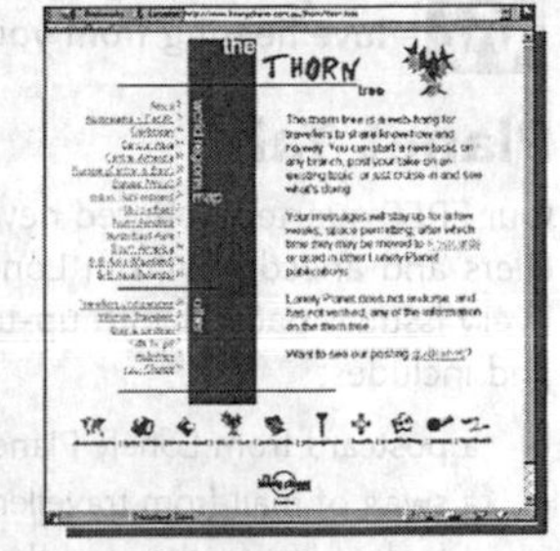

Whether you've just begun planning your next trip, or you're chasing down specific info on currency regulations or visa requirements, check out Lonely Planet Online for up-to-the-minute travel information.

As well as miniguides to more than 250 destinations, you'll find maps, photos, travel news, health and visa updates, travel advisories and discussion of the ecological and political issues you need to be aware of as you travel. You'll also find timely upgrades to popular guidebooks that you can print out and stick in the back of your book.

There's an online travellers' forum (The Thorn Tree) where you can share your experience of life on the road, meet travel companions and ask other travellers for their recommendations and advice.

There's also a complete and up-to-date list of all Lonely Planet travel products including travel guides, diving and snorkeling guides, phrasebooks, atlases, travel literature and videos, and a simple online ordering facility if you can't find the book you want elsewhere.

Lonely Planet Diving & Snorkeling Guides

Beautifully illustrated with full-colour photos throughout, Lonely Planet's Pisces books explore the world's best diving and snorkeling areas and prepare divers for what to expect when they get there, both topside and underwater.

Dive sites are described in detail with specifics on depths, visibility, level of difficulty, special conditions, underwater photography tips and common and unusual marine life present. You'll also find practical logistical information and coverage on topside activities and attractions, sections on diving health and safety, plus listings for diving services, live-aboards, dive resorts and tourist offices.

FREE Lonely Planet Newsletters

We love hearing from you and think you'd like to hear from us.

Planet Talk

Our FREE quarterly printed newsletter is full of tips from travellers and anecdotes from Lonely Planet guidebook authors. Every issue is packed with up-to-date travel news and advice, and includes:

- a postcard from Lonely Planet co-founder Tony Wheeler
- a swag of mail from travellers
- a look at life on the road through the eyes of a Lonely Planet author
- topical health advice
- prizes for the best travel yarn
- news about forthcoming Lonely Planet events
- a complete list of Lonely Planet books and other titles

To join our mailing list, residents of the UK, Europe and Africa can email us at go@lonelyplanet.co.uk; residents of North and South America can email us at info@lonelyplanet.com; the rest of the world can email us at talk2us@lonelyplanet.com.au, or contact any Lonely Planet office.

Comet

Our FREE monthly email newsletter brings you all the latest travel news, features, interviews, competitions, destination ideas, travellers' tips & tales, Q&As, raging debates and related links. Find out what's new on the Lonely Planet Web site and which books are about to hit the shelves.

Subscribe from your desktop: www.lonelyplanet.com/comet

Index

Abbreviations

Belarus – B　　Russia – R　　Ukraine – U

Text

Bold indicates maps.

Bold indicates maps.

Bold indicates maps.

Boxed Text

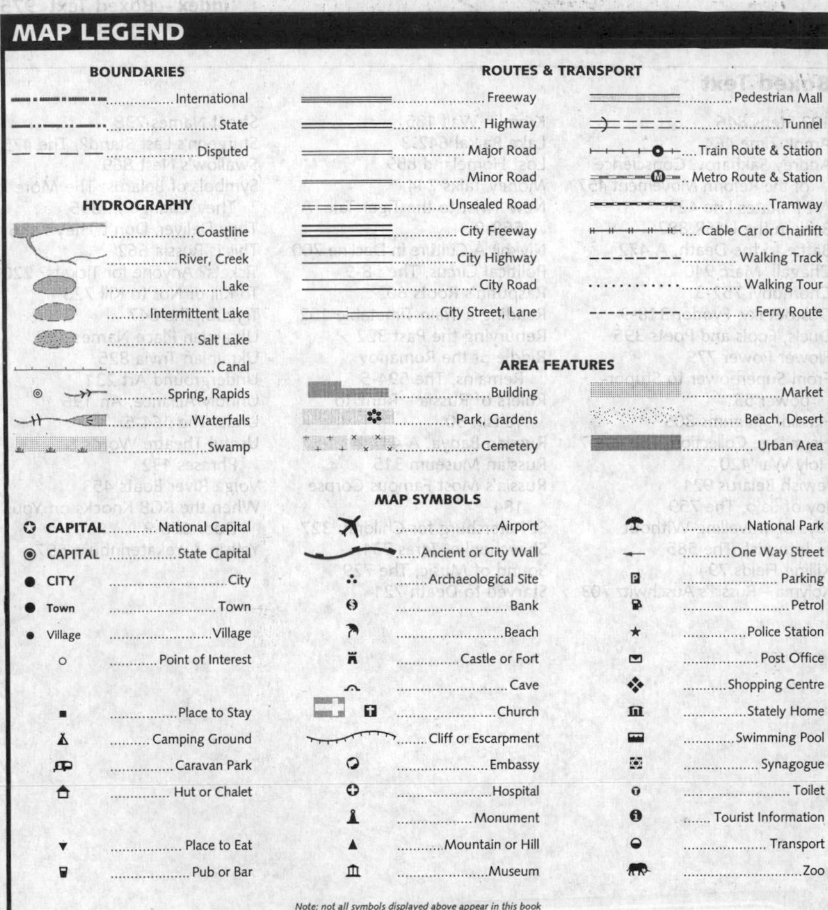

LONELY PLANET OFFICES

Australia
PO Box 617, Hawthorn, Victoria 3122
☎ 03 9819 1877 fax 03 9819 6459
email: talk2us@lonelyplanet.com.au

USA
150 Linden St, Oakland, CA 94607
☎ 510 893 8555 TOLL FREE: 800 275 8555
fax 510 893 8572
email: info@lonelyplanet.com

UK
10a Spring Place, London NW5 3BH
☎ 020 7428 4800 fax 020 7428 4828
email: go@lonelyplanet.co.uk

France
1 rue du Dahomey, 75011 Paris
☎ 01 55 25 33 00 fax 01 55 25 33 01
email: bip@lonelyplanet.fr
www.lonelyplanet.fr

World Wide Web: www.lonelyplanet.com *or* AOL keyword: lp
Lonely Planet Images: lpi@lonelyplanet.com.au